A MODERN VIEW OF THEODORE THEODORSEN

Theodore Theodorsen ♦ 1897-1978

Chief, Physical Research Division
NASA Langley Memorial Aeronautical Laboratory

Chief Scientist, U.S. Air Force

Chief of Research, Republic Aviation Corp.

Consultant, United Aircraft Corp.
Sikorsky Aircraft and Hamilton
Standard Divisions

American Institute of Aeronautics and Astronautics, Inc.
The Aerospace Center
370 L'Enfant Promenade, SW
Washington, DC 20024-2518

Library of Congress Cataloging in Publication Data

ISBN 0-930403-85-1

design • Sara Bluestone
• John Newbauer
composition • Simki Michael
• Eric Sorenson
editing • Earl Dowell, John Newbauer
production • Tom Walsh
type • Garamond • Avant Garde
body paper • 70# Matte

Printed in the United States of America

FOREWORD

It has been a distinct honor and pleasure to serve as the editor for this volume. Never has an editor had more enthusiastic and helpful contributors. Professors Holt Ashely, Anthony Perry and Robert Scanlan, Dr. Donald Hanson, Mr. John Newbauer and Mrs. Muriel Theodorsen Williams have been exceptional in their efforts. It has been truly a labor of love for all of us.

Much the most important reason for this is the subject of our book, Dr. Theodore Theodorsen. A giant of the youthful days of aeronautics, he still stands tall among all of those who have followed him. By this book we hope to bring to this and succeeding generations of aeronautical engineers and scientists an appreciation of the person and the age in which he was so notable a figure.

The broader context of NASA Langley Research Center history has been admirably captured in "Engineer in Charge: A History of the Langley Aeronautical Laboratory, 1917–1958," by James R. Hansen (NASA Scientific and Technical Information Office, Washington, DC, 1987). Our focus here will be on Theodorsen's research contributions through a reprinting of selected papers and appreciations authored by notable scholars in several of the fields in which he was active.

A special treat is a reprinting of the remembrance by his long-time colleague, Dr. I. Edward Garrick, and also the new biographical sketch by his daughter, Mrs. Muriel Theodorsen Williams.

Finally, I would like to thank Willaree Curtis and the library staff of the NASA Langley Research Center for helping us obtain the best copies available of Dr. Theodorsen's papers for reprinting in this volume.

We all hope that you will enjoy reading this volume as much as we have enjoyed preparing it.

Earl H. Dowell
Professor and Dean
School of Engineering, Duke University

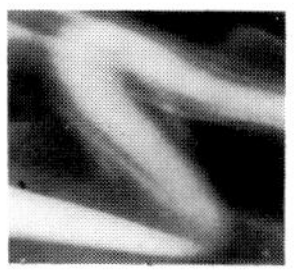

A MODERN VIEW AND APPRECIATION OF THE WORKS OF

THEODORE THEODORSEN

PHYSICIST AND ENGINEER

Critical Essays By

I. E. GARRICK

HOLT ASHLEY

DONALD B. HANSON

ANTHONY E. PERRY

ROBERT H. SCANLAN

Together with reprintings of his chief works and a biographical reminiscence by **Muriel Theodorsen Williams**

Edited by **EARL H. DOWELL**
Duke University

AIAA

Published by the
American Institute of Aeronautics and Astronautics

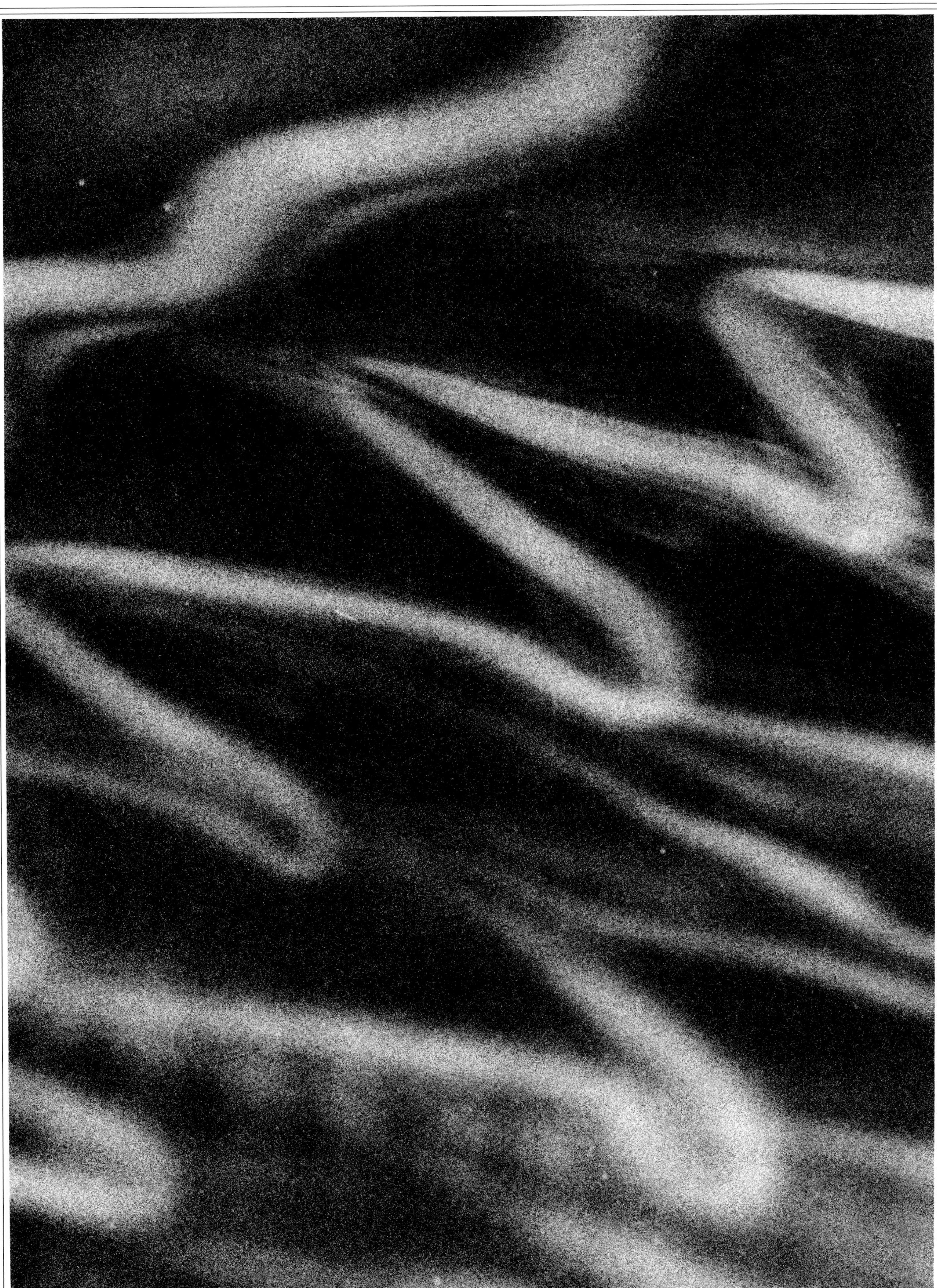

Contents

An Appreciation
of the Contributions of

THEODORE THEODORSEN

Introduction

Sharing His Insights and Innovations
(with a chronological list of his works)

I. E. Garrick

Long a stellar figure at the NACA (now NASA) Langley Research Center, in part through his role as Chief of the Dynamic Loads Division. A protege of Theodorsen, his research encompassed aerodynamics, emphasized aeroelasticity.

Critical Essays

Inspired Aerodynamics of Wing Sections

Holt Ashley

Professor of Aeronautics and Astronautics at Stanford University; previously a member of the MIT faculty. A leading figure in aerodynamics and aeroelasticity.

Remarkable Legacy in Propeller Aerodynamics

Donald B. Hanson

Senior member of the research staff of Hamilton Standard Division of United Technologies. His research includes aerodynamics and acoustics.

His Modern View of Turbulence

Anthony E. Perry

Professor of Engineering at the University of Melbourne, a leader in contemporary fluid mechanics and turbulence.

Pioneering in Aeroelasticity

Robert H. Scanlan

Professor of Civil Engineering at the Johns Hopkins University; previously a faculty member at Princeton and Case Western Reserve. His research spans acoustics, aeroelasticity, applied mechanics, and wind engineering.

Biographical Reminiscence

About My Father

Muriel Theodorsen Williams

Introduction

SHARING HIS INSIGHTS AND INNOVATIONS

by I. E. Garrick

It has been my special privilege to have worked under Dr. Theodorsen for more than 15 years, from 1930 to 1946, at the Langley Memorial Aeronautical Laboratory (LMAL) of the U. S. National Advisory Committee for Aeronautics (NACA), predecessor to the National Aeronautics and Space Administration (NASA). LMAL is now the Langley Research Center, and it was the mother laboratory from which at least five of the major NASA centers were spun off, now known as Ames Research Center (California), Lewis Research Center (Ohio), Dryden Flight Center (California), Johnson Space Center (Texas), and Wallops Flight Center (Virginia). Only about 200 were employed by NACA when Theodorsen came to Langley in 1929, and his role in helping establish the great scientific and engineering traditions of NACA, which became the cornerstone of NASA, was a distinguished one of major importance. I hope to give herein a brief account of the contributions of Theodorsen to science and technology and to impart a fleeting glimpse of the unique flavor and stimulation of those early pioneering NACA days.

Theodorsen followed his engineering degree from the Norwegian Institute of Technology at Trondheim in 1922 with a doctoral degree in physics from Johns Hopkins University. His thesis,[1] under the supervision of the eminent physicist Professor K. F. Hertzfeld, dealt with thermodynamic and aerodynamic themes that were to permeate much of his later work, and was developed in two parts: 1) shock waves and explosions and 2) combustion and detonation. Through the urging of Dr. Joseph S. Ames, President of Johns Hopkins University and Chairman of the Executive Committee of NACA, Theodorsen came to LMAL in 1929 as an associate physicist. Langley was then the only in-house research arm of NACA and had a highly motivated young staff. The work atmosphere was very informal, though competitive, with much open stimulating discussion. [One may note, in passing, that the annual budget then was about $500,000, whereas by contrast at the peak of the Apollo program (1965–66) NASA's budget was approaching $6,000,000,000, supporting an in-house staff of about 40,000 and some 200,000 in industry.] However, conditions were rather primitive; for example, the "library" consisted of one small shelf of books. Theodorsen used as his mainstays his old reliable Hütte mechanical engineering handbook and a set of the marvelous 1929 edition of *Handbuch der Physik*, which he acquired for his use.

Within a short time, Theodorsen was made head of the Physical Research Division, the other research divisions being Engine Research and Aerodynamics, the largest division, which included structures and flight research. Langley was then in the process of expanding its experimental facilities to include the Full-Scale Wind Tunnel

---

†Presented at the colloquium honoring Theodore Theodorsen, on the occasion of his 80th year, by the Royal Norwegian Society of Science, Trondheim, Norway, September 1–4, 1976. In the absence of Dr. Garrick, the paper was read by Associate Professor Helge Nörstrud.

and the Hydrodynamic Towing Basin. One of the first activities of Theodorsen was the developing of an instrument for detecting buried metals,[2,3] and on its very first use it picked up a live bomb on a former bombing range, the site of the new hydrodynamic tank.

The ensuing years were highly productive ones for Theodorsen in a great variety of experimental and theoretical areas, as the list of publications, arranged chronologically and appended herein, discloses. As an overview, Theodorsen improved thin-airfoil theory by introducing the angle of best streamlining,[4] went on to develop the now classical and elegant theory of arbitrary wing sections,[11] performed the first NACA in-house noise research,[7] worked on fire prevention in aircraft and on means of icing removal and prevention, contributed to the theory of open, closed and partially open wind-tunnel test sections,[10] developed the basic theory of aircraft flutter and its verification,[17] made improvements to NACA engine cowlings and ducted propellers, added to our knowledge of stall flutter of propellers, developed scaling laws for propeller vibrations, made early measurements of skin friction at transonic and supersonic speeds,[45] developed the use of freon (dicholoro-difluoro-methane) for experimental aeroelastic work, gave damping properties of structure, and expanded general propeller theory. During World War (WW) II, Theodorsen was called on for the analysis and troubleshooting of many aircraft problems and to help devise necessary modifications.

After leaving Langley, Theodorsen helped to organize and administer an aeronautical institute in Brazil (1947–50). Then he served as Chief Scientist for the U. S. Air Force (1950–54), during which time he did important work on the structure of turbulence. Theodorsen became Chief of Research for the Republic Aviation Corporation (1955–62), a post from which he retired in 1962 when he became an active consultant to the United Aircraft Corporation, where he specialized on ducted propeller work. Apparently, he also found time to ponder relativity theory.

We may extract from the above list of Theodorsen's activities a few topics for brief expanded discussion, subjects that have been especially significant and that play important roles in current research and technology. Before doing so, I feel I should not neglect to emphasize that Theodorsen helped to establish a pattern for productive research for the associates in his small group and that several of these worked jointly with him as coauthors and otherwise became productive in their own names. Among these are: Carl Kaplan, who specialized in theoretical compressible-flow aerodynamics; A. A. Regier, a highly capable experimentalist, now deceased, who did important work on noise, flutter, and vibration; U.T. Joyner, a versatile physicist, who specialized on heat exchangers and landing-loads dynamics; M.J. Brevoort, a physicist, and G.W. Stickle, an engineer, who did research on instrumentaion, engine cowlings, and aircraft performance; R.P. Coleman, who made contributions to helicopter stability and rotor dynamics; and I.E. Garrick, who has specialized in applied mathematics and aeroelasticity.

A word or two on Theodorsen's method of working. When a problem captured his attention, he would work on it during relatively short periods of intense concentrated activity, almost incommunicado, followed by periods of apparent desultory inactivity. Often, some of us would walk with him among trees and orchards then still existing at Langley, and he would discuss foibles of mankind. As head of a division, he had the major virtue, now rare, of protecting his staff from routine and time-draining demands of management, allowing a person to develop his own talents and resources. When one had a finished or semifinished product, Theodorsen would then be a helpful though severe critic.

The theory of arbitrary airfoils based on conformal mapping developed by Theodorsen[11] is a model of classical applied mathematics. There is no need to go over this work in any detail, as it is now described in many textbooks. However, I do wish to point out two key concepts that made Theodorsen's approach different from and a clear improvement on methods that preceded it, such as that of von Mises or of von Kármán and Trefftz. One was the important use of the complex variable transformation, not in the usual form of a polynomial or power series, but in the form of an exponential to power series, as follows:

$$z' = z \exp\left[\sum_{1}^{\infty}\left(\frac{a_n}{z^n}\right)\right]$$

This integral transcendental form, for which no zeros other than $z = 0$ can occur, automatically removes singularities from the flow region; and, as the second point, led directly to the basic boundary value equation of the form—

$$\epsilon(\phi') = \frac{1}{2\pi}\int_{0}^{2\pi} \psi(\phi) \cot\left(\frac{\varphi - \varphi'}{2}\right) d\varphi$$

which, as an integral equation, represents an exact solution of the problem in terms of the given airfoil data. Many methods for its numerical solution have developed, but I believe a most useful and elegant one is given in a paper of mine, "Conformal Mapping in Aerodynamics with Emphasis on the Method of Successive Conjugates" in Vol. 18 of the Applied Mathematics Series of the Bureau of Standards (1952). The intriguing connections of this integral equation with wide vistas of mathematics and mathematical transforms have been indicated here and in the literature. (See also D. Gaier, *Konstruktive Methoden der Konformen Abbildung*, Springer, 1964.) Connections of the numerical method with the Fast Fourier Transform method of Cooley-Tukey have also been indicated. The method has been automated so that complete pressure distributions for a given airfoil section can be obtained in a matter of seconds. The philosophy in Theodorsen's approach was that an exact formulation is often simpler and preferable to an approximate one, and that while approximations are essential in applied mathematics, they should be delayed as far as possible. This work led me to generalize it to biplane sections, a most beautiful application of elliptic functions, and has also led to many other airfoil studies including multiple interfering airfoils, and the development of wing sections with desirable drag and moment properties. Theodorsen's method now often has a prime role in general numerical flow studies, a currently prominent domain of fluid dynamics utilizing the most modern high-speed computers, where, for example, for the Navier-Stokes equation it may allow the obtaining of the simplest choice of coordinates in which to treat a given problem.

Another topic that merits further discussion is the work of Theodorsen on flutter, particularly.[17] The approach here is again direct and clean, leading to an explicit exact solution as contrasted with previous implicit and approximate results. The unsteady aerodynamics for an oscillatory two-dimensional airfoil in incompressible flow is developed in two parts: noncirculatory potentials involving no wake effects and circulatory potentials for the wake effects. The classical trailing-edge flow condition immediately gave an integral relation between their flow potentials, which Theodorsen assigned to me to evaluate, first by purely numerical methods, then by analytical means, yielding the famous important function of Theodorsen:

$$C(k) = F(k) + iG(k) = \frac{H_1^{(2)}(k)}{H_1^{(2)}(k) + iH_0^{(2)}(k)}$$

This exact flutter solution, including results for control surfaces, has had a keystone role in the development of flutter methods in the United States. It has enabled an engineering feel for effects of variables and parameters in complex situations and has been available as a model against which approximate solutions utilizing numerical methods for rotors or for three-dimensional airfoils and for subsonic Mach numbers could be compared. It is of interest to remark that Theodorsen's function $C(k)$ also occurs prominently in the theory of propulsion of birds and fish. (Here a leading-edge condition must supplement the trailing-edge relation as indicated in NACA TR-567.) Lighthill's recent book *Mathematical Biofluiddynamics* represents a new field that in its theoretical aspects makes some contact with the work of Theodorsen.

Although Theodorsen has leaned strongly toward basic theoretical analysis, he has usually accompanied his work with experimental verification. He has also been highly innovative in engineering and experimental activities where he has always sought a theoretical framework or has been guided by physical intuition. He was responsible for proposing a wind tunnel for flutter work, which employed a mixture of air and freon ($C\ Cl_2\ F_2$) with variable pressure to greatly increase the scope of research with aeroelastic models throughout the Mach range and with lowered horsepower requirements. The Transonic Dynamics Tunnel now used exclusively for aeroelastic research and development at Langley is based on the use of the same principles plus the use of a slotted-throat test section. Another unique facility due to Theodorsen was the helicopter rotor tower for aerodynamic and noise rotor research. In the area of propeller vibrations he developed, from nondimensional reasoning, new methods of simulating vibrations for rotating propellers employing reduced-thickness models; gave the mechanism of stall flutter of propellers; developed methods for obtaining structural damping of propellers of various materials; and improved engine cowlings and ducted propellers. Ideal propeller aerodynamics was given a definitive treatment in several reports and a book; Theodorsen utilized electric potential differences across nonconducting helical models to evaluate necessary mathematical functions that occur for both single and counterrotating propellers. By measurement over spinning disks, Theodorsen was among the earliest to obtain reliable skin-friction drag data at subsonic, transonic, and supersonic speeds.

A question raised by Lamb in his *Hydrodynamics* (6th edition, p. 161) about the indeterminacy of certain momentum integrals for a body in an infinite fluid is put to rest by Theodorsen in a small paper in a volume published in honor of von Kármán's 60th anniversary.[29] Theodorsen shows that the problem is resolved by considering the relative shape (or solid angle) of the distant control surface with respect to the origin in the flow direction. A more significant development is his contribution to the structure of turbulence in a paper honoring Prandtl's 75th anniversary.[56,59] The universality of turbulence from microphenomena to astrophysics is well known, as for example, the hypothesis that the planets have condensed from a gaseous cloud and that the angular momentum of the solar system is a result of the action of viscosity in the nebula. Turbulence remains as the major unsolved domain of fluid dynamics. Theodorsen identifies main turbulence-creating terms in the equations of motion ($q \times \text{curl}\ q \cdot \text{curl curl}\ q$); he shows that two-dimensional turbulence cannot exist; that vortex line stretching and bending is the important mechanism and ingredient of turbulence; and discusses the hierarchy of vortices (Kolmogorov). While this work of Theodorsen has not met with full approval by turbulence specialists, I cannot help but feel that it will repay deeper study.

In closing this brief (and, I am sure, inadequate) review of Theodorsen's accomplishments, may I state on my own behalf, and on behalf of his associates of former NACA days, how greatly pleased we are at the honoring of Dr. Theodorsen by his Alma Mater on his approaching 80th birthday, and wish him healthful and happy years ahead.

Bibliography by Date

[1]"On the Propagation of Large Disturbances in a Gas; on the Combustion of Oil," Ph.D. Thesis, The Johns Hopkins University, 1929.

[2]"A Sensitive Induction Balance for the Purpose of Detecting Unexploded Bombs," NACA Memo, 1930.

[3]"Instrument for Detecting Metallic Bodies Buried in the Earth," *Journal of the Franklin*

Institute, 1930, pp. 311–326.
[4]"On the Theory of Wing Sections With Particular Reference to the Lift Distribution," NACA TR-383, 1931.
[5]"Investigation of the Diaphragm-Type Pressure Cell," NACA TR-388, 1931.
[6]"Prevention of Ice Formulation on Gasoline Tank Vents" (with William C. Clay), NACA TN-394, 1931.
[7]"A New Principle of Sound Frequency Analysis," NACA TR-395, 1931.
[8]"Ice Prevention on Aircraft by Means of Engine Exhaust Heat and a Technical Study of Heat Transmission from a Clark Y Airfoil" (with William C. Clay), NACA TR-403, 1931.
[9]"Elimination of Fire Hazard Due to Back Fires" (with Ira M. Freeman), NACA TR-409, 1931.
[10]"Theory of Wind-Tunnel Wall Interference," NACA TR-410, 1931.
[11]"Theory of Wing Sections of Arbitrary Shape," NACA TR-411, 1931.
[12]"General Potential Theory of Arbitrary Wing Sections" (with I. E. Garrick), NACA TR-452, 1933.
[13]"Interference on an Airfoil of Finite Span in an Open Rectangular Wind Tunnel," NACA TR-461, 1933.
[14]"Experimental Verification of the Theory of Wind-Tunnel Boundary Interference" (with A. Silverstein), NACA TR-478, 1934.
[15]"Vibration Response of Airplane Structures" (with A. G. Gelalles), NACA TR-491, 1934.
[16]"Propeller Vibrations and the Effect of the Centrifugal Force," NACA TN-516, 1935.
[17]"General Theory of Aerodynamic Instability and the Mechanism of Flutter," NACA TR-496, 1935 (reprinted in 1940).
[18]"Full-Scale Test of NACA Cowlings" (with M. J. Brevoort and G. W. Stickle), NACA TR-592, 1937.
[19]"Cooling of Airplane Engines at Low Air Speeds" (with M. J. Brevoort and G. W. Stickle), NACA TR-593, 1937.
[20]"Characteristics of Six Propellers Including the High-Speed Range" (with G. W. Stickle and M.J. Brevoort), NACA TR-594, 1937.
[21]"Full-Scale Test of a New Type NACA Nose-Slot Cowling" (with M. J. Brevoort, G. W. Stickle, and M. N. Gough), NACA TR-595, 1937.
[22]"The Reaction of a Body in a Compressible Fluid," *Journal of the Aeronautical Sciences*, 1937, pp. 239–40.
[23]"The Fundamental Principles of NACA Cowling," *Journal of the Aeronautical Sciences*, 1938, pp. 169–174.
[24]"Test of Nose-Slot Cowling Installed on SB2U-1 Airplane" (with G. W. Stickle and W. H. McAvoy), NACA Memo, Dec 1938.
[25]"The Flutter Problem," *Fifth International Congress on Applied Mechanics*, Cambridge, MA, 1938.
[26]"Investigation of XPBM Wing-Flutter Model," NACA Memo for the U. S. Naval Bureau of Aeronautics, 1939.
[27]"Flutter Analysis on the Brewster XF2A-2 Airplane," NACA Memo for the U. S. Naval Bureau of Aeronautics, May 1940.
[28]"Mechanism of Flutter—A Theoretical and Experimental Investigation of the Flutter Problem" (with I. E. Garrick), NACA TR-685, 1940.
[29]Impulse and Momentum in a Infinite Fluid," article in memorial volume in honor of the 60th birthday of Theodore von Kármán, 1941.
[30]"Non-Stationary Flow About a Wing-Aileron-Tab Combination Including Aerodynamic Balance" (with I. E. Garrick), NACA TR-736, 1942.
[31]"Flutter Calculations in Three Degrees of Freedom" (with I. E. Garrick) NACA TR-741, 1942.
[32]"Miscellaneous Tests in Vacuum Sphere on Structural Damping of Airplane Wing Panels," NACA R. B., Oct 1942.
[33]"Preliminary Vibration and Flutter Studies on P-47 Tail," NACA WR L-654, Aug. 1943.
[34]"Flutter Test on SB2U Model in 16-foot Tunnel" (with R. P. Coleman and N. H. Smith), NACA WR-657, Feb 1943.
[35]"Flutter Tests of Modified SB2U Model in 16-foot Tunnel" (with R. P. Coleman and N. H. Smith), NACA WR-742, Aug 1943.
[36]"Vibration Surveys of the P-40 Rudder and Fin-Rudder Assembly" (with A. A. Regier), NACA WR-L-652, April 1943.

[37]"Vibration Surveys of the P-47-B Rudder and Fin-Rudder Assembly" (with A. A. Regier), NACA WR L-653, April 1943.
[38]"Vibration-Response Tests of a 1/5 Scale Model of the Grumman F6F Airplane in the Langley 16-foot High-Speed Tunnel" (with A. A. Regier), NACA WR L-743, 1944.
[39]"Flutter Tests of B-34 Fin-Rudder-Tab System" (with N. H. Smith), NACA WR L-679, Sep 1944.
[40]"Airfoil-Contour Modifications Based on ϵ-Curve Method of Calculating Pressure Distribution," NACA WR L-135, Jul 1944.
[41]"The Theory of Propellers: I. Determination of the Circulation Function and the Mass Coefficient for Dual-Rotating Propellers," NACA TR-775, 1944.
[42]"The Theory of Propellers: II. Method for Calculating the Axial Interference Velocity," NACA TR-776, 1944.
[43]"Effect of a Trailing-Edge Extension of the Characteristics of a Propeller Section" (with G. W. Stickle), NACA WR L-637, 1944.
[44]"The Theory of Propellers: III. Slipstream Contraction with Numerical Values for Two-Blade and Four-Blade Propellers," NACA TR-777, 1944.
[45]"The Theory of Propellers: IV. Thrust, Energy, and Efficiency Formulas for Single and Dual Rotating Propellers with Ideal Circulation Distribution," NACA TR-778, 1944.
[46]"Experiments on Drag of Revolving Disks, Cylinders, and Streamline Rods at High Speeds" (with A. A. Regier), NACA TR-793, 1944.
[47]"Effect of the Lift Coefficient on Propeller Flutter" (with A. A. Regier), NACA WR L-161, Jul 1945.
[48]"Measurements of Pressure Distribution on an Airfoil in the Mach-Number Range Near Unity" (with A. A. Regier), NACA MR. L5H17b AAF, for U. S. Navy Bureau of Aircraft, 1945.
[49]"Pressure Distributions for Representative Airfoils and Related Profiles" (with I. Naiman), NACA TN-1016, Feb 1946.
[50]"Extension of the Chaplygin Proofs on the Existence of Compressible-Flow Solutions to the Supersonic Region," NACA TN-1028, Mar 1946.
[51]"A Condition on the Initial Shock," NACA TN-1029, Mar 1946.
[52]"Note on the Theorems of Bjerkness and Crocco," TN-1073, May 1946.
[53]"The Problem of Noise Reduction in Airplanes" (with A. A. Regier), NACA TN-1145, Aug 1946.
[54]*Theory of Propellers*, McGraw-Hill, New York, 1948.
[55]"Note of the Theory of Hurricanes," Reader's Forum, *Journal of the Aerospace Sciences*, 1952, p. 645.
[56]"Mechanism of Turbulence," *Proceedings of the Second Midwestern Conference on Fluid Mechanics,* Ohio State Univ., 1952, pp. 1–18.
[57]"Limits and Classification of Supersonic Flows," Office of Scientific Research, U. S. Air Force; Univ. of Maryland Institute for Fluid Dynamics and Applied Mathematics, TN BN-23, Mar 1954.
[58]"The Structure of Turbulence," Office of Scientific Research, U. S. Air Force; Univ. of Maryland Institute for Fluid Dynamics and Applied Mathematics, TN BN-31, May 1954.
[59]"The Structure of Turbulence," in *50 Jahre Grenzschichts-forschung*, an anniversary volume for Ludwig Prandtl, Vieweg, Brauschweig, 1955, pp. 55–62.
[60]"Operation Analysis—Optimum Path of an Airplane; Minimum Time to Climb," Republic Aviation Corp. Rept., Feb 1, 1958; revised May 1, 1958.
[61]"Minimuim Take-Off Distance of a Jet Propelled Airplane," Republic Aviation Corp. Rept. Dec 1959.
[62]"Theoretical Investigation of Ducted Propeller Aerodynamics," U. S. Army Transportation Research Command Contract DA 44-177-TC-606, Vol. I and II, Aug 10, 1960.
[63]"Ramjet Compression, Combustion, and Cycle Efficiency at Hypersonic Inlet Velocities," Republic Aviation Corp. Rept., Mar 17, 1961.
[64]"The Stucture of Turbulence," Republic Aviation Corp. Rept., April 10, 1961.
[65]"Theoretical Investigation of Ducted Propeller Aerodynamics," U. S. Army Transportation Research Command Contract DA 44-177-TC-674, Vol. III and IV, Aug 10, 1961.
[66]"Theory of Static Propellers and Helicopter Rotors," United Aircraft Rept., Sikorsky Div. Sep 1968.

Critical Essays

INSPIRED AERODYNAMICS OF WING SECTIONS

by Holt Ashley

The determination of pressure distribution and aerodynamic loads on an airfoil exposed to a two-dimensional uniform stream of incompressible fluid was a much more central problem in aeronautics of the early '30s than it is today. Flight speeds were "microsonic," sweepback was yet to be discovered, and wing aspect ratios were as large as structural considerations would permit. True cantilever monoplanes, however, were a relative novelty, and they required profiles of much higher thickness ratio than biplanes to accommodate load-carrying structure. Thus the stage was set for a general "thick-airfoil" theory. Theodorsen was the man who provided it.

The method of analysis may be regarded as a synthesis of two research streams.[2,3] (Superscripts refer to works listed in the Bibliography by Subject; "Ref." numbers to the publications listed at the end of this essay.) The first went back to the late 19th Century and involved the use of simple conformal transformations to construct parallel flows past specific airfoils from flows around circles, with circulation added to satisfy the "Kutta condition" of smooth fluid departure from the sharp trailing edge. Important examples are associated with the names of Joukowsky, von Mises, and von Kármán and Trefftz. These profiles are not limited to small thickness or camber, but experience showed that the practical needs of structural and aerodynamic designers were not optimally met from the available catalogue.

The other stream—often characterized "thin-airfoil theory"—employed superposition of sources, vortices, and/or doublets to create small perturbations on the uniform flow, cleverly arranged to simulate the effects of actual thickness, camber, and angle of attack. Betz, Munk, Glauert and many other "giants" of early aeronautics contributed.

The evolution of Theodorsen's published work begins with NACA TR-383 of 1931,[1] where he adapts a method that he attributes to Glauert (Ref. 1), who in turn recognized Munk (Ref. 2). The given profile is located on a plane associated with the complex variable ζ, with its leading and trailing edges suitably close to the singular points of the transformation (due to Joukowsky):

$$\zeta = z' + (a^2/z') \tag{1}$$

The corresponding figure in the z' plane turns out to be nearly a circle. A second transformation to the z plane is then carried out, by equating z' with an inverse power series in z, so that the result is a nearly perfect circle centered at the z-origin. Both transformations preserve the uniform stream at infinity and the circulation, whereupon the Kutta condition and angle-of-attack adjustments are easy to accomplish. The whole formulation remains limited to small disturbances, however, since no exact account is taken of the thickness. Pressure distributions over the upper and lower surfaces can be calculated approximately, and in this connection an important feature of TR-383 is the clear separation between the basic loading at the "ideal angle of attack" and the additional loading due to changes from this angle. Experiments on three popular current airfoils show that the former is well predicted by theory. It should be mentioned, incidentally, that the extension of all these methods to find loading on wings of finite span was universally assigned to that durable product of another aeronautical genius: Prandtl's lifting-line theory.

The closely related reports TR-411 (1931 also) and TR-452 (1933) break cleanly from the past by systematically accounting for "arbitrary" thickness, camber, and incidence.[2,3] The only limitations remain those imposed by viscous effects, like flow separation, which invalidate potential theory itself. Transformation (1) is retained, but with the profile carefully placed on the z plane so that the singular points at $\zeta = \pm 2a$ bisect, respectively, lines between the leading and trailing edges and their centers of curvature. Often called a "pseudocircle," the z' figure is then transformed to a true z circle by means of the following:

$$z' = z \exp\left[\sum_{n=1}^{\infty} c_n / z^n\right] \tag{2}$$

Garrick, who was a frequent collaborator in Theodorsen's research, once marked Eq. (2) with an exclamation point (!), comparing it, as a move in development, with a common practice employed during analysis of chess games. The real and imaginary parts of the sum in the Eq. (2) brackets are associated, respectively, with a small number ψ, which fixes the radius distribution of the "pseudocircle," and the "conformal angular distortion" ϵ. These are conjugate quantities in the terminology of complex algebra. Through the use of sums of Fourier-series representations, Theodorsen was able to derive a simple integral relation [Eq. (13) in TR-452[3]] between ϵ and ψ. In turn, this facilitated a rapidly-convergent iterative scheme for evaluating the transformation of Eq. (2). The resulting functions then provide everything needed for efficiently computing pressures and resultant aerodynamic loads, given only the upper- and lower-surface ordinates and the angle of attack.

It is hard to overestimate the impact of Theodorsen's method on subsequent airfoil development in the United States. Through modifications of what came to be known as the "ϵ curve," the designer could make favorable adjustments to the pressure distribution and thus influence boundary-layer transition/separation. It is well known that the problem of finding exact profile shapes, which support prescribed pressure variations, had not been properly posed. But efficient approximate means were in hand,[4] and from them arose the "laminar flow" airfoils and the other NACA series, which played a significant role in improving aircraft designs of the '30s and '40s. The story of their evolution is told, along with a compendium of measured data, by Abbott and von Doenhoff (Ref. 3). A useful by-product of TR-411 and TR-452 was the ability to produce what Theodorsen called "synthetic airfoils"—the profiles generated by selecting appropriate individual terms in the Fourier series for ϵ.[6] Some of them turned out to be quite interesting in their own right; others furnished the starting points for more refined designs. One can speculate that these developments might have taken place, to some degree, without the basic contributions of TR-411 and TR-452. Unless someone else with Theodorsen's insight had supplied an equivalent theory, however, the signposts would not have been as clear and the necessary computations would have been much more difficult.

Lifting-surface flutter is discussed in another section of this volume; but in connection with the aerodynamics of wing sections, Theodorsen's work on the oscillating airfoil deserves special recognition.

Flutter was first encountered on tailplanes and wings during World War I, but rigorous theory for its prediction took many years to evolve. The greatest challenge was to supply aerodynamic terms for the governing equation. Along with aircraft response to atmospheric turbulence, this was the strongest motivation for research on airloads experienced by wings and airfoils performing time-dependent or "unsteady" motions. Early investigators recognized that the first step would be to adapt the methods of thin-airfoil theory so as to account for phenomena such as small oscillations normal to the direction of flight and impulsive changes in angle of attack. For incompressible fluid, Wagner dealt rather completely with the latter problem in 1925 (Ref. 4), and significant contributions to the former during the '20s came from Birnbaum (Ref. 5) and Glauert (Ref. 6). Their approaches were valid but required considerable computation and were approximate in the sense that limitations were placed on the size of the "reduced frequency" k of the oscillation and on the mode of motion. Defined as follows, this k plays a central role in unsteady aerodynamics: $k = \Omega b / V$, where Ω is the circular frequency, b the airfoil semichord, and V the airstream speed (or speed of flight).

Mathematically what needed to be done was clearly defined. In the mid-'30s, just as rapidly-increasing performance of monoplane aircraft exacerbated the threat of flutter, aerodynamicists in several countries independently and almost simultaneously published the solution. At least five names could be mentioned, but the significant fact is that Theodorsen is usually accorded priority.[12] (When listing the order of publication, the noted authority E. Reissner names Theodorsen first—e.g., "On the General Theory of Thin Airfoils for Nonuniform Motion," NACA TN-946, 1944, p. 35.)

The analytical scheme set forth in TR-496[12]—and then elaborated with applications to various types of airfoil-flap motion[14-16]—was complicated. Heavy reliance was placed on the Joukowsky transformation between parallel-stream flows past a circle and a zero-thickness flat plate. At first glance, this may seem an oversimplification, but Theodorsen knew that, within the framework of thin-airfoil theory, the steady-flow problems of thickness and camber can be rigorously separated from the unsteady case on which he focused. He also separated the airloads due to "apparent mass" effects from the "circulatory" phenomena, and he correctly enforced the Kutta condition in the presence of an infinite wake of trailing vortices, whose existence is required as "countervortices" due to changes in the circulation bound to the airfoil (and its transformed circular image). Space considerations prevent even a summary of the mathematical details.

The final product of TR-496 can be described as a set of complex frequency-response functions connecting vertical translation (or bending), angle of attack (or torsion), and aileron rotation angle as "inputs" with unsteady lift, pitching moment, and aileron hinge moment as "outputs." The aileron or trailing-edge flap was aerodynamically unbalanced, with sealed gap, but its chord could be an arbitrary fraction of the airfoil's. Later, with Garrick as coauthor, a trailing-edge tab was added as a fourth degree of freedom.[15] Perhaps the most important discovery of the entire investigation was that, regardless of the nature of the (small) oscillation or of the "output" quantity to be calculated, only a single transcendental function of k appears in their relationship. This is the famous "Theodorsen Function," as follows[12]:

$$C(k) \equiv F + iG = \frac{-J_1 + iY_1}{-(J_1 + Y_0) + i(Y_1 - J_0)} \tag{3}$$

Here J_i and Y_i are Bessel functions of the first and second kinds and order i. Later their complex combinations were also identified with Bessel functions of imaginary argument or with Hankel functions of the second kind. Since suitable tables were available in the 1930s, the calculation of the airloads for arbitrary values of k was greatly facilitated.

The appearance of $C(k)$ as a unique response function was a truly extraordinary result. For airfoils oscillating in a compressible airstream and for three-dimensional lifting surfaces, there is, in essence, a distinct transcendental relation between each type of motion and each aerodynamic generalized force. TR-496 contains other surprises.[12] For example, the unsteady lift associated with the circulatory part of the flow unexpectedly acts exactly through the quarter-chordline for all three types of motion considered.

The main works on flutter[12-16] include, of course, the complete methodology of calculation for the "typical section" idealization of a wing, along with numerous details about the influence of various system parameters on its aeroelastic performance. As time passed and experience accumulated in the aircraft industry, confidence grew in the use of aerodynamic "strip theory" for finite wings and tails. With aerodynamic terms in the equations of motion constructed by adapting the formulas of TR-496, predicted critical "flutter boundaries" proved often to be quite accurate and usually somewhat conservative. The extra "margin of safety" for avoiding this dangerous instability was appreciated. A final measure of the lasting vitality of Theodorsen's contribution is that, even today, more than half a century later, his theory is frequently employed for design calculations on subsonic airplanes.

Not so familiar as his research on airfoils, propellers, and wing flutter are three of Theodorsen's early papers[57-59] dealing with the effects of rectangular wind-tunnel boundaries on tests of lifting surfaces. In TR-410,[57], he credits Glauert's use of the "method of images" to predict the correction that must be made to the measured angle of attack so that the lift is representative of flight in an unbounded airstream. Glauert did this only for a solid set of rectangular walls, with height h and width b. He discovered—as did Theodorsen for other tunnel configurations—that this correction is proportional to lift coefficient times wing plan area divided by test-section cross-sectional area. The factor of proportionality depends on geometry.

Theodorsen's novel inspiration was to extend the analysis to tunnels whose boundaries were partially open to the surrounding chamber. He covered the completely open rectangle,[58] then did cases like closed sidewalls, top and bottom. In most calculations, the wingspan was assumed to be small, so that its lift and that of the image array could be idealized by single centered doublets with their axes horizontal. But he examined "large wing span" with a pair of trailing vortices whose span was three-quarters of the tunnel width; this was done only for closed walls and for open vertical boundaries.[57] Attempts were made to validate some of the results experimentally.[59] Those comparisons were only partially successful, but their failure belies the great assistance that Theodorsen's calculations have furnished over subsequent years to the operators of subsonic test facilities the world around.

The most interesting discovery of TR-410 was perhaps that certain arrangements of boundaries give rise to small or zero "wall corrections" when compared either with solid or entirely open test sections. For instance, the small-wingspan correction is predicted to be zero for a square tunnel with open sidewalls but solid floor and ceiling, as well as zero at $(b/h) = 1.9$ when the open and solid boundaries are interchanged. May we speculate that his proposal for cancelling wall effects was the earliest precursor of the slots and permeable boundaries that later proved so essential for testing in the transonic speed range?

References

1. Glauert, H., "A Theory of Thin Airfoils," Aeronautical Research Council Report and Memoranda 910, 1924.

2. Munk, M. M., "General Theory of Thin Wing Sections," NACA Rept. 142, 1921.

3. Abbot, I. H., and von Doenhoff, A. E., *Theory of Wing Sections,* Dover, New York, 1959.

4. Wagner, H., "Über die Entstehung des dynamischer Augtriebes von Tragflügeln," *Zeitschrift auf M. und M.,* Vol. 5, 1925, pp. 17–35.

5. Birnbaum, W., "Das ebene Problem des schlagenden Flügels," *Zeitschrift auf M. und M.,* Vol. 3, 1923, pp. 290–297.

6. Glauert, H., "The Force and Moment of an Oscillating Airfoil," Aeronautical Research Council Reports and Memoranda 1242, 1929.

REMARKABLE LEGACY IN PROPELLER AERODYNAMICS

by Donald B. Hanson

Propeller analysis and design rank among the richest fields of aerodynamics. There can be little argument on this point when one recognizes that propellers include all of the challenges of wing and airfoil aerodynamics plus those associated with propulsion. Theodorsen's contributions to propeller technology ranged from generation of clear and definitive test reports to development of complete and novel design methodologies for ducted and unducted propellers, and further to solution of mathematical boundary-value problems requiring the most difficult forms of classical analysis. This characteristic of giving equal emphasis to the theoretical and the practical stands out as one of his most remarkable attributes.

Theodorsen's work on propeller aerodynamics fell into three periods. While he was at NACA's Langley Memorial Aeronautical Laboratory, he developed his theory for unducted single and counter-rotating propellers. This culminated in a series of four NACA reports[31–34] published in 1944 that formed the basis for his book *Theory of Propellers*.[36] (Superscripts refer to works listed in the Bibliography by Subject.) In the late '50s and early '60s, he held the post of Director of Scientific Research at Republic Aviation Corporation on Long Island, where he developed his theory for ducted propellers in support of the company's activities with vertical-takeoff airplanes. This work also culminated in a four-volume report published by the U.S. Army in 1960 and 1961.[37,38] Theodorsen's third period of propeller work came later in the 1960s, during his consulting contract at Sikorsky Aircraft, a division of United Aircraft Corporation (now United Technologies). As an extension of his helicopter work, he developed a method to design propellers for static thrust in support of the VTOL (vertical takeoff and landing) work at Hamilton Standard, another division of United Aircraft.

To introduce Theodorsen's propeller work, it is useful to review the concepts of lifting lines and actuator disks. Propeller blades can be treated with good accuracy as lifting lines because of their high aspect ratio and because, in most cases, they are unswept. In a lifting-line analytical method, three-dimensional theory is used to compute the induction, or induced flow angle, at each airfoil section along the span of the blade based on an estimated load distribution. Blade geometry and the induced angles are then used with two-dimensional airfoil data to refine the load estimate in an iterative procedure. The design objective is to stack airfoils along the line in a manner that optimizes performance at a specified condition. Computation of induction for a general loading distribution is difficult. A simple method will be mentioned here, not because it is recommended for design work, but because it actually includes much of the physics of the problem and because it can be used to describe where Theodorsen's work fits into the spectrum of propeller theory in his time.

The simplest induction model of any value for unducted propellers is, of course, the actuator disk. The effect of a delta pressure representing the propeller thrust is analyzed with the help of Bernoulli's equation and conservation of mass, with the result—

$$T = \rho A_{pd}(V + w/2)\, w$$

where V is the forward flight speed, A_{pd} the propeller disk area, and ρ the density. Equation (1) can be read simplistically as thrust $T =$ mass flux $\rho A_{pd}(V + w/2)$ times velocity change w in the ultimate wake.

Propeller operating regimes can be defined according to the magnitude of the induction at the propeller $w/2$ compared with the flight speed V:

1) For light loading and moderate to high flight speed, $w/2$ will be small compared to V and can therefore be neglected in the parentheses of Eq. (1), linearizing the thrust-induction relationship.

2) For high loading or low flight speed, $w/2$ and V will be comparable and thus nonlinear effects must be taken into account.

3) For the static condition, $V = 0$, the thrust-induction relationship is fundamentally nonlinear and analysis by classical means becomes very difficult.

The first (light-loading) regime was analyzed by the English applied mathematician Sydney Goldstein ("On the Vortex Theory of Screw Propellers," *Proceedings of the Royal Society* (London), Series A, Vol. 123, No. 792, 1929, pp. 440–465). By applying Betz's theorem, that the optimum propeller circulation distribution resulted in a far wake of helicoidal vortex sheets convected rearward as a rigid surface, Goldstein solved for his circulation, or K, factors. These give the spanwise distribution of circulation per unit induced flow for a propeller optimized in terms of induced loss. The factors $K(x)$ vary with radius ratio x but otherwise depend only on blade number and advance ratio (ratio of flight speed to blade tip-speed). The Betz/Goldstein work was the foundation that Theodorsen used to reach into operating regimes 2 and 3 in the list above. In fact, in the introduction to his book,[36] Theodorsen described the Goldstein work as "unquestionably the greatest single step in the evolution of propeller theory."

However, the accuracy of Goldstein's analysis deteriorates at high advance ratio and does not apply at all to dual (counter-rotating) propellers. Recognizing that design tables were needed for these applications, which were too difficult for the computational means of the day, and pressed by the urgency of the war effort, Theodorsen

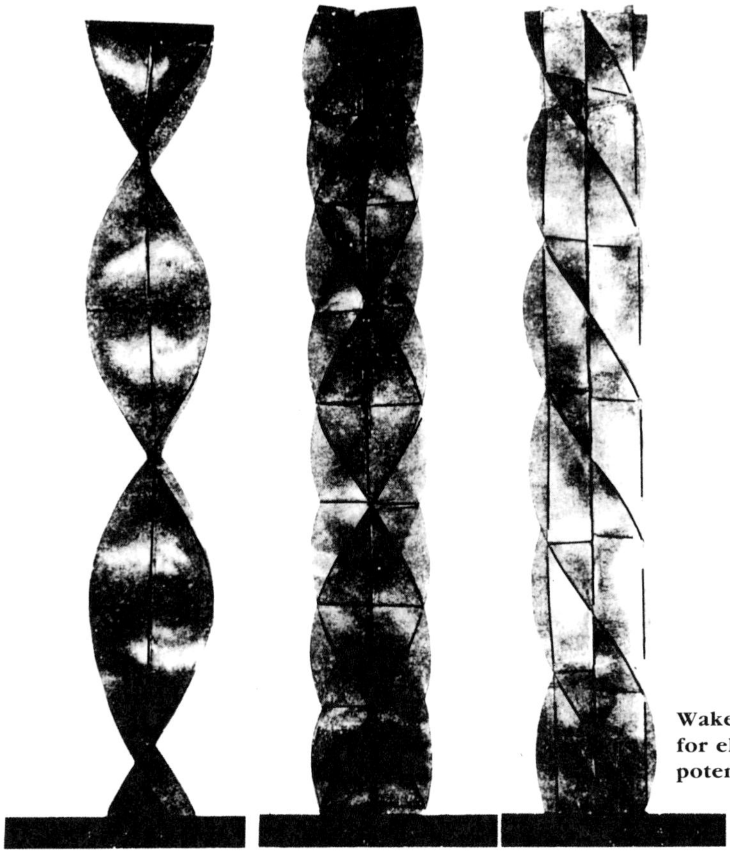

Wake-sheet models for electrolytic tank potential measures.[31, 36]

resorted to other than computational methods. In a major experimental effort at Langley, he developed an electrolytic tank measurement method based on the analogy between electric current and fluid flow fields.[31] He modeled the vortex wakes with twisted celluloid sheets, samples of which are shown here. The models were immersed in a cylindrical tube of tap water, which acted as the electrolyte, and an electric voltage was imposed along the length of the tube. Since celluloid is an insulator, it represented the impervious nature of vortex sheets. The potential drop across the sheets, corresponding to the circulation, was found by probing around the sheets with an electrode. In these experiments, Theodorsen first verified the K factors computed by Goldstein and then filled in data needed for single-rotation propellers at the higher advance ratios. Next, he tested models of dual-rotation wakes, as with the left two panels in the figure, and finally tested a configuration representing a propeller with exit guide vanes, as in the right panel of the figure. Some 60 wake models were evaluated to cover all regimes of interest. (Theodorsen would be pleased to know that a wind-tunnel model of a propfan with guide vanes was tested at NASA Lewis Research Center in 1989.)

Theodorsen's most significant contribution to propeller aerodynamics was to show that, with the correct interpretation, Goldstein's optimum loading method could be extended to the heavy loading case (regime 2 in the list above). This is done by referencing the helicoid parameters (diameter and advance ratio) to the ultimate (contracted) wake values, rather than to conditions at the propeller disk. Theodorsen's book presents proof of this heavy-loading result and provides a detailed methodology with many charts and tables for applying it to the design problem.

Use of this design method is facilitated by special coefficients defined for the purpose. Theodorsen had a wonderful knack for reducing complex analyses to simple formulas containing these coefficienсts and then plotting them in a form that could be interpolated by the designer. The best known of these are the mass coefficient κ and the axial energy-loss factor ϵ. The mass coefficient is Goldstein's K factor averaged over the cross-sectional area of the wake:

$$\kappa = 2\int_0^1 K(x)x\,\mathrm{d}x$$

In one interpretation, κ is the ratio of the rearward displacement velocity at the vortex sheet (or blade) to the displacement velocity averaged over the disk. The value of this interpretation is that it can be used as a correction to actuator-disk induction values. The ϵ gives the axial energy loss between a pair of vortex sheets and appears in many of Theodorsen's working fomulas; and ϵ appears also in his discussion of partition of energy losses between axial, radial, and tangential velocity components and a pressure loss that had been overlooked by previous investigators. With these two coefficients, Theodorsen was able to rewrite the thrust-axial induction relationship as follows:

$$T = \rho A_{wd}[V + w(1/2 + \epsilon/\kappa)]\ \kappa w$$

where A_{wd} is the cross-sectional area of the wake disk. This is an exact result, still in the form of the actuator-disk formula in Eq. (1), that gives induction at the blade, as needed for design work, rather than induction averaged over the disk. His book and reports give graphs of κ and ϵ covering the ranges of interest for design applications.

At the time of his book's publication, Theodorsen felt that the heavy-loading design cruise condition (regime 2 in the list above) was the limit of theoretical analysis. On page 7 of the book, he makes this statement: "For the take-off condition, the [wake] contraction is very large. A propeller is not and cannot be designed for the take-off conditions, however. Estimates of take-off characteristics may most easily be based on available test data or experience with similar designs." The static condition (regime 3) is even more difficult and seemed unapproachable at the time. Nevertheless, the static-thrust problem for helicopters and VTOL propellers was precisely the subject of Theodorsen's final propeller studies. Once again, Theodorsen showed that the Goldstein factors could be applied to the static propeller problem if they were properly reflected from the ultimate wake to the propeller disk. This proof is given in one of his consulting reports to Sikorsky Aircraft.[39] Again, he gives a complete design methodology, including numerous charts and graphs computed numerically.

The above discussion all relates to unducted propellers. However, in his middle period of propeller activity at Republic Aviation, Theodorsen concentrated on ducted propellers for VTOL aircraft. One of the motivations for this work was a "Flying Jeep" for the U. S. Army. The Goldstein factors obviously no longer applied because of the different boundary conditions at the blade tips. As might be guessed, Theodorsen approached this problem by reworking the Goldstein analysis with modified boundary conditions. This significant feat of applied mathematics produced Theodorsen's own induction factors, which are published in his report to the Army as the basis of a design methodology for VTOL's and other lift-fan applications.[37,38] The Army report in four volumes contains several model problems related to vertical-take-off configurations that Theodorsen treated with methods of classical analysis. In addition to the induction-factor analysis, these include the flow field of a nonuniform sink distribution in a circular disk, a wing with a line sink on the upper surface and a jet on the lower surface, flow field for a cylindrical nonuniform vortex sheet, and velocity field and forces on a flat plate due to a cylindrical jet. The Army report also includes a great deal of design information for the deflection vanes and baffle systems needed for VTOL's as well as for the propellers.

Theodorsen's propeller aerodynamic theories and design methodologies form a remarkable legacy. In his consulting days at United Aircraft, he often expressed frustration that computers were not more advanced. He could write out the equations for the full static-thrust problem, but the required computational power had not yet become available. It is interesting to speculate what Theodorsen's contributions would have been if he had had today's supercomputers at his disposal.

HIS MODERN VIEW OF TURBULENCE

by Anthony E. Perry

Theodore Theodorsen published only a few papers on turbulence. However, one can see from the titles he used, such as "The Mechanism of Turbulence" and "The Structure of Turbulence," that he was concerned very much with the heart of the turbulence problem.

His work was done between 1952 and 1961, and for its day was quite revolutionary.[46,48,49] (Superscripts refer to works listed in the Bibliography by Subject; "Ref." refers to works at the end of this essay.) One could probably say that Theodorsen was one of the early pioneers seeking a structure of turbulence. As he pointed out, because of the complexity and lack of any convincing mathematical solutions, many decades of turbulence research did not even consider the possibility of structure. "The situation was further aggravated," he said, "by the fact that most authors were accustomed to the idea that there was a perfectly random motion of particles and that no basic pattern should or could exist."[48] In today's terminology, Theodorsen was one of the early pioneers of the "coherent structure" concept and was seeking a mechanism for turbulent shear flow that would replace the crude and arbitrary gradient-diffusion models for momentum transport. This was an activity that did not become fashionable throughout the world until the mid-to-late '70s; it is still very much a growing activity.

One wonders why it took the world so long to follow Theodorsen's approach and why he did not receive more adequate recognition. I think the world was simply not ready for his ideas. The classical mixing-length theories and eddy-viscosity formulations had yet to run their courses. Computers, which arrived on the scene in the '60s, were very primitive and the simple mixing-length and eddy-viscosity closure models were perfectly suited to the capabilities of the early machines. Theodorsen's conjectures and ideas are more in tune with the turbulence-structure research being pursued today, which in part requires supercomputers. His main problem was that he lived in the wrong era.

How does Theodorsen's contribution fit current thinking? His work and ideas are based primarily on his consideration of the Navier-Stokes equations expressed in a form that gave the material derivative of the square of vorticity. For equilibrium turbulence, he showed that a "creative" term had to be in balance with a "destructive" term, which involved viscous diffusion. The creative term had to be positive, and from this he concluded that an essential element in turbulence was vortex stretching. By intuition, this led him to propose that there exists a definite structure characterized by a universal element of turbulence. This element, because of an obvious resemblance in form, he called the "horseshoe."[48]

The intuitive argument used by Theodorsen involved concepts of lift and drag on vortex tubes. A more rigorous approach adopted many years later (1982) by Perry and Chong (Ref. 1) using Biot-Savart-law computation, showed that a simple isolated horshoe-like vortex, together with its image in the wall, does indeed produce a self-induced stretching of its vortex tubes, just as envisaged by Theodorsen. Such horseshoe structures were observed experimentally by Weske and Plankholt in early transitional stages of turbulence, and photographs are given in one of Theodorsen's papers.[48] The more recent photo here from Perry, Lim and Teh (Ref. 2) shows vortices coming from a tripwire immersed in a laminar boundary layer, and it is quite obvious that these vortices with spanwise waviness rapidly turn into horseshoe-like structures. Perry et al postulated with some experimental support that turbulent spots consist of an array of hairpin or horseshoe-like vortices arranged in staggered rows (Ref. 3). Theodorsen emphasized the importance of three-dimensionality in the transition

Theodorsen's "horseshoe" vortices coming from a tripwire immersed in a laminar boundary layer—from Perry, Lim, and Teh (Ref. 2).

process, and said that a horseshoe vortex did not have "ends" but was really a "bent vortex line."

For fully turbulent flow, the drawing here shows the conjectured structure given by Theodorsen.[48] This is the structure that he claimed produces the momentum exchange responsible for the Reynolds shear stress. He was obviously aware of the need to have an hierarchy of eddy scales to explain the Kolmogorov spectral region, and that dissipation must occur with fine-scale motions. To account for this, he very creatively proposed a primary horseshoe (responsible for the Reynolds shear stress) with "lower order" horseshoes, i.e., secondary and tertiary horseshoes riding on the surface of the primary horseshoe and "orbiting" it.

In today's modeling, many workers have adopted the primary horseshoe model; e.g., in Townsend's attached-eddy hypothesis (of 1976) the horseshoe model would be a perfect candidate (Ref. 4). However, instead of considering only one scale of attached eddy proportional to the boundary-layer width or thickness, as Theodorsen

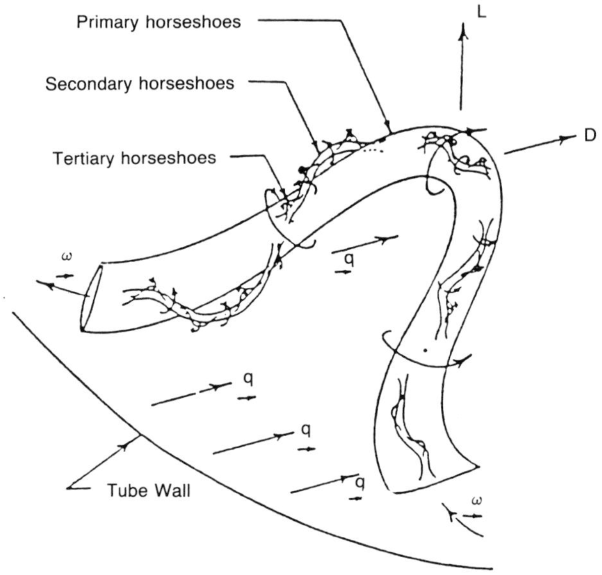

Theodorsen's depiction of a horseshoe at large Reynolds number.[48] Note the lift (L) and drag (D) and the lower-order horsehoes.

had done, Townsend models a range of scales of geometrically similar eddies attached to the boundary. As Perry and Chong (Ref. 1) and Perry, Henbest and Chong (Ref. 3) have pointed out, such a range of scales is necessary for explaining spectral scaling laws at moderate to low wave-numbers, the logarithmic mean velocity profiles and the broad-band turbulence intensity distributions, and the Reynolds shear stress. In fact, the use of horseshoe vortices enables a link to be established between the mean flow, Reynolds shear stress, turbulence intensity, and spectra. This shows great promise for leading to a closure hypothesis in the future. That, of course, must have been the dream of Theodorsen.

At high wave-numbers, the secondary and tertiary vortices of Theodorsen are currently replaced in Perry et al (Ref. 3) by fine-scale detached eddy motions, which are statistically isotropic and surround the attached eddies, and these give rise to the Kolmogov region. This, of course, is just as speculative as the suggestion by Theodorsen of lower-order horseshoes, and more work is required to clarify this aspect of the turbulence problem. In fully turbulent flow, the attached eddies are very difficult to see clearly using fluid markers. Head and Bandyopadhyay used smoke-filled layers and sheets of laser light to show that structures exist that roughly resembled horseshoe vortices, with their planes approximately 45 deg to the wall in the downstream direction (Ref. 5). This angle, amazingly enough, was the same as the one conjectured by Theodorsen. However, the structures are very jumbled and complex, as indeed are those that have been produced using the full-direction simulations of wall turbulence on supercomputers at NASA Ames Research Center [see Kim and Moin (Ref. 6) and Spalart (Ref. 7)]. The attached eddies of the simple horseshoe type should really be regarded as "representative" or "statistical" abstractions, which can be adduced only by some sort of conditional averaging process—if indeed such a process could be discovered or devised. Work along these lines has been pursued at NASA-Ames [see Kim (Ref. 8)].

In his papers, Theodorsen does not give clear mathematical interpretations; his reasoning is intuitive, much is conjecture. Nevertheless, the picture he creates bears a remarkable similarity to the picture emerging from work being carried out today. His paper "The Structure of Turbulence," published in *50 Jahre Grenzschichtforshung*, has been an inspiratiion to me since my days as a Ph.D. candidate, and it has been a favorite article read and well-thumbed by my many research students over the years.

References

1. Perry, A. E., and Chong, M. S., "On the Mechanism of Wall Turbulence," *Journal of Fluid Mechanics*, Vol. 119, 1982, pp. 173–217.

2. Perry A. E., Lim, T. T., and Teh, E. W., "A Visual Study of Turbulent Spots," *Journal of Fluid Mechanics,* Vol. 104, 1981, pp. 387–405.

3. Perry, A. E., Henbest, S. M., and Chong, M. S., "A Theoretical and Experimental Study of Wall Turbulence," *Journal of Fluid Mechanics*, Vol. 165, 1986, pp. 163–199.

4. Townsend, A. A., *The Structure of Turbulent Sheer Flow*, 2nd edition, Cambridge Univ. Press, Cambridge, England, 1976.

5. Head, M. R., and Bandyopadhyay, P. R., "New Aspects of Turbulent Boundary Layer Structure," *Journal of Fluid Mechanics*, Vol. 107, 1981, pp. 297–338.

6. Kim, J., and Moin, P., "The Structure of the Vorticity Field in Turbulent Channel Flow: Part 2. Study of Ensembled Average Fields," *Journal of Fluid Mechanics*, Vol. 162, 1985, pp. 339–363.

7. Spalart, P. R., "Direct Simulation of a Turbulent Boundary Layer up to $R_\theta = 1410$," *Journal of Fluid Mechanics,* Vol. 187, pp. 61–98.

8. Kim, J., "Evolution of a Vortical Structure Associated with the Bursting Event in a Channel Flow," *Fifth Symposium on Turbulent Shear Flow*, Cornell Univ., Ithaca, NY, 1985, p. 9.23.

PIONEERING IN AEROELASTICITY

by Robert H. Scanlan

It is enlightening, as a way of fully appreciating Theodorsen's major contributions to aeroelasticity, to take a brief look at the early stages of his preparation for a career in engineering. In particular, his solid training in fluid mechanics and thermodynamics played a key role in his subsequent professional work.

His primary studies were in mechanical engineering at the Norwegian Institute of Technology in Trondheim. In 1921, he received the highest obtainable grade for his student project, "Heat Transfer in a Smoke Pipe." After graduation he was appointed research fellow, then later an instructor, in mechanical engineering, carrying out heat-transfer, vibration and other studies under Professor A. Watzinger. The following year he became an instructor in mechanical engineering at The Johns Hopkins University.

While teaching engineering mechanics and thermodynamics at Johns Hopkins from 1924 to 1929, Theodorsen carried out extensive experimental research on the combustion of oil in small furnaces. He also registered in 1928 as a graduate student in the Dept. of Physics, pursuing courses in physical optics, X-rays, thermodynamics, heat conduction, hydrodynamics, atomic theory, theoretical physics and applied mathematics, this last under F. D. Murnaghan. His doctoral dissertation[62] consisted of two parts—"On Propagation of Large Disturbances in a Gas" and "On the Combustion of Oil." (Superscripts key references in the Bibliography by Subject; "Ref." numbers give references at the end of this essay.) The former was primarily theoretical, written under the general direction of K. F. Herzfeld of the Physics Dept. The latter was largely experimental, reflecting his strong mechanical-engineering interests. Fluid mechanics and thermodynamics were dissertation themes that would reappear in his later work.

Through the urging of Joseph S. Ames, then president of Hopkins and chairman of the Executive Committee of the National Advisory Committee for Aeronautics (NACA), Theodoresn joined the Langley Laboratory, which was then an NACA organization of relatively modest size. Within a short time he was appointed head of its Physical Research Division, where he directed the work of several highly qualified and enthusiastic researchers, whose work later became a credit both to NACA and to themselves. It was here that he came to collaborate, in particular, with I. E. Garrick, who specialized in applied mathematics and aeroelasticity.

As his doctoral dissertation and his subsequent publications readily reveal, Theodorsen was not confined in his interests to pure theory, nor exclusively to aerodynamics. He sustained a strong interest in experiments and their normative value for theory. While, as his personal history shows, he was an accomplished theoretician, he remained very much the engineer, ready to put theory to arduous test or to present theoretical ideas in ways calculated to aid practitioners.

At NACA, Theodorsen tackled one of the agency's more practical immediate problems: the determination of the pressure distribution on an airfoil of arbitrary camber and thickness. The problem was fully susceptible to theoretical fluid-mechanical treatment, and he approached it with insight, and notable success. By the time he worked on this problem, he had clearly acquired an unusual fluency in the techniques of complex flow potentials and conformal mappings applied to (and extending) the analytic airfoil theory of Munk, Glauert, and Joukowsky. This fluency was certainly amply demonstrated later in his brilliant analysis of airfoil flutter. His work on predicting the pressure distributions on airfoils of arbitrary profile (not the immediate subject of this essay) was among the several notable and long-lasting contributions he made to aeronautics.

The late '20s and early '30s saw great ferment in the field of what much later acquired the name "aeroelasticity." In the broadest terms, at the then ever-increasing flight speeds, aircraft lifting surfaces were exhibiting dangerous vibrations in flight, and existing theory was inadequate to cope with the phenomena witnessed. The carefully measured static-force coefficients obtained for the steady-state conditions of the airfoils were proving unequal to the task of characterizing the evolution of forces upon them as they deflected rapidly in the passing airstream. While the force acting on an airfoil fixed in an airstream is steady and proportional to the strength of its "starting vortex," the force on a moving airfoil is variable, lagging behind the movement and depending importantly on the vorticity shed into the near wake.

As early as 1924, two researchers in Germany, Birnbaum (Ref. 1) at Göttingen and Wagner (Ref. 2) at Charlottenburg, had produced dissertations mathematically describing the force evolution on an airfoil undergoing, in the one case, sinusoidal oscillations and, in the other, a step change in angle of attack. By 1929, English researchers, notably Bairstow (Ref. 3), Lamb (Ref. 4), and Glauert (Ref. 5), had discussed theoretical forces on the oscillating airfoil. Again in Germany, Küssner (Ref. 6) had analyzed fluctuating forces on a vibrating airfoil by that same year.

Theodorsen set to work on the oscillating-airfoil (flutter) problem quite independently. In 1934 he completed the manuscript for what became Technical Report 496, one of the most widely disseminated and quoted reports from NACA.[12] This remarkable report constitutes the centerpiece of Theodorsen's contribution to aeroelasticity. In it, he first treats the moving airfoil in two dimensions, under a relative horizontal wind velocity v, as a flat plate (straight line), thus capturing the primary effects of its motion. He then proceeds to define the velocity potentials for the noncirculatory flow due to the position and vertical velocity of the individual parts of a wing-aileron system represented by the straight line that coincides with the diameter of a unit circle. The aileron was assumed to be attached at its leading edge to the main portion of the airfoil; all deflections away from the horizontal axis were assumed small.

Next, the velocity potentials corresponding to the defined motions, and to a distributed surface of discontinuity extending infinitely rearward in the wake from the trailing edge, were defined for the circulatory flow, the magnitude of the circulation being determined by the Kutta condition proscribing infinite velocity at the trailing edge. When the defined motions of the airfoil components and the wake vorticity distribution were all specified as being sinusoidal based on the airfoil circular frequency ω, some remarkable results emerged: all circulation-related forces act through the forward one-quarter-chord point of the chord of width $2b$ of the airfoil—as in steady-state theory—and both forces and moments depend upon the product CQ, where, defining the key dimensionless reduced frequency parameter as $k = (b\omega)/v$, the function $C = C(k)$ is given as follows (the integrals being over the dimensionless airfoil wake region):

$$C(k) = \frac{\displaystyle\int_1^\infty \frac{x}{\sqrt{x^2-1}}\, e^{-ikx}\, dx}{\displaystyle\int_1^\infty \frac{x+1}{\sqrt{x^2-1}}\, e^{-ikx}\, dx} \qquad (1)$$

For the case of undeflected aileron, Q can be recognized as the vertical velocity of the rearward 1/4-chord point of the airfoil.

According to I. E. Garrick (see page 21), Theodorsen assigned the integral relation leading to the function $C(k)$ to him to be evaluated, first by numerical means and later analytically. The analytical form, after some questions of the convergence of the integrals are resolved, may be given as follows:

$$C(k) = F(k) + iG(k) = \frac{H_1^{(2)}(k)}{H_1^{(2)}(k) + iH_0^{(2)}(k)} \tag{2}$$

where $H_i^{(2)}$ are Hänkel functions of k.

This now-famous function, corroborated by the parallel work of Küssner and others, has gone on to an almost independent life of its own. It has been featured centrally in countless practical calculations of the flutter susceptibility of aircraft lifting surfaces in subsonic flow up to Mach numbers as high as 0.65—even up to the present day. It has been generalized to cases of finite aspect ratio (Ref. 7); it figures in propulsion analyses of the flapping flight of birds and the swimming of fish; and it and its generic cousins have been featured in the oscillation of airfoils in compressible flow.

Garrick (Ref. 8) demonstrated the Fourier transform relationship of $C(k)$ to the Wagner indicial function $\phi(vt/b)$ defining the evolution of circulatory lift following an impulsive change in airfoil angle of attack; and to the Küssner function $\psi(vt/b)$ describing the lift evolution of an airfoil penetrating a vertical gust "wall." Sears (Ref. 9) described the force evolution on a thin airfoil penetrating a sinusoidal vertical gust and demonstrated its relation too to $C(k)$. Thus, of the "four famous functions" of motional airfoil incompressible lift theory: Wagner, Küssner, Theodorsen, and Sears, all are generically tied together via $C(k)$. This remarkably coherent system of results emphasizes the penetrating insight of Theodorsen in his primary treatment of the flutter problem.

It should be underscored here that the fundamental requirement that culminated in these succinct characterizations of airfoil forces via $C(k)$ was the satisfaction of the Kutta trailing-edge condition. Thus, generic relatives of $C(k)$ can be anticipated wherever the Kutta condition remains in force. Where this condition is absent—as in the cases of bluff bodies with strongly separated flow—a circulation function like $C(k)$ becomes inapplicable. This is mentioned here because, like many another broadly applicable analytical device (one recalls *Mc/I* in the stress-analysis field!), the function $C(k)$ has, in the last 50 years, received its share of abuse, notable cases being attempts to apply it or its implications to the aerodynamics of bridge decks (Refs. 10–12), which are decidedly bluff bodies. Scanlan and Tomko (Refs. 13 and 14) and Försching (Ref. 15) have responded to this misuse, although misapplications appear even now, with continuing momentum of their own.

After completion of NACA TR-496, Theodorsen collaborated with Garrick on three more important contributions to incompressible-flow flutter analysis.[14–16] Report 685 pursued calculational aspects of three-degree-of-freedom flutter together with some experimental corroborations; Report 736 added a tab degree of freedom to the theoretical analysis; and Report 741 returned to problems of practical calculation, including the effects of structural damping. All of these studies were carried out with the meticulous care and insightful responsibility of these two remarkable collaborators.

After his excursions into basic flutter theory, in the 1940s Theodorsen became involved in many aspects of its practical application. He was in particular associated with research into the nature and amount of structural damping in models, the three-dimensional vibration modes of models and full-scale aircraft, and applied flutter analyses of specific U.S. aircraft of importance in World War II, notably the PBM, P-40, P-47, SB2U, and F6F.

Theodorsen's original analytical method in TR-496 has since been more succinctly summarized (Ref. 16). (This reference also treats many new developments in the field.) Küssner later completed a parallel theory taking airfoil thickness effects into account (Ref. 17). The entire field has in fact been extended to all flight speed regimes, into three dimensions, and into nonlinear effects, with modern high-speed computing figuring prominently. By 1976 Försching had already commented on some of these developments (Ref. 18). (The reader may also wish to peruse Ref. 19–22.)

It is a paradigm of technical development that once a landmark understanding is achieved others benefit by and extend the accomplishment. An original breakthrough provides subsequent researchers with the comforting reassurance that the landmark is there to lend validity to their points of departure. So it has been in the field of aeroelasticity, where the insistent drive toward ever-greater flight vehicle performance has pushed aeroelastic research far beyond the plateau upon which Theodorsen's pioneering work placed it in 1934. Without exception, however, the newer contributors appear to have been fully aware of—and have acknowledged—the "giant shoulders" upon which they have stood to launch their own contributions.

References

1. Birnbaum, W., "Das ebene Problem des schlagenden Flügels," *Zeitschrift für angewandte Mathematik und Mechanik*, Vol. 4, 1924.

2. Wagner, H., "Über die Enstehung des dynamischen Auftriebes von Tragflügeln," *Zeitschrift für angewandte Mathematik und Mechanik*, Vol. 5, 1925.

3. Bairstow, L., "The Theory of Wing Flutter, *Br. ARC G24.18*, Oct. 1925.

4. Lamb, H., "Flutter Theory—Note on Dimensions," *Br. ARC Ft. 17*, June 1927.

5. Glauert, H., "The Force and Moment of an Oscillating Airfoil," *BR. ARC, R&M 1216*, Nov. 1928.

6. Küssner, H. G., "Schwingungen von Flugzeugflügeln," *DLV Jahrbuch*, 1929, pp. 3413–334; also, *Luftfarhtforschung,* Vol. 4, No. 44, 1929.

7. Reissner, E., "Effect of Finite Span on the Airload Distributions for Oscillating Wings: I—Aerodynamic Theory of Oscillating Wings of Finite Span," NACA TN-1194, 1947.

8. Garrick, I. E., "On Some Fourier Transforms in the Theory of Nonstationary Flows," *Proceedings of the Fifth International Congress for Applied Mechanics*, Wiley, New York, 1939, pp. 590–593.

9. Sears, W. R., "Some Aspects of Nonstationary Airfoil Theory and Its Practical Application," *Journal of the Aeronautical Sciences*, Vol. 8, No. 3, 1941, pp., 104–108.

10. Bleich, F., "Dynamic Instability of Truss-Stiffened Suspension Bridges under Wind Action," *Proceedings of the ASCE*, Vol. 74, No. 8, 1948, pp. 1269–1314; Vol. 75, No. 3, 1949, pp. 413–416; Vol. 75, No. 6, 1949, pp., 855–865.

11. Rocard, Y., *L'instabilité en mécanique*, Masson & Cie, Paris, 1945, Chap. 4.

12. Selberg, A., and Hjorth-Hansen, E., "The Fate of Flat-Plate Aerodynamics in the World of Bridge Decks," *Proceedings of the Theodorsen Colloquium, Det Kongelige Norske Videnskabers Selskab*, Trodheim, 1976, pp. 101–113.

13. Scanlan, R. H., and Tomko, J. J. "Airfoil and Bridge-Deck Flutter Derivatives," *Journal of Engineering Mechanics Division, ASCE,* Vol., 97, No. EM6, Dec. 1971, pp. 1717–1737.

14. Scanlan, R. H., "On the State of Stability Considerations for Suspended-Span Bridges under Wind," *Practical Experiences with Flow-Induced Vibrations*, edited by E. Naudascher and D. Rockwell, Springer-Verlag, New York, 1980, pp. 595–618.

15. Försching, H. W., *Grundlagen der Aeroelastik,* Springer-Verlag, Berlin, 1974, pp. 597.

16. Dowell, E. H., et al, *A Modern Course in Aeroelasticity*, 2nd edition, Kluwer, Dordrecht, The Netherlands, 1989.

17. Küssner, H. G., and von Gorup, G., "Instationäre Linearisierte Theorie der Flügelprofile endlicher Dicke in inkompressible Strömung," *Mitt. MPI für Strömungsforschung, Aerodyn. Versuchsanstalt Göttingen*, No. 26, 1960.

18. Förschung, H. W., "Unsteady Airload Measurements on Oscillating Lifting Systems and Bodies," *Proceedings of the Theodorsen Colloquium, Det Kongelige Norske Videnskabers Selskob,* Trondheim, 1976, pp. 36–53.

19. Hajela, P., "Recent Trends in Aeroelasticity, Structures, and Structural Dynamics," *Proceedings of the Bisplinghoff Symposium,* Univ. of Florida, Gainesville, FL, 1987.

20. Krothapalli, A., and Smith, C., eds., *Recent Advances in Aerodynamics,* Springer-Verlag, New York, 1984.

21. McCroskey, W. J., "Unsteady Airfoils," *Annual Review of Fluid Mechanics,* Vol. 14, 1982, p. 285–311.

22. Dowell, E. H., and Ilgamov, M., *Studies in Nonlinear Aeroelasticity,* Springer-Verlag, New York, 1988.

A BIOGRAPHICAL REMINISCENCE

THEODORE THEODORSEN

OVER THE YEARS -
***from the left* -**
student at Trondheim
with grandson, John
with his daughter
a spry step on 79th birthday
at ease at home

Theodore Theodorsen (Jan. 8, 1897–Nov. 6, 1978)

ABOUT MY FATHER

by Muriel Theodorsen Williams, B.S.E.E.

A friend of that brilliant inventor Nikola Tesla opined that he never quite left his own world of thought and technical problems. This could be said of my father too. Men like them are often insufficiently acclaimed for their achievements, but they are compensated to some extent by the pleasure and excitement they experience in exercising their God-given powers of intellect. Tesla said that in his lifetime he had had "more than his full measure of this exquisite enjoyment." Father himself declared that it was in a mental state of deep concentration that he was the happiest. Both men, from what I have read of Tesla and learned about Father, made a conscious and concientious effort to keep a part of their mind clear and uncluttered and receptive. Father purposefully seldom read anything technical. He relied chiefly on two books: Hutte's *Des Ingenieurs Taschenbuch* from student days and the *Handbuch Der Physik*. He had a prodigious memory and recall. When pondering a problem, and even when working on something else, a part of his mind was always seeking for the key to the solution; waiting, waiting for a flash of inspiration. This period could span several years. Then inspiration came as a clear signal. It was as though he had been expecting a message.

When he arrived at the Langley Memorial Aeronautical Laboratory of the National Advisory Committee for Aeronautics (NACA) in 1929, immediately after getting a Ph.D. in physics from Johns Hopkins University, the young engineer-physicist was assigned to solve an unusual and pressing problem. Langley Laboratory was expanding rapidly and a new test facility was to be constructed on a site which had been used as a practice bombing range in World War (WW) I. When an undetonated bomb was unearthed, the general contractor refused to proceed until the area was cleared of this potential danger to the workmen. Various organizations were asked for advice. When no proposed methods proved satisfactory, the problem was given to Father, who in his usual quiet and seemingly effortless way devised an instrument to detect metals. On the first day the grounds were scanned with it, the detector located several hidden bombs. One was live! This device was certainly one of the earliest metal detectors invented, if not the very first one.

Soon after, Father was appointed Chief Physicist of Langley Laboratory with the title Chief of the Physical Research Division. He remained in this position until he resigned in 1946 to participate in the organization of an aeronautical institution in Brazil.

At Langley he did a prodigious amount of work. Aerodynamicists know him best, perhaps, for his work on flutter. The paper NACA published on this subject in 1935 proved to be of such importance that it had the distinction (rare in technical literature) of being reprinted five years later.[12] Flutter was a mysterious phenomenon in those days. It was the unrecognized cause of many airplane crashes. His basic flutter theory resolved the mystery and had the practical result of providing a means to calculate the flutter speed of almost any structure. It was a breakthrough in aerodynamics. The risk of producing airplanes or components that fluttered in flight could be almost entirely circumvented by applying his theory at the drafting-board stage. All large manufacturers established sections on flutter in their engineering departments; and Father was in great demand as a consultant. Flutter of course remains an important field.

In an attempt to solve the problem of determining airfoil profiles with laminar flow and consequent low drag, Father developed what has become known as the "exact theory of wing sections of arbitrary shape." His NACA publication predicts the pressure distribution along an airfoil of arbitrary shape, providing the flow is laminar.[2] Various authors have termed this paper elegant and classic. Theoreticians Sydney Goldstein and M. J. Lighthill have worked out approximations and variations on this theme.

The inverse of this theory—that is, working from an established pressure distribution to determine the corresponding shape of an airfoil having laminar flow—would be a most effective way to design airfoils. But according to Bryan Twaites in *Incompressible Aerodynamics* (1960, p. 143), "No full solution of the inverse problem has yet been given." Nevertheless, engineers at NACA in the late Thirties attempted to do this. Apparently by rough approximations and considerable wind-tunnel testing they, led by Eastman Jacobs, produced a series of airfoils superior to earlier ones as regards drag. In WW II, the P-51 Mustang fighter was the first plane to be equipped with wings of one of these designs. It was this now famous paper on exact wing section theory that provided the inspiration for the development of NACA low-drag or laminar-flow airfoils (see *Engineer-in-Charge* by James R. Hansen, NASA, Washington, D.C., 1987).

In propeller design, problems, and theory, Father was also expert. In 1948, McGraw-Hill published a text written by him on the theory of propellers. Throughout his life he was a consultant in this field. His practice related to single, dual-rotation, and ducted propellers, helicopter rotors, VTOL propellers and ship propellers. His clients included Fairchild, Northrop, Sikorsky, Hamilton Standard, Republic Aviation (where in later years he was Chief of Research), Stanley Works, Newport News Shipbuilding, Norfolk Naval Shipyard, and New York Shipbuilding.

Father made refinements of the famous NACA cowling initially developed by Fred Weick and his associates at NACA. Their excellent work had been chiefly empirical. With his analytical approach Father was able to establish certain principles of cowling design, and consequently to add improvements.[10] The cowling based on his patent (No. 2270912) is the one used on most radial aircraft engines since 1940. Although NACA, as is routine, retained the U. S. patent rights, Father retained rights to the British patent. During WW II the British used this cowling on the Bristol Beau fighter plane without license. For this infringement, he and a friend, E. F. Andrews of Chicago, who handled the litigation, received a substantial settlement.

Later in life, Father attacked the two areas that interested him the most, fluid turbulence and relativity. Sir Horace Lamb, the noted English theoretician in fluid mechanics, is quoted in *Technology Review* (April 1983, p. 81) as having said: "I am an old man. When I die and go to heaven there are two matters on which I wish enlightenment. One is the [Theory of Relativity], and the other, the theory of turbulence. About the former, I am really rather optimistic!" Father's papers on these subjects appear in this volume; in view of this comment by Sir Horace, it would appear that he would have been interested in reading them.

Lamb may have had a more personal interest in the solution to a particular problem that he posed in his well-known textbook *Hydrodynamics* (6th ed., p. 161) regarding the indeterminacy of certain momentum integrals for a body in an infinite fluid. The solution was given by Father in 1941 in a paper published in a volume honoring Theodore von Kármán's 60th birthday.[64]

Father's paper (this volume, p. 332) on a proposed mechanism of fluid turbulence maintains that the structure of turbulent flow is a horseshoe-shaped vortex and that turbulence may exist only in a three-dimensional pattern (two-dimensional flows are stable); it was first presented at a conference on fluid mechanics at Ohio State University in 1952. Another paper[48] on the subject was published in an anniversary volume for Ludwig Prandtl in 1955. Father states that hurricanes and tornadoes are examples of large-scale turbulence, and that such storms have the same horeshoe-vortex structure (Coriolis forces dissipate one side of the horseshoe-vortex storm in most but not all cases) and creative mechanism as any turbulent flow. These papers have not had wide circulation as they are not readily accessible to readers. Through greater exposure and further investigation, his theory may yet provide an important clue, if not the solution, to the problem of turbulence.

Father posed for only one portrait-photograph in his lifetime, and that was at the behest of Mother. He was not a vain man, though he was handsome, tall, and gracefully built, and women found him attractive. He was quiet, courteous with a shy courtliness, sensitive and unassuming. He had refined taste in music, art and literature, had a good sense of humor, and was generally light-hearted and contented, although he had times of great sadness, as when a brother died in Norway during the German occupation and when my younger brother John succumbed at the age of twenty-one during heart-valve surgery. He had private moments of frustration, too, in reaction to the inconsiderate caricaturizations by some NACA associates of his gentle demeanor, and awkward attempts at correcting this image in his younger days. Through his work he gained stature and respect and sophistication. In outward appearance he became a polished gentleman, but remained a country boy at heart.

In his younger years, Father paid little attention to dress, often putting on trousers belonging to one suit and the coat of another. (Mother interceded and saw to it that he was always well dressed.) This lack of attention was due to lack of interest and to absent-mindedness. Some of the heartiest laughs enjoyed by our family of mother, father, two brothers and myself were focused on the incident (which we rehashed many times) when, on leaving a dinner party, Father made a determined and successful attempt to squeeze himself into a lady's overcoat of the same color as his. It was a tight fit and very short! He frequently came home with table napkins in his coat pockets, thinking, I suppose, that they were handkerchiefs. Once he unintentionally left us children behind in a hardware store while he continued on alone to another one, lost in thought. He laughed readily at his absent-minded-professor behavior when it was pointed out.

But in an emergency that required presence of mind and quick physical response he functioned effectively. There was the time when he was driving the car, and we were discussing our reactions to the typhoid shots we had all just received, that he fainted, the first and only time in his life. But just before this happened, he turned off the ignition key, applied the brakes and gave the wheel a turn so that the car drifted safely to a halt on the side of the road.

Father was alert to the practicalities of everyday living and acted constructively. As an example, during the depression of the Thirties, when he was forever borrowing from and repaying the bank, as were so many people, he and his associates were heavily dependent on their paychecks. One day a rumor began to circulate that the local bank was failing and was going to close a few days before checks were due to be distributed. People felt helpless and full of fear about losing their pay. But Father realized that if the funds from payroll headquarters in Washington were not transferred to the bank, the money would be saved. Although having nothing to do with general administration at NACA, he had the presence of mind to alert management to telephone Washington and stop delivery of funds. The bank failed, the money was saved, and Father was a hero to those who would have lost out at least temporarily if this transaction had been completed as scheduled.

His respect for nature may have contributed to his ability as a scientist. Once, on a visit to his home, he took me from a family gathering out to the porch to show me a strand of ivy that had entered through a hole in the screen, traveled about five feet along the porch floor, and climbed up the leg of a table. "Do you see anything strange?" he asked. "Do you see that in its travel across the floor the vine took a straightline course direct to the leg nearest the entry point? It did not deviate left or right. It *knew* precisely where the leg was. *How* did it know? Plants to our knowledge don't have brains or eyes or nervous system; by what mechanism did it know about the leg and how to direct itself toward it?" Father held nature in wonder; most of us take it for granted.

Interestingly, in the March 1979 *Smithsonian Magazine* I came across an article on the *skototropism* of certain plants. This is the term for the ability of climbing vines to find vertical supports. The author, Thomas S. Ray, Jr., claimed the original discovery of this phenomenon in conjunction with a friend in 1974. That was the year Father showed it to me! Ray is a botanist. Father had no particular knowledge of this field; but he was a true scientist, alert, observant and receptive. He died in 1978 before the article appeared. I wish he had seen it.

Father was a good psychologist. One evening at dinner my older brother, Ted, then twelve years old, angry because of a reprimand from Mother, stood up from the table and defiantly announced that he was leaving home, that he was going to find a job and be on his own. Father spoke up in a calm voice and said he thought Ted was capable of doing this, but if he was really going he was to leave *now,* right away, *without* finishing his meal. Brother reconsidered and immediately abandoned the notion.

He was a good teacher. He never did any of our homework for us. We were welcome to ask questions at any time, but he never gave direct answers. He responded by asking questions which directed us towards the solution if it was a mathematics, physics or chemistry problem; if composition, he analyzed and criticized if we wished, but he never wrote a word.

With advice mostly, and some physical participation when strength was needed, Father helped my brothers with projects they found interesting such as building tree huts and working on old cars. He taught them how to use guns, and all of us about safety measures of all sorts. At dinner we discussed interesting problems or strange phenomena or world history. He wanted us to think independently and to be self-reliant. He taught us to be this way not by an organized program, but by setting the example himself, imbuing us with this desire, and by abandoning us to our own resources whenever it was presumably safe, thus allowing natural forces to act and us to react and learn.

Father's health was excellent. Trite as it may sound, one could say he was as healthy as a horse and as strong as an ox, although rather slender. He was athletic and rugged partly as a result of endowment and partly as a consequence of years of running or skiing cross-country to and from the one-room rural schoolhouse of his boyhood. Though he seldom exercised except for short walks in his mature years, he retained a youthful agility until late in life. On his sixty-fifth birthday, at our request he demonstrated this by walking on his hands, feet straight up in the air, for five or six yards before quitting.

He was a member of only one social club, the exclusive Cosmos Club of Washington, D.C. He treated everyone with deference, including little children, who responded to his charm spontaneously. He enjoyed a small party with friends occasionally, but he was at heart a homebody. He loved the domestic hearthside, his family, and Mother's home-cooking. Fish and potatoes, potatoes and fish, the ubiquitous fare of his native Norway, were without reservation his dish.

He was by inheritance Norwegian to the bone. In the records of the churches of his hometown area, the names, and sometimes the occupations, of his ancestors can be traced in unbroken line back to the late 1500's. He was proud of this "Viking" heritage. As a child, the eldest of six children, he used to fish in a pond in Sandar where the remains of a Viking king and his handsome Gokstad ship dating from 900 A.D. were unearthed a few years before Father's birth. It was in this county of Vestfold that the famous Vikings Harold Fairhair, the leader first to unite the independent earldoms of Norway, and Halvdan the Dark lived. As a child he was steeped in the lore of those ancient days.

In his bones he was a Norwegian, but in his heart Father belonged to Virginia. He considered the years he lived there the best of his life. The climate was easy, the way of life was easy. The neighbors were genteel and hospitable and tolerant of others with accents and eccentric ways. (In Hampton, where we lived, NACA scientists were familiarly, but not disrespectfully, referred to as NACA nuts.) And from adjacent Chesapeake Bay, fresh fish and other seafood, his favorite fare, were available in endless abundance.

While he was quietly proud of his origins, he loved America. He loved the vastness of the country and the optimism of the people. He admired our technological competence and our efficiency in farming, manufacturing and distribution. He was awed at the wealth of the country, which most of us are not even aware of, we take so much for granted.

When he was eight in Stokke, a rural area near Sandefjord in Norway where he was born, his father, who had been studying to be a ship's engineer, was home one evening after having taken the qualification examination that day. He had made the best grade of all the candidates and furthermore had been the only one to solve an especially difficult problem. Young Theodore also solved it all by himself. In later years, with his knowledge and insight, he overwhelmed his middle-school teachers, who consequently allowed him to study whatever and whenever he wished.

In Norway, public education was of the highest quality. In 1921 Father graduated from the Royal Technical Insitute in Trondheim (which, because of his high grades at Larvik Real Gymnasium, he and all others of high scholastic rank attended tuition-free) with a master's degree in mechanical engineering. By then he was a superb mathematician, and was proficient in two foreign languages, English and German. He knew world geography, the history of exploration, world history, literature, and art. He was a natural mechanic and a skilled carpenter. In later years, after he became a theoretical physicist, Father was quick to point out that he was an engineer also. He thought a physicist who could not apply his abstract ideas in a practical way was of little value to society.

This engineering school is known today as the Norwegian Institute of Technology, a part of the University of Trondheim. It was established in 1910, similar German institutions serving as a model. The first permanent professorship was held by a German researcher of international standing, W. J. Watzinger. (His son was with Heyerdahl on the Kon-Tiki expedition in 1952.) He was Father's principal teacher. Many of the teaching staff were English or German. Consequently, some courses were given in each language. An institution of the highest standards, today the institute offers degrees in architecture, metallurgy, civil, electrical, mechanical and chemical engineering, engineering physics, naval architecture and marine engineering. It has about eight-thousand students.

While a student there, Father lived in a rented garret at Bahusgate 14 and took his meals of pea soup and other spare fare nearby. (Food was in short supply during this period following the war.) He borrowed money for living expenses. He fell in love with a pretty girl from the town named Johanne Hoem. Johanne was the city sophisticate who had learned English in England, and he was the naive country boy who had been nowhere. She was charmed. They were married shortly after he graduated. Her loving care and attention provided a comfortable haven for him the rest of his life.

The Lutheran marriage ceremony was held in Nidaros cathedral, a large gothic structure which was begun in the year 1070 A.D. when Norway was a Catholic nation. Nearby stood, and stands today, the archbishop's palace, a rustic stone building constructed in 1180 to house the first archbishop of this far northern country. One of the oldest functioning buildings in Western Europe, it is used today for important affairs and functions of state. The wedding couple traveled through the snow to the cathedral in a fancy sleigh drawn by horses.

It was Mother who persuaded Father that they should be venturesome and try their future in America. (Almost all of Father's fellow graduates emigrated owing to the lack of engineering jobs in Norway.) Though the school wished to keep him on the teaching staff, Mother's wishes prevailed. Father was told that a position would always be open to him should he return.

In 1976, the Norwegian Institute of Techology, his *alma mater*, awarded Father the great honor of its degree of Doctor Technicae Honoris Causa for his enduring contributions to aerodynamics and fluid mechanics. It had previously, in 1935, recognized Ludwig Prandtl with this honorary degree, and in 1960 likewise honored Yale professor Lars Onsager, who later, in 1968, won the Nobel prize for chemistry. As part of the week-long program of lectures by speakers from several countries, an elegant dinner was served in the Valhalla-like hall of the ancient stone residence of the archbishop. Father was very touched by this recognition of his work.

Coincidentally, Lars Onsager, a life-long friend, also attended the Royal Technical Institute of Norway in the years just after Father graduated. He, like Father, became an instructor at Johns Hopkins just one year before Father left to go to NACA as an associate physicist, the year during which he obtained a Ph.D. degree in physics. About that time in the late Twenties, Harold C. Urey, later to become a Nobel laureate in chemistry, was also teaching at Johns Hopkins—a school with a remarkable teaching staff then. Father said it was then the only school in the country to offer a Ph.D. degree in physics.

This was Father's first employment in the United States. When he applied at Johns Hopkins the school was in need of a technical translator from German into English. Having this facility and a high academic rating, Father was hired to do the work and to serve as an instructor in mechanical engineering. Joseph Ames, then president of Johns Hopkins and also chairman of the Executive Committee of NACA, was impressed with Father's talents and suggested that he join NACA. For 16 years thereafter, from 1930 to 1946, Father served as Chief Physicist (after a year of being in the atmospheric wind tunnel division) at NACA-Langley.

In 1947, Richard Smith of MIT in conjunction with the Brazilian government invited Father to participate in organizing an institute of aeronautics in Brazil. Father was vice-president and dean of engineering of this organization until he resigned in 1951. He was asked to return in 1958 but by then he was heavily involved in consulting work. From 1951–54 he had served as contract administrator of the applied mechanics division of the USAF Office of Scientific Research. His last project was in 1970 with the Hamilton Standard Division of United Aircraft (now United Technologies) consulting on the design of static propellers.

After that he retired and was able to spend more time trying to get the tangle of relativity untied. He had never felt comfortable with a large part of Einstein's famous work and had been pondering the problem for years. The inspiration to the solution came sometime in the Sixties. By 1976, in time for the colloquium at the University of Trondheim, he had written a short paper, which is reproduced with some revision and editing in this volume. This is essentially an extension of Newtonian physics encompassing certain verified aspects of relativity theory and is a consequent new theory of light and the universe.

Sadly, by then Father was sick. His robust health had begun to fail in 1974. The next year his gall bladder was removed, but recovery from the operation was slow and he was never really vital and strong after that. I believe he thought he had cancer and, not wanting to upset mother and us, avoided discussing his health. One night in September 1978, in terrible pain he was taken to a hospital. Tests and an exploratory operation showed that he had an inflamed pancreas. On November 6, 1978, my dear father died after enduring silently two months of terrible suffering in a hospital near his house in Centerport, New York. Had he been able to speak at the end it would have been characteristic of him to say that he had had a good life.

Father lacked the time and the taste, and indeed the ability, to promote himself or his ideas. The accomplishments that became known and applied succeeded by their merits alone. They have been published in various textbooks and technical journals, presented at international scientific meetings, and taught in universtiy classrooms. In time some of his other work, such as the horseshoe-vortex turbulence theory and his theory of relativity, light and the universe, will, I believe, be seen to out-rank in importance his other notable accomplishments in aerodynamics and flutter. They are products of a brilliant mind that was, according to his associates, intuitive and creative, yet rigorously analytical and critical. Father was a true scientist.

Selected Reprints

NACA Aeronautical Symbols

Instrument for Detecting Metallic Bodies Buried in the Earth
Theodore Theodorsen, 1930

The Theory of Wind-Tunnel Wall Interference
Theodore Theodorsen, 1931

Theory of Wing Sections of Arbitrary Shape
Theodore Theodorsen, 1931

General Potential Theory of Arbitrary Wing Sections
Theodore Theodorsen and I. E. Garrick, 1933

Experimental Verification of the Theory of Wind-Tunnel Boundary Interference
Theodore Theodorsen and Abe Silverstein, 1934

Vibration Response of Airplane Structures
Theodore Theodorsen and A. G. Gelalles, 1934

General Theory of Aerodynamic Instability and the Mechanism of Flutter
Theodore Theodorsen, 1935

The Fundamental Principles of the N.A.C.A. Cowling
Theodore Theodorsen, 1938

The Flutter Problem
Theodore Theodorsen, 1939

Mechanism of Flutter—A Theoretical and Experimental Investigation of the Flutter Problem
Theodore Theodorsen and I. E. Garrick, 1940

Nonstationary Flow About a Wing-Aileron-Tab Combination Including Aerodynamic Balance
Theodore Theodorsen and I. E. Garrick, 1942

Flutter Calculations in Three Degrees of Freedom
Theodore Theodorsen and I. E. Garrick, 1942

The Theory of Propellers I—Determination of the Circulation Function and the Mass Coefficient for Dual-Rotating Propellers
Theodore Theodorsen, 1944

The Theory of Propellers II—Method for Calculating the Axial Interference Velocity
Theodore Theodorsen, 1944

The Theory of Propellers III—The Slipstream Contraction with Numerical Values for Two-Blade and Four-Blade Propellers
Theodore Theodorsen, 1944

The Theory of Propellers IV—Thrust, Energy, and Efficiency Formulas for Single- and Dual-Rotating Propellers with Ideal Circulation Distribution
Theodore Theodorsen, 1944

Note on the Theorems of Bjerknes and Crocco
Theodore Theodorsen, 1946

Note on the Theory of Hurricanes
Theodore Theodorsen, 1952

Mechanism of Turbulence
Theodore Theodorsen, 1952

The Structure of Turbulence
Theodore Theodorsen, 1955

The Structure of Turbulence
Theodore Theodorsen, 1962

Relativity and Classical Physics
Theodore Theodorsen, 1976

AERONAUTICAL SYMBOLS

1. FUNDAMENTAL AND DERIVED UNITS

Item	Symbol	Metric Unit	Metric Symbol	English Unit	English Symbol
Length	l	meter	m	foot (or mile)	ft. (or mi.)
Time	t	second	s	second (or hour)	sec. (or hr.)
Force	F	weight of one kilogram	kg	weight of one pound	lb.
Power	P	kg/m/s		horsepower	hp
Speed		km/h	k.p.h.	mi./hr	m.p.h.
		m/s	m.p.s.	ft./sec.	f.p.s

2. GENERAL SYMBOLS, ETC.

W Weight $= mg$

g Standard acceleration of gravity $= 9.80665$ m/s^2 $= 32.1740$ ft./sec.^{2}

m Mass $= \frac{W}{g}$

ρ Density (mass per unit volume)

Standard density of dry air, 0.12497 (kg-m^{-4} s^2) at 15°C. and 760 mm = 0.002378 (lb.-ft.$^{-4}$ sec.^{2})

Specific weight of "standard" air, 1.2255 kg/m^3 = 0.07651 lb./ft.^{3}

mk^2 Moment of intertia (indicate axis of the radius of gyration k, by proper subscript)

S Area

S_w Wing area, etc.

G Gap

b Span

c Chord

$\frac{b^2}{S}$ Aspect ratio

μ Coefficient of viscosity

3. AERODYNAMICAL SYMBOLS

V True air speed

q Dynamic (or impact) pressure $= \frac{1}{2}\rho V^2$

L Lift, absolute coefficient $C_L = \frac{L}{qS}$

D Drag, absolute coefficient $C_D = \frac{D}{qS}$

D_0 Profile drag, absolute coefficient $C_{D_0} = \frac{D_0}{qS}$

D_i Induced drag, absolute coefficient $C_{D_i} = \frac{D_i}{qS}$

D_p Parasite drag, absolute coefficient $C_{D_p} = \frac{D_p}{qS}$

C Cross-wind force, absolute coefficient $C_C = \frac{C}{qS}$

R Resultant force

i_w Angle of setting of wings (relative to thrust line)

i_t Angle of stabilizer setting (relative to thrust line)

Q Resultant moment

Ω Resultant angular velocity

$\rho\frac{Vl}{\mu}$ Reynolds Number, where l is a linear dimension

e.g., for a model airfoil 3 in. chord, 100 mi./hr. normal pressure, at 15°C., the corresponding number is 234,000;

or for a model of 10 cm chord 40 m/s, the corresponding number is 274,000

C_p Center of pressure coefficient (ratio of distance of $c.p.$ from leading edge to chord length)

α Angle of attack

ϵ Angle of downwash

α_0 Angle of attack, infinite aspect ratio

α_i Angle of attack, induced

α_a Angle of attack, absolute (measured from zero lift position)

γ Flight path angle

AERONAUTICAL SYMBOLS (cont'd.)

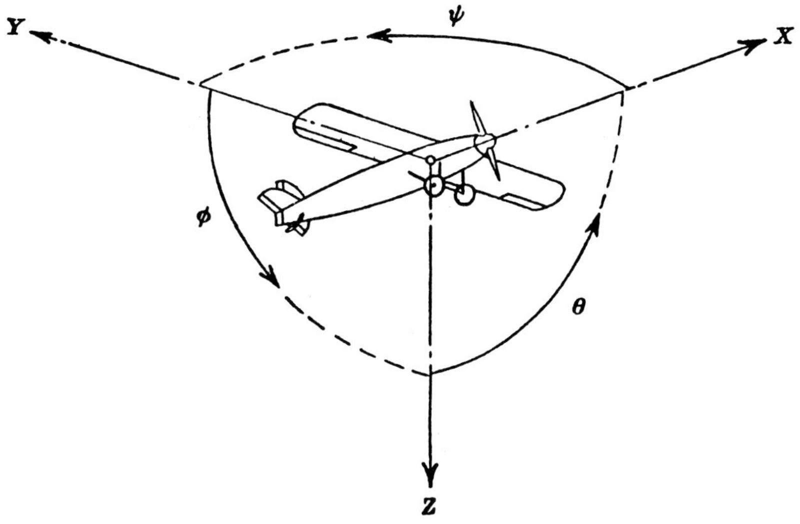

Positive directions of axes and angles (forces and moments) are shown by arrows

Axis		Force (parallel to axis)	Moment about axis			Angle		Velocities	
Designation	Symbol	symbol	Designation	Symbol	Positive direction	Designation	Symbol	Linear (component along axis)	Angular
Longitudinal	X	X	rolling	L	$Y \rightarrow Z$	roll	ϕ	u	p
Lateral	Y	Y	pitching	M	$Z \rightarrow X$	pitch	θ	v	q
Normal	Z	Z	yawing	N	$X \rightarrow Y$	yaw	ψ	w	r

Absolute coefficients of moment:

$$C_l = \frac{L}{qbS} \qquad C_m = \frac{M}{qcS} \qquad C_n = \frac{N}{qbS}$$

Angle of set of control surface (relative to neutral position), δ. (Indicate surface by proper subscript.)

4. PROPELLER SYMBOLS

D Diameter

p Geometric pitch

p/D Pitch ratio

V' Inflow velocity

V_s Slipstream velocity

T Thrust, absolute coefficient $C_T = \frac{T}{\rho n^2 D^4}$

Q Torque, absolute coefficient $C_Q = \frac{Q}{\rho n^2 D^5}$

P Power, absolute coefficient $C_P = \frac{P}{\rho n^3 D^5}$

C_S Speed power coefficient $= \sqrt[5]{\frac{\rho V^5}{P n^2}}$

η Efficiency

n Revolutions per second, r.p.s.

Φ Effective helix angle $= \tan^{-1}\left(\frac{V}{2\pi r n}\right)$

5. NUMERICAL RELATIONS

1 hp = 76.04 kg/m/s = 550 lb./ft./sec.

1 kg/m/s/ = 0.01315 hp

1 mi./hr. = 0.44704 m/s

1 m/s = 2.23693 mi./hr.

1 lb. = 0.4535924277 kg.

1 kg = 2.2046224 lb.

1 mi. = 1609.35 m = 5280 ft.

1 m = 3.2808333 ft.

INSTRUMENT FOR DETECTING METALLIC BODIES BURIED IN THE EARTH

BY THEODORE THEODORSEN

National Advisory Committee for Aeronautics

Published in *Journal of the Franklin Institute,* 1930, pp. 311–326.

SUMMARY.

This paper gives a description of a new instrument recently developed by the National Advisory Committee for Aeronautics at the Langley Memorial Aeronautical Laboratory. The instrument was made for the immediate purpose of locating unexploded bombs which were known to have been dropped from airplanes at targets in close proximity of the site of the new Seaplane Towing Channel at Langley Field, Virginia. The new "detector" successfully located a number of bombs buried on and near the projected site. It is of a simple design and requires no skilled operators.

The author gives a brief theoretical survey of the general nature of the difficulties encountered in the design of sensitive detectors of this type. He points, in particular, to the importance of avoiding capacity and resistance effects, and outlines other essential factors contributing to the success of the new detector.

INTRODUCTION.

This work was undertaken by the National Advisory Committee for Aeronautics for the purpose of detecting and removing unexploded bombs from the site to be occupied by the Seaplane Towing Channel. It was known that the projected channel was to pass through an area near one which had been used for bombing practice, and the Committee desired to take every precaution in order to avoid dangerous explosions of live bombs during the construction.

The problem was to obtain some instrument which could do the work; that is, which could locate the bombs that might be buried in the area referred to. It was desired that a layer of several feet in depth might be searched at one time.

While some experimental work has been done along such lines, no information of successful bomb detection is available, or has come to the author's notice.

An inquiry by the Committee at the Bureau of Mines resulted in an investigation of the practicability of employing an ultra-sensitive magnetometer. The scheme was, however, abandoned. It was found that the method was not sufficiently convenient for the purpose, and that in any case, the amount of labor involved would be prohibitive. Five minutes were required at each setup of the instrument, covering an area of possibly not more than from 10 to 15 square feet of the surroundings, and highly trained operators were required for such work.

A similar inquiry at the Bureau of Standards disclosed the fact that some attention had been paid to this question during the war. A brief résumé of work relating to this subject is published in the "War Works" of the Bureau. No record of instruments employed for actual field use is found, however.

The Bureau recommended the use of a Maxwell or Andersen bridge in connection with a large "search coil" of several henrys as being possibly the most sensitive method. The Committee tried this scheme:

A coil 8 feet in diameter containing 1300 turns of No. 21 wire was made up and inserted in a Maxwell bridge circuit.[1] The result was negative. It was found that the self-capacity of the coil, being of the order of 0.01–0.02 microfarad, was entirely too large to permit even an approach to the balancing of the bridge without extraordinary means. Being pressed for time, the Committee was forced to abandon the attempt, having in the meantime succeeded in developing an instrument of its own, which type in the following will be referred to as the N. A. C. A. Bomb Detector.

While it is too early to claim any absolute superiority of this instrument or of the principles involved as compared with others, the Committee feels, on the basis of the practical results obtained and the great simplicity of the scheme, that a description of this device might be of benefit to others. Several bombs were located after the first day's work, one of them being a live T.N.T. 17 pounder buried with its center of gravity approximately 2 feet below the surface. While the exploded bombs all were found in holes of considerable size, no visible evidence disclosed the presence of the unexploded ones. The above bomb was set off on the following day, and a systematic scanning of the entire field taken up as a result. This work is completed at the writing of this article.

[1] For description of this circuit see, for instance, "Dictionary of Applied Physics," Vol. II, "Electricity," page 436, etc.

DESCRIPTION OF THE N. A. C. A. INSTRUMENT.

The diagram of the electrical system of the N. A. C. A. instrument is shown in Fig. 1. *G* is a high frequency generator working on a power coil *A*. *T* is a telephone supplied from the two opposing pick-up coils, *B* and *C*.

FIG. 1.

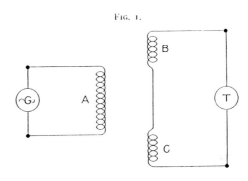

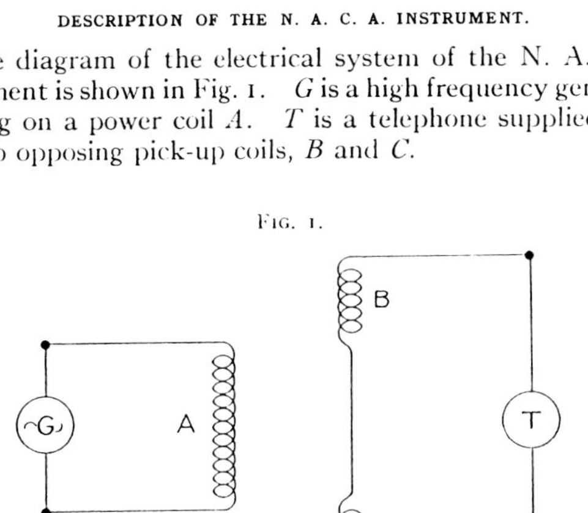

The three coils, *A*, *B*, and *C* are mounted symmetrically on a cylindrical wooden frame. A comparatively loose magnetic interlinking of the central power coil *A* and the two opposing pick-up coils, *B* and *C*, is employed. See Fig. 2. This feature is essential for the instrument and the reason for its importance is given in the following. The pick-up coils contain each 100 turns of No. 21 wire, while the power coil has about 75 turns of the same size. The coils are wound in a single layer in order to keep the self-capacity down.

The generator *G* supplied 500-cycle per sec. current, which frequency is probably the most satisfactory for the purpose. It was capable of supplying about 6 amperes at 110 volts.

The power coil was attached to this source of current by means of a step-up transformer.

The telephone *T* was specially designed to suit the low impedance of the pick-up coils. It consisted of a sensitive

Fig. 2.

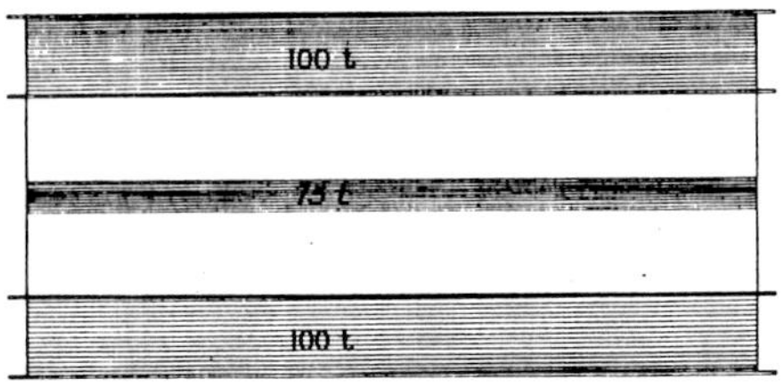

Fig. 3.

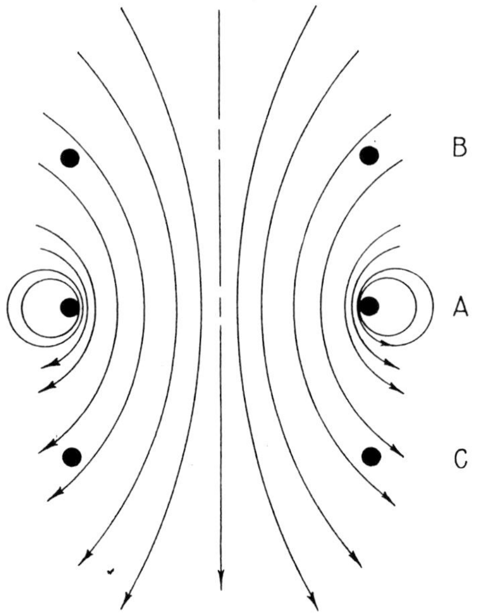

Diagram showing field in balance.

Baldwin head set rewound with about 100 turns of heavy wire. The operation of the instrument will be readily understood from the simple wiring diagram in Fig. 1. The "power" coil *A* supplies a strong alternating field. The electromotive forces set up in the two pick-up coils are in opposition to each other, so that only the difference appears across the telephone. In balanced condition *B* should be an "image" of *A* with respect to the central coil. When this image is perfect there is no current through the telephone. This condition is indicated in Fig. 3. If the instrument is brought close to a piece of

Fig. 4.

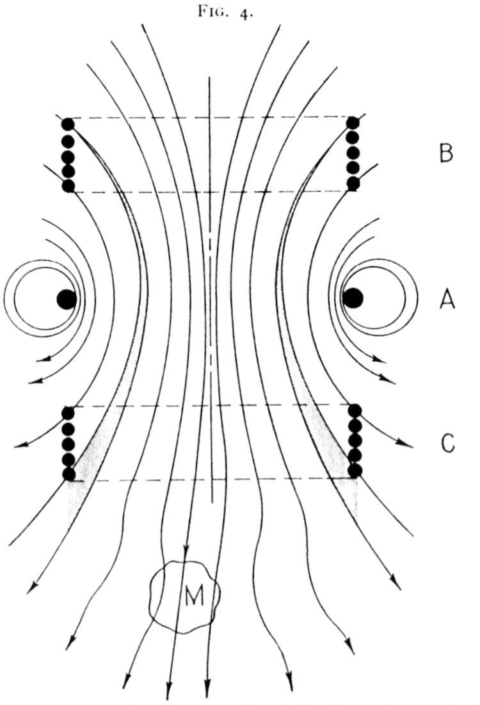

Diagram showing distortion of field due to introduction of magnetic material at M. The shaded portion is "audible."

magnetic material, like a bomb, a distortion of the magnetic field lines takes place. This condition is shown exaggerated in Fig. 4. The shaded portion indicates the difference in magnetic flux through the two telephone coils *B* and *C*. This difference is consequently "audible" in the telephone. Care should be taken that the wooden frame be extremely rigid and the coils securely stretched and glued onto it. For this reason the three circular bobbins comprising the N. A. C. A. instrument were all glued together, forming a rigid cylindrical body. No nails or other metal parts should be used. To avoid local bending moments the handles were not directly fastened to the body. The latter was carried by four ropes fastened so as to minimize structural deflections. A "close up" of the design and method of suspension is shown in Fig. 5. *A* is the power coil, *B* and *C* the pick-up coils. A sketch of the frame giving dimensions is shown in Fig. 6.

Fig. 5.

N. A. C. A. bomb detector.

It was on basis of experience gathered from a preliminary design shown in Fig. 13 that the above method of construction was adopted. The picture shown in Fig. 13 reproduces only what we have been referring to as the "power" coil, while the two pick-up coils had been removed before the photograph was taken.

This method of fastening the handles proved to be entirely unsatisfactory. The instrument was thrown greatly out of balance on picking it up by the handles.

Fig. 6.

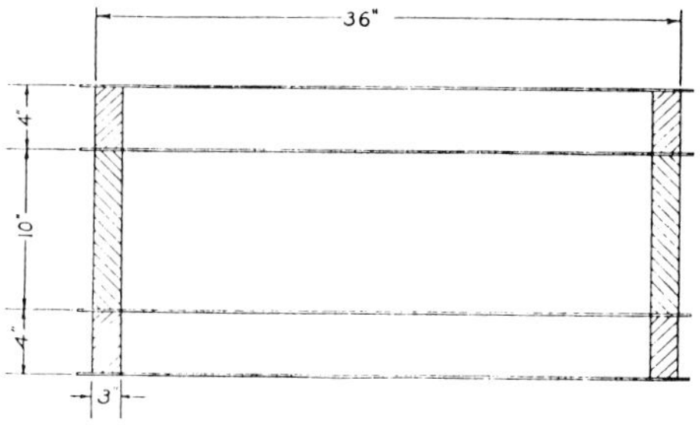

This larger coil of 5 1/2 feet in diameter was also somewhat too heavy for convenient operation.

DISCUSSION OF METHODS OF DETECTION.

It is hoped that the following analysis of the general difficulties involved in the design of an instrument of the present kind will serve to promote its further development.

Looking for some means of detecting a piece of iron, or other metals, several feet below the surface of the earth, the only conspicuous property of such material as distinguished from that of the soil is its effect on a magnetic field.

If a coil of a diameter which is comparable in magnitude to the depth desired is brought close to the ground above the buried metal, a definite change in the value of the self-inductance of the coil takes place. The power factor is also changed, due to the eddy currents set up within the metal. The change looked for is, however, so small (say 1 : 10,000) that any use of measuring instruments to indicate directly changes in current consumption or power factor of the coil is out of question.

The next step is to employ bridges as usually employed for such purposes. The Maxwell bridge and the Hughes bridge will both serve the purpose.

The bridge systems are, however, apparently too complicated in adjustment. It must be appreciated that the value of the bridge as indicator depends entirely on the possibility of obtaining "zero" adjustment of the telephone or bridge current. This is not so easy. The question of securing absolute silence is an interesting one. A bridge contains four arms. Each arm contains its ohmic resistance, its capacitance, and its inductance.

It may be possible to make up resistances comparatively free from inductance. The condition of minimum self-capacity may then be greatly violated, etc.

It is further not possible to make inductances entirely free from self-capacity, etc.

The result is that each bridge arm actually is composed of a complicated arrangement of resistances, inductances, and capacities. In order to obtain zero current through the telephone, it is in consequence necessary to balance for ohmic resistance, for capacity, and for inductance. How this may be done is in itself a difficult mathematical and experimental problem, subject only to approximate solutions and trials. It may be done in the laboratory for a single frequency. If the imposed frequency is slightly changed, a new adjustment is, however, in general, necessary.

The problem is not so serious when it comes to measurement of comparatively large changes of say 1:500 or more in the value of the unknown inductance, particularly if a source of power of a wave-form as free as possible from harmonics is employed.

When it comes to greater accuracy, slight changes in the ohmic resistances due to temperature effects, small changes in the desired, or undesired, capacities and inductances associated with each arm of the bridge, are detrimental to the sensitivity of the method. The adjustment for silence is as mentioned only possible for one frequency which, of course, may be the most pronounced note, while all other disturbances, in general, pass through the telephone. Unavoidable changes in frequency, wave form and intensity of the source continuously tend to upset the balance. With a powerful source of power which ought to be employed, the ear may not even be able to detect any definite minimum.

This strict requirement of an absolute "zero" current in the telephone at balance is brought about by the fact that the ear is able to distinguish between sounds of intensity 0 and 1, while no difference may be detected between sounds of intensity 10 and 11.

A great step forward in the direction of increased sensitivity is shown in the scheme disclosed in Drawing No. 583B of the Bureau of Standards, termed "Induction Balance for Detecting Metallic Bodies" and dated June 16, 1922. This type makes use of two transformers each in the form of coils of 5 feet in diameter. The system is shown in Fig. 9. It employs a separate variable mutual inductor and variable and fixed resistances for adjustments. Possibly the greatest objection to the scheme is the apparent close coupling between the primary and the secondary of the two transformers employed. This brings about considerable charging current between the two windings, apparently necessitating some means of compensation of the "out-of-phase" currents as evidenced by the interposed variable resistance.

A French article by M. C. Gutton entitled "Sur une Balance destinée a la Recherche des Obus enterrés dans les Terrains a mettre en Culture," published in *Comptes Rendus*, Volume 161, page 71, 1915, describes an instrument which is similar, with the exception that the resistances *AB* and *CD* of Fig. 9 are omitted. Mr. Gutton experiences, however, apparently the same trouble of not being able to obtain perfect silence, due to the same close coupling between primary and secondary of the two transformers, and probably also due to self-capacity of the coils. He avoids the trouble by cutting the power, as may be seen from the following quotation:

"La expérience m'a montré que, dans le large limites, cette sensibilité dépend du trembleur, qui doit donner un son musical aigu et avoir une trés petite amplitude d'oscillation." [2]

Both the French paper and the Bureau of Standards description given in the "War Works" of the Bureau indicate that primary and secondary of each transformer are wound

[2] "The sensitivity depends on the vibrator which should produce a distinct musical sound of a very small amplitude."

on common bobbins with the distance between the inside edges of the two coils equal to 1 centimeter.

The N. A. C. A. instrument employs only a single power coil which may be termed a primary with two opposing pick-up coils, both of which are in loose magnetic coupling with the former.

Since there is only a negligible change taking place in the force lines running close around the power coil when a piece of metal is introduced in the field, it will be seen that practically all of the change of the field is imposed on the pick-up coils. In fact, the system seems to be superior for the purpose for which it is intended, since the disturbing effect of a small piece of iron on the surface is almost avoided, while the full effect of a larger piece at a great distance is retained.

We will now indicate numerically the importance of avoiding the capacity effects between power and pick-up coils by a reference to the Bureau of Standards induction balance shown systematically in Fig. 9. With P_1 and S_1 5 feet in diameter and 1 centimeter apart and, for instance, wound with multiple layers, the capacity amounts to the order of 30 centimeters e.s.u. With a voltage of 300 and a frequency of 500 the current leaking across and going partly through the phones is of the order of some hundredths of a milliampere.

Now the 500 cycle current usually contains higher harmonics, and the condition is further aggravated, in particular, because the 1,000 and the 2,000 cycles are more "audible" than the fundamental, and the receiver, in addition, may "peak" at high frequencies.

It is evident that, as this charging current is avoided the sensitivity is increased, and the question of balancing greatly simplified. The N. A. C. A. Bomb Detector could be brought to perfect silence by means of one adjustment. In fact, the balancing was so good that the operator had a tendency to "forget" the note and actually preferred to keep the instrument slightly out of balance. The self-capacity of the pick-up coils is brought down to a negligible nagnitude by employing a single layer coil. The instrument is thus not sensitive to changes in generator frequency nor to irregularities in wave form. This simplifies the requirement as to the source of power.

The instrument is independent also of temperature differences and temperature changes.

The practical value of this latter fact can only be appreciated if one attempts to design bridge circuits having the same characteristics.

The instrument was adjusted by changing the position of the power coil or, in fact, by touching slightly *one* of its 75 turns, which acted as a very good vernier. The stability of the instrument was, however, so nearly perfect that on starting out for field work new adjustment was not always needed.

PRACTICAL CONSIDERATIONS REGARDING THE DESIGN OF THE N. A. C. A. TYPE.

The design of this instrument is so simple that anybody having at his disposal a small high frequency generator and a telephone receiver will have no difficulty in making up such a device. A few points to be taken in consideration will be brought up briefly in the following:

The N. A. C. A. Detector was operated satisfactorily in the field with one ampere through the power coil. If there is sufficient power available, there is no reason why the number of ampere turns should not be increased. The sensitivity of the instrument increases noticeably with the number of ampere turns employed in the primary. This is due to the fact, as brought out before, that perfect balancing is approached quite closely with this instrument.

The problem is thus to make up the power coil with as few turns as the available generator will permit.

The instrument should, for the sake of safety, not be operated in the field with more than a few hundred volts on the power coil; preferably with much less, depending on the necessary length of the supply line.

Regarding the question of "power" actually required for the instrument, it will be observed that, since no resistances form part of the circuit, the only energy consumption taking place is theoretically occuring in the telephone membrane.

In other words, if the coils were made of wire having no resistance, all of the power supplied to the Detector would appear in the telephone and as heat in the object.

Considerations of weight will, however, limit the size of

Fig. 7.

Fig. 8.

Fig. 9.

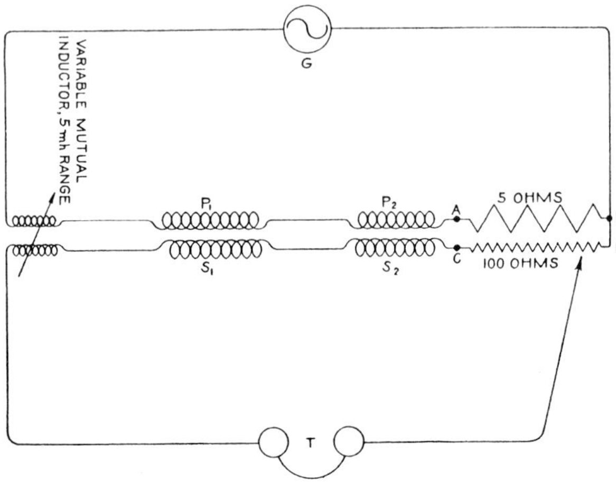

the wire to a reasonable magnitude and the actual efficiency is lowered accordingly.

Regarding the pick-up system, it will be noticed from the wiring in Fig. 1 that there exists no connection to the power coil or high potential side of the system, incidentally protecting the operator from receiving shocks through the telephone.

It is not necessary to employ more than approximately 100 turns of wire in each of the pick-up coils and the impedance of the telephone should not differ too much from the impedance of the coils for best results. The length of the telephone-connection line should be at least 20 feet.

Fig. 10.

Upper picture shows the hole left by one of the bombs as it was destroyed.

The practicability of connecting the low-impedance pick-up system to an audio-amplifier has been given some consideration. More experimental work, however, is necessary in order to perfect the arrangement to such a degree that the added complications of the scheme may be justified by improved performance.

It is important to notice that the individual connections to the coils must not be allowed to hang loose, but must be carefully twisted together to neutralize the effect of the field and carefully secured to the frame. Notice also in Fig. 5, how the leads are brought out of the field.

Fig. 11.

Bomb uncovered in path of sea plane towing channel.

Regarding the structural design of the instrument, it must be made as rigid as possible and at the same time it should not be heavier than can be carried by two men with ease. Not a single nail or screw should be used, since this will make perfect balancing by the simple means referred to above impossible. The method of construction is quite evident from Fig. 5 and 13.

FIELD OPERATION OF THE INSTRUMENT.

The site of the new Seaplane Towing Channel is a strip of land about 20–30 feet wide and more than 2,000 feet long, located to the north of the present buildings of the Langley Memorial Aeronautical Laboratory.

The generator was put at one end of the field and a supply line of 500-cycle current was run from this point to the instrument. Some photographs of the instrument in operation on the site are reproduced in Fig. 7 and 8.

Fig. 12.

Two men carried the Detector with the bottom coil a few inches above the ground. The operator walked behind or to one side at a distance of about 20 feet or more.

No difficulty was experienced in operation. The instrument showed no tendency to get out of balance, nor was the balancing in itself more difficult than the tuning of a single dial radio. This simplicity in operation is of considerable practical value.

Fig. 13.

Experimental power coil.

Fig. 10 is a photograph of the first bomb hole. Figure 11 shows a newly uncovered bomb, the tail and part of the body being visible. Note the peculiar method of digging employed. Figure 12 shows the explosion from a bomb being destroyed.

Langley Field, Va.,
March 18, 1930.

THE THEORY OF WIND-TUNNEL WALL INTERFERENCE

BY THEODORE THEODORSEN

National Advisory Committee for Aeronautics

Report No. 410, 1931

SUMMARY

This paper outlines the development of a general theory for the calculation of the effect of the boundaries of the air stream on the flow past an airfoil. An analytical treatment of the conventional closed and open jet types of rectangular wind tunnels disclosed the possibility of devising three distinctly new types: Tunnels with horizontal boundaries only, with vertical boundaries only, and with a bottom boundary only. Formulas are developed for the tunnel wall interference in each case for an airfoil located at the center of the tunnel. The correction is given as a function of the width to height ratio of the tunnel. The formulas are exact for infinitely small airfoils only, but give good approximations for spans up to about three-quarters of the tunnel width.

The surprising result is obtained that the three last-mentioned nonconventional types of wind tunnels all are superior to the conventional open or closed tunnels as regards wall interference. It is, indeed, possible to design two distinct types of semiclosed wind tunnels having no wall interference; namely, a square tunnel with horizontal boundaries and no side walls, and a rectangular type of a width to height ratio of slightly less than 2 : 1 and equipped with vertical boundaries only.

The author goes on to show that instabilities in the flow may occur for the free jet and the open bottom type tunnels, impairing the predictability of the tunnel wall corrections. A tunnel with a jet free on three sides and restricted only by a lower horizontal boundary extending along the test section from the entrance to the exit cone, is finally recommended as the most promising choice. The correction for this type is from five to eight times smaller than that of the corresponding free jet type.

INTRODUCTION

The two main factors of concern as regards the application of wind-tunnel data to free-flight conditions are the Reynolds Number and the tunnel wall interference. The finite cross section of the stream of air in a wind tunnel gives rise to a flow past an airfoil or other body which differs distinctly from the flow at "free" air conditions. In the language of mathematics, the solution of the problem of the air flow past the body must satisfy the boundary conditions at the surface of the stream. For tunnels having a closed working section the solution must be such that the component of the velocity normal to the boundary must be zero. For jet-type wind tunnels the condition to be satisfied at the surface is that of an unaltered or constant flow velocity. Considering a thin layer of air at the outer boundary, this layer will not experience any relative distortion of its individual elements because each element is progressing at a fixed velocity of translation. This statement is, however, only true as regards first order effects. It is, in particular, apparent that the surfaces are distorted in a normal direction. Surface elements originally plane will thus not remain plane.

In the particular types of wind tunnels proposed by the author in the following, both kinds of boundary conditions have to be satisfied simultaneously, inasmuch as the working section is composed of "free" surfaces as well as fixed walls.

It is possible to introduce a third kind of boundary condition; namely, one depicting the condition of a flexible boundary, but this case is solely of mathematical interest.

The construction of the tunnel may be considered as an independent task; the main concern is to produce a flow in the test chamber which is parallel to itself and constant in magnitude. No theoretical reasons exist to preclude the achievement of such an end. Of considerable consequence as regards the operating flow characteristics is the choice of tunnel type and the geometrical shape of its cross section.

A number of cases can fortunately be treated with mathematical stringency. The airfoil is considered to be small compared with the cross section of the tunnel, and is mathematically represented for this purpose by a vortex doublet line through the center of the cross section and extending from the plane of the test section to infinity in the direction of the flow. This simplified assumption yields results which are substantially correct for airfoils extending across as much as three-quarters of the tunnel width. For larger spans the treatment is complicated by the fact that the effect of the interference varies noticeably along the span.

The interference in an open or closed circular tunnel is known from classical hydrodynamics. The effects are numerically identical, but of opposite sign. The closed rectangular tunnel has been treated by Glauert.

(Reference 1.) The present paper is devoted to a systematic analytical treatment of the properties and relative advantages of the several possible arrangements of rectangular tunnels, including the conventional types.

WIND-TUNNEL INTERFERENCE

The wind-tunnel wall interference is obtained analytically by arranging a series of vortices in such a manner that the given boundary conditions are satisfied. The problem of the circular cross section is a case of elementary hydrodynamics, and the textbooks will be referred to. Let C be the cross-sectional area of the tunnel, S the area of the airfoil, and ϵ the *upward* inclination of the air stream due to the interference at the boundary.

The case of the circle is then given by

$$\epsilon = \pm \frac{1}{8} \frac{S}{C} C_L$$

where the upper sign refers to a closed and the lower sign to an open tunnel. The magnitude ϵ is dimensionless and represents an angle of "up-flow." The angle is numerically of some consequence; the ratio $\frac{S}{C}$ may reach a value of $\frac{1}{6}$, C_L may reach, say, 1.5, while the

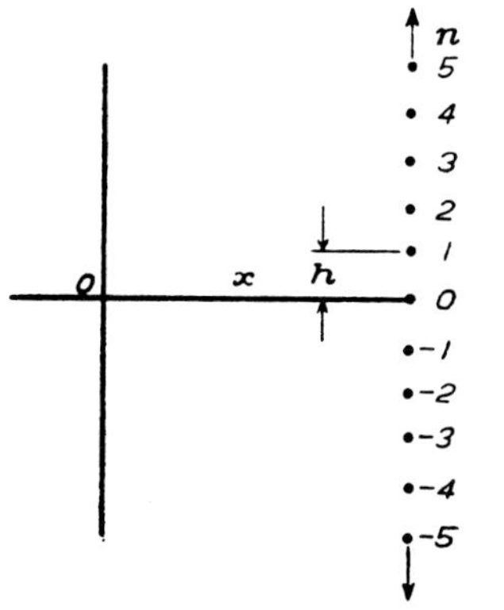

FIGURE 1.—Vertical row of equidistant vortices

constant of proportionality in the most unfavorable case of an open rectangular jet of a 2 : 1 ratio is equal to 0.26. This gives a value of ϵ equal to about 3.7°.

Several interesting arrangements of rectangular cross sections will now be treated. For the sake of uniformity in presentation, the case of a closed rectangular section, which is the only type studied in the previous literature, will be included. Consider the following problem. Let **0** be the origin of a rectangualr system of coordinates. (Fig. 1.) At x is arranged a vertical column of equidistant line vortices of strength Γ perpendicular to the x–y plane, the vortices extending from the x–y plane to infinity in one direction. What is the value of the disturbance at $x=0$ caused by a vertical column of such vortices extending from $y=-\infty$ to $y=+\infty$?

If the distance between the vortices be designated h, we have for the nth unit above the x-axis the velocity at the origin perpendicular to the radius vector from that point,

$$v = \frac{\Gamma}{4\pi} \frac{1}{\sqrt{x^2+n^2h^2}}$$

and for the vertical component,

$$v_n = \frac{\Gamma}{4\pi} \frac{x}{x^2+n^2h^2}$$

The velocity due to *all* the vortices at x is parallel to the y-axis and equal to

$$v_T = \sum_{-\infty}^{+\infty} \frac{\Gamma}{4\pi} \frac{x}{x^2+n^2h^2} = \frac{\Gamma}{4\pi} \sum_{-\infty}^{+\infty} \frac{x}{x^2+n^2h^2}$$

This expression may be brought into a very simple form:

$$\sum_{-\infty}^{+\infty} \frac{x}{x^2+n^2h^2} = \frac{\pi}{h} \sum_{-\infty}^{+\infty} \frac{\frac{\pi x}{h}}{\left(\frac{\pi x}{h}\right)^2 + n^2\pi^2} =$$

$$\frac{\pi}{h}\left[\frac{1}{\frac{\pi x}{h}} + 2\sum_{1}^{\infty} \frac{\frac{\pi x}{h}}{\left(\frac{\pi x}{h}\right)^2 + n^2\pi^2}\right] = \frac{\pi}{h} \coth \frac{\pi x}{h}$$ (see reference 3, page 135)

or

$$\frac{4\pi v_T}{\Gamma} = \frac{\pi}{h} \coth \frac{\pi x}{h} \qquad \text{(I)}$$

If the vortices are of alternating signs, starting with $+\Gamma$ at $y=0$, a corresponding expression is obtained:

$$\frac{4\pi v_T}{\Gamma} = \frac{\pi}{h}\left[\frac{1}{\frac{\pi x}{h}} + 2\sum_{1}^{\infty} \frac{(-1)^n \frac{\pi x}{h}}{\left(\frac{\pi x}{h}\right)^2 + n^2\pi^2}\right] = \frac{\pi}{h} \operatorname{cosech} \frac{\pi x}{h} \qquad \text{(II)}$$

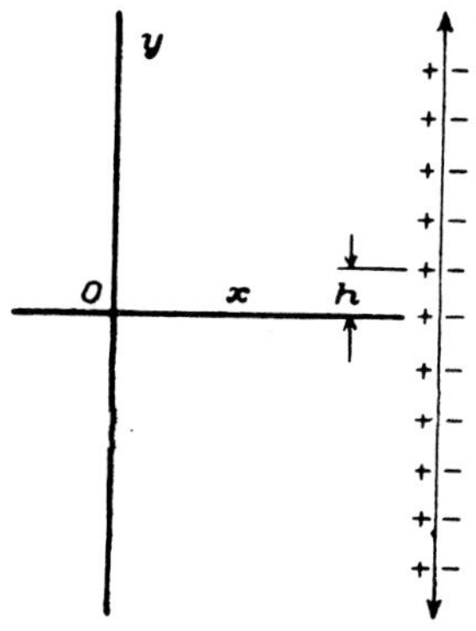

FIGURE 2.—Vertical row of equidistant doublets

The next step is to study the effect of doublets instead of single vortices as in Figure 2. Let the strength of the doublet be $\Gamma \Delta l$. The doublets, which in the following discussion are termed positive, are so arranged as to correspond to the vortices of an airfoil at a positive angle of attack and facing the reader; that is, with the air stream down toward the paper.

From the definition of the derivative of $F(x)$ as

$\lim_{\Delta x \to 0} \frac{F(x+\Delta x)-F(x)}{\Delta x}$, it will be seen that the effect of the doublet is readily obtained as the negative of the derivatives of the expressions already determined, multiplied by Δl.

Hence the flow velocity at **0** in the positive y direction is, from equation (I),

$$v_T = -\frac{\Gamma\Delta l}{4\pi}\frac{d}{dx}\left[\frac{\pi}{h}\coth\frac{\pi x}{h}\right] = \frac{\Gamma\Delta l}{4\pi}\left(\frac{\pi}{h}\right)^2\frac{1}{\sinh^2\frac{\pi x}{h}} \qquad \text{(III)}$$

and in the second case, equation (II), with alternating signs

$$v_T = -\frac{\Gamma\Delta l}{4\pi}\frac{d}{dx}\left[\frac{\pi}{h}\operatorname{cosech}\frac{\pi x}{h}\right] = \frac{\Gamma\Delta l}{4\pi}\left(\frac{\pi}{h}\right)^2\frac{\cosh\frac{\pi x}{h}}{\sinh^2\frac{\pi x}{h}} \qquad \text{(IV)}$$

The effect of a row of doublets arranged along the y-axis must be treated separately. We are interested in the effect of the row extending from minus to plus infinity minus the unit located at the origin (**0**, **0**). From formula (I) we have for this case with $x=\Delta x$

$$\frac{4\pi v_T}{\Gamma} = \frac{\pi}{h}\coth\frac{\pi\Delta x}{h} - \frac{1}{\Delta x}$$

where $\frac{1}{\Delta x}$ is the effect of the doublet at the origin. This expression may be expanded in a series as follows:

$$\frac{\pi}{h}\left[\frac{1}{\frac{\pi\Delta x}{h}} + \frac{1}{3}\left(\frac{\pi\Delta x}{h}\right)^2 - \frac{1}{45}\left(\frac{\pi\Delta x}{h}\right)^4 + \right] - \frac{1}{\Delta x} =$$

$$\frac{\pi}{h}\left[\frac{1}{3}\left(\frac{\pi\Delta x}{h}\right) - \frac{1}{45}\left(\frac{\pi\Delta x}{h}\right)^3 + \ldots\right]$$

The negative derivative of this expression times $\frac{\Gamma\Delta l}{4\pi}$ gives the induced velocity of a series of positive double sources located at $x=0$ and $y=nh$ where n assumes all positive and negative integral values excepting zero. Hence

$$v_T = -\frac{\Gamma\Delta l}{4\pi}\frac{d}{dx}\frac{\pi}{h}\left[\frac{1}{3}\frac{\pi\Delta x}{h} - \frac{1}{45}\left(\frac{\pi\Delta x}{h}\right)^2 + \ldots\right]$$

$$= -\frac{\Gamma\Delta l}{4\pi}\left(\frac{\pi}{h}\right)^2\left(\frac{1}{3} - \frac{2}{45}\frac{\pi\Delta x}{h} + \ldots\right)$$

or for small values of Δx

$$v_T = -\frac{1}{3}\left(\frac{\pi}{h}\right)^2\frac{\Gamma\Delta l}{4\pi} \qquad \text{(V)}$$

and similarly for a row of doublets on the y-axis with *alternating* signs

$$v_T = +\frac{1}{6}\left(\frac{\pi}{h}\right)^2\frac{\Gamma\Delta l}{4\pi} \qquad \text{(VI)}$$

By means of the above formulas the interference caused by rectangular tunnels can be determined. The following five cases are investigated:

I. Tunnel entirely enclosed.
II. Free jet.
III. Horizontal boundaries only.
IV. Vertical boundaries only.
V. Bottom boundary only.

The wing will be represented by a positive double source, which is equivalent to considering the airfoil small compared with the cross section C of the tunnel. The conditions for which this assumption is permissible or of value will be specified later.

Case I—Closed tunnel.—The images of the airfoil are conveniently represented by the schematic diagram of Figure 3.[1] Let h be the height of the tunnel and b the width. The upflow velocity caused by a row of doublets located at $x=mb$ is from (IV) for alternating signs

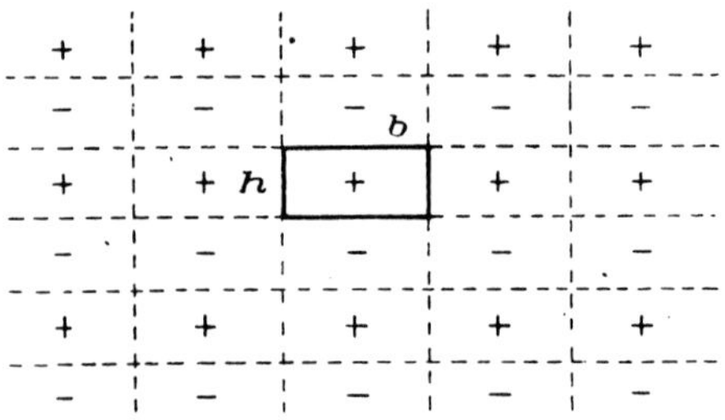

FIGURE 3.—Vortex arrangement for closed tunnel

$$v_T = \frac{\Gamma\Delta l}{4\pi}\left(\frac{\pi}{h}\right)^2\frac{\cosh\frac{\pi mb}{h}}{\sinh^2\frac{\pi mb}{h}}$$

For the row at $x=0$, from (VI)

$$v_T = \frac{1}{6}\left(\frac{\pi}{h}\right)^2\frac{\Gamma\Delta l}{4\pi}$$

By summing up the effect of all rows from $x=-\infty$ to $x=+\infty$ the total interference effect at the origin is obtained as

$$v_T = \frac{\Gamma\Delta l}{2\pi}\left(\frac{\pi}{h}\right)^2\left(\frac{1}{12} + \sum_{m=1}^{\infty}\frac{\cosh\frac{\pi mb}{h}}{\sinh^2\frac{\pi mb}{h}}\right)$$

$$= \frac{\Gamma\Delta l}{2\pi}\left(\frac{\pi}{h}\right)^2\left(\frac{1}{12} + S_1\right) \qquad \text{(VII)}$$

[1] The doublets in Figures 3 to 7 are indicated by single signs.

The series term in the above expression converges rapidly. We have to consider, however, a large number of small terms all of the same sign. A little farther on it will be shown how the value of the expression can be obtained with better than 1 per cent accuracy by the use of an expression representing *all* terms of the series beyond the first.

Case II—Free jet.—The images of the airfoil are, for analytical purposes, represented by the schematic

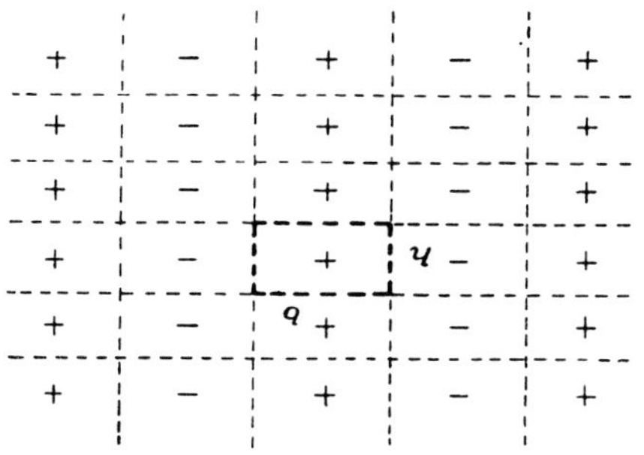

FIGURE 4.—Vortex arrangement for free jet

diagram of Figure 4. For a vertical row located at $x=mb$ one obtains correspondingly from Formula (III)

$$v_T=\frac{\Gamma\Delta l}{4\pi}\left(\frac{\pi}{h}\right)^2\frac{1}{\sinh^2\frac{\pi mb}{h}}(-1)^m$$

where the factor $(-1)^m$ takes care of the alternating signs of each row. For the row at $x=0$ from (V)

$$v_T=-\frac{1}{3}\left(\frac{\pi}{h}\right)^2\frac{\Gamma\Delta l}{4\pi}$$

By summing up for all integral values of m from minus to plus infinity there results

$$v_T=\frac{\Gamma\Delta l}{2\pi}\left(\frac{\pi}{h}\right)^2\left[-\frac{1}{6}+\sum_{1}^{\infty}\frac{(-1)^m}{\sinh^2\frac{\pi mb}{h}}\right]$$

$$=\frac{\Gamma\Delta l}{2\pi}\left(\frac{\pi}{h}\right)^2\left(-\frac{1}{6}+S_2\right) \qquad \text{(VIII)}$$

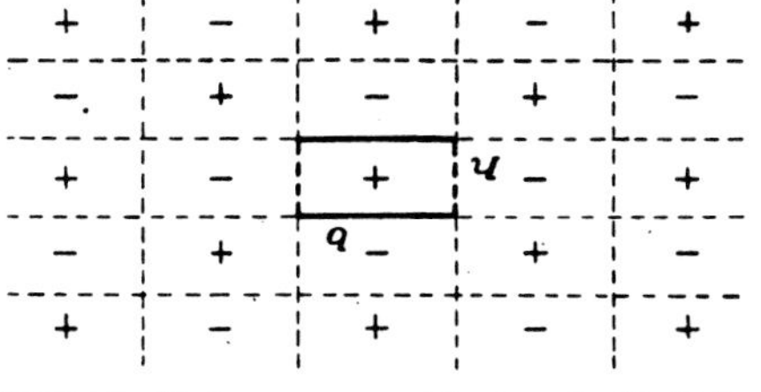

FIGURE 5.—Vortex arrangement for tunnel with horizontal boundaries

Case III—Top and bottom closed, sides free.—The arrangement of images is as indicated in Figure 5. The flow at $x=0$, due to an alternating row at $x=mb$, is again given by Formula (IV) as

$$v_T=\frac{\Gamma\Delta l}{4\pi}\left(\frac{\pi}{h}\right)^2\frac{\cosh\frac{\pi mb}{h}}{\sinh^2\frac{\pi mb}{h}}(-1)^m$$

and for the zero row from Formula (VI) as

$$v_T=\frac{1}{6}\left(\frac{\pi}{h}\right)^2\frac{\Gamma\Delta l}{4\pi}$$

The total interference is thus given as

$$v_T=\frac{\Gamma\Delta l}{2\pi}\left(\frac{\pi}{h}\right)^2\left[\frac{1}{12}+\sum_{m=1}^{\infty}\frac{\cosh\frac{\pi mb}{h}}{\sinh^2\frac{\pi mb}{h}}(-1^m)\right]$$

$$=\frac{\Gamma\Delta l}{2\pi}\left(\frac{\pi}{h}\right)^2\left(\frac{1}{12}+S_3\right) \qquad \text{(IX)}$$

Case IV—Sides closed, top and bottom open.—The arrangement of images is here as indicated in Figure 6

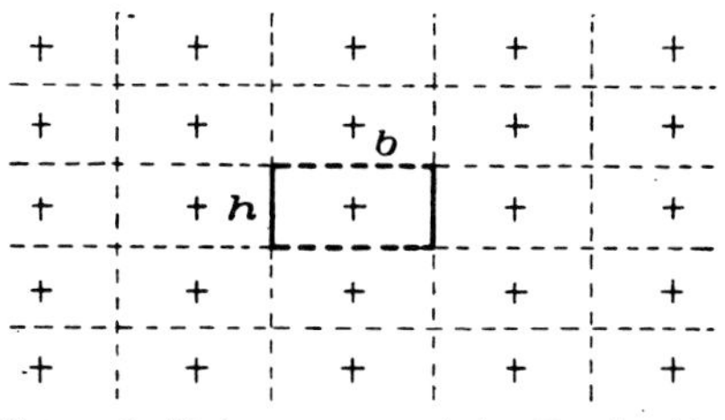

FIGURE 6.—Vortex arrangement for tunnel with vertical boundaries

Notice that all images are positive. The flow at the origin due to a row at $x=mb$ is from (III)

$$v_T=\frac{\Gamma\Delta l}{4\pi}\left(\frac{\pi}{h}\right)^2\frac{\cosh\frac{\pi mb}{h}}{\sinh^2\frac{\pi mb}{h}}$$

except for the row at $x=0$, which is given by

$$v_T=-\frac{1}{3}\left(\frac{\pi}{h}\right)^2\frac{\Gamma\Delta l}{4\pi}$$

Again by summation

$$v_T=\frac{\Gamma\Delta l}{2\pi}\left(\frac{\pi}{h}\right)^2\left(-\frac{1}{6}+\sum_{m=1}^{\infty}\frac{\cosh\frac{\pi mb}{h}}{\sinh^2\frac{\pi mb}{h}}\right)$$

$$=\frac{\Gamma\Delta l}{2\pi}\left(\frac{\pi}{h}\right)^2\left(-\frac{1}{6}+S_4\right) \qquad \text{(X)}$$

The labor of summing up the rather slowly converging series S_4 can again be avoided, as will be shown.

Case V—Bottom or top boundary only.—The arrangement of images is as shown in Figure 7 for bottom boundary only. The flow at the origin due

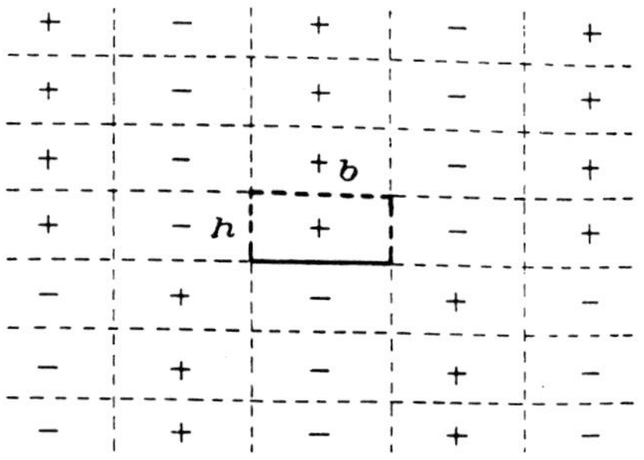

FIGURE 7.—Vortex arrangement for tunnel with bottom boundary only

to the mth vertical row at $x=mb$ is simply equal to the flow caused by the doublet located at $y=0$, since all the other doublets cancel each other in pairs. Or

$$v_T=\frac{\Gamma\Delta l}{4\pi}\,2\sum_{m=1}^{\infty}\frac{(-1)^m}{m^2\,b^2}$$

But

$$\sum_{m=1}^{\infty}\frac{(-1)^m}{m^2}=-\frac{\pi^2}{12}$$

Hence,

$$\begin{aligned}v_T&=-\frac{\Gamma\Delta l}{2\pi}\cdot\frac{1}{b^2}\cdot\frac{\pi^2}{12}\\&=-\frac{\Gamma\Delta l}{2\pi}\left(\frac{\pi}{h}\right)^2\cdot\left(\frac{h}{\pi}\right)^2\frac{1}{b^2}\cdot\frac{\pi^2}{12}\\&=-\frac{\Gamma\Delta l}{2\pi}\cdot\left(\frac{\pi}{h}\right)^2\cdot\left(\frac{h}{b}\right)^2\cdot\frac{1}{12}\qquad\text{(XI)}\end{aligned}$$

The process of evaluating the two rather slowly converging series S_1 and S_4 will now be indicated. The individual terms represent, as shown, the interference due to a row of doublets at $x=mb$. For large values of m it does not matter whether a doublet of strength $\Gamma\Delta l$ is arranged at $x=mb$ or whether two vortices of opposite sign and of strength $\frac{\Gamma\Delta l}{b}$ are substituted at $x=\left(m-\frac{1}{2}\right)b$ and $x=\left(m+\frac{1}{2}\right)b$, respectively. By the second arrangement all vortices except the one nearest the origin are cancelled by being superimposed on one of opposite sign. The entire effect of all vertical rows of positive doublets extending from $x=mb$ to infinity is thus represented by the effect of a single positive vortex row of a strength $\frac{\Gamma\Delta l}{b}$ located at $x=\left(p+\frac{1}{2}\right)b$ where p is the number of the last doublet taken into account. The accuracy is the greater, the greater the chosen value of p. Fortunately, it is found that it is sufficient to make $p=1$ and still retain an accuracy of better than 1 per cent. The numerical evaluation of the expressions is thus greatly simplified.

The effect of *single* sources is given by (I) for rows of the same sign as

$$v_T=\frac{\Gamma}{4\pi}\left(\frac{\pi}{h}\right)\coth\frac{\pi x}{h}$$

and by (II) for rows of alternating signs as

$$v_T=\frac{\Gamma}{4\pi}\left(\frac{\pi}{h}\right)\operatorname{cosech}\frac{\pi x}{h}$$

The series $S_1=\sum_{1}^{\infty}\frac{\cosh\frac{\pi m b}{h}}{\sinh^2\frac{\pi m b}{h}}$ may then accordingly be written as $S_1=\sum_{m=1}^{m=p}\frac{\cosh\frac{\pi m b}{h}}{\sinh^2\frac{\pi m b}{h}}$

$$+\frac{1}{b}\left(\frac{\pi}{h}\right)^{-1}\operatorname{cosech}\frac{\pi\left(p+\frac{1}{2}\right)b}{h}$$

and $S_4=\sum_{1}^{\infty}\frac{1}{\sinh^2\frac{\pi m b}{h}}$ may be written as

$$S_4=\sum_{m=1}^{m=p}\frac{1}{\sinh^2\frac{\pi m b}{h}}+\frac{1}{b}\left(\frac{\pi}{h}\right)^{-1}\coth\frac{\pi\left(p+\frac{1}{2}\right)b}{h}$$

As mentioned above, we obtain accuracy greater than is needed for any practical purposes by making $p=1$ in the above finite series expression. The remaining series S_2 and S_3 are obtained without any difficulties.

The expressions (VII) to (X) giving the induced flow at $x=0$ are all of the form

$$v_T=\frac{\Gamma\Delta l}{2\pi}\left(\frac{\pi}{h}\right)^2(a+\Sigma)$$

where Σ stands for S_1, S_2, S_3, or S_4, and a is a numerical constant. By means of the aerodynamical relation

$$\Gamma\Delta l\rho V=\frac{1}{2}C_L\rho V^2 S$$

where ρ is the density and V the velocity of the medium, and by putting

$$\frac{v_T}{V}=\epsilon,$$

the upward inclination of the air stream, there results

$$\epsilon=\frac{C_L S}{4\pi}\left(\frac{\pi}{h}\right)^2(a+\Sigma)$$

or with $bh=C$ and $\frac{b}{h}=r$

$$\epsilon=\frac{C_L S}{C}\frac{\pi r}{4}(a+\Sigma)_n$$

On writing

$$\epsilon=\frac{C_L S}{C}\delta\qquad\text{(XII)}$$

where

$$\delta=\frac{\pi r}{4}(a+\Sigma)\qquad\text{(XIII)}$$

it is noticed that the angle of up-flow ϵ is proportional to the lift coefficient C_L, to the ratio of wing area to tunnel cross section $\frac{S}{C}$, and to the quantity δ which in turn is seen to be a function solely of the width to height ratio $\frac{b}{h}$ or r.

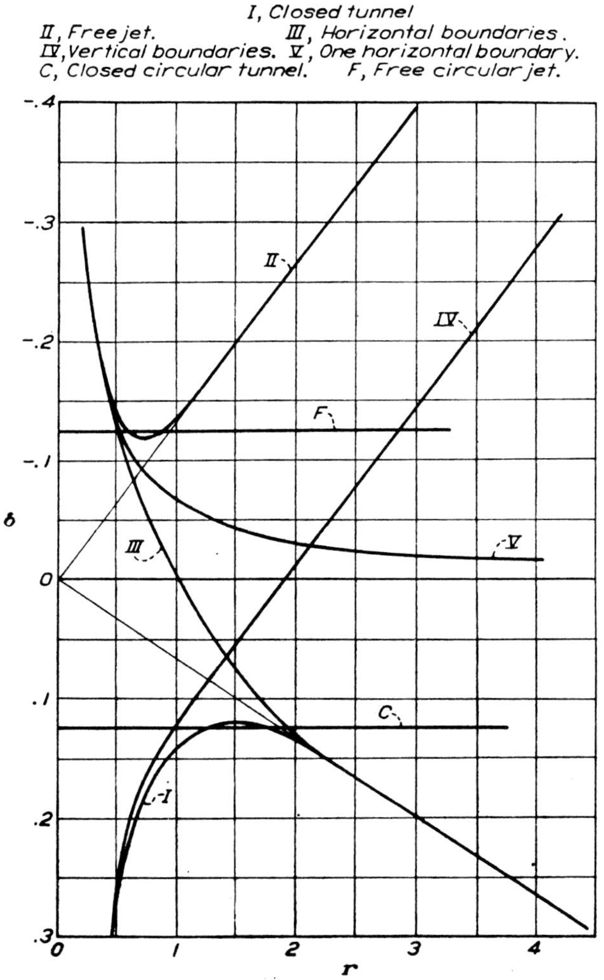

FIGURE 8.—Tunnel-wall correction δ for five types of rectangular tunnels of width-height ratio r

The values of δ for the five cases considered are given below:

$$\text{I.}\quad \delta=\frac{\pi r}{4}\left(\frac{1}{12}+S_1\right)$$

$$\text{II.}\quad \delta=\frac{\pi r}{4}\left(-\frac{1}{6}+S_2\right)$$

$$\text{III.}\quad \delta=\frac{\pi r}{4}\left(\frac{1}{12}+S_3\right)$$

$$\text{IV.}\quad \delta=\frac{\pi r}{4}\left(-\frac{1}{6}+S_4\right)$$

$$\text{V.}\quad \delta=\frac{\pi r}{4}\left(-\frac{1}{12}\frac{1}{r^2}\right)$$

These values are given in Table I and also plotted in Figure 8 against the single variable r as abscissa. This figure gives in a convenient way the essential results of the preceding analysis.

The square tunnel, $\frac{b}{h}=1$, gives identical numerical values of the interference whether it is open or closed, as is also the case for the circle. The square tunnel with horizontal boundaries shows no interference. A rather interesting result! Notice also that the open tunnels of the conventional width to height ratio exhibit a much larger correction factor than the closed type. Notice further that all of the proposed types are superior to the conventional ones and in particular the surprisingly beneficial effect of a lower horizontal boundary on an otherwise free jet.

WIND TUNNELS FREE FROM WALL INTERFERENCE

Inasmuch as wind-tunnel testing is largely concerned with the prediction of free-flight performance of aircraft, it is highly desirable to employ a wind tunnel having no wall interference. Such a tunnel is in this respect entirely equivalent to an air stream of infinite cross section.

The results of the preceding analysis as represented in Figure 8 show that we are perfectly able to devise such a tunnel. Curve III, which corresponds to Case III, crosses the $\delta=0$ line at $r=1$, showing that a square tunnel with walls at top and bottom and both sides removed has zero wall interference. Such a type of tunnel exhibits the particular advantages of the open-jet tunnel and is distinctly superior to both of the conventional types by reason of the fact that it has zero wall interference, or stated otherwise, that it is equivalent to an infinite jet of air.

It is further noticed that the curve IV representing the tunnel with closed sides crosses the $\delta=0$ line at $r=1.9$, showing that a rectangular jet of a width to height ratio of a little less than 2:1 and equipped only with vertical walls exhibits zero wall interference. There is, however, a condition which renders the use of a tunnel wall correction in this particular case rather questionable.

A single fixed horizontal boundary has also a surprisingly beneficial guiding effect. The interference in the case of a 2:1 tunnel is seen from Figure 8 to be reduced from $\delta=0.262$ for a free jet to $\delta=0.033$ for curve V representing a tunnel equipped with a bottom boundary only. The interference is still of the same sign, but eight times smaller. Whether a fixed bottom or top boundary is employed is immaterial, since the result of the analysis in both cases is the same. As regards the accurate prediction of the interference effect, it will be pointed out, however, that it is necessary to employ a tunnel with a fixed *bottom*.

EFFECT OF THE EXIT CONE

The preceding Case II refers strictly to a *free* jet. As such is defined a jet which meets no obstructions behind the model body. Correspondingly, in Case IV there must be no obstruction to prevent the free flow of the air in a vertical direction.

The main effect of the exit cone as regards the wall interference is to guide the air back into its original direction. In a well-designed cone with a small angle of divergence and sufficient bell we may assume this end to be achieved completely, as indicated in Figure 9.

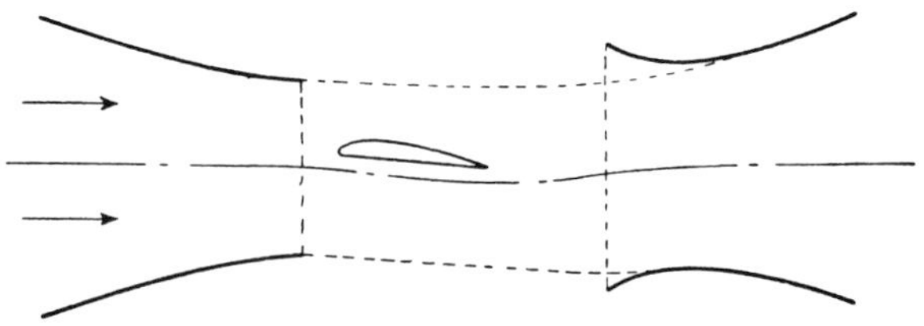

FIGURE 9.—Showing guiding effect of exit cone

The effect of the cone may then, as far as the interference goes, be equivalent to the creation of a countercirculation of magnitude $-\Gamma$ located some distance behind the entrance of the cone. The "trailing" vortices will thus not extend from the plane of the airfoil to infinity, as was assumed in the earlier cases, but will close themselves in the exit cone. The numerical value of the interference can readily be found in each particular case, although the method is rather cumbersome.

The solution is mathematically obtainable; there exist, however, some practical difficulties concerning the assumption of the type of flow to be expected in the exit cone. If the cone is rather large and of poor efficiency, a condition similar to Case II, that of an entirely free jet, may actually occur. When the downflow becomes large, the possibility exists that the jet may break loose from the upper side of the cone and follow along the lower. Not only that, but, if the exit cone has an entrance too slightly belled or with no bell at all, the air may *spill* underneath the exit cone. It is entirely possible to imagine that the jet is deflected downward to such an extent that the correction will exceed that of a free jet. The difficulty in these several cases is that the correction factor δ is dependent on the amount of the downflow and on factors of rather vaguely definable and unstable nature. In fact, it is probable that the interference is not even a continuous function of the downflow, but is subject to abrupt changes at certain critical values.

If the tunnel is closed entirely or on the top and bottom sides, this difficulty is dispensed with and the exact mathematical prediction of the tunnel wall correction is possible. This fact is essential, since there exists no experimental method by which the existing angle of downflow of the air current *at* the location of the test model can be obtained.

Attention is, therefore, again directed to the tunnels which have already been referred to as having no wall interference. One of these is of a square cross section with two horizontal fixed boundaries. In contrast to the second type of tunnel with no wall interference, there is in this case no possibility of spillage. The lateral deflection of the air stream is negligible, compared with the vertical, and since the air stream enters the diffuser cone in perfect alignment no radical changes in the type of flow in the cone are to be expected. The third type of the proposed tunnels, the one with a lower boundary only, will obviously achieve the same end. Because a more efficient utilization of the cross section of this tunnel is possible, and since the interference for a 2:1 tunnel is eight times smaller than that for the free jet type of the same side ratio, the superiority of this latter type is obvious.

EFFECT OF LARGE WING SPAN

The effect of the airfoil has hitherto been represented by vortex doublets. The permissibility of this purely mathematical simplification will now be given some attention. Let us consider the airfoil to be represented by a vortex pair located a distance apart comparable to the width of the tunnel.

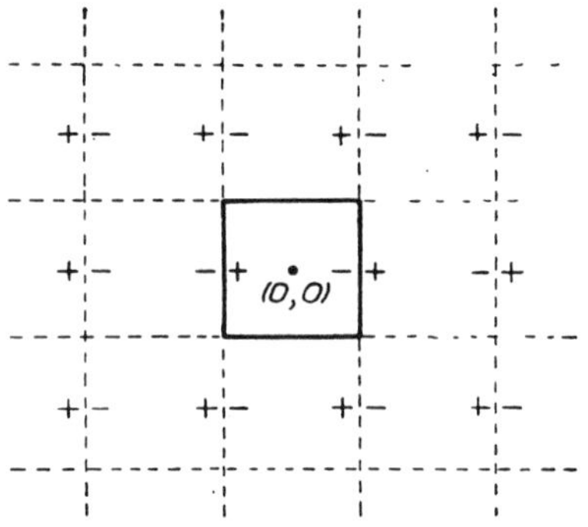

FIGURE 10.—Vortex arrangement in closed square tunnel with airfoil span three-fourths tunnel width

Let Figure 10 represent a closed tunnel. For single alternating vortices in a vertical row, Equation (II) gives

$$\frac{4\pi v_n}{\Gamma}=\frac{\pi}{h}\operatorname{cosech}\frac{\pi x}{h}$$

But

$$\Gamma\cdot\Delta l\rho V=\frac{1}{2}\rho V^2 SC_L$$

Hence

$$\epsilon=\frac{v_n}{V}=\frac{SC_L}{8\Delta lh}\operatorname{cosech}\frac{\pi x}{h} \qquad \text{(XIV)}$$

For the *first* row on either side of the origin, however, it is necessary to omit the vortex located on the x-axis, or

$$\epsilon=\frac{SC_L}{8\Delta lh}\cdot\left(\operatorname{cosech}\frac{\pi x}{h}-\frac{1}{\frac{\pi x}{h}}\right) \qquad \text{(XV)}$$

These formulas will be applied to the square tunnel with $\Delta l=\frac{3}{4}b$ or the span of the airfoil equal to three-quarters of the tunnel width. The interference at the center ($x=0$) is

$$\delta=\frac{1}{3}\left(-\frac{1}{\sinh\frac{3}{8}\pi}+\frac{1}{\frac{3}{8}\pi}+\frac{1}{\sinh\frac{5}{8}\pi}-\frac{1}{\sinh\frac{11}{8}\pi}+\frac{1}{\sinh\frac{13}{8}\pi}+\dots\right)=0.147$$

and the interference at the tip

$$\delta=\frac{1}{6}\left(-\frac{1}{\sinh\frac{3}{4}\pi}+\frac{1}{\frac{3}{4}\pi}+\frac{1}{\sinh\frac{1}{4}\pi}-\frac{1}{\sinh\pi}+\frac{1}{\sinh\frac{5}{4}\pi}+\frac{1}{\sinh\pi}-\frac{1}{\sinh\frac{7}{4}\pi}+\dots\right)=0.239$$

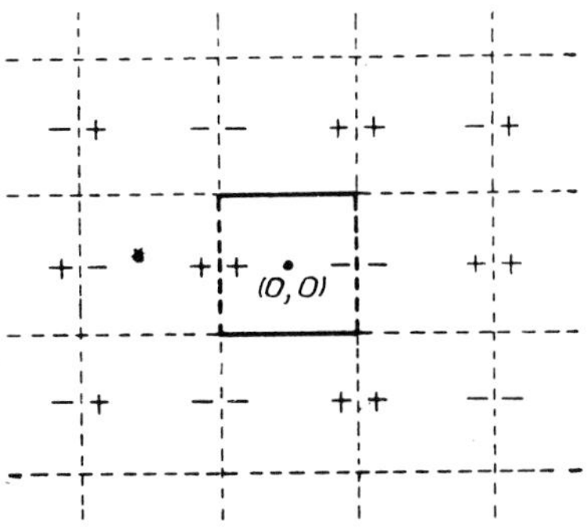

FIGURE 11.—Vortex arrangement in square tunnel with horizontal boundaries with airfoil span three-fourths tunnel width

The next important case, III, horizontal boundaries only, is shown in Figure 11. At the center

$$\delta=\frac{1}{3}\left(-\frac{1}{\sinh\frac{3}{8}\pi}+\frac{1}{\frac{3}{8}\pi}-\frac{1}{\sinh\frac{5}{8}\pi}+\frac{1}{\sinh\frac{11}{8}\pi}+\dots\right)=-0.028$$

At the tip

$$\delta=\frac{1}{6}\left(-\frac{1}{\sinh\frac{3}{4}\pi}+\frac{1}{\frac{3}{4}\pi}-\frac{1}{\sinh\frac{1}{4}\pi}+\frac{1}{\sinh\pi}+\frac{1}{\sinh\frac{5}{4}\pi},-\frac{1}{\sinh\pi}+\frac{1}{\sinh\frac{7}{4}\pi}+\dots\right)=-0.148$$

This calculation can be easily performed for any particular case by means of the formulas (XIV) and (XV). It is left to the reader, therefore, to check any case with which he is concerned. Notice from the preceding examples that it is undesirable to use an airfoil which has an equivalent span of three-quarters of the width of a square tunnel because the interference differs too much over the span. The flow at the center does not, however, differ materially from the flow at shorter spans. It is thus possible to study the flow near the fuselage of an airplane or model which may otherwise be too large for the tunnel.

WING INTERCEPTING THE TEST TUNNEL

The undesirable condition of unequal interference along the span is still more pronounced when the wing span exceeds the width of the tunnel. In the limiting case, let the circulation along the wing be constant. The trailing vortices are then, mathematically speaking, located at $x=\pm\frac{b}{2}$. Considering the case of a closed tunnel, we can readily see that the real and a corresponding pair of virtual vortices cancel each other and that all the remaining virtual vortices cancel each other in pairs. On the other hand, for a free jet the interference near the vertical surface approaches theoretically an infinite value due to the nearness of the first image. The flow near the center, however, remains finite.

It is difficult to imagine that tests on airfoils intercepting a free test jet would be of any value whatsoever except in the study of local conditions. The prediction of the lift distribution is mathematically of great difficulty, and moreover, the distribution differs too greatly along the span to permit the application of the results to other conditions. It may be postulated that the interference effect along the span must be nearly a constant. Only in this case can a correction be applied that is of sufficient simplicity and accuracy.

CONCLUSIONS

Several rectangular wind tunnel arrangements that exhibit zero or negligible wall interference have been brought out by a mathematical analysis of the general problem of tunnel interference. Uniform formulas have been presented for the calculation of the wall interference for the conventional as well as for the newly proposed wind tunnels.

It has been indicated that the exact prediction of the interference for tunnels with no lower horizontal boundaries is greatly impaired by the inherent instability of the flow in the exit cone. Attention has been brought to the importance of employing an exit cone with a small angle of divergence, and also to the importance of having the air stream properly centered at the entrance of the jet. A tunnel with a jet free on three sides and restricted only by a lower horizontal boundary extending along the test section from the entrance to the exit cone, is finally recommended as the most promising choice. The correction for this type is from five to eight times smaller than that of the corresponding free jet type.

LANGLEY MEMORIAL AERONAUTICAL LABORATORY,
NATIONAL ADVISORY COMMITTEE FOR AERONAUTICS,
LANGLEY FIELD, VA., *October 9, 1931.*

REFERENCES

1. Glauert, H.: The Elements of Aerofoil and Airscrew Theory. Cambridge University Press, 1926.
2. Prandtl, L., and Betz, A.: Vier Abhandlungen zur Hydrodynamik und Aerodynamik. Göttingen, 1927.
3. Smithsonian Mathematical Formulae and Tables of Elliptic Functions. Publication 2672, Smithsonian Institution, 1922.

TABLE I

VALUES OF SINH πr, COSH, πr AND δ

$$\delta_1=\frac{\pi}{4}r\left(\sum_1^p\frac{\cosh n\pi r}{\sinh^2 n\pi r}+\frac{1}{12}\right)+\frac{1}{4\sinh\left(p+\frac{1}{2}\right)\pi r}\quad\text{closed tunnel}$$

$$\delta_2=\frac{\pi}{4}r\left(\sum_1^\infty\frac{(-1)^n}{\sinh^2 n\pi r}-\frac{1}{6}\right)\quad\text{free jet}$$

$$\delta_3=\frac{\pi}{4}r\left(\sum_1^\infty\frac{(-1)^n\cosh n\pi r}{\sinh^2 n\pi r}+\frac{1}{12}\right)\quad\text{horizontal boundaries}$$

$$\delta_4=\frac{\pi}{4}r\left(\sum_1^p\frac{1}{\sinh^2 n\pi r}-\frac{1}{6}\right)+\frac{1}{4}\coth\left(p+\frac{1}{2}\right)\pi r,\quad\text{vertical boundaries}$$

$$\delta_5=\frac{\pi}{4}r\left(-\frac{1}{12r^2}\right)=-\frac{\pi}{48}\cdot\frac{1}{r}\quad\text{one horizontal boundary}$$

r	sinh πr	cosh πr	r	δ_1	δ_2	δ_3	δ_4	δ_5
0	0	1. 00	0	∞	— ∞	— ∞	+ ∞	— ∞
. 125	. 4032	1. 078	. 125	1. 055	−0. 524	−0. 524	+1. 051	−0. 524
. 250	. 8686	1. 324	. 25	. 523	—. 262	—. 262	+. 524	—. 262
. 375	1. 4702	1. 778	. 50	. 263	—. 137	—. 127	+. 262	—. 131
. 500	2. 299	2. 507	. 625	. 213	—. 122	—. 089	+. 210	—. 105
. 625	3. 492	3. 632	. 75	. 175	—. 120	—. 056	+. 161	—. 087
. 750	5. 227	5. 322	1. 00	. 138	—. 137	. 000	+. 124	—. 066
1. 00	11. 530	11. 574	1. 50	. 120	—. 197	+. 077	+. 054	—. 044
1. 50	55. 52	55. 53	2. 00	. 137	—. 262	+. 126	—. 012	—. 033
2. 0	267	267	4. 00	. 262	—. 524	+. 262	—. 276	—. 016
∞	∞	∞	∞	∞	— ∞	+ ∞	— ∞	. 000

THEORY OF WING SECTIONS OF ARBITRARY SHAPE

BY THEODORE THEODORSEN

National Advisory Committee for Aeronautics

Report No. 411, 1931

SUMMARY

This paper presents a solution of the problem of the theoretical flow of a frictionless incompressible fluid past airfoils of arbitrary forms. The velocity of the 2-dimensional flow is explicitly expressed for any point at the surface, and for any orientation, by an exact expression containing a number of parameters which are functions of the form only and which may be evaluated by convenient graphical methods. The method is particularly simple and convenient for bodies of streamline forms. The results have been applied to typical airfoils and compared with experimental data.

INTRODUCTION

The theory of airfoils is of vital importance in aeronautics. It is true that the limit of perfection as regards efficiency has almost been reached. This attainment is a result of persistent and extensive testing by a large number of institutions rather than of the fact that the important design factors are known. Without the knowledge of the theory of the air flow around airfoils it is well-nigh impossible to judge or interpret the results of experimental work intelligently or to make other than random improvements at the expense of much useless testing.

A science can develop on a purely experimental basis only for a certain time. Theory is a process of systematic arrangement and simplification of known facts. As long as the facts are few and obvious no theory is necessary, but when they become many and less simple theory is needed. Although the experimenting itself may require little effort, it is, however, often exceedingly difficult to analyze the results of even simple experiments. There exists, therefore, always a tendency to produce more test results than can be digested by theory or applied by industry. A large number of investigations are carried on with little regard for the theory and much testing of airfoils is done with insufficient knowledge of the ultimate possibilities. This state of affairs is due largely to the very common belief that the theory of the actual airfoil necessarily would be approximate, clumsy, and awkward, and therefore useless for nearly all purposes.

The various types of airfoils exhibit quite different properties, and it is one of the objects of aerodynamical science to detect and define in precise manner the factors contributing to the perfection of the airfoil. Above all, we must work toward the end of obtaining a thorough understanding of the ideal case, which is the ultimate limit of performance. We may then attempt to specify and define the nature of the deviations from the ideal case.

No method has been available for the determination of the potential flow around an arbitrary thick wing section. The exclusive object of the following report is to present a method by which the flow velocity at any point along the surface of a thick airfoil may be determined with any desired accuracy. The velocity of the potential flow around the thick airfoil has been expressed by an exact formula, no approximation having been made in the analysis. The evaluation for specific cases, however, requires a graphical determination of some auxiliary parameters. Since the airfoil is perfectly arbitrary, it is, of course, obvious that graphical methods are to some extent unavoidable.

Curiously enough, the theory of actual airfoils as presented in this report has been brought into a much simpler form than has hitherto been the case with the theory of thin airfoils. In the theory of thin airfoils certain approximations have restricted its application to small cambers only. This undesirable feature has been avoided, and the results obtained in this report have a complete applicability to airfoils of any camber and thickness.

The author has pointed out in an earlier report that another difficulty exists in the theory of thin airfoils. It consists in the fact that in potential flow the velocity at the leading edge is infinite at all angles except one. This particular angle at which the theory actually applies has been defined as the ideal angle of attack. In the present work we shall not go any further into this theory, since it is included in the following theory as a special case of rather limited practical importance.

THEORY OF THICK AIRFOILS

In the theory of functions there is a theorem by Riemann[1] which shows that it is always possible to transform the potential field around any closed contour into the potential field around a circle. The direct transformation of an airfoil into a circle may,

[1] Handbuch der Physik, Band III, p. 245, Fundamentalsatz der konformen Abbildung.

for analytical purposes, conveniently be performed in two steps. The first step is to transform the airfoil into a curve which ordinarily does not differ greatly from a circle by the transformation

$$\zeta = z' + \frac{a^2}{z'} \tag{I}$$

where ζ is a complex quantity defining the points in the plane describing the flow around the airfoil and z' is another complex quantity defining the points in the plane describing the flow around the almost circular curve. The constant a is of dimension length and is merely a geometrical scale factor. In the following theory, attention is directed to the fact that the shape of the curve resulting from transformation (I) is arbitrary, since the airfoil shape is arbitrary. At a later point we shall transform this curve into a circle.

The z' and the ζ planes are shown superposed in Figure 1. It will be noticed that at great distances

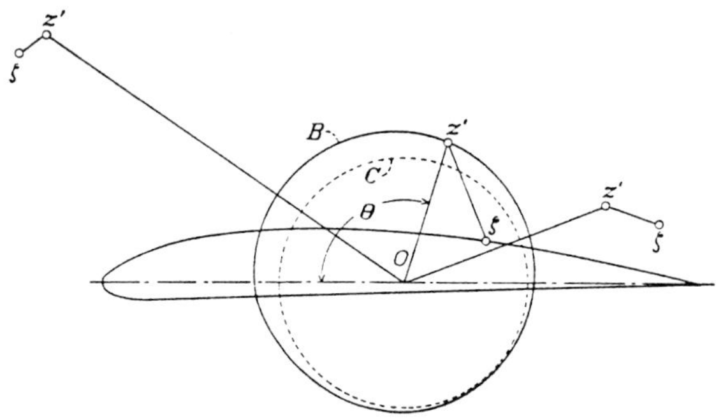

FIGURE 1.—Showing the transformation from a noncircular curve B into an airfoil

from the origin $z' \to \zeta$; that is, both flows are similar at infinity. In particular, the "angle of attack," defined as the direction of flow at infinitity with respect to some fixed reference line in the body, is identical in both flows. Near the origin the two flows are entirely different; one value of z' is, however, uniquely associated with a given value of ζ by the relation (I).

We shall, at a later point, determine the flow in the z' plane. At present we shall determine the appearance of the airfoil when the almost circular curve B is given, or what amounts to the same thing, we shall determine the curve B when the airfoil is given. In Figure 1, C is a circle of unit radius. Since the matter of dimensions is rather important, we shall avoid confusion in the following by adhering to this length as unity. The curve B is uniquely given by the relation $z' = ae^{\psi + i\theta}$ where ψ is a known or unknown real function of the angle θ where θ varies from zero to 2π and i is the imaginary unit. Since the airfoil surface corresponds to the surface of the curve, the former is given from relation (I) as

$$\zeta = a\ e^{\psi + i\theta} + a\ e^{-\psi - i\theta}$$

or

$$\zeta = a(e^{\psi} + e^{-\psi})\cos\theta + i\ a(e^{\psi} - e^{-\psi})\sin\theta$$

This relation may further be conveniently expressed in hyperbolic functions

$$\zeta = 2a \cosh\psi \cos\theta + 2ia \sinh\psi \sin\theta$$

Since $\zeta = x + iy$, the coordinates of the airfoil (x, y) are given by

$$\begin{aligned} x &= 2a \cosh\psi \cos\theta \\ y &= 2a \sinh\psi \sin\theta \end{aligned} \tag{II}$$

We obtain a relation between θ and the coordinates of the airfoil as follows:

$$\cosh\psi = \frac{x}{2a\cos\theta}$$

$$\sinh\psi = \frac{y}{2a\sin\theta}$$

and since $\cosh^2\psi - \sinh^2\psi = 1$

$$\left(\frac{x}{2a\cos\theta}\right)^2 - \left(\frac{y}{2a\sin\theta}\right)^2 = 1$$

or developed

$$2\sin^2\theta = p + \sqrt{p^2 + \left(\frac{y}{a}\right)^2} \tag{III}$$

where

$$p = 1 - \left(\frac{x}{2a}\right)^2 - \left(\frac{y}{2a}\right)^2$$

Similarly we obtain a relation between ψ and the coordinates of the airfoil by using the equation

$$\left(\frac{x}{2a\cosh\psi}\right)^2 + \left(\frac{y}{2a\sinh\psi}\right)^2 = 1$$

or developed

$$2\sinh^2\psi = -p + \sqrt{p^2 + \left(\frac{y}{a}\right)^2} \tag{IV}$$

Since ψ is generally small for wing sections it may be more conveniently expressed for purposes of calculation as a series in terms of $\frac{y}{2a\sin\theta}$, as follows:

We have

$$\begin{aligned} e^{\psi} &= \sinh\psi + \cosh\psi \\ &= \sinh\psi + \sqrt{1 + \sinh^2\psi} \\ &= 1 + \sinh\psi + \frac{1}{2}\sinh^2\psi + \cdots \\ \psi &= \log_e\left(1 + \sinh\psi + \frac{1}{2}\sinh^2\psi + \cdots\right) \\ &= \sinh\psi - \frac{1}{6}\sinh^3\psi + \cdots \\ &= \frac{y}{2a\sin\theta} - \frac{1}{6}\left(\frac{y}{2a\sin\theta}\right)^3 + \cdots \end{aligned} \tag{IVa}$$

$$[\text{for } \psi < \log_e 2]$$

We are now in a position to reproduce the conformal representation of an airfoil in the z' plane, since for each point of the airfoil (x, y) both θ and ψ have been determined.

The curves ψ = constant are ellipses in the ζ plane

$$\left(\frac{x}{2a\cosh\psi}\right)^2+\left(\frac{y}{2a\sinh\psi}\right)^2=1$$

The foci are located at $(\pm 2a, 0)$. The radius of curvature at the end of the major axis is $\rho=\frac{(2a\sinh\psi)^2}{2a\cosh\psi}$

or $$\frac{\rho}{2a}=\frac{(\sinh\psi)^2}{\cosh\psi}\cong\psi^2$$

$$\psi\cong\sqrt{\frac{\rho}{2a}}\text{ (for small }\psi)$$

This relation is useful for the determination of ψ near the nose and the tail.

The leading edge, corresponding to $\theta=0$, is located at

$$2a\cosh\cong\psi 2a\left(1+\frac{\psi^2}{2}\right)=2a+a\psi^2=2a+\frac{1}{2}\rho$$

Thus we see that the length $4a$ corresponds to the distance between the point midway between the nose and the center of curvature of the leading edge to the point midway between the tail and the center of curvature of the trailing edge.[2]

To establish the magnitude of the velocity at any point (x, y) on the airfoil, we start in customary manner with the velocity around a circle in 2-dimensional flow. Contrary to usual practice we will, however, make the radius of the circle equal to ae^{ψ_0} where ψ_0 is a small constant quantity. This quantity is shown later in this report (equation (e)), to represent the average value of ψ taken around the circle C.

The potential function of the flow past this circle is

$$w=-V\left(z+\frac{a^2e^{2\psi_0}}{z}\right)-\frac{i\Gamma}{2\pi}\log\frac{z}{ae^{\psi_0}} \qquad \text{(V)}$$

(reference 1, p. 83) and the velocity[3]

$$\frac{dw}{dz}=-V\left(1-\frac{a^2e^{2\psi_0}}{z^2}\right)-\frac{i\Gamma}{2\pi z} \qquad \text{(VI)}$$

where Γ is the circulation. This expression must vanish at the rear stagnation point[4] (Kutta condition) whose coordinate is $z=-ae^{\psi_0+i(\alpha+\epsilon_T)}$, where α is the angle of attack and ϵ_T is shown to be the angle of zero lift.

[2] The choice of axes is entirely arbitrary. It is a matter of convenience only to choose the axes so that the airfoil appears as nearly elliptical as possible, thereby making the "almost circular" curve B as nearly circular as possible by means of the single transformation I. It will be seen that the evaluation of the important integral appearing in the appendix is then most easily accomplished. In fact, the transformation I itself is only a matter of convenience to permit the ready evaluation of this integral.

[3] $\frac{dw}{dz}$ actually equals $u-iv$, the image of the velocity vector about the x-axis.

[4] It is worthy of mention to note that the theory outlined in this report may actually be applied to smooth *bodies* of arbitrary shape if the *circulation* is specified. The term "wing sections" has been used in the title to imply bodies with sharp (or nearly sharp) trailing edges, whose circulation is or may be considered fixed by the Kutta condition or some equivalent assumption.

149900—33——16

We obtain $\Gamma=-\frac{2\pi z}{i}V\left(1-\frac{a^2e^{2\psi_0}}{z^2}\right)$

$$=4\pi Vae^{\psi_0}\left(\frac{e^{i(\alpha+\epsilon_T)}-e^{-i(\alpha+\epsilon_T)}}{2i}\right)$$

$$=4\pi Vae^{\psi_0}\sin(\alpha+\epsilon_T) \qquad \text{(VII)}$$

This flow around the circle may now be transformed into the flow around any other body. In the particular case in which the flow at infinity is not altered the circulation will not be altered and the force experienced by a body at the origin will remain at the fixed value $L=\rho V\Gamma$.

We will now transform this circle, defined as $z=ae^{\psi_0+i\varphi}$ into our curve B defined by the relation $z'=ae^{\psi+i\theta}$. For this purpose we employ the general transformation $z'=ze^{\sum_n (A_n+iB_n)\frac{1}{z^n}}$ which leaves the flow at infinity unaltered, the constants being determined by the boundary conditions. By definition

$$z'=ze^{\psi-\psi_0+i(\theta-\varphi)}.$$

Consequently

$$\psi-\psi_0+i(\theta-\varphi)=\sum_n (A_n+iB_n)\frac{1}{z^n} \qquad \text{or}$$

$$\psi-\psi_0+i(\theta-\varphi)=\sum_n (A_n+iB_n)\frac{1}{r^n}(\cos n\varphi-i\sin n\varphi)$$

where z has been expressed in polar form

$$z=r(\cos\varphi+i\sin\varphi)$$

and by De Moivre's theorem

$$\frac{1}{z^n}=\frac{1}{r^n}(\cos n\varphi-i\sin n\varphi)$$

Equating the real and imaginary parts we obtain the two Fourier expansions:

$$\psi-\psi_0=\sum_n\left[\frac{A_n}{r^n}\cos n\varphi+\frac{B_n}{r^n}\sin n\varphi\right] \qquad \text{(a)}$$

and

$$\theta-\varphi=\sum_n\left[\frac{B_n}{r^n}\cos n\varphi-\frac{A_n}{r^n}\sin n\varphi\right] \qquad \text{(b)}$$

The values of the coefficients $\frac{A_n}{r^n}$, $\frac{B_n}{r^n}$, as well as the quantity ψ_0, may be determined from (a) as follows:

$$\frac{A_n}{r^n}=\frac{1}{\pi}\int_0^{2\pi}\psi\cos n\varphi\, d\varphi \qquad \text{(c)}$$

$$\frac{B_n}{r^n}=\frac{1}{\pi}\int_0^{2\pi}\psi\sin n\varphi\, d\varphi \qquad \text{(d)}$$

and

$$\psi_0=\frac{1}{2\pi}\int_0^{2\pi}\psi\, d\varphi \qquad \text{(e)}$$

The quantity $\theta-\varphi$ is necessary in the following analysis. Let us eliminate the coefficient $\frac{A_n}{r^n}$ and $\frac{B_n}{r^n}$ in (b) by means of (c) and (d).
We obtain

$$(\theta-\varphi)_c=\sum_n \cos n\varphi_c \frac{1}{\pi}\int_0^{2\pi}\psi \sin n\varphi d\varphi$$
$$-\sin n\varphi_c \frac{1}{\pi}\int_0^{2\pi}\psi \cos n\varphi d\varphi$$

The subscript c is added to indicate that the angles so distinguished are kept constant while the integrations are performed. The expression may be simplified

$$(\theta-\varphi)_c=\frac{1}{\pi}\sum_n\int_0^{2\pi}\psi\,(\sin n\varphi \cos n\varphi_c-\cos n\varphi \sin n\varphi_c)\,d\varphi$$
$$=\frac{1}{\pi}\sum_n\int_0^{2\pi}\psi \sin n(\varphi-\varphi_c)\,d\varphi$$

But

$$\sum_n \sin n\,(\varphi-\varphi_c)=\frac{1}{2}\cot\frac{(\varphi-\varphi_c)}{2}-\frac{\cos\,(2n+1)\frac{(\varphi-\varphi_c)}{2}}{2\sin\frac{\varphi-\varphi_c}{2}}$$

Therefore,

$$(\theta-\varphi)_c=\frac{1}{2\pi}\int_0^{2\pi}\psi\cot\frac{(\varphi-\varphi_c)}{2}d\varphi$$
$$-\frac{1}{2\pi}\int_0^{2\pi}\psi\frac{\cos\,(2n+1)\frac{(\varphi-\varphi_c)}{2}}{2\sin\frac{(\varphi-\varphi_c)}{2}}d\varphi$$

The latter integral is identically zero. (See Wilson, E. B. Advanced Calculus, p. 368. Follow method of exercise 10.)
Then

$$(\theta-\varphi)_c=\frac{1}{2\pi}\int_0^{2\pi}\psi\cot\frac{(\varphi-\varphi_c)}{2}d\varphi \qquad \text{(VIII)}$$

For purposes of calculation this integral is expressed in convenient form in the appendix.

We shall now resume the task of determining the velocity at any point of the surface of the airfoil.

The velocity at the surface of the circle is $\frac{dw}{dz}$ (see equation (VI) and footnote). For corresponding points on the curve B in the z' plane and on the airfoil in the ζ plane the velocities are respectively $\frac{dw}{dz}\cdot\frac{dz}{dz'}$ and $\frac{dw}{dz}\cdot\frac{dz}{dz'}\cdot\frac{dz'}{d\zeta}$.

The quantities ζ and z' are related by the expression

$$\zeta=z'+\frac{a^2}{z'}$$

Hence

$$\frac{d\zeta}{dz'}=1-\frac{a^2}{z'^2}=\frac{1}{z'}\left(z'-\frac{a^2}{z'}\right)=\frac{1}{z'}\,(ae^{\psi+i\theta}-ae^{-\psi-i\theta})$$
$$=\frac{1}{z'}\,[a(e^{\psi}-e^{-\psi})\cos\theta+ia\,(e^{\psi}+e^{-\psi})\sin\theta]$$
$$=\frac{1}{z'}\,[2a\sinh\psi\cos\theta+2ia\cosh\psi\sin\theta]$$

Using the relations (II),

$$2a\sinh\psi=\frac{y}{\sin\theta}\text{ and }2a\cosh\psi=\frac{x}{\cos\theta}$$

we obtain

$$\frac{d\zeta}{dz'}=\frac{1}{z'}\,(y\cot\theta+i\,x\tan\theta). \qquad \text{(IX)}$$

It now remains to find the ratio $\frac{dz}{dz'}$. From the relation

$$z'=z\,e^{\sum(A_n+iB_n)\frac{1}{z^n}}$$

we obtain

$$\frac{dz'}{dz}=z'\left[\frac{1}{z}+\frac{d}{dz}\sum_n(A_n+i\,B_n)\frac{1}{z^n}\right]$$

or

$$\frac{dz'}{dz}=z'\left(\frac{1}{z}+\frac{d}{dz}[(\psi-\psi_0)+i\,(\theta-\varphi)]\right)$$
$$=z'\frac{d}{dz}\,(\psi+i\,(\theta-\varphi)+\log z)$$

But

$$z=ae^{\psi_0+i\varphi}$$

from which,

$$\frac{1}{z}=\frac{d}{dz}\,(\log z)=\frac{d}{dz}\,(\log a+\psi_0+i\varphi)=\frac{d}{dz}\,(i\varphi)$$

Therefore

$$\frac{dz'}{dz}=z'\frac{d}{dz}\,(\psi+i\,(\theta-\varphi)+i\varphi)$$
$$=z'\frac{d}{dz}\,(\psi+i\theta)$$

This expression may be written

$$\frac{dz'}{dz}=z'\frac{d}{d\theta}\,(\psi+i\theta)\cdot\frac{d\theta}{dz}$$

But we have

$$\frac{1}{z}=i\frac{d\varphi}{dz}$$

or

$$\frac{dz}{z}=id\,\varphi=i\,d(\varphi-\theta)+i\,d\theta$$

and

$$\frac{dz}{d\theta}=i\,z\left(1+\frac{d(\varphi-\theta)}{d\theta}\right)$$

Hence

$$\frac{dz'}{dz}=\frac{z'}{z}\frac{d}{d\theta}(-i\psi+\theta).\frac{1}{1+\frac{d\epsilon}{d\theta}}$$

where

$$\epsilon=\varphi-\theta$$

or

$$\frac{dz'}{dz}=\frac{z'}{z}\frac{1-i\psi'}{1+\epsilon'} \qquad (X)$$

where ϵ' and ψ' indicate $\frac{d\epsilon}{d\theta}$ and $\frac{d\psi}{d\theta}$, respectively.

Equations (IX) and (X) give now

$$\frac{d\zeta}{dz'}\cdot\frac{dz'}{dz}=\frac{d\zeta}{dz}=\frac{1}{z'}(y\cot\theta+ix\tan\theta)\frac{z'}{z}\frac{1-i\psi'}{1+\epsilon'}$$

$$=(y\cot\theta+ix\tan\theta)\frac{1}{z}\frac{1-i\psi'}{1+\epsilon'} \qquad (XI)$$

Because we are interested more in the magnitude than in the direction of the velocity we will write for the numerical value of this expression

$$\frac{d\zeta}{dz}=\frac{\sqrt{(y^2\cot^2\theta+x^2\tan^2\theta)(1+\psi'^2)}}{ae^{\psi_0}(1+\epsilon')} \qquad (XIa)$$

The quantity $\left(\frac{y}{2a}\right)^2\cot^2\theta+\left(\frac{x}{2a}\right)^2\tan^2\theta$ is readily seen to be equal to (by relation (II))

$$\left(\frac{y}{2a\sin\theta}\right)^2+\sin^2\theta$$

or also

$$\sinh^2\psi+\sin^2\theta$$

Hence

$$\frac{d\zeta}{dz}=2\frac{\sqrt{\left[\left(\frac{y}{2a\sin\theta}\right)^2+\sin^2\theta\right](1+\psi'^2)}}{e^{\psi_0}(1+\epsilon')} \qquad (XIb)$$

The numerical value of the velocity at the surface of the circle is obtained by equations (VI) and (VII) as follows:

Substituting the general point $z=ae^{\psi_0+i(\alpha+\varphi)}$, where α is the angle of attack as measured from the axis of coordinates, in equation (VI)

$$\frac{dw}{dz}=-V(1-e^{-2i(\alpha+\varphi)})-2iV\sin(\alpha+\epsilon_T)e^{-i(\alpha+\varphi)}$$
$$=-V[1-\cos 2(\alpha+\varphi)+2\sin(\alpha+\epsilon_T)\sin(\alpha+\varphi)$$
$$+i(\sin 2(\alpha+\varphi)+2\sin(\alpha+\epsilon_T)\cos(\alpha+\varphi))]$$

$$\left|\frac{dw}{dz}\right|^2=V^2[4\sin^2(\alpha+\epsilon_T)+8\sin(\alpha+\epsilon_T)\sin(\alpha+\varphi)$$
$$+4\sin^2(\alpha+\varphi)]$$

$$\left|\frac{dw}{dz}\right|=2V[\sin(\alpha+\varphi)+\sin(\alpha+\epsilon_T)]$$

Replacing φ by $\theta+\epsilon$ (ϵ_T, the angle of zero lift, is the value of $\varphi-\theta$ at the tail[5]), we have

$$\left|\frac{dw}{dz}\right|=2V[\sin(\alpha+\theta+\epsilon)+\sin(\alpha+\epsilon_T)]$$

For a point on the airfoil we have, then,

$$v=\left|\frac{dw}{dz}\right|\cdot\left|\frac{dz}{d\zeta}\right| \text{ and from (XI), finally}$$

$$v=V\frac{[\sin(\alpha+\theta+\epsilon)+\sin(\alpha+\epsilon_T)](1+\epsilon')e^{\psi_0}}{\sqrt{(\sinh^2\psi+\sin^2\theta)(1+\psi'^2)}} \qquad (XII)$$

where the various symbols have the following significance:

- v is the velocity at any point (x, y) of the airfoil.
- V is the uniform velocity of flow at infinity.
- y is the ordinate of the airfoil as measured from the x-axis, where to fix the system of coordinates $(2a, 0)$ is the point midway between nose and center of curvature of the nose, and $(-2a, 0)$ is the point midway between the tail and center of curvature of the tail.
- α is the angle of attack as measured from the x-axis as indicated in Figure 6.
- y, θ, ψ, ψ', ϵ, and ϵ' are all functions of x.

Equation (XII), expressing the value of the velocity at any point of an airfoil of any shape, is surprisingly simple when the complex nature of the problem is considered. It has the distinct advantage of being exact; no approximations have been made in the preceding analysis.

We shall note some of the properties of this important relation. Because y is generally small, the term $\frac{y}{2a\sin\theta}$ is of influence chiefly near the leading edge, where $\sin\theta$ is small. It is noticed, however, that if $\frac{y}{\sin\theta}=0$ for $\theta=0$, equation (XII) yields in all cases $v=\infty$. This means that the velocity at the nose becomes infinite for $\sinh\psi=0$ (thin airfoils). This fact has been pointed out in an earlier report. (Reference 2.) The quantity $\frac{y}{2a\sin\theta}$ or $\sinh\psi$ is thus of considerable significance in the theory of thick airfoils.

The velocity near the tail is obtained by putting $\theta=\pi+\Delta\theta$ and $\epsilon=\epsilon_T+\epsilon'\Delta\theta$. Where $\Delta\theta$ is a small angle, in equation (XII)

$$\left|\frac{v}{V}\right|=\frac{e^{\psi_0}(1+\epsilon')[\sin(\theta+\alpha+\epsilon)+\sin(\alpha+\epsilon_T)]}{\sqrt{(\sinh^2\psi+\sin^2\theta)(1+\psi'^2)}}$$

we get

$$\left|\frac{v}{V}\right|\cong\frac{e^{\psi_0}(1+\epsilon')[-\Delta\theta+\alpha+\epsilon_T+\epsilon'\Delta\theta+\alpha+\epsilon_T]}{\sqrt{(\psi^2+\Delta\theta^2)(1+\psi'^2)}}$$

$$=\frac{e^{\psi_0}(1+\epsilon')^2\Delta\theta}{\sqrt{(\psi^2+\Delta\theta^2)(1+\psi'^2)}}$$

$$=\frac{e^{\psi_0}(1+\epsilon')^2}{\sqrt{\left[1+\left(\frac{\psi}{\Delta\theta}\right)^2\right](1+\psi'^2)}} \qquad (f)$$

[5] It should be pointed out that the rear stagnation point is *chosen* to be on the x-axis at $\theta=\pi$. The curvature at the tail is, as far as the specification of the ideal circulation is concerned, to be considered as a mechanical imperfection.

ψ near the tail may be expressed as

$$\psi_T+\psi'\,\Delta\theta+\frac{1}{2}\psi''(\Delta\theta)^2+\quad\cdot\quad\cdot\quad\cdot$$

or

$$\frac{\psi}{\Delta\theta}=\frac{\psi_T}{\Delta\theta}+\psi'+\frac{1}{2}\psi''\Delta\theta+\quad\cdot\quad\cdot\quad\cdot$$

The quantity $\frac{\psi_T}{\Delta\theta}$ is infinite if ψ_T is different from zero at $\Delta\theta=0$. The velocity is in this case zero, indicating the presence of the rear stagnation point. If, on the other hand, ψ_T is zero, that is, if the tail is perfectly sharp,

$$\frac{\psi}{\Delta\theta}=\psi' \text{ for } \Delta\theta=0$$

and the velocity at the tail is

$$v_T=V\frac{e^{\psi_0}(1+\epsilon')^2}{(1+\psi'^2)}$$

or

$$v_T^2=V^2\frac{e^{2\psi_0}(1+\epsilon')^4}{(1+\psi'^2)^2} \qquad \text{(g)}$$

(For the Clark Y, v_T^2 is about 0.88 V^2 near the tail.)

We obtain the front stagnation point by letting $v=0$ in equation (XII). Hence

$$\alpha+\theta+\epsilon_N=-(\alpha+\epsilon_T)$$

$$\theta=-(2\alpha+\epsilon_N+\epsilon_T)$$

In a previous report (reference 2)

$$\alpha_I=-\frac{\epsilon_N+\epsilon_T}{2}$$

has been defined as the ideal angle of attack. It is seen that, for this angle of attack, θ is zero or the stagnation point occurs directly at the nose.

Equation (XII) may also be applied to strut forms, and for such symmetrical shapes takes even a simpler form.

PRACTICAL APPLICATION OF RESULTS

We will now apply Formula (XII) to the typical case of the Clark Y airfoil and calculate the velocities at points of the airfoil surface. The detailed method of procedure is as follows.

1. The axis of coordinates is drawn through the points $(2a, 0)$ and $(-2a, 0)$ located respectively at the point midway between the nose and the center of curvature of the nose and the point midway between the tail and the center of curvature of the tail. (See fig. 6.) The radius of curvature at the leading edge is 1.75 per cent chord.

2. The points (x, y) of the upper and lower surfaces of the airfoil are determined with respect to this axis.

3. Sin $^2\theta$, sin θ, and θ are determined by the relation

$$2\sin^2\theta=p+\sqrt{p^2+\left(\frac{y}{a}\right)^2} \qquad \text{where } p=1-\left(\frac{x}{2a}\right)^2-\left(\frac{y}{2a}\right)^2$$

4. ψ is given by the relation

$$\psi=\left(\frac{y}{2a\sin\theta}\right)-\frac{1}{6}\left(\frac{y}{2a\sin\theta}\right)^3+\quad\cdot\quad\cdot\quad\cdot\quad\cdot\quad\cdot$$

5. ψ is plotted as a function of θ

$$\psi_0=\frac{1}{2\pi}\int_0^{2\pi}\psi d\varphi \quad\cong\quad \frac{1}{2\pi}\int_0^{2\pi}\psi d\theta$$

6. Determine $\epsilon_c=-\frac{1}{2\pi}\int_0^{2\pi}\psi\cot\frac{(\varphi-\varphi_c)}{2}d\varphi$ by formula shown in the appendix:

$$\epsilon_c=-\frac{1}{\pi}[0.628\psi'_c+1.065(\psi_1-\psi_{-1})+0.445(\psi_2-\psi_{-2})$$
$$+0.231(\psi_3-\psi_{-3})+0.104(\psi_4-\psi_{-4})]$$

where ψ'_c is the slope of the ψ curve at $\varphi=\varphi_c$ ψ_1 the value of ψ at $\varphi=\varphi_c+\frac{\pi}{5}$, ψ_2 at $\varphi=\varphi_c+\frac{2\pi}{5}$, etc.

ψ_{-1} the value of ψ at $\varphi=\varphi_c-\frac{\pi}{5}$, etc.

7. From the ϵ versus θ curve and from the ψ versus θ curves ϵ' and ψ' are determined.

8. Determine F by the relation

$$F=\frac{(1+\epsilon')e^{\psi_0}}{\sqrt{\left[\left(\frac{y}{2a\sin\theta}\right)^2+\sin^2\theta\right](1+\psi'^2)}}$$

9. $(\theta+\epsilon)$ is determined in radians and degrees.

10. $\text{Sin}(\theta+\alpha+\epsilon)+\sin(\alpha+\epsilon_T)$ is now calculated where α is the angle of attack as measured from the axis of coordinates.

11. $\frac{v}{V}=F\cdot[\sin(\theta+\alpha+\epsilon)+\sin(\alpha+\epsilon_T)]$

12. $\frac{P}{q}=1-\left(\frac{v}{V}\right)^2$ (pressure)

The entire calculation, properly arranged, can be quite accurately obtained in a very short time.

COMPARISON WITH EXPERIMENTAL RESULTS

In order to compare the theory with experimental results, the geometric angle of attack α_G as measured in the wind tunnel must be corrected for a number of items, such as finite span and effect of wall interference. We may, however, obtain approximately the apparent or effective angle of attack α_A (in radians as measured from the angle of zero lift) by taking the quotient of the area of the pressure-distribution curve and 5.5, since it is known that this value of the lift coeffi-

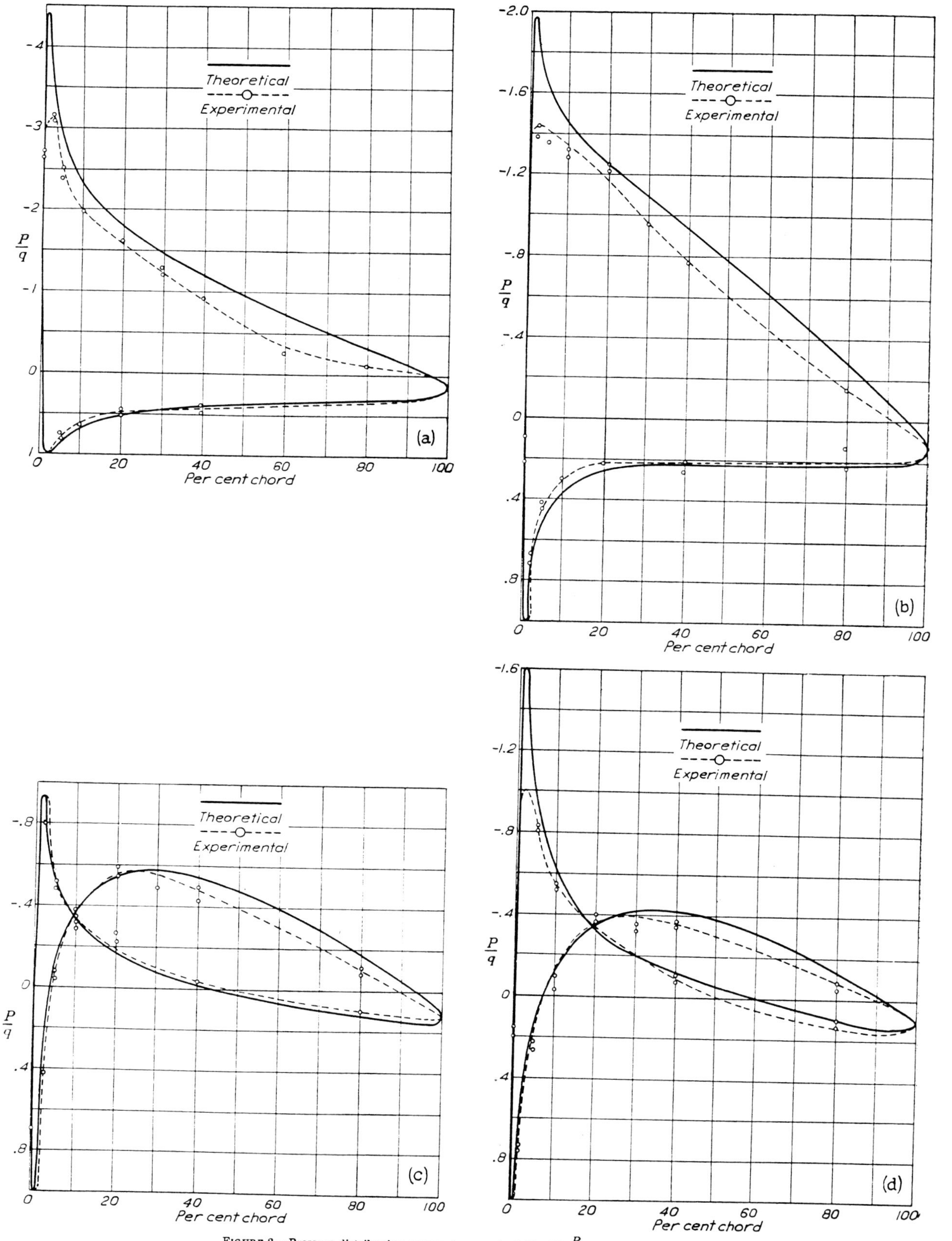

FIGURE 2.—Pressure-distribution curves along x-axis of Clark Y; $\frac{P}{q}$ against per cent chord

(a) $\alpha=9°33'$. (b) $\alpha=5°\ 19'$. (c) $\alpha=-1°\ 16'$. (d) $\alpha=-3°\ 15'$

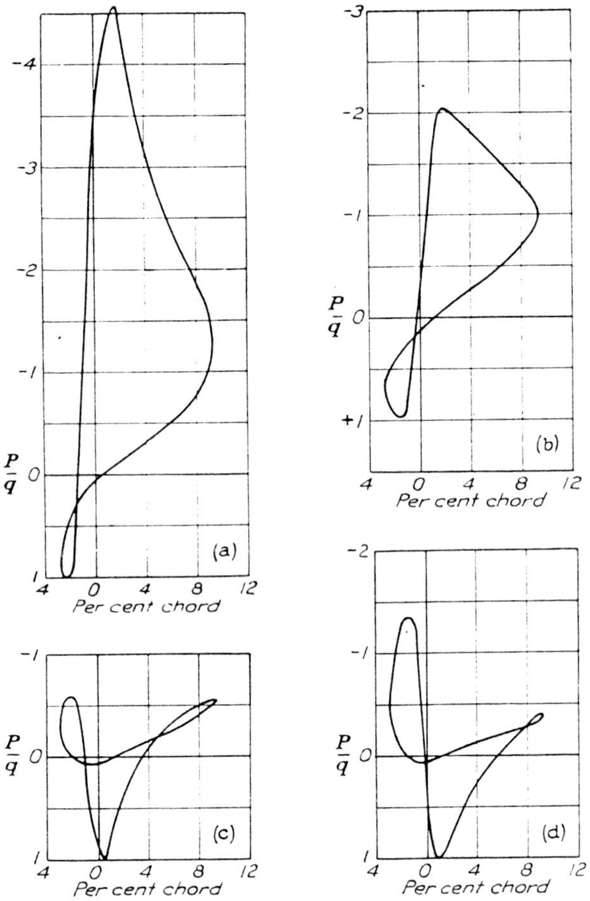

FIGURE 3.—Theoretical pressure distribution along y-axis of Clark Y
(a) $\alpha=9°\ 33'$. (b) $\alpha=5°\ 19'$. (c) $\alpha=-1°\ 16'$. (d) $\alpha=-3°\ 15'$

cient is very nearly realized in most cases. This has been done in Table III, and the angle of attack α, which should be substituted in the Equation (XII), is given in the last column. The pressure distribution curves, Figures 2a, b, c, d, and 3a, b, c, d, were obtained by application of Equation (XII) to the Clark Y airfoil. Numerical results are shown in Tables I, II, and III. The experimental values are from original data sheets for N. A. C. A. Technical Report No. 353, and are not entirely consistent due to difficulties experienced in these experiments. After the theoretical pressure distribution curves have been obtained, the moments about any required axis may be found. Table IV

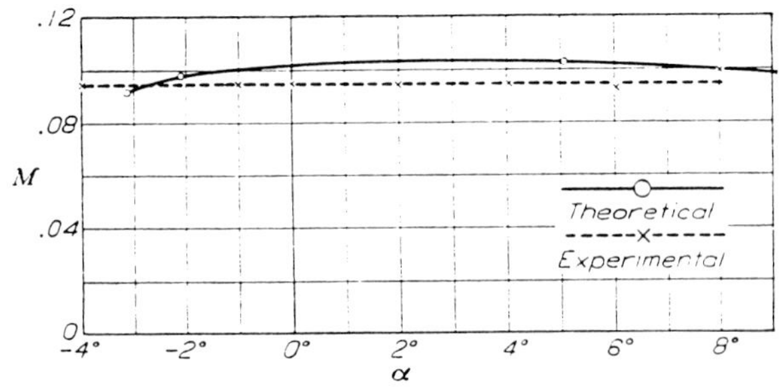

FIGURE 4.—Moment against angle of attack

gives some of these results and Figure 4 shows the comparison with experimental data taken from N. A. C. A. Technical Report No. 312.

LANGLEY MEMORIAL AERONAUTICAL LABORATORY,
NATIONAL ADVISORY COMMITTEE FOR AERONAUTICS,
LANGLEY FIELD, VA., *October 15, 1931.*

APPENDIX

EVALUATION OF THE FORMULA

$$\epsilon_c = (\varphi - \theta)_c = -\frac{1}{2\pi}\int_0^{2\pi} \psi \cot \frac{(\varphi - \varphi_c)}{2} \, d\varphi$$

Although the above integrand becomes positively and negatively infinite around $\varphi = \varphi_c$, it is readily verified that for ψ finite, throughout the range $0 - 2\pi$, the integral remains finite, the positive and negative infinite strips exactly canceling each other.

The value of the integral for any point φ_c may be accurately obtained by the following device. We know that if ψ is a continuous function and the range φ_2 to φ_2 not too large

$$\frac{1}{2}\int_{\varphi_1}^{\varphi_2} \psi \cot \frac{(\varphi - \varphi_c)}{2} \, d\varphi \text{ is very nearly } \psi_A \log \frac{\sin \frac{\varphi_2 - \varphi_c}{2}}{\sin \frac{\varphi_1 - \varphi_c}{2}}$$

where ψ_A is the average value of ψ in the range φ_1 to φ_2. Also near $\varphi = \varphi_c$ we may write

$$\psi = \psi_c + (\varphi - \varphi_c)\,\psi'_c + (\varphi - \varphi_c)^2 \frac{\psi''_c}{2} + \quad . \quad . \quad . \quad .$$

Then for s a small quantity

$$\int_{\varphi_c - s}^{\varphi_c + s} \psi \cot \frac{(\varphi - \varphi_c)}{2} \, d\varphi = 2\int_{\varphi_c - s}^{\varphi_c + s} \psi'_c \frac{(\varphi - \varphi_c)}{2} \cdot \cot \frac{(\varphi - \varphi_c)}{2} \, d\varphi$$
$$= 4\, s\psi'_c$$

(Since the even powers drop out and the $\lim_{\varphi \to 0} \varphi \cot \varphi = 1$).

Let us now divide the interval $0 - 2\pi$ into 10 parts, starting with φ_c as a reference point. (See fig. 5.)

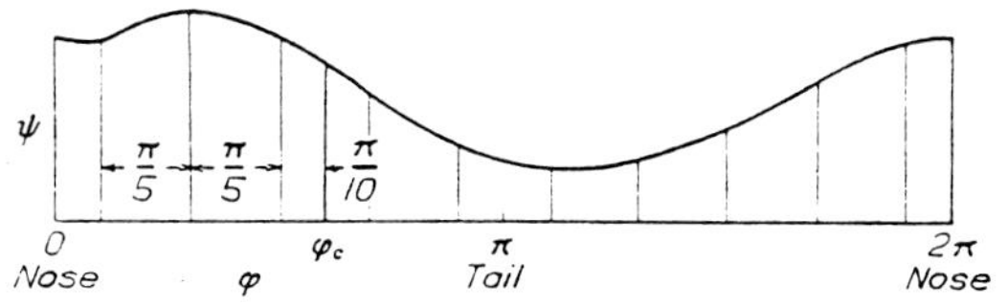

FIGURE 5.—The ψ against φ curve, illustrating method of evaluation of ϵ_c

$$\varphi_c - \frac{\pi}{10} \text{ to } \varphi_c + \frac{\pi}{10}, \varphi_c + \frac{\pi}{10} \text{ to } \varphi_c + \frac{3\pi}{10}, \varphi_c + \frac{3\pi}{10} \text{ to}$$

$$\varphi_c + \frac{5\pi}{10}, \varphi_c + \frac{5\pi}{10} \text{ to } \varphi_c + \frac{7\pi}{10}, \varphi_c + \frac{7\pi}{10} \text{ to } \varphi_c + \frac{9\pi}{10},$$

$$\varphi_c + \frac{9\pi}{10} \text{ to } \varphi_c - \frac{9\pi}{10}, \varphi_c - \frac{9\pi}{10} \text{ to } \varphi_c - \frac{7\pi}{10}, \varphi_c - \frac{7\pi}{10} \text{ to}$$

$$\varphi_c - \frac{5\pi}{10}, \varphi_c - \frac{5\pi}{10} \text{ to } \varphi_c - \frac{3\pi}{10} \text{ and } \varphi_c - \frac{3\pi}{10} \text{ to } \varphi_c - \frac{\pi}{10}.$$

Then,

$$\epsilon_c = -\frac{1}{2\pi}\int_0^{2\pi} \psi \cot \frac{(\varphi - \varphi_c)}{2} \, d\varphi$$

$$\cong -\frac{1}{\pi}\Bigg[\frac{\pi}{5}\psi'_c + (\psi_1 - \psi_{-1}) \log \frac{\sin \frac{3\pi}{20}}{\sin \frac{\pi}{20}}$$

$$+ (\psi_2 - \psi_{-2}) \log \frac{\sin \frac{5\pi}{20}}{\sin \frac{3\pi}{20}} + (\psi_3 - \psi_{-3}) \log \frac{\sin \frac{7\pi}{20}}{\sin \frac{5\pi}{20}}$$

$$+ (\psi_4 - \psi_{-4}) \log \frac{\sin \frac{9\pi}{20}}{\sin \frac{7\pi}{20}}\Bigg]$$

$$= -\frac{1}{\pi}[0.628\,\psi'_c + 1.065\,(\psi_1 - \psi_{-1}) + 0.445\,(\psi_2 - \psi_{-2})$$
$$+ 0.231\,(\psi_3 - \psi_{-3}) + 0.104\,(\psi_4 - \psi_{-4})]$$

where ψ'_c is the slope of the ψ curve at $\varphi = \varphi_c$

ψ_1 value of ψ at $\varphi = \varphi_c + \frac{\pi}{5}$, ψ_{-1} at $\varphi = \varphi_c - \frac{\pi}{5}$,

ψ_2 at $\varphi = \varphi_c + \frac{2\pi}{5}$, ψ_3 at $\varphi = \varphi_c + \frac{3\pi}{5}$, etc.

To evaluate the above integral it is, strictly speaking, necessary to know ψ as a function of φ rather than of θ.[1] We have $\varphi = \theta + \epsilon$. For all flattened or streamline bodies, however, ϵ is small; for ordinary airfoils it is, in fact, so small that $\psi(\theta)$ may unconditionally be considered equal to $\psi(\phi)$. For the sake of mathematical accuracy we will, however, indicate how the problem may be solved also for bodies of more irregular contour by successive approximations. We have

$$\psi(\varphi) = \psi(\theta) + \epsilon\,\psi'(\theta) + \quad . \quad . \quad .$$

As a first approximation we neglect the second and all following terms of this expression. The value of ϵ thus obtained by graphical integration or otherwise is then used in the expression for $\psi(\varphi)$ and a second integration is performed, etc.

[1] The equation for ϵ is a nonlinear integral equation and to obtain its exact solution is a difficult matter; fortunately because of the small magnitude of ϵ the solution is obtainable to any desired accuracy by ordinary definite integrals.

APPLICATION OF FLOW FORMULA TO THE SPECIAL CASE OF AN ELLIPTIC CYLINDER

As a matter of interest we will assume the form of the body to be the ellipse $\left(\frac{x}{2a\cosh\psi}\right)^2+\left(\frac{y}{2a\sinh\psi}\right)^2=1$ and find $\frac{v}{V}$ for zero angle of attack, i. e., we have $\psi=\psi_o=$constant, $\psi'=0$, $\epsilon=0$, $\epsilon'=0$, $\alpha=0$. Equation (XII) becomes

$$\left(\frac{v}{V}\right)=\frac{\sin\theta\cdot e^{\psi}}{\sqrt{\sinh^2\psi+\sin^2\theta}}=\frac{\dfrac{y\cdot e^{\psi}}{2a\sinh\psi}}{\sqrt{\sinh^2\psi+\left(\dfrac{y}{2a\sinh\psi}\right)^2}}$$

and

$$\frac{p}{q}=1-\left(\frac{v}{V}\right)^2=1-\frac{e^{2\psi}\,(2ay)^2}{(2a\sinh\psi)^4+(2ay)^2}$$

This result checks exactly with the form given by Dr. A. F. Zahm in N. A. C. A. Technical Report No. 253, Flow and Drag Formulas for Simple Quadrics, equation 14.

REFERENCES

1. Glauert, H.: Elements of Airfoil and Air-Screw Theory. Cambridge University Press, 1926.
2. Theodorsen, Theodore: On the Theory of Wing Sections with Particular Reference to the Lift Distribution. T. R. No. 383, N. A. C. A., 1931.

EXPLANATION OF THE TABLES

The first part of Table I refers to the upper surface or to positive ordinates of the Clark Y, the second part to the lower surface or to negative ordinates. Column 1 gives the location in per cent of the chord; 2 gives the ordinates with respect to the x-axis in this same unit; 3 and 4 give x and y in the present system of coordinates; 5, 6, and 7 give $\sin^2\theta$, $\sin\theta$, and θ, respectively (Equation (III)); 8 gives ψ (by equation (IVa)); 9 gives ϵ (appendix); 10 and 11 give $\frac{d\psi}{d\theta}$ and $\frac{d\epsilon}{d\theta}$ as obtained from ψ against θ and ϵ against θ curves; (See figs. 7 and 8). Column 12 gives the quantity

$$F=\frac{(1+\epsilon')\,e^{\psi_0}}{\sqrt{\left[\left(\dfrac{y}{2\sin\theta}\right)^2+\sin^2\theta\right](1+\psi'^2)}}\quad(e^{\psi_0}=1.11);$$

Column 14 gives $\theta+\epsilon$ in degrees. The velocity at any point x and angle of attack α is given by $v=V\,[\sin(\alpha+\theta+\epsilon)+\sin(\alpha+\epsilon_T)]\cdot F$ and the pressure, by $\frac{P}{q}=1-\left(\frac{v}{V}\right)^2$

It must be noted that α is measured from the line of

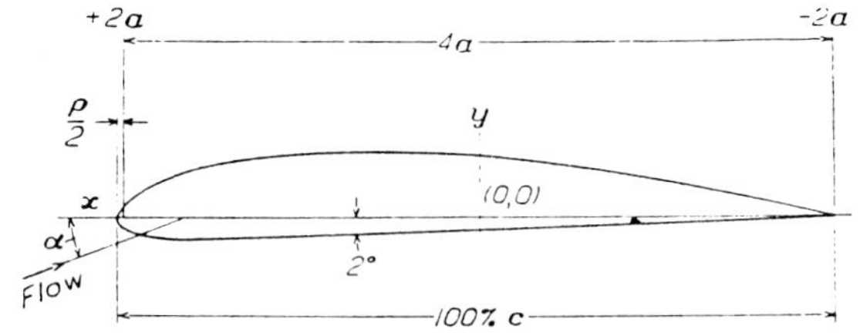

FIGURE 6.—Clark Y airfoil—showing system of coordinates

flow to the x-axis as shown in Figure 6, and if otherwise measured, must be reduced to this basis.

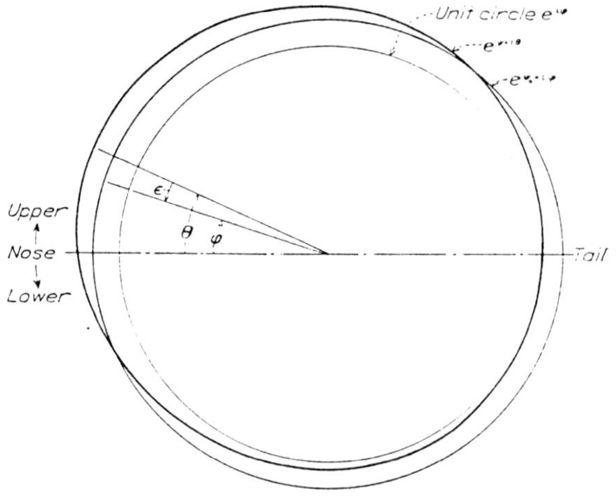

FIGURE 7.—The unit circle $z=e^{i\varphi}$, the circle $z=e^{\psi_0+i\varphi}$, and the corresponding curve $z'=e^{\psi+i\theta}$

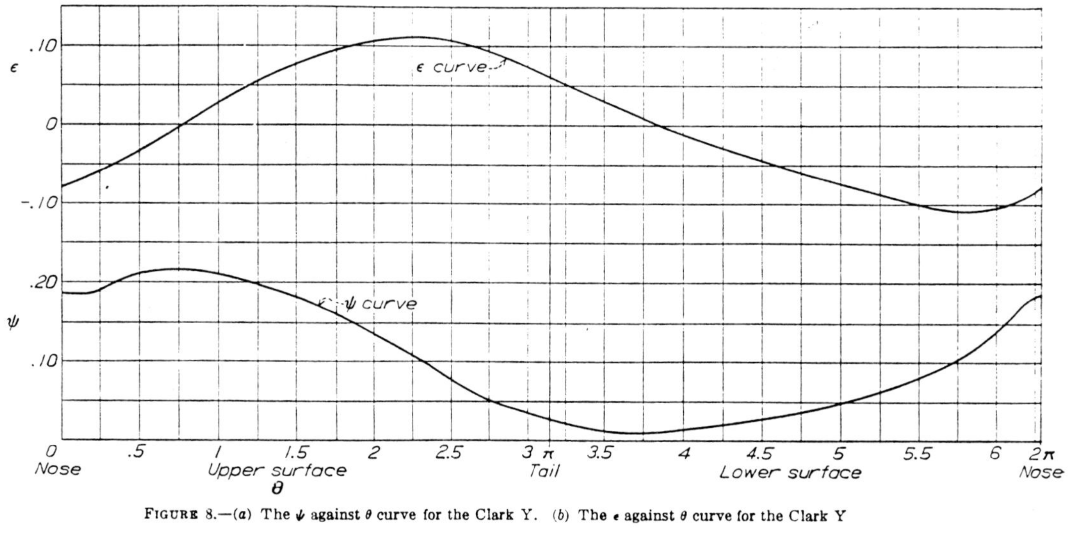

FIGURE 8.—(a) The ψ against θ curve for the Clark Y. (b) The ϵ against θ curve for the Clark Y

TABLE I

CLARK Y

UPPER SURFACE

% c	y in % c	x	y	$\sin^2\theta$	$\sin\theta$	θ radians	ψ	ϵ	ψ'	ϵ'	F	$\theta+\epsilon$ radians	$\theta+\epsilon$ (° ′)
0	0	2.035	0.000	0.000	0.000	0.000	0.188	−0.079(ϵ_N)	0.000	0.075	6.33	−0.079	−4 32
1.25	1.99	1.985	.0804	.0474	.218	.220	.184	−.067	.035	.080	4.20	.153	8 47
2.50	3.08	1.934	.124	.0994	.315	.321	.198	−.055	.075	.105	3.28	.266	15 17
5.0	4.59	1.833	.185	.195	.442	.458	.208	−.038	.060	.115	2.52	.420	24 4
7.5	5.61	1.732	.226	.282	.531	.559	.213	−.026	.030	.115	2.16	.533	30 33
10	6.45	1.631	.260	.365	.605	.649	.214	−.016	.020	.120	1.92	.633	36 16
15	7.70	1.430	.311	.512	.716	.798	.216	.003	.000	.120	1.66	.801	45 53
20	8.55	1.228	.345	.640	.801	.929	.214	.020	−.030	.120	1.48	.949	54 22
30	9.23	.824	.372	.837	.915	1.156	.202	.044	−.060	.105	1.30	1.200	68 45
40	9.28	.421	.374	.957	.978	1.361	.190	.063	−.065	.091	1.21	1.424	81 35
50	8.74	.0175	.353	1.000	1.000	1.571	.176	.080	−.085	.078	1.17	1.651	94 35
60	7.77	−.386	.313	.963	.982	1.761	.159	.094	−.100	.070	1.18	1.855	106 16
70	6.32	−.790	.255	.847	.920	1.972	.137	.106	−.104	.025	1.22	2.078	119 3
80	4.48	−1.193	.181	.649	.806	2.204	.112	.110	−.107	.004	1.36	2.314	132 34
90	2.40	−1.596	.097	.368	.606	2.490	.080	.106	−.110	−.015	1.78	2.596	148 43
95	1.25	−1.798	.050	.195	.443	2.683	.056	.095	−.080	−.075	2.30	2.778	159 10
100	.06	−2.001	.002	.000	.000	3.142	.030	.062(ϵ_T)	−.053	−.080	Large	3.204	183 33

LOWER SURFACE

% c	y in % c	x	y	$\sin^2\theta$	$\sin\theta$	θ radians	ψ	ϵ	ψ'	ϵ'	F	$\theta+\epsilon$ radians	$\theta+\epsilon$ (° ′)
0	0	2.035	0.000	0.000	0.000	6.283	0.188	−0.079	0.000	0.075	6.33	6.204	−4 32
1.25	1.53	1.985	−.0617	.0387	−.197	6.085	.156	−.100	.170	.085	4.71	5.985	−17 5
2.50	1.95	1.934	−.0787	.0822	−.287	5.992	.137	−.105	.162	.055	3.64	5.887	−22 41
5.0	2.38	1.833	−.0960	.171	−.414	5.857	.116	−.110	.130	.000	2.55	5.747	−30 43
7.5	2.61	1.732	−.105	.258	−.508	5.750	.103	−.107	.110	−.015	2.09	5.643	−36 40
10	2.73	1.631	−.110	.342	−.585	5.658	.094	−.105	.093	−.032	1.81	5.553	−41 50
15	2.84	1.430	−.115	.492	−.702	5.505	.082	−.100	.080	−.046	1.49	5.399	−50 40
20	2.78	1.228	−.112	.625	−.791	5.371	.071	−.093	.075	−.048	1.33	5.278	−57 35
30	2.47	.824	−.0996	.831	−.912	5.135	.055	−.081	.058	−.050	1.15	5.054	−71 0
40	2.12	.421	−.0885	.956	−.978	4.922	.045	−.072	.043	−.050	1.075	4.850	−82 6
50	1.78	.0175	−.0720	1.000	−1.000	4.712	.036	−.058	.040	−.060	1.04	4.654	−93 21
60	1.38	−.386	−.0556	.962	−.981	4.518	.028	−.045	.030	−.060	1.06	4.473	−103 40
70	1.03	−.790	−.0416	.844	−.919	4.306	.023	−.034	.025	−.060	1.13	4.272	−115 14
80	.74	−1.193	−.0295	.645	−.803	4.075	.018	−.019	.022	−.070	1.275	4.055	−127 39
90	.40	−1.596	−.0161	.364	−.604	3.790	.013	.000	.018	−.082	1.685	3.790	−142 51
95	.24	−1.798	− 0097	.191	−.438	3.595	.011	.023	−.017	−.090	2.30	3.618	−152 43
100	.06	−2.001	−.002	.000	−.000	3.142	.030	.062	−.053	−.080	Large	3.204	−176 27

TABLE II

CLARK Y

$$\frac{v}{V}=[\sin(\theta+\alpha+\epsilon)+\sin(\alpha+\epsilon_T)]\cdot F \qquad \frac{P}{q}=1-\left(\frac{v}{V}\right)^2$$

$\alpha=9°\ 33'$

$\epsilon_T=3°\ 33'$ $\sin(\alpha+\epsilon_T)=\sin 13°\ 6'=0.2267$

	Upper surface						Lower surface					
% c	$\theta+\alpha+\epsilon$ (° ′)	$\sin(\theta+\alpha+\epsilon)$	$\sin(\theta+\alpha+\epsilon)+\sin(\alpha+\epsilon_T)$	$\frac{v}{V}$	$\left(\frac{v}{V}\right)^2$	$\frac{P}{q}$	$\theta+\alpha+\epsilon$ (° ′)	$\sin(\theta+\alpha+\epsilon)$	$\sin(\theta+\alpha+\epsilon)+\sin(\alpha+\epsilon_T)$	$\frac{v}{V}$	$\left(\frac{v}{V}\right)^2$	$\frac{P}{q}$
0	5 1	0.0875	0.3142	1.99	3.96	−2.96	5 1	0.0875	0.3142	1.99	3.96	−2.96
1.25	18 20	.3145	.5412	2.26	5.12	−4.12	−7 32	−.1311	.0956	.450	.203	.797
2.50	24 50	.4200	.6467	2.12	4.49	−3.39	−13 8	−.2272	.0005	.002	.000	1.000
5.0	33 37	.5537	.7804	1.97	3.87	−2.87	−21 10	−.3611	−.1344	.343	.117	.883
7.5	40 6	.6441	.8708	1.88	3.55	−2.55	−27 7	−.4558	−.2291	.479	.229	.771
10	45 49	.7171	.9438	1.82	3.30	−2.30	−32 17	−.5341	−.3074	.556	.308	.692
15	55 26	.8235	1.0502	1.74	3.04	−2.04	−41 7	−.6576	−.4307	.643	.414	.586
20	63 55	.8981	1.1248	1.68	2.83	−1.83	−48 2	−.7435	−.5168	.685	.469	.531
30	78 18	.9792	1.2059	1.57	2.47	−1.47	−61 27	−.8784	−.6517	.748	.558	.442
40	91 8	.9998	1.2265	1.49	2.22	−1.22	−72 33	−.9540	−.7273	.788	.621	.379
50	104 8	.9697	1.1964	1.40	1.98	−0.98	−83 48	−.9941	−.7674	.800	.640	.360
60	115 49	.9000	1.1267	1.33	1.76	−0.76	−94 7	−.9974	−.7707	.821	.674	.326
70	128 36	.7815	1.0082	1.23	1.51	−0.51	−105 41	−.9627	−.7357	.834	.696	.304
80	142 7	.6141	.8408	1.14	1.31	−0.31	−118 6	−.8821	−.6554	.836	.698	.302
90	158 16	.3703	.5970	1.06	1.13	−0.13	−133 18	−.7278	−.5011	.844	.711	.289
95	168 43	.1957	.4224	.97	.95	0.05	−143 10	−.5995	−.3728	.857	.735	.265
100								Formula (g)		.935	.875	.125

Table II gives the numerical values for Figure 2a in detail as an example. See also Table I.

TABLE III

Figure	Geometric angle as measured from chord line experimentally α_G (° ′)	Area of experimental pressure distribution curve A	$\frac{A}{5.5}=\alpha_A$ radians	Apparent angle measured from zero lift $\alpha_A=\alpha+\epsilon_T$ degrees (° ′)	Angle measured from chord line (to be used as a basis for comparison with α_G) $\alpha=\alpha_A-3°\ 33'$ (° ′)
2a	13 25	1.260	0.229	13 6	9 33
2b	7 25	.855	.155	8 52	5 19
2c	−1 40	.221	.040	2 17	−1 16
2d	−4 35	.030	.0053	0 18	−3 15

TABLE IV

Figure	M_x Moment about line $x=25$ per cent chord	M_y Moment about line $y=0$	M_T Moment about point $x=25$ per cent chord, $y=0$
2a	−0.0896	−0.0085	−0.098
2b	−.098	−.005	−.103
2c	−.098	.000	−.098
2d	−.093	.0015	−.091

GENERAL POTENTIAL THEORY OF ARBITRARY WING SECTIONS

BY THEODORE THEODORSEN
AND I.E. GARRICK

National Advisory Committee for Aeronautics

Report No. 452, 1933

SUMMARY

This report gives an exact treatment of the problem of determining the 2-dimensional potential flow around wing sections of any shape. The treatment is based directly on the solution of this problem as advanced by Theodorsen in N.A.C.A. Technical Report No. 411. The problem condenses into the compact form of an integral equation capable of yielding numerical solutions by a direct process.

An attempt has been made to analyze and coordinate the results of earlier studies relating to properties of wing sections. The existing approximate theory of thin wing sections and the Joukowsky theory with its numerous generalizations are reduced to special cases of the general theory of arbitrary sections, permitting a clearer perspective of the entire field. The method not only permits the determination of the velocity at any point of an arbitrary section and the associated lift and moments, but furnishes also a scheme for developing new shapes of preassigned aerodynamical properties. The theory applies also to bodies that are not airfoils, and is of importance in other branches of physics involving potential theory.

INTRODUCTION

The solution of the problem of determining the 2-dimensional potential flow of a nonviscous incompressible fluid around bodies of arbitrary shape can be made to depend on a theorem in conformal representation stated by Riemann almost a century ago, known as the fundamental theorem of conformal representation. This theorem is equivalent to the statement that it is possible to transform the region bounded by a simple curve into the region bounded by a circle in such a way that all equipotential lines and streamlines of the first region transform respectively into those of the circle. The theorem will be stated more precisely in the body of this report and its significance for wing section theory shown—suffice it at present to state that if the analytic transformation by which the one region is transformed conformally into the region bounded by the circle is known, the potential field of this region is readily obtained in terms of the potential field of the circle.

A number of transformations have been found by means of which it is possible to transform a circle into a contour resembling an airfoil shape. It is obviously true that such *theoretical* airfoils possess no particular qualities which make them superior to the types of more empirical origin. It was probably primarily because of the difficulty encountered in the inverse problem, viz, the problem of transforming an airfoil into a circle (which we shall denote as the direct process) that such artificial types came into existence. The 2-dimensional theoretical velocity distribution, or what is called the flow pattern, is known only for some special symmetrical bodies and for the particular class of Joukowsky airfoils and their extensions, the outstanding investigators[1] being Kutta, Joukowsky, and von Mises. Although useful in the development of airfoil theory, these theoretical airfoils are based solely on special transformations employing only a small part of the freedom permitted in the general case. However, they still form the subject of numerous isolated investigations.

The direct process has been used in the theory of thin airfoils with some success. An approximate theory of thin wing sections applicable only to the mean camber line has been developed[2] by Munk and Birnbaum, and extended by others. However, attempts[3] which have been made to solve the general case of an arbitrary airfoil by direct processes have resulted in intricate and practically unmanageable solutions. Lamb, in his "Hydrodynamics" (Ref. 1, p. 77), referring to this problem as dependent upon the determi-

[1]See bibliography given in Ref. 9, pp. 24, 84, and 583.
[2]Cf. footnote 1.
[3]See Appendix II of this paper.

nation of the complex coefficients of a conformal transformation, states: "The difficulty, however, of determining these coefficients so as to satisfy given boundary conditions is now so great as to render this method of very limited application. Indeed, the determination of the irrotational motion of a liquid subject to given boundary conditions is a problem whose exact solution can be effected by direct processes in only a very few cases. Most of the cases for which we know the solution have been obtained by an inverse process; viz, instead of trying to find a value of ϕ or ψ which satisfies the [Laplacian] $\nabla^2\phi = 0$ or $\nabla^2\psi = 0$ and given boundary conditions, we take some known solution of these differential equations and inquire what boundary conditions it can be made to satisfy."

In a report (Ref. 2) recently published by the National Advisory Committee for Aeronautics a general solution employing a direct method was briefly given. It was shown that the problem could be stated in a condensed form as an integral equation and also that it was possible to effect the practical solution on this equation for the case of any given airfoil. A formula giving the velocity at any point on the surface of an arbitrary airfoil was developed. The first part of the present paper includes the essential developments of Ref. 2 and is devoted to a more complete and precise treatment of the method, in particular with respect to the evaluation of the integral equation.

In a later part of this paper, a geometric treatment of arbitrary airfoils, coordinating the results of earlier investigations, is given. Special airfoil types have also been studied on the basis of the general method and their relations to arbitrary airfoils have been analyzed. The solution of the inverse problem of creating airfoils of special types, in particular, types of specified aerodynamical properties, is indicated.

It is hoped that this paper will serve as a step toward the unification and ultimate simplification of the theory of the airfoil.

TRANSFORMATION OF AN ARBITRARY AIRFOIL INTO A CIRCLE

Statement of the problem

The problem which this report proposes to treat may be formulated as follows. Given an arbitrary airfoil[4] inclined at a specific angle in a nonviscous incompressible fluid and translated with uniform velocity V, to determine the theoretical 2-dimensional velocity and pressure distribution at all points of the surface for all orientations, and to investigate the properties of the field of flow surrounding the airfoil. Also, to determine the important aerodynamical parameters of the airfoil. Of further interest, too, is the problem of finding shapes with given aerodynamical properties.

Principles of the theory of fluid flow

We shall first briefly recall the known basic principles of the theory of the irrotational flow of a frictionless incompressible fluid in two dimensions. A flow is termed "2-dimensional" when the motion is the same in all planes parallel to a definite one, say, xy. In this case the linear velocity components u and v of a fluid element are functions of x, y, and t only.

The differential equation of the lines of flow in this case is

$$v\,dx - u\,dy = 0$$

and the equation of continuity is

$$\frac{\partial u}{\partial x} + \frac{\partial v}{\partial y} = 0 \quad \text{or} \quad \frac{\partial u}{\partial x} = \frac{\partial(-v)}{\partial y}$$

which shows that the above first equation is an exact differential.

If $Q = c$ is the integral, then

$$u = \frac{\partial Q}{\partial y} \quad \text{and} \quad v = -\frac{\partial Q}{\partial x}$$

This function Q is called the stream function, and the lines of flow, or streamlines, are given by the equation $Q = c$, where c is in general an arbitrary function of time.

Furthermore, we note that the existence of the stream function does not depend on whether the motion is irrotational or rotational. When rotational its vorticity is

$$\zeta = \frac{\partial v}{\partial x} - \frac{\partial u}{\partial y} = \frac{\partial^2 Q}{\partial x^2} + \frac{\partial^2 Q}{\partial y^2}$$

which is twice the mean angular velocity or "rotation" of the fluid element. Hence, in irrotational flow the stream function has to satisfy

$$\frac{\partial^2 Q}{\partial x^2} + \frac{\partial^2 Q}{\partial y^2} = 0 \tag{2'}$$

Then there exists a velocity potential P and we have

$$\left.\begin{aligned} \frac{\partial P}{\partial x} &= u = \frac{\partial Q}{\partial y} \\ \frac{\partial P}{\partial y} &= v = -\frac{\partial Q}{\partial x} \end{aligned}\right\} \tag{1}$$

The equation of continuity is now

$$\frac{\partial^2 P}{\partial x^2} + \frac{\partial^2 Q}{\partial y^2} = 0 \tag{2}$$

[4]By an airfoil shape, or wing section, is roughly meant an elongated smooth shape rounded at the leading edge and ending in a sharp edge at the rear. All practical airfoils are characterized by a lack of abrupt change of curvature except for a rounded nose and small radius of curvature at the tail.

Equations (1) show that

$$\frac{\partial P}{\partial x}\frac{\partial Q}{\partial x} + \frac{\partial P}{\partial y}\frac{\partial Q}{\partial y} = 0$$

so that the family of curves P = constant, Q = constant cut orthogonally at all their points of intersection.

For steady flows, that is, flows that do not vary with time, the paths of the particles coincide with the streamlines so that no fluid passes normal to them. The Bernoulli formula then holds and the total pressure head H along a streamline is a constant, that is—

$$\tfrac{1}{2}\rho v^2 + p' = H$$

where p' is the static pressure, v the velocity, and ρ the density. If we denote the undisturbed velocity at infinity by V, the quantities $p'_\infty - p'_0$ by p, and $\tfrac{1}{2}\rho V^2$ by q, the Bernoulli formula may be expressed as

$$\frac{p}{q} = 1 - \left(\frac{v}{V}\right)^2 \qquad (3)$$

The solutions of Eq. (2) and (2′), infinite in number, represent all possible types of irrotational motion of a nonviscous incompressible fluid in two dimensions. For a given problem, there are usually certain specified boundary conditions to be satisfied which may be sufficient to fix a unique solution or a family of solutions. The problem of an airfoil moving uniformly at a fixed angle of incidence in a fluid field is identical with that of an airfoil fixed in position and fluid streaming uniformly past it. Our problem is then to determine the functions P and Q so that the velocity at each point of the airfoil profile has a direction tangential to the surface (that is, the airfoil contour is itself a streamline) so that at infinite distance from the airfoil the fluid has constant velocity and direction.

The introduction of the complex variable $z = x + iy$ simplifies the problem of determining P and Q. Any analytic function $w(z)$ of a complex variable z, that is, a function of z possessing a unique derivative in a region of the complex plane, may be separated into its real and imaginary parts as $w(z) \equiv w(x + iy) = P(x,y) + iQ(x,y)$, determining functions P and Q which may represent the velocity potential and stream function of a possible fluid motion. Thus, analytic functions of a complex variable possess the special property that the component functions P and Q satisfy the Cauchy-Riemann equations Eq. (1), and each therefore also satisfies the equation of Laplace Eq. (2). Conversely, any function $P(x,y) + iQ(x,y)$ for which P and Q satisfy relations (1) and (2) may be written as $w(x + iy) \equiv w(z)$. The essential difficulty of the problem is to find the particular function $w(z)$ which satisfies the special boundary-flow conditions mentioned above for a specified airfoil.

The method of conformal representation, a geometric application of the complex variable, is well adapted to this problem. The fundamental properties of transformations of this type may be stated as follows: Consider a function of a complex variable $z = x + iy$, say, $w(z)$ analytic in a given region, such that for each value of z, $w(z)$ is uniquely defined. The function $w(z)$ may be expressed as $w = \xi + i\eta$, where ξ and η are each real functions of x and y. Suppose now in the xy complex plane there is traced a simple curve $f(z)$ (Fig. 1). Each value of z along the curve defines a point w in the w plane and $f(z)$ maps into a curve $f(w)$ or $F(z)$. Because of the special properties of analytic functions of a complex variable, there exist certain special relations between $f(z)$ and $F(z)$.

The outstanding property of functions of a complex variable analytic in a region is the existence of a unique derivative at every point of the region:

$$\frac{dw}{dz} = \lim_{z \to z'} \frac{w - w'}{z - z'} = \rho e^{i\gamma}$$

or

$$du = \rho e^{i\gamma}\, dz$$

This relation expresses the fact that any small curve zz' through the point z is transformed into a small curve ww' through the point w by a magnification ρ and a rotation γ; i.e., in Fig. 1 the tangent t will coincide in direction with T by a rotation $\gamma = \beta - \alpha$. This is also true for any other pair of corresponding curves through z and u, so that in general, angles between corresponding curves are preserved. In particular, a curve zz'' orthogonal to zz' transforms into a curve ww'' orthogonal to ww'.

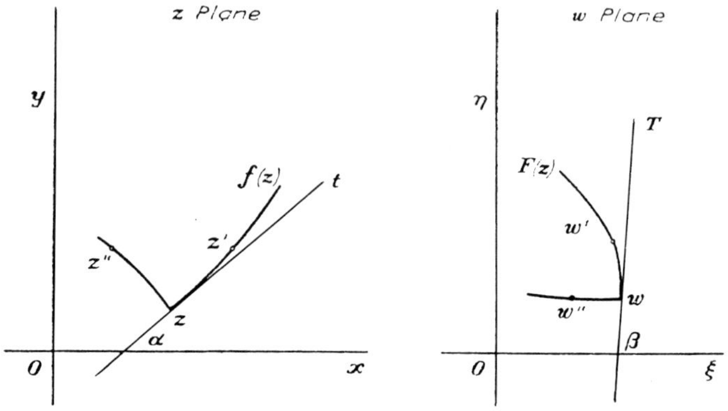

Fig. 1 Conformal property of analytic functions.

It has been seen that an analytic function $f(z)$ may be written $P(x,y) + iQ(x,y)$, where the curves P = constant and Q = constant form an orthogonal system. If, then, $f(z)$ is transformed conformally into $f(w) = P(\xi, \eta) + iQ(\xi, \eta)$, that is, into $f[w\,|(z)] \equiv F(z) = R(x,y) + iS(x,y)$, the curves $P(x,y)$ = constant,

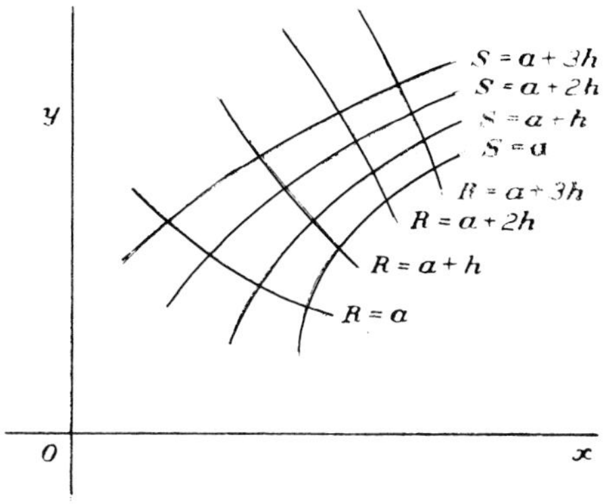

Fig. 2 Orthogonal network obtained by a conformal transformation.

$Q(x,y) =$ constant map into the orthogonal network of curves $R(x,y) =$ constant, $S(x,y) =$ constant (Fig. 2). If the magnification $|dw/dz| = \rho$ is zero at a point w, the transformation at that point is singular and ceases to be conformal.

We may use the method of conformal transformations to find the motion about a complicated boundary from that of a simpler boundary. Suppose $w(z)$ is a function which corresponds to any definite fluid motion in the z plane, for instance, to that around a circle. Now, if a new variable ξ is introduced and z set equal to any analytic function of ζ, say, $z = f(\zeta)$, then $w(z)$ becomes $w[f(\zeta)]$ or $W(\zeta)$ representing a new motion in the ζ plane. This new motion is, as has been seen, related to that in the z plane in such a way that the streamlines of the z plane are transformed by $z = f(\zeta)$ into the streamlines of the ζ plane. Thus, the contour into which the circle is transformed represents the profile around which the motion $W(\zeta)$ exists. The problem of determining the flow around an airfoil is now reduced to finding the proper conformal transformation which maps a curve for which the flow is known into the airfoil. The *existence* of such a function was first shown by Riemann.

We shall first formulate the theorem for a simply connected region[5] bounded by a closed curve, and then show how it is readily applied to the region external to the closed curve. The guiding thought leading to the theorem is simple. We have seen that an analytic function may transform a given closed region into another closed region. But suppose we are given two separate regions bounded by closed curves—does there exist an analytic transformation which transforms one region conformally into the other? This question is answered by Riemann's theorem as follows.

Riemann's theorem

The interior T of any simply connected region [whose boundary contains more than one point, but we shall be concerned only with regions having closed boundaries, the boundary curve being composed of piecewise differentiable curves (Jordan curve), corners at which two tangents exist being permitted] can be mapped in a one-to-one conformal manner on the interior of the unit circle, and the analytic[6] function $\zeta = f(z)$ which consummates this transformation becomes *unique* when a given interior point z_0 of T and a direction through z_0 are chosen to correspond, respectively, to the center of the circle and a given direction through it. By this transformation the boundary of T is transformed uniquely and continuously into the circumference of the unit circle.

The unit circle in this theorem is, of course, only a convenient normalized region. For suppose the regions T_1 in the ζ plane and T_2 in the w plane are transformed into the unit circle in the z plane by $\zeta = f(z)$ and $w = F(z)$, respectively, then T_1 is transformed into T_2 by $\zeta = \Phi(w)$, obtained by eliminating z from the two transformation equations.

In airfoil theory it is in the region external to a closed curve that we are interested. Such a region can be readily transformed conformally into the region internal to a closed curve by an inversion. Thus, let us suppose a point z_0 to be within a closed curve B whose external region is Γ, and then choose a constant k such that for every point z on the boundary of Γ, $|z - z_0| > k$. Then the inversion transformation $w = k/z - z_0$ will transform every point in the external region Γ into a point internal to a closed region Γ' lying entirely within B, the boundary B mapping into the boundary of Γ', the region at infinity into the region near z_0. We may now restate Riemann's theorem as follows:

One and only one analytic function $\zeta = f(z)$ exists by means of which the region Γ external to a given curve B in the ζ plane is transformed conformally into the region external to a circle C in the z plane (center at $z = 0$) such that the point $z = \infty$ goes into the point $\zeta = \infty$ and also $df(z)/dz = 1$ at infinity. This function can be developed in the external region of C in a uniformly convergent series with complex coefficients of the form

$$\zeta - m = f(z) - m = z + \frac{c_1}{z} + \frac{c_2}{z^2} + \frac{c_3}{z^3} + \cdots \quad (4)$$

by means of which the radius R and also the constant m are completely determined. Also, the boundary B of Γ is transformed continuously and uniquely into the circumference of C.

It should be noticed that the transformation (4) is a normalized form of a more general series

[5] A region of the complex plane is simply connected when any closed countour lying entirely within the region may be shrunk to a point without passing out of the region. Cf. Ref. 3, p. 367, where a proof of the theorem based on Green's function is given.

[6] Attention is here directed to the fact that an analytic function is developable at a point in a power series convergent in any circle about the point and entirely within the region.

$$\zeta - m = a_0 + a_{-1}z + \frac{a_1}{z} + \frac{a_2}{z_2} + \cdots$$

and is obtained from it by a finite translation by the vector a_0 and a rotation and expansion of the entire field depending on the cofficient a_{-1}. The condition $a_{-1} = 1$ is necessary and sufficient for the fields at infinity to coincide in magnitude and direction.

The constants c_1 of the transformation are functions of the shape of the boundary curve alone and our problem is, really, to determine the complex coefficients defining a given shape. With this in view, we proceed first to a convenient intermediate transformation.

The transformation $\zeta = z' + \dfrac{a^2}{z'}$

This initial transformation, although not essential to a purely mathematical solution, is nevertheless very useful and important, as will be seen. It represents also the key transformation leading to Joukowsky airfoils, and is the basis of nearly all approximate theories.

Let us define the points in the ζ plane and $\zeta = x + iy$ using rectangular coordinates (x,y), and the points in the z' plane by $z' = ae^{\psi\ \theta}$ using polar coordinates (ae^{ψ},θ). The constant a may conveniently be considered unity and is added to preserve dimensions. We have

$$\zeta = z' + \frac{a^2}{z'} \tag{5}$$

and substituting $z' = ae^{\psi + i\theta}$ we obtain $\zeta = 2a\cosh(\psi + i\theta)$ or $\zeta = 2a \cosh\psi \cos\theta + 2ia \sinh\psi \sin\theta$. Since $\zeta = x + iy$, the coordinates (x,y) are given by

$$\left.\begin{aligned} x &= 2a \cosh\psi \cos\theta \\ y &= 2a \sinh\psi \sin\theta \end{aligned}\right\} \tag{6}$$

If $\psi = 0$, then $z' = ae^{i\theta}$ and $\zeta = 2a\cos\theta$. That is, if P and P' are corresponding points in the ζ and z' planes, respectively, then as P traverses the x axis from $2a$ to $-2a$, P' traverses the circle $ae^{i\theta}$ from $\theta = 0$ to $\theta = \pi$, and as P retraces its path to $\zeta = 2a$, P' completes the circle. The transformation (5) then may be seen to map the entire ζ plane external to the line

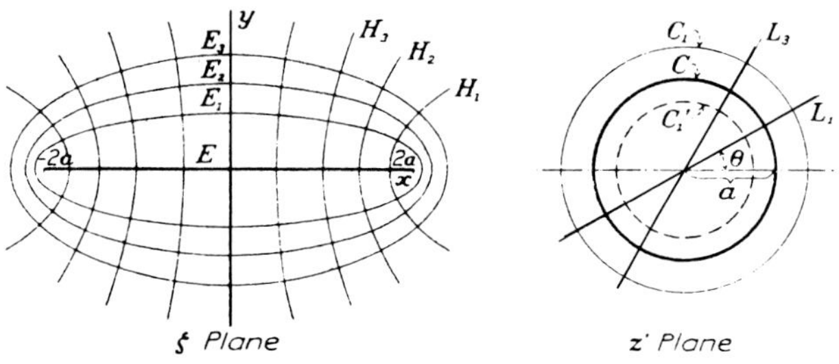

Fig. 3 Transformation by elliptic coordinates.

$4a$ uniquely into the region external (or internal) to the circle of radius a about the origin in the z' plane.

Let us invert Eq. (6) and solve for the elliptic coordinates ψ and θ (Fig. 3). We have

$$\cosh\psi = \frac{x}{2a\cos\theta}$$

$$\sinh\psi = \frac{y}{2a\sin\theta}$$

and since $\cosh^2\psi \sinh^2\psi - 1$

$$\left(\frac{x}{2a\cos\theta}\right)^2 - \left(\frac{y}{2a\sin\theta}\right)^2 - 1$$

or solving for $\sin^2\theta$ (which cannot become negative),

$$2\sin^2\theta = p + \sqrt{p^2 + \left(\frac{y}{a}\right)^2} \tag{7}$$

where

$$p = 1 - \left(\frac{x}{2a}\right)^2 - \left(\frac{y}{2a}\right)^2$$

Similarly, we obtain

$$\left(\frac{x}{2a\cosh\psi}\right)^2 + \left(\frac{y}{2a\cosh\psi}\right)^2 = 1$$

or solving for $\sinh^2\psi$,

$$2\sinh^2\psi = -p + \sqrt{p^2 + \left(\frac{y}{a}\right)^2} \tag{8}$$

We note that the system of radial lines $\theta =$ constant become confocal hyperbolas in the ζ plane. The circles $\psi =$ constant become ellipses in the ζ plane with major axis $2a\cosh\psi$ and minor axis $2a\sinh\eta$. These orthogonal systems of curves represent the potential lines and streamlines in the two planes. The foci of these two confocal systems are located at $(\pm 2a, 0)$.

Equation (8) yields two values of ψ for a given point (x,y), and one set of these values refers to the correspondence of (x,y) to the point (ae^{ψ}, θ) external to a curve and the other set to the correspondence of (x,y) to the point $(ae^{-\psi}, -\theta)$ internal to another curve. Thus, in Fig. 3, for every point external to the ellipse E_1 there is a corresponding point external to the circle C_1, and also one internal to C_1'.

The radius of curvature of the ellipse at the end of the major axis is $\rho = 2a \times (\sinh^2\psi/\cosh\psi)$ or for small values of ψ, $\rho \cong 2a\psi^2$. The leading edge is at

$$2a\cosh\psi \cong 2a\left(1 + \frac{\psi^2}{2}\right) \cong 2a + \frac{\rho}{2}$$

Now, if there is given an airfoil in the ζ plane (Fig. 4), and it is desired to transform the airfoil profile into a curve as nearly circular as possible in the z' plane by using only transformation (5), it is clear that the axes of coordinates should be chosen so that the airfoil appears as nearly elliptical as possible with respect to the chosen axes. It was seen that a focus of an elongated ellipse very nearly bisects the line joining the end of the major axis and the center of curvature of this point; thus, we arrive at a convenient choice of origin for the airfoil as the point bisecting the line of length $4a$, which extends from the point midway between the leading edge and the center of curvature of the leading edge to a point midway between the center of curvature of the trailing edge and the trailing edge. This latter point practically coincides with the trailing edge.

The curve B, defined by $ae^{\psi + i\theta}$, resulting in the z' plane, and the inverse and reflected curve B', defined

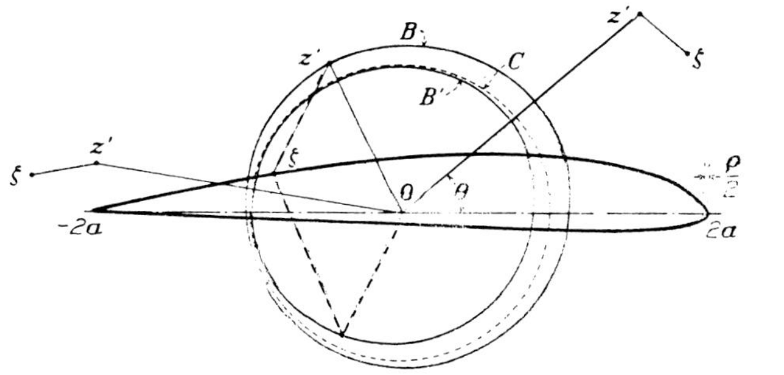

Fig. 4 Transformation of airfoil into a nearly circular contour.

by $ae^{-\psi + i\theta}$, are shown superimposed on the ζ plane in Fig. 4. The convenience and usefulness of transformation (5) and the choice of axes of coordinates will become evident after our next transformation.

The transformation $z' = ze^{\sum_0^\infty \frac{c_n}{z^n}}$

Consider the transformation $z' = ze^{f(z)}$, where

$$f(z) = \sum_0^\infty \frac{c_n}{z^n}$$

Each exponential term

$$e^{\frac{c_n}{z^n}}$$

represents the uniformly convergent series

$$1 + \frac{c_n}{z^n} + \frac{1}{2!}\left(\frac{c_n}{z^n}\right)^2 + \cdots \frac{1}{m!}\left(\frac{c_n}{z^n}\right)^m + \cdots \qquad (9)$$

where the coefficients $c_n = A_n + iB_n$ are complex numbers. For $f(z)$ convergent at all points in a region external to a certain circle, z' has a unique real absolute value $|z|e^{|f(z)|}$ in the region and its imaginary part is definitely defined except for integral multiples of $2\pi i$. When $z = \infty$, $z' = ze^{c_0}$. The constant $c_0 = A_0 + iB_0$ is then the determining factor at infinity, for the field at infinity is magnified by e^{A_0} and rotated by the angle B_0. It is thus clear that if it is desired that the regions at infinity be identical, that is, $z' = z$ at infinity, the constant c_0 must be zero. The constants c_1 and c_2 also play important roles, as will be shown later.

We shall now transform the closed curve[7] $z' = ae^{\psi + i\theta}$ into the circle $z = ae^{\psi_0 + i\varphi}$ (radius ae^{ψ_0}, origin at center) by means of the general transformation (Ref. 2)—

$$z' = ze^{\sum_1^\infty \frac{c_n}{z^n}} \qquad (10)$$

which leaves the fields at infinity unaltered, and we shall obtain expressions for the constants A_n, B_n, and ψ_0. The justification of the solution will be assured by the actual convergence of

$$\sum_1^\infty \frac{c_n}{z^n}$$

since if the solution exists it is unique.

By definition, for the correspondence of the boundary points, we have

$$z' = ze^{\psi - \psi_0 + i(\theta - \varphi)} \qquad (10')$$

Also

$$z' = ze^{\sum_1^\infty (A_n + iB_n)\frac{1}{z^n}}$$

Consequently

$$\psi - \psi_0 + i(\theta - \varphi) = \sum_1^\infty (A_n + iB_n)\frac{1}{z^n}$$

where

$$z = ae^{\psi_0 + i\varphi}$$

On writing $z = R(\cos\varphi + i\sin\varphi)$ where $R = ae^{\psi_0}$, we have

$$\psi - \psi_0 + i(\theta - \varphi) = \sum_1^\infty (A_n + iB_n)\frac{1}{R^n} \times (\cos n\varphi - i\sin n\varphi)$$

Equating the real and imaginary parts of this relation, we obtain the two conjugate Fourier expansions:

$$\psi - \psi_0 = \sum_1^\infty \left[\frac{A_n}{R^n}\cos n\varphi + \frac{B_n}{R^n}\sin n\varphi\right] \qquad (11)$$

$$\theta - \varphi = \sum_1^\infty \left[\frac{B_n}{R^n}\cos n\varphi + \frac{A_n}{R^n}\sin n\varphi\right] \qquad (12)$$

From Eq. (11), the values of the coefficients A_n/R^n, B_n/R^n, and the constant ψ_0 are obtained as follows:

[7]Unless otherwise stated, ψ and θ will now be used in the restricted sense, i.e., as defining the boundary curve itself, and not all points in the z′ plane.

$$\frac{A_n}{R^n} = \frac{1}{\pi}\int_0^{2\pi} \psi \cos n\varphi \, d\varphi \qquad \text{(a)}$$

$$\frac{B_n}{R^n} = \frac{1}{\pi}\int_0^{2\pi} \psi \sin n\varphi \, d\varphi \qquad \text{(b)}$$

$$\psi_0 = \frac{1}{2\pi}\int_0^{2\pi} \psi \, d\varphi \qquad \text{(c)}$$

The evaluation of the infinite number of constants as represented by equations (a) and (b) can be made to depend upon an important single equation, which we shall obtain by eliminating these constants from Eq. (12).

Substitution of (a) and (b) for the coefficients of Eq. (12) gives—

$$(\theta - \varphi)' = \frac{1}{\pi}\sum_1^\infty \left[\cos n\varphi' \int_0^{2\pi} \psi(\varphi) \sin n\varphi \, d\varphi - \sin n\varphi' \int_0^{2\pi} \psi(\varphi) \cos n\varphi \, d\varphi \right]$$

where $\psi(\varphi) = \psi$ and $(\theta - \varphi)'$ represents $\theta - \varphi$ as a function of φ', and where φ' is used to distinguish the angle kept constant while the integrations are performed. The expression may be readily rewritten as

$$(\theta - \varphi)' = \frac{1}{\pi}\sum_1^\infty \int_0^{2\pi} \psi(\varphi)(\sin n\varphi \cos n\varphi' - \cos n\varphi \sin n\varphi') \, d\varphi$$

$$= \frac{1}{\pi}\sum_1^\infty \int_0^{2\pi} \psi(\varphi) \sin n(\varphi - \varphi') \, d\varphi$$

But

$$\sum_1^\infty \sin n(\varphi - \varphi') = \frac{1}{2}\cot\frac{(\varphi - \varphi')}{2} - \frac{\cos(2n+1)\dfrac{(\varphi - \varphi')}{2}}{2\sin\dfrac{\varphi - \varphi'}{2}}$$

Then

$$(\theta - \varphi)' = \lim_{n\to\infty} \left\{ \frac{1}{2\pi}\int_0^{2\pi} \psi(\varphi) \cot\frac{(\varphi - \varphi')}{2} \, d\varphi - \frac{1}{2\pi}\int_0^{2\pi} \psi(\varphi) \frac{\cos(2n+1)\dfrac{(\varphi - \varphi')}{2}}{\sin\dfrac{(\varphi - \varphi')}{2}} \, d\varphi \right\}$$

The first integral is independent of n, whereas the latter one becomes identically zero.

Finally, representing $\varphi - \theta$ by a single quantity ϵ, viz, $\varphi - \theta \equiv \epsilon \equiv \epsilon(\varphi)$, we have

$$\epsilon(\varphi') = -\frac{1}{2\pi}\int_0^{2\pi} \psi(\varphi) \cot\frac{(\varphi - \varphi')}{2} \, d\varphi \qquad (13)$$

By solving for the coefficients in Eq. (12) and substituting these in Eq. (11) it may be seen that a similar relation to Eq. (13) holds for the function $\psi(\varphi)$:

$$\psi(\varphi') = \frac{1}{2\pi}\int_0^{2\pi} \epsilon(\varphi) \cot\frac{\varphi - \varphi'}{2} \, d\varphi + \frac{1}{2\pi}\int_0^{2\pi} \psi(\varphi) \, d\varphi \quad (14)$$

The last term is merely the constant ψ_0, which is, as has been shown, determined by the condition of magnification of the z and z' fields at infinity. The corresponding integral

$$\frac{1}{2\pi}\int_0^{2\pi} \epsilon(\varphi) \, d\varphi$$

does not appear in Eq. (13), being zero as a necessary consequence of the coincidence of directions at infinity and, in general, if the region at infinity is rotated, is a constant different from zero.

Investigation of Eq. (13)

This equation is of fundamental importance. A discussion of some of its properties is therefore of interest. First it should be noted that when the function $\psi(\varphi)$ is considered known, the equation reduces to a definite integral. The function[8] $\epsilon(\varphi)$ obtained by this evaluation is the "conjugate" function to $\psi(\varphi)$, so called because of the relations existing between the coefficients of the Fourier expansions as given by Eq. (11) and (12). For the existence of the integral it is only necessary that $\psi(\varphi)$ be piecewise continuous and differentiable, and may even have infinities which must be below first order. We shall, however, be interested only in continuous single-valued functions having a period 2π, of a type which results from continuous closed curves with a proper choice of origin.

If Eq. (13) is regarded as a definite integral, it is seen to be related to the well-known Poisson integral which solves the following boundary-value problem of the circle (Ref. 3). Given, say, for the z plane a single-valued function $u(R, \tau)$ for points on the circumference of a circle $w = Re^{i\tau}$ (center at origin), then the single-valued continuous potential function $u(r, \sigma)$ in the external region $z = re^{i\sigma}$ of the circle which assumes the values $u(R, \tau)$ on the circumferene is given by

[8]This function will be called "conformal angular distortion" function, for reasons evident later.

$$u(r, \sigma) = \frac{1}{2\pi}\int_0^{2\pi} u(R, \tau)\,\frac{r^2 - R^2}{R^2 + r^2 - 2Rr\cos(\sigma - \tau)}\,d\tau$$

and similarly for the conjugate function $v(r, \sigma)$

$$v(r, \sigma) = \frac{1}{2\pi}\int_0^{2\pi} v(R, \tau)\,\frac{r^2 - R^2}{R^2 + r^2 - 2Rr\cos(\sigma - \tau)}\,d\tau$$

These may be written as a single equation:

$$u(r,\sigma) + iv(r,\alpha) = f(z) = \frac{1}{2\pi}\int_C f(w)\,\frac{z + w}{z - w}\,dw$$

where the value $f(z)$ at a point of the external region $z = re^{i\sigma}$ is expressed in terms of the known values $f(w)$ along the circumference $w = Re^{i\tau}$. In particular, we may note that at the boundary itself, since

$$i\frac{e^{i\sigma} + e^{i\tau}}{e^{i\sigma} - e^{i\tau}} = \cot\frac{(\sigma - \tau)}{2}$$

we have

$$u(R,\sigma) + iv(R,\sigma) = -\frac{1}{2\pi}\int_0^{2\pi} [u(R,\tau) + iv(R, \tau)]\cot\frac{(\sigma - \tau)}{2}\,d\tau$$

which is a special form of Eq. (13) and (14).

The quantity ψ is immediatly given as a function of θ when a particular closed curve is preassigned, and this is our starting point in the direct process of transforming from airfoil to circle. We desire, then, to find the quantity η as a function of φ from Eq. (13), and this equation is no longer a definite integral but an integral equation whose process of solution becomes more intricate. It would be surprising, indeed, if anything less than a functional or integral equation were involved in the solution of the general problem stated. The evaluation of the solution of Eq. (13) is readily accomplished by a powerful method of successive approximations. It will be seen that the nearness of the curve $ae^{\psi + i\theta}$ to a circle is very significant, and in practice, for airfoil shapes, one or at most two steps in the process is found to be sufficient for great accuracy.

The quantities ψ and ϵ considered as functions of φ have been denoted by $\psi(\varphi)$ and $\epsilon(\varphi)$, respectively. When these quantities are thought of as functions of θ they shall be written as $\bar{\psi}(\theta)$ and $\bar{\epsilon}(\theta)$, respectively.

Then, by definition

$$\bar{\psi}(\theta) \equiv \psi[\varphi(\theta)]$$

and (15)

$$\bar{\epsilon}(\theta) \equiv \epsilon[\varphi(\theta)]$$

Since $\varphi - \theta = \epsilon$, we have

$$\left.\begin{aligned} \theta(\varphi) &= \varphi - \epsilon(\varphi) \\ \varphi(\theta) &= \theta + \bar{\epsilon}(\theta) \end{aligned}\right\} \qquad (16)$$

We are seeking, then, two functions, $\psi(\varphi)$ and $\epsilon(\varphi)$, conjugate in the sense that their Fourier series expansions are given by Eq. (11) and (12), such that $\psi[\varphi(\theta)] = \bar{\psi}(\theta)$, where $\bar{\psi}(\theta)$ is a *known* single-valued function of period 2π.

Integrating Eq. (13) by parts, we have

$$\epsilon(\varphi') = \frac{1}{\pi}\int_0^{2\pi} \log\sin\frac{\varphi - \varphi'}{2}\,\frac{d\psi(\varphi)}{d\varphi}\,d\varphi \qquad (13')$$

The term $\log\sin(\varphi - \varphi')/2$ is real only in the range $\varphi = \varphi'$ to $\varphi = 2\pi + \varphi'$, but we may use the interval 0 to 2π for φ with the understanding that only the real part of the logarithm is retained.

Let us write down the following identity:

$$\begin{aligned}
\log\sin\frac{\varphi - \varphi'}{2} \equiv{}& \log\sin\frac{\theta - \theta'}{2} \\
&+ \log\frac{\sin\dfrac{(\theta + \bar{\epsilon}_1) - (\theta + \bar{\epsilon}_1)'}{2}}{\sin\dfrac{\theta - \theta'}{2}} \\
&+ \log\frac{\sin\dfrac{(\theta + \bar{\epsilon}_2) - (\theta + \bar{\epsilon}_2)'}{2}}{\sin\dfrac{(\theta + \bar{\epsilon}_1) - (\theta + \bar{\epsilon}_1)'}{2}} \\
&+ \log\frac{\sin\dfrac{(\theta + \bar{\epsilon}_k) - (\theta + \bar{\epsilon}_k)'}{2}}{\sin\dfrac{(\theta + \bar{\epsilon}_{k-1}) - (\theta + \bar{\epsilon}_{k-1})'}{2}} \\
&+ \log\frac{\sin\dfrac{(\theta + \bar{\epsilon}_n) - (\theta + \bar{\epsilon}_n)'}{2}}{\sin\dfrac{(\theta + \bar{\epsilon}_{n-1}) - (\theta + \bar{\epsilon}_{n-1})'}{2}} \\
&+ \log\frac{\sin\dfrac{(\theta + \bar{\epsilon}) - (\theta + \bar{\epsilon})'}{2}}{\sin\dfrac{(\theta + \bar{\epsilon}_n) - (\theta + \bar{\epsilon}_n)'}{2}} \qquad (17)
\end{aligned}$$

where in the last term we recall that $\theta + \bar{\epsilon}(\theta) = \varphi(\theta)$; and where it may be noted that each denominator is the numerator of the preceding term. The symbols ϵ_k $(k = 1, 2, \cdots, n)$ represent functions of θ, which thus far are arbitrary.[9]

Since by Eq. (15) $\bar{\psi}(\theta) \equiv \psi[\varphi(\theta)]$ we have for corresponding elements $d\theta$ and $d\varphi$

[9]The symbol $(\theta + \bar{\epsilon}_k)'$ represents $\theta' + \bar{\epsilon}_k(\theta')$ and is used to denote the same function of θ' that $\theta + \epsilon_b(\theta)$ is of θ. The variables θ and θ' are regarded as independent of each other.

$$\frac{d\psi(\varphi)}{d\varphi}\,d\varphi = \frac{d\bar{\psi}(\theta)}{d\theta}\,d\theta$$

Then, multiplying the left side of Eq. (17) by $\frac{1}{\pi}\frac{d\psi(\varphi)}{d\varphi}\,d\varphi$ and the right side by $\frac{1}{\pi}\frac{d\psi(\theta)}{d\theta}\,d\theta$ and integrating over the period 0 to 2π we obtain—

$$\epsilon[\varphi(\theta')] \equiv \bar{\epsilon}(\theta') = \frac{1}{\pi}\int_0^{2\pi} \log \sin\frac{\theta-\theta'}{2}\,\frac{d\bar{\psi}(\theta)}{d\theta}\,d\theta$$

$$+\frac{1}{\pi}\int_0^{2\pi} \log \frac{\sin\dfrac{(\theta+\bar{\epsilon}_k)-(\theta+\bar{\epsilon}_k)'}{2}}{\sin\dfrac{(\theta+\bar{\epsilon}_{k-1})-(\theta+\bar{\epsilon}_{k-1})'}{2}}\,\frac{d\bar{\psi}(\theta)}{d\theta}\,d\theta$$

$$+\frac{1}{\pi}\int_0^{2\pi} \log \frac{\sin\dfrac{[\theta+\bar{\epsilon}(\theta)]-[\theta+\bar{\epsilon}(\theta)]'}{2}}{\sin\dfrac{(\theta+\bar{\epsilon}_n)-(\theta+\bar{\epsilon}_n)'}{2}}\,\frac{d\bar{\psi}(\theta)}{d\theta}\,d\theta \qquad (18)$$

where $k = 1, 2, \cdots, n$.

We now choose the arbitrary functions $\bar{\epsilon}_k(\theta')$ so that $\bar{\epsilon}_0(\theta') = 0$ and

$$\bar{\epsilon}_k(\theta') = \frac{1}{\pi}\int_0^{2\pi} \log \sin\frac{(\theta+\bar{\epsilon}_{k-1})-(\theta+\bar{\epsilon}_{k-1})'}{2}\,\frac{d\bar{\psi}(\theta)}{d\theta}\,d\theta \qquad (19)$$

where $k = 1, 2, \cdots, n$.

Equation (18) may then be written—

$$\bar{\epsilon}(\theta') = \bar{\epsilon}_0 + \bar{\epsilon}_1 + (\bar{\epsilon}_2 - \bar{\epsilon}_1) + \cdots + (\bar{\epsilon} - \bar{\epsilon}_{n-1}) + (\bar{\epsilon} - \bar{\epsilon}_n) \qquad (20)$$

or

$$\bar{\epsilon}(\theta') = \lambda_1 + \lambda_2 + \cdots \lambda_n + \lambda$$

where $\lambda_k(\theta') = \bar{\epsilon}_{k-1}$ and is in fact the kth term of Eq. (18). The last term we denote by λ.

From Eq. (19) we see that the function $\bar{\epsilon}_k(\theta')$ is obtained by a knowledge of the preceding function $\bar{\epsilon}_{k-1}(\theta')$. For convenience in the evalution of these functions, say

$$\bar{\epsilon}_{k-1}(\theta') = \frac{1}{\pi}\int_0^{2\pi} \log \sin\frac{(\theta+\bar{\epsilon}_k)-(\theta+\bar{\epsilon}_k)'}{2}\,\frac{d\bar{\psi}(\theta)}{d\theta}\,d\theta$$

we introduce a new variable φ_k defined by

$$\varphi_k(\theta) = \theta + \bar{\epsilon}_k(\theta) \qquad (k = 1, 2, \ldots, n)$$

Then

$$\bar{\epsilon}_{k+1}[\theta(\varphi'_{k+1})] \equiv \epsilon^*_{k+1}(\varphi'_k)$$

$$= \frac{1}{\pi}\int_0^{2\pi} \log \sin\frac{(\varphi_k - \varphi'_k)}{2}\,\frac{d\bar{\psi}[\theta(\varphi_k)]}{d\varphi_k}\,d\varphi_k \qquad (21)$$

From the definition of φ_k as $\varphi_k(\theta) = \theta + \bar{\epsilon}_k(\theta)$ we may also define the symbol $\epsilon_k(\varphi_k)$ by $\theta(\varphi_k) = \varphi_k - \epsilon_k(\varphi_k)$ where $\bar{\epsilon}_k(\theta) \equiv \epsilon_k[\varphi_k(\theta)]$. It is important to note that the symbols $\bar{\epsilon}_k$, ϵ_k, ϵ^*_k denote the same quantity considered, however, as a function of θ, φ_k, φ_{k-1}, respectively.

The quantities $(\bar{\epsilon}_k - \bar{\epsilon}_{k-1})$ in Eq. (20) rapidly approach zero for wide classes of initial curves $\psi(\theta)$, i.e., $\bar{\psi}[\theta(\varphi_k)]$ very nearly equals $\bar{\psi}[\theta(\varphi_{k+1})]$ for even small k. The process of solution of our problem is then one of obtaining successively the functions $\bar{\psi}(\theta)$, $\bar{\psi}[\theta(\varphi_1)]$, $\bar{\psi}[\theta(\varphi_2)]$, $\ldots$ $\bar{\psi}[\theta(\varphi_n)]$ where $\bar{\psi}[\theta(\varphi_n)]$ and $\bar{\epsilon}_n[\theta(\varphi_n)]$ become more and more "conjugate." The process of obtaining the successive conjugates in practice is explained in a later paragraph. We first pause to state the conditions which the functions φ_k are subject to, necessary for a one-to-one correspondence of the boundary points, and for a one-to-one correspondence of points of the external regions, i.e., the conditions which are necessary in order that the transformations be conformal.

In order that the correspondence between boundary points of the circle in the z plane and boundary points of the contour in the z' plane be one-to-one, it is necessary that $\theta(\varphi)$ be a monotonic increasing function of its argument. This statement requires a word of explanation. We consider only values of the angles between 0 and 2π. For a point of the circle boundary, that is, for one value of φ there can be only one value of θ, i.e., $\theta(\varphi)$ is always single-valued. However, $\varphi(\theta)$, in general, does not need to be, as for example, by a poor choice of origin it may be many valued, a radius vector from the origin intersecting the boundary more than once; but since we have already postulated that $\psi(\theta)$ is single-valued this case cannot occur, and $\varphi(\theta)$ is also single-valued. If we decide on a definite direction of rotation, then the inequality $d\theta/d\varphi \geq 0$ expresses the statement that as the radius vector from the origin sweeps over the boundary of the circle C, the radius vector in the z' plane sweeps over the boundary of B and never retraces its path.

The inequality

$$\frac{d\theta}{d\varphi} = 1 - \frac{d\epsilon(\varphi)}{d\varphi} \geq 0$$

corresponds to

$$\frac{d\epsilon(\varphi)}{d\varphi} \leq 1$$

Also, the condition

$$\frac{d\varphi}{d\theta} = 1 + \frac{d\bar{\epsilon}(\theta)}{d\theta} \geq 0$$

corresponds to

$$\frac{d\bar{\epsilon}(\varphi)}{d\varphi} \geq -1$$

Multiplying $d\theta/d\varphi$ by $d\varphi/d\theta$ we get

$$\left(1 - \frac{d\epsilon(\varphi)}{d\varphi}\right)\left(1 + \frac{d\bar{\epsilon}(\theta)}{d\theta}\right) = 1$$

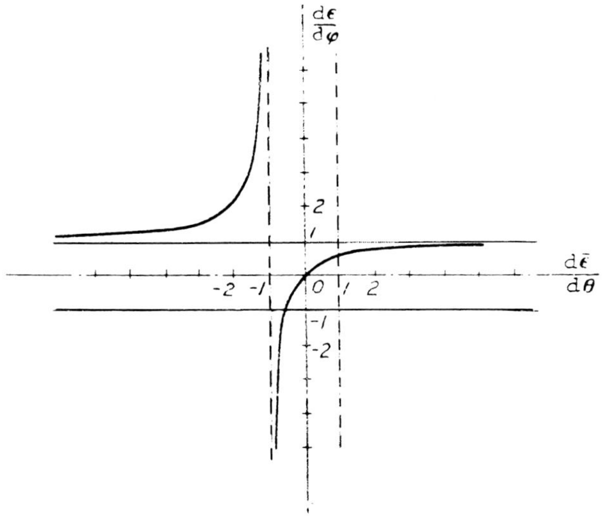

Fig. 5 The quantity $\frac{d\epsilon}{d\psi}$ as a function of $\frac{d\epsilon}{d\theta}$.

This relation is shown in Fig. 5 as a rectangular hyperbola. We may notice, then, that the monotonic behavior of $\varphi(\theta)$ and $\theta(\varphi)$ requires that $d\epsilon/d\varphi$ remain on the *lower* branch[10] of the hyperbola, i.e.,

$$-\infty \leq \frac{d\epsilon}{d\varphi} \leq 1 \qquad (22)$$

It will be seen later that the limiting values

$$\frac{d\epsilon(\varphi)}{d\varphi} = 1, \frac{d\epsilon(\varphi)}{d\varphi} = -\infty\left(\text{i.e., } \frac{d\bar{\epsilon}}{d\theta} = \infty, \frac{d\bar{\epsilon}}{d\theta} = -1\right)$$

correspond to points of infinite velocity and of zero velocity, respectively, arising from sharp corners in the original curve.

The condition for a one-to-one conformal correspondence between points of the external region of the circle and of the external region of the contour in the z' plane may be given (Ref. 5, p. 98, and Ref. 6, Pt. II) as follows: There must be a one-to-one boundary point correspondence and the derivative of the analytic function

$$z' = z e^{\sum_1^\infty \frac{c_n}{z^n}}$$

given by Eq. (10) must not vanish in the region. That is, writing $g(z)$ for $\sum_1^\infty \frac{c_n}{z^n}$ we have

$$\frac{dz'}{dz} = e^{g(z)}\left(1 + z\frac{dg(z)}{dz}\right) \neq 0 \qquad \text{for} \qquad |z| > R$$

or since the integral transcendental function $e^{g(z)}$ does not vanish in the entire plane, the condition is equivalent to $[z\, dg(z)]/dz \neq -1$ for $|z| > R$.

By Eq. (10′) we have on the boundary of the circle, $g(Re^{i\varphi}) = \psi - \psi_0 - i\epsilon$, and

$$z\frac{dg(z)}{dz} = (Re^{i\varphi})\frac{d[\psi(\varphi) - i\epsilon(\varphi)]}{i(Re^{i\varphi})\,d\varphi} = \frac{d\epsilon(\varphi)}{d\varphi} - i\frac{d\psi(\varphi)}{d\varphi}$$

the first term on the right-hand side being real and the last term imaginary. We have already postulated the condition $-\infty \leq d\epsilon/d\varphi \leq 1$ as necessary for a one-to-one boundary point correspondence. Now, by writing $z = \xi + i\eta$ and

$$z\frac{dg(z)}{dz} = P(\xi,\eta) + iQ(\xi,\eta)$$

we note that $d\epsilon(\varphi)/d\varphi$ gives the boundary values of a harmonic function $P(\xi,\eta)$ and therefore this function assumes its maximum and minimum values on the boundary of the circle itself (Ref. 3, p. 223). Hence $z[dg(z)]/dz$ can never become -1 in the external region, i.e., dz'/dz can never vanish in this region.

At each step in the process of obtaining the successive conjugates we desire to maintain a one-to-one correspondence between θ and φ_k; i.e., the functions $\theta(\varphi_k)$ and $\varphi_k(\theta)$ should be monotonic increasing and are hence subject to a restriction similar to Eq. (22):

$$-\infty \leq \frac{d\epsilon_k}{d\varphi_k} \leq 1 \qquad (22')$$

The process may be summed up as follows: We consider the function $\bar{\psi}(\theta)$ as known, where $\bar{\psi}(\theta)$ is the functional relation between ψ and θ defining a closed curve $ae^{\psi + i\theta}$. The conjugate of $\bar{\psi}(\theta)$ with respect to θ is $\bar{\epsilon}_1(\theta)$. We form the variable $\varphi_1 = \theta + \epsilon_1(\theta)$ and also the function $\bar{\psi}[\theta\varphi_1)]$. The conjugate of $\bar{\psi}[\theta(\varphi_1)]$ with respect to φ_1 is $\epsilon_2^*(\varphi_1)$ which expressed as a function of θ is $\bar{\epsilon}_2(\theta)$. We form the variable $\varphi_2 = \theta + \bar{\epsilon}_2(\theta)$ and the function $\bar{\psi}[\theta(\varphi_2)]$. The conjugate of $\bar{\psi}[\theta(\varphi_2)]$ is $\epsilon_3^*(\varphi_2)$, which as a function of θ is $\epsilon_3(\theta)$, etc. The graphical criterion for convergence is, of course, reached when the function $\bar{\psi}[\theta(\varphi_n)]$ is no longer altered by the pro-

[10] The values of the upper branch of the hyperbola arise when the region internal to the curve $ae^{\psi + i\theta}$ is transformed into the external region of a circle, but may also there be avoided by defining $\epsilon = \varphi + \theta$ instead of $\varphi - \theta$.

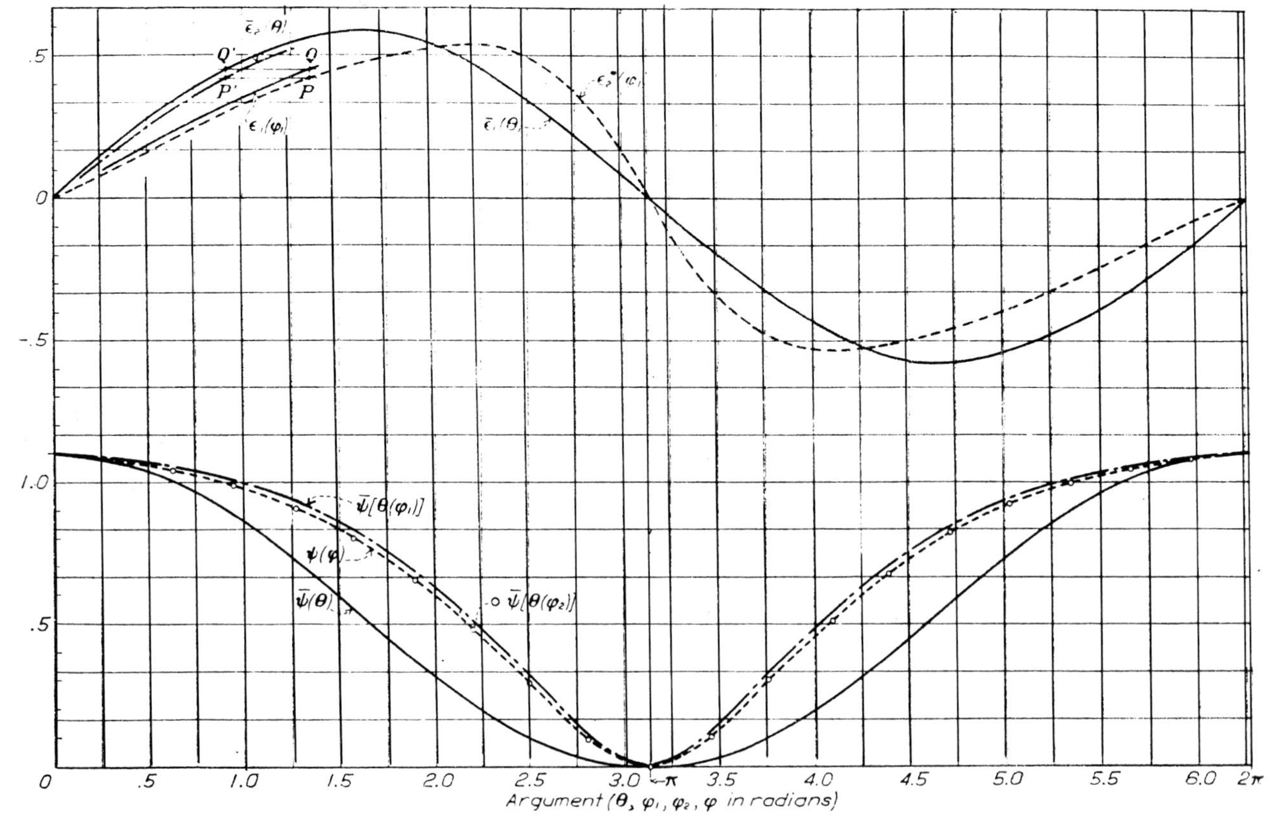

Fig. 6 The process of obtaining successive conjugates.

cess. The following figures illustrate the method and exhibit vividly the rapidity of convergence. The numerical calculations of the various conjugates are obtained from formula I of Appendix I.

In Fig. 6, the $\bar{\psi}(\theta)$ curve represents a circle referred to an origin which bisects a radius (obtained from an extremely thick Joukowsky airfoil) (see p. 26; all page references here cite the pagination in the original paper, and "page 00" means no page number was given in the original) and has numerical values approximately five times greater than those that occur for common airfoils. The $\psi(\varphi)$ curve is known independently and is represented by the dashed curve. The process of going from $\bar{\psi}(\theta)$ to $\psi(\varphi)$ assuming $\psi(\varphi)$ as unknown is as follows: The function $\bar{\epsilon}_1(\theta)$, the conjugate function of $\bar{\psi}(\theta)$, is found. The quantity ψ is then plotted against the new variable $\varphi_1 = \theta + \bar{\epsilon}_1(\theta)$ (i.e., each point of $\bar{\psi}(\theta)$ is displaced horizontally a distance $\bar{\epsilon}_1$) and yields the curve $\bar{\psi}[\theta(\varphi_1)]$. Likewise, $\bar{\epsilon}_1(\theta)$ plotted vs. φ_1 yields $\epsilon_1(\varphi_1)$.

The function $\epsilon_2^*(\varphi_1)$ is now determined as the conjugate function of $\psi[\theta(\varphi_1)]$. It is plotted as follows: At a point P of $\epsilon_2^*(\varphi_1)$ and Q of $\epsilon_1(\varphi_1)$ corresponding to a definite value of φ_1, one finds the value of θ which

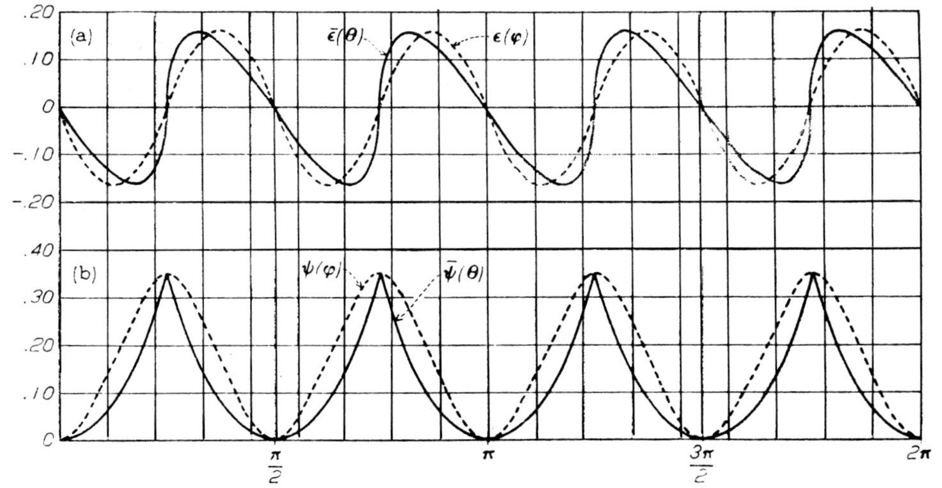

Fig. 7 Process applied to transforming a square into a circle.

corresponds to φ_1 by a horizontal line through Q meeting $\bar{\epsilon}_1(\theta)$ in Q'; for this value of θ, the quantity ϵ_2 at P is drawn at P'. This process yields the function $\bar{\epsilon}_2(\theta)$. The quantity ψ is now plotted against the new variable $\varphi_2 = \theta + \bar{\epsilon}_2(\theta)$ [i.e., each point of $\bar{\psi}(\theta)$ is displaced horizontally a distance $\bar{\epsilon}_2$] giving the function $\bar{\psi}[\theta(\varphi_2)]$. This curve is shown with small circles and coincides with $\psi(\varphi)$. Further application of the process can yield no change in this curve. It may be remarked here that for nearly all airfoils used in practice one step in the process is sufficient for very accurate results.

As another example we shall show how a square (origin at center) is transformed into a circle by this method. In Fig. 7 the $\bar{\psi}(\theta)$ curve is shown, and in Fig. 8 it is reproduced for one octant.[11] The value is $\bar{\psi}(\theta) = \log \sec\theta$. The function $\bar{\psi}[\theta\varphi_1)]$ is shown dashed; the function $\bar{\psi}[\theta\varphi_2)]$ is shown with small crosses; and $\bar{\psi}[\theta\varphi_2)]$ is shown with small circles. The solution $\psi(\varphi)$ is represented by the curve with small triangles and is obtained independently by the known transformation (Ref. 3, p. 375) which transforms the external region of a square into the external region of the unit circle, as follows:

$$w(z) = \int_{z_0}^{z} \frac{\sqrt{z^4 - 1}}{z_2}\, dz = z\left[1 + P\left(\frac{1}{z}\right)\right]$$

$$\epsilon(\varphi') = -\frac{1}{2\pi}\int_0^{2\pi} \psi(\varphi) \cot\frac{(\varphi - \varphi')}{2}\, d\varphi$$

$$= -\frac{2}{\pi}\int_0^{\pi/4} \psi(\varphi)\, [\cot 2(\varphi - \varphi') - \cot 2(\varphi + \varphi')\, d\varphi$$

where $P(1/z)$ denotes a power series. Comparing this with Eq. (10), we find that $\psi(\varphi)$ except for the constant ψ_0 is given as the real part of $\log[1 + P(1/z)]$ evaluated for $z = e^{i\varphi}$, and that $\epsilon(\varphi)$ is given as the negative of the

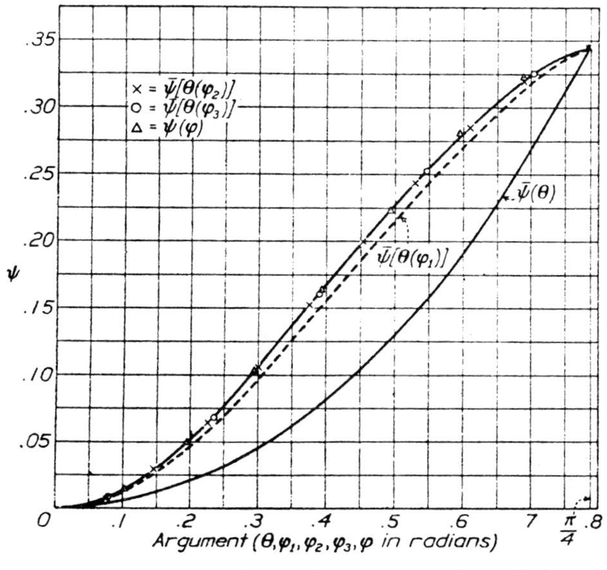

Fig. 8 Process applied to transforming a square into a circle.

imaginary part. It may be observed in Fig. 8 that the function $\bar{\psi}[\theta\varphi_3)]$ very nearly equals $\psi(\varphi)$. The functions $\epsilon(\varphi)$ and $\bar{\epsilon}(\theta)$ are shown in Fig. 7(a); we may note that at $\varphi = \pi/4$, which corresponds to a corner of the square, $d\epsilon/d\varphi = 1$ or also, $d\bar{\epsilon}/d\theta = \infty$.

It may be remarked that the rapidity of convergence is influenced by certain factors. It is noticeably affected by the initial choice of $\bar{\epsilon}_0(\theta)$. The choice $\bar{\epsilon}_0(\theta) = 0$ implies that θ and φ are considered to be very nearly equal, i.e., that $ae^{\psi + i\theta}$ represents a nearly circular curve. The initial transformation given by Eq. (5) and the choice of axes and origin were adapted for the purpose of obtaining a nearly circular curve for airfoil shapes. If we should be concerned with other classes of contours, more appropriate initial transformations can be developed. If, however, for a curve $ae^{\psi + i\theta}$ the quantity $\epsilon = \varphi - \theta$ has large values, either because of a poor initial transformation or because of an unfavorable choice of origin, it may occur that the choice $\bar{\epsilon}_0(\theta) = 0$ will yield a function $\epsilon_1(\varphi_1)$ for which $d\epsilon_1/d\varphi_1$ may exceed unity at some points, thus violating condition (22′). Such slopes can be replaced by slopes less than unity, the resulting *function* chosen as $\bar{\epsilon}_0(\theta)$ and the process continued as before.[12] Indeed, the closer the choice of the function $\bar{\epsilon}_0(\theta)$ is to the final solution $\bar{\epsilon}_0(\theta)$, the more rapid is the convergence. The case of the square illustrates that even the relatively poor choice $\bar{\epsilon}_0(\theta) = 0$ does not appreciably defer the convergence.

The translation $z_1 = z + c_1$

Let us divert our attention momentarily to another transformation which will prove useful. We recall that the initial transformation [Eq. (5)] applied to an airfoil in the ζ plane gives a curve B in the z' plane shown schematically in Fig. 9(a). Equation (10) transforms this curve into a circle C about the origin 0 as center and yields in fact small values of the quantity $\varphi - \theta$.

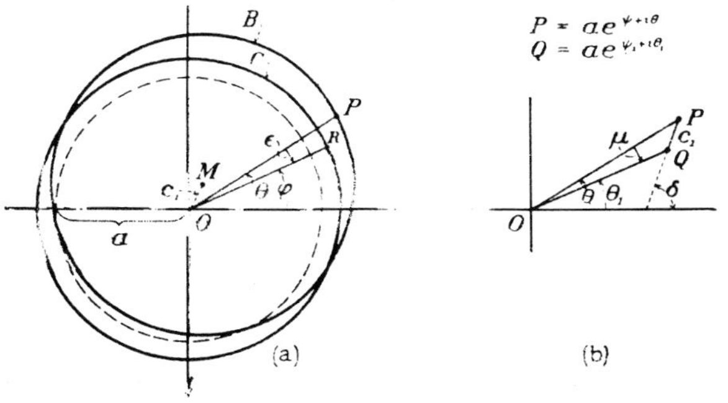

Fig. 9 Translation by the distance *OM*.

[11]Because of the symmetry involved, only the interval 0 to $\pi/4$ need be used. The integral in Appendix I can be treated as

[12]The first step in the process is now to define $\varphi_0 = \theta + \epsilon_0(\theta)$ and form the function $\bar{\psi}[\theta(\varphi_0)]$. The conjugate function of $\bar{\psi}[\theta(\varphi_0)]$ is $\epsilon_0^*(\varphi_0)$, which expressed as a function of θ is $\bar{\epsilon}_1(\theta)$, etc.

We are, however, in a position to introduce a convenient transformation, namely, to translate the circle C into a most favorable position with respect to the curve B (or vice versa). These qualitative remarks admit of a mathematical formulation. It is clear that, if the curve B itself happens to be a circle,[13] the vector by which the circle C should be translated is exactly the distance between the centers. It is readily shown that then Eq. (10) should contain no constant term. We have—

$$z' = ze^{\sum_1^\infty \frac{c_n}{z^n}} \tag{10}$$

$$= e\left(1 + \frac{z_1}{z} + \frac{1}{2!}\left(\frac{c_1}{z}\right)^2 + \cdots\right)$$

$$\times\left(1 + \frac{c_2}{z^2} + \cdots\right)\left(1 + \frac{c_3}{z^3} + \cdots\right), \text{ etc.}$$

$$= z\left(1 + \frac{k_1}{z} + \frac{k_2}{z^2} + \cdots\right) \tag{10a}$$

where[14]

$$k_1 = c_1$$

$$k_2 = c_2 + \frac{c_1^2}{2}$$

$$k_3 = c_3 + c_2 c_1 + \frac{c_1^3}{6}$$

$$\cdots\cdots\cdots\cdots$$

It is thus apparent that if Eq. (10) contains no first-harmonic term, i.e., if—

$$c_1 = A_1 + iB1 = \frac{R}{\pi}\int_0^{2\pi} \psi e^{i\varphi}\, d\varphi = 0$$

the transformation is obtained in the so-called normal form

$$z' = z_1 + \frac{d_1}{z_1} + \frac{d_2}{z_1^2} + \cdots \tag{23}$$

This translation can be effected either by substituting a new variable $z_1 = z + c_1$ or a new variable $z_1' = z' - c_1$. This latter substitution will be more convenient at this time. Writing

$$z_1' = ae^{\psi_1 + i\theta_1}, \quad c_1 = ae^{\gamma + i\delta}, \quad \text{and} \quad z' = ae^{\psi + i\theta}$$

we have

$$ae^{\psi_1 + i\theta_1} = ae^{\psi + i\theta} - ae^{\gamma + i\delta}$$

The variables ψ_1 and θ_1 can be expressed in terms of ψ, θ, γ, and δ. In Fig. 9(b), P is a point on the B curve, i.e., $OP = ae^{\psi}$, PQ represents the translation vector $c_1 = ae^{\gamma + i\delta}$, OQ is $ae^{\psi_1 + i\theta_1}$, and angle POQ is denoted by μ. Then by the law of cosines

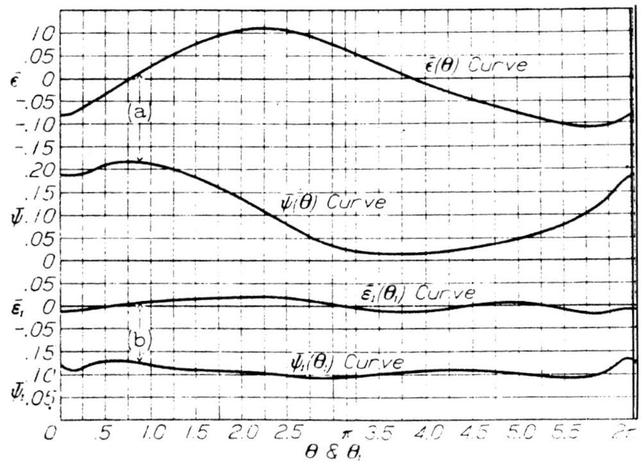

Fig. 10 The $\bar{\psi}(\theta)$ and $\bar{\psi}_1(\theta_1)$ curves (for Clark Y airfoil).

$$e^{2\psi_1} = e^{2\psi} + e^{2\gamma} - 2e^{\psi}e^{\gamma}\cos(\theta - \delta) \tag{a}$$

and by the law of sines

$$\sin\mu = \frac{e^{\gamma}\sin(\theta - \delta)}{e^{\psi_1}}$$

or

$$\theta_1 = \theta + \mu = \theta + \tan^{-1}\frac{e^{\gamma - \psi}\sin(\theta - \delta)}{1 - e^{\gamma - \psi}\cos(\theta - \delta)} \tag{b}$$

In Fig. 10 are shown the $\bar{\psi}(\theta)$ and $\bar{\epsilon}(\theta)$ curves for the Clark Y airfoil (shown in Fig. 4) and $\bar{\psi}_1(\theta_1)$ and $\epsilon_1(\theta_1)$ curves which result when the origin is moved from 0 to M. It may be noted that $\epsilon_1(\theta_1)$ is indeed considerably small than $\bar{\epsilon}(\theta)$. It is obtained from

$$(\varphi - \theta_1)' = -\frac{1}{2\pi}\int_0^{2\pi} \psi_1(\varphi)\cot\frac{(\varphi - \varphi')}{2}\, d\varphi$$

and the constant ψ_0 is given[15] by

$$\psi_0 = \frac{1}{2\pi}\int_0^{2\pi} \psi_1(\varphi)\, d\varphi$$

The combined transformations

It will be useful to combine the various transformations into one. We obtain from Eq. (5) and (10) an expression as follows:

$$\zeta = 2a\cosh\left(\log z + \sum_1^\infty \frac{c_n}{z^n}\right) \tag{24}$$

[13]See p. 26.

[14]These constants can be obtained in a recursion form. See footnote 16.

[15]The constant ψ_0 is invariant to change of origin (see p. 26). It should be remarked that the translation by the vector c_1 is only a matter of convenience and is especially useful for very irregular shapes. For a study of the properties of airfoil shapes we shall use only the original $\epsilon(\varphi)$ curve [Fig. 10(a)].

or we can also obtain a power-series development in z:

$$\zeta = c_1 + z + \frac{a_1}{z} + \frac{a_2}{z^2} + \frac{a_3}{z^3} + \cdots \tag{25}$$

where[16]

$$a^n = k_{n+1} + a^2 b_{n-1}$$

The constants k_n may be obtained in a convenient recursion form as

$$\begin{aligned} k_1 &= c_1 \\ 2k_2 &= k_1 c_1 + 2c_2 \\ 3k_3 &= k_2 c_1 + 2k_1 c_2 + 3c_3 \\ 4k_4 &= k_3 c_1 + 2k_2 c_2 + 3k_1 c_3 + 4c_4 \\ &\cdots\cdots\cdots\cdots \end{aligned}$$

The constants b_n have the same form as k_n but with *each* c_1 replaced by $-c_1$ (and $b_0 = 1$). It will be recalled that the values of c_n are given by the coefficients of the Fourier expansion of $\psi(\varphi)$ as

$$\frac{c_n}{R^n} = \frac{1}{\pi}\int_0^{2\pi} \psi(\varphi) e^{in\varphi}\, d\varphi$$

where $R = ae^{\psi_0}$ and

$$\psi_0 = \frac{1}{2\pi}\int_0^{2\pi} \psi(\varphi)\, d\varphi$$

The first few terms of Eq. (25) are then as follows:

$$\zeta = z + c_1 + \frac{c_2 + \dfrac{c_1^2}{2} + a^2}{z} + \frac{c_3 + c_2 c_1 + \dfrac{c_1^3}{6} - c_1 a^2}{z^2} + \cdots \tag{25'}$$

By writing $z_1 = z + c_1$, Eq. (25) is cast into the normal form:

$$\zeta - z_1 + \frac{b_1}{z_1} + \frac{b_2}{z_2} + \cdots \tag{26}$$

The constants b_n may be evaluated directly in terms of a_n or may be obtained merely by replacing $\psi(\varphi)$ by $\psi_1(\varphi)$ in the foregoing values for a_n.

The series given by Eq. (25) and (26) may be inverted and z or z_1 developed as a power series in ζ. Then—

$$z(\zeta) = \zeta - c_1 \frac{a_1}{\zeta} - \frac{a_2 + a_1 c_1}{\zeta^2} - \frac{a_1 c_1^2 + 2a_2 c_1 + a_3 + a_1^2}{\zeta^3} \cdots \tag{27}$$

and

$$z_1(\zeta) = \zeta - \frac{b_1}{\zeta} - \frac{b_2}{\zeta^2} - \frac{b_3 + b_1^2}{\zeta^3} \cdots \tag{28}$$

The various transformations have been performed for the purpose of transforming the flow pattern of a circle into the flow pattern of an airfoil. We are thus led immediately to the well-known problem of determining the most general type of irrotational flow around a circle satisfying certain specified boundary conditions.

The flow about a circle

The boundary conditions to be satisfied consist of the following: The circle must be a streamline of flow and, at infinity, the velocity must have a given magnitude and direction. Let us choose the ξ axis as corresponding to the direction of the velocity at infinity. Then the problem stated is equivalent to that of an infinite circular cylinder moving parallel to the ξ axis with velocity V in a fluid at rest at infinity.

The general complex flow potential[17] for a circle of radius R and velocity at infinity V parallel to the x axis will be—

$$w(z) = -V\left(z + \frac{R^2}{z}\right) - \frac{i\Gamma}{2\pi}\log\frac{z}{R} \tag{29}$$

where Γ is a real constant parameter, known as the circulation. It is defined as $\oint v_z ds$ along any closed curve enclosing the cylinder, v_s being the velocity along the tangent at each point.

Writing $z = Re^{\mu + i\varphi}$ and $w = P + iQ$, Eq. (29) becomes

$$w = -V\cosh(\mu + i\varphi) - \frac{i\Gamma}{2\pi}(\mu + i\varphi) \tag{29'}$$

or

$$\left.\begin{aligned} P &= -V\cosh\mu\,\cos\varphi + \frac{\Gamma}{2\pi}\varphi \\ Q &= -V\sinh\mu\,\sin\varphi + \frac{\Gamma}{2\pi}\mu \end{aligned}\right\}$$

For the velocity components, we have

$$\frac{dw}{dz} = u - iv = -V\left(1 - \frac{R^2}{z^2}\right) - \frac{i\Gamma}{2\pi z} \tag{30}$$

---

[16]By Eq. (5) and (10) we have

$$\zeta = ze^{\sum_1^\infty \frac{c_n}{z^n}} + \frac{a^2}{z} e^{-\sum_1^\infty \frac{c_n}{z^n}}$$

The constant k_n is thus the coefficient of $1/z^n$ in the expansion of

$$e^{\sum_1^\infty \frac{c_n}{z^n}}$$

and the constant b_n the coefficient of z^n in the expansion of

$$e^{-\sum_1^\infty \frac{c_n}{z^n}}$$

For the recursion form for k_n see *Smithsonian Mathematical Formulae and Tables of Elliptic Functions,* p. 120.

[17]Reference 4, p. 56, or Ref. 5, p. 118. The log term must be added because the region outside the infinite cylinder (the point at infinity excluded) is doubly connected and therefore we must include the possibility of cyclic motion.

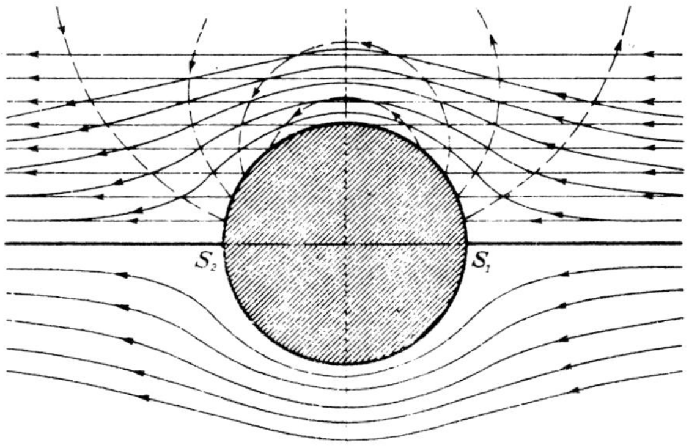

Fig. 11 **Streamlines about circle with zero circulation (shown by the full lines) $Q = -V \sinh \mu \sin \varphi =$ constant.**

In Fig. 11 and 12 are shown the streamlines for the cases $\Gamma = 0$ and $V = 0$, respectively. The cylinder experiences no resultant force in these cases since all streamlines are symmetrical with respect to it.

The stagnation points, that is, points for which u and r are both zero, are obtained as the roots of $dw/dz = 0$. This equation has two roots:

$$z_0 = \frac{i\Gamma \pm \sqrt{16\pi^2R^2V^2 - \Gamma^2}}{4\pi V}$$

and we may distinguish different types of flow according to the discriminant $16\pi^2R^2V^2 - \Gamma^2$ is positive, zero, or negative. We recall here that a conformal transformation $w = f(z)$ ceases to be conformal at points where dw/dx vanishes, and at a stagnation point the flow divides and the streamline possesses a singularity.

The different types of flow that result according to the parameter

$$\Gamma^2 \begin{smallmatrix}>\\=\\<\end{smallmatrix} 6\pi^2R^2V^2$$

are represented in Fig. 13. In the first case [Fig. 13(a)], which will not interest us later, the stagnation point occurs as a double point in the fluid on the η axis, and all fluid within this streamline circulates in closed orbits around the circle, while the rest of the fluid passes downstream. In the second case [Fig. (13b)],

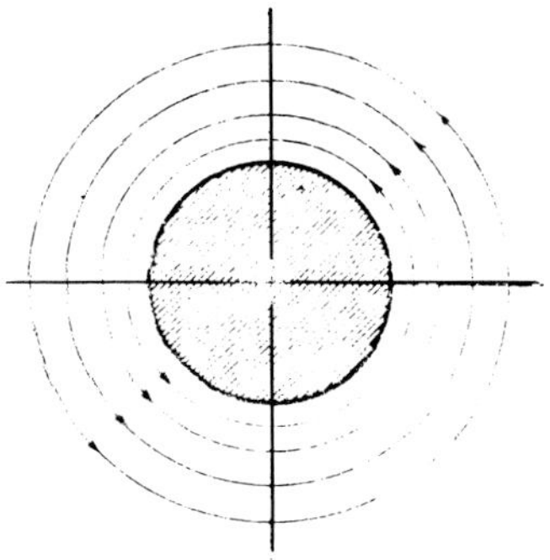

Fig. 12 **Streamlines about circle for $V = 0$ $Q = -\frac{V}{2\pi}\mu =$ constant.**

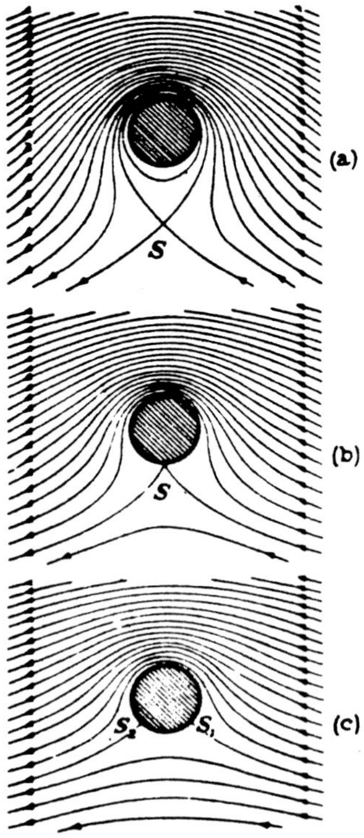

Fig. 13 **Streamlines about circle [from Lagally-Handbuch der Physik Bd. VII] $Q = V \sinh \mu \sin \varphi - \frac{\Gamma}{2\pi}\mu =$ constant (a) $\Gamma^2 > 16\pi^2R^2V^2$(b) $\Gamma^2 = 16\pi^2R^2V^2$ (c) $\Gamma^2 < 16\pi^2R^2V^2$.**

the stagnation points are together at S on the circle $Re^{i\varphi}$, and in the third case [Fig. (13c)] they are symmetrically located on the circle. We have noted then that as Γ increases from 0 to $4\pi RV$ the stagnation points move downward on the circle $Re^{i\varphi}$ from the ξ axis toward the η axis. Upon further increase in Γ they leave the circle and are located on the η axis in the fluid.

Conversely, it is clear that the position of the stagnation points can determine the circulation Γ. This fact will be shown to be significant for wing-section theory. At present, we note that when both Γ and $V \neq 0$ a marked dissymmetry exists in the streamlines with respect to the circle. They are symmetrical about the η axis but are not symmetrical about the ξ axis. Since they are closer together on the upper side of the circle than on the lower side, a resultant force exists perpendicular to the motion.

We shall now combine the transformation (27) and the flow formula for the circle of Eq. (29) and obtain the general complex flow giving the 2-dimensional irrotational flow about an airfoil shape, and indeed, about any closed curve for which the Riemann theorem applies.

The flow around the airfoil

In Fig. 14 are given, in a convenient way, the different complex planes and transformations used thus far.

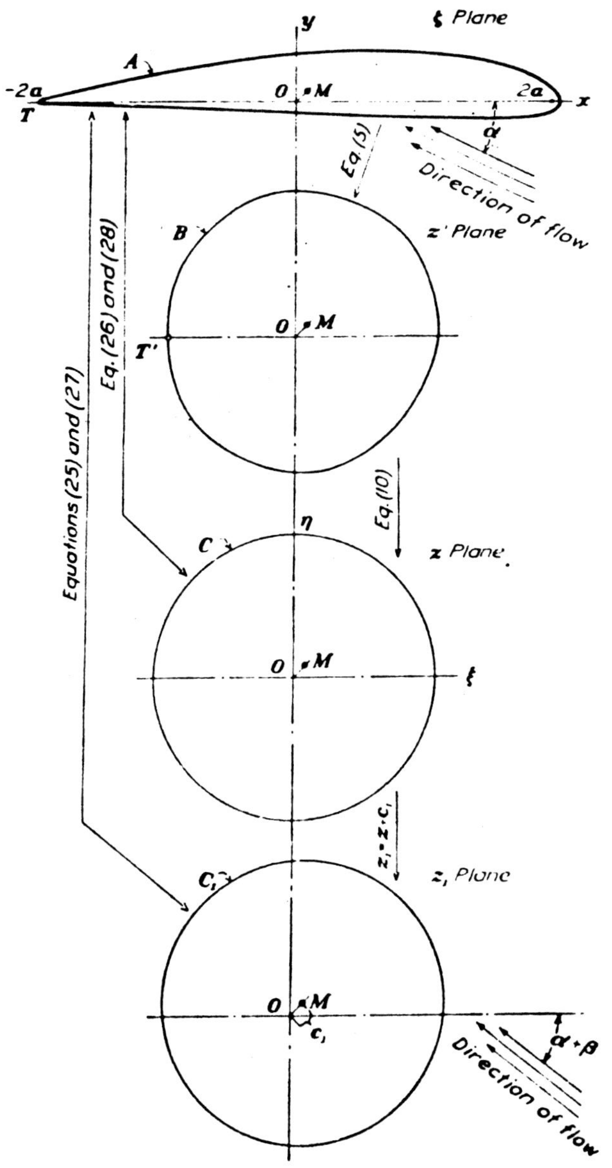

Fig. 14 The collected transformations.

The complex flow potential in the z plane for a circle of radius R origin at the center has been given as

$$w(z) = -V\left(z + \frac{R^2}{z}\right) - \frac{i\Gamma}{2\pi}\log z \qquad (29)$$

where V, the velocity at infinity, is in the direction of the negative ξ axis. Let us introduce a parameter to permit a change in the direction of flow at infinity by the angle α which will be designated *angle of attack* and defined by the direction of flow at infinity with respect to a fixed axis on the body, in this case the axis $\varphi = 0$. This flow is obtained simply by writing $ze^{i\alpha}$ *for* z in Eq. (29) and represents a rotation of the entire flowfield about the circle by angle α. We have

$$w(z) = -V\left(ze^{i\alpha} + \frac{R_2}{z}e^{-i\alpha}\right) - \frac{i\Gamma}{2\pi}\log z \qquad (31)$$

$$\frac{dw}{dz} = u - iv$$

$$= -Ve^{i\alpha}\left(1 - \frac{R^2}{z^2}e^{-2i\alpha}\right) - \frac{i\Gamma}{2\pi z} \qquad (32)$$

Since a conformal transformation maps streamlines and potential lines into streamlines and potential lines, we may obtain the complex flow potential in the various planes by substitutions. For the flow about the circle in the z_1 plane, z is replaced by $z_1 - c_1$:

$$w(z_1) = -V\left[(z_1 - c_1)e^{i\alpha} + \frac{R^2e^{-i\alpha}}{(z_1 - c_1)}\right]\frac{i\Gamma}{2\pi}\log(z_1 - c_1) \qquad (31')$$

$$\frac{dw}{dz_1} = -Ve^{i\alpha}\left[1 - \frac{R^2e^{-i\alpha}}{(z_1 - c_1)^2}\right]\frac{i\Gamma}{2\pi(z_1 - c_1)} \qquad (32')$$

For the flow about the B curve in the z' plane, z is replaced by $z(z')$ [the inverse of Eq. (10a)] and for the flow about the airfoil in the ζ plane z is replaced by $z(\zeta)$ from Eq. (27):

$$W(\zeta) = -V\left[z(\zeta)e^{i\alpha} + \frac{R^2}{z(\zeta)}e^{-i\alpha}\right]\frac{i\Gamma}{2\pi}\log z(\zeta) \qquad (33)$$

$$\frac{dW}{d\zeta} = \left[-Ve^{i\alpha}\left(1 + \frac{R^2e^{-2i\alpha}}{[z(\zeta)]^2}\right)\frac{i\Gamma}{2\pi[z(\zeta)]}\right]\frac{dz(\zeta)}{d\zeta} \qquad (34)$$

The flowfields at infinity for all these transformations have been made to coincide in magnitude and direction.

At this point attention is directed to two important facts. First, in the previous analysis the original closed curve may differ from an airfoil shape. The formulas, when convergent, are applicable to any closed curve satisfying the general requirements of the Riemann theorem. However, the peculiar case of numerical evaluations for streamline shapes is noteworthy and significant. The second important fact is that the parameter Γ which as yet is completely undetermined is readily determined for airfoils, and the next section is devoted to a discussion of this statement. It will be seen that airfoils may be regarded as fixing their own circulation.

Kutta-Joukowsky method for fixing the circulation

All contours used in practice as airfoil profiles possess the common property of terminating in either a cusp or sharp corner at the trailing edge (a point of two tangents). Upon transforming the circle into an airfoil by $\zeta f(z)$, we shall find that $dz/d\zeta$ is infinite at the trailing edge if the tail is perfectly sharp (or very large if the tail is almost sharp). This implies that the numerical value of the velocity $|dw/dz|\,|dz/d\zeta| = r$ is infinite (or extremely large) provided the factor $|dw/dz|$ is not zero at the tail. There is but one value of the circulation that avoids infinite velocities or gradients of pressure at the tail and this fact gives a practical basis for fixing the circulation.

The concept of the ideal fluid in irrotational potential flow implies no dissipation of energy, however large the velocity at any point. The circulation being a measure of the energy in a fluid is unaltered and independent of time. In particular, if the circulation is zero to begin with, it can never be different from zero.

However, since all real fluids have viscosity, a better physical concept of the ideal fluid is to endow the fluid with infinitesimal viscosity so that there is then no dissipation of energy for finite velocities and pressure gradients, but for infinite velocities, energy losses would result. Moreover, by Bernoulli's principle the pressure would become infinitely negative, whereas a real fluid cannot sustain absolute negative pressures and the assumption of incompressibility becomes invalid long before this condition is reached. It should then be postulated that nowhere in the ideal fluid from the physical concept should the velocity become infinite. It is clear that the factor dw/dz must then be zero at the trailing edge in order to avoid infinite velocities. It is then precisely the sharpness of the trailing edge which furnishes us with the following basis for fixing the circulation.

It will be recalled that the equation $dw/dz = 0$ determines two stagnation points symmetrically located on the circle, the position of which varies with the value of the circulation and conversely the position of a stagnation point determines the circulation. In this paper the x axis of the airfoil has been chosen so that the negative end $(\theta = \pi)$ passes through the trailing edge. From the calculation of $\epsilon = \varphi - \theta$ [by Eq. (13)] the value of φ corresponding to any value of θ is determined as $\varphi = \theta + \epsilon$, in particular at $\theta = \pi$, $\varphi + \beta$, where β is the value of ϵ at the tail and for a given airfoil is a geometric constant (although numerically it varies with the choice of axes). This angle β is of considerable significance and for good reasons is called the angle of zero lift. The substance of the foregoing discussion indicates that the point $z = Re^{i(\pi+\beta)} = -Re^{i\beta}$ is a stagnation point on the circle. Then for this value of z, by Eq. (32) we have

$$\frac{dw}{dz} = -Ve^{i\alpha}\left(\frac{1 - R^2e^{-2i\alpha}}{z^2}\right) - \frac{i\Gamma}{2\pi z} = 0$$

or

$$\Gamma = 2\pi RVie^{\alpha+\beta}(1 - e^{-2i(\alpha+\beta)})$$

$$= 4\pi RV\left(\frac{e^{i(\alpha+\beta)} - e^{-i(\alpha+\beta)}}{2i}\right)$$

$$= 4\pi RV\sin(\alpha+\beta) \qquad (35)$$

This value of the circulation is then sufficient to make the trailing edge a stagnation point for any value of α. The airfoil may be considered to equip itself with that amount of circulation which enables the fluid to flow past the airfoil with a minimum energy loss, just as electricity flowing in a flat plate will distribute itself so that the heat loss is a minimum. The final justification for the Kutta assumption is not only its plausibility, but also the comparatively good agreement with experimental results. Figure 15(b) shows the streamlines around an airfoil for a flow satisfying the Kutta condition, and Fig. 15(a) and 15(c) illustrate cases for which the circulation is, respectively, too small and

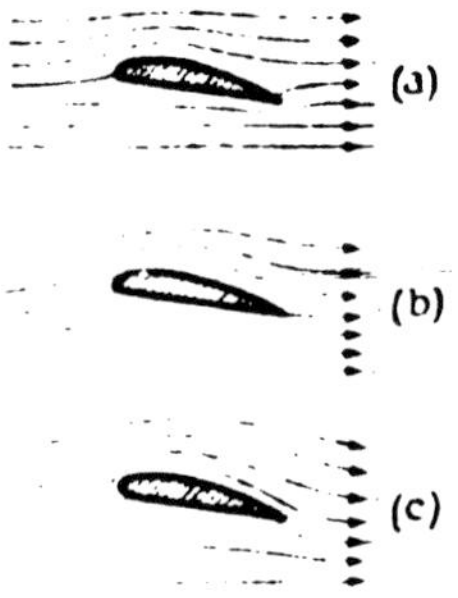

Fig. 15 (a) Flow with circulation smaller than for Kutta condition; (b) flow satisfying Kutta condition; (c) flow with circulation greater than for Kutta condition.

too large, the stagnation point being then on the upper and lower surfaces, respectively. For these latter cases, the complete flow is determinable only if, together with the angle of attack, the circulation or a stagnation point is specified.

Velocity at the surface

The flow formulas for the entire field are now uniquely determined by substituting the value of Γ in Eq. (33) and (34). We are, however, in a position to obtain much simpler and more convenient relations for the boundary curves themselves. Indeed, we are chiefly interested in the velocity at the surface of the airfoil, which velocity is tangential to the surface, since the airfoil contour is a streamline of flow. The numerical value of the velocity at the surface of the airfoil is

$$v = \sqrt{v_x^2 + v_y^2} = |v_x - iv_y| = \left|\frac{dw}{d\zeta}\right|$$

$$= \left|\frac{dw}{dz}\right| \cdot \left|\frac{dz}{dz'}\right| \cdot \left|\frac{dz'}{d\zeta}\right|$$

We shall evaluate each of these factors in turn. From Eq. (32) and (35)—

$$\frac{dw}{dz} = -Ve^{i\alpha}\left(1 - \frac{R^2}{z_2}e^{-2i\alpha}\right) - \frac{i4\pi RV\sin(\alpha+\beta)}{2\pi z}$$

At the boundary surface $z = Re^{i\varphi}$, and

$$\frac{dw}{dz} = -Ve^{i\alpha}(1 + e^{-2i(\alpha+\varphi)}) - 2iVe^{-i\varphi}\sin(\alpha+\beta)$$

or

$$\frac{dw}{dz} = -Ve^{i\varphi}[(e^{i(\alpha+\varphi)} - e^{i(\alpha+\varphi)}) + 2i\sin(\alpha+\beta)]$$

$$= -2iVe^{i\varphi}[\sin(\alpha+\varphi) + \sin(\alpha+\beta)]$$

and

$$\left|\frac{dw}{dz}\right| = 2V[\sin(\alpha+\varphi) + \sin(\alpha+\beta)] \qquad (36)$$

In general, for arbitrary Γ we find that

$$\left|\frac{dw}{dz}\right| = 2V\sin(\alpha+\varphi) + \frac{\Gamma}{2\pi R} \qquad (36')$$

To evaluate $|dw/dz'|$ we start with relation (10):

$$z' = ze^{\sum_1^\infty \frac{c_n}{z^n}}$$

At the boundary surface

$z' = ze^{\psi-\psi_0-i\epsilon}$ where $\epsilon = \varphi - \theta$ and $z = ae^{\psi_0+i\varphi}$

$$\frac{dz'}{dz} = \frac{z'}{z}\left(1 + z\frac{d(\varphi - i\epsilon)}{dz}\right)$$

$$= \frac{z'}{z}\left(1 + \frac{d(\psi - i\epsilon)}{i\,d\varphi}\right) \qquad (37')$$

$$= \frac{z'}{z}\left(1 - \frac{\frac{d\varphi}{d\theta} - \frac{d\epsilon}{d\theta} - i\frac{d\bar{\psi}}{d\theta}}{\frac{d\varphi}{d\theta}}\right) = \frac{z'}{z}\left(\frac{1 - i\frac{d\psi}{d\theta}}{1 - \frac{d\bar{\epsilon}}{d\theta}}\right)$$

Then

$$\left|\frac{dz'}{dz}\right| = e^{\psi-\psi_0}\frac{\sqrt{1 + \left(\frac{d\bar{\psi}}{d\theta}\right)^2}}{1 + \frac{d\epsilon}{d\theta}} \qquad (37)$$

By Eq. (5)—

$$\zeta = z' + \frac{a^2}{z'}$$

and at the boundary $z' = ae^{\psi+i\theta}$, or

$$\zeta = 2a\cosh(\psi + i\theta)$$

$$\frac{d\zeta}{dz'} = 2a\sinh(\psi + i\theta)\frac{d(\psi + i\theta)}{dz'}$$

$$= 2a\sinh(\psi + i\theta)\,e^{-(\psi+i\theta)}$$

Then

$$\left|\frac{d\zeta}{dz'}\right|^2 = 4e^{-2\psi}(\sinh^2\psi\cos^2\theta + \cosh^2\psi\sin^2\theta)$$

$$= 4e^{-2\psi}(\sinh^2\psi + \sin^2\theta)$$

and

$$\left|\frac{d\zeta}{dz'}\right| = 2e^{-\psi}\sqrt{\sinh^2\psi + \sin^2\theta)} \qquad (38)$$

Then finally:

$$v = \left|\frac{dw}{d\zeta}\right| = \left|\frac{dw}{dz}\right| \cdot \left|\frac{dz}{dz'}\right| \cdot \left|\frac{dz'}{d\zeta}\right|$$

$$= \frac{V[\sin(\alpha+\varphi) + \sin(\alpha+\beta)]\left(1 + \frac{d\bar{\epsilon}}{d\theta}\right)e^{\psi_0}}{\sqrt{(\sinh^2\psi + \sin^2\theta)\left[1 + \left(\frac{d\bar{\psi}}{d\theta}\right)^2\right]}} \qquad (39)$$

In this formula the circulation is given by Eq. (35). In general, for an arbitrary value of Γ [see Eq. (36′)], the equation retains its form and is given by

$$v = \frac{V\left[\sin(\alpha+\varphi) + \frac{\Gamma}{4\pi RV}\right]\left(1 + \frac{d\bar{\epsilon}}{d\theta}\right)e^{\psi_0}}{\sqrt{(\sinh^2\psi + \sin^2\theta)\left[1 + \left(\frac{d\bar{\psi}}{d\theta}\right)^2\right]}} \qquad (40)$$

For the special case $\Gamma = 0$, we get

$$v = \frac{V\sin(\alpha+\varphi)\left(1 + \frac{d\bar{\epsilon}}{d\theta}\right)e^{\psi_0}}{\sqrt{(\sinh^2\psi + \sin^2\theta)\left[1 + \left(\frac{d\bar{\psi}}{d\theta}\right)^2\right]}} \qquad (41)$$

Equation (40) is a general result giving the velocity at any point of the surface of an arbitrary airfoil section, with *arbitrary* circulation for any angle of attack α. Equation (39) represents the important special case in which the circulation is specified by the Kutta condition. The various symbols are functions only of the coordinates (r,y) of the airfoil boundary and expressions for them have already been given. In Tables I and II numerical results for different airfoils are given, and explanations are made of the methods of calculation and use of the formulas is developed.

We have immediately by Eq. (3) the value of the pressure p at any point of the surface in terms of the pressure at infinity as

$$\frac{p}{q} = 1 - \left(\frac{v}{V}\right)^2$$

Some theoretical pressure distribution curves are given at the end of this report and comparison is made with experimental results. These comparisons, it will be seen, within a large range of angles of attack, are strikingly good.[15]

TABLE I
N.A.C.A.—M6
UPPER SURFACE

Per cent c	y in per cent c	x	y	sin θ	sinh ψ	θ radians	ψ	ϵ	$\frac{d\psi}{d\theta}$	$\frac{d\epsilon}{d\theta}$	k	$\varphi=\theta+\epsilon$ (° ′)
0	0	2.037	0.000	0.000	0.0373	0.000	0.192	−0.0457	0.000	0.085	6.280	−2 37
1.25	1.97	1.986	.0796	.0465	.0341	.217	.184	−.0276	−.010	.080	4.249	10 52
2.50	2.81	1.936	.1135	.0941	.0342	.312	.184	−.0205	.009	.080	3.368	16 41
5.0	4.03	1.835	.163	.187	.0354	.447	.187	−.0098	.022	.080	2.557	25 4
7.5	4.94	1.734	.200	.275	.0363	.551	.189	−.0015	.022	.080	2.163	31 31
10	5.71	1.633	.231	.357	.0373	.640	.192	.0063	.020	.085	1.929	37 3
15	6.82	1.431	.276	.507	.0375	.792	.193	.0188	−.009	.095	1.660	46 27
20	7.55	1.229	.305	.636	.0366	.923	.190	.0310	−.031	.100	1.498	54 38
30	8.22	.825	332	.835	.0330	1.153	.181	.0549	−.066	.107	1.324	69 11
40	8.05	.421	.325	.957	.0276	1.361	.165	.0717	−.085	.088	1.220	82 7
50	7.26	.017	.293	1.000	.0215	1.571	.146	.0856	−.100	.060	1.166	94 55
60	6.03	−.387	.244	.963	.0154	1.764	.124	.0932	−.100	.025	1.152	106 25
70	4.58	−.791	.185	.845	.0101	1.975	.100	.0920	−.100	−.029	1.167	118 28
80	3.06	−1.195	.124	.645	.0059	2.209	.077	.0828	−.088	−.056	1.302	131 19
90	1.55	−1.599	.063	.363	.0027	2.495	.052	.0617	−.067	−.085	1.687	146 30
95	.88	−1.801	.036	.191	.0016	2.690	.040	.0419	−.035	−.080	2.340	156 28
100	.26	−2.003	.000	.000	.0030	3.142	.055	.0105	.000	−.027	19.83	180 36

LOWER SURFACE

Per cent c	y in per cent c	x	y	sin θ	sinh ψ	θ radians	ψ	ϵ	$\frac{d\psi}{d\theta}$	$\frac{d\epsilon}{d\theta}$	k	$\varphi=\theta+\epsilon$ (° ′)
0	0	2.037	0.000	0.000	0.0373	6.283	0.192	−0.0457	0.000	0.085	6.280	−2 37
1.25	1.76	1.986	−.071	.0425	.0297	6.075	.172	−.0781	.133	.120	4.615	−16 21
2.50	2.20	1.936	−.089	.0844	.0234	5.989	.152	−.0850	.160	.050	3.525	−21 43
5.0	2.73	1.835	−.110	.173	.0176	5.855	.132	−.0882	.133	−.010	2.510	−29 35
7.5	3.03	1.734	−.122	.259	.0144	5.749	.120	−.0850	.109	−.035	2.025	−35 28
10	3.24	1.633	−.131	.342	.0125	5.659	.112	−.0811	.080	−.057	1.764	−40 24
15	3.47	1.431	−.140	.494	.0099	5.505	.099	−.0723	.069	−.067	1.466	−48 44
20	3.62	1.229	−.146	.626	.0085	5.371	.092	−.0637	.057	−.067	1.307	−55 54
30	3.79	.825	−.153	.831	.0070	5.136	.084	−.0516	.025	−.052	1.156	−68 39
40	3.90	.421	−.158	.956	.0065	4.924	.081	−.0421	.008	−.036	1.098	−80 17
50	3.94	.017	−.159	1.000	.0063	4.712	.079	−.0350	.000	−.029	1.081	−91 59
60	3.82	−.387	−.154	.963	.0062	4.518	.0785	−.0310	.010	−.013	1.120	−102 53
70	3.48	−.791	−.141	.847	.0058	4.307	.076	−.0300	.019	.000	1.211	−114 55
80	2.83	−1.195	−.114	.645	.0050	4.074	.071	−.0295	.036	−.011	1.370	−128 14
90	1.77	−1.599	−.072	.363	.0035	3.788	.059	−.0235	.044	−.040	1.769	−144 16
95	1.08	−1.801	−.044	.191	.0025	3.594	.050	−.0140	.020	−.067	2.368	−154 50
100	.26	−2.003	.000	.000	.0030	3.142	.055	.0105	.000	−.027	19.83	−179 24

TABLE II

$\epsilon(\varphi) = 0.1 \sin(\varphi - 45^\circ) \quad \psi_0 = 0.10 \quad \beta = \epsilon(\pi) = 0.0657 = 3^\circ 47'$

UPPER SURFACE

φ Degrees	φ Radians	ϵ	θ Radians	θ Degrees (° ′)	ψ	$\frac{d\epsilon}{d\phi}$	$\frac{d\psi}{d\phi}$	cosh ψ	sinh ψ	cos θ	sin θ	$\frac{x}{2}$	$\frac{y}{2}$	k
0	0.0000	−0.0707	0.0707	4 3	0.1707	0.0707	0.0707	1.0146	0.1715	0.9975	0.0706	1.0121	0.0121	6.3941
5	.0873	−.0643	.1516	8 41	.1766	.0766	.0643	1.0156	.1775	.9885	.1510	1.0039	.0268	5.1215
10	.1745	−.0574	.2319	13 17	.1819	.0819	.0574	1.0166	.1826	.9732	.2298	.9895	.0420	4.0960
15	.2618	−.0500	.3118	17 52	.1866	.0866	.0500	1.0175	.1877	.9518	.3068	.9685	.0576	3.3902
20	.3491	−.0423	.3914	22 26	.1906	.0906	.0423	1.0182	.1918	.9243	.3816	.9411	.0732	2.8421
25	.4363	−.0342	.4705	26 57	.1940	.0940	.0342	1.0189	.1952	.8914	.4532	.9082	.0885	2.4704
30	.5236	−.0259	.5495	31 29	.1966	.0966	.0259	1.0194	.1979	.8528	.5223	.8693	.1034	2.1892
35	.6109	−.0174	.6283	36 0	.1985	.0985	.0174	1.0198	.1997	.8090	.5878	.8250	.1174	1.9746
45	.7854	.0000	.7854	45 0	.2000	.1000	.0000	1.0201	.2013	.7071	.7071	.7213	.1423	1.6689
55	.9599	.0174	.9425	54 0	.1985	.0985	−.0174	1.0198	.1998	.5878	.8090	.5994	.1616	1.4709
70	1.2217	.0423	1.1794	67 35	.1906	.0906	−.0423	1.0182	.1918	.3813	.9244	.3882	.1773	1.2859
80	1.3963	.0574	1.3390	76 43	.1819	.0819	−.0574	1.0166	.1826	.2298	.9733	.2336	.1777	1.2133
90	1.5708	.0707	1.5001	85 57	.1707	.0707	−.0707	1.0146	.1715	.0706	.9975	.0716	.1711	1.1717
100	1.7453	.0819	1.6634	95 18	.1574	.0574	−.0819	1.0124	.1581	−.0924	.9957	−.0935	.1574	1.1586
110	1.9199	.0906	1.8293	104 49	.1423	.0423	−.0906	1.0101	.1428	−.2557	.9668	−.2583	.1381	1.1756
125	2.1817	.0985	2.0832	119 22	.1174	.0174	−.0985	1.0069	.1177	−.4904	.8715	−.4938	.1026	1.2727
135	2.3562	.1000	2.2562	129 16	.1000	.0000	−.1000	1.0050	.1002	−.6329	.7742	−.6361	.0776	1.4088
150	2.6180	.0966	2.5214	144 28	.0741	−.0259	−.0966	1.0028	.0742	−.8138	.5812	−.8161	.0431	1.8306
160	2.7925	.0906	2.7019	154 48	.0577	−.0423	−.0906	1.0017	.0577	−.9048	.4258	−.9063	.0246	2.4584
170	2.9671	.0819	2.8852	165 19	.0426	−.0574	−.0819	1.0009	.0426	−.9673	.2538	−.9682	.0108	4.0496
180	3.1416	.0707	3.0709	175 57	.0293	−.0707	−.0707	1.0004	.0293	−.9975	.0706	−.9979	.0021	13.4411

LOWER SURFACE

φ Degrees	φ Radians	ϵ	θ Radians	θ Degrees (° ′)	ψ	$\frac{d\epsilon}{d\phi}$	$\frac{d\psi}{d\phi}$	cosh ψ	sinh ψ	cos θ	sin θ	$\frac{x}{2}$	$\frac{y}{2}$	k
0	0.0000	−0.0707	0.0707	4 3	0.1707	0.0707	.0707	1.0146	0.1715	0.9975	0.0706	1.0121	0.0121	6.3941
−5	−.0873	−.0766	−.0107	−0 37	.1643	.0643	.0766	1.0135	.1650	.9999	−.0108	1.0134	−.0018	7.1236
−10	−.1745	−.0819	−.0925	−5 18	.1574	.0574	.0819	1.0124	.1581	.9957	−.0924	1.0090	−.0146	6.3827
−15	−.2618	−.0866	−.1752	−10 2	.1500	.0500	.0866	1.0113	.1506	.9847	−.1742	.9958	−.0262	5.0338
−20	−.3491	−.0906	−.2585	−14 49	.1423	.0423	.0906	1.0101	.1428	.9668	−.2557	.9766	−.0365	3.9225
−25	−.4363	−.0940	−.3423	−19 37	.1342	.0342	.0940	1.0090	.1346	.9420	−.3357	.9505	−.0452	3.1489
−30	−.5236	−.0966	−.4270	−24 28	.1259	.0259	.0966	1.0079	.1262	.9102	−.4142	.9171	−.0523	2.6077
−35	−.6109	−.0985	−.5124	−29 21	.1174	.0174	.0985	1.0069	.1177	.8716	−.4901	.8776	−.0577	2.2203
−45	−.7854	−.1000	−.6854	−39 16	.1000	.0000	.1000	1.0050	.1002	.7742	−.6329	.7781	−.0634	1.7161
−55	−.9599	−.0985	−.8614	−49 21	.0826	−.0174	.0985	1.0034	.0827	.6514	−.7587	.6536	−.0627	1.4168
−70	−1.2217	−.0906	−1.1311	−64 48	.0577	−.0423	.0906	1.0017	.0577	.4258	−.9048	.4265	−.0522	1.1650
−80	−1.3963	−.0819	−1.3144	−75 19	.0426	−.0574	.0819	1.0009	.0426	.2545	−.9673	.2537	−.0412	1.0763
−90	−1.5708	−.0707	−1.5001	−85 57	.0293	−.0707	.0707	1.0004	.0293	.0706	−.9975	.0706	−.0292	1.0322
−100	−1.7453	−.0574	−1.6879	−96 43	.0181	−.0819	.0574	1.0002	.0181	−.1170	−.9931	−.1170	−.0180	1.0270
−110	−1.9199	−.0423	−1.8776	−107 3	.0094	−.0906	.0423	1.0000	.0094	−.3021	−.9533	−.3021	−.0090	1.0616
−125	−2.1817	−.0174	−2.1643	−124 1	.0015	−.0985	.0174	1.0000	.0015	−.5594	−.8289	−.5594	−.0012	1.2136
−135	−2.3562	.0000	−2.3562	−135 0	.0000	−.1000	.0000	1.0000	.0000	−.7071	−.7071	−.7071	.0000	1.4200
−150	−2.6180	.0259	−2.6439	−151 29	.0034	−.0966	−.0259	1.0000	.0034	−.8787	−.4774	−.8787	−.0016	2.1106
−160	−2.7925	.0423	−2.8348	−162 25	.0094	−.0906	−.0423	1.0000	.0094	−.9533	−.3021	−.9533	−.0028	3.3501
−170	−2.9671	.0574	−3.0245	−173 18	.0181	−.0819	−.0574	1.0002	.0181	−.9932	−.1167	−.9934	−.0021	8.0641
−180	−3.1416	.0707	−3.2123	−184 3	.0293	−.0707	−.0707	1.0004	.0293	−.9975	+.0706	−.9979	+.0021	13.4411

GENERAL WING-SECTION CHARACTERISTICS

The remainder of this report will be devoted to a discussion of the parameters of the airfoil shape affecting aerodynamic properties with a view to determining airfoil shapes satisfying preassigned properties. This discussion wil not only furnish an illuminating sequel to the foregoing analysis leading to a number of new results, but will also unify much of the existing theory of the airfoil. In the next section we shall obtain some expressions for the integrated characteristics of the airfoil. We start with the expressions for total lift and total moment, first developed by Blasius.

Blasius' fomulas

Let C in Fig. 16 represent a closed streamline contour in an irrotational fluid field. Blasius' formulas give expressions for the total force and moment experienced by C in terms of the complex velocity potential. They may be obtained in the following simple way. We have for the total forces in the x and y directions

$$P_z = -\int_C p_x \, ds = -\int_C p \, dy$$

$$P_y = \int_C p_y \, ds = -\int_C p \, dx$$

$$P_z - iP_y = -\int_C p(dy + i \, dx)$$

The pressure at any point is

$$p = p_0 - \tfrac{1}{2}\rho v^2$$

Then

$$P_x - iP_y = \frac{\rho}{2}\int_C v^2 \, (dy + i dx)$$

$$= \frac{i\rho}{2}\int_C \frac{dw}{dz}\overline{\frac{dw}{dz}}\,\overline{dz}$$

where the bar denotes conjugate complex quantities. Since C is a streamline, $v_x \, dy - v_y \, dx = 0$. Adding the quantity

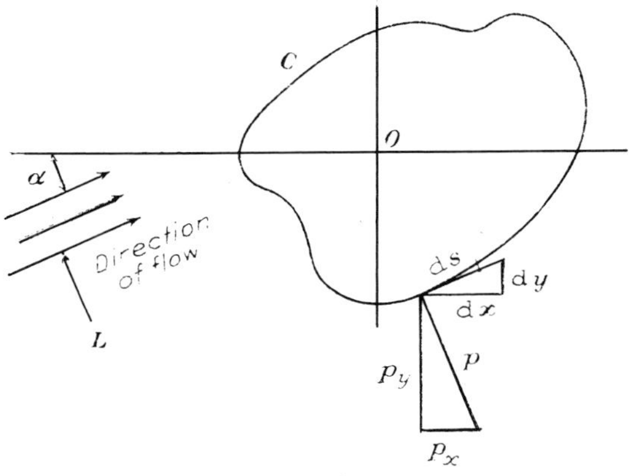

Fig. 16

$$i\rho \int_C (v_y + iv_x)(v_x \, dy - v_y \, dx) = 0$$

to the last equation, we get[19]

$$P_x - iP_y = \frac{i\rho}{2}\int_C (v_x - iv_y)^2(dx + i \, dy)$$

$$= \frac{i\rho}{2}\int_C \left(\frac{dw}{dz}\right)^2 dz \qquad (42)$$

The differential of the moment of the resultant force about the origin is

$$dM_0 = p(x \, dx + y \, dy)$$

$$= R.P. \quad \text{of} \quad p[x \, dx + y \, dy(y \, dx - x \, dy)]$$

$$= R.P. \quad \text{of} \quad pz \, dz$$

where "*R.P.* of" denotes the real part of the complex quantity. We have from the pervious results

$$d(P_x - iP_y) = ip \, \overline{dz} = \frac{i\rho}{2}\left(\frac{dw}{dz}\right)^2 dz$$

Then

$$dM_0 = -R.P. \quad \text{of} \quad \frac{i\rho}{2}\left(\frac{dw}{dz}\right)^2 z \, dz$$

and

$$M_0 = -R.P. \quad \text{of} \quad \frac{\rho}{2}\int_C \left(\frac{dw}{dz}\right)^2 z \, dz \qquad (43)$$

Let us now for completeness apply these formulas to the airfoil A in the ζ plane (Fig. 14) to derive the Kutta-Joukowsky classical formula for the lift force. By Eq. (32) we have

$$\frac{dw}{dz} = -Ve^{i\alpha} - \frac{i\Gamma}{2\pi z} + \frac{R^2 Ve^{-i\alpha}}{z^2}$$

and by Eq. (25)

$$\frac{d\zeta}{dz} = 1 - \frac{a_1}{z^2} - \frac{a_2}{z^3} - \cdots$$

[18]A paper devoted to more extensive applications to present-day airfoils is in progress.

[19]Cf. Blasius, H., *Zs. f. Math. u. Phys.*, Bd. 58 S. 93 and Bd. 59 S. 43, 1910. Similarly,

$$P_z + iP_y = -\frac{i\rho}{2}\int_C \left(\frac{dw}{d\theta}\right)^2 dz$$

a less convenient relation to use than Eq. (42).

Note that when the region about C is regular the value of the integral of Eq. (42) remains unchanged by integrating about any other curve enclosing C.

Then

$$\frac{\mathrm{d}w}{\mathrm{d}\zeta} = \mathrm{d}w\,\mathrm{d}z \cdot \frac{\mathrm{d}z}{\mathrm{d}\zeta}$$

$$= -Ve^{i\alpha} - \frac{i\Gamma}{2\pi}\frac{1}{z} + (R^2Ve^{-i\alpha} - a_1Ve^{i\alpha})\frac{1}{z^2} + \cdots$$

and

$$\left(\frac{\mathrm{d}w}{\mathrm{d}\zeta}\right) = A_0 + \frac{A_1}{z} + \frac{A_2}{z^2} + \cdots$$

where

$$A_0 = V^2e^{2i\alpha}$$

$$A_1 = iVe^{i\alpha}\frac{\Gamma}{\pi}$$

$$A_2 = -2\mathrm{R}^2V^2 + 2a_1V^2e^{2i\alpha} - \frac{\Gamma^2}{4\pi^2}$$

Then

$$P_x - iP_y = \frac{i\rho}{2}\int_A \left(\frac{\mathrm{d}w}{\mathrm{d}\zeta}\right)^2 \mathrm{d}\zeta$$

$$= \frac{i\rho}{2}\int_C \left(\frac{\mathrm{d}w}{\mathrm{d}\zeta}\right)^2 \frac{\mathrm{d}\zeta}{\mathrm{d}z}\,\mathrm{d}\zeta$$

$$= \frac{i\rho}{2}(2\pi i A_1)$$

$$= -ie^{i\alpha}\rho V\Gamma$$

Therefore

$$\left.\begin{aligned} P_x &= \rho V\Gamma \sin\alpha \\ P_y &= \rho V\Gamma \cos\alpha \end{aligned}\right\} \qquad (6)$$

and are the components of a force $\rho V\Gamma$ which is perpendicular to the direction of the stream at infinity. Thus the resultant lift force experienced by the airfoil is

$$L = \rho V\Gamma \qquad (44)$$

and writing for the circulation Γ the value given by Eq. (35)

$$L = 4\pi R\rho V^2 \sin(\alpha + \beta) \qquad (45)$$

The moment of the resultant lift force about the origin $\zeta = 0$ is obtained as

$$M_0 = R.P. \text{ of } -\frac{\rho}{2}\int_A \left(\frac{\mathrm{d}w}{\mathrm{d}z}\right)^2 \zeta\,\mathrm{d}\zeta$$

$$= R.P. \text{ of } -\frac{\rho}{2}\int_C \left(\frac{\mathrm{d}w}{\mathrm{d}\zeta}\right)^2 \zeta\,\frac{\mathrm{d}\zeta}{\mathrm{d}z}\,\mathrm{d}\zeta$$

$$= R.P. \text{ of } -\frac{\rho}{2}\int_C \left(A_0 + \frac{A_1}{z} + \frac{A_2}{z^2} + \cdots\right)$$

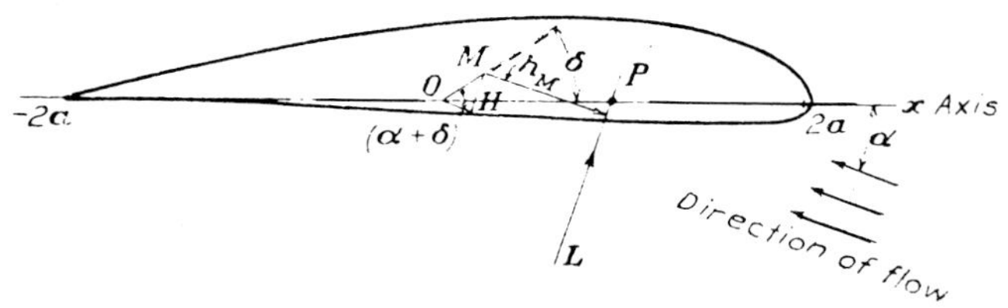

Fig. 17 Moment arm from *M* onto the lift vector.

$$\times\left(c_1 + z + \frac{a_1}{z} + \frac{a_2}{z^2} + \cdots\right)\left(1 - \frac{a_1}{z^1} + \cdots\right)\mathrm{d}z$$

$$= R.P. \text{ of } -\frac{\rho}{2}2\pi i \quad (\text{coefficient of } z^{-1})$$

$$= R.P. \text{ of } -\frac{\rho}{2}2\pi i\,(A_2 + A_1c_1)$$

or M_0 is the imaginary part of $\rho(A_2 + A_1c_1)$. After putting[20] $c_1 = me^{i\delta}$ and $a_1 = b^2e^{2i\gamma}$ we get

$$M_0 = 2\pi\rho V_2b_2 \sin2(\alpha + \gamma) + \rho V\Gamma\, m \cos(\alpha + \delta) \quad (46)$$

The results given by Eq. (44) and (46) have physical significance and are invariant to a transformation of origin as may be readily verified by employing Eq. (26) and (32′) and integrating around the C_1 circle in the z_1 plane. It is indeed a remarkable fact that the total integrated characteristics, lift and location of lift, of the airfoil depend on so few parameters of the transformation as to be almost independent of the shape of the contour. The parameters R, β, a_1, and c_1 involved in these relations will be discussed in a later paragraph.

We shall obtain an interesting result[21] by taking moments about the point $\zeta = c_1$ instead of the origin (M in Fig. 17). By Eq. (25) we have

$$\zeta - c_1 = z + \frac{a_1}{z} + \frac{a_1}{z^2} + \cdots$$

and by Eq. (43)

$$M_M = R.P. \text{ of } -\frac{\rho}{2}\int_A \left[\frac{\mathrm{d}w}{\mathrm{d}(\zeta - c_1)}\right]^2 (\zeta - c_1)\mathrm{d}\zeta$$

$$= R.P. \text{ of } -\frac{\rho}{2}\int_C \left(A_0 + \frac{A_1}{z} + \frac{A_2}{z^2} + \ldots\right) \times$$

$$\left(z + \frac{a_1}{z} + \frac{a_2}{z^2} + \ldots\right)\left(1 - \frac{a_1}{z^2} + \ldots\right)\mathrm{d}z$$

[20]It may be recalled that $c_1 = \frac{R}{\pi}\int_0^{2\pi} \psi(\varphi)^{i\varphi}\,\mathrm{d}\varphi$ and $a_1 = \eta^2 + \frac{c_1^2}{2} + c_2$ [see Eq. (25′)].

[21]First obtained by R. von Mises (Ref. 6). The work of von Mises forms an elegant geometrical study of the airfoil.

$$= R.P. \text{ of } -i\pi\rho A_2$$

or

$$M_M = 2\pi b^2 \rho V^2 \sin 2(\alpha + \gamma) \tag{47}$$

This result could have been obtained directly from Eq. (46) by noticing that $\rho V\Gamma$ in the second term is the resultant lift force L and that $Lm\cos(\alpha+\delta)$ represents a moment which vanishes at M for all values of α. [In Fig. 17 the complex coordinate of M is $\zeta - me^{i\delta}$, and the arm OH is $m\cos(\alpha+\delta)$.] The perpendicular b_M from M onto the resultant lift vector is simply obtained from $M_M = Lb_M$:

$$b_M = \frac{b^2 \sin 2(\alpha+\gamma)}{2R\sin(\alpha+\beta)} \tag{48}$$

The intersection of the resultant lift vector with the chord or axis of the airfoil locates a point which may be considered the center of pressure. The amount of travel of the center of pressure with change in angle of attack is an important characteristic of airfoils, especially for considerations of stability, and will be discussed in a later paragraph.

The lift force has been found to be proportional to $\sin(\alpha+\beta)$ or writing $\alpha + \beta = \alpha_1$:

$$L = 4\pi\rho RV^2 \sin\alpha_1 \tag{49}$$

where α_1 may be termed the absolute angle of attack. Similarly, writing $\alpha + \gamma = \alpha_2$:

$$M_M = 2\pi b^2 \rho V^2 \sin 2\alpha_2 \tag{50}$$

With von Mises (Ref. 6, Pt. II) we shall denote the axes determined by passing lines through M at angles β and γ to the x axis as the first and second axes of the airfoil, respectively (Fig. 18). The directions of these axes alone are important and these are fixed with respect to a given airfoil. Then the lift L is proportional to the sine of the angle of attack with respect to the first axis and the moment about M to the sine of twice the angle of attack with respect to the second axis.

From Eq. (47) we note that the moment at any point Q whose radius vector from M is $re^{i\sigma}$ is given by

$$M_Q = 2\pi\rho b^2 V^2 \sin 2(\alpha+\gamma) - Lr\cos(\alpha+\sigma)$$

Let us determine whether there exist particular values of r and σ for which M_Q is independent of the angle of attack α. Writing for L its value given by Eq. (45)—

$$M_Q = 2\pi\rho b^2 V^2 \sin 2(\alpha+\gamma) - 4\pi\rho RrV^2 \sin(\alpha+\beta)\cos(\alpha+\sigma)$$

And separating this trigonometrically:

$$M_Q = 2\pi\rho^2 V^2 \,[(b^2\cos 2\gamma - Rr\cos(\beta+\sigma))\sin 2\alpha + (b^2 \sin 2\gamma - Rr\sin(\beta+\sigma))\cos 2\alpha - Rr\sin(\beta-\sigma)]$$

If this moment is to be independent of α_1, the coefficients of $\sin 2\alpha$ and $\cos 2\alpha$ must vanish. Then—

$$b^2 \cos 2\gamma = Rr\cos(\beta+\sigma)$$

and

$$b^2 \sin 2\gamma = Rr\sin(\beta+\sigma)$$

Hence,

$$r = \frac{b^2}{R} \quad \text{and} \quad \sigma = 2\gamma - \beta$$

Then, if we move the reference point of the mo-

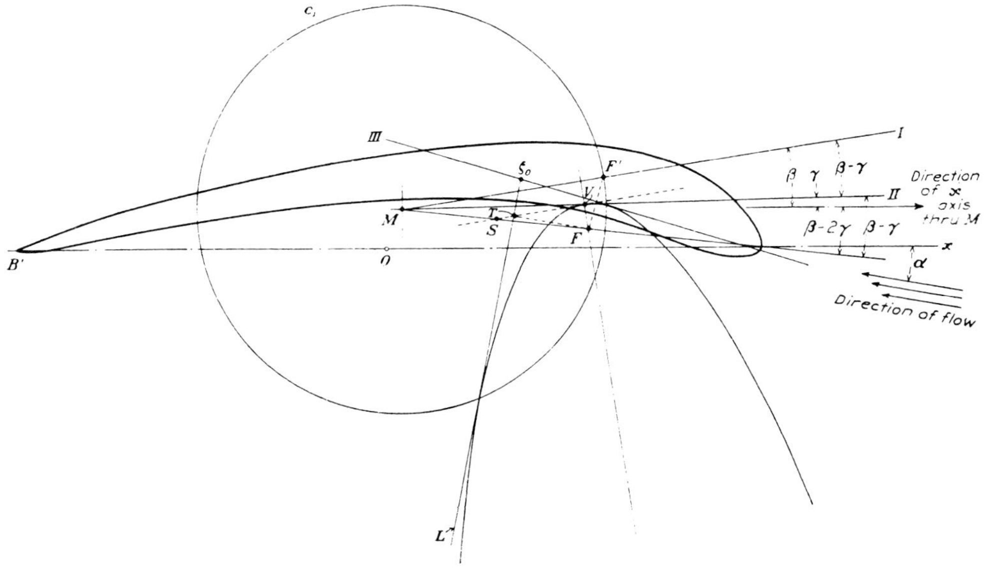

Fig. 18

ment to a point F whose radius vector from M is $(b^2/R)e^{2\gamma-\beta}$, the moment existing at F is for all angles of attack constant, given by

$$M_F = 2\pi\rho b^2 V^2 \sin 2(\gamma - \beta) \qquad (51)$$

It has thus been shown that with every airfoil profile there is associated a point F for which the moment is independent of the angle of attack. A change in the lift force resulting from a change in angle of attack distributes itself so that its moment about F is zero.

From Eq. (47) it may be noted that at zero lift (i.e., $\alpha = -\beta$) the airfoil is subject to a moment couple which is, in fact, equal to M_F. This moment is often termed "dividing moment" or "moment for zero lift." If M_F is zero, the resultant lift force must pass through F for all angles of attack and we thus have the statement that the airfoil has a constant center of pressure, if and only if the moment for zero lift is zero.

The point F, denoted by von Mises as the focus of the airfoil, will be seen to have other interesting properties. We note here that its construction is very simple. It lies at a distance b^2/R from M on a line making angle $2\gamma - \beta$ with respect to the x axis. From Fig. 18 we see that the angle between this line and the first axis is bisected by the second axis.

The arm h_F from F onto the resultant lift vector L (h_F is designated FT in Fig. 18.) Note also that FT, being perpendicular to L, must be parallel to the direction of flow; the line TV is drawn parallel to the first axis and therefore angle $VTF = (\alpha + \beta)$ is obtained as

$$h_F = \frac{M_F}{L} = \frac{-b^2 \sin 2(\beta - \gamma)}{2R \quad \sin(\alpha + \beta)}$$

or setting

$$h = \frac{b^2}{2R}\sin 2(\beta - \gamma)$$

$$h_F = -\frac{h}{\sin(\alpha + \beta)} \qquad (52)$$

But h_F is parallel to the direction of α, and the relation $h = -h_F \sin(\alpha + \beta)$ states, then, that the projection of h_F onto the line through F perpendicular to the first axis is equal to the constant h (h is designated FV in the figure) for all angles of attack. In other words, the pedal points T determined by the interesction of h_F and L for *all* positions of the lift vector L lie on a straight line. (The line is determined by T and V in Fig. 18.) The parabola is the only curve having the property that pedal points of the perpendiculars dropped from its focus onto any tangent lie on a straight line, that line being the tangent at the vertex. This may be shown analytically by noting that the equation of L for a coordinate system having F as origin and FV as negative x axis is

$$x \sin\alpha_1 + y \cos\alpha_1 = h_F = -\frac{h}{\sin(\alpha + \beta)}$$

By differentiating with respect to $\alpha_1 = (\alpha + \beta)$ and eliminating α_1 we get the equation of the curve which the lines L envelop as $y^2 = 4h(x + h)$. From triangle FVS in Fig. 18, it may be seen that the distance $MF = (b^2/R)$ is bisected at S by the line TV; for, since $FV = h = (b^2/2R)\sin 2(\gamma - \beta)$ and angle $FSV = 2(\beta - \gamma)$, then $SF = b^2/2R$. It has thus been shown that the resultant lift vectors envelop, in general, a parabola whose focus is at F and whose directrix is the first axis. The second axis and its perpendicular at M, it may be noted, are also tangents to the parabola being, by definition, the resultant lift vectors for $\alpha = -\gamma$ and $\alpha = (\pi/2) - \gamma$, respectively.

If the constant h reduces to zero, the lift vectors reduce to a pencil of lines through F. Thus a constant center of pressure is given by $h = 0$ or $\sin 2(\beta - \gamma) = 0$ which is equivalent to stating that the first and second axes coincide. The lift parabola opens downward when the first axis is above the second axis ($\beta > \gamma$); it reduces to a pencil of lines when the two axes are coincident ($\beta = \gamma$) and opens upward when the second axis is above the first ($\beta < \gamma$).

W. Müller[22] introduced a third axis which has some interesting properties. Defining the complex coordinate ζ_0 as the centroid of the circulation by

$$\Gamma\zeta_0 = \int_A \zeta\left(\frac{dw}{d\zeta}\right) d\zeta$$

and using Eq. (25) and (32) one obtains

$$\zeta_0 - c_1 = x_0 + iy_0$$

where

$$\left.\begin{aligned} x_0 &= \frac{1}{2\sin(\alpha + \beta)}\left[R \sin\alpha + \frac{b^2}{R}\sin(\alpha + 2\gamma)\right] \\ y_0 &= \frac{1}{2\sin(\alpha + \beta)}\left[R \cos\alpha - \frac{b^2}{R}\cos(\alpha + 2\gamma)\right] \end{aligned}\right\} \qquad (53)$$

The equation of the lift-vector lines referred to the origin at M and x axis drawn through M is

$$x \cos\alpha - y \sin\alpha = \frac{b^2 \sin(\alpha + \gamma)}{2R \sin(\alpha + \beta)} \qquad (54)$$

and it may be seen that the point (x_0, y_0) will be—

[22]Reference 7, p. 169. Also *Zs. für Ang. Math. u. Mech*. Bd 3.8, S–117, 1923. Airfoils having the same first, second, and third axes are alike theoretically in total lift properties and also in travel of the center of pressure, i.e., they have the same lift parabola.

$$2x_0[R\cos\beta - \frac{b^2}{R}\cos(\beta - 2\gamma)]$$
$$+ 2y_0\,[R\sin\beta + \frac{b^2}{R}\sin(\beta - 2\gamma)] = R^2 - \frac{b^4}{R^2}$$

which is the equation of a line, the third axis, and proves to be a tangent to the lift parabola. Geometrically, it is the perpendicular bisector of the line *FF′* joining the focus to the point of intersection of the first axis with the circle (Fig. 18).

The conformal centroid of the contour

It has already been seen that the point M has special interesting properties. The transformation from the airfoil to the circle having M as center was expressed in the normal form and permitted a very small $\epsilon(\varphi)$ curve (see p. 00). It was also shown that the movement with respect to M is simply proportional to the sine of twice the angle of attack with respect to the second axis. We may note, too, that in the presentation of this report the coordinate of M—

$$\zeta = c_1 = \frac{R}{\pi}\int_0^{2\pi} \psi e^{i\varphi} \mathrm{d}\varphi$$

is a function only of the first harmonic of the $\psi(\varphi)$ curve.

We shall now obtain a significant property of M invariant with respect to the transformation from airfoil to circle. We start with the evaluation of the integral

$$\int_A \zeta \left|\frac{\mathrm{d}z}{\mathrm{d}\zeta}\right| \mathrm{d}s \qquad (55)$$

where A is the airfoil contour, ds is the differential of arc along A, and $|\mathrm{d}z/\mathrm{d}\zeta|$, as will be recalled, is the magnification factor of the transformation $\zeta = f(z)$ mapping airfoil into circle; i.e., each element ds of A when magnified by $|\mathrm{d}z/\mathrm{d}\zeta|$ gives dS the differential of arc in the plane of the circle, i.e., $|\mathrm{d}z|$. Then we have

$$\int_A \zeta \left|\frac{\mathrm{d}z}{\mathrm{d}\zeta}\right| \mathrm{d}s = \int_C \zeta(z)\,|\mathrm{d}z|$$

and by Eq. (25)

$$= \int_C \left(c_1 + z + \frac{a_1}{z} + \frac{a_2}{z^2} + \cdots\right) |\mathrm{d}z|$$

$$= \int_0^{2\pi} \left(c_1 + Re^{i\varphi} + \frac{a_1}{R}\, e^{-i\varphi} + \frac{a_2}{R^2} e^{-2i\varphi} + \cdots\right) R\,\mathrm{d}\varphi$$

$$= 2\pi R c_1$$

$$= c_1 \int_C \mathrm{d}S = c_1 \int_A \left|\frac{\mathrm{d}z}{\mathrm{d}\zeta}\right| \mathrm{d}s$$

Then

$$c_1 = \frac{\int_A \zeta \left|\frac{\mathrm{d}z}{\mathrm{d}\zeta}\right| \mathrm{d}s}{\int_A \zeta \left|\frac{\mathrm{d}z}{\mathrm{d}\zeta}\right| \mathrm{d}s} \qquad (56)$$

The point M of the airfoil is thus the conformal centroid obtained by giving each element of the contour a weight equal to the magnification of that element, which results when the airfoil is transformed into a circle, the region at infinity being unaltered. It lies within any convex region enclosing the airfoil contour.[23]

ARBITRARY AIRFOILS AND THEIR RELATION TO SPECIAL TYPES

The total lift and moment experienced by the airfoil have been seen to depend on but a few parameters of the airfoil shape. The resultant lift force is completely determined for a particuar angle of attack by only the radius R and the angle of zero lift β. The moment about the origin depends, in addition, on the complex constants c_1 and a_1 or, what is the same, on the position of the conformal centroid M and the focus F. The constants c_1 and a_1 or, what is the same, on the position of the conformal centroid M and the focus F. The constants c_1 and a_1 were also shown (see footnote 20) to depend only on the first and second harmonics of the $\epsilon(\varphi)$ curve. Before studying these parameters for point of view of the "conformal angular distortion" $[\epsilon(\varphi)]$ curve.

Flow about the straight line or flat plate

As a first approximation to the theory of actual airfoils, there is the one which considers the airfoil section to be a straight line. It has been seen that the line of length $4a$ is obtained by transforming a circle of radius a, center at the origin, by $\zeta = z + a^2/z$. The region external to the line $4a$ in the ζ plane maps uniquely into the region external to the circle $|z| = a$. A point Q of the line corresponding to a point P at $ae^{i\theta}$ is obtained by simply adding the vectors $a(e^{i\theta} + e^{-i\theta})$ or completing the parallelogram *OPQP′*

For $\psi = O$, we have from Eq. (6):

$$x = 2a\cosh\psi\,\cos\theta = 2a\cos\theta$$

$$y = 2a\sinh\psi\,\sin\theta = 0$$

Then the parameters for this case are $R = a$, $\beta = 0$, $a_1 = a^2$ (i.e., $b = a$, $\gamma = 0$), and M is at the origin O.

[23]Cf. P. Frank and K. Lowner, *Math. Zs.* Bd. 3, S. 78, 1919. Also Ref. 5, p. 146.

Taking the Kutta assumption for determining the circulation we have

$$\left.\begin{array}{lll} \text{the circulation} & \Gamma = 4\pi a V \sin\alpha \\ \text{the lift} & L = 4\pi a \rho V^2 \sin\alpha \\ \text{moment about } M & M_M = 2\pi a^2 \rho V^2 \sin 2\alpha \\ \text{position of } F \text{ is at} & z_F = c_1 + \dfrac{b^2}{R} e^{i(2\gamma - \beta)} = a \end{array}\right\} \quad (57)$$

Since $\beta = \gamma$, we know that the travel of the center of pressure vanishes and that the center of pressure is at F or at one-fourth the length of the line from the leading edge. The complex flow potential for this case is

$$w(\zeta) = -V[z(\zeta)e^{i\alpha} + \frac{a^2}{z(\zeta)} e^{i\alpha}] + \frac{i\Gamma}{2\pi} \log z(\xi) \quad (58)$$

where

$$z(\zeta) = \frac{\zeta}{2} \pm \sqrt{\left(\frac{\zeta}{2}\right)^2 + a_2}$$

is the inverse of Eq. (5). Since $\psi(\varphi) = \epsilon(\varphi) = 0$ for this case, Eq. (39) giving velocity at the surface reduces to

$$v = V\left[\frac{\sin\left(\dfrac{\varphi}{2} + \alpha\right)}{\sin\dfrac{\varphi}{2}}\right] \quad \text{for } \Gamma = 4\pi a V \sin\alpha$$

and by Eq. (41) $v = V(\sin(\varphi + \alpha)/\sin\varphi)$ for $\Gamma = 0$.

Flow about the elliptic cylinder

If Eq. (5) is applied to a circle with center at the origin and radius a^{ψ}, the ellipse (Fig. 19)

$$\frac{x^2}{(2a \cosh\psi)^2} + \frac{y^2}{(2a \sinh\psi)^2} = 1$$

is obtained in the ζ plane and the region external to this ellipse is mapped uniquely into the region external to the circle. The same transformation also transforms this external region into the region internal to the inverse circle, radius $ae^{-\psi}$. We note that a point Q of the ellipse corresponding to P at $ae^{\psi + i\theta}$ is obtained

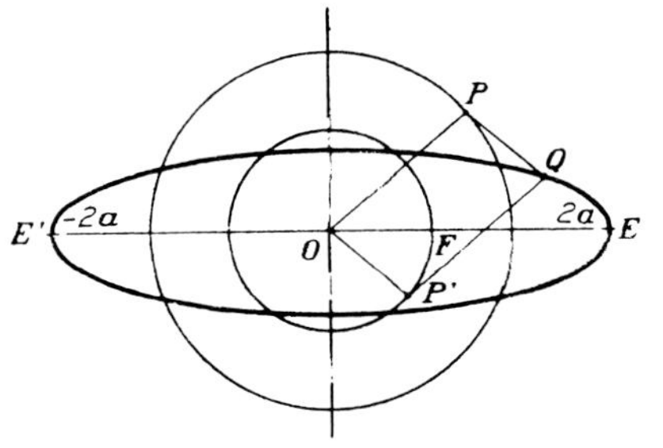

Fig. 19

by simply completing the parallelogram $OPQP'$ (Fig. 19) where P' now terminates on the circle $ae^{-\psi}$. The parameters are obtained as $R = ae^{\psi}$, $\beta = 0$, $a_1 = a_2$; M is at the origin O. Then, assuming the rear stagnation point at the end of the major axis—

$$\Gamma = 4\pi a e^{\psi} V \sin\alpha$$

$$L = 4\pi a e^{\psi} V^2 \sin\alpha$$

$$M_M = 2\pi a^2 \rho V^2 \sin 2\alpha$$

Since $\beta = \gamma$, the point F is the center of pressure for all angles of attack and is located at $z_F = ae^{-\psi}$ from O or a distance ae^{ψ} from the leading edge. The quantity

$$\frac{EF}{EE'} = \frac{ae^{\psi}}{2a(e^{\psi} + e^{-\psi})} = \frac{\cosh\psi + \sinh\psi}{4\cosh\psi} = \frac{1}{4}(1 + \tanh\psi)$$

represents the ratio of the distance of F from the leading edge to the major diameter of the ellipse.

The complex flow potential is identical with that given by Eq. (58) for the flat plate, except that the quantity a^2 in the numerator of the second term is replaced by the constant $a^2e^{2\psi}$. Since $\psi(\varphi)$ = constant, $\epsilon(\varphi) = 0$ and Eq. (39) giving the velocity at each point of the surface for a stagnation point at end of major axis becomes

$$v = V\frac{[\sin(\varphi + \alpha) + \sin\alpha]e^{\psi}}{\sqrt{\sinh^2\psi + \sin^2\varphi}} \quad (59)$$

and for zero circulation by Eq. (41)

$$v = V\frac{\sin(\varphi + \alpha)e^{\psi}}{\sqrt{\sinh^2\psi + \sin^2\varphi}} \quad (59')$$

Circular-arc sections

It has been shown that the transformation $\zeta = z + a^2/z$ applied to a circle with center at $z = 0$ and radius a gives a straight line in the ζ plane, and when applied to a circle with center $z = 0$ and radius different from a gives an ellipse in the ζ plane. We now show that if it is used to transform a circle with center at $z = is$ (s being a real number) and radius $\sqrt{a^2 + s^2}$, a circular arc results. The coordinates of the transform of the circle C in the z plane are given by Eq. (6) as

$$x = 2a \cosh\psi \cos\theta$$

$$y = 2a \cosh\psi \cos\theta$$

A relation between ψ and θ can be readily obtained. In right triangle OMD (Fig. 20), $OM = s$, angle $OMD = \theta$, and, recalling that the product of segments of any chord through O is equal to a^2, $OD = \frac{1}{2}(OP - OP_1) = a(e^{\psi} - e^{-\psi})/2 = a \sinh\psi$. Then $s \sin\theta =$

$= a\sinh\psi$, and from the equation for y, $y = 2s\sin^2\theta$. Eliminating both θ and ψ in Eq. (6) we get

$$x^2 + \left(y + \left(\frac{a^2 - s^2}{s}\right)\right)^2 = \left(\frac{a^2 + s^2}{s}\right)^2 \qquad (60)$$

the equation of a circle; but since y can have only positive values, we are limited to a circular arc. In fact, as the point P in Fig. 20 moves from A' to A on the circle, the point Q traverses the arc $A_1' A_1$ and as P completes the circuit AA' the arc is traversed in the opposite direction. As in the previous cases, we note that the point Q corresponding to either P or to the inverse and reflected point P' is obtained by completing the parallelogram $OPQP'$. We may also note that had the arc $A_1 A_1'$ been preassigned with the requirement of transforming it into the circle, the most convenient choice of origin of coordinates would be the midpoint of the line, length $4a$, joining the end points. The curve B then resulting from using transformation (5) would be a circle in the z' plane, center at $z' = is$, and the theory developed in the report could be directly applied to this continuous closed B curve. Had another axis and origin been chosen, e.g., as in Fig. 21, the B curve resulting would have finite discontinuities at A and A', although the arc $A_1 A_1'$ of chord length $4a$ and maximum height $2s$ are then $R = \sqrt{a^2 + s^2}$, $\beta = \tan^{-1}(s/a)$. The focus F may be constructed by erecting a perpendicular to the chord at A' of length s and projecting its extremity on MA'. The center M' of the arc also lies on this line.

The infinite sheet having the circular arc as cross section contains as a special case the flat plate, and thus permits a better approximation to the mean camber line of actual airfoils. The complex flow potential and the formulas for the velocity at the surface for the

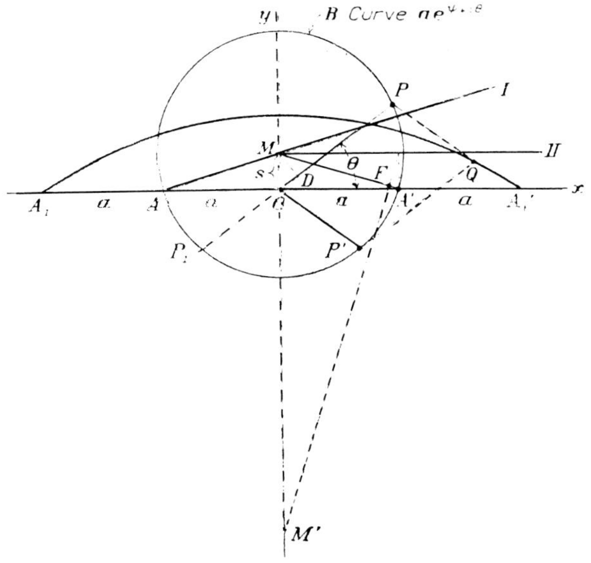

Fig. 20 The circular arc airfoil.

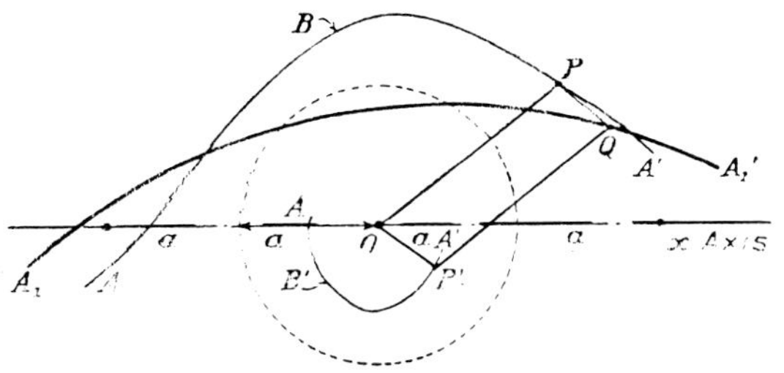

Fig. 21 Discontinuous *B* curve.

circular arc are of the same form as those given in the next section for the Joukowsky airfoil, where also a simple geometric interpretation of the parameters ϵ and ψ are given.

Joukowsky airfoils

If Eq. (5) is applied to a circle with center at $z = s$, s being a real number, and with radius $R = a + s$, a symmetrical Joukowsky airfoil (or strut form) is obtained. The general Joukowsky airfoil is obtained when the transformation $\zeta = z(a^2/z)$ is applied to a circle C passing through the point $z = -a$ and containing $z = a$ (near the circumference usually), and whose center M is not limited to either the x or y axes, but may be on a line OM inclined to the axes (Fig. 22). The parametric equations of the shape are as before:

$$\left.\begin{aligned} x &= 2a\cosh\psi\cos\theta \\ y &= 2a\sinh\psi\sin\theta \end{aligned}\right\} \qquad (6)$$

Geometrically, a point Q of the airfoil is obtained by adding the vectors $ae^{\psi + i\theta}$ and $ae^{-\psi - i\theta}$ or by completing the parallelogram $OPQP'$ as before, but now P' lies on another circle B' defined as $z = ae^{-\psi - i\theta}$, the inverse and reflected circle of B with respect to the circle of radius a at the origin (obtained by the transformation of reciprocal radii and subsequent reflection in the x axis). Thus $OP \cdot OP' = a^2$ for all positions of P, and OP' is readily constructed. The center M_1 of the circle B' may be located on the line AM by drawing OM_1 symmetrically to OM with respect to the y axis. Let the coordinate of M be $z = is + de^{i\varphi}$, where d, s, and β are real quantities. The circle of radius a, with center M_0 at $z = is$, is transformed into a circular arc through $A_1 A_1'$ which may be considered the mean camber line of the airfoil. At the tail the Joukowsky airfoil has a cusp and the upper and lower surfaces include a zero angle. The lift parameters are $R = \sqrt{a^2 + s^2} + d$, $\beta = \tan^{-1}(s/a)$, $a_1 = a^2 = b^2 e^{2i\gamma}$ or $b = a$ and $\gamma = 0$. Since $\gamma = 0$, the second axis has the direction of the x axis. The focus F is determined by laying off the segment $MF = a^2/R$ on the line MA'. This quantity, it may be noted, is obtained easily by the following construction. In triangle MDC', $MD = R$, MC' and MC are made equal to a, then CF drawn parallel to DC' determines $MF = a^2/R$. The lift

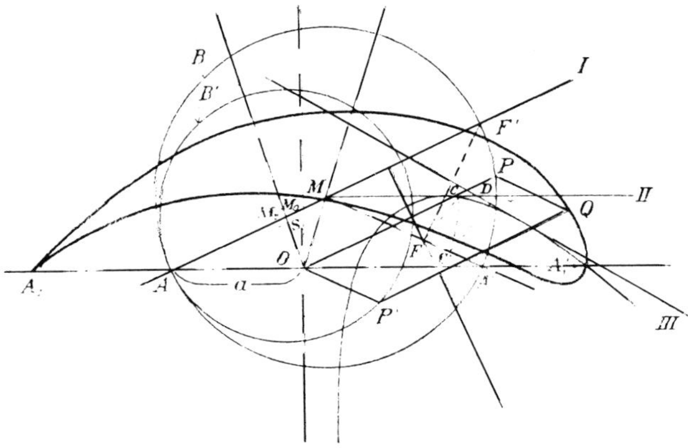

Fig. 22 The Joukowsky airfoil.

parabola may be now determined uniquely since its directrix AM and focus F are known.

It may be observed that if it is desired to transform a preassigned Joukowsky profile into a circle, there exists a choice of axis and origin for the airfoil such that the inverse of transformation (5) will map the airfoil directly into a circle. This axis is very approximately given by designating the tail as $(-2a, 0)$ and the point midway between the leading edge and the center of curvature of the leading edge as $(+2a, 0)$, the origin then bisecting the line joining these points.

The complex potential flow function for the Joukowsky airfoil is

$$w(\zeta) = -V\left[g(\zeta)e^{i\alpha} + \frac{R^2e^{-i\alpha}}{g(\zeta)}\right] + \frac{i\Gamma}{2\pi}\log g(\zeta) \qquad (61)$$

where

$$g(\zeta) = \pm\frac{\zeta}{2}\sqrt{\left(\frac{\zeta}{2}\right)^2 + a^2 - m}$$

By Eq. (39) we have for the velocity at the surface

$$v = \frac{V[\sin(\alpha+\varphi) + \sin(\alpha+\beta)]\left(1 + \frac{d\bar{\epsilon}}{d\theta}\right)e^{\psi_0}}{\sqrt{(\sinh^2\psi + \sin^2\theta)\left(1 + \left(\frac{d\bar{\psi}}{d\theta}\right)^2\right)}}$$

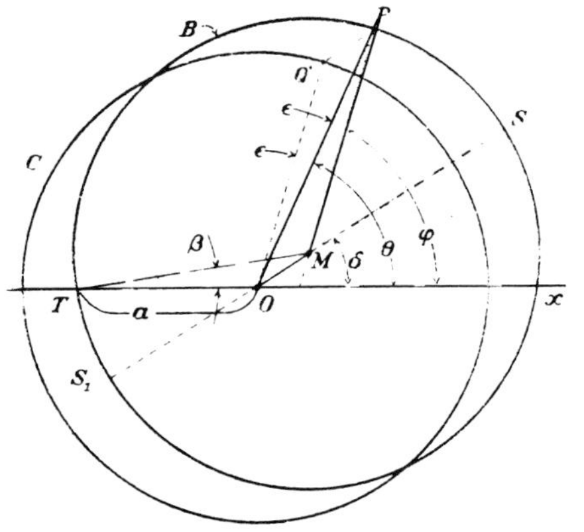

Fig. 23 Geometrical representation of ϵ and ψ for Joukowsky airfoils.

This formula was obtained by transforming the flow around C into that around B and then into that around A. Since we know that B is itself a circle for this case, we can simply use the latter two transformations alone. We get

$$v = \frac{V[\sin(\alpha+\varphi) + \sin(\alpha+\beta)]\,e^{\psi}}{\sqrt{\sinh^2\psi + \sin^2\theta}} \qquad (62)$$

That these formulas are equivalent is immediately evident since the quantity

$$\frac{e^{\psi_0-\psi}\left(1 + \frac{d\bar{\epsilon}}{d\theta}\right)}{\sqrt{1 + \left(\frac{d\bar{\psi}}{d\theta}\right)^2}}$$

is unity, being the ratio of the magnification of each arc element of C to that of B [see Eq. (37)].

A very simple geometrical picture of the parameters ϵ and ψ exists for the cases discussed. In Fig. 23 the value of ϵ or $\varphi - \theta$ at the point P is simply angle OPM, i.e., the angle subtended at P by the origin O and the center M. The angle of zero lift is the value of ϵ for $\theta = \pi$; i.e., $\epsilon_{\text{Tail}} = \beta = OTM$. In particular, we may note that $\epsilon = 0$ at S and S_1 which are on the straight line OM. Consider the triangle OMP, where $OP = ae^{\psi}$, $MP = R = ae^{\psi_0}$, $OM/MP = \rho$, angle $OPM = \epsilon$; also, $MOX = \delta$, $MOP = \theta - \delta$, $OMP = \pi - (\varphi - \delta)$. Then by the law of cosines we have

$$e^{2(\psi-\psi_0)} = 1 + 2\rho\cos(\varphi-\delta) + \rho^2$$

or

$$\psi - \psi_0 = \frac{1}{2}\log(1 + 2\rho\cos(\varphi-\delta) + \rho^2) \qquad (63)$$

$$= \sum_1^{\infty}(-1)^{n-1}\frac{\cos n(\varphi-\delta)}{n}\rho^n$$

and by the law of sines

$$\sin\epsilon = \frac{\rho\sin(\varphi-\delta)}{(1 + 2\rho\cos(\varphi-\delta) + \rho^2)^{1/2}}$$

or

$$\epsilon(\varphi) = \tan^{-1}\frac{\rho\sin(\varphi-\delta)}{1 + 2\rho\cos(\varphi-\delta)}$$

$$= \sum_1^{\infty}(-1)^{n-1}\frac{\sin n(\varphi-\delta)}{n}\rho^n \qquad (64)$$

We see that, as required, the expressions for the "radial distortion" $\psi(\varphi)$ and the "angular distortion" $\epsilon(\varphi)$ are conjugate Fourier series and may be expressed as a single complex quantity:

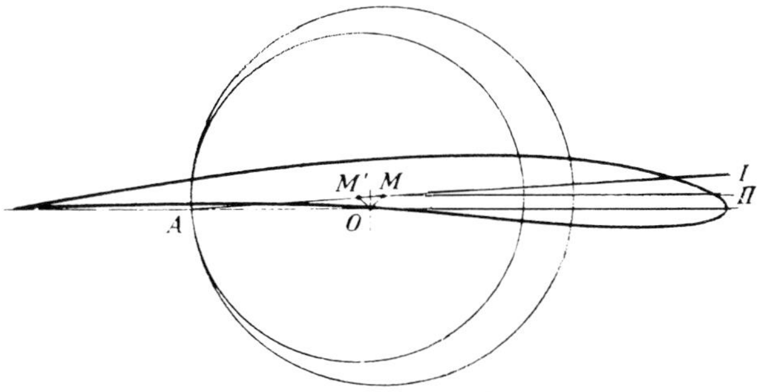

Fig. 24 The Joukowsky airfoil $\rho = 0.10$, $\delta = 45°$.

$$(\psi - \psi_0) - i\epsilon = \sum_1^\infty \frac{(-1)^{n-1}}{n} \rho^n e^{-in(\varphi - \delta)}$$

$$= -\log [1 + \rho e^{-1(\varphi - \delta)}]$$

It is evident also that the coefficient for $n = 1$ or the "first-harmonic term" is simply $\rho e^{i\delta}$ and a translation by this quantity brings the circle C into coincidence with B as was pointed out on page 13.

The constant

$$\psi_0 = \frac{1}{2\pi}\int_0^{2\pi} \psi \, d\varphi$$

is readily shown to be invariant to the choice of origin O, as long as O is within B. We have

$$\frac{1}{2\pi}\int_0^{2\pi} \psi \, d\varphi = \frac{1}{2\pi}\int_0^{2\pi} \frac{1}{2} \log$$

$$\times (1 + 2\rho \cos(\varphi - \delta) + \rho^2)e^{2\psi_0} \, d\varphi$$

$$= \frac{1}{2\pi}\int_0^{2\pi} \left(\psi_0 + \sum_1^\infty (-1)^{(n-1)} \frac{\cos n(\varphi - \delta)}{n}\right) d\varphi = \psi_0$$

Figure 24 shows the Joukowsky airfoil defined by $\rho = 0.10$ and $\delta = 45°$, and Fig. 25 shows the $\bar{\psi}(\theta)$, $\psi(\varphi)$, $\bar{\epsilon}(\theta)$, and $\epsilon(\theta)$ curves for this airfoil.

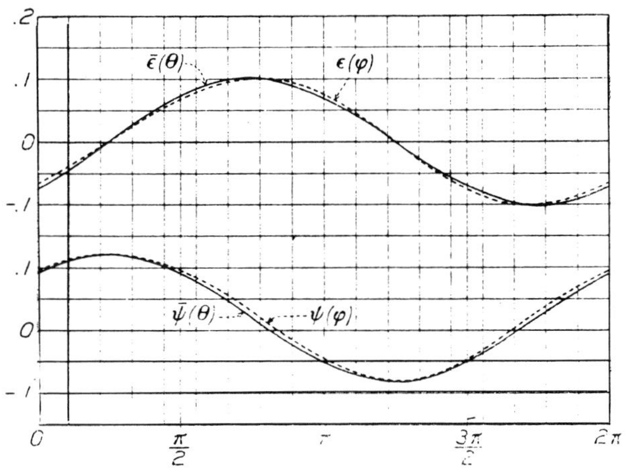

Fig. 25 The $\bar{\epsilon}(\theta)$ and $\bar{\psi}(\theta)$ curves for the airfoil in Figure 24.

Arbitrary sections

In order to obtain the lift parameters of an arbitrary airfoil, a convenient choice of coordinate axes is first made as indicated for the Joukowsky airfoil and as stated previously (page 00). The curve resulting from the use of transformation (5) will yield an arbitrary curve $ae^{\psi + i\theta}$ which will, in general, differ very little from a circle. The inverse and reflected curve $ae^{-\psi - i\theta}$ will also be almost circular. The transition from the curve $ae^{\psi + i\theta}$ to a circle is reached by obtaining the solution $\epsilon(\varphi)$ of Eq. (13). The method of obtaining this solution as already given converges with extreme rapidity for nearly circular curves.

The geometrical picture is analogous to that given for the special cases. In Fig. 26 it may be seen that a point Q on the airfoil (N.A.C.A.–M6) corresponding to P on the B curve (or P' on the B' curve) is obtained by constructing parallelogram $OPQP'$. The $\bar{\psi}(\theta)$ and $\bar{\epsilon}(\theta)$ curves are shown in Fig. 27 for this airfoil. The complex velocity potential and the expression for velocity at the surface are given, respectively, by Eq. (33) and (39). The lift parameters are

$$R = ae^{\psi_0}, \ \beta = \epsilon_{\text{Tail}}$$

(at $\theta = \pi$),

$$M \text{ is at } z = c_1 = \frac{R}{\pi}\int_0^\pi \psi(\varphi)e^{i\varphi} \, d\varphi$$

and F is at $z = c_1 + (a_1/R)$ where a_1 is given in Eq. (25′).

The first and second axes for the N.A.C.A.–M6 airfoil are found to coincide and this airfoil has then a constant center of pressure at F. Figures 28(a) to 28(l) give the pressure distribution (along the x axis) for a series of angles of attack as calculated by this theory and as obtained by experiment.[24] Table I contains the essential numerical data for this airfoil.

The method used for arbitrary airfoils is readily applied to arbitrary thin arcs or to broken lines such as the sections of tail surfaces form approximately. In Fig. 26 the part of the airfoil boundary above the x axis transforms by Eq. (5) into the two discontinuous arcs shown by full lines, while the lower boundary transforms into the arcs shown by dashed lines. If the upper boundary surface is given alone (thin airfoil), we may obtain a closed curve $ae^{\psi + i\theta}$ only by joining the end points by a chord of length $4a$ and choosing

[24]The experimental results are taken from test No. 323 of the N.A.C.A., variable-density wind tunnel. The angle of attack α substituted in Eq. (39) has been modified arbitrarily to take account of the effects of finite span, tunnel-wall interference, and viscosity, by choosing it so that the theoretical lift is about 10 per cent more than the corresponding experimental value. The actual values of the lift coefficients are given in the figures.

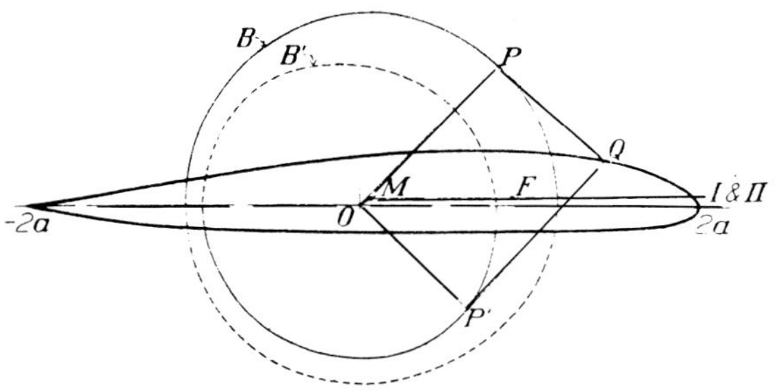

Fig. 26 The N.A.C.A.–M6 airfoil.

the origin at its midpoint.[25] The resulting curve has two double points for which the first derivative is not uniquely defined; and, in general, it may be seen that infinite velocities correspond to such points.

At a point of the $\bar{\psi}(\theta)$ curve corresponding to a mathematically sharp corner, there exist two tangents, that is, the slope $d\bar{\psi}(\theta)/d\theta$ is finitely discontinuous. The curve $\bar{\epsilon}(\theta)$ must have an infinite slope at such a point for according to a theorem in the theory of Fourier series, at a point of discontinuity of a F.S., the conjugate F.S. is properly divergent. This manifests itself in the velocity-formula, Eq. (39), in the factor $[1 + (d\bar{\epsilon}/d\theta)]$ which is infinite at these sharp corners. For practical purposes, however, a rounding of the sharp edge, however small, considerably alters the slope $d\bar{\epsilon}(\theta)/d\theta$ at this point.

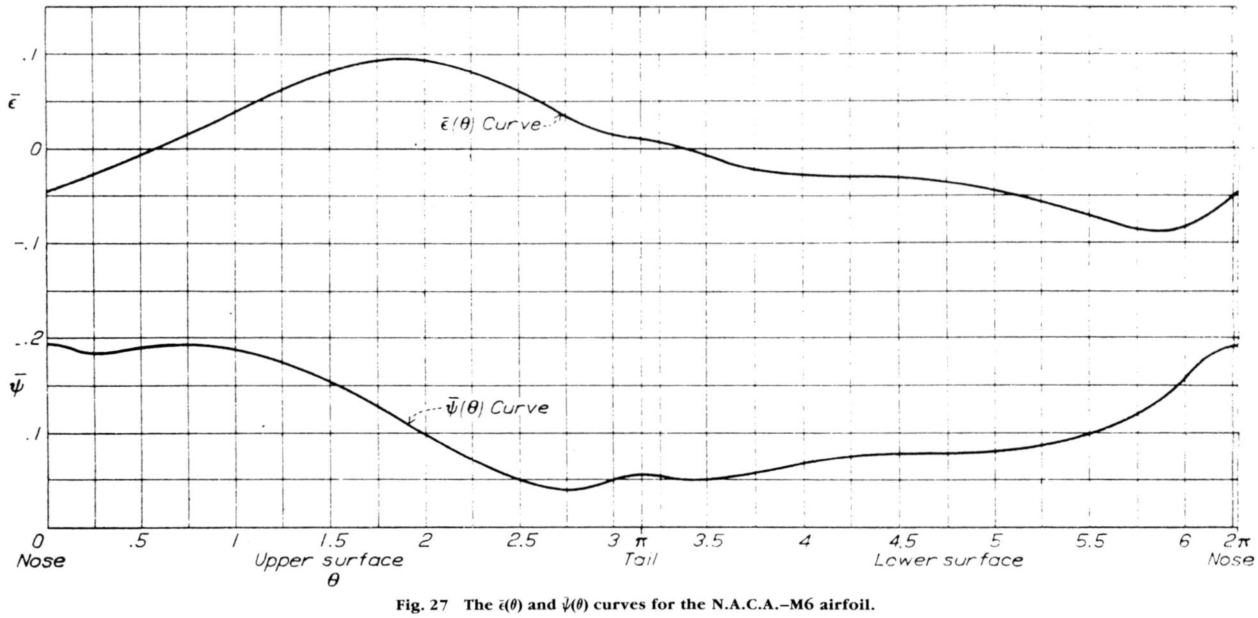

Fig. 27 The $\bar{\epsilon}(\theta)$ and $\bar{\psi}(\theta)$ curves for the N.A.C.A.–M6 airfoil.

Ideal angle of attack

A thin airfoil, represented by a line arc, has both sharp leading edge and sharp trailing edge. The Kutta assumption for fixing the circulation places a stagnation point at the tail for all angles of attack. At the leading edge, however, the velocity is infinite at all angles of attack except one, namely, that angle for which the other stagnation point is at the leading edge. It is natural to expect that for this angle of attack in actual cases the frictional losses are at or near a minimum, and thus arises the concept of "ideal" angle of attack introduced by Theodorsen (Ref. 8) and which has also been designated "angle of best streamlining." The definition for the ideal angle may be extended to thick airfoils, as that angle for which a stagnation point occurs directly at the foremost point of the mean camber line.

The lift at the leading edge vanishes and the change from velocity to pressure along the airfoil surface is usually more gradual than at any other angle of attack. The minimum profile drag of airfoils actually occurs very close to this angle. At the ideal angle, which we denote by α_I, the factor $[\sin(\alpha + \varphi) + \sin(\alpha + \beta)]$ in Eq. (39) is zero not only for $\theta = \pi$ or $\epsilon = \epsilon_T = \beta$ but also for $\theta = 0$ or $\epsilon = \epsilon_N$. We get

$$\alpha_I + \epsilon_N = -(\alpha_I + \epsilon_T)$$

or

$$\alpha_I = -\frac{(\epsilon_N + \epsilon_T)}{2} \tag{65}$$

CREATION OF FAMILIES OF WING SECTIONS

The process of transforming a circle into an airfoil is inherently less difficult than the inverse process of transforming an airfoil into a circle. By a direct application of previous results we can derive a powerful and flexible method for the creation of general families of airfoils. Instead of assuming that the $\bar{\psi}(\theta)$ curve is preassigned (that is, instead of a given airfoil),

[25] Note that $\bar{\psi}(\theta + \pi) = -\bar{\psi}(\theta)$ for this case.

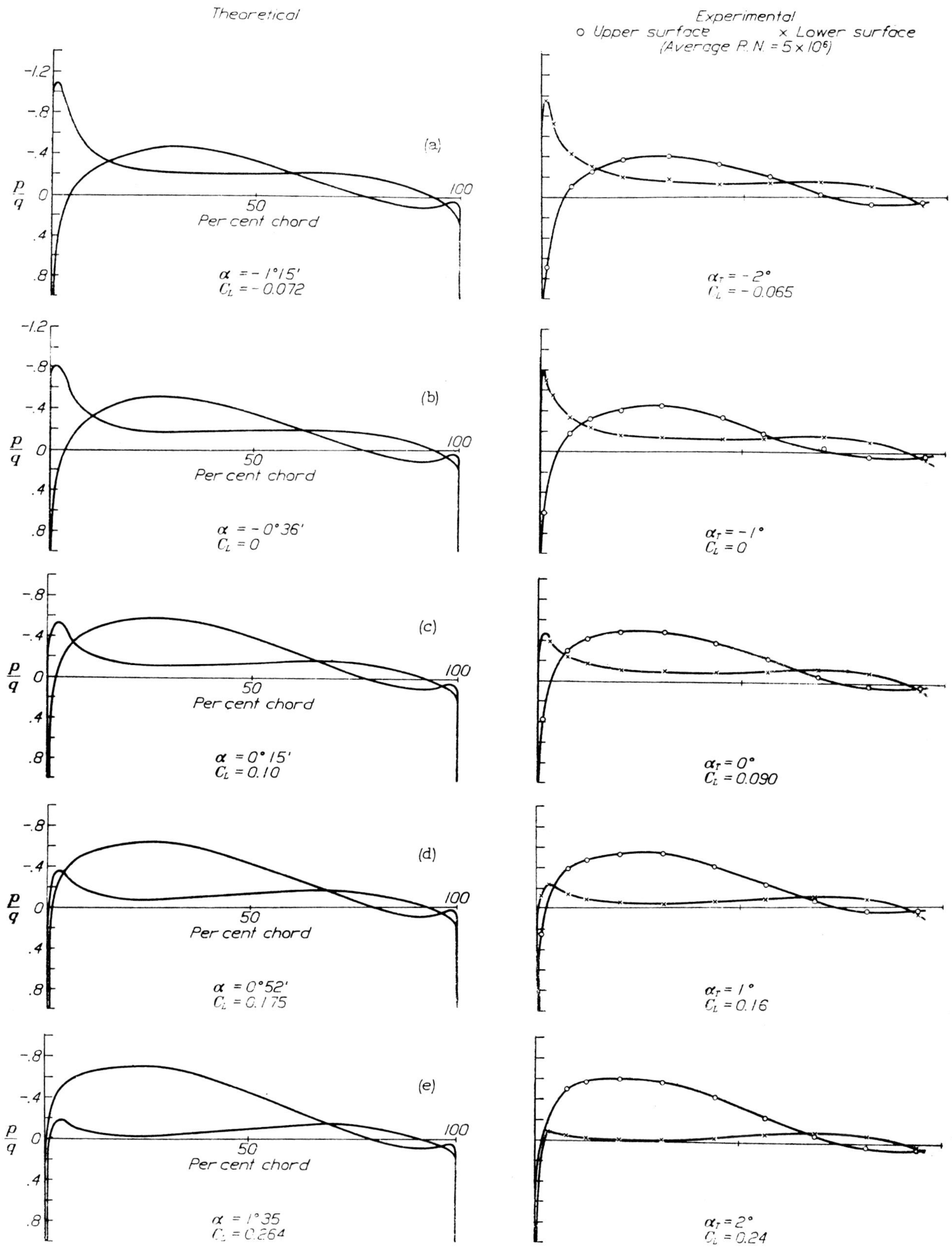

Fig. 28 a to e.—Theoretical and experimental pressure distribution for the M6 airfoil at various angles of attack.

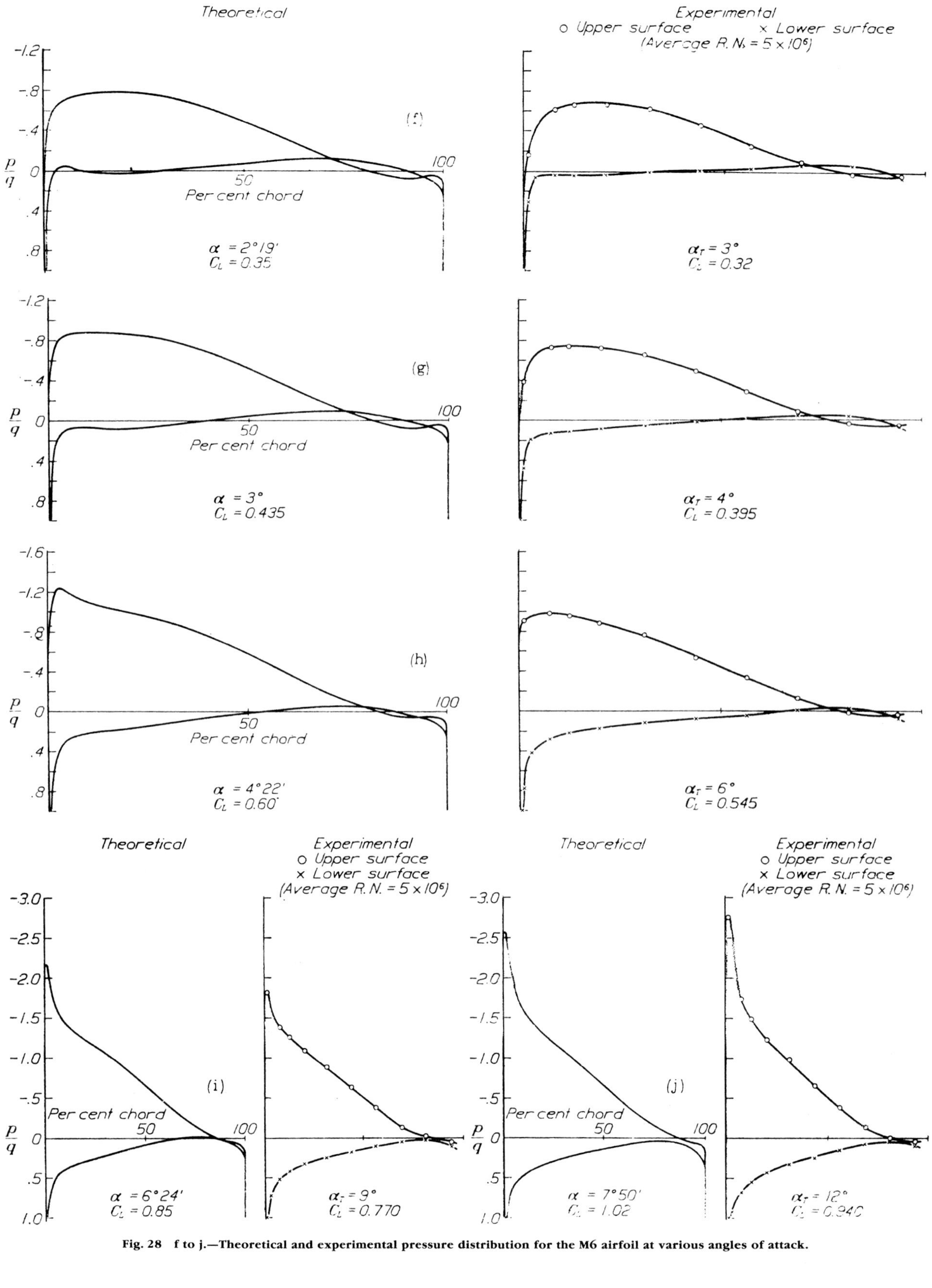

Fig. 28 f to j.—Theoretical and experimental pressure distribution for the M6 airfoil at various angles of attack.

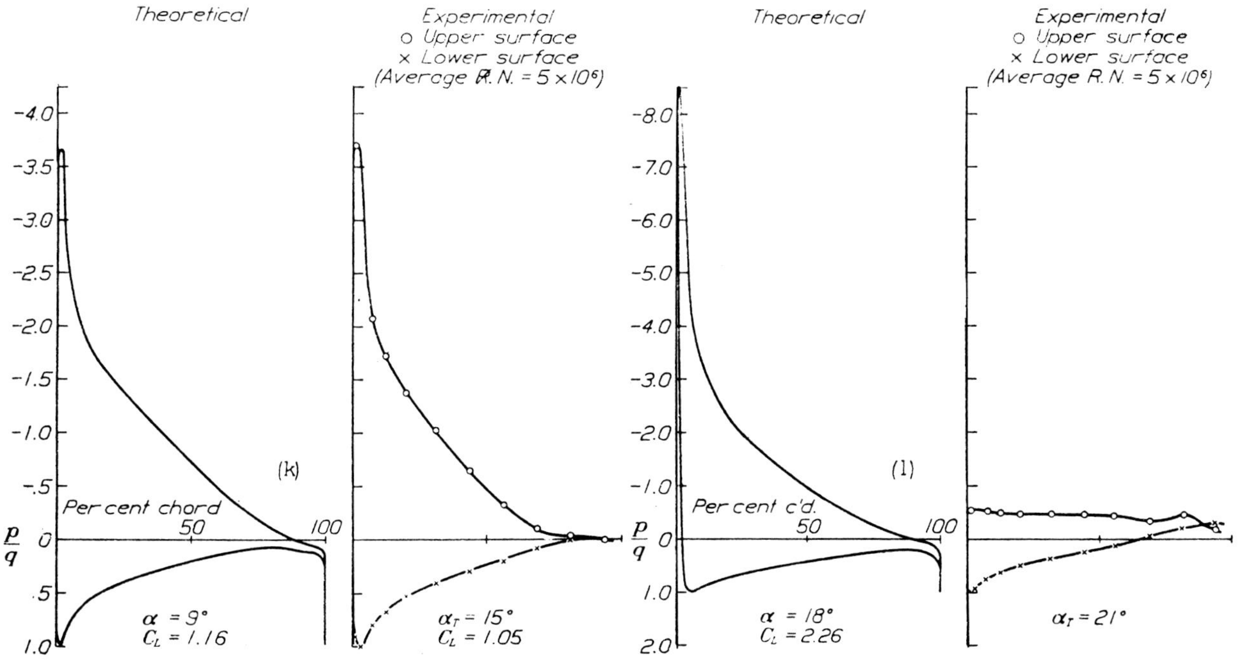

Fig. 28 k to l.—Theoretical and experimental pressure distribution for the M6 airfoil at various angles of attack.

we assume an arbitrary $\psi(\varphi)$ or $\epsilon(\varphi)$ curve[26] as given. This is equivalent to assuming as known a boundary-value function along a circle and, by the proper choice of this function, one can determine airfoil shapes of definite properties. The $\epsilon(\varphi)$ function, which we have designated conformal angular distortion function, will be seen to determine not only the shape but also to give easily all the theoretical aerodynamic characteristics of the airfoil.

An arbitary $\epsilon(\varphi)$ curve is chosen, single-valued, of period 2π, of zero area, and such that $-\infty \leq d\epsilon/d\varphi \leq 1$. These limiting values of $d\epsilon/d\varphi$ are far beyond values yielding airfoil shapes.[27] The $\psi(\varphi)$ function, except for the constant ψ_0, is given by the conjugate of the Fourier expansion of $\epsilon(\theta)$ or, what is the same, by evaluating Eq. (14) as a definite integral. The constant ψ_0 is an important arbitrary[28] parameter which permits changes in the shape and for a certain range of values may determine the sharpness of the trailing edge.

We first obtain the variable θ as $\theta(\varphi) = \varphi - \epsilon(\varphi)$, so that the quantity ψ considered as a function of θ is $\bar{\psi}(\theta) = \psi[\varphi(\theta)]$. The coordinates of the airfoil surface are then

$$\left.\begin{aligned} x &= 2a \cosh\psi \cos\theta \\ y &= 2a \sinh\psi \sin\theta \end{aligned}\right\} \qquad (6)$$

The velocity at the surface is

$$v = V \frac{[\sin(\alpha + \varphi) + \sin(\alpha + \beta)]\, e^{\psi_0}}{\sqrt{(\sinh^2\psi + \sin^2\theta)\left[1 - \left(\frac{d\epsilon}{d\varphi}\right)^2 + \left(\frac{d\psi}{d\varphi}\right)^2\right]}} \qquad (39')$$

and is obtained by using Eq. (37′) instead of (37) in deriving (39). Then angle of zero lift β is given by

$$\varphi(\theta) = \theta + \bar{\epsilon}(\theta) \quad \text{for } \theta = \pi, \qquad \text{i.e., } \varphi(\pi) = \pi + \beta$$

The following figures and examples will make the process clear. We may first note that the most natural method of specifying the $\epsilon(\varphi)$ function is by a Fourier series expansion. In this sense then the elementary types of $\epsilon(\varphi)$ functions are the individual terms of this expansion.

Consider first the effect of the first-harmonic term

$$\epsilon(\varphi) = A_1 \sin(\varphi - \delta_1), \qquad \psi_0 = c$$

In Fig. 29(a) to 29(g) may be seen the shapes resulting by displacing δ_1 successively by intervals of 15° and

[26]Subject to some general restrictions given in the next paragraph.

[27]For common airfoils, with a proper choice of orgin, $|d\epsilon/d\varphi| \ll 0.30$.

[28]For common airfoils ψ_0 is usually between 0.05 and 0.15. The constant ψ_0 is not, however, completely arbitrary. We have seen that the condition given by Eq. (22) is sufficient to yield a contour free from double points in the z' plane. We may also state the criterion that the inverse of Eq. (5) applied to this contour shall yield a contour in the ζ plane free from double points. Consider the function $\bar{\psi}(\theta)$ for θ varying from 0 to π only. The negative of each value of $\bar{\psi}(\theta)$ in this range is considered associated with $-\theta$, i.e., $\pi \leq \theta \leq 2\pi$. Designate the function thus formed from $\theta = 0$ to 2π by $\bar{\psi}(\theta)^*$. Then $\bar{\psi}(\theta)^*$ represents a line arc in the ζ plane, i.e., the upper surface of a contour. (See footnote 25.) Then for the entire contour to be free from double points it is necessary that the lower surface should not cross the upper, that is, the *original* $\bar{\psi}(\theta)$ curve for θ varying from π to 2π must not cross below $\bar{\psi}(\theta)^*$.

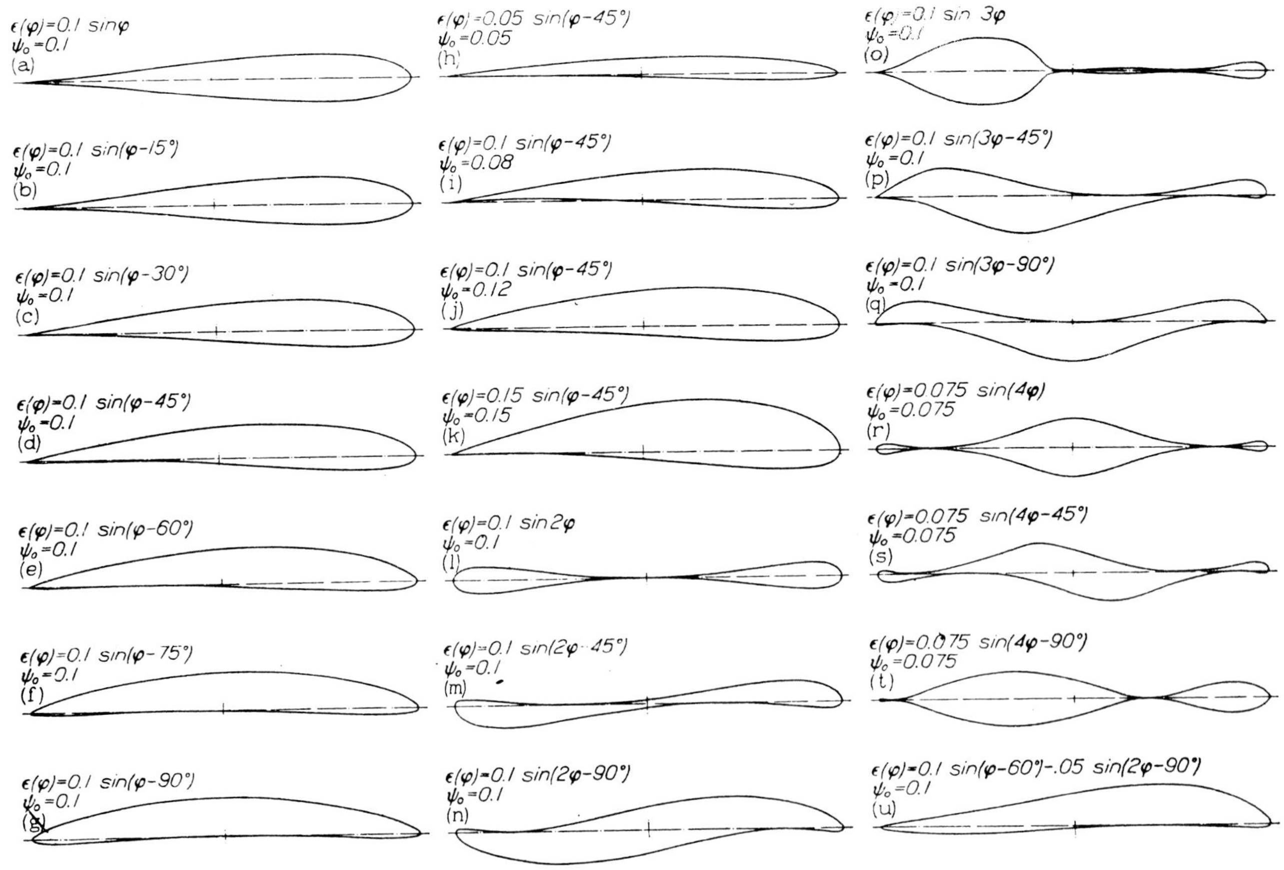

Fig. 29 Airfoils created by varying $\epsilon(\varphi)$.

keeping the constants $A_1 = 0.10$ and $\psi_0 = 0.10$. The first harmonic term is of chief influence in determining the airfoil shape. The case $\epsilon(\varphi) = 0.1\ \sin(\varphi - 45°)$ is detailed in Table II. (This airfoil is remarkably close to the commonly used Clark Y airfoil.) The entire calculations are characterized by their simplicity and, as may be noted, are completely free from the necessity of any graphical evaluations or constructions.

The effect of the second and higher harmonics as well as the constant ψ_0 may be observed in Fig. 29(h) to 29(t). In particular, the second-harmonic term may yield S shapes, and by a proper combination of first- and second-harmonic terms, i.e., by a proper choice of the constants A_1, A_2, δ_1, and δ_2 in the relation

$$\epsilon(\varphi) = A_1\ \sin(\varphi - \delta_1) + A_2\ \sin(2\varphi - \delta_2)$$

it is possible to fix the focus F of the lift parabola as the center of pressure for all angles of attack.[29] The equation

$$\epsilon(\varphi) = 0.1\ \sin(\varphi - 60°) + 0.05\ \cos 2\varphi$$

represents such an airfoil and is shown in Fig. 29(u).

The general process will yield infinite varieties of contours by superposition of sine functions; in fact, if the process is thought of as a boundary-value problem of the circle, it is seen that it is sufficiently general to yield every closed curve for which Riemann's theorem applies.

Langley Memorial Aeronautical Laboratory
National Advisory Committee for Aeronautics
Langley Field, Va., November 4, 1932.

---

[29]This is accomplished as follows: We seek to determine the constants A_1, A_2, δ_1, and δ_2 so that $\beta = \gamma$, where γ is obtained from Eq. (25′) as $a_1 = b^2e^{2i\gamma} = a^2 + (c_1{}^2/2) + c_2$ and we may note that $(c_1/ae^{\psi_0}) = A_1e^{i\delta_1}$ and $(c_1/a^2e^{2\psi_0}) = A_2e^{i\delta_2}$. These relations are transcendental; however, with but a few practice trials, solutions can be obtained at will. Addition of higher harmonics will yield further shapes having the same center-of-pressure properties if β is kept unchanged.

APPENDIX

I. EVALUATION OF THE INTEGRAL

$$\epsilon(\varphi') = -\frac{1}{2\pi}\int_0^{2\pi} \psi(\varphi)\cot\frac{\varphi-\varphi'}{2}\,d\varphi \qquad (13)$$

$$= \frac{1}{\pi}\int_0^{2\pi} \frac{d\psi(\varphi)}{d\varphi}\log\left|\sin\frac{\varphi-\varphi'}{2}\right| d\varphi \qquad (13')$$

The function $\psi(\varphi)$ is of period 2π and is considered known. (Note that the variables φ and φ' are replaced by θ and θ', φ_1', φ_2 and φ_2', etc., in Eq. (21) and that the following formula is applicable for all these cases.)

A 20-point method for evaluating Eq. (13) as a definite integral gives

$$\epsilon(\varphi') \simeq -\frac{1}{\pi}\left[a_0\frac{d\psi(\varphi)}{d\varphi} + a_1(\psi_1 - \psi_{-1}) + a_2(\psi_2 - \psi_{-2}) + \cdots + a_9(\psi_9 - \psi_{-9})\right]_{\varphi=\varphi'} \qquad (I)$$

where

$$\psi_1 = \text{value of } \psi(\varphi) \text{ at } \varphi = \varphi' + \frac{\pi}{10}$$

$$\cdots\cdots$$

$$\psi_n = \text{value of } \psi(\varphi) \text{ at } \varphi = \varphi' + \frac{n\pi}{10}$$

$$(n = 1, -1, 2, -2, \ldots 9, -9).$$

and the constants a_n are as folows: $a_0 = \pi/10 = 0.3142$; $a_1 = 1.091$; $a_2 = 0.494$; $a_3 = 0.313$; $a_4 = 0.217$; $a_5 = 0.158$; $a_6 = 0.115$; $a_7 = 0.0884$; $a_8 = 0.0511$; and $a_9 = 0.0251$.

This formula may be derived directly from the definition of the definite integral. The 20 intervals[1] chosen are $\varphi - \pi/20$ to $\varphi + \pi/20$, $\varphi + \pi/20$ to $\varphi + 3\pi/20$, etc. It is only necessary to note that by expanding $\psi(\varphi)$ in a Taylor series around $\varphi = \varphi'$ we get

$$\frac{1}{2}\int_{\varphi'-s}^{\varphi'+s} \psi(\varphi)\cot\frac{\varphi-\varphi'}{2}\,d\varphi \simeq -2s\left[\frac{d\psi(\varphi)}{d\varphi}\right]_{\varphi=\varphi'}$$

where the interval $\varphi - s$ to $\varphi' + s$ is small; and, in general—

$$\frac{1}{2}\int_{\varphi_s}^{\varphi_s} \psi(\varphi)\cot\frac{\varphi-\varphi'}{2}\,d\varphi \simeq -2s\left[\frac{d\psi(\varphi)}{d\varphi}\right]_{\varphi=\varphi'}$$

is very nearly

$$-\psi_A \log\left|\frac{\sin\dfrac{\varphi-\varphi_2}{2}}{\sin\dfrac{\varphi-\varphi_1}{2}}\right|$$

where the range $\varphi_2 - \varphi_1$ is small and ψ_A is the average value of $\psi(\varphi)$ in this range. The constants a_n for the 20 divisions chosen above are actually

$$a_n = \log\left|\frac{\sin\pi\dfrac{2n+1}{40}}{\sin\pi\dfrac{2n-1}{40}}\right| \quad (n = -9, \ldots +9)$$

As an example of the calculation of $\bar{\epsilon}(\theta)$ we may refer to Table I and Fig. 26 and 27 for the N.A.C.A. –M6 airfoil. From the $\bar{\psi}(\theta)$ curve (Fig. 27) we obtain the 20 values of ψ and $d\bar{\psi}/d\theta$ for 20 equal intervals of θ. For the airfoil (Fig. 26) we get the following values:

(Upper θ surface)	ψ	$\frac{d\bar{\psi}}{d\theta}$	(Lower θ surface)	ψ	$\frac{d\bar{\psi}}{d\theta}$
0 (nose)	0. 192	0. 000	$\frac{11\pi}{10}$	0. 049	−0. 002
$\frac{\pi}{10}$	. 185	. 027	$\frac{12\pi}{10}$	. 057	. 050
$\frac{2\pi}{10}$	. 192	. 000	$\frac{13\pi}{10}$	. 071	. 030
$\frac{3\pi}{10}$	. 189	−. 030	$\frac{14\pi}{10}$	. 077	. 011
$\frac{4\pi}{10}$	. 174	−. 064	$\frac{15\pi}{10}$	. 079	. 000
$\frac{5\pi}{10}$	. 146	−. 095	$\frac{16\pi}{10}$	. 082	. 016
$\frac{6\pi}{10}$	. 110	−. 114	$\frac{17\pi}{10}$	. 090	. 039
$\frac{7\pi}{10}$	. 077	−. 086	$\frac{18\pi}{10}$	. 111	. 091
$\frac{8\pi}{10}$	. 052	−. 066	$\frac{19\pi}{10}$	. 150	. 154
$\frac{9\pi}{10}$	. 041	. 025	2π (nose)	. 192	. 000
π (tail)	. 055	. 000			

The value of ϵ at the tail (i.e., the angle of zero lift) is, for example, using formula I:

$$\epsilon = -\frac{1}{\pi}\left[\frac{\pi}{10}\times 0 \right.$$
$$+ 1.091(.049 - .041)$$
$$+ .494(.057 - .052)$$
$$+ .313(.071 - .077)$$
$$+ .217(.077 - .110)$$
$$+ .158(.079 - .146)$$
$$+ .115(.082 - .174)$$
$$+ .0884(.090 - .189)$$
$$+ .0511(.111 - .192)$$
$$+ .0251(.150 - .185) = .0105$$

[1]Reference 2, p. 11, gives a 10-point-method result.

The value of ϵ for $\theta = 3\pi/10$, for example, is obtained by a cyclic rearrangement. Thus:

$$\epsilon = -\frac{1}{\pi}\left[\frac{\pi}{10}(.030)\right.$$
$$+ 1.091(.174 - .192)$$
$$+ .494(.146 - .185)$$
$$+ .313(.110 - .192)$$
$$+ .217(.077 - .150)$$
$$+ .158(.052 - .111)$$
$$+ .115(.041 - .090)$$
$$+ .0884(.055 - .082)$$
$$+ .0511(.049 - .079)$$
$$+ .0251(.057 - .077) = .0347$$

The 20 values obtained in this way form the $\bar{\epsilon}_1(\theta)$ curve, which, for all practical purposes for the airfoil considered, is actually identical with the final $\bar{\epsilon}(\theta)$ curve.

II. NOTES ON THE TRANSFORMATION

$$\zeta = f(z) = c_1 + z + \frac{a_1}{z} + \frac{a_2}{z^2} + \cdots \qquad (4')$$

There exist a number of theorems giving general limiting values for the coefficients of the transformation [Eq. (4)] that are interesting and to some extent useful. If $\zeta = f(z)$ transforms the external region of the circle C of radius R in the z plane, into the external region of a contour A in the ζ plane in a one-to-one conformal manner and the origin $\zeta = 0$ lies *within* the contour A (and $f'(\infty) = 1$), then the area S enclosed by A is given by the Faber-Bieberbach theorem as[2]

$$S = R^2\pi - \sum_{n=1}^{\infty} \frac{n\,|a_n|^2}{R^{2(n+1)}}$$

Since all members of the above series term are positive, it is observed that the area of C is greater than that enclosed by any contour A in the ζ plane (or, at most, equal to the area enclosed by A if A is a circle).

This theorem leads to the following results:

$$|a_1| \le R^2 \qquad \text{(a)}$$

$$|c_1| \le 2R \qquad \text{(b)}$$

Let us designate the circle of radius R about the conformal centroid M as center as C_1 (i.e., the center is at $\zeta = c_1$; this circle has been called the "Grundkreis" or "basic" circle by von Mises). Then since $|a_1|/R$ represents the distance of the focus F from M, the relation (a) states that the focus is always within C_1. In fact, a further extension shows that if r_0 is the radius of the largest circle that can be enclosed within A, then F is removed from C_1 by at least r_0^2/R.

From relation (b) may be derived the statement that if any circle within A is concentrically double in radius it is contained entirely within a circle about M as center of radius $2R$. Also, if we designate by c the largest diameter of A (this is usually the "chord" of the airfoil), then the following limits can be derived:

$$R \ge \frac{1}{4}c$$

$$R \le \frac{1}{2}c$$

These inequalities lead to interesting limits for the lift coefficient. Writing the lift coefficient as

$$C_L = \frac{L}{½\rho V^2 c}$$

where by Eq. (45) the lift force is given by

$$L = 4\pi R \rho V^2 \sin(\alpha + \beta)$$

we have

$$\pi \sin(\alpha + \beta) \le C_L = \frac{8\pi R}{c} \sin(\alpha + \beta) \le 4\pi \sin(\alpha + \beta) \qquad \text{(II)}$$

The flat plate is the only case where the lower limit is reached, while the upper limit is attained for the circular cylinder only. We may observe that a curved thin plate has a lift coefficient which exceeds $2\pi \sin(\alpha + \beta)$ by a very small amount. In general, the thickness has a much greater effect on the value of the lift coefficient than the camber. For common airfoils the lift coefficient is but slightly greater than the lower limit and is approximately $1.1 \times 2\pi \sin(\alpha + \beta)$.

Another theorem, similar to the Faber-Bieberbach

[2]For details of this and following statements see Ref. 5, p. 100 and p. 147, an also Ref. 6, P II.

[3]Müller, W., *Zs. f. angew. Math. u. Mech.* Bd. 5, S. 397, 1925. Höhndorf, F., *Zs. f. angew. Math. u. Mech.* Bd. 6, S. 265, 1926. Also Ref. 5, p. 185.

area theorem, states that if the equation $\zeta = f(z)$ transforms the internal region of a circle in the ζ plane into the internal region of a contour B in the ζ plane in a one-to-one conformal manner and $f'(0) = 1$ (the origins are within the contours) then the area of the circle is less than that contained by any contour B. This theorem, extended by Bieberbach, has been used in an attempt to solve the arbitrary airfoil.[3] The process used is one in which the area theorem is a criterion as to the direction in which the convergence proceeds. Although theoretically sound, the process is, when applied, extremely laborious and very slowly convergent. It cannot be said to have yielded as yet really satisfactory results.

III. LOCATION OF THE CENTER OF PRESSURE FOR AN ARBITRARY AIRFOIL

It is of some interest to know the exact location of the center of pressure *on the x axis* as a function of the angle of attack. In Fig. 30, O is the origin, M the conformal centroid, L the line of action of the lift force for angle of attack α. Let us designate the intersection of L with the x axis of the airfoil as the center of pressure P. In the right ΔONM we have

$$OM = c_1 = me^{i\delta} = A_1 + iB_1$$

$$ON = m\cos\delta = A_1$$

$$MN = m\sin\delta = B_1$$

and in the right ΔJKM—

$$KM = \frac{MJ}{\sin\alpha} = \frac{h_M}{\sin\alpha}$$

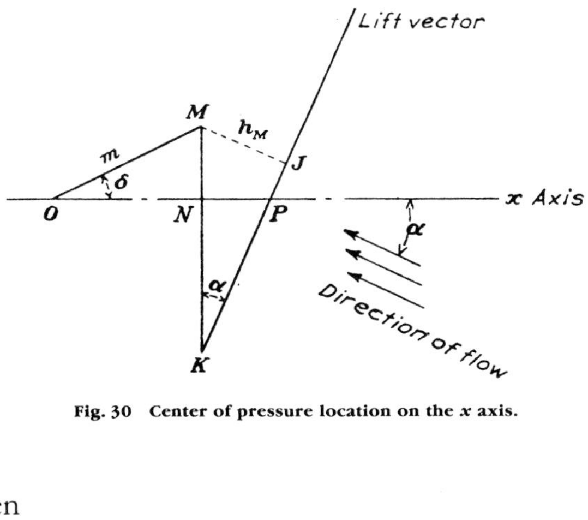

Fig. 30 Center of pressure location on the x axis.

Then

$$KN = \frac{h_M}{\sin\alpha} - B_1$$

and

$$NP = KN\tan\alpha = h_M\sec\alpha - B_1\tan\alpha$$

By Eq. (48):

$$h_M = \frac{M_M}{L} = \frac{b^2}{2R}\frac{\sin 2(\alpha+\gamma)}{\sin(\alpha+\beta)}$$

Then the distance from the origin to the center of pressure P is

$$OP = ON + NP = A_1 - B_1\tan\alpha$$

$$+ \frac{b^2}{2R}\frac{\sin 2(\alpha+\gamma)}{\cos\alpha\sin(\alpha+\beta)} \qquad \text{(III)}$$

EXPLANATION OF THE TABLES

Table I gives the essential data for transformation of the N.A.C.A.–M6 airfoil (shown in Fig. 26) into a circle, and yields readily the complete theoretical aerodynamical characteristics. Columns (1) and (2) define the airfoil surface in per cent chord; (3) and (4) are the coordinates after choosing a convenient origin (p. 7); (5) and (6) are obtained from Eq. (7) and (8) of the report; (9) is the evaluation of Eq. (13) (see Appendix); (10) and (11) are the slopes, obtained graphically, of the ψ against θ, and ϵ against θ curves, respectively; (12) is given by—

$$\frac{\left(1 + \frac{d\bar\epsilon}{d\theta}\right)e^{\psi_0}}{\sqrt{(\sinh^2\psi + \sin^2\theta)\left(1 + \left(\frac{d\bar\psi}{d\theta}\right)^2\right)}}$$

where

$$\psi_0 = \frac{1}{2\pi}\int_0^{2\pi}\psi(\varphi)\,d\varphi$$

and may be obtained graphically or numerically; column (13) gives $\varphi = \theta + \epsilon$. The velocity v, for any angle of attack, is by Eq. (39)

$$v = Vk\,[\sin(\alpha+\varphi) + \sin(\alpha+\beta)]$$

and the pressure is given by Eq. (3). The angle of zero lift β is the value of ϵ at the tail; i.e., the value of ϵ for $\theta = \pi$.

Table II gives numerical data for the inverse process

to that given in Table I; viz, the transformation of a circle into an airfoil (see Fig. 29). The function $\epsilon(\varphi) = 0.1\sin(\varphi - 45°)$ and constant $\psi_0 = 0.10$ are chosen for this case. Then $\psi(\varphi) = 0.1\cos(\varphi - 45°) + 0.10$. It may be observed that columns (11) and (12) giving the coordinates of the airfoil surface are obtained from Eq. (6) of the report. Column (13) is given by

$$k = \frac{e^{\psi_0}}{\sqrt{(\sinh^2\psi + \sin^2\theta)\left[\left(1 + \frac{d\epsilon}{d\varphi}\right)^2 + \left(\frac{d\psi}{d\varphi}\right)^2\right]}}$$

and from Eq. (39′) the velocity at the surface is

$$v = Vk\,[\sin(\alpha + \varphi) + \sin(\alpha + \beta)]$$

REFERENCES

1. Lamb, H., *Hydrodynamics,* Fifth Edition, Cambridge University Press, 1924.

2. Theodorsen, Theodore, "Theory of Wing Sections of Arbitrary Shape," T.R. No. 411, N.A.C.A., 1931.

3. Kellogg, O.D., *Foundations of Potential Theory,* J. Springer, Berlin, 1929.

4. Glauert, H., *The Elements of Aerofoil and Airscrew Theory,* Cambridge University Press, 1926.

5. Schmidt, H., *Aerodynamik des Fluges,* W. de Gryter, Berlin, 1929.

6. von Mises, R., "Zur Theorie des Tragflächenauftriebs," *Zeitschr. f. Flugtechn. u. Motorluftschiffarhrt,* First Part: (23–24) Bd. 8, 1917; Second Part: (5–6) Bd. 11, 1920.

7. Müller, W., *Mathematische Strömungslehre,* J. Springer, Berlin, 1928.

8. Theodorsen, Theodore, "Theory of Wing Sections with Particular Reference to the Lift Distribution," T.R. No. 383, N.A.C.A., 1931.

9. Dryden, Murnaghan, and Bateman, *Hydrodynamics,* National Research Council, Washington, 1932.

EXPERIMENTAL VERIFICATION OF THE THEORY OF WIND-TUNNEL BOUNDARY INTERFERENCE

BY THEODORE THEODORSEN
AND ABE SILVERSTEIN

National Advisory Committee for Aeronautics

Report No. 478, 1934

SUMMARY

The results of an experimental investigation on the boundary-correction factor, conducted at the N.A.C.A. laboratories at Langley Field, Va., are presented in this report. The values of the boundary-correction factor from the theory, which at the present time is virtually completed, are given in the paper for all conventional types of tunnels.

With the isolation of certain disturbing effects, the experimental boundary-correction factor was found to be in satisfactory agreement with the theoretically predicted values, thus verifying the soundness and sufficiency of the theoretical analysis. The establishment of a considerable velocity distortion, in the nature of a unique blocking effect, constitutes a principal result of the investigation.

The major portion of the investigation was carried on in the N.A.C.A. full-scale wind tunnel, which afforded the unusual opportunity of a direct comparison with flight results as a final verification.

INTRODUCTION

A number of theoretical papers have recently appeared on the subject of wind-tunnel interference. The theory has in particular been extended to include the effect of a finite airfoil span. The correction factors are available for all ordinary types of tunnels and all airfoil spans. The curves presented in figure 1 embrace virtually all important results on the boundary-correction factors. The curves for the open and closed elliptical sections are taken from a recent paper by Tani and Sanuki (reference 1); the curve for the correction factor of the closed rectangular tunnel from a paper by Glauert (reference 2), the results of which have been extended to cover intermediate cases; while the final case of the open rectangular tunnel is taken from a paper by one of the authors (reference 3).

It remained to be shown whether experimental agreement with the theory existed. A paper by Knight and Harris on open-throat wind tunnels (reference 4), which was the only extensive experimental material available on the subject, gave an indication of conflicting results, inasmuch as the drag correction seemed to differ from the lift correction and no consistent agreement with the theory was obtained.

About 2 years ago a paper by one of the authors (reference 5) appeared on the correction factor for several special types of rectangular tunnels. Cases of zero wall interference were predicted [1] (fig. 2), and it was at the time decided to subject not only these, but the entire problem of boundary interference, to an extensive experimental study to verify the theory. This information became even more desirable with the construction of the full-scale tunnel.

This tunnel (reference 6) afforded the unique opportunity of measuring characteristics of airplanes at large Reynolds Numbers. The fact that accurate flight results were available for these airplanes permitted a critical checking of the corrected wind-tunnel characteristics. Any test errors or disregarded influences immediately revealed themselves, which served materially to guide the course and nature of the following investigations, and led to important conclusions.

The experiments on the boundary-interference factor were started originally in a 2- by 4-foot experimental model of the N.A.C.A. full-scale tunnel. The model tunnel was rebuilt with various modifications of the test section. Some tests were also conducted with the airfoils at various heights in the original open-throat model tunnel. This case has also been treated theoretically in reference 1, and typical numerical examples have been worked out in figure 3, which refers to airfoils of 40, 50, 60, and 70 percent spans at various heights in the full-scale tunnel and its model.

The experimental results from the model tunnel showed conflicting tendencies similar to those observed in reference 4. It is obvious that in tests of this nature the greatest accuracy is required; however, the inconsistencies persisted in spite of numerous refinements and checkings. The investigation was next extended to the full-scale tunnel. The preliminary results in the full-scale tunnel again conflicted with the theory;

[1] Glauert called attention to certain errors in these results; for the corrected values, see Rosenhead: Interference Due to a Wind Tunnel. Proceedings of the Royal Society, Oct. 2, 1933.

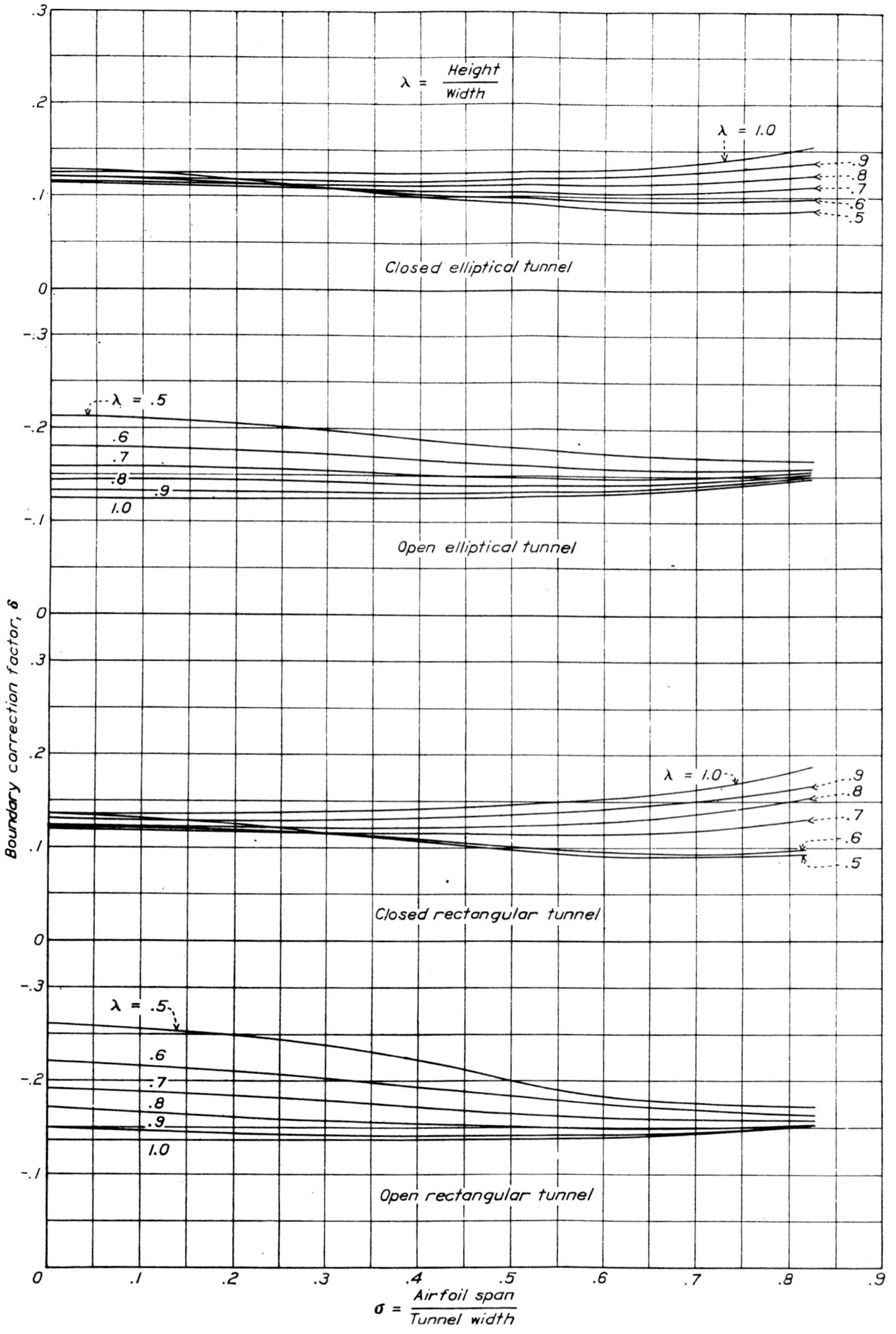

FIGURE 1.—Theoretical boundary correction factors for airfoils of finite span in conventional tunnel sections.

moreover, the corrected characteristics did not agree with flight results, indicating the presence of certain disturbing influences. The nature of these was finally disclosed and their effects are included in the results. The material is presented in chronological order.

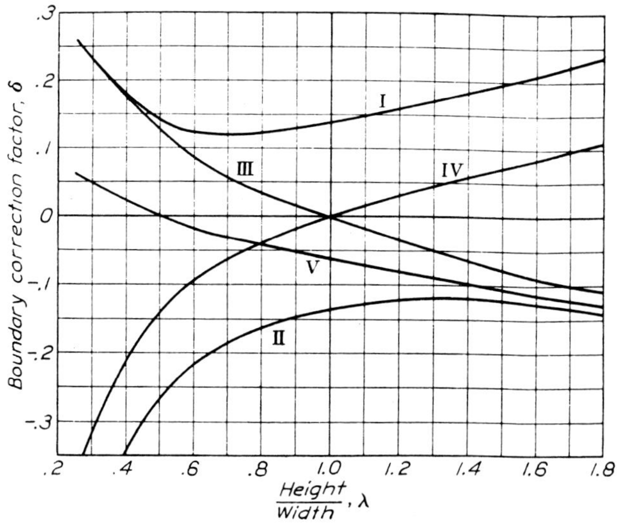

FIGURE 2.—Theoretical boundary correction factors for five types of rectangular tunnels (infinitely small airfoils). I, closed tunnel; II, free jet; III, horizontal boundaries; IV, vertical boundaries; V, one horizontal boundary.

The authors wish to extend their acknowledgment to Mr. Smith J. DeFrance, under whose supervision the tests in the full-scale tunnel were conducted and whose generous cooperation greatly facilitated the work.

MODEL TUNNEL INVESTIGATION

Tunnel and equipment.—The 1/15-scale model of the full-scale wind tunnel, in which the first test series was conducted, was built at the time the large tunnel was being designed to provide general knowledge of the air-flow characteristics and design information. The model tunnel is not an exact scale model of the final full-scale tunnel, owing to changes incorporated into the design of the large tunnel as a result of experience

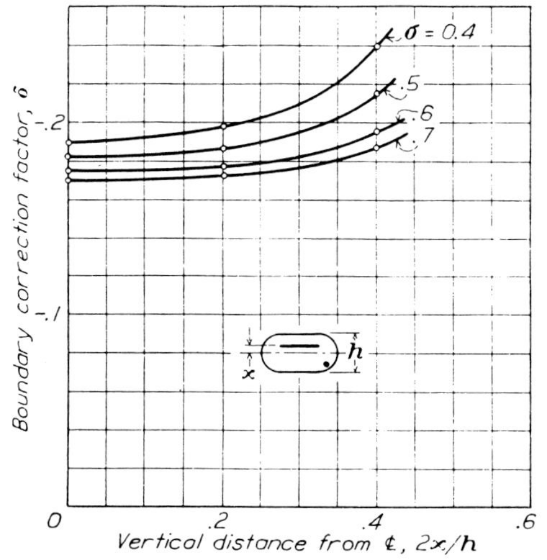

FIGURE 3.—Theoretical boundary correction factor for off-center positions of airfoils with σ=0.4, 0.5, 0.6, and 0.7 in an open elliptical tunnel (2:1 ellipse).

with the model. The entrance and exit cones of the model are, however, geometrically similar to those of the full-scale tunnel.

The model is an open-throat double-return-passage tunnel (fig. 4) with a jet cross section of 2 by 4 feet with parallel top and bottom and semicircular ends (fig. 5). The air is circulated by two propellers, each absorbing 15 horsepower at full load, driven by 2 direct-current motors. An area reduction of approximately 5 : 1 is effected in the double curved entrance cone. A collector bell is attached to the mouth of the exit cone, and the tunnel cross section increases almost uniformly from this point to the mouth of the entrance cone. A maximum velocity of about 85 miles per hour

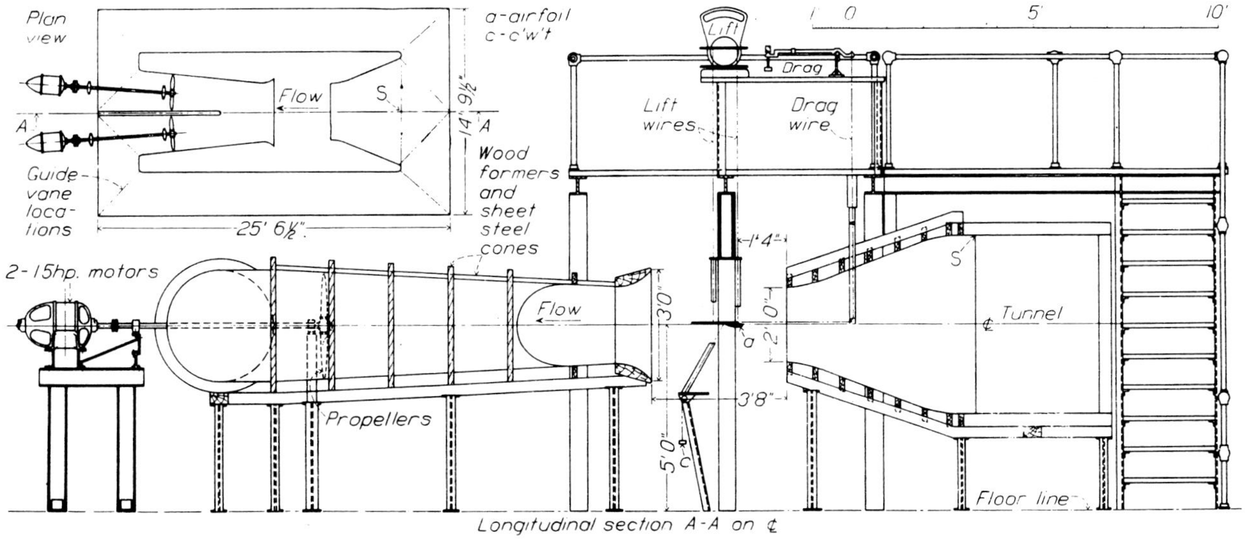

FIGURE 4.—Plan and elevation of model tunnel.

is attainable, and rheostats on the motors permit control to a minimum speed of 5 miles per hour. The energy ratio at maximum speed is 1.5. The dynamic

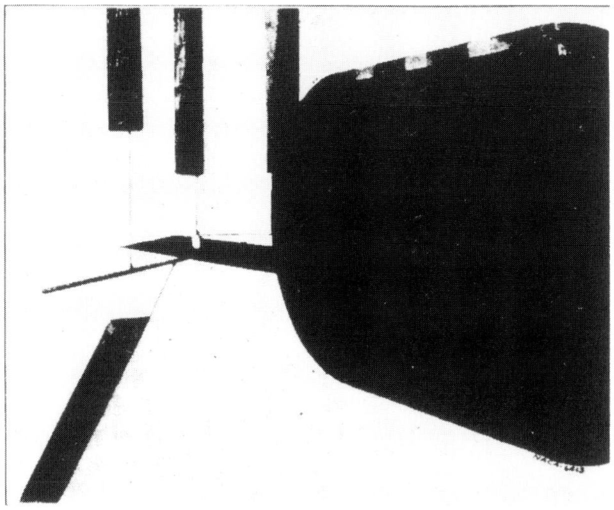

FIGURE 5.—Experimental set-up of Clark Y airfoil in model tunnel.

pressure at any point within the working portion of the jet is within 1 percent of the average value, and the direction of flow is within ±½° of the tunnel axis. The static pressure gradient along the axis of the jet is approximately zero in the region in which the airfoils were tested. The dynamic pressure at the test body is indicated by means of the differential pressure existing between a static pressure orifice in the entrance cone and the room pressure, which differential is measured on a standard N.A.C.A. micromanometer. The dynamic pressure is obtained by calibration of this differential pressure against a standard pitot tube; with the fairings for particular set-ups in position, pitot surveys are made across the area to be occupied by the airfoil and from an average of these surveys the calibration factor computed. The location of the static orifice is shown by S in figure 4.

A wire balance (figs. 5 and 6) is used to measure the forces on the airfoils. The vertical forces are transmitted to the lift scale overhead by three wires, the front two of which are connected by streamline lugs to the airfoil proper and the rear one is connected to a sting. A V-wire yoke connected to the same lugs and extending forward into the entrance cone is used to transmit the drag force. A single wire is connected between the apex of the V and the bell crank in the drag strut, from which point the drag force is transmitted upward to the scale. A counterweight, used to hold the proper tension in the wires, is connected through a wire to the airfoil sting. A pendulum-type dial scale is used to measure the lift, and a beam scale is used for the drag. The angle of attack is measured by a sensitive inclinometer, the precision being in the order of ±0.05°. The tare drag is reduced to a minimum by the use of fairings over the wires. These fairings are dimensioned in sizes proportional to the

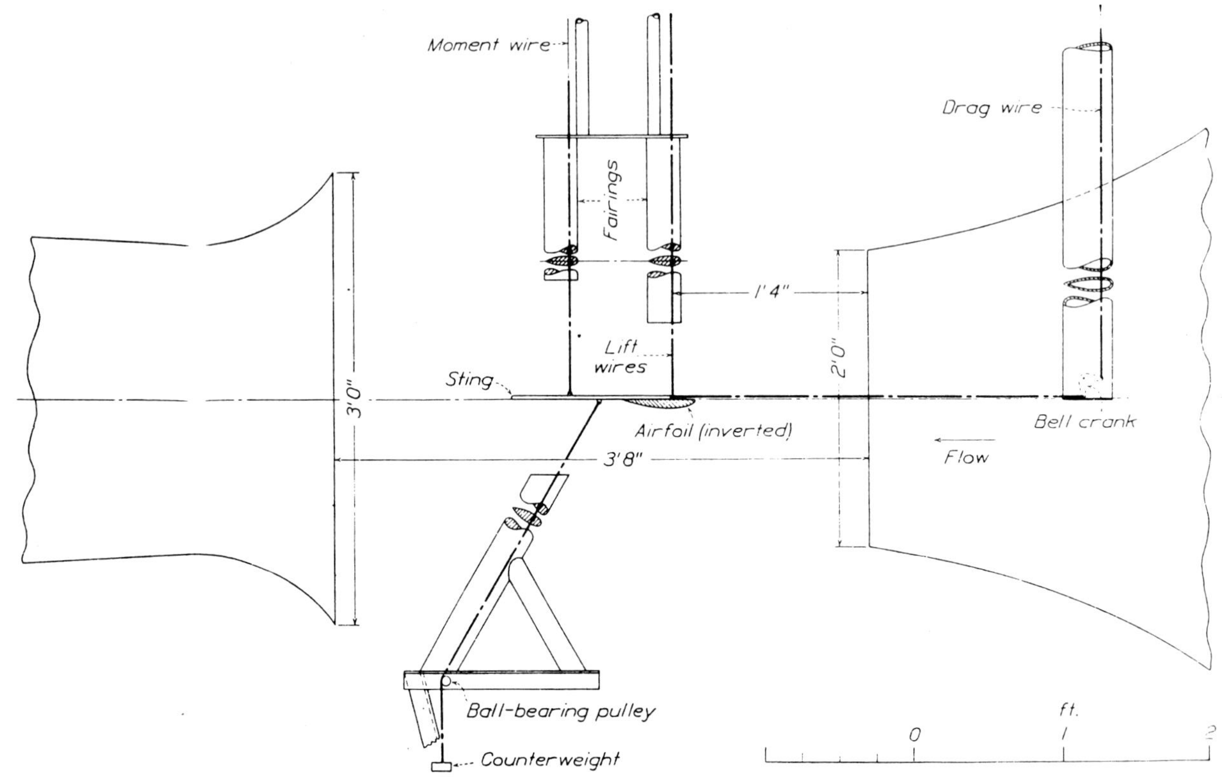

FIGURE 6.—Arrangement of airfoil on balance in model tunnel.

airfoil chords and, through the additional precaution of scaling all wires and fittings in these same proportions, practically the same tare drag coefficient is present with all set-ups.

Four duralumin Clark Y airfoils were used as standards throughout the entire test series in the model tunnel. These airfoils were of 3-, 4-, 5-, and 6-inch chords, and of aspect ratio 6. Since small inaccuracies in the airfoil sections in certain critical locations are detrimental to the precision of the tests, the airfoils were carefully inspected and measured and no serious irregularities were disclosed.

Tests and results.—The boundary correction factor δ is conventionally defined by the relations,

$$\Delta\alpha = \delta \times \frac{S}{C} \times C_L \tag{1}$$

and

$$\Delta C_D = \delta \times \frac{S}{C} \times C_L^2 \tag{2}$$

where $\Delta\alpha$ is the *upward* deflection of the air stream at the airfoil and ΔC_D is the corresponding *decrease* in the drag caused by the presence of the boundaries. S is the airfoil area and C is the cross-sectional area of the jet. In accordance with this definition, the values of $\Delta\alpha$, ΔC_D, and the correction factor δ are positive for the closed tunnel and negative for the open.

The routine procedure for obtaining the experimental boundary correction δ involves the plotting of characteristics with the extrapolation to free-air conditions. These plots for the model-tunnel tests have not been included and, in order to illustrate the method of derivation of the boundary factors, the corresponding plots for the full-scale tunnel will temporarily be made use of here. Figure 27 shows lift and drag against the geometric angle of attack measured from zero lift for the series of four Clark Y airfoils in the full-scale tunnel. The results are extrapolated to a zero value of $\frac{S}{C}$ as illustrated in figure 28. The zero value of $\frac{S}{C}$ corresponds to the free-air condition or the case of zero boundary correction.

It is then possible to plot directly the stream deflection $\Delta\alpha$ and drag decrease ΔC_D against C_L and C_L^2, respectively (fig. 29). Equations (1) and (2) furnish by substitution the experimentally derived values of δ.

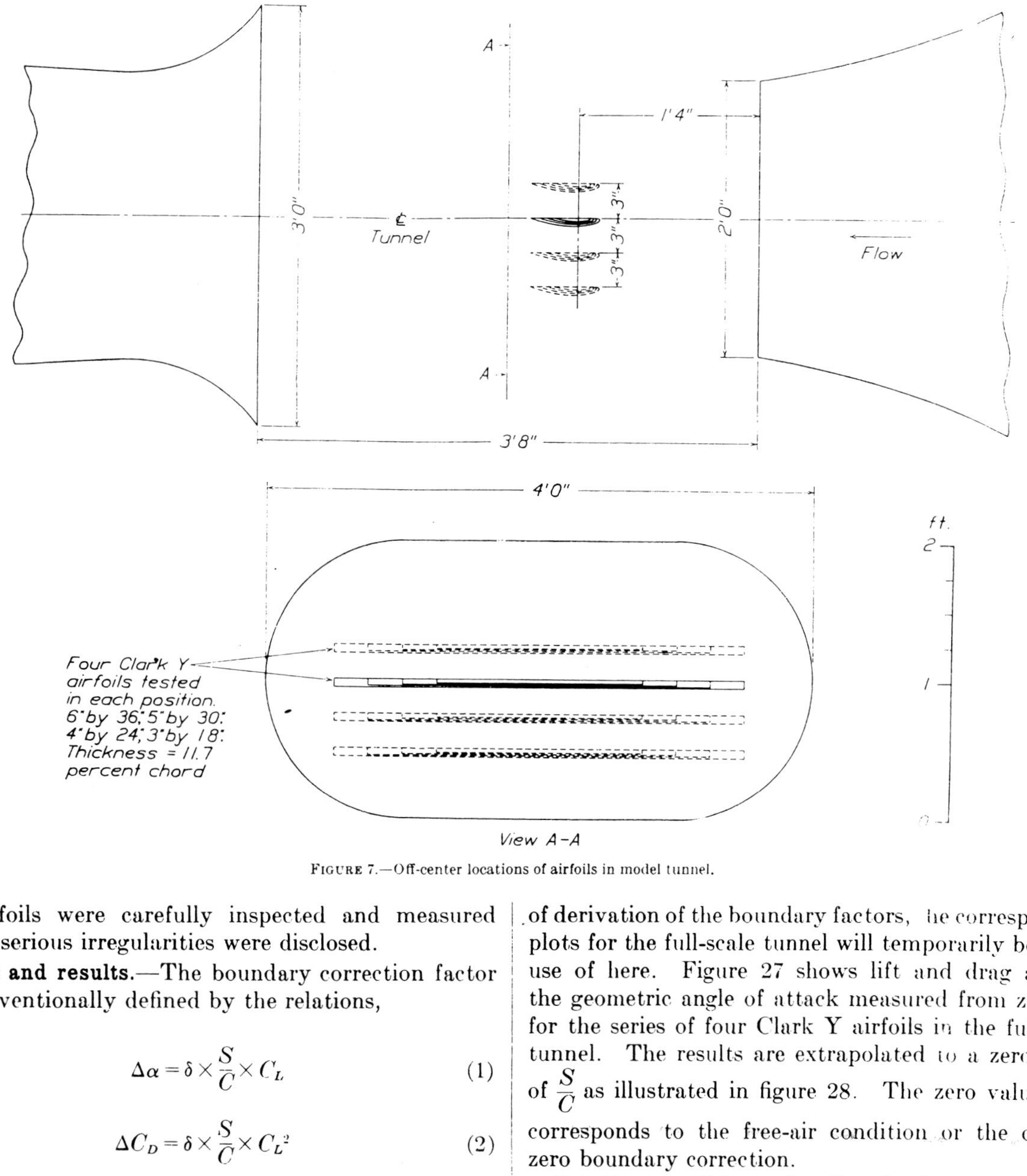

FIGURE 7.—Off-center locations of airfoils in model tunnel.

It is mentioned at this point that the possible effect of scale was eliminated by using tests of the same Reynolds Number throughout the preceding analysis. The velocities used were 80, 60, 48, and 40 miles per hour for the 3-, 4-, 5-, and 6-inch chord airfoils, respectively. Upright and inverted tests were made for each airfoil to determine the effective tunnel axis.

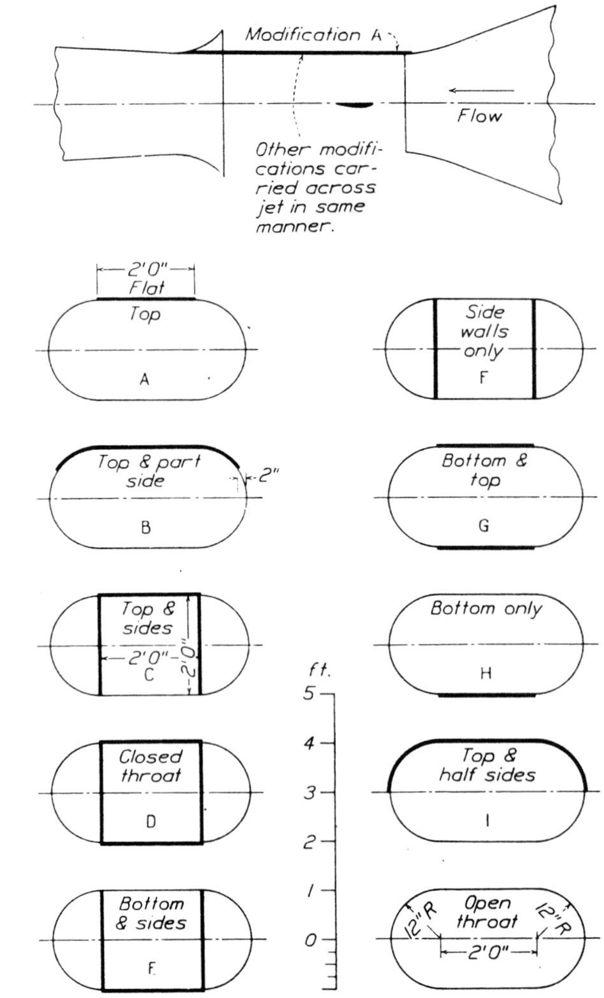

FIGURE 8.—Modifications of model tunnel test chamber.

A total of 29 tests was made in the model tunnel to obtain the desired data. These consisted of the following:

(a) Sixteen tests on the four airfoils, each being tested in four positions in the original tunnel. (Fig. 7 shows positions.)

(b) Thirteen tests to verify the effects of various boundary restraints as predicted in reference 5. These tests were performed in nine modified tunnel types, as lettered from A to I in figure 8. It was necessary in several of the types to restrict the tests to the 3-inch airfoil, inasmuch as the limited width of the tunnel in these cases prohibited the use of an airfoil span in excess of 18 inches.

The results of the tests under (a) are given in figure 9, in which δ_α is the correction factor obtained from equation (1) and δ_D is the correction factor as obtained from equation (2). The curves 1 to 4 refer to the center position in the tunnel. The correction factors δ_α and δ_D are not identical in value. According to theory, no such duplexity is conceded, the values δ in equations (1) and (2) being identical. The remaining tests, 5 to 16, give results for various off-center positions.

The main conclusion to be extracted from this rather chaotic evidence is the fact that the drag correction factors compare, at least approximately, with the theoretical value for the open elliptical tunnel (fig. 1), while the angle correction factors attain entirely too large values. The explanation and detection of the causes of this contradictory result presented themselves as the main objects of the subsequent research.

The results of the tests under (b) are given in figure 10. The tests 1 to 4 have again been included. The airfoils were tested *inverted* in the model tunnel, and this fact should be kept in mind in connection with the tunnel modifications. Test 17 refers to a tunnel with a top boundary only (or bottom with reference to the airfoil), designated modification A on figure 8. Test 18 is taken with the top extended somewhat farther (modification B). It appears from figure 2 that the expected boundary correction in these cases, more particularly the latter, should approximate zero. The experimental results show fair agreement; modification B shows a zero δ_D within experimental error and only a small discrepancy in δ_α at the higher lift coefficients.

Test 20 refers to modification D, which is a closed square tunnel. Figure 1 shows a theoretical value of 1.70 for a square closed tunnel $\lambda = 1$ with a span ratio $\sigma = 0.75$. The experimental result is in perfect agreement for the angle correction factor, δ_α, the value being exactly 1.70; although the drag correction factor, δ_D, is not constant, its average value is close to 1.70.

Test 23 on modification G with top and bottom boundaries shows a theoretical value from figure 2 of approximately zero. The experimental check is not as good, the angle and drag correction factors being of opposite sign and numerically too large.

Tests 24 and 25, representing modifications H and A, must theoretically lie somewhere between the value for a free jet and the value for case V in figure 2. It can be seen that test 24, with a small airfoil, approaches the case of a single horizontal boundary (V), inasmuch as the corrections are both close to zero, while test 25 with a larger airfoil shows values which approach more closely the values for a free jet.

The remaining tunnel modifications show, in general, the expected trends, but since some of these were not treated theoretically and are only of an academic interest, we shall present the results of these cases with no further comment.

A noteworthy feature of these experiments on modified tunnels is that the deviation from the predicted values becomes larger for partially and fully open tunnels, while quite close agreement is obtained for the closed type. The drag coefficient shows again the best agreement with the predicted values. The open tunnel (tests 1 to 4) shows the largest corrections.

A further peculiar result is shown in figure 11, which shows that the maximum lift coefficients for the airfoils tested in the open tunnel decrease with an increase in size. This result was rather unexpected since the tests were conducted at a given Reynolds Number and in the same tunnel. Obviously, some influence is present which has not formerly been considered.

It is evident from the preceding paragraphs that no really satisfactory agreement was obtained between

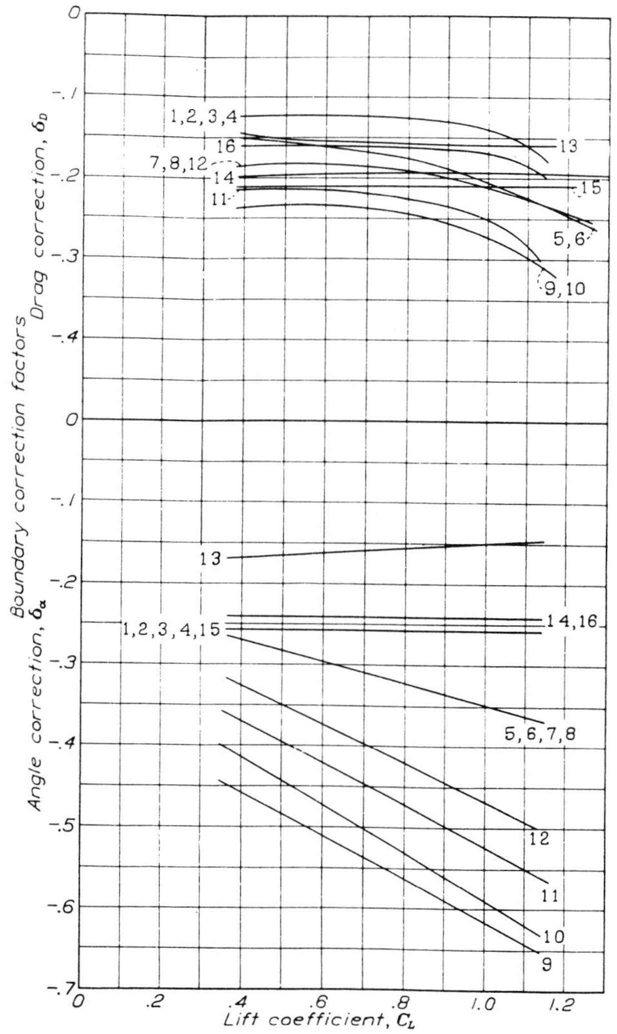

TABLE I

Test no.	1	2	3	4	5	6	7	8	9	10	11	12	13	14	15	16
Airfoil	3″	4″	5″	6″	3″	4″	5″	6″	3″	4″	5″	6″	[illegible]	4″	5″	6″
Position	c.l.[1]	c.l.	c.l.	c.l.	3″ below c.l.				6″ below c.l.				3″ above c.l.			
S/C	0.053	0.094	0.146	0.210	0.053	0.094	0.146	0.210	0.053	0.094	0.146	0.210	0.053	0.094	0.146	0.210

[1] Center line.

NOTE.—Airfoils tested in inverted position for above test.

FIGURE 9.—Angle and drag correction factors for the original model tunnel. (See table I.)

43860—34——2

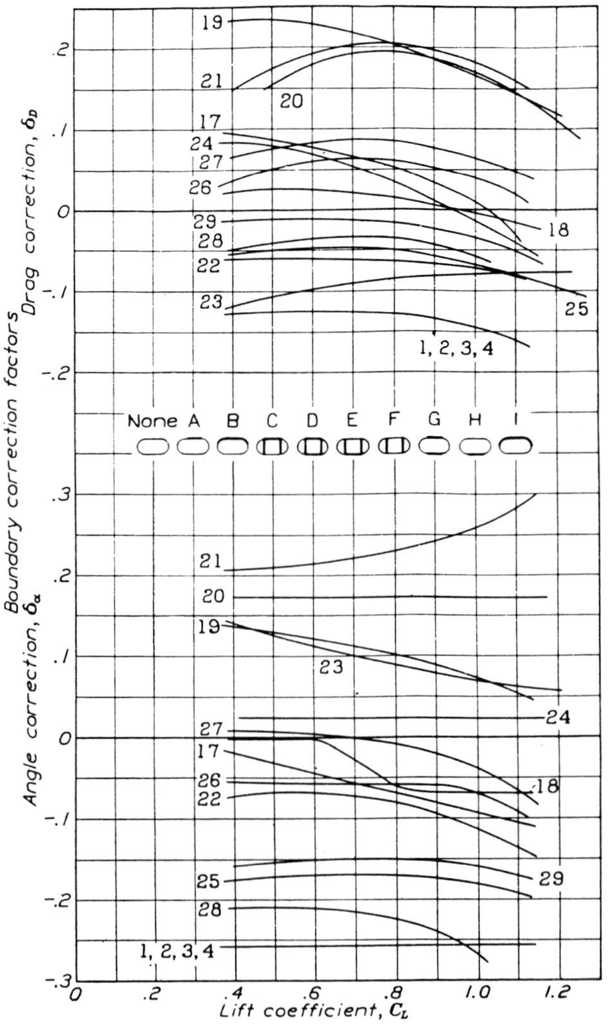

TABLE II

Test no.	1	2	3	4	17	18	19	20	21
Airfoil	3″	4″	5″	6″	3″	3″	3″	3″	3″
Position	c.l.[1]	c.l.	c.l.	c.l.	c.l.	c.l.	c.l.	c.l.	c.l.
Type of tunnel wall [2]	None	None	None	None	Top	Top and part side.	Top and sides	Closed tunnel	Bottom and sides.
Modification					A	B	C	D	E

Test no.	22	23	24	25	26	27	28	29
Airfoil	3″	3″	3″	6″	6″	6″	6″	4″
Position	c.l.	c.l.	c.l.	c.l.	c.l.	c.l.	c.l.	c.l.
Type of tunnel wall [2]	Sides	Top and bottom.	Bottom	Top	Top and part sides.	Top and half sides.	Top and half sides.	Top.
Modification	F	G	H	A	B	I	I	A

[1] Center line. [2] See fig. 8 for descriptive drawings.

NOTE.—Airfoils in inverted position for above-tests.

FIGURE 10.—Angle and drag correction factors for various modifications of the model tunnel. (See table II.)

the experimental and the theoretically predicted boundary correction factors of the model tunnel. It was at the time believed that the low Reynolds Number might have had an objectionable effect on the results, and also that the test accuracy in this small tunnel might not have been sufficient. The unexpected effect on the maximum lift and the consistently larger errors in the boundary factors for the open tunnels rather tended to indicate that a more fundamental cause was to be suspected.

FULL-SCALE TUNNEL INVESTIGATION

Tunnel and equipment.—The full-scale tunnel and its equipment have been fully described in reference 6. The cross section of the jet, which is similar to that of the model tunnel, is of a width/height ratio of 2, with parallel top and bottom and semicircular ends (figs. 12 and 13). The jet is 60 feet wide and 30 feet high, and has a free length of 56 feet between entrance and exit cones. Two electric motors enclosed in streamline nacelles circulate the air through the tunnel. A 6-component electrically recording balance measures

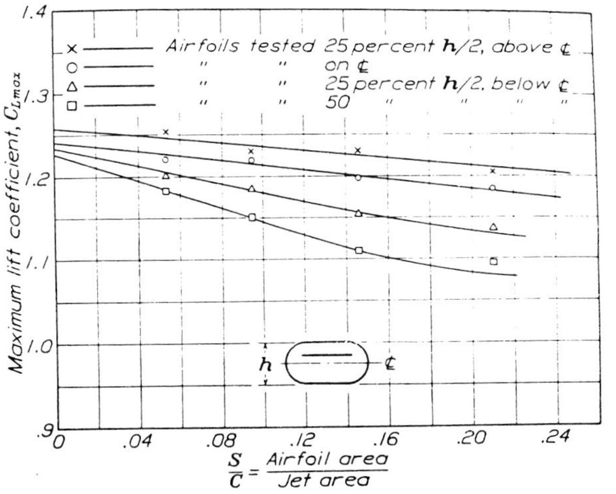

FIGURE 11.—Variation in maximum lift coefficient in model tunnel for various positions of airfoils.

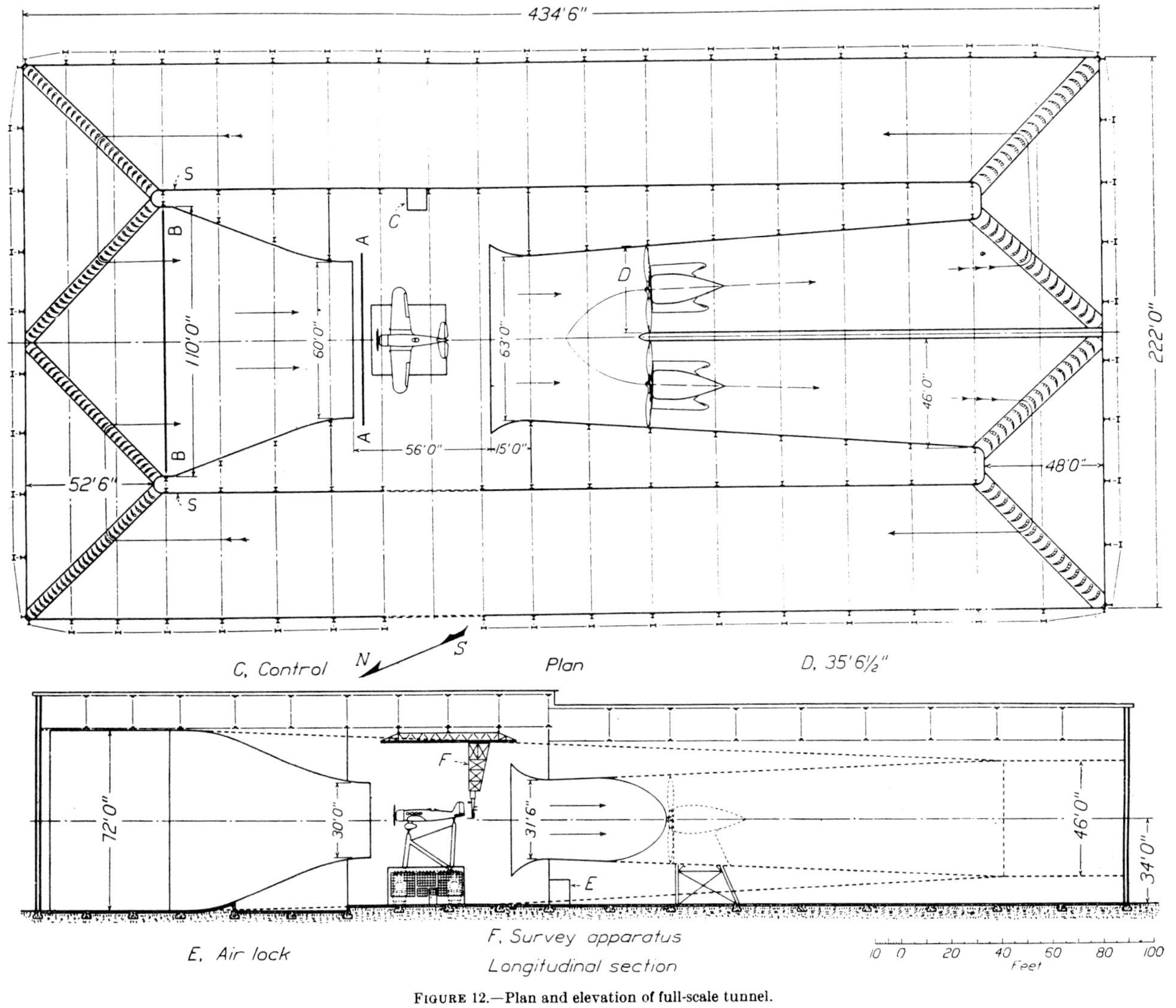

FIGURE 12.—Plan and elevation of full-scale tunnel.

and records the forces and moments. The airfoil is supported in the air stream on the balance frame by streamlined struts (fig. 13). Careful shielding of the

FIGURE 13.—Experimental set-up of Clark Y airfoil in full-scale tunnel.

major portion of these supporting struts and streamlining of all exposed surfaces reduce the tare drag to a low value (about one third of the minimum airfoil drag for the smallest airfoil and one fiftieth of the

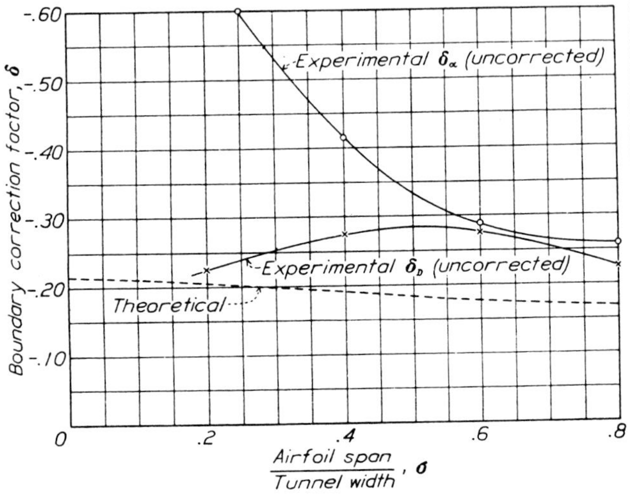

FIGURE 14.—Preliminary results on the boundary corrections for the full-scale tunnel

minimum drag of the largest airfoil). The arrangement and method of measuring dynamic pressures are similar to those of the model. The location of the static pressure orifices is shown at S on figure 12.

Four Clark Y airfoils, which were especially built for the purpose, were used as standards throughout the entire series of tests. These served, in addition, the important purpose of furnishing the full-scale characteristics of the Clark Y airfoil. The airfoils are of 12-, 24-, 36-, and 48-foot span, all with an aspect ratio of 6, constructed with steel spars and aluminum sheet covering. These airfoils were also subjected to a careful inspection and checking, and were found to comply with the stringent requirements of this type of experiment.

Preliminary results.—The initial results from the full-scale tunnel boundary correction tests are shown in figure 14. The extrapolation process and detailed procedure are the same as those outlined for the model-tunnel tests. It is observed that the agreement with the predicted theoretical value is no better than in the case of the model tunnel. It became evident at this point that the difficulty could not all be due to scale effect or test inaccuracy, as the experimental test accuracy of the full-scale tunnel was considerably

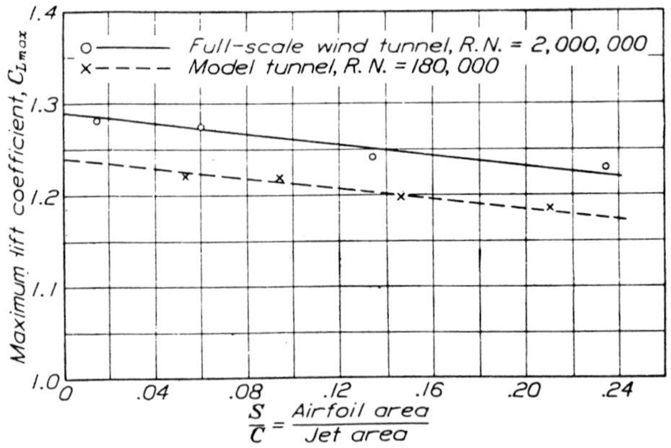

FIGURE 15.—Variation of maximum lift with airfoil size in full-scale tunnel.

greater than that of the model tunnel, and the Reynolds Number about 15 times larger.

Considerable time and effort were spent in arriving at the correct explanation of the large discrepancy with the theoretically predicted results. The possible effect of the load distribution over the airfoil was considered, but discarded as being of negligible importance. A number of possible effects, such as curvature of the stream, length of the free jet, the effect of the exit cone restraint, and spillage, were theoretically considered; but none of them was found to be of appreciable concern.

A further definite agreement with the results from the model tunnel in regard to maximum lift coefficient is shown in figure 15, in which the upper curve shows the results in the full-scale tunnel. The values of the maximum lift coefficient in the large tunnel are greater, as expected, but the considerable drop in the maximum lift with increase in airfoil size persists. From the earlier results in the model tunnel it was already established (fig. 11) that certain off-center stations of the airfoil resulted in still smaller lift coefficients. It was suspected that this effect was intimately related to the discrepancies in the boundary correction factors.

Dynamic pressure or q correction.—It was recognized at this time that an error in the measurement of the velocity head might account not only for the drop in maximum lift but also for the discrepancies in the boundary correction factors. The calibration of the tunnel had been, as is conventional, performed with the jet *empty*, with the tacit assumption that this cali-

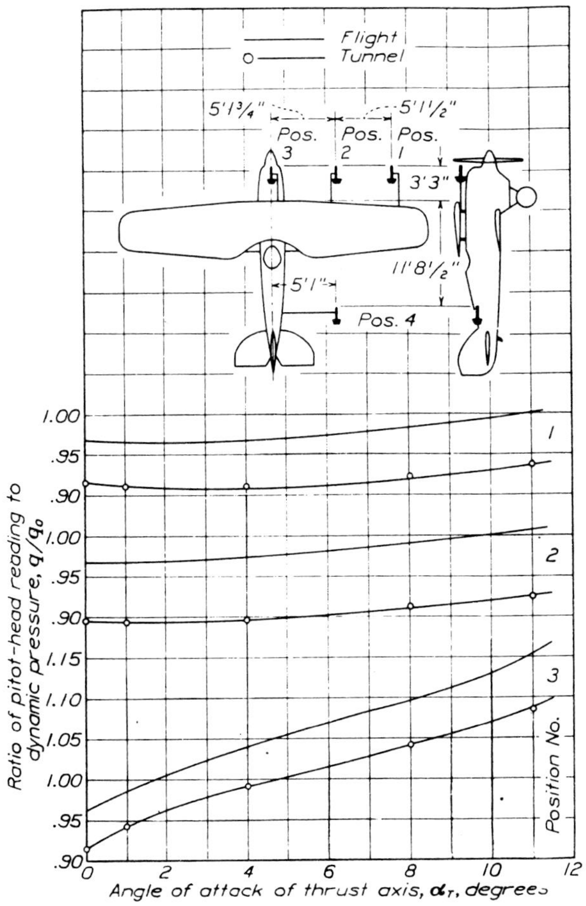

FIGURE 16.—Dynamic pressure at three locations on the PW-9 airplane in flight and in the full-scale tunnel. q_o, dynamic pressure in flight or in the tunnel; q, local dynamic pressure.

bration sufficed for the tests with a body in the air stream. Although nothing but the ordinary displacement blocking was anticipated it was decided to subject the problem to an exhaustive investigation.

Figure 12 shows the location of a full-size airplane in the large tunnel. A pitot tube was attached to the wing of an airplane in the full-scale tunnel, well in front of the wing and clear of the body. The indicated dynamic pressure on this pitot head showed the astonishing result of reading about 7 percent below the estimated theoretical value, apparently indicating a considerable decrease in velocity in the region around the airplane.

In order to substantiate this finding and to avoid the necessity of theoretical estimates of the velocity field, it was decided to obtain a direct comparison with flight. A PW-9 airplane was equipped with four pitot heads, as shown in figure 16, and observations of the dynamic and static pressures at these locations were taken in flight over a large angle-of-attack range. The airplane was then installed in the tunnel and identical observations taken. The results, shown in figures 16 and 17, confirm beyond question the existence of a considerable distortion of the velocity field in the tunnel. Figure 16 shows the dynamic pressure for three front locations. Figure 17 shows the static pressure for the same three locations, using the static

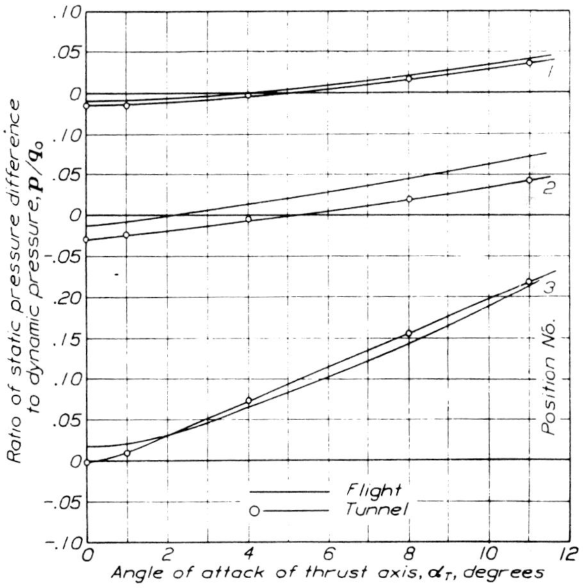

FIGURE 17.—Static pressure at three locations on the PW-9 airplane in flight and in the full-scale tunnel. Static pressure at rear pitot head no. 4 used as reference. q_o, dynamic pressure in flight or in the tunnel; p, local static pressure minus the static pressure at head no. 4.

head at the fourth (rear) pitot tube as a reference pressure. The differences between the static pressures taken in flight and in the tunnel are shown plotted along the span in figure 18. Observe that the average dynamic pressure in the region around the airplane is about 6 percent lower than that of flight, when the indicated tunnel velocity is equal to the flight speed. Observe also that there is a static gradient in the tunnel acting in a direction so as to increase the drag force. This latter effect is of the order of 5 percent of the minimum drag.

The velocity field in the tunnel was subsequently studied in greater detail. Figures 19, 20, and 21 show, respectively, the dynamic, static, and total pressures taken with the full-scale tunnel survey equipment (reference 6) at position A (fig. 12) approximately 13 feet ahead of the PW-9 airplane, which has a 32-foot span. Notice the large velocity drop in the central part of the jet in figure 19 and the static pressure increase in figure 20. The reference pressure for static measurement is the pressure in the tunnel test chamber. The total head in figure 21 shows a definite decrease toward the center of the air stream, indicating

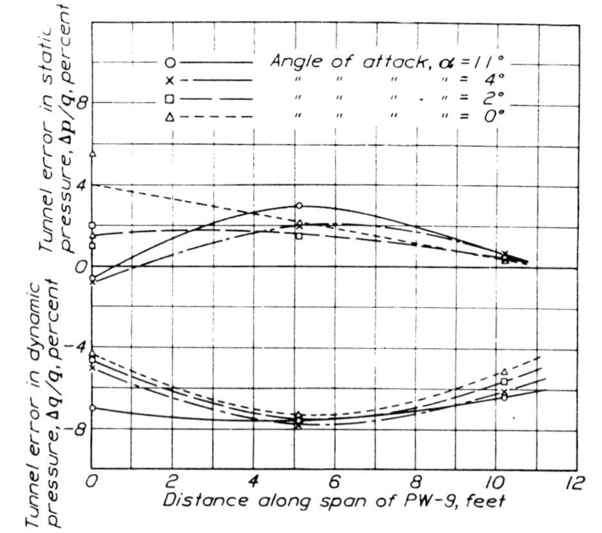

FIGURE 18.—Blocking errors along the span of the PW-9 airplane at different angles of attack in the jet of the full-scale tunnel.

that the energy in the region around the airplane is below that of the exterior jet from which the indicated tunnel velocity is obtained.

This decrease in velocity head obtained with the survey apparatus is within about 1 percent of that indicated by the pitot heads on the airplane, showing

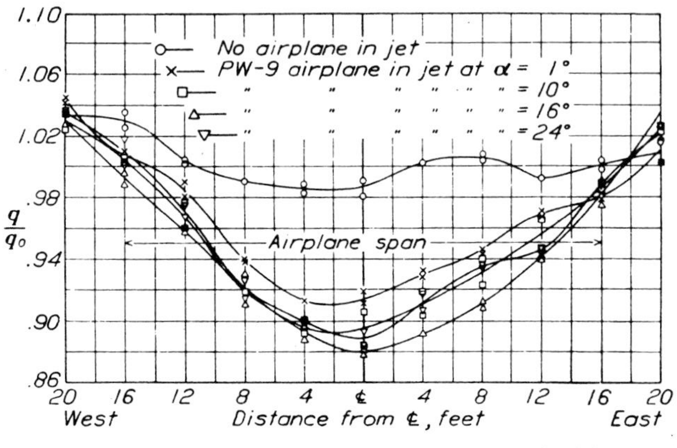

FIGURE 19.—Dynamic-pressure surveys at wing height and two chords in front of the PW-9 airplane in the full-scale tunnel. q_o, average dynamic pressure along the span with jet empty; q, dynamic pressure with the airplane in the tunnel.

that the effect is not localized to the immediate vicinity of the airplane. It was therefore suspected that the effect might extend much farther in the forward direction. This suspicion was substantiated. Figure 22 shows the velocity distribution at the large end of the entrance cone (at section B–B in fig. 12) resulting from the PW-9 at several angles of attack, as compared with that of the empty tunnel. It becomes obvious that the characteristics of an airplane determined with disregard of this considerable field distortion are in error. Both the slope of the lift curve and the maximum lift coefficient become too low, simply because they are computed on the basis of a velocity

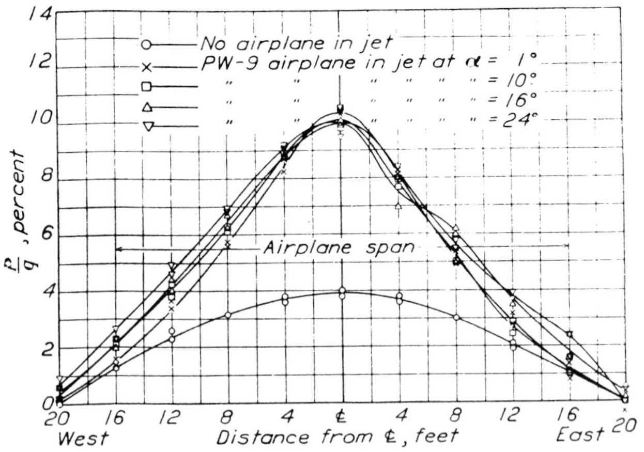

FIGURE 20.—Static-pressure surveys at wing height and two chords in front of the PW-9 airplane in the full-scale tunnel. p, static pressure in jet with reference to the test chanber; q, dynamic pressure in the jet.

higher than that existing. The drag coefficients are affected in essentially the same manner; however, the effect of the static pressure gradient must also be included.

The definition of the true velocity in a distorted field of this nature becomes quite difficult. A permissible approximation may be to use the average velocity

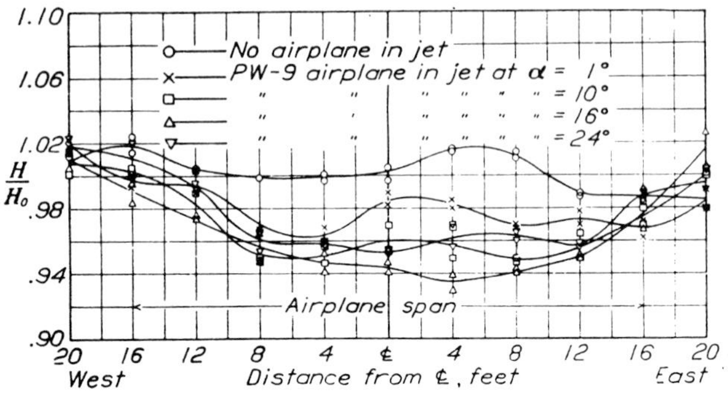

FIGURE 21.—Total-pressure surveys at wing height and two chords in front of the PW-9 airplane in the full-scale tunnel. H_o, average total pressure along the span with jet empty; H, total pressure with the airplane in the tunnel.

along the span taken at some distance in front of the airplane. This average velocity is, as pointed out, considerably below the indicated tunnel velocity, necessitating a considerable correction to the latter. It will in the following be referred to as a "q" correction.

Support interference.—The necessity in a problem of this nature for reducing all errors to an absolute minimum forced a further inquiry. When comparing tests with airfoils in upright and inverted positions, that is, with the supports attached to the lower and upper surfaces respectively, it was observed that a good agreement in the characteristics of the smaller airfoils did not result. The drag of the supports was measured separately with the airfoil in position, but

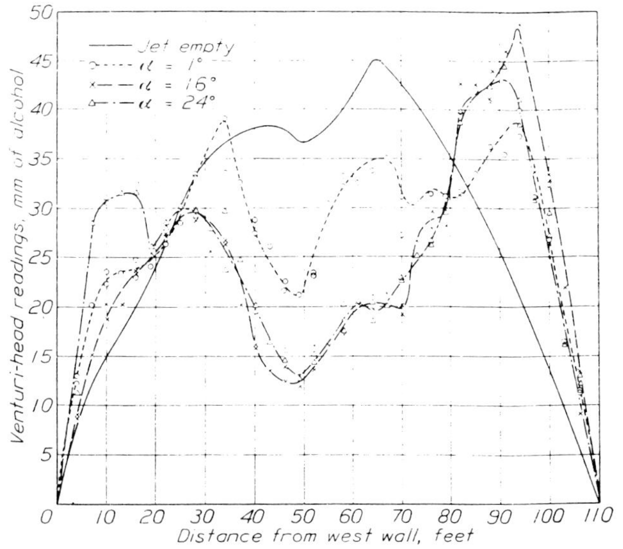

FIGURE 22.—Velocity distribution showing the blocking effect extending into the mouth of the entrance cone.

supported by wires. This drag of the exposed struts, which included the interference of the wing upon them, was subtracted from the drag of the total set-up.

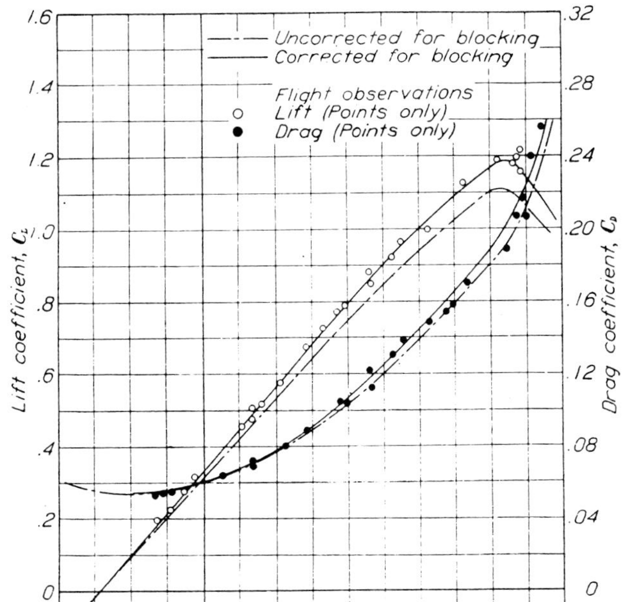

FIGURE 23.—Characteristics of the PW-9 airplane obtained in the full-scale tunnel, corrected for blocking and boundary interference, and compared with flight results.

It was acknowledged that the difference in the results was due to the interference of the supports upon the airfoil, although at first it was difficult to imagine that the effect of these unusually small and carefully streamlined supports (fig. 13) could be of any consequence. It was found that in the *upright* position the drag at zero lift was increased by a large unfavorable interference effect due to the struts. The *inverted* position showed an apparent, although small, favorable interference. This latter result was found to be produced by a virtual straightening of the effective mean camber line of the airfoil. It was necessary to resort to the refinement of adding dummy supports to the opposite side of the airfoil. The results from the upright and inverted tests were thus brought into satisfactory agreement. Details of these tests will be published in a future paper.

Boundary-correction factor.—With the establishment of the existence of the q correction for the full-scale tunnel, the predicted boundary correction factors were successfully applied to a number of airplanes for which flight data were available. Figure 23, showing

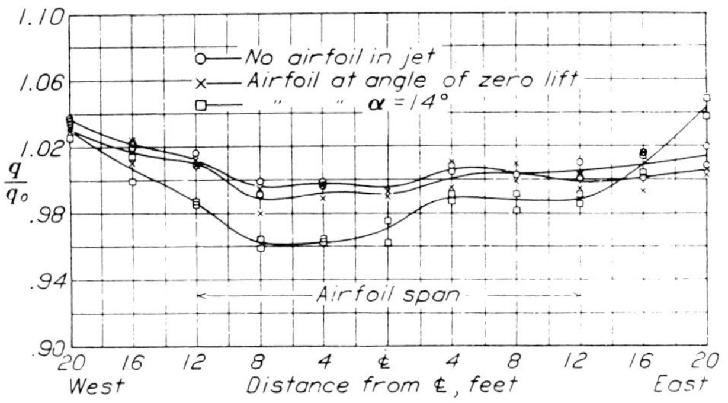

FIGURE 24.—Dynamic-pressure surveys level with and approximately three chords in front of the by 4- by 24-foot airfoil. q_0, average dynamic pressure along the span with jet empty; q, dynamic pressure with the airfoil in the tunnel.

comparative results of the characteristics of the PW-9 airplane from tunnel and flight tests, is presented as an example. The lift and drag values obtained in flight are shown with points only. The broken curves show the wind-tunnel tests corrected for jet boundaries, while the continuous curves take the q correction also into account. The agreement is striking.

Similar results giving the comparison between flight and tunnel tests on the Fairchild F-22 airplane are presented in reference 6. Good agreement has also been obtained on the YO-31A and several other airplanes employing an estimated value of the q correction. It is worthy of notice that the maximum lifts in all cases were brought into close agreement with flight results by means of the q correction.

It was of interest to determine the q correction to be applied to the standard airfoil series. It was necessary, of course, to make a theoretical estimate of the undisturbed field around the airfoil, as no flight observations could possibly be obtained. The 24- and the 48-foot airfoils were checked.

Figures 24, 25, and 26 show the dynamic pressure, static head, and total head as measured approximately

12 feet ahead of the 4- by 24-foot airfoil. The average drop in the dynamic pressure across the span varies from a negligible quantity at low angles to about

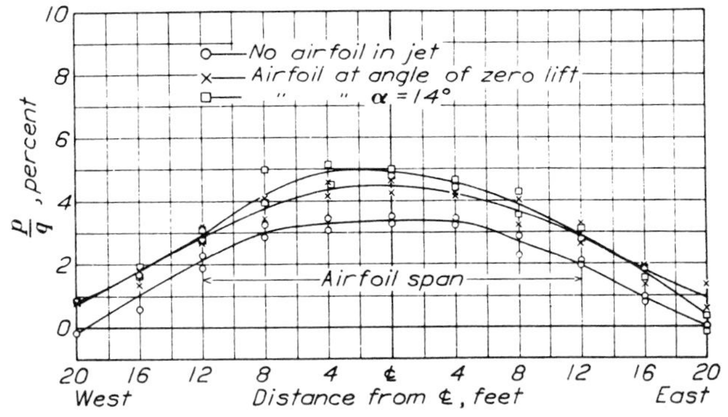

FIGURE 25.—Static-pressure surveys level with and approximately three chords in front of the 4- by 24-foot airfoil. p, static pressure in jet with reference to the test chamber; q, dynamic pressure in the jet.

3 percent at high angles. The experimental angle and drag correction factors were found to be equal and to fall close to the predicted curve. (See circles in fig. 30.)

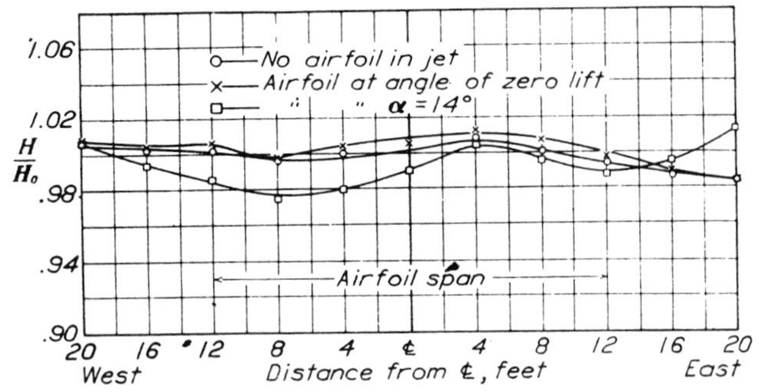

FIGURE 26.—Total-pressure surveys level with and approximately three chords in front of the 4- by 24-foot airfoil. H_o, average total pressure along the span with jet empty; H, total pressure with the airfoil in the tunnel.

An explanation of the curious drop in maximum lift with the size of the airfoil (fig. 15) is available. By introducing the correct value of the velocity for the 4 by 24 and 8 by 48 airfoils from the surveys, no drop in maximum lift is obtained. On assuming a direct relationship between the velocity decrease and the decrease in maximum lift for the remaining airfoils, the boundary correction factors fall into agreement with the theory (fig. 30). Figures 27, 28, and 29 show the intermediate steps in the derivation.

CONCLUDING REMARKS

It has thus been shown that the predicted boundary factors are confirmed, provided that proper account is taken of strut interference and velocity errors. The adequacy of the theory has thus been verified.

Regarding the real nature of the q correction, it is recognized that it differs from the usual displacement

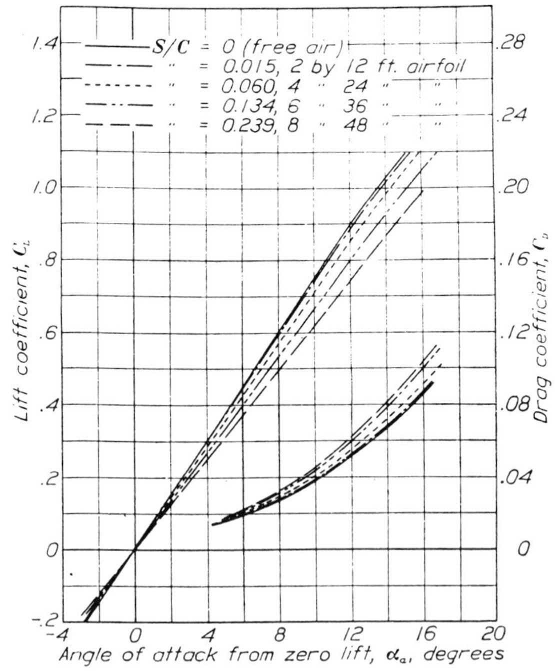

FIGURE 27.—Lift and drag coefficients of four Clark Y airfoils obtained in the full-scale tunnel, corrected for tunnel blocking.

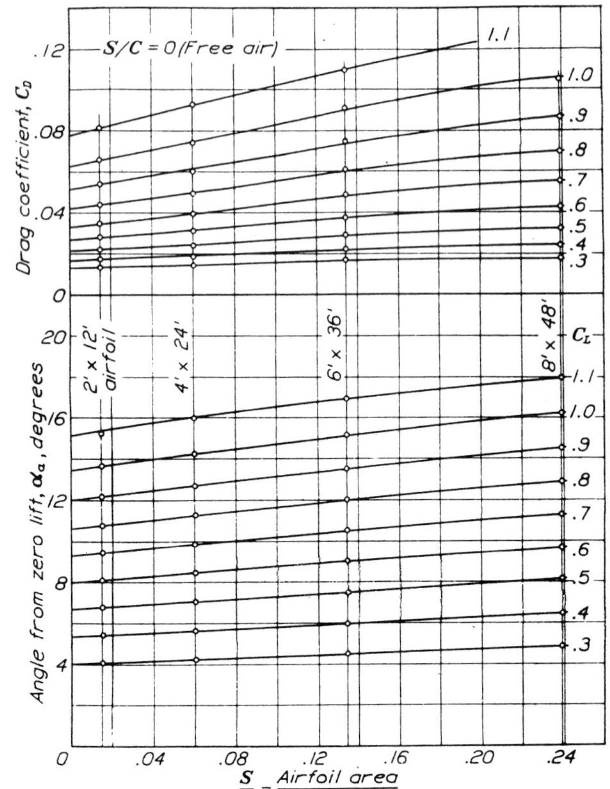

FIGURE 28.—Extrapolation of corrected airfoil characteristics to free-air condition.

blocking. The large distortion at the mouth of the entrance cone, almost 100 feet ahead of the test section, excludes the possibility that this is the normal type of blocking, since the effect of the normal displacement blocking is confined to the immediate vicinity of the object. The decrease in dynamic pressure observed in front of the test body is associated with a corresponding, but much smaller, increase in static pressure, resulting in a deficiency of total head.

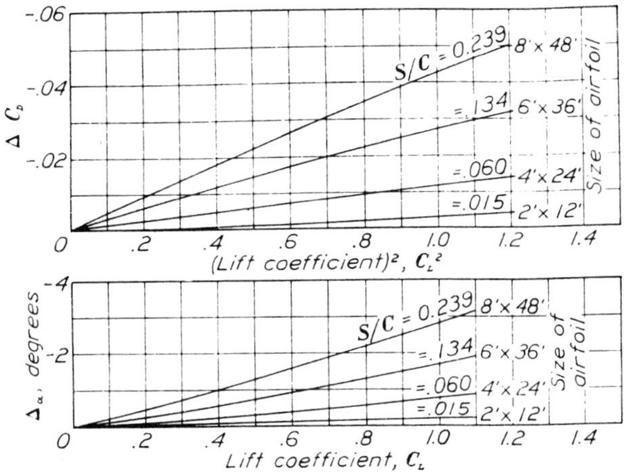

FIGURE 29.—Down-flow angle and drag increment against lift coefficient.

The loss in total head seems to account for the greater part of the q correction. Quite evidently the pattern, or wake of the body, is carried around the tunnel. It is not inconceivable that this considerable wake might be responsible for a further distortion of the flow in the entrance cone. It is realized that the flow in a short entrance cone is of a rather unstable nature, and that the introduction of a slower moving core might tend to upset the normal flow.

While it is believed that a wake could build up and persist in a tunnel with small inherent turbulence, it is obvious that such a pattern would be rapidly dissipated in a more turbulent tunnel. It is probable that a velocity distortion of this kind might be a contributing factor to the differences in maximum lift coefficients observed in various tunnels.

No attempt has been made to extend this study to provide a basis for the prediction of the q correction or to the avoidance of this phenomenon. It will be a problem for future experience and research to determine

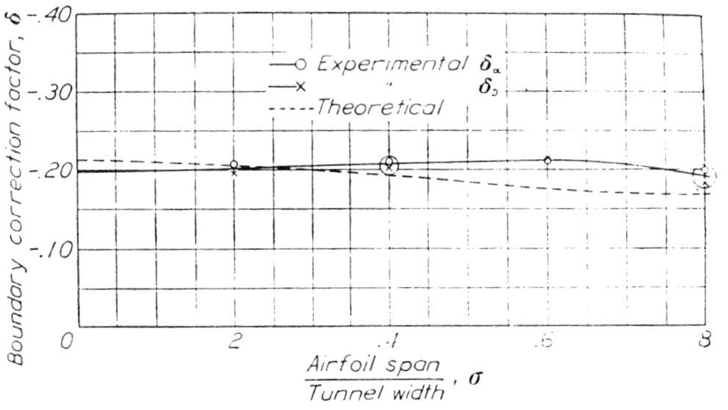

FIGURE 30.—Experimental and theoretical boundary-correction factors for the full-scale tunnel. Points in large circles obtained by direct measurement of blocking. Remaining points obtained on basis of blocking as indicated by drop in maximum lift.

in what manner the velocity distortion depends on the characteristics of the body and the tunnel.

LANGLEY MEMORIAL AERONAUTICAL LABORATORY,
NATIONAL ADVISORY COMMITTEE FOR AERONAUTICS,
LANGLEY FIELD, VA., *May 18, 1933.*

REFERENCES

1. Tani, Itiro, and Sanuki, Matao: The Wall Interference of a Wind Tunnel of Elliptic Cross-Section. Proceedings of the Physics-Math. Soc. of Japan, 3d Series, vol. 14, no. 10, 1932.
2. Glauert, H.: Interference on Characteristics of Aerofoil in Wind Tunnel of Rectangular Section. R. & M. No. 1459, British A.R.C., 1932.
3. Theodorsen, Theodore: Interference on an Airfoil of Finite Span in an Open Rectangular Wind Tunnel. T.R. No. 461, N.A.C.A., 1933.
4. Knight, Montgomery, and Harris, Thomas A.: Experimental Determination of Jet Boundary Corrections for Airfoil Tests in Four Open Wind Tunnel Jets of Different Shapes. T.R. No. 361, N.A.C.A., 1930.
5. Theodorsen, Theodore: The Theory of Wind-Tunnel Wall Interference. T.R. No. 410, N.A.C.A., 1931.
6. DeFrance, Smith J.: The N.A.C.A. Full-Scale Wind Tunnel. T.R. No. 459, N.A.C.A., 1933.

VIBRATION RESPONSE OF AIRPLANE STRUCTURES

BY THEODORE THEODORSEN
AND A. G. GELALLES

National Advisory Committee for Aeronautics

Report No. 491, 1934

SUMMARY

This report presents test results of experiments on the vibration-response characteristics of airplane structures on the ground and in flight. It also gives details regarding the construction and operation of vibration instruments developed by the National Advisory Committee for Aeronautics.

In the ground tests a study was made of the vibration response of the fuselage, wings, and tail by applying sinusoidal forces and couples at different parts of the fuselages of two airplanes. The amplitudes of vibration along the fuselage and wings at various frequencies were measured and plotted, and the important natural modes of vibration were determined.

In the flight tests vibration records were taken in the cockpits and the tails of two airplanes. The vibrograms obtained in flight tests were analyzed and the amplitudes of the fundamental frequencies and the most important harmonics were plotted.

INTRODUCTION

Important contributions to knowledge on the subject of vibration in aircraft have been made by Constant (references 1 and 2). In his papers an exposition is given of the physiological effect of the vibration as dependent on amplitude and frequency, and consideration is given to the importance of the various sources of vibration and their effects on the aircraft structure. Of interest is his establishment of a curve of amplitude against frequency that defines the limits beyond which an unpleasant sensation is experienced. The amplitude limit varies from about 0.003 inch at a frequency of 5,000 per minute to about 0.006 inch at a frequency of 1,000 per minute, with permissible amplitude increasing sharply toward the lower range.

The sources of vibration in an airplane are the engine, the propeller, and the aerodynamic effects. Vibrations originating in either the engine or the propeller have frequencies that are related to the engine speed. The frequencies of vibrations of aerodynamic origin, in general, bear no relation to the engine speed.

Vibrations having their origin in the engine may be due to unbalance of rotating and reciprocating parts or to fluctuations in the torque. In the conventional aviation engines, inertia and torque resultants higher than the second order of the engine speed are usually of small magnitude, as far as causing vibration in the fuselage and wing structure, and are therefore of no consequence. No inertia unbalance of the second order or lower should be present in multicylinder engines except in 4-cylinder in-line and in radial engines. Computations by a method given by Tanaka (reference 3) show the secondary unbalance of some American single-bank radial engines as varying from about 200 pounds in a 5-cylinder engine to 800 pounds or more in a 9-cylinder radial engine at rated speeds. Torque resultants lower than the second order are present chiefly because of the unequal contribution in mean torque by each cylinder. In some instances torque resultants of the 1/2 and the first orders may vary from a few hundred to several thousand pound-inches.

Vibrations in the aircraft attributed to the propeller are usually of the first and second orders of the engine speed. Large unbalanced gyroscopic and aerodynamic couples (that may cause large amplitudes of vibration of the structure) may be induced by rapid changing of the direction of flight—as in turning or looping—especially in airplanes with 2-bladed propellers.

The aerodynamic disturbances, flutter and those resulting from tail buffeting, are sources of dangerous vibration. Flutter may be described as an unstable flight condition. Wings, tail planes, and propellers are susceptible to flutter. The speed at which flutter occurs is dependent on a large number of factors, including the frequencies of the responding parts in the various degrees of freedom. Buffeting of the airplane tail is often considered to be the result of vortices originating at the wings and impinging on the horizontal tail surfaces. Buffeting is more prevalent in low-wing monoplanes than in high-wing monoplanes or in biplanes. Treatments of aerodynamic disturbances will be found in references 4, 5, 6, and elsewhere.

In dealing with the vibration problem, the aircraft designer is required (1) to eliminate as far as practicable the sources of vibration; (2) to reduce the transmissibility to the structure by isolating the sources; and (3) to avoid resonant response of the structure.

The undesirable effects on the structure of unbalanced forces or couples in the engines or propellers are well recognized by designers. Their elimination is carried out as far as possible or practicable, however, recourse must often be had to the other two alternatives. It is possible that the isolation of the engine-propeller unit from the aircraft structure in many cases is very helpful; but good results would be obtained only if the problem were sufficiently well understood.

The purpose of this report is to present the vibration-response characteristics of fuselages, wings, and tails of airplanes so as to convey some idea of what frequencies might be expected in the general case or, at least, in related designs. Obviously a great deal is to be gained by avoiding resonant responses of the fuselage-tail unit or the wing structure. If the engine is running at 1,800 revolutions per minute, it is evidently not desirable to have the main response of the fuselage at 900 vibrations per minute or to have a critical response of the wing tips at 1,800 vibrations per minute. A summary of the tests conducted, i.e., airplanes tested, type of tests, and response measured, are given in table I. The tests conducted herein were made at Langley Field, Va., during 1932 and 1933.

N.A.C.A. VIBRATION INSTRUMENTS

At the beginning of this study the necessity arose for developing instruments capable of conveniently and accurately recording the large number of vibration characteristics desired. Three instruments, using the seismograph principle of operation, were developed. One of these instruments, the vibrograph, records flexural vibrations in any given direction; another, the torsiograph, records torsional vibrations about any given axis; the third instrument, the vibration indicator, indicates effective amplitudes of vibration in any given direction and is used for a rapid survey of magnitudes of vibration. In order to permit recording of vibrations in all parts of the aircraft in flight, the additional feature of remote operation was incorporated in all three instruments.

VIBROGRAPH

A sectional view of the vibrograph is shown in figure 1. This instrument consists chiefly of a short piece of shafting A attached to the vibrating body, and a casing B with a film drum C mounted on the shaft through a helical spring. Floating bearings permit a sliding motion between the shaft and the casing. The casing with film drum and accessories constitutes the suspended weight.

An optical method is used for recording the vibration and for timing. A mirror D, held between the shaft and the casing by a spring E, is rocked along the shaft axis as the shaft vibrates. A light beam directed onto the mirror through a lens and then reflected back to a film drum records the rocking motion of the mirror; only vibrations parallel to the shaft are recorded. Similarly, a light beam, from a lamp not shown, is directed onto a mirror F, which is mounted on a high-frequency vibrating reed and records the timing along the lower edge of the film. The frequency of vibration of the reed is controlled by an independent timer which makes and breaks the circuit of the magnetic coil G at definite intervals.

Damping is obtained by means of the dashpot H. Liquids of varying viscosities are used in the dashpot, depending on the temperature at which the tests are conducted. A small shaft I, with a roller properly fitted in a slot in the casing, limits the circumferential and the maximum axial motion of the suspended casing. A locking device (not shown), which is simply a spring-loaded latch, locks the casing rigidly to the shaft when the instrument is not in use.

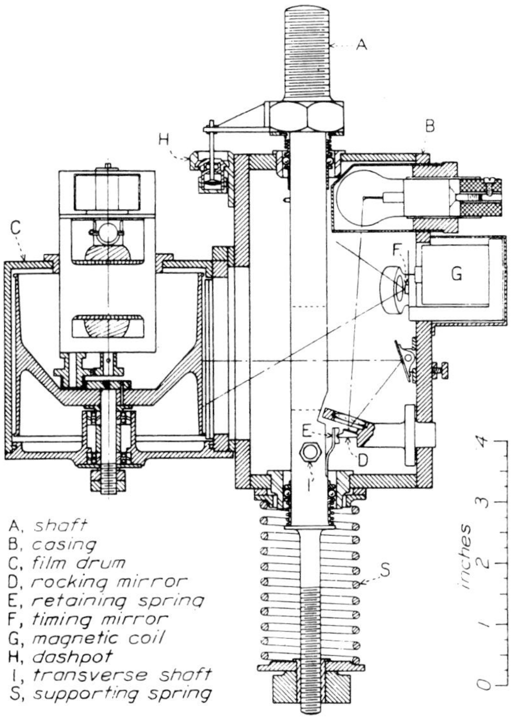

FIGURE 1.—Diagrammatic sketch of N.A.C.A. vibrograph.

The vibrograph, like all instruments of its type, has a definite frequency range of applicability. The lower limit of its reliability depends upon the natural frequency of the suspended weight, and on the amount and type of damping. The upper limit is determined only by the restoring force of the spring E, which holds the mirror in place. The calibration curve for the vibrograph is given in figure 2. Amplitudes of vibration at frequencies below about 600 vibrations per minute need a correction. Frequencies as low as 350 vibrations per minute are, however, obtained with accuracy. The instrument was calibrated and found to be accurate at frequencies up to 4,000 per minute. Computations indicate that the range extends to frequencies up to 15,000 per minute.

The sensitivity of the vibrograph depends mainly on the distance between the knife-edge pivots of mirror D. For the tests presented in this report 2 mirrors having 2 different widths between knife-edges were used. The sensitivity with the smaller mirror

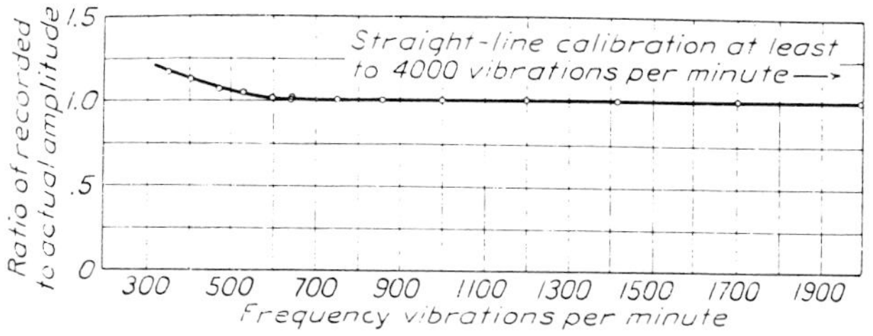

FIGURE 2.—Calibration curve of N.A.C.A. vibrograph.

was of the order of 0.50-inch amplitude recorded for 0.01-inch actual amplitude. With the larger mirror the ratio was 0.27 to 0.01. This sensitivity was constant over the whole range of amplitudes.

TORSIOGRAPH

Sectional views of the torsiograph are shown in figure 3. With this instrument torsional vibrations

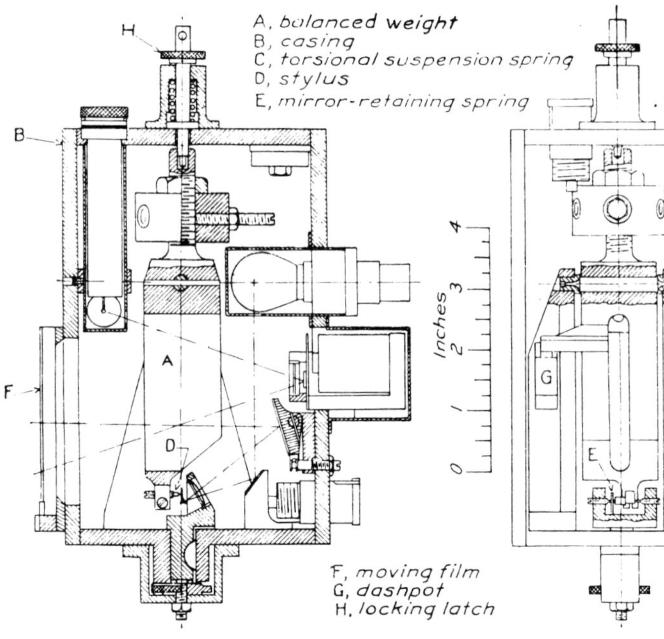

FIGURE 3.—Diagrammatic sketch of N.A.C.A. torsiograph.

in any given plane may be recorded. Like the vibrograph, it consists primarily of a suspended weight A and a casing B, which in this case is attached to the vibrating body. The weight A is suspended as a perfectly balanced flywheel and is held in its zero setting by the spiral spring C. For the useful range of torsional-vibration frequencies the casing vibrates with the body, while the suspended weight or flywheel remains stationary in its center position. Only torsional relative motion is possible between the weight and the casing. A stylus D at the lower end of the suspended weight rocks a mirror mounted on pivots. A spiral spring E retains the mirror in continuous contact with the stylus. The recording of the torsional motion and timing is accomplished optically in the same manner as that of the vibrograph. The motion recorded on the moving film F is proportional to the angular twist of the casing with respect to the stationary flywheel. Liquid damping is obtained by means of the dashpot G. A spring-loaded latch H holds the suspended weight rigidly to the casing when the instrument is not in use and limits the angular motion when it is operating.

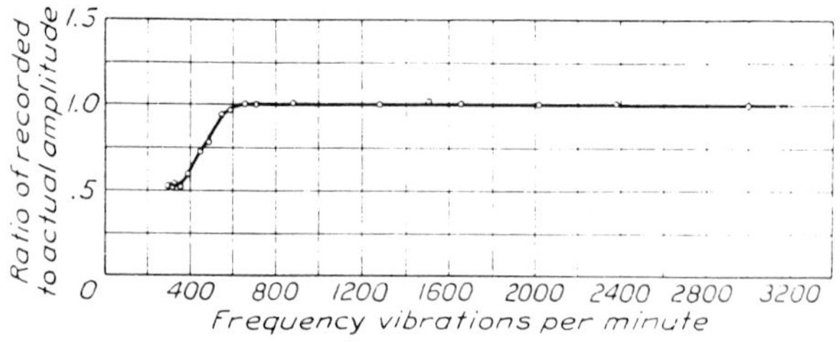

FIGURE 4.—Calibration curve of N.A.C.A. torsiograph.

The lower limit of reliability of the torsiograph, as for the vibrograph, depends largely on the natural frequency in torsion of the suspended weight, or flywheel, and on the type and amount of damping. The upper limit of this instrument is reached when the restoring acceleration of the mirror spring E is exceeded by that of the stylus D, i.e., when the mirror spring is no longer able to retain the mirror in continuous contact with the stylus.

A calibration curve of the torsiograph is shown in figure 4. From this curve it is seen that for frequencies below about 600 vibrations per minute corrections must be applied to the amplitude recorded by the torsiograph. Frequencies as low as 400 per minute may be recorded if proper corrections are applied to the amplitudes. No vibration tests were conducted to determine the upper limit of reliability of the torsiograph, as the calibration table in use was not suitable for very high frequencies. The natural frequency of the mirror-staff unit, which is the limiting factor for the upper range of the instrument, was determined by tests to be about 9,000 per minute.

The sensitivity of the torsiograph depends on the distance at which the stylus D acts from the pivot axis of the mirror staff. This distance can be varied. The sensitivity is constant for the whole amplitude range of the instrument for any given setting of this distance. Magnifications of 40, 55, and 70 were used for the tests of this investigation.

VIBRATION INDICATOR

A photograph of the vibration indicator is given in figure 5, and figure 6 is a sketch of the "feeler" unit of the indicator and a diagram of the wiring. With this instrument a quick survey of the effective amplitude of vibration in any part of the structure may be made. In common with the other two instruments, the underlying principle of its operation is the seismograph; but the hot-wire principle is utilized for recording the vibration.

FIGURE 5.—N.A.C.A. vibration indicator.

The vibration indicator consists of two separate units—the feeler unit, which may be held with a slight pressure or clamped to any part of the aircraft; and the recording unit, in which the observer may read the effective magnitude of vibration. As shown in figure 6 (a), the feeler unit consists of a weight A suspended on a spring B, a piston C connected rigidly to the weight, a nozzle D, and two hot-wire elements E and F of the same electrical resistance. In the recording unit are housed electrical resistances, flashlight batteries, a voltmeter, and a milliammeter.

The method of operation is indicated in figure 6 (b). The hot-wire element E and a similar element F constitute 2 arms of a Wheatstone bridge, and a fixed resistance G and a variable resistance H constitute the other 2 arms of the bridge. The variable resistance I controls the voltage across the bridge; the voltage is held constant for any desired calibration. When the feeler unit is held onto the vibrating body, its casing vibrates with the body. The weight A and the piston C, by virtue of their inertia, remain practically stationary for the range of frequencies for which the instrument is designed. As a result of this relative motion an air blast hits the element E, or air is drawn in through the nozzle D. This cooling effect changes the resistance of the element, the balance of the Wheatstone bridge is disturbed, and the effect is indicated by the milliammeter.

The principal problem in the early development of this instrument was to make the indicated amplitudes independent of the frequency and to obtain a calibration curve of satisfactory form. These difficulties were overcome by a systematic study of the functioning of all elements, and a final design was evolved. The development proceeded along a line similar to that of the development of a microphone of corresponding characteristics. The error in determining the effective amplitudes with this instrument at any frequency in the range does not exceed ±3 percent. In figure 7 are shown the calibration curves of the instrument used in the tests of this report.

In the calibration of this instrument, frequencies as high as 10,000 vibrations per minute were used and the independence of amplitude and frequency was found to hold true. The lower frequency limit of the reliability of this instrument also depends largely on the natural frequency of the suspended weight. From the amplitude-frequency curve of figure 7 it is seen that the range of this particular instrument extends down to about 600 per minute; at this point the curve drops off sharply. The range of usefulness can easily be extended to lower frequencies by using a larger suspended weight or a more flexible spring.

The sensitivity of the instrument depends also on the dimensions of the various parts of the feeler unit and, in particular, on the resistances employed. The sensitivity in the lower range of the indicated amplitudes in this investigation amounts to about 1 milliampere per 0.01 inch amplitude, the actual ratio of the travel of the pointer to the vibration amplitude being of the order of 200:1. For larger amplitudes the sensitivity is gradually reduced. This latter property is very useful and was obtained only after considerable work. The absence of a response peak, common to all other vibration instruments at the natural frequency of the suspended mass, is a very desirable attribute. The instrument exhibits a very sharp cut-off in the fashion of a high-pass filter—a property that is inherent in the method.

engine block the forces applied, varying as the square of the frequency, were 28 pounds at a frequency of 600 per minute and 770 pounds at 3,200 vibrations per minute. These values are comparable with the

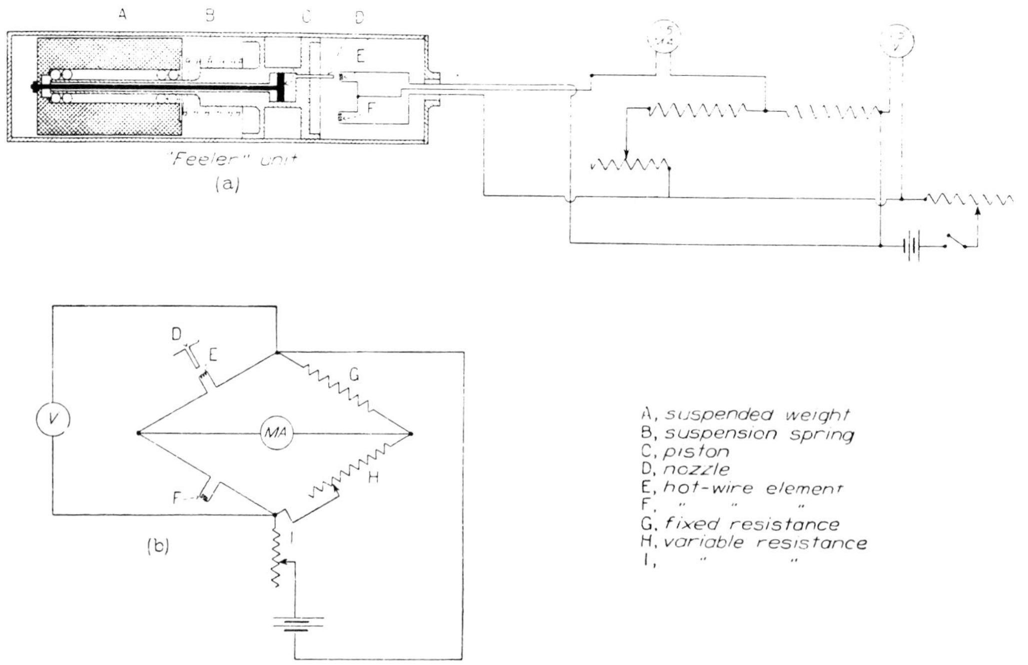

FIGURE 6.—Diagrammatic detailed sketch of N.A.C.A. vibration indicator.

VIBRATION TESTS ON THE RESPONSE OF AIRPLANE STRUCTURES

METHODS AND EQUIPMENT

The vibration response of the fuselage and wings of an airplane were determined by mounting the airplane on springs to obtain a floating suspension that would approximate conditions obtaining in flight. Forced vibrations of magnitude and frequencies comparable to those existing in aircraft were applied at different parts of the fuselage and the response was recorded with either the vibration indicator or the vibrograph. Tests were conducted on the Boeing PW-9, an Army pursuit airplane, and on the N2Y-1, a Navy training airplane.

Figure 8 is a photograph of the PW-9 mounted for the vibration-response tests. The weight of this airplane is approximately 3,100 pounds. Automobile springs were substituted for the landing wheels and the tail skid, as shown. The frequency of free vibrations of the airplane on the springs in the vertical direction was about 100 vibrations per minute.

A vibrator externally driven through a cog-belt by a motor on a separate stand was mounted successively at the top of the engine block, at the center of gravity of the airplane, and at the fuselage near the tail. With this vibrator sinusoidal forces and couples of varying magnitude and frequency could be impressed on the fuselage. With the vibrator on the secondary unbalanced inertia forces existing in present-day radial engines. Because of the much larger response with the vibrator mounted at the center of gravity and at the tail, smaller forces had to be used there.

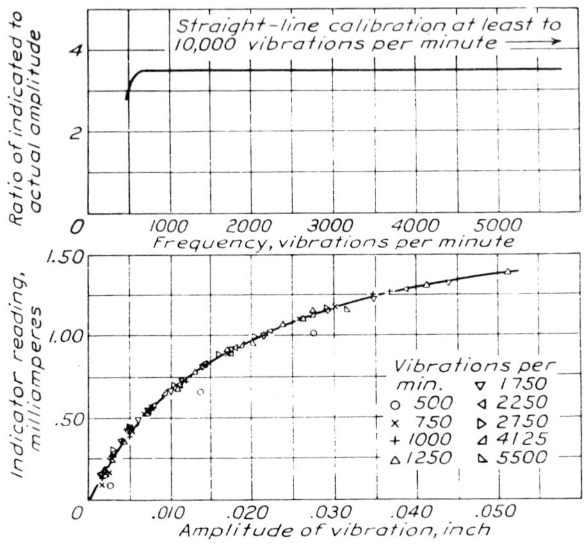

FIGURE 7.—Calibration curves for the N.A.C.A. vibration indicator.

For nearly all the vibration-response tests the hot-wire indicator was used in connection with an "automatic observer" to take simultaneous pictures of the readings of the vibration indicator and of a tachometer indicating the frequency of the imposed vibrations. This automatic observer consists of a light-tight box with the tachometer and vibration indicator mounted on one side and a motor-driven motion-picture camera mounted on the opposite side. Electric lamps within the camera box are timed to switch on and off at regular intervals and provide the illumination necessary for taking records of the instrument readings. Readings of the amplitude [1] of vibration were taken along the length of the fuselage and wing every 6 to 12 inches, and a complete record of the vibration in any one position was obtained for the frequency range of 500 to 3,200 vibrations per minute in about 15 to 20 minutes. Check tests were made to verify the positions of the nodal points.

Because of the multiplicity of test points and the number of curves plotted together, the points have been omitted from the experimental curves for the convenience of easier reading. Although the amplitude of vibration as determined from these particular tests did not deviate from the drawn curves more than about 0.0003 inch, the amplitude response at any one position was observed to vary as much as 10 percent for duplicate test conditions. The form of the elastic curve, however, was identical under all duplicate test conditions.

Previous to the tests on the PW–9, a series of tests were conducted of the vibration-response characteristics of the fuselage of the Consolidated N2Y–1, a 5-cylinder Navy training airplane weighing about 1,500 pounds. This airplane was also mounted on leaf springs. The vibration indicator not having been developed at the time, the vibrograph was used in recording the vibration. The vibrator was mounted on the top cylinder in the place of the removed cylinder head.

FIGURE 8.—Flexible mounting of PW–9 airplane for vibration-response tests.

In the flight tests two Navy biplanes were used—an N2Y–1, similar to that used in the response tests, and an NY–2. The N2Y–1 is powered with a 5-cylinder Kinner radial engine, and the NY–2 with a 9-cylinder Wright J–5 radial engine. The framework of each of the airplanes tested was of welded tubular steel. The engines of these two airplanes and that of the PW–9 used in the vibrator tests were either

[1] Amplitude throughout this paper refers to the single amplitude, i.e., the distance from the mean position to the extreme.

rigidly mounted, or very nearly so, with only a thin layer of cushioning material between the clamps and the fuselage, chiefly used to prevent abrasion of the structural members. All three types of engines were equipped with 2-bladed direct-driven propellers.

When vibration records were taken at the front or rear cockpits, the vibrograph was mounted on the upper longeron of the fuselage on, or close to, the bulkheads. The torsiograph was mounted along the thrust axis of the airplane. Particular care had to be taken to mount the instruments rigidly and in such a manner that no local vibrations of the mounting interfered with the actual vibration at the point. In the tests at the tail of the airplane the instruments were mounted on the upper longerons, slightly back of the tail skid. Electric connections and a wire cable for operating and for locking and unlocking the instruments permitted remote operation from the cockpit.

Timing was obtained directly from the engine. A unit consisting of a commutator and a brush was attached to the camshaft connection of the tachometer drive. By means of this device, together with a magnetic coil and a high-frequency reed, four timing marks were made on the recording film for each revolution of the camshaft simultaneously with the recording of the vibration. The pilot observed the engine speed during the interval the record was taken, which lasted from one-third to one-half second. This timing was found satisfactory for the tests in the cockpit, as the vibrations there were found to be exact multiples of the engine speed. An independent chronometric timer is more convenient, however, when vibrations of frequencies other than multiples of engine speed are recorded, especially when records are taken during maneuvers and when the engine speed is continually changing.

Fourier's analysis was applied to separate the harmonic components of the vibrograph and torsiograph flight records. By the use of Runge's method of tabulation on prepared printed standard forms, an analysis could be made in less than 3 hours per record.

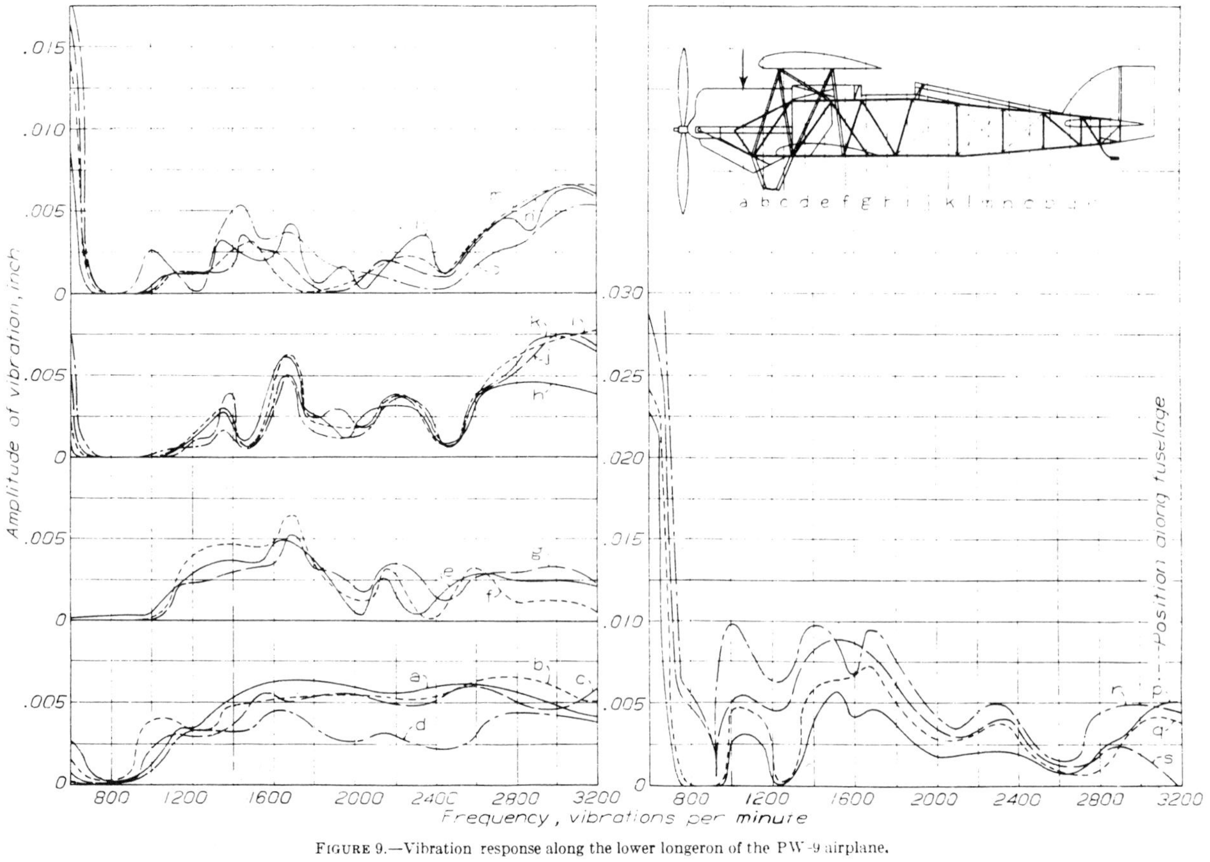

FIGURE 9.—Vibration response along the lower longeron of the PW-9 airplane.

TEST RESULTS AND DISCUSSION

Vibration response of PW-9 fuselage.—Figures 9 and 10 show the response of the fuselage of the PW-9 to a vertical sinusoidal force applied on the engine block with the airplane mounted on springs as shown in figure 8. In figure 9 the amplitude in the vertical direction as measured at points a to s along the lower longeron is plotted against the frequency of vibration, and in figure 10 the amplitude is plotted against position along the fuselage or distance from the plane of rotation of the propeller. These curves show peaks at approximate frequencies of 600, 1,400 1,680, 2,250, and 3,100 per minute, the largest response occurring

70089—34——2

at the frequencies of 600 and 3,100 vibrations per minute.

From subsequent experimental observations, the disturbance at the frequency of 1,400 vibrations per minute was traced to a resonant vibration of the trailing edge of the lower wing, that at 1,670 to one of the wing spans, and that at 2,200 to the bench supporting the rear spring. The disturbance due to the supporting bench was eliminated in all subsequent tests. The two main disturbances, that at 600 and that at 3,100 per minute, were identified as the resonant vibrations of the fuselage.

Because limitations of the vibrator unit did not permit a lengthy running at higher speeds, no record readings were taken with the automatic observer at the frequencies above 3,200 per minute. The elastic curves of the fuselage at any one frequency, however, could be determined approximately by observing amplitudes at different positions. The elastic curve at 4,000 per minute is shown in figure 10. No other amplitude peaks, small or large, were observed at the range of frequencies between 3,200 and 4,500 per minute.

Vibration response of the fuselage with the wings removed, and with the vibrator mounted at the center of gravity of the airplane.—The vibration tests on the PW-9 fuselage were continued with the vibrator mounted on the upper longerons immediately above the center of gravity of the airplane, with the wings and stabilizer replaced by equivalent weights located at their respective centers of gravity. Because of the very large response of the fuselage at the frequency of 2,500 vibrations per minute when the unbalanced weights used at the engine block were applied at this position, weights of less than one-third the magnitude were used in these tests. The results are given in figures 11 and 12. No vibration was observed at frequencies below about 1,800 and only small response immediately above 3,000 per minute. A pronounced maximum response was obtained at 2,500 per minute.

Only by using the larger weights was it possible to obtain even a small response at 600 per minute of the form given in figure 10, because the forces were applied immediately above the nodal point of the elastic curve at this frequency.

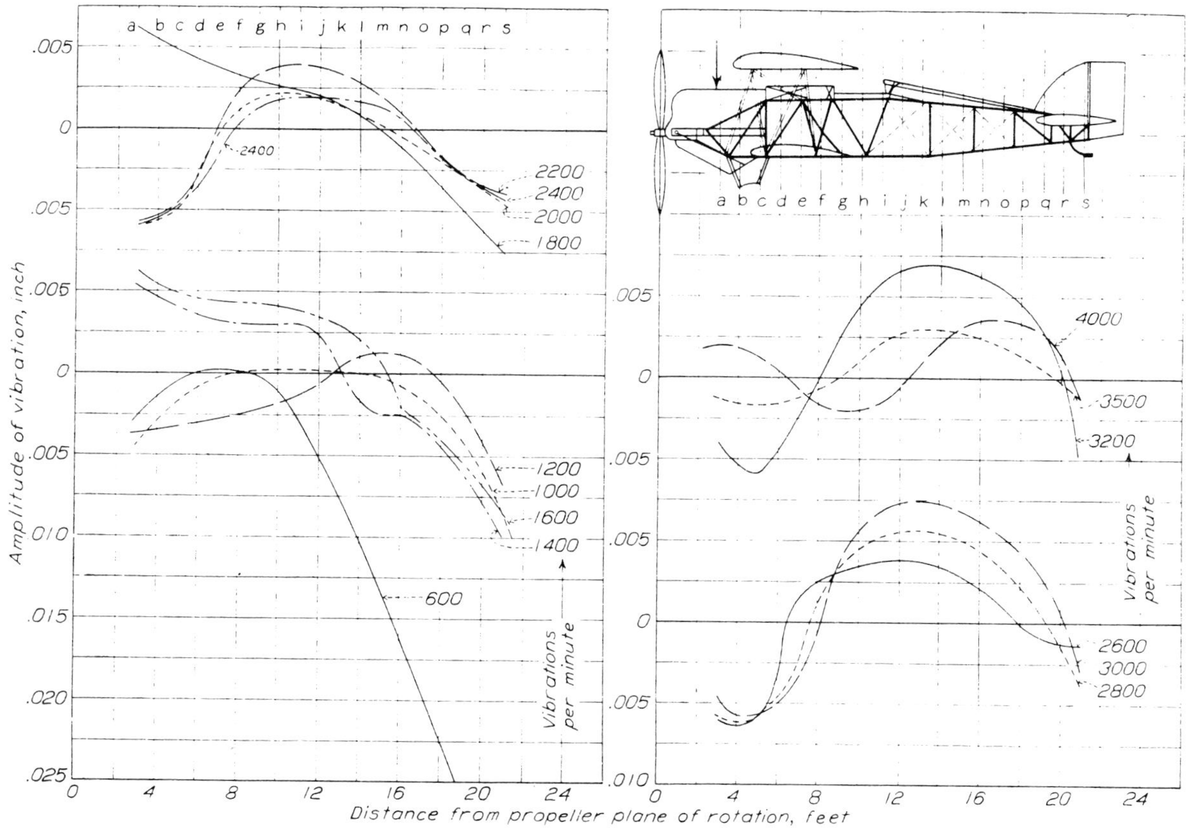

FIGURE 10.—Elastic curves of the lower longeron of the PW-9 airplane at different frequencies.

The unmistakable response at a frequency of 2,500 vibrations per minute was similar to that expected from a comparatively clean undamped structure. The form of the elastic curve at this critical frequency corresponds to that of a frequency of 3,100 vibrations per minute in the vibration results with the wings on. (See fig. 10.) The lowering in frequency of this mode of vibration from 3,100 with the wings on to 2,500 vibrations per minute without the wings may be attributed to the loss of the stiffening effect of the wing bracing. A smaller response at the frequency of about

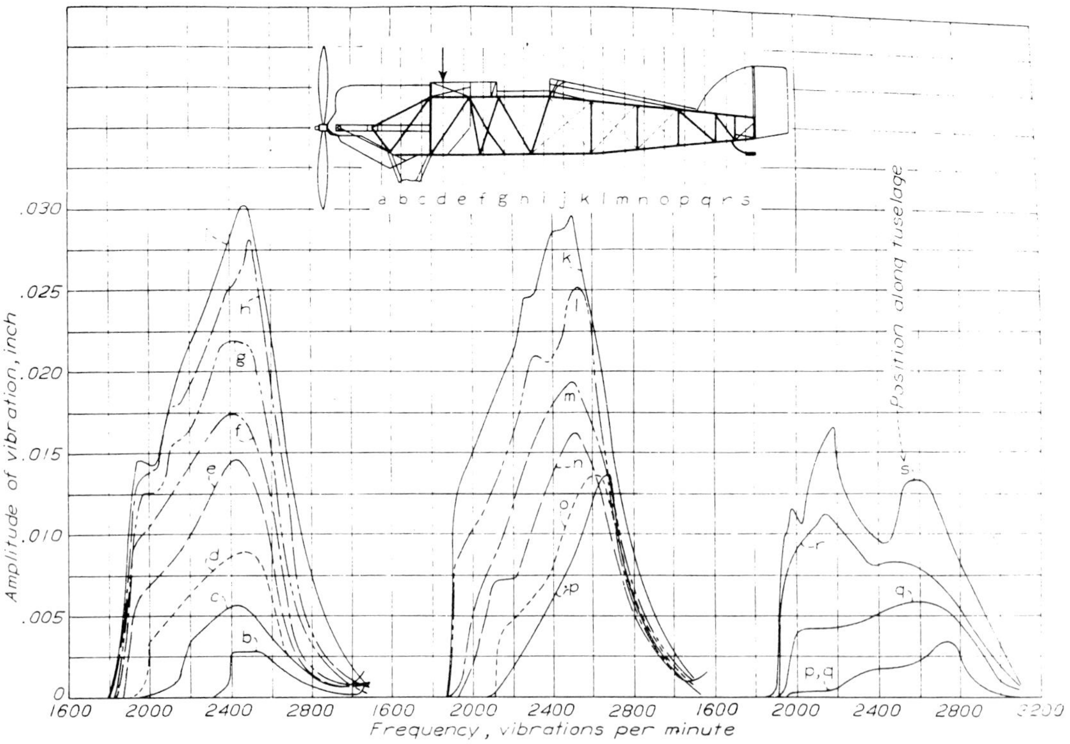

FIGURE 11.—Vibration response along the lower longeron of the PW-9 airplane. No wings nor stabilizer. Vibrator mounted at the center of gravity of the airplane.

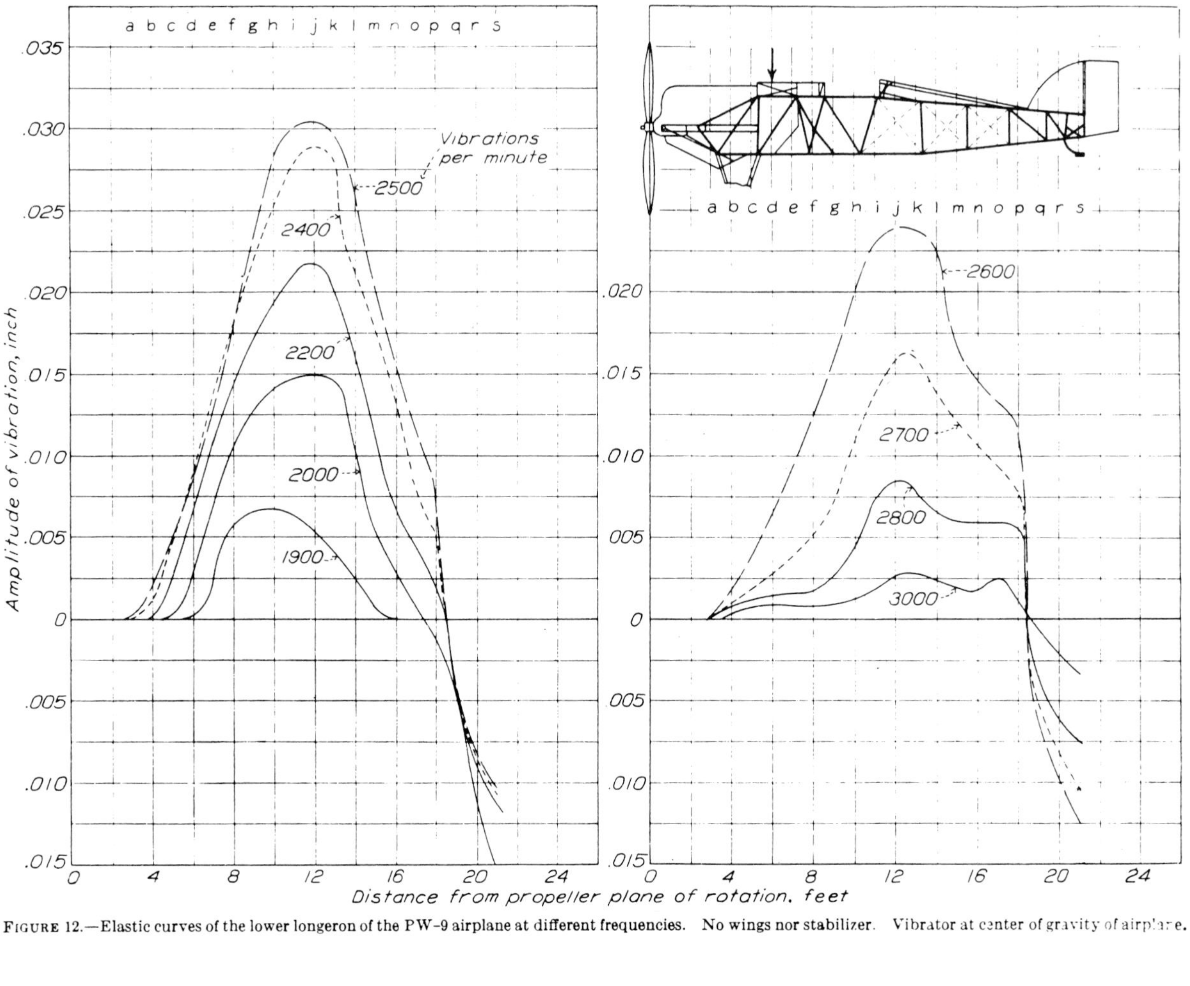

FIGURE 12.—Elastic curves of the lower longeron of the PW-9 airplane at different frequencies. No wings nor stabilizer. Vibrator at center of gravity of airplane.

2,100 per minute, localized at the span of the upper longerons on which the vibrator was mounted, was also observed. This response was found to be a resonant vibration of this span brought within the range of recording due to the added weight of the vibrator. The effect of this local disturbance is noticeable in the shape of the curves of figure 12. No other resonant vibrations were observed up to 4,000 vibrations per minute. The amplitude of vibration along the fuselage remained below about 0.0025 inch at these higher speeds, even though the force applied increased as the square of the speed.

Additional tests for the determination of the fundamental mode of the PW–9 fuselage.—The results of figures 9 to 12 have shown two critical frequencies of the fuselage, one at 600 vibrations per minute and the other at 3,100 with the wings attached, or at 2,500 with the wings replaced by an equivalent weight. Theoretical considerations show that the airplane being flexibly mounted, the fuselage may be considered as a free-end beam of nonuniform elasticity and weight distribution. The elastic curve of a free, uniform beam gives for the mode of lowest frequency very nearly three-fourths of a full wave corresponding to $3\pi/2$ radians, the second mode $5\pi/2$, the third $7\pi/2$, etc. The frequencies of these 2-, 3-, 4-node, etc., vibrations bear the relation to each other of 1, $(5/3)^2$, $(7/3)^2$, etc., or 1, 2.77, 5.44, etc. Beams having stiffness and weight distributions comparable to those of an airplane fuselage are expected to give larger frequency ratios between the fundamental and the higher principal modes of vibration. The ratio of the lower to the higher critical frequency for the fuselage of the PW–9 (figs. 9 to 12) was found to be 5.1 with the wings on and 4.1 without the wings. Further tests on other airplanes supplementing these results are considered desirable.

In order to obtain an unquestionable evidence whether the disturbance at 600 vibrations per minute was the fundamental mode of vibration of the fuselage, tests were conducted with a wooden-beam model of proportional elasticity and weight distribution. In figure 13 the forms of vibration obtained at different conditions are given. Weights were mounted on the forward part to represent the power-plant unit and wings, and a small weight on the other extreme end to represent the tail unit. With the amount and location of fixed weights, given in the figure, a fundamental mode of vibration of two nodes was obtained at the frequency of 460 per minute, and a second mode of three nodes at 1,550 per minute. These values give the ratio of the fundamental to the second mode as 3.4. One of the nodes of the fundamental frequency was located near the center of gravity of the forward weights, and the other one about two-thirds the distance toward the tail. As the ratio of the weights of the forward part to those at the tail was increased, however, the node nearer the tail of the fundamental mode moved forward and approached the second. Simultaneously, the amplitude of vibration under the larger weights diminished considerably. This form of vibration duplicated approximately the form that was obtained with the fuselage of the PW–9 at 600 per minute.

Supplementary static tests were made by supporting the fuselage under the center of gravity and applying weights at both ends and at only the tail end of the PW–9 fuselage. Computations made from the observed deflections gave the frequency of the fundamental mode as being within 50 cycles of 600 vibrations per minute.

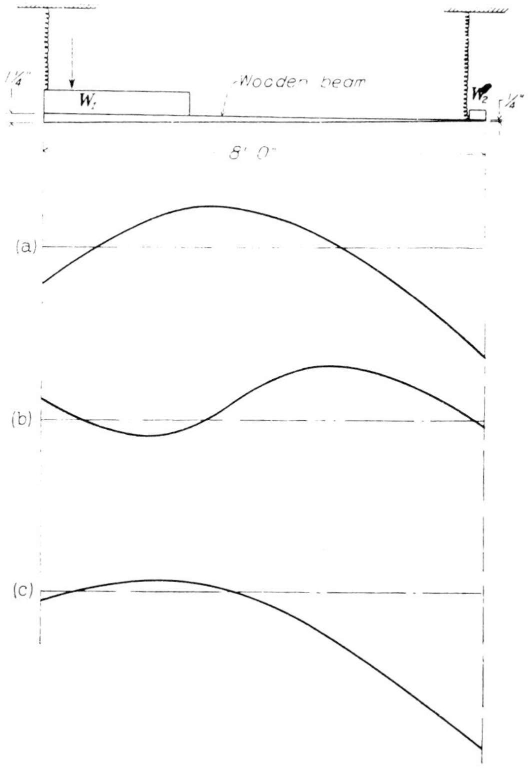

FIGURE 13.—Test results with a model beam.
a. Fundamental mode of vibration—W_1=70 pounds, W_2=2.5 pounds. Frequency=460 vibrations per minute.
b. Second principal mode—W_1=70 pounds, W_2=2.5 pounds. Frequency=1,550 vibrations per minute.
c. Fundamental mode—W_1=150 pounds, W_2=1 pound. Frequency=650 vibrations per minute.

The model and static tests proved beyond doubt that the 2-noded fundamental mode of vibration of this particular fuselage is at 600 per minute. The elastic curves of figure 10 indicate that the 3-noded second principal mode of vibration must lie in the range of frequencies between 2,500 and 4,500 per minute. Since no critical frequencies other than that at 3,100 per minute with the wings and 2,500 without the wings were observed up to frequencies of 4,500 per minute, it is logical to conclude that these frequencies are the second principal modes of vibration of the fuselage, although some doubt still exists as to the location of their nodes.

Vibration response with the vibrator mounted near the tail of the PW-9 airplane.—The studies of the fuselage vibration were further pursued by mounting the vibrator on the fuselage immediately forward of the fin. Both forces and moments were applied. Different methods of suspension were employed to eliminate any possible effects of the supports and in particular to

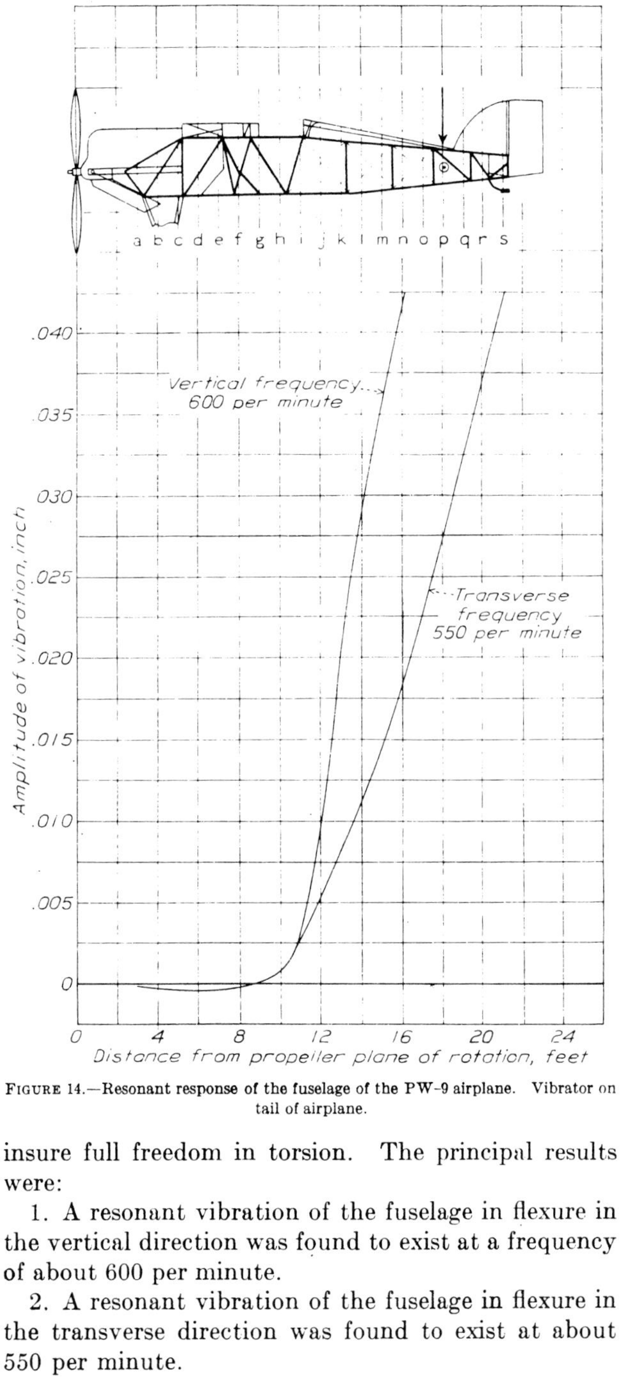

FIGURE 14.—Resonant response of the fuselage of the PW-9 airplane. Vibrator on tail of airplane.

insure full freedom in torsion. The principal results were:

1. A resonant vibration of the fuselage in flexure in the vertical direction was found to exist at a frequency of about 600 per minute.

2. A resonant vibration of the fuselage in flexure in the transverse direction was found to exist at about 550 per minute.

3. A resonant vibration of the fuselage in torsion was found to exist at a frequency slightly under 500 per minute.

4. A resonant vibration of the stabilizer in torsion about an axis transverse to the fore-and-aft axis at about 1,900 per minute.

5. A resonant torsional vibration of the fuselage alone with the fin and rudder and without the stabilizer at the frequency of about 1,700 per minute. Because of the play in the controlling gear between the stabilizer and the fuselage, the fuselage executed a torsional vibration of its own as though the stabilizer did not exist. The vibration, although damped by the large inertia of the stabilizer, was relatively noticeable. It was definitely identified only after the tests were conducted with the stabilizer removed.

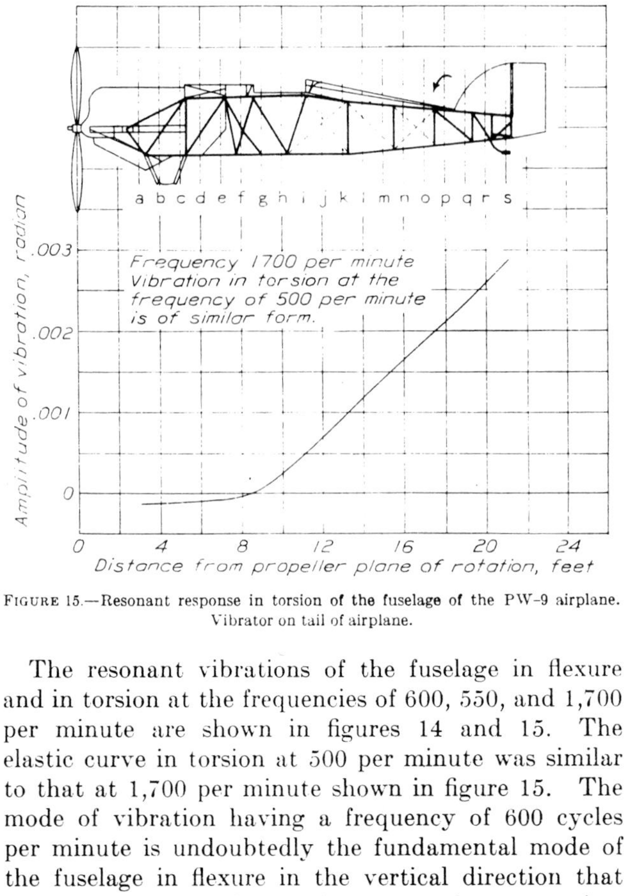

FIGURE 15.—Resonant response in torsion of the fuselage of the PW-9 airplane. Vibrator on tail of airplane.

The resonant vibrations of the fuselage in flexure and in torsion at the frequencies of 600, 550, and 1,700 per minute are shown in figures 14 and 15. The elastic curve in torsion at 500 per minute was similar to that at 1,700 per minute shown in figure 15. The mode of vibration having a frequency of 600 cycles per minute is undoubtedly the fundamental mode of the fuselage in flexure in the vertical direction that was determined in the previous tests; that at 550 is a flexure in the transverse direction; and that at 500 a torsion. It was practically impossible to distinguish the nodes of vibration forward of about 9 feet from the propeller axis, the vibration amplitudes being very small and within the limits of experimental error. The large inertia of the engine block, accessories, and wings damped any normal response of the fuselage structure.

Vibration response of N2Y-1 fuselage.—Another set of curves of flexural vibration of the lower longeron in the vertical direction, which were obtained with the vibrograph in its early stages of development, is shown in figure 16. The N2Y-1, a Naval training airplane weighing approximately 1,600 pounds, was used in these tests, and was mounted in a manner similar to the PW-9. Owing to the high magnification and the relatively high error in the instrument at the time, some difficulty was experienced in recording the response curves at the critical frequencies and in determining the exact mode of vibration of the structure. In general, however, the modes of vibration are identical with those obtained with the PW-9. From these instrumental and also from visual observations, principal modes of vibration were noted at the approximate frequencies of 750, 1,100, 1,900, and 2,900 vibrations per minute. The mode at 750, judging from the results obtained with the PW-9 tests, is the fundamental mode of vibration of the fuselage in flexure in the vertical direction. The disturbances at 1,100 and 1,900 per minute were found to be resonant vibrations of the upper wing tips and what appeared to be a response of the inner bay spans of both wings, respectively. The resonant vibration at 2,900 per minute is undoubtedly the second principal mode of vibration of the fuselage in the vertical direction, and corresponds to that at 3,100 per minute for the PW-9 fuselage.

Vibration response of upper and lower wings of the PW-9.—In figures 17 to 20, the vibration responses of the upper and lower wings of the PW-9 airplane in the vertical direction are shown. A vertical force was applied at the engine block, as for the tests on the fuselage. The amplitudes were measured along the front spar of the right wings. Check tests on the left half of the wings indicated that there was no appreciable difference in the deflections at corresponding symmetrical positions. Particular attention was given to the location of nodal points. With the exception of frequencies above about 2,500 vibrations per minute, it was quite difficult to determine the exact location of the nodal points because of superimposed disturbances. At the nodal points shown in figure 18, the amplitudes actually did not fall below the values of 0.0005 to 0.0015 inch.

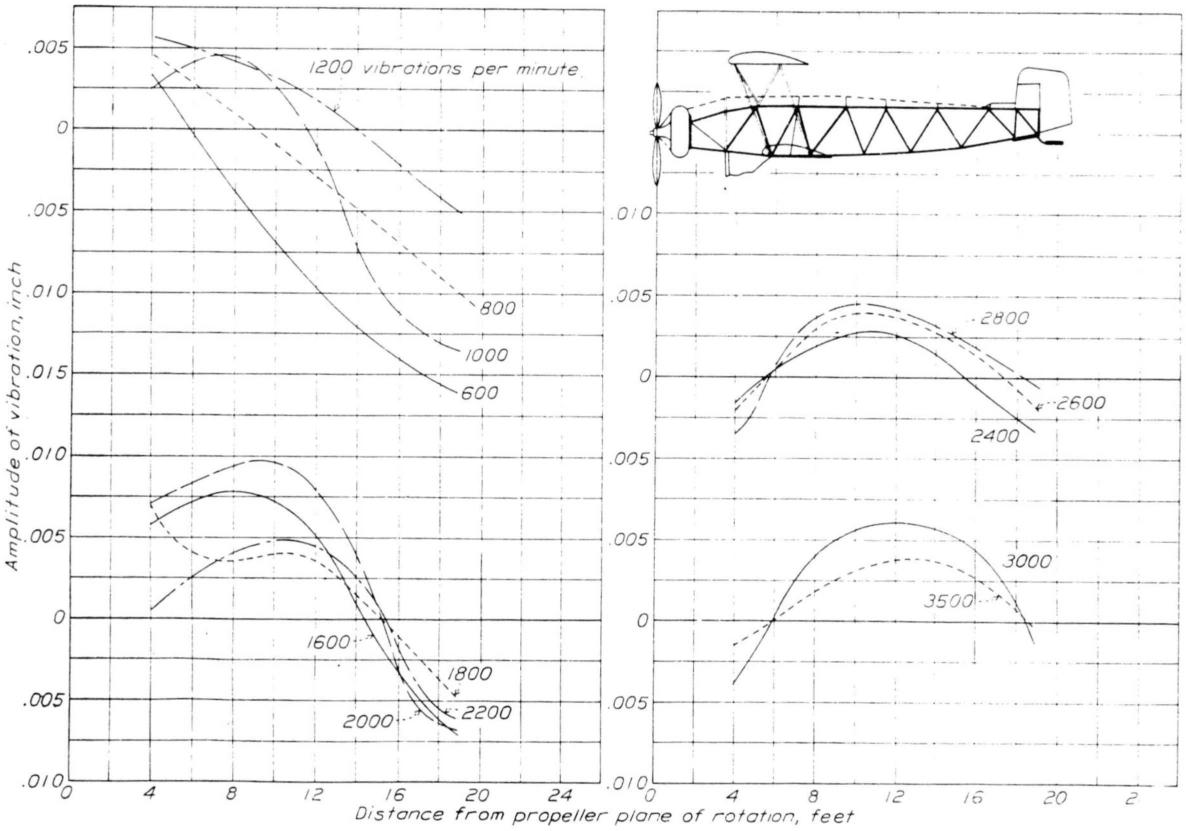

FIGURE 16.—Elastic curves of the lower longeron of N2Y-1 airplane.

The principal amplitude peaks indicating resonant vibrations in the upper wing (fig. 17) are at the approximate frequencies of 800, 1,650, 2,350, and 2,850 vibrations per minute. In addition, there are smaller peaks at 1,050, 1,400, and 2,100 per minute. The principal amplitude peaks in the lower wing (figs.

19 and 20) exist at the approximate frequencies of 1,650 and 2,350 per minute. In addition, there are small peaks at the frequencies of 1,400 and 2,800 per minute. It is difficult to attribute definitely any one of these resonant vibrations to any one of the wings, for they appear in both upper and lower wings. Close examination of the figure and visual observation, however, indicate a resonant vibration of the upper wing tip at a frequency of about 800 per minute, a resonance in the inner bay span at 2,350 per minute, and a resonance mode in mid-span at 2,800 per minute. In the lower wing the indications are that there is a resonant vibration of the wing tip at a frequency of 1,650 per minute and one in the trailing edge at 1,400 per minute. Although the effect of the vibration of the trailing edge of the lower wing is not marked by excessively high amplitudes at the leading edge, the observed amplitudes at the trailing edge at the frequency of 1,400 per minute exceeded the range of the available instruments. From figures 19 and 20 it is seen that the vibration of the entire lower wing appears to be largely influenced by vibrations in the upper wing and the fuselage. The tips of both wings are in a state of continual disturbance throughout almost the whole range of speeds.

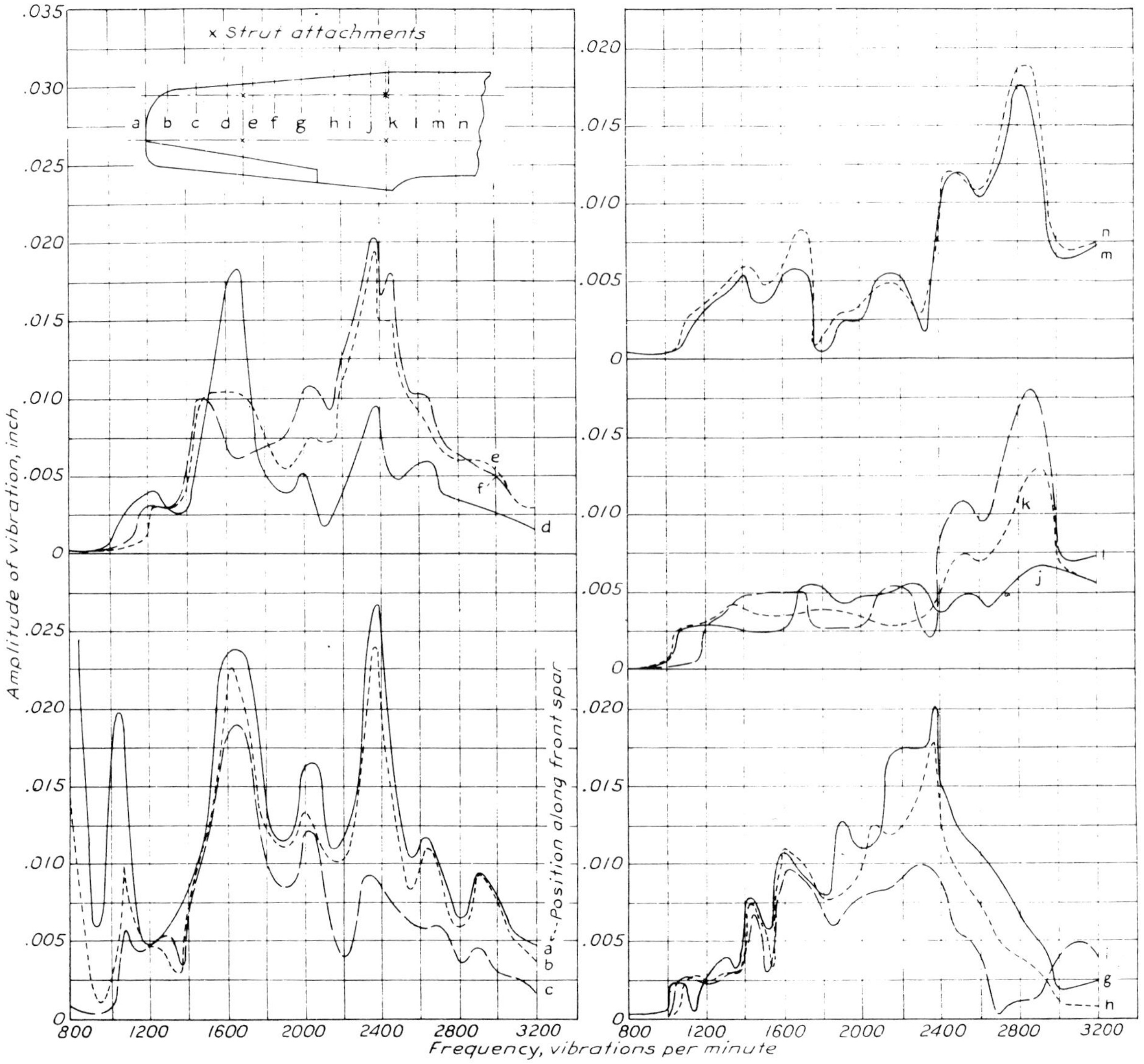

FIGURE 17.—Vibration response along the front spar of the upper wing of the PW-9 airplane.

General discussion of the vibrator tests.—A summary of the principal response of the PW-9 structure is given in table II. It may be concluded that the fuselage of an airplane usually has the fundamental modes of vibration in flexure and in torsion within the range of possible buffeting frequencies and possibly within the range of the 1/2 harmonic of the engine speed. Flight tests showed buffeting frequencies to vary from a few hundred to 1,200 vibrations per

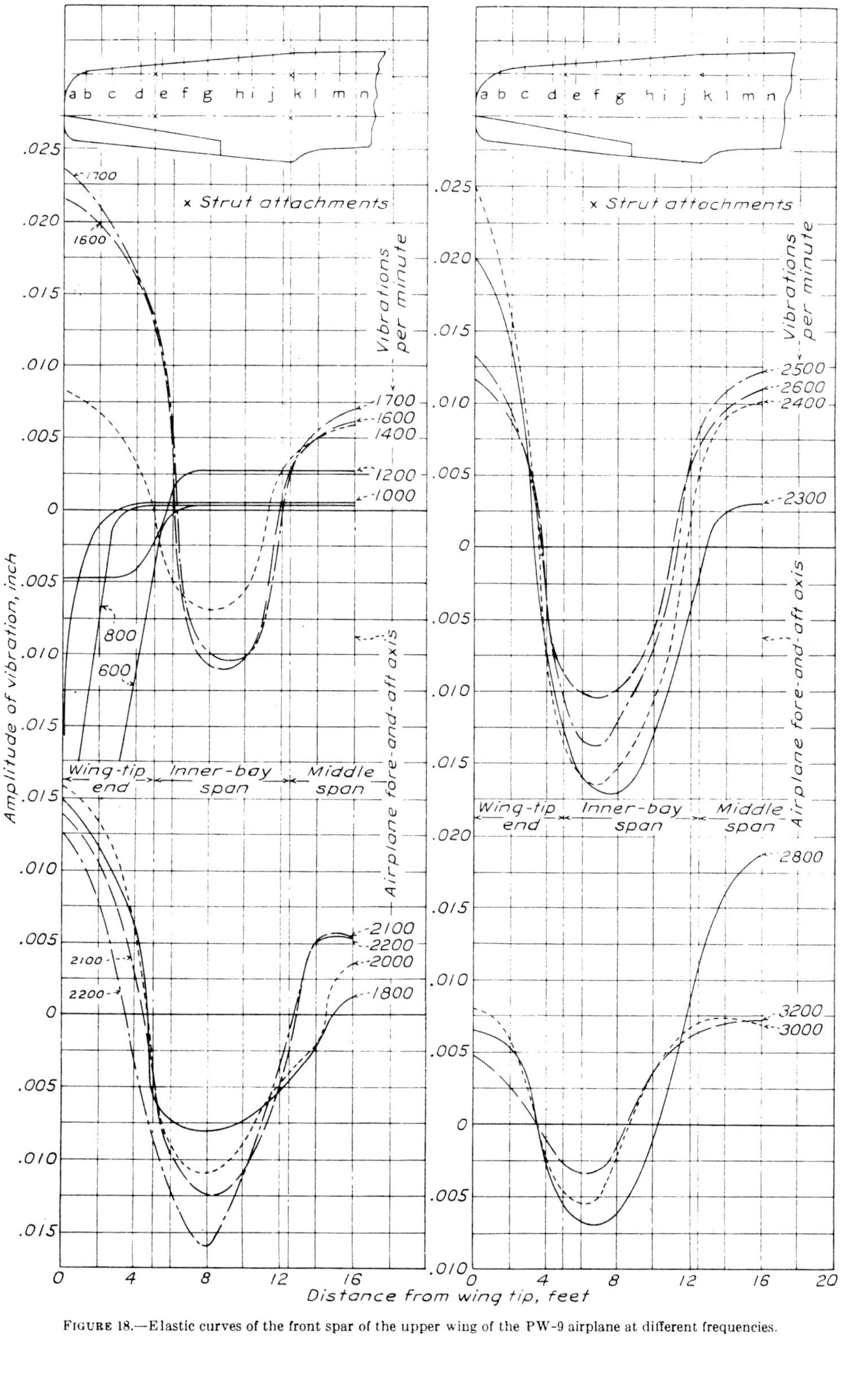

FIGURE 18.—Elastic curves of the front spar of the upper wing of the PW-9 airplane at different frequencies.

minute (reference 5). In order to avoid resonance, the fuselage, especially back of the cockpit, may have to be stiffened in order that its fundamental mode of vibration falls above these frequencies. If the operating range of the engine is between 1,500 and 1,900 revolutions per minute, the logical range of the fundamental mode of vibration of the fuselage is

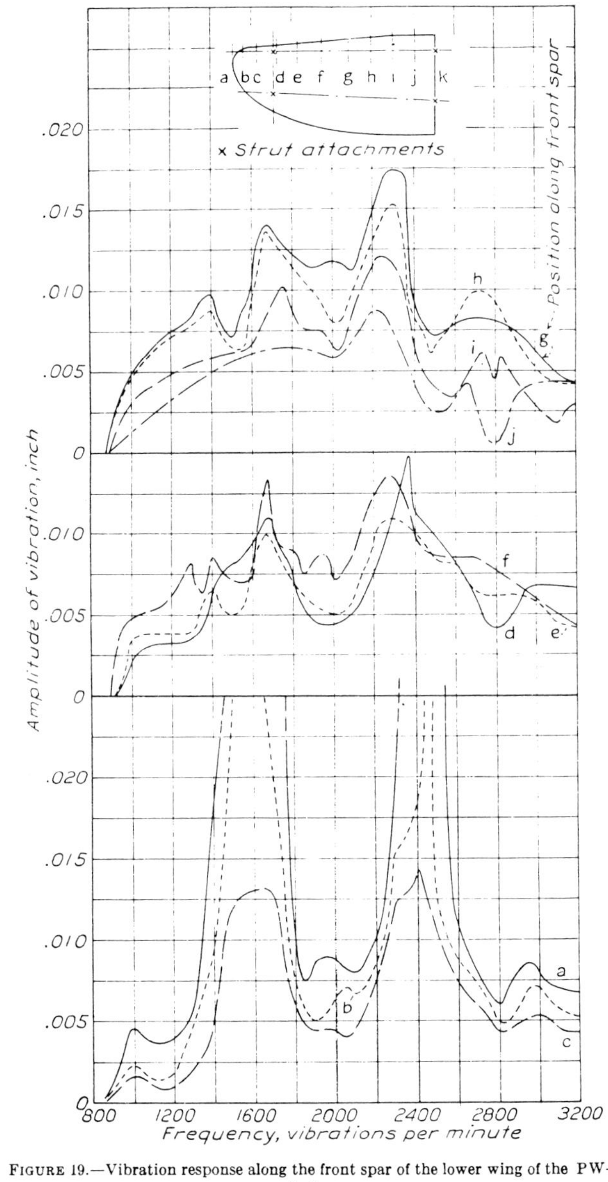

FIGURE 19.—Vibration response along the front spar of the lower wing of the PW-9 airplane.

between 1,200 and 1,500 per minute. Since the other parts of the tail structure besides the fuselage are affected by buffeting impulses as well, these also must be designed to avoid resonance.

The second principal modes of vibration of the fuselage in flexure or in torsion may fall at frequencies higher than the first order of the engine speed. For both airplanes tested, in which the frequency of the second principal mode of vibration of the fuselage in flexure in the vertical direction was found to be close to 3,000 per minute, the possibility exists that the fuselage may resonate either in flexure or in torsion with a possible exciting force of the second order of the inertia unbalance and the torque resultant of the same order from the engine or propeller.

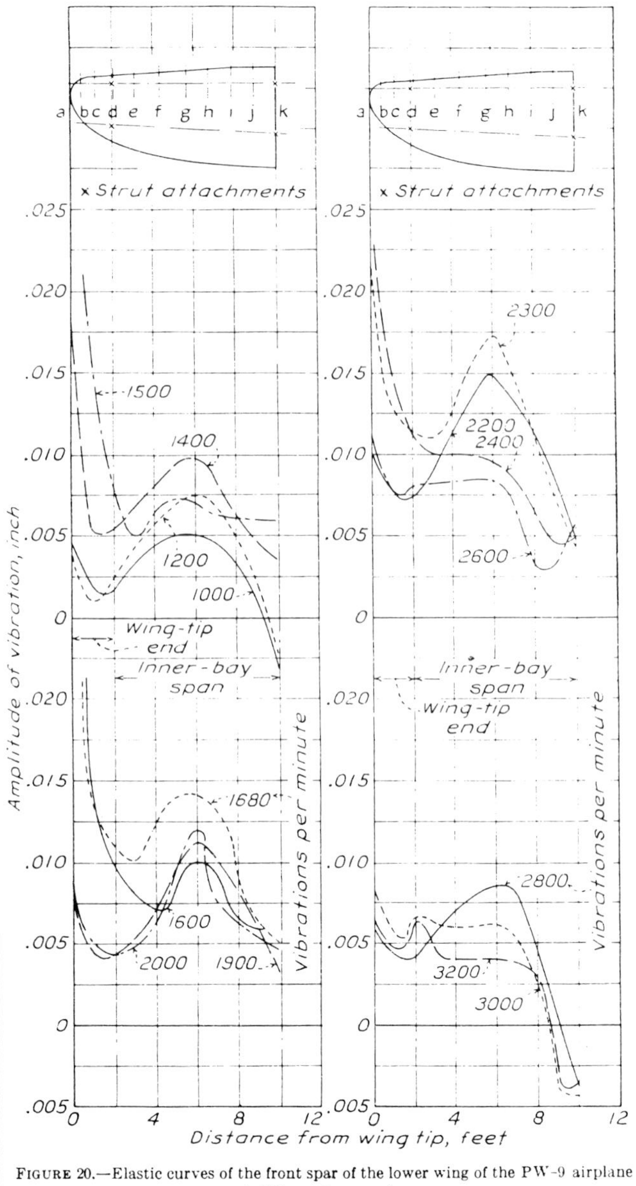

FIGURE 20.—Elastic curves of the front spar of the lower wing of the PW-9 airplane at different frequencies.

Although no tests were conducted to determine the second principal mode of vibration in flexure in the transverse direction, these are believed to be at slightly lower frequencies than that in the vertical direction, as the stiffness of the structure is usually made somewhat less in these directions.

Similar considerations apply to the design of the aircraft wings. It would seem from these tests that the vibrations transmitted to the fuselage because of resonant responses in the wings are of sufficient magnitude to be a source of discomfort to passengers, although they may not endanger the structure. In biplanes there is a considerable likelihood that the principal modes of vibration of the several wing spans will be distributed over a wide range of frequencies. Considerable caution must therefore be exercised in designing the wings to avoid a resonant response by any of their spans with exciting sources in the engine or propeller.

In general, in the design of the aircraft structure, it is necessary first to design for strength and lightness,

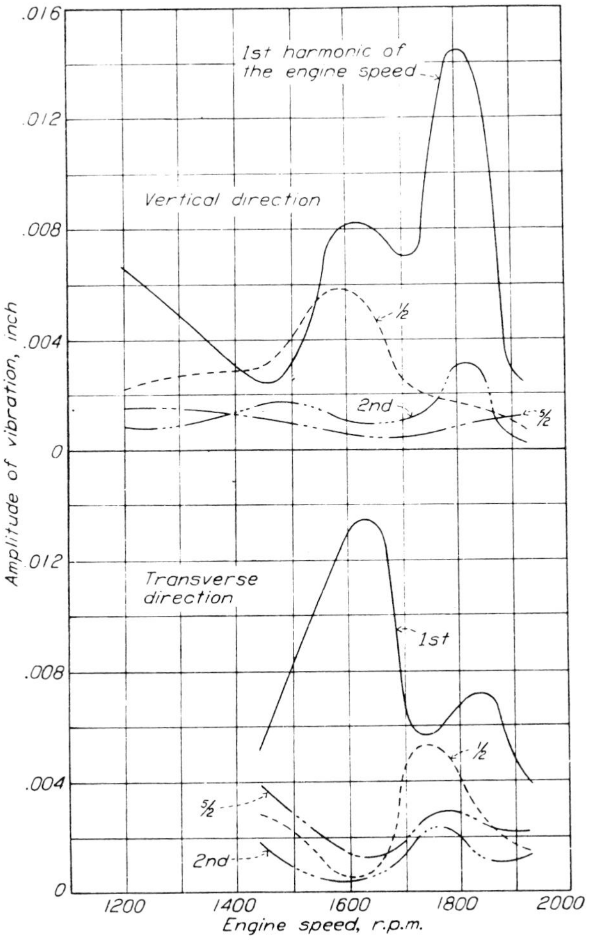

FIGURE 21.—Vibration in the rear cockpit of the N2Y-1 airplane in flight.

to obtain the minimum possible weight, and then to determine the natural modes of vibration of the various members of the structure by computation or by other means. If, in normal operating conditions of the aircraft, the frequency of any of these modes synchronizes with any of the exciting frequencies, the logical course is to change the design of the member, provided that the change does not conflict too much with other requirements.

Flight tests with vibration recorders in rear cockpit of N2Y-1.—The results of tests made with the N2Y-1 are shown in figures 21 and 22. This airplane was similar to the one that was used to determine the vibration response of the fuselage given in figure 16.

In figure 21 the vibration of the upper longeron in the rear cockpit in the vertical and transverse directions is given. The flights were made with the airplane in a level attitude. The principal amplitude peaks are at 1,630 and 1,800 revolutions per minute. Since the frequency of these peaks coincides with the engine speed, the cause of the excessive vibration at these speeds can confidently be attributed to the engine or propeller.

The amplitude peak at 1,800 revolutions per minute was determined by visual observations to be due to a flexure in the inner bay span of the wings in

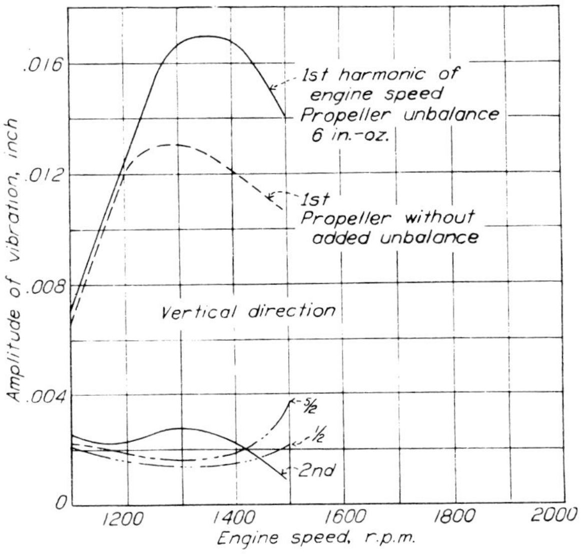

FIGURE 22.—Vibration of engine block of N2Y-1 airplane on the ground with propeller unbalance.

the vertical direction. In the description of the vibration-response tests for an N2Y-1 airplane it was explained that a resonant vibration existed in the wings at 1,950 vibrations per minute. In this airplane, which is very similar to the one used to obtain the results of figure 16, a corresponding mode of vibration cannot be far from the above frequency. The peak of the first harmonic at 1,630 is probably mostly due to a torsional disturbance, for the vibration is noticeable in both the vertical and transverse directions.

Figure 21 shows that in addition to the first, only the 1/2, 2, and 5/2 harmonics are of importance. The other amplitudes were much less than 0.001 inch. The 1/2 and 5/2 harmonics must be attributed to the engine torque alone, as it is not possible for inertia forces or other couples of these orders to exist in either the engine, the propeller, or any other source in level flight. A resultant couple in torsion of the 1/2 order is usually caused by the unequal contribution of mean torque by each cylinder of the engine, which, in turn, is the result either of faulty ignition of one or more cylinders or of difference in the mixture strength. A resultant couple of the 5/2 order, inherent in the torque of this engine, is large for a 5-cylinder engine because the torque components of this order are in phase. The second harmonics can be attributed mostly to second-order inertia unbalance due to articulation, which is known to exist in all radial engines.

Neither the second nor the 5/2 harmonics cause any appreciable disturbance in the rear cockpit. The 1/2 harmonic shows amplitude peaks at engine speeds of 1,600 and 1,740 revolutions per minute in the vertical and transverse directions, respectively. The increase of vibration at these engine speeds is a possible indication that the 1/2-order resultant engine torque is in

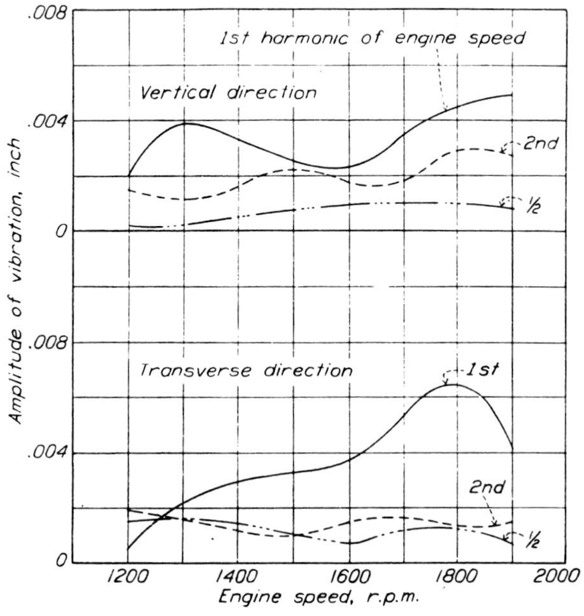

FIGURE 23.—Vibration forward of the front cockpit of the NY-2 airplane in flight.

or near resonance with a resonant vibration of some part of the aircraft structure in torsion—possibly the fuselage, of which the frequency of the fundamental mode of vibration is usually low, as seen from the PW-9 tests.

In figure 22 is shown the vibration of the engine block with added propeller static unbalance. The tests were run on the ground with vibrograph mounted on the engine block so as to record vibration in the vertical direction. There is a peak of vibration of the first harmonic, for both unbalances used, at about 1,300 revolutions per minute. Apparently, a mode of free vibrations of the engine mounting occurs at that frequency. The amplitudes of the other harmonics are not appreciable.

The magnitude of vibration over the entire operating range of this airplane is far beyond the 0.004-inch limit of amplitude for comfortable riding, set by the test results obtained by Constant (reference 1). The explanation of repeated complaints that the N2Y-1 airplane was "rough" and somewhat uncomfortable in the air becomes obvious upon examination of the results of figures 21 and 22.

Flight tests with vibration recorders in front and rear cockpits of NY-2.—In figures 23 and 24 are shown the results obtained with the vibrograph mounted in the front and rear cockpits, respectively, of the NY-2 airplane. The vibrations shown in these figures are those of the upper left longeron.

In flexure, the vibration is hardly noticeable at 1,800 revolutions per minute. The maximum amplitude of 0.006 inch is recorded in the front cockpit and is that of the first harmonic. There appears to be a peak in the amplitude of the first harmonic in the vertical direction at 1,900 revolutions per minute and in the transverse direction at 1,800 revolutions per

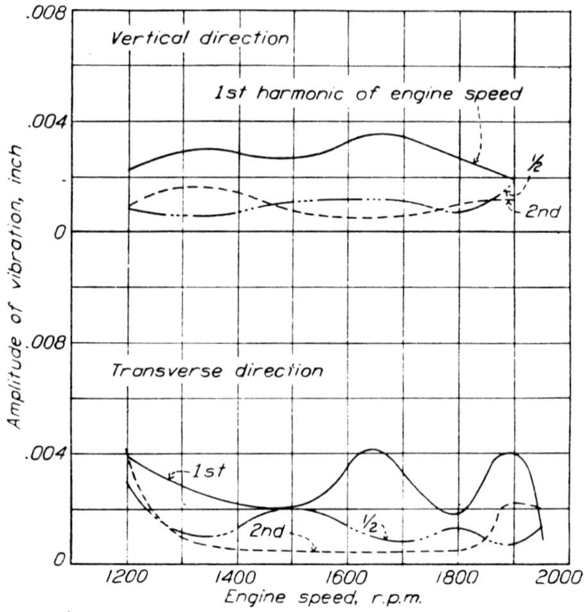

FIGURE 24.—Vibration in the rear cockpit of the NY-2 airplane in flight.

minute, but the vibration is well damped and no definite statement can be made as to whether a mode of vibration in any part of the airplane structure in flexure is of either of these frequencies.

In figure 25 are shown the results obtained with the torsiograph in the front and rear cockpits of the NY-2. The instrument was mounted on the bulkhead along the thrust axis of the airplane. There are amplitude peaks of the 1/2 and second harmonics at 1,800 revolutions per minute and of the first harmonic at 1,900 revolutions per minute or slightly above.

The pilot reported that the vibration in this airplane was noticeable at speeds between 1,800 and 1,900 revolutions per minute and became somewhat disagreeable as the airplane was nosed slightly down at engine speeds slightly above 1,900 revolutions per minute.

Flight tests with vibration recorders on tail of NY-2.—A number of tests of a preliminary nature were made with the vibration recorders mounted on the tail of the airplane. The information obtained thus far is given in tables III and IV. The angles of attack were estimated from aerodynamic data with a probable error of less than 1°. A complete analysis of the records by Fourier series was found somewhat impracticable

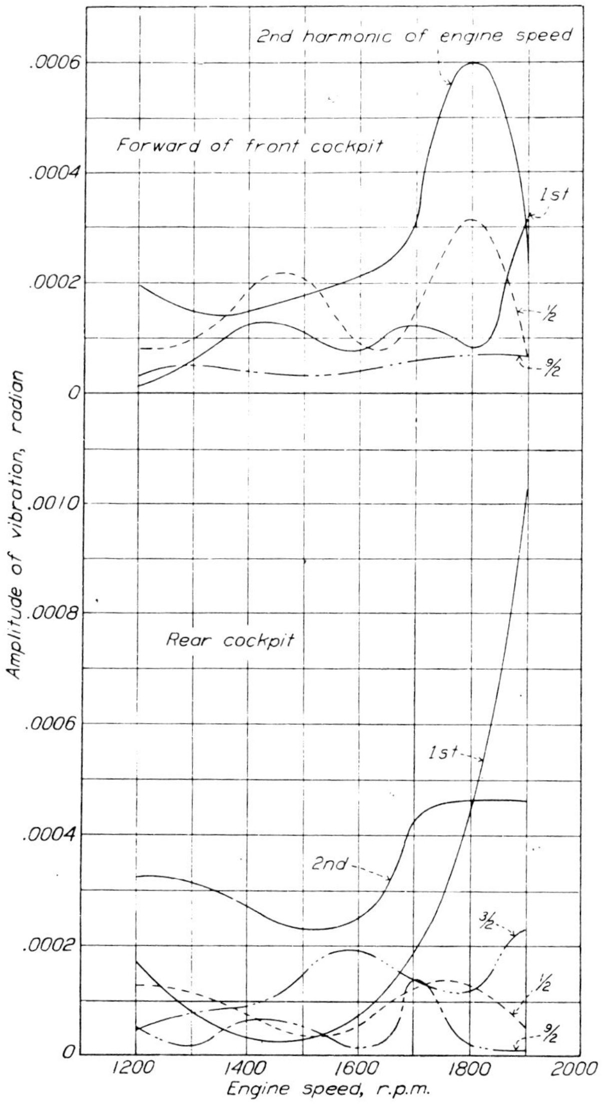

FIGURE 25.—Torsional vibration in the front and rear cockpits of the NY-2 airplane in flight.

and unnecessary in these tests in which the determination of the frequencies of vibration was of more importance. The few superimposed harmonics could be readily separated by an approximate graphical method. The frequencies could be determined to within an accuracy of 10 vibrations per minute. The amplitudes given contain a possible error of 25 percent.

An examination of the frequency column in both the tables shows that a frequency of about 670 vibrations per minute appears often in both flexure and torsion. This vibration made its appearance and was damped out within half a second, sometimes in less time. Since it appears in flexure as well as in torsion, it is reasonable to conclude that it is a torsional frequency of free vibrations of the horizontal tail plane or possibly the fundamental mode of vibration of the fuselage.

In the comparison of the frequencies, air speeds, and angles of attack it is noticed that, in addition to the vibrations whose frequencies are multiples of engine speed, forced vibrations of frequencies in the range of 400 to 650 vibrations per minute make their appearance. These vibrations can only be of aerodynamic origin. Supplementary tests have shown these low-frequency vibrations to be a maximum near the stern post, but decreasing rapidly forward of the tail; and they were hardly noticeable immediately back of the cockpit.

CONCLUSIONS

The results of the ground and flight tests with specially designed vibration instruments to determine the response of the several parts of the airplane structure to the forces encountered in flight may be summarized as follows:

1. In ground tests with a vibrator, the frequencies of the fundamental modes of vibration of the fuselages of the two biplanes tested were found to lie between 500 and 750 vibrations per minute for both flexure and torsion. The frequency of the second principal mode of vibration of the fuselages in flexure in the vertical direction was found to be close to 3,000 per minute. The wings vibrated approximately as multispan beams having the supports close to the strut attachments, and the natural frequencies of the several spans ranged from about 800 to 2,800 per minute.

2. In flight tests with airplanes equipped with radial engines, vibrations at, or forward of, the rear cockpit were found to be of frequencies that were multiples of the engine speed, a positive indication of their origin being in the engine or the propeller. In addition, vibrations of low frequencies were found to be present in the part of the fuselage back of the cockpits. These vibrations were of maximum intensity near the stern post. Some of these low frequencies were not multiples of the engine speed, apparently being of aerodynamic origin.

3. Ground and flight tests indicate that unless resonance occurs between a free mode of vibration of the airplane structure and the exciting source, the magnitude of vibration is usually of no practical consequence. It follows that considerable reduction of vibration may be obtained by avoiding a resonance of

a mode of free vibration of the structure and the exciting sources. Because of the large number of independent degrees of freedom of the several parts of the structure, however, the reduction can only be accomplished after close study of the response characteristics of the particular type of structure in connection with a knowledge of the exciting forces.

LANGLEY MEMORIAL AERONAUTICAL LABORATORY,
NATIONAL ADVISORY COMMITTEE FOR AERONAUTICS,
LANGLEY FIELD, VA., *May 10, 1934.*

REFERENCES

1. Constant, H.: Aircraft Vibration. Roy. Aero. Soc. Jour., March 1932, pp. 205–250.
2. Constant, Hayne: Torque Reaction and Vibration. Aircraft Eng., June 1932, pp. 146–149.
3. Tanaka, Keikichi: The Inertia Forces and Couples and Their Balancing of the Star Type Engine. Aero. Research Inst., Tokyo Imperial Univ., vol. 1, no. 10, 1925, pp. 247–304.
4. Roche, J. A.; Airplane Vibrations and Flutter Controllable by Design. S.A.E. Jour., September 1933, pp. 305–312.
5. Blenk, Hermann, Hertel, Heinrich, and Thalau, Karl: The German Investigation of the Accident at Meopham (England). T.M. No. 669, N.A.C.A., 1932.
6. Biechteler, Curt: Tests for the Elimination of Tail Flutter. T.M. No. 710, N.A.C.A., 1933.

TABLE I.—TYPES OF TESTS AND AIRPLANES USED

Airplane tested	Type of tests	Vibration measured
PW-9; pursuit biplane; 12-cylinder Curtiss engine.	Stationary tests with vibrator on engine block, *c.g.* of airplane, and tail.	Along lower longeron and front spar of both wings.
	Tests with wings on and without the wings	Along lower longeron.
N2Y-1; training biplane; 5-cylinder radial Kinner engine.	Stationary tests with vibrator on engine block	Do.
	Ground tests engine running	Of engine block.
	Flight tests	In rear cockpit.
NY-2; training biplane; 9-cylinder radial, Wright engine.	do	In front cockpit.
	do	In rear cockpit.
	do	On tail.

TABLE II.—SUMMARY OF PRINCIPAL RESPONSES OF THE PW-9 STRUCTURE AS DETERMINED IN THE VIBRATOR TESTS

Member responding	Type of response	Frequency vibrations per minute	Mode of vibration
Fuselage	Flexure in vertical direction	600	Fundamental.
Fuselage with wings	do	3, 100	Second principal mode.
Fuselage without wings	do	2, 500	Do.
Do	Flexure in transverse direction	550	Fundamental.
Do	Torsion about fore-and-aft axis	500	Do.
Upper wing:			
Wing tip or outer bay span	Flexure in vertical direction	800	Do.
Inner bay span	do	2, 350	Do.
Middle span	do	2, 800	Do.
Lower wing:			
Outer bay span	do	1, 650	Do.
Inner bay span	do	2, 300	Do.
Trailing edge	Torsion about axis along spar	1, 400	Do.
Stabilizer	Torsion about axis transversely to fore-and-aft axis	1, 850	Do.

TABLE III.—NY-2 TAIL VIBRATIONS IN THE VERTICAL DIRECTION VIBROGRAPH TEST IN FLIGHT

Record no.	Approximate angle of attack	Air speed	Engine speed	Frequency, vibrations per minute	Amplitude of vibrations
	°	M.p.h.	R.p.m.		Inch
1	0.0	75	1,650	1,650	0.005
				825	.014
				670	.015
2	−.5	80	1,700	1,700	.006
				850	.010
3	1.2	70	1,600	1,600	.008
				800	.007
4	−1.0	84	1,700	1,700	.008
				850	.011
				670	.017
5	−1.7	92	1,800	1,800	.010
				900	.013
6	3.2	61	1,500	1,500	.005
				750	.008
				670	.011
7	[1] −2.6	107	1,900	1,900	.005
				950	.012
				670	.034
8	[1] −2.7	109	1,900	1,900	.008
				950	.012
				640	.018
				490	.024
9	8.2	46	1,300	2,600	.004
				1,300	.008
				650	.013
10	11.4	40	1,200	1,200	.008
				600	.016
				670	.024

Record no.	Approximate angle of attack	Air speed	Engine speed	Frequency, vibrations per minute	Amplitude of vibrations
	°	M.p.h.	R.p.m.		Inch
11	11.4	40	1,200	2,400	0.003
				1,200	.008
				600	.012
12	11.4	40	1,500	1,500	.005
				750	.012
13	10.2	43	1,300	2,600	.004
				1,300	.005
				650	.008
14	10.8	43	1,480	1,480	.007
				740	.012
15	13.0	38	1,500	1,500	.003
				750	.013
16	[2] 16.0	37	1,600	1,600	.0025
				800	.016
				600	.028
				400	.027
17	[2] 16.0	37	1,600	800	.013
				550	.044
18	[3] 18.0	36	1,600	800	.010
				640	.013
19	[4] −3.4	127	1,950	1,940	.009
				970	.013
				550	.032
20	[4] −2.4	104	1,200	600	.008
				480	.015
				390	.021
21	[4] −2.4	104	1,200	1,200	.011
				600	.019
				400	.021

[1] Slight diving angle.
[2] Stall, or slightly above.
[3] Above stall.
[4] Dive.

TABLE IV.—TORSIONAL VIBRATIONS OF THE NY-2 TAIL[1] TORSIOGRAPH TEST IN FLIGHT

Record no.	Approximate angle of attack	Air speed	Engine speed	Frequency, vibrations per minute	Amplitude of vibrations	Record no.	Approximate angle of attack	Air speed	Engine speed	Frequency, vibrations per minute	Amplitude of vibrations
	°	M.p.h.	R.p.m.		Radian		°	M.p.h.	R.p.m.		Radian
1	0.6	73	1,600	670	0.00063	8	−3.0	115	1,810	600	0.00059
2	−1.0	84	1,700	680	.00091	9	−3.2	121	1,800	620	.00063
3	−1.6	92	1,800	680	.00031	10	−3.6	132	1,900	480	.00123
4	10.2	43	1,400	700	.00063	11	−3.4	127	1,600	560	.00086
5	13.0	38	1,510	640	.00118	12	−4.0	150	1,600	550	.00078
6	16.0	37	1,600	580	.00137					570	.00088
7	16.0	37	1,560	780	.00101	13	−4.0	150	1,800	600	.00080
				620	.00084					620	.00080
				480	.00096						

[1] Amplitudes of most frequency multiples of engine speed are not included because their low magnitudes were not easily determinable.

GENERAL THEORY OF AERODYNAMIC INSTABILITY AND THE MECHANISM OF FLUTTER

BY THEODORE THEODORSEN

National Advisory Committee for Aeronautics

Report No. 496, 1935

SUMMARY

The aerodynamic forces on an oscillating airfoil or airfoil-aileron combination of three independent degrees of freedom have been determined. The problem resolves itself into the solution of certain definite integrals, which have been identified as Bessel functions of the first and second kind and of zero and first order. The theory, being based on potential flow and the Kutta condition, is fundamentally equivalent to the conventional wing-section theory relating to the steady case.

The air forces being known, the mechanism of aerodynamic instability has been analyzed in detail. An exact solution, involving potential flow and the adoption of the Kutta condition, has been arrived at. The solution is of a simple form and is expressed by means of an auxiliary parameter k. The mathematical treatment also provides a convenient cyclic arrangement permitting a uniform treatment of all subcases of two degrees of freedom. The flutter velocity, defined as the air velocity at which flutter starts, and which is treated as the unknown quantity, is determined as a function of a certain ratio of the frequencies in the separate degrees of freedom for any magnitudes and combinations of the airfoil-aileron parameters.

For those interested solely or particularly in the numerical solutions Appendix I has been prepared. The routine procedure in solving numerical examples is put down detached from the theoretical background of the paper. It first is necessary to determine a certain number of constants pertaining to the case, then to perform a few routine calculations as indicated. The result is readily obtained in the form of a plot of flutter velocity against frequency for any values of the other parameters chosen. The numerical work of calculating the constants is simplified by referring to a number of tables, which are included in Appendix I. A number of illustrative examples and experimental results are given in Appendix II.

INTRODUCTION

It has been known that a wing or wing-aileron structurally restrained to a certain position of equilibrium becomes unstable under certain conditions. At least two degrees of freedom are required to create a condition of instability, as it can be shown that vibrations of a single degree of freedom would be damped out by the air forces. The air forces, defined as the forces due to the air pressure acting on the wing or wing-aileron in an arbitrary oscillatory motion of several degrees of freedom, are in this paper treated on the basis of the theory of nonstationary potential flow. A wing-section theory and, by analogy, a wing theory shall be thus developed that applies to the case of oscillatory motion, not only of the wing as a whole but also to that of an aileron. It is of considerable importance that large oscillations may be neglected; in fact, only infinitely small oscillations about the position of equilibrium need be considered. Large oscillations are of no interest since the sole attempt is to specify one or more conditions of instability. Indeed, no particular type or shape of airfoil shall be of concern, the treatment being restricted to primary effects. The differential equations for the several degrees of freedom will be put down. Each of these equations contains a statement regarding the equilibrium of a system of forces. The forces are of three kinds: (1) The inertia forces, (2) the restraining forces, and (3) the air forces.

There is presumably no necessity of solving a general case of damped or divergent motion, but only the border case of a pure sinusoidal motion, applying to the case of unstable equilibrium. This restriction is particularly important as the expressions for the air force developed for oscillatory motion can thus be employed. Imagine a case that is unstable to a very slight degree; the amplitudes will then increase very slowly and the expressions developed for the air forces will be applicable. It is of interest simply to know under what circumstances this condition may obtain and cases in which the amplitudes are decreasing or increasing at a finite rate need not be treated or specified. Although it is possible to treat the latter cases, they are of no concern in the present problem. Nor is the internal or solid friction of the structure of primary concern. The fortunate situation exists that the effect of the solid friction is *favorable*. Knowledge is desired concerning the condition as existing in the absence of the internal friction, as this case constitutes a sort of lower limit, which it is not always desirable to exceed.

Owing to the rather extensive field covered in the paper it has been considered necessary to omit many elementary proofs, it being left to the reader to verify certain specific statements. In the first part of the paper, the velocity potentials due to the flow around the airfoil-aileron are developed. These potentials are treated in two classes: The noncirculating flow potentials, and those due to the surface of discontinuity behind the wing, referred to as "circulatory" potentials. The magnitude of the circulation for an oscillating wing-aileron is determined next. The

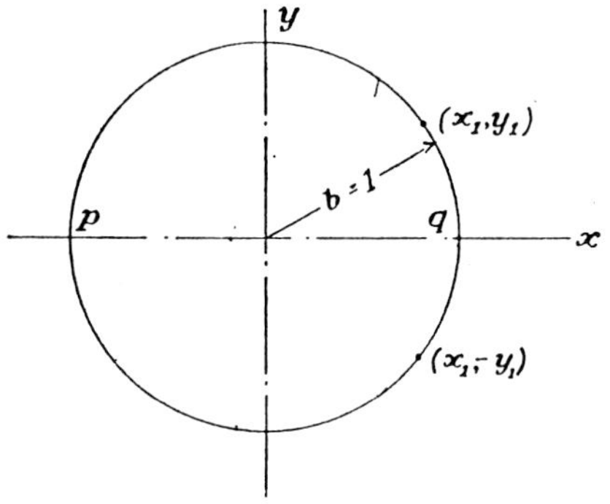

FIGURE 1.—Conformal representation of the wing profile by a circle.

forces and moments acting on the airfoil are then obtained by integration. In the latter part of the paper the differential equations of motion are put down and the particular and important case of unstable equilibrium is treated in detail. The solution of the problem of determining the flutter speed is finally given in the form of an equation expressing a relationship between the various parameters. The three subcases of two degrees of freedom are treated in detail.

The paper proposes to disclose the basic nature of the mechanism of flutter, leaving modifications of the primary results by secondary effects for future investigations.[1] Such secondary effects are: The effects of a finite span, of section shape, of deviations from potential flow, including also modifications of results to include twisting and bending of actual wing sections instead of pure torsion and deflection as considered in this paper.

The supplementary experimental work included in Appendix II similarly refers to well-defined elementary cases, the wing employed being of a large aspect ratio, nondeformable, and given definite degrees of freedom by a supporting mechanism, with external springs maintaining the equilibrium positions of wing or wing-aileron. The experimental work was carried on largely to verify the general shape of and the approximate magnitudes involved in the theoretically predicted response characteristics. As the present report is limited to the mathematical aspects of the flutter problem, specific recommendations in regard to practical applications are not given in this paper.

[1] The effect of internal friction is in some cases essential; this subject will be contained in a subsequent paper.

VELOCITY POTENTIALS, FORCES, AND MOMENTS OF THE NONCIRCULATORY FLOW

We shall proceed to calculate the various velocity potentials due to position and velocity of the individual parts in the whole of the wing-aileron system. Let us temporarily represent the wing by a circle (fig. 1). The potential of a source ϵ at the origin is given by

$$\varphi=\frac{\epsilon}{4\pi}\log\,(x^2+y^2)$$

For a source ϵ at (x_1, y_1) on the circle

$$\varphi=\frac{\epsilon}{4\pi}\log\,\{(x-x_1)^2+(y-y_1)^2\}$$

Putting a double source 2ϵ at (x_1,y_1) and a double negative source -2ϵ at $(x_1, -y_1)$ we obtain for the flow around the circle

$$\varphi=\frac{\epsilon}{2\pi}\log\frac{(x-x_1)^2+(y-y_1)^2}{(x-x_1)^2+(y+y_1)^2}$$

The function φ on the circle gives directly the surface potential of a straight line pq, the projection of the circle on the horizontal diameter. (See fig. 1.) In this case $y=\sqrt{1-x^2}$ and φ is a function of x only.

We shall need the integrals:

$$\int_c^1\log\frac{(x-x_1)^2+(y-y_1)^2}{(x-x_1)^2+(y+y_1)^2}dx_1=2(x-c)\log N-2\sqrt{1-x^2}\cos^{-1}c$$

and

$$\int_c^1\log\frac{(x-x_1)^2+(y-y_1)^2}{(x-x_1)^2+(y+y_1)^2}(x_1-c)dx_1=-\sqrt{1-c^2}\sqrt{1-x^2}$$
$$-\cos^{-1}c(x-2c)\sqrt{1-x^2}+(x-c)^2\log N$$

where $$N=\frac{1-cx-\sqrt{1-x^2}\sqrt{1-c^2}}{x-c}$$

The location of the center of gravity of the wing-aileron x_α is measured from a, the coordinate of the axis of rotation (fig. 2); x_β the location of the center

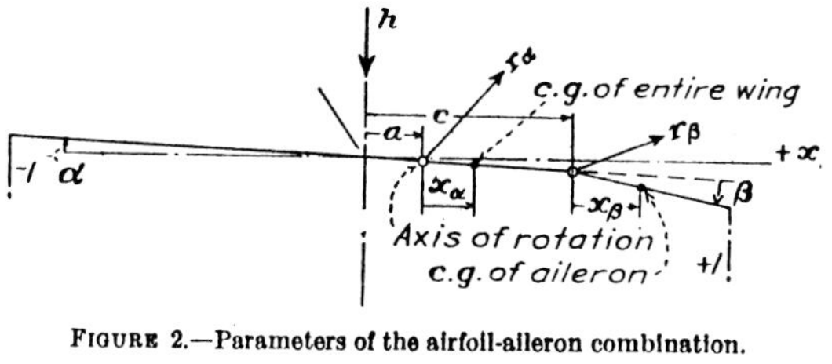

FIGURE 2.—Parameters of the airfoil-aileron combination.

of gravity of the aileron is measured from c, the coordinate of the hinge; and r_α and r_β are the radii of gyration of the wing-aileron referred to a, and of the aileron referred to the hinge. The quantities x_β and r_β are "reduced" values, as defined later in the paper. The quantities a, x_α, c, and x_β are positive toward the rear (right), h is the vertical coordinate of the axis of rotation at a with respect to a fixed reference frame and is positive downward. The angles α and β are positive clockwise (right-hand turn). The wind velocity v is to the right and horizontal. The angle (of attack) α refers to the direction of v, the aileron angle β refers to the undeflected position and *not* to the wind direction. The quantities r_α and r_β always occur as squares. Observe that the leading edge is located at -1, the trailing edge at $+1$. The quantities a, c, x_α, x_β, r_α, and r_β, which are repeatedly used in the following treatment, are all dimensionless with the half chord b as reference unit.

The effect of a flap bent down at an angle β (see fig. 2) is seen to give rise to a function φ obtained by substituting $-v\beta b$ for ϵ; hence

$$\varphi_\beta = \frac{v\beta b}{\pi}[\sqrt{1-x^2}\cos^{-1}c - (x-c)\log N]$$

To obtain the effect of the flap going down at an angular velocity $\dot\beta$, we put $\epsilon = -(x_1-c)\dot\beta b^2$ and get

$$\varphi_{\dot\beta} = \frac{\dot\beta b^2}{2\pi}[\sqrt{1-c^2}\sqrt{1-x^2} + \cos^{-1}c(x-2c)\sqrt{1-x^2} - (x-c)^2\log N]$$

To obtain the effect of an angle α of the entire airfoil, we put $c=-1$ in the expression for φ_β, hence

$$\varphi_\alpha = v\alpha b\sqrt{1-x^2}$$

To depict the airfoil in downward motion with a velocity $\dot h$ (+ down), we need only introduce $\frac{\dot h}{v}$ instead of α. Thus

$$\varphi_{\dot h} = \dot h b\sqrt{1-x^2}$$

Finally, to describe a rotation around point a at an angular velocity $\dot\alpha$, we notice that this motion may be taken to consist of a rotation around the leading edge $c=-1$ at an angular velocity $\dot\alpha$ plus a vertical motion with a velocity $-\dot\alpha(1+a)b$. Then

$$\varphi_{\dot\alpha} = \frac{\dot\alpha b^2}{2\pi}\pi(x+2)\sqrt{1-x^2} - \dot\alpha(1+a)b^2\sqrt{1-x^2} = \dot\alpha b^2\left(\frac{1}{2}x-a\right)\sqrt{1-x^2}$$

The following tables give in succession the velocity potentials and a set of integrals [2] with associated constants, which we will need in the calculation of the air forces and moments.

VELOCITY POTENTIALS

$$\varphi_\alpha = v\alpha b\sqrt{1-x^2}$$

$$\varphi_{\dot h} = \dot h b\sqrt{1-x^2}$$

$$\varphi_{\dot\alpha} = \dot\alpha b^2\left(\frac{1}{2}x-a\right)\sqrt{1-x^2}$$

$$\varphi_\beta = \frac{1}{\pi}v\beta b[\sqrt{1-x^2}\cos^{-1}c - (x-c)\log N]$$

$$\varphi_{\dot\beta} = \frac{1}{2\pi}\dot\beta b^2[\sqrt{1-c^2}\sqrt{1-x^2} + (x-2c)\sqrt{1-x^2}\cos^{-1}c - (x-c)^2\log N]$$

where

$$N = \frac{1-cx-\sqrt{1-x^2}\sqrt{1-c^2}}{x-c}$$

[2] Some of the more difficult integral evaluations are given in Appendix III.

INTEGRALS

$\int_c^1 \varphi_\alpha dx = -\frac{b}{2}v\alpha T_4$	$\int_{-1}^{+1} \varphi_\alpha dx = \frac{b}{2}v\alpha\pi$
$\int_c^1 \varphi_{\dot h} dx = -\frac{b}{2}\dot h T_4$	$\int_{-1}^{+1} \varphi_{\dot h} dx = \frac{b}{2}\dot h\pi$
$\int_c^1 \varphi_{\dot\alpha} dx = \dot\alpha b^2 T_9$	$\int_{-1}^{+1} \varphi_{\dot\alpha} dx = -\dot\alpha b^2\frac{\pi a}{2}$
$\int_c^1 \varphi_\beta dx = -\frac{b}{2\pi}v\beta T_5$	$\int_{-1}^{+1} \varphi_\beta dx = -\frac{b}{2}v\beta T_4$
$\int_c^1 \varphi_{\dot\beta} dx = -\frac{b^2}{2\pi}\dot\beta T_2$	$\int_{-1}^{+1} \varphi_{\dot\beta} dx = -\frac{b^2}{2}\dot\beta T_1$
$\int_c^1 \varphi_\alpha(x-c) dx = -\frac{b}{2}v\alpha T_1$	$\int_{-1}^{+1} \varphi_\alpha(x-c) dx = -\frac{b}{2}v\alpha c\pi$
$\int_c^1 \varphi_{\dot h}(x-c) dx = -\frac{b}{2}\dot h T_1$	$\int_{-1}^{+1} \varphi_{\dot h}(x-c) dx = -\frac{b}{2}\dot h c\pi$
$\int_c^1 \varphi_{\dot\alpha}(x-c) dx = \dot\alpha b^2 T_{13}$	$\int_{-1}^{+1} \varphi_{\dot\alpha}(x-c) dx = \dot\alpha b^2 T_{14}\pi$
$\int_c^1 \varphi_\beta(x-c) dx = -\frac{b}{2\pi}v\beta T_2$	$\int_{-1}^{+1} \varphi_\beta(x-c) dx = -\frac{b}{2}v\beta T_8$
$\int_c^1 \varphi_{\dot\beta}(x-c) dx = -\frac{b^2}{2\pi}\dot\beta T_3$	$\int_{-1}^{+1} \varphi_{\dot\beta}(x-c) dx = -\frac{b^2\dot\beta T_7}{2}$

CONSTANTS

$$T_1 = -\frac{1}{3}\sqrt{1-c^2}(2+c^2) + c\cos^{-1}c$$

$$T_2 = c(1-c^2) - \sqrt{1-c^2}(1+c^2)\cos^{-1}c + c(\cos^{-1}c)^2$$

$$T_3 = -\left(\frac{1}{8}+c^2\right)(\cos^{-1}c)^2 + \frac{1}{4}c\sqrt{1-c^2}\cos^{-1}c(7+2c^2) - \frac{1}{8}(1-c^2)(5c^2+4)$$

$$T_4 = -\cos^{-1}c + c\sqrt{1-c^2}$$

$$T_5 = -(1-c^2) - (\cos^{-1}c)^2 + 2c\sqrt{1-c^2}\cos^{-1}c$$

$$T_6 = T_2$$

$$T_7 = -\left(\frac{1}{8}+c^2\right)\cos^{-1}c + \frac{1}{8}c\sqrt{1-c^2}(7+2c^2)$$

$$T_8 = -\frac{1}{3}\sqrt{1-c^2}(2c^2+1) + c\cos^{-1}c$$

$$T_9 = \frac{1}{2}\left[\frac{1}{3}\left(\sqrt{1-c^2}\right)^3 + aT_4\right] = \frac{1}{2}(-p+aT_4)$$

where $p = -\frac{1}{3}\left(\sqrt{1-c^2}\right)^3$

$$T_{10} = \sqrt{1-c^2} + \cos^{-1}c$$

$$T_{11} = \cos^{-1}c\,(1-2c) + \sqrt{1-c^2}\,(2-c)$$

$$T_{12} = \sqrt{1-c^2}\,(2+c) - \cos^{-1}c\,(2c+1)$$

$$T_{13} = \frac{1}{2}[-T_7 - (c-a)T_1]$$

$$T_{14} = \frac{1}{16} + \frac{1}{2}ac$$

FORCES AND MOMENTS

The velocity potentials being known, we are able to calculate local pressures and by integration to obtain the forces and moments acting on the airfoil and aileron.

Employing the extended Bernoulli Theorem for unsteady flow, the local pressure is, except for a constant

$$p_h = -\rho\left(\frac{w^2}{2} + \frac{\partial\varphi}{\partial t}\right)$$

where w is the local velocity and φ the velocity potential at the point. Substituting $w = v + \frac{\partial\varphi}{\partial x}$ we obtain ultimately for the pressure difference between the upper and lower surface at x

$$p = -2\rho\left(v\frac{\partial\varphi}{\partial x} + \frac{\partial\varphi}{\partial t}\right)$$

where v is the constant velocity of the fluid relative to the airfoil at infinity. Putting down the integrals for the force on the entire airfoil, the moment on the flap

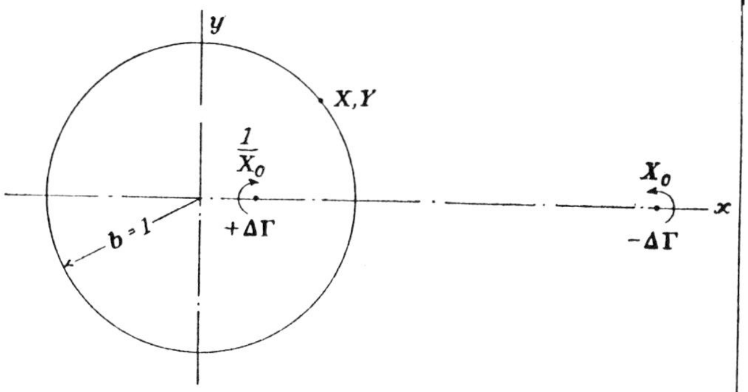

FIGURE 3.—Conformal representation of the wing profile with reference to the circulatory flow.

around the hinge, and the moment on the entire airfoil, we obtain by means of partial integrations

$$P = -2\rho b\int_{-1}^{+1}\dot{\varphi}\,\mathrm{d}x$$

$$M_\beta = -2\rho b^2\int_c^1\dot{\varphi}(x-c)\,\mathrm{d}x + 2\rho v b\int_c^1\varphi\,\mathrm{d}x$$

$$M_\alpha = -2\rho b^2\int_{-1}^{+1}\dot{\varphi}\,(x-c)\,\mathrm{d}x + 2\rho v b\int_{-1}^{+1}\varphi\,\mathrm{d}x$$

$$-2\rho b^2\int_{-1}^{+1}\dot{\varphi}\,(c-a)\,\mathrm{d}x$$

Or, on introducing the individual velocity potentials from page 5,

$$P = -\rho b^2\left[v\pi\dot{\alpha} + \pi\ddot{h} - b\pi a\ddot{\alpha} - vT_4\dot{\beta} - bT_1\ddot{\beta}\right] \tag{I}$$

$$M_\beta = -\rho b^3\left[-vT_1\dot{\alpha} - T_1\ddot{h} + 2T_{13}b\ddot{\alpha} - \frac{1}{\pi}vT_2\dot{\beta} - \frac{1}{\pi}T_3 b\ddot{\beta}\right]$$
$$+\rho v b^2\left[-vT_4\alpha - T_4\dot{h} + 2T_9 b\dot{\alpha} - \frac{1}{\pi}vT_5\beta - \frac{1}{\pi}T_2 b\dot{\beta}\right]$$
$$= -\rho b^2\left[T_4 v^2\alpha - (2T_9 + T_1)bv\dot{\alpha} + 2T_{13}b^2\ddot{\alpha} + \frac{1}{\pi}T_5 v^2\beta\right.$$
$$\left.+\left(\frac{1}{\pi}T_2 - \frac{1}{\pi}T_2\right)bv\dot{\beta} - \frac{1}{\pi}b^2T_3\ddot{\beta} + T_4 v\dot{h} - T_1 b\ddot{h}\right] \tag{II}$$

$$M_\alpha = -\rho b^2\left[-\pi v^2\alpha + \pi\left(\frac{1}{8} + a^2\right)b^2\ddot{\alpha} + v^2T_4\beta + \{T_1 - T_{\dot{3}}\right.$$
$$-(c-a)T_4\}b\dot{\beta}v + \{-T_7 - (c-a)T_1\}b^2\ddot{\beta}$$
$$\left.-ba\pi\ddot{h} - \pi v\dot{h}\right] \tag{III}$$

VELOCITY POTENTIALS, FORCES, AND MOMENTS OF THE CIRCULATORY FLOW

In the following we shall determine the velocity potentials and associated forces and moments due to a surface of discontinuity of strength U extending along the positive x axis from the wing to infinity. The velocity potential of the flow around the circle (fig. 3) resulting from the vortex element $-\Delta\Gamma$ at (X_0, O) is

$$\varphi_\Gamma = \frac{\Delta\Gamma}{2\pi}\left[\tan^{-1}\frac{Y}{X - X_0} - \tan^{-1}\frac{Y}{X - \frac{1}{X_0}}\right]$$

$$= \frac{\Delta\Gamma}{2\pi}\tan^{-1}\frac{\left(-\frac{1}{X_0} + X_0\right)Y}{X^2 - \left(X_0 + \frac{1}{X_0}\right)X + Y^2 + 1}$$

where (X, Y) are the coordinates of the variable and X_0 is the coordinate of $-\Delta\Gamma$ on the x axis.

Introducing $X_0 + \frac{1}{X_0} = 2x_0$

or $X_0 = x_0 + \sqrt{x_0^2 - 1}$ on the x axis

and $X = x$ and $Y = \sqrt{1 - x^2}$ on the circle

the equation becomes

$$\varphi_{xx_0} = -\frac{\Delta\Gamma}{2\pi}\tan^{-1}\frac{\sqrt{1-x^2}\sqrt{x_0^2-1}}{1 - xx_0}$$

This expression gives the clockwise circulation around the airfoil due to the element $-\Delta\Gamma$ at x_0.

We have: $p = -2\rho\left(\frac{\partial\varphi}{\partial t} + v\frac{\partial\varphi}{\partial x}\right)$

But, since the element $-\Delta\Gamma$ will now be regarded as moving to the right relative to the airfoil with a velocity v

$$\frac{\partial\varphi}{\partial t} = \frac{\partial\varphi}{\partial x_0}v$$

Hence, $p = -2\rho v\left(\frac{\partial\varphi}{\partial x} + \frac{\partial\varphi}{\partial x_0}\right)$

Further

$$\frac{2\pi}{\Delta\Gamma}\frac{\partial\varphi}{\partial x} = \sqrt{x_0^2 - 1}\,\frac{\frac{x}{(1 - xx_0)\sqrt{1-x^2}} + \frac{x_0\sqrt{1-x^2}}{(1-xx_0)^2}}{1 + \frac{(1-x^2)(x_0^2-1)}{(1-xx_0)^2}}$$

$$= \frac{\sqrt{x_0^2-1}}{\sqrt{1-x^2}}\,\frac{1}{(x_0 - x)}$$

and

$$\frac{2\pi}{\Delta\Gamma}\frac{\partial\varphi}{\partial x_0} = \sqrt{1-x^2}\,\frac{\frac{1}{(1 - xx_0)}\,\frac{x_0}{\sqrt{x_0^2-1}} + \sqrt{x_0^2-1}\,\frac{x}{(1-xx_0)^2}}{1 + \frac{(1-x^2)(x_0^2-1)}{(1-xx_0)^2}}$$

$$= \frac{\sqrt{1-x^2}}{\sqrt{x_0^2-1}}\,\frac{1}{(x_0 - x)}$$

By addition:

$$\frac{\partial\varphi}{\partial x} + \frac{\partial\varphi}{\partial x_0} = \frac{\Delta\Gamma}{2\pi}\,\frac{x_0 + x}{\sqrt{1-x^2}\sqrt{x_0^2-1}}$$

To obtain the force on the aileron, we need the integral

$$\int_c^1\left(\frac{\partial\varphi}{\partial x}+\frac{\partial\varphi}{\partial x_0}\right)dx=\frac{\Delta\Gamma}{2\pi}\int_c^1\frac{x_0+x}{\sqrt{x_0^2-1}\sqrt{1-x^2}}dx$$

$$=-\frac{\Delta\Gamma}{2\pi}\left[\frac{x_0}{\sqrt{x_0^2-1}}\cos^{-1}x+\frac{\sqrt{1-x^2}}{\sqrt{x_0^2-1}}\right]_c^1$$

$$=\frac{\Delta\Gamma}{2\pi}\left[\frac{x_0}{\sqrt{x_0^2-1}}\cos^{-1}c+\frac{\sqrt{1-c^2}}{\sqrt{x_0^2-1}}\right]$$

Thus, for the force on the aileron

$$\Delta P_{c1}=-\rho vb\frac{\Delta\Gamma}{\pi}\left(\frac{x_0}{\sqrt{x_0^2-1}}\cos^{-1}c+\frac{1}{\sqrt{x_0^2-1}}\sqrt{1-c^2}\right)\quad\text{or}$$

$$\Delta P_{c1}=-\rho vb\frac{\Delta\Gamma}{\pi}\left[\frac{x_0}{\sqrt{x_0^2-1}}\left(\cos^{-1}c-\sqrt{1-c^2}\right)+\sqrt{\frac{x_0+1}{x_0-1}}\sqrt{1-c^2}\right]$$

Integrated, with $\Delta\Gamma=U dx_0$

$$P_{c1}=-\frac{\rho vb}{\pi}\left[\left(\cos^{-1}c-\sqrt{1-c^2}\right)\int_1^\infty\frac{x_0}{\sqrt{x_0^2-1}}U dx_0+\sqrt{1-c^2}\int_1^\infty\sqrt{\frac{x_0+1}{x_0-1}}U dx_0\right]$$

for $c=-1$ we obtain the expression for P, the force on the *whole* airfoil

$$P=-\rho vb\int_1^\infty\frac{x_0}{\sqrt{x_0^2-1}}U dx_0\qquad\text{(IV)}$$

Since U is considered stationary with respect to the fluid elements

$$U=f(vt-x_0)$$

where t is the time since the beginning of the motion. U is thus a function of the *distance* from the location of the *first* vortex element or, referred to a system moving with the fluid, U is *stationary* in value.

Similarly we obtain for the moment on the *aileron*

$$\int_c^1\left(\frac{\partial\varphi}{\partial x}+\frac{\partial\varphi}{\partial x_0}\right)(x-c)dx=\frac{\Delta\Gamma}{2\pi}\int_c^1\frac{(x-c)\,(x_0+x)}{\sqrt{1-x^2}\sqrt{x_0^2-1}}dx$$

$$=-\frac{\Delta\Gamma}{2\pi}\frac{1}{\sqrt{x_0^2-1}}\left[x_0\sqrt{1-x^2}+\frac{x\sqrt{1-x^2}}{2}-c\sqrt{1-x^2}+\left(\frac{1}{2}-x_0c\right)\cos^{-1}x\right]_c^1$$

$$=+\frac{\Delta\Gamma}{2\pi}\frac{1}{\sqrt{x_0^2-1}}\left[\left(x_0+\frac{c}{2}-c\right)\sqrt{1-c^2}+\frac{1}{2}\left(1-2x_0c\right)\cos^{-1}c\right]$$

$$=+\frac{\Delta\Gamma}{2\pi}\left[\frac{x_0}{\sqrt{x_0^2-1}}\left(\sqrt{1-c^2}-c\cos^{-1}c\right)+\frac{\frac{1}{2}}{\sqrt{x_0^2-1}}\left(\cos^{-1}c-c\sqrt{1-c^2}\right)\right]$$

Finally

$$\Delta M_\beta=-\rho vb^2\frac{\Delta\Gamma}{\pi}\left[\frac{x_0}{\sqrt{x_0^2-1}}\left\{\sqrt{1-c^2}\left(1+\frac{c}{2}\right)-\cos^{-1}c\left(c+\frac{1}{2}\right)\right\}+\frac{1}{2}\sqrt{\frac{x_0+1}{x_0-1}}\left(\cos^{-1}c-c\sqrt{1-c^2}\right)\right]$$

Putting $\Delta\Gamma=U dx_0$ and integrating

$$M_\beta=-\frac{\rho vb^2}{\pi}\left[\left\{\sqrt{1-c^2}\left(1+\frac{c}{2}\right)-\cos^{-1}c\left(c+\frac{1}{2}\right)\right\}\int_1^\infty\frac{x_0}{\sqrt{x_0^2-1}}U dx_0+\left(\cos^{-1}c-c\sqrt{(1-c^2)}\right)\frac{1}{2}\int_1^\infty\sqrt{\frac{x_0+1}{x_0-1}}U dx_0\right]\qquad\text{(V)}$$

Further, for the moment on the entire airfoil around a

$$\int_{-1}^{+1}\left(\frac{\partial\varphi}{\partial x}+\frac{\partial\varphi}{\partial x_0}\right)(x-a)dx=-\frac{\Delta\Gamma}{2\pi}\frac{1}{\sqrt{x_0^2-1}}\left[\left(x_0+\frac{x}{2}-a\right)\sqrt{1-x^2}+\left(\frac{1}{2}-x_0a\right)\cos^{-1}x\right]_{-1}^{+1}=+\frac{\Delta\Gamma}{2\pi}\frac{1}{\sqrt{x_0^2-1}}\left(\frac{1}{2}-x_0a\right)\pi$$

and

$$\Delta M_\alpha=-\rho vb^2\Delta\Gamma\frac{\frac{1}{2}-x_0a}{\sqrt{x_0^2-1}}$$

Integrated, this becomes

$$M_\alpha=-\rho vb^2\int_1^\infty\frac{\frac{1}{2}-x_0a}{\sqrt{x_0^2-1}}U dx_0$$

$$=-\rho vb^2\int_1^\infty\left\{\frac{\frac{1}{2}+\frac{1}{2}x_0}{\sqrt{x_0^2-1}}-\frac{x_0\left(a+\frac{1}{2}\right)}{\sqrt{x_0^2-1}}\right\}U dx_0$$

$$=-\rho vb^2\int_1^\infty\left\{\frac{1}{2}\sqrt{\frac{x_0+1}{x_0-1}}-\left(a+\frac{1}{2}\right)\frac{x_0}{\sqrt{x_0^2-1}}\right\}U dx_0\qquad\text{(VI)}$$

THE MAGNITUDE OF THE CIRCULATION

The magnitude of the circulation is determined by the Kutta condition, which requires that no infinite velocities exist at the trailing edge, or, at $x=1$

$$\frac{\partial}{\partial x}(\varphi_\Gamma+\varphi_\alpha+\varphi_{\dot h}+\varphi_{\dot\alpha}+\varphi_\beta+\varphi_{\dot\beta})=\text{finite}$$

Introducing the values of φ_α, etc. from page 5 and φ_Γ from $\frac{\partial\varphi}{\partial x}$ page 6 gives the important relation:

$$\frac{1}{2\pi}\int_1^\infty\frac{\sqrt{x_0+1}}{\sqrt{x_0-1}}U dx_0=v\alpha+\dot h+b\left(\frac{1}{2}-a\right)\dot\alpha+\frac{T_{10}}{\pi}v\beta+b\frac{T_{11}}{2\pi}\dot\beta\qquad\text{(VII)}$$

This relation must be satisfied to comply with the Kutta condition, which states that the flow shall leave the airfoil at the trailing edge.

It is observed that the relation reduces to that of the Kutta condition for stationary flow on putting $x_0=\infty$, and in subsequence omitting the variable parameters $\dot{\alpha}$, $\dot{\beta}$, and $\dot{h}$.

Let us write

$$\frac{1}{2\pi}\int_1^\infty \sqrt{\frac{x_0+1}{x_0-1}}\,U\mathrm{d}x_0 = v\alpha + \dot{h} + b\left(\frac{1}{2}-a\right)\dot{\alpha} + \frac{T_{10}}{\pi}v\beta + b\frac{T_{11}}{2\pi}\dot{\beta} = Q$$

Introduced in (IV)

$$P = -2\pi\rho v b Q \frac{\int_1^\infty \frac{x_0}{\sqrt{x_0^2-1}}U\mathrm{d}x_0}{\int_1^\infty \sqrt{\frac{x_0+1}{x_0-1}}\,U\mathrm{d}x_0}$$

from (V)

$$M_\beta = -2\rho v b^2\left[\left(\sqrt{1-c^2}\left(1+\frac{c}{2}\right)-\cos^{-1}c\left(c+\frac{1}{2}\right)\right)\frac{\int_1^\infty \frac{x_0}{\sqrt{x_0^2-1}}U\mathrm{d}x_0}{\int_1^\infty \sqrt{\frac{x_0+1}{x_0-1}}\,U\mathrm{d}x_0} + \frac{1}{2}\left(\cos^{-1}c - c\sqrt{1-c^2}\right)\right]Q$$

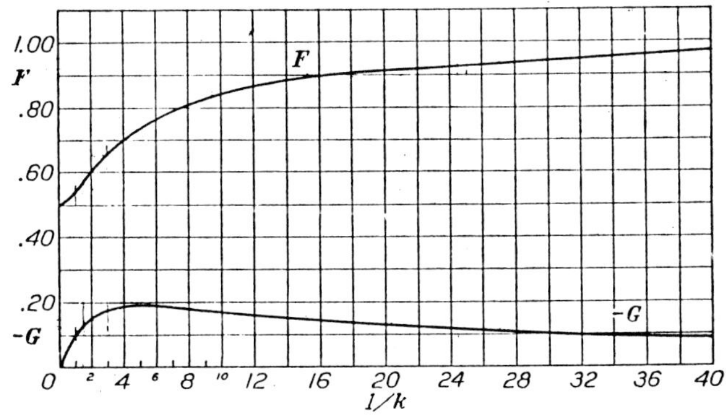

FIGURE 4.—The functions F and G against $\frac{1}{k}$.

and from (VI)

$$M_\alpha = -2\pi\rho v b^2\left[\frac{1}{2}-\left(a+\frac{1}{2}\right)\frac{\int_1^\infty \frac{x_0}{\sqrt{x_0^2-1}}U\mathrm{d}x_0}{\int_1^\infty \sqrt{\frac{x_0+1}{x_0-1}}\,U\mathrm{d}x_0}\right]Q$$

Introducing

$$C = \frac{\int_1^\infty \frac{x_0}{\sqrt{x_0^2-1}}U\mathrm{d}x_0}{\int_1^\infty \sqrt{\frac{x_0+1}{x_0-1}}\,U\mathrm{d}x_0}$$

we obtain finally

$$P = -2\rho v b\pi C Q \qquad \text{(VIII)}$$

$$M_\beta = -2\rho v b^2\left[\left(\sqrt{1-c^2}\left(1+\frac{c}{2}\right)-\cos^{-1}c\left(c+\frac{1}{2}\right)\right)C + \frac{1}{2}\left(\cos^{-1}c - c\sqrt{1-c^2}\right)\right]Q = -\rho v b^2(T_{12}C - T_4)Q \qquad \text{(IX)}$$

$$M_\alpha = 2\pi\rho v b^2\left[\left(a+\frac{1}{2}\right)C - \frac{1}{2}\right]Q \qquad \text{(X)}$$

where Q is given above and $C=C(k)$ will be treated in the following section.

VALUE OF THE FUNCTION $C(k)$

Put $U = U_0 e^{i\left[k\left(\frac{s}{b}-x_0\right)+\varphi\right]}$

where $s=vt$ $(s\to\infty)$, the distance from the *first* vortex element to the airfoil, and k a positive constant determining the wave length,

then

$$C(k) = \frac{\int_1^\infty \frac{x_0}{\sqrt{x_0^2-1}}e^{-ikx_0}\mathrm{d}x_0}{\int_1^\infty \frac{x_0+1}{\sqrt{x_0^2-1}}e^{-ikx_0}\mathrm{d}x_0} \qquad \text{(XI)}$$

These integrals are known, see next part, formulas (XIV)—(XVII) and we obtain [3]

$$C(k) = \frac{-\frac{\pi}{2}J_1 + i\frac{\pi}{2}Y_1}{-\frac{\pi}{2}J_1 - \frac{\pi}{2}Y_0 + i\frac{\pi}{2}Y_1 - i\frac{\pi}{2}J_0} = \frac{-J_1+iY_1}{-(J_1+Y_0)+i(Y_1-J_0)}$$

$$= \frac{(-J_1+iY_1)[-(J_1+Y_0)-i(Y_1-J_0)]}{(J_1+Y_0)^2+(Y_1-J_0)^2}$$

$$= \frac{J_1(J_1+Y_0)+Y_1(Y_1-J_0)}{(J_1+Y_0)^2+(Y_1-J_0)^2} - i\frac{Y_1(J_1+Y_0)-J_1(Y_1-J_0)}{(J_1+Y_0)^2+(Y_1-J_0)^2} = F+iG$$

where

$$F = \frac{J_1(J_1+Y_0)+Y_1(Y_1-J_0)}{(J_1+Y_0)^2+(Y_1-J_0)^2} \qquad \text{(XII)}$$

$$G = -\frac{Y_1Y_0+J_1J_0}{(J_1+Y_0)^2+(Y_1-J_0)^2} \qquad \text{(XIII)}$$

These functions, which are of fundamental importance in the theory of the oscillating airfoil are given graphically against the argument $\frac{1}{k}$ in figure 4.

SOLUTION OF THE DEFINITE INTEGRALS IN C BY MEANS OF BESSEL FUNCTIONS

We have

$$K_n(z) = \int_0^\infty e^{-z\cosh t}\cosh nt\,\mathrm{d}t$$

(Formula (34), p. 51—Gray, Mathews & MacRobert: Treatise on Bessel Functions. London, 1922)

where

$$K_n(t) = e^{\frac{in\pi}{2}}G_n(it)$$

(Eq. (28), sec. 3, p. 23, same reference)

and

$$G_n(x) = -\overline{Y_n}(x) + \left[\log 2 - \gamma + \frac{i\pi}{2}\right]J_n(x)$$

but

$$\overline{Y_n}(x) = \frac{\pi}{2}Y_n(x) + (\log 2 - \gamma)J_n(x)$$

(where $Y_n(x)$ is from N. Nielsen: Handbuch der Theorie der Cylinderfunktionen. Leipzig, 1904).

[3] This may also be expressed in Hänkel functions, $C = \frac{H_1^{(2)}}{H_1^{(2)}+i\,H_0^{(2)}}$

Thus,

$$G_n(x) = -\frac{\pi}{2}[Y_n(x) - iJ_n(x)]$$

We have

$$K_0(-ik) = \int_0^\infty e^{ik\cosh t}\,dt = \int_1^\infty \frac{e^{ikx}}{\sqrt{x^2-1}}\,dx$$

or

$$-\frac{\pi}{2}Y_0(k) + i\frac{\pi}{2}J_0(k) = \int_1^\infty \frac{\cos kx\,dx}{\sqrt{x^2-1}} + i\int_1^\infty \frac{\sin kx\,dx}{\sqrt{x^2-1}}$$

Thus,

$$\int_1^\infty \frac{\cos kx\,dx}{\sqrt{x^2-1}} = -\frac{\pi}{2}Y_0(k) \qquad \text{(XIV)}$$

$$\int_1^\infty \frac{\sin kx\,dx}{\sqrt{x^2-1}} = \frac{\pi}{2}J_0(k) \qquad \text{(XV)}$$

Further,

$$K_1(-ik) = \int_0^\infty e^{ik\cosh t}\cosh t\,dt = \int_1^\infty \frac{e^{ikx}\,x\,dx}{\sqrt{x^2-1}}$$

$$iG_1(k) = -i\frac{\pi}{2}Y_1(k) - \frac{\pi}{2}J_1(k)$$

$$= \int_1^\infty \frac{x}{\sqrt{x^2-1}}(\cos kx + i\sin kx)\,dx$$

Thus,

$$\int_1^\infty \frac{x\cos kx\,dx}{\sqrt{x^2-1}} = -\frac{\pi}{2}J_1(k) \qquad \text{(XVI)}$$

$$\int_1^\infty \frac{x\sin kx\,dx}{\sqrt{x^2-1}} = -\frac{\pi}{2}Y_1(k) \qquad \text{(XVII)}$$

TOTAL AERODYNAMIC FORCES AND MOMENTS

TOTAL FORCE

From equations (I) and (VIII) we obtain

$$P = -\rho b^2(v\pi\dot\alpha + \pi\ddot h - \pi ba\ddot\alpha - vT_4\dot\beta - T_1 b\ddot\beta)$$
$$-2\pi\rho vbC\left\{v\alpha + \dot h + b\left(\frac{1}{2}-a\right)\dot\alpha + \frac{1}{\pi}T_{10}v\beta + b\frac{1}{2\pi}T_{11}\dot\beta\right\} \qquad \text{(XVIII)}$$

TOTAL MOMENTS

From equations (II) and (IX) we obtain similarly

$$M_\beta = -\rho b^2\Big[\Big\{-2T_9 - T_1 + T_4\left(a-\frac{1}{2}\right)\Big\}vb\dot\alpha + 2T_{13}b^2\ddot\alpha + \frac{1}{\pi}v^2\beta(T_5 - T_4T_{10}) - \frac{1}{2\pi}vb\dot\beta T_4T_{11} - \frac{1}{\pi}T_3b^2\ddot\beta - T_1b\ddot h\Big] - \rho vb^2T_{12}C\left\{v\alpha + \dot h + b\left(\frac{1}{2}-a\right)\dot\alpha + \frac{1}{\pi}T_{10}v\beta + b\frac{1}{2\pi}T_{11}\dot\beta\right\} \qquad \text{(XIX)}$$

From equations (III) and (X)

$$M_\alpha = -\rho b^2\Big[\pi\left(\frac{1}{2}-a\right)vb\dot\alpha + \pi b^2\left(\frac{1}{8}+a^2\right)\ddot\alpha + (T_4+T_{10})v^2\beta + \left(T_1 - T_8 - (c-a)T_4 + \frac{1}{2}T_{11}\right)vb\dot\beta - \left(T_7 + (c-a)T_1\right)b^2\ddot\beta - a\pi b\ddot h\Big] + 2\rho vb^2\pi\left(a+\frac{1}{2}\right)C\left\{v\alpha + \dot h + b\left(\frac{1}{2}-a\right)\dot\alpha + \frac{1}{\pi}T_{10}v\beta + b\frac{1}{2\pi}T_{11}\dot\beta\right\} \qquad \text{(XX)}$$

DIFFERENTIAL EQUATIONS OF MOTION

Expressing the equilibrium of the moments about a of the entire airfoil, of the moments on the aileron about c, and of the vertical forces, we obtain, respectively, the following three equations:

α: $\quad -I_\alpha\ddot\alpha - I_\beta\beta - b(c-a)S_\beta\ddot\beta - S_\alpha\ddot h - \alpha C_\alpha + M_\alpha = 0$

β: $\quad -I_\beta\ddot\beta - I_\beta\ddot\alpha - b(c-a)\ddot\alpha S_\beta - \ddot h S_\beta - \beta C_\beta + M_\beta = 0$

h: $\quad -\ddot hM - \ddot\alpha S_\alpha - \ddot\beta S_\beta - hC_h + P = 0$

Rearranged:

α: $\quad \ddot\alpha I_\alpha + \ddot\beta(I_\beta + b(c-a)S_\beta) + \ddot hS_\alpha + \alpha C_\alpha - M_\alpha = 0$

β: $\quad \ddot\alpha(I_\beta + b(c-a)S_\beta) + \ddot\beta I_\beta + hS_\beta + \beta C_\beta - M_\beta = 0$

h: $\quad \ddot\alpha S_\alpha + \ddot\beta S_\beta + \ddot hM + hC_h - P = 0$

The constants are defined as follows:

ρ, mass of air per unit of volume.

b, half chord of wing.

M, mass of wing per unit of length.

S_α, S_β, static moments of wing (in slugs-feet) per unit length of wing-aileron and aileron, respectively. The former is referred to the axis a; the latter, to the hinge c.

I_α, I_β, moments of inertia per unit length of wing-aileron and aileron about a and c, respectively.

C_α, torsional stiffness of wing around a, corresponding to unit length.

C_β, torsional stiffness of aileron around c, corresponding to unit length.

C_h, stiffness of wing in deflection, corresponding to unit length.

DEFINITION OF PARAMETERS USED IN EQUATIONS

$\kappa = \dfrac{\pi\rho b^2}{M}$, the ratio of the mass of a cylinder of air of a diameter equal to the chord of the wing to the mass of the wing, both taken for equal length along span.

$r_\alpha=\sqrt{\frac{I_\alpha}{Mb^2}}$, the radius of gyration divided by b.

$x_\alpha=\frac{S_\alpha}{Mb}$, the center of gravity distance of the wing from a, divided by b.

$\omega_\alpha=\sqrt{\frac{C_\alpha}{I_\alpha}}$, the frequency of torsional vibration around a.

$r_\beta=\sqrt{\frac{I_\beta}{Mb^2}}$, *reduced* radius of gyration of aileron divided by b, that is, the radius at which the entire mass of the airfoil would have to be concentrated to give the moment of inertia of the aileron I_β.

$x_\beta=\frac{S_\beta}{Mb}$, *reduced* center of gravity distance from c.

$\omega_\beta=\sqrt{\frac{C_\beta}{I_\beta}}$, frequency of torsional vibration of aileron around c.

$\omega_h=\sqrt{\frac{C_h}{M}}$, frequency of wing in deflection.

FINAL EQUATIONS IN NONDIMENSIONAL FORM

On introducing the quantities M_α, M_β, and P, replacing T_9 and T_{13} from page 5, and reducing to nondimensional form, we obtain the following system of equations:

$$\text{(A)}\quad \ddot{\alpha}\left[r_\alpha^2+\kappa\left(\frac{1}{8}+a^2\right)\right]+\dot{\alpha}\frac{v}{b}\kappa\left(\frac{1}{2}-a\right)+\alpha\frac{C_\alpha}{Mb^2}+\ddot{\beta}\left[r_\beta^2+(c-a)x_\beta-\frac{T_7}{\pi}\kappa-(c-a)\frac{T_1}{\pi}\kappa\right]+\frac{1}{\pi}\dot{\beta}\kappa\frac{v}{b}\left[-2p-\left(\frac{1}{2}-a\right)T_4\right]$$

$$+\beta\kappa\frac{v^2}{b^2}\frac{1}{\pi}(T_4+T_{10})+\ddot{h}\left(x_\alpha-a\kappa\right)\frac{1}{b}-2\kappa\left(a+\frac{1}{2}\right)\frac{vC(k)}{b}\left[\frac{v\alpha}{b}+\frac{\dot{h}}{b}+\left(\frac{1}{2}-a\right)\dot{\alpha}+\frac{T_{10}}{\pi}\frac{v}{b}\beta+\frac{T_{11}}{2\pi}\dot{\beta}\right]=0$$

$$\text{(B)}\quad \ddot{\alpha}\left[r_\beta^2+(c-a)x_\beta-\kappa\frac{T_7}{\pi}-(c-a)\frac{T_1}{\pi}\kappa\right]+\dot{\alpha}\left(p-T_1-\frac{1}{2}T_4\right)\frac{v}{b}\frac{\kappa}{\pi}+\ddot{\beta}\left(r_\beta^2-\frac{1}{\pi^2}\kappa T_3\right)-\frac{1}{2\pi^2}\dot{\beta}T_4T_{11}\frac{v}{b}\kappa$$

$$+\beta\left[\frac{C_\beta}{Mb^2}+\frac{1}{\pi^2}\frac{v^2}{b^2}\kappa(T_5-T_4T_{10})\right]+\ddot{h}\left(x_\beta-\frac{1}{\pi}\kappa T_1\right)\frac{1}{b}+\frac{T_{12}}{\pi}\kappa\frac{vC(k)}{b}\left[\frac{v\alpha}{b}+\frac{\dot{h}}{b}+\left(\frac{1}{2}-a\right)\dot{\alpha}+\frac{T_{10}}{\pi}\frac{v}{b}\beta+\frac{T_{11}}{2\pi}\dot{\beta}\right]=0$$

$$\text{(C)}\quad \ddot{\alpha}\left(x_\alpha-\kappa a\right)+\dot{\alpha}\frac{v}{b}\kappa+\ddot{\beta}\left(x_\beta-\frac{1}{\pi}T_1\kappa\right)-\dot{\beta}\frac{v}{b}T_4\kappa\frac{1}{\pi}+\ddot{h}(1+\kappa)\frac{1}{b}+h\frac{C_h}{M}\frac{1}{b}$$

$$+2\kappa\frac{vC(k)}{b}\left[\frac{v\alpha}{b}+\frac{\dot{h}}{b}+\left(\frac{1}{2}-a\right)\dot{\alpha}+\frac{T_{10}}{\pi}\frac{v}{b}\beta+\frac{T_{11}}{2\pi}\dot{\beta}\right]=0$$

SOLUTION OF EQUATIONS

As mentioned in the introduction, we shall only have to specify the conditions under which an unstable equilibrium may exist, no general solution being needed. We shall therefore introduce the variables at once as sine functions of the distance s or, in complex form with $\frac{1}{k}$ as an auxiliary parameter, giving the ratio of the wave length to 2π times the half chord b:

$$\alpha=\alpha_0 e^{ik\frac{s}{b}}$$

$$\beta=\beta_0 e^{i\left(k\frac{s}{b}+\varphi_1\right)}$$

and

$$h=h_0 e^{i\left(k\frac{s}{b}+\varphi_2\right)}$$

where s is the distance from the airfoil to the *first* vortex element, $\frac{ds}{dt}=v$, and φ_1 and φ_2 are phase angles of β and h with respect to α.

Having introduced these quantities in our system of equations, we shall divide through by $\left(\frac{v}{b}k\right)^2\kappa$.

We observe that the velocity v is then contained in only *one* term of each equation. We shall consider this term containing v as the unknown parameter ΩX. To distinguish terms containing X we shall employ a bar; terms without bars do not contain X.

We shall resort to the following notation, taking care to retain a perfectly cyclic arrangement. Let the letter A refer to the coefficients in the first equation not containing $C(k)$ or X, B to similar coefficients of the second equation, and C to those in the third equation. Let the first subscript α refer to the first variable α, the subscript β to the second, and h to the third. Let the second subscripts 1, 2, 3 refer to the second derivative, the first derivative, and the argument of each variable, respectively. $A_{\alpha 1}$ thus refers to the coefficient in the first equation associated with the second derivative of α and not containing $C(k)$ or

X; C_{h3} to the constant in the third equation attached to h, etc. These coefficients[4] are as follows:

$$A_{\alpha 1}=\frac{r_\alpha^2}{\kappa}+\left(\frac{1}{8}+a^2\right)$$

$$A_{\alpha 2}=\left(\frac{1}{2}-a\right)$$

$$A_{\alpha 3}=0$$

$$A_{\beta 1}=\frac{r_\beta^2}{\kappa}-\frac{T_7}{\pi}+(c-a)\left(\frac{x_\beta}{\kappa}-\frac{T_1}{\pi}\right)$$

$$A_{\beta 2}=\frac{1}{\pi}\left[-2p-\left(\frac{1}{2}-a\right)T_4\right]$$

$$A_{\beta 3}=\frac{1}{\pi}(T_4+T_{10})$$

$$A_{h1}=\frac{x_\alpha}{\kappa}-a$$

$$A_{h2}=0$$

$$A_{h3}=0$$

$$B_{\alpha 1}=\frac{r_\beta^2}{\kappa}-\frac{T_7}{\pi}+(c-a)\left(\frac{x_\beta}{\kappa}-\frac{T_1}{\pi}\right) \qquad (=A_{\beta 1})$$

$$B_{\alpha 2}=\frac{1}{\pi}\left(p-T_1-\frac{1}{2}T_4\right)$$

$$B_{\alpha 3}=0$$

$$B_{\beta 1}=\frac{r_\beta^2}{\kappa}-\frac{1}{\pi^2}T_3$$

$$B_{\beta 2}=-\frac{1}{2\pi^2}T_4T_{11}$$

$$B_{\beta 3}=\frac{1}{\pi^2}(T_5-T_4T_{10})$$

$$B_{h1}=\frac{x_\beta}{\kappa}-\frac{1}{\pi}T_1$$

$$B_{h2}=0$$

$$B_{h3}=0$$

$$C_{\alpha 1}=\frac{x_\alpha}{\kappa}-a \qquad (=A_{h1})$$

$$C_{\alpha 2}=1$$

$$C_{\alpha 3}=0$$

$$C_{\beta 1}=\frac{x_\beta}{\kappa}-\frac{1}{\pi}T_1 \qquad (=B_{h1})$$

$$C_{\beta 2}=-\frac{1}{\pi}T_4$$

$$C_{\beta 3}=0$$

$$C_{h1}=\frac{1}{\kappa}+1$$

$$C_{h2}=0$$

$$C_{h3}=0$$

[4] The factor $\frac{1}{k}$ or $\frac{1}{k^2}$ is not included in these constants. See the expressions for the R's and I's on next page.

The solution of the instability problem as contained in the system of three equations A, B, and C is given by the vanishing of a third-order determinant of complex numbers representing the coefficients. The solution of particular subcases of two degrees of freedom is given by the minors involving the particular coefficients. We shall denote the case *torsion-aileron* (α, β) as case 3, *aileron-deflection* (β, h) as case 2, and *deflection-torsion* (h, α) as case 1. The determinant form of the solution is given in the major case and in the three possible subcases, respectively, by:

$$\bar{D}=\begin{vmatrix}\bar{R}_{a\alpha}+iI_{a\alpha}, & R_{a\beta}+iI_{a\beta}, & R_{ah}+iI_{ah}\\ R_{b\alpha}+iI_{b\alpha}, & \bar{R}_{b\beta}+iI_{b\beta}, & R_{bh}+iI_{bh}\\ R_{c\alpha}+iI_{c\alpha}, & R_{c\beta}+iI_{c\beta}, & \bar{R}_{ch}+iI_{ch}\end{vmatrix}=0$$

and

$$\bar{M}_{ch}=\begin{vmatrix}\bar{R}_{a\alpha}+iI_{a\alpha}, & R_{a\beta}+iI_{a\beta}\\ R_{b\alpha}+iI_{b\alpha}, & \bar{R}_{b\beta}+iI_{b\beta}\end{vmatrix}=0 \qquad \text{Case 3}$$

$$\bar{M}_{a\alpha}=\begin{vmatrix}\bar{R}_{b\beta}+iI_{b\beta}, & R_{bh}+iI_{bh}\\ R_{c\beta}+iI_{c\beta}, & \bar{R}_{ch}+iI_{ch}\end{vmatrix}=0 \qquad \text{Case 2}$$

$$\bar{M}_{b\beta}=\begin{vmatrix}\bar{R}_{ch}+iI_{ch}, & R_{c\alpha}+iI_{c\alpha}\\ R_{ah}+iI_{ah}, & \bar{R}_{a\alpha}+iI_{a\alpha}\end{vmatrix}=0 \qquad \text{Case 1}$$

REAL EQUATIONS — IMAGINARY EQUATIONS

$$\begin{vmatrix}\bar{R}_{a\alpha}R_{a\beta}\\ R_{b\alpha}\bar{R}_{b\beta}\end{vmatrix}-\begin{vmatrix}I_{a\alpha}I_{a\beta}\\ I_{b\alpha}I_{b\beta}\end{vmatrix}=0 \quad \begin{vmatrix}\bar{R}_{a\alpha}R_{a\beta}\\ I_{b\alpha}I_{b\beta}\end{vmatrix}+\begin{vmatrix}I_{a\alpha}I_{a\beta}\\ R_{b\alpha}\bar{R}_{b\beta}\end{vmatrix}=0 \quad \text{Case 3}$$

$$\begin{vmatrix}\bar{R}_{b\beta}R_{bh}\\ R_{c\beta}\bar{R}_{ch}\end{vmatrix}-\begin{vmatrix}I_{b\beta}I_{bh}\\ I_{c\beta}I_{ch}\end{vmatrix}=0 \quad \begin{vmatrix}\bar{R}_{b\beta}R_{bh}\\ I_{c\beta}I_{ch}\end{vmatrix}+\begin{vmatrix}I_{b\beta}I_{bh}\\ R_{c\beta}\bar{R}_{ch}\end{vmatrix}=0 \quad \text{Case 2}$$

$$\begin{vmatrix}\bar{R}_{ch}R_{c\alpha}\\ R_{ah}\bar{R}_{a\alpha}\end{vmatrix}-\begin{vmatrix}I_{ch}I_{c\alpha}\\ I_{ah}I_{a\alpha}\end{vmatrix}=0 \quad \begin{vmatrix}\bar{R}_{ch}R_{c\alpha}\\ I_{ah}I_{a\alpha}\end{vmatrix}+\begin{vmatrix}I_{ch}I_{c\alpha}\\ R_{ah}\bar{R}_{a\alpha}\end{vmatrix}=0 \quad \text{Case 1}$$

NOTE.—Terms with bars contain X; terms without bars do not contain X.

The 9 quantities $R_{a\alpha}$, $R_{a\beta}$, etc., refer to the real parts and the 9 quantities $I_{a\alpha}$, $I_{a\beta}$, etc., to the imaginary parts of the coefficients of the 3 variables α, β, and h in the 3 equations A, B, C on page 10. Denoting the coefficients of $\ddot{\alpha}$, $\dot{\alpha}$, and α in the first equation by p, q, and r,

$$R_{a\alpha}+iI_{a\alpha}=\frac{1}{\kappa}\left[-p+iq\frac{b}{kv}+r\left(\frac{b}{kv}\right)^2\right]$$

which, separated in real and imaginary parts, gives the quantities $R_{a\alpha}$ and $I_{a\alpha}$. Similarly, the remaining quantities R and I are obtained. They are all functions of k or $C(k)$. The terms with bars $\bar{R}_{a\alpha}$, $\bar{R}_{b\beta}$, and $\bar{R}_{ch}$ are seen to be the only ones containing the unknown X. The quantities Ω and X will be defined shortly. The quantities R and I are given in the following list:

$$\begin{cases} \bar{R}_{a\alpha}=-A_{\alpha 1}+\Omega_\alpha X+\frac{1}{k}2\left(\frac{1}{2}+a\right)\left[\left(\frac{1}{2}-a\right)G-\frac{1}{k}F\right] & (1)\\ R_{a\beta}=-A_{\beta 1}+\frac{1}{k^2}A_{\beta 3}+\frac{1}{k}\frac{1}{\pi}\left(a+\frac{1}{2}\right)\left[T_{11}G-2\frac{1}{k}T_{10}F\right] & (2)\\ R_{ah}=-A_{h1}+\frac{1}{k}2\left(a+\frac{1}{2}\right)G & (3)\end{cases}$$

$$\begin{cases} R_{b\alpha}=-B_{\alpha 1}-\frac{1}{k}\frac{T_{12}}{\pi}\left[\left(\frac{1}{2}-a\right)G-\frac{1}{k}F\right] & (4)\\ \bar{R}_{b\beta}=-B_{\beta 1}+\frac{1}{k^2}B_{\beta 3}+\Omega_\beta X-\frac{1}{k}\frac{T_{12}}{2\pi^2}\left[T_{11}G-2T_{10}\frac{1}{k}F\right] & (5)\\ R_{bh}=-B_{h1}-\frac{1}{k}\frac{T_{12}}{\pi}G & (6)\end{cases}$$

$$\begin{cases} R_{c\alpha}=-C_{\alpha 1}-\frac{1}{k}2\left[\left(\frac{1}{2}-a\right)G-\frac{1}{k}F\right] & (7)\\ R_{c\beta}=-C_{\beta 1}-\frac{1}{k}\frac{1}{\pi}\left[T_{11}G-2T_{10}\frac{1}{k}F\right] & (8)\\ \bar{R}_{ch}=-C_{h1}+\Omega_h X-\frac{1}{k}2G & (9)\end{cases}$$

$$\begin{cases} I_{a\alpha}=-\frac{1}{k}\left[2\left(a+\frac{1}{2}\right)\left\{\left(\frac{1}{2}-a\right)F+\frac{1}{k}G\right\}-A_{\alpha 2}\right] & (11)\\ I_{a\beta}=-\frac{1}{k}\left[\frac{1}{\pi}\left(a+\frac{1}{2}\right)\left(T_{11}F+2\frac{1}{k}T_{10}G\right)-A_{\beta 2}\right] & (12)\\ I_{ah}=-\frac{1}{k}2\left(a+\frac{1}{2}\right)F & (13)\end{cases}$$

$$\begin{cases} I_{b\alpha}=\frac{1}{k}\left[\frac{T_{12}}{\pi}\left\{\left(\frac{1}{2}-a\right)F+\frac{1}{k}G\right\}+B_{\alpha 2}\right] & (14)\\ I_{b\beta}=\frac{1}{k}\left[\frac{T_{12}}{2\pi^2}\left(T_{11}F+2\frac{1}{k}T_{10}G\right)+B_{\beta 2}\right] & (15)\\ I_{bh}=\frac{1}{k}\frac{T_{12}}{\pi}F & (16)\end{cases}$$

$$\begin{cases} I_{c\alpha}=\frac{1}{k}\left[2\left\{\left(\frac{1}{2}-a\right)F+\frac{1}{k}G\right\}+C_{\alpha 2}\right] & (17)\\ I_{c\beta}=\frac{1}{k}\left[\frac{1}{\pi}\left(T_{11}F+2\frac{1}{k}T_{10}G\right)+C_{\beta 2}\right] & (18)\\ I_{ch}=\frac{1}{k}2F & (19)\end{cases}$$

The solution as given by the three-row determinant shall be written explicitly in X. We are immediately able to put down for the general case a cubic equation in X with complex coefficients and can easily segregate the three subcases. The quantity D is as before the value of the determinant, but with the term containing X missing. The quantities $M_{a\alpha}$, $M_{b\beta}$, and M_{ch} are the minors of the elements in the diagonal squares $a\alpha$, $b\beta$, and ch, respectively. They are expressed explicitly in terms of R and I under the subcases treated in the following paragraphs.

$$\bar{D}=\begin{vmatrix} \boldsymbol{A}_{a\alpha}+\Omega_\alpha X & \boldsymbol{A}_{a\beta} & \boldsymbol{A}_{ah}\\ \boldsymbol{A}_{b\alpha} & \boldsymbol{A}_{b\beta}+\Omega_\beta X & \boldsymbol{A}_{bh}\\ \boldsymbol{A}_{c\alpha} & \boldsymbol{A}_{c\beta} & \boldsymbol{A}_{ch}+\Omega_h X\end{vmatrix}=0$$

where $\boldsymbol{A}_{a\alpha}=R_{a\alpha}+iI_{a\alpha}$ etc.

Complex cubic equation in X:

$$\Omega_\alpha\Omega_\beta\Omega_h X^3+(\Omega_\alpha\Omega_\beta\boldsymbol{A}_{ch}+\Omega_\beta\Omega_h\boldsymbol{A}_{a\alpha}+\Omega_h\Omega_\alpha\boldsymbol{A}_{b\beta})X^2 +(\Omega_\alpha M_{a\alpha}+\Omega_\beta M_{b\beta}+\Omega_h M_{ch})X+D=0 \qquad \text{(XXI)}$$

Case 3, (α, β):

$$\Omega_\alpha\Omega_\beta X^2+(\Omega_\alpha\boldsymbol{A}_{b\beta}+\Omega_\beta\boldsymbol{A}_{a\alpha})X+M_{ch}=0 \qquad \text{(XXII)}$$

Case 2, (β, h):

$$\Omega_\beta\Omega_h X^2+(\Omega_\beta\boldsymbol{A}_{ch}+\Omega_h\boldsymbol{A}_{b\beta})X+M_{a\alpha}=0 \qquad \text{(XXIII)}$$

Case 1, (h, α):

$$\Omega_h\Omega_\alpha X^2+(\Omega_h\boldsymbol{A}_{a\alpha}+\Omega_\alpha\boldsymbol{A}_{ch})X+M_{b\beta}=0 \qquad \text{(XXIV)}$$

$$\Omega_\alpha X=\frac{C_\alpha}{k^2 M v^2 \kappa}=\left(\frac{\omega_\alpha r_\alpha}{\omega_r r_r}\right)^2\frac{1}{\kappa}\left(\frac{b r_r \omega_r}{vk}\right)^2$$

$$\Omega_\beta X=\frac{C_\beta}{k^2 M v^2 \kappa}=\left(\frac{\omega_\beta r_\beta}{\omega_r r_r}\right)^2\frac{1}{\kappa}\left(\frac{b r_r \omega_r}{vk}\right)^2$$

$$\Omega_h X=\frac{C_h b^2}{k^2 M v^2 \kappa}=\left(\frac{\omega_h}{\omega_r r_r}\right)^2\frac{1}{\kappa}\left(\frac{b r_r \omega_r}{vk}\right)^2$$

and finally

$$X=\frac{1}{\kappa}\left(\frac{b r_r \omega_r}{vk}\right)^2$$

We are at liberty to introduce the reference parameters ω_r and r_r, and the convention adopted is: ω_r is the last ω in cyclic order in each of the subcases 3, 2, and 1.

Then $\Omega_n=\left(\frac{\omega_n r_n}{\omega_{n+1} r_{n+1}}\right)^2$ and $\Omega_{n+1}=1$, thus for

$$\textit{Case 3, } \Omega_\alpha=\left(\frac{\omega_\alpha r_\alpha}{\omega_\beta r_\beta}\right)^2 \text{ and } \Omega_\beta=1$$

$$\textit{Case 2, } \Omega_\beta=\left(\frac{\omega_\beta r_\beta}{\omega_h}\right)^2 \text{ and } \Omega_h=1$$

$$\textit{Case 1, } \Omega_h=\left(\frac{\omega_h}{\omega_\alpha r_\alpha}\right)^2 \text{ and } \Omega_\alpha=1$$

To treat the general case of three degrees of freedom (equation (XXI)), it is observed that the real part of the equation is of third degree while the imaginary part furnishes an equation of second degree. The problem is to find values of X satisfying both equations. We shall adopt the following procedure: Plot graphically X against $\frac{1}{k}$ for both equations. The points of intersection are the solutions. We are only concerned with positive values of $\frac{1}{k}$ and positive values of X. Observe that we do not have to solve for k, but may reverse the process by choosing a number of values of k and solve for X. The plotting of X against $\frac{1}{k}$ for the second-degree equation is simple enough, whereas the task of course is somewhat more laborious for the third-degree equation. However, the general case is of less practical importance than are the three subcases. The equation simplifies considerably, becoming of second degree in X.

We shall now proceed to consider these three subcases. By virtue of the cyclic arrangement, we need only consider the first case (α, β). The complex quadratic equations (XXII)–(XXIV) all resolve themselves into two independent statements, which we shall for convenience denote "Imaginary equation" and "Real equation", the former being of first and the latter of second degree in X. All constants are to be resolved into their real and imaginary parts, denoted by an upper index R or I, respectively.

Let $M_{a\alpha}=M^R{}_{a\alpha}+iM^I{}_{a\alpha}$ and let similar expressions denote $M_{b\beta}$ and M_{ch}

Case 3, (α,β). Separating equation (XXII) we obtain.
(1) Imaginary equation:

$$(\Omega_\alpha I_{b\beta}+\Omega_\beta I_{a\alpha})X+M^I{}_{ch}=0$$

$$X=-\frac{M^I{}_{ch}}{\Omega_\alpha I_{b\beta}+\Omega_\beta I_{a\alpha}}$$

(2) Real equation:

$$\Omega_\alpha\Omega_\beta X^2+(\Omega_\alpha R_{b\beta}+\Omega_\beta R_{a\alpha})X+M^R{}_{ch}=0$$

Eliminating X we get

$$\Omega_\alpha\Omega_\beta(M^I{}_{ch})^2-(\Omega_\alpha R_{b\beta}+\Omega_\beta R_{a\alpha})(\Omega_\alpha I_{b\beta}+\Omega_\beta I_{a\alpha})M^I{}_{ch}$$
$$+M^R{}_{ch}(\Omega_\alpha I_{b\beta}+\Omega_\beta I_{a\alpha})^2=0$$

By the convention adopted we have in this case:

$$\omega_r=\omega_\beta,\qquad \Omega_\alpha=\left(\frac{\omega_\alpha}{\omega_\beta}\right)^2\left(\frac{r_\alpha}{r_\beta}\right)^2,\qquad \text{and } \Omega_\beta=1$$

Arranging the equation in powers of Ω_α we have:

$$\Omega_\alpha^2[-M^I{}_{ch}(R_{b\beta}I_{b\beta})+M^R{}_{ch}I_{b\beta}{}^2]+\Omega_\alpha[(M^I{}_{ch})^2$$
$$-M^I{}_{ch}(R_{a\alpha}I_{b\beta}+I_{a\alpha}R_{b\beta})+2M^R{}_{ch}I_{a\alpha}I_{b\beta}]$$
$$+[-M^I{}_{ch}R_{a\alpha}I_{a\alpha}+M^R{}_{ch}I_{a\alpha}{}^2]=0$$

But we have

$$(M^I{}_{ch})^2-M^I{}_{ch}(R_{a\alpha}I_{b\beta}+I_{a\alpha}R_{b\beta})$$
$$=M^I{}_{ch}[R_{a\alpha}I_{b\beta}-R_{a\beta}I_{b\alpha}+R_{b\beta}I_{a\alpha}-R_{b\alpha}I_{a\beta}-R_{a\alpha}I_{b\beta}-R_{b\beta}I_{a\alpha}]$$
$$=-M^I{}_{ch}(R_{a\beta}I_{b\alpha}+I_{a\beta}R_{b\alpha})$$

Finally, the equation for Case 3 (α, β) becomes:

$$\Omega_\alpha^2(M^R{}_{ch}I_{b\beta}{}^2-M^I{}_{ch}R_{b\beta}I_{b\beta})+\Omega_\alpha[-M^I{}_{ch}(R_{a\beta}I_{b\alpha}+I_{a\beta}R_{b\alpha})$$
$$+2M^R{}_{ch}I_{a\alpha}I_{b\beta}]+M^R{}_{ch}I_{a\alpha}{}^2-M^I{}_{ch}R_{a\alpha}I_{a\alpha}=0 \quad \text{(XXV)}$$

where

$$M^R{}_{ch}=R_{a\alpha}R_{b\beta}-R_{a\beta}R_{b\alpha}-I_{a\alpha}I_{b\beta}+I_{a\beta}I_{b\alpha}$$
$$M^I{}_{ch}=R_{a\alpha}I_{b\beta}-R_{a\beta}I_{b\alpha}+I_{a\alpha}R_{b\beta}-I_{a\beta}R_{b\alpha}$$

The remaining cases may be obtained by cyclic rearrangement:

Case 2, (β,h) $\qquad \omega_r=\omega_h \qquad \Omega_\beta=\left(\frac{\omega_\beta}{\omega_h}\right)^2 r_\beta{}^2 \qquad \Omega_h=1$

$$\Omega_\beta^2(M^R_{a\alpha}I_{ch}{}^2-M^I_{a\alpha}R_{ch}I_{ch})+\Omega_\beta[-M^I_{a\alpha}(R_{bh}I_{c\beta}+I_{bh}R_{c\beta})$$
$$+2M^R_{a\alpha}I_{b\beta}I_{ch}]+M^R_{a\alpha}I_{b\beta}{}^2-M^I_{a\alpha}R_{b\beta}I_{b\beta}=0 \quad (XXVI)$$

where $\quad M^R{}_{a\alpha}=R_{b\beta}R_{ch}-R_{bh}R_{c\beta}-I_{b\beta}I_{ch}+I_{bh}I_{c\beta}$

$\qquad\qquad M^I_{a\alpha}=R_{b\beta}I_{ch}-R_{bh}I_{c\beta}+I_{b\beta}R_{ch}-I_{bh}R_{c\beta}$

Case 1, (h,α) $\qquad \omega_r=\omega_\alpha \qquad \Omega_h=\left(\frac{\omega_h}{\omega_\alpha}\right)^2\frac{1}{r_\alpha{}^2} \qquad \Omega_\alpha=1$

$$\Omega_h^2(M^R_{b\beta}I_{a\alpha}{}^2-M^I_{b\beta}R_{a\alpha}I_{a\alpha})+\Omega_h[-M^I_{b\beta}(R_{c\alpha}I_{\alpha h}+I_{c\alpha}R_{\alpha h})$$
$$+2M^R_{b\beta}I_{ch}I_{a\alpha}]+M^R_{b\beta}I_{ch}{}^2-M^I_{b\beta}R_{ch}I_{ch}=0 \quad (XXVII)$$

where $\quad M^R_{b\beta}=R_{ch}R_{a\alpha}-R_{c\alpha}R_{ah}-I_{ch}I_{a\alpha}+I_{c\alpha}I_{ah}$

$\qquad\qquad M^I_{b\beta}=R_{ch}I_{a\alpha}-R_{c\alpha}I_{ah}+I_{ch}R_{a\alpha}-I_{c\alpha}R_{ah}$

Equations (XXV), (XXVI), and (XXVII) thus give the solutions of the cases: *torsion-aileron*, *aileron-deflection*, and *deflection-torsion*, respectively. The quantity Ω may immediately be plotted against $\frac{1}{k}$ for any value of the independent parameters. The coefficients in the equations are all given in terms of R and I, which quantities have been defined above. Routine calculations and graphs giving Ω against $\frac{1}{k}$ are contained in Appendix I and Appendix II. Knowing related values of Ω and $\frac{1}{k}$, X is immediately expressed as a function of Ω by means of the first-degree equation. The definition of X and Ω for each subcase is given above. The cyclic arrangement of all quantities is very convenient as it permits identical treatment of the three subcases.

It shall finally be repeated that the above solutions represent the *border case* of unstable equilibrium. The plot of X against Ω gives a boundary curve between the stable and the unstable regions in the $X\Omega$ plane. It is preferable, however, to plot the quantity $\frac{1}{k^2}\frac{1}{X}$ instead of X, since this quantity is proportional to the square of the flutter speed. The stable area can easily be identified by inspection as it will contain the axis $\frac{1}{k^2}\frac{1}{X}=0$, if the combination is stable for zero velocity.

Langley Memorial Aeronautical Laboratory,
National Advisory Committee for Aeronautics,
Langley Field, Va., *May 2, 1934.*

APPENDIX I

PROCEDURE IN SOLVING NUMERICAL EXAMPLES

(1) Determine the R's and I's, nine of each for a major case of three degrees of freedom, or those pertaining to a particular subcase, 4 R's and 4 I's. Refer to the following for the R's and I's involved in each case:

The numerals 1 to 9 and 11 to 19 are used for convenience.

(Major case) Three degrees of freedom

1	$R_{a\alpha}$	$I_{a\alpha}$	11
2	$R_{a\beta}$	$I_{a\beta}$	12
3	R_{ah}	I_{ah}	13
4	$R_{b\alpha}$	$I_{b\alpha}$	14
5	$R_{b\beta}$	$I_{b\beta}$	15
6	R_{bh}	I_{bh}	16
7	$R_{c\alpha}$	$I_{c\alpha}$	17
8	$R_{c\beta}$	$I_{c\beta}$	18
9	R_{ch}	I_{ch}	19

(Case 3) Torsional-aileron (α, β)

1	$R_{a\alpha}$	$I_{a\alpha}$	11
2	$R_{a\beta}$	$I_{a\beta}$	12
4	$R_{b\alpha}$	$I_{b\alpha}$	14
5	$R_{b\beta}$	$I_{b\beta}$	15

(Case 2) Aileron-deflection (β, h)

5	$R_{b\beta}$	$I_{b\beta}$	15
6	R_{bh}	I_{bh}	16
8	$R_{c\beta}$	$I_{c\beta}$	18
9	R_{ch}	I_{ch}	19

(Case 1) Deflection-torsion (h, α)

7	$R_{c\alpha}$	$I_{c\alpha}$	17
9	R_{ch}	I_{ch}	19
1	$R_{a\alpha}$	$I_{a\alpha}$	11
3	R_{ah}	I_{ah}	13

It has been found convenient to split the R's in two parts $R=R'+R''$, the former being independent of the argument $\frac{1}{k}$. The quantities I and R'' are functions of the two independent parameters a and c only.[5] The formulas are given in the following list.

$$R''_{a\alpha}=\frac{1}{k}2\left(a+\frac{1}{2}\right)\left\{\left(\frac{1}{2}-a\right)G-\frac{F}{k}\right\} \tag{1}$$

$$R''_{a\beta}=\frac{1}{k}\frac{1}{\pi}\left\{(T_4+T_{10})\frac{1}{k}+\left(a+\frac{1}{2}\right)\left(T_{11}G-\frac{2}{k}T_{10}F\right)\right\} \tag{2}$$

$$R''_{ah}=\frac{1}{k}2\left(a+\frac{1}{2}\right)G \tag{3}$$

$$R''_{b\alpha}=-\frac{1}{k}\frac{T_{12}}{\pi}\left\{\left(\frac{1}{2}-a\right)G-\frac{F}{k}\right\} \tag{4}$$

$$R''_{b\beta}=-\frac{1}{k}\frac{1}{\pi^2}\left\{\frac{T_{12}}{2}\left(T_{11}G-\frac{2}{k}T_{10}F\right)-\frac{1}{k}(T_5-T_4T_{10})\right\} \tag{5}$$

$$R''_{bh}=-\frac{1}{k}\frac{T_{12}}{\pi}G \tag{6}$$

$$R''_{c\alpha}=-\frac{1}{k}2\left\{\left(\frac{1}{2}-a\right)G-\frac{F}{k}\right\} \tag{7}$$

$$R''_{c\beta}=-\frac{1}{k}\frac{1}{\pi}\left(T_{11}G-2T_{10}\frac{F}{k}\right) \tag{8}$$

$$R''_{ch}=-\frac{1}{k}2\,G \tag{9}$$

$$I_{a\alpha}=-2\left(a+\frac{1}{2}\right)\left\{\left(\frac{1}{2}-a\right)F+\frac{1}{k}G\right\}+\frac{1}{2}-a \tag{11}$$

$$I_{a\beta}=-\frac{1}{\pi}\left\{\left(a+\frac{1}{2}\right)\left(T_{11}F+\frac{2}{k}T_{10}G\right)+2p+\left(\frac{1}{2}-a\right)T_4\right\} \tag{12}$$

$$I_{ah}=-2\left(a+\frac{1}{2}\right)F \tag{13}$$

$$I_{b\alpha}=\frac{T_{12}}{\pi}\left\{\left(\frac{1}{2}-a\right)F+\frac{1}{k}G\right\}+\frac{1}{\pi}\left(p-T_1-\frac{1}{2}T_4\right) \tag{14}$$

Where $p=-\frac{1}{3}(1-c^2)^{3/2}$

$$I_{b\beta}=\frac{1}{2\pi^2}\left\{T_{12}\left(T_{11}F+\frac{2}{k}T_{10}G\right)-T_4T_{11}\right\} \tag{15}$$

$$I_{bh}=\frac{T_{12}}{\pi}F \tag{16}$$

$$I_{c\alpha}=2\left\{\left(\frac{1}{2}-a\right)F+\frac{1}{k}G\right\}+1 \tag{17}$$

$$I_{c\beta}=\frac{1}{\pi}\left\{\left(T_{11}F+\frac{2}{k}T_{10}G\right)-T_4\right\} \tag{18}$$

$$I_{ch}=2F \tag{19}$$

[5] The quantities I given in the appendix and used in the following calculations are seen to differ from the I's given in the body of the paper by the factor $\frac{1}{k}$. It may be noticed that this factor drops out in the first-degree equations.

Choosing certain values of a and c and employing the values of the T's given by the formulas of the report (p. 5) or in table I and also using the values of F and G (formulas (XII) and (XIII)) or table II, we evaluate the quantities I and R'' for a certain number of $\frac{1}{k}$ values. The results of this evaluation are given in tables III and IV, which have been worked out for $a=0, -0.2$, and -0.4, and for $c=0.5$ and $c=0$. The range of $\frac{1}{k}$ is from 0 to 40. These tables save the work of calculating the I's and R'''s for almost all cases of practical importance. Interpolation may be used for intermediate values. This leaves the quantities R' to be determined. These, being independent of $\frac{1}{k}$, are as a result easy to obtain. Their values, using the same system of numbers for identification, and referring to the definition of the original independent variables on pages 9 and 10, are given as follows:

$$R'_{a\alpha}=-\frac{r_\alpha^2}{\kappa}-\left(\frac{1}{8}+a^2\right) \qquad (1)$$

$$R'_{a\beta}=-\frac{r_\beta^2}{\kappa}-(c-a)\frac{x_\beta}{\kappa}+\frac{T_7}{\pi}+(c-a)\frac{T_1}{\pi} \qquad (2)$$

$$R'_{ah}=-\frac{x_\alpha}{\kappa}+a \qquad (3)$$

$$R'_{b\alpha}=\text{same as } R'_{a\beta} \qquad (4)$$

$$R'_{b\beta}=-\frac{r_\beta^2}{\kappa}+\frac{1}{\pi^2}T_3 \qquad (5)$$

$$R'_{bh}=-\frac{x_\beta}{\kappa}+\frac{1}{\pi}T_1 \qquad (6)$$

$$R'_{c\alpha}=\text{same as } R'_{ah} \qquad (7)$$

$$R'_{c\beta}=\text{same as } R'_{bh} \qquad (8)$$

$$R'_{ch}=-\frac{1}{\kappa}-1 \qquad (9)$$

Because of the symmetrical arrangement in the determinant, the 9 quantities are seen to reduce to 6 quantities to be calculated. It is very fortunate, indeed, that all the remaining variables segregate themselves in the 6 values of R' which are independent of $\frac{1}{k}$, while the more complicated I and R'' are functions solely of c and a. In order to solve any problem it is therefore only necessary to refer to tables III and IV and then to calculate the 6 values of R'.

The quantities (1) to (9) and (11) to (19) thus having been determined, the plot of Ω against $\frac{1}{k}$, which constitutes our method of solution, is obtained by solving the equation $a\Omega^2+b\Omega+c=0$. The constants a, b, and c are obtained automatically by computation according to the following scheme:

Case 3

Find products 1.5 2.4 11.15 12.14

Then $M^R_{ch}=1.5-2.4-\frac{1}{k^2}(11.15-12.14)$

Find products 1.15 2.14 11.5 12.4

Then $M^I_{ch}=1.15-2.14+11.5-12.4$

and $a=M^R_{ch}(15)^2-M^I_{ch}(5.15)$

$b=-M^I_{ch}(2.14+12.4)+2M^R_{ch}(11.15)$

$c=M^R_{ch}(11)^2-M^I_{ch}(1.11)$ Find Ω_α

Solution: $\frac{1}{X}=-\frac{\Omega_\alpha(15)+11}{M^I_{ch}}$

Similarly

Case 2

5.9 6.8 15.19 16.18

$M^R_{a\alpha}=5.9-6.8-\frac{1}{k^2}(15.19-16.18)$

5.19 6.18 15.9 16.8

$M^I_{a\alpha}=5.19-6.18+15.9-16.8$

$a=M^R_{a\alpha}(19)^2-M^I_{a\alpha}(9.19)$

$b=-M^I_{a\alpha}(6.18+16.8)$

$+2M^R_{a\alpha}(6.18+16.8)$

$c=M^R_{a\alpha}(15)^2-M^I_{a\alpha}(5.15)$ Find Ω_β

$\frac{1}{X}=\frac{\Omega_\beta(19)+15}{M^I_{a\alpha}}$

and

Case 1

9.1 7.3 19.11 17.13

$M^R_{b\beta}=9.1-7.3-\frac{1}{k^2}(19.11-17.13)$

9.11 7.13 19.1 17.3

$M^I_{b\beta}=9.11-7.13+19.1-17.3$

$a=M^R_{b\beta}(11)^2-M^I_{b\beta}(1.11)$

$b=-M^I_{b\beta}(7.13+17.3)+2M^R_{b\beta}(19.11)$

$c=M^R_{b\beta}(19)^2-M^I_{b\beta}(9.19)$ Find Ω_h

$\frac{1}{X}=\frac{\Omega_h(11)+19}{M^I_{b\beta}}$

Ω_α is defined as $\left(\frac{\omega_\alpha r_\alpha}{\omega_\beta r_\beta}\right)^2$ for case 3;

Ω_β is defined as $\left(\frac{\omega_\beta r_\beta}{\omega_h}\right)^2$ for case 2; and

Ω_h is defined as $\left(\frac{\omega_h}{\omega_\alpha r_\alpha}\right)^2$ for case 1.

The quantity $\frac{1}{X}$ is $\kappa\left(\frac{vk}{b\omega_r r_r}\right)^2$ by definition.

Since both Ω and $\frac{1}{X}$ are calculated for each value of $\frac{1}{k}$, we may plot $\frac{1}{k^2}\frac{1}{X}$ directly as a function of Ω. This quantity, which is proportional to the square of the flutter speed, represents the solution.

We shall sometimes use the square root of the above quantity, viz, $\frac{1}{k}\sqrt{\frac{1}{X}}=\frac{\sqrt{\kappa}\,v}{b\omega_r r_r}$, and will denote this quantity by F, which we shall term the "flutter factor." The flutter velocity is consequently obtained as

$$v=F\frac{b\omega_r r_r}{\sqrt{\kappa}}$$

Since F is nondimensional, the quantity $\frac{b\omega_r r_r}{\sqrt{\kappa}}$ must obviously be a velocity. It is useful to establish the significance of this velocity, with reference to which the flutter speed, so to speak, is measured. Observing that $\kappa=\frac{\pi\rho b^2}{M}$ and that the stiffness in case 1 is given by $\omega_\alpha=\sqrt{\frac{C_\alpha}{Mb^2r_\alpha^2}}$ this reference velocity may be written:

$$v_R=\frac{b\omega_\alpha r_\alpha}{\sqrt{\kappa}}=\frac{1}{b}\sqrt{\frac{C_\alpha}{\pi\rho}} \text{ or}$$

$$\pi\rho v_R^2b^2=C_\alpha$$

The velocity v_R is thus the velocity at which the total force on the airfoil $\pi\rho v_R^2 2b$ attacking with an arm $\frac{b}{2}$ equals the torsional stiffness C_α of the wing. This statement means, in case 1, that the reference velocity used is equal to the "divergence" velocity obtained with the torsional axis in the middle of the chord. This velocity is considerably smaller than the usual divergence velocity, which may be expressed as

$$v_D=v_R\frac{1}{\frac{1}{2}+a}$$

where a ranges from 0 to $-\frac{1}{2}$. We may thus express the flutter velocity as

$$v_F=v_RF$$

In case 3 the reference velocity has a similar significance, that is, it is the velocity at which the entire lift of the airfoil attacking with a leverage $\frac{1}{2}b$ equals numerically the torsional stiffness C_β of the aileron or movable tail surface.

In case 2, no suitable or useful significance of the reference velocity is available.

TABLE I.—VALUES OF T

	$c=1$	$c=\frac{1}{2}$	$c=0$	$c=-\frac{1}{2}$	$c=-1$
T_1	0	−0.1259	−0.6667	−1.6967	−3.1416
T_2	0	−0.2103	−1.5707	−4.8356	−9.8697
T_3	0	−.05313	−.8084	−3.8375	−11.1034
T_4	0	−.6142	−1.5708	−4.6614	−3.1416
T_5	0	−.9398	−3.4674	−6.9503	−9.8697
T_6	0	−0.2103	−1.5707	−4.8356	−9.8697
T_7	0	.0132	−.1964	−1.1913	−3.5343
T_8	0	.0903	−.3333	−1.4805	−3.1416
T_{10}	0	1.9132	2.5708	2.9604	3.1416
T_{11}	0	1.2000	3.5708	6.3538	9.4218
T_{12}	0	.07066	.4292	1.2000	3.1416

TABLE II.—TABLE OF THE BESSEL FUNCTIONS J_0, J_1 Y_0, Y_1 AND THE FUNCTIONS F AND G

$$F(k)=\frac{J_1(J_1+Y_0)+Y_1(Y_1-J_0)}{(J_1+Y_0)^2+(Y_1-J_0)^2}$$

$$-G(k)=\frac{Y_1(J_1+Y_0)-J_1(Y_1-J_0)}{(J_1+Y_0)^2+(Y_1-J_0)^2}$$

k	$\frac{1}{k}$	J_0	J_1	Y_0	Y_1	F	$-G$
∞	0	----	----	----	----	0.5000	0
10	1/10	−0.2159	0.0435	0.0557	0.2490	.5006	0.0126
6	1/6	.1506	−.2767	−.2882	−.1750	.5018	.0207
4	1/4	−.3972	−.0660	−.0170	.3979	.5037	.0305
2	1/2	.2239	.5767	.5104	−.1071	.5129	.0577
1	1	.7652	.4401	.0882	−.7813	.5395	.1003
.8	1 1/4	.8463	.3688	−.0868	−.9780	.5541	.1165
.6	1 2/3	.9120	.2867	−.3085	−1.2604	.5788	.1378
.5	2	.9385	.2423	−.4444	−1.4714	.6030	.151
.4	2 1/2	.9604	.1960	−.6060	−1.7808	.6245	.166
.3	3 1/3	.9776	.1483	−.8072	−2.2929	.6650	.180
.2	5	.9900	.0995	−1.0810	−3.3235	.7276	.1886
.1	10	.9975	.0499	−1.5342	−7.0317	.8457	.1626
.05	20	----	----	----	----	.911	.132
.025	40	----	----	----	----	.965	.090
0	∞	----	----	----	----	1.000	0

TABLE III.—VALUES OF R

	c	a	1/k = 0	1/10	1/6	1/4	1/2	1	1 1/4	1 2/3	2	2 1/2	3 1/3	5	10	20	40
$R''_{a\alpha}$	(1)	0	0	−0. 00564	−0. 01566	−0. 03529	−0. 14265	−0. 58965	−0. 93656	−1. 72330	−2. 56300	−4. 11000	−7. 68720	−18. 66150	−85. 38300	−365. 72000	−1, 528. 2000
		−. 2	0	−. 00353	−. 00981	−. 02208	−. 08905	−. 36586	−. 58061	−1. 06158	−1. 57400	−2. 51580	−4. 68430	−11. 31010	−51. 42490	−219. 74900	−917. 3520
		−. 4	0	−. 00123	−. 00341	−. 00767	−. 03084	−. 12595	−. 19936	−. 36305	−. 53676	−. 85520	−1. 58540	−3. 80774	−17. 20670	−73. 35520	−305. 9280
$R''_{a\beta}$	0	0	0	−. 00163	−. 00452	−. 01020	−. 04175	−. 18016	−. 29384	−. 56223	−. 87212	−1. 43983	−2. 84988	−7. 46300	−38. 29650	−172. 36360	−741. 7972
		−. 2	0	. 00030	. 00083	. 00184	. 00679	. 01922	. 02266	. 01629	−. 01400	−. 06803	−. 29517	−1. 29480	−10. 24590	−52. 49020	−241. 3664
		−. 4	0	. 00222	. 00617	. 01388	. 05531	. 21861	. 33914	. 59499	. 84414	1. 30365	2. 25914	4. 87340	17. 80470	67. 38320	259. 0648
	0. 5	0	0	. 00083	. 00229	. 00510	. 01932	. 06419	. 08876	. 12176	. 12260	. 12205	−. 02900	−. 93535	−10. 48970	−59. 16180	−268. 7236
		−. 2	0	. 00214	. 00595	. 01336	. 05278	. 20325	. 31065	. 53062	. 73222	1. 10233	1. 81135	3. 55230	10. 14740	31. 49620	101. 6340
		−. 4	0	. 00347	. 00965	. 02170	. 08656	. 34361	. 53463	. 94336	1. 34762	2. 09190	3. 66913	8. 08235	30. 97980	120. 89760	475. 2592
R''_{ah}	(1)	0	0	−. 00125	−. 00345	−. 00763	−. 02890	−. 10030	−. 14560	−. 22470	−. 30200	−. 41500	−. 60000	−. 94300	−1. 62600	−2. 64000	−3. 6000
		−. 2	0	−. 00075	−. 00207	−. 00426	−. 01734	−. 06018	−. 08736	−. 13482	−. 18120	−. 24900	−. 36000	−. 56580	−. 97560	−1. 58400	−2. 1600
		−. 4	0	−. 00201	−. 00334	−. 00502	−. 01003	−. 02006	−. 02508	−. 03236	−. 04012	−. 05015	−. 06683	−. 10030	−. 20060	−. 40120	−. 8024
$R''_{b\alpha}$	0	0	0	. 00077	. 00214	. 00482	. 01949	. 08055	. 12821	. 23541	. 35010	. 56143	1. 05008	2. 54920	11. 66330	49. 95700	208. 7520
		−. 2	0	. 00080	. 00223	. 00503	. 02027	. 08329	. 13219	. 24169	. 35836	. 57276	1. 06650	2. 57490	11. 70770	50. 03000	208. 8500
		−. 4	0	. 00084	. 00233	. 00523	. 02106	. 08603	. 13616	. 24796	. 36661	. 58410	1. 08286	2. 60069	11. 75220	50. 10160	208. 9490
	0. 5	0	0	. 00013	. 00035	. 00079	. 00321	. 01327	. 02112	. 03878	. 05767	. 09248	. 17296	. 41988	1. 92110	8. 22870	34. 3850
		−. 2	0	. 00013	. 00037	. 00083	. 00334	. 01372	. 02177	. 03981	. 05903	. 09434	. 17566	. 42413	1. 92840	8. 24060	34. 4007
		−. 4	0	. 00014	. 00038	. 00086	. 00347	. 01417	. 02243	. 04084	. 06039	. 09621	. 17836	. 42837	1. 93575	8. 25246	34. 4169
$R''_{b\beta}$	0	(2)	0	. 00124	. 00343	. 00772	. 03101	. 12642	. 19830	. 35807	. 52400	. 82930	1. 51630	3. 54970	15. 35120	64. 02240	263. 2340
	. 5		0	. 00031	. 00087	. 00196	. 00785	. 03170	. 04980	. 08935	. 13000	. 20440	. 36940	. 84970	3. 55050	14. 56740	59. 3188
R''_{bh}	0	(2)	0	. 00017	. 00047	. 00104	. 00394	. 01370	. 01989	. 03177	. 04125	. 05669	. 08196	. 12881	. 22211	. 36062	. 4918
	. 5		0	. 00003	. 00008	. 00016	. 00065	. 00226	. 00328	. 00506	. 00680	. 00934	. 01350	. 02122	. 03659	. 05940	. 0810
$R''_{c\alpha}$	(1)	0	0	. 01128	. 03132	. 07058	. 28530	1. 17930	1. 87710	3. 44670	5. 12600	8. 22000	15. 37450	37. 32300	170. 76600	731. 44000	3, 056. 4000
		−. 2	0	. 01178	. 03270	. 07362	. 29684	1. 21954	1. 93540	3. 53860	5. 24680	8. 38600	15. 61440	37. 70020	171. 41640	732. 49600	3, 057. 8400
		−. 4	0	. 01228	. 03408	. 07668	. 30838	1. 25950	1. 99360	3. 63050	5. 36760	8. 55200	15. 85440	38. 07740	172. 06680	733. 55200	3, 059. 2800
$R''_{c\beta}$	0	(2)	0	−. 00963	−. 02673	−. 06018	−. 24266	−1. 00561	−1. 58246	−2. 89371	−4. 29100	−6. 85898	−15. 49965	−30. 84330	−140. 26370	−599. 41300	−2, 502. 3470
	. 5		0	. 00660	. 01840	. 04150	. 16810	. 69850	1. 11453	2. 05320	3. 06224	4. 92530	9. 24438	22. 54400	103. 67300	444. 86400	1, 881. 9900
R''_{ch}	(1)	(2)	0	. 00250	. 00690	. 01420	. 05780	. 20060	. 29120	. 44940	. 60400	. 83000	1. 20000	1. 88600	3. 25200	5. 28000	7. 2000

[1] Independent of *c*. [2] Independent of *a*.

TABLE IV.—VALUES OF I

	c	a	1/k = 0	1/10	1/6	1/4	1/2	1	1 1/4	1 2/3	2	2 1/2	3 1/3	5	10	20	40
$I_{a\alpha}$	(1)	0	0. 25000	0. 25096	0. 25255	0. 25578	0. 27240	0. 33055	0. 36855	0. 44030	0. 50050	0. 60275	0. 76750	1. 07920	1. 70320	2. 68450	3. 61750
		−. 2	. 49000	. 49050	. 49131	. 49302	. 50189	. 53359	. 55464	. 59472	. 62794	. 68671	. 78070	. 96021	1. 32040	1. 90140	2. 45470
		−. 4	. 81000	. 81014	. 81037	. 81086	. 81145	. 82395	. 82938	. 84176	. 85186	. 87059	. 90030	. 95763	1. 07300	1. 26400	1. 44630
$I_{a\beta}$	0	0	. 17805	. 17874	. 17985	. 18219	. 19433	. 23768	. 26645	. 32132	. 36664	. 44690	. 57526	. 82035	1. 31213	2. 10476	2. 85963
		−. 2	. 39170	. 39212	. 39278	. 39418	. 40147	. 42748	. 44474	. 47761	. 50485	. 55300	. 63002	. 77708	1. 07215	1. 54773	2. 00065
		−. 4	. 60531	. 60545	. 60567	. 60614	. 60857	. 61724	. 62299	. 63395	. 64303	. 65908	. 68475	. 73377	. 82313	. 99065	1. 14163
	0. 5	0	. 13252	. 13317	. 13425	. 13640	. 14742	. 18544	. 20914	. 25611	. 29514	. 35951	. 46379	. 65973	1. 05124	1. 65524	2. 22869
		−. 2	. 21297	. 21336	. 21401	. 21530	. 22191	. 24472	. 25894	. 28712	. 31054	. 34916	. 41173	. 52929	. 76420	1. 12651	1. 47067
		−. 4	. 29342	. 29354	. 29376	. 29419	. 29640	. 30400	. 30891	. 31813	. 32594	. 33881	. 35966	. 39884	. 47714	. 59792	. 71260
I_{ah}	(1)	0	−. 50000	−. 50060	−. 50180	−. 50370	−. 51290	−. 53950	−. 55410	−. 57880	−. 60300	−. 62450	−. 66500	−. 72760	−. 84570	−. 94100	−. 96500
		−. 2	−. 30000	−. 30036	−. 30108	−. 30222	−. 30774	−. 32370	−. 33246	−. 34728	−. 36180	−. 37470	−. 39900	−. 43656	−. 50752	−. 56460	−. 57900
		−. 4	−. 10000	−. 10012	−. 10036	−. 10074	−. 10258	−. 10790	−. 11082	−. 11576	−. 12060	−. 12490	−. 13300	−. 14552	−. 16914	−. 18220	−. 19300
$I_{b\alpha}$	0	0	. 39023	. 39010	. 38988	. 38944	. 38717	. 37923	. 37404	. 36424	. 35601	. 34204	. 31954	. 27696	. 19172	. 05766	−. 06980
		−. 2	. 40389	. 40378	. 40359	. 40320	. 40119	. 39397	. 38918	. 38005	. 37249	. 35911	. 33771	. 29683	. 21469	. 08255	−. 04344
		−. 4	. 41755	. 41746	. 41730	. 41697	. 41520	. 40871	. 40432	. 39586	. 38896	. 37617	. 35598	. 31671	. 23793	. 10744	−. 01707
	0. 5	0	. 07438	. 07435	. 07433	. 07424	. 07387	. 07256	. 07171	. 07009	. 06874	. 06644	. 06273	. 05572	. 04168	. 01960	−. 00327
		−. 2	. 07663	. 07661	. 07658	. 07651	. 07618	. 07499	. 07420	. 07270	. 07145	. 06925	. 06572	. 05899	. 04548	. 02370	. 00295
		−. 4	. 07887	. 07885	. 07882	. 07867	. 07848	. 07741	. 07668	. 07529	. 07416	. 07205	. 06871	. 06226	. 04928	. 02779	. 00728
$I_{b\beta}$	0	(2)	. 32297	. 32288	. 32273	. 32241	. 32075	. 31483	. 31090	. 30342	. 29721	. 28625	. 26872	. 23524	. 16806	. 05979	−. 04333
	. 5		. 04270	. 04270	. 04270	. 04270	. 04240	. 04150	. 04095	. 03930	. 03904	. 03760	. 03386	. 03080	. 02200	. 00845	−. 00470
I_{bh}	0	(2)	. 06830	. 06840	. 06850	. 06880	. 07010	. 07370	. 07570	. 07910	. 08240	. 08530	. 09080	. 09940	. 11550	. 12440	. 13180
	. 5		. 01125	. 01126	. 01129	. 01133	. 01154	. 01214	. 01247	. 01302	. 01357	. 01405	. 01496	. 01637	. 01903	. 02117	. 02171
$I_{c\alpha}$	(1)	0	1. 50000	1. 49808	1. 49490	1. 48844	1. 45520	1. 33890	1. 26290	1. 11940	. 99900	. 74950	. 46500	−. 15840	−1. 40630	−3. 36900	−5. 23500
		−. 2	1. 70000	1. 69832	1. 69562	1. 68992	1. 66036	1. 55470	1. 48454	1. 35092	1. 24020	1. 04130	. 73100	. 13264	−1. 06802	−3. 00460	−4. 84900
		−. 4	1. 90000	1. 89856	1. 89634	1. 89140	1. 88552	1. 77050	1. 70618	1. 58244	1. 48410	1. 31410	. 99700	. 42370	−. 72974	−2. 64020	−4. 46300
$I_{c\beta}$	0	(2)	1. 06830	1. 06690	1. 06470	1. 06000	1. 03580	. 94900	. 89150	. 78190	. 69110	. 52840	. 27380	−. 21640	−1. 20010	−2. 78550	−4. 29530
	. 5		. 40220	. 40100	. 39880	. 39450	. 37240	. 29640	. 24640	. 15510	. 07610	−. 05180	−. 26030	−. 65220	−1. 43520	−2. 64380	−3. 79010
I_{ch}	(1)	(2)	1. 00000	1. 00120	1. 00360	1. 00740	1. 02580	1. 07900	1. 10820	1. 15760	1. 20600	1. 24900	1. 33000	1. 45520	1. 69140	1. 82200	1. 93000

[1] Independent of *c*. [2] Independent of *a*.

APPENDIX II

NUMERICAL CALCULATIONS

A number of routine examples have been worked out to illustrate typical results. A "standard" case has been chosen, represented by the following constants:

$$\kappa=0.1,\ c=0.5,\ a=-0.4,\ x_\alpha=0.2,$$

$$r_\alpha^2=0.25,\ x_\beta=\frac{1}{80},\ r_\beta^2=\frac{1}{160}$$

$$\omega_\alpha,\ \omega_\beta,\ \omega_h \text{ variable.}$$

We will show the results of a numerical computation of the three possible subcases in succession.

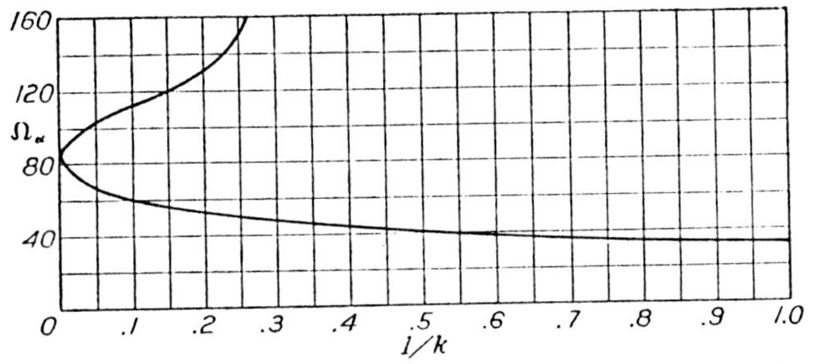

FIGURE 5. –Case 3, Torsion-aileron (α,β): Standard case. Showing Ω_α against $\frac{1}{k}$.

Case 3, Torsion-aileron (α,β): Figure 5 shows the Ω_α against $\frac{1}{k}$ relation and figure 6 the final curve

$$F=\kappa\left(\frac{v}{\omega_\beta r_\beta b}\right)^2 \text{ against } \Omega_\alpha=\left(\frac{\omega_\alpha r_\alpha}{\omega_\beta r_\beta}\right)^2=40\left(\frac{\omega_\alpha}{\omega_\beta}\right)^2$$

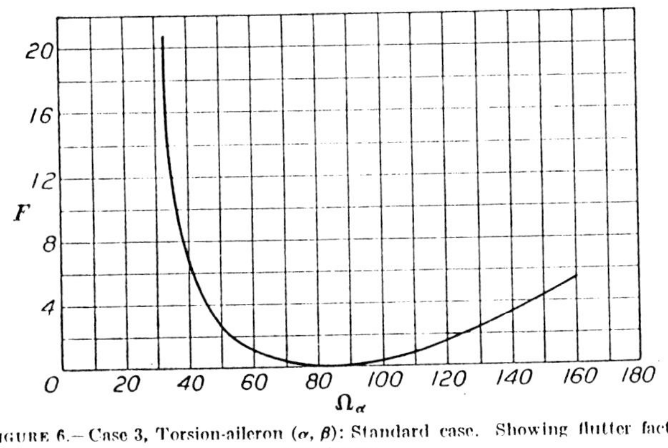

FIGURE 6.–Case 3, Torsion-aileron (α,β): Standard case. Showing flutter factor F against Ω_α.

Case 2, Aileron-flexure (β, h): Figure 7 shows the Ω_β against $\frac{1}{k}$ relation[6] and figure 8 the final curve $\kappa\left(\frac{v}{\omega_h b}\right)^2$ against $\Omega_\beta=\left(\frac{\omega_\beta r_\beta}{\omega_h}\right)^2=\frac{1}{160}\left(\frac{\omega_\beta}{\omega_h}\right)^2$

[6] It is realized that considerable care must be exercised to get these curves reasonably accurate.

The heavy line shows the standard case, while the remaining curves show the effect of a change in the value of x_β to $\frac{1}{40}$ and $\frac{1}{160}$.

Case 1, Flexure-torsion (h, α): Figure 9 shows again

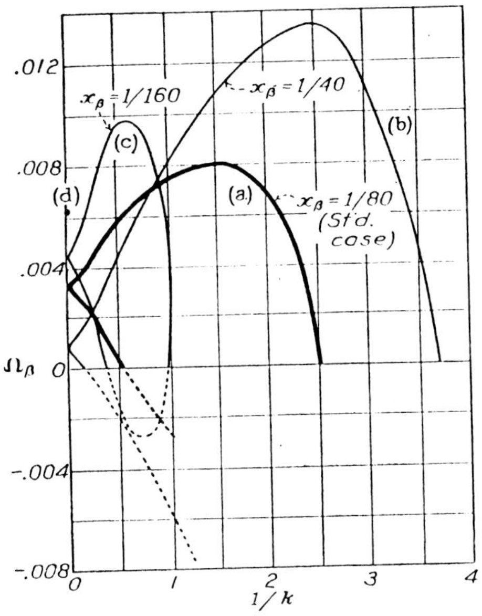

FIGURE 7.–Case 2, Aileron-deflection (β, h): (a) Standard case. (b), (c), (d) indicate dependency on x_β. Case (d), $x_\beta=-0.004$, reduces to a point.

the Ω_h against $\frac{1}{k}$ relation and figure 10 the final result

$$\kappa\left(\frac{v}{\omega_\alpha r_\alpha b}\right)^2 \text{ against } \Omega_h=\left(\frac{\omega_h}{\omega_\alpha r_\alpha}\right)^2=4\left(\frac{\omega_h}{\omega_\alpha}\right)^2$$

Case 1, which is of importance in the propeller theory, has been treated in more detail. The quantity F shown in the figures is $\sqrt{\kappa}\ \frac{v}{\omega_\alpha r_\alpha b}$.

Figure 11 shows the dependency on $\frac{\omega_h}{\omega_\alpha}=\frac{\omega_1}{\omega_2}$; figure 12 shows the dependency on the location of the axis a; figure 13 shows the dependency on the radius of gyration $r_\alpha=r$; and figure 14 shows the dependency on the location of the center of gravity x, for three different combinations of constants.

EXPERIMENTAL RESULTS

Detailed discussion of the experimental work will not be given in this paper, but shall be reserved for a later report. The experiments given in the following are restricted to wings of a large aspect ratio, arranged with two or three degrees of freedom in accordance with the

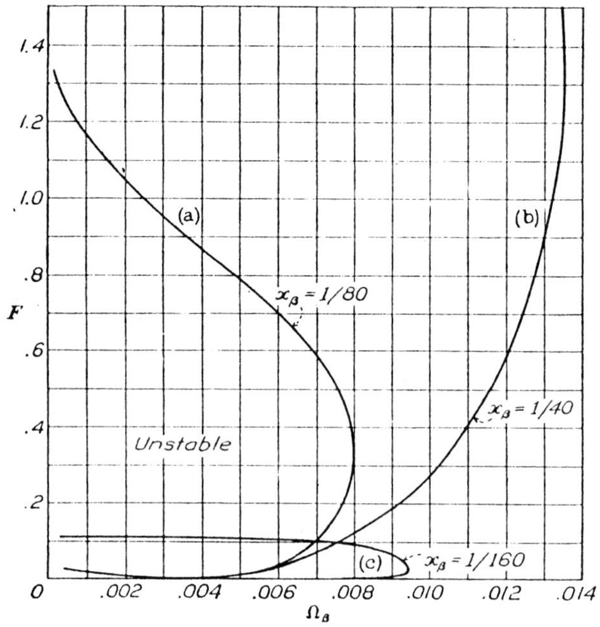

FIGURE 8. Case 2, Aileron-deflection (β, h): Final curves giving flutter factor F against Ω_β corresponding to cases shown in figure 7.

theoretical cases. The wing is free to move parallel to itself in a vertical direction (h); is equipped with an

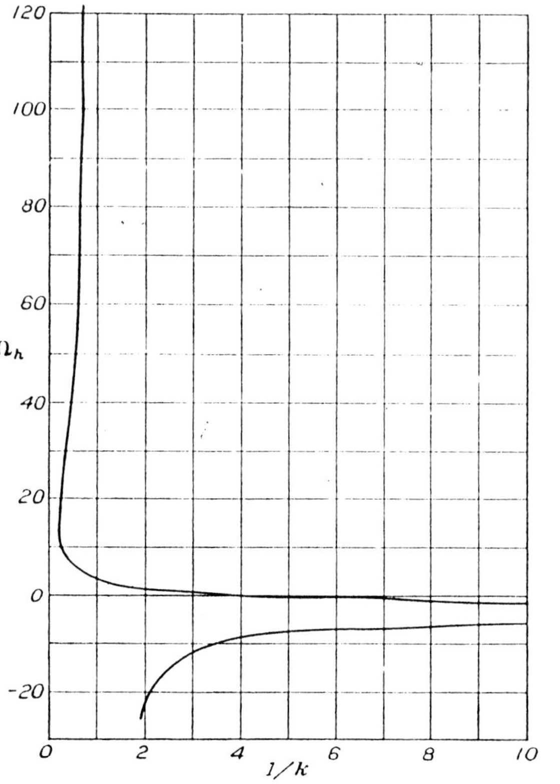

FIGURE 9.—Case 1. Flexure-torsion (h, α): Standard case. Showing Ω_h against $\frac{1}{k}$.

axis in roller bearings at (a) (fig. 2) for torsion, and with an aileron hinged at (c). Variable or exchangeable springs restrain the wing to its equilibrium position.

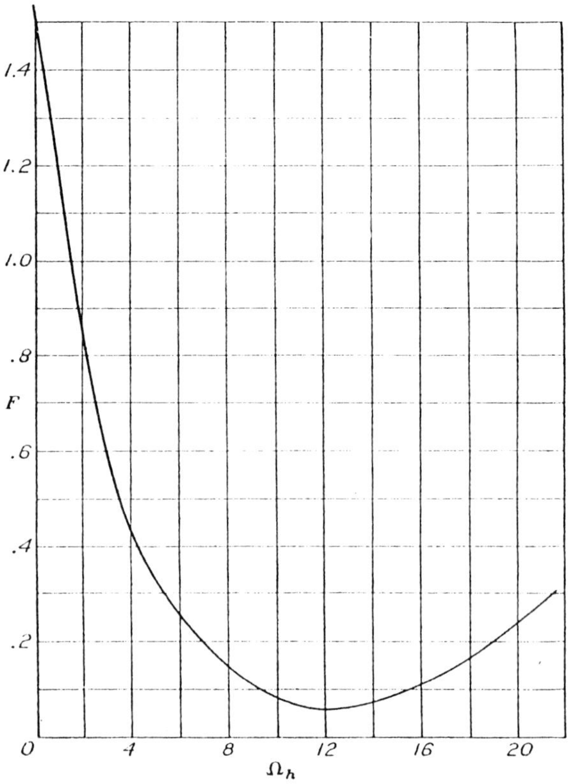

FIGURE 10.—Case 1, Flexure-torsion (h, α): Standard case. Showing flutter factor F against Ω_h.

We shall present results obtained on two wings, both of symmetrical cross section 12 percent thick, and with chord $2b=12.7$ cm, tested at 0°.

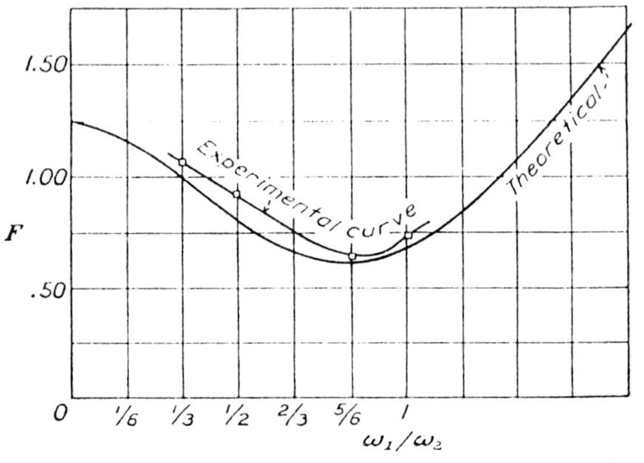

FIGURE 11.—Case 1, Flexure-torsion (h, α): Showing dependency of F on $\frac{\omega_h}{\omega_\alpha}$. The upper curve is experimental. Airfoil with $r=\frac{1}{2}$; $a=-0.4$; $x=0.2$; $\kappa=.01$; $\frac{\omega_1}{\omega_2}$ variable.

Wing A, aluminum, with the following constants:

$$\kappa=\frac{1}{416},\ a=-0.4,\ x_\alpha=0.31,\ 0.173,\text{ and }0.038,$$

respectively;

$$r_\alpha^2=0.33\text{ and }\omega_\alpha=7\times 2\pi$$

Wing B, wood, with flap, and the constants:

$\kappa=\frac{1}{100}$, $c=0.5$, $a=-0.4$, $x_\alpha=0.192$, $r_\alpha^2=0.178$, $x_\beta=0.019$, $r_\beta^2=0.0079$, and ω_α kept constant $=17.6\times 2\pi$

The results for wing A, case 1, are given in figure 15; and those for wing B, cases 2 and 3, are given in figures 16 and 17, respectively. The abscissas are the frequency ratios and the ordinates are the velocities in cm/sec. Compared with the theoretical results calculated for the three test cases, there is an almost perfect

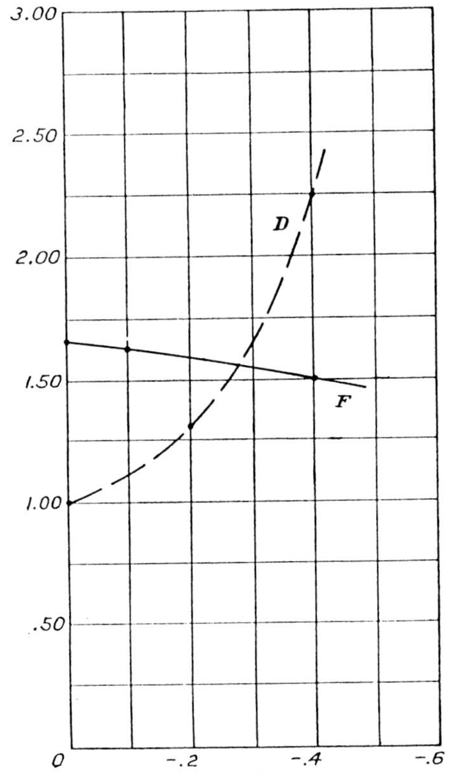

FIGURE 12.—Case 1, Flexure-torsion (h, α): Showing dependency of F on location of axis of rotation a. Airfoil with $r=\frac{1}{2}$; $x=0.2$; $\kappa=\frac{1}{4}$; $\frac{\omega_1}{\omega_2}=\frac{1}{6}$; a variable.

agreement in case 1 (fig. 15). Not only is the minimum velocity found near the same frequency ratio, but the experimental and theoretical values are, furthermore, very nearly alike. Very important is also the fact that the peculiar shape of the response curve in case 2, predicted by the theory, repeats itself experimentally. The theory predicts a *range* of instabilities extending from a small value of the velocity to a definite upper limit. It was very gratifying to observe that the upper branch of the curve not only existed but that it was remarkably definite. A small increase in speed near this upper limit would suffice to change the condition from violent flutter to complete rest, no range of transition being observed. The experimental cases 2 and 3 are compared with theoretical results given by the dotted lines in both figures (figs. 16 and 17).

The conclusion from the experiments is briefly that the general shapes of the predicted response curves re-

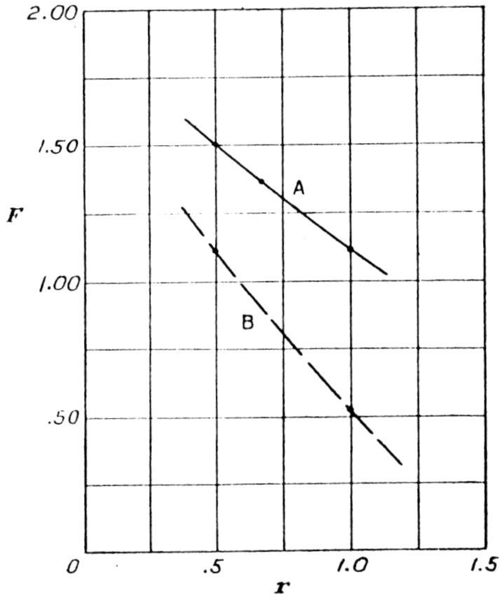

FIGURE 13.—Case 1, Flexure-torsion (h, α): Showing dependency of F on the radius of gyration $r_\alpha=r$.

A, airfoil with $a=-0.4$; $\kappa=\frac{1}{4}$; $x=0.2$; $\frac{\omega_1}{\omega_2}=\frac{1}{6}$; r variable.

B, airfoil with $a=-0.4$; $\kappa=\frac{1}{4}$; $x=0.2$; $\frac{\omega_1}{\omega_2}=1.00$; r variable.

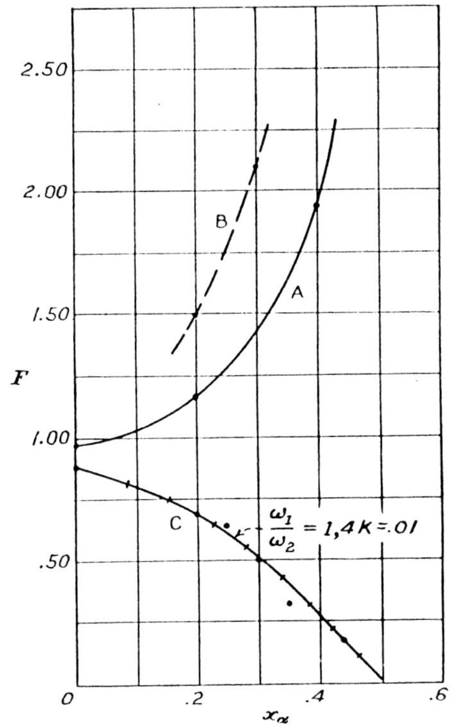

FIGURE 14.—Case 1, Flexure-torsion (h, α): Showing dependency of F on x_α, the location of the center of gravity.

A, airfoil with $r=\frac{1}{2}$; $a=-0.4$; $\kappa=\frac{1}{400}$; $\frac{\omega_1}{\omega_2}=\frac{1}{6}$; x variable.

B, airfoil with $r=\frac{1}{2}$; $a=-0.4$; $\kappa=\frac{1}{4}$; $\frac{\omega_1}{\omega_2}=\frac{1}{6}$; x variable.

C, airfoil with $r=\frac{1}{2}$; $a=-0.4$; $\kappa=\frac{1}{100}$; $\frac{\omega_1}{\omega_2}=1$; x variable.

peat themselves satisfactorily. Next, that the influence of the internal friction[7] obviously is quite appreci-

[7] This matter is the subject of a paper now in preparation.

able in case 3. This could have been expected since the predicted velocities and thus also the air forces on the aileron are very low, and no steps were taken to eliminate the friction in the hinge. The outline of the stable region is rather vague, and the wing is subject

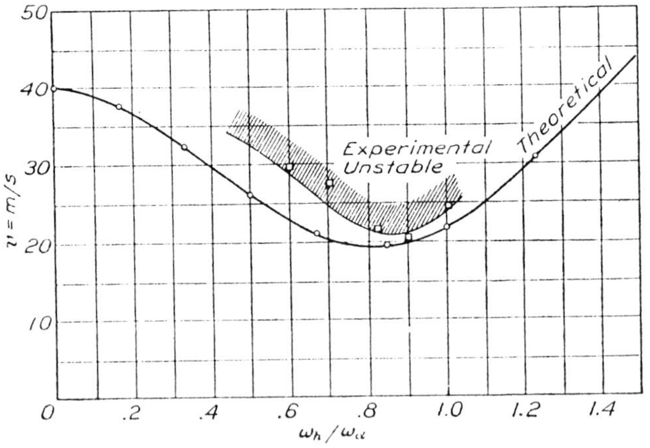

FIGURE 15.—Case 1. Wing A. Theoretical and experimental curves giving flutter velocity v against frequency ratio $\frac{\omega_h}{\omega_\alpha}$. Deflection-torsion.

to temporary vibrations at much lower speeds than that at which the violent flutter starts. The above experiments are seen to refer to cases of exaggerated unbalance, and therefore of low flutter speeds. It is evident that the internal friction is less important at larger velocities. The friction does in all cases *increase* the speed at which flutter starts.

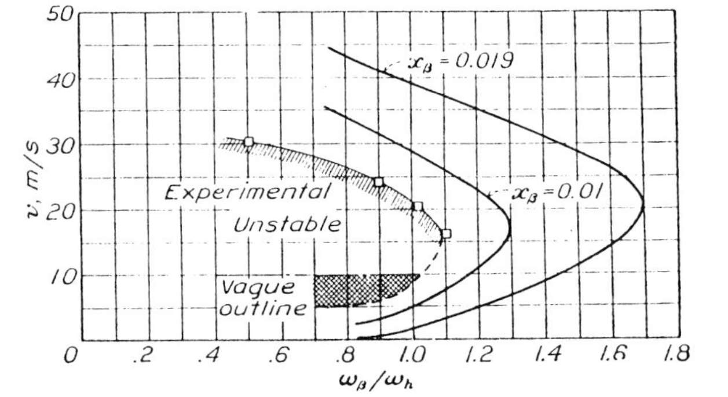

FIGURE 16.—Case 2. Wing B. Theoretical and experimental curves giving flutter velocity v against frequency ratio $\frac{\omega_\beta}{\omega_h}$. Aileron-deflection ($\beta$, h).

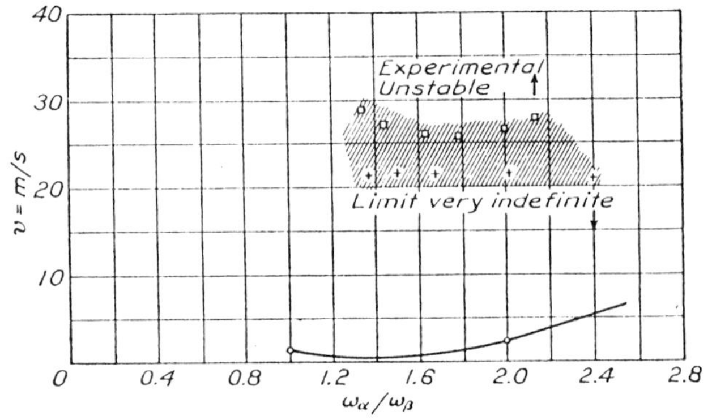

FIGURE 17.—Case 3. Theoretical curve giving flutter velocity against the frequency ratio $\frac{\omega_\alpha}{\omega_\beta}$. The experimental unstable area is indefinite due to the importance of internal friction at very small velocities. Torsion-aileron (α, β).

APPENDIX III

EVALUATION OF φ_α

$$\int_c^1 \log\frac{(x-x_1)^2+(y-y_1)^2}{(x-x_1)^2+(y+y_1)^2}\,dx_1$$

$$=\left[x_1\log\frac{(x-x_1)^2+(y-y_1)^2}{(x-x_1)^2+(y+y_1)^2}\right]_c^1-2y\int_c^1\frac{x_1dx_1}{y_1(x-x_1)}$$

$$=-2c\log\frac{1-xc-y\sqrt{1-c^2}}{(x-c)}-2y\int_c^1\frac{x_1dx_1}{\sqrt{1-x_1^2}(x-x_1)}$$

$$+\int_c^1\frac{x_1dx_1}{\sqrt{1-x_1^2}(x-x_1)}=\int\frac{dx_1}{\sqrt{1-x_1^2}}$$

$$+x\int\frac{dx_1}{(x_1-x)\sqrt{1-x_1^2}}\ \text{[Putting } x_1=\cos\theta]$$

$$=-\theta-\frac{x}{\sqrt{1-x^2}}\log\frac{1-x\cos\theta+\sqrt{1-x^2}\sin\theta}{\cos\theta-x}\Bigg|_{\cos\theta=c}^{\cos\theta=1}$$

$$=\cos^{-1}c+\frac{x}{\sqrt{1-x^2}}\log\frac{1-cx+\sqrt{1-x^2}\sqrt{1-c^2}}{c-x}$$

$$=\cos^{-1}c+\frac{x}{\sqrt{1-x^2}}\log\frac{c-x}{1-cx-\sqrt{1-x^2}\sqrt{1-c^2}}$$

$$\varphi\frac{2\pi}{\epsilon}=-2c\log\left(1-cx-\sqrt{1-x^2}\sqrt{1-c^2}\right)+2c\log(x-c)$$

$$-2\sqrt{1-x^2}\cos^{-1}c-2x\log(c-x)$$

$$+2x\log\left(1-cx-\sqrt{1-x^2}\sqrt{1-c^2}\right)$$

$$=2(x-c)\log\left(\frac{1-cx-\sqrt{1-x^2}\sqrt{1-c^2}}{x-c}\right)$$

$$-2\sqrt{1-x^2}\cos^{-1}c$$

EVALUATION OF φ_β

$$\varphi_x=\int_c^1\{\log[(x-x_1)^2+(y-y_1)^2]$$

$$-\log[(x-x_1)^2+(y+y_1)^2]\}(x_1-c)dx_1$$

$$=\frac{(x_1-c)^2}{2}\{\log[(x-x_1)^2+(y-y_1)^2]$$

$$-\log[(x-x_1)^2+(y+y_1)^2]\}\Big|_c^1$$

$$+y\int_c^1(x_1-c)^2\frac{dx_1}{y_1(x-x_1)}$$

$$\int_c^1\frac{(x_1-c)^2dx_1}{y_1(x-x_1)}=\int_c^1\frac{(x_1-c)^2dx_1}{\sqrt{1-x_1^2}(x-x_1)}=-\int\frac{(\cos\theta-c)^2d\theta}{x-\cos\theta}$$

$$x_1=\cos\theta,\ y_1=\sin\theta,\ dx_1=-\sin\theta d\theta$$

$$\int_c^1\frac{(x_1-c)^2dx_1}{y_1(x-x_1)}=\sin\theta+(x-2c)\theta-(x-c)^2\int_c^1\frac{d\theta}{x-\cos\theta}$$

$$\int_c^1\frac{d\theta}{x-\cos\theta}=\int_c^1\frac{d(\pi+\theta)}{x+\cos(\pi+\theta)}$$

$$=-\frac{1}{\sqrt{1-x^2}}\log\frac{1-x\cos\theta-\sqrt{1-x^2}\sin\theta}{x-\cos\theta}\Bigg|_{\cos\theta=c}^{\cos\theta=1}$$

$$=-\frac{1}{\sqrt{1-x^2}}\left[\log\frac{1-x}{x-1}-\log\frac{1-cx-\sqrt{1-x^2}\sqrt{1-c^2}}{x-c}\right]$$

$$=-\frac{1}{\sqrt{1-x^2}}\log\left(1-cx-\sqrt{1-x^2}\sqrt{1-c^2}\right)$$

$$+\frac{1}{\sqrt{1-x^2}}\log(x-c)$$

$$\frac{2\pi}{\epsilon}\varphi_x=\sqrt{1-x^2}\Big[-\sqrt{1-c^2}-(x-2c)\cos^{-1}c$$

$$+\frac{(x-c)^2}{\sqrt{1-x^2}}\log\left(1-cx-\sqrt{1-x^2}\sqrt{1-c^2}\right)$$

$$-\frac{(x-c)^2}{\sqrt{1-x^2}}\log(x-c)\Big]$$

$$\frac{2\pi}{\epsilon}\varphi_x=-\sqrt{1-c^2}\sqrt{1-x^2}-\cos^{-1}c(x-2c)\sqrt{1-x^2}$$

$$+(x-c)^2\log\left(1-cx-\sqrt{1-x^2}\sqrt{1-c^2}\right)$$

$$-(x-c)^2\log(x-c)$$

EVALUATION OF T_3

$$\int_c^1\frac{2\pi}{\epsilon}\varphi_x(x-c)dx=-\sqrt{1-c^2}\int(x-c)\sqrt{1-x^2}\,dx$$

$$-\cos^{-1}c\int(x-c)(x-2c)\sqrt{1-x^2}\,dx$$

$$+\frac{(x-c)^4}{4}\log\left(1-cx-\sqrt{1-x^2}\sqrt{1-c^2}\right)$$

$$-\frac{1}{4}\int(x-c)^3dx-\sqrt{\frac{1-c^2}{4}}\frac{(x-c)^3}{\sqrt{1-x^2}}dx$$

$$-\int(x-c)^3\log(x-c)dx;\ x=\cos\theta,\ dx=-\sin\theta d\theta$$

$$\frac{2\pi}{\epsilon}\int_c^1\varphi_x(x-c)dx=\sqrt{1-c^2}\int(\cos\theta-c)\sin^2\theta d\theta$$

$$+\cos^{-1}c\int(\cos\theta-c)(\cos\theta-2c)\sin^2\theta d\theta$$

$$+\frac{(x-c)^4}{4}\log\left(1-cx-\sqrt{1-x^2}\sqrt{1-c^2}\right)$$

$$-\frac{1}{4}\int(x-c)^3dx+\frac{\sqrt{1-c^2}}{4}\int(\cos\theta-c)^3d\theta$$

$$-\frac{(x-c)^4}{4}\log(x-c)+\frac{1}{4}\int(x-c)^3dx$$

$$\frac{2\pi}{\epsilon}\int_c^1\varphi_x(x-c)dx=-\cos^{-1}c\int\cos^4\theta d\theta$$

$$+\left(3c\cos^{-1}c-\sqrt{1-c^2}+\frac{\sqrt{1-c^2}}{4}\right)\int\cos^3\theta d\theta$$

$$+\left(\cos^{-1}c-2c^2\cos^{-1}c+c\sqrt{1-c^2}-\frac{3}{4}c\sqrt{1-c^2}\right)\int\cos^2\theta d\theta$$

$$+\left(-3c\cos^{-1}c+\sqrt{1-c^2}+\frac{3c^2\sqrt{1-c^2}}{4}\right)\int\cos\theta d\theta$$

$$+\left(2c^2\cos^{-1}c-c\sqrt{1-c^2}-\frac{c^3\sqrt{1-c^2}}{4}\right)\int d\theta$$

$$\cos^{-1}c\left[\frac{\cos^3\theta\sin\theta}{4}+\frac{3}{4}\left(\frac{\theta}{2}+\frac{\sin\theta\cos\theta}{2}\right)\right]$$

$$+\frac{1}{3}\left(3c\cos^{-1}c-\frac{3}{4}\sqrt{1-c^2}\right)\sin\theta(\cos^2\theta+2)$$

$$+\left(\cos^{-1}c-2c^2\cos^{-1}c+\frac{c\sqrt{1-c^2}}{4}\right)\left(\frac{\theta}{2}+\frac{\sin\theta\cos\theta}{2}\right)$$

$$+\left(-3c\cos^{-1}c+\sqrt{1-c^2}+\frac{3c^2\sqrt{1-c^2}}{4}\right)\sin\theta$$

$$+\left(2c^2\cos^{-1}c-c\sqrt{1-c^2}-\frac{c^3\sqrt{1-c^2}}{4}\right)\theta$$

$$=\cos^{-1}c\left(\frac{3}{8}\pi+\frac{\pi}{2}-3\pi\right)=-\frac{9}{8}\pi\cos^{-1}c$$

$$\frac{2\pi}{\epsilon}\int_c^1\varphi_x(x-c)\,\mathrm{d}x$$

$$=\cos^{-1}c\left[\frac{c^3\sqrt{1-c^2}}{4}+\frac{3\cos^{-1}c}{8}+\frac{3c\sqrt{1-c^2}}{8}\right]$$

$$-\left[c\cos^{-1}c-\frac{\sqrt{1-c^2}}{4}\right](c^2\sqrt{1-c^2}+2\sqrt{1-c^2})$$

$$-\left(\cos^{-1}c-2c^2\cos^{-1}c+\frac{c\sqrt{1-c^2}}{4}\right)\left(\frac{\cos^{-1}c+c\sqrt{1-c^2}}{2}\right)$$

$$-\left(-3c\cos^{-1}c+\sqrt{1-c^2}+\frac{3c^2\sqrt{1-c^2}}{4}\right)\sqrt{1-c^2}$$

$$-\left(2c^2\cos^{-1}c-c\sqrt{1-c^2}-\frac{c^3\sqrt{1-c^2}}{4}\right)\cos^{-1}c$$

$$=\cos^{-1}c\left[\frac{3}{8}-\frac{1}{2}+c^2-2c^2\right]$$

$$+\sqrt{1-c^2}\cos^{-1}c\left[\frac{c^3}{4}+\frac{3c}{8}-c^3-2c-\frac{c}{2}+c^3+3c+c\right.$$

$$\left.+\frac{c^3}{4}-\frac{c}{8}\right]+\frac{c^2(1-c^2)}{4}+\frac{(1-c^2)}{2}-\frac{c^2(1-c^2)}{8}$$

$$-(1-c^2)-\frac{3c^2(1-c^2)}{4}=-\left(\frac{1}{8}+c^2\right)(\cos^{-1}c)^2$$

$$+\frac{c\sqrt{1-c^2}\cos^{-1}c}{4}(7+2c^2)-\frac{(1-c^2)}{8}(5c^2+4)\quad(=T_3)$$

EVALUATION OF T_5

$$\int_c^1\left\{2(x-c)\log\frac{1-cx-\sqrt{1-x^2}\sqrt{1-c^2}}{x-c}\right.$$

$$\left.-2\sqrt{1-x^2}\cos^{-1}c\right\}\mathrm{d}x=T_5=-2\int(x-c)\log(x-c)\,\mathrm{d}x$$

$$+2\int(x-c)\log(1-cx-\sqrt{1-x^2}\sqrt{1-c^2})\,\mathrm{d}x$$

$$-2\cos^{-1}c\int\sqrt{1-x^2}\,\mathrm{d}x=-\frac{2(x-c)^2}{2}\log(x-c)$$

$$+\int(x-c)\,\mathrm{d}x+2\cos^{-1}c\int\sin^2\theta\,\mathrm{d}\theta$$

$$+(x-c)^2\log(1-cx-\sqrt{1-x^2}\sqrt{1-c^2})$$

$$-\int(x-c)^2\frac{-c+x\dfrac{\sqrt{1-c^2}}{\sqrt{1-x^2}}}{1-cx-\sqrt{1-x^2}\sqrt{1-c^2}}\mathrm{d}x$$

Now

$$\int(x-c)^2\frac{-c+x\dfrac{\sqrt{1-c^2}}{\sqrt{1-x^2}}}{1-cx-\sqrt{1-x^2}\sqrt{1-c^2}}\,\mathrm{d}x$$

$$=\int\left\{-c+c^2x-c\sqrt{1-c^2}\sqrt{1-x^2}+x\frac{\sqrt{1-c^2}}{\sqrt{1-x^2}}-cx^2\frac{\sqrt{1-c^2}}{\sqrt{1-x^2}}\right.$$

$$\left.+(1-c^2)x\right\}\mathrm{d}x=\int\frac{(x-c)\sqrt{1-x^2}+(x-c)\sqrt{1-c^2}}{\sqrt{1-x^2}}\,\mathrm{d}x$$

$$=\int(x-c)\,\mathrm{d}x+\sqrt{1-c^2}\int\frac{(x-c)}{\sqrt{1-x^2}}\,\mathrm{d}x$$

$$T_5=-(x-c)^2\log(x-c)+2\cos^{-1}c\int\sin^2\theta\,\mathrm{d}\theta$$

$$+(x-c)^2\log(1-cx-\sqrt{1-x^2}\sqrt{1-c^2})$$

$$+\sqrt{1-c^2}\int(\cos\theta-c)\,\mathrm{d}\theta$$

$$=\frac{2\cos^{-1}c}{2}(\theta-\sin\theta\cos\theta)+\sqrt{1-c^2}\sin\theta$$

$$-c\sqrt{1-c^2}\,\theta\Big|_{\cos\theta=c}^{\cos\theta=1}$$

$$=-(1-c^2)-(\cos^{-1}c)^2+2c\sqrt{1-c^2}\cos^{-1}c$$

THE FUNDAMENTAL PRINCIPLES OF THE N.A.C.A. COWLING

BY THEODORE THEODORSEN

National Advisory Committee for Aeronautics

Presented at the Aerodynamics Session, Sixth Annual Meeting, I.Ae.S., January 26, 1938; published in *Journal of the Aeronautical Sciences,* Vol. 5, No. 5, March 1938.

Introduction

THE present paper presents a discussion of the underlying principles of operation of the N.A.C.A. cowling. The information upon which the following analysis is based was obtained from large-scale wind-tunnel tests (Fig. 1) conducted systematically on a large variety of cowling combinations during 1935–36. The history of the early development of the N.A.C.A. cowling and the status of the design information prior to 1935 is well given in E. P. Warner's "*Airplane Design,*" pages 368–382. Detail technical information of this latest investigation has also been made available through the regular N.A.C.A. reports.[1,2,3,4] Therefore no attempt shall be made to go into the history, nor to give many details of the results. On the other hand an attempt shall be made to present the basic information gained in their relation to our present knowledge of aerodynamics. Many results become obvious, once their nature has been established and the facts have been made to fit the laws of nature, as they are seen. A few of the more essential or illustrative results and the main conclusions will be presented.

As a preliminary orientation for the following discussion, it is pointed out that it is useful to separate the problem into as many distinct parts as possible. To start with, the cowling itself actually performs two distinct functions: (1) it provides a streamline enclosure of minimum drag, and (2) it provides a certain pressure difference across the engine. It shall be shown how the drag coefficient correspondingly consists of a form drag coefficient and a cooling drag coefficient and rules will be given as to how to estimate both with sufficient accuracy. Several constants will be introduced relating to specific physical quantities and essential relationships between the quantities involved, governing the design and operation of an N.A.C.A. cowling, will be presented.

FIG. 1. Photograph of full-scale test installation.

Conductivity

One readily recognizes the fact that as far as the aerodynamic performance of the cowling is concerned, the engine might just as well be replaced by a certain fixed resistance. To indicate the magnitude of this resistance, or rather its reciprocal, the term conductivity, designated by K, has been introduced for convenience.

There is the relation

$$\Delta p = \xi\ (v_1^2/2g)\gamma$$

where Δp is the pressure drop across the resistance

v_1, *any representative* velocity

γ, specific weight

ξ, a fixed constant

also

$$\Delta p = \xi \cdot q_1$$

where

$$q_1 = (v_1^2/2g)\gamma$$

If F_1 is the *representative* cross-section, for the volume passing through in unit time

$$Q = F_1 \sqrt{2gq_1/\gamma} = F_1 \sqrt{2g\Delta p/\gamma\xi}$$

To obtain non-dimensional relations another volume given by the full stream velocity and the cross-section of the nacelle is introduced.

$$Q_R = F\sqrt{2gq/\gamma}$$

dividing:

$$Q/Q_R = (F_1/F)\sqrt{q_1/q} = (F_1/F)\sqrt{\Delta p/(\xi \cdot q)} = (F_1/F)(1/\sqrt{\xi})\sqrt{\Delta p/q}$$

The quantity $(F_1/F)(1/\sqrt{\xi})$may be seen to be a *constant* which depends on the geometrical and physical properties of the engine; this is what has been termed the conductivity K.

Hence

$$Q/Q_R = K \cdot \sqrt{\Delta p/q}$$

where

$$K = (F_1/F)(1/\sqrt{\xi})$$

Experimentally then, K may be obtained simply by measuring volume passing through for a given pressure drop. Fortunately this experiment is not absolutely necessary since it is found that the value ξ lies within fairly narrow limits. In fact $1/\sqrt{\xi} = 0.65$ for sharp-edged holes and is found to be of about the same value for baffles with poor exit expansion and to reach about 0.9 for well-designed expanding exits, as in Fig. 6.

The following simple rule may therefore be expressed: *The conductivity of the engine is a number expressing the area of the free passage in ratio to the nacelle cross-section. The free passage may be considered equal to about* 60 *to* 90 *percent of the free minimum cross-section.*

For single-row engines the value of the conductivity is about 0.05 and probably reaches 0.07 for the more modern, deeper fins. For double-row engines the values are about double since the flow is in parallel.

For many purposes of experimentation on the cowling, the engine may readily be replaced by an orifice plate. For instance, for a 50 in. diameter nacelle each one inch hole would represent a conductivity of (1/2500) × 0.65 and 250 holes would give the approximate conductivity of a single-row engine, or 0.065.

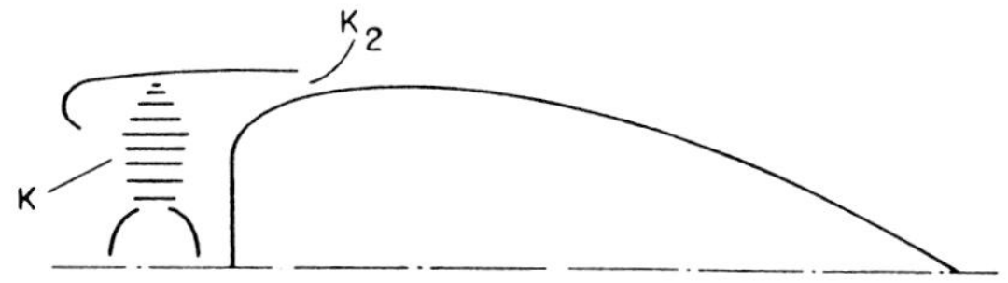

$$\frac{\Delta P}{q} = \left(\frac{Q}{FV}\right)^2 \left[\frac{1}{K^2} + \frac{1}{K_2^2}\right]$$

FIG. 2. Equation of flow regulation.

FLOW REGULATION

Referring to Fig. 2, one may write $\Delta P = \Delta p + \Delta p_2$, where ΔP is the total available pressure difference created by the cowling, or the static pressure ahead of the engine minus the static pressure in the exit slot. The static pressure in front was found to be almost exactly $1q$ for the smaller conductivities of the one-row engine, and about $0.9q$ for a conductivity corresponding to a modern two-row engine. The static pressure behind may be put equal to zero or -0.1 for well-designed and efficient exits. Thus ΔP *is for all practical purposes equal to one velocity head q in good cowling designs.* It should be noted that ΔP is not the pressure difference across the engine, but the *total* created by the cowling. Part of the available pressure, namely Δp_2, is used to get the air through the relatively narrow exit slot.

The friction loss in the exit slot of normal good design is found to be negligible, so that

$$\Delta p_2 = \gamma\ V_2^2/2g$$

Introduce $V_2 = Q/A_2$, where Q is the volume in unit time and A_2 the effective cross-section of the exit slot. Further, put $A_2 = K_2 \cdot F$ where F, as above, is the representative cross-sectional area of the nacelle and K_2 the "conductivity" of the exit slot. With $q = \gamma\ V^2/2g$ this gives

$$\Delta p_2/q = (Q/K_2FV)^2$$

Using the relation already developed for Δp, the pressure drop across the engine,

$$\Delta P/q = (Q/FV)^2\ [(1/K^2) + (1/K_2^2)]$$

This equation has been called the equation of flow regulation. It is the basic equation governing the flow of the cooling air. As could have been expected, the relation was found to hold for the entire range; in other words, there is no appreciable Reynolds Number effect on K, K_2, or the available pressure.

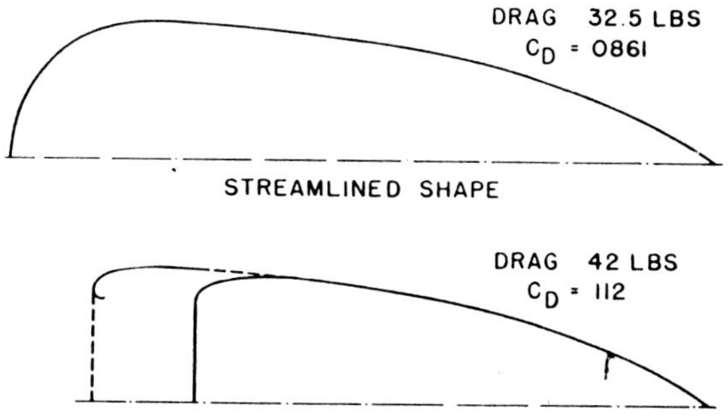

FIG. 3. Basic shape. N.A.C.A. cowling tests. In this figure C_D should equal .0861 and .112, respectively, for the upper and lower figures.

The left side of this equation gives the available pressure in non-dimensional form; its value is, furthermore, for all practical purposes, equal to unity. The first term on the right side is the square of the flow, also in non-dimensional form, simply as the fraction of the air column FV. The last term on the right side is seen to represent two resistances in series, also non-dimensional.

Take an example to show the use of this equation. Assume an engine with a conductivity of $K = 0.15$, cooling satisfactorily at 20 lbs. per sq.ft. pressure difference across the baffles. What should be the area of the exit slot at 300 m.p.h. to prevent waste of cooling power? First, for the pressure drop across the engine, one has

$$\Delta p/q = (Q/FV)^2 \cdot (1/K^2)$$

or

$$(Q/FV)^2 = (\Delta p/q) \cdot K^2 = (20/230) \cdot 0.15^2 = 0.00195$$

and from the main equation

$$1 = 0.00195\ [(1/0.15^2) + (1/K_2{}^2)]$$

which gives $K_2 = 0.046$, or an opening of $A_2 = 0.046$ $(\pi/4)\ D^2$ where D is the cowling diameter. It is seen that this opening corresponds to a little more than $^1/_2$ in. effective gap for conventional cowling sizes. Again, referring to the equation of flow regulation, if the engine requires 20 lbs. per sq.ft. across the engine for continuous cooling, the required exit opening gradually increases as the air speed is decreased. At 125 m.p.h. the conductivities K and K_2 are approximately equal, the required effective gap on a 50 in. diameter cowling being then

$$(1/4) \cdot 50 \cdot 0.15 = 1.9 \text{ in.}$$

At still lower air speeds the simple widening of the exit gap is no longer effective; a speed of 100 m.p.h. is in the present example the lower limit.

The only other possibility for increasing the cooling flow is to increase the generated pressure $\Delta P/q$. This calls for very special measures. It must be realized that even for a flat circular disk the average pressure differential is only about $1.2\,q$ in spite of the enormous drag. The use of cowl flaps is an attempt in this direction. The present investigation showed that flaps actually increase the $\Delta P/q$ from unity, its normal value, to a maximum of 1.3. This would permit a lowering of the minimum air speed in the above example to a little less than 90 m.p.h. The increase in drag is, however, considerable. Another attempt to increase the available $\Delta P/q$ has been undertaken in an N.A.C.A. nose-cowl investigation, the early results of which are given in Technical Report No. 595.[4]

Pump Efficiency

So far the drag associated with the cooling has only occasionally been referred to. It is realized that it is not only necessary to have sufficient head available to cool the engine but that this cooling must be done at the minimum expense of power. For this consideration the concept *"pump efficiency"* has been introduced. The pump efficiency is simply the ratio of the work expended for cooling, $Q\Delta p$ in previous notation, divided by the work due to the increased drag of the cowling, $D - D_0$, at the velocity V, or

$$\eta_p = Q\Delta p/(D - D_0)V.$$

It is interesting to remark at once that the cowling constitutes a remarkably good pump. Efficiencies of around 90 percent may be regarded as normal. There is, of course, a certain ambiguity in regard to the definition of D_0, which is considered to be the drag of a similar cowl performing *the function of streamlining the power plant but not the function of cooling.* (See Fig. 3.)

Since the engine cowling nacelle is not usually of the best streamline form, this imperfection in form must not be charged against the cooling. The quantity D_0 is therefore the drag of the basic form of the same general contour as the cowling considered, but with the cooling ducts closed by the best possible fairings. This "basic shape" by stippled lines closing the frontal cavity and the exit ducts is shown in Fig. 3.

By referring again to Fig. 3, it can be seen that the drag of the "flat-nosed" cowling at 100 m.p.h. in the wind tunnel is 42 lbs. as against 32.5 lbs. for the semi-spherical nose shown above. However, the difference is not at all a total loss, as shall be seen later. The value of D_0 of 42 lbs. is therefore used in calculating pump efficiencies. In the tests referred to, it soon became evident that the pump efficiency is an excellent figure of merit; and further, that its value depends largely on the flow condition at the exit. A design embodying a smooth external contour line is always distinctly superior. Also, it was found that a large exit velocity is favorable. The dependence on the exit velocity is, however, not large, unless this approaches zero.

The formula for the pump efficiency shall now be rewritten in a somewhat different form

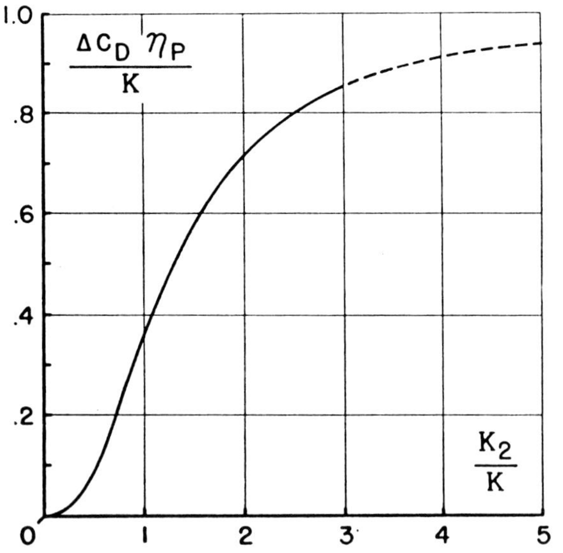

FIG. 4. Drag coefficient *versus* conductivity. Note that the equation of the ordinate should read: $\Delta C_D \eta_p / K$.

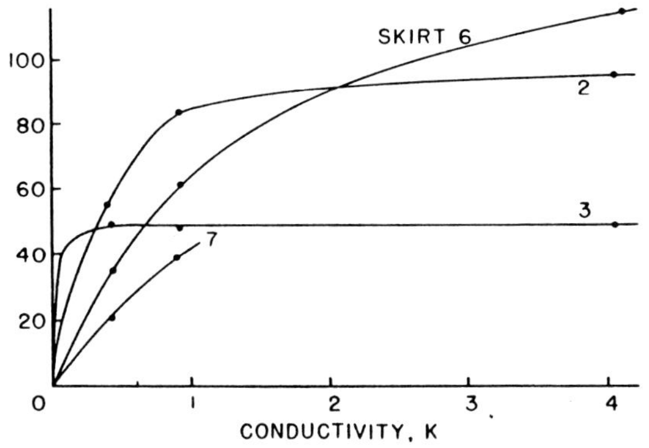

FIG. 5. Pump efficiency. N.A.C.A. cowling tests. The ordinate in the above figure represents percentages.

$$\eta_p = Q \Delta p / (D - D_0) V$$

By putting

$$D - D_0 = \Delta C_D F q$$

where ΔC_D is the increase in the drag coefficient due to cooling, as before referred to the nacelle cross-section. Also introduce

$$Q / VF = \sqrt{\Delta p / q} \cdot K$$

Then

$$\eta_p = (1/\Delta C_D)\, K \cdot (\Delta p / q)^{3/2}$$

or also

$$\Delta C_D = (1/\eta_p)\, K \cdot (\Delta p / q)^{3/2}$$

From the equation of flow regulation for conventional cowlings ($\Delta P / q = 1$)

$$\Delta p / q = \frac{1/K^2}{(1/K^2) + (1/K_2{}^2)} = \frac{1}{1 + (K/K_2)^2}$$

and finally for the cooling drag coefficient

$$\Delta C_D = (1/\eta_p) \cdot K\, [1 + (K/K_2)^2]^{-3/2}$$

This relation gives a very convenient formula for the drag increase. The relation lends itself to a plot of the form

$$(\Delta C_D \cdot \eta_p)/K = 1/[1 + (1/p^2)]^{3/2}$$

where $p = K_2/K$ is simply the ratio of the exit opening to the equivalent free engine flow cross-section as already defined.

Fig. 4 gives this relation in the form

$$(\Delta C_D \cdot \eta_p)/K = f(K_2/K)$$

The value of η_p (for the optimum design) is somewhat dependent on the abscissa K_2/K. It is close to 100 percent, however, over most of the range, dropping to around 80 percent at $K_2/K = 3$ and dropping further beyond this point due to the low exit velocity. For inefficient exits, of course, these values do not apply. Typical test results on the pump efficiency are shown in Fig. 5. (See reference 1.)

As an example, refer to the case already given with $K = 0.15$, $K_2 = 0.15$. From the plot one immediately obtains

$$\Delta C_D\, \eta_p / K = 0.353$$

or using $\eta_p = 0.90$

$$\Delta C_D = 0.353 \cdot 0.15/0.90 = 0.059$$

This value is probably within ± 10 percent, provided the design is the best possible.

Mechanism of Frontal Cooling

The body shown in the lower part of Fig. 3 represents the basic form of the nacelle used in this investigation. Its drag coefficient is $C_D = 0.112$; removing the flat plate (shown by stippled line, Fig. 3) and thus exposing the frontal cavity to the air stream, increases the drag coefficient to $C_D = 0.119$. These figures compare with a drag coefficient of only 0.086 found for the same body equipped with a spherical nose as shown in the upper part of Fig. 3. This drag increase of 0.026–0.033 over the drag of a better streamlined body is typical of the normal present-day cowling, and can consequently be partly reclaimed by using a more spherical nose with a longer propeller shaft. However, this loss manifests itself in a large turbulence of the air striking the front of the engine, and is thus responsible for the excellent cooling observed on the frontal unbaffled halves of the cylinders.

In fact, at speeds below 150 m.p.h. it is probably not possible to provide a more efficient cooling by any other means. Returning to the example, it was found that the normal cooling drag ΔC_D was equal to 0.059 at

FIG. 6. N.A.C.A. baffle design for double-row radial.

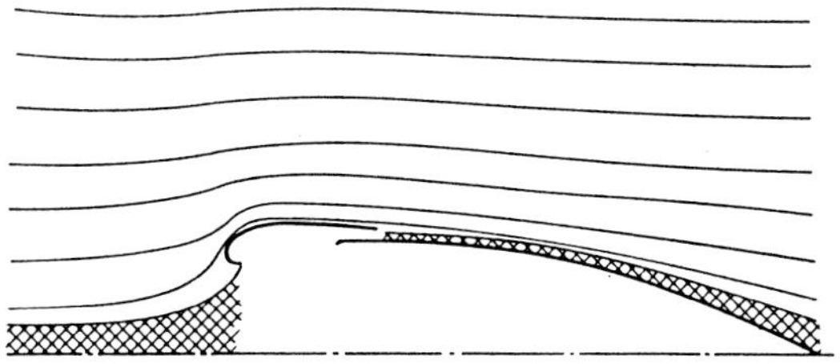

FIG. 7. Streamlines. N.A.C.A. cowling tests.

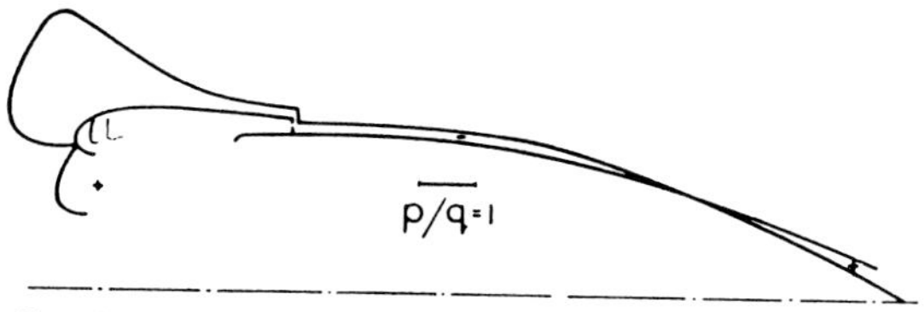

FIG. 8. Typical pressure distribution. N.A.C.A. cowling tests.

a speed of 125 m.p.h. This drag accounts for the cooling within the narrow baffle channels but hardly for any of the front cooling, which fact can be demonstrated by a simple experiment. The cost of the frontal cooling may therefore be considered to be no more than the drag difference 0.033. To recapitulate: The poor shape of the front cowling contours is responsible for a drag increase of 0.033, manifesting itself as a result of an unstable and turbulent flow in front of the cowling resulting, of course, in an earlier transition into fine-grain surface turbulence; but this unstable and turbulent flow in front of the engine may at the same time be credited with a large heat-absorbing ability. Comparing the two figures just mentioned, one is tempted to state that the front cooling is as efficient as the cooling in the ducts. It must be noticed, however, that the cooling drag coefficient ΔC_D may be reduced as much as desired at higher air speeds, so as to provide just the right amount of pressure differential, but that that there are no provisions for decreasing the drag relating to the flat nose. For high speeds a better streamlined nose, permitting some sort of regulation, is obviously desirable.

A direct effect of recognizing the importance of the front turbulence is the baffle design shown for a double-row engine in Fig. 6. Note the spacious entrance to the rear bank. The baffle design shall otherwise be considered to be beyond the scope of this paper.

Effects of Propeller

For normal flight conditions the effect of the propeller is found to be a minor one. The main table in reference 1 shows that the propeller causes a slight decrease in pump efficiency compensated by a corresponding slight improvement in the cooling. The net effect of the propeller on the main flow is a slight convergence of the streamlines in front of the cowling, as compared with the flow around the cowling alone, and by a comparatively small velocity increase. This slight convergence of the frontal streamlines due to the propeller may paradoxically convert a poor cowling (nose 1 in reference 1) into a comparatively good one; that is, the presence of the propeller actually decreased the drag of the cowling. This fact is, of course, only of incidental interest insofar as it confirms the expected change in the flow lines. The actual appearance of the streamlines with propeller on is shown as an illustration in Fig. 7. Note the very divergent flow in front of the cowling.

At low air speeds, particularly for the case of ground cooling, there is quite a different problem. The inherent deficiency of the normal propeller to produce a pressure differential near the hub is here a serious problem. As a measure of the blower action of the propeller, the *blower constant* $\Delta p/n^2$, has been introduced, which is actually the resulting pressure differential available for cooling behind the propeller in lbs. per sq.ft. at a speed of one r.p.s. As expected, the blower constant depends on the size and perfection of the shank cross-section immediately in front of the cowling and also on the diameter of the opening. For detail information, the reader is referred to reference 2. It will just be mentioned that the value of $\Delta p/n^2$ in lbs./ft.^{2} r.p.s.^{2} ranges from a minimum of 0.01 observed for a propeller with a poor shank section on a cowling with the smallest front opening to a maximum of 0.04 for a propeller with a pronounced airfoil section near the hub on a cowling with a front opening somewhat larger than the one considered optimum for normal conditions of flight. The latter showed a constant of 0.036.

Other Problems and Further Research

Another investigation which has been carried on in parallel is the development of the nose cowling, so called to indicate that the exit is located near the front of the cowling. The typical pressure distribution shown for a conventional cowling in Fig. 8 reveals the existence of a large negative pressure near the front. Preliminary tests[4] employing, however, very small values of K, showed large pump efficiencies. Realizing the possibility of utilizing this greater pressure differential for cooling, the work on the nose cowling has been continued. The final outcome will be available through the regular reports.

The use of much larger engine conductivities employed on recent design calls for a certain extension of the original research here reported. The possible interference effect of the cooling air and the "flat" nose on the characteristics of a wing of which the nacelle is an integral part is also an important problem, as of course the nacelle is expected to merge into the wing with the greatest possible perfection in all respects.

General Considerations of Cowling Design

As a summary based on the experience gained in the N.A.C.A. cowling investigation, the essential design considerations shall be given briefly.

(1) *Nose design*. Not critical; should on the whole resemble the design given in Fig. 9, which is the number 7 of the original test series. The angle of the front camber line should be of the order of 45° with the axis. The area of the opening should merely be as large as consistent with these requirements.

(2) *Skirt design*. Rather critical; the area is to be determined by the equation of flow regulation and is consequently dependent on the engine conductivity and the pressure required across the engine. The skirt edge should not project into the external airstream but permit the external streamlines to remain smooth, nor should the edge project inward. The opening should therefore be formed by means of the inner cowl to permit a gradual velocity increase from the low velocity behind the engine. The mean flow line must be essentially parallel to the external flow lines, or at least not point too much outward at the point of exit. The skirt design should embody some provision for regulating the flow of cooling air, to prevent excessive losses at high speed, preferably by mechanical means for changing the location or contour of the inner cowl so as to increase or decrease the exit conductivity as conditions require.

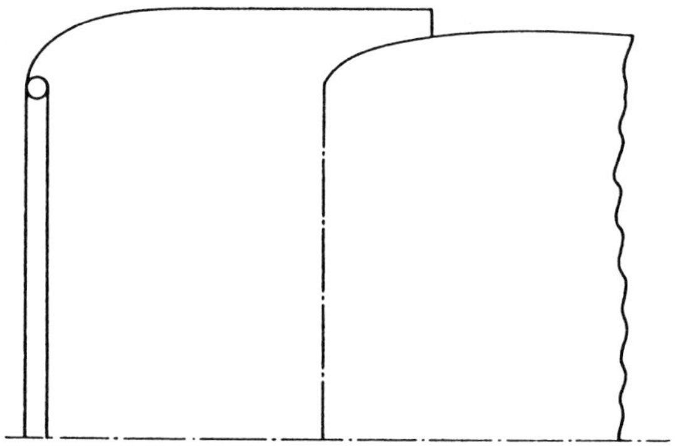

Fig. 9. N.A.C.A. cowling design.

The general appearance of the N.A.C.A. cowling is finally indicated in Fig. 9.

References

[1] Theodorsen, Theodore, Brevoort, M. J., and Stickle, George W., *Full-Scale Tests of N.A.C.A. Cowlings*, Technical Report No. 592, *N.A.C.A.*, 1937.

[2] Theodorsen, Theodore, Brevoort, M. J., and Stickle, George W., *Cooling of Airplane Engines at Low Air Speeds*, Technical Report No. 593, *N.A.C.A.*, 1937.

[3] Theodorsen, Theodore, Stickle, George W., and Brevoort, M. J., *Characteristics of Six Propellers Including the High-Speed Range*, Technical Report No. 594, *N.A.C.A.*, 1937.

[4] Theodorsen, Theodore, Brevoort, M. J., Stickle, George W., and Gough, M. N., *Full-Scale Tests of a New Type N.A.C.A. Nose-Slot Cowling*, Technical Report No. 595, *N.A.C.A.*, 1937.

[5] General literature: Edward P. Warner, *Airplane Design, Performance*, McGraw-Hill Book Co., New York and London, 1936, pp. 368, etc.

THE FLUTTER PROBLEM

BY THEODORE THEODORSEN

National Advisory Committee for Aeronautics

Presented at the 5th International Congress for Applied Mechanics held at Harvard University and the Massachusetts Institute of Technology, Cambridge, Mass., September 12–16, 1938; published in *Proceedings of the 5th International Congress for Applied Mechanics,* Wiley, New York, 1939.

The problem of flutter has found itself in a status of rapid development since 1930. It is of interest to observe that the theory of this nonstationary type of flow appears to describe the real condition much closer than does the theory of the stationary case. Numerous experiments conducted by NACA and which are not yet published show a consistent and remarkably close agreement between predicted and observed flutter speeds.

The theoretical problem reduces itself to the solution of a system of differential equations, each specifying the equilibrium in a separate degree of freedom. No difficulty is involved in writing these equations except for the term representing the aerodynamic forces. It was therefore a step forward when the author in the spring of 1934 published the exact two-dimensional expressions for the air forces for wings with ailerons in the most general form (Ref. 1). The derivation of this expression is of no great concern at the present time since it is well known and since furthermore every author seems to employ his preferred method. The expression of the air forces, except for the classical inertia terms, is given by means of the significant function—

$$C(k) = \frac{-\frac{\pi}{2}J_1 + i\frac{\pi}{2}Y_1}{-\frac{\pi}{2}J_1 - \frac{\pi}{2}Y_0 + i\frac{\pi}{2}Y_1 - i\frac{\pi}{2}J_0}$$

$$= \frac{-J_1 + iY_i}{-(J_1 + Y_0) + i(Y_1 - J_0)}$$

$$= \frac{(-J_1 + iY_1)[-(J_1 + Y_0) - i(Y_1 - J_0)]}{(J_1 + Y_0)^2 + (Y_1 - J_0)^2}$$

$$= \frac{J_1(J_1 + Y_0) + Y_1(Y_1 - J_0)}{(J_1 + Y_0)^2 + (Y_1 - J_0)^2}$$

$$- i\frac{Y_1(J_1 + Y_0) - J_1(Y_1 - J_0)}{(J_1 + Y_0)^2 + (Y_1 - J_0)^2} = F + iG$$

where

$$F = \frac{J_1(J_1 + Y_0) + Y_1(Y_I - J_0)}{(J_1 + Y_0)^2 + (Y_1 - J_0)^2}$$

$$G = -\frac{Y_1 Y_0 + J_1 J_0}{(J_1 + Y_0)^2 + (Y_1 - J_0)^2}$$

where J_0, J_1, Y_0, and Y_1 are Bessel functions of the argument k.

This argument k is really a reduced frequency, which is very conveniently considered as the independent variable in the treatment of the flutter problem. The actual flutter frequency is given by the relation—

$$\omega = \frac{kv}{b}$$

where v is the critical velocity and b the semichord of the wing section, used as unity in Fig. 1.

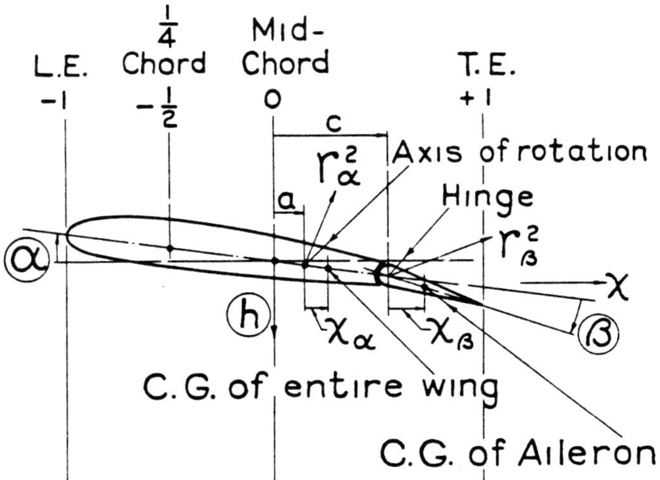

Fig. 1. Variables and parameters used. The positive direction of α, β, and h, etc. are indicated by arrows. Note that a is measured from midchord, and X_α is measured from the axis of rotation; r_β is a "reduced" radius of gyration, X_β a reduced center of gravity distance.

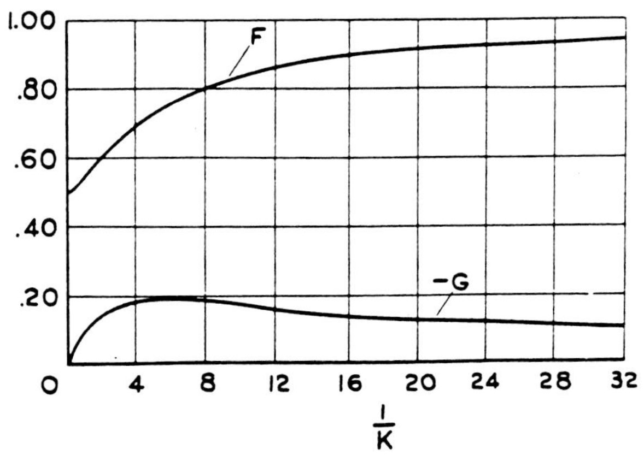

Fig. 2. The functions F and $-G$ against $1/k$. (reduced wavelength).

The functions F and G are shown in Fig. 2 against the argument $1/k$ with the values given in Table II of the original paper. This function has been abundantly verified and rederived by several later writers, particularly Cicala, 1935 (Ref. 2), Kassner and Fingado, 1936 (Ref. 3), and finally by Küssner (Ref. 4), who shows the identity in details by comparing with the author's original paper.

We shall mention briefly the main results of the flutter theory. The force due to circulation of an airfoil in a two-dimensional flow is given simply as—

$$P = -2\pi\rho v b Q \cdot C(k)$$

and the moment as—

$$M_\alpha = -2\pi\rho v b^2\left[\frac{1}{2} - \left(a + \frac{1}{2}\right)C(k)\right] Q$$

The moment on the aileron is given similarly by

$$M_\beta = -\rho v b^2 (T_{12} C - T_4)\, Q$$

where the Ts are simple functions of the hinge location and are listed in the original report. The quantity Q is a velocity given by—

$$Q = v\alpha + \dot{h} + b\left(\frac{1}{2} - a\right)\dot{\alpha} + \frac{T_{10}}{\pi} v\beta + b\,\frac{T_{11}}{2\pi}\dot{\beta}$$

This velocity may be called the significant velocity. In the simple case without aileron, it is simply the vertical velocity at the rear three-quarter point of the airfoil.

The quantities defining the three degrees of freedom α, β, and h and the constant parameters may be obtained from Fig. 1.

In a stationary (slow) case $C(k)$ approaches unity. The force and moment are then recognized as those of a stationary airfoil in two dimensions, generalized to include the effect of the aileron. In this case, the force and moment are in phase with the velocity Q. If the airfoil, however, executes sinusoidal motions (flutter) it is convenient to express Q by a complex quantity in the solution of the problem. It is then noticed that the air force, which is obtained by a multiplication with the function $C(k)$, lags in phase with respect to the impressed velocity Q. The maximum angle of lag is about 15 deg and occurs at a value of $k = \sim 0.3$. It is further noticed that the magnitude of the air force is decreased as the frequency is increased; at the highest frequency it reduces to one-half of its stationary (low-frequency) value. The moments exhibit essentially a similar effect. It should be mentioned that the out-of-phase component of the air force is important in the flutter theory since the solution is found to be sensitive to the forces at right angles to the restoring forces, particularly in the case involving ailerons. Stated otherwise, wherever the solution is critical in regard to structural damping, the frequency effect of the air forces must be properly included. The equations of motion are then, using the above expression for air forces and moments, and expressing in succession the equilibrium of the entire airfoil about the torsional axis a (see Fig. 1), the moment of the aileron about the hinge C, and the vertical equilibrium of the entire airfoil:

$$\text{(A)}\ \ddot{\alpha}A + \dot{\alpha}\frac{v}{b}B + \alpha\bar{C} + \ddot{\beta}D + \dot{\beta}\frac{v}{b}E + \beta\frac{v^2}{b}F + \ddot{h}G - 2\kappa\left(a + \frac{1}{2}\right)\frac{v}{b}C(k)\,Q = 0$$

$$\text{(B)}\ \ddot{\alpha}H + \dot{\alpha}\frac{v}{b}I + \ddot{\beta}J + \dot{\beta}\frac{v}{b}K + \beta L + \ddot{h}M + \frac{T_{12}}{\pi}\kappa\frac{v}{b}C(k)\,Q = 0$$

$$\text{(C)}\ \ddot{\alpha}N + \dot{\alpha}\frac{v}{b}O + \beta P + \dot{\beta}\frac{v}{b}\bar{Q} + \ddot{h}R + hS + 2\kappa\frac{v}{b}C(k)\,Q = 0$$

where A, B, $\bar{C}$, etc. are given in TR 496.

$$Q = \frac{v}{b}\alpha + \frac{\dot{h}}{b} + \left(\frac{1}{2} - a\right)\dot{\alpha} + \frac{T_{10}}{\pi}\frac{v}{b}\beta + \frac{T_{11}}{2\pi}\dot{\beta}$$

and

$$C(k) = F(k) + iG(k)$$

The original parameters needed in the constants A, B, C, etc. are all given in Fig. 1 in their nondimensional forms, defined in Ref. 1. It should be noted, however, that the constants giving the restoring forces C_α, C_β, and C_h are used in complex form to include the effect of structural damping. This type of damping, represented simply by a phase shift of the restoring force, has been used by several writers. On putting—

$$\alpha = \alpha_0 \, e^{i(\omega t + \varphi_0)}$$

$$\beta = \beta_0 \, e^{i(\omega t + \varphi_1)}$$

$$h = h_0 \, e^{i(\omega t + \varphi_2)}$$

the determinant of the coefficients of α_0, β_0, and h_0 is—

$$\kappa\omega^2 \begin{vmatrix} \bar{R}_{a\alpha} + iI_{a\alpha}, & R_{a\beta} + iI_{a\beta}, & R_{ah} + iI_{ah} \\ R_{b\alpha} + iI_{b\alpha}, & \bar{R}_{b\beta} + iI_{b\beta}, & R_{bh} + iI_{bh} \\ R_{c\alpha} + iI_{c\alpha}, & R_{c\beta} + iI_{c\beta}, & \bar{R}_{ch} + iI_{ch} \end{vmatrix}$$

where the Rs and Is are listed in Ref. 1.

The condition of unstable equilibrium, or the flutter point, is simply obtained by putting the above determinant equal to zero. The three terms with bars are the only ones containing the (unknown) flutter velocity in the form—

$$X = \text{const} \left(\frac{1}{vk}\right)^2$$

The Rs and Is are known functions of the original parameters and the quantity k.

This equation is then separated into its real and imaginary parts, and each equation is plotted by giving the value of X against the reduced frequency k or rather the reduced wavelength $(1/k)$. The intersection of the two curves then gives the flutter point or points. This point determines both the flutter speed and the flutter frequency.

The complete three-degree-of-freedom case involves the solution of the two equations of the third degree in X for each chosen value of k. The actual method of numerical solution, which will not be shown here, has been arranged, however, as a perfectly simple routine method. The only judgment required at all is the proper choice of the range of the reduced frequency, or independent variable k. The intersection (or intersections) furnishes a set of values X and k, and the critical speed and frequency are then given by the above relations.

Fortunately, it is not usually necessary to solve a complete case of three degrees of freedom. A study of the three subcases involving two degrees of freedom at a time will in most cases furnish the necessary information. These are much simpler to handle as the unknown X occurs at most in the second degree in each of the two equations.

These subcases are:

Case 1—Deflection-torsion ($h\alpha$)

Case 2—Aileron-deflection (βh)

Case 3—Torsion-aileron ($\alpha\beta$)

A typical solution of Case 1 is shown in Fig. 3, in which the critical speed is plotted against the frequency ratio. This case is treated extensively by several authors. Less known are the two other cases involving aileron flutter. A typical solution of Case 2, deflection-aileron, is finally shown in Fig. 4, in which the flutter speed is again plotted against the frequency ratio ω_β/ω_h. The flutter is here limited to a certain range of speed, below or above which the combination is stable. It is interesting to observe that a sufficiently high aileron frequency eliminates the flutter entirely. The "flutter area" in the diagram can be reduced or eliminated at will by mass balancing or the introduction of structural damping.

Case 3 is of an intermediate type—in fact more related to Case 1.

In the transition to actual cases which are more or less three-dimensional problems, there are some im-

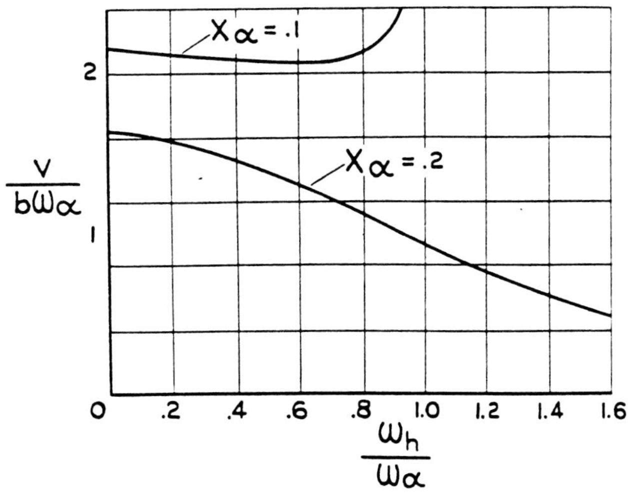

Fig. 3. Typical example of case 1 (torsion-deflection) with $X = 1/4$, $a = -0.4$, $r_\alpha^2 = 1/4$. Flutter coefficient is plotted against frequency ratio for two values of X_α.

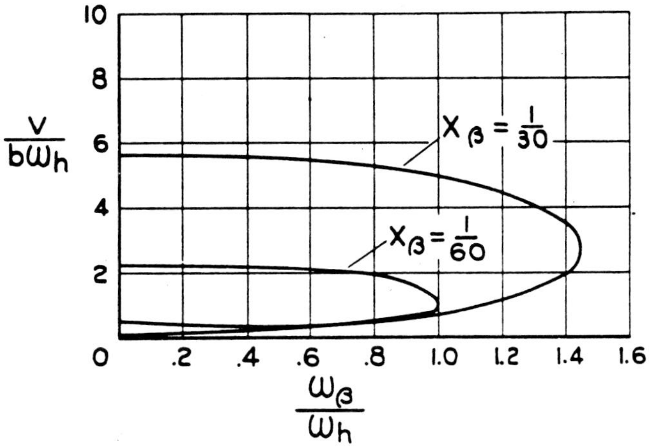

Fig. 4. Typical case 2 (deflection-aileron) with $C = 0.5$, $X = 1/5$, $r_\beta^2 = 1/120$. Flutter coefficient plotted against frequency-ratio for two values of X_β.

portant considerations. In the first place, the wing is not of infinite length. Fortunately, the aspect-ratio effect is not as great as in the stationary case. This problem can therefore be taken care of by a small correction factor. A far more important problem is the question of "flutter modes," particularly in regard to bending. There are usually one or more bending modes with a frequency lower than that of the torsional response. Can the wing flutter in a higher bending mode? Does it flutter in the lowest (stationary) mode? Is there any relation between the "flutter modes" and the ordinary vibration modes? To answer these questions it is useful to consider the two-dimensional case as the "averages" of a certain three-dimensional one. The "average" bending deflection h is thus very small for a high bending mode, even though the deflections in the loops are large. This condition is equivalent to a large effective internal damping, since the work lost per cycle refers to a small "average" h. The effective friction in fact rapidly approaches infinity as the number of the mode n is increased.

Now the structural friction is known to displace the location of the critical point toward the lowest bending frequency. With no internal friction the lowest flutter speed is usually located near unity value of the ratio of bending frequency to torsion frequency.

The wing will, of course, select the response corresponding to the lowest flutter speed. We get an interesting minimum condition: the wing will not flutter in a mode corresponding to the lowest stationary frequency; structural damping will prevent the selection of a high bending mode; some intermediate bending mode must therefore be preferred. How close this is to the lowest mode depends on the damping. We shall advance the hypothesis:

From among the possible mode or modes, the flutter will select the particular response which corresponds to the lowest critical speed.

In the case of ordinary wings, the flutter speed calculated on basis of the lowest (stationary) bending mode is a few per cent too high. The actual bending response in flutter is therefore fairly close in appearance to the lowest stationary mode. With very small internal damping, the appearance of the flutter mode approaches that of the second stationary mode.

To recapitulate:

1) The flutter speed calculated on basis of the two-dimensional theory is slightly too low because of the aspect-ratio effect.

2) The bending frequency involved in the flutter of a cantilever wing is greater than that of the lowest stationary mode. The flutter speed calculated on basis of the lowest bending mode is therefore too high.

The corrections under 1) and 2) are fairly small—say, 1–5%, for ordinary wings, and also are of opposite sign so that they tend to cancel.

In regard to the practical solution of the flutter problem, one is immediately confronted with the problem of indentifying the various possible combinations in which a particular structure may flutter. Very often a structure is capable of executing two torsional modes and it may furthermore have a succession of bending modes. It is a fairly safe rule that the lowest torsional mode together with a bending mode of a frequency somewhat in excess of the lowest will show the lowest flutter speed.

Another problem of concern, and probably the most difficult one, is the technical determination of the structural parameters. It is necessary to obtain reasonable averages, properly weighted, or what might be called "representative" values. The flutter speed is a rather critical function of some of these parameters, e.g., the location of the center of gravity, but depends much less on others, which may then be estimated. The theory is very useful in showing the expected dependency and thus to determine the required accuracy in the determination of these parameters. The theory is also useful in indicating flutter remedies. It must be realized, however, that the whole problem is one of compromise. One can not simply have a flutter-free structure since this may, and usually does, involve undesirable features in other respects. Detailed knowledge of the whole flutter problem is therefore desirable.

References

1. Theodorsen, T., "General Theory of Aerodynamic Instability and the Mechanicsm of Flutter," NACA TR 496, 1935.

2. Cicala, P., "Le Azioni Aerodinamiche sul Profili di Ala Oscillanti in Presenza di Corrente Uniforme," Royal Academy of Sciences, Torino, 1935.

3. Kassner, R., and Fingado, H., "Das ebene Problem der Flügel-Schwingung," Luftfahrtforschung, Vol. 13, No. 11, 1936, pp. 374–387.

4. Küssner, H. G., "Zusammenfassender Bericht übewr den instationären Auftrieb von Flügeln," Luft.-Forshung, Bd. 13, No. 13, 1935, pp. 410–424.

MECHANISM OF FLUTTER

A THEORETICAL AND EXPERIMENTAL INVESTIGATION OF THE FLUTTER PROBLEM

BY THEODORE THEODORSEN
AND I. E. GARRICK

National Advisory Committee for Aeronautics

Report No. 685, 1940

SUMMARY

The results of the basic flutter theory originally devised in 1934 and published as N. A. C. A. Technical Report No. 496 are presented in a simpler and more complete form convenient for further studies. The paper attempts to facilitate the judgment of flutter problems by a systematic survey of the theoretical effects of the various parameters. A large number of experiments were conducted on cantilever wings, with and without ailerons, in the N. A. C. A. high-speed wind tunnel for the purpose of verifying the theory and to study its adaptability to three-dimensional problems. The experiments included studies on wing taper ratios, nacelles, attached floats, and external bracings. The essential effects in the transition to the three-dimensional problem have been established. Of particular interest is the existence of specific flutter modes as distinguished from ordinary vibration modes. On the basis of the concepts introduced, results that are apparently paradoxical could logically be brought into conformity with the theory. In fact, it is shown that there exists a rather remarkable agreement between theoretical and experimental results. A simple method is presented for numerical calculations of the flutter speed by routine operations, requiring no reference to the theory. Application is made to a complete numerical example. The matter of identifying possible types of flutter in an airplane and of determining the parameters is briefly discussed. A section treating the subject of forced vibrations of a wing in an air stream and the question of air damping in its relation to flutter is included.

INTRODUCTION

The theory of flutter.—The problem of flutter is passing through a period of rapid development. Full cognizance is taken of the value of the theory; a simple or an empirical understanding of this problem is not available and could, at best, be of value only to the investigator. An exact treatment of the basic flutter problem in two-dimensional flow, involving the important functions F and G relating to the air forces, was given by Theodorsen in 1934. (See reference 1.) These functions are simple combinations of Bessel functions; they have been rederived in related form by Cicala (reference 2) in 1935, by Kassner and Fingado (reference 3) in 1936, and also by Küssner (reference 4) in 1936, who pointed out the identity of the functions. At about this time, Garrick (reference 5) also established a check on the general functions F and G by comparing them with expressions by Wagner, Glauert, and von Kármán and Burgers for special cases.

The system of equations as given in the original paper is

$$(A)\quad \ddot{\alpha}A+\dot{\alpha}\frac{v}{b}B+\alpha C+\ddot{\beta}D+\dot{\beta}\frac{v}{b}E+\beta\frac{v^2}{b^2}F+\ddot{h}G$$

$$-2\left(a+\frac{1}{2}\right)\frac{v}{b}C(k)Z=0$$

$$(B)\quad \ddot{\alpha}H+\dot{\alpha}\frac{v}{b}I+\ddot{\beta}J+\dot{\beta}\frac{v}{b}K+\beta L+\ddot{h}M+\frac{T_{12}}{\pi}\kappa\frac{v}{b}C(k)Z=0$$

$$(C)\quad \ddot{\alpha}N+\dot{\alpha}\frac{v}{b}O+\ddot{\beta}P+\dot{\beta}\frac{v}{b}Q+\ddot{h}R+hS+2\kappa\frac{v}{b}C(k)Z=0$$

where A, B, C, etc., are given on page 10 of reference 1.

$$Z=\frac{v}{b}\alpha+\frac{\dot{h}}{b}+\left(\frac{1}{2}-a\right)\dot{\alpha}+\frac{T_{10}v}{\pi\, b}\beta+\frac{T_{11}}{2\pi}\dot{\beta}$$

and (table 1)

$$C(k)=F(k)+iG(k)$$

Putting

$$\alpha=\alpha_0e^{i(\omega t+\varphi_0)}$$

$$\beta=\beta_0e^{i(\omega t+\varphi_1)}$$

$$h=h_0e^{i(\omega t+\varphi_2)}$$

where

$$\omega=\frac{kv}{b}$$

the determinant of the coefficients of α_0, β_0, and h_0 becomes

$$\kappa\omega^2\begin{vmatrix}\overline{R}_{a\alpha}+i\bar{I}_{a\alpha} & R_{a\beta}+iI_{a\beta} & R_{ah}+iI_{ah}\\ R_{b\alpha}+iI_{b\alpha} & \overline{R}_{b\beta}+i\bar{I}_{b\beta} & R_{bh}+iI_{bh}\\ R_{c\alpha}+iI_{c\alpha} & R_{c\beta}+iI_{c\beta} & \overline{R}_{ch}+i\bar{I}_{ch}\end{vmatrix}$$

where the R's and I's are listed in the appendix.

This determinant put equal to zero contains two simultaneous equations, the solution of which determines X and $1/k$ from which the (unknowns) flutter velocity and flutter frequency are obtained. Only the diagonal terms with bars contain the quantity X. All terms contain or are functions of $1/k$.

The work of numerous investigators, notably Becker and Föppl, has shown that the structural friction is mainly a function of amplitude, not of frequency. The structural friction can be described by a force in phase with the velocity but of a magnitude proportional to the restoring force. With each restoring-force term, say αC_α, there will be a friction term $i\alpha\ g_\alpha\ C_\alpha$, in which g_α is the damping coefficient. The net result is very simply that the restoring-force terms αC_α, βC_β, and hC_h have been replaced by terms of the form $\alpha C_\alpha (1+ig_\alpha)$, $\beta C_\beta(1+ig_\beta)$, $hC_h(1+ig_h)$. These friction coefficients occur only in the diagonal $\bar{I}$ terms of the determinant.

Technical flutter problems and the flutter parameters.—Experimental evidence, some of which is presented later, has been accumulated which indicates that, in the two-dimensional problem, the flutter speed can be closely predicted from the theory if the parameters are given with accuracy. (In fact, it seems that in some cases the flutter speed can be used to determine some parameters more precisely than by a direct method.) In the two-dimensional problem of flexure-torsion-aileron flutter, about a dozen different quantities are required to calculate the flutter speed. The determination of these parameters requires technical skill and experience and is perhaps the most difficult step in the solution of the flutter problem. A knowledge of the functional dependency of the flutter speed on each parameter is essential in order to obtain sufficient accuracy in the determination of the important ones and to prevent waste of time on those of less influence. This need is partly the purpose of the material given in this paper.

One of the problems in connection with an actual airplane is the identification of the combination of vibration modes that may cause flutter. In regard to wing flutter, in the case of flexure-torsion, the situation is fairly clear. It will be shown that normally the most important parameter is the center-of-gravity location. This constant can be obtained with considerable accuracy in the design stage. An accurate value of this parameter can also be experimentally obtained as the "dynamic" torsion axis, that is, the axis around which the wing, owing to the low bending frequency, oscillates when put into torsional resonance. The location of the (static) torsional stiffness axis is much more difficult to calculate or to determine experimentally but fortunately, as will be observed, its effect on the flutter velocity is small.

The internal damping coefficients are, moreover, of fairly small influence in flexure-torsion flutter; these parameters are also fairly difficult to obtain. On the whole, however, it may be said that this case of flutter can be fairly well handled.

Another important case, that of the combination flexure-aileron, was shown by the original study (reference 1) to be an essentially different type of flutter from flexure-torsion. Its primary characteristic is that, normally, the flutter is limited to a *range* of speeds. Below and above the extremes of this speed range there is aerodynamic stability. A reduction of the static moment of the aileron with respect to the hinge (balancing) reduces the range; that is, the lower limit is raised and the upper limit is lowered. Damping in the structure is found to have the same general effect. Sufficient internal friction will, in fact, completely eliminate the danger of flutter, as will also complete mass balance or the proper combination of both. The structural friction of a wing system, although not readily predictable, can be obtained by a ground test.

In regard to the tail assembly, the difficulty is somewhat greater since it may not be easy to identify the most dangerous combination or to predict or even to measure the necessary parameters, including the structural damping. It therefore seems that certain empirical or semiempirical aids will be required and that it will be necessary, for a time at least, to resort to flight-test methods as a final assurance against tail flutter.

The transition to the three-dimensional case of actual flutter is quite complex. It is necessary to consider an aerodynamic span effect (which fortunately is very small, see reference 6); the variation of the parameters along the span; the possibility of higher-order deflection modes; and, in certain cases, fractional span effects, as for partial ailerons. The most promising manner of attack on such problems is by means of the two-dimensional treatment with the introduction of certain weight functions and average parameters in conjunction with a study of representative models of reasonable simplicity, followed by a crystallization of the collected experience into generally applicable semiempirical correction factors. The present paper makes initial studies with this purpose in mind.

It is realized that, for high values of the flutter speed, a correction must be made for the effect of compressibility. In the first order, this effect is due to a change in the slope of the lift curve. The air forces in the steady case are known to be increased approximately in the ratio $1/\sqrt{1-M^2}$, where M is the Mach number. Consequently, a decrease in the flutter speed, roughly as $(1-M^2)^{1/4}$, is expected. This correction, although small through the usual flight range, becomes appreciable for speeds near sound speed. Until experimental verification is available, such correction is preferable to none and should be applied for high-speed airplanes. (See footnote 2, p. 9, for details.)

Content of paper.—A straightforward scheme is presented in the first section for routine calculation of the flutter speeds in the two-dimensional types; case 1, flexure-torsion; case 2, flexure-aileron; and case 3, torsion-aileron; and in the three-degrees-of-freedom type, flexure-torsion-aileron. A numerical example, referring to a modern large airplane, is included.

The second section deals with a survey of the effect of the flutter parameters on the critical velocity. The effect of changing the parameters within certain practical limits in cases 1, 2, and 3 is shown by a number of charts.

The discussion in the third section deals with the transition to a three-dimensional case, showing how a "representative" two-dimensional wing may be used to give the essential results. Both uniform and tapered cantilever wings are included. The question of the probable occurrence of higher-order bending modes in flutter is also discussed. The effects of "friction" and "coupling" are especially pronounced in higher-order flutter.

It is pointed out that the deflection mode occurring in flutter is quite different from that of the static condition and that the lowest bending frequency involved in flutter is greater than that of the lowest ordinary vibration mode. A new concept of flutter, that the mode arising in flutter is such that the flutter speed is a minimum, is then introduced. In other words, if *all* primary variables including friction could be included in the analysis, the actual mode would be determined from all possible modes as the one giving the minimum critical speed. This concept is useful in explaining certain otherwise paradoxical, experimental facts. The extreme difficulty of a direct analytic attack on the general case, even if all the physical parameters were specified, justifies the adapting of the two-dimensional treatment supplemented by empirical information obtained on actual wings. In fact, as will later be shown, the corrections are small.

Almost 100 separate experiments were conducted in the 8-foot high-speed tunnel. The fourth section deals with the experimental tests and results. About one-half of these tests pertain to flutter of wings in flexure-torsion; the rest pertain to aileron flutter. Cantilever wings of aluminum and of built-up wood construction were used. The tests were performed on a conveniently large scale, most of the wings having a chord of 1 foot and a span of about 7 feet. The air speeds ranged from 50 to about 300 miles per hour. A number of safety devices had to be employed to prevent the ruin of the tunnel equipment.

A section is included showing the theoretical effects of the air damping on the forced vibrations of a two-dimensional wing system. This study leads to a more comprehensive understanding of the flutter condition, since it studies not only the critical speed but also the approach to this speed. A number of figures are presented that show the nature of the response curves in both one and two degrees of freedom. It is perhaps worth mentioning that von Schlippe (reference 7) has employed an experimental flight method for determining the critical flutter speed, which is based upon the use of an impressed alternating exciting force. The practical value of experiments of this nature is yet somewhat doubtful since the flutter usually comes on rather explosively. In any case, the theoretical results are of interest because they indicate the critical frequency as well as the growth of the maximum response as the critical speed is approached.

METHOD FOR ROUTINE CALCULATION OF FLUTTER SPEED

The calculation of the flutter speed can be reduced to a routine procedure by the following scheme. Nothing more involved arises than the calculation of the numerical values of double and triple determinants.

Given are a maximum of seven original parameters κ, r_α^2, a, x_α, r_β^2, x_β, c, from which are formed the 18 constants $A_{\alpha1}$, $A_{\alpha2}$, $A_{\beta1}$, $A_{\beta2}$, etc., defined as follows:

$$A_{\alpha1}=\frac{r_\alpha^2}{\kappa}+\left(\frac{1}{8}+a^2\right)$$

$$A_{\alpha2}=\left(\frac{1}{2}-a\right)$$

$$A_{\beta1}=\frac{r_\beta^2}{\kappa}-\frac{T_7}{\pi}+(c-a)\left(\frac{x_\beta}{\kappa}-\frac{T_1}{\pi}\right)$$

$$A_{\beta2}=\frac{1}{\pi}\left[-2p-\left(\frac{1}{2}-a\right)T_4\right]$$

$$A_{\beta3}=\frac{1}{\pi}(T_4+T_{10})$$

$$A_{h1}=\frac{x_\alpha}{\kappa}-a$$

$$B_{\alpha1}=\frac{r_\beta^2}{\kappa}-\frac{T_7}{\pi}+(c-a)\left(\frac{x_\beta}{\kappa}-\frac{T_1}{\pi}\right)(=A_{\beta1})$$

$$B_{\alpha2}=\frac{1}{\pi}\left(p-T_1-\frac{1}{2}T_4\right)$$

$$B_{\beta1}=\frac{r_\beta^2}{\kappa}-\frac{1}{\pi^2}T_3$$

$$B_{\beta2}=-\frac{1}{2\pi^2}T_4T_{11}$$

$$B_{\beta3}=\frac{1}{\pi^2}(T_5-T_4T_{10})$$

$$B_{h1}=\frac{x_\beta}{\kappa}-\frac{1}{\pi}T_1$$

$$C_{\alpha1}=\frac{x_\alpha}{\kappa}-a(=A_{h1})$$

$$C_{\alpha2}=1$$

$$C_{\beta1}=\frac{x_\beta}{\kappa}-\frac{1}{\pi}T_1(=B_{h1})$$

$$C_{\beta2}=-\frac{1}{\pi}T_4$$

$$C_{\beta3}=0$$

$$C_{h1}=\frac{1}{\kappa}+1$$

These constants are obtained from the original variables and from the T table (table 2) given at the end of the report.

Another set of quantities $R_{a\alpha}$, $I_{a\alpha}$, etc., will be needed; their expressions are as follows:

$$R_{a\alpha}=-A_{\alpha 1}+\left(\frac{1}{4}-a^2\right)\frac{2G}{k}-\left(\frac{1}{2}+a\right)\frac{2F}{k^2}$$

$$I_{a\alpha}=\frac{1}{k}\left[A_{\alpha 2}-\left(\frac{1}{2}+a\right)\frac{2G}{k}-\left(\frac{1}{4}-a^2\right)2F\right]$$

$$R_{b\beta}=-B_{\beta 1}+\frac{1}{k^2}B_{\beta 3}-\frac{T_{12}}{2\pi}\frac{T_{11}}{2\pi}\frac{2G}{k}+\frac{T_{12}}{2\pi}\frac{T_{10}}{\pi}\frac{2F}{k^2}$$

$$I_{b\beta}=\frac{1}{k}\left(B_{\beta 2}+\frac{T_{12}}{2\pi}\frac{T_{10}}{\pi}\frac{2G}{k}+\frac{T_{12}}{2\pi}\frac{T_{11}}{2\pi}2F\right)$$

$$R_{ch}=-C_{h1}-\frac{2G}{k}$$

$$I_{ch}=\frac{1}{k}2F$$

These six quantities are derived from the constants already given and from two additional quantities F and G, which are functions of $1/k$. The quantity $1/k$ is, in reality, the independent variable in the problem. The quantities F and G occur in the forms $2F$, $2F/k^2$, and $2G/k$; their values are given in table 1 for different values of $1/k$. In order to facilitate the calculation of these quantities, the parts depending on $1/k$ are given in tables 3 and 4.

Additional constants involved are the frequencies Ω_α, Ω_β, and Ω_h, defined under the scheme for each case, and three damping constants g_α, g_β, and g_h. Generally all these constants are not simultaneously needed. The four cases will next be solved.

Case 1.—The problem is given by two quadratic equations, for convenience referred to as the "real" and the "imaginary" equations. The coefficients of each are given in the calculation scheme presented in the following section. The coefficient of the first term in each equation involves the constants g_α and g_h, the coefficients of internal friction or structural damping, which are given as original constants. The coefficient of the second term of each equation involves the g's and the R's and I's, just defined. The constant term in each of the equations is obtained by the schematic arrangement shown in the calculation scheme; it is made up from certain constants A_1, B_1, C_1, and D_1 together with the quantities $2F$, $2F/k^2$, and $2G/k$. The quantities A_1, B_1, C_1, and D_1 are simple determinants built up from the constants $A_{\alpha 1}$, etc.

The coefficients of the two equations must be calculated for a fixed value of $1/k$; these coefficients are then substituted into the equations and the solution, that is, the value of X, is found. The real equation usually has two solutions, and the imaginary equation usually has one. The values of X, or preferably of $\sqrt{X}$, are then plotted against $1/k$, and the procedure is repeated until continuous curves representing the two equations are obtained. (Attained judgment or the knowledge of the solution of similar cases may considerably reduce the labor involved because it is then possible to choose reasonable values of $1/k$ at the start. For wings and ailerons, $1/k$ is usually less than 5, very often around 1 or 2.) The point of intersection of the two curves represents the flutter point. Read off the values of X and $1/k$. The flutter speed is then given by the expression

$$v=\frac{r_\alpha\omega_\alpha b}{\sqrt{\kappa}}\frac{1}{k}\frac{1}{\sqrt{X}}$$

Case 2.—The coefficient of the first term in each of the two quadratic equations again involves the constants of internal friction g_β and g_h. The coefficient of the second terms is built up as in case 1. The constant term is built up likewise. Proceed as outlined for case 1. The critical speed is then

$$v=\frac{\omega_h b}{\sqrt{\kappa}}\frac{1}{k}\frac{1}{\sqrt{X}}$$

where $1/k$ and X are the values at the intersection point of the curves representing the real and the imaginary equations, respectively. There are usually two critical speeds.

Case 3.—Case 3 requires a more laborious calculation of the constant terms; otherwise, the procedure is the same as for cases 1 and 2. The flutter speed is given by

$$v=\frac{r_\alpha\omega_\alpha b}{\sqrt{\kappa}}\frac{1}{k}\frac{1}{\sqrt{X}}$$

Three degrees of freedom.—The case of three degrees of freedom requires the solution of two third-degree equations in X. The constants of the first, the second, and the third terms are readily recognized as containing only quantities already used under cases 1, 2, and 3. The expressions for the constant terms of the two equations, D^R and D^I, involve three-row determinants but can be obtained by straightforward calculations for each value of $1/k$. The point or points of intersection of the two curves representing the equations are again representative of the critical speed, which is given by

$$v=\frac{r_\alpha\omega_\alpha b}{\sqrt{\kappa}}\frac{1}{k}\frac{1}{\sqrt{X}}$$

CALCULATION SCHEME

Case 1 (h, α).—

Real equation:

Coefficient of X^2: $\Omega_h\Omega_\alpha(1-g_h g_\alpha)$

Coefficient of X: $\Omega_h(R_{a\alpha}-g_h I_{a\alpha})+\Omega_\alpha(R_{ch}-g_\alpha I_{ch})$

Constant: $M_1{}^R=A_1+B_1\frac{2G}{k}+C_1\frac{2F}{k^2}$

Imaginary equation: [1]

Coefficient of X^2: $\Omega_h\Omega_\alpha(g_h+g_\alpha)$

Coefficient of X: $\Omega_h(R_{a\alpha}g_h+I_{a\alpha})+\Omega_\alpha(R_{ch}g_\alpha+I_{ch})$

Constant: $M_1{}^I=\frac{1}{k}\left(D_1+C_1\frac{2G}{k}-B_1 2F\right)$

$$A_1=\begin{vmatrix}A_{\alpha 1} & A_{h1}\\ C_{\alpha 1} & C_{h1}\end{vmatrix}$$

$$B_1=\begin{vmatrix}A_{\alpha 1} & -(\frac{1}{2}+a)\\ C_{\alpha 1} & 1\end{vmatrix}+(\tfrac{1}{2}-a)\begin{vmatrix}-(\frac{1}{2}+a) & A_{h1}\\ 1 & C_{h1}\end{vmatrix}$$

$$C_1=-\begin{vmatrix}-(\frac{1}{2}+a) & A_{h1}\\ 1 & C_{h1}\end{vmatrix}-\begin{vmatrix}A_{\alpha 2} & -(\frac{1}{2}+a)\\ C_{\alpha 2} & 1\end{vmatrix}$$

$$=\begin{vmatrix}A_{h1}-A_{\alpha 2} & -(\frac{1}{2}+a)\\ C_{h1}-C_{\alpha 2} & 1\end{vmatrix}$$

$$D_1=-\begin{vmatrix}A_{\alpha 2} & A_{h1}\\ C_{\alpha 2} & C_{h1}\end{vmatrix}$$

$$\Omega_\alpha=1$$

$$\Omega_h=\left(\frac{\omega_h}{\omega_\alpha}\right)^2\frac{1}{r_\alpha{}^2}$$

$$X=\frac{r_\alpha{}^2}{\kappa}\left(\frac{\omega_\alpha}{\omega}\right)^2$$

$$v=\frac{r_\alpha\omega_\alpha b}{\sqrt{\kappa}}\,\frac{1}{k}\,\frac{1}{\sqrt{X}}$$

Case 2.— (h, β).—

Real equation:

Coefficient of X^2: $\Omega_\beta\Omega_h(1-g_\beta g_h)$

Coefficient of X: $\Omega_\beta(R_{ch}-g_\beta I_{ch})+\Omega_h(R_{b\beta}-g_h I_{b\beta})$

Constant: $M_2{}^R=A_2+\overline{A}_2\frac{1}{k^2}+\left(B_2+\overline{B}_2\frac{1}{k^2}\right)\frac{2G}{k}+C_2\frac{2F}{k^2}$

Imaginary equation:

Coefficient of X^2: $\Omega_\beta\Omega_h(g_\beta+g_h)$

Coefficient of X: $\Omega_\beta(R_{ch}g_\beta+I_{ch})+\Omega_h(R_{b\beta}g_h+I_{b\beta})$

[1] Note that when the friction coefficients g are zero, a factor $1/k$ can be canceled out of all terms in all imaginary equations.

Constant: $M_2{}^I=\frac{1}{k}\left[D_2+C_2\frac{2G}{k}-\left(B_2+\overline{B}_2\frac{1}{k^2}\right)2F\right]$

$$A_2=\begin{vmatrix}B_{\beta 1} & B_{h1}\\ C_{\beta 1} & C_{h1}\end{vmatrix}$$

$$\overline{A}_2=-\begin{vmatrix}B_{\beta 3} & B_{h1}\\ C_{\beta 3} & C_{h1}\end{vmatrix}$$

$$B_2=\begin{vmatrix}B_{\beta 1} & \frac{T_{12}}{2\pi}\\ C_{\beta 1} & 1\end{vmatrix}+\frac{T_{11}}{2\pi}\begin{vmatrix}\frac{T_{12}}{2\pi} & B_{h1}\\ 1 & C_{h1}\end{vmatrix}$$

$$\overline{B}_2=-\begin{vmatrix}B_{\beta 3} & \frac{T_{12}}{2\pi}\\ C_{\beta 3} & 1\end{vmatrix}$$

$$C_2=-\begin{vmatrix}B_{\beta 2} & \frac{T_{12}}{2\pi}\\ C_{\beta 2} & 1\end{vmatrix}-\frac{T_{10}}{\pi}\begin{vmatrix}\frac{T_{12}}{2\pi} & B_{h1}\\ 1 & C_{h1}\end{vmatrix}$$

$$D_2=-\begin{vmatrix}B_{\beta 2} & B_{h1}\\ C_{\beta 2} & C_{h1}\end{vmatrix}$$

$$\Omega_h=1$$

$$\Omega_\beta=\left(\frac{\omega_\beta}{\omega_h}\right)^2 r_\beta{}^2$$

$$X=\frac{1}{\kappa}\left(\frac{\omega_h}{\omega}\right)^2$$

$$v=\frac{\omega_h b}{\sqrt{\kappa}}\,\frac{1}{k}\,\frac{1}{\sqrt{X}}$$

Case 3 (α, β).—

Real equation:

Coefficient of X^2: $\Omega_\alpha\Omega_\beta(1-g_\alpha g_\beta)$

Coefficient of X: $\Omega_\alpha(R_{b\beta}-g_\alpha I_{b\beta})+\Omega_\beta(R_{a\alpha}-g_\beta I_{a\alpha})$

Constant: $M_3{}^R=A_3+\overline{A}_3\frac{1}{k^2}+\left(B_3+\overline{B}_3\frac{1}{k^2}\right)\frac{2G}{k}$
$+\left(C_3+\overline{C}_3\frac{1}{k^2}\right)\frac{2F}{k^2}$

Imaginary equation:

Coefficient of X^2: $\Omega_\alpha\Omega_\beta(g_\alpha+g_\beta)$

Coefficient of X: $\Omega_\alpha(R_{b\beta}g_\alpha+I_{b\beta})+\Omega_\beta(R_{a\alpha}g_\beta+I_{a\alpha})$

Constant: $M_3{}^I=\frac{1}{k}\left[D_3+\overline{D}_3\frac{1}{k^2}+\left(C_3+\overline{C}_3\frac{1}{k^2}\right)\frac{2G}{k}\right.$
$\left.-\left(B_3+\overline{B}_3\frac{1}{k^2}\right)2F\right]$

$$A_3=\begin{vmatrix}A_{\alpha 1} & A_{\beta_1}\\ B_{\alpha 1} & B_{\beta 1}\end{vmatrix}$$

$$\overline{A}_3=-\begin{vmatrix}A_{\alpha 1} & A_{\beta 3}\\ B_{\alpha 1} & B_{\beta 3}\end{vmatrix}-\begin{vmatrix}A_{\alpha 2} & A_{\beta_2}\\ B_{\alpha 2} & B_{\beta 2}\end{vmatrix}$$

$$B_3=(\tfrac{1}{2}-a)\begin{vmatrix}-(\tfrac{1}{2}+a) & A_{\beta 1}\\ \frac{T_{12}}{2\pi} & B_{\beta 1}\end{vmatrix}+\frac{T_{11}}{2\pi}\begin{vmatrix}A_{\alpha 1} & -(\tfrac{1}{2}+a)\\ B_{\alpha 1} & \frac{T_{12}}{2\pi}\end{vmatrix}$$

$$\overline{B}_3=-(\tfrac{1}{2}-a)\begin{vmatrix}-(\tfrac{1}{2}+a) & A_{\beta 3}\\ \frac{T_{12}}{2\pi} & B_{\beta 3}\end{vmatrix}-\frac{T_{10}}{\pi}\begin{vmatrix}A_{\alpha 2} & -(\tfrac{1}{2}+a)\\ B_{\alpha 2} & \frac{T_{12}}{2\pi}\end{vmatrix}-\begin{vmatrix}-(\tfrac{1}{2}+a) & A_{\beta 2}\\ \frac{T_{12}}{2\pi} & B_{\beta 2}\end{vmatrix}$$

$$C_3=-(\tfrac{1}{2}-a)\begin{vmatrix}-(\tfrac{1}{2}+a) & A_{\beta 2}\\ \frac{T_{12}}{2\pi} & B_{\beta 2}\end{vmatrix}-\frac{T_{11}}{2\pi}\begin{vmatrix}A_{\alpha 2} & -(\tfrac{1}{2}+a)\\ B_{\alpha 2} & \frac{T_{12}}{2\pi}\end{vmatrix}-\frac{T_{10}}{\pi}\begin{vmatrix}A_{\alpha 1} & -(\tfrac{1}{2}+a)\\ B_{\alpha 1} & \frac{T_{12}}{2\pi}\end{vmatrix}-\begin{vmatrix}-(\tfrac{1}{2}+a) & A_{\beta 1}\\ \frac{T_{12}}{2\pi} & B_{\beta 1}\end{vmatrix}$$

$$\overline{C}_3=\begin{vmatrix}-(\tfrac{1}{2}+a) & A_{\beta 3}\\ \frac{T_{12}}{2\pi} & B_{\beta 3}\end{vmatrix}$$

$$D_3=-\begin{vmatrix}A_{\alpha 1} & A_{\beta 2}\\ B_{\alpha 1} & B_{\beta 2}\end{vmatrix}-\begin{vmatrix}A_{\alpha 2} & A_{\beta 1}\\ B_{\alpha 2} & B_{\beta 1}\end{vmatrix}$$

$$\overline{D}_3=\begin{vmatrix}A_{\alpha 2} & A_{\beta 3}\\ B_{\alpha 2} & B_{\beta 3}\end{vmatrix}$$

$$\Omega_\alpha=1$$

$$\Omega_\beta=\left(\frac{\omega_\beta}{\omega_\alpha}\right)^2\left(\frac{r_\beta}{r_\alpha}\right)^2$$

$$X=\frac{r_\alpha^2}{\kappa}\left(\frac{\omega_\alpha}{\omega}\right)^2$$

$$v=\frac{r_\alpha\omega_\alpha b}{\sqrt{\kappa}}\frac{1}{k}\frac{1}{\sqrt{X}}$$

Three degrees of freedom with friction.—

Real equation:

Coefficient of X^3: $\Omega_\alpha\Omega_\beta\Omega_h(1-g_\alpha g_\beta-g_\beta g_h-g_h g_\alpha)$

Coefficient of X^2: $\Omega_\alpha\Omega_\beta[(1-g_\alpha g_\beta)R_{ch}-(g_\alpha+g_\beta)I_{ch}]+\Omega_\beta\Omega_h[(1-g_\beta g_h)R_{a\alpha}-(g_\beta+g_h)I_{a\alpha}]$
$+\Omega_h\Omega_\alpha[(1-g_h g_\alpha)R_{b\beta}-(g_h+g_\alpha)I_{b\beta}]$

Coefficient of X: $\Omega_\alpha(M_2^R-g_\alpha M_2^I)+\Omega_\beta(M_1^R-g_\beta M_1^I)+\Omega_h(M_3^R-g_h M_3^I)$

Constant: $D^R=R+\overline{R}\frac{1}{k^2}+\left(S+\overline{S}\frac{1}{k^2}\right)\frac{2G}{k}+\left(T+\overline{T}\frac{1}{k^2}\right)\frac{2F}{k^2}$

Imaginary equation:

Coefficient of X^3: $\Omega_\alpha\Omega_\beta\Omega_h(g_\alpha+g_\beta+g_h+g_\alpha g_\beta g_h)$

Coefficient of X^2: $\Omega_\alpha\Omega_\beta[(1-g_\alpha g_\beta)I_{ch}+(g_\alpha+g_\beta)R_{ch}]+\Omega_\beta\Omega_h[(1-g_\beta g_h)I_{a\alpha}+(g_\beta+g_h)R_{a\alpha}]$
$+\Omega_h\Omega_\alpha[(1-g_h g_\alpha)I_{b\beta}+(g_h+g_\alpha)R_{b\beta}]$

Coefficient of X: $\Omega_\alpha(M_2^I+g_\alpha M_2^R)+\Omega_\beta(M_1^I+g_\beta M_1^R)+\Omega_h(M_3^I+g_h M_3^R)$

Constant: $D^I=\frac{1}{k}\left[U+\overline{U}\frac{1}{k^2}+\left(T+\overline{T}\frac{1}{k^2}\right)\frac{2G}{k}-\left(S+\overline{S}\frac{1}{k^2}\right)2F\right]$

$$R=-\begin{vmatrix} A_{\alpha 1} & A_{\beta 1} & A_{h1} \\ B_{\alpha 1} & B_{\beta 1} & B_{h1} \\ C_{\alpha 1} & C_{\beta 1} & C_{h1} \end{vmatrix}$$

$$\overline{R}=\begin{vmatrix} A_{\alpha 1} & A_{\beta 3} & A_{h1} \\ B_{\alpha 1} & B_{\beta 3} & B_{h1} \\ C_{\alpha 1} & C_{\beta 3} & C_{h1} \end{vmatrix}+\begin{vmatrix} A_{\alpha 2} & A_{\beta} & A_{h1} \\ B_{\alpha 2} & B_{\beta 2} & B_{h1} \\ C_{\alpha 2} & C_{\beta 2} & C_{h1} \end{vmatrix}$$

$$S=-\begin{vmatrix} A_{\alpha 1} & A_{\beta 1} & -(\tfrac{1}{2}+a) \\ B_{\alpha 1} & B_{\beta 1} & \dfrac{T_{12}}{2\pi} \\ C_{\alpha 1} & C_{\beta 1} & 1 \end{vmatrix}-(\tfrac{1}{2}-a)\begin{vmatrix} -(\tfrac{1}{2}+a) & A_{\beta 1} & A_{h1} \\ \dfrac{T_{12}}{2\pi} & B_{\beta 1} & B_{h1} \\ 1 & C_{\beta 1} & C_{h1} \end{vmatrix}-\frac{T_{11}}{2\pi}\begin{vmatrix} A_{\alpha 1} & -(\tfrac{1}{2}+a) & A_{h1} \\ B_{\alpha 1} & \dfrac{T_{12}}{2\pi} & B_{h1} \\ C_{\alpha 1} & 1 & C_{h1} \end{vmatrix}$$

$$\overline{S}=\begin{vmatrix} A_{\alpha 1} & A_{\beta 3} & -(\tfrac{1}{2}+a) \\ B_{\alpha 1} & B_{\beta 3} & \dfrac{T_{12}}{2\pi} \\ C_{\alpha 1} & C_{\beta 3} & 1 \end{vmatrix}+\begin{vmatrix} -(\tfrac{1}{2}+a) & A_{\beta 2} & A_{h1} \\ \dfrac{T_{12}}{2\pi} & B_{\beta 2} & B_{h1} \\ 1 & C_{\beta 2} & C_{h1} \end{vmatrix}+\begin{vmatrix} A_{\alpha 2} & A_{\beta 2} & -(\tfrac{1}{2}+a) \\ B_{\alpha 2} & B_{\beta 2} & \dfrac{T_{12}}{2\pi} \\ C_{\alpha 2} & C_{\beta 2} & 1 \end{vmatrix}+\frac{T_{10}}{\pi}\begin{vmatrix} A_{\alpha 2} & -(\tfrac{1}{2}+a) & A_{h1} \\ B_{\alpha 2} & \dfrac{T_{12}}{2\pi} & B_{h1} \\ C_{\alpha 2} & 1 & C_{h1} \end{vmatrix}$$
$$+(\tfrac{1}{2}-a)\begin{vmatrix} -(\tfrac{1}{2}+a) & A_{\beta 3} & A_{h1} \\ \dfrac{T_{12}}{2\pi} & B_{\beta 3} & B_{h1} \\ 1 & C_{\beta 3} & C_{h1} \end{vmatrix}$$

$$T=\begin{vmatrix} A_{\alpha 1} & A_{\beta 2} & -(\tfrac{1}{2}+a) \\ B_{\alpha 1} & B_{\beta 2} & \dfrac{T_{12}}{2\pi} \\ C_{\alpha 1} & C_{\beta 2} & 1 \end{vmatrix}+\begin{vmatrix} A_{\alpha 2} & A_{\beta 1} & -(\tfrac{1}{2}+a) \\ B_{\alpha 2} & B_{\beta 1} & \dfrac{T_{12}}{2\pi} \\ C_{\alpha 2} & C_{\beta 1} & 1 \end{vmatrix}+\begin{vmatrix} -(\tfrac{1}{2}+a) & A_{\beta 1} & A_{h1} \\ \dfrac{T_{12}}{2\pi} & B_{\beta 1} & B_{h1} \\ 1 & C_{\beta 1} & C_{h1} \end{vmatrix}+(\tfrac{1}{2}-a)\begin{vmatrix} -(\tfrac{1}{2}+a) & A_{\beta 2} & A_{h1} \\ \dfrac{T_{12}}{2\pi} & B_{\beta 2} & B_{h1} \\ 1 & C_{\beta 2} & C_{h1} \end{vmatrix}$$
$$+\frac{T_{10}}{\pi}\begin{vmatrix} A_{\alpha 1} & -(\tfrac{1}{2}+a) & A_{h1} \\ B_{\alpha 1} & \dfrac{T_{12}}{2\pi} & B_{h1} \\ C_{\alpha 1} & 1 & C_{h1} \end{vmatrix}+\frac{T_{11}}{2\pi}\begin{vmatrix} A_{\alpha 2} & -(\tfrac{1}{2}+a) & A_{h1} \\ B_{\alpha 2} & \dfrac{T_{12}}{2\pi} & B_{h1} \\ C_{\alpha 2} & 1 & C_{h1} \end{vmatrix}$$

$$\overline{T}=-\begin{vmatrix} -(\tfrac{1}{2}+a) & A_{\beta 3} & A_{h1} \\ \dfrac{T_{12}}{2\pi} & B_{\beta 3} & B_{h1} \\ 1 & C_{\beta 3} & C_{h1} \end{vmatrix}-\begin{vmatrix} A_{\alpha 2} & A_{\beta 3} & -(\tfrac{1}{2}+a) \\ B_{\alpha 2} & B_{\beta 3} & \dfrac{T_{12}}{2\pi} \\ C_{\alpha 2} & C_{\beta 3} & 1 \end{vmatrix}$$

$$U=\begin{vmatrix}A_{\alpha1} & A_{\beta2} & A_{h1}\\ B_{\alpha1} & B_{\beta2} & B_{h1}\\ C_{\alpha1} & C_{\beta2} & C_{h1}\end{vmatrix}+\begin{vmatrix}A_{\alpha2} & A_{\beta1} & A_{h1}\\ B_{\alpha2} & B_{\beta1} & B_{h1}\\ C_{\alpha2} & C_{\beta1} & C_{h1}\end{vmatrix}$$

$$\bar{U}=-\begin{vmatrix}A_{\alpha2} & A_{\beta3} & A_{h1}\\ B_{\alpha2} & B_{\beta3} & B_{h1}\\ C_{\alpha2} & C_{\beta3} & C_{h1}\end{vmatrix}$$

Note that five of the determinants occurring in the expressions for T and $\bar{T}$ occur also in the expressions for S and $\bar{S}$.

$$\Omega_\alpha=1$$

$$\Omega_\beta=\left(\frac{\omega_\beta}{\omega_\alpha}\right)^2\left(\frac{r_\beta}{r_\alpha}\right)^2$$

$$\Omega_h=\left(\frac{\omega_h}{\omega_\alpha}\right)^2\frac{1}{r_\alpha^2}$$

$$X=\frac{r_\alpha^2}{\kappa}\left(\frac{\omega_\alpha}{\omega}\right)^2$$

$$v=\frac{r_\alpha\omega_\alpha b}{\sqrt{\kappa}}\,\frac{1}{k}\,\frac{1}{\sqrt{X}}$$

NUMERICAL EXAMPLE

The following example refers to a modern large airplane. The parameters, which were furnished by the manufacturer, are:

$\kappa=0.25$	$r_\alpha^2=0.25$
$a=-0.4$	$c=0.6$
$x_\alpha=0.2$	$x_\beta=0$
	$r_\beta^2=0.0012$

A verbal description of the representative parameters used in the example is: wing density, σ, about 2.5 pounds per square foot per chord length (in ft); stiffness-axis location, 30 percent of the chord from the leading edge; center-of-gravity location, 40 percent of the chord from the leading edge; aileron length, one-fifth of the total chord; balanced aileron (center of gravity of aileron at hinge axis, $x_\beta=0$). (The structural damping coefficients g_α, g_β, and g_h will be kept zero, corresponding to a safety factor.) It is not necessary to specify the chord length $2b$ and the torsional frequency ω_α until the final step. The following frequency ratios, however, are specified:

$$\left(\frac{\omega_h}{\omega_\alpha}\right)^2=1/16$$

$$\left(\frac{\omega_\beta}{\omega_h}\right)^2=3/2$$

That is, the torsional frequency is four times the bending frequency and the aileron frequency is 1.22 times the bending frequency. The constants from which are composed all the determinants in the calculation scheme are tabulated as follows:

$A_{\alpha1}=1.285$ $A_{\alpha2}=.9$ $A_{\beta1}=.02374$ $A_{\beta2}=.23679$ $A_{\beta3}=.40744$ $A_{h1}=1.2$	$B_{\alpha1}=0.02374$ $B_{\alpha2}=.04009$ $B_{\beta1}=.007028$ $B_{\beta2}=.021177$ $B_{\beta3}=.01651$ $B_{h1}=.02322$	$C_{\alpha1}=1.2$ $C_{\alpha2}=1$ $C_{\beta1}=.02322$ $C_{\beta2}=.14238$ $C_{\beta3}=0$ $C_{h1}=5.0$
$-\left(\frac{1}{2}+a\right)=-0.1$	$\frac{T_{12}}{2\pi}=0.006357$	1

The equations are written explicitly for $1/k=1$, that is, $2G/k=-0.2006$, $2F=1.0788$, $2F/k^2=1.0788$.

Case 1 (flexure-torsion).—

Real equation:

The coefficient of X^2 is

$$\frac{1}{16}\times4\times1=\frac{1}{4}$$

The coefficient of X is

$$\frac{1}{4}(-1.285-0.12593)+1(-5.0+0.2006)=-5.15213$$

The constants

$$A_1=4.985$$
$$B_1=-0.125$$
$$C_1=0.7$$
$$D_1=-3.3$$

Hence the constant term is

$$M_1^R=4.985+(-0.125)\ (-0.2006)+0.7(1.0788)=5.76524$$

The real equation is then

$$\frac{1}{4}X^2-5.15213X+5.76524=0$$

Imaginary equation:

The coefficient of X is

$$\frac{1}{4}(0.9-0.07703)+1(1.0788)=1.28454$$

The constant term M_1^I is

$$-3.3+0.7(-0.2006)-(-0.125)(1.0788)=-3.30557$$

The imaginary equation is then

$$1.28454X-3.30557=0$$

The roots of the real equation are $X=1.187$ and 19.421, and the root of the imaginary equation is $X=2.573$, or

$$\sqrt{X}=1.089,\ 4.407,\ \text{and}\ 1.604$$

These values of $\sqrt{X}$ are plotted against $1/k$ in figure 1. The curves traced by plotting the roots are shown in the figure. The intersection is at $\sqrt{X}=1.594$, $1/k=2.46$. The flutter speed is then

$$v=\frac{1}{2}\times2\times\frac{2.46}{1.594}b\omega_\alpha=1.542b\omega_\alpha$$

In the present example, the chord $2b$ is 12 feet and ω_α is 90 (corresponding to a torsional frequency of 859 cyles per minute); $b\omega_\alpha$ is then 540 feet per second or

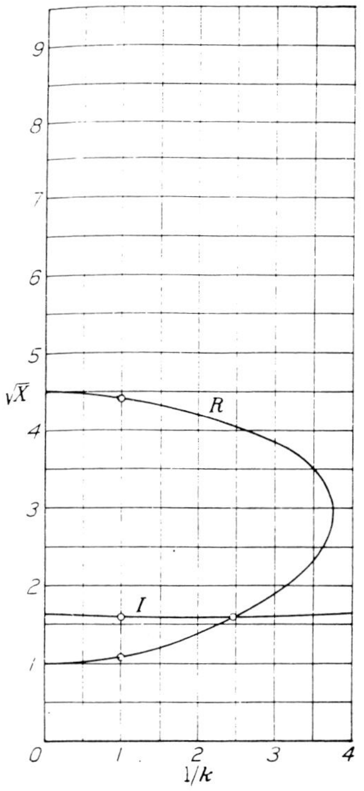

FIGURE 1.—Case 1. Numerical example. The roots $\sqrt{X}$ of the real and the imaginary equations against $1/k$.

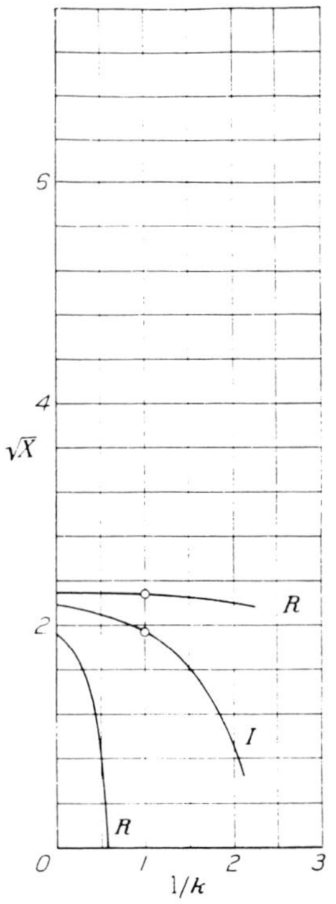

FIGURE 2.—Case 2. Numerical example. The roots $\sqrt{X}$ of the real and the imaginary equations against $1/k$.

about 368 miles per hour. Hence the flutter speed is, for this case, 567 miles per hour.[2]

Case 2 (flexure aileron).—

Real equation:

The coefficient of X^2 is

$$\frac{3}{2}\times 0.0012\times 1=0.0018$$

The coefficient of X is

$$0.0018(-5+0.2006)+1(-0.007028+0.020470)=0.004803$$

The constants

$$A_2=0.034601$$
$$\overline{A}_2=-0.08255$$
$$B_2=0.008154$$
$$\overline{B}_2=-0.016510$$
$$C_2=-0.024980$$
$$D_2=-0.10258$$

The constant term $M_2^R=-0.07322$.

The real equation is then

$$0.0018X^2+0.004803X-0.07322=0$$

Imaginary equation:

The coefficient of X is

$$0.0018\times 1.0788+1(0.021177+0.0003184)=0.023437$$

The constant term $M_2^I=-0.088554$

The imaginary equation is then

$$0.023437X-0.088554=0$$

The roots of the real equation are $X=5.182$ and -7.85 and the root of the imaginary equation is $X=3.778$ or (for the positive roots) $\sqrt{X}=2.276$ and 1.944. These values of $\sqrt{X}$ are plotted against $1/k$ in figure 2. The curves traced by the roots are shown in the figure. Since no intersection exists, this case is stable.

Case 3 (torsion-aileron).—

Real equation:

The coefficient of X^2 is

$$1\times\frac{3}{32}\times\frac{0.0012}{0.25}=0.00045$$

The coefficient of X is

$$1(-0.007028+0.020470)+0.00045(-1.285-0.12593)=0.012807$$

The constants

$A_3=0.008468$	$C_3=-0.003129$
$\overline{A}_3=-0.021110$	$\overline{C}_3=-0.004241$
$B_3=0.000799$	$D_3=-0.026964$
$\overline{B}_3=0.002090$	$\overline{D}_3=-0.001474$

The constant term $M_3^R=-0.021173$

The real equation is then

$$0.00045X^2+0.012807X-0.021173=0$$

Imaginary equation:

The coefficient of X is

$$(0.021177+0.0003184)+0.00045(0.9-0.07703)=0.021865$$

The constant term $M_3^I=-0.030076$

The imaginary equation is then

$$0.021865X-0.030076=0$$

The roots of the real equation are $X=1.567$ and -30.03 and the root of the imaginary equation is $X=1.375$ or (for the positive roots) $\sqrt{X}=1.252$ and 1.173. These values for the $\sqrt{X}$ are plotted against $1/k$ in figure 3. The curve traced by the roots is shown in the figure. Since no intersection exists, this case is also stable.

Three degrees of freedom (flexure-torsion-aileron).—

Real equation:

The coefficient of X^3 is

$$1\times 0.00045\times \tfrac{1}{4}=0.0001125$$

[2] The compressibility correction: Let the calculated flutter speed for the incompressible fluid be v_i and let the corresponding speed for the compressible fluid be v_c Denote v_i/c by M_i and v_c/c by M_c, where c is the velocity of sound. Then (see Introduction)

$$M_c^2\frac{1}{\sqrt{1-M_c^2}}=M_i^2$$

or, on solving for M_c^2,

$$M_c^2=M_i^2\left(\sqrt{1+\frac{M_i^4}{4}}-\frac{M_i^2}{2}\right)$$
$$\cong M_i^2\left(1-\frac{M_i^2}{2}+\frac{M_i^4}{8}-\ \ldots\right)$$

For example, with $v_i=567$ m. p. h., $M_i=567/760=0.746$, $M_c=0.650$, and $v_c=494$ m. p. h. Note that the example given refers to sea level; at altitude, the example should be based on another value of κ and an appropriate value of the velocity of sound.

The coefficient of X^2 is

$$0.00045(-4.7994)+0.0001125(-1.41093)+\tfrac{1}{4}(0.013442)=0.001042$$

The coefficient of X is

$$1(-0.07322)+0.00045(5.76524)+\tfrac{1}{4}(-0.021173)=-0.07592$$

The constants are

$R=-0.032848$ $\quad T=0.017042$

$\overline{R}=\ 0.077092$ $\quad \overline{T}=0.028790$

$S=-0.004381$ $\quad U=0.103485$

$\overline{S}=-0.000344$ $\quad \overline{U}=0.017720$

The constant term $D^R=0.094635$

The real equation is then

$$0.0001125X^3+0.001042X^2-0.07592X+0.094635=0$$

Imaginary equation:

The coefficient of X^2 is

$$0.00045(1.0788)+0.0001125(0.82297)+\tfrac{1}{4}(0.021495)=0.005952$$

The coefficient of X is

$$1(-0.088554)+0.00045(-3.30557)+\tfrac{1}{4}(-0.030076)=-0.097561$$

The constant term $D^I=0.11711$

The imaginary equation is then

$$0.005952X^2-0.097561X+0.1171=0$$

The positive roots of the real equation are $X=1.270$ and 21.0 and the roots of the imaginary equation are 1.302 and 15.08, or $\sqrt{X}=1.126$ and 4.58, and 1.141 and 3.883. These values of $\sqrt{X}$ are plotted against $1/k$ in figure 4. The curves traced by the roots against $1/k$ are shown in the figure. The intersection is at $\sqrt{X}=1.06$, $1/k=0.875$. Hence

$$v=\tfrac{1}{2}\times 2\times\frac{0.875}{1.06}b\omega_\alpha=0.826b\omega_\alpha$$

For $2b=12$ feet and $\omega_\alpha=90$, the flutter speed is 304 miles per hour.

These examples have been selected from several listed under the last part of the following section, to which the reader may refer for other examples, including the case of an unbalanced aileron.

THEORETICAL SURVEY OF THE EFFECT OF THE FLUTTER PARAMETERS

The purpose of this section is the study of the effect on the critical speed of the various independent variables. Although the theory in itself permits the solution of any particular case without difficulty, it is somewhat difficult to obtain a perspective of the effects of the parameters. Because of the many variables, this survey has been limited to the magnitudes and the ranges of most practical interest. It is realized that the effect of increasing or decreasing a certain parameter is dependent on the values chosen for the others. As a mathematical experiment, it is possible to change one variable and to keep *all* the others constant. With reference to practical problems, however, the change of one parameter is usually accompanied by unavoidable changes in several of the others. This fact must be kept in mind when actual or proposed changes intended to increase the flutter speed of airplanes are considered. This discussion is intended to give only the salient facts; the charts contain the complete data.

CASE 1 (FLEXURE-TORSION)

The flutter speed for case 1 is plotted in the coefficient form $v/b\omega_\alpha$. In the following graphs, the frequency ratio ω_h/ω_α is generally used as abscissa and the critical flutter coefficient $v/b\omega_\alpha$, as ordinate.

The graphs under each of the following sections of case 1 are arranged in order of decreasing values of κ

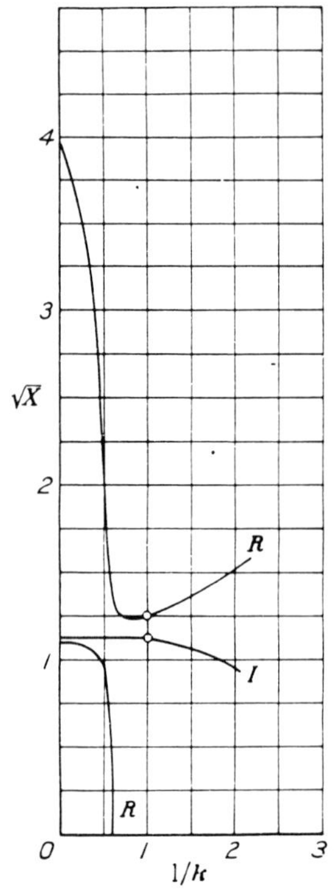

FIGURE 3.—Case 3. Numerical example. The roots $\sqrt{X}$ of the real and the imaginary equations against $1/k$.

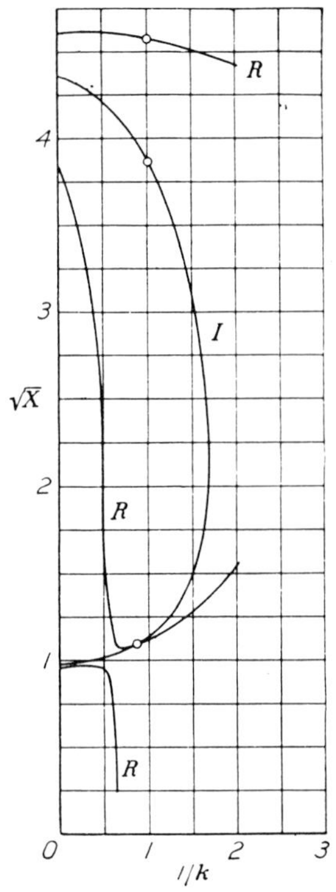

FIGURE 4.—Three degrees of freedom. Numerical example. The roots $\sqrt{X}$ of the real and the imaginary equations against $1/k$.

starting with $\kappa=1/2$ (lightest wings) and ending with $\kappa=1/20$ (heaviest). The range of κ for present-day airplanes is approximately $\kappa=1/3$ to $\kappa=1/15$. The graphs are further arranged in order of increasing values of a, starting with the smallest values of a (stiffness axis in the most forward location). In most cases, the radius of gyration is kept at a fixed value $r_\alpha^2=1/4$.

Effect of center of gravity x_α.—The effect of x_α on flutter speed is given in graph I–A. It may be observed that there is usually a decrease in the critical speed as the frequency ratio ω_h/ω_α is increased from zero and that the curves tend to a minimum near the frequency ratio $\omega_h/\omega_\alpha=1$. There are cases, however, in which the minimum critical speed lies at $\omega_h/\omega_\alpha=0$. The transition takes place for a certain small value of x_α.

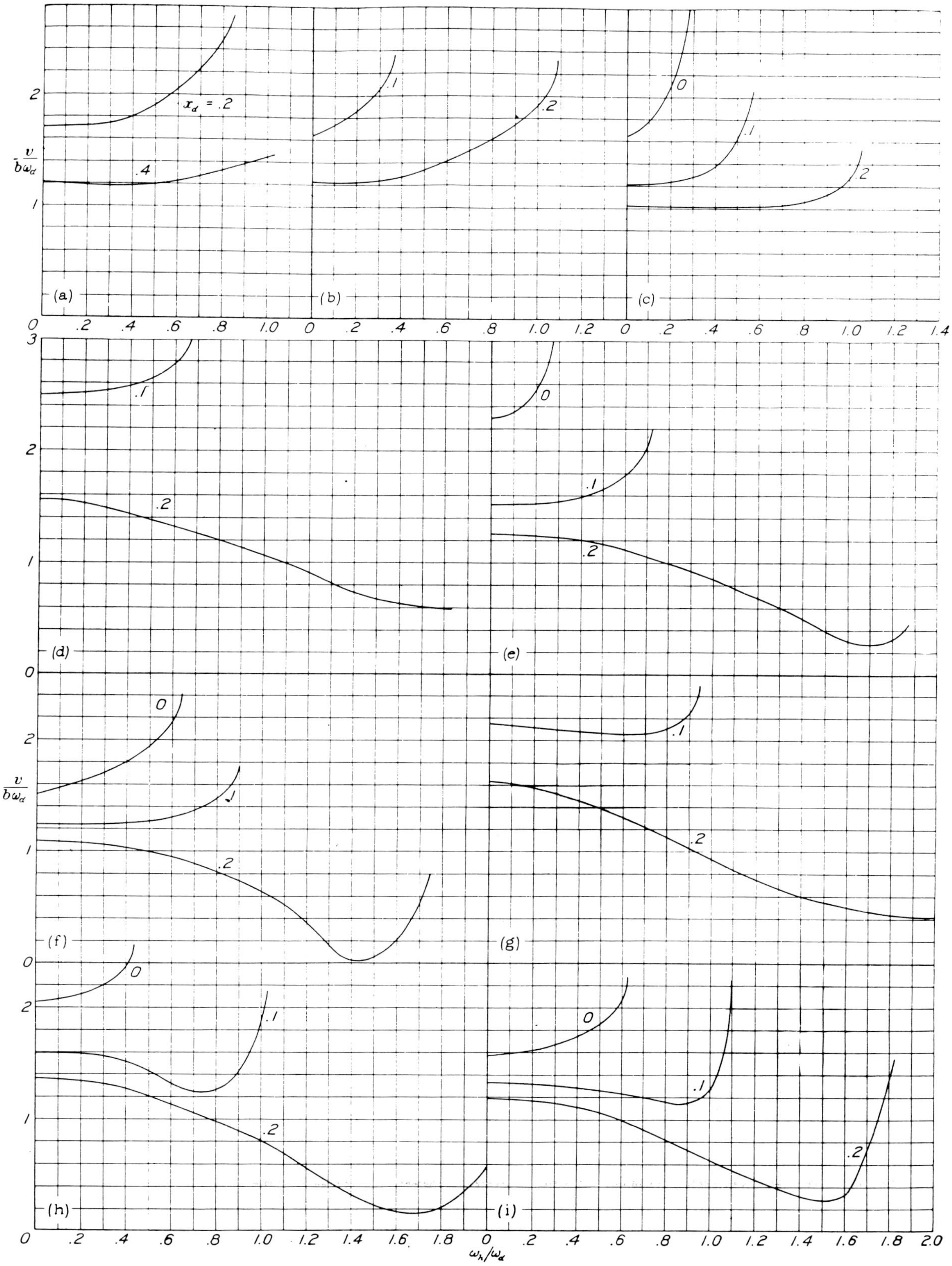

(a) $\kappa = 1/2$; $a = -0.4$; $x_\alpha = 0$ stable; $x_\alpha = 0.1$ stable; $v_D/b\omega_\alpha = 1.58$. (b) $\kappa = 1/2$; $a = -0.3$; $x_\alpha = 0$ stable; $v_D/b\omega_\alpha = 1.12$. (c) $\kappa = 1/2$; $a = -0.2$; $v_D/b\omega_\alpha = 0.913$.
(d) $\kappa = 1/3$; $a = -0.4$; $x_\alpha = 0$ stable; $v_D/b\omega_\alpha = 1.94$. (e) $\kappa = 1/3$; $a = -0.3$; $v_D/b\omega_\alpha = 1.37$.
(f) $\kappa = 1/3$; $a = -0.2$; $v_D/b\omega_\alpha = 1.12$. (g) $\kappa = 1/4$; $a = -0.4$; $x_\alpha = 0$ stable; $v_D/b\omega_\alpha = 2.24$.
(h) $\kappa = 1/4$; $a = -0.3$; $v_D/b\omega_\alpha = 1.58$. (i) $\kappa = 1/4$; $a = -0.2$; $v_D/b\omega_\alpha = 1.29$.

Graph I-A (a-i).—The effect of x_α; the flutter coefficient against the frequency ratio; $r_\alpha^2 = 1/4$. Case 1 (h, α).

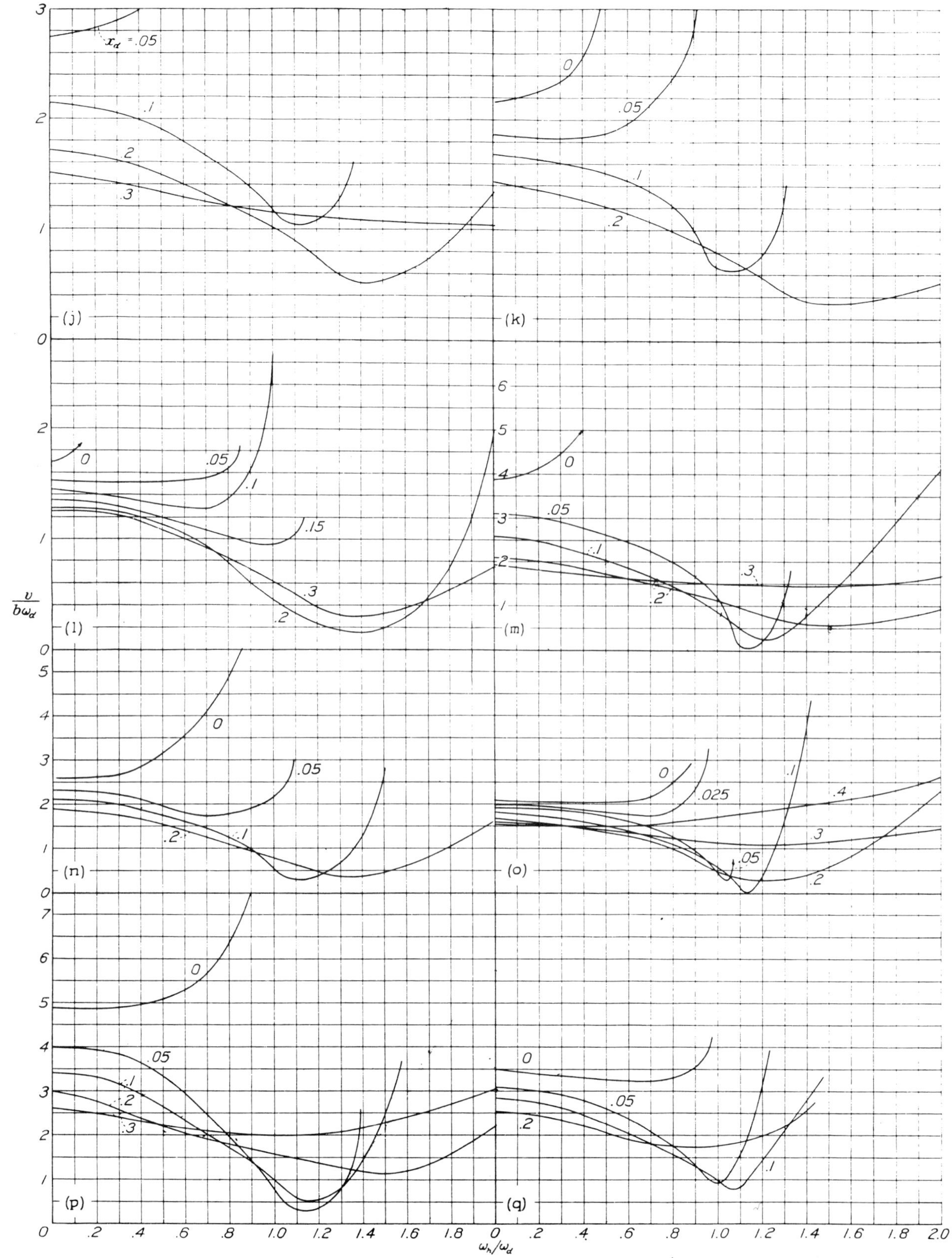

(j) $\kappa=1/5$; $a=-0.4$; $v_D/b\omega_\alpha=2.5$; $x_\alpha=0$, starts at ordinate 6.9.
(l) $\kappa=1/5$; $a=-0.2$; $v_D/b\omega_\alpha=1.45$.
(n) $\kappa=1/10$; $a=-0.3$; $v_D/b\omega_\alpha=2.5$.
(p) $\kappa=1/20$; $a=-0.4$; $v_D/b\omega_\alpha=5.0$.

(k) $\kappa=1/5$; $a=-0.3$; $v_D/b\omega_\alpha=1.77$.
(m) $\kappa=1/10$; $a=-0.4$; $v_D/b\omega_\alpha=3.54$.
(o) $\kappa=1/10$; $a=-0.2$; $v_D/b\omega_\alpha=2.05$.
(q) $\kappa=1/20$; $a=-0.3$; $v_D/b\omega_\alpha=3.54$.

Graph 1-A (j-q).—The effect of x_α; the flutter coefficient against the frequency ratio; $r_\alpha^2=1/4$. Case 1 (h, α).

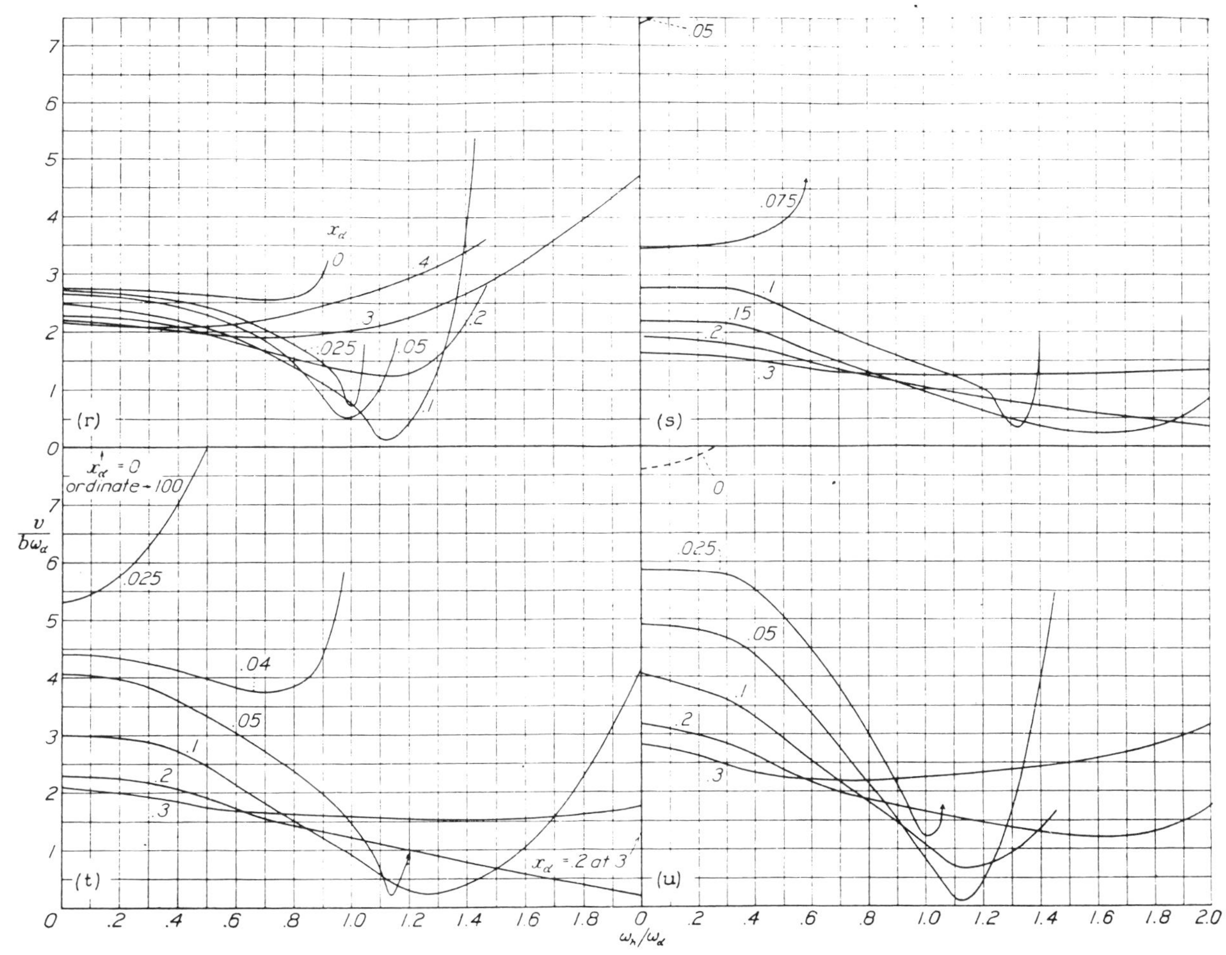

(r) $\kappa=1/20$; $a=-0.2$; $v_D/b\omega_\alpha=2.88$.
(t) $\kappa=1/10$; $a=-0.45$; $v_D/b\omega_\alpha=5.0$.
(s) $\kappa=1/5$; $a=-0.45$; $v_D/b\omega_\alpha=3.54$.
(u) $\kappa=1/20$; $a=-0.45$; $v_D/b\omega_\alpha=7.07$.

Graph I-A (r-u).—The effect of x_α; the flutter coefficient against the frequency ratio; $r_\alpha^2=1/4$. Case 1 (h, α).

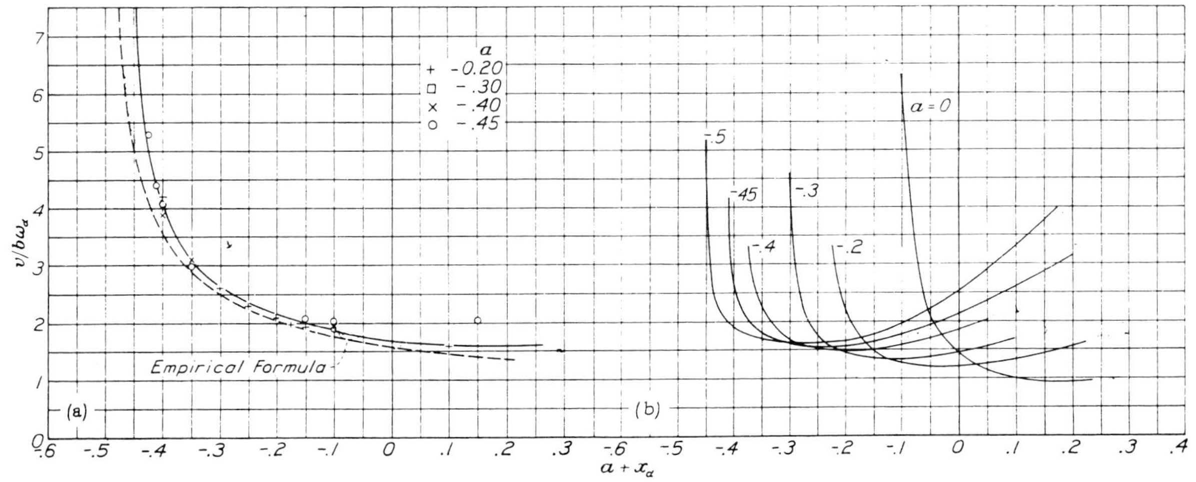

(a) $\kappa=1/10$; $\left(\frac{\omega_h}{\omega_\alpha}\right)^2=0$. (b) $\kappa=1/10$; $\left(\frac{\omega_h}{\omega_\alpha}\right)^2=1/2$.

Graph I-B.—The effect of the stiffness axis; the flutter coefficient against the center-of-gravity location; $r_\alpha^2=1/4$. Case 1 (h, α).

This value is greater the larger the values of κ (light wings). For instance, when $\kappa=1/4$, a value of $x_\alpha=$ about 0.1 (graph I–A (g)) brings the minimum near the speed near unity frequency ratio from zero to infinity. As may be observed later, structural damping will greatly alter the shape of the curve in this range.

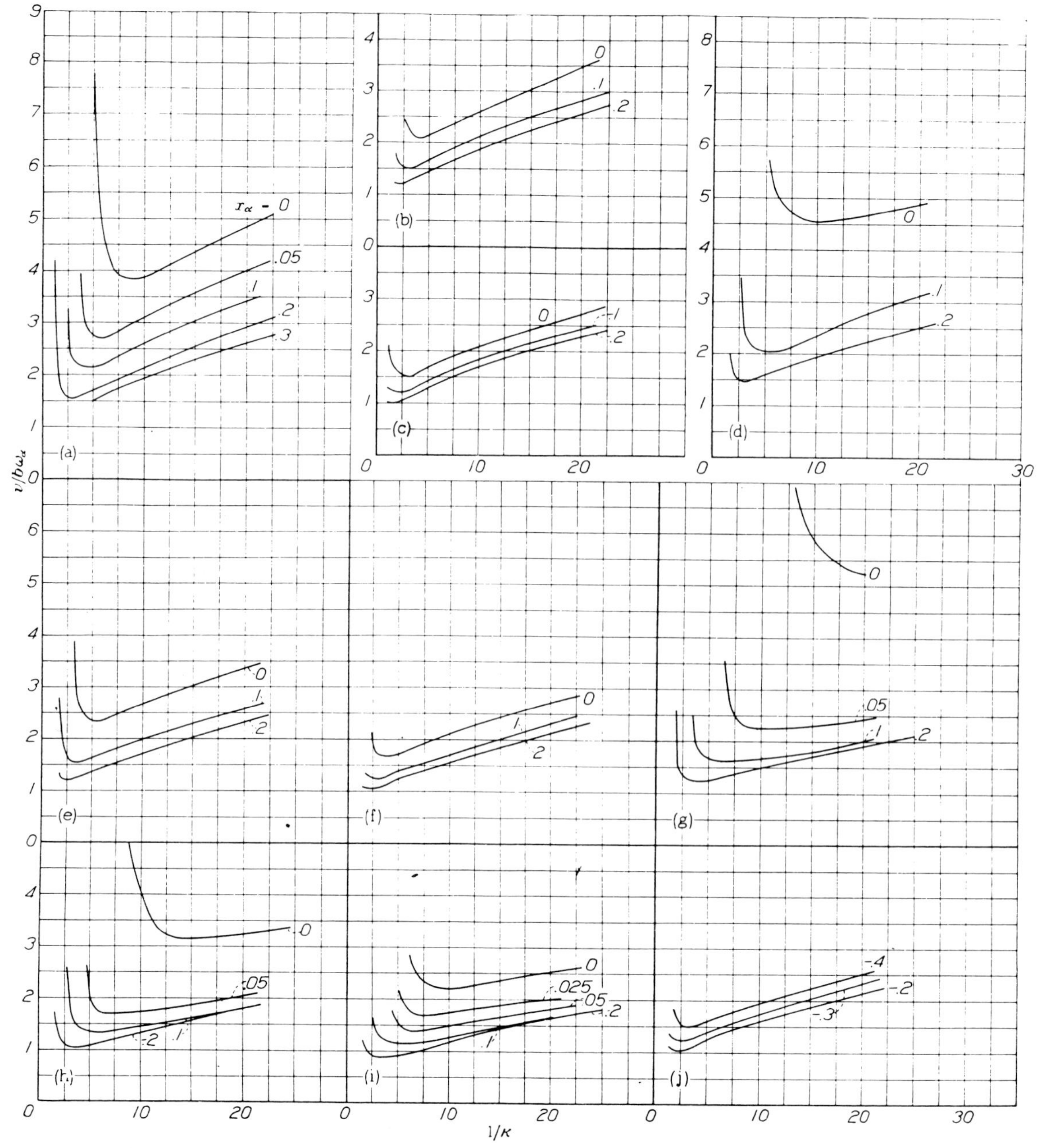

(a) $\left(\frac{\omega_h}{\omega_\alpha}\right)^2=0$; $a=-0.4$.

(b) $\left(\frac{\omega_h}{\omega_\alpha}\right)^2=0$; $a=-0.3$.

(c) $\left(\frac{\omega_h}{\omega_\alpha}\right)^2=0$; $a=-0.2$.

(d) $\left(\frac{\omega_h}{\omega_\alpha}\right)^2=1/10$; $a=-0.4$.

(e) $\left(\frac{\omega_h}{\omega_\alpha}\right)^2=1/10$; $a=-0.3$.

(f) $\left(\frac{\omega_h}{\omega_\alpha}\right)^2=1/10$; $a=-0.2$.

(g) $\left(\frac{\omega_h}{\omega_\alpha}\right)^2=1/2$; $a=-0.4$.

(h) $\left(\frac{\omega_h}{\omega_\alpha}\right)^2=1/2$; $a=-0.3$.

(i) $\left(\frac{\omega_h}{\omega_\alpha}\right)^2=1/2$; $a=-0.2$.

(j) $\left(\frac{\omega_h}{\omega_\alpha}\right)^2=1/10$; $x_\alpha=0.2$. In this section of the graph, the values on the curves refer to a, not to x_α as in sections (a) to (i).

Graph I–C (a–j).—The effect of x_α; the flutter coefficient against $1/\kappa$; $r_\alpha^2=1/4$. Case 1 (h, α).

origin. For $\kappa=1/10$, x_α must be close to zero (graph I–A (m)) to cause transition. The transition is critical; graph I–A (m) shows that a 2.5-percent change in the position of the center of gravity changes the flutter

The range of most practical importance is, however, the neighborhood of the zero frequency ratio. (For wings, the ratio is approximately 1/4.) In this range, the parameter of greatest significance is really the combination $\frac{1}{2}+a+x_\alpha$. In other words, the flutter speed is very nearly a function of the location of the center of gravity with respect to the forward quarter-chord position and not of the distance relative to the stiffness axis. Graph I–B (a) shows clearly that the value of a actually has no influence on the flutter speed. Outside of this range, that is, for larger values of ω_h/ω_α, the relationship is less simple. Graph I–B (b) shows the dependency on the center-of-gravity location for various positions of the stiffness axis a. For a constant x_α, that is, for a constant distance between the stiffness axis and the center of gravity, the flutter speed is increased as the stiffness axis (and center of gravity) is moved forward.

Graph I–C shows the flutter coefficient plotted against $1/\kappa$. The normal range of wings is included in the diagram (the heaviest wings to the right). The diagrams are arranged in order of increasing values of $(\omega_h/\omega_\alpha)^2$ and of a. An interesting result is the existence of a minimum critical speed that falls in the range of light wings ($\kappa=1/3$ to $1/5$). Graph I–C (d) gives very normal values of the parameters as used for most wings. These curves, for a *given* wing, may be taken to give the effect of altitude. Note that, for a given wing with $\kappa=1/5$ at sea level, κ becomes 1/10 at approximately 15,000 feet, with a resulting increase in the flutter speed under normal circumstances. For the case with $x_\alpha=0.2$ given in graph I–C (d), the increase in the flutter coefficient is from 1.6 to 1.95, or about 20 percent. It is possible that, for very light wings, the flutter speed might decrease with altitude until a certain altitude is reached. For high values of $1/\kappa$ (heavy wings), the flutter speed increases nearly as the square root of the wing density, $1/\kappa$.

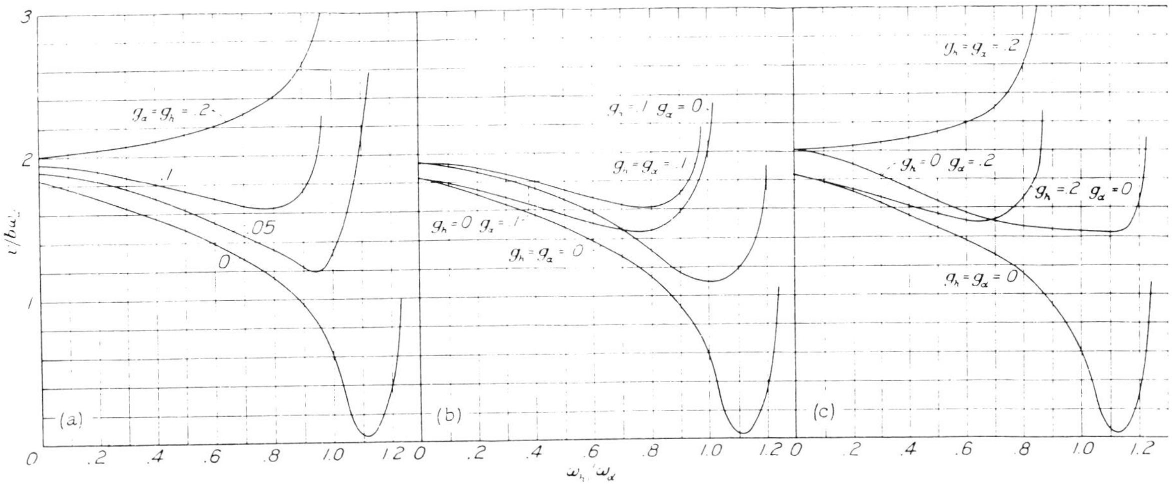

Graph I–D (a–c).—The effect of structural friction; the flutter coefficient against the frequency ratio; $\kappa=1/10$; $a=-0.2$; $x_\alpha=0.1$. Case 1 (h, α).

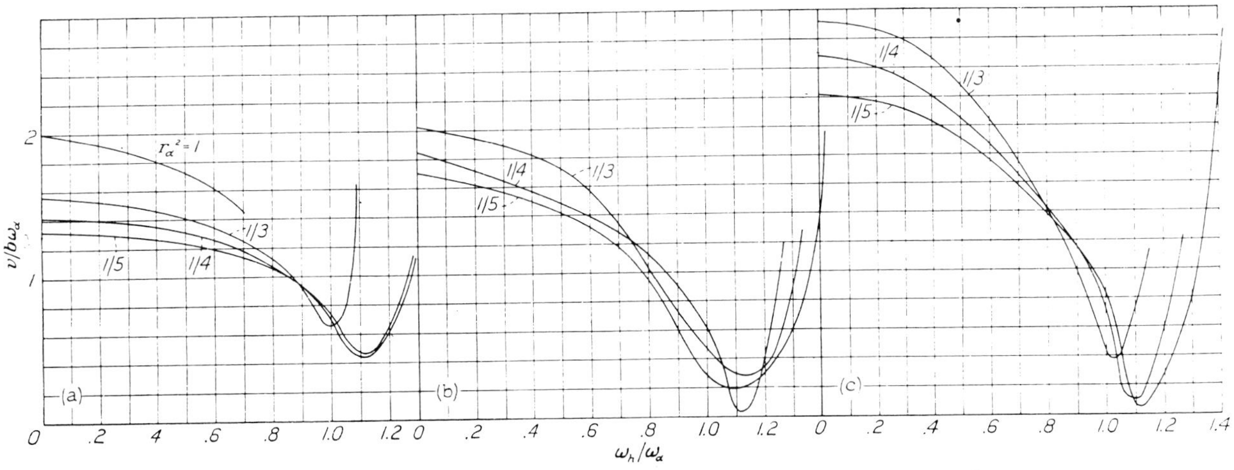

(a) $\kappa=1/5$. (b) $\kappa=1/10$ (c) $\kappa=1/20$.

Graph I–E (a–c).—The effect of radius of gyration; the flutter coefficient against the frequency ratio; $a=-0.2$, $x_\alpha=0.1$. Case 1 (h, α).

Effect of structural friction g_α, g_h.—Graph I–D is intended to show the effect of the structural friction on the critical speed. As the coefficients of friction are increased, there is a definite tendency for the often pronounced minimum flutter speed near $\omega_h/\omega_\alpha\cong1.0$ to disappear and to produce response curves of the type

207726—40—3

obtained for negative value of x_α. In the range of most practical interest ($\omega_h/\omega_\alpha \cong 0$), the torsional friction is the more important.

Effect of radius of gyration r_α.—Graph I–E is arranged in conventional order. Note that the flutter coefficient in the low ω_h/ω_α range increases with increase in the radius of gyration. This increase in the flutter coefficient does not necessarily correspond to an increase in the flutter speed; it *does* if the torsional frequency ω_α is kept constant. If the *stiffness* is kept constant, which means that ω_α is decreased as $1/r_\alpha$, the flutter speed is actually decreased, as is shown in the following table.

FLUTTER SPEED FOR CONSTANT TORSIONAL STIFFNESS

[$a=-0.2$, $x_\alpha=0.1$, $(\omega_h/\omega_\alpha)^2=0$]

κ \ r_α^2	1/5	1/4	1/3
1/5	100	97.6	92.4
1/10	91.2	88.6	84.8
1/20	84	83.2	80.2

(Values in the preceding table are given in relation to the value for $\kappa=1/5$, $r_\alpha^2=1/5$, which is the case of lowest wing density and smallest radius of gyration.) The speed corresponding to given stiffness drops if any mass is added so that r_α, the density $1/\kappa$, or both are increased. Hence, any mass added not for the purpose of increasing the stiffness or moving the center of gravity forward is detrimental.

Flutter frequency.—The flutter frequency is shown in graph I–F. It is seen, for instance, that for small values of ω_h/ω_α, the flutter frequency is around 60 percent of the torsional frequency ω_α; for higher values of the flexural frequency, the flutter frequency approaches or exceeds the torsional. This graph is primarily of interest in connection with experimental flutter research.

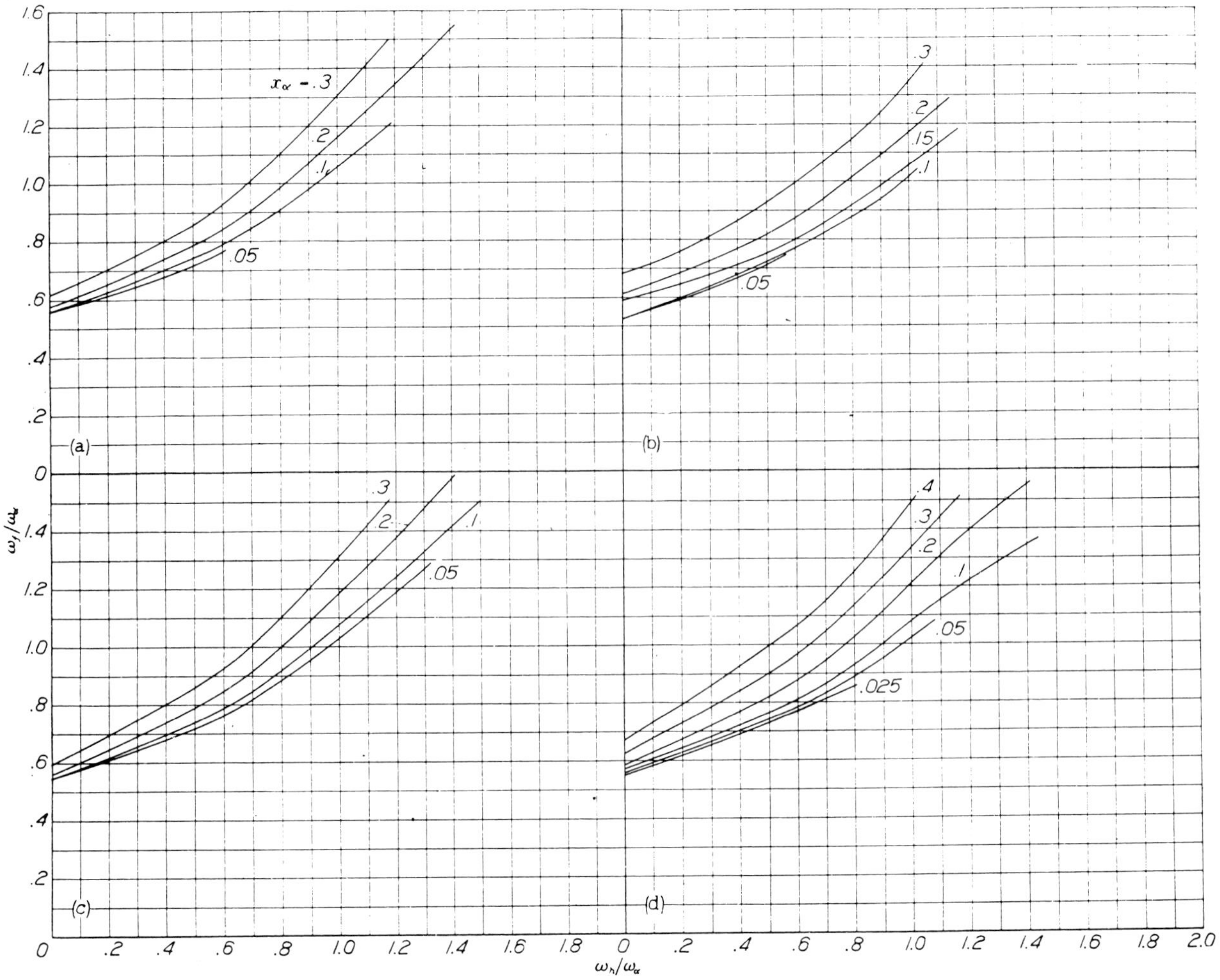

(a) $\kappa=1/5$; $a=-0.4$.
(c) $\kappa=1/10$; $a=-0.4$.
(b) $\kappa=1/5$; $a=-0.2$.
(d) $\kappa=1/10$; $a=-0.2$.

Graph I-F (a-d).—Flutter frequency ratio as dependent on x_α against frequency ratio; $r_\alpha^2=1/4$. Case 1 (h, α).

Coupling factor ξ.—Consider a two-dimensional case of flutter in which only a *part* of the total length of the (infinitely long) wing is given the second degree of freedom. This arrangement, because of the deficient coupling, exhibits a higher critical speed. Call the fraction having *both* degrees of freedom, ξ. The results are shown for several values of ξ in graph I–G.

Divergence velocity and approximate flutter formula.—It can be shown that the divergence velocity may be expressed in nondimensional form as

$$\frac{v_D}{b\omega_\alpha}=\sqrt{\frac{r_\alpha^2}{\kappa}\,\frac{\frac{1}{2}}{\frac{1}{2}+a}}$$

The divergence velocity $v_D/b\omega_\alpha$ is given in graphs I–A. This velocity is usually higher than the flutter velocity.

An empirical expression, which is useful in quickly obtaining the order of magnitude of the flutter speed for small values of ω_h/ω_α and which appears to hold very well for heavy wings (with $\kappa<1/10$) is given by

$$\frac{v_f}{b\omega_\alpha}\approx\sqrt{\frac{r_\alpha^2}{\kappa}\,\frac{\frac{1}{2}}{\frac{1}{2}+a+x_\alpha}}$$

Graph I–B (a) shows the curve obtained from the empirical expression (dashed) and a curve based on the exact values (in full lines).

CASE 2 (FLEXURE-AILERON)

The flutter coefficient for case 2 is $v/b\omega_h$. The frequency ratio ω_β/ω_h is ordinarily used as abscissa. The graphs are again arranged in order of increasing wing density. Two values of the location of the aileron hinge axis c have been included. The first value, $c=\frac{1}{2}$, or the aileron chord equal to 25 percent of the total chord, is intended to represent a wing-aileron combination; the second value, $c=0$, or the aileron chord equal to 50 percent of the total chord represents a stabilizer-elevator or a fin-rudder combination. Several values of x_β and r_β^2 and of the damping coefficients g_β and g_h have been included.

It should be mentioned that ordinarily, as shown in reference 1, case 2 differs basically from case 1 by the

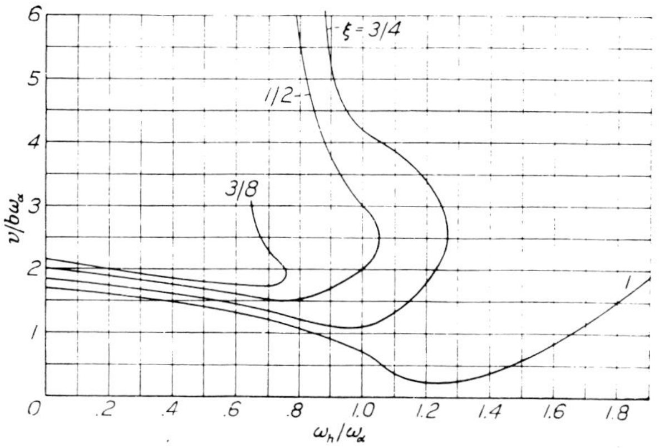

Graph I–G.—The effect of the coupling factor ξ; the flutter coefficient against the frequency ratio; $\kappa=1/10$; $a=-0.2$; $x_\alpha=0.2$.

existence of a *flutter range* extending between a lower and an upper flutter speed. This range of flutter can be reduced or eliminated by various means. It is important also to notice that, beyond a certain value of the frequency ratio ω_β/ω_h, in fact, for a value slightly greater than unity, no critical speed exists, since the critical area does not extend much beyond this point. The reduction of the center-of-gravity distance from the

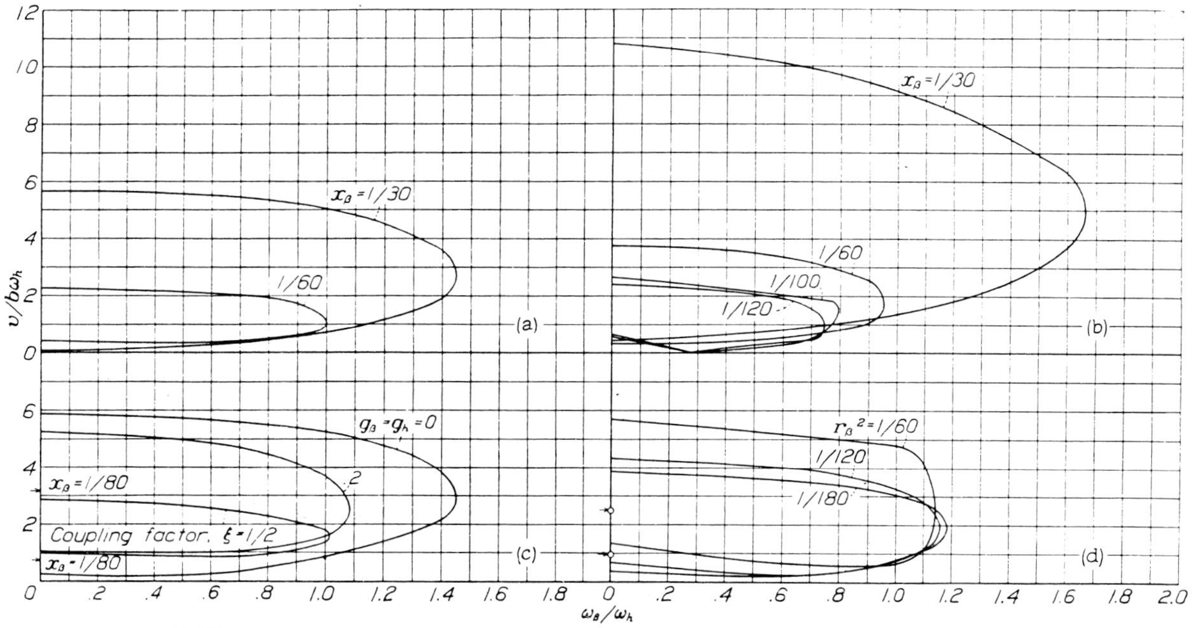

(a) Effect of x_β; $\kappa=1/5$; $r_\beta^2=1/120$.
(b) Effect of x_β; $\kappa=1/10$; $r_\beta^2=1/120$.
(c) Effect of g_β and g_h; $\kappa=1/10$; $r_\beta^2=1/60$; $x_\beta=1/40$.
(d) Effect of r_β^2; $\kappa=1/10$; $x_\beta=1/60$.

Graph II–A (a–d).—Flutter coefficient against frequency ratio; $c=\frac{1}{2}$. Case 2 (β, h).

hinge has the effect of reducing and finally eliminating the critical flutter area. Internal damping shows the same general effect. The fact that the aileron extends effectively over a shorter length is theoretically expressed by a "coupling factor" ξ, which is the length of the aileron divided by the total length of the wing executing deflection. The effect of ξ is shown in some of the graphs.

Effect of frequency ω_β/ω_h ($c=\frac{1}{2}$).—Graphs II–A (a) and (b) show the effect of varying x_β in reducing the critical area. The effect of damping is shown in graph II–A (c) and, finally, the effect of r_β^2 in graph II–A (d).

Effect of center of gravity x_β ($c=\frac{1}{2}$).—Graph II–B shows the flutter coefficient against the center-of-gravity distance x_β, giving, for two values of κ, the

be defined for each value of the frequency ratio. It is necessary then to choose the largest frequency ratio or the smallest unbalance, then to calculate the other value, and finally to choose the most practical combination, using a margin of safety.

Effect of radius of gyration r_β ($c=\frac{1}{2}$).—Graph II–C shows, for a typical wing-aileron case, the effect of changing the radius of gyration for various values of the frequency ratio.

Effect of frequency ω_β/ω_h ($c=0$).—In the preceding graphs, the hinge axis was at $c=\frac{1}{2}$. Graphs II–D, II–E, and II–F show the results for $c=0$. The curves are arranged in order and show the effect of x_β, r_β^2, g_h, and g_β for $\kappa=\frac{1}{5}$ and $\frac{1}{10}$. One curve is also included for $\kappa=\frac{1}{2}$ (graph II–D (d)).

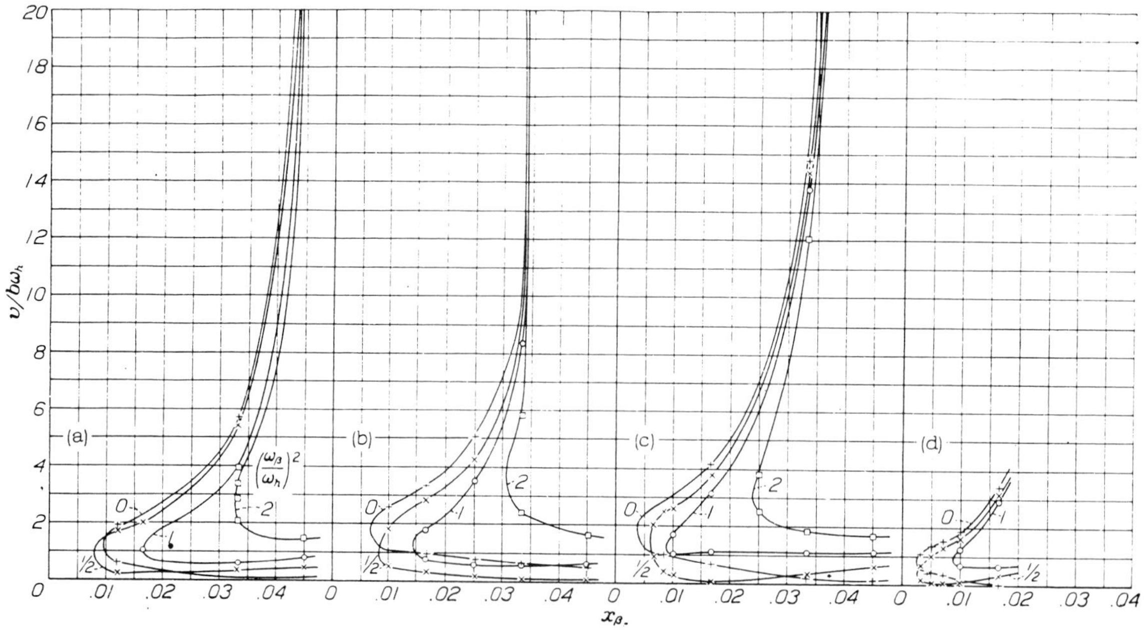

(a) $c=\frac{1}{2}$; $\kappa=\frac{1}{5}$; $r_\beta^2=\frac{1}{120}$. (b) $c=\frac{1}{2}$; $\kappa=\frac{1}{5}$; $r_\beta^2=\frac{1}{60}$. (c) $c=\frac{1}{2}$; $\kappa=\frac{1}{10}$; $r_\beta^2=\frac{1}{120}$. (d) $c=\frac{2}{3}$; $\kappa=\frac{1}{5}$; $r_\beta^2=\frac{1}{500}$.

Graph II–B (a–d).—Flutter coefficient against x_β for various frequency ratios. Case 2 (β, h).

effect of varying the frequency ratio ω_β/ω_h at three values of r_β^2. Note that for large x_β (beyond normal range) the type of flutter reverts to that of case 1; that is, the upper flutter speed becomes infinite for a certain value of x_β.

It is important to notice, by considering each curve in this figure, that x_β must be decreased below a certain value, which is rather critical, in order to avoid flutter. If x_β is larger than this value, the lower flutter speed remains at a virtually constant, small value. The frequency ratio exhibits a similar effect; that is, flutter is eliminated beyond a certain frequency ratio often greater than unity, whereas for smaller ratios, the lower flutter speed remains at a low, nearly constant value. In other words, a critical frequency ratio can be defined for each value of the unbalance and, inversely, a definite critical value of the unbalance can

Effect of center of gravity x_β ($c=0$).—The figures are given in graph II–E, arranged as usual.

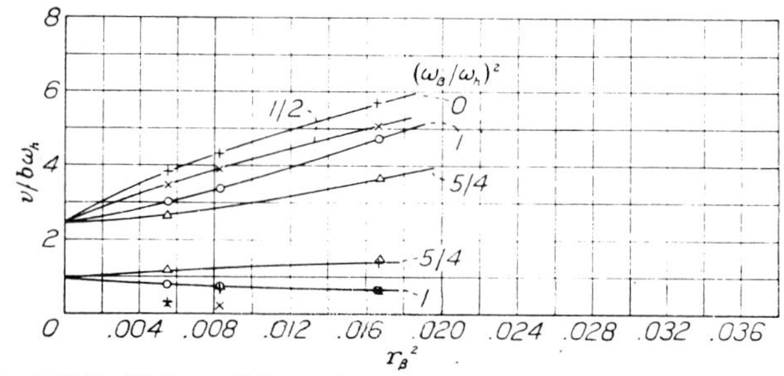

Graph II–C.—Flutter coefficient against r_β^2 for various frequency ratios; $c=\frac{1}{2}$; $\kappa=\frac{1}{10}$; $x_\beta=\frac{1}{60}$. Case 2 (β, h).

Effect of coupling factor ($c=0$) —In graph II–F the effect of the coupling factor ξ is shown for an extreme case of unbalance (x_β large). The superimposed effect

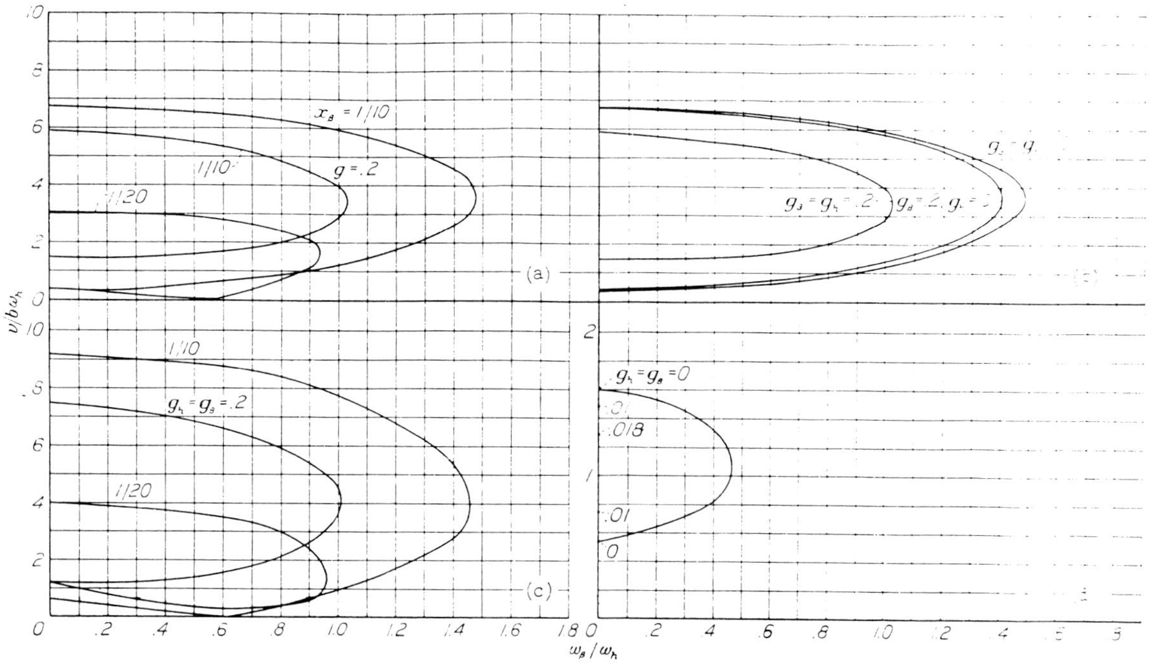

(a) $\kappa = 1/5$; $r_\beta^2 = 1/20$; $x_\beta = 1/10, 1/20$.
(b) $\kappa = 1/5$; $r_\beta^2 = 1/20$; $x_\beta = 1/10$.
(c) $\kappa = 1/5$; $r_\beta^2 = 1/10$; $x_\beta = 1/10, 1/20$.
(d) $\kappa = 1/2$; $r_\beta^2 = 1/20$.

Graph II-D (a-d).—Flutter coefficient against frequency ratio, showing effect of x_β, g_β, and g_h; $c=0$. Case 2 (β, h).

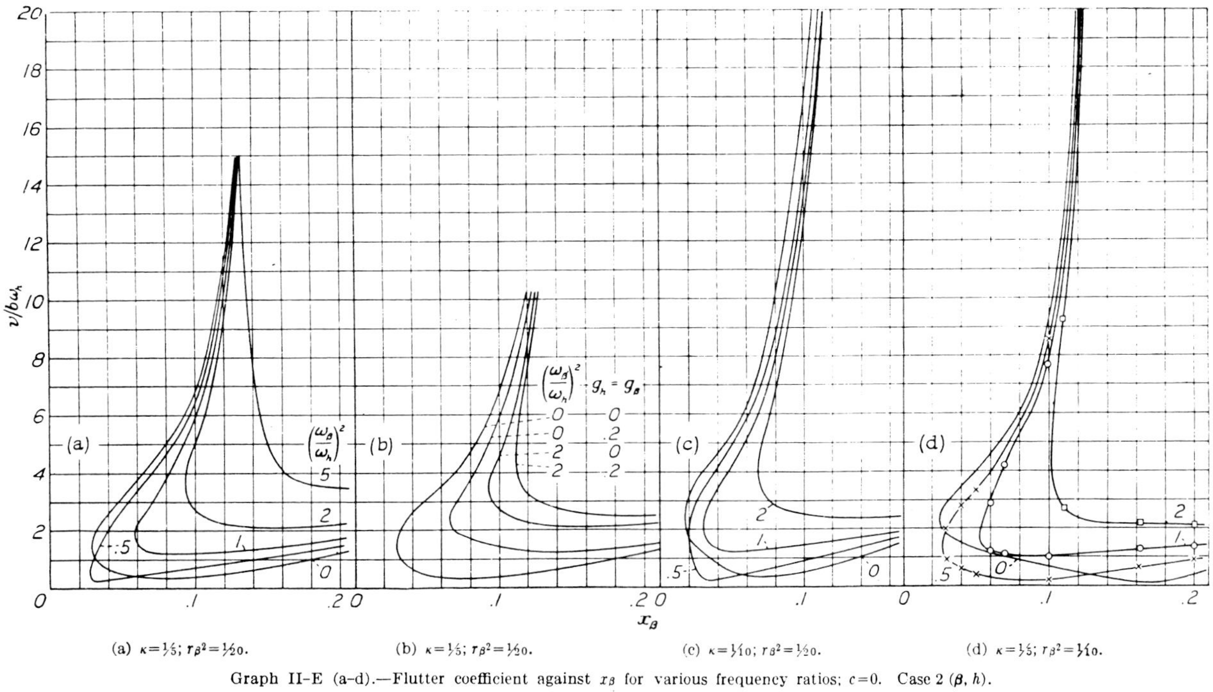

(a) $\kappa = 1/5$; $r_\beta^2 = 1/20$.
(b) $\kappa = 1/5$; $r_\beta^2 = 1/20$.
(c) $\kappa = 1/10$; $r_\beta^2 = 1/20$.
(d) $\kappa = 1/5$; $r_\beta^2 = 1/10$.

Graph II-E (a-d).—Flutter coefficient against x_β for various frequency ratios; $c=0$. Case 2 (β, h).

of damping is shown for the zero frequency ratio. Notice how the coupling factor ($\xi \rightarrow 0$) gradually eliminates the flutter area.

CASE 3 (TORSION-AILERON)

Three graphs, III–A, III–B, and III–C, are presented. There is a similarity to case 2. Graph III–A shows how the internal damping increases the lower flutter

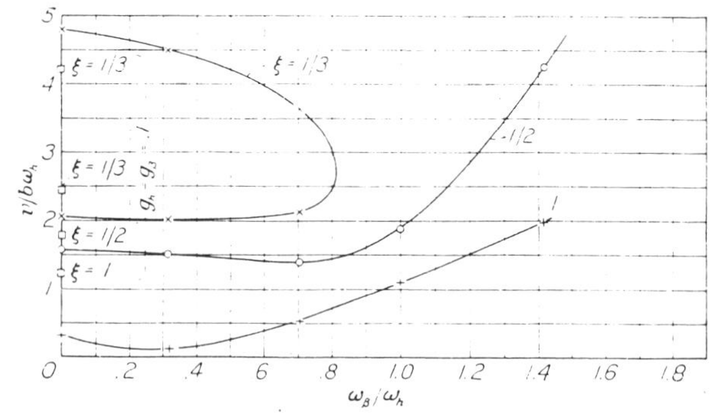

Graph II-F.—Effect of coupling factor ξ; flutter coefficient against frequency ratio; $c=0$; $\kappa=1/5$; $r_\beta^2=1/6$; $x_\beta=1/4$ (an extreme case of unbalance). Also effect of friction for $\omega_\beta/\omega_h=0$.

speed. Graph III–B represents data taken from an actual case of a light wing with a smaller aileron. Note the striking similarity to case 2. For the value $x_\beta=0.0066$ (completely unbalanced aileron), $\omega_\beta/\omega_\alpha$ must be greater than 0.6 to avoid flutter; for the more normal value $x_\beta=0.002$, $\omega_\beta/\omega_\alpha$ need only be $\geqq 0.1$. The flutter area is eliminated by reducing x_β to a slightly smaller value.

Case 3 (torsion-aileron) is probably of less practical importance because the elimination of flutter for case

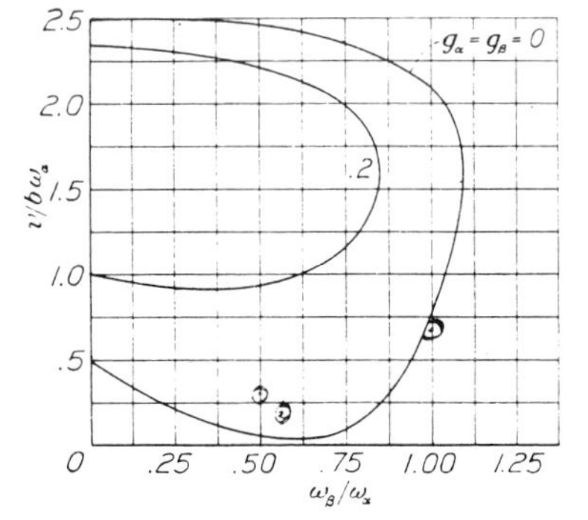

Graph III-A.—Effect of friction coefficients g_α, g_β; flutter coefficient against frequency ratio; $c=0.5$; $\kappa=1/10$; $a=-0.4$; $r_\alpha^2=1/4$; $x_\beta=1/80$; $r_\beta^2=1/160$. Case 3.

2 ordinarily excludes the possibility of flutter in case 3; but it is noted that, in order to eliminate mass coupling in the torsion-aileron case, a complete balance of the aileron in the ordinary sense ($x_\beta=0$) is not quite sufficient. It is actually found in the case of a heavy wing and no internal friction (with $x_\beta=0$) that the flutter speed is low, particularly near $\omega_\beta=\omega_\alpha$. Even a slight amount of friction, however, is sufficient to cancel the cause of this flutter. Graph III–C (fairly heavy wing) shows that, for no friction, a small overbalance ($x_\beta<0$) is necessary to eliminate flutter. For light wings, the effect is less pronounced and $x_\beta=0$ is usually sufficient. It may be observed from the original set of equations that true balance against rotation implies $r_\beta^2+(c-a)\,x_\beta=0$.

THREE DEGREES OF FREEDOM

In order to familiarize the reader with the complete case of three degrees of freedom and its relationship to the three subcases, a set of typical figures is shown. The constants used are the same as those in the numerical example (p. 8) with some additions. Case

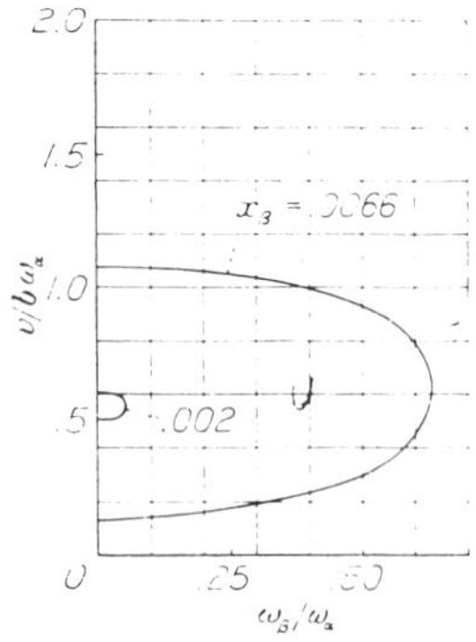

Graph III-B.—Effect of x_β; flutter coefficient against frequency ratio; $c=0.6$; $\kappa=1/4$; $a=-0.4$; $r_\alpha^2=1/4$; $r_\beta^2=0.0012$. Case 3(α, β).

1 is shown in figure 1 under the numerical example. The flutter coefficient $v/b\omega_\alpha=1.542$.

Case 2 is shown in figure 5; each part of the figure refers to different combinations of x_β and ω_β/ω_h. No flutter occurs for the combinations shown in figures 5 (a) and 5 (b) because of the balanced aileron and none in figure 5 (d) because of the large aileron frequency. For the combination shown in figure 5 (c), there is a normal range of flutter with two flutter points shown.

Case 3 is shown in figure 6; each part refers, respectively, to the same aileron parameters used in case 2. (Note that ω_h/ω_α is 1/4 in all cases.) The combinations

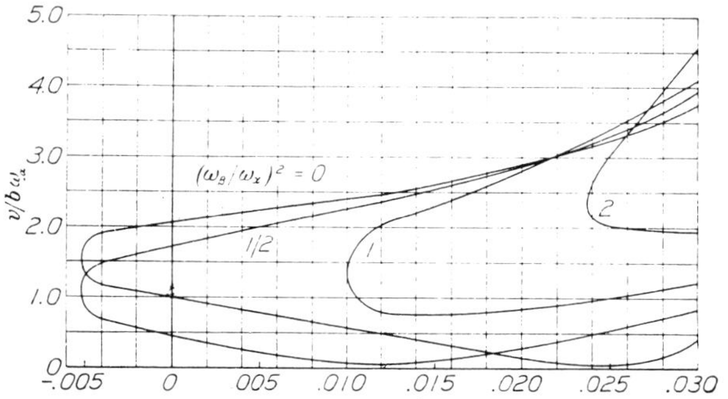

Graph III-C.—Flutter coefficient against x_β for various frequency ratios. $c=0.5$; $\kappa=1/10$; $r_\alpha^2=1/4$; $r_\beta^2=1/160$; $a=-0.4$. Case 3.

shown in figures 6 (a) and 6 (b) are again stable because of the aileron mass balance. For the arrangement shown in figure 6 (d), the aileron frequency is not high enough to prevent flutter as it did in case 2. Conditions are still worse for the combination shown in figure 6 (c).

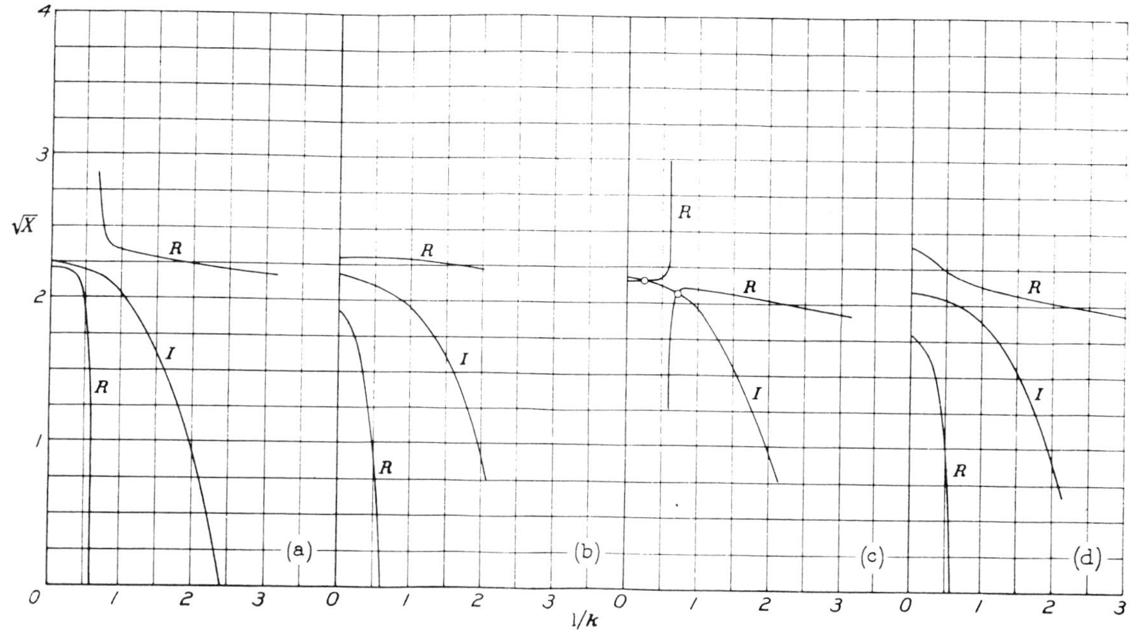

(a) $\left(\frac{\omega_\beta}{\omega_h}\right)^2=0;\ x_\beta=0.$ (b) $\left(\frac{\omega_\beta}{\omega_h}\right)^2=3/2;\ x_\beta=0.$ (c) $\left(\frac{\omega_\beta}{\omega_h}\right)^2=0;\ x_\beta=0.0066.$ (d) $\left(\frac{\omega_\beta}{\omega_h}\right)^2=3/2;\ x_\beta=0.0066.$

FIGURE 5.—Case 2. The roots $\sqrt{X}$ of the real and the imaginary equations against $1/k$. Same parameters as in numerical example except as indicated.

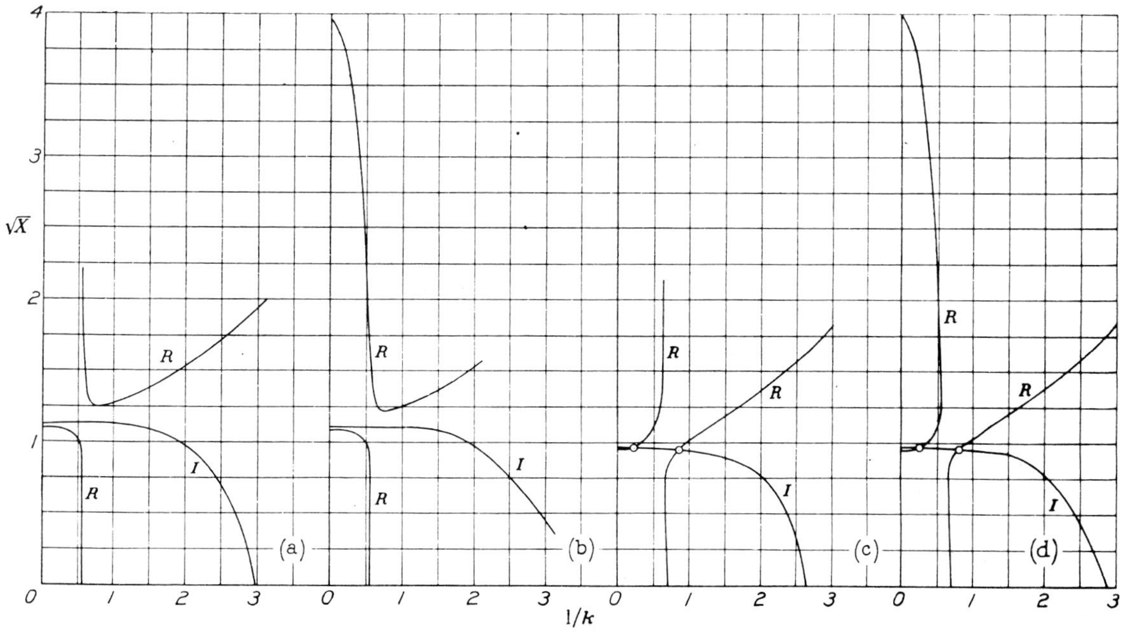

(a) $\left(\frac{\omega_\beta}{\omega_\alpha}\right)^2=0;\ x_\beta=0.$ (b) $\left(\frac{\omega_\beta}{\omega_\alpha}\right)^2=3/32;\ x_\beta=0.$ (c) $\left(\frac{\omega_\beta}{\omega_\alpha}\right)^2=0;\ x_\beta=0.0066.$ (d) $\left(\frac{\omega_\beta}{\omega_\alpha}\right)^2=3/32;\ x_\beta=0.0066.$

FIGURE 6.—Case 3. The roots $\sqrt{X}$ of the real and the imaginary equations against $1/k$. Same parameters in numerical example except as indicated.

For the case of three degrees of freedom, figure 7 shows the results arranged in the same order as under cases 2 and 3. For the conditions given in figures 7 (a) and 7 (b), flutter existed only in case 1. The flutter point shown is therefore essentially case 1 flutter. The value of the flutter coefficient, however, has actually *decreased* from its case 1 value of 1.542 to 0.70 and 0.825, respectively.

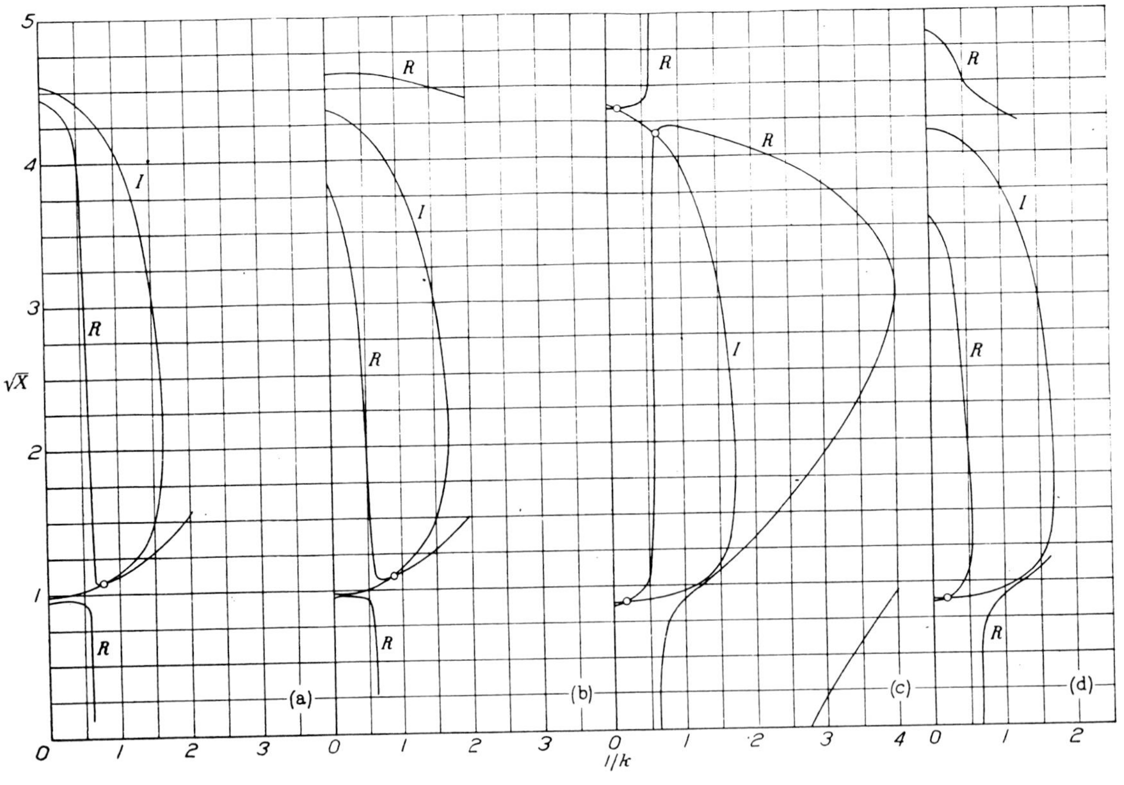

(a) $\left(\frac{\omega_\beta}{\omega_h}\right)^2=0$; $x_\beta=0$. (b) $\left(\frac{\omega_\beta}{\omega_h}\right)^2=3/2$; $x_\beta=0$. (c) $\left(\frac{\omega_\beta}{\omega_h}\right)^2=0$; $x_\beta=0.0066$. (d) $\left(\frac{\omega_\beta}{\omega_h}\right)^2=3/2$; $x_\beta=0.0066$.

FIGURE 7.—Three degrees of freedom. The roots $\sqrt{X}$ of the real and the imaginary equations against $1/k$. Same parameters as in numerical example except as indicated.

For the arrangement shown in figure 7 (d), flutter exists in cases 1 and 3. Here the ranges completely merge, indicating stability at only very low speed. Flutter exists in all three cases for the combination shown in figure 7 (c). The case 2 flutter can be recognized, almost unchanged, while again the flutter ranges of case 1 and case 3 have merged, as in figure 7 (d).

Figure 8 has been included to show that there is a considerable lowering of the flutter speed for low values of the aileron frequency even though the aileron is balanced. This condition is probably not of primary concern because a small amount of friction, particularly g_α, will restore the flutter speed to its full (case 1) value. It is to be noted, however, that a slight overbalance ($x_\beta<0$) may be desirable.

TRANSITION TO THREE-DIMENSIONAL FLUTTER PROBLEMS

The previous theory relates to two-dimensional flutter and, strictly, to a wing of infinite length. The second restriction is not very troublesome, the aspect-ratio, or span, effect being relatively unimportant and by no means as great as the aspect-ratio effect associated with stationary flows. It may be disregarded

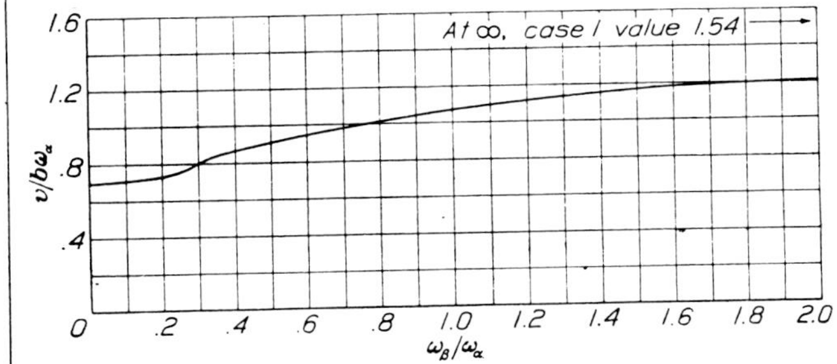

FIGURE 8.—Flutter coefficient against frequency ratio $\omega_\beta/\omega_\alpha$. Three degrees of freedom. $\kappa=0.25$; $a=-0.4$; $x_\alpha=0.2$; $r_\alpha^2=1/4$; $c=0.6$; $x_\beta=0$; $r_\beta^2=0.0012$; $g_\alpha=g_h=0$.

and tacitly considered as a safety factor, since an air speed of the order of a few percent more than that in two-dimensional flow is necessary to cause flutter.

Consider the case of a rectangular cantilever wing. Some authors have attempted a solution on the assumption that the response curves in torsion and deflection under normal conditions (zero air speed) may be used in the flutter theory. It is contended that this assumption is false. Several rather interesting experimental results will be presented in the next section, which show directly and indirectly that the modes in flutter differ radically from the ordinary ones. The following questions arise: (1) Does the wing flutter in the first, second, or third, etc., bending "mode"? (2) Are these modes in any way related to the ordinary types of vibration modes?

Consider first the case of a very high bending mode. It is useful to consider the two-dimensional case as representing the "averages" of parameters and variables of the three-dimensional case. The variable h now appearing in the (two-dimensional) equations refers to the "average" h which approaches zero even though the local h in the loops is very large. It is, furthermore, evident that the average curvatures are greater, the greater the mode. Both these conditions are equivalent to a large coefficient of internal damping, since the work lost per cycle refers to a very small average h.

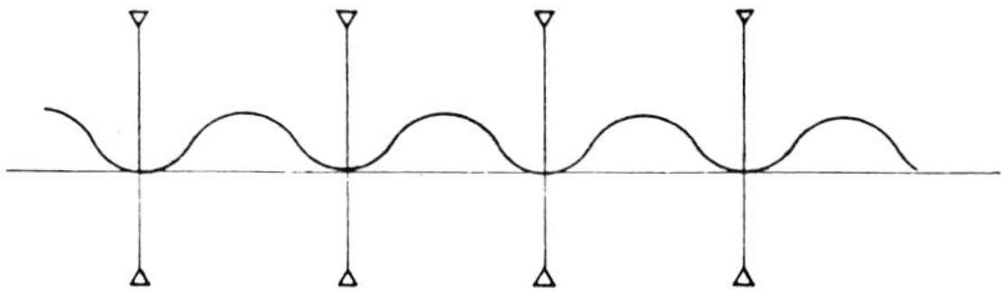

FIGURE 9.—Schematic figure for higher-order bending mode of cantilever wing restrained by wires and with deflections in phase.

The coefficient, in fact, rapidly approaches an infinite value as the number n of the mode is increased. It is probable that the second "flutter" mode involves a coefficient of damping 20 to 50 times larger than that of the first.

A study of the graphs with specific reference to the effect of damping shows that higher flutter modes can be expected only under very special circumstances. This fact does not mean that flutter occurs in the lowest (zero air speed) bending mode.

The bending frequency in flutter of a cantilever beam is determined by a certain minimum condition. The wing will, of course, flutter at the lowest speed possible. It will, therefore, not assume its lowest (stationary) bending mode but will tend to assume a mode of a higher frequency. Since this higher frequency tends to uncouple the h degree of freedom, the actual response ordinarily happens to be a cross between the first and the second modes. Large internal friction will tend to push the response closer to the first mode. The result is a flutter speed distinctly lower than that calculated on the basis of the frequency of the ordinary fundamental bending mode. The flutter speed calculated by using the lowest bending frequency is too favorable. In the case of wings of small internal friction (solid metal wings), the actual flutter speed is only about 0.9, the speed calculated on the basis of the lowest bending frequency. In the case of conventional wings, the error is apparently in the order of only 1 or 2 percent, a fortunate coincidence because it permits the use of a small experimental-empirical correction. This point of view is in harmony with the Rayleigh principle, which states that any response function whatsoever corresponds to a frequency higher than that of the fundamental.

To recapitulate: *The bending frequency involved in the flutter of a cantilever wing is greater than that observed at zero air speed; the more so, the lower the internal damping of the wing structure.*

This interesting phenomenon is demonstrated by the photograph of the flutter of a uniform cantilever beam (see fig. 18) presented in the experimental section, which shows that the maximum amplitude is not at the tip but is rather close to the middle of the span.

Another very convincing experimental proof of this phenomenon, given in the experimental section of this paper, is that a counterweight at the tip section in front of the center of gravity actually *lowers* the flutter speed of a uniform cantilever wing. For a relatively small counterweight, the tip section is beyond a node in the h curve. In this same connection, another rather remarkable experiment was made: A cantilever wing flutters at about 200 miles per hour. The point where the node of the second bending mode (at zero air speed) intersects the torsional stiffness axis was fixed by connecting this point by wires to the tunnel walls. The wing subsequently fluttered at 150 miles per hour. The flutter stopped when the wire broke! The explanation is that the bracing wires "couple" a bending mode that was previously entirely "uncoupled." It should be noted that the frequency actually involved in this flutter is again in excess of that of the second bending mode (at zero air speed); large forces are therefore transmitted through the wire supports from the walls.

In order to illustrate more convincingly how the support wires lower the flutter speed, reference is made to figure 9, which shows a high-order bending mode of a wing. If this bending frequency is about equal to the torsional frequency, the lowest flutter speed is obtained. When the support wires are removed, the wing will tend to vibrate about a fixed mass center line, with the result that the average h deflection becomes zero and all h couplings disappear. The α moments and the h forces transmitted to the support are good measures of what may be called the effective values of α and h when the two-dimensional theory is applied to three-dimensional cases. For instance, the transmittal of a small h force to the support indicates that the positive and the negative h values very nearly cancel. The h effect, although locally large, may very nearly cancel itself. This fact does not prevent the use of a certain (small) average or effective h in the calculations. With no internal friction, the flutter speed is not changed. As was pointed out before, the use of the small effective h for higher modes is, in reality, equivalent to employing a greatly increased coefficient of internal friction.

This discussion and associated experiments lead to the important conclusion: A bracing wire *may* lower the critical speed of a cantilever wing or fin. It usually does lower the critical speed when the internal damping in the structure is low.

For a rectangular cantilever wing, there is no difficulty in regard to the other parameters. With the bending modes considered known, the variables α, β, and h were given simply as average values and used in the two-dimensional solution. Inspection shows that the flutter speed of a uniform cantilever wing is essentially that of the two-dimensional case involving the same parameters and the proper frequency ratio.

A cantilever wing of normal tapered shape will next be considered. It is assumed that there is a similarity in construction along the span for each cross section. The mass is put equal to a constant times the square of the chord; static moments, to the third power; and the moments of inertia, to the fourth power of the chord. Further, the air force is proportional to the chord and the acting moments are proportional to the second power.

Various weight factors of the form $(b/b_r)^n f(x)dx$ are obtained, where $f(x)$ is a weighted wing parameter and x is measured along the span. If the reference section is chosen in such a location that, for a particular $n=m$,

$$\int_0^t \left(\frac{b}{b_r}\right)^m f(x)dx = \int_0^t f(x)dx$$

which is always possible, then

$$\int \left(\frac{b}{b_r}\right)^{m+1} f(x)dx \cong \int f(x)dx$$

In other words, the proper choice of a reference section renders the weight factors of approximately equal magnitudes. If the reference section is taken too close to the tip of the wing, there will be a certain positive correction; if chosen too close inboard, there will be a negative correction. The correct value is thus virtually confined between definite limits. The most representative section will lie close to the three-quarter semispan location.

In the two-dimensional case, the length along the span is considered to be equal to unity and this unity is treated as being large as far as span effects are concerned. If the length is different for the two variables considered, a slight modification of the theory is necessary. Each length is considered to be long enough to permit disregard of aspect-ratio corrections for the air forces.

This sort of consideration is of interest chiefly in the case of ailerons and tail surfaces. The equation giving the equilibrium of the ailerons refers only to the length of the aileron. The included area of the h curve is sometimes a small fraction of the total area under the h curve. This fraction will be called ξ.

The solution of the deflection-aileron case is given in reference 1 by

$$\overline{M}_{a\alpha} = \begin{vmatrix} \overline{R}_{b\beta}+iI_{b\beta} & R_{bh}+iI_{bh} \\ R_{c\beta}+iI_{c\beta} & R_{ch}+iI_{ch} \end{vmatrix} = 0$$

and with the effect of ξ:

$$\overline{M}_{a_\alpha} = \begin{vmatrix} \overline{R}_{b\beta}+iI_{b\beta} & \xi(R_{bh}+iI_{bh}) \\ R_{c\beta}+iI_{c\beta} & R_{ch}+iI_{ch} \end{vmatrix} = 0$$

It is noticed that the factor $\xi<1$ describes a certain uncoupling of the system. The calculation of flutter speed can be performed for any coupling factor ξ. Again it should be remembered that the free-vibration modes are not identical with the flutter modes. A tendency exists for ξ to approach unity since the aileron forces the motion of the wing.

EXPERIMENTAL FLUTTER RESEARCH

GENERAL

The purpose of the experimental research was, first, to check the theory as regards accuracy and, second, to provide a basis for an understanding of problems met with in airplanes.

These tests, about one hundred in all, were conducted in the N. A. C. A. 8-foot high-speed tunnel. (See fig. 10.) In order to protect the propeller, a heavy wire screen was inserted in the test section immediately behind the flutter model. For convenience, models having a flutter speed below 300 miles per hour were tested.

The procedure followed was to increase the tunnel speed slowly until flutter appeared. If the flutter was of a violent type, the load was immediately dropped to save the model. In the tests on ailerons, the lower branch of the flutter curve was similarly obtained. The upper end of the range was obtained by the following method: The aileron was kept in place by restraining wires attached to its rear end and running across the tunnel. By manual operation of the wires from the outside, the arrangement could be conveyed through the dangerous range; on slackening the wires, the operator would receive indication of incipient flutter until the speed had increased above the dangerous range. When the upper stable region had been reached, the wires were completely released and the conventional flutter-test procedure was reversed; that is, the tunnel speed was slowly decreased until the violent flutter appeared. The restraining wires were then immediately tightened, and the speed was noted. The effect of the very fine wire was shown to be negligible in the released condition.

DESCRIPTION OF WING FLUTTER MODELS

All wings tested were cantilever wings and are based on the section given in the following table.

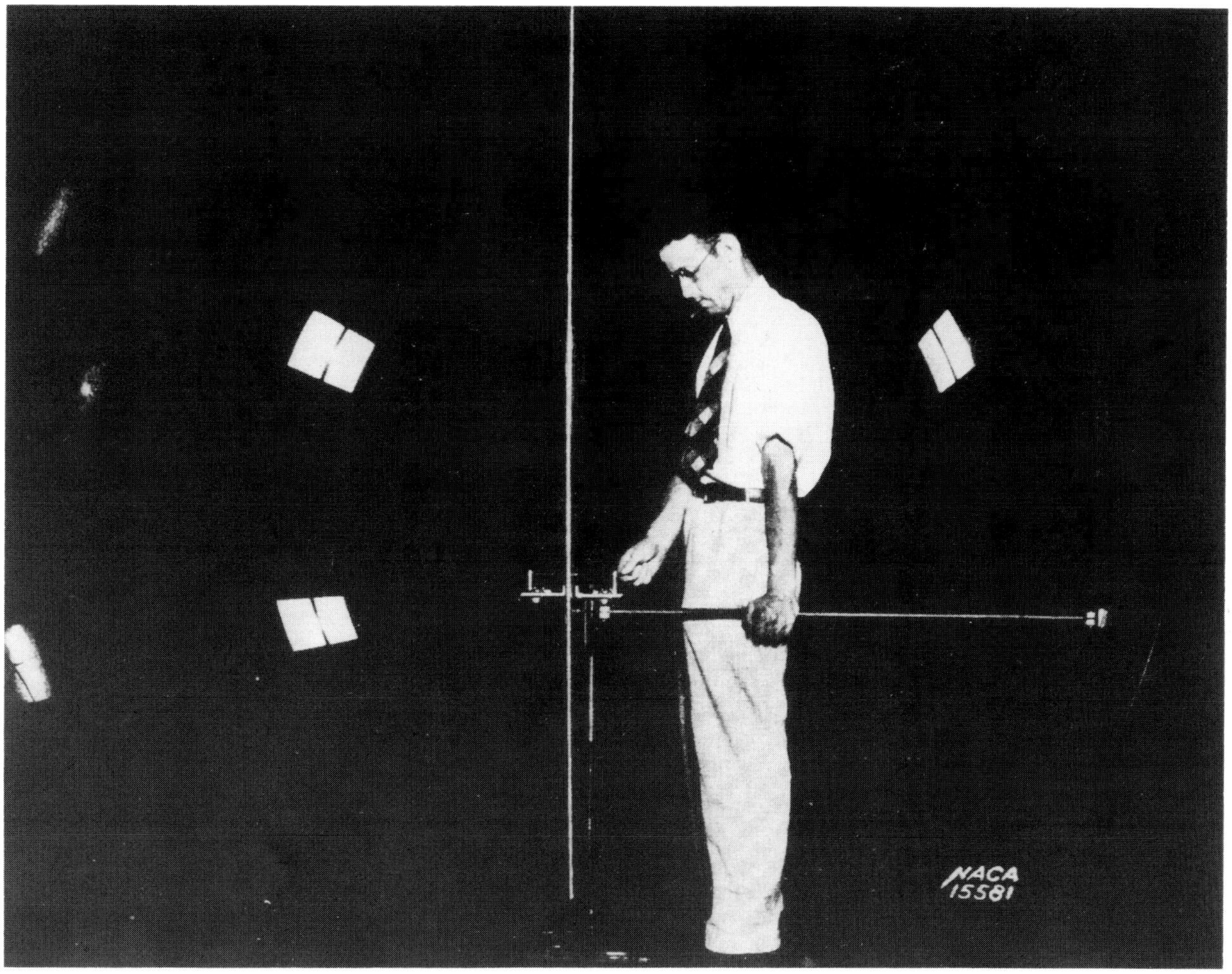

FIGURE 10.—Installation of wing 1 in 8-foot high-speed tunnel. The stop shown was used in only a few initial tests.

AIRFOIL SHAPE USED IN FLUTTER TESTS

Station x (percent chord)	Ordinate y (maximum thickness = 1)
0	0
1.25	.460
2.5	.600
5	.740
7.5	.820
10	.880
15	.940
20	.960
30	1.000
40	.960
50	.900
60	.780
70	.620
80	.440
90	.240
95	.132
100	.020

The frequencies of the various wings are given in the main table of experimental data (table I). All section constants were obtained both by calculation and by direct testing. The basic section has its center of gravity at 42.5 percent from the leading edge. The stiffness axis is at 32 percent but was artificially put at 30 percent in the case 1 tests by chordwise cuts. (See figs. 11 to 13.)

In addition to obtaining the flutter speed of the plain wings, the effects of restraining wires, of mass balancing counterweights in various locations, and of large nacelles both at the wing and some distance away from it were studied. Experimental data are included in table I. In the aileron tests, the effects of mass balancing, hinge location, frequency, and friction were investigated.

Wing 1.—Wing 1 (see fig. 10) was a rectangular cantilever wing model of ½-inch duralumin plate of 12-inch chord by ½-inch thickness by a free length of 6 feet 9 inches perforated with closely drilled ½-inch holes and covered by a $\frac{6}{1000}$-inch sheet of duralumin to give a smooth surface. The constants can be obtained from data in the experimental table.

Wings 2, 3, and 4.—Wings 2, 3, and 4 represent a series of cantilever wings of the same root section (1-foot chord by ½ inch thick), the same span (6 feet 9 inches), but having taper ratios, respectively, of 1:1, 2:1 and 4:1. (See figs. 11, 12, and 13.) The wings are made of duralumin and are constructed to give similarity in strength and mass distribution. Note that the detail at or near the tips is a scaled-down replica of the detail at the root. The stiffness axis a is put at 30 percent chord or $a=-0.4$ by means of chordwise cuts.

The three types of wing 2 (2A, 2B, and 2C) were so designated because the first one, 2A, finally showed a

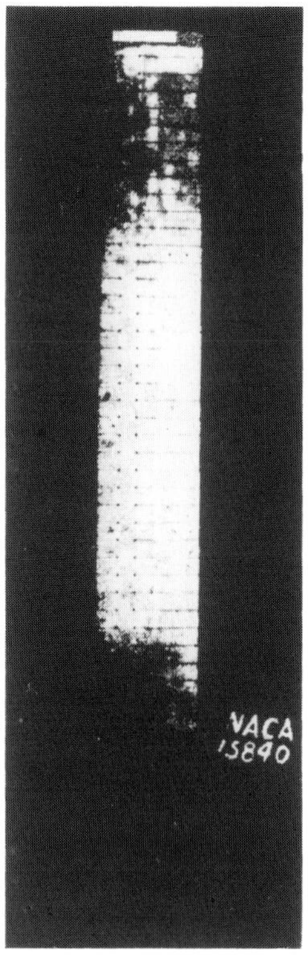

FIGURE 11.—Rectangular cantilever wing 2A. Note chordwise cuts used for purpose of lowering torsional frequency and for placing stiffness axis at 30 percent chord from leading edge.

crack and had to be replaced with 2B, which is almost identical. Wing 2B finally broke at the root, was repaired by shortening it, and was used for some tests under the designation 2C.

Wing 5.—Wing 5 was also a solid duralumin rectangular cantilever wing of 1-foot chord, 4-foot length, and 1-inch thickness at the maximum ordinate; it was used for aileron testing. (See fig. 14) Three ailerons were tested, 14, 24, and 34 inches long with 2, 3, and 4 hinges, respectively. Most of the tests were performed on the 24-inch aileron (aileron A II).

Tests were made for different spring-restraints on the hinge, with a balance counterweight on the outboard end (fig. 15) and with a special arrangement permitting the changing of the hinge axis from the forward edge of the aileron to about 30 percent of the aileron chord behind the center of gravity.

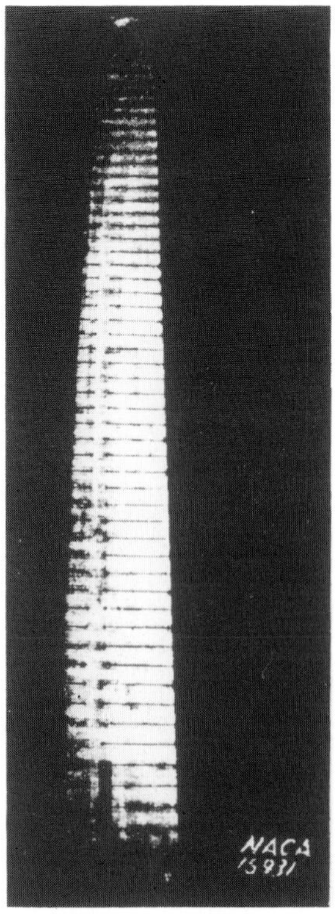

FIGURE 12.—Tapered cantilever wing 3; taper ratio both in chord and thickness is 2:1. Dimensional similarity of cross section and cuts.

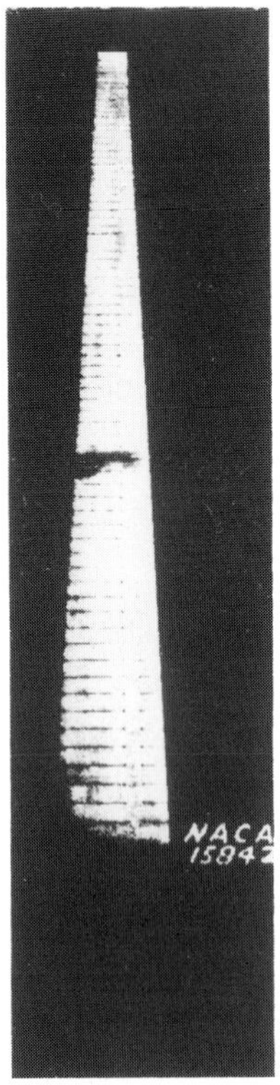

FIGURE 13.—Tapered cantilever wing 4; taper ratio, 4:1.

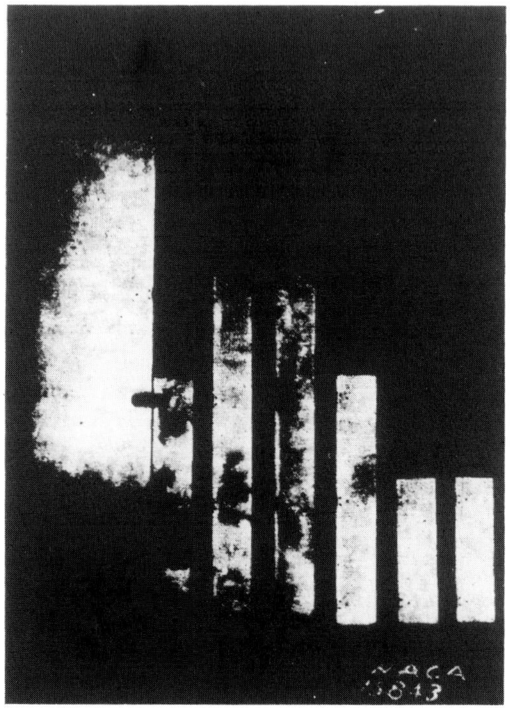

FIGURE 14.—Cantilever wing 5 used for aileron tests.

Wings 6 and 7.—Wings 6 and 7 are model wings of normal density built by covering a balsa structure with 1/16-inch mahogany. Wing 6 has the same external dimensions as wing 2 (fig. 16). Wing 7 has a root chord of 18 inches, a maximum thickness of 1.5 inches, and a taper ratio of 3:2 (fig. 16). All tapered wings were tapered equally in chord and thickness.

DISCUSSION OF EXPERIMENTAL RESULTS

The scheme already discussed of introducing flutter-bending modes completely fits the experimental results into the theoretical picture. Figure 17 shows the theoretical flutter speed for wings 2A, 2B, 3, and 4 with the experimental points plotted. Wing 2A with

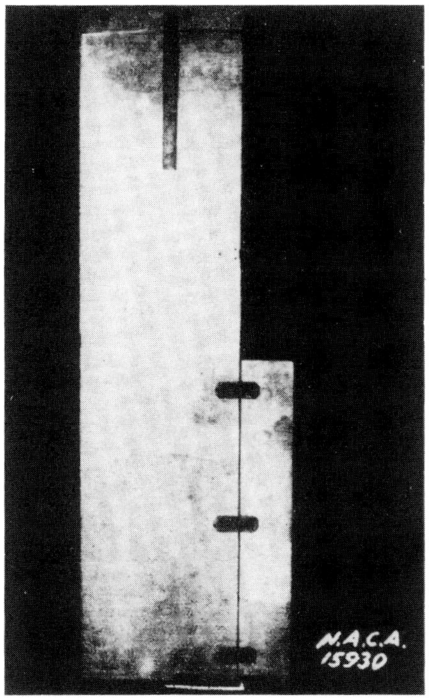

FIGURE 15.—Wing 5 with aileron mass balanced by counterweight at outboard end.

a flutter speed of 202 miles per hour obviously bends in a "first" flutter mode that approaches the second bending mode in appearance and frequency (fig. 18). The flutter frequency calculated on the basis of this bending mode closely checks the measured flutter frequency (fig. 19). Wing 3 checks equally well; its bending frequencies are noted in table I. Wing 4, the most tapered one, obviously collapsed (fig. 20) in the second flutter mode. (See fig. 17.) On this assumption, its experimental flutter speed also fits well in figure 17.

Since the effect of the bending mode was brought so strongly into the picture, an independent study was made on the rectangular wing 2B and on the tapered wing 3 by attaching one point of the torsional axis rigidly to the tunnel walls by restraining wires. The results are shown in figures 21 and 22. Note that the wire attached to the tip had no effect on the flutter speed, which fact again tends to prove the contention that the flutter bending response is closely related to

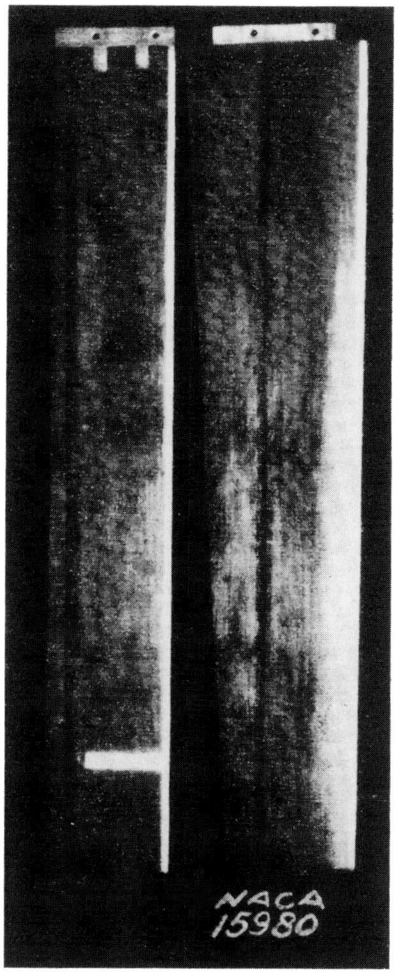

FIGURE 16.—Rectangular wooden wing 6 (left) and tapered wooden wing 7 (right); taper ratio, 3:2.

the second ordinary bending mode. Note also that the observed minimum speeds correspond very nearly to

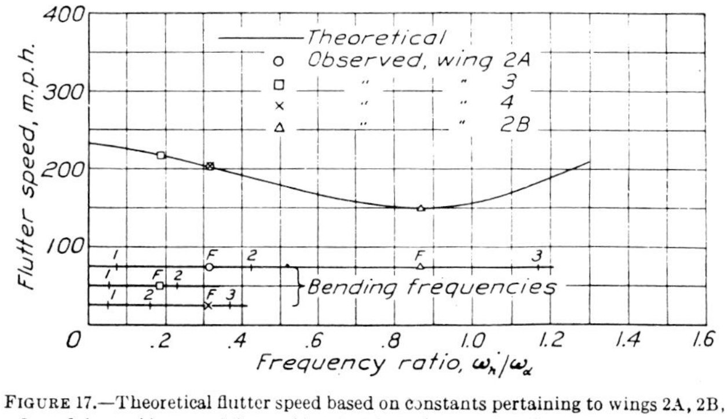

FIGURE 17.—Theoretical flutter speed based on constants pertaining to wings 2A, 2B, 3, and 4. $\kappa = 1/60$; $a = -0.4$; $x_\alpha = 1/4$; $r_\alpha^2 = 0.3125$; $b\omega_\alpha = 38.8$ miles per hour. Experimental test points are also shown, and flutter modes and frequencies are indicated.

the minimum theoretical speed. (See fig. 17.) Of practical importance is the fact that a stay near the root of a wing gave a higher bending frequency and

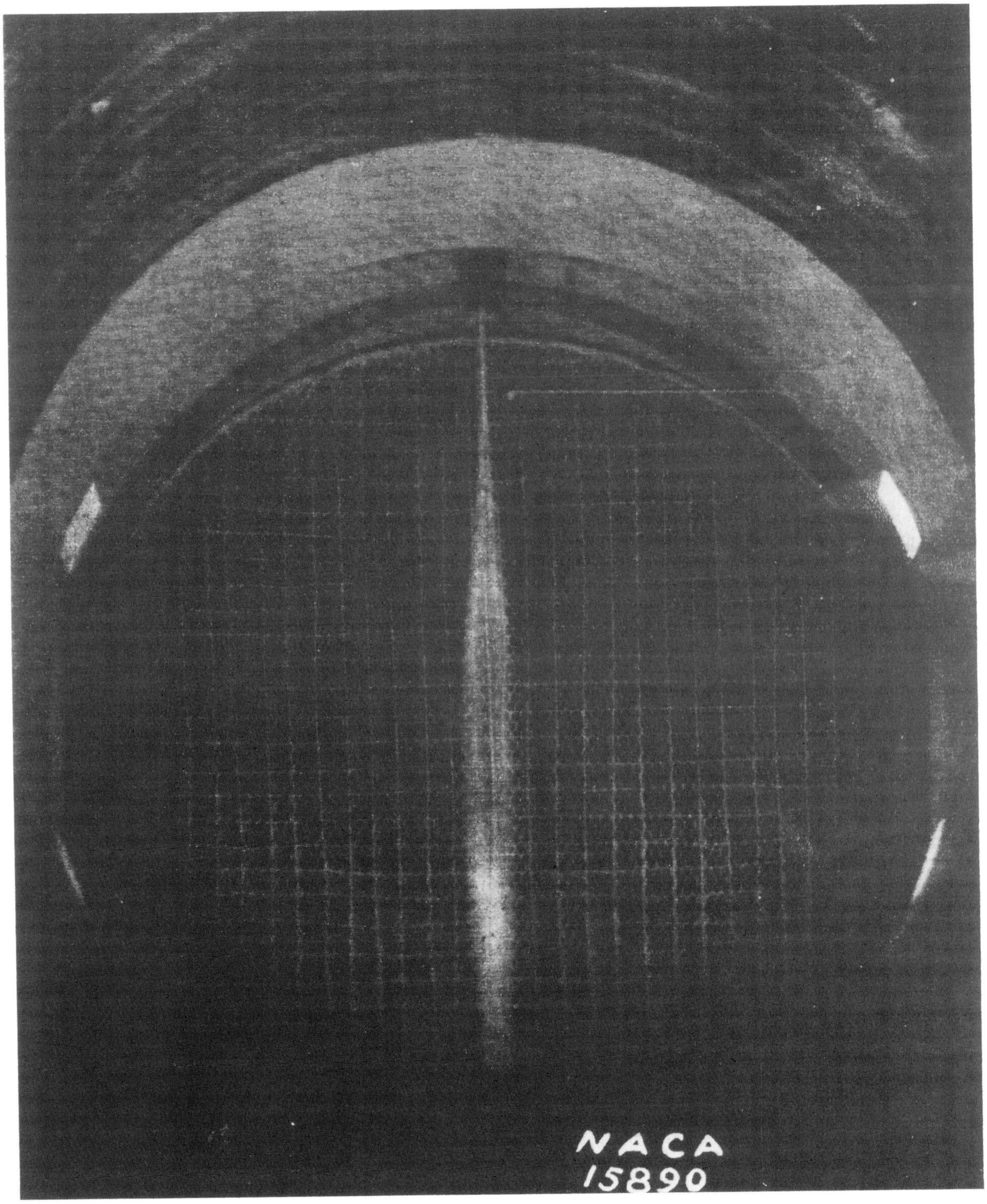

FIGURE 18.—Wing 2A in flutter, demonstrating first flutter mode. Note tendency for node at tip and maximum amplitude near middle.

definitely lowered the critical speed. There existed points, however, near the middle of both wings for

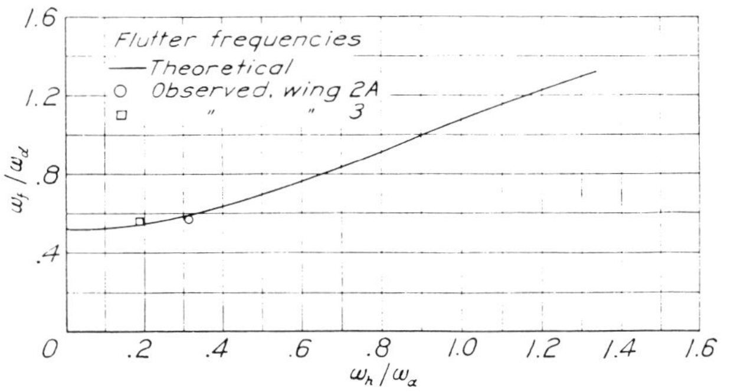

FIGURE 19.—Theoretical flutter frequencies based on constants for wings 2, 3, and 4 with experimentally observed values for wings 2A and 3. $\kappa=1/60$; $a=-0.4$; $x\alpha=1/4$; $r_\alpha^2=0.3125$. Case 1(h, α).

which the stays caused the flutter speed to attain a large value. The explanation is that, with this point fixed, the average h value becomes very small and the h deflection becomes "ineffective." A relatively high flutter speed results.

The matter of leading-edge counterweights has been investigated, in particular on wing 2C. Figure 23 shows the effect of moving a counterweight along the span. The weight has a rather surprising *negative* effect near the tip, indicating that, in this case, there must be an h node inside the tip and again substantiating the theory of the flutter modes. Farther in along the wing there was an expected increase in the flutter speed. When all three weights were applied at the same time, the flutter speed for wing 2C was increased to 295 miles per hour, which is in good agreement with the calculated value.

A large nacelle at an inboard position (fig. 24) increased the flutter speed from 202 to 216 miles per hour when in the forward position and decreased it to 197 when in the rearward position.

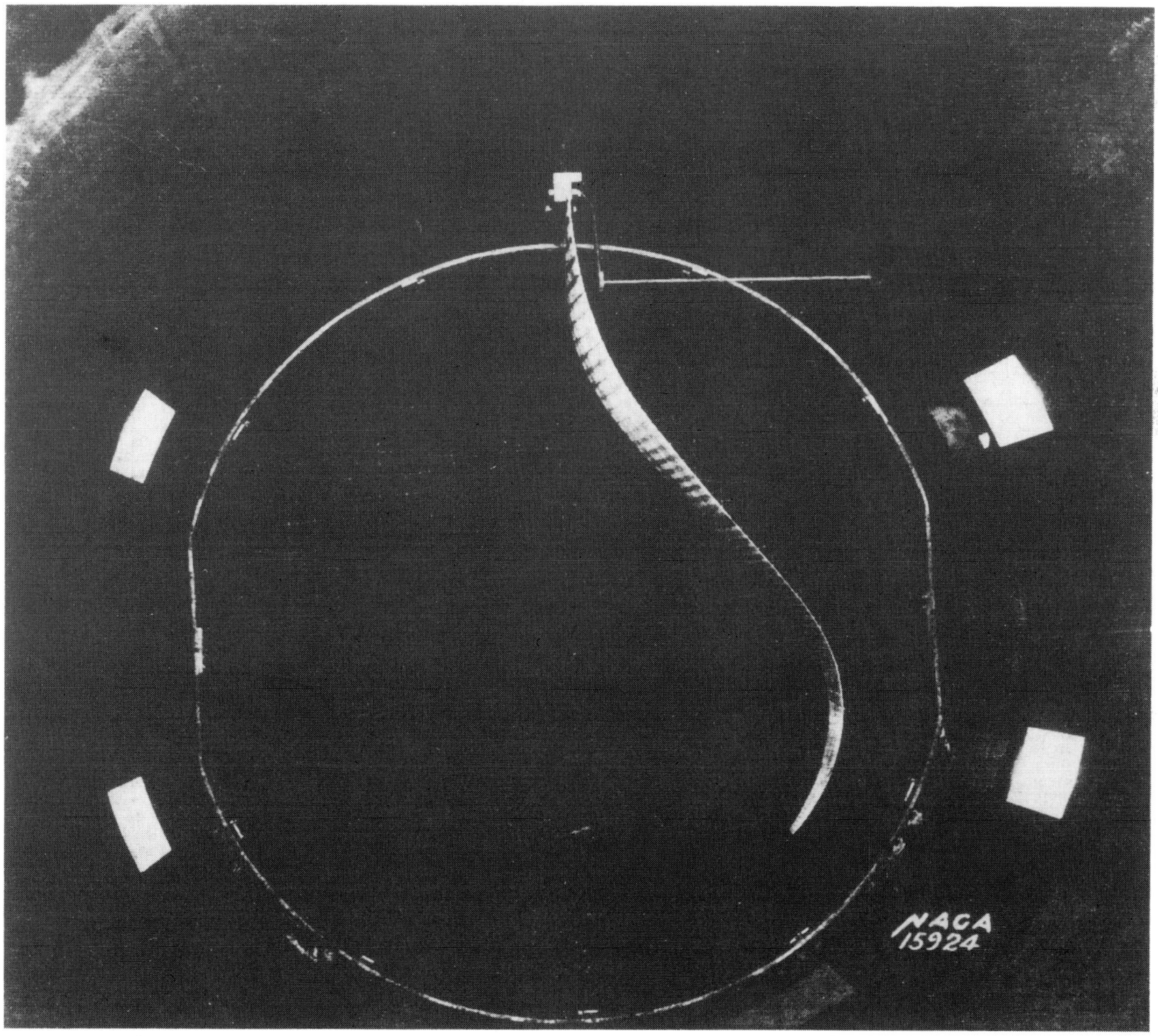

FIGURE 20.—The effect of violent flutter (in second mode) on wing 4.

Large bodies disposed at some distance from the wing, such as floats, were very detrimental as regards the critical speed. (See fig. 25.)

Wing 1 showed a flutter speed that is in agreement with the predicted value within about 1 percent. This agreement is due to the considerable internal damping of this wing. Wing 6, a rectangular wing of the same plan dimensions as wings 1, 2, 3, and 4, but of low density, showed a flutter speed about 3 percent below the theoretical value based on the measured parameters and the lowest ordinary bending mode. This result indicates that, for damped, low-density structures, the flutter mode approaches the first bending mode somewhat more than hitherto indicated.

Wing-aileron flutter has been studied on wing 5. (See fig. 14 and table IA.) The theoretical response is

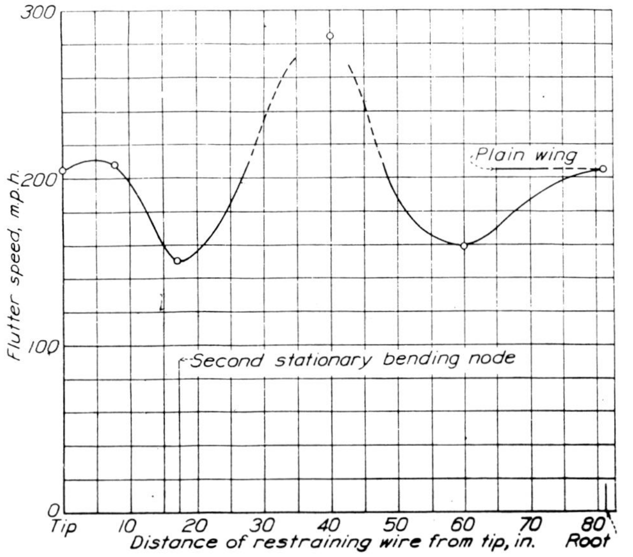

FIGURE 21.—Experimentally observed flutter speed as depending on location of restraining wire along axis of wing 2B.

shown with proper constants in figure 26 for the most representative aileron AII, upon which most of the tests were made. A number of test points have been directly plotted in this figure. In order to obtain internal friction, a lead hinge was used in some tests. It is rather remarkable how well the theory is reaffirmed by the test data. Apparently, if all parameters could be satisfactorily determined, no flutter testing would be necessary. Tests in which the hinge axis (fig. 27) was changed show the beneficial effect of decreasing the aerodynamic moment around the hinge. The lower flutter speed, which is the one of practical importance, is considerably increased as the hinge axis is moved backward. This increase is not only a center-of-gravity effect but is also caused by the decrease in the aerodynamic moment around the hinge. Note that, as the center of gravity is approached, the flutter speed rather suddenly becomes infinite.

AIR DAMPING OF FORCED VIBRATIONS

This report has heretofore been concerned with a study of a border velocity separating stable and unstable velocity regions. Further light on the whole matter of flutter is given by a study of the vibration response of the wing system to impressed forces and moments, that is, generalizing the point of view

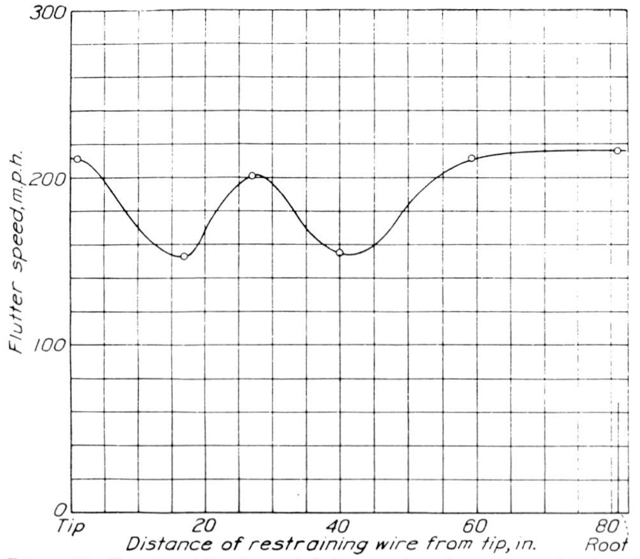

FIGURE 22.—Experimentally observed flutter speed as depending on location of restraining wire along axis of wing 3.

from free vibrations to forced vibrations. Instead of the homogeneous system of equations (A), (B), and (C) (see Introduction), impressed exciting forces and moments introduced on the right-hand side of these equations are considered. In equation (A) a

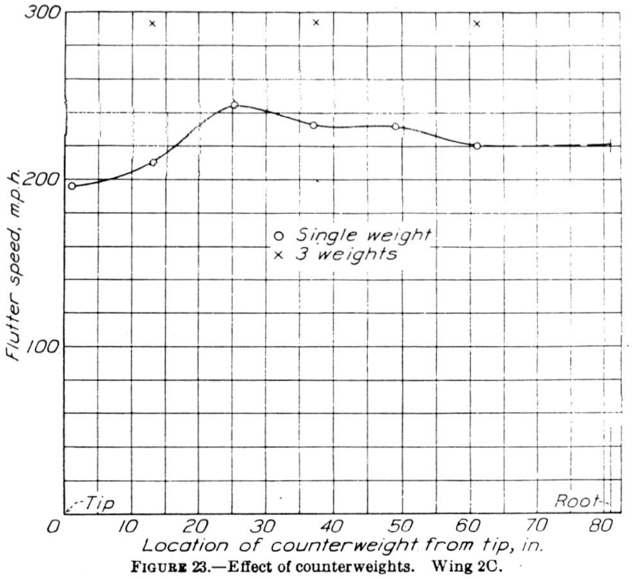

FIGURE 23.—Effect of counterweights. Wing 2C.

term $M_\alpha e^{i(\omega t+\psi_0)}/Mb^2$, in equation (B) a term $M_\beta e^{i(\omega t+\psi_1)}/Mb^2$, and, in equation (C) a term $P_0 e^{i(\omega t+\psi_2)}/Mb$ are introduced. Here M_α and M_β are the magnitudes of the sinusoidal impressed torques in the α and β degrees of freedom, P_0 is the magnitude of the impressed force in the h degree of freedom, ω is the circular frequency of the forced vibrations, and the ψ's are certain phase angles.

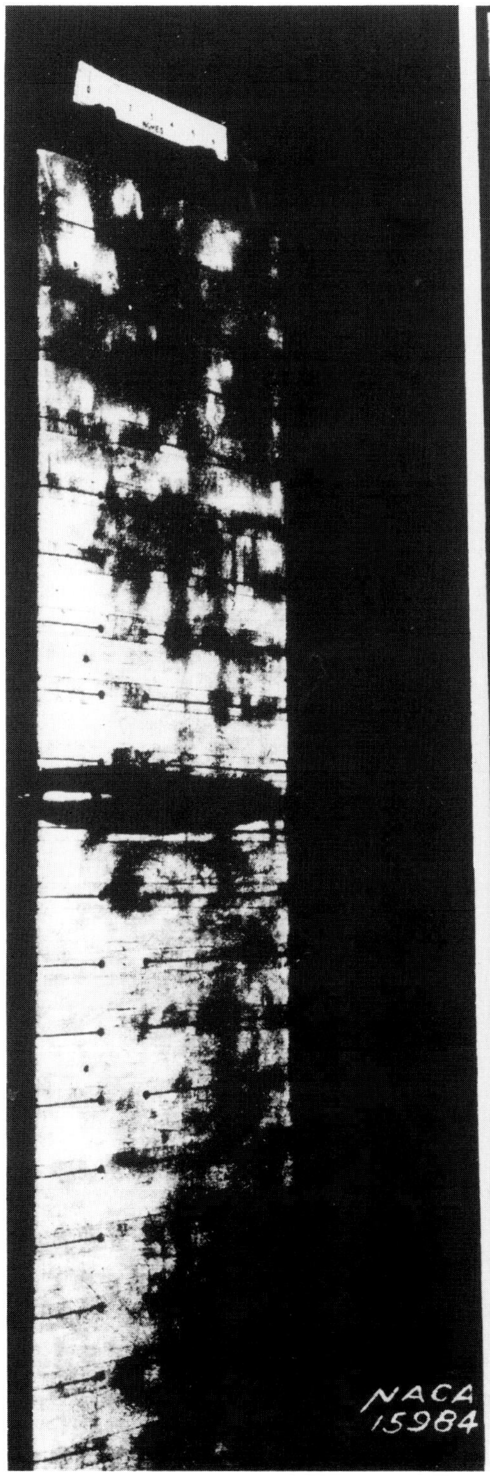

FIGURE 24.—Nacelle on wing 2A.

FIGURE 25.—Float attached to wing 3.

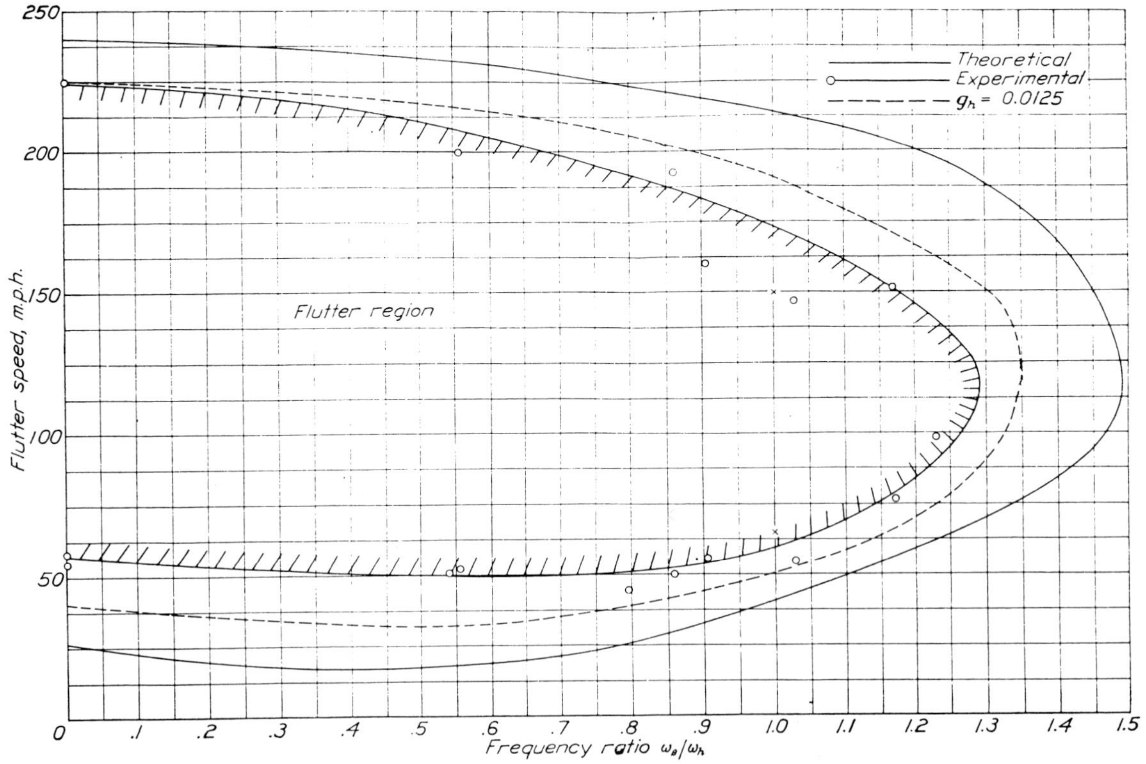

FIGURE 26.—Theoretical flutter speed based on constants pertaining to wing 5 with aileron AII. ($c=\frac{1}{2}$; $x_\beta=0.0076$; $r_\beta^2=0.0019$; $\kappa=\frac{1}{105}$; $b\omega_h=30.5$ m. p. h.) Experimental values are shown; flutter region is shaded. Dashed (theoretical) curve corresponds to friction coefficient $g_h=0.0125$.

CASE 1 (h, α)

By substitution of $\alpha=\alpha_0 e^{i(\omega t+\varphi_0)}$, $\frac{h}{b}=\frac{h_0}{b}\, e^{i(\omega t+\varphi_2)}$, in equations (A) and (C) and solving for $\left(\frac{h_0}{b}\right)e^{i\varphi_2}$ and $\alpha_0 e^{i\varphi_0}$ (put $M_\alpha=P_0\, bm$), there results

$$\frac{h_0}{b}\, e^{i\varphi_2}=\frac{P_0 e^{i\psi_2}}{bM\kappa\omega^2}\,\frac{\begin{vmatrix}\bar{R}_{a\alpha}+i\bar{I}_{a\alpha} & me^{i(\psi_0-\psi_2)}\\ R_{c\alpha}+iI_{c\alpha} & 1\end{vmatrix}}{\Delta_1^R+i\Delta_1^I}$$

$$\alpha_0 e^{i\varphi_0}=\frac{P_0 e^{i\psi_2}}{bM\kappa\omega^2}\,\frac{\begin{vmatrix}me^{i(\psi_0-\psi_2)} & R_{ah}+iI_{ah}\\ 1 & \bar{R}_{ch}+i\bar{I}_{ch}\end{vmatrix}}{\Delta_1^R+i\Delta_1^I}$$

from which both the amplitudes and the phases may be obtained. The R's and the I's are listed in the appendix and Δ_1^R and Δ_1^I represent the real and the imaginary equations listed under the calculation scheme for case 1.

Consider the equation for $h_0 e^{i\varphi_2}$ and denote the determinant in the numerator by N_h, i. e.,

$$N_h=\begin{vmatrix}\bar{R}_{a\alpha}+i\bar{I}_{a\alpha} & me^{i(\psi_0-\psi_2)}\\ R_{c\alpha}+iI_{c\alpha} & 1\end{vmatrix}$$

If the excitation is only in the h degree of freedom $m=0$, i. e., there is no impressed torque about the elastic axis. If a single exciter were placed, for example, 25 percent of the chord in front of the elastic axis, $m=-0.5$.

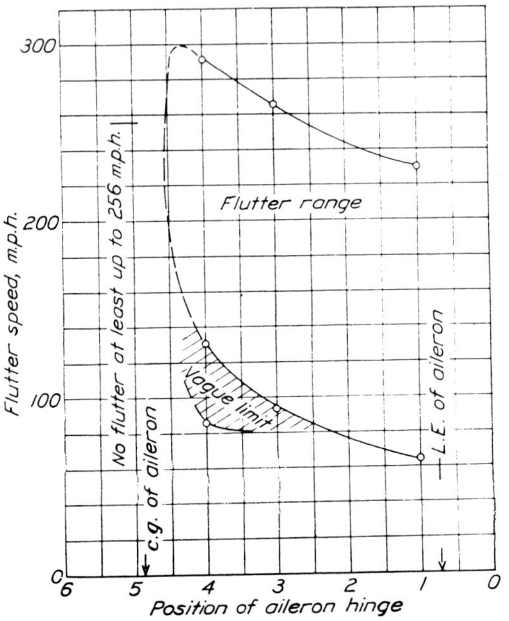

FIGURE 27.—Flutter speed as depending on position of aileron hinge. Observe that no flutter exists when the hinge approaches the center-of-gravity location. Aileron AVIII.

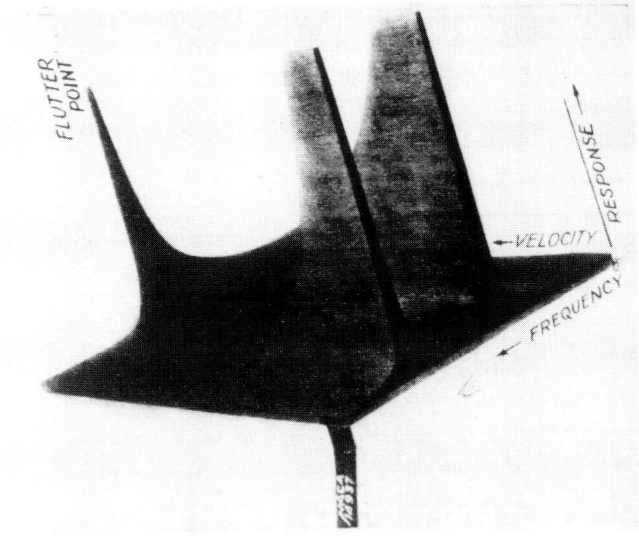

FIGURE 28.—Photograph of model showing forced vibration response in two degrees of freedom as depending on air speed. Note flutter point.

It is convenient to define a certain static deflection h_{st}, which is the deflection due to force P_0,

$$h_{st}=\frac{P_0}{C_h}=\frac{P_0}{M\omega_h^2}$$

Define α_{st} as the static torsional response to an impressed moment P_0b

$$\alpha_{st}=\frac{P_0b}{C_\alpha}$$

Then

$$\left|\frac{\alpha_0}{\alpha_{st}}\right|=\frac{\omega_\alpha^2}{\omega^2}\left|\frac{N_\alpha}{\Delta}\right|\frac{1}{\kappa}$$

Figure 28 is a photograph of a three-dimensional model of the response ratio h_0/h_{st} as a function of the exciting frequency ratio ω/ω_α and of the speed ratio $v/b\omega_\alpha$ for a case of deflection-torsion for which a critical flutter speed exists. In this example, the exciting force has been assumed to act in the deflection degree of freedom alone ($m=0$). At zero speed there exist two resonant frequencies corresponding to the natural frequencies in the separate degree of freedom. The air damping due to speed is zero and the response is infinite at these frequencies. (With friction g_α and g_h, the responses are approximately $1/g_\alpha$ and $1/g_h$, respectively.) As the speed increases, the air damping increases and the response diminishes until, along one frequency branch (the ω_α branch) the response becomes negligibly small. Along the other frequency branch, however, a minimum response is reached, after which

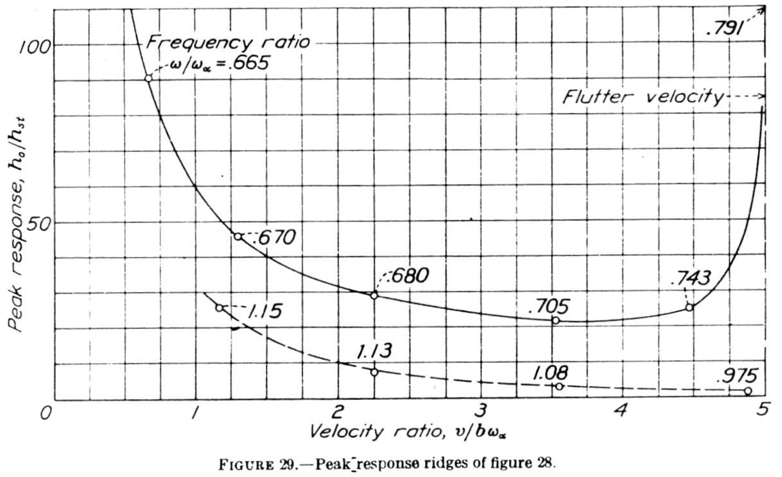

FIGURE 29.—Peak response ridges of figure 28.

Then

$$\left|\frac{h_0}{h_{st}}\right|=\frac{\omega_h^2}{\omega^2}\left|\frac{N_h}{\Delta}\right|\frac{1}{\kappa}$$

where

$$\Delta=\sqrt{(\Delta_1^R)^2+(\Delta_1^I)^2}$$

This result gives the steady-state deflection response h_0 in terms of the static deflection h_{st} due to an impressed force or moment. The results of some numerical calculations will shortly be presented.

The torsional response can be similarly calculated. Let N_α represent the determinant in the numerator of the expression for $\alpha_0e^{i\psi_0}$:

$$N_\alpha=\begin{vmatrix} me^{i(\psi_0-\psi_2)} & R_{ah}+iI_{ah} \\ 1 & \overline{R}_{ch}+i\overline{I}_{ch} \end{vmatrix}$$

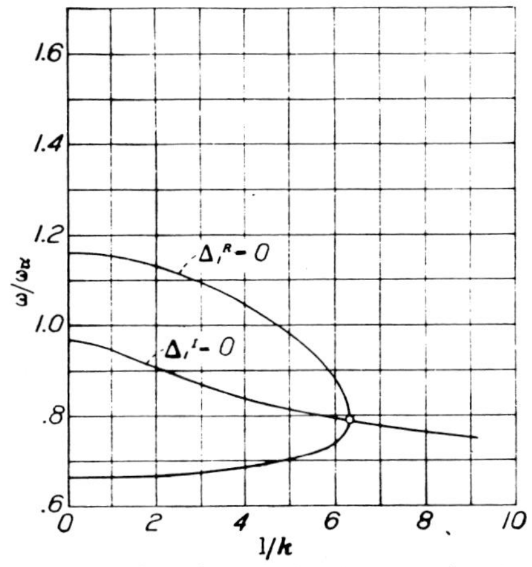

FIGURE 30.—The roots of the real and the imaginary equations (pertaining to case shown in fig. 28) against 1/k.

the air damping decreases and the response increases (usually rapidly) until the flutter point is reached. The critical flutter frequency lies between the two critical frequencies that exist at zero speed. The two peak response ridges for this case are shown in figure 29. These curves, it may be observed, illustrate the essential characteristics of the three-dimensional figure. The procedure of calculation is as follows:

The equations $\Delta_1^R=0$, $\Delta_1^I=0$ are solved for ω/ω_α for various fixed values of $1/k$, as already discussed, in order to locate the flutter point. This plot, for the example cited, is shown in figure 30. The value of Δ_1^I is then obtained for various selected points $(1/k, \omega/\omega_\alpha)$ along $\Delta_1^R=0$. These values may be employed to determine Δ. The numerator is easily evaluated for these same values of $1/k$, ω/ω_α. This process determines the *peak* response with sufficient accuracy for a given value of $1/k$ and conversion to speed is obtained by the relation $v/b\omega_\alpha=(\omega/\omega_\alpha)(1/k)$. Such response curves, calculated with and without the effect of friction, are given in figures 31 and 32.

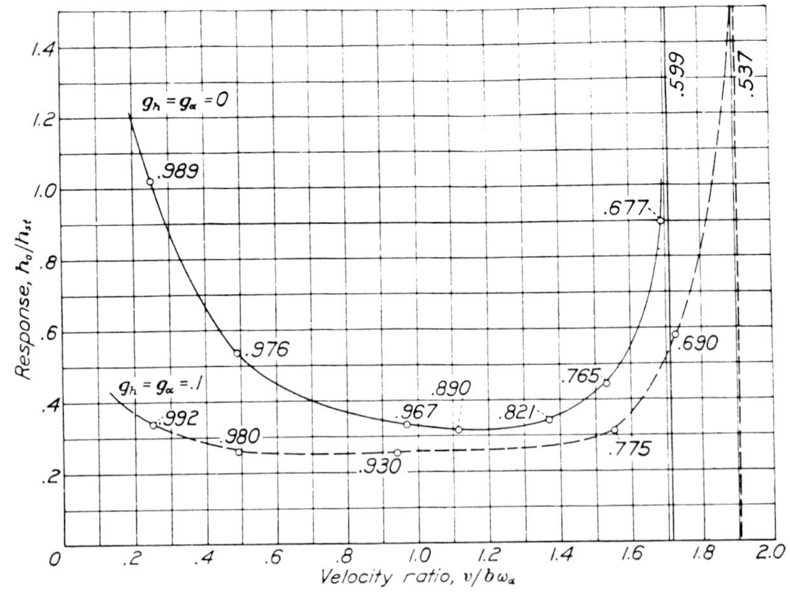

FIGURE 31.—Peak response h_0/h_{st} against velocity $v/b\omega_\alpha$ for the case $\kappa=1/10$; $a=-0.2$; $x_\alpha=0.1$; $m=0$; $(\omega_h/\omega_\alpha)^2=1/25$. The full curve refers to friction coefficients $g_h=g_\alpha=0$; the dashed curve, to $g_h=g_\alpha=0.1$. Case 1 (h, α).

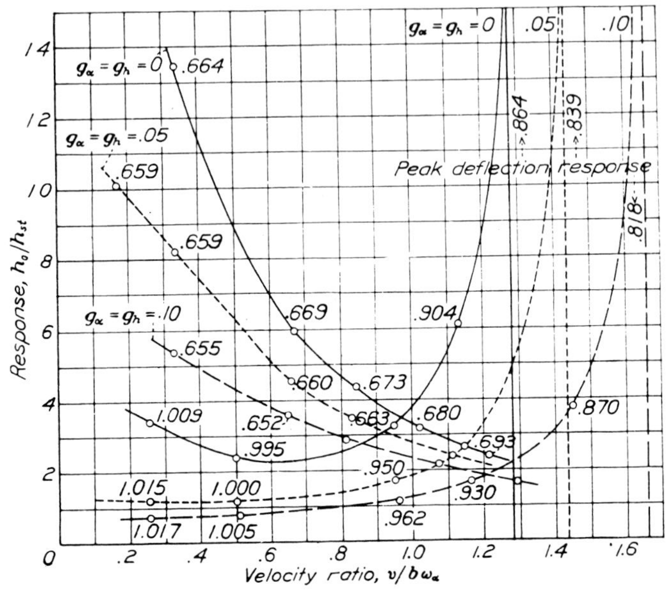

FIGURE 32.—Peak-response ridges for three values of friction coefficients $g_\alpha=g_h=0$, 0.05, and 0.10. ($\kappa=1/10$; $a=-0.2$; $x_\alpha=0.1$; $(\omega_h/\omega_\alpha)^2=1/2$). Case 1.

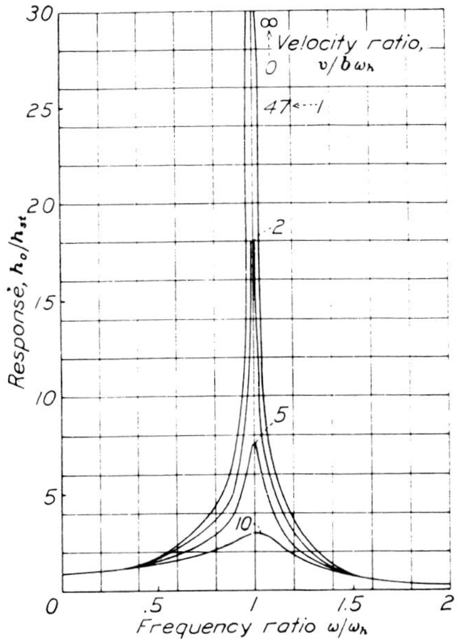

FIGURE 33.—Forced vibration response for deflection degree of freedom ($g_h=0$).

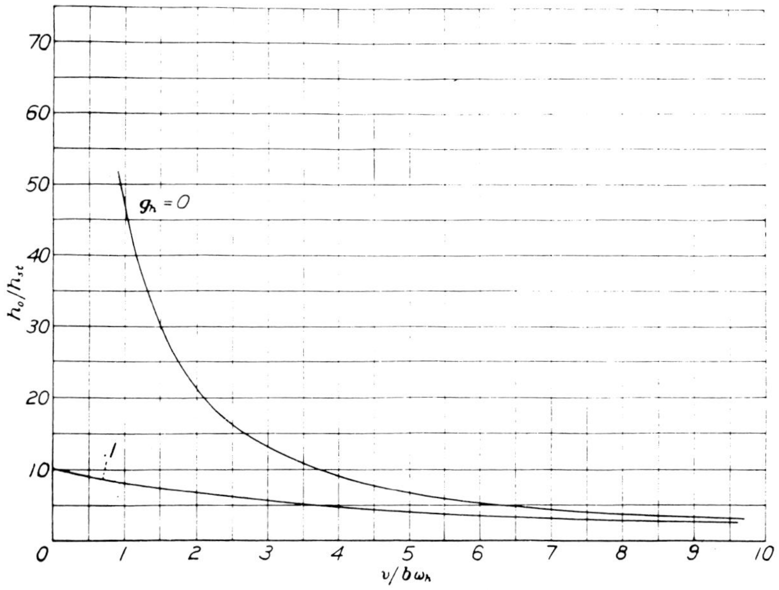

FIGURE 34.—Peak response h_0/h_{st} against velocity ratio $v/b\omega_h$ for two values of the friction coefficient $g_h=0$ and $g_h=0.1$. $\kappa=1/50$.

One degree of freedom (deflection).—Further light on the two-degree-of-freedom case, deflection-torsion, may be obtained by a discussion of the one-degree-of-freedom cases, deflection alone and torsion alone.

When $h=h_0e^{i(\omega t+\varphi_2)}$ is substituted in the deflection equation of motion,

$$h_0e^{i\varphi_2}(\overline{R}_{ch}+i\overline{I}_{ch})\kappa\omega^2=\frac{P_0}{M}e^{i\psi_2}$$

On the introduction of $h_{st}=P_0/C_h$ (static response in deflection to impressed force P_0), it follows that

$$\frac{h_0}{h_{st}}=\frac{1}{\kappa}\left(\frac{\omega_h}{\omega}\right)^2\frac{1}{(R_{ch}^2+I_{ch}^2)^{\frac{1}{2}}}=\frac{\Gamma_h}{[(\Gamma_h-A_h)^2+(g_h\Gamma_h+B_h)^2]^{\frac{1}{2}}}$$

where

$$\Gamma_h=\left(\frac{\omega_h}{\omega}\right)^2$$

$$A_h=1+\kappa\left(1+\frac{2G}{k}\right)$$

$$B_h=\kappa\frac{2F}{k}$$

g_h is the friction coefficient.

It is observed that the speed is determined by $v/b\omega_h=(\omega/\omega_h)(1/k)$.

The resonance response is obtained by putting $\partial/\partial\Gamma_h|h_0/h_{st}|=0$ and solving for Γ_h. There results

$$\Gamma_{res}=\left(\frac{\omega_h}{\omega}\right)^2_{res}=\frac{A_h^2+B_h^2}{A_h-g_hB_h}$$

or

$$\left(\frac{\omega}{\omega_h}\right)_{res}=\left(\frac{A_h-g_hB_h}{A_h^2+B_h^2}\right)^{\frac{1}{2}}$$

The maximum response is then

$$\left(\frac{h_0}{h_{st}}\right)_{res}=\frac{(A_h^2+B_h^2)^{\frac{1}{2}}}{B_h+g_hA_h}$$

Figures 33 and 34 pertain to this case. The results may be summarized as follows: The resonant frequency is practically constant and is approximately $\omega=\omega_h$. The air damping at the maximum response is proportional to $B_h=\kappa\frac{2F}{k}$ or, since the frequency is nearly constant, the air damping at the maximum response is proportional to κv. Away from the resonant frequency, however, the response quickly becomes independent of κ. No flutter or self-excitation exists in this case. At zero air speed, the maximum response ratio is simply $1/g_h$.

One degree of freedom (torsion).—When $\alpha=\alpha_0e^{i(\omega t+\varphi_0)}$ is substituted into the α equation of motion

$$\alpha_0e^{i\varphi_0}(\overline{R}_{a\alpha}+i\overline{I}_{a\alpha})\kappa\omega^2=\frac{M_\alpha}{Mb^2}e^{i\psi_0}$$

On the introduction of $\alpha_{st}=M_\alpha/C_\alpha$ (static response in torsion to impressed torque M_α), it follows that

$$\left|\frac{\alpha_0}{\alpha_{st}}\right|=\frac{r_\alpha^2}{\kappa}\left(\frac{\omega_\alpha}{\omega}\right)^2\frac{1}{(R_{a\alpha}^2+I_{a\alpha}^2)^{\frac{1}{2}}}$$

$$=\frac{\Gamma_\alpha}{[(\Gamma_\alpha-A_\alpha)^2+(g_\alpha\Gamma_\alpha+B_\alpha)^2]^{\frac{1}{2}}}$$

where

$$\Gamma_\alpha=\left(\frac{\omega_\alpha}{\omega}\right)^2$$

$$A_\alpha=1+\frac{\kappa}{r_\alpha^2}\left[\frac{1}{8}+a^2-\left(\frac{1}{4}-a^2\right)\frac{2G}{k}+\left(\frac{1}{2}+a\right)\frac{2F}{k^2}\right]$$

$$B_\alpha=\frac{\kappa}{r_\alpha^2}\frac{1}{k}\left[\frac{1}{2}-a-\left(\frac{1}{2}+a\right)\frac{2G}{k}-\left(\frac{1}{4}-a^2\right)2F\right]$$

g_α is the friction coefficient.

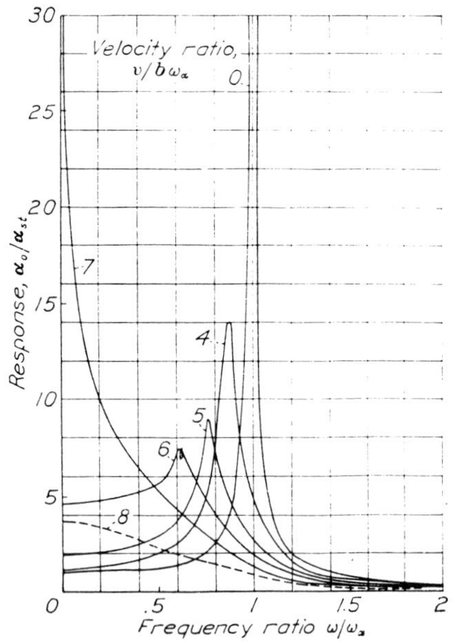

FIGURE 35.—Forced vibration response for torsion degree of freedom (axis at $a=0$; $\kappa/r_\alpha^2=1/50$; $g_\alpha=0$).

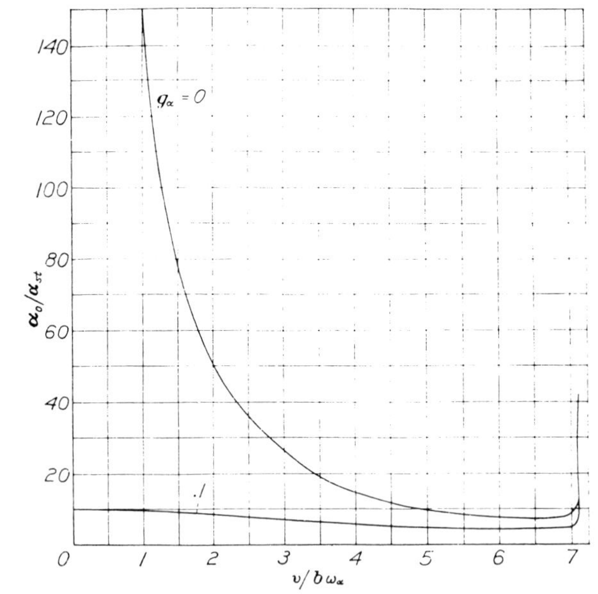

FIGURE 36.—Peak response α_0/α_{st} against velocity ratio $v/b\omega_\alpha$ for two values of the friction coefficient $g_\alpha=0$ and $g_\alpha=0.1$. $a=0$; $\kappa/r_\alpha^2=1/50$.

It is observed that the speed is determined by $v/b\omega_\alpha=(\omega/\omega_\alpha)\ (1/k)$. Put $\partial/\partial\Gamma_\alpha|\alpha_0/\alpha_{st}|=0$. Then

$$\Gamma_{res}=\left(\frac{\omega_\alpha}{\omega}\right)^2_{res}=\frac{A_\alpha^2+B_\alpha^2}{A_\alpha-g_\alpha B_\alpha}$$

or

$$\left(\frac{\omega}{\omega_\alpha}\right)_{res}=\left(\frac{A_\alpha-g_\alpha B_\alpha}{A_\alpha^2+B_\alpha^2}\right)^{\frac{1}{2}}$$

of the torsional axis. The air damping at resonance is essentially proportional to κ/r_α^2 and to the wave-length parameter $1/k$. For the quarter-chord position of the axis, $a=-0.5$, the response α_0/α_{st} is very similar to the deflection response h_0/h_{st} in the preceding case (fig. 33). For any position of the torsional axis back of the quarter-chord point, however, a peculiar result

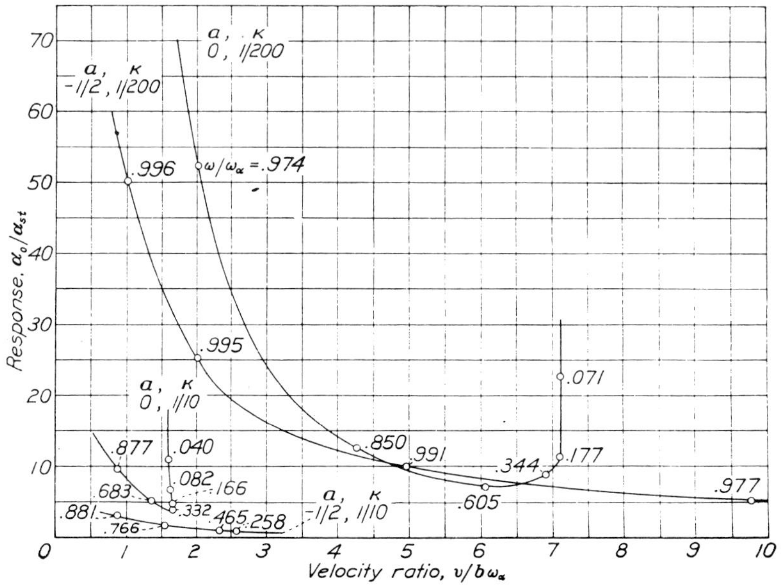

FIGURE 37.—Peak response α_0/α_{st} against velocity ratio $v/b\omega_\alpha$ for two values of a (0 and $-\frac{1}{2}$) and two values of κ ($\frac{1}{10}$ and $\frac{1}{200}$). Case 1 (h, α).

The maximum response is then

$$\left(\frac{\alpha_0}{\alpha_{st}}\right)_{res}=\frac{(A_\alpha^2+B_\alpha^2)^{\frac{1}{2}}}{B_\alpha+g_\alpha A_\alpha}$$

Figures 35, 36, and 37 pertain to this case. The resonant frequency is strongly affected by the position is obtained. The air damping increases with increase in speed and the resonant frequency decreases; but a speed is ultimately reached where the response increases again until, at a vanishingly small resonant frequency, the response is very large. In figure 35, which illustrates a case for the midchord position of the axis,

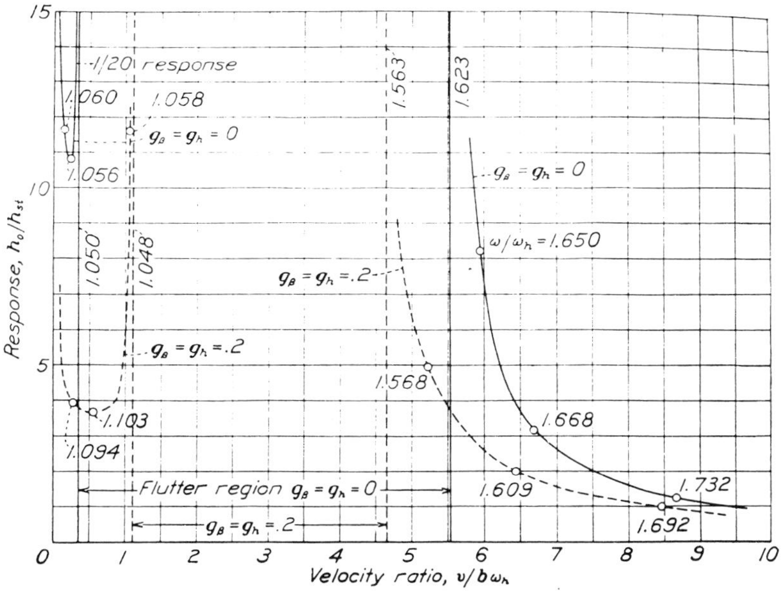

FIGURE 38.—Peak response h_0/h_{st} against velocity ratio $v/b\omega_h$ for a case of flexure-aileron flutter, showing effect of changing friction coefficients $g_h=g_\beta=0$ to $g_h=g_\beta=0.2$. (Other parameters are $c=0.5$; $\kappa=1/10$; $r_\beta^2=1/160$; $x_\beta=1/40$; $(\omega_\beta/\omega_h)^2=1/2$).

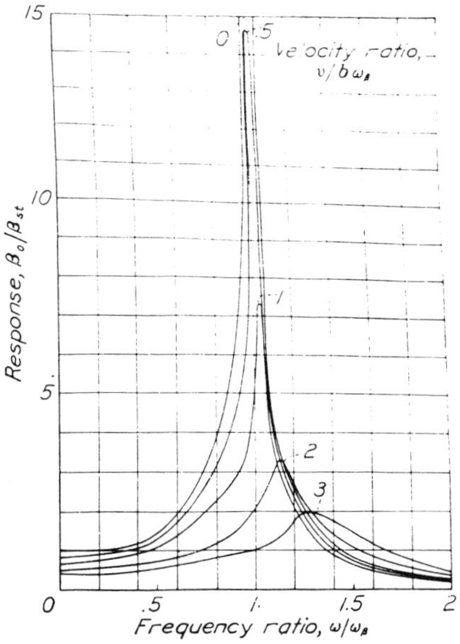

FIGURE 39.—Forced vibration response of aileron alone against frequency and velocity; friction coefficient $g_\beta=0$.

$a=0$, the peak response occurs at $v/b\omega_\alpha=7.10$. This sort of instability has been called divergence. The divergence velocity can be easily calculated as follows:

Let $\omega/\omega_\alpha \rightarrow 0$, $1/k \rightarrow \infty$ in the expression for α_0/α_{st}. Then

$$\underset{1/k\rightarrow\infty}{\text{Limit}}\left(\frac{\alpha}{\alpha_{st}}\right)_{res}=\frac{1}{1-\frac{\kappa}{r_\alpha^2}2\left(\frac{1}{2}+a\right)\left(\frac{v}{b\omega_\alpha}\right)^2}$$

or

$$\left(\frac{v}{b\omega_\alpha}\right)^2_{div}=\frac{r_\alpha^2}{\kappa}\,\frac{1/2}{\frac{1}{2}+a}$$

CASE 2 (β, h)

A study of the response characteristics to forced vibrations is also of some interest in the case of flexure-aileron. The details are omitted here. Two figures are presented. An illustration showing the peak response ratio h_0/h_{st} in this case with and without friction is presented in figure 38. A response for one degree of freedom of the aileron alone is shown in figure 39.

REMARKS ON FLUTTER IN AIRPLANES

WING FLUTTER

The wing may flutter as a whole in torsion-flexure. This case is the most easily treated. Experience with models indicates that this flutter speed may be calculated on the basis of the measured constants with an accuracy of a few percent. The actual bending frequency involved in flutter is apparently not exactly the lowest ordinary bending frequency but a slightly higher value.

Probably the most common type of wing flutter is case 2 (flexure-aileron). This type, as well as that involving torsion-flexure, is evidently symmetrical with respect to the fuselage. The ailerons would therefore be in phase and have a frequency considerably in excess of the wing-bending frequency. This condition is favorable. Any slack in the aileron cables, however, permits a motion that may cause a mild type of flutter, which should not be permitted for too long a time.

A nonsymmetrical aileron motion would involve a second bending mode (nonsymmetrical). It is probable that, in most cases, the node would be close to the middle of the aileron and therefore poorly coupled.

There remains to consider a complete case of flutter (torsion-flexure-aileron). Apparently cases do exist in which this type would appear at the lowest speed. The effect of the additional degree of freedom can probably be taken care of by a safety factor applied to the flutter speed obtained for two degrees of freedom. The calculation of the case of three degrees of freedom is perfectly straightforward although more lengthy than the simple cases.

TAIL FLUTTER

In regard to tail flutter, the situation is more complex. The possible combinations are subdivided as follows into three main groups, which will be separately analyzed:

(1) Vertical flexure of tail assembly.
(2) Horizontal flexure of tail assembly.
(3) Torsion of tail assembly.

Vertical flexure.—It is possible, in general, to identify two responses in vertical flexure; one corresponding to the fundamental bending mode of the fuselage and the other, to the bending mode of the horizontal-fin arrangement. The frequency of the fin arrangement is slightly greater than the one obtained with the rear end of the fuselage fixed in space. It is probable that the fuselage bending mode need not be considered. In any case, the flutter speed calculated for each of the two cases will not differ very much because the density involved is about in the same ratio as the squares of the frequencies involved. Only the vertical fundamental bending frequency of the horizontal fin will therefore be considered. This bending frequency may couple with fin torsion and elevator motion. This motion is necessarily symmetrical and simulates the motion of the main wing system. Since the elevator has no particular restraint to this motion, it is evident that an unbalanced elevator is highly undesirable. As in the case of the wing system, the most frequent cause of flutter is also the flexure-aileron combination.

Horizontal flexure.—Horizontal flexure affects the vertical fin or fins and may be separately considered as a cantilever wing with an aileron. The rudder, which takes the place of the aileron, has no particular restraint to this motion and must therefore be carefully mass balanced.

Torsion.—Torsion is composed of a relatively low-frequency type of flutter involving the fuselage and a higher frequency type involving the fin tips, which may be considered as fin flexure in opposite phase. This type of flutter is not common because the great stiffness of the torque tube prevents its occurrence (β large). The rudder is affected in the same manner as for horizontal flexure.

In summary, it may be said that the expected causes of flutter are the in-phase motion of the horizontal fins as flexure-elevator and the motion of the vertical fin in flexure with rudder motions.

With two rudders disposed at the ends of the horizontal fins, care must be taken that the flexure frequency is sufficiently high. The mass of the rudders at the ends of the horizontal fins also affects the parameters used in the fin-stability calculation; that is, the density of the fins and the radius of gyration are increased. The center-of-gravity location may also be changed.

GROUND TESTS

DETERMINATION OF CENTER-OF-GRAVITY LOCATION

From the theory, it may be observed that the location of the torsional stiffness axis is of fairly secondary importance. The location of the center-of-gravity axis, on the other hand, is of great importance. The application of a very low-frequency (zero) torque will rotate the wing around the torsional stiffness axis a; the application of a very high frequency (infinity) torque will cause the mass center line to remain stationary. As the torsional frequency for wings is several times larger than the lowest bending frequency, it can be shown with all desired accuracy that the axis observed for the torsional frequency is the center-of-gravity line.

Assume the wing to be vibrating around an axis at a distance d behind the stiffness axis. The moment of inertia reduced to the center of gravity is

$$I=M(r_\alpha^2-x_\alpha^2)b^2$$

Moving the axis to d increases the moment of inertia to

$$M(r_\alpha^2-x_\alpha^2)b^2+M(x_\alpha-d)^2b^2=M(r_\alpha^2+d^2-2dx_\alpha)b^2$$

The corresponding torsional stiffness is $C_\alpha+d^2C_h$.

The frequency is consequently

$$\omega^2=\frac{(C_\alpha+d^2C_h)b^2}{M(r_\alpha^2+d^2-2dx_\alpha)b^2}$$

Then

$$2\log\omega=\log(C_\alpha+d^2C_h)b^2-\log Mb^2(r_\alpha^2+d^2-2dx_\alpha)$$

The wing will assume the state of vibration giving the greatest frequency. By derivation, with respect to d,

$$\frac{dC_h}{C_\alpha+d^2C_h}-\frac{d-x_\alpha}{r_\alpha^2+d^2-2dx_\alpha}=0$$

or

$$\frac{dC_h}{d-x_\alpha}=\omega^2M$$

Then

$$d=x_\alpha\frac{1}{1-(\omega_h/\omega)^2}$$

or, with d known,

$$x_\alpha=d[1-(\omega_h/\omega)^2]\cong d\text{ for }\omega_h/\omega\longrightarrow0$$

That is, the center-of-gravity axis is slightly ahead of the dynamic axis (assuming both axes to be normally behind the stiffness axis). If the torsional frequency is very large, they coincide ($d=x_\alpha$). (If the torsional frequency is very low, $d=0$, giving the stiffness axis.)

In other words, the center-of-gravity location along a finished wing can be determined by establishing the dynamic torsional axis.

DIMENSIONAL CONSIDERATIONS

Proportionally increasing all dimensions of a wing while retaining all details lowers the frequencies in inverse proportion to the size. The reference speed ωb therefore always remains the same, as do all other parameters including the wing density. The actual flutter speed therefore depends on the shape but not on the size. It is important to keep in mind, however, that the reference is to wings or tails similar in all respects. In reality, a lighter contruction is necessarily employed in larger wing sizes, resulting in a weaker structure and a general lowering of the critical flutter speed.

The foregoing considerations are significant in the testing of models. Thus a true model constructed of the same material as the full-scale airplane will have the same flutter speed. For testing purposes, it is very desirable to have a fairly low flutter speed. This end may be achieved by employing models of special materials related to celluloid, which have a value of $\sqrt{E/\rho}$ nearly five times smaller than that of materials normally used in airplane construction.

The most desirable condition would be to use a material with the same density ρ as the airplane and with the moduli E and G, say, $1/n$ times the original values. Fortunately, the density of the model wing can be very simply corrected by using a suitable thickness of the materials. Thus, if the density of the material used is three times lower than that of the original, the thickness of the skin and all the internal members is increased by a factor of 3.

It should be further noted that the model can be critically checked as to accuracy of reproduction by direct measurements of its mechanical properties. In other words, all the parameters, including the reference quantity ωb, are directly measured on the model itself. The value of ωb is usually close to the predicted value. The important point, however, is that it is not necessary to depend on a predicted theoretical value.

Thus the feasibility of conducting direct flutter tests on models of actual airplanes or of its component parts is indicated. Some work of this nature is now being undertaken. The procedure may be of value in cases that are difficult to treat theoretically and should be of value in accumulating useful experience on special designs.

GENERAL CONCLUSIONS

1. The two-dimensional theory has been verified within the limits of error in the determination of the primary parameters.

2. The most essential three-dimensional effect is the occurrence of distinct flutter bending modes, which differ from the ordinary vibration modes in that they tend to assume a form which approaches the next higher vibration mode and exhibit a correspondingly higher frequency. The flutter speed is consequently lower than that calculated on the basis of the lowest vibration frequency and the flutter frequency itself is higher. For ordinary damped structures, this effect lowers the flutter speed calculated on the basis of the lowest bending mode by only a few percent.

3. A cantilever wing flutters at a speed calculated by using the constants for the most representative section, which is located at approximately three-quarters of the semispan.

4. Aspect ratio and structural damping effects tend to *increase* the flutter speed by a few percent above that calculated for infinite aspect ratio and zero internal damping.

5. The effect of mass balancing to bring the center of gravity forward is essentially as predicted by theory. The effect of nacelles is of lesser importance, but large weights located at some distance away from the wing and attached to it show a very detrimental effect on the flutter speed.

6. Wing-aileron experimental studies show that the characteristic flutter *range* predicted by the theory exists and is in substantial agreement with the predicted values. A decrease in the unbalance and an increase in the frequency ratio are both beneficial. There exists, for each value of the unbalance, a certain critical frequency ratio and, inversely, for each frequency ratio, a certain critical value of the unbalance.

7. The considerable difficulty involved in the determination of the primary structural parameters including the damping is recognized and will constitute one of the chief problems of future flutter research.

LANGLEY MEMORIAL AERONAUTICAL LABORATORY,
NATIONAL ADVISORY COMMITTEE FOR AERONAUTICS,
LANGLEY FIELD, VA., *September 22, 1938.*

APPENDIX

LIST OF NOTATION

α, angle of attack (fig. 40).

β, aileron angle (fig. 40).

h, vertical distance (fig. 40).

$\dot{\alpha}=\frac{d\alpha}{dt}$, $\ddot{\alpha}=\frac{d^2\alpha}{dt^2}$, etc.

α_0, β_0, h_0, φ_1, φ_2, amplitudes and phase angles.

b, half chord, used as reference unit length.

a, coordinate of axis of rotation (torsional axis) (fig. 40). Location of stiffness axis in percentage total chord measured from the leading edge is $100\frac{1+a}{2}$ or $a=\frac{2\ (\text{stiffness axis})}{100}-1$.

c, coordinate of aileron hinge axis (fig. 40). Location of aileron hinge axis in percentage total chord measured from leading edge is $100\frac{1+c}{2}$ or $c=\frac{2\ (\text{aileron hinge})}{100}-1$.

ρ, mass of air per unit of volume.

M, mass of wing per unit span length.

$\kappa=\frac{\pi\rho b^2}{M}$, the ratio of the mass of a cylinder of air of a diameter equal to the chord of the wing to the mass of the wing, both taken for equal length along the span; this ratio may be expressed as $\kappa=0.24(b^2/W)\ (\rho/\rho_0)$ where W is weight in pounds per foot span, b is in feet, and ρ/ρ_0 is ratio of air density to standard air. [The quantity $\sigma=W/4b^3$ (weight per square foot per chord in feet) has been used by British writers. Thus, $\kappa=(0.06/\sigma)\ (\rho/\rho_0)$.]

$x_\alpha=\frac{S_\alpha}{Mb}$, location of center of gravity of wing-aileron system *measured from* a (fig. 40); S_α, static moment of wing-aileron per unit span length referred to a. Location of center of gravity in percentage total chord measured from the leading edge is $100\frac{1+a+x_\alpha}{2}$ or $a+x_\alpha=\frac{2\ (\text{center of gravity})}{100}-1$.

$x_\beta=\frac{S_\beta}{Mb}$, *reduced* location of center of gravity of aileron referred to c (fig. 40). S_β, static moment of aileron per unit span length referred to c.[3]

$r_\alpha=\sqrt{\frac{I_\alpha}{Mb^2}}$, radius of gyration of wing aileron referred to a (fig. 40). I_α, moment of inertia of wing aileron about the elastic axis per unit span length.

$r_\beta=\sqrt{\frac{I_\beta}{Mb^2}}$, *reduced* radius of gyration of aileron referred to c (fig. 40). I_β, moment of inertia of aileron about c per unit span length.

[3] Note that M refers to the total wing mass and not to the mass of the aileron alone.

C_α, torsional stiffness of wing around a per unit span length.

C_β, torsional stiffness of aileron around c per unit span length.

C_h, stiffness of wing in deflection per unit span length.

$\omega_\alpha=\sqrt{\frac{C_\alpha}{I_\alpha}}$, natural angular frequency of torsional vibration around a in vacuum ($\omega_\alpha=2\pi f_\alpha$, where f_α is in cycles per second).

$\omega_\beta=\sqrt{\frac{C_\beta}{I_\beta}}$, natural angular frequency of torsional vibrations of aileron about c.

$\omega_h=\sqrt{\frac{C_h}{M}}$, natural angular frequency of wing in deflection.

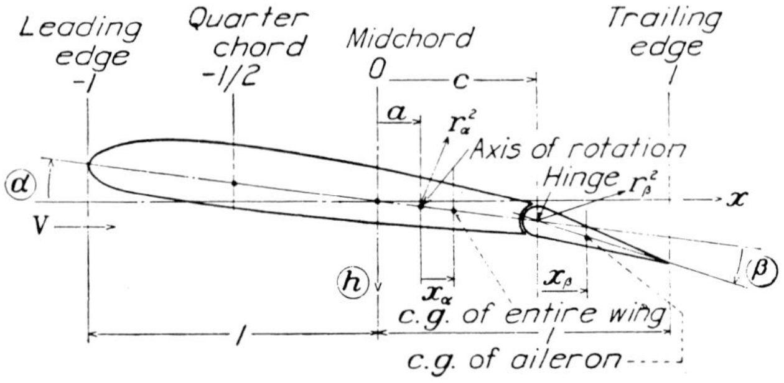

FIGURE 40.—Half chord b is used as the unit length. The positive directions of α, β, and h are indicated by arrows. Note that a is measured from midchord and that x_α is measured from the elastic axis positive to the right. Also note that r_β is a "reduced" parameter and not the actual distance from the hinge to the c. g. of the aileron.

t, time.

v, speed of forward motion.

v_f, flutter or critical speed.

ω, circular frequency of wing vibrations.

$k=\frac{b\omega}{v}$, *reduced* frequency=number of waves in the wake in a distance equal to the semichord$\times 2\pi$.

$1/k$, reduced wave length=length of one wave of the wake in terms of a distance equal to the semichord$\times 2\pi$.

F and G, functions of k in table 2.

$$\begin{cases} R_{a\alpha}=-A_{\alpha 1}+\left(\frac{1}{4}-a^2\right)\frac{2G}{k}-\left(\frac{1}{2}+a\right)\frac{2F}{k^2} \\ R_{a\beta}=-A_{\beta 1}+\frac{1}{k^2}A_{\beta 3}+\left(\frac{1}{2}+a\right)\left(\frac{T_{11}}{2\pi}\frac{2G}{k}-\frac{T_{10}}{\pi}\frac{2F}{k^2}\right) \\ R_{ah}=-A_{h1}+\left(\frac{1}{2}+a\right)\frac{2G}{k} \end{cases}$$

$$\begin{cases} R_{b\alpha}=-B_{\alpha 1}-\dfrac{T_{12}}{2\pi}\left[\left(\dfrac{1}{2}-a\right)\dfrac{2G}{k}-\dfrac{2F}{k^2}\right] \\ R_{b\beta}=-B_{\beta 1}+\dfrac{1}{k^2}B_{\beta 3}-\dfrac{T_{12}}{2\pi}\left(\dfrac{T_{11}}{2\pi}\dfrac{2G}{k}-\dfrac{T_{10}}{\pi}\dfrac{2F}{k^2}\right) \\ R_{bh}=-B_{h1}-\dfrac{T_{12}}{2\pi}\dfrac{2G}{k} \end{cases}$$

$$\begin{cases} R_{c\alpha}=-C_{\alpha 1}-\left(\dfrac{1}{2}-a\right)\dfrac{2G}{k}+\dfrac{2F}{k^2} \\ R_{c\beta}=-C_{\beta 1}-\dfrac{T_{11}}{2\pi}\dfrac{2G}{k}+\dfrac{T_{10}}{\pi}\dfrac{2F}{k^2} \\ R_{ch}=-C_{h1}-\dfrac{2G}{k} \end{cases}$$

$$\begin{cases} I_{a\alpha}=\dfrac{1}{k}\left[-\left(\dfrac{1}{2}+a\right)\dfrac{2G}{k}-\left(\dfrac{1}{4}-a^2\right)2F+A_{\alpha 2}\right] \\ I_{a\beta}=\dfrac{1}{k}\left[-\left(\dfrac{1}{2}+a\right)\left(\dfrac{T_{10}}{\pi}\dfrac{2G}{k}+\dfrac{T_{11}}{2\pi}2F\right)+A_{\beta 2}\right] \\ I_{ah}=\dfrac{1}{k}\left[-\left(\dfrac{1}{2}+a\right)2F\right] \end{cases}$$

$$\begin{cases} I_{b\alpha}=\dfrac{1}{k}\left\{\dfrac{T_{12}}{2\pi}\left[\dfrac{2G}{k}+\left(\dfrac{1}{2}-a\right)2F\right]+B_{\alpha 2}\right\} \\ I_{b\beta}=\dfrac{1}{k}\left[\dfrac{T_{12}}{2\pi}\left(\dfrac{T_{10}}{\pi}\dfrac{2G}{k}+\dfrac{T_{11}}{2\pi}2F\right)+B_{\beta 2}\right] \\ I_{bh}=\dfrac{1}{k}\left(\dfrac{T_{12}}{2\pi}2F\right) \end{cases}$$

$$\begin{cases} I_{c\alpha}=\dfrac{1}{k}\left[\dfrac{2G}{k}+\left(\dfrac{1}{2}-a\right)2F+C_{\alpha 2}\right] \\ I_{c\beta}=\dfrac{1}{k}\left(\dfrac{T_{10}}{\pi}\dfrac{2G}{k}+\dfrac{T_{11}}{2\pi}2F+C_{\beta 2}\right) \\ I_{ch}=\dfrac{1}{k}2F \end{cases}$$

$$\overline{R}_{a\alpha}=R_{a\alpha}+\Omega_\alpha X \qquad \Omega_\alpha X=\frac{r_\alpha^2}{\kappa}\left(\frac{\omega_\alpha}{\omega}\right)^2$$

$$\overline{R}_{b\beta}=R_{b\beta}+\Omega_\beta X \qquad \Omega_\beta X=\frac{r_\beta^2}{\kappa}\left(\frac{\omega_\beta}{\omega}\right)^2$$

$$\overline{R}_{ch}=R_{ch}+\Omega_h X \qquad \Omega_h X=\frac{1}{\kappa}\left(\frac{\omega_h}{\omega}\right)^2$$

$$\overline{I}_{a\alpha}=I_{a\alpha}+g_\alpha\Omega_\alpha X$$

$$\overline{I}_{b\beta}=I_{b\beta}+g_\beta\Omega_\beta X$$

$$\overline{I}_{ch}=I_{ch}+g_h\Omega_h X$$

The quantities $A_{\alpha 1}$, $A_{\beta 1}$, etc. and $\Omega_\alpha X$, $\Omega_\beta X$, etc. are defined under the calculation scheme (pp. 5–7). The T's are listed in table 2. The definitions of the T's are given in reference 1, page 5, should other values than those listed in the table be required.

$v/b\omega_\alpha$, flutter-speed coefficient (cases 1 and 3).
$v/b\omega_h$, flutter-speed coefficient (case 2).
ω_h/ω_α, frequency ratio (case 1).
ω_β/ω_h, frequency ratio (case 2).
$\omega_\beta/\omega_\alpha$, frequency ratio (case 3).

$$v_D=b\omega_\alpha\sqrt{\frac{r_\alpha^2}{\kappa}\,\frac{1/2}{(1/2)+a}},\ \text{divergence velocity.}$$

g_α, g_β, g_h, structural damping coefficients; πg corresponds approximately to the usual logarithmic decrement.
M_α, M_β, magnitude of sinusoidal impressed torques in the α and β degrees of freedom.
P_0, magnitude of impressed force in the h degree of freedom.
ψ, phase angle.
α_0/α_{st}, β_0/β_{st}, h_0/h_{st}, peak response for the various degrees of freedom.

REFERENCES

1. Theodorsen, Theodore: General Theory of Aerodynamic Instability and the Mechanism of Flutter. T. R. No. 496, N. A. C. A., 1935.
2. Cicala, Placido: Le Azioni aerodinamiche sui profili di ala oscillanti in presenza di corrente uniforme. Mem. R. Accad. Sci. Torino, ser. 2, pt. I, t. 68, 1934–1935, pp. 73–98.
3. Kassner, R., and Fingado, H.: Das ebene Problem der Flügelschwingung. Luftfahrtforschung, Bd. 13, Nr. 11, 20.Nov. 1936, S. 374–387.
4. Küssner, H. G.: Zusammenfassender Bericht über den instationären Auftrieb von Flügeln. Luftfahrtforschung, Bd. 13, Nr. 12, 20.Dec. 1936, S. 410–424.
5. Garrick, I. E.: Propulsion of a Flapping and Oscillating Airfoil. T. R. No. 567, N. A. C. A., 1936.
6. Voigt, H.: Wind-Tunnel Investigations on Flexural-Torsional Wing Flutter. T. M. No. 877, N. A. C. A. 1938.
7. von Schlippe, B.: The Question of Spontaneous Wing Oscillations. T. M. No. 806, N. A. C. A., 1936.

TABLE 1

k	$1/k$	F	$-G$	$-2G/k$	$2F/k^2$
∞	0.000	0.5000	0	0	0
10	.100	.5006	.0124	.00248	.010012
6	.16667	.5017	.0206	.00686	.02787
4	.250	.5037	.0305	.01525	.06296
3	.33333	.5063	.0400	.02667	.1125
2	.500	.5129	.0577	.0577	.2565
1.5	.66667	.5210	.0736	.0948	.4631
1.2	.83333	.5300	.0877	.1462	.7361
1.0	1.000	.5394	.1003	.2006	1.0788
.80	1.250	.5541	.1165	.2912	1.7316
.66	1.51516	.5699	.1308	.3964	2.6166
.60	1.66667	.5788	.1378	.4593	3.2156
.56	1.78572	.5857	.1428	.5100	3.7353
.50	2.000	.5979	.1507	.6028	4.7832
.44	2.27273	.6130	.1592	.7236	6.3326
.40	2.500	.6250	.1650	.8250	7.8125
.34	2.94118	.6469	.1738	1.022	11.192
.30	3.33333	.6650	.1793	1.195	14.778
.24	4.16667	.6989	.1862	1.552	24.267
.20	5.000	.7276	.1886	1.886	36.380
.16	6.250	.7628	.1876	2.345	59.592
.12	8.33333	.8063	.1801	3.002	111.99
.10	10.000	.8320	.1723	3.446	166.4
.08	12.500	.8604	.1604	4.010	268.9
.06	16.66667	.8920	.1426	4.753	495.6
.05	20.000	.9090	.1305	5.220	727.2
.04	25.000	.9267	.1160	5.800	1158.3
.025	40.000	.9545	.0872	6.976	3054.4
.01	100.000	.9824	.0482	9.640	19648
0	∞	1.000	0	∞	∞

TABLE 2

Values of T

$c \longrightarrow$	−1	−0.5	0	0.1	0.2	0.3
T_1/π	−1.00000	−0.54008	−0.21221	−0.16539	−0.12490	−0.09064
T_3/π^2	−1.25000	−.38882	−.08191	−.05434	−.03429	−.02031
$T_4/\pi(=-C_{\beta 2})$	−1.00000	−.80450	−.50000	−.43644	−.37353	−.31192
T_7/π	−1.12500	−.37922	−.06250	−.03540	−.01672	−.00489
T_{10}/π	1.00000	.94233	.81831	.78483	.74779	.70666
$T_{11}/2\pi$	1.50000	1.01125	.56831	.48813	.41146	.33870
$T_{12}/2\pi$	.50000	.20675	.06831	.05168	.03793	.02679
p/π	0	−.06891	−.10610	−.10452	−.09980	−.09105
$A_{\beta 3}=\frac{T_4+T_{10}}{\pi}$	0	.13783	.31831	.34789	.37426	.39474
$B_{\alpha 2}=\frac{1}{\pi}\left(p-T_1-\frac{T_4}{2}\right)$	1.50000	.87342	.35611	.27909	.21187	.15555
$B_{\beta 2}=-\frac{T_4 T_{11}}{2\pi^2}$	1.50000	.81355	.28416	.21304	.15369	.10565
$B_{\beta 3}=\frac{T_5-T_4 T_{10}}{\pi^2}$	0	.05376	.05783	.05275	.04643	.03922

$c \longrightarrow$	0.4	0.5	0.6	0.7	0.8	0.9	1.0
T_1/π	−0.06238	−0.04008	−0.02322	−0.01145	−0.00420	−0.00076	0
T_3/π^2	−.01107	−.00539	−.00223	−.00071	−.00014	−.00001	0
$T_4/\pi(=-C_{\beta 2})$	−.25231	−.19550	−.14238	−.09406	−.05204	−.01868	0
T_7/π	−.00161	.00421	.00428	.00302	.00144	.00032	0
T_{10}/π	.66075	.60900	.54982	.48050	.39582	.28231	0
$T_{11}/2\pi$	.27029	.20675	.14874	.09712	.05314	.01889	0
$T_{12}/2\pi$	.01798	.01125	.00636	.00306	.00110	.00020	0
p/π	−.08169	−.06891	−.05433	−.03864	−.02292	−.00879	0
$A_{\beta 3}=\frac{T_4+T_{10}}{\pi}$	.40844	.41350	.40744	.38644	.34378	.26843	0
$B_{\alpha 2}=\frac{1}{\pi}\left(p-T_1-\frac{T_4}{2}\right)$	.10685	.06892	.04008	.01984	.00830	.00131	0
$B_{\beta 2}=-\frac{T_4 T_{11}}{2\pi^2}$	.06820	.04042	.02118	.00914	.00277	.00035	0
$B_{\beta 3}=\frac{T_5-T_4 T_{10}}{\pi^2}$	.03156	.02384	.01651	.00999	.00476	.00127	0

The expressions for the T's are listed in reference 1, page 5.

TABLE 3

Values of $R_{a\alpha}''$

$$R_{a\alpha}=-A_{\alpha 1}+R_{a\alpha}''$$

$1/k$ \ a	−0.5	−0.45	−0.4	−0.3	−0.2	−0.1	0
0	0	0	0	0	0	0	0
.100	0	−.00061840	−.00122	−.00240	−.00352	−.00460	−.00563
.16667	0	−.0017193	−.00341	−.00567	−.00980	−.01079	−.01566
.250	0	−.0038724	−.00767	−.01503	−.02209	−.02884	−.03539
.33333	0	−.0068918	−.01365	−.02677	−.03935	−.05140	−.06292
.500	0	−.015566	−.03084	−.06053	−.08907	−.11645	−.14268
.66667	0	−.027658	−.05484	−.10779	−.15884	−.20799	−.25525
.83333	0	−.043749	−.08677	−.17061	−.25153	−.32953	−.40460
1.000	0	−.063468	−.12593	−.24786	−.36577	−.47966	−.58955
1.250	0	−.10041	−.19937	−.39291	−.58063	−.76253	−.93860
1.51516	0	−.14966	−.29734	−.58674	−.86822	−1.14178	−1.40740
1.66667	0	−.18260	−.36290	−.71661	−1.06113	−1.39647	−1.72263
1.78572	0	−.21098	−.41943	−.82866	−1.22769	−1.61652	−1.99515
2.000	0	−.26779	−.53257	−1.05309	−1.56125	−2.05795	−2.54230
2.27273	0	−.35100	−.69838	−1.38230	−2.05174	−2.70670	−3.34720
2.500	0	−.42981	−.85555	−1.69450	−2.51700	−3.32300	−4.11250
2.94118	0	−.60814	−1.21120	−2.40192	−3.57222	−4.72208	−5.85150
3.33333	0	−.79566	−1.58535	−3.14680	−4.68435	−6.19800	−7.68775
4.16667	0	−1.2871	−2.56638	−5.10072	−7.60602	−10.07728	−12.52150
5.000	0	−1.9086	−3.80774	−7.57776	−11.31006	−15.00464	−18.66150
6.250	0	−3.0910	−6.17025	−12.29360	−18.37005	−24.39960	−30.38225
8.33333	0	−5.7421	−11.46918	−22.87832	−34.22742	−45.51648	−56.74550
10.000	0	−8.4837	−16.95014	−33.83136	−50.64366	−67.38704	−84.06150
12.500	0	−13.635	−27.25090	−54.42160	−81.51210	−108.52240	−135.45250
16.66667	0	−25.006	−49.98777	−99.88048	−149.67813	−199.38072	−248.98825
20.000	0	−36.608	−73.18980	−146.27520	−219.25620	−292.13280	−364.90500

TABLE 3—Continued

Values of $I_{a\alpha}''$

$I_{a\alpha}=1/k\ I_{a\alpha}''$

1/k \ a	−0.5	−0.45	−0.4	−0.3	−0.2	−0.1	0
0	1. 00000	0. 90250	0. 81000	0. 64000	0. 49000	0. 36000	0. 25000
. 100	1. 00000	. 90256	. 81014	. 64031	. 49049	. 36070	. 25094
. 16667	1. 00000	. 90268	. 81038	. 64083	. 49135	. 36192	. 25258
. 250	1. 00000	. 90291	. 81086	. 64187	. 49303	. 36432	. 25578
. 33333	1. 00000	. 90323	. 81154	. 64331	. 49535	. 36764	. 26019
. 500	1. 00000	. 90415	. 81345	. 64741	. 50189	. 37689	. 27240
. 66667	1. 00000	. 90524	. 81570	. 65224	. 50962	. 38784	. 28690
. 83333	1. 00000	. 90696	. 81922	. 65962	. 52126	. 40404	. 30810
1. 000	1. 00000	. 90879	. 82297	. 66751	. 53363	. 42133	. 33060
1. 250	1. 00000	. 91192	. 82938	. 68093	. 55464	. 45051	. 36855
1. 51516	1. 00000	. 91568	. 83706	. 69691	. 57956	. 48501	. 40325
1. 66667	1. 00000	. 91797	. 84175	. 70664	. 59469	. 50590	. 44025
1. 78572	1. 00000	. 91986	. 84557	. 71457	. 60701	. 52286	. 46215
2. 000	1. 00000	. 92334	. 85266	. 72923	. 62972	. 55413	. 50245
2. 27273	1. 00000	. 92794	. 86202	. 74856	. 65962	. 59520	. 55530
2. 500	1. 00000	. 93187	. 87000	. 76500	. 68500	. 63000	. 60000
2. 94118	1. 00000	. 93964	. 88576	. 79739	. 73490	. 69829	. 68755
3. 33333	1. 00000	. 94657	. 89980	. 82620	. 77920	. 75960	. 76500
4. 16667	1. 00000	. 96120	. 92949	. 88675	. 87206	. 88533	. 92655
5. 000	1. 00000	. 97518	. 95763	. 94437	. 96021	1. 00515	1. 07920
6. 250	1. 00000	. 99478	. 99720	1. 02490	1. 08312	1. 17186	1. 29110
8. 33333	1. 00000	1. 0235	1. 05507	1. 24238	1. 26195	1. 41378	1. 59785
10. 000	1. 00000	1. 0433	1. 09484	1. 32296	1. 38436	1. 57904	1. 80700
12. 500	1. 00000	1. 0688	1. 14613	1. 42667	1. 54163	1. 79101	2. 07480
16. 66667	1. 00000	1. 1029	1. 21474	1. 56516	1. 75126	2. 07304	2. 43050
20. 000	1. 00000	1. 1246	1. 25838	1. 65312	1. 88422	2. 25168	2. 65550

TABLE 4

Values of $R_{b\beta}''$

$R\beta=-B_{\beta 1}+R_{b\beta}''$

1/k \ c	0	0. 1	0. 2	0. 3	0. 4	0. 5	0. 6	0. 7	0. 8	0. 9	1. 0
0	0	0	0	0	0	0	0	0	0	0	0
. 100	. 00123	. 00100	. 00078	. 00060	. 00045	. 00032	. 00021	. 00011	. 00005	. 00001	0
. 16667	. 00342	. 00267	. 00219	. 00168	. 00124	. 00087	. 00057	. 00032	. 00014	. 00004	0
. 250	. 00768	. 00623	. 00493	. 00378	. 00279	. 00196	. 00126	. 00071	. 00032	. 00008	0
. 33333	. 01367	. 01109	. 00877	. 00673	. 00498	. 00349	. 00225	. 00119	. 00056	. 00015	0
. 500	. 03085	. 02505	. 01978	. 01519	. 01122	. 00787	. 00507	. 00290	. 00126	. 00033	0
. 66667	. 05494	. 04461	. 03525	. 02706	. 01999	. 01402	. 00905	. 00515	. 00225	. 00059	0
. 83333	. 08647	. 07018	. 05540	. 04250	. 03137	. 02236	. 01419	. 00806	. 00352	. 00092	0
1. 000	. 12517	. 10158	. 08015	. 06146	. 04535	. 03177	. 02048	. 01164	. 00510	. 00133	0
1. 250	. 19729	. 16000	. 12621	. 09670	. 07130	. 04990	. 03214	. 01825	. 00798	. 00208	0
1. 51516	. 29270	. 23723	. 18699	. 14317	. 10547	. 07373	. 04744	. 02690	. 01175	. 00307	0
1. 66667	. 35614	. 28854	. 22733	. 17398	. 12810	. 08952	. 05755	. 03262	. 01425	. 00371	0
1. 78572	. 41062	. 33258	. 26195	. 20040	. 14750	. 10302	. 06620	. 03750	. 01637	. 00426	0
2. 000	. 51910	. 42022	. 33078	. 25290	. 18595	. 12980	. 08335	. 04717	. 02058	. 00535	0
2. 27273	. 67692	. 54753	. 43071	. 32902	. 24177	. 16857	. 10813	. 06113	. 02664	. 00691	0
2. 500	. 82550	. 66738	. 52463	. 40050	. 29407	. 20488	. 13131	. 07417	. 03230	. 00838	0
2. 94118	1. 15907	. 93605	. 73500	. 56040	. 41094	. 28588	. 18296	. 10318	. 04486	. 01162	0
3. 33333	1. 50670	1. 21566	. 95364	. 72637	. 53204	. 36968	. 23630	. 13308	. 05779	. 01495	0
4. 16667	2. 40775	1. 93923	1. 51852	1. 15435	. 84375	. 58495	. 37303	. 20958	. 09080	. 02342	0
5. 000	3. 53385	2. 84190	2. 22193	1. 68628	1. 23036	. 85134	. 54187	. 30380	. 13137	. 03380	0
6. 250	5. 65191	4. 00926	3. 54031	2. 68138	1. 95216	1. 34764	. 85572	. 47853	. 20644	. 05296	0
8. 33333	10. 34067	8. 28124	6. 44720	4. 87081	3. 53670	2. 43454	1. 54135	. 85928	. 36960	. 09447	0
10. 000	15. 14353	12. 11112	9. 41589	7. 10321	5. 14958	3. 53887	2. 23667	1. 24464	. 53443	. 13633	0

TABLE 4—Continued

Values of $I_{b\beta}''$

$I_{b\beta}=1/k\ I_{b\beta}''$

1/k \ c	0	0. 1	0. 2	0. 3	0. 4	0. 5	0. 6	0. 7	0. 8	0. 9	1. 0
0	0. 32298	0. 23827	0. 16930	0. 11472	0. 07306	0. 04275	0. 02213	0. 00944	0. 00283	0. 00035	0
. 100	. 32289	. 23820	. 16925	. 11468	. 07304	. 04273	. 02212	. 00944	. 00283	. 00035	0
. 16667	. 32273	. 23808	. 16916	. 11462	. 07300	. 04269	. 02211	. 00943	. 00283	. 00035	0
. 250	. 32242	. 23784	. 16899	. 11450	. 07292	. 04260	. 02209	. 00942	. 00282	. 00035	0
. 33333	. 32198	. 23751	. 16874	. 11433	. 07280	. 04243	. 02205	. 00940	. 00282	. 00035	0
. 500	. 32075	. 23658	. 16806	. 11386	. 07250	. 04241	. 02195	. 00937	. 00280	. 00035	0
. 66667	. 31931	. 23548	. 16727	. 11331	. 07213	. 04220	. 02184	. 00931	. 00279	. 00034	0
. 83333	. 31714	. 23385	. 16609	. 11249	. 07161	. 04183	. 02168	. 00925	. 00277	. 00034	0
1. 000	. 31483	. 23212	. 16484	. 11163	. 07106	. 04156	. 02150	. 00917	. 00274	. 00034	0
1. 250	. 31090	. 22919	. 16273	. 11019	. 07013	. 04101	. 02121	. 00904	. 00271	. 00034	0
1. 51516	. 30625	. 22572	. 16024	. 10849	. 06903	. 04036	. 02087	. 00890	. 00267	. 00033	0
1. 66667	. 30343	. 22362	. 15873	. 10746	. 06837	. 03997	. 02067	. 00881	. 00264	. 00033	0
1. 78572	. 30112	. 22190	. 15752	. 10662	. 06783	. 03966	. 02050	. 00874	. 00262	. 00033	0
2. 000	. 29688	. 21876	. 15526	. 10509	. 06685	. 03908	. 02021	. 00861	. 00257	. 00033	0
2. 27273	. 29130	. 21462	. 15231	. 10307	. 06556	. 03832	. 01981	. 00845	. 00252	. 00032	0
2. 500	. 28657	. 21112	. 14980	. 10137	. 06448	. 03768	. 01948	. 00831	. 00249	. 00031	0
2. 94118	. 27726	. 20423	. 14491	. 09803	. 06235	. 03643	. 01883	. 00803	. 00240	. 00030	0
3. 33333	. 26899	. 19813	. 14056	. 09509	. 06046	. 03533	. 01826	. 00778	. 00232	. 00029	0
4. 16667	. 25166	. 18536	. 13152	. 08894	. 05655	. 03305	. 01708	. 00728	. 00217	. 00027	0
5. 000	. 23522	. 17325	. 12292	. 08315	. 05286	. 03089	. 01596	. 00681	. 00203	. 00025	0
6. 250	. 21229	. 15642	. 11100	. 07510	. 04775	. 02791	. 01442	. 00615	. 00183	. 00023	0
8. 33333	. 17895	. 13197	. 09372	. 06345	. 04038	. 02362	. 01220	. 00521	. 00155	. 00019	0
10. 000	. 15613	. 11525	. 08194	. 05551	. 03535	. 02069	. 01070	. 00457	. 00135	. 00017	0

TABLE I.—EXPERIMENTAL RESULTS OF FLUTTER INVESTIGATION

Figure number	Wing model	Wing dimensions	First bending (cycles/sec.)	Second bending (cycles/sec.)	Third bending (cycles/sec.)	Fourth bending (cycles/sec.)	First torsion (cycles/sec.)	Second torsion (cycles/sec.)	c. g. location (percent chord from L. E.): Calculated	c. g. location (percent chord from L. E.): Observed	Stiffness axis (percent chord from L. E.)	r_a^2 (radius of gyration)² (cf. notation)	Wing weight (lb.)	Test conditions and remarks	Run	Air density, ρ	Flutter frequency (cycles/sec.)	Flutter velocity (m. p. h.)	Theoretical results
10	1	Rectangular: 12-in. chord; 6-ft. 9-in. span	1.09	6.8	19.7	-----	15.0	-----	41.2	41.2	30.0	0.3125	7.32	Tests on wing 1 were preliminary. A stop was used.	20-2	2.283×10^{-3}	-----	97.1	-----
														Later tests employed a screen instead	20-3	2.278		99.2	100
														Damping test	20-4				
														Run 20-3 repeated	20-5	2.274		98.5	
														Weight, 0.028 lb. on L. E. 18 in. from tip.	20-8	2.265		114.4	
11	2A	Rectangular: 12-in. chord; 6-ft. 9-in. span	1.29	7.7	21.0	-----	18.1	-----	41.2	42.3	30.0	0.3125	36.50	Stop used; all other tests screen used (tip flutter).	20-10	2.256	15.0	188.0	Figs. 17 and 19
														Model support fractured	20-11			203.0	
														Model repaired	20-15	2.154	10.2	202.0	
														Restraining wires 17 in. from tip, 3.6 in. from L. E.	20-16	2.216		151.0	
							16.7							Nacelle 6.10 lb. placed 2 ft. from top, 2.70 in. ahead of c. g.	20-17	2.116	9.45	216.0	
							17.0							Nacelle placed 2 ft. from top, 1.34 in. back of c. g.	20-18	2.170		197.0	
														Run 20-16 repeated	20-19	2.225		154.0	
							14.8							Counterweight 3.07 lb. at L. E. 13 in. from tip.	20-20	2.173		197.0	
														Run 20-20 repeated	20-21	2.174		202.0	
11	2B	Same as 2A	1.31	7.7	20.8	-----	17.8	-----	42.5	-----	30.0	-----	35.95	Plain; no weight attached	20-23	2.159	10.2	205.9	Figs. 17 and 19
														Disk 12.77 lb. 12-in. diam. on bottom; c. g. of disk on c. g. of airfoil.	20-24	2.204	8.35	154.2	
														Disk 12.45 lb. 17-in. diam. in same position as 20-24.	20-25	2.228	7.35	121.5	
														Disk as in 20-25 placed 1 in. ahead of c. g.	20-26	2.232	7.48	116.2	
														Disk as in 20-25 placed 1 in. back of c. g.	20-27	2.214	7.25	131.9	
														Run 20-23 repeated	20-28	2.149		205.0	
														Airfoil tip restrained by wires	20-29	2.154		205.1	
														Run 20-25 repeated	20-30	2.232		120.7	
														Run 20-23 repeated	20-31	2.146		199.3	
														Same as 20-31, movies taken	20-32	2.144		198.7	Fig. 21
														Plain; restraining wires 8 in. from tip	20-33	2.122	10.8	208.0	
														Plain; restraining wires 60 in. from tip	20-34	2.171	13.1	159.5	
														Restraining wires 40 in. from tip; model broke near tip.	20-35	2.053	8.24	284.7	
11	2C	Rectangular: 12-in. chord; 6-ft. 4-in. span	1.40	8.2	22.5	-----	18.8	-----	42.5	-----	30.0	-----	-----	Model 2B repaired	20-73	2.133×10^{-3}	-----	220.4	Fig. 23
			1.22	7.2	20.8	-----	16.2							With 3.05-lb. counterweight 1 in. from tip at L. E.	20-74	2.169		196.8	
			1.29	8.2	22.4	-----	15.8							Counterweight 13 in. from tip at L. E.	20-75	2.152		210.5	
			1.34	8.0	22.2	-----	16.0							Counterweight 25 in. from tip at L. E.	20-76	2.101		244.6	
			1.38	7.6	22.5	-----	16.8							Counterweight 37 in. from tip at L. E.	20-77	2.119		235.7	
			1.39	7.8	22.0	-----	17.4							Counterweight 49 in. from tip at L. E.	20-78	2.122		232.2	
			1.39	8.0	21.2	-----	18.2							Counterweight 61 in. from tip at L. E.	20-79	2.136		219.8	
			1.24	7.7	19.8	-----	13.8							With weights simultaneously at 13 in., 37 in., and 61 in. from tip.	20-81	2.056		294.3	
12	3	Taper ratio, 2:1	1.65	6.8	16.5	30.7	29.1	-----	42.5	42.0	30.0	-----	20.48	Plain tapered wing	20-22	2.160	16.4	216.0	
														Run 20-22 repeated	20-68	2.150		214.9	
			1.64	5.2	13.1	28.4	8.9	37.8						Nacelle 6.10 lb.; c. g. 3.10 in. back of c. g. of airfoil.	20-69	2.232		109.2	
							9.1							Nacelle placed 1.10 in. back of c. g. Fig. 25.	20-70	2.245		91.0	
							8.8							Nacelle placed 2.80 in. ahead of c. g.	20-71	2.240	8.50	90.4	
														Run 20-68 repeated	20-72	2.149	14.0	213.3	
13	4	Taper ratio, 4:1	2.07	6.0	13.3	24.0	36.2	-----	41.2	41.5	-----	-----	16.88	Violent flutter suddenly. Wing bent out of shape. Fig. 20.	20-67	2.174	-----	203.9	Fig. 17
12	3	Taper ratio, 2:1	1.65	6.8	16.5	30.7	29.1	-----	42.5	42.0	-----	-----	20.48	Restraining wires 59 in. from tip at stiffness axis.	20-89	2.187	-----	211.1	Fig. 22
														Same except wires 2 in. ahead of stiffness axis.	20-90	2.200	-----	204.4	
														Same except wires 4 in. back of stiffness axis.	20-91	-----	-----	-----	
														Restraining wires 40 in. from tip at stiffness axis.	20-93	2.234	-----	155.8	
														Restraining wires 17 in. from tip at stiffness axis.	20-94	2.229	-----	152.9	
														Restraining wires 1 in. from tip at stiffness axis.	20-95	2.182	-----	211.4	
														Restraining wires 27 in. from tip at stiffness axis.	20-96	2.202	-----	200.8	
16	6	-----	2.30	12.8	31.2	-----	19.2	-----	42.5	45.2	-----	-----	3.45	Rectangular wooden model; 81-in. span.	20-82	2.268	-----	73.8	
16	7	-----	4.92	25.0	67.2	-----	35.8	-----	42.5	43.9	-----	-----	6.01	Tapered wooden model; completely destroyed by violent flutter.	20-92	2.199	-----	205.6	

TABLE IA.—WING-AILERON FLUTTER TESTS

Wing model	Aileron (see fig. 14)	Wing weight (lb.)	Aileron weight (lb.)	First bending (cycles/sec.)	Aileron frequency (cycles/sec.)	r_β^2 (cf. notation)	Test conditions and remarks	Run	Air density, ρ	Lower critical velocity (m. p. h.)	Air density, ρ	Upper critical velocity (m. p. h.)
5	AII	44.84	0.950	10.68	0	0.0019	Aileron with 3 free hinges	20-36	2.273×10^{-3}	53.9		
	AV		.618		0			20-37	2.278	50.7		
	AII		.950		5.75		Aileron with springs	20-38	2.273	50.4		
	AV		.618		7.91			20-39	2.271	42.4		
	AII		.950		12.5			20-40	2.269	76.8		
	AII				8.50		Theoretical results for aileron AII shown in fig. 26	20-41	2.306	44.8		
	AII				11.0			20-42	2.301	55.4		
	AII				11.0			20-43			2.240×10^{-3}	147.0
	AII				12.5			20-44			2.229	151.6
	AII				13.1			20-45	2.259	98.4		
	AII				9.67			20-46	2.283	57.4	2.236	159.3
	AII				9.17			20-47	2.268	50.0	2.162	193.0
	AII				5.75			20-48	2.245	52.6	2.165	199.9
	AII				0		Hinges free	20-49	2.242	58.3	2.138	225.1
	AII				13.3			20-50	2.242	60.3	2.200	125.7
	AII				10.8			20-51	2.240	65.0	2.199	149.9
	AII				0		3 free hinges with aileron counterweight, 0.557 lb., Fig. 15.	20-52		No flutter		
	AII				0		Counterweight, 0.452 lb	20-53		No flutter		
	AII				0		Counterweight, 0.346 lb	20-54	2.249	75.2	2.243	206.1
	AII				0		Counterweight, 0.398 lb	20-55	2.243	99.5	2.173	197.8
	AII				3.00		do	20-56	2.243	99.9	2.193	167.3
	AII				6.92		do	20-57	2.262	62.8	2.218	147.1
	AI		.567		0		2 free hinges	20-58	2.262	65.3	2.163	218.7
	AVII		.300		0		3 free hinges	20-59	2.259	57.8	2.221	105.7
	AIII		1.43		0		4 free hinges	20-60	2.250	60.2	2.161	205.3
	AIII				0		4 free hinges with lead for damping	20-61	2.251	52.2	2.199	145.3
	AIII				0		do	20-63	2.261	78.0	2.171	199.5
	AIII				0		do	20-64	2.255	97.8	2.150	223.2
	AIII				4.67		do	20-65	2.259	67.3	2.178	166.8
	AIII				6.00		do	20-66	2.260	63.8	2.210	161.6
	AVIII		2.01		0		Hinge-pin position varied as shown in fig. 27	20-83	2.285	64.4	2.178	230.5
	AVIII				0		do	20-84	2.281	93.6	2.143	266.0
	AVIII				0		do	20-86		No flutter		
	AVIII				0		do	20-87	2.250	85.5	2.098	290.8
	AVIII				7.00		do	20-88	2.259	41.1	2.130	264.1

NONSTATIONARY FLOW ABOUT A WING-AILERON-TAB COMBINATION INCLUDING AERODYNAMIC BALANCE

BY THEODORE THEODORSEN
AND I.E. GARRICK

National Advisory Committee for Aeronautics

Report No. 736, 1942

SUMMARY

The present paper presents a continuation of the work published in Report No. 496. The results of that paper have been extended to include the effect of aerodynamic balance and the effect of a tab added to the aileron. The aerodynamic coefficients are presented in a form convenient for application to the flutter problem.

INTRODUCTION

It is the object of this paper to present theoretical expressions for the forces and the moments in a uniform horizontal air stream on a plane airfoil performing small sinusoidal motions in several degrees of freedom: vertical motion, torsional movement about an arbitrary spanwise axis, aileron movement about a hinge axis not necessarily located at the leading edge of the aileron, and tab movement similar to the aileron movement. The solution of this problem has direct application to the larger problem of flutter involving these various degrees of freedom and, in particular, to flutter of tails with control surfaces, including servocontrols.

The development of the theory is analogous with that of Theodorsen (reference 1) who treats explicitly the case of three degrees of freedom: vertical motion, torsional movement about an arbitrary spanwise axis, and an aileron movement about a hinge axis located at the leading edge of the aileron.

Since this work was originally begun, there have appeared two German papers, one by Küssner and Schwarz (reference 2) and one by Dietze (reference 3), that bear directly on the problem. A comparison of the results of this paper with the results of Küssner and Schwarz, obtained by a different development, is given in appendix A.

AIR FORCES AND MOMENTS

Figure 1 represents a wing section with two hinges, an aileron (rudder) hinge at $x=e$ and a tab hinge at $x=f$. The leading edge of the wing is at $x=-1$ and the trailing edge at $x=1$. The leading edge of the aileron is at $x=c$ and the distance from the hinge to the aileron leading edge $e-c$ is denoted by l. The leading edge of the tab is at $x=d$ and the distance from the tab hinge to the tab leading edge $f-d$ is denoted by m. The wing is undergoing the following motions with small amplitudes: a displacement h (velocity $\dot{h}$) in a vertical direction downward; a turning about $x=a$, the instantaneous angle of attack being α; a rotation of the aileron about $x=e$, the angle of the aileron or rudder being β measured with respect to the wing; and a rotation of the tab about $x=f$, the angle of the tab being γ measured with respect to the aileron. The

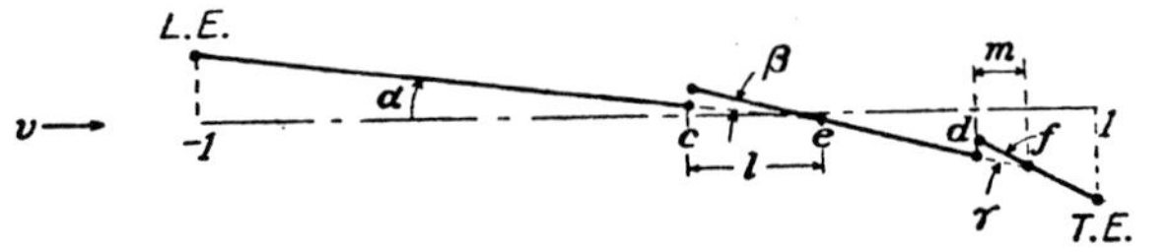

FIGURE 1.—Representation of wing section with aileron and tab showing main parameters.

actual chord is considered to be of length $2b$, so that b is used throughout the analysis as a reference length.

The procedure and method follow those of reference 1. In order to avoid needless repetition of certain expressions contained in this reference, the following notation is frequently used. A symbol or equation followed by (reference 1) denotes the corresponding expression of reference 1. The final results will, however, be explicitly given independently of reference 1.

The air forces and the moments are treated in two groups: the noncirculatory and the circulatory. The expressions for the noncirculatory part consist of apparent-mass terms, which do not depend on the vorticity in the wake. The circulatory part takes account of the vorticity in the wake generated at the trailing edge.

Noncirculatory forces and moments.—The noncirculatory velocity potential at the surface, associated with the various motions of the airfoil, is

$$\phi=\phi_{\dot{h}}+\phi_\alpha+\phi_{\dot{\alpha}}+\phi_\beta+\phi_{\dot{\beta}}+\phi_\gamma+\phi_{\dot{\gamma}} \qquad (1)$$

where only ϕ_β, $\phi_{\dot{\beta}}$, ϕ_γ, and $\phi_{\dot{\gamma}}$ need be given here.[1]

$$\phi_\beta=\phi_\beta\text{ (reference 1)}+v\beta lb\frac{1}{\pi}\log N(x,c) \qquad (2)$$

$$\phi_{\dot{\beta}}=\phi_{\dot{\beta}}\text{ (reference 1)}$$
$$-\beta lb^2\frac{1}{\pi}\left[\sqrt{1-x^2}\cos^{-1}c-(x-c)\log N(x,c)\right] \qquad (3)$$

and

$$\left.\begin{aligned}\phi_\gamma&=\phi_\beta\\ \phi_{\dot{\gamma}}&=\phi_{\dot{\beta}}\end{aligned}\right\} \qquad (4)$$

with β, c, and l replaced by γ, d, and m, respectively. The two extra terms appearing in ϕ_β and $\phi_{\dot{\beta}}$, which contain the coefficient l, arise from the aerodynamic-balance effect, that is, the offset of the aileron hinge position from the aileron leading edge. The derivation is as follows:

The motion of the aileron around $x=e$ is considered separated into two parts, a turning around the aileron leading edge plus a vertical displacement of the aileron relative to the wing (fig. 2). The amplitude of the first type of motion is β and of the second type of motion is $bH=b\beta(e-c)=b\beta l$. The additional potentials referred to are then due to the effect of the vertical displacement bH and the associated vertical velocity $b\dot{H}$.

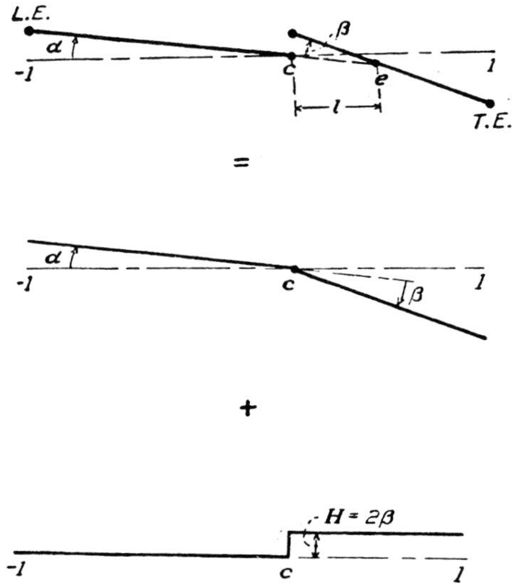

FIGURE 2.—Representation of the motion of the aileron around $x=e$ as separated into a turning around $x=c$ plus a vertical displacement.

The potential associated with bH is determined from a limiting case (as $c'\rightarrow c$) of a shape (fig. 3) located on the x axis from $x=-1$ to $x=c$ and at ordinate H from $x=c'$ to $x=1$ and joined by a straight-line segment from $x=c$ to $x=c'$. This potential is associated with a vertical-velocity distribution:

$$\begin{aligned} w(x_1)&=0 && -1<x_1<c\\ &=v_H=\frac{vH}{c'-c} && c<x_1<c'\\ &=0 && c'<x_1<1\end{aligned}$$

The surface potential associated with a vertical upward velocity of the air of magnitude w at the element located at $x=x_1$ is

$$\Delta\phi=\frac{bw}{2\pi}\log\frac{(x-x_1)^2+(y-y_1)^2}{(x-x_1)^2+(y+y_1)^2}dx_1 \qquad (5)$$

where

$$y=\sqrt{1-x^2}\text{ and }y_1=\sqrt{1-x_1{}^2}$$

Equation (5) is fundamental to the description of the noncirculatory flow pattern since, by integration with respect to x_1, any admissible potential distribution may be obtained. The integrated result desired in this case as $c'\rightarrow c$ is simply

$$\phi_H=\frac{bvH}{2\pi}\log\frac{(x-c)^2+(\sqrt{1-x^2}-\sqrt{1-c^2})^2}{(x-c)^2+(\sqrt{1-x^2}+\sqrt{1-c^2})^2}$$
$$=vb\beta l\frac{1}{\pi}\log N(x,c) \qquad (6)$$

where

$$N(x,c)=\left|\frac{1-xc-\sqrt{1-x^2}\sqrt{1-c^2}}{c-x}\right|$$

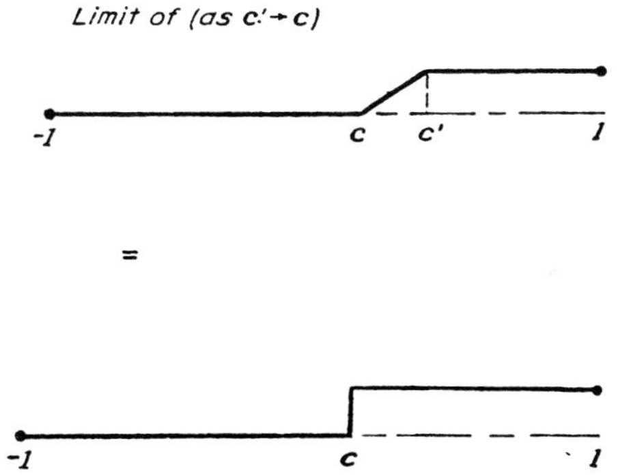

FIGURE 3.—Representation of the sharp vertical displacement as a limit.

The potential associated with $b\dot{H}$ is due to a vertical velocity distribution

$$\begin{aligned} w&=0 && -1<x_1<c\\ &=\dot{\beta}lb && c<x_1<1\end{aligned}$$

and is (see ϕ_β, reference 1, p. 5)

$$\phi_{\dot{H}}=\int_{x_1=-1}^{1}\Delta\phi$$
$$=-\beta lb^2\frac{1}{\pi}[\sqrt{1-x^2}\cos^{-1}c-(x-c)\log N(x,c)] \qquad (7)$$

Exactly similar considerations were made for the tab and lead to equations (4).

It may be remarked that the analysis assumes no leak of fluid in the gap between the aileron and the wing; that is, the gap is considered sealed.

The following new sets of integral evaluations will be required. The expressions for the T and Y terms are listed in appendix B. The T terms are functions of c or of d only. When no explicit mention is made, c is

[1] The expressions for the ϕ values are to be understood prefixed by $\pm$ signs: by $+$ for the upper side of the line segment and by $-$ for the lower side.

to be understood. The Y terms are functions of both c and d.

$$\int_c^1 \phi_\beta dx = -\frac{bv\beta}{2\pi}(T_5 + 2l\sqrt{1-c^2}\cos^{-1}c)$$

$$\int_c^1 \phi_{\dot\beta} dx = -\frac{b^2\dot\beta}{2\pi}(T_2 - lT_5)$$

$$\int_c^1 \phi_\beta (x-c)dx = -\frac{bv\beta}{2\pi}(T_2 - lT_0)$$

$$\int_c^1 \phi_{\dot\beta}(x-c)dx = -\frac{b^2\dot\beta}{2\pi}(T_3 - lT_2)$$

$$\int_1^1 \phi_\beta dx = -\frac{bv\beta}{2}(T_4 + 2\sqrt{1-c^2})$$

$$\int_{-1}^1 \phi_{\dot\beta} dx = -\frac{b^2\dot\beta}{2}(T_1 - lT_4)$$

$$\int_{-1}^1 \phi_\beta (x-c)dx = -\frac{bv\beta}{2}(T_8 - lc\sqrt{1-c^2})$$

$$\int_{-1}^1 \phi_{\dot\beta}(x-c)dx = -\frac{b^2\dot\beta}{2}(T_7 - lT_8)$$

$$\int_c^1 \phi_\gamma dx = -\frac{bv\gamma}{2\pi}(Y_1 + mY_2)$$

$$\int_c^1 \phi_{\dot\gamma} dx = -\frac{b^2\dot\gamma}{2\pi}(Y_3 - mY_1)$$

$$\int_c^1 \phi_\gamma (x-c)dx = -\frac{bv\gamma}{2\pi}(Y_4 - mY_5)$$

$$\int_c^1 \phi_{\dot\gamma}(x-c)dx = -\frac{b^2\dot\gamma}{2\pi}(Y_6 - mY_4)$$

$$\int_d^1 \phi_\beta dx = -\frac{bv\beta}{2\pi}(Y_1 + lY_7)$$

$$\int_d^1 \phi_{\dot\beta} dx = -\frac{b^2\dot\beta}{2\pi}(Y_4 - lY_1)$$

$$\int_d^1 \phi_\beta (x-d)dx = -\frac{bv\beta}{2\pi}(Y_3 - lY_8)$$

$$\int_d^1 \phi_{\dot\beta}(x-d)dx = -\frac{b^2\dot\beta}{2\pi}(Y_6 - lY_3)$$

The pressure difference on an element of the airfoil located at x is

$$p = -2\rho\left(\frac{v}{b}\frac{\partial\phi}{\partial x} + \frac{\partial\phi}{\partial t}\right) \tag{8}$$

and the total force (positive downward) is therefore

$$P = -2\rho b\int_{-1}^1 \dot\phi dx \tag{9}$$

The moment on the airfoil (positive clockwise) about $x=a$ is

$$M_\alpha = b^2\int_{-1}^1 (x-a)p dx$$

$$= -2\rho b\int_{-1}^1 \dot\phi(x-c)dx + 2\rho vb\int_{-1}^1 \phi dx$$

$$-2\rho b^2(c-a)\int_{-1}^1 \dot\phi dx \tag{10}$$

The moment on the aileron (positive clockwise) about the hinge $x=e$ is

$$M_\beta = b^2\int_c^1 (x-e)p dx$$

This moment may be written

$$M_\beta = -2\rho b^2\int_c^1 \dot\phi(x-c)dx + 2\rho vb\int_c^1 \phi dx$$

$$+2\rho b^2 l\int_c^1 \phi dx + 2\rho vbl[\phi]_c^1 \tag{11}$$

Similarly, for the moment on the tab about the hinge $x=f$,

$$M_\gamma = -2\rho b^2\int_d^1 \dot\phi(x-d)dx + 2\rho vb\int_d^1 \phi dx$$

$$+2\rho b^2 m\int_d^1 \dot\phi dx + 2\rho vbm[\phi]_d^1 \tag{12}$$

Circulatory terms.—The potential at the surface of the airfoil associated with an element (counterclockwise) of vorticity in the wake at x_0 of magnitude $\Delta\Gamma = Ubdx_0$ is (reference 1, p. 6)

$$\phi_\Gamma dx_0 = \frac{\Delta\Gamma}{2\pi}\tan^{-1}\frac{\sqrt{1-x^2}\sqrt{x_0^2-1}}{1-xx_0} \tag{13}$$

where $|x|<1$ and $x_0>1$.

The potential for the entire wake is

$$\Phi_\Gamma = \int_1^\infty \phi_\Gamma dx_0 \tag{14}$$

With the assumption that the wake remains where formed, the expression for the pressure at x (equation (8)) becomes

$$p = -2\rho\frac{v}{b}\left(\frac{\partial\Phi_\Gamma}{\partial x} + \frac{\partial\Phi_\Gamma}{\partial x_0}\right)$$

$$= -2\rho v\int_1^\infty \frac{U}{2\pi}\frac{x_0+x}{\sqrt{1-x^2}\sqrt{x_0^2-1}}dx_0 \tag{15}$$

The Kutta condition for smooth flow at the trailing edge, which requires that $\partial/\partial x(\Phi_\Gamma + \phi)$ must remain finite for $x=1$, leads to the result

$$\frac{1}{2\pi}\int_1^\infty U\sqrt{\frac{x_0+1}{x_0-1}}dx_0 = v\alpha + \dot h + b\left(\frac{1}{2}-a\right)\dot\alpha + \frac{1}{\pi}(T_{10} - lT_{21})v\beta$$

$$+\frac{1}{2\pi}(T_{11} - 2lT_{10})b\dot\beta + \frac{1}{\pi}(T_{10}(d) - mT_{21}(d))v\gamma$$

$$+\frac{1}{2\pi}(T_{11}(d) - 2mT_{10}(d))b\dot\gamma \tag{16}$$

This quantity will be denoted by Q.

When the various degrees of freedom of the airfoil are undergoing sinusoidal motions of the form $e^{i\omega t}$ for a long period of time, the wake is also sinusoidal and it is convenient to introduce the parameter k defined by the relation

$$\omega t = ks = k\frac{vt}{b}$$

or

$$k = \frac{\omega b}{v} \tag{17}$$

The force (negative lift) on the airfoil due to vorticity is

$$P=b\int_{-1}^{1} p\,dx=-2\pi\rho v b C(k) Q \tag{18}$$

where $C(k)=F(k)+iG(k)$ denotes the fundamental function introduced by Theodorsen (reference 1, p. 8).

The moment about $x=a$ is

$$M_\alpha=b^2\int_{-1}^{1} p(x-a)\,dx=2\pi\rho v b^2\left[\left(a+\frac{1}{2}\right)C(k)-\frac{1}{2}\right]Q \tag{19}$$

The hinge moment on the aileron about $x=e$ is

$$M_\beta=b^2\int_{c}^{1} p(x-e)\,dx=b^2\int_{c}^{1} p(x-c)\,dx+b^2(c-e)\int_{c}^{1} p\,dx$$
$$=-\rho v b^2(T_{12}C(k)-T_4)Q+\rho v b^2 l(2T_{20}C(k)+2\sqrt{1-c^2})Q \tag{20}$$

Similarly, the moment on the tab around its hinge, $x=f$, is

$$M_\gamma=-\rho v b^2(T_{12}(d)C(k)-T_4(d))Q$$
$$+\rho v b^2 m(2T_{20}(d)C(k)+2\sqrt{1-d^2})Q \tag{21}$$

Finally, when both the noncirculatory and the circulatory terms are combined, there result the following expressions for the force and moments.

TOTAL FORCE

$$P=-\rho b^2(\pi\ddot{h}+v\pi\dot{\alpha}-\pi ba\ddot{\alpha}-vT_4\dot{\beta}-T_1 b\ddot{\beta}-vT_4(d)\dot{\gamma}-T_1(d)b\ddot{\gamma})-\rho b^2 l(-2\sqrt{1-c^2}v\dot{\beta}+bT_4\ddot{\beta})$$
$$-\rho b^2 m(-2\sqrt{1-d^2}v\dot{\gamma}+bT_4(d)\ddot{\gamma})-2\pi\rho v b C Q \tag{22}$$

where

$$Q=v\alpha+\dot{h}+b\left(\frac{1}{2}-a\right)\dot{\alpha}+\frac{1}{\pi}(T_{10}-lT_{21})v\beta+\frac{1}{2\pi}(T_{11}-2lT_{10})b\dot{\beta}+\frac{1}{\pi}(T_{10}(d)-mT_{21}(d))v\gamma+\frac{1}{2\pi}(T_{11}(d)-2mT_{10}(d))b\dot{\gamma}$$

TOTAL MOMENT ABOUT $x=a$

$$M_\alpha=-\rho b^2\left[-a\pi b\ddot{h}+\pi\left(\frac{1}{2}-a\right)vb\dot{\alpha}+\pi b^2\left(\frac{1}{8}+a^2\right)\ddot{\alpha}+T_{15}v^2\beta+T_{16}vb\dot{\beta}+2T_{13}b^2\ddot{\beta}+T_{15}(d)v^2\gamma+T_{16}(d)vb\dot{\gamma}\right.$$
$$\left.+2T_{13}(d)b^2\ddot{\gamma}\right]-\rho b^2 l(T_{22}v^2\beta+T_{23}vb\dot{\beta}+T_{24}b^2\ddot{\beta})-\rho b^2 m(T_{22}(d)v^2\gamma+T_{23}(d)vb\dot{\gamma}+T_{24}(d)b^2\ddot{\gamma})+2\pi\rho v b^2\left(a+\frac{1}{2}\right)CQ \tag{23}$$

TOTAL AILERON HINGE MOMENT

$$M_\beta=-\rho b^2\left(-T_1 b\ddot{h}+T_{17}vb\dot{\alpha}+2T_{13}b^2\ddot{\alpha}+\frac{1}{\pi}T_{18}v^2\beta+\frac{1}{\pi}T_{19}vb\dot{\beta}-\frac{1}{\pi}T_3 b^2\ddot{\beta}+\frac{1}{\pi}Y_9 v^2\gamma+\frac{1}{\pi}Y_{10}vb\dot{\gamma}-\frac{1}{\pi}Y_6 b^2\ddot{\gamma}\right)$$
$$-\rho b^2 l\left(T_4 b\ddot{h}+T_{25}vb\dot{\alpha}+T_{24}b^2\ddot{\alpha}+\frac{1}{\pi}T_{26}v^2\beta+\frac{1}{\pi}T_{27}bv\dot{\beta}+\frac{2}{\pi}T_2 b^2\ddot{\beta}+\frac{1}{\pi}Y_{11}v^2\gamma+\frac{1}{\pi}Y_{12}bv\dot{\gamma}+\frac{1}{\pi}Y_3 b^2\ddot{\gamma}\right)$$
$$-\rho b^2 l^2\left(\frac{1}{\pi}T_{28}v^2\beta+\frac{1}{\pi}T_{29}bv\dot{\beta}-\frac{1}{\pi}T_5 b^2\ddot{\beta}\right)-\rho b^2 m\left(\frac{1}{\pi}Y_{13}v^2\gamma+\frac{1}{\pi}Y_{14}bv\dot{\gamma}+\frac{1}{\pi}Y_4 b^2\ddot{\gamma}\right)$$
$$-\rho b^2 lm\left(\frac{1}{\pi}Y_{15}v^2\gamma+\frac{1}{\pi}Y_{16}bv\dot{\gamma}-\frac{1}{\pi}Y_1 b^2\ddot{\gamma}\right)-\rho v b^2(T_{12}-2lT_{20})CQ \tag{24}$$

TOTAL TAB MOMENT

$$M_\gamma=-\rho b^2\left(-T_1(d)b\ddot{h}+T_{17}(d)vb\dot{\alpha}+2T_{13}(d)b^2\ddot{\alpha}+\frac{1}{\pi}Y_{17}v^2\beta+\frac{1}{\pi}Y_{18}vb\dot{\beta}-\frac{1}{\pi}Y_6 b^2\ddot{\beta}+\frac{1}{\pi}T_{18}(d)v^2\gamma+\frac{1}{\pi}T_{19}(d)vb\dot{\gamma}\right.$$
$$\left.-\frac{1}{\pi}T_3(d)b^2\ddot{\gamma}\right)-\rho b^2 m\left(T_4(d)b\ddot{h}+T_{25}(d)vb\dot{\alpha}+T_{24}(d)b^2\ddot{\alpha}+\frac{1}{\pi}Y_{19}v^2\beta+\frac{1}{\pi}Y_{20}vb\dot{\beta}+\frac{1}{\pi}Y_4 b\ddot{\beta}\right.$$
$$\left.+\frac{1}{\pi}T_{26}(d)v^2\gamma+\frac{1}{\pi}T_{27}(d)bv\dot{\gamma}+\frac{2}{\pi}T_2(d)b^2\ddot{\gamma}\right)-\rho b^2 m^2\left(\frac{1}{\pi}T_{28}(d)v^2\gamma+\frac{1}{\pi}T_{29}(d)bv\dot{\gamma}-\frac{1}{\pi}T_5(d)b^2\ddot{\gamma}\right)$$
$$-\rho b^2 l\left(\frac{1}{\pi}Y_{21}v^2\beta+\frac{1}{\pi}Y_{22}bv\dot{\beta}+\frac{1}{\pi}Y_3 b^2\ddot{\beta}\right)-\rho b^2 lm\left(\frac{1}{\pi}Y_{23}v^2\beta+\frac{1}{\pi}Y_{24}bv\dot{\beta}-\frac{1}{\pi}Y_1 b^2\ddot{\beta}\right)-\rho v b^2(T_{12}(d)-2mT_{20}(d))CQ \tag{25}$$

Discussion of the term T_{28}.—The concentrated sink-source representing the steep break (fig. 3) properly describes the main flow pattern, but the local flow pattern at the break is incorrect. The underlying theory excludes the possibility of representing the flow at a steep break. The limiting process therefore cannot be used in this simple theory, as far as the local flow is concerned.

There is one term that depends on the local flow condition at the break. This term arises in the evalua-

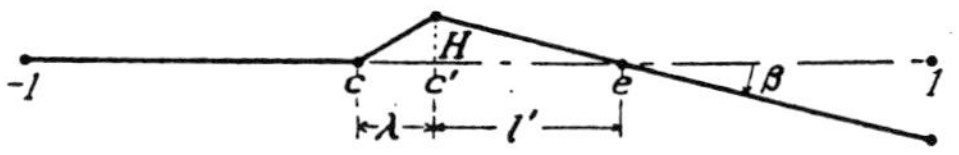

FIGURE 4.—Representation of the effective mean camber line for a displaced aileron with hinge position at $x=e$ as depending upon an additional parameter c'.

tion of $[\phi_\beta]_c^1$ (equation (11)) and is present in the expression for the force on the aileron. It occurs, then, in the expression for hinge moment M_β in the term T_{28} associated with the coefficient $l^2\beta$.

In order to picture the local flow and, at the same time, retain physical reality, it is necessary either to disregard a certain small neighborhood of the break or to spread the concentrated sink-source over a certain finite area. This end may be accomplished by regarding the mean camber line of the displaced aileron with rounded leading edge as depending on an additional parameter c' (fig. 4). Let $e-c'=l'$ and $c'-c=\lambda$. The velocity potential at the surface replacing equation (2) is then

$$\phi_\beta=\phi_{\beta,c'}+\frac{l'}{\lambda}(\phi_{\beta,c'}-\phi_{\beta,c})$$

where $\phi_{\beta,c}$ denotes $\frac{v b\beta}{\pi}[\sqrt{1-x^2}\cos^{-1}c-(x-c)\log N(x,c)]$

The analysis can be performed by use of this equation and a similar one for $\phi_{\dot\beta}$ instead of equations (2) and (3). The result will, however, differ essentially from that already presented in two respects: (1) The average value of l will be slightly less than $e-c$ and will be nearly $e-\frac{c+c'}{2}$. (2) The term $\log N(c,c')$ will occur in T_{28} to replace the infinite term $\log N(c,c)$.

An effective value of c' may be estimated in any given case or may be determined by experiment. The essential point is that the difference $c'-c$ cannot become zero. It appears probable that $c'-c$ is greater than, say, 0.05 $(e-c)$ and less than 0.40 $(e-c)$. As an average value 0.25 $(e-c)$ appears good. Within these limits the value of the term $\log N(c,c')$ is fairly independent of the selection of c'. The effect of the choice of c' in the steady case on the hinge moment is illustrated in figure 5. Conversely, the experimental hinge-moment values may be used to estimate c'.

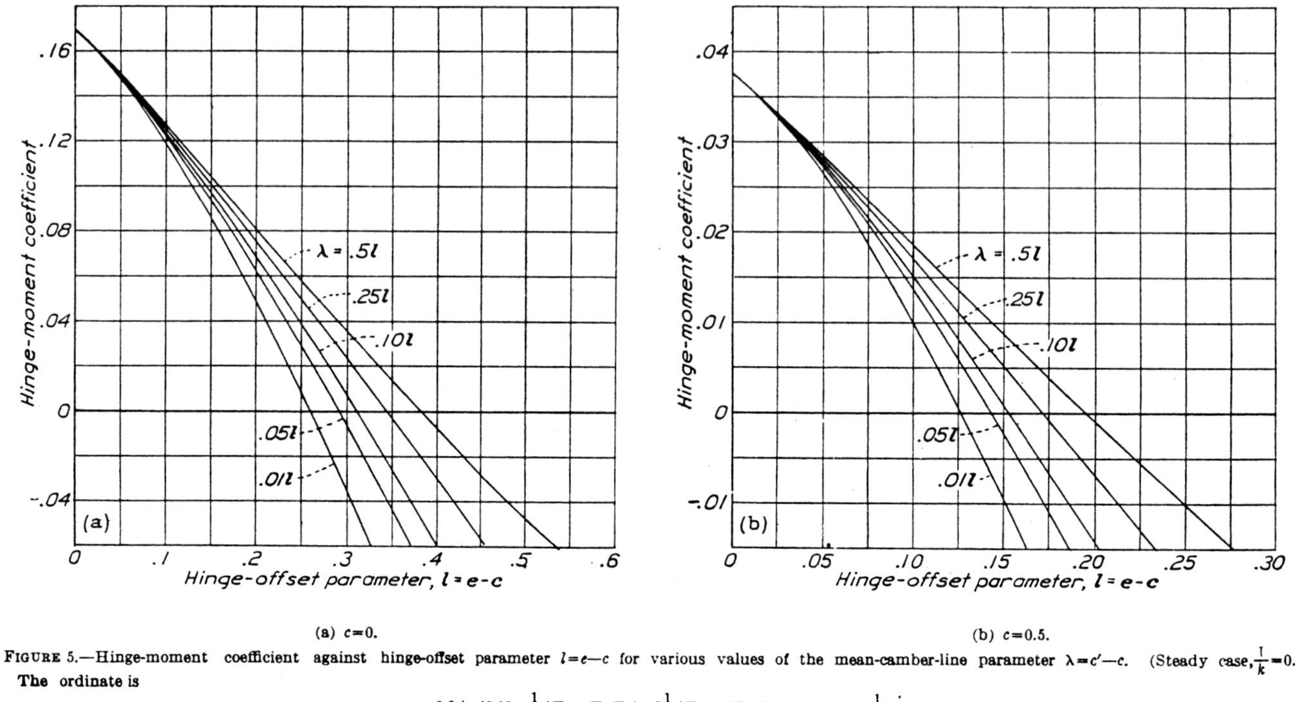

(a) $c=0$. (b) $c=0.5$.

FIGURE 5.—Hinge-moment coefficient against hinge-offset parameter $l=e-c$ for various values of the mean-camber-line parameter $\lambda=c'-c$. (Steady case, $\frac{1}{k}=0$.) The ordinate is

$$-M_\beta/\pi\rho b^2v^2\beta=\frac{1}{\pi^2}(T_{18}+T_{10}T_{12})+l\frac{1}{\pi^2}(T_{26}-2T_{10}T_{20}-T_{12}T_{21})+l^2\frac{1}{\pi^2}(\dot T_{28}+2T_{20}T_{21})$$

Equations (22) to (25) may be conveniently expressed in a coefficient form:

$$P=-\pi\rho\omega^2b^3\left(\frac{h}{b}A_{ch}+\alpha A_{c\alpha}+\beta A_{c\beta}+\gamma A_{c\gamma}\right) \quad (22')$$

$$M_\alpha=-\pi\rho\omega^2b^4\left(\frac{h}{b}A_{ah}+\alpha A_{a\alpha}+\beta A_{a\beta}+\gamma A_{a\gamma}\right) \quad (23')$$

$$M_\beta=-\pi\rho\omega^2b^4\left(\frac{h}{b}A_{bh}+\alpha A_{b\alpha}+\beta A_{b\beta}+\gamma A_{b\gamma}\right) \quad (24')$$

$$M_\gamma=-\pi\rho\omega^2b^4\left(\frac{h}{b}A_{dh}+\alpha A_{d\alpha}+\beta A_{d\beta}+\gamma A_{d\gamma}\right) \quad (25')$$

where

$$\omega=kv/b,\quad A_{ch}=R_{ch}+iI_{ch},\ A_{c\alpha}=R_{c\alpha}+iI_{c\alpha},\ \text{etc.}$$

and where

$$R_{a\alpha}=-A_{\alpha1}+\left(\frac{1}{4}-a^2\right)\frac{2G}{k}-\left(\frac{1}{2}+a\right)\frac{2F}{k^2}$$

$$R_{a\beta}=-A_{\beta1}+\frac{1}{k^2}A_{\beta3}+\left(\frac{1}{2}+a\right)\left[\left(\frac{T_{11}-2lT_{10}}{2\pi}\right)\frac{2G}{k}-\left(\frac{T_{10}-lT_{21}}{\pi}\right)\frac{2F}{k^2}\right]$$

$$R_{ah}=-A_{h1}+\left(\frac{1}{2}+a\right)\frac{2G}{k}$$

$$R_{a\gamma}=-A_{\gamma1}+\frac{1}{k^2}A_{\gamma3}+\left(\frac{1}{2}+a\right)\left[\frac{1}{2\pi}(T_{11}(d)-2mT_{10}(d))\frac{2G}{k}-\frac{1}{\pi}(T_{10}(d)-mT_{21}(d))\frac{2F}{k^2}\right]$$

$$R_{b\alpha}=-B_{\alpha1}-\frac{1}{2\pi}(T_{12}-2lT_{20})\left[\left(\frac{1}{2}-a\right)\frac{2G}{k}-\frac{2F}{k^2}\right]$$

$$R_{b\beta}=-B_{\beta1}+\frac{1}{k^2}B_{\beta3}-\frac{1}{2\pi}(T_{12}-2lT_{20})\left[\frac{1}{2\pi}(T_{11}-2lT_{10})\frac{2G}{k}-\frac{1}{\pi}(T_{10}-lT_{21})\frac{2F}{k^2}\right]$$

$$R_{bh}=-B_{h1}-\frac{1}{2\pi}(T_{12}-2lT_{20})\frac{2G}{k}$$

$$R_{b\gamma}=-B_{\gamma1}+\frac{1}{k^2}B_{\gamma3}-\frac{1}{2\pi}(T_{12}-2lT_{20})\left[\frac{1}{2\pi}(T_{11}(d)-2mT_{10}(d))\frac{2G}{k}-\frac{1}{\pi}(T_{10}(d)-mT_{21}(d))\frac{2F}{k^2}\right]$$

$$R_{c\alpha}=-C_{\alpha1}-\left(\frac{1}{2}-a\right)\frac{2G}{k}+\frac{2F}{k^2}$$

$$R_{c\beta}=-C_{\beta1}-\frac{1}{2\pi}(T_{11}-2lT_{10})\frac{2G}{k}+\frac{1}{\pi}(T_{10}-lT_{21})\frac{2F}{k^2}$$

$$R_{ch}=-C_{h1}-\frac{2G}{k}$$

$$R_{c\gamma}=-C_{\gamma1}-\frac{1}{2\pi}(T_{11}(d)-2mT_{10}(d))\frac{2G}{k}+\frac{1}{\pi}(T_{10}(d)-mT_{21}(d))\frac{2F}{k^2}$$

$$R_{d\alpha}=-D_{\alpha1}-\frac{1}{2\pi}(T_{12}(d)-2mT_{20}(d))\left[\left(\frac{1}{2}-a\right)\frac{2G}{k}-\frac{2F}{k^2}\right]$$

$$R_{d\beta}=-D_{\beta1}+\frac{1}{k^2}D_{\beta3}-\frac{1}{2\pi}(T_{12}(d)-2mT_{20}(d))\left[\frac{1}{2\pi}(T_{11}-2lT_{10})\frac{2G}{k}-\frac{1}{\pi}(T_{10}-lT_{21})\frac{2F}{k^2}\right]$$

$$R_{dh}=-D_{h1}-\frac{1}{2\pi}(T_{12}(d)-2mT_{20}(d))\frac{2G}{k}$$

$$R_{d\gamma}=-D_{\gamma1}+\frac{1}{k^2}D_{\gamma3}-\frac{1}{2\pi}(T_{12}(d)-2mT_{20}(d))\left[\frac{1}{2\pi}(T_{11}(d)-2mT_{10}(d))\frac{2G}{k}-\frac{1}{\pi}(T_{10}(d)-mT_{21}(d))\frac{2F}{k^2}\right]$$

$$I_{a\alpha}=\frac{1}{k}\left[A_{\alpha2}-\left(\frac{1}{2}+a\right)\frac{2G}{k}-\left(\frac{1}{4}-a^2\right)2F\right]$$

$$I_{a\beta}=\frac{1}{k}\left\{A_{\beta2}-\left(\frac{1}{2}+a\right)\left[\frac{1}{\pi}(T_{10}-lT_{21})\frac{2G}{k}+\frac{1}{2\pi}(T_{11}-2lT_{10})2F\right]\right\}$$

$$I_{ah}=\frac{1}{k}\left[-\left(\frac{1}{2}+a\right)2F\right]$$

$$I_{a\gamma}=\frac{1}{k}\left\{A_{\gamma2}-\left(\frac{1}{2}+a\right)\left[\frac{1}{\pi}(T_{10}(d)-mT_{21}(d))\frac{2G}{k}+\frac{1}{2\pi}(T_{11}(d)-2mT_{10}(d))2F\right]\right\}$$

$$I_{b\alpha}=\frac{1}{k}\left\{B_{\alpha 2}+\frac{1}{2\pi}(T_{12}-2lT_{20})\left[\frac{2G}{k}+\left(\frac{1}{2}-a\right)2F\right]\right\}$$

$$I_{b\beta}=\frac{1}{k}\left\{B_{\beta 2}+\frac{1}{2\pi}(T_{12}-2lT_{20})\left[\frac{1}{\pi}(T_{10}-lT_{21})\frac{2G}{k}+\frac{1}{2\pi}(T_{11}-2lT_{10})2F\right]\right\}$$

$$I_{bh}=\frac{1}{k}\frac{1}{2\pi}(T_{12}-2lT_{20})2F$$

$$I_{b\gamma}=\frac{1}{k}\left\{B_{\gamma 2}+\frac{1}{2\pi}(T_{12}-2lT_{20})\left[\frac{1}{\pi}(T_{10}(d)-mT_{21}(d))\frac{2G}{k}+\frac{1}{2\pi}(T_{11}(d)-2mT_{10}(d))2F\right]\right\}$$

$$I_{c\alpha}=\frac{1}{k}\left[C_{\alpha 2}+\frac{2G}{k}+\left(\frac{1}{2}-a\right)2F\right]$$

$$I_{c\beta}=\frac{1}{k}\left[C_{\beta 2}+\frac{1}{\pi}(T_{10}-lT_{21})\frac{2G}{k}+\frac{1}{2\pi}(T_{11}-2lT_{10})2F\right]$$

$$I_{ch}=\frac{1}{k}2F$$

$$I_{c\gamma}=\frac{1}{k}\left[C_{\gamma 2}+\frac{1}{\pi}(T_{10}(d)-mT_{21}(d))\frac{2G}{k}+\frac{1}{2\pi}(T_{11}(d)-2mT_{10}(d))2F\right]$$

$$I_{d\alpha}=\frac{1}{k}\left\{D_{\alpha 2}+\frac{1}{2\pi}(T_{12}(d)-2mT_{20}(d))\left[\frac{2G}{k}+\left(\frac{1}{2}-a\right)2F\right]\right\}$$

$$I_{d\beta}=\frac{1}{k}\left\{D_{\beta 2}+\frac{1}{2\pi}(T_{12}(d)-2mT_{20}(d))\left[\frac{1}{\pi}(T_{10}-lT_{21})\frac{2G}{k}+\frac{1}{2\pi}(T_{11}-2lT_{10})2F\right]\right\}$$

$$I_{dh}=\frac{1}{k}\frac{1}{2\pi}(T_{12}(d)-2mT_{20}(d))2F$$

$$I_{d\gamma}=\frac{1}{k}\left\{D_{\gamma 2}+\frac{1}{2\pi}(T_{12}(d)-2mT_{20}(d))\left[\frac{1}{\pi}(T_{10}(d)-mT_{21}(d))\frac{2G}{k}+\frac{1}{2\pi}(T_{11}(d)-2mT_{10}(d))2F\right]\right\}$$

$$A_{\alpha 1}=\frac{1}{8}+a^2$$

$$A_{\alpha 2}=\frac{1}{2}-a$$

$$A_{\beta 1}=\frac{2T_{13}}{\pi}+l\frac{T_{24}}{\pi}$$

$$A_{\beta 2}=\frac{1}{\pi}(T_{16}+lT_{23})$$

$$A_{\beta 3}=\frac{1}{\pi}(T_{15}+lT_{22})$$

$$A_{h1}=-a$$

$$A_{\gamma 1}=\frac{1}{\pi}(2T_{13}(d)+mT_{24}(d))$$

$$A_{\gamma 2}=\frac{1}{\pi}(T_{16}(d)+mT_{23}(d))$$

$$A_{\gamma 3}=\frac{1}{\pi}(T_{15}(d)+mT_{22}(d))$$

$$B_{\alpha 1}=A_{\beta 1}$$

$$B_{\alpha 2}=\frac{1}{\pi}(T_{17}+lT_{25})$$

$$B_{\beta 1}=\frac{1}{\pi^2}(-T_3+2lT_2-l^2T_5)$$

$$B_{\beta 2}=\frac{1}{\pi^2}(T_{19}+lT_{27}+l^2T_{29})$$

$$B_{\beta 3}=\frac{1}{\pi^2}(T_{18}+lT_{26}+l^2T_{28})$$

$$B_{h1}=\frac{1}{\pi}(-T_1+lT_4)$$

$$B_{\gamma 1}=\frac{1}{\pi^2}(-Y_6+lY_3+mY_4-lmY_1)$$

$$B_{\gamma 2}=\frac{1}{\pi^2}(Y_{10}+lY_{12}+mY_{14}+lmY_{16})$$

$$B_{\gamma 3}=\frac{1}{\pi^2}(Y_9+lY_{11}+mY_{13}+lmY_{15})$$

$$C_{\alpha 1}=A_{h1}$$

$$C_{\alpha 2}=1$$

$$C_{\beta 1}=B_{h1}$$

$$C_{\beta 2}=\frac{1}{\pi}(-T_4-2l\sqrt{1-c^2})$$

$$C_{h1}=1$$

$$C_{\gamma 1}=D_{h1}$$

$$C_{\gamma 2}=\frac{1}{\pi}(-T_4(d)-2m\sqrt{1-d^2})$$

705899 O - 46 - 10

$$D_{\alpha 1}=A_{\gamma 1}$$

$$D_{\alpha 2}=\frac{1}{\pi}(T_{17}(d)+mT_{25}(d))$$

$$D_{\beta 1}=B_{\gamma 1}$$

$$D_{\beta 2}=\frac{1}{\pi^2}(Y_{18}+mY_{20}+lY_{22}+lmY_{24})$$

$$D_{\beta 3}=\frac{1}{\pi^2}(Y_{17}+mY_{19}+lY_{21}+lmY_{23})$$

$$D_{h1}=\frac{1}{\pi}(-T_1(d)+mT_4(d))$$

$$D_{\gamma 1}=\frac{1}{\pi^2}(-T_3(d)+2mT_2(d)-m^2T_5(d))$$

$$D_{\gamma 2}=\frac{1}{\pi^2}(T_{19}(d)+mT_{27}(d)+m^2T_{29}(d))$$

$$D_{\gamma 3}=\frac{1}{\pi^2}(T_{18}(d)+mT_{26}(d)+m^2T_{28}(d))$$

CONCLUDING REMARKS

The material presented in the preceding pages represents an extension of the work published in reference 1, which has been expanded to include the tab functions and the effect of aerodynamic balance. Inasmuch as this addition fits in with the general arrangement of the earlier report, reference should be made to that report, and also to reference 4, for the application to the flutter problem.

Langley Memorial Aeronautical Laboratory,
National Advisory Committe for Aeronautics,
Langley Field, Va., *December 16, 1941.*

APPENDIX A

COMPARISON WITH REFERENCE 2

In order to compare the results of this report with those of Küssner and Schwarz (reference 2), the following relationships are noted:

$$c=-\cos\varphi$$

$$d=-\cos\psi$$

$$k=-i\omega$$

$$C(k)=1+2T(-i\omega)$$

$$a=-\frac{1}{2}$$

$$T_1=-\frac{1}{2}\Phi_4$$

$$T_2=-\frac{1}{2}\Phi_{37}$$

$$T_3=-\frac{1}{4}\Phi_{12}$$

$$T_4=-\Phi_3$$

$$T_5=-\Phi_{17}$$

$$T_9=\frac{1}{8}\Phi_6$$

$$T_{10}=\Phi_1$$

$$T_{11}=\Phi_2$$

$$T_{12}=\Phi_8$$

$$T_{13}=\frac{1}{8}\Phi_7$$

$$T_{15}=\Phi_5$$

$$T_{16}=\frac{1}{2}\Phi_6$$

$$T_{17}=\frac{1}{2}\Phi_9$$

$$T_{18}=\Phi_{10}$$

$$T_{19}=\frac{1}{2}\Phi_{11}$$

$$T_{20}=\Phi_{31}$$

$$T_{21}=\Phi_{13}$$

$$T_{22}=-\Phi_{15}$$

$$T_{23}=-2\Phi_5$$

$$T_{24}=-\frac{1}{4}\Phi_8$$

$$T_{25}=-\Phi_{32}$$

$$T_{26}=-(\Phi_{18}+\Phi_{35})^1$$

$$T_{27}=-(\Phi_{19}+\Phi_{36})$$

$$T_{28}=\pi^2 r_d{}^*$$

$$T_{29}=\Phi_{16}$$

$$\log N(c,d)=-L(\varphi,\psi)$$

$$Y_1(c,d)=-X_{14}(\varphi,\psi)$$

$$Y_2(c,d)=Y_{13}(c,d)-T_4(c)\,T_{21}(d)$$

$$Y_3(c,d)=-X_{18}(\varphi,\psi)$$

$$Y_4(c,d)=-X_5(\varphi,\psi)$$

$$Y_8(c,d)=Y_5(d,c)=X_8(\varphi,\psi)-X_{17}(\varphi,\psi)$$

$$Y_6(c,d)=-X_{10}(\varphi,\psi)$$

$$Y_7(c,d)=X_3(\varphi,\psi)+\Phi_{14}(\varphi)\Phi_{31}(\psi)$$

$$Y_{17}(c,d)=Y_9(d,c)=X_8(\varphi,\psi)$$

$$Y_{18}(c,d)=Y_{10}(d,c)=X_9(\varphi,\psi)$$

$$Y_{19}(c,d)=Y_{11}(d,c)=-X_3(\varphi,\psi)$$

$$Y_{20}(c,d)=Y_{12}(d,c)=-X_4(\varphi,\psi)$$

$$Y_{21}(c,d)=Y_{13}(d,c)=-X_{16}(\varphi,\psi)$$

$$Y_{22}(c,d)=Y_{14}(d,c)=-X_{17}(\varphi,\psi)$$

$$Y_{23}(c,d)=Y_{15}(d,c)=X_{12}(\varphi,\psi)$$

$$Y_{24}(c,d)=Y_{16}(d,c)=X_{13}(\varphi,\psi)$$

[1] There appears to be an error in the sign of the numerical values for Φ_{18} in table 3 of reference 2.

APPENDIX B

EXPRESSION FOR THE T AND Y FUNCTIONS

T FUNCTIONS

$$T_0 = c\sqrt{1-c^2}\cos^{-1}c - (1-c^2)$$
$$= \sqrt{1-c^2}\,(c\cos^{-1}c - \sqrt{1-c^2})$$

$$T_1 = -\frac{1}{3}(2+c^2)\sqrt{1-c^2} + c\cos^{-1}c$$

$$T_2 = c(1-c^2) - (1+c^2)\sqrt{1-c^2}\cos^{-1}c + c(\cos^{-1}c)^2$$

$$T_3 = -\frac{1}{8}(1-c^2)(5c^2+4) + \frac{1}{4}c(7+2c^2)\sqrt{1-c^2}\cos^{-1}c$$
$$-\left(\frac{1}{8}+c^2\right)(\cos^{-1}c)^2$$

$$T_4 = c\sqrt{1-c^2} - \cos^{-1}c$$

$$T_5 = -(1-c^2) + 2c\sqrt{1-c^2}\cos^{-1}c - (\cos^{-1}c)^2$$

$$T_6 = T_2$$

$$T_7 = -\frac{1}{8}c(7+2c^2)\sqrt{1-c^2} - \left(\frac{1}{8}+c^2\right)\cos^{-1}c$$

$$T_8 = -\frac{1}{3}(1+2c^2)\sqrt{1-c^2} + c\cos^{-1}c = -\frac{1}{3}(1-c^2)^{3/2} - cT_4$$

$$T_9 = \frac{1}{2}\left[\frac{1}{3}(1-c^2)^{3/2} + aT_4\right]$$

$$T_{10} = \sqrt{1-c^2} + \cos^{-1}c$$

$$T_{11} = (2-c)\sqrt{1-c^2} + (1-2c)\cos^{-1}c$$

$$T_{12} = (2+c)\sqrt{1-c^2} - (1+2c)\cos^{-1}c$$

$$T_{13} = -\frac{1}{2}(T_7 + (c-a)T_1)$$

$$T_{14} = \frac{1}{16} + \frac{1}{2}ac$$

$$T_{15} = T_4 + T_{10} = (1+c)\sqrt{1-c^2}$$

$$T_{16} = T_1 - T_8 - (c-a)T_4 + \frac{1}{2}T_{11} = \frac{2}{3}(1-c^2)^{3/2} - \left(\frac{1}{2}-a\right)T_4$$

$$T_{17} = -2T_9 - T_1 + \left(a-\frac{1}{2}\right)T_4 = -\frac{1}{3}(1-c^2)^{3/2} - T_1 - \frac{1}{2}T_4$$

$$T_{18} = T_5 - T_4T_{10}$$

$$T_{19} = -\frac{1}{2}T_4T_{11}$$

$$T_{20} = -\sqrt{1-c^2} + \cos^{-1}c$$

$$T_{21} = \sqrt{\frac{1+c}{1-c}}$$

$$T_{22} = 2\sqrt{1-c^2} - \sqrt{\frac{1+c}{1-c}}$$

$$T_{23} = (-1-2c+2a)\sqrt{1-c^2}$$

$$T_{24} = T_8 + (c-a)T_4 = -2T_9$$

$$T_{25} = T_4 - (1-c)\sqrt{1-c^2}$$

$$T_{26} = 2\sqrt{1-c^2}T_{20} + T_4\sqrt{\frac{1+c}{1-c}}$$

$$T_{27} = T_4T_{10} - \sqrt{1-c^2}T_{11}$$

$$T_{28} = 2(1+c+\log N(c,c'))$$

$$T_{29} = 2\sqrt{1-c^2}T_{10}$$

The term T_{28} is discussed separately in the paper.. The variable c is to be understood when no explicit variable is indicated for the T terms.

Y FUNCTIONS

$$Y_1(c,d) = -\sqrt{1-c^2}\sqrt{1-d^2} - \cos^{-1}c\cos^{-1}d$$
$$+ d\sqrt{1-d^2}\cos^{-1}c + c\sqrt{1-c^2}\cos^{-1}d - (d-c)^2\log N(c,d)$$

where

$$N(c,d) = \left|\frac{1-cd-\sqrt{1-c^2}\sqrt{1-d^2}}{d-c}\right|$$

$$Y_2(c,d) = 2\sqrt{1-d^2}\cos^{-1}c - 2(d-c)\log N(c,d)$$

$$Y_3(c,d) = \frac{1}{3}(c+2d)\sqrt{1-c^2}\sqrt{1-d^2} + d\cos^{-1}c\cos^{-1}d$$
$$-\frac{1}{3}(2+d^2)\sqrt{1-d^2}\cos^{-1}c$$
$$-\frac{1}{3}(1+3cd-c^2)\sqrt{1-c^2}\cos^{-1}d$$
$$+\frac{1}{3}(d-c)^3\log N(c,d)$$

$$Y_4(c,d) = Y_3(d,c)$$
$$= \frac{1}{3}(d+2c)\sqrt{1-c^2}\sqrt{1-d^2} + c\cos^{-1}c\cos^{-1}d$$
$$-\frac{1}{3}(2+c^2)\sqrt{1-c^2}\cos^{-1}d$$
$$-\frac{1}{3}(1+3cd-d^2)\sqrt{1-d^2}\cos^{-1}c$$
$$-\frac{1}{3}(d-c)^3\log N(c,d)$$

$$Y_5(c,d) = -\sqrt{1-c^2}\sqrt{1-d^2} + (2c-d)\sqrt{1-d^2}\cos^{-1}c$$
$$+ (d-c)^2\log N(c,d)$$

$$Y_6(c,d) = -\frac{1}{2}\sqrt{1-c^2}\sqrt{1-d^2}\left(1+\frac{1}{6}c^2+\frac{1}{6}d^2+\frac{11}{12}cd\right)$$
$$-\left(\frac{1}{8}+cd\right)\cos^{-1}c\cos^{-1}d$$
$$+\frac{1}{3}\left[\frac{d}{4}\left(\frac{5}{2}-d^2\right)+c(2+d^2)\right]\sqrt{1-d^2}\cos^{-1}c$$
$$+\frac{1}{3}\left[\frac{c}{4}\left(\frac{5}{2}-c^2\right)+d(2+c^2)\right]\sqrt{1-c^2}\cos^{-1}d$$
$$+\frac{(d-c)^4}{12}\log N(c,d)$$

$$Y_7(c,d)=2\sqrt{1-c^2}\cos^{-1}d+2(d-c)\log N(c,d)$$
$$=Y_2(d,c)$$
$$Y_8(c,d)=-\sqrt{1-c^2}\sqrt{1-d^2}+(2d-c)\sqrt{1-c^2}\cos^{-1}d$$
$$+(d-c)^2\log N(c,d)=Y_5(d,c)$$
$$Y_9(c,d)=Y_1-T_4(c)T_{10}(d)$$
$$Y_{10}(c,d)=Y_3-Y_4-\frac{1}{2}T_4(c)T_{11}(d)$$
$$Y_{11}(c,d)=Y_7-2\sqrt{1-c^2}T_{10}(d)$$
$$Y_{12}(c,d)=Y_1-Y_8-\sqrt{1-c^2}T_{11}(d)$$
$$Y_{13}(c,d)=Y_2+T_4(c)T_{21}(d)$$
$$Y_{14}(c,d)=Y_5-Y_9$$
$$Y_{15}(c,d)=2\sqrt{1-c^2}T_{21}(d)+2\log N(c,d)$$
$$Y_{16}(c,d)=Y_2-Y_7+2\sqrt{1-c^2}T_{10}(d)$$
$$Y_{17}(c,d)=Y_1-T_4(d)T_{10}(c)=Y_9(d,c)$$
$$Y_{18}(c,d)=Y_4-Y_3-\frac{1}{2}T_4(d)T_{11}(c)=Y_{10}(d,c)$$
$$Y_{19}(c,d)=Y_2-2\sqrt{1-d^2}T_{10}=Y_{11}(d,c)$$
$$Y_{20}(c,d)=Y_1-Y_5-\sqrt{1-d^2}T_{11}=Y_{12}(d,c)$$
$$Y_{21}(c,d)=Y_7+T_4(d)T_{21}(c)=Y_{13}(d,c)$$
$$Y_{22}(c,d)=-Y_1+Y_8+T_{10}(c)T_4(d)=Y_{14}(d,c)$$
$$Y_{23}(c,d)=2\sqrt{1-d^2}T_{21}(c)+2\log N(c,d)=Y_{15}(d,c)$$
$$Y_{24}(c,d)=Y_7-Y_2+2\sqrt{1-d^2}T_{10}=Y_{16}(d,c)$$

In the evaluation of the Y terms the following pertinent integrals occur:

$$\int (x-c)^n \log N\,dx=\frac{(x-c)^{n+1}}{n+1}\log N$$
$$-\frac{\sqrt{1-c^2}}{n+1}\int\frac{(x-c)^n}{\sqrt{1-x^2}}dx$$

where

$$N=\left|\frac{1-cx-\sqrt{1-x^2}\sqrt{1-c^2}}{x-c}\right|$$

In order to evaluate the last integral put $x=\cos\theta$; for example, consider $n=1$:

$$\int_d^1 (x-c)\log N\,dx=-\frac{(d-c)^2}{2}\log N(c,d)$$
$$-\frac{\sqrt{1-c^2}}{2}(\sqrt{1-d^2}-c\cos^{-1}d)$$

REFERENCES

1. Theodorsen, Theodore: General Theory of Aerodynamic Instability and the Mechanism of Flutter. Rep. No. 496, NACA, 1935.
2. Küssner, H. G., and Schwarz, L.: The Oscillating Wing with Aerodynamically Balanced Elevator. T. M. No. 991, NACA, 1941.
3. Dietze, F.: Die Luftkräfte der harmonisch schwingenden, in sich verformbaren Platte (Ebenes Problem). Luftfahrtforschung, Bd. 16, Lfg. 2, 20. Feb. 1939, pp. 84–96.
4. Theodorsen, Theodore, and Garrick, I. E.: Mechanism of Flutter—A Theoretical and Experimental Investigation of the Flutter Problem. Rep. No. 685, NACA, 1940.

FLUTTER CALCULATIONS IN THREE DEGREES OF FREEDOM

BY THEODORE THEODORSEN
AND I. E. GARRICK

National Advisory Committee for Aeronautics

Report No. 741, 1942

SUMMARY

The present paper is a continuation of the general study of flutter published in NACA Reports Nos. 496 and 685. The paper is mainly devoted to flutter in three degrees of freedom (bending, torsion, and aileron), for which a number of selected cases have been calculated and presented in graphical form. The results are analyzed and discussed with regard to the effects of structural damping, of fractional-span ailerons, and of mass-balancing. The analysis shows that more emphasis should be put on the effect of structural damping and less on mass-balancing. The conclusion is drawn that a definite minimum amount of structural damping, which is usually found to be present, is essential in the calculations for an adequate description of the flutter case. Theoretical flutter predictions are thus brought into closer agreement with the facts of experience.

A brief discussion is included of a particular biplane that had experienced flutter at about 200 miles per hour. Some simplifications have been achieved in the method of calculation.

INTRODUCTION

Since the publication of the previous flutter papers, the necessity of considering complete cases of three degrees of freedom including the effect of structural damping has become evident. The purpose of the present paper is therefore to present such extensions of general applicability. The calculations herein reported are directly based on methods already given in references 1 and 2. The earlier papers deal, to some extent, with cases of three degrees of freedom and also indicate that the internal structural damping in some cases has a great effect on the flutter velocity; a small value of the internal damping may suffice to bring the flutter velocity from nearly zero to a normal value. Thus, in order to obtain better agreement with practice, the existence of a certain amount of internal damping must be recognized.

A separate investigation on the subject of hysteresis in airplane structures, which has been conducted in the meantime and will be reported in detail elsewhere, shows that a significant amount of internal damping ($g_\alpha > 0.01$) is present, usually with considerable margin. This low value of $g_\alpha \approx 0.01$ is found to be effective in smoothing out the low-velocity flutter values appearing in flutter curves calculated for the case of zero internal damping. A similar effect of different origin is the so-called fractional aileron-span effect. This effect was noted in reference 1 for binary cases and is here also treated for ternary cases. Strangely enough, a reduction in the length of the aileron from that of the full span to a shorter length has a disproportionally large effect on the flutter velocity. Thus, the calculated flutter speed for a full-span aileron may be of a low value; whereas, for a half-span or even a three-quarter-span aileron, it may be nearly normal.

It is of interest to note in connection with the study of three degrees of freedom that the addition of the third degree is the cause of a reduction in the flutter speed based on only two degrees. If a control surface is mass-balanced, is reasonably stiff, and a certain minimum amount of torsional damping is present, the bending-torsion value of the flutter speed will be closely approached.

The following study originated in an investigation of a certain biplane in which flutter had been experienced on a number of occasions. Two of these biplanes were made available at Langley Field for the purpose of the investigation. These biplanes were subjected to the conventional vibration tests in order to obtain the flutter parameters, and the flutter speed was calculated. These calculations were used as the nucleus in the following study of flutter in three degrees of freedom. For readers particularly interested in the biplane mentioned, an appendix (appendix C) has been prepared.

It should further be mentioned that some simplification has been achieved in the method of calculation. This simplification is based on an analogy with Sylvester's method of elimination and reduces quite noticeably the labor of calculating the flutter speed for three degrees of freedom. Appendix B presents a summary of this method.

RESULTS

The results of the flutter calculations are presented in figures 1 to 40. In tables I to IX the constant parameters and the variable parameters are arranged to serve as a key to the figures. In order further to assist the reader in the study of the curves, a brief description of the figures will be given.

It will be noticed that the ordinate for all the curves is the flutter speed in the coefficient form $v/b\omega_\alpha$. The product $b\omega_\alpha$ is thus used as a reference velocity throughout. The symbols used in this paper are defined in appendix A.

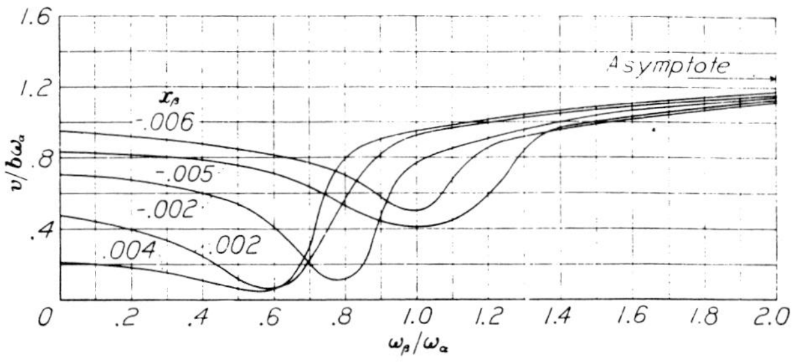

FIGURE 1.—Flutter coefficient $v/b\omega_\alpha$ against frequency ratio $\omega_\beta/\omega_\alpha$ for several values of the aileron unbalance, x_β. x_α,0.2; r_α^2, 1; no damping.

The figures are arranged according to the values of r_α^2: figures 1 to 11, $r_\alpha^2=1$ (biplane case); figures 12 to 28, $r_\alpha^2=0.5$; figures 29 to 36, $r_\alpha^2=0.25$ (monoplane case). Within each group a further arrangement is made according to the value of κ, the wing-density parameter.

Figure 1 shows a number of curves plotted against the aileron frequency ratio $\omega_\beta/\omega_\alpha$, with ω_α thus used as a reference frequency. The wing bending-frequency ratio ω_h/ω_α is kept constant. The curves differ only in the value of x_β, which determines the degree of aileron mass balance. Note the low dips present near $\omega_\beta/\omega_\alpha=1.0$ and the shifting of these low spots with the value of x_β. All the curves approach an asymptote for $\omega_\beta/\omega_\alpha\rightarrow\infty$, which corresponds to the bending-torsion binary flutter value.

Figure 2 shows the effect of the torsional structural damping coefficient $g_\alpha=0.01$ on some of the curves of figure 1. Note that the dip in the flutter curves is now eliminated and that the flutter coefficient does not differ by much from its bending-torsion value.

Figure 3 shows the individual effects of the structural damping coefficients g_α, g_β, and g_h on the flutter coefficient for the constant parameters $x_\beta=0.002$ and $\omega_\beta/\omega_\alpha=0.833$. Note that g_α has the greatest effect in increasing the flutter speed.

The parameters for the next set of curves (fig. 4) differ from those of figure 1 only in the value of x_α, which is now 0; that is, the center of gravity of the main wing coincides with the elastic axis at the 40-percent-chord position. Again, for values of x_β of 0 and 0.002, low dips exist near $\omega_\beta/\omega_\alpha=1.0$. For $x_\beta=-0.002$, the low dip does not exist. The bending-torsion flutter value at $\omega_\beta/\omega_\alpha=\infty$ is considerably increased over that for $x_\alpha=0.2$ in figure 1.

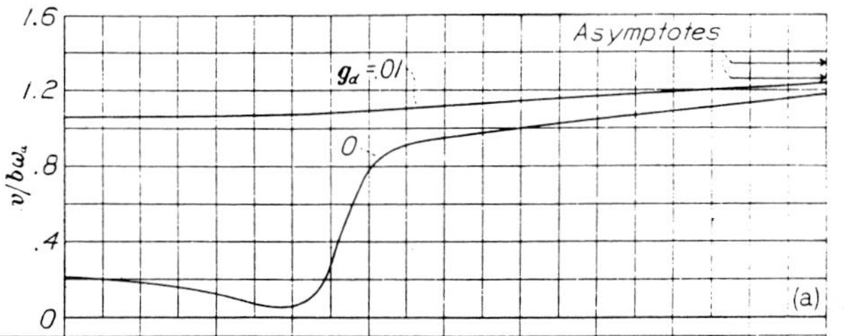

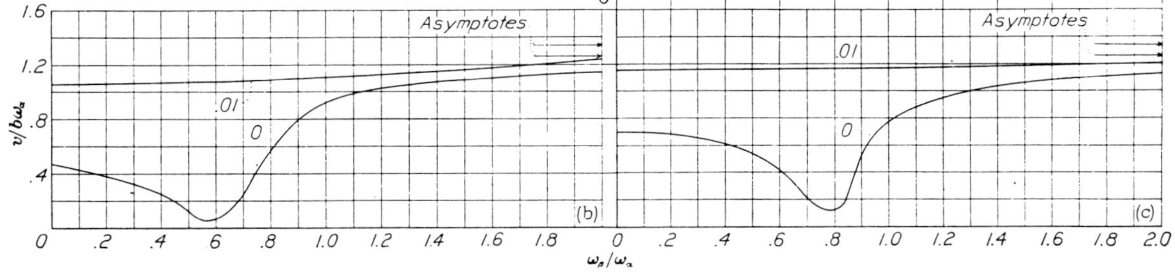

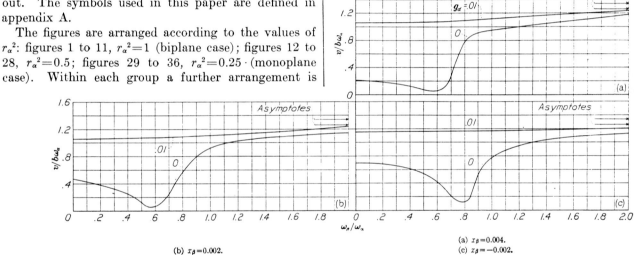

(a) $x_\beta=0.004$.
(b) $x_\beta=0.002$.
(c) $x_\beta=-0.002$.

FIGURE 2.—Flutter coefficient $v/b\omega_\alpha$ against frequency ratio $\omega_\beta/\omega_\alpha$ with and without structural torsional damping. x_α, 0.2; r_α^2, 1.

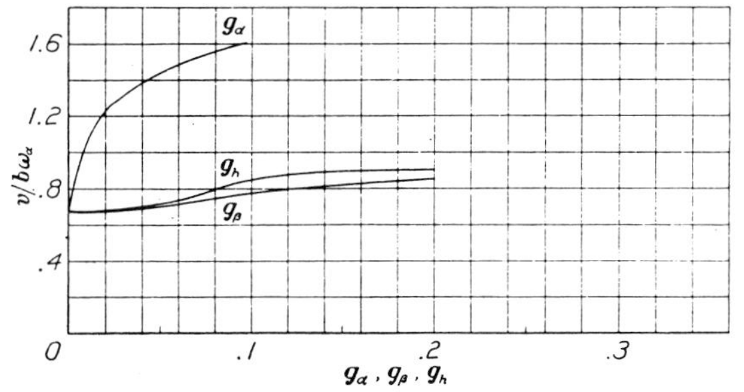

FIGURE 3.—Flutter coefficient $v/b\omega_\alpha$ against structural damping coefficients g_α, g_β, and g_h. $\omega_\beta/\omega_\alpha$, 0.833; x_β, 0.002; r_α^2, 1.

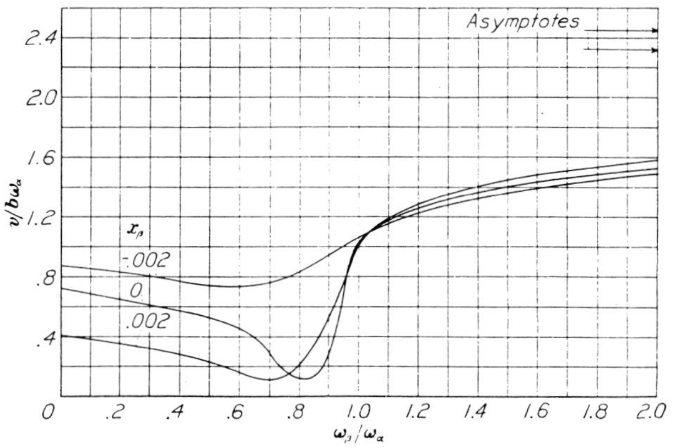

FIGURE 4.—Flutter coefficient $v/b\omega_\alpha$ against frequency ratio $\omega_\beta/\omega_\alpha$ for several values of the aileron unbalance x_β. x_β, 0; r_α^2, 1; no damping.

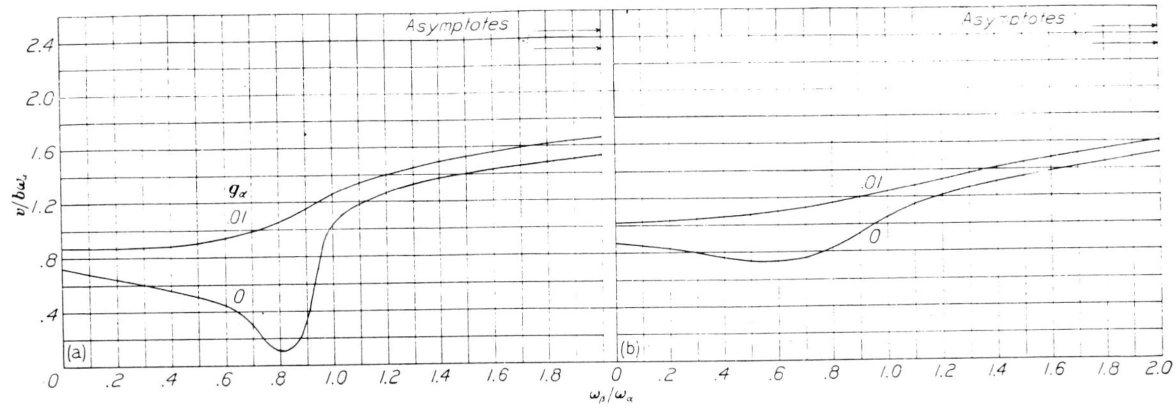

(a) $x_\beta = 0$. (b) $x_\beta = -0.002$.

FIGURE 5.—Flutter coefficient $v/b\omega_\alpha$ against frequency ratio $\omega_\beta/\omega_\alpha$, with and without structural torsional damping. x_α, 0; r_α^2, 1.

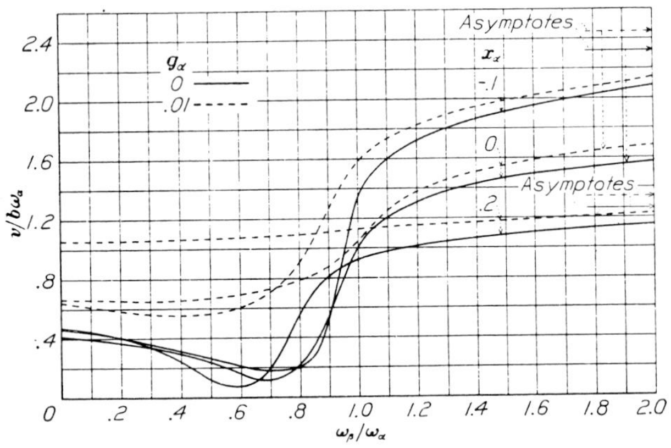

FIGURE 6.—Flutter coefficient $v/b\omega_\alpha$ against frequency ratio $\omega_\beta/\omega_\alpha$ for several values of the wing unbalance x_α, with and without structural torsional damping. x_β, 0.002; r_α^2, 1.

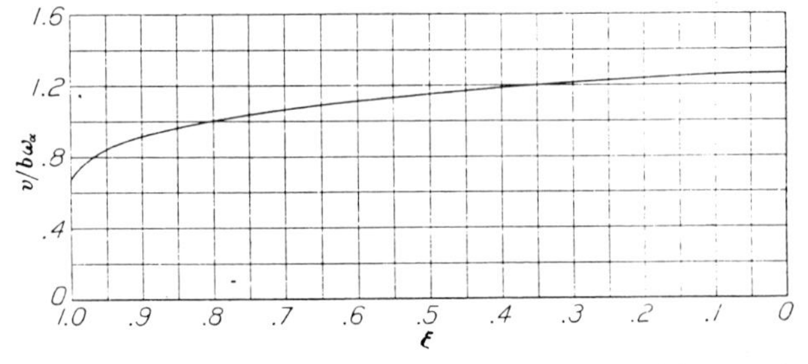

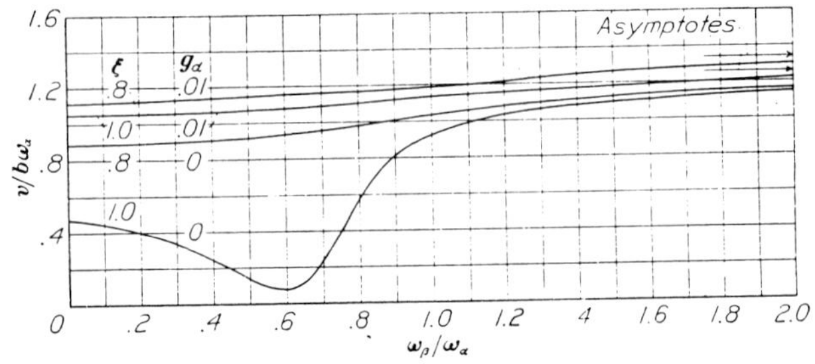

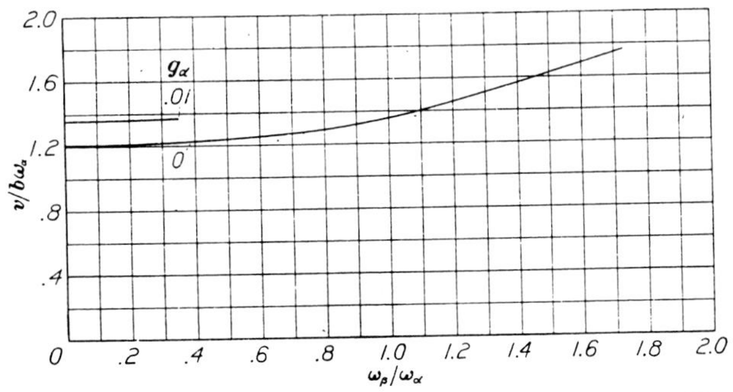

FIGURE 7.—Flutter coefficient $v/b\omega_\alpha$ against frequency ratio $\omega_\beta/\omega_\alpha$ with and without structural torsional damping. x_α, -0.1; x_β, -0.005; r_α^2, 1.

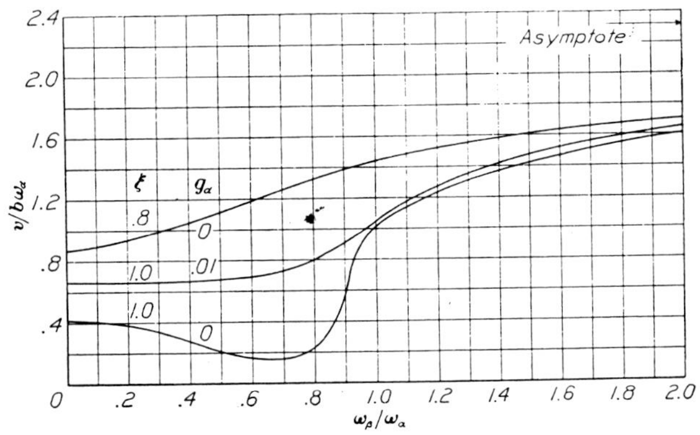

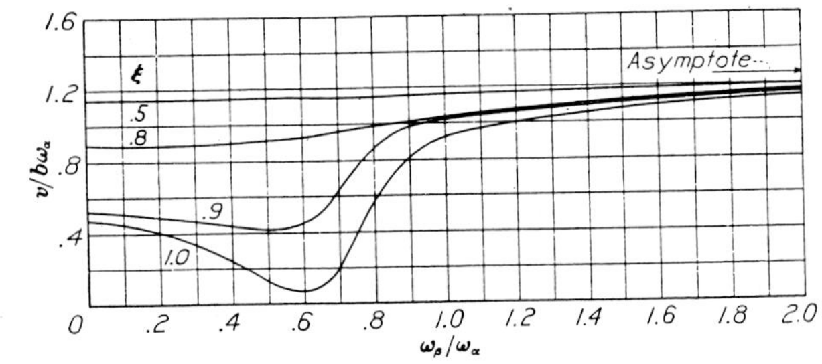

FIGURE 8.—Flutter coefficient $v/b\omega_\alpha$ against frequency ratio $\omega_\beta/\omega_\alpha$ showing the effect of partial-span aileron coefficient ξ. x_β, 0.002; r_α^2, 1.

FIGURE 9.—Flutter coefficient $v/b\omega_\alpha$ against partial-span aileron coefficient ξ. $\omega_\beta/\omega_\alpha$, 0.833; r_α^2, 1.

FIGURE 10.—Flutter coefficient $v/b\omega_\alpha$ against frequency ratio $\omega_\beta/\omega_\alpha$ showing the combined effect of structural damping coefficient g_α and partial-span aileron coefficient ξ. x_β, 0.002; r_α^2, 1.

FIGURE 11.—Flutter coefficient $v/b\omega_\alpha$ against frequency ratio $\omega_\beta/\omega_\alpha$ showing the combined effect of the structural damping coefficient g_α and partial-span aileron coefficient ξ. x_β, 0.002; r_α^2, 1.

Figure 5 shows the effect of the torsional structural damping coefficient $g_\alpha=0.01$ in increasing the value of the flutter speed. Figure 6 gives several curves for a curves presented in figure 4 ($x_\alpha=0$, $x_\beta=0.002$). The effect of $g_\alpha=0.01$ is shown for comparison. It is interesting to observe that in the range $\omega_\beta/\omega_\alpha<1.0$ the effect of ξ is significant. In the comparison of this case with figure 10 ($x_\alpha=0.2$), it appears that $\xi=0.8$ is of more influence on the case $x_\alpha=0$ while $g_\alpha=0.01$ is more effective on the case $x_\alpha=0.2$.

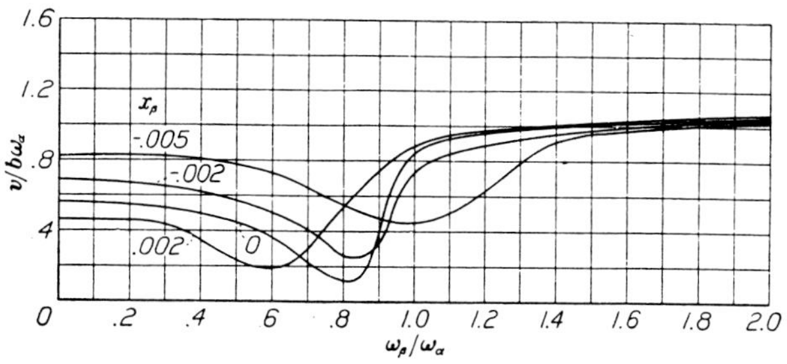

FIGURE 12.—Flutter coefficient $v/b\omega_\alpha$ against frequency ratio $\omega_\beta/\omega_\alpha$ for several values of the aileron unbalance x_β. x_α, 0.2; r_α^2, 0.5; no damping.

The next set of figures (figs. 12 to 28) has been calculated with $r_\alpha^2=0.5$. Figure 12 is similar to figure 1 and shows the flutter-speed coefficient plotted against aileron frequency ratio for several values of x_β. The effect of structural damping is included in figure 13. Figure 14 is a cross plot (similar to fig. 3) against the structural damping coefficients g_α, g_β, and g_h. Figure 15 extends the cases given in figures 13 (a) and 13 (c) to include other values of the frequency ratio ω_h/ω_α. Figure 16 represents a case of a lighter wing for which κ is 0.25 instead of 0.2. The value of x_β is 0.002; curves with and without structural damping are given. Figure 17 has the same conditions presented in figure 16 except that x_α is equal to 0 instead of 0.2.

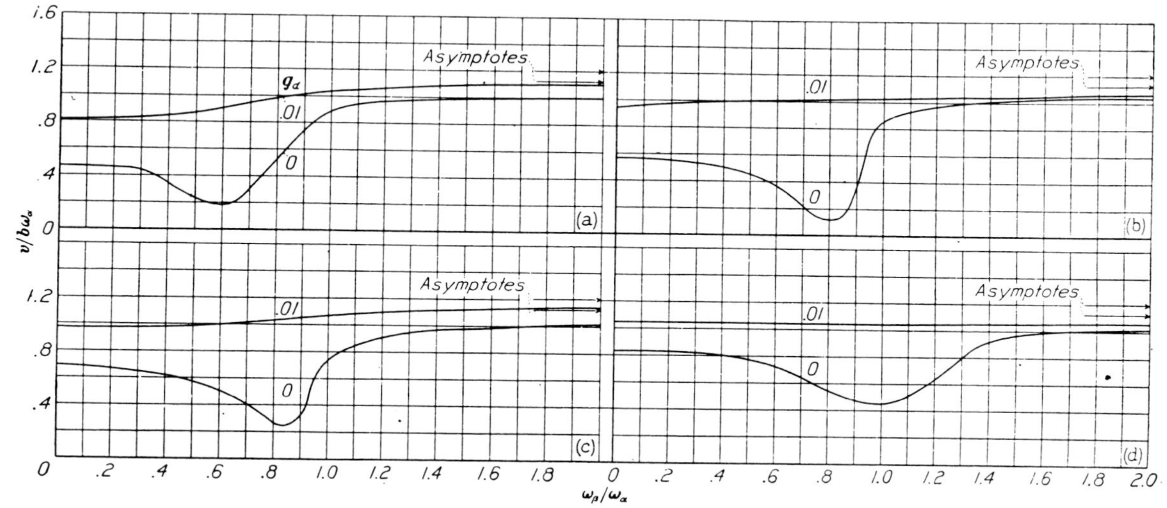

(a) $x_\beta=0.002$. (b) $x_\beta=0$.
(c) $x_\beta=-0.002$. (d) $x_\beta=-0.005$.

FIGURE 13.—Flutter coefficient $v/b\omega_\alpha$ against frequency ratio $\omega_\beta/\omega_\alpha$ with and without structural torsional damping. x_α, 0.2; r_α^2, 0.5; ω_h/ω_α, 0.607.

constant value of x_β of 0.002 and for different values of x_α (0.2, 0, and -0.1), with and without structural damping.

Figure 7 represents a case for which $x_\alpha=-0.1$ and $x_\beta=-0.005$. Case 1 (bending-torsion) is completely stable.

Figure 8 shows the effect of ξ, the partial-span aileron coefficient. The curve $\xi=1.0$ is taken from figure 1 ($x_\beta=0.002$) and is the case of the full-span aileron. Note that even a small reduction to $\xi=0.8$ has a marked favorable effect, especially in the range of frequencies $\omega_\beta/\omega_\alpha<1.0$. As $\xi\rightarrow0$ (no aileron), the curves approach the bending-torsion flutter value.

Figure 9 represents a plot against ξ for a constant value of $\omega_\beta/\omega_\alpha$ of 0.833. Figure 10 is intended to show a combined effect of $\xi=0.8$ and $g_\alpha=0.01$. For comparison the separate combinations $\xi=1.0$, $g_\alpha=0$; $\xi=1.0$, $g_\alpha=0.01$; and $\xi=0.8$, $g_\alpha=0$ are also shown.

Figure 11 shows the effect of $\xi=0.8$ on one of the

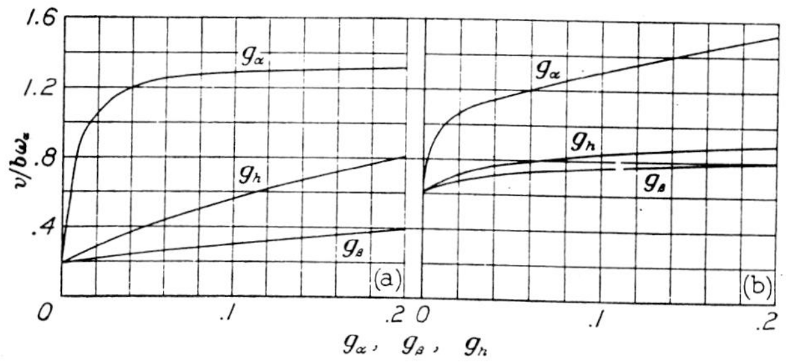

(a) $\omega_\beta/\omega_\alpha$, 0.607. (b) $\omega_\beta/\omega_\alpha$, 0.833.

FIGURE 14.—Flutter coefficient $v/b\omega_\alpha$ against structural damping coefficients g_α, g_β, and g_h. x_β, 0.002; r_α^2, 0.5.

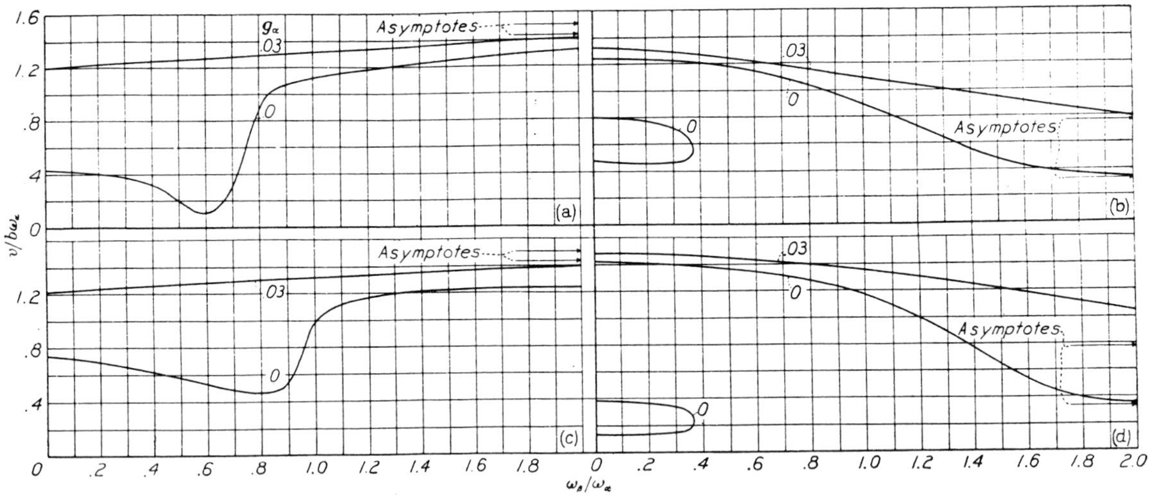

(a) x_β, 0.002; ω_h/ω_α, 0.316.
(c) x_β, −0.002; ω_h/ω_α, 0.316.

(b) x_β, 0.002; ω_h/ω_α, 1.0.
(d) x_β, −0.002; ω_h/ω_α, 1.0.

FIGURE 15.—Flutter coefficient $v/b\omega_\alpha$ against frequency ratio $\omega_\beta/\omega_\alpha$ with and without structural torsional damping. x_α, 0.2; r_α^2, 0.5; (cf. figs. 13 (a) and 13 (c)).

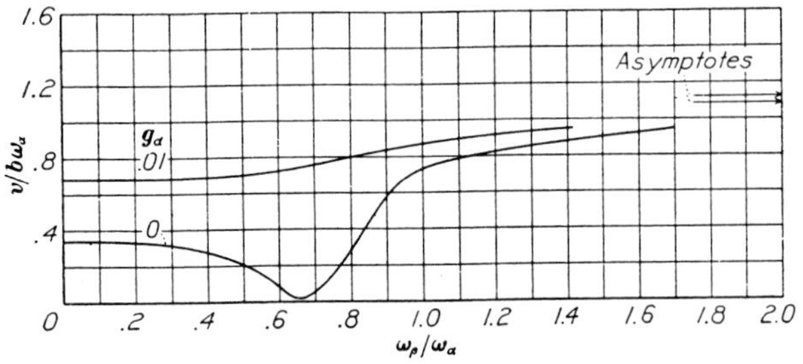

FIGURE 16.—Flutter coefficient $v/b\omega_\alpha$ against frequency ratio $\omega_\beta/\omega_\alpha$ with and without structural torsional damping. x_α, 0.2; x_β, 0.002; κ, 0.25; r_α^2, 0.5.

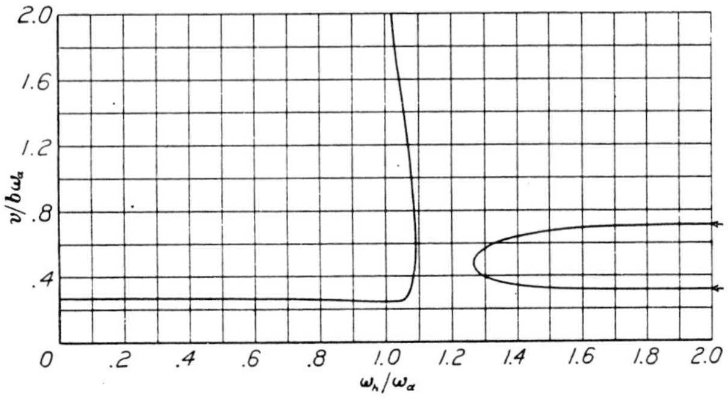

FIGURE 18.—Flutter coefficient $v/b\omega_\alpha$ against wing bending-frequency ratio ω_h/ω_α. $\omega_\beta/\omega_\alpha$, 0.5; x_β, 0.002; κ, 0.25; r_α^2, 0.5; no damping.

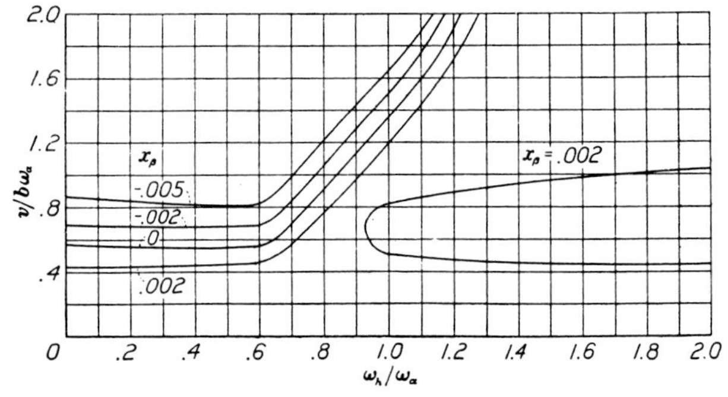

FIGURE 20.—Flutter coefficient $v/b\omega_\alpha$ against wing bending-frequency ratio ω_h/ω_α for several values of the aileron unbalance x_β. $\omega_\beta/\omega_\alpha$, 0; κ, 0.2; r_α^2, 0.5; no damping.

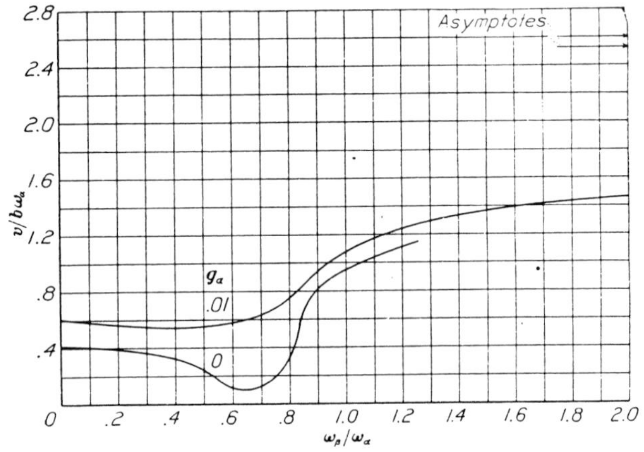

FIGURE 17.—Flutter coefficient $v/b\omega_\alpha$ against frequency ratio $\omega_\beta/\omega_\alpha$ with and without structural torsional damping. x_α, 0; x_β, 0.002; κ, 0.25; r_α^2, 0.5.

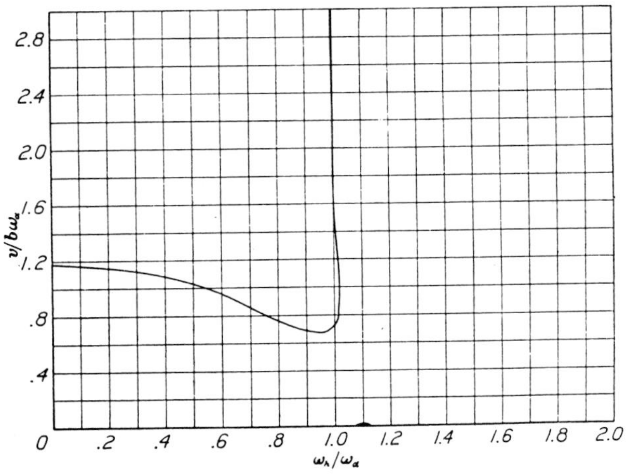

FIGURE 19.—Flutter coefficient $v/b\omega_\alpha$ against wing bending-frequency ratio ω_h/ω_α. $\omega_\beta/\omega_\alpha$, 1.0; x_β, 0.002; κ, 0.25; r_α^2, 0.5; no damping.

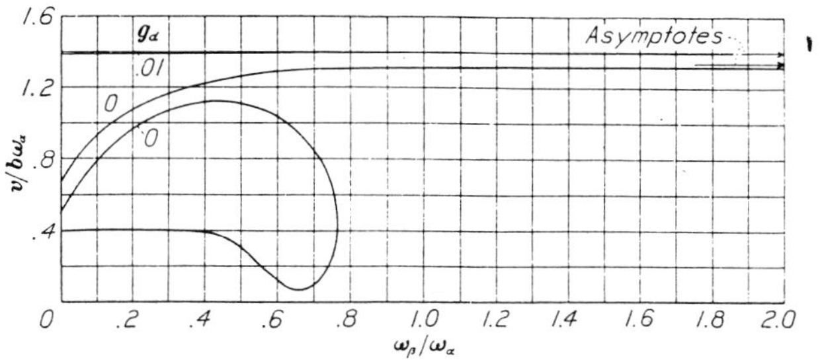

FIGURE 21.—Flutter coefficient $v/b\omega_\alpha$ against frequency ratio $\omega_\beta/\omega_\alpha$ with and without structural torsional damping. x_β, 0.002; κ, 0.125; r_α^2, 0.5; ω_h/ω_α, 0.607.

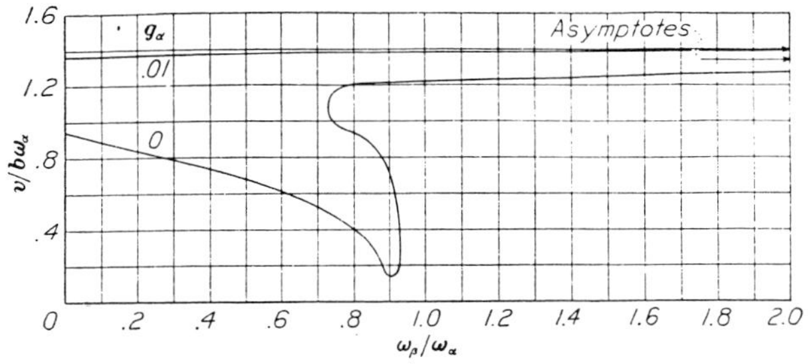

FIGURE 22.—Flutter coefficient $v/b\omega_\alpha$ against frequency ratio $\omega_\beta/\omega_\alpha$ with and without structural torsional damping. x_β, −0.002; κ, 0.125; r_α^2, 0.5; ω_h/ω_α, 0.607.

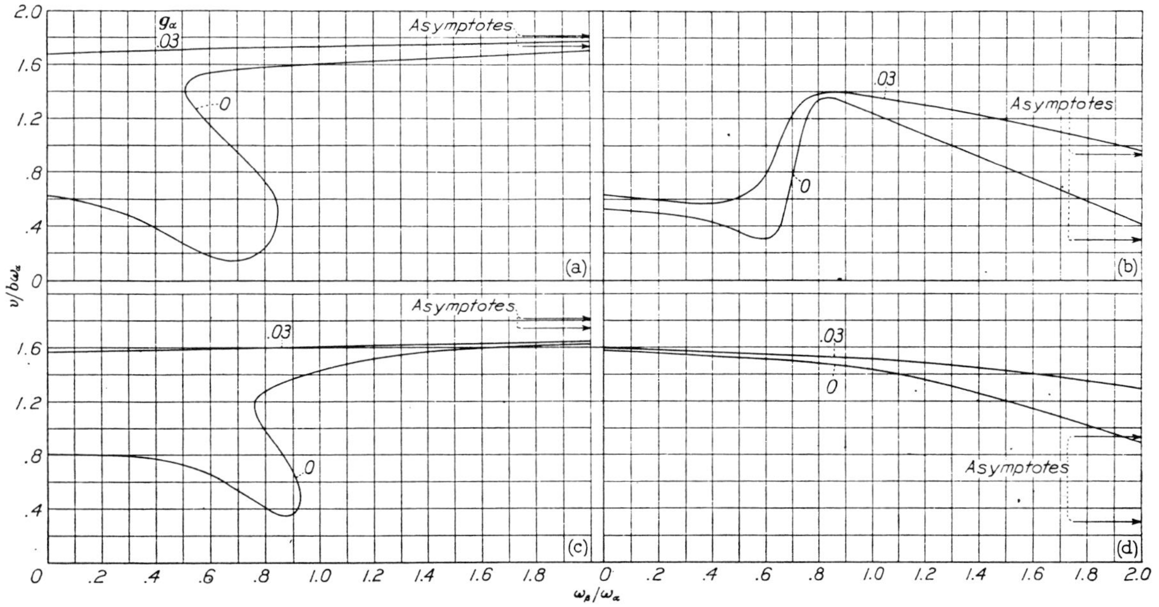

(a) x_β=0.002; ω_h/ω_α=0.316.
(b) x_β=0.002; ω_h/ω_α=1.0.
(c) x_β=−0.002; ω_h/ω_α=0.316.
(d) x_β=−0.002; ω_h/ω_α=1.0.

FIGURE 23.—Flutter coefficient $v/b\omega_\alpha$ against frequency ratio $\omega_\beta/\omega_\alpha$ with and without structural torsional damping. (See also figs. 21 and 22.) κ, 0.125; r_α^2, 0.5.

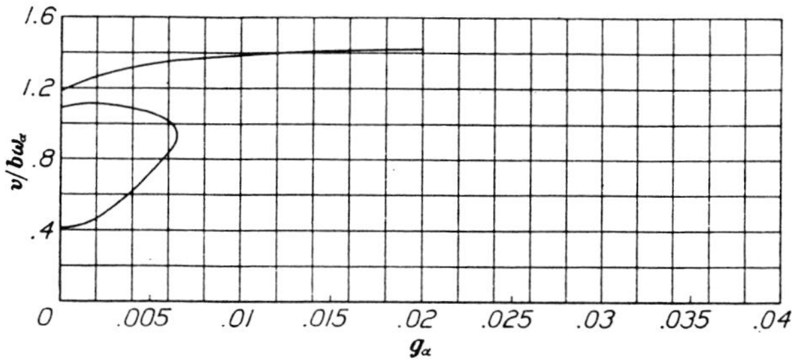

FIGURE 24.—Flutter coefficient $v/b\omega_\alpha$ against structural damping coefficient g_α. $\omega_\beta/\omega_\alpha$, 0.316; x_β, 0.002; κ, 0.125; r_α^2, 0.5.

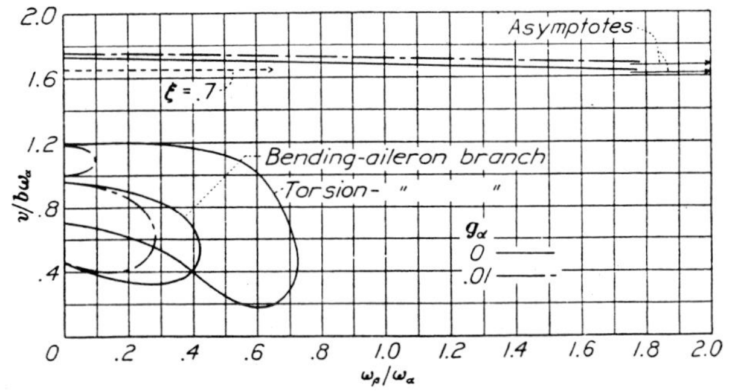

FIGURE 25.—Flutter coefficient $v/b\omega_\alpha$ against frequency ratio $\omega_\beta/\omega_\alpha$ showing the combined effect of the structural damping coefficient g_α and partial-span aileron coefficient ξ. x_β, 0.002; κ, 0.083; r_α^2, 0.5.

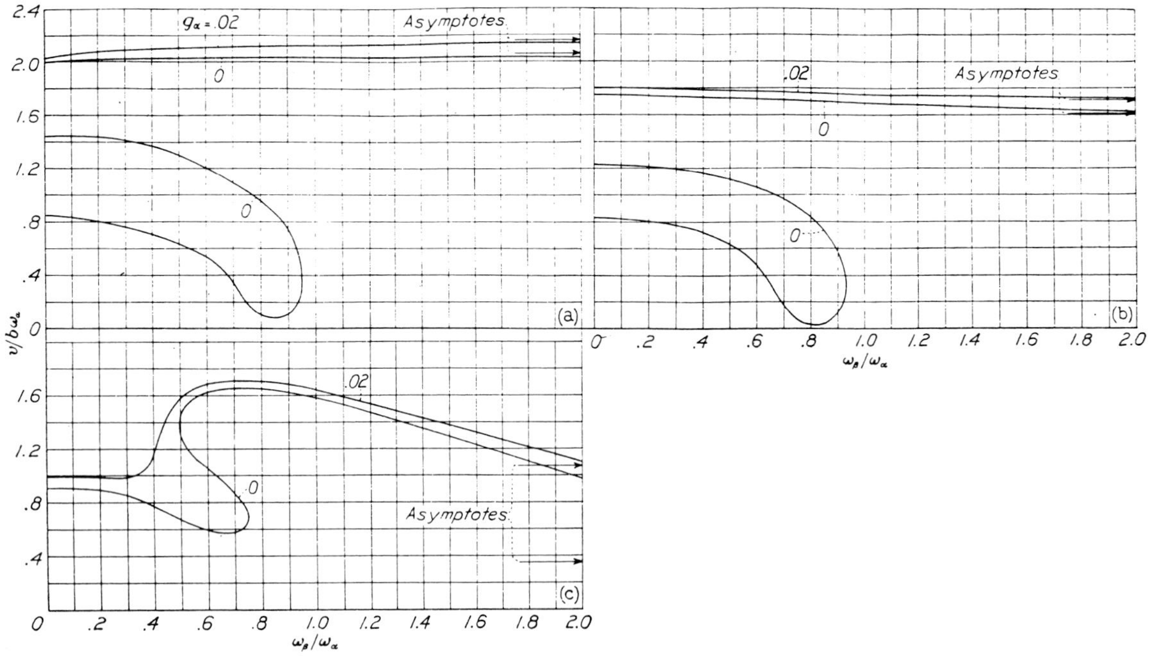

(a) ω_h/ω_α, 0.316.
(c) ω_h/ω_α, 1.0.

(b) ω_h/ω_α, 0.607.

FIGURE 26.—Flutter coefficient $v/b\omega_\alpha$ against frequency ratio $\omega_\beta/\omega_\alpha$ with and without structural torsional damping. x_β, 0; x_α, 0.2; κ, 0.083; r_α^2, 0.5.

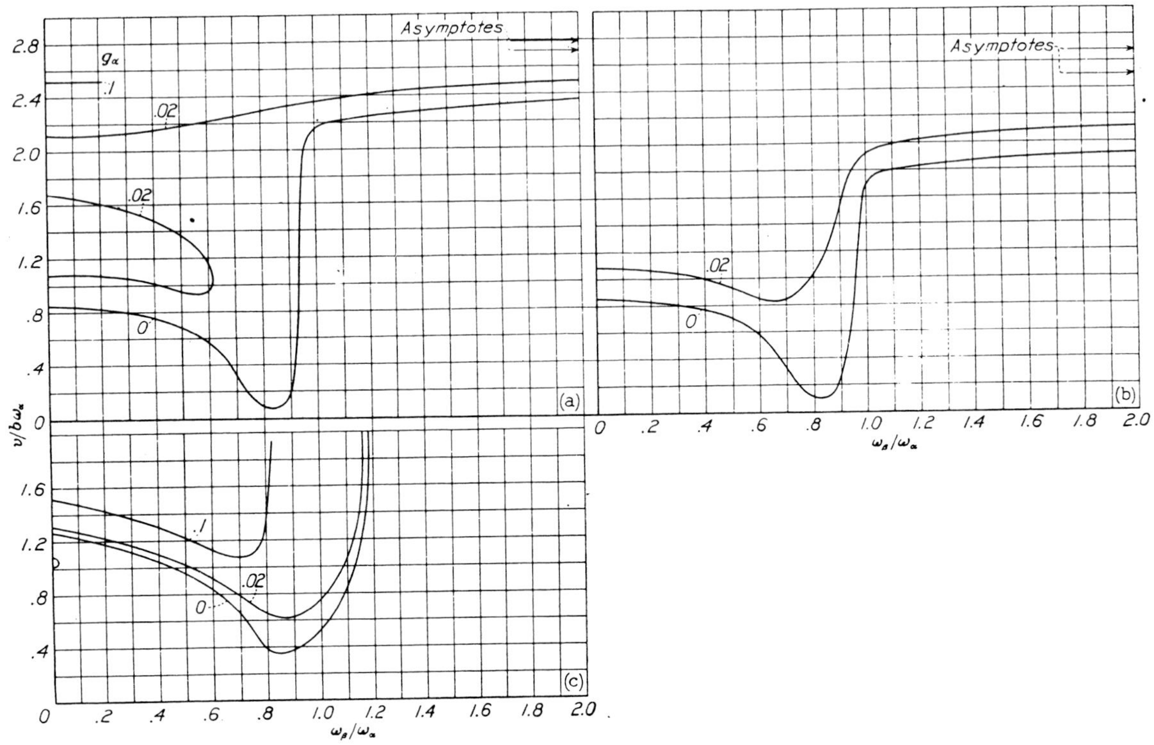

(a) ω_h/ω_α, 0.316.
(c) ω_h/ω_α, 1.0.

(b) ω_h/ω_α, 0.607.

FIGURE 27.—Flutter coefficient $v/b\omega_\alpha$ against frequency ratio $\omega_\beta/\omega_\alpha$ with and without structural torsional damping. x_β, 0; x_α, 0; κ, 0.083; r_α^2, 0.5.

477642—43——2

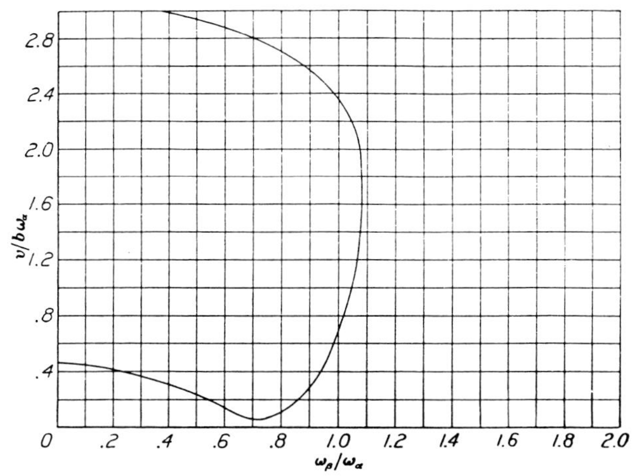

FIGURE 28.—Flutter coefficient $v/b\omega_\alpha$ against frequency ratio $\omega_\beta/\omega_\alpha$. ω_h/ω_α, 1.0; x_α, 0; κ, 0.25; r_α^2, 0.5; no damping.

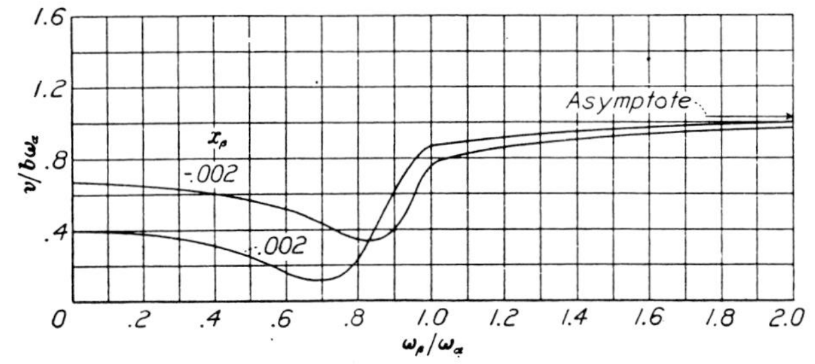

FIGURE 29.—Flutter coefficient $v/b\omega_\alpha$ against frequency ratio $\omega_\beta/\omega_\alpha$ for two values of aileron unbalance x_β. r_α^2, 0.25; no damping.

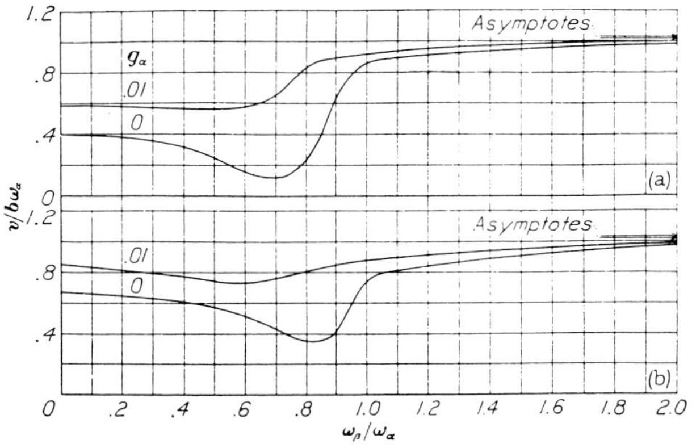

(a) x_β, 0.002. (b) x_β, −0.002.

FIGURE 30.—Flutter coefficient $v/b\omega_\alpha$ against frequency ratio $\omega_\beta/\omega_\alpha$ with and without structural torsional damping. r_α^2, 0.25; ω_h/ω_α, 0.607.

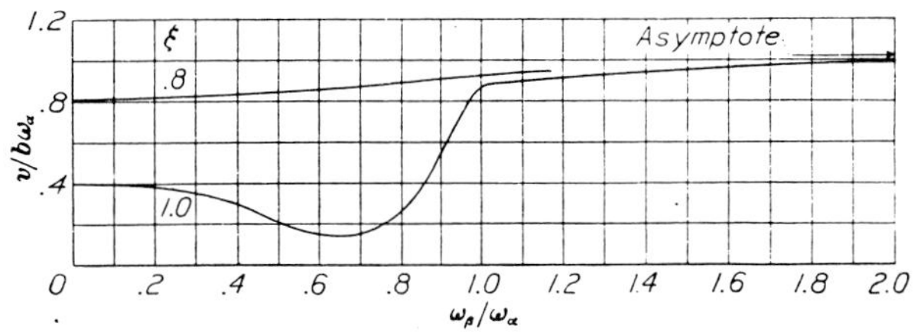

FIGURE 31.—Flutter coefficient $v/b\omega_\alpha$ against frequency ratio $\omega_\beta/\omega_\alpha$ for two values of the partial-span aileron coefficient ξ. x_β, 0.002; r_α^2, 0.25.

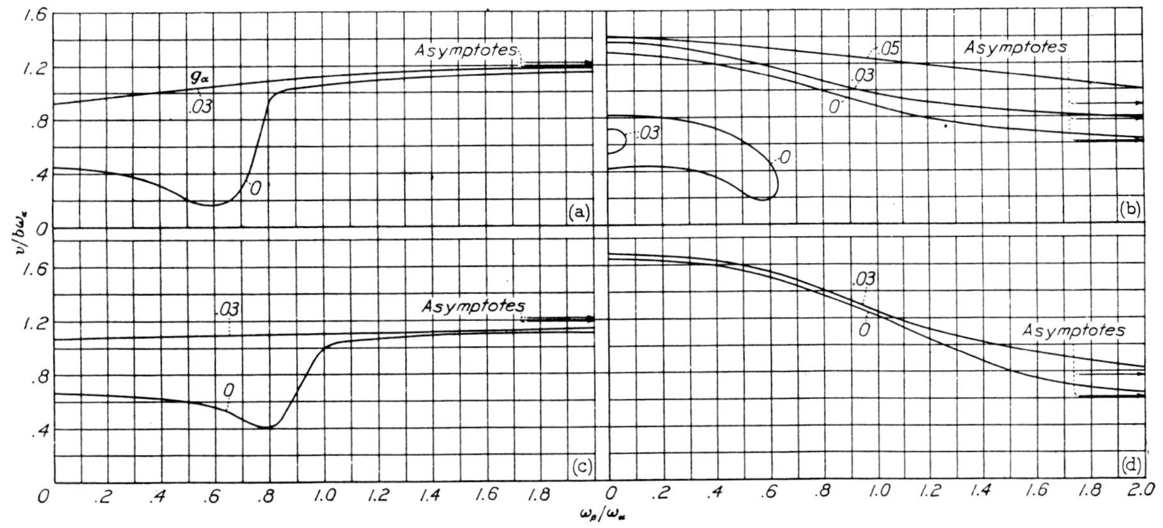

(a) x_β, 0.002; ω_h/ω_α, 0.316. (b) x_β, 0.002; ω_h/ω_α, 1.0.
(c) x_β, −0.002; ω_h/ω_α, 0.316. (d) x_β, −0.002; ω_h/ω_α, 1.0.

FIGURE 32.—Flutter coefficient $v/b\omega_\alpha$ against frequency ratio $\omega_\beta/\omega_\alpha$ with and without structural torsional damping. (See also fig. 30.) κ, 0.2; r_α^2, 0.25.

Figure 18 is a plot of the flutter coefficient against the wing bending-frequency ratio, for a constant value of $\omega_\beta/\omega_\alpha = 0.5$. The case $\omega_h/\omega_\alpha = \infty$ corresponds now to the binary case, torsion-aileron. The branch representing essentially this case is easily evident. Figure 19 differs from figure 18 only in the value of $\omega_\beta/\omega_\alpha$, which is now 1.0. The branch representing torsion-aileron is now gone. (The small singular branch on the axis near $\omega_h/\omega_\alpha = 1.1$ can be shown to disappear completely with a very small amount of friction.)

Figure 20 differs from figure 18 in the value of κ, which is now 0.2, and also in the value of $\omega_\beta/\omega_\alpha$, which is now 0. In addition, several values of x_β have been employed. Note that the aileron-torsion branch beyond $\omega_h/\omega_\alpha=1.0$ exists only for the largest unbalance, $x_\beta=0.002$.

Figure 21 differs from the parallel cases shown by curves $x_\beta=0.002$ in figures 12 and 16 only in the value of κ, which is now 0.125; that is, it represents a heavier wing or a higher altitude. Note that $x_\beta=0.002$ does not eliminate the torsion-aileron branch. The effect of $g_\alpha=0.01$ produces a flutter curve, the ordinate of which is remarkably near the bending-torsion value.

Figure 22 differs from figure 21 in the value of x_β, which is now -0.002. The low dip near $\omega_\beta/\omega_\alpha=1.0$ is eliminated for a value of $g_\alpha=0.01$. Figure 23 extends the cases of figures 21 and 22 to two other values of the frequency ratio ω_h/ω_α.

Figure 24 is a plot of the flutter coefficient against g_α for the constant value of $x_\beta=0.002$ and $\omega_\beta/\omega_\alpha=0.316$. (See fig. 21.) Note that the torsion-aileron branch is gradually eliminated and vanishes for $g_\alpha \approx 0.006$.

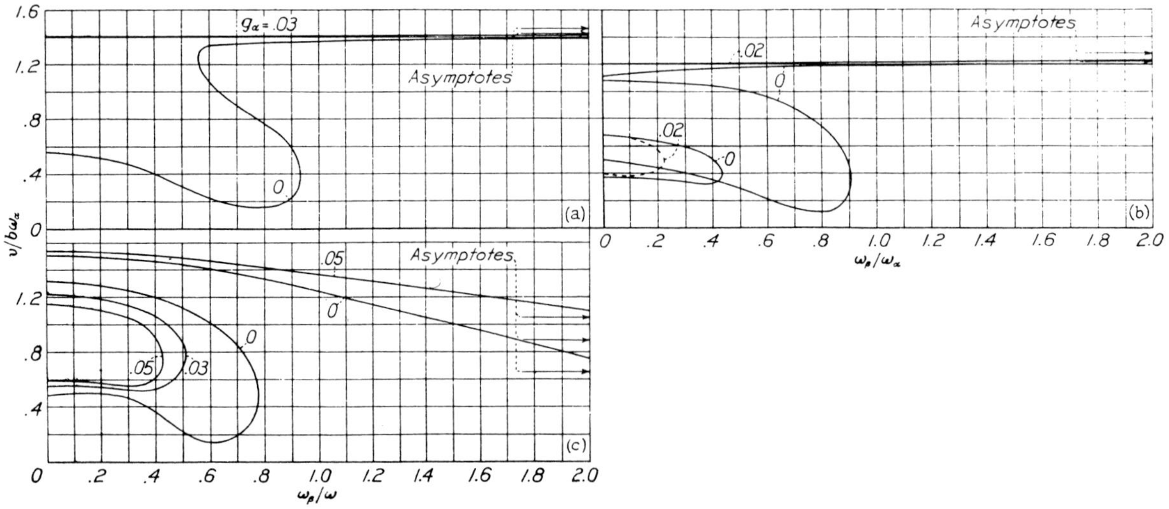

(a) ω_h/ω_α, 0.316.
(b) ω_h/ω_α, 0.607.
(c) ω_h/ω_α, 1.0.

FIGURE 33.—Flutter coefficient $v/b\omega_\alpha$ against frequency ratio $\omega_\beta/\omega_\alpha$ with and without structural torsional damping. κ, 0.125; r_α^2, 0.25; x_β, 0.002.

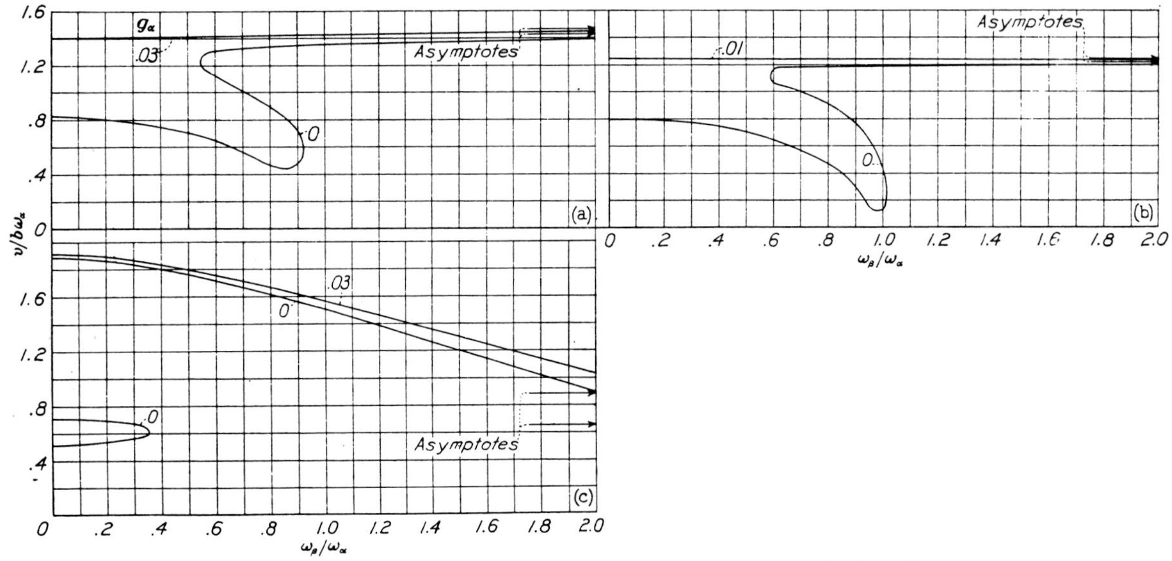

(a) ω_h/ω_α, 0.316.
(b) ω_h/ω_α, 0.607.
(c) ω_h/ω_α, 1.0.

FIGURE 34.—Flutter coefficient $v/b\omega_\alpha$ against frequency ratio $\omega_\beta/\omega_\alpha$ with and without structural torsional damping. κ, 0.125; r_α^2, 0.25; x_β, -0.002.

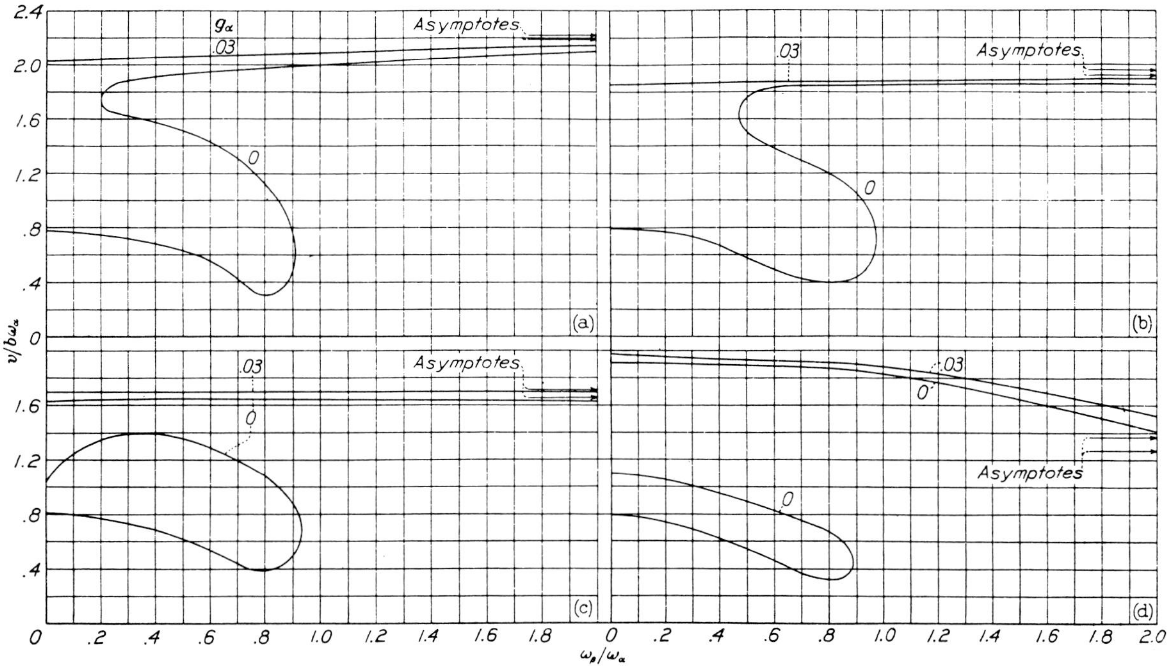

(a) ω_h/ω_α, 0.316.
(b) ω_h/ω_α, 0.5.
(c) ω_h/ω_α, 0.707.
(d) ω_h/ω_α, 1.0.

FIGURE 35.—Flutter coefficient $v/b\omega_\alpha$ against frequency ratio $\omega_\beta/\omega_\alpha$ with and without structural torsional damping. κ, 0.0752; r_α^2, 0.25; x_β,0.

Figure 25 represents a still heavier wing (κ=0.083). This curve shows that x_β=0.002 does not eliminate either the torsion-aileron branch or the bending-aileron branch for low values of $\omega_\beta/\omega_\alpha$. The value ξ=0.7 as shown eliminates the low branches. The value g_α=0.02 eliminates the torsion-aileron branch but has little influence on the bending-aileron branch. Figures 26 and 27 represent similar cases with x_β=0 and with several values of the frequency ratio ω_h/ω_α. In the cases represented by figure 26 (x_α=0.2) the center of gravity of the wing is at 50-percent chord and for those of figure 27 (x_α=0) the center of gravity is at 40-percent chord.

Figure 28 represents a case in which κ=0.25, x_α=0, and ω_h/ω_α=1.0. The figure shows that the bending-torsion flutter branch is eliminated and only the torsion-aileron branch exists. This branch can also be eliminated by increasing the value of g_α.

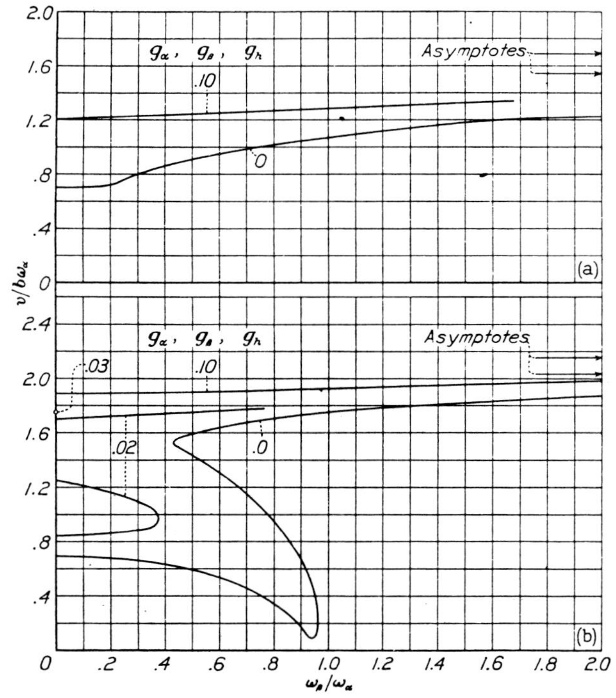

(a) κ, 0.25.
(b) κ, 0.1.

FIGURE 36.—Flutter coefficient $v/b\omega_\alpha$ against frequency ratio $\omega_\beta/\omega_\alpha$. x_α, 0.2; r_α^2, 0.25.

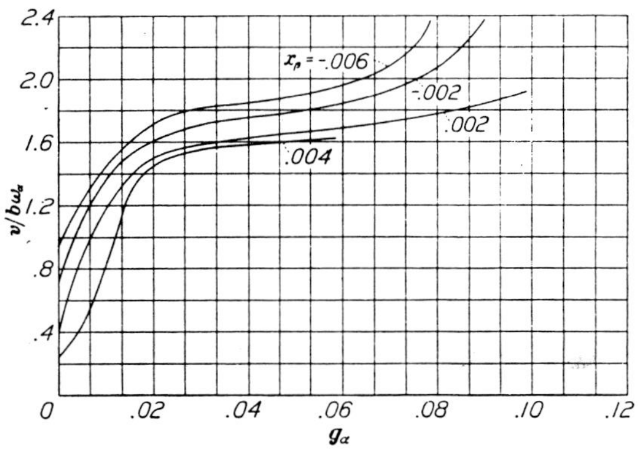

FIGURE 37.—Flutter coefficient $v/b\omega_\alpha$ against the structural damping coefficient g_α in antisymmetrical cases for several values of the aileron unbalance x_β. $\omega_\beta/\omega_\alpha$, 0; ω_h/ω_α, 0.

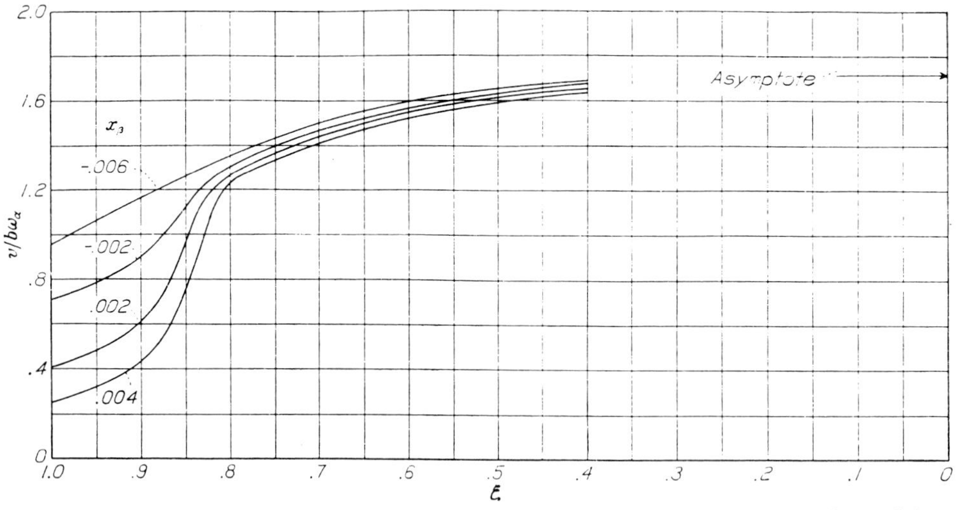

FIGURE 38.—Flutter coefficient $v/b\omega_\alpha$ against partial-span aileron coefficient ξ in the antisymmetrical cases for several values of the aileron unbalance x_β. $\omega_\beta/\omega_\alpha$, 0; ω_h/ω_α, 0.

The next set of figures (figs. 29 to 36) have been calculated with $r_\alpha^2=0.25$ (monoplane case). Figure 29 shows the flutter coefficient plotted against $\omega_\beta/\omega_\alpha$ for two values of x_β: 0.002 and -0.002. The effect of structural damping, $g_\alpha=0.01$, is shown in figure 30 and the effect of the partial-span aileron coefficient ξ is shown in figure 31. Figure 32 extends the cases of figure 30 to other values of the bending-frequency ratio ω_h/ω_α; figures 33 and 34 represent parallel cases for a heavier wing, $\kappa=0.125$.

Figure 35 represents a monoplane case with parameters based on a modern heavy pursuit airplane. For completeness, several curves are shown with different values of the bending-frequency ratio ω_h/ω_α. Figure 36 is based on the parameters for a modern large airplane. Two values of κ are presented: 0.25 and 0.1.

The rest of the figures were calculated for two constant values: $\omega_\beta/\omega_\alpha=0$ and $\omega_h/\omega_\alpha=0$ (antisymmetrical flutter cases). Figure 37 shows the flutter coefficient plotted against g_α for four values of x_β (0.004, 0.002, -0.002, and -0.006). It is observed that the effect of g_α is quite significant. Figure 38 shows the flutter coefficient plotted against ξ for the same values of x_β that were used in figure 37. The effect of ξ in figure 38 is rather large. Figure 39 is a cross plot of figure 38, with x_β as the abscissa. Figure 40 is a plot of the flutter coefficient against g_α for three values of r_α^2 (1, 0.5, and 0.25) and for two values of x_β (0.002 and -0.002).

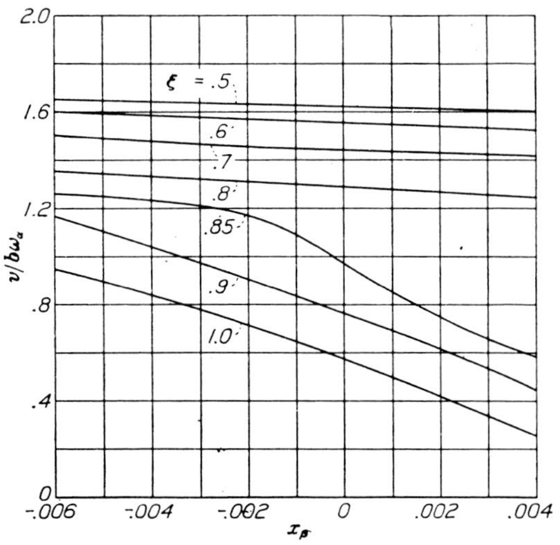

FIGURE 39.—Flutter coefficient $v/b\omega_\alpha$ against aileron unbalance x_β in the antisymmetrical cases for several values of the partial-span aileron coefficient ξ. $\omega_\beta/\omega_\alpha$, 0; ω_h/ω_α, 0.

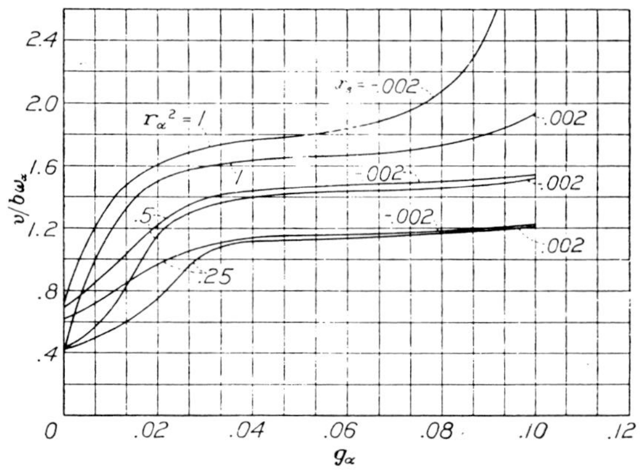

FIGURE 40.—Flutter coefficient $v/b\omega_\alpha$ against the structural damping coefficient g_α in the antisymmetrical cases for three values of r_α^2 and two values of aileron unbalance x_β. $\omega_\beta/\omega_\alpha$, 0; ω_h/ω_α, 0.

DISCUSSION

The first noteworthy observation in the case of three degrees of freedom is the distinct dip in the flutter curve at values of $\omega_\beta/\omega_\alpha$ somewhat less than unity when structural damping is neglected. Apparently the aileron under these circumstances is very nearly in mechanical resonance with the wing in torsion. It is further observed that the flutter velocity remains rather low in this range of values of the aileron frequency. Since the aileron frequency in most practical cases is definitely less than that of the wing torsion, the region below unity is of the most significance.

There are two types of aileron response: One type corresponds to symmetrical wing motion and the other type corresponds to an antisymmetrical motion. The frequency of the first type is of the order of one-half to three-fourths of the torsion frequency and the frequency of the second type is zero. It is noted that the elimination by mass-balancing of flutter resulting from the symmetrical type of response may be difficult, particularly if the aileron frequency is close to the wing-torsion frequency; whereas, the antisymmetrical type is more favorably affected by normal mass-balancing of the aileron. It is also to be noted that the wing damping is unusually effective in removing the dip in the flutter curve. Indeed, for comparatively light structures a value of the torsional damping coefficient g_α of 0.01 brings the flutter velocity almost back to its full bending-torsion value. Significantly, the torsional damping seems to be the most effective. Heavier structures appear to be less susceptible to the effect of damping. In fact, a larger value of g_α is needed and apparently it may be necessary also to provide damping in one or both of the other degrees of freedom (fig. 25).

A partial-span aileron has a rather profound effect on the dip in the flutter curve, which is similar to the effect of the damping. A reduction of the effective aileron length ξ from 1.0 to 0.8 practically restores the normal value of the flutter speed.

It is rather evident from the present study that the effect of mass-balancing has been overemphasized in the earlier literature. Of significance is the fact that a pronounced dip exists in the flutter curve even for an overbalanced aileron (fig. 1). The aileron balancing seems to become most effective for the case in which the wing itself is overbalanced (fig. 7). This case is only of academic interest. Overbalancing alone does not present a solution of the general case of three degrees of freedom; the appropriate value of the flutter speed cannot be obtained solely by any practicable method of balancing.

On the other hand, the greatest beneficial effect of damping is obtained for the unbalanced, that is, the normal wing (fig. 6). Only in this case is the full bending-torsion value nearly reached. In the range of frequencies $\omega_\beta/\omega_\alpha < 1$ the flutter speed of the overbalanced wing remains much lower than that of the normal wing. It is further noted that the beneficial effect of aileron balance is small when a small amount of damping is present (fig. 2).

For the antisymmetrical case with no damping present, $\omega_h=0$, it is observed that the balancing of the aileron is more effective. For a given value of the torsional damping coefficient ($g_\alpha=0.01$) the gain from balancing is not large. The effect of the fractional aileron is very marked. At $\xi=0.8$ the flutter velocity equals the torsion-bending value independently of the balance coefficient.

CONCLUSION

It has been shown that mass-balancing is of less significance than has heretofore been attributed to it. The profound effect of internal structural damping has been shown. For the normal, unbalanced wing a small amount of damping removes the dip in the flutter curve and substantially yields the torsion-bending value of the flutter velocity. The large beneficial effect of the fractional-span aileron has been indicated. These statements apply to light, low-density structures and apply to a lesser degree as the wing density is increased. Because of the complexity of the problem, too general conclusions cannot be safely made and detailed calculations of individual cases are still needed. The included graphs, which cover a fairly representative field, should be of value for specific studies and should furnish numerical solutions in a number of cases.

Langley Memorial Aeronautical Laboratory,
National Advisory Committee for Aeronautics,
Langley Field, Va., *June 7, 1941.*

APPENDIX A

LIST OF NOTATION

α — angle of attack (fig. 41)

β — aileron angle (fig. 41)

h — vertical distance (fig. 41)

b — half chord, used as reference unit length

a — coordinate of elastic axis (also called axis of rotation or torsional axis) (fig. 41). Location of elastic axis in percentage total chord measured from leading edge is

$$100\,\frac{1+a}{2}\text{ or }a=\frac{2\text{ (elastic axis)}}{100}-1$$

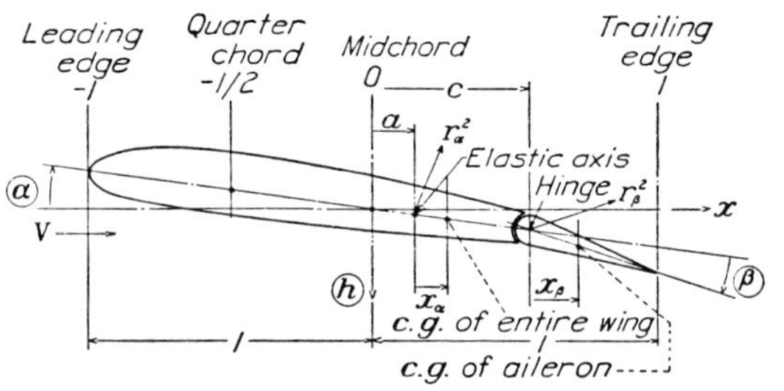

FIGURE 41.—Half chord b is used as the unit length. The positive directions of α, β, and h are indicated by arrows. Note that a is measured from midchord and x_α is measured from the elastic axis positive to the right. Also note that x_β is a "reduced" parameter and not the actual distance from the hinge to the center of gravity of the aileron.

c — coordinate of aileron hinge axis (fig. 41). Location of aileron hinge axis in percentage total chord measured from leading edge is

$$100\,\frac{1+c}{2}\text{ or }c=\frac{2\text{ (aileron hinge)}}{100}-1$$

ρ — mass of air per unit volume

M — mass of wing per unit span length

$\kappa=\frac{\pi\rho b^2}{M}$ — ratio of mass of cylinder of air of diameter equal to chord of wing to mass of wing, both taken for equal length along the span; this ratio may be expressed as $\kappa=0.24\,(b^2/W)\,(\rho/\rho_0)$ where W is weight in pounds per foot span, b is in feet, and ρ/ρ_0 is ratio of air density to standard air

$x_\alpha=\frac{S_\alpha}{Mb}$ — location of center of gravity of wing-aileron system *measured from a* (fig. 41); S_α, static moment of wing-aileron per unit span length referred to a. Location of center of gravity in percentage total chord measured from the leading edge is

$$100\,\frac{1+a+x_\alpha}{2}\text{ or}$$

$$a+x_\alpha=\frac{2\text{(center of gravity)}}{100}-1$$

$x_\beta=\frac{S_\beta}{Mb}$ — *reduced* location of center of gravity of aileron referred to c (fig. 41); S_β, static moment of aileron per unit span length referred to c. M refers to total wing mass and not to mass of aileron alone

$r_\alpha=\sqrt{\frac{I_\alpha}{Mb^2}}$ — radius of gyration of wing aileron referred to a (fig. 41); I_α, moment of inertia of wing aileron about elastic axis per unit span length

$r_\beta=\sqrt{\frac{I_\beta}{Mb^2}}$ — *reduced* radius of gyration of aileron referred to c (fig. 41); I_β, moment of inertia of aileron about c per unit span length

C_α — torsional stiffness of wing around a per unit span length

C_β — torsional stiffness of aileron around c per unit span length

C_h — stiffness of wing in bending per unit span length

$\omega_\alpha=\sqrt{\frac{C_\alpha}{I_\alpha}}$ — natural angular frequency of torsional vibrations around a in vacuum ($\omega_\alpha=2\pi f_\alpha$, where f_α is in cycles per sec)

$\omega_\beta=\sqrt{\frac{C_\beta}{I_\beta}}$ — natural angular frequency of torsional vibrations of aileron around c

$\omega_h=\sqrt{\frac{C_h}{M}}$ — natural angular frequency of wing in bending

t — time

v — speed of forward motion

ω — angular frequency of wing vibrations

$k=\frac{\omega b}{v}$ — *reduced* frequency=number of waves in wake in a distance equal to semichord$\times 2\pi$

$1/k$ — reduced wave length—length of one wave of wake in terms of a distance equal to semichord$\times 2\pi$

$v/b\omega_\alpha$ — flutter-speed coefficient

g_α, g_β, g_h — structural damping coefficients; πg corresponds approximately to the usual logarithmic decrement

ξ — partial-span aileron coefficient. Note that this coefficient is not the geometric ratio but an "effective" value of the order of $[\int f(\alpha)dz]^2/\int f^2(\alpha)dz$, where the integral in the numerator is taken over the aileron span and that in the denominator is taken over the full span; $f(\alpha)$ represents the spanwise amplitude of (flutter) torsion mode

APPENDIX B

METHOD OF ELIMINATION AS APPLIED TO FLUTTER CALCULATIONS

The treatment of the flutter problem (references 1 and 2) leads to the simultaneous solution of two equations. The degree of each of these equations in the general case of three degrees of freedom (flexure, torsion, and aileron) is three. If, in addition, the effect of a tab motion or a float is desired, the degree of the equations may be more than three. The numerical calculations involving the plotting of roots becomes laborious and time-consuming. A method of elimination for obtaining common roots of two simultaneous equations may be used, which does away with the necessity for any root extractions. (See, for example, reference 3.) The procedure results in the saving of considerable effort, particularly when more than two degrees of freedom are involved. The Sylvester method of obtaining the condition that two simultaneous equations have a common root completely eliminates the unknown quantity. It is feasible, however, to terminate the process of elimination with two equations of the first or second degree. The choice made in the following sections is the use of two equations of the first degree.

The equations arising in the calculations in the case of three degrees of freedom are of the form:

$$\left.\begin{aligned} A_3X^3+A_2X^2+A_1X+A_0=0 \\ B_3X^3+B_2X^2+B_1X+B_0=0 \end{aligned}\right\} \qquad (1)$$

where in special cases the degrees of the equations [(3,3) in equation (1)] may be (3,2), (2,2), (2,1), or (1,1). The quantity X is an unknown frequency parameter, and the coefficients A and B are functions of a large number of parameters: structural parameters a, b, c, x_α, x_β, r_α^2, r_β^2, κ, g_α, g_β, and g_h; frequency parameters Ω_h, Ω_α, Ω_β; and the reduced frequency $1/k$. For a particular aircraft structure represented by given parameters there corresponds a flutter velocity and a frequency determined from X and $1/k$. Expressions for the quantities A and B are listed in references 1 and 2. In the following discussion it is assumed that these quantities are available.

The common solution of equations (1) can be obtained from the common solution of

$$\left.\begin{aligned} a_1X+a_0=0 \\ b_1X+b_0=0 \end{aligned}\right\} \qquad (2)$$

where a_1, a_0, b_1, and b_0 are functions, listed later, of the A's and B's in equations (1). Now, from equations (2) it is evident that the common solution exists if and only if

$$X_1=-a_0/a_1 \text{ is also equal to } X_2=-b_0/b_1$$

Then, if all the parameters but one are kept constant, for instance $1/k$, and X_1 and X_2 are plotted against $1/k$, the intersection (or intersections) determines the common root (or roots) X and the value (or values) of $1/k$ for which this common solution occurs, and X and $1/k$ together determine the flutter solution for the particular structure.

Another possibility, namely, keeping $1/k$ fixed and plotting X against one of the structural or frequency parameters, will yield as a flutter solution the necessary structural parameter. Many variations are possible.

The Sylvester resultant of equations (2) is the determinant $\begin{vmatrix} a_1 & a_0 \\ b_1 & b_0 \end{vmatrix}$ and its vanishing is the condition for the existence of a common root. If this quantity is plotted against $1/k$ as the abscissa, for instance, the intersection with the $1/k$ axis gives the required value of $1/k$. The first-mentioned method involving two parameters is preferable, however, because the two curves are simpler and yield both X and $1/k$ simultaneously.

There remains, then, only the task of listing the expressions for a_1, a_0, b_1, and b_0. It is convenient to list these expressions separately for the cases in which the degree of the equation is (2, 2), (3, 2), and (3, 3).

In order to obtain a_0, a_1, b_0, and b_1 for the case of two quadratics, multiply the first of equations (1) by B_2 and the second equation by A_2 and subtract; and similarly multiply the first of equations (1) by B_2X+B_1 and the second by A_2X+A_1 and subtract. Then

$$a_0=\begin{vmatrix} A_0 & A_2 \\ B_0 & B_2 \end{vmatrix}$$

$$a_1=\begin{vmatrix} A_1 & A_2 \\ B_1 & B_2 \end{vmatrix}$$

$$b_0=\begin{vmatrix} A_0 & A_1 \\ B_0 & B_1 \end{vmatrix}$$

$$b_1=\begin{vmatrix} A_0 & A_2 \\ B_0 & B_2 \end{vmatrix}=a_0$$

Similarly, for one cubic and one quadratic (3, 2):

$$a_0=\begin{vmatrix} A_0B_1-A_1B_0 & -B_0A_3 \\ B_0 & B_2 \end{vmatrix}$$

$$a_1=\begin{vmatrix} A_0B_2-A_2B_0 & -B_0A_3 \\ B_1 & B_2 \end{vmatrix}$$

$$b_0=\begin{vmatrix} A_0B_1-A_1B_0 & A_0B_2-A_2B_0 \\ B_0 & B_1 \end{vmatrix}$$

$$b_1=a_0$$

In the case of two cubics

$$a_0=\begin{vmatrix} \begin{vmatrix} A_0 & A_1 \\ B_0 & B_1 \end{vmatrix} & \begin{vmatrix} A_0 & A_3 \\ B_0 & B_3 \end{vmatrix} \\ \begin{vmatrix} A_0 & A_3 \\ B_0 & B_3 \end{vmatrix} & \begin{vmatrix} A_2 & A_3 \\ B_2 & B_3 \end{vmatrix} \end{vmatrix}$$

$$a_1=\begin{vmatrix} \begin{vmatrix} A_0 & A_2 \\ B_0 & B_2 \end{vmatrix} & \begin{vmatrix} A_0 & A_3 \\ B_0 & B_3 \end{vmatrix} \\ \begin{vmatrix} A_1 & A_3 \\ B_1 & B_3 \end{vmatrix} & \begin{vmatrix} A_2 & A_3 \\ B_2 & B_3 \end{vmatrix} \end{vmatrix}$$

$$b_0=\begin{vmatrix} \begin{vmatrix} A_0 & A_1 \\ B_0 & B_1 \end{vmatrix} & \begin{vmatrix} A_0 & A_2 \\ B_0 & B_2 \end{vmatrix} \\ \begin{vmatrix} A_0 & A_3 \\ B_0 & B_3 \end{vmatrix} & \begin{vmatrix} A_1 & A_3 \\ B_1 & B_3 \end{vmatrix} \end{vmatrix}$$

$$b_1=a_0$$

In the use of this method it is sometimes found that the common intersection is not obtained with precision without the use of many values of $1/k$. It may then appear to be more convenient to employ a different form. Thus, in the case of two cubics, there are three possible forms for a_0, a_1, b_0, and b_1 and a second form is

$$a_0=\begin{vmatrix} \begin{vmatrix} A_0 & A_3 \\ B_0 & B_3 \end{vmatrix} & \begin{vmatrix} A_2 & A_3 \\ B_2 & B_3 \end{vmatrix} \\ \begin{vmatrix} A_0 & A_2 \\ B_0 & B_2 \end{vmatrix} & \begin{vmatrix} A_1 & A_3 \\ B_1 & B_3 \end{vmatrix} \end{vmatrix}$$

$$a_1=\begin{vmatrix} \begin{vmatrix} A_1 & A_3 \\ B_1 & B_3 \end{vmatrix} & \begin{vmatrix} A_2 & A_3 \\ B_2 & B_3 \end{vmatrix} \\ \begin{vmatrix} A_0 & A_3 \\ B_0 & B_3 \end{vmatrix} + \begin{vmatrix} A_1 & A_2 \\ B_1 & B_2 \end{vmatrix}, & \begin{vmatrix} A_1 & A_3 \\ B_1 & B_3 \end{vmatrix} \end{vmatrix}$$

$$b_0=\begin{vmatrix} \begin{vmatrix} A_0 & A_3 \\ B_0 & B_3 \end{vmatrix} & \begin{vmatrix} A_1 & A_3 \\ B_1 & B_3 \end{vmatrix} \\ \begin{vmatrix} A_0 & A_2 \\ B_0 & B_2 \end{vmatrix}, & \begin{vmatrix} A_0 & A_3 \\ B_0 & B_3 \end{vmatrix} + \begin{vmatrix} A_1 & A_2 \\ B_1 & B_2 \end{vmatrix} \end{vmatrix}$$

$$b_1=a_0$$

The method is not limited to the original form of the equations. Assume, for example, that *both* X and $1/k$ are preassigned and that it is required to know the values of two parameters, say u_1 and u_2, which have as the flutter solution the preassigned values of X and $1/k$. The original equations can be considered as equations in u_1 and u_2 whose common solution is determined by

$$a_1u_1+a_0=0$$
$$b_1u_1+b_0=0$$

where a_1, a_0, b_1, and b_0 are known (calculable) functions of all the other parameters. If the two roots are plotted against u_2, the intersections (if any) will give the required values of u_1 and u_2.

APPENDIX C

EXAMPLE ON FLUTTER OF BIPLANE

Experiments on the vibration frequencies showed the following results (values given in cycles per min):

1. Antisymmetrical torsion of wing-cellule system	1300
2. Symmetrical bending of wing-cellule system	800
3. Symmetrical torsion of wing-cellule system	1300
4. Local wing bending:	
a. Lower wing, with node at or near interplane strut	1300
b. Upper wing, with node at or near interplane strut	1100
5. Aileron against controls	1100
6. Local torsion in aileron	1800
7. Local torsion in flap	1100
8. Engine rocking	830

There are two possible types of ternary flutter:

a. Symmetrical torsion-symmetrical bending-symmetrical aileron motion. The frequencies are 1300, 800, and 1100, respectively.

b. Antisymmetrical torsion-antisymmetrical bending-antisymmetrical aileron motion. The frequencies are 1300, 0, and 0, respectively.

The other parameters were used as follows: $a=-0.2$ (elastic axis at 40-percent chord); $x_\alpha=0.2$ (center of gravity at 50-percent chord; the actual center of gravity was near 48-percent chord); $r_\alpha^2=1$; $\kappa=0.2$ (this value of the wing-density parameter corresponds not to sea level but to an altitude of approximately 10,000 ft); $2b=4$ feet 9 inches (reference chord).

With the use of these parameters, there is obtained for the torsion-bending (case 1) flutter-speed coefficient $v/b\omega_\alpha$ from figure 1 a value of 1.26. The reference velocity $b\omega_\alpha$ is equal to 221 miles per hour. Thus the flutter speed V_F is equal to 278 miles per hour. Because the observed flutter speed on this biplane was lower than this value, (about 200 mph), the aileron was evidently involved. The parameters relating to the aileron were assumed to be as follows:

Location of the center of gravity, x_β	0.002
Radius of gyration, r_β^2	0.002
Chord location, c	0.6

The aileron was considered a full-span aileron. This assumption is fairly reasonable because the lower wing flap was almost identical with the aileron. These values were used in the results shown in figure 1, which was based on the biplane. The ratio $\omega_\beta/\omega_\alpha=0.833$ gives, for the assumed unbalance $x_\beta=0.002$, a value of the flutter coefficient $v/b\omega_\alpha$ of 0.68 or a speed of 151 miles per hour.

For the antisymmetrical case, if a full-span aileron and zero damping are conservatively considered, there is obtained from figure 37 the value $v/b\omega_\alpha=0.41$. A value of the internal damping g_α of 0.01, however, increases the flutter coefficient to 1.18, which is equal to 261 miles per hour (true speed). Notice that this value is calculated without the benefit of a fractional aileron. If there is used in the symmetrical case a small value of the internal damping g_α of 0.01, it is seen from figure 2 (b) that there is only a slight favorable effect from mass-balancing. The flutter coefficient $v/b\omega_\alpha$ is equal to 1.10 for $x_\beta=0.002$ and increases to 1.16 for $x_\beta=-0.002$. With the use of $v/b\omega_\alpha=1.1$, there is obtained a flutter speed of 243 miles per hour (true speed). From later experiments it has been found that the value $g_\alpha=0.01$ is evidently a safe value to use in such calculations. It is thus noted that the flutter speed, because of this effect, approaches the torsion-bending value. It is further observed that with this amount or a larger amount of damping the mass-balancing of the aileron becomes fairly ineffective.

Since the calculation for the symmetrical case based on $g_\alpha=0.01$ gives values of the flutter velocity in the order of 240 miles per hour, true speed (corresponding to an indicated speed of approximately 206 mph), it is probable that this case describes the observed flutter, which was known to be symmetrical.

This biplane was aerodynamically cleaner than many of the earlier types and it is possible that the absence of numerous interplane wires and struts contributed to a lowering of the torsional damping effect to such an extent that flutter was invited. No doubt, many of the older types of biplane were safe from flutter because of their large structural damping.

REFERENCES

1. Theodorsen, Theodore, and Garrick, I. E.: Mechanism of Flutter—A Theoretical and Experimental Investigation of the Flutter Problem. Rep. No. 685, NACA, 1940.
2. Theodorsen, Theodore: General Theory of Aerodynamic Instability and the Mechanism of Flutter. Rep. No. 496, NACA, 1935.
3. Dickson, Leonard Eugene: First Course in the Theory of Equations. John Wiley & Sons, Inc., 1922, ch. X.

FLUTTER CALCULATIONS IN THREE DEGREES OF FREEDOM

TABLE I

[r_α^2, 1; κ, 0.2; c, 0.6; a, −0.2; x_α, 0.2; r_β^2, 0.002; ξ, 1.0]

Figure	$\omega_\beta/\omega_\alpha$	ω_h/ω_α	x_β	g_α	g_β	g_h
1	Variable	0.607	−0.006	0	0	0
	do	.607	−.005	0	0	0
	do	.607	−.002	0	0	0
	do	.607	.002	0	0	0
	do	.607	.004	0	0	0
2 (a)	do	.607	.004	0	0	0
	do	.607	.004	.01	0	0
2 (b)	do	.607	.002	0	0	0
	do	.607	.002	.01	0	0
2 (c)	do	.607	−.002	0	0	0
	do	.607	−.002	.01	0	0
3	0.833	.607	.002		Variable	

TABLE II

[r_α^2, 1; κ, 0.2; c, 0.6; a, −0.2; r_β^2, 0.002; ξ, 1.0]

Figure	$\omega_\beta/\omega_\alpha$	ω_h/ω_α	x_β	x_α	g_α
4	Variable	0.607	−0.002	0	0
	do	.607	0	0	0
	do	.607	.002	0	0
5 (a)	do	.607	0	0	0
	do	.607	0	0	.01
5 (b)	do	.607	−.002	0	0
	do	.607	−.002	0	.01
6	do	.607	.002	.2	0
	do	.607	.002	.2	.01
	do	.607	.002	0	0
	do	.607	.002	0	.01
	do	.607	.002	−.1	0
	do	.607	.002	−.1	.01
7	do	.607	−.005	−.1	0
	do	.607	−.005	−.1	.01

TABLE III

[r_α^2, 1; κ, 0.2; c, 0.6; a, −0.2; x_β, 0.002; r_β^2, 0.002]

Figure	$\omega_\beta/\omega_\alpha$	ω_h/ω_α	x_α	ξ	g_α
8	Variable	0.607	0.2	0.5	0
	do	.607	.2	.8	0
	do	.607	.2	.9	0
	do	.607	.2	1.0	0
9	0.833	.607	.2	Variable	0
10	Variable	.607	.2	.8	.01
	do	.607	.2	1.0	.01
	do	.607	.2	.8	0
	do	.607	.2	1.0	0
11	do	.607	0	.8	0
	do	.607	0	1.0	.01
	do	.607	0	1.0	0

TABLE IV

[r_α^2, 0.5; κ, 0.2; c, 0.6; a, −0.2; x_α, 0.2; r_β^2, 0.002; ξ, 1.0]

Figure	$\omega_\beta/\omega_\alpha$	ω_h/ω_α	x_β	g_α	g_β	g_h
12	Variable	0.607	−0.005	0	0	0
	do	.607	−.002	0	0	0
	do	.607	0	0	0	0
	do	.607	.002	0	0	0
13 (a)	do	.607	.002	0	0	0
	do	.607	.002	.01	0	0
13 (b)	do	.607	0	0	0	0
	do	.607	0	.01	0	0
13 (c)	do	.607	−.002	0	0	0
	do	.607	−.002	.01	0	0
13 (d)	do	.607	−.005	0	0	0
	do	.607	−.005	.01	0	0
14 (a)	0.607	.607	.002	Variable	Variable	Variable
14 (b)	.833	.607	.002	Variable	Variable	Variable
15 (a)	Variable	.316	.002	0	0	0
	do	.316	.002	.03	0	0
15 (b)	do	1.0	.002	0	0	0
	do	1.0	.002	.03	0	0
15 (c)	do	.316	−.002	0	0	0
	do	.316	−.002	.03	0	0
15 (d)	do	1.0	−.002	0	0	0
	do	1.0	−.002	.03	0	0

TABLE V

[r_α^2, 0.5; c, 0.6; a, −0.2; r_β^2, 0.002; ξ, 1.0]

Figure	$\omega_\beta/\omega_\alpha$	ω_h/ω_α	κ	x_β	x_α	g_α
16	Variable	0.607	0.25	0.002	0.2	0
	do	.607	.25	.002	.2	.01
17	do	.607	.25	.002	0	0
	do	.607	.25	.002	0	.01
18	0.5	Variable	.25	.002	0	0
19	1	do	.25	.002	0	0
20	0	do	.2	.002	.2	0
	0	do	.2	0	.2	0
	0	do	.2	−.002	.2	0
	0	do	.2	−.005	.2	0
21	Variable	.607	.125	.002	.2	0
	do	.607	.125	.002	.2	.01
22	do	.607	.125	−.002	.2	0
	do	.607	.125	−.002	.2	.01
23 (a)	do	.316	.125	.002	.2	0
	do	.316	.125	.002	.2	.03
23 (b)	do	1.0	.125	.002	.2	0
	do	1.0	.125	.002	.2	.03
23 (c)	do	.316	.125	−.002	.2	0
	do	.316	.125	−.002	.2	.03
23 (d)	do	1.0	.125	−.002	.2	0
	do	1.0	.125	−.002	.2	.03
24	0.316	.607	.125	.002	.2	Variable
25	Variable	.607	.083	.002	.2	0
	do	.607	.083	.002	.2	.01
26 (a)	do	.316	.083	0	.2	0
	do	.316	.083	0	.2	.02
26 (b)	do	.607	.083	0	.2	0
	do	.607	.083	[illegible]	.2	.02
26 (c)	do	1.0	.083	0	.2	0
	do	1.0	.083	0	.2	.02
27 (a)	do	.316	.083	0	0	0
	do	.316	.083	0	0	.02
27 (b)	do	.607	.083	0	0	0
	do	.607	.083	0	0	.02
27 (c)	do	1.0	.083	0	0	0
	do	1.0	.083	0	0	.02
	do	1.0	.083	0	0	.10
28	do	1.0	.25	.002	0	0

TABLE VI

[r_α^2, 0.25; c, 0.6; a, −0.2; x_α, 0.2; r_β^2, 0.002]

Figure	$\omega_\beta/\omega_\alpha$	ω_h/ω_α	κ	x_β	ξ	g_α
29	Variable	0.607	0.2	0.002	1.0	0
	do	.607	.2	−.002	1.0	0
30 (a)	do	.607	.2	.002	1.0	0
	do	.607	.2	.002	1.0	.01
30 (b)	do	.607	.2	−.002	1.0	0
	do	.607	.2	−.002	1.0	.01
31	do	.607	.2	.002	1.0	0
	do	.607	.2	.002	.8	0
32 (a)	do	.316	.2	.002	1.0	0
	do	.316	.2	.002	1.0	.03
32 (b)	do	1.0	.2	.002	1.0	0
	do	1.0	.2	.002	1.0	.03
32 (c)	do	.316	.2	−.002	1.0	0
	do	.316	.2	−.002	1.0	.03
32 (d)	do	1.0	.2	−.002	1.0	0
	do	1.0	.2	−.002	1.0	.03
33 (a)	do	.316	.125	.002	1.0	0
	do	.316	.125	.002	1.0	.03
33 (b)	do	.607	.125	.002	1.0	0
	do	.607	.125	.002	1.0	.02
33 (c)	do	1.0	.125	.002	1.0	0
	do	1.0	.125	.002	1.0	.05
	do	1.0	.125	.002	1.0	.03
34 (a)	do	.316	.125	−.002	1.0	0
	do	.316	.125	−.002	1.0	.03
34 (b)	do	.607	.125	−.002	1.0	0
	do	.607	.125	−.002	1.0	.01
34 (c)	do	1.0	.125	−.002	1.0	0
	do	1.0	.125	−.002	1.0	.03

TABLE VII

[r_α^2, 0.25; κ, 0.0752; c, 0.5; a, − 0.4; x_α, 0.2; x_β, 0; r_β^2, 0.002]

Figure	$\omega_\beta/\omega_\alpha$	ω_h/ω_α	g_α
35 (a)	Variable	0.316	0
	do	.316	.03
35 (b)	do	.500	0
	do	.500	.03
35 (c)	do	.707	0
	do	.707	.03
35 (d)	do	1.0	0
	do	1.0	.03

TABLE VIII

[r_α^2, 0.25; c, 0.6; a, − 0.4; x_α, 0.2; x_β, 0; r_β^2, 0.0012]

Figure	$\omega_\beta/\omega_\alpha$	ω_h/ω_α	κ	g_α	g_β	g_h
36 (a)	Variable	0.25	0.25	0	0	0
	do	.25	.25	.10	.10	.10
36 (b)	do	.25	.1	0	0	0
	do	.25	.1	.02	.02	.02
	do	.25	.1	.10	.10	.10

TABLE IX

[$\omega_\beta/\omega_\alpha$, 0; ω_h/ω_α, 0; κ, 0.2; c, 0.6; a, − 0.2; x_α, 0.2; r_β^2, 0.002]

Figure	r_α^2	x_β	ξ	g_α
37	1	0.004	1.0	Variable.
	1	.002	1.0	Do.
	1	−.002	1.0	Do.
	1	−.006	1.0	Do.
38	1	.004	Variable	0
	1	.002	do	0
	1	−.002	do	0
	1	−.006	do	0
39	1	Variable	.5	0
	1	do	.6	0
	1	do	.7	0
	1	do	.8	0
	1	do	.85	0
	1	do	.9	0
	1	do	1.0	0
40	.5	.002	1.0	Variable
	.5	−0.002	1.0	Do.
	1	.002	1.0	Do.
	1	−0.002	1.0	Do.
	.25	.002	1.0	Do.
	.25	−.002	1.0	Do.

THE THEORY OF PROPELLERS

I—DETERMINATON OF THE CIRCULATION FUNCTION AND THE MASS COEFFICIENT FOR DUAL-ROTATING PROPELLERS

BY THEODORE THEODORSEN

National Advisory Committee for Aeronautics

Report No. 775, 1944

SUMMARY

Values of the circulation function have been obtained for dual-rotating propellers. Numerical values are given for four-, eight-, and twelve-blade dual-rotating propellers and for advance ratios from 2 to about 6. In addition, the circulation function has been determined for single-rotating propellers for the higher values of the advance ratio. The mass coefficient, another quantity of significance in propeller theory, has been introduced. This mass coefficient, which is actually the mean value of the circulation coefficient, expresses the effective area of the column of the medium acted upon by the propeller in terms of the propeller-disk area. Values of the mass coefficient, which have been determined directly by special measurements and also by integration of the circulation function, are given for the four-, eight-, and twelve-blade dual-rotating propellers. The mass coefficient has also been determined for several cases of single-rotating propellers, partly for the purpose of comparing such experimental values with theoretical results in the known range of low advance ratios and partly to extend the results to include a range of high advance ratios. The effect of stationary countervanes on the mass coefficient has also been determined for several cases of practical interest.

INTRODUCTION

CIRCULATION FUNCTION $K(x)$

In 1929 Goldstein (reference 1) succeeded in solving the problem of the ideal lift distribution of single-rotating propellers. Goldstein's work is restricted to the case of a light loading and also, in effect, to a small advance ratio. Numerical values given by Goldstein for the optimum circulation distribution are reproduced in table I and figure 1. Some additional values calculated by Kramer (reference 2) for higher advance ratios are given in table I and have been superimposed on the Goldstein results in figure 1. Numerical results by Lock and Yeatman (reference 3) for the four-blade propeller are reproduced in table II and figure 2. The parameter λ used in tables I and II is the tangent of the tip vortex angle in the ultimate wake

$$\lambda=\frac{1}{\pi}\frac{V+w}{nD}$$

where w is the rearward displacement velocity of the helical vortex surface at infinity. (A list of the symbols used throughout the paper is given in the appendix.) These data have been used for comparison with results contained in the present paper.

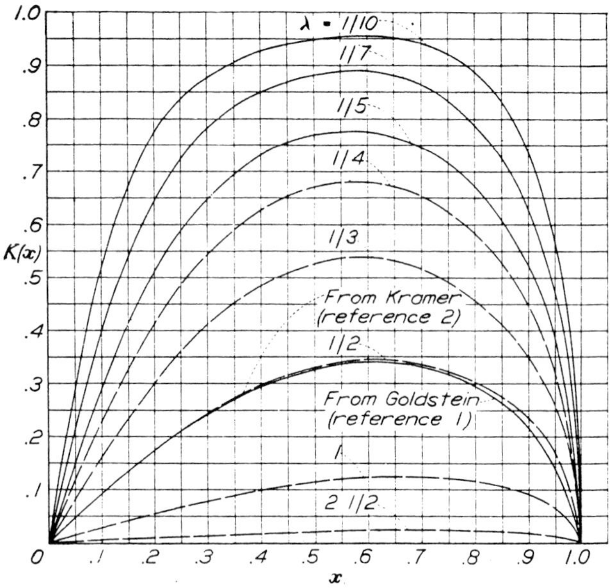

FIGURE 1.—The function $K(x)$ for several values of λ for two-blade propellers.

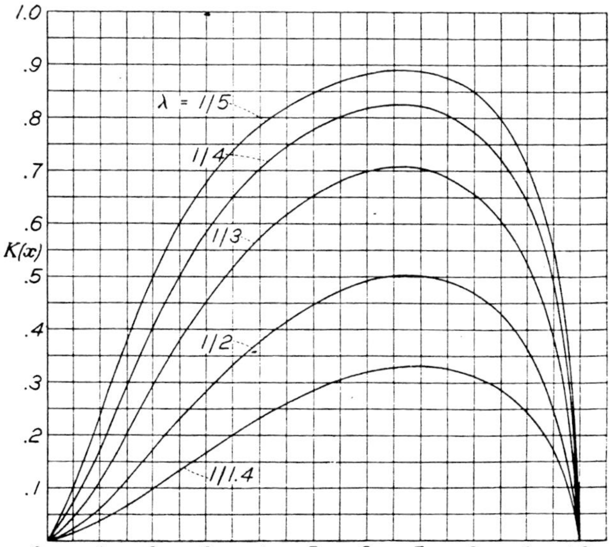

FIGURE 2.—The function $K(x)$ for several values of λ for four-blade propellers.

TABLE I

OPTIMUM CIRCULATION DISTRIBUTION FOR THE TWO-BLADE PROPELLER

Calculated by Goldstein (reference 1, p. 450)

x	$\lambda=\frac{1}{20}$	x	$\lambda=\frac{1}{[illegible]}$	x	$\lambda=\frac{1}{5}$	x	$\lambda=\frac{1}{4}$	x	$\lambda=\frac{1}{3}$	x	$\lambda=\frac{1}{2}$
0.020	0.125	0.029	0.126	0.040	0.124	0.050	0.120	0.067	0.111	0.100	0.092
.040	.245	.057	.215	.080	.240	.100	.232	.133	.213	.200	.175
.060	.372	.086	.331	.120	.344	.150	.331	.200	.303	.300	.243
.080	.445	.114	.445	.160	.434	.200	.418	.267	.379	.400	.295
.100	.526	.143	.523	.200	.511	.250	.489	.333	.440	.500	.329
.120	.583	.171	.590	.240	.575	.300	.548	.400	.485	.600	.341
.140	.650	.200	.646	.280	.626	.350	.592	.467	.514	.700	.331
.160	.698	.229	.691	.320	.669	.400	.628	.533	.533	.800	.295
.180	.738	.257	.732	.360	.704	.450	.654	.600	.537	.900	.220
.200	.772	.286	.766	.400	.731	.500	.670	.667	.525	----	----
.250	.836	.357	.826	.500	.770	.625	.676	.833	.427	----	----
.280	----	----			----	----	----	.933	.303	----	----
.300	.878	.429	.863	.600	.775	.750	.621	----	----	----	----
.350	.908	.509	.884	.700	.747	.875	.486	----	----	----	----
.380	----	----			----	.950	.334	----	----	----	----
.400	.927	.571	.890	.800	.671	----	----	----	----	----	----
.450	.940	.643	.882	.900	.519	----	----	----	----	----	----
.480	----	----		.950	.351	----	----	----	----	----	----
.500	.950	.714	.858		----	----	----	----	----	----	----
.600	.955	.857	.71[illegible]		----	----	----	----	----	----	----
.650	----	.929	.554		----	----	----	----	----	----	----
.680	----	.971	.376		----	----	----	----	----	----	----
.700	.941	----			----	----	----	----	----	----	----
.800	.890	----	----		----	----	----	----	----	----	----
.900	.738	----	----		----	----	----	----	----	----	----
.950	.589	----	----		----	----	----	----	----	----	----
.980	.388	----	----		----	----	----	----	----	----	----

Calculated by Kramer (reference 2, p. 23)

x	$\lambda=\frac{1}{4}$	$\lambda=\frac{1}{3}$	$\lambda=\frac{1}{2}$	$\lambda=1.0$	$\lambda=2.5$
0.1	0.232	0.164	0.0919	0.0283	0.00494
.2	.418	.303	.1758	.0552	.00974
.3	.548	.412	.246	.0795	.01415
.4	.629	.486	.297	.0999	.01806
.45	.655	.510	------	.1082	.01976
.5	.671	.528	.331	.1155	.02124
.6	.679	.540	.345	.1239	.02342
.7	.654	.517	.338	.1243	.02423
.75	.623	.493	.325	.1213	.02396
.8	.580	.457	.305	.1156	.02310
.85	.528	.413	.276	.1061	.02147
.9	.449	.351	.235	.0919	.0187
.925	.395	.311	------	.0817	.0168
.95	.329	.260	.173	.0687	.0141
.975	------	.190	------	.0497	.0103

TABLE II

OPTIMUM CIRCULATION DISTRIBUTION FOR THE FOUR-BLADE PROPELLER

Calculated by Lock and Yeatman (reference 3)

x	$\lambda=\frac{1}{5}$	x	$\lambda=\frac{1}{4}$	x	$\lambda=\frac{1}{3}$	x	$\lambda=\frac{1}{2}$	x	$\lambda=\frac{1}{1.4}$
0.1200	0.300	0.150	0.299	0.0667	0.066	0.100	0.064	0.1429	0.061
.2000	.506	.250	.505	.1333	.179	.200	.173	.2857	.159
.3200	.706	.350	.619	.2000	.297	.300	.283	.4286	.249
.4000	.786	.400	.702	.2667	.405	.400	.377	.5714	.310
.5000	.848	.450	.744	.3333	.497	.500	.449	.7143	.329
.5600	.871	.500	.776	.4000	.572	.600	.492	.7857	.317
.6000	.881	.625	.821	.4667	.630	.700	.501	.8571	.282
.7000	.887	.700	.821	.5333	.672	.800	.469	.9286	.213
.7600	.872	.750	.806	.6000	.698	.900	.370	------	------
.8000	.850	.875	.689	.6667	.706	-----	-----	------	------
.9000	.714	.950	.488	.8333	.627	-----	-----	------	------
.9600	.503	-----		.9333	.445	-----	-----	------	------

It should be emphasized that a distinction has been made between dimensions and conditions of the slipstream at the propeller and those in the ultimate wake, a distinction that does not occur in the treatment of lightly loaded propellers. The present paper is concerned exclusively with conditions in the ultimate wake; in fact, it can be shown that thrust, torque, and efficiency are all uniquely given as functions of the ultimate wake only, no knowledge of the propeller being necessary except for purposes of actual design. It should be pointed out that both the diameter and the advance angle of the ultimate helix are different from the values at the propeller, the diameter being smaller and the advance ratio larger. It can be shown that the distribution function depends on the advance angle only. The ideal distribution function is therefore identical for light and heavy loadings provided both refer to identical helix angles in the ultimate wake.

In figures 1 and 2 the quantity $K(x)$ is a characteristic function related to the circulation $\Gamma(x)$ along the blade as follows:

$$K(x)\equiv\frac{p\Gamma\omega}{2\pi(V+w)w}$$

where Γ is the potential difference across the helix surface at a radius x, p is the number of blades, and ω is the angular velocity of the propeller. The quantity

$$w\frac{V+w}{p\frac{\omega}{2\pi}}$$

is the potential drop for a velocity w through a length

$$\frac{H}{p}=\frac{V+w}{p\frac{\omega}{2\pi}}.$$

which is the axial distance between two successive vortex sheets. Each sheet has $\frac{\omega}{2\pi}$ turns corresponding to a time of 1 second and there are p separate sheets corresponding to p blades. The quantity $K(x)$ is thus the nondimensional expression for the potential drop across the surface of discontinuity as a fraction of the available drop in the direction of the helix axis.

It should be noted that the coefficient $K(x)$ differs from the Goldstein coefficient

$$\frac{p\Gamma\omega}{2\pi Vw}$$

in which the velocity w has been disregarded in comparison with the advance velocity V. The coefficients are identical if referred to the same helix angle of the ultimate wake.

MASS COEFFICIENT κ

A significant coefficient, which will be termed the mass coefficient κ and which may be shown to be one of the basic parameters in the propeller theory, is now introduced. It is given here merely by definition

$$\kappa\equiv2\int_0^1 K(x)x\,dx$$

where x is the radius and the integral is taken from $x=0$ to $x=1$. By inspection it is noted that κ is really the mean value of the coefficient $K(x)$ over the disk area. If $K(x)\equiv1$, then $\kappa=1$, which is the limiting value of κ.

A physical interpretation of κ is interesting. It is possible to show that κ represents the effective cross-section of the column of the medium "pushed" by the propeller divided by the projected propeller-wake area. In other words, the propeller imparts the full interference velocity w to a column of air of cross-section κ per unit area of the ultimate propeller wake. The diameter of such a column is therefore $\sqrt{\kappa}$ for a propeller wake of unit diameter. Although mathematical refinements will not be considered in the present paper, this physical interpretation should suffice to indicate the nature of the coefficient and the designation adopted. It will be shown herein that the coefficient κ is readily obtained by direct measurements, to be described later.

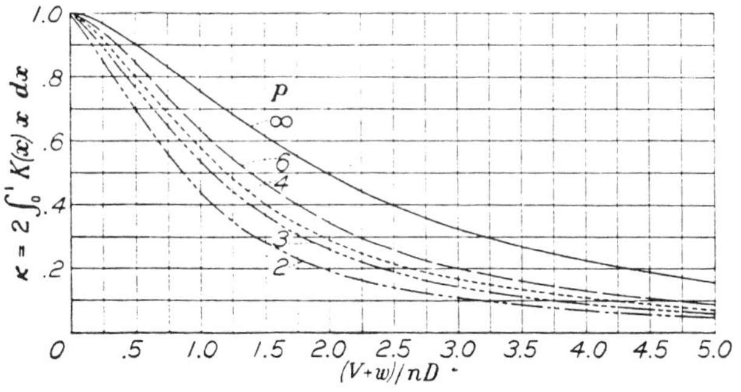

FIGURE 3.—Mass coefficient κ against $\frac{V+w}{nD}$ for various numbers of blades for single-rotating propellers.

Figure 3 shows curves for various values of the mass coefficient κ for the cases for which $K(x)$ is known—that is, for the single-rotating two- and four-blade propellers from tables I and II—as well as for the limiting case of an infinite number of blades. This latter case is readily obtained by integration. With

$$K(x)=\frac{x^2}{\lambda^2+x^2}$$

$$\kappa=2\int_0^1 \frac{x^2}{\lambda^2+x^2}x\,dx$$

is obtained or, after integration,

$$\kappa=1-\lambda^2 \log\left(1+\frac{1}{\lambda^2}\right)$$

The curve for this equation is shown as the upper limit line in figure 3. Values for three- and six-blade propellers, which were calculated from data by Lock and Yeatman (reference 3), are also shown in figure 3. The curves in figure 3 are used later for comparison with data obtained in the present investigation.

ELECTRICAL METHOD AND EQUIPMENT FOR MEASURING $K(x)$ AND κ

DESCRIPTION

It is well known that the flow of electric currents in a field of uniform resistance is mathematically identical with the flow of a perfect fluid. The velocity potential may be perfectly reproduced by an electrical potential, provided the boundary conditions are identical.

843110—50——4

For the present problem a direct measurement of the aerodynamic field behind a propeller presents insurmountable difficulties; in contradistinction, the electrical method of measurement is convenient and accurate and, in addition, permits the determination of local as well as integrated effects. The arrangement may, in fact, be considered a special calculating machine for sol ing the differential equation for given boundary conditions rather than a means for obtaining experimental solutions.

Since the ideal flow (far behind the propeller) is identical with the flow around a rigid helix moving at a constant velocity in the direction of its axis, the corresponding electric field is obtained very simply by inserting an insulating helix surface in a conducting liquid and applying a uniform field in the direction of the helix axis. The vessel confining the liquid is a long cylindrical shell, also of insulating material. The vessel is closed at both ends by copper end plates that are used as electrodes to apply the potential. The test-specimen helix is placed coaxially with the shell. The confining shell is considerably larger in diameter than the test helix.

Figure 4 is a photograph of the test setup for the direct determination of the mass coefficient κ. The cylinder on the right constitutes a dummy compensating resistance. The electrolyte used in these experiments consisted of tap water from the local water-supply system. The source of current was a 1000-cycle alternating-current generator producing a rather pure wave form at an available voltage of about 100 volts, which was applied to the electrodes. An exploring device consisting of a fine glass-insulated platinum wire with an exposed tip was used to determine the voltage at any point on the helix surface. This pickup device formed a part of a potentiometer circuit used in a Wheatstone bridge arrangement with a sensitive telephone as a zero indicator. When voltage readings were taken, no current passed through the telephone and the exploration wire. This type of measurement is inherently accurate; the error in the electrical measurements is estimated as not more than one part in 10,000.

Figure 5, also a photograph, shows the equipment used in the manufacture of the helix surfaces. The vertical insulated cylinder is an electrically heated oil tank. To the top center of this tank is attached a simple die or guiding device with a spiral slit through which the heated plastic sheet material is pulled at a uniform rate. A fan is used to supply cooling air at a uniform rate. With certain precautions an almost perfect helix is produced. Two models of single helix surfaces thus obtained are shown at the left and center in figure 6. A preliminary type of built-up model of laminated construction, which was abandoned as too inaccurate and expensive to build, is shown on the right in figure 6.

In figure 7(a) are shown examples of dual helix surfaces used for the main investigation. A four-blade dual-wake model is shown on the left and a six-blade dual-wake model is shown in the center. On the right is a four-blade single-rotation helix surface with four-blade "guide vanes." In figure 7(b) are other examples of high-order multiple dual-rotation wake models. Some additional examples of single-rotation wake models with guide vanes are shown in figure 8.

The method of building the dual helix models is indicated in figure 9. Unit surfaces were cut from right- and left-handed helix surfaces and glued together to form a multiple dual helix. Fortunately these complex built-up dual models were needed only for determining the mass coefficient κ and did not have to be too accurate in detail.

For the dual-rotating-propeller field a significant property is to be noted: The field repeats itself not only along the axis but also circumferentially. A "unit cell" consisting of the helix surface between two successive lines of intersection is representative of the entire helix. It may be seen that the boundary condition is taken care of by inserting two insulating planes containing the axis and the two intersecting lines, respectively, and by using conducting end planes perpendicular to the axis which contain the same two intersecting lines. The vessel may therefore be given the form of an open V-shape tray with the electrodes at each end. The representative helix may be obtained simply by stretching a rubber membrane from one corner of the tray to the opposite corner at the other end. The membrane is equipped with stiff radial spokes and is securely clamped in place. It automatically assumes a spiral shape, the effects of gravity being of secondary order. The entire tray is arranged on a machine lathe with the helix axis along the center line and the exploring needle is attached to the carriage. This arrangement affords convenient reading of the voltage at any point on the spiral surface. In order to increase accuracy, the trays were made of considerable size, 6 to 10 feet long. By changing the length and the angle of the tray, all values of λ and the effect of the number of blades could be investigated.

In figures 10 and 11 are shown experimental setups for measuring the potential distribution $K(x)$. The connections leading to the exploring needle may be seen in figure 11.

Figures 12, 13, and 14 show the general arrangement for determination of the potential distribution on dual wake models. Figure 12 shows a unit cell for very low advance ratio. Note the V-shape test tank and the adjustable end plate to change the advance ratio. Note, also, the rubber membrane stretched between opposite corners. Figure 13 shows the arrangement for supporting the exploring needle. In figure 14 is finally shown the complete experimental setup for dual helix surfaces of very high pitch.

WALL, END, AND THICKNESS CORRECTIONS

The similarity between the electrical test method and the conventional wind-tunnel method may be extended also to include certain corrections. Obviously there is a correction that corresponds to the customary wall correction. This correction is readily ascertained by use of vessels of different

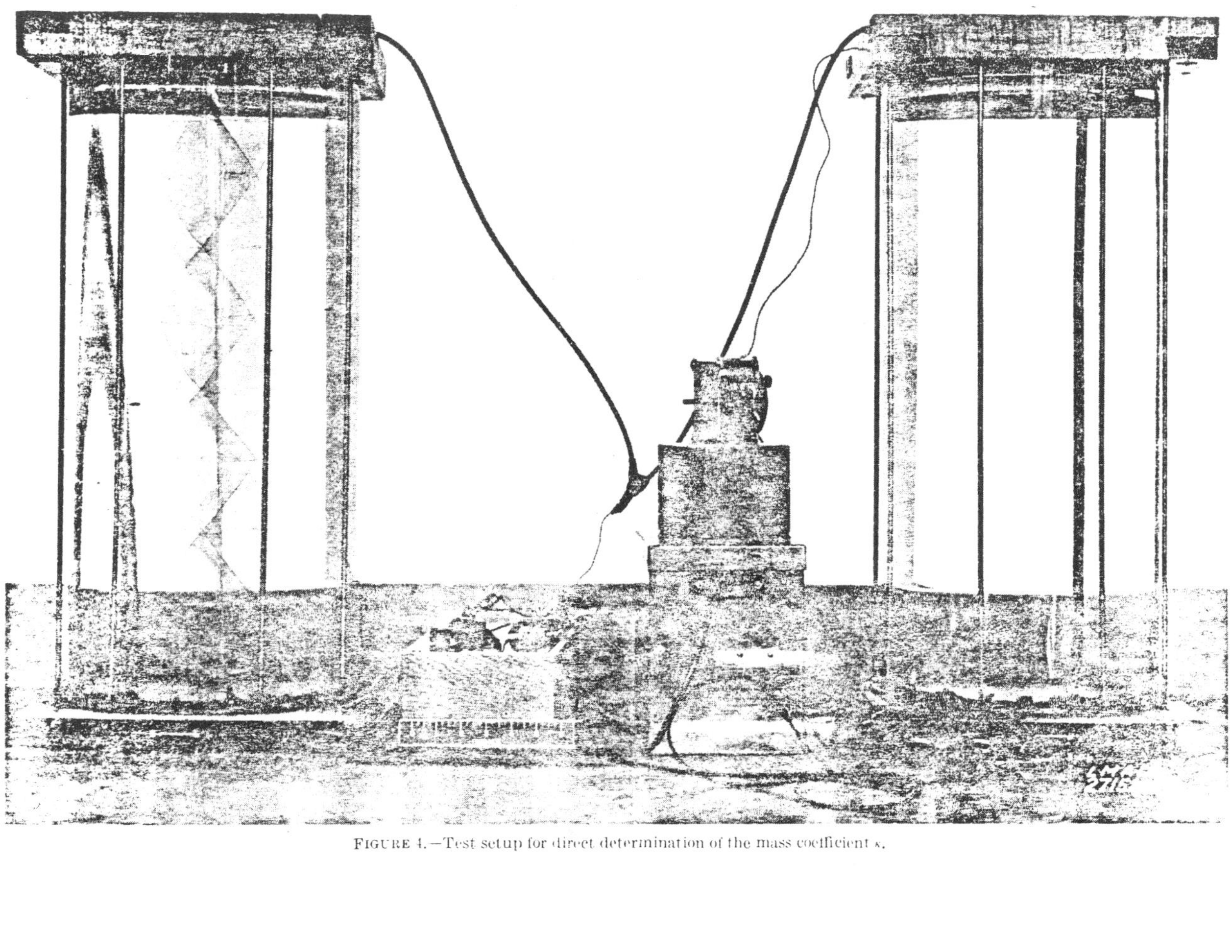

FIGURE 4.—Test setup for direct determination of the mass coefficient κ.

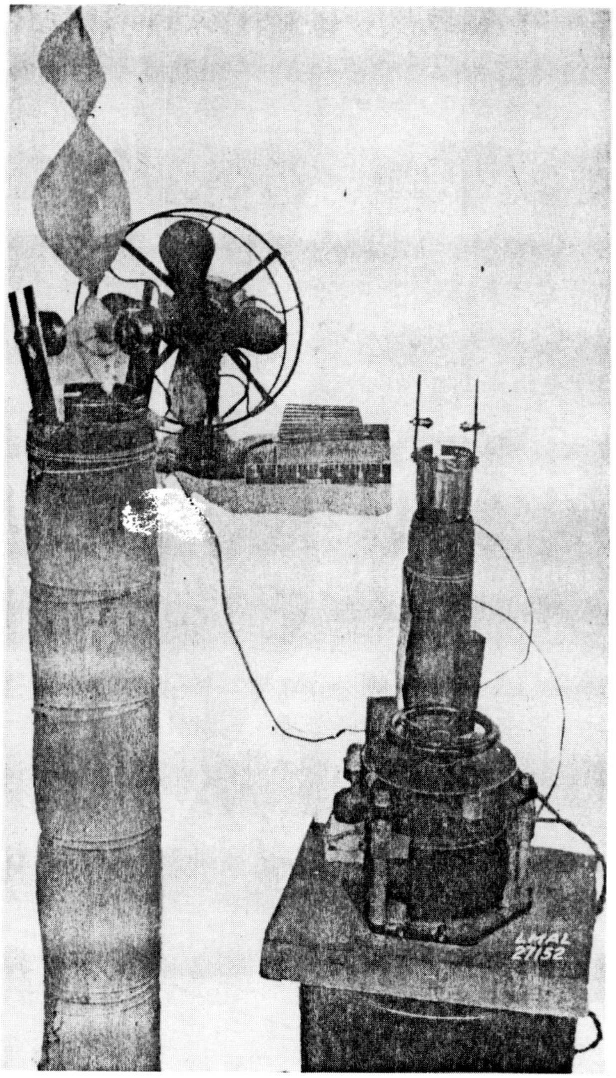

Fig. 5 Equipment for constructing celluloid helix surfaces.

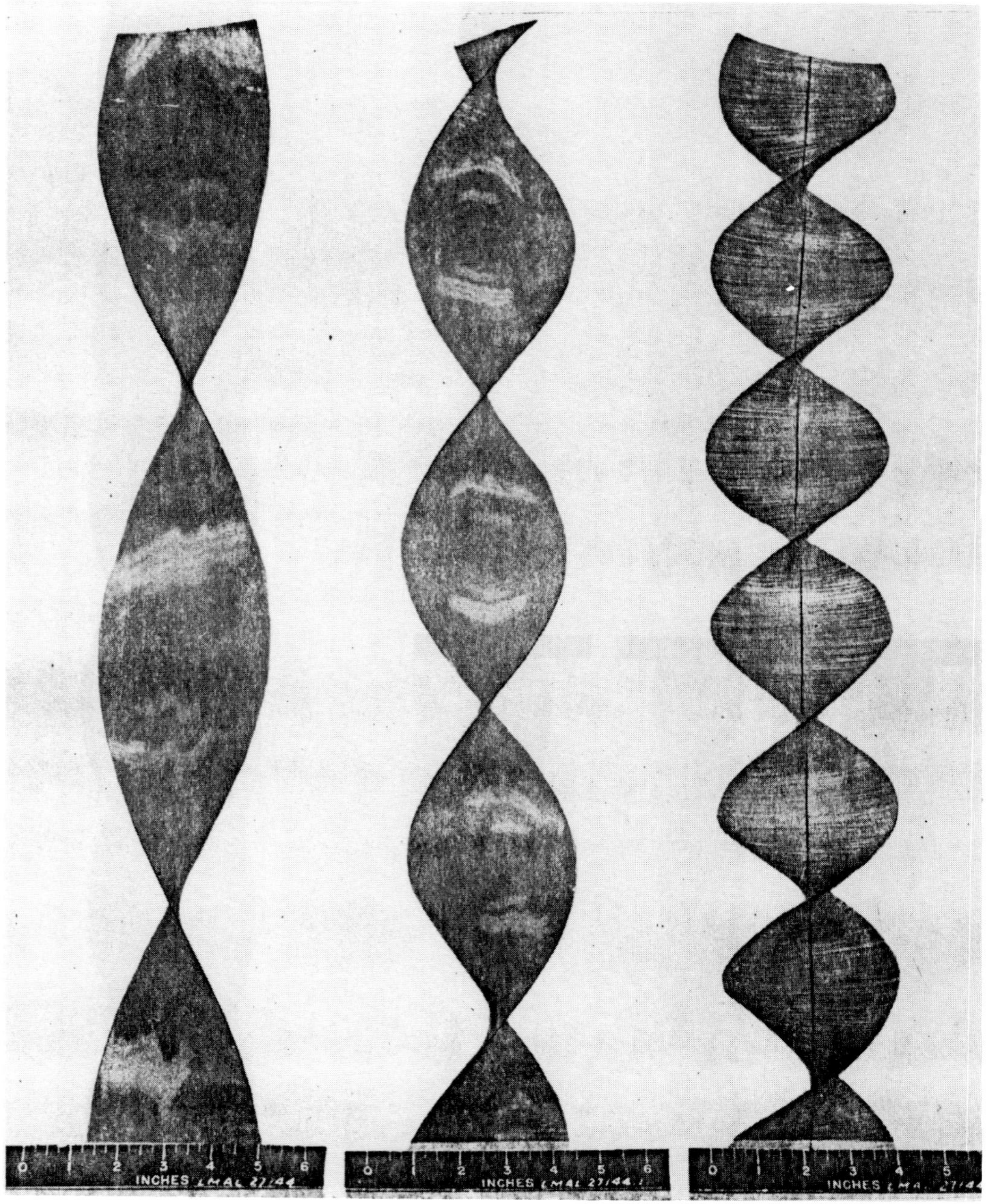

Fig. 6 Celluloid single helix surfaces. (On right, preliminary laminated construction.)

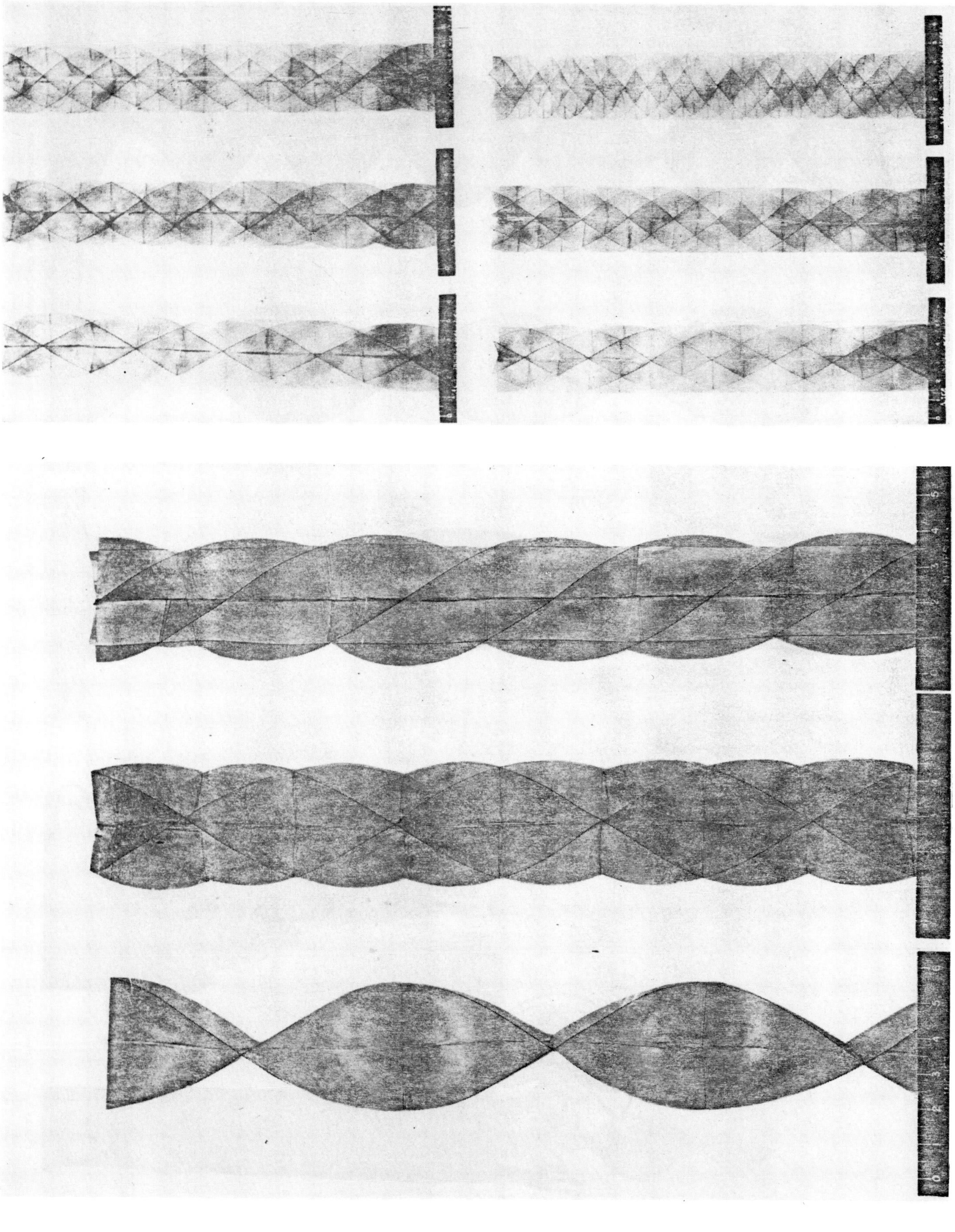

b) High-order multiple blades, dual-rotation.

a) Left and center—for four and six blades, dual-rotation.
Right—for four blades, single rotation, with four-blade guide vanes.

Fig. 7 Dual helix surfaces.

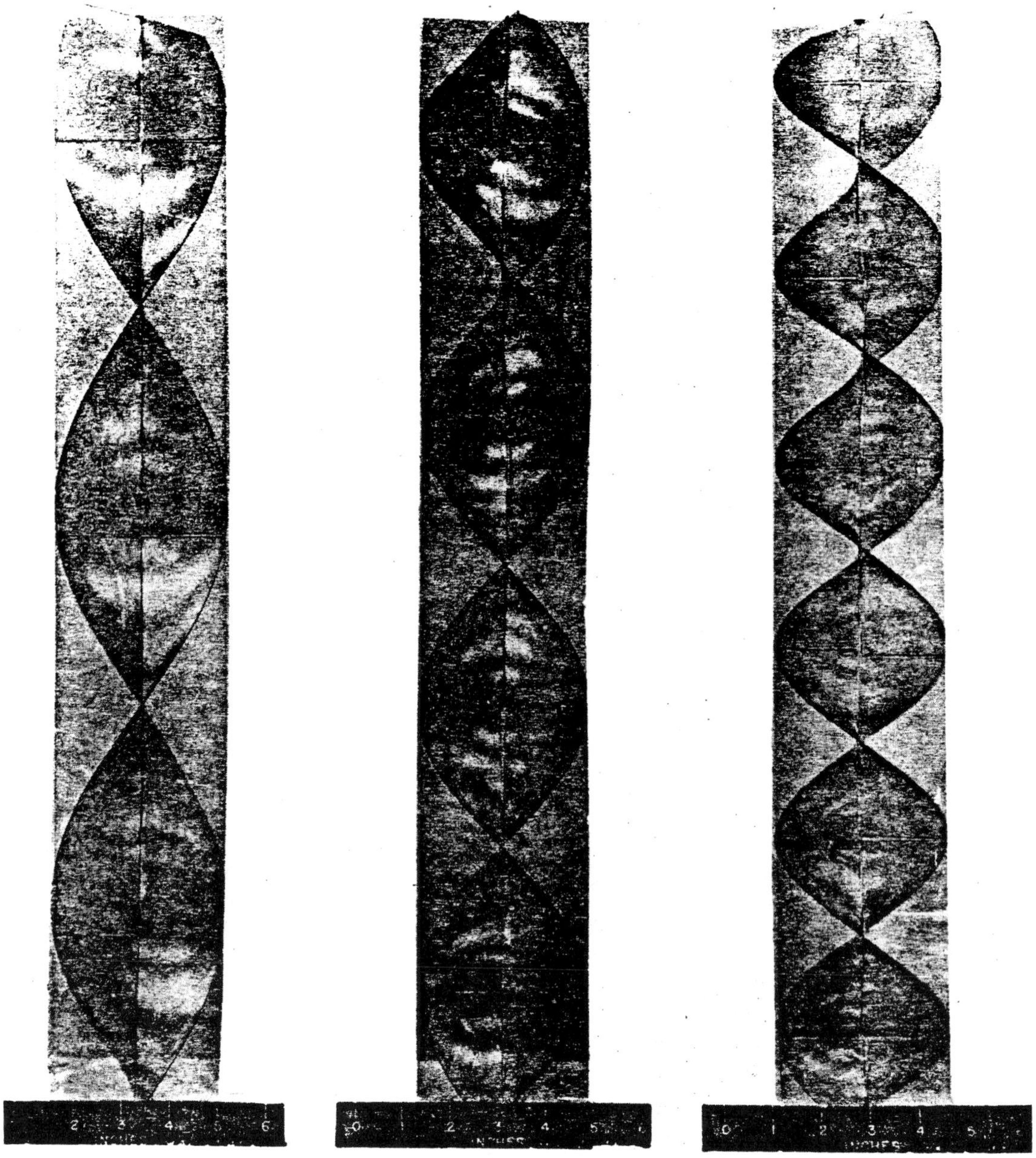

FIGURE 8.—Two-blade single-rotation helix surfaces with guide vanes.

diameters, a procedure that cannot be easily utilized in wind-tunnel practice. It should be noted further that the wall corrections are obtained with great accuracy since each reading by the electrical method is more precise than its aerodynamic counterpart. By using tube diameters about three times the diameter of the test spiral the error in the results was reduced to less than ½ percent.

A correction not appearing in aerodynamic practice is the end correction. This correction occurs only with single-rotating propellers and is therefore of minor importance in the present investigation. Dual-rotating propellers possess planes of constant potential perpendicular to their axes, and the ends therefore cause no difficulties. By cutting the dual helix at a plane of constant potential and by inserting a conducting end plate in the cylinder the boundary condition is satisfied. For single helix surfaces, tests on two lengths of the same helix must be used and the difference observed. This procedure was used to measure the mass coefficient κ. To measure the potential distribution $K(x)$ a long helix is required, the measurements to be made near the middle.

Another source of error exists for which the correction has been referred to as the thickness correction. This error results from the fact that the material of the helix sheet must have a finite thickness. This error may be determined by using sheets of two or more thicknesses. It is readily seen from theoretical considerations that approximately one-half the thickness of the sheet must be added to the diameter in order to obtain an equivalent infinitely thin sheet.

It should be mentioned finally that there is an error resulting from inaccuracies in the model vortex sheets. The error in $K(x)$ can be minimized by using mean values from a large number of readings over a considerable portion of the helix. Fortunately, there is no effect on the mass coefficient κ since this coefficient is a mean-value parameter.

PROOF THAT THE MASS COEFFICIENT κ IS THE BLOCKING EFFECT OF THE (INFINITELY LONG) HELIX SURFACE

The mass coefficient κ is obtained experimentally by measuring the change in resistance caused by the helix surface when inserted in the cylindrical container. On inserting the (infinitely long) helix in the container, the current between the end plates I_0 is decreased by a definite amount ΔI, and it can be proved that

$$\frac{\kappa F}{S}=\frac{\Delta I}{I_0}$$

or

$$\kappa=\frac{\Delta I}{I_0}\frac{S}{F}$$

where F is the projected cross section of the helix and S is the cross section of the cylindrical container.

By Green's theorem

$$\int_\sigma (U\nabla W-W\nabla U)d\sigma=\int_\tau (U\nabla^2 W-W\nabla^2 U)d\tau$$

If

$$\nabla^2 U=\nabla^2 W=0$$

it follows that

$$\int_\sigma (U\nabla W-W\nabla U)d\sigma=0$$

Let W be the distance z along the helix axis measured from a reference plane perpendicular to the axis; ∇W is therefore a unit vector in the direction z. Let U be the potential resulting from the applied voltage and the local gradient ∇U may be written

$$\nabla U=\frac{U_0}{L}\frac{i}{i_0}$$

Figure 9.—Steps in the construction of the more complicated helix surfaces.

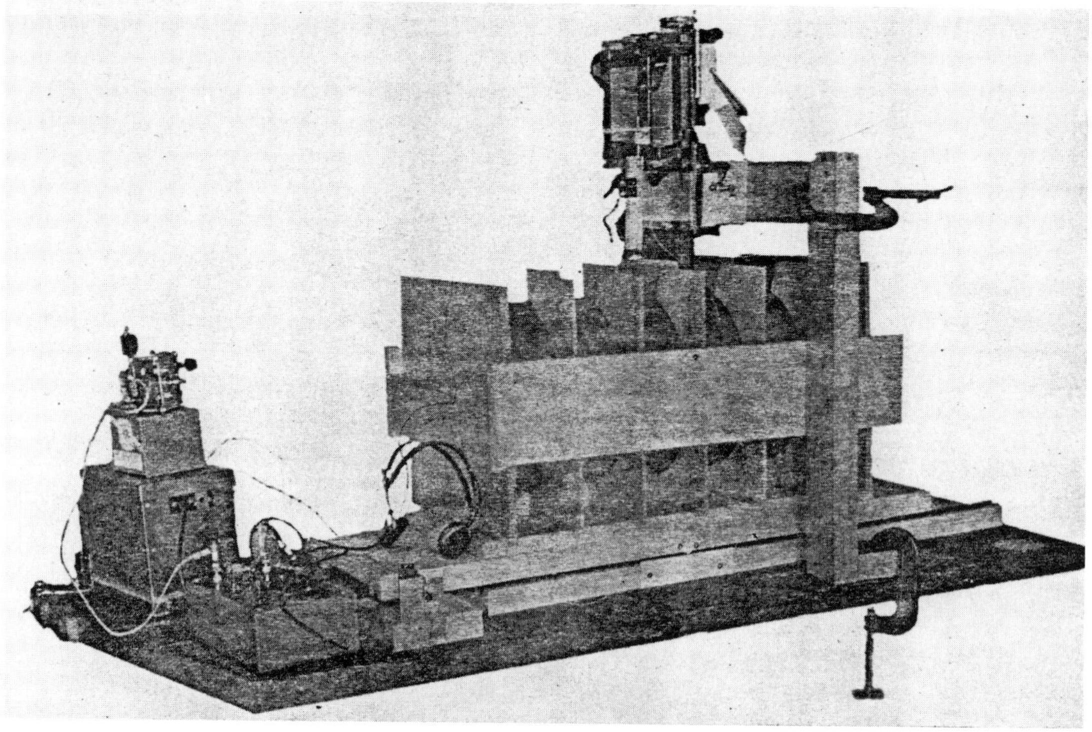

Fig. 10 Setup for measuring the potential distribution $K(x)$ for single-rotation wake models.

Fig. 11 Setup for measuring potential distribution $K(x)$ for single-rotation wake models, showing detail of exploring device.

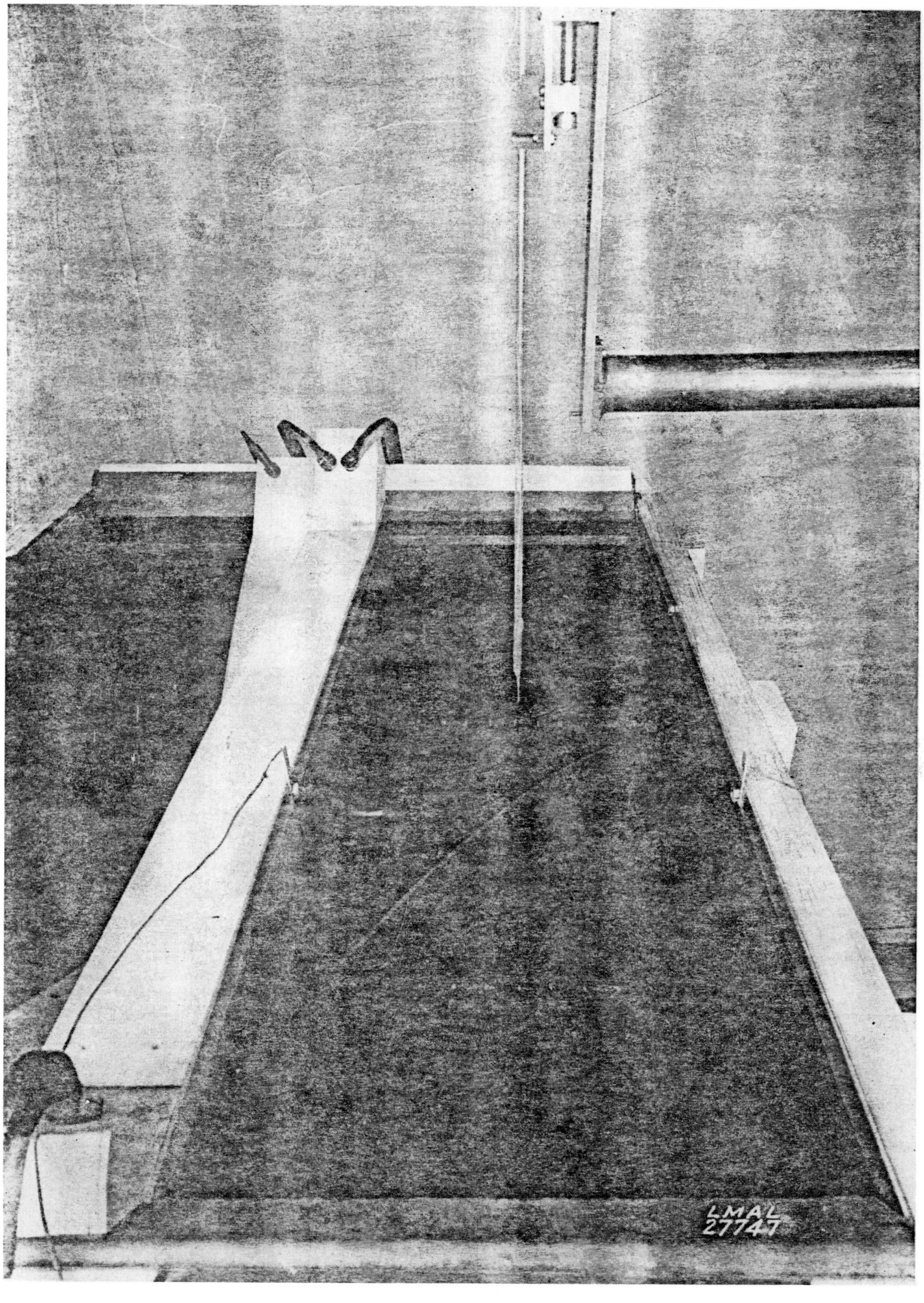

Fig 12 Unit cell for very low advance ratio.

where U_0 is the constant voltage difference between the end plates, which are placed at an axial distance L apart, and i is the local current and i_0 the current at infinity. If the surface integrals for the entire enclosed helix surface A and the end surfaces S, respectively, are taken, the following relation is obtained

$$\int_A U\,dA_z = \int_S \left(U - z\frac{U_0}{L}\frac{i}{i_0}\right) dS$$

or

$$\frac{1}{U_0}\int_A U\,dA_z = \int_S \left(\frac{U}{U_0} - \frac{z}{L}\frac{i}{i_0}\right) dS$$

where the integrals are to be taken over both sides of the p helix surfaces and over both end plates. However,

$$\frac{1}{U_0}\int_A U\,dA_z$$

may be written in the form

$$\frac{pL}{U_0 H}\int (U_1 - U_2) dF$$

where the integral is taken over one turn of one helix for one side only, as $U_1 - U_2$ is the difference potential between the two sides of the sheet. The voltage drop per sheet is

$$\frac{U_0}{L}\frac{H}{p}$$

FIGURE 13.—Unit cell for very low advance ratio, showing arrangement of exploring device.

FIGURE 14.—Unit cell for high pitch.

By definition

$$K(x)=\frac{U_1-U_2}{\frac{U_0}{L}\frac{H}{p}}$$

Thus

$$\frac{1}{U_0}\int_{1} U\,dA_2=\int_F K(x)\;dF=2F\int_0^1 K(x)x\;dx=\kappa F$$

Also,

$$\int_S\left(\frac{U}{U_0}-\frac{z}{L}\frac{i}{i_0}\right)dS=\int_S\left(1-\frac{i}{i_0}\right)dS=\frac{\Delta I}{I_0}\;S$$

and therefore

$$\frac{\kappa F}{S}=\frac{\Delta I}{I_0}$$

where I_0 is the total current between the end plates with a uniform gradient $\frac{U_0}{L}$ in the field.

EXPERIMENTAL DATA

MASS COEFFICIENT κ

Numerical values for the mass coefficient κ, obtained on dual-rotation wake models, are shown in figure 15. This chart is probably adequate for all practical purposes, as a large range of advance ratio has been covered. The designation used for the propellers comprises three digits: The first digit refers to the number of right-handed blades, the middle digit to the number of guide vanes, and the last digit to the number of left-handed blades—for instance, 3–0–3 represents a dual-rotating propeller with three right-handed and three left-handed blades. The highest number of blades tested was for a 6–0–6 or twelve-blade propeller.

As a matter of interest, it is very fortunate that the method and equipment could be tried out in all its ramifications on the known case of the Goldstein curve for a two-blade propeller. The Goldstein curve is the curve in figure 15 marked "Theoretical." The test points, which have been corrected for wall, thickness, and end effects, are shown. Except in a very few cases, the test points lie on the theoretical curve for the two-blade propellers. The somewhat lesser consistency in the cases of dual-rotating propellers is not due to inherent test inaccuracy but rather to a necessary limitation on time and equipment for making the models, performing the tests, and obtaining the corrections. The thickness correction for the high advance ratios is considerable. Note that three thicknesses have been used for many of the test points. A glance at one of the composite models shown in figure 7(b) will suffice to indicate the labor involved in producing the models. Each test point in figure 15 represents a different complete model; some fifty models thus are represented by the results shown. This number was necessary in order to include all propellers and all advance ratios of interest at present and in the future.

Results for single-rotation wake models with guide vanes are shown in figure 16 for two-, three-, and four-blade propellers, respectively. Such guide vanes are supposed to represent stationary vanes arranged immediately in front of or behind the propeller to straighten the flow. It should be noted that the cases shown correspond to those of an ideal thrust distribution both on the propeller and on the guide vanes. The uppermost curve in each part of figure 16 is reproduced for purposes of comparison with the corresponding dual case.

DISTRIBUTION FUNCTION $K(x,\theta)$

The measured potential distributions on dual wake models are shown in figure 17. These tests were made on large-scale unit cells of the type described earlier. Figure 17 contains results on 2–0–2, 4–0–4, and 6–0–6 dual-rotating propellers, in each case for three advance ratios. The potential drop is given in nondimensional form and is plotted against the radius. Each curve represents a radial line on the helix. The angular position of the radial line is given as a fraction of the cell semiangle measured from the middle or symmetry line of the cell.

Figure 18 shows $K(x)$ as the potential difference at the zero angle or midway between two successive intersecting lines. The results are arranged in order showing the four-, eight-, and twelve-blade dual-rotating propellers at three advance ratios.

The function $K(\theta)$ is shown in figure 19 plotted against the angle measured from the same zero reference angle. Results are shown for the same three propellers at the same three advance ratios. Curves are shown for three values of the radial distance $x=\frac{1}{4}, \frac{1}{2}$, and $\frac{3}{4}$.

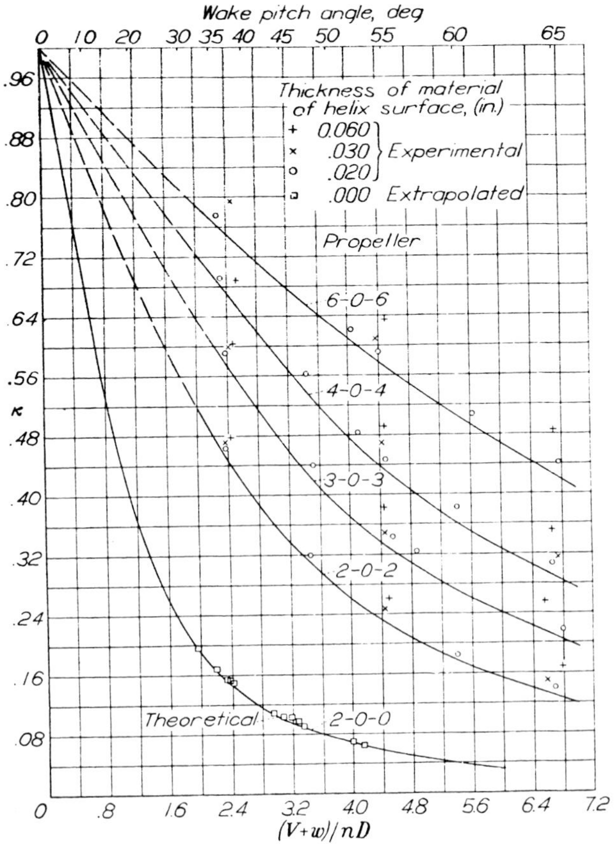

FIGURE 15.—Measured values of mass coefficient κ for dual-rotating propellers with various numbers of blades.

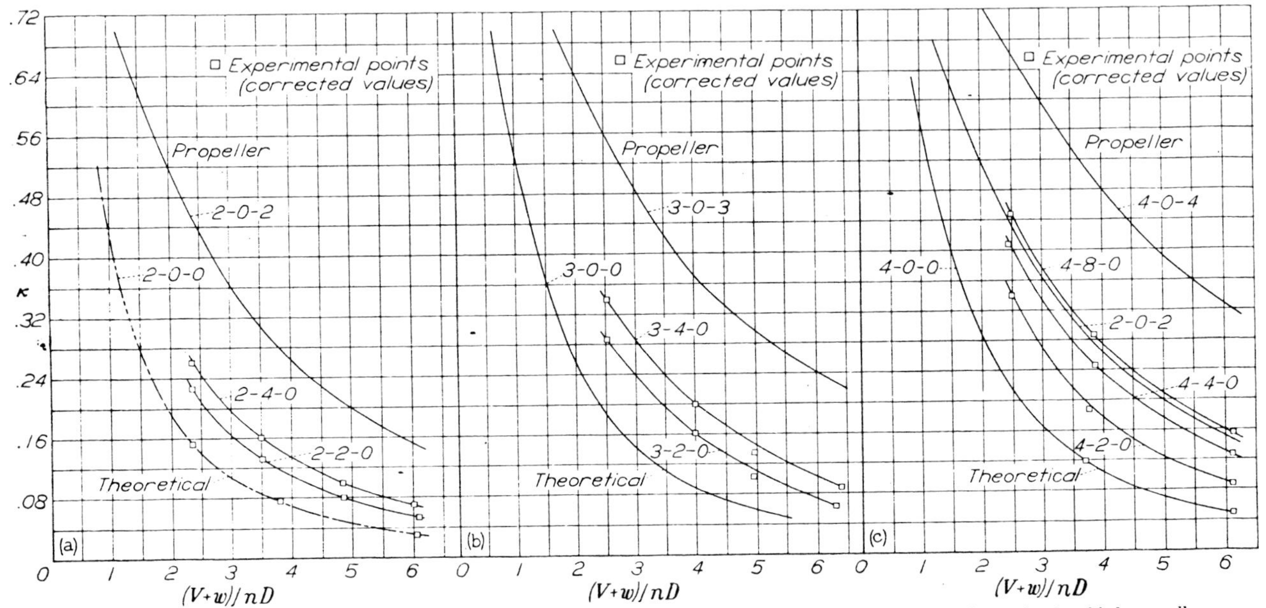

(a) Single-rotating two-blade propellers. (b) Single-rotating three-blade propellers. (c) Single-rotating four-blade propellers.

FIGURE 16.—Measured values of mass coefficient κ against $\frac{V+w}{nD}$ showing the effect of guide vanes.

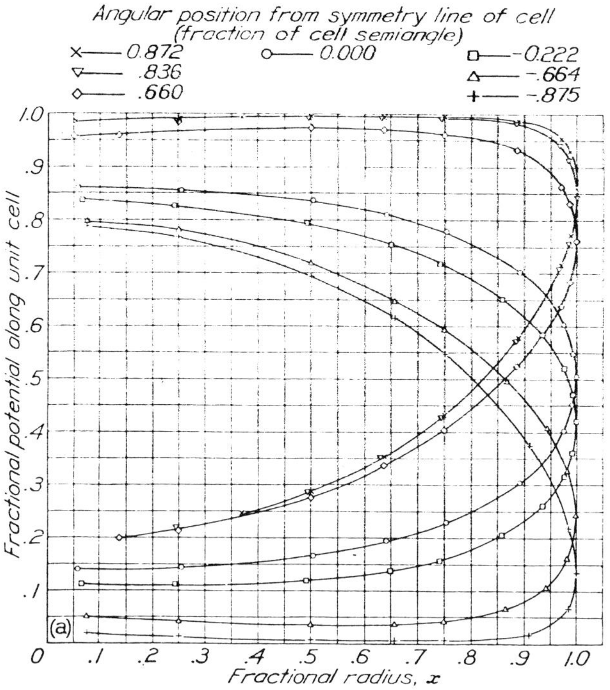

(a) 2-0-2 unit cell; $\frac{V+w}{nD}=1.89$.

FIGURE 17.—Variation of potential along a radius for various angular positions.

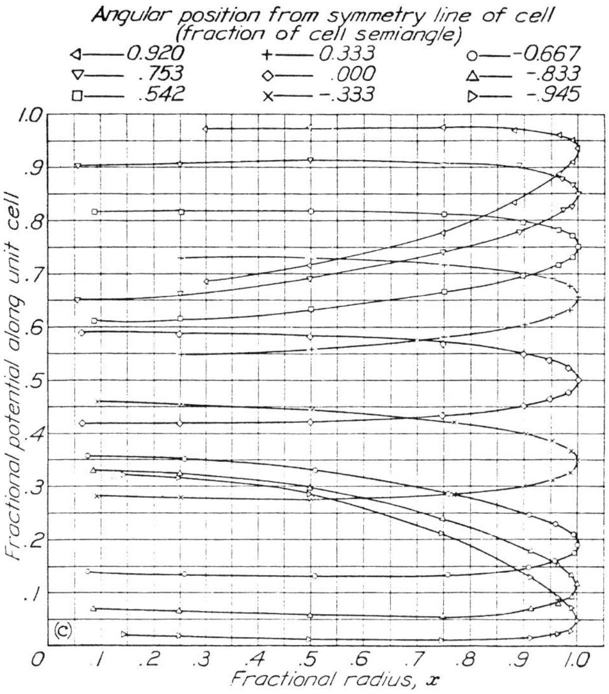

(c) 2-0-2 unit cell; $\frac{V+w}{nD}=6$.

FIGURE 17.—Continued.

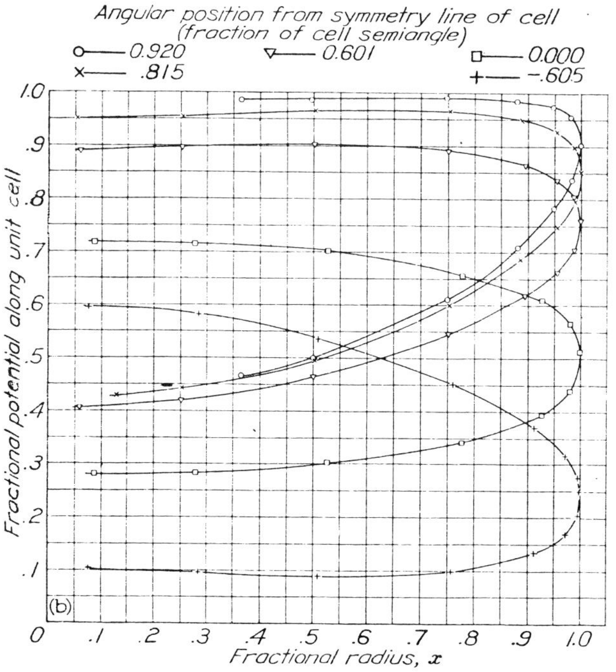

(b) 2-0-2 unit cell; $\frac{V+w}{nD}=3.14$.

FIGURE 17.—Continued.

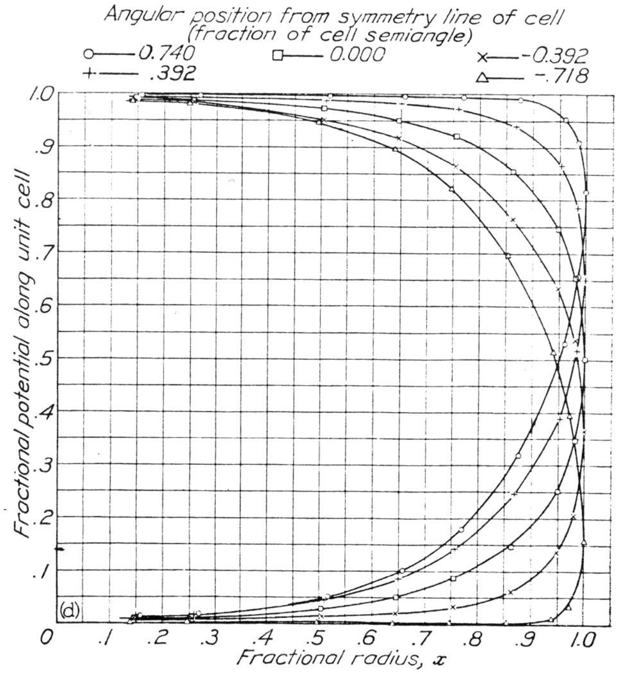

(d) 4-0-4 unit cell; $\frac{V+w}{nD}=1.55$.

FIGURE 17.—Continued.

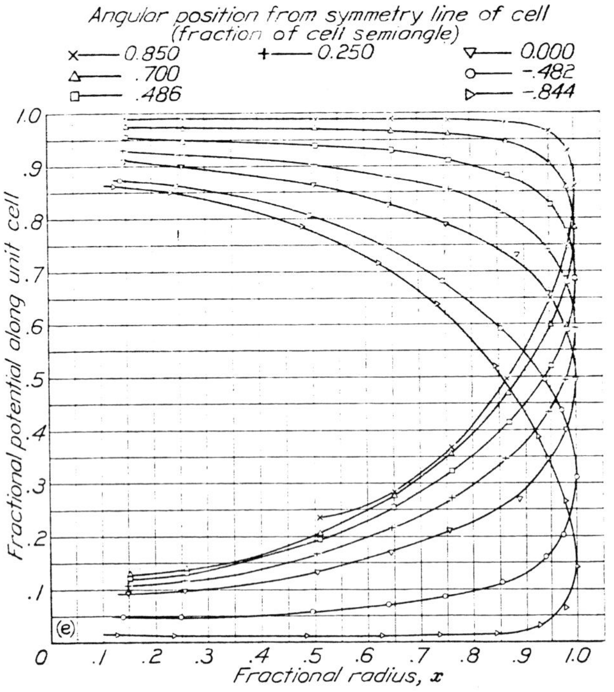

(e) 4-0-4 unit cell; $\frac{V+w}{nD}=3.11$.

FIGURE 17.—Continued

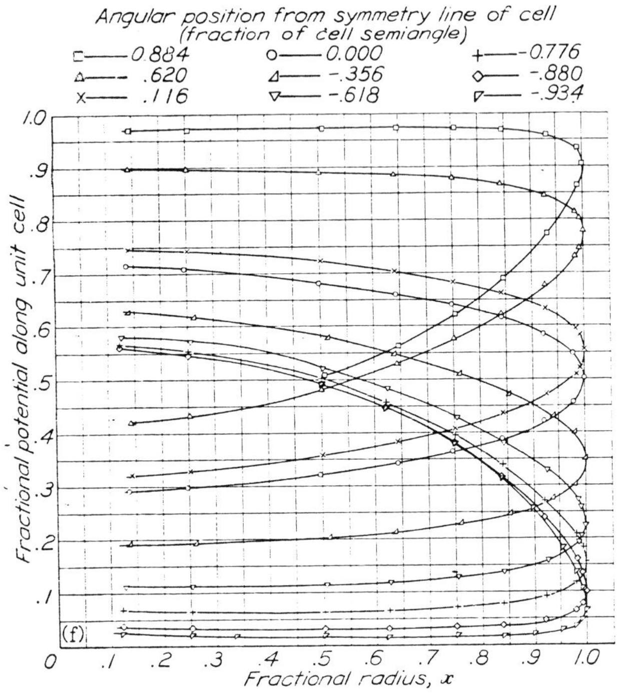

(f) 4-0-4 unit cell; $\frac{V+w}{nD}=6.34$.

FIGURE 17.—Continued.

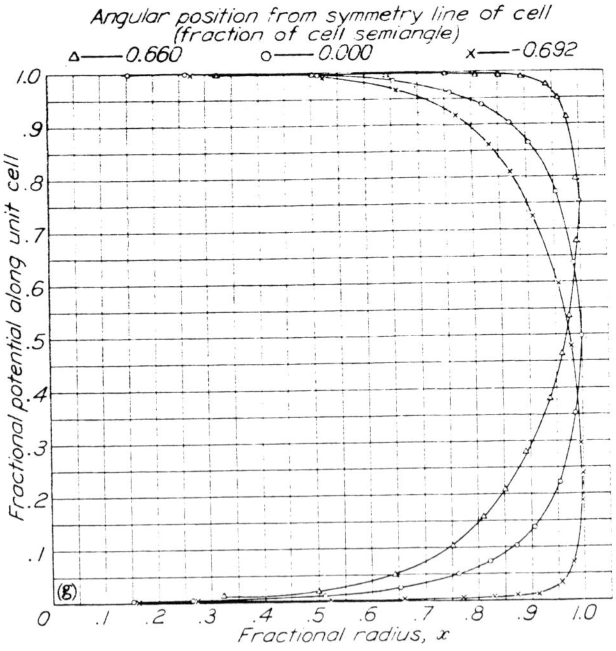

(g) 6-0-6 unit cell; $\frac{V+w}{nD}=1.55$.

FIGURE 17.—Continued.

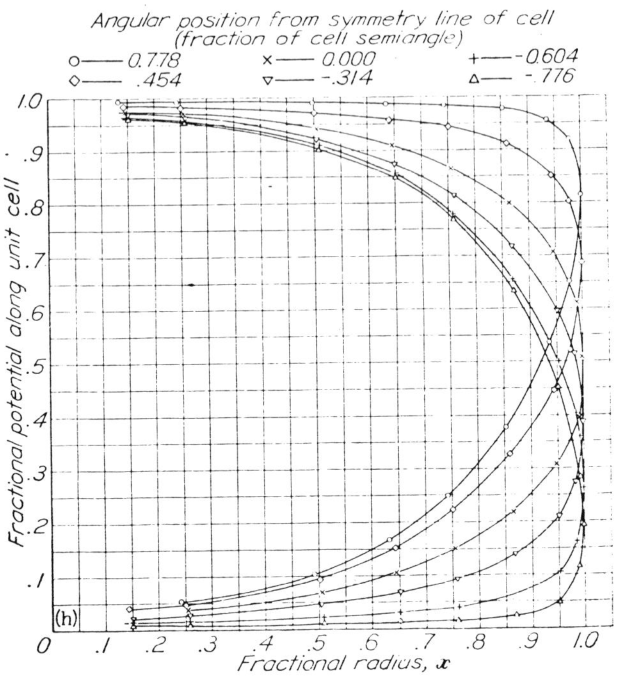

(h) 6-0-6 unit cell; $\frac{V+w}{nD}=3.12$.

FIGURE 17.—Continued

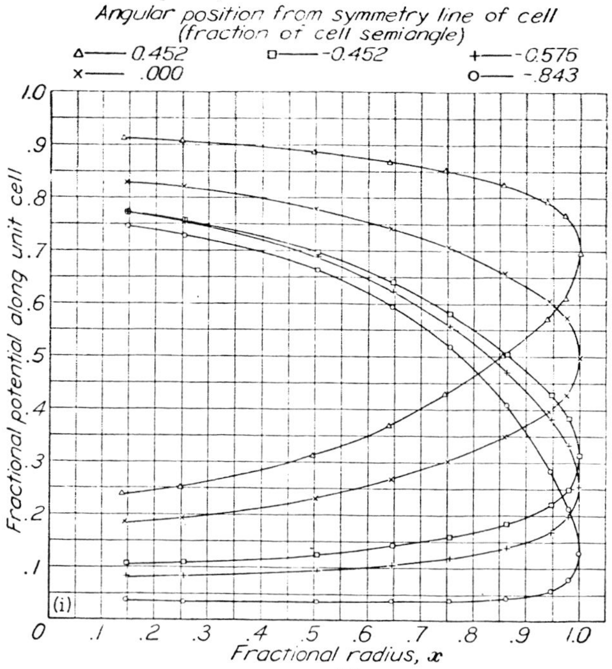

(i) 6-0-6 unit cell; $\frac{V+w}{nD}=6.41$.

FIGURE 17.—Concluded.

DISCUSSION

The concept of a mass coefficient κ defined as

$$\kappa \equiv 2\int_0^1 K(x)x\,dx$$

has been introduced, where $K(x)$ is a nondimensional distribution function and x is the nondimensional radius. Numerical values of κ for the known cases of single-rotating propellers are shown in figure 3. It is noted that the mass coefficient drops rapidly with the advance ratio. For $\frac{V+w}{nD}=2$, the value of κ is less than 0.5 even for an infinite number of blades and is less than 0.2 for the two-blade single-rotating propeller.

For dual-rotating propellers the mass coefficient defined a

$$\kappa=\frac{1}{\pi}\int_0^1\int_0^{2\pi} K(x,\theta)x\,dx\,d\theta$$

is considerably larger. A 2-0-2 propeller has, in fact, a larger mass coefficient at $\frac{V+w}{nD}=2$ than the single-rotating propeller with an infinite number of blades. The 6-0-6 propeller at the same advance ratio has a mass coefficient $\kappa=0.79$ or near unity. (See fig. 15.)

The effect of guide vanes is of considerable practical interest. These vanes are stationary and are arranged either immediately in front of or behind the propeller. The question is whether such a stationary system in some cases may be more acceptable than a dual arrangement of counterrotating propellers. As an example, consider a three-blade single-rotating propeller at an advance ratio of 3. (See fig. 16(b).) The mass coefficient κ of the propeller alone is seen to be 0.142; the 3-2-0 propeller with two guide vanes shows a value of κ of 0.238, and the 3-4-0 propeller with four guide vanes shows a value of κ of 0.286. For comparison, the

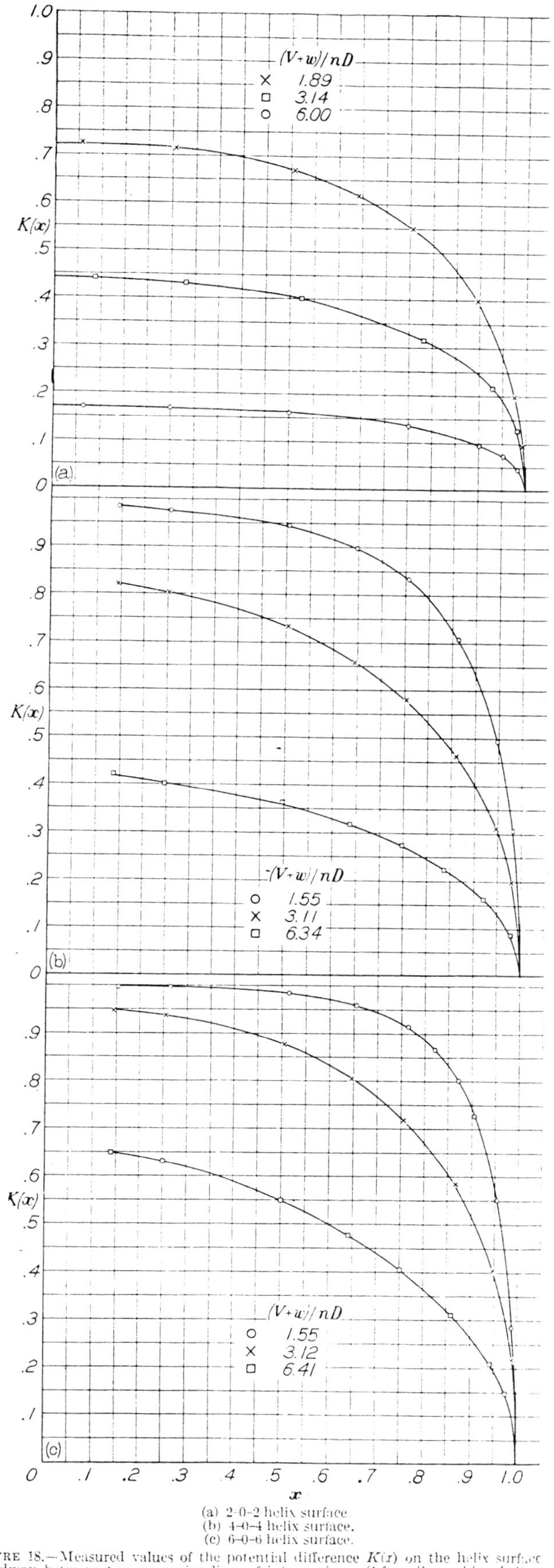

(a) 2-0-2 helix surface.
(b) 4-0-4 helix surface.
(c) 6-0-6 helix surface.

FIGURE 18.—Measured values of the potential difference $K(x)$ on the helix surface midway between two successive lines of intersection. (1-ft radius rubber helix see figs. 12, 13, and 14.)

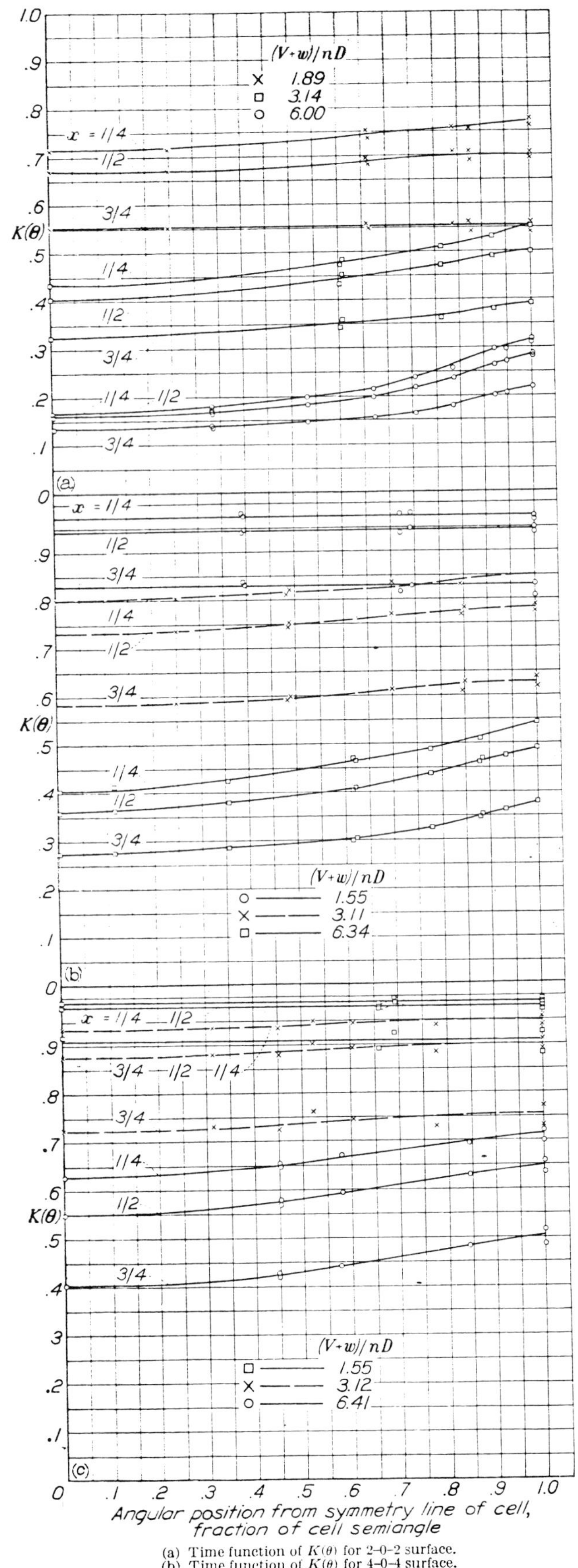

(a) Time function of $K(\theta)$ for 2–0–2 surface.
(b) Time function of $K(\theta)$ for 4–0–4 surface.
(c) Time function of $K(\theta)$ for 6–0–6 surface.

FIGURE 19.—Measured values of the potential difference at various radii and distances along the helix surface.

six-blade dual-rotating propeller shows a value of κ of 0.486 at the same advance ratio. If a dual-rotating propeller is not used, the double guide vane is undoubtedly desirable in some cases. Actually, the induced loss is reduced to about half as compared with the loss in the case without vanes. The difference in the effect of two or four vanes is relatively small.

LANGLEY MEMORIAL AERONAUTICAL LABORATORY,
NATIONAL ADVISORY COMMITTEE FOR AERONAUTICS,
LANGLEY FIELD, VA., *May 27, 1944.*

APPENDIX

SYMBOLS

V	advance velocity of propeller
w	rearward displacement velocity of helical vortex surface (at infinity)
n	rotational speed of propeller, revolutions per second
ω	angular velocity of propeller $(2\pi n)$
D	diameter of vortex sheet
$\frac{V+w}{nD}$	advance ratio of wake helix
$\lambda=\frac{1}{\pi}\frac{V+w}{nD}$	
H	pitch of wake helix $\left(\frac{V+w}{n}\right)$
Γ	circulation at radius r
$K(x)$	circulation function for single rotation $\left(\frac{p\Gamma\omega}{2\pi(V+w)w}\right)$
$K(x,\theta)$	circulation function for dual rotation
p	number of blades of propeller or separate helix surfaces
κ	mass coefficient $\left(2\int_0^1 K(x)x\,dx \text{ or } \frac{1}{\pi}\int_0^1\int_0^{2\pi}K(x,\theta)x\,dx\,d\theta\right)$
x	ratio of radius of element to tip radius of vortex sheet (r/R)
r	radius of element of vortex sheet
R	tip radius of vortex sheet $\left(\frac{1}{2}D\right)$
θ	angular coordinate on vortex sheet
F	projected area of helix (πR^2)
S	area of end plates of cylindrical test tank
I_0	current through test tank with helix removed
ΔI	reduction in current due to presence of helix

REFERENCES

1. Goldstein, Sidney: On the Vortex Theory of Screw Propellers Proc. Roy. Soc. (London), ser. A, vol. 123, no. 792, April 6, 1929, pp. 440–465.
2. Kramer, K. N.: The Induced Efficiency of Optimum Propellers Having a Finite Number of Blades. NACA TM No. 884, 1939.
3. Lock, C. N. H., and Yeatman, D.: Tables for Use in an Improved Method of Airscrew Strip Theory Calculation. R. & M. No 1674, British A. R. C., 1935.

THE THEORY OF PROPELLERS

II—METHOD FOR CALCULATING THE AXIAL INTERFERENCE VELOCITY

BY THEODORE THEODORSEN

National Advisory Committee for Aeronautics

Report No. 776, 1944

SUMMARY

A technical method is given for calculating the axial interference velocity of a propeller. The method involves the use of certain weight functions P, Q, and F. Numerical values for the weight functions are given for two-blade, three-blade, and six-blade propellers.

INTRODUCTION

It has formerly been the practice to use the Glauert-Lock simplified assumption that the interference velocity is proportional to the loading at the point considered. This assumption is obviously inadequate since the interference flow depends on the slope and curvature of the loading function as well as on the local magnitude. A method is developed herein for calculating the axial interference flow for any loading. The method is accurate to the first order and therefore gives the interference flow in ratio to the loading for small loadings. It can be shown that this accuracy is adequate for all technical applications.

The present paper is the second in a series on the theory of propellers. Part I deals with a method for obtaining the circulation function for dual-rotating propellers. (See reference 1.)

SYMBOLS

v_1	axial interference velocity at x_1 $[v_z(x_1)]$
w	rearward displacement velocity of helical vortex surface (at infinity)
V	advance velocity of propeller
p	number of blades
n	order number of blade $(0 \leqq n \leqq p-1)$
ω	angular velocity of propeller
Γ	circulation at radius x
K	circulation coefficient to first order $\left(\frac{p\Gamma\omega}{2\pi Vw}\right)$
x	nondimensional radius in terms of tip radius
x_1	reference point at which interference velocity is calculated
θ	angular distance of vortex element from propeller
λ	advance ratio $(V/\omega R)$
R	tip radius of propeller
$P_1(x)$	function defined in equation (1)
$Q_1(x)$	function defined in equation (3)
P	used for $P_1(x)$ in tables and figures; refers to other blades $(n \neq 0)$
Q	used for $Q_1(x)$ in tables and figures; refers to blade itself $(n=0)$
τ	phase angle of nth blade $\left(\frac{2n\pi}{p}\right)$
φ_1	helix angle at x_1 $\left(\tan^{-1}\frac{\lambda}{x_1}\right)$

WEIGHT FUNCTION $P_1(x)$

It can be shown that the axial interference flow is given by the expression

$$\frac{v_1}{\frac{1}{2}w}=\frac{1}{p}\sum_n\int\frac{dK}{dx}x\frac{dP_1(x)}{dx}dx$$

where the summation is over the number of blades 0 to $p-1$. The important function $P_1(x)$ is defined as

$$P_1(x)=\int_0^\infty\frac{d\frac{\theta}{2\pi}}{\sqrt{\frac{1}{4\pi^2\lambda^2}\left[x^2+x_1^2-2xx_1\cos\left(\theta+\frac{2n\pi}{p}\right)\right]+\left(\frac{\theta}{2\pi}\right)^2}}$$

where $n=0, 1, 2, \ldots p-1$, the number of the particular blade. The problem is thus essentially solved by giving the function $P_1(x)$ for each point along the radius.

It is convenient to make $P_1(x)$ finite by subtracting a quantity that is independent of x. The function $P_1(x)$ may therefore be redefined as

$$P_1(x)=\int_0^\infty\left\{\frac{1}{\sqrt{\frac{1}{4\pi^2\lambda^2}\left[x^2+x_1^2-2xx_1\cos\left(\theta+\frac{2n\pi}{p}\right)\right]+\left(\frac{\theta}{2\pi}\right)^2}}-\frac{1}{\sqrt{1+\left(\frac{\theta}{2\pi}\right)^2}}\right\}d\frac{\theta}{2\pi} \qquad (1)$$

It is noticed that, in the integral $P_1(x)$, the integrand changes from $+\infty$ to $-\infty$ at $x=x_1$ for $\theta=0$. This difficulty, which occurs only for $n=0$ (that is, for the blade itself), is overcome in the following manner: The expression

$$\int_0^\infty\left[\frac{1}{\sqrt{\frac{1}{4\pi^2\lambda^2}(x-x_1)^2+\left(\frac{xx_1}{\lambda^2}+1\right)\left(\frac{\theta}{2\pi}\right)^2}}-\frac{1}{\sqrt{\frac{1}{4\pi^2\lambda^2}+\left(\frac{xx_1}{\lambda^2}+1\right)\left(\frac{\theta}{2\pi}\right)^2}}\right]d\frac{\theta}{2\pi} \qquad (2)$$

which is integrable and equal to

$$-\sqrt{\frac{\lambda^2}{\lambda^2+xx_1}}\log|x-x_1|$$

may be subtracted from $P_1(x)$ to yield a finite and smooth integrand. Thus, by subtraction, a quantity

$$Q_1(x)=\int_0^\infty\left[\frac{1}{\sqrt{\frac{1}{4\pi^2\lambda^2}(x^2+x_1^2-2xx_1\cos\theta)+\left(\frac{\theta}{2\pi}\right)^2}}-\frac{1}{\sqrt{1+\left(\frac{\theta}{2\pi}\right)^2}}-\frac{1}{\sqrt{\frac{1}{4\pi^2\lambda^2}(x-x_1)^2+\left(\frac{xx_1}{\lambda^2}+1\right)\left(\frac{\theta}{2\pi}\right)^2}}+\frac{1}{\sqrt{\frac{1}{4\pi^2\lambda^2}+\left(\frac{xx_1}{\lambda^2}+1\right)\left(\frac{\theta}{2\pi}\right)^2}}\right]d\frac{\theta}{2\pi} \quad (3)$$

is obtained. Finally, for the blade itself ($n=0$),

$$P_1(x)=Q_1(x)+F$$

where

$$F=-\sqrt{\frac{\lambda^2}{\lambda^2+xx_1}}\log|x-x_1|$$

The integral $Q_1(x)$ is convenient for graphical integration and is, in fact, small in comparison with the function F.

No discontinuities arise in the P functions for the other blades ($n\neq 0$). The P functions are therefore used directly in the calculation for the other blades. It should be noted that the functions P, Q, and F are all symmetrical in x and x_1. The use of the subscript, which has been used to indicate reference to the point x_1, is therefore discontinued. In the following discussion, the functions Q and F refer to the blade itself and P refers to the other blades.

Since the weight function is needed in the form $x\frac{dP}{dx}$, it is written as

$$x\frac{dP}{dx}=x\frac{dQ}{dx}+x\frac{dF}{dx}$$

It is to be noted that by far the largest contribution comes from the logarithmic function F since it really represents the entire field in the neighborhood of the point considered. In developed form,

$$x\frac{dF}{dx}=-\frac{1}{\sqrt{1+\frac{xx_1}{\lambda^2}}}\frac{x}{x-x_1}+\frac{1}{2}\frac{\frac{xx_1}{\lambda^2}}{\sqrt{\left(1+\frac{xx_1}{\lambda^2}\right)^3}}\log|x-x_1| \quad (4)$$

NUMERICAL EVALUATION OF WEIGHT FUNCTIONS *Q*, *F*, AND *P*

The weight functions Q, F, and P are shown in a series of tables and figures. The first step of integrating against the angle θ is omitted for simplicity. The functions $\frac{dQ}{dx}$ and $\frac{dP}{dx}$ have been obtained by graphical differentiation of the Q and P functions with actual calculation at the end points $x=0$ and 1 for accuracy. It should be noted that these functions and their derivatives are continuous and smooth. The results are given in the following order:

(1) Table I and figure 1: Q against x ($0\leqq x\leqq 1.00$; $0.1564\leqq x_1\leqq 1.00$; $\lambda=\frac{1}{2}$, 1, and 2), obtained from equation (3)

(2) Table II and figure 2: $\frac{dQ}{dx}$ against x ($0\leqq x\leqq 1.00$; $0.1564\leqq x_1\leqq 1.00$; $\lambda=\frac{1}{2}$, 1, and 2), where $\frac{dQ}{dx}$ is obtained by graphical differentiation of Q except for $x=0$ and 1, for which $\frac{dQ}{dx}$ is obtained analytically

(3) Table III and figure 3: $-x\frac{dQ}{dx}$ against x ($0\leqq x\leqq 1.00$; $0.1564\leqq x_1\leqq 1.00$; $\lambda=\frac{1}{2}$, 1, and 2), obtained by multiplying values in table II by $-x$

(4) Table IV: $x\frac{dF}{dx}$ against x ($0\leqq x\leqq 1.00$; $0\leqq x_1\leqq 1.00$; $\lambda=\frac{1}{2}$, 1, and 2), obtained from equation (4)

(5a) Table V: P against x for $\tau=60°$ ($0\leqq x\leqq 1.00$; $0.1564\leqq x_1\leqq 1.00$; $\lambda=\frac{1}{2}$, 1, and 2), obtained from equation (1)

(5b) Figure 4: $P(x)-P(1)$ against x for $\tau=60°$ ($0\leqq x\leqq 1.00$; $0.1564\leqq x_1\leqq 1.00$; $\lambda=\frac{1}{2}$, 1, and 2)

(6a) Table VI: same as table V for $\tau=120°$

(6b) Figure 5: same as figure 4 for $\tau=120°$

(7a) Table VII: same as table V for $\tau=180°$

(7b) Figure 6: same as figure 4 for $\tau=180°$

(8a) Table VIII: same as table V for $\tau=240°$

(8b) Figure 7: same as figure 4 for $\tau=240°$

(9a) Table IX: same as table V for $\tau=300°$

(9b) Figure 8: same as figure 4 for $\tau=300°$

(10) Table X: $\frac{dP}{dx}$ against τ for $\lambda=\frac{1}{2}$ ($\tau=60°$, 120°, 180°, 240°, and 300°; $x=0$ and 1.00; $0.1564\leqq x_1\leqq 1.00$), obtained analytically

(11) Table XI: same as table X for $\lambda=1$

(12) Table XII: same as table X for $\lambda=2$

(13) Table XIII and figure 9: $-x\frac{dP}{dx}$ against x for $\lambda=\frac{1}{2}$ ($\tau=60°$, 120°, 180°, 240°, and 300°; $0.1564\leqq x\leqq 1.00$; $0.1564\leqq x_1\leqq 1.00$), obtained by multiplying values in table X by $-x$

(14) Table XIV and figure 10: same as table XIII and figure 9 for $\lambda=1$

(15) Table XV and figure 11: same as table XIII and figure 9 for $\lambda=2$

(16) Table XVI and figure 12: $\sum -x\frac{dP}{dx}$ against x for three-blade and six-blade propellers ($\tau=120°$ and 240° for three-blade propeller; $\tau=60°$, 120°, 180°, 240°, and 300° for six-blade propeller; $0.1564\leqq x\leqq 1.00$; $0\leqq x_1\leqq 1.00$; $\lambda=\frac{1}{2}$, 1, and 2); it may be noted that these values for two-blade propellers are given by $-x\frac{dP}{dx}$ for $\tau=180°$ in tables XIII to XV and in figures 9 to 11

APPLICATION OF METHOD

Steps to obtain the induced velocity expressed as $\frac{v_1}{\frac{1}{2}w}$ are as follows:

(1) Plot the quantity $x\frac{dQ}{dx}$ against the circulation coefficient K and perform graphically the integration

$$\int x\frac{dQ}{dx}dK$$

(2a) Plot similarly the functions $x\frac{dF}{dx}$ against K and perform the integration

$$\int x\frac{dF}{dx}dK$$

Since $x\frac{dF}{dx}$ becomes infinite at $x=x_1$, it is necessary to exclude a gap from $x_1-\frac{1}{2}\Delta x$ to $x_1+\frac{1}{2}\Delta x$ and to consider this gap separately by use of a Taylor expansion.

(2b) The contribution from the gap Δx becomes

$$\Delta=-b\left[x_1K''+\left(1-\frac{1}{2}c\log\frac{\Delta x}{2}\right)K'\right]\Delta x$$

where

$$\Delta x=2|x-x_1|$$

$$b=\frac{\lambda}{\sqrt{\lambda^2+x_1^2}}=\sin\phi_1$$

$$c=\frac{x_1^2}{\lambda^2+x_1^2}=\cos^2\phi_1$$

and K' and K'' are the derivatives of K with respect to x.

(3) Finally, there is a contribution from the other blades. This contribution is obtained by plotting $x\frac{dP}{dx}$ against K for the other blades. Since the value $\sum -x\frac{dP}{dx}$ can be taken directly from the tables, this work contains only one step with a single graphical integration

$$\int\sum x\frac{dP}{dx}\,dK$$

By addition of the results of steps (1) to (3), the total interference velocity v_1 in the axial direction is obtained. The relationship between the axial interference velocity v_1 at the radius x_1 to the axial displacement velocity w of the vortex sheet may be seen from the sketch in figure 13. The relation is

$$v_1=\frac{1}{2}w\cos^2\phi_1$$

or, conversely, the displacement velocity w of the vortex sheet may be obtained from the calculated axial interference velocity v_1 by the relation

$$\frac{1}{2}w=\frac{v_1}{\cos^2\phi_1}$$

which gives the axial displacement velocity at the propeller disk. For the case of the ideal loading this axial displacement velocity must come out as a constant, thus permitting a check on the weight functions. Cases of nonideal loading are evidently of more practical concern. It is the purpose of this paper to give a method for calculation of the axial interference and displacement velocity for any (light) loading.

LANGLEY MEMORIAL AERONAUTICAL LABORATORY,
NATIONAL ADVISORY COMMITTEE FOR AERONAUTICS,
LANGLEY FIELD, VA., *September 19, 1944.*

REFERENCE

1. Theodorsen, Theodore: The Theory of Propellers. I—Determination of the Circulation Function and the Mass Coefficient for Dual-Rotating Propellers. NACA Rep. No. 775, 1944.

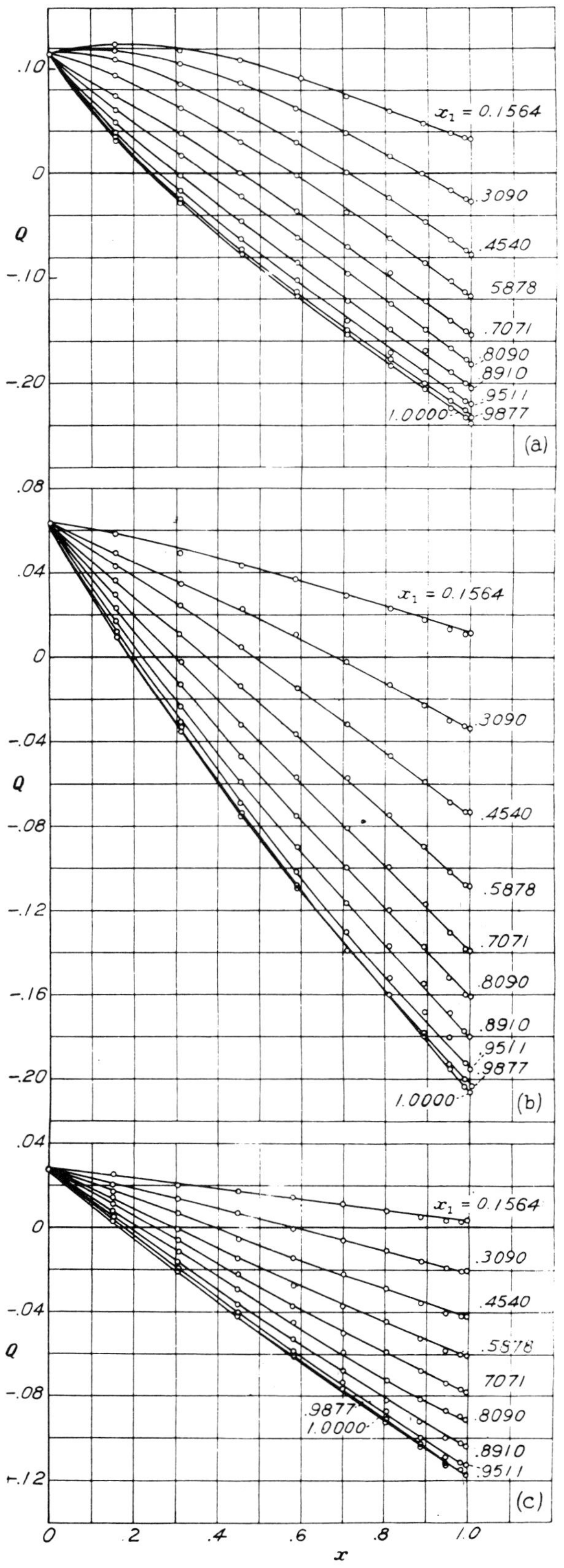

(a) $\lambda=\frac{1}{2}$. (b) $\lambda=1$. (c) $\lambda=2$.

FIGURE 1.—Function Q against x.

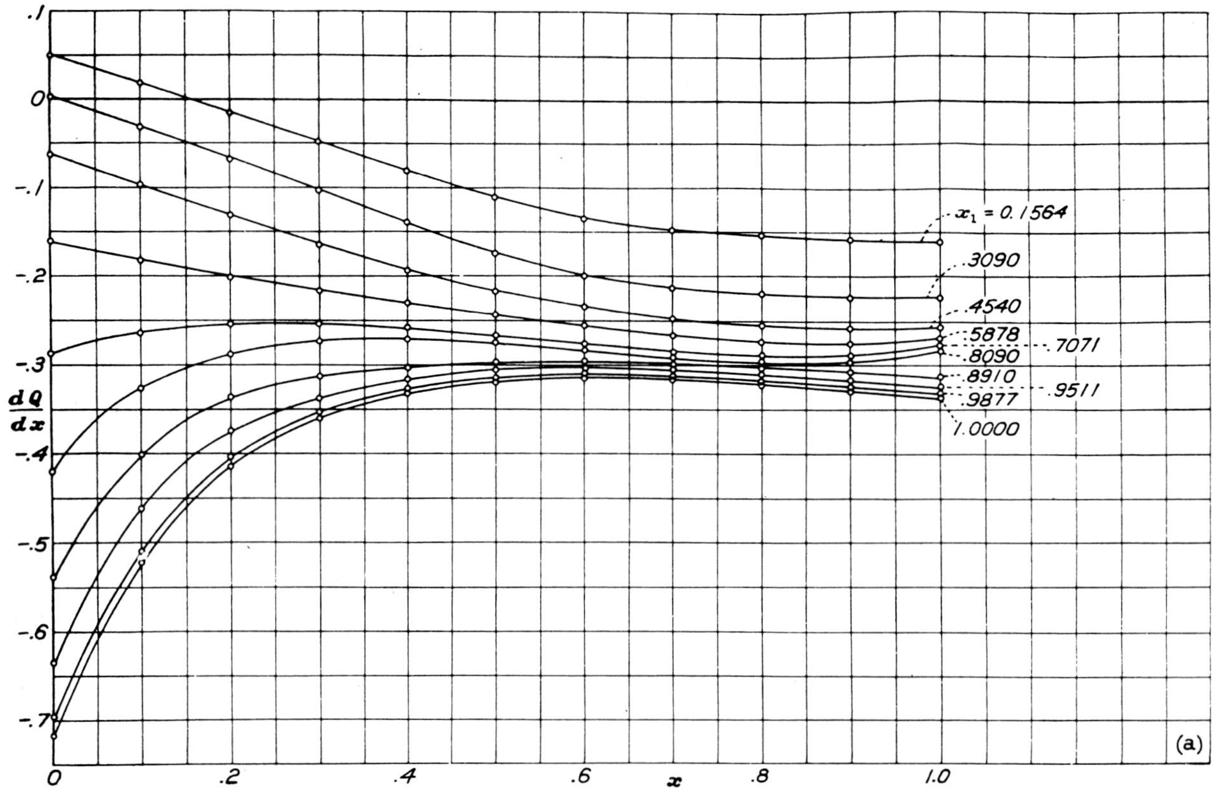

(a) $\lambda=\frac{1}{2}$.

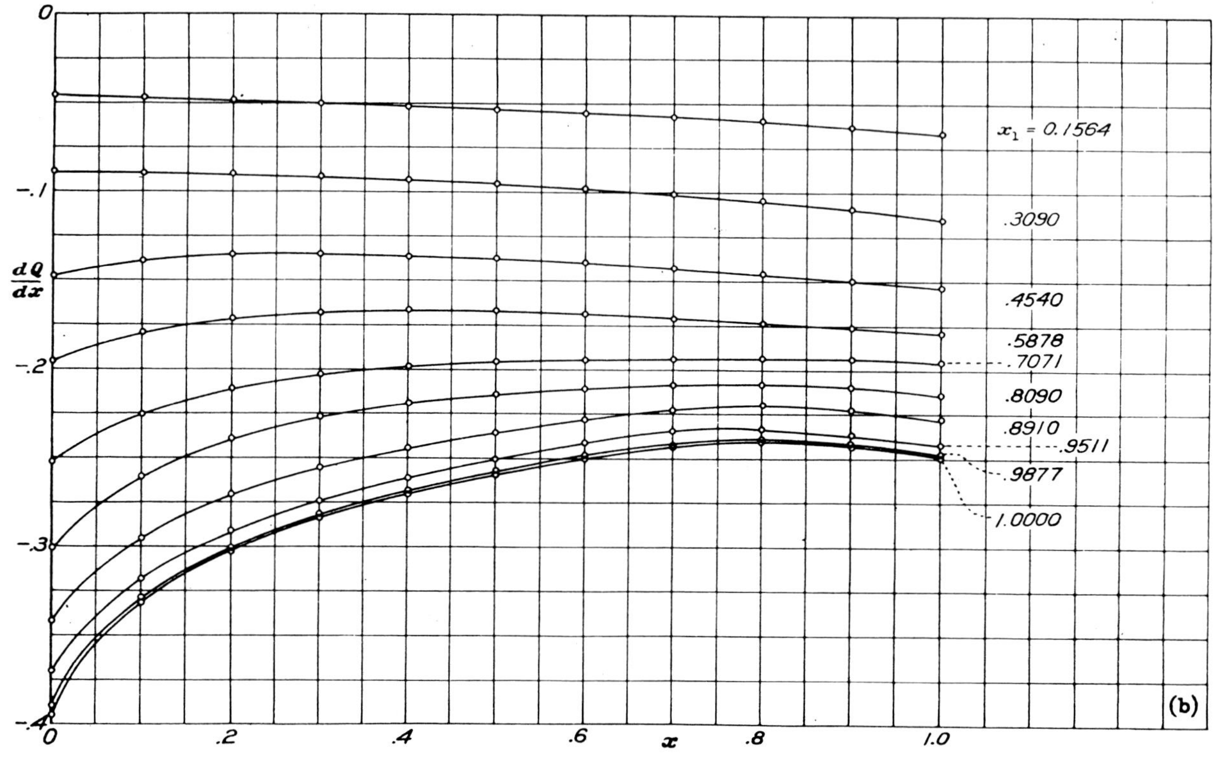

(b) $\lambda=1$.

FIGURE 2.—Function dQ/dx against x.

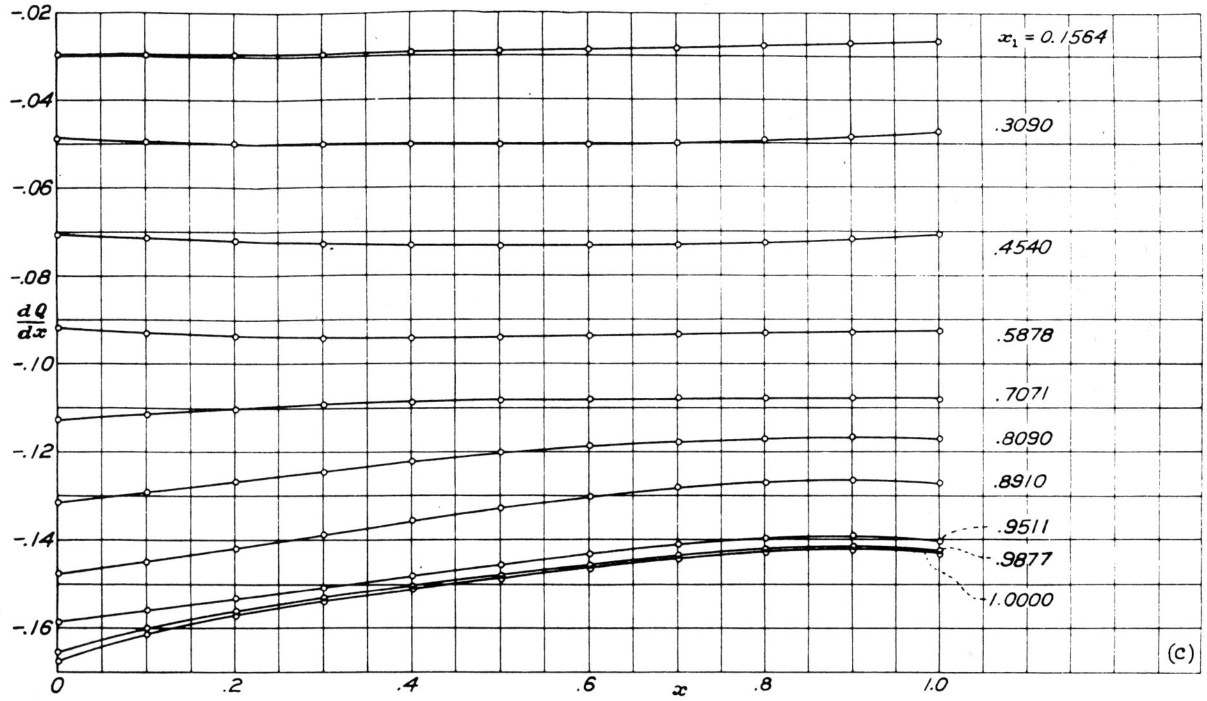

(c) $\lambda=2$.

FIGURE 2.—Concluded.

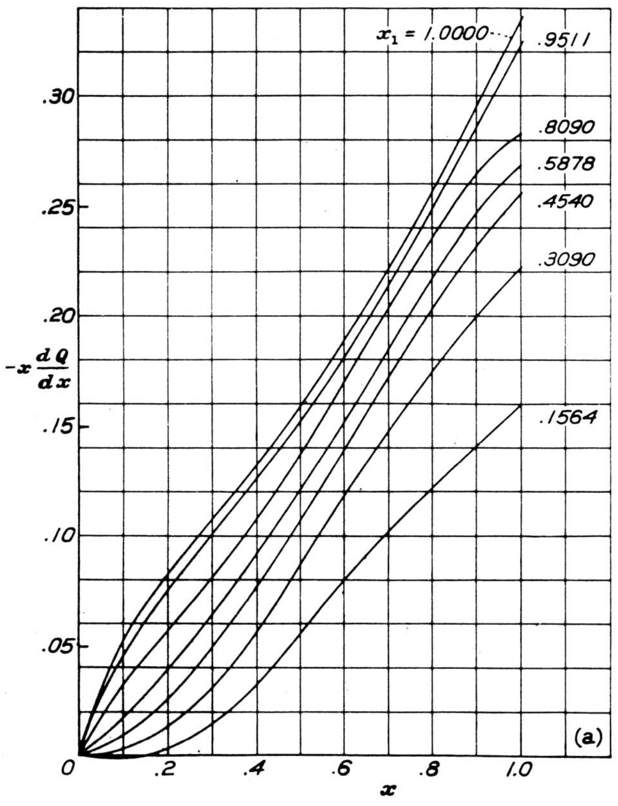

(a) $\lambda=\frac{1}{2}$.

FIGURE 3.—Function $-x\frac{dQ}{dx}$ against x.

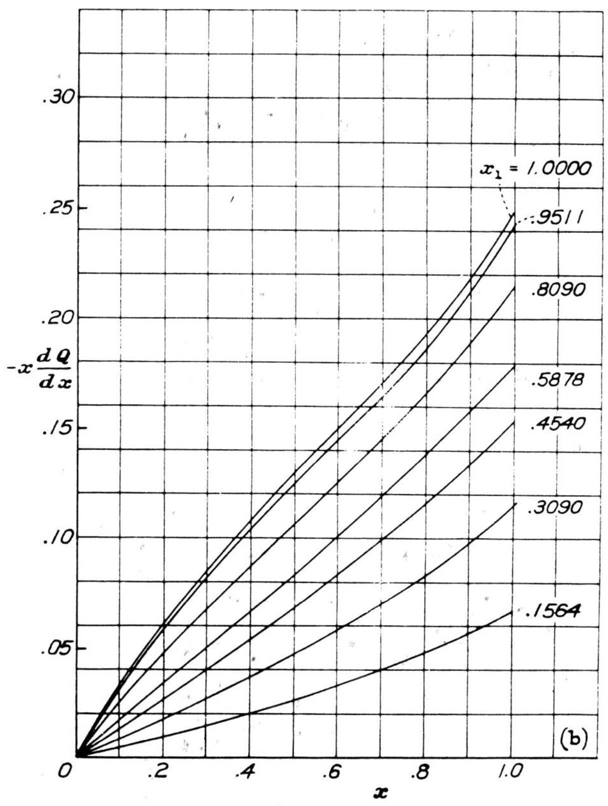

(b) $\lambda=1$.

FIGURE 3.—Continued.

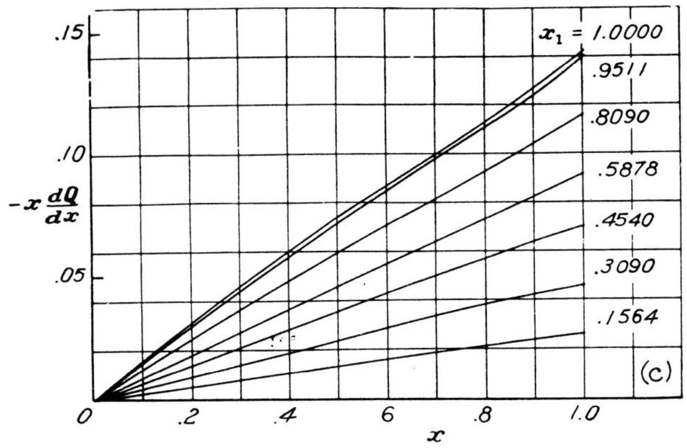

(c) $\lambda=2$.
FIGURE 3.—Concluded.

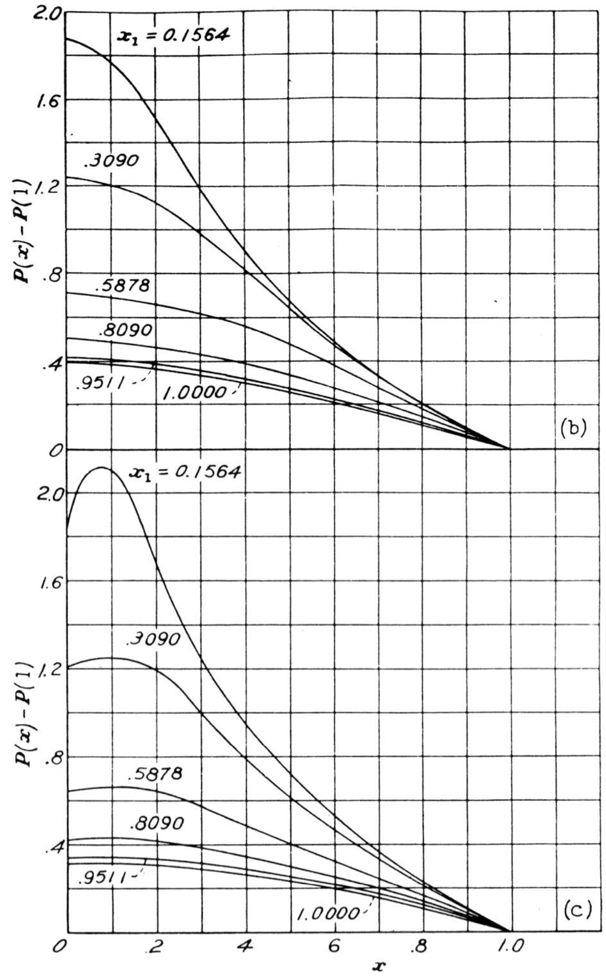

(b) $\lambda=1$. (c) $\lambda=2$.
FIGURE 4.—Continued.

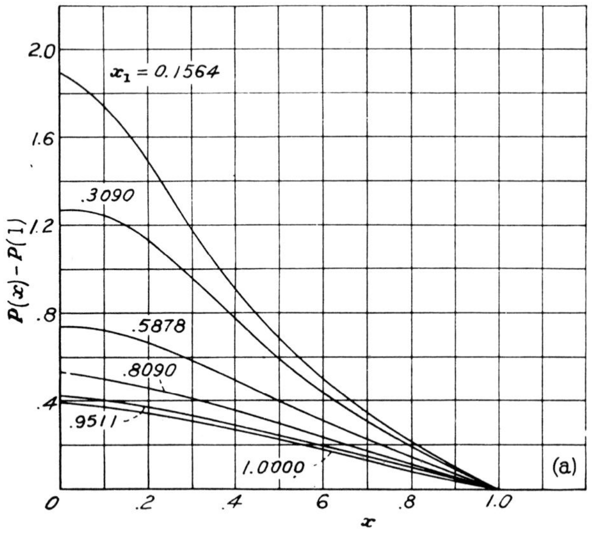

(a) $\lambda=\frac{1}{2}$.
FIGURE 4.—$P(x)-P(1)$ against x for $\tau=60°$.

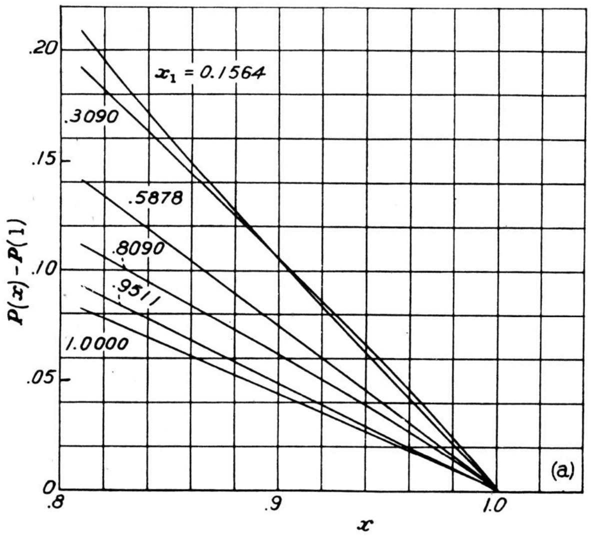

(a) $\lambda=\frac{1}{2}$—Concluded.
FIGURE 4.—Continued.

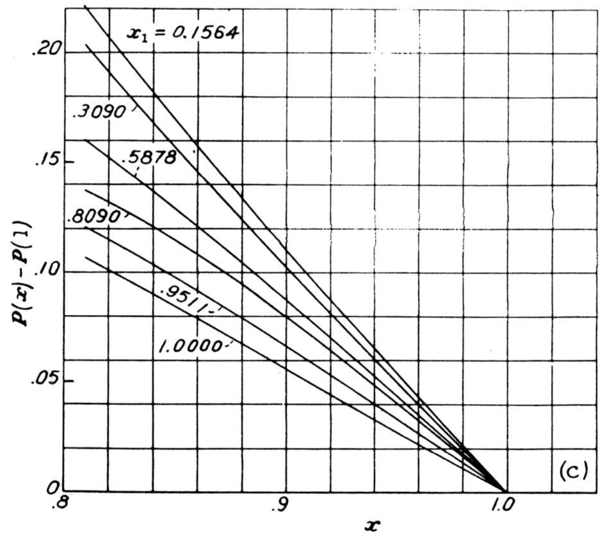

(c) $\lambda=2$—Concluded.
FIGURE 4.—Concluded.

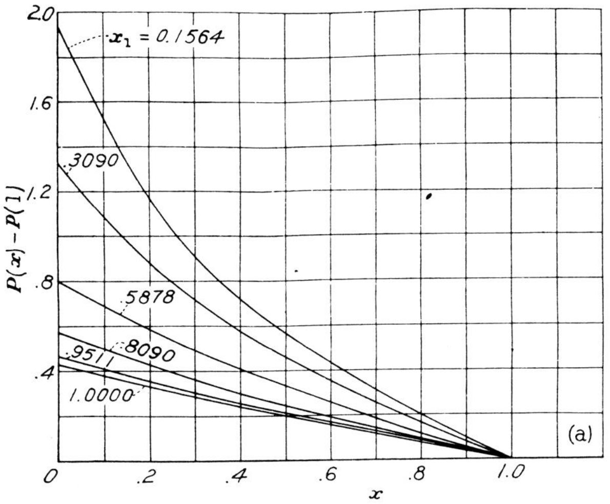

(a) $\lambda=\frac{1}{2}$.
FIGURE 5.—$P(x)-P(1)$ against x for $\tau=120°$.

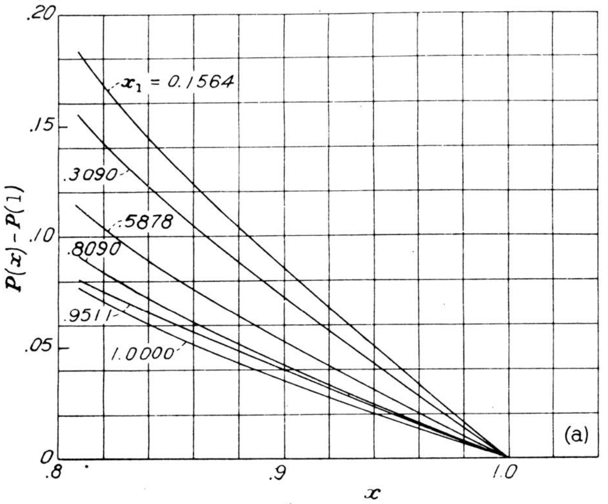

(a) $\lambda=\frac{1}{2}$—Concluded.
FIGURE 5.—Continued.

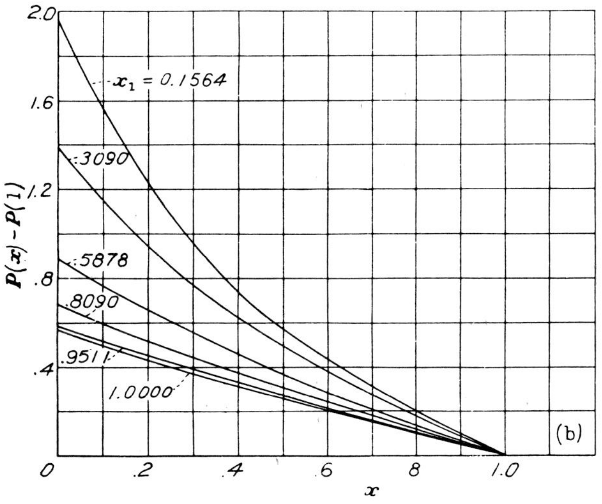

(b) $\lambda=1$.
FIGURE 5.—Continued.

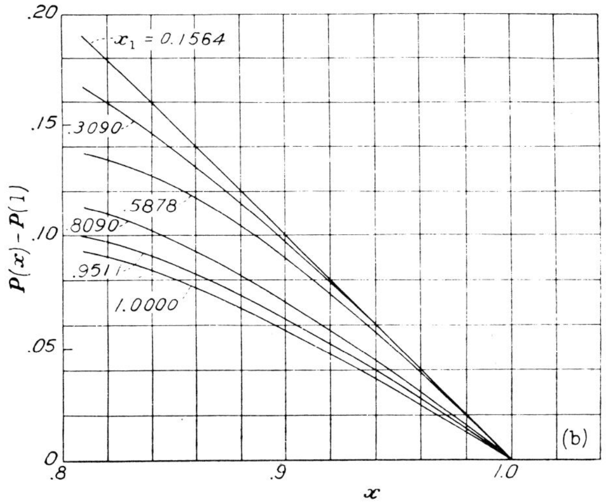

(b) $\lambda=1$—Concluded.
FIGURE 5.—Continued.

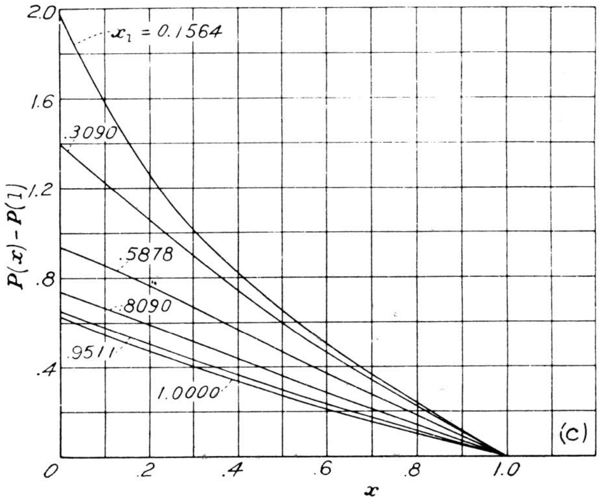

(c) $\lambda=2$.
FIGURE 5.—Continued.

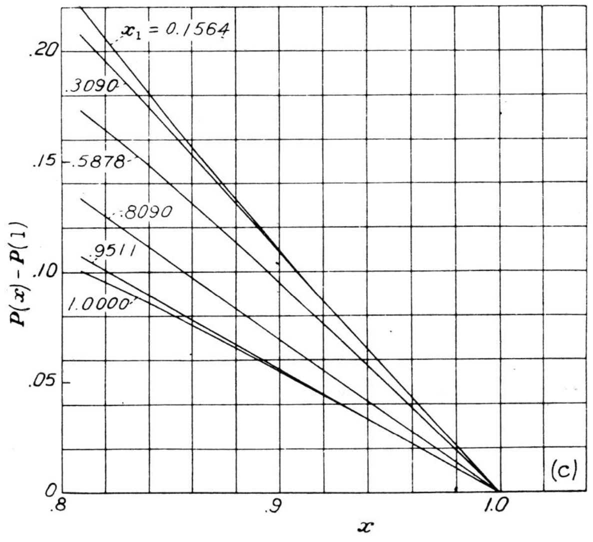

(c) $\lambda=2$—Concluded.
FIGURE 5.—Concluded.

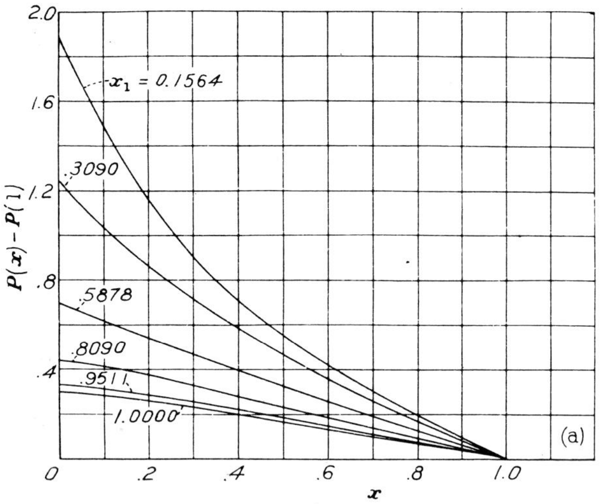

(a) $\lambda=\frac{1}{2}$.
FIGURE 6.—$P(x)-P(1)$ against x for $\tau=180°$.

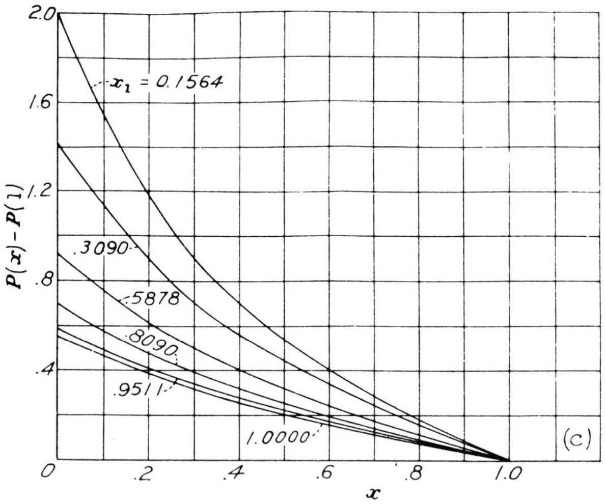

(c) $\lambda=2$.
FIGURE 6.—Continued.

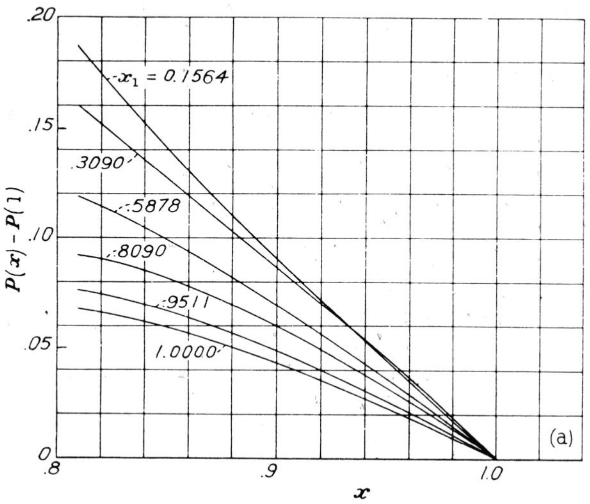

(a) $\lambda=\frac{1}{2}$—Concluded.
FIGURE 6.—Continued.

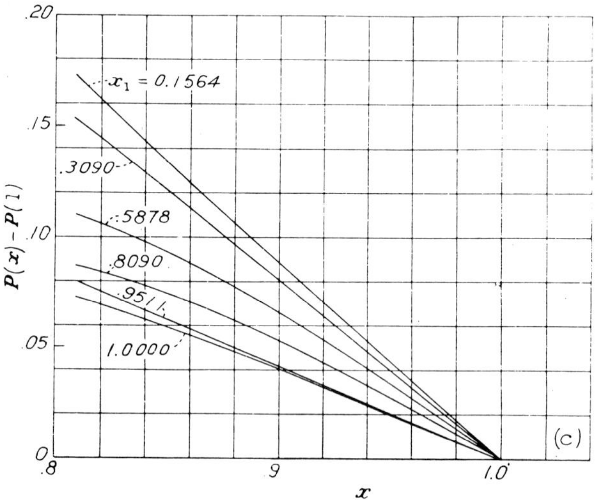

(c) $\lambda=2$—Concluded.
FIGURE 6.—Concluded.

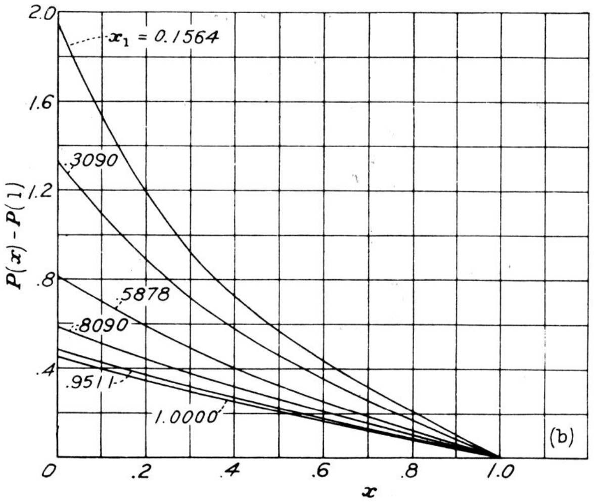

(b) $\lambda=1$.
FIGURE 6.—Continued.

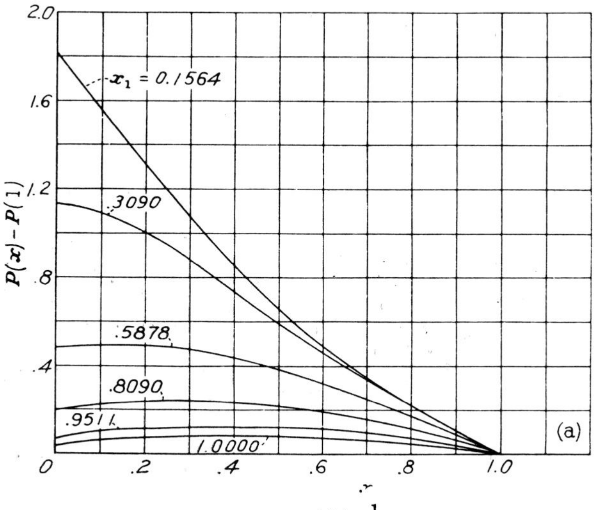

(a) $\lambda=\frac{1}{2}$.
FIGURE 7.—$P(x)-P(1)$ against x for $\tau=240°$.

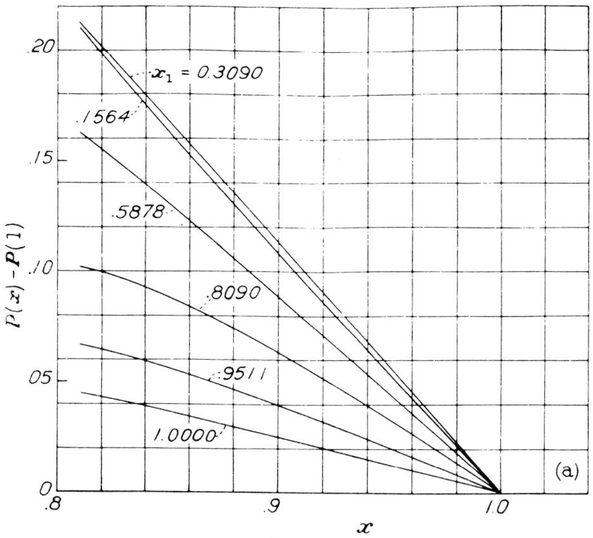

(a) $\lambda=\frac{1}{2}$—Concluded.
FIGURE 7.—Continued.

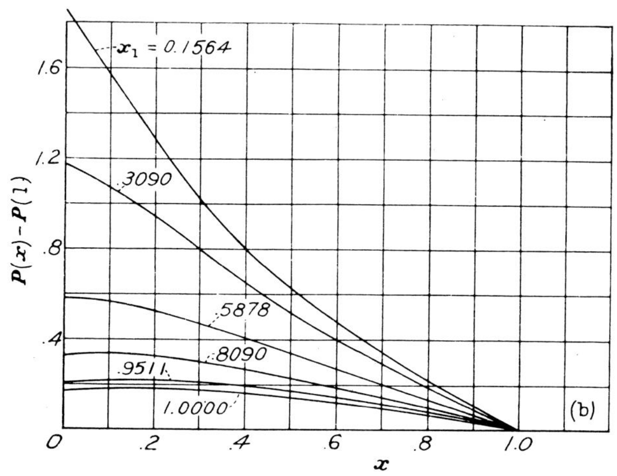

(b) $\lambda=1$.
FIGURE 7.—Continued.

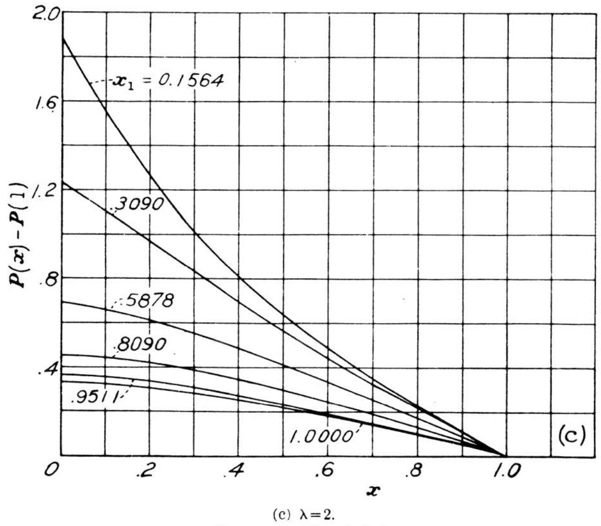

(c) $\lambda=2$.
FIGURE 7.—Concluded.

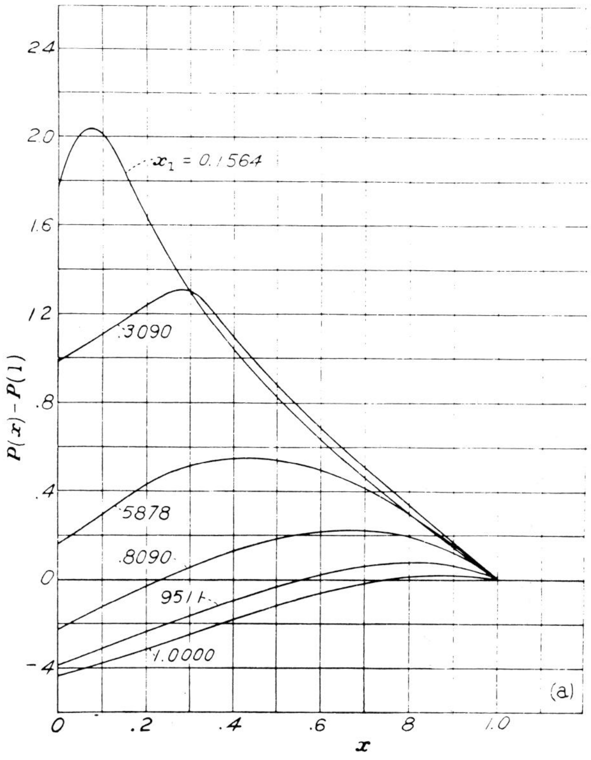

(a) $\lambda=\frac{1}{2}$.
FIGURE 8.—$P(x)-P(1)$ against x for $\tau=300°$.

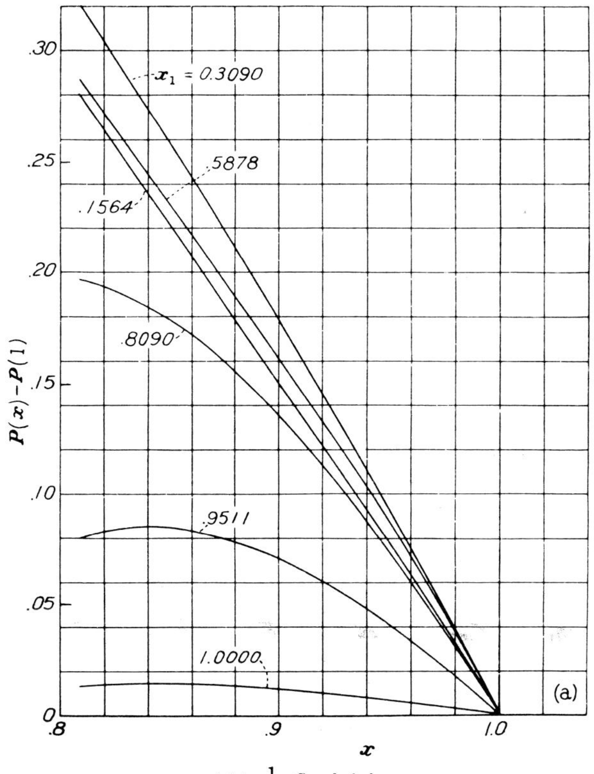

(a) $\lambda=\frac{1}{2}$—Concluded.
FIGURE 8.—Continued.

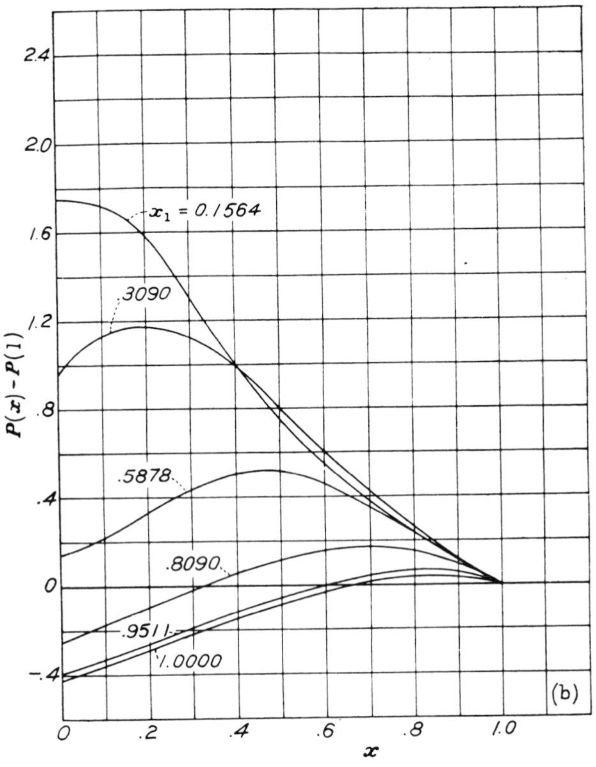

(b) $\lambda=1$.
FIGURE 8.—Continued.

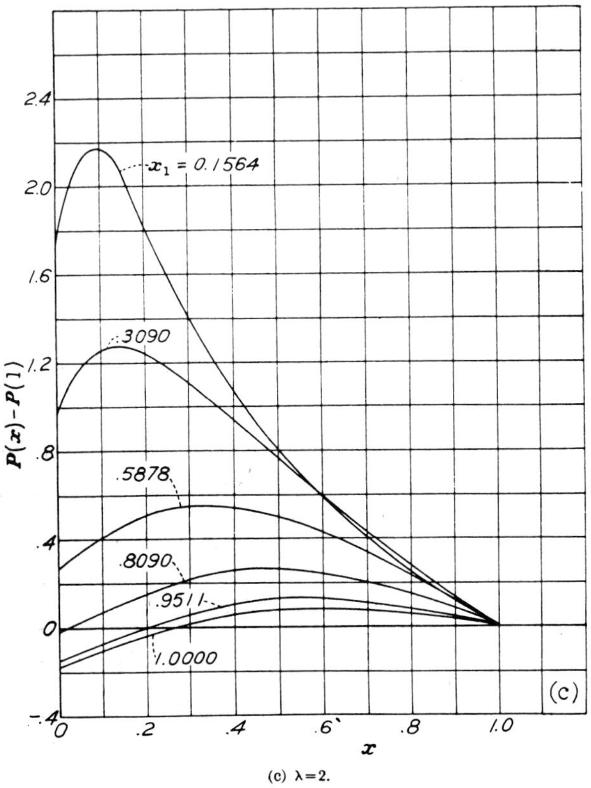

(c) $\lambda=2$.
FIGURE 8.—Concluded.

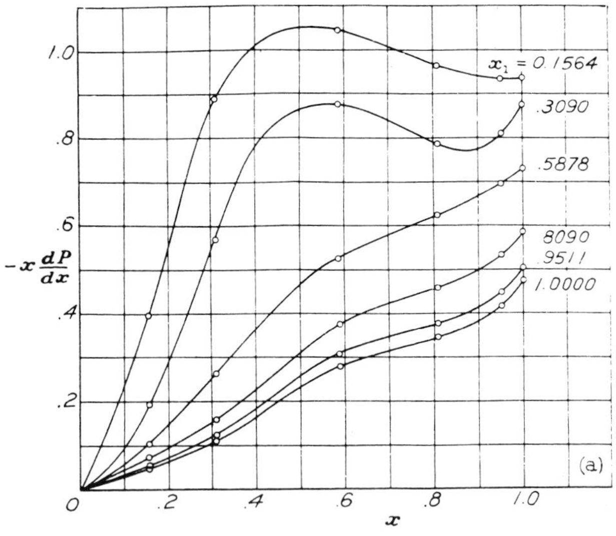

(a) $\tau=60°$.
FIGURE 9.—Function $-x\frac{dP}{dx}$ against x for $\lambda=\frac{1}{2}$.

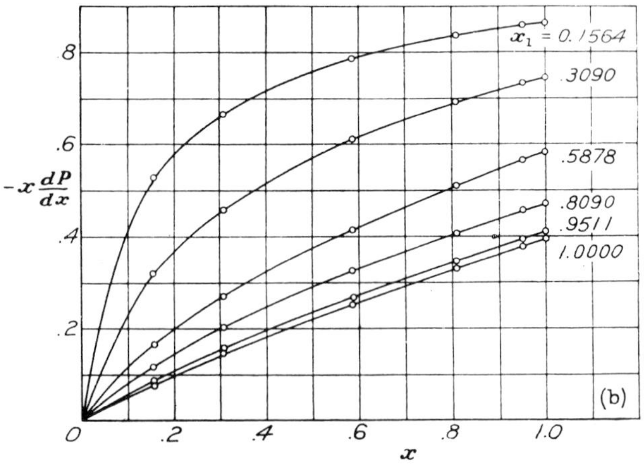

(b) $\tau=120°$.
FIGURE 9.—Continued.

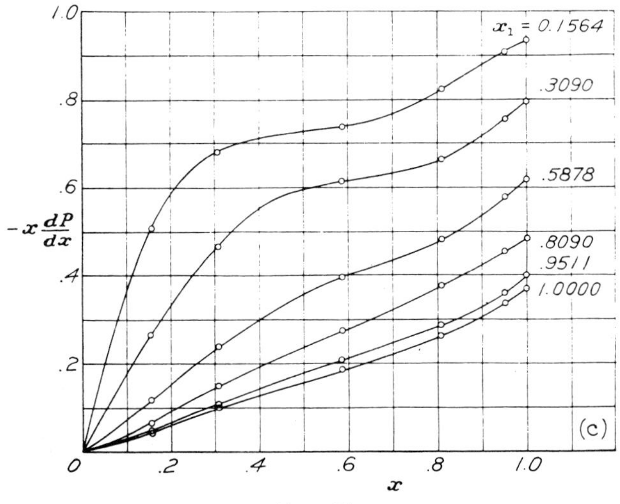

(c) $\tau=180°$.
FIGURE 9.—Continued.

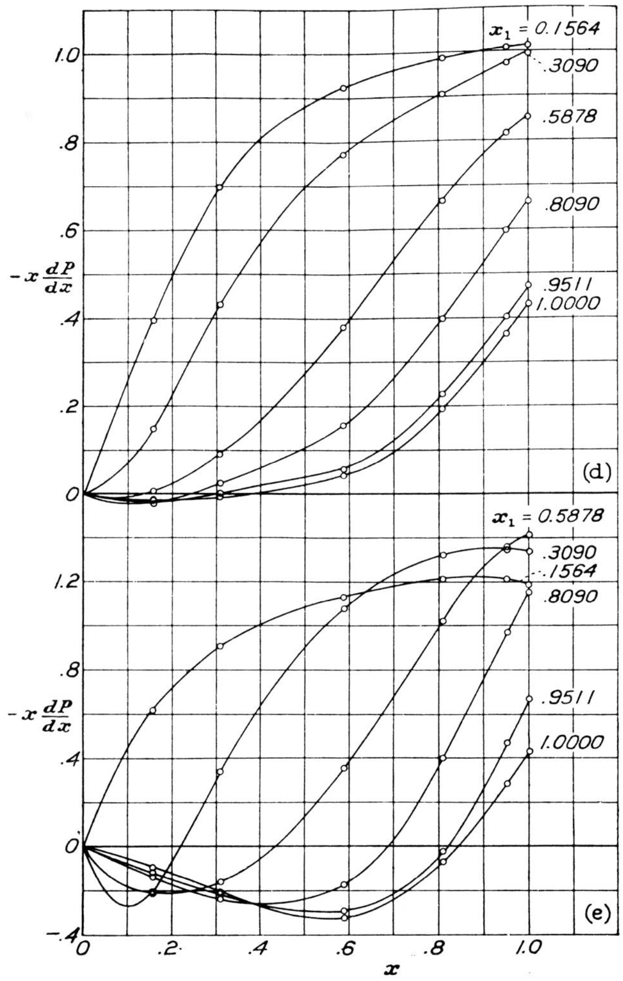

(d) $\tau=240°$. (e) $\tau=300°$.
FIGURE 9.—Concluded.

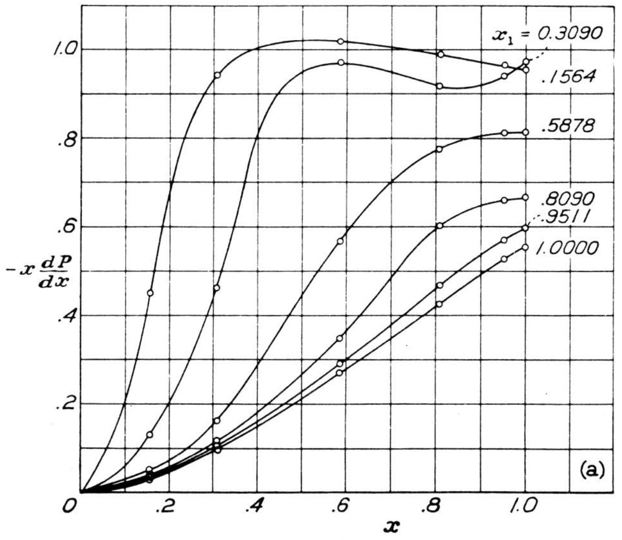

(a) $\tau=60°$.
FIGURE 10.—Function $-\frac{dP}{dx}$ against x for $\lambda=1$.

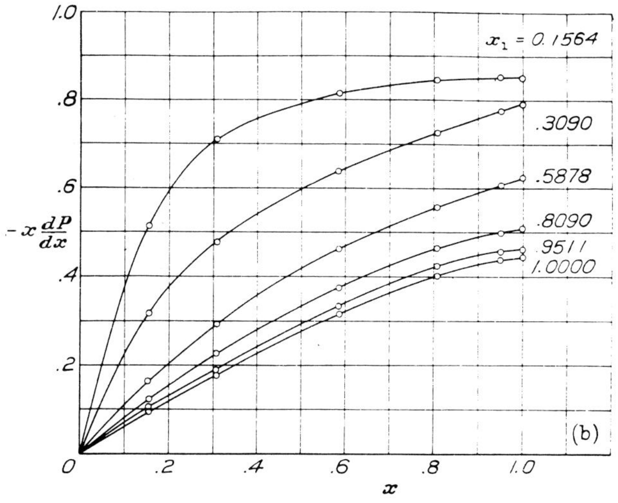

(b) $\tau=120°$.
FIGURE 10.—Continued.

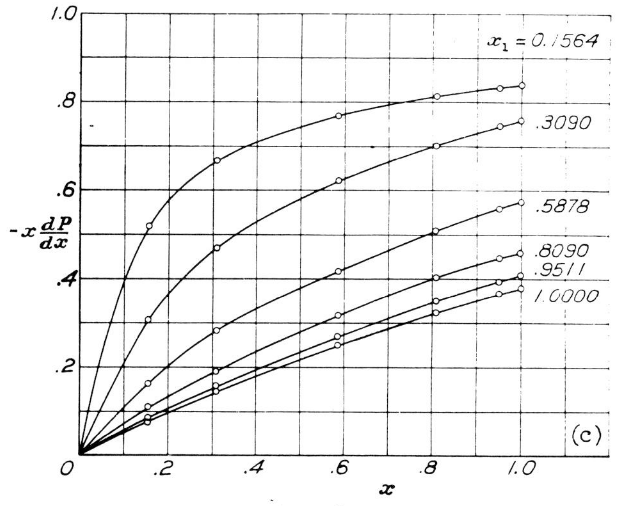

(c) $\tau=180°$.
FIGURE 10.—Continued.

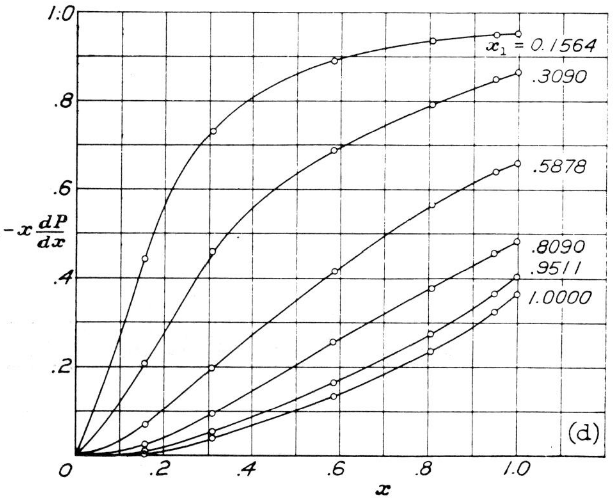

(d) $\tau=240°$.
FIGURE 10.—Continued.

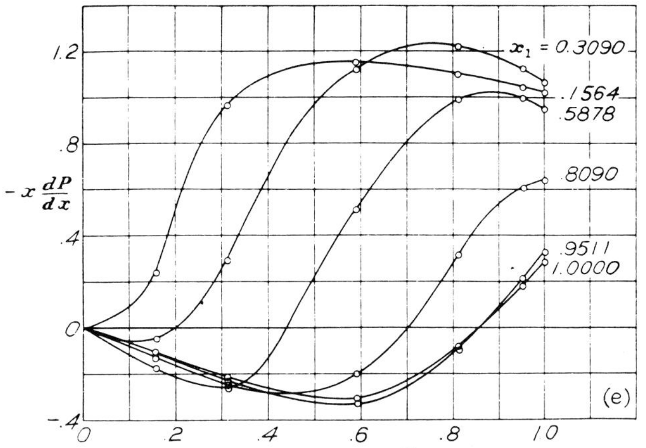

(e) $\tau=300°$.
FIGURE 10.—Concluded.

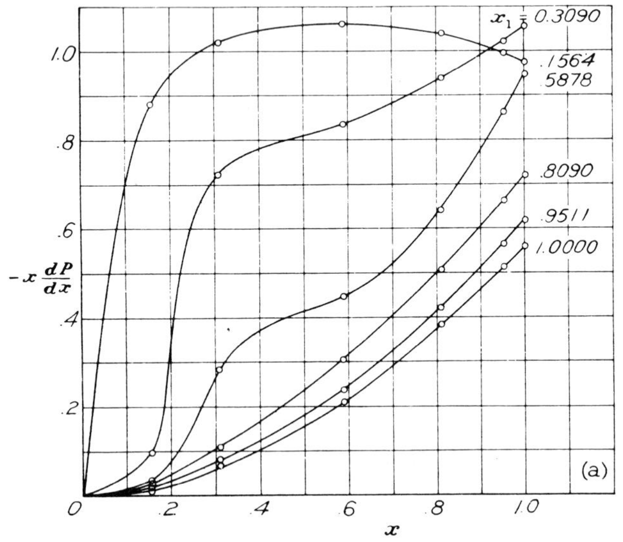

(a) $\tau=60°$.
FIGURE 11.—Function $-x\frac{dP}{dx}$ against x for $\lambda=2$.

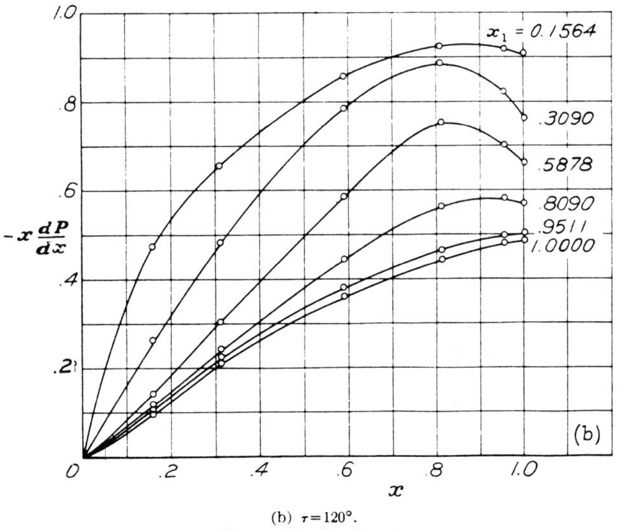

(b) $\tau=120°$.
FIGURE 11.—Continued.

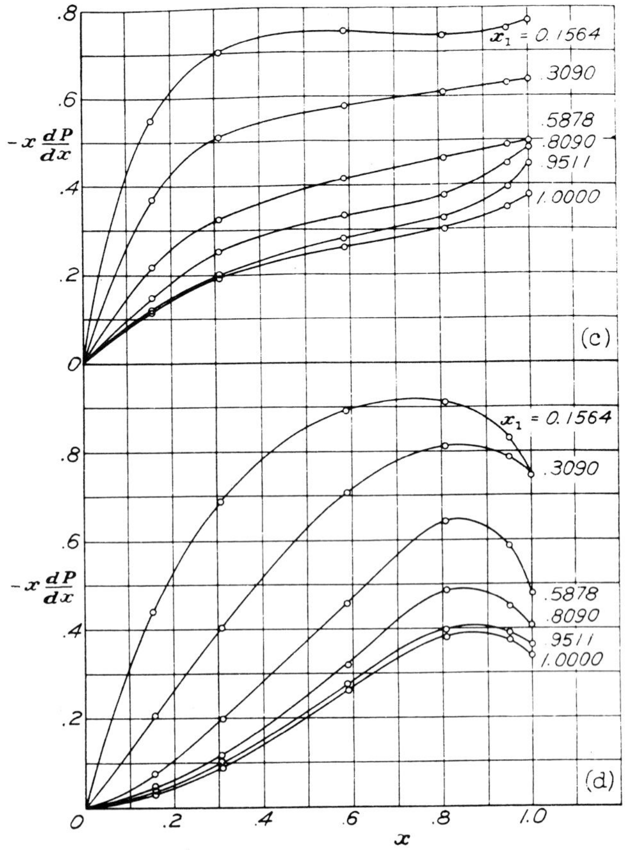

(c) $\tau=180°$. (d) $\tau=240°$.
FIGURE 11.—Continued.

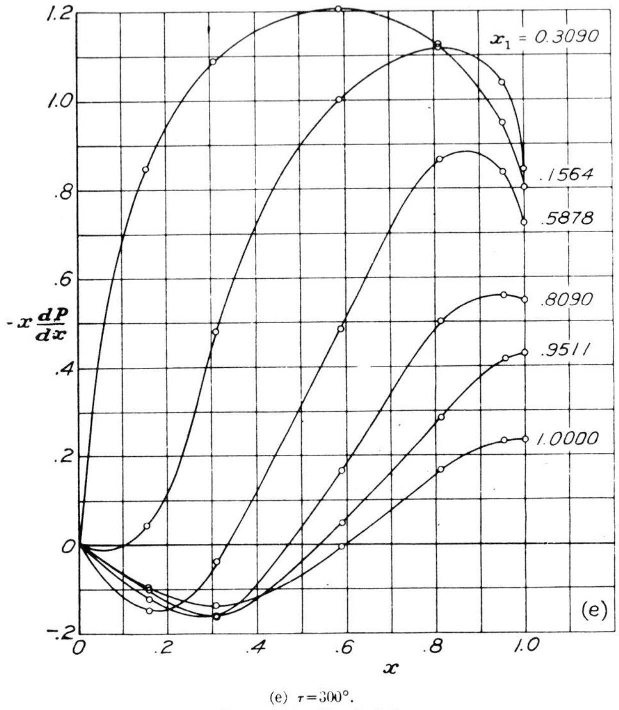

(e) $\tau=300°$.
FIGURE 11.—Concluded.

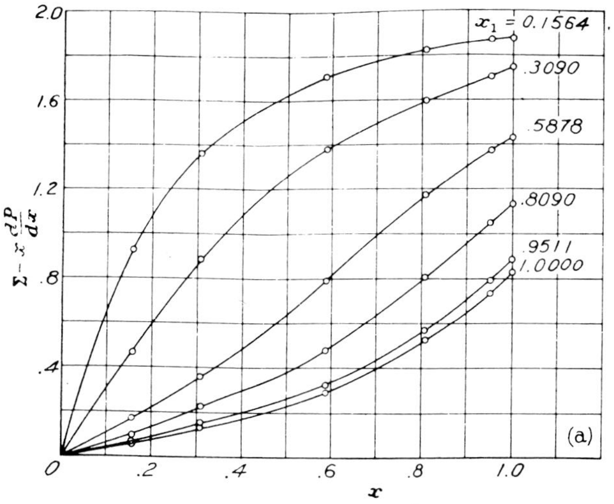

(a) Three-blade propeller; $\lambda = \frac{1}{2}$.
FIGURE 12.—Values of $\sum -x\frac{dP}{dx}$ against x for three-blade and six-blade propellers.

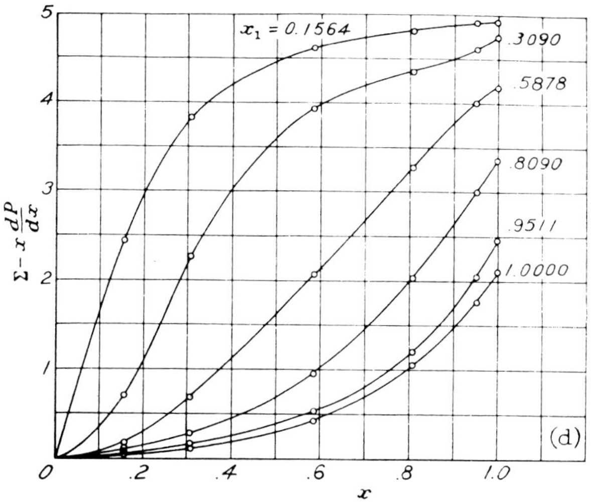

(d) Six-blade propeller; $\lambda = \frac{1}{2}$.
FIGURE 12.—Continued.

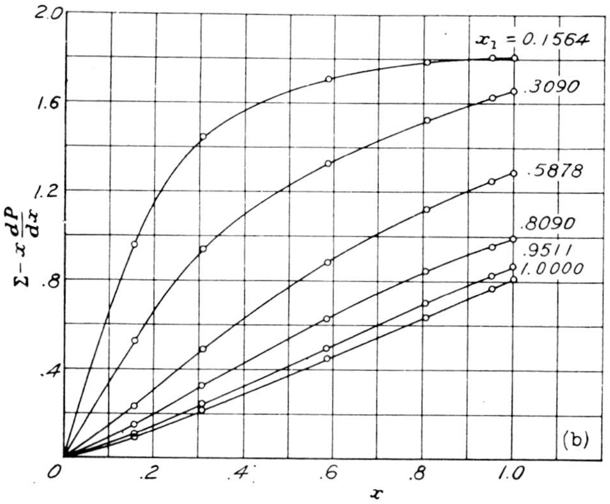

(b) Three-blade propeller; $\lambda = 1$.
FIGURE 12.—Continued.

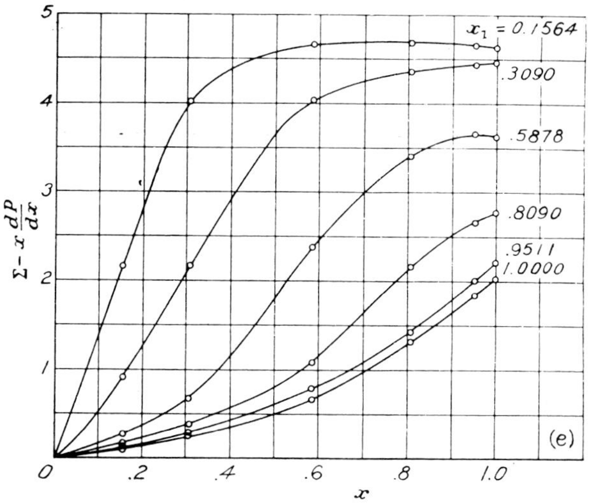

(e) Six-blade propeller; $\lambda = 1$.
FIGURE 12.—Continued.

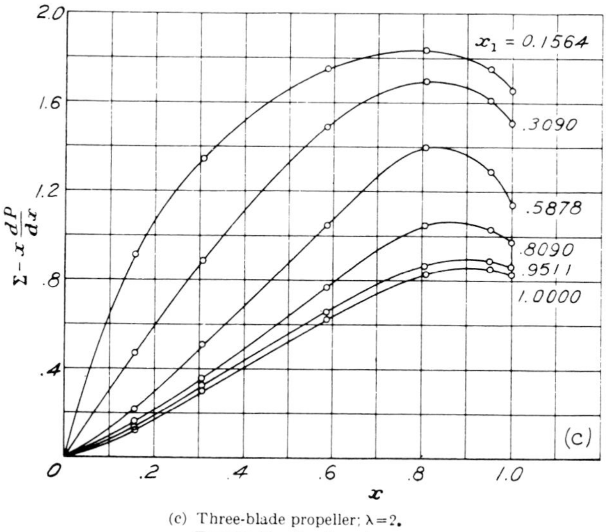

(c) Three-blade propeller; $\lambda = 2$.
FIGURE 12.—Continued.

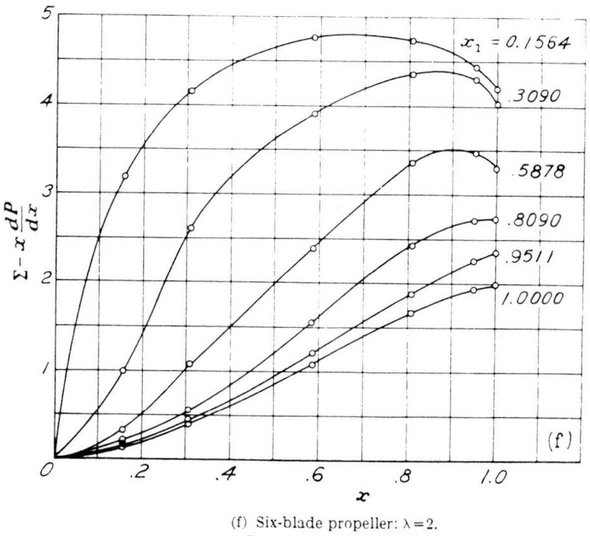

(f) Six-blade propeller; $\lambda = 2$.
FIGURE 12.—Concluded.

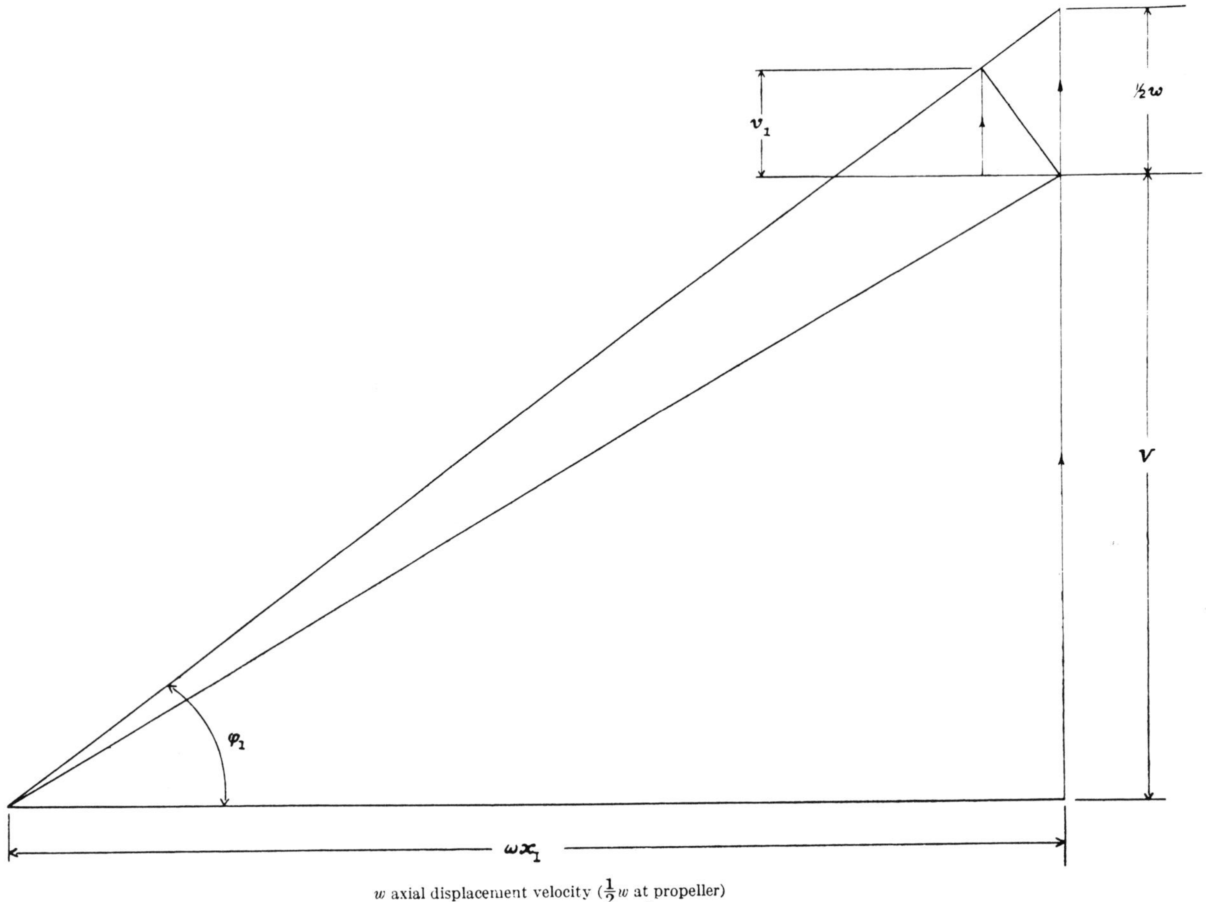

w axial displacement velocity ($\frac{1}{2}w$ at propeller)
v_1 actual axial interference velocity ($\frac{1}{2}w\ \cos^2\varphi_1$ at propeller)
φ_1 helix angle at radius x

FIGURE 13.—Velocity diagram.

TABLE I.—FUNCTION Q AGAINST x

x_1 \ x	0	0.1564	0.3090	0.4540	0.5878	0.7071	0.8090	0.8910	0.9511	0.9877	1.00
$\lambda=\frac{1}{2}$											
0.1564	0.11826	0.12420	0.11817	0.10898	0.09334	0.07351	0.06051	0.04820	0.03937	0.03429	0.03252
.3090	.11826	.11817	.10580	.08696	.06259	.03851	.01679	−.00264	−.01646	−.02407	−.02729
.4540	.11826	.10898	.08696	.06101	.02926	−.00072	−.02257	−.04633	−.06370	−.07355	−.07720
.5878	.11826	.09334	.06259	.02926	−.00169	−.03644	−.06191	−.08528	−.10315	−.11315	−.11755
.7071	.11826	.07351	.03851	.00072	−.03644	−.07081	−.09533	−.12238	−.14059	−.15029	−.15430
.8090	.11826	.06051	.01679	−.02257	−.06191	−.09533	−.12420	−.14934	−.16703	−.17761	−.18246
.8910	.11826	.04820	−.00264	−.04633	−.08528	−.12238	−.14934	−.16900	−.18837	−.20063	−.20496
.9511	.11826	.03937	−.01646	−.06370	−.10315	−.14059	−.16703	−.18837	−.20752	−.21634	−.22098
.9877	.11826	.03429	−.02407	−.07355	−.11315	−.15029	−.17761	−.20003	−.21634	−.22633	−.23283
1.00	.11826	.03252	−.02729	−.07720	−.11755	−.15430	−.18246	−.20496	−.22098	−.23283	−.23724
$\lambda=1$											
0.1564	0.06390	0.05804	0.04915	0.04323	0.03635	0.02954	0.02318	0.01727	0.01236	0.01021	0.01111
.3090	.06390	.04915	.03428	.02244	.01054	−.00262	−.01301	−.02336	−.03059	−.03352	−.03425
.4540	.06390	.04323	.02244	.00444	−.01419	−.03213	−.04733	−.05956	−.06941	−.07376	−.07401
.5878	.06390	.03635	.01054	−.01419	−.03715	−.05761	−.07560	−.09053	−.10235	−.10847	−.10903
.7071	.06390	.02954	−.00262	−.03213	−.05761	−.08155	−.10030	−.11704	−.13087	−.13861	−.13974
.8090	.06390	.02318	−.01301	−.04733	−.07560	−.10030	−.12049	−.13758	−.15259	−.16012	−.16143
.8910	.06390	.01727	−.02336	−.05956	−.09053	−.11704	−.13758	−.15528	−.16920	−.17850	−.18026
.9511	.06390	.01236	−.03059	−.06941	−.10235	−.13087	−.15259	−.16920	−.18140	−.19344	−.19590
.9877	.06390	.01021	−.03352	−.07376	−.10847	−.13861	−.16012	−.17850	−.19344	−.20407	−.20496
1.00	.06390	.01111	−.03425	−.07401	−.10903	−.13974	−.16140	−.18026	−.19590	−.20496	−.20486
$\lambda=2$											
0.1564	0.02794	0.02524	0.02008	0.01748	0.01426	0.01102	0.00792	0.00521	0.00301	0.00305	0.00310
.3090	.02794	.02008	.01370	.00697	−.00084	−.00624	−.01128	−.01605	−.01970	−.02072	−.02064
.4540	.02794	.01748	.00697	−.00182	−.01432	−.02246	−.02941	−.03612	−.04060	−.04210	−.04251
.5878	.02794	.01426	−.00084	−.01432	−.02785	−.03786	−.04536	−.05329	−.05897	−.06081	−.06145
.7071	.02794	.01102	−.00624	−.02246	−.03786	−.05035	−.05964	−.06815	−.07407	−.07713	−.07820
.8090	.02794	.00792	−.01128	−.02941	−.04536	−.05964	−.07814	−.08246	−.08781	−.09040	−.09199
.8910	.02794	.00521	−.01605	−.03612	−.05329	−.06815	−.08246	−.09277	−.10019	−.10284	−.10437
.9511	.02794	.00301	−.01970	−.04060	−.05897	−.07407	−.08781	−.10019	−.10970	−.11211	−.11318
.9877	.02794	.00305	−.02072	−.04210	−.06081	−.07713	−.09040	−.10284	−.11211	−.11582	−.11708
1.00	.02794	.00310	−.02064	−.04251	−.06145	−.07820	−.09199	−.10437	−.11318	−.11708	−.11779

TABLE II.—FUNCTION $\frac{dQ}{dx}$ AGAINST x

x_1 \ x	0	0.1	0.2	0.3	0.4	0.5	0.6	0.7	0.8	0.9	1.0
$\lambda=\frac{1}{2}$											
0.1564	0.05000	0.0175	−0.0150	−0.0470	−0.0800	−0.1100	−0.1340	−0.1470	−0.1520	−0.1568	−0.15974
.3090	.00250	−.0320	−.0672	−.1025	−.1396	−.1748	−.1984	−.2120	−.2184	−.2220	−.22254
.4540	−.06293	−.0975	−.1300	−.1648	−.1928	−.2168	−.2340	−.2448	−.2544	−.2578	−.25584
.5878	−.16149	−.1825	−.2000	−.2150	−.2300	−.2425	−.2555	−.2655	−.2720	−.2750	−.26922
.7071	−.28838	−.2648	−.2550	−.2548	−.2576	−.2665	−.2752	−.2840	−.2880	−.2875	−.27642
.8090	−.42088	−.3255	−.2880	−.2740	−.2700	−.2750	−.2840	−.2915	−.2952	−.2950	−.28349
.8910	−.53863	−.4000	−.3352	−.3140	−.3024	−.2970	−.2952	−.2978	−.3020	−.3068	−.31319
.9511	−.63559	−.4620	−.3744	−.3375	−.3160	−.3050	−.3020	−.3060	−.3100	−.3160	−.32400
.9877	−.69631	−.5100	−.4040	−.3525	−.3264	−.3150	−.3100	−.3135	−.3165	−.3248	−.33100
1.00	−.71759	−.5240	−.4144	−.3590	−.3320	−.3190	−.3150	−.3160	−.3220	−.3290	−.3360
$\lambda=1$											
0.1564	−0.04690	−0.0475	−0.0480	−0.0500	−0.0520	−0.0530	−0.0550	−0.0575	−0.0600	−0.0630	−0.06727
.3090	−.08960	−.0900	−.0902	−.0920	−.0930	−.0955	−.0980	−.1014	−.1050	−.1090	−.11586
.4540	−.14818	−.1390	−.1360	−.1350	−.1370	−.1375	−.1400	−.1426	−.1465	−.1500	−.15343
.5878	−.19684	−.1800	−.1720	−.1680	−.1670	−.1675	−.1685	−.1712	−.1740	−.1770	−.17918
.7071	−.25298	−.2265	−.2120	−.2030	−.1980	−.1960	−.1950	−.1940	−.1936	−.1936	−.19592
.8090	−.30136	−.2620	−.2396	−.2270	−.2196	−.2140	−.2108	−.2090	−.2080	−.2100	−.21471
.8910	−.34255	−.2955	−.2712	−.2560	−.2450	−.2380	−.2280	−.2225	−.2200	−.2225	−.22800
.9511	−.37091	−.3187	−.2920	−.2748	−.2620	−.2508	−.2416	−.2350	−.2336	−.2370	−.24250
.9877	−.39041	−.3298	−.3010	−.2822	−.2680	−.2575	−.2480	−.2420	−.2390	−.2420	−.24700
1.00	−.39689	−.3322	−.3025	−.2837	−.2700	−.2600	−.2505	−.2438	−.2410	−.2435	−.24850
$\lambda=2$											
0.1564	−0.02960	−0.0295	−0.0294	−0.0291	−0.0290	−0.0288	−0.0284	−0.0280	−0.0276	−0.0270	−0.02641
.3090	−.04857	−.0492	−.0499	−.0500	−.0500	−.0500	−.0500	−.0498	−.0491	−.0482	−.04712
.4540	−.07063	−.0712	−.0720	−.0725	−.0730	−.0730	−.0730	−.0730	−.0725	−.0715	−.07058
.5878	−.09199	−.0929	−.0937	−.0940	−.0940	−.0939	−.0936	−.0931	−.0930	−.0929	−.09270
.7071	−.11265	−.1114	−.1100	−.1090	−.1084	−.1080	−.1078	−.1078	−.1078	−.1078	−.10800
.8090	−.13155	−.1291	−.1269	−.1243	−.1220	−.1200	−.1188	−.1178	−.1170	−.1167	−.11700
.8910	−.14748	−.1450	−.1420	−.1387	−.1356	−.1327	−.1300	−.1281	−.1270	−.1266	−.12705
.9511	−.15874	−.1560	−.1534	−.1508	−.1480	−.1454	−.1430	−.1410	−.1396	−.1390	−.14034
.9877	−.16554	−.1600	−.1561	−.1530	−.1501	−.1478	−.1456	−.1434	−.1420	−.1416	−.14240
1.00	−.16757	−.1616	−.1571	−.1538	−.1510	−.1486	−.1460	−.1440	−.1428	−.1420	−.14320

TABLE II.—FUNCTION $\frac{dQ}{dx}$ AGAINST x—CONCLUDED

x_1 \ x	0	0.1564	0.3090	0.4540	0.5878	0.7071	0.8090	0.8910	0.9511	0.9877	1.00
$\lambda=\frac{1}{2}$											
0.1564	0.05000	−0.0010	−0.0501	−0.0970	−0.1315	−0.1475	−0.1540	−0.1565	−0.1595	−0.1600	−0.15974
.3090	.00250	−.0520	−.1060	−.1598	−.1960	−.2130	−.2200	−.2220	−.2240	−.2235	−.22254
.4540	−.06293	−.1165	−.1665	−.2065	−.2330	−.2470	−.2551	−.2580	−.2575	−.2565	−.25584
.5878	−.16149	−.1930	−.2170	−.2370	−.2545	−.2665	−.2740	−.2750	−.2735	−.2700	−.26922
.7071	−.28838	−.2580	−.2540	−.2630	−.2750	−.2840	−.2880	−.2890	−.2845	−.2780	−.27642
.8090	−.42088	−.3010	−.2735	−.2730	−.2830	−.2925	−.2965	−.2955	−.2915	−.2860	−.28349
.8910	−.53863	−.3575	−.3120	−.2990	−.2950	−.2980	−.3025	−.3060	−.3110	−.3115	−.31319
.9511	−.63559	−.4040	−.3350	−.3085	−.3020	−.3060	−.3100	−.3155	−.3200	−.3235	−.32400
.9877	−.69631	−.4420	−.3495	−.3190	−.3100	−.3135	−.3185	−.3240	−.3280	−.3301	−.33100
1.00	−.71759	−.4535	−.3560	−.3240	−.3150	−.3175	−.3230	−.3280	−.3325	−.3350	−.33600
$\lambda=1$											
0.1564	−0.04690	−0.0477	−0.0505	−0.0526	−0.0550	−0.0575	−0.0600	−0.0625	−0.0650	−0.0669	−0.06727
.3090	−.08960	−.0900	−.0922	−.0947	−.0978	−.1020	−.1051	−.1085	−.1123	−.1149	−.11586
.4540	−.14818	−.1368	−.1351	−.1373	−.1398	−.1430	−.1468	−.1498	−.1522	−.1530	−.15343
.5878	−.19684	−.1748	−.1678	−.1670	−.1683	−.1718	−.1742	−.1765	−.1776	−.1790	−.17918
.7071	−.25298	−.2170	−.2027	−.1972	−.1950	−.1940	−.1936	−.1936	−.1949	−.1952	−.19592
.8090	−.30136	−.2475	−.2265	−.2168	−.2110	−.2088	−.2080	−.2098	−.2120	−.2132	−.21471
.8910	−.34255	−.2805	−.2550	−.2395	−.2285	−.2225	−.2200	−.2223	−.2250	−.2275	−.22800
.9511	−.37091	−.3020	−.2732	−.2560	−.2423	−.2345	−.2336	−.2365	−.2400	−.2420	−.24250
.9877	−.39041	−.3123	−.2810	−.2625	−.2495	−.2418	−.2390	−.2412	−.2445	−.2465	−.24700
1.00	−.39689	−.3135	−.2822	−.2645	−.2518	−.2436	−.2410	−.2428	−.2465	−.2480	−.24850
$\lambda=2$											
0.1564	−0.02960	−0.0295	−0.0291	−0.0290	−0.0285	−0.0280	−0.0273	−0.0270	−0.0267	−0.0264	−0.02641
.3090	−.04857	−.0497	−.0500	−.0500	−.0500	−.0498	−.0490	−.0483	−.0478	−.0472	−.04712
.4540	−.07063	−.0718	−.0726	−.0730	−.0730	−.0730	−.0723	−.0718	−.0711	−.0708	−.07058
.5878	−.09199	−.0933	−.0940	−.0940	−.0937	−.0931	−.0930	−.0929	−.0928	−.0927	−.09270
.7071	−.11265	−.1108	−.1090	−.1081	−.1078	−.1078	−.1078	−.1078	−.1080	−.1080	−.10800
.8090	−.13155	−.1279	−.1241	−.1210	−.1189	−.1177	−.1169	−.1167	−.1168	−.1170	−.11700
.8910	−.14748	−.1432	−.1384	−.1340	−.1304	−.1280	−.1269	−.1266	−.1268	−.1270	−.12705
.9511	−.15874	−.1546	−.1505	−.1467	−.1432	−.1409	−.1396	−.1390	−.1393	−.1400	−.14034
.9877	−.16554	−.1578	−.1528	−.1490	−.1459	−.1433	−.1420	−.1416	−.1419	−.1422	−.14240
1.00	−.16757	−.1589	−.1534	−.1497	−.1463	−.1439	−.1428	−.1420	−.1424	−.1429	−.14320

TABLE III.—FUNCTION $-x\frac{dQ}{dx}$ AGAINST x

x_1 \ x	0	0.1	0.2	0.3	0.4	0.5	0.6	0.7	0.8	0.9	1.0
$\lambda=\frac{1}{2}$											
0.1564	0	−0.00175	0.00300	0.01410	0.03200	0.05500	0.08040	0.10290	0.12160	0.14112	0.15974
.3090	0	.00320	.01344	.03075	.05584	.08740	.11904	.14840	.17472	.19980	.22254
.4540	0	.00975	.02600	.04944	.07712	.10840	.14040	.17136	.20352	.23202	.25584
.5878	0	.01825	.04000	.06450	.09200	.12125	.15192	.18585	.21760	.24750	.26922
.7071	0	.02648	.05100	.07644	.10304	.13325	.16512	.19880	.23040	.25875	.27642
.8090	0	.03255	.05760	.08220	.10800	.13750	.17040	.20405	.23616	.26550	.28349
.8910	0	.04000	.06704	.09420	.12096	.14850	.17712	.20846	.24160	.27612	.31319
.9511	0	.04620	.07488	.10125	.12640	.15250	.18120	.21420	.24800	.28440	.32400
.9877	0	.05100	.08080	.10575	.13056	.15750	.18600	.21945	.25320	.29232	.33100
1.00	0	.05240	.08288	.10770	.13280	.15950	.18900	.22120	.25760	.29610	.33600
$\lambda=1$											
0.1564	0	0.00475	0.00960	0.01500	0.02080	0.02650	0.03300	0.04025	0.04800	0.05670	0.06727
.3090	0	.00900	.01804	.02760	.03720	.04775	.05880	.07098	.08400	.09810	.11586
.4540	0	.01390	.02720	.04050	.05480	.06875	.08400	.09982	.11720	.13500	.15343
.5878	0	.01800	.03440	.05040	.06680	.08375	.10110	.11984	.13920	.15930	.17918
.7071	0	.02265	.04240	.06090	.07920	.09800	.11700	.13580	.15488	.17424	.19592
.8090	0	.02620	.04792	.06810	.08784	.10700	.12648	.14630	.16640	.18900	.21471
.8910	0	.02955	.05424	.07680	.09800	.11900	.13680	.15575	.17600	.20025	.22800
.9511	0	.03187	.05840	.08244	.10480	.12540	.14496	.16450	.18688	.21330	.24250
.9877	0	.03298	.06020	.08466	.10720	.12875	.14880	.16940	.19120	.21780	.24700
1.00	0	.03322	.06050	.08511	.10800	.13000	.15030	.17066	.19280	.21915	.24850
$\lambda=2$											
0.1564	0	0.00295	0.00588	0.00873	0.01160	0.01440	0.01704	0.01960	0.02208	0.02430	0.02641
.3090	0	.00492	.00998	.01500	.02000	.02500	.03000	.03486	.03928	.04338	.04712
.4540	0	.00712	.01440	.02175	.02920	.03650	.04380	.05110	.05800	.06435	.07058
.5878	0	.00929	.01874	.02820	.03760	.04695	.05616	.06517	.07440	.08361	.09270
.7071	0	.01114	.02200	.03270	.04336	.05400	.06468	.07546	.08624	.09702	.10800
.8090	0	.01291	.02538	.03729	.04880	.06000	.07128	.08246	.09360	.10503	.11700
.8910	0	.01450	.02840	.04161	.05424	.06635	.07800	.08967	.10160	.11394	.12705
.9511	0	.01560	.03068	.04524	.05920	.07270	.08580	.09870	.11168	.12510	.14034
.9877	0	.01600	.03122	.04590	.06004	.07390	.08736	.10038	.11360	.12744	.14240
1.00	0	.01616	.03142	.04614	.06040	.07430	.08760	.10080	.11424	.12780	.14320

TABLE III.—FUNCTION $-x\frac{dQ}{dx}$ AGAINST x—CONCLUDED

x_1 \ x	0	0.1564	0.3090	0.4540	0.5878	0.7071	0.8090	0.8910	0.9511	0.9877	1.00
$\lambda=\frac{1}{2}$											
0.1564	0	0.00016	0.01548	0.04404	0.07730	0.10430	0.12459	0.13944	0.15170	0.15803	0.15974
.3090	0	.00813	.03275	.07255	.11521	.15061	.17798	.19780	.21305	.22075	.22254
.4540	0	.01822	.05145	.09375	.13696	.17465	.20638	.22988	.24491	.25335	.25584
.5878	0	.03019	.06705	.10760	.14960	.18844	.22167	.24502	.26013	.26668	.26922
.7071	0	.04035	.07849	.11940	.16164	.20082	.23299	.25750	.27059	.27458	.27642
.8090	0	.04708	.08451	.12394	.16635	.20683	.23987	.26329	.27725	.28248	.28349
.8910	0	.05591	.09641	.13575	.17340	.21072	.24472	.27265	.29579	.30767	.31319
.9511	0	.05319	.10351	.14006	.17752	.21637	.25079	.28111	.30435	.31952	.32400
.9877	0	.06913	.10800	.14483	.18222	.22168	.25767	.28868	.31196	.32604	.33100
1.00	0	.07093	.11000	.14710	.18516	.22450	.26131	.29225	.31624	.33088	.33600
$\lambda=1$											
0.1564	0	0.00746	0.01560	0.02388	0.03233	0.04066	0.04854	0.05569	0.06182	0.06608	0.06727
.3090	0	.01408	.02849	.04299	.05749	.07212	.08503	.09667	.10681	.11349	.11586
.4540	0	.02140	.04175	.06233	.08217	.10112	.11876	.13347	.14476	.15112	.15343
.5878	0	.02734	.05185	.07582	.09893	.12148	.14093	.15726	.16892	.17680	.17918
.7071	0	.03394	.06263	.08953	.11462	.13718	.15662	.17250	.18537	.19280	.19592
.8090	0	.03871	.06999	.09843	.12403	.14764	.16827	.18693	.20163	.21058	.21471
.8910	0	.04387	.07880	.10873	.13431	.15733	.17798	.19807	.21400	.22470	.22800
.9511	0	.04723	.08442	.11622	.14242	.16581	.18898	.21072	.22826	.23902	.24250
.9877	0	.04884	.08683	.11917	.14666	.17098	.19335	.21491	.23254	.24347	.24700
1.00	0	.04903	.08720	.12008	.14801	.17225	.19497	.21633	.23445	.24495	.24850
$\lambda=2$											
0.1564	0	0.00461	0.00899	0.01317	0.01675	0.01980	0.02209	0.02406	0.02539	0.02608	0.02641
.3090	0	.00777	.01545	.02270	.02939	.03521	.03964	.04304	.04546	.04662	.04712
.4540	0	.01123	.02243	.03314	.04291	.05162	.05849	.06397	.06762	.06993	.07058
.5878	0	.01459	.02905	.04268	.05508	.06583	.07524	.08277	.08826	.09156	.09270
.7071	0	.01733	.03368	.04908	.06336	.07623	.08721	.09605	.10272	.10667	.10800
.8090	0	.02000	.03835	.05493	.06989	.08323	.09457	.10398	.11109	.11556	.11700
.8910	0	.02240	.04277	.06084	.07665	.09051	.10266	.11280	.12060	.12544	.12705
.9511	0	.02418	.04650	.06660	.08417	.09963	.11294	.12385	.13249	.13828	.14034
.9877	0	.02468	.04722	.06765	.08576	.10133	.11488	.12617	.13496	.14045	.14240
1.00	0	.02485	.04740	.06796	.08600	.10175	.11553	.12652	.13544	.14114	.14320

TABLE IV.—FUNCTION $x\frac{dF}{dx}$ AGAINST x

x_1 \ x	0	0.1564	0.3090	0.4540	0.5878	0.7071	0.8030	0.8910	0.9511	0.9877	1.00
$\lambda=\frac{1}{2}$											
0		−1.00	−1.00	−1.00	−1.00	−1.00	−1.00	−1.00	−1.00	−1.00	−1.00
.1564	0	±∞	−1.99303	−1.46458	−1.26170	−1.19621	−1.06855	−1.01614	−.98157	−.96187	−.95540
.3090	0	.79883	±∞	−2.78366	−1.80906	−1.45440	−1.26665	−1.15397	−1.08539	−1.04803	−1.03613
.4540	0	.34549	1.42781	±∞	−3.41645	−2.10410	−1.64634	−1.41821	−1.29261	−1.22783	−1.20769
.5878	0	.21336	.63897	1.99871	±∞	−4.03919	−2.43710	−1.89999	−1.64972	−1.53080	−1.49506
.7071	0	.16030	.41011	.93133	2.61274	±∞	−4.81641	−2.90544	−2.29684	−2.04745	−1.97675
.8090	0	.13685	.31447	.61779	1.26965	3.38854	±∞	−5.98509	−3.67916	−3.01834	−2.85105
.8910	0	.12638	.26841	.48398	.87241	1.72629	4.53529	±∞	−8.07131	−5.23205	−4.69950
.9511	0	.12189	.24512	.41901	.70492	1.24095	2.45465	6.55772	±∞	−12.97115	−9.87489
.9877	0	.12017	.23403	.38579	.63067	1.05355	1.88986	3.90597	11.31495	±∞	−37.32797
1.00	0	.11974	.23074	.37922	.60914	1.00201	1.75072	3.12125	8.32837	35.30113	∞
$\lambda=1$											
0		−1.00	−1.00	−1.00	−1.00	−1.00	−1.00	−1.00	−1.00	−1.00	−1.00
.1564	0	∞	−2.02000	−1.51292	−1.33779	−1.24658	−1.19054	−1.15399	−1.13052	−1.11731	−1.11302
.3090	0	.95868	∞	−3.04334	−2.02983	−1.68390	−1.50919	−1.40738	−1.34642	−1.31349	−1.30302
.4540	0	.46900	1.88440	∞	−4.09131	−2.72121	−2.06744	−1.82101	−1.68705	−1.61849	−1.59724
.5878	0	.31308	.92928	2.82641	∞	−5.50622	−3.21099	−2.54678	−2.24206	−2.09846	−2.05546
.7071	0	.24131	.62835	1.41541	3.87876	∞	−6.66344	−4.05123	−3.23335	−2.90145	−2.80771
.8090	0	.20322	.49077	.97474	1.98748	5.20307	∞	−8.68248	−5.35062	−4.40589	−4.16788
.8910	0	.18179	.41840	.77603	1.40438	2.75532	7.12155	∞	−12.11751	−7.84804	−7.05128
.9511	0	.16974	.37883	.67518	1.15039	2.02152	3.96099	10.43287	∞	−19.95323	−15.16694
.9877	0	.16360	.35885	.62606	1.03526	1.73314	3.09010	6.32119	18.08469	∞	−58.44076
1.00	0	.16171	.35272	.61123	1.00149	1.65306	2.87394	5.56464	13.39780	56.18133	∞
$\lambda=2$											
0		−1.00	−1.00	−1.00	−1.00	−1.00	−1.00	−1.00	−1.00	−1.00	−1.00
.1564	0	∞	−2.02393	−1.52266	−1.35649	−1.27453	−1.22695	−1.19742	−1.17919	−1.16922	−1.16602
.3090	0	1.00761	∞	−3.10970	−2.08915	−1.75281	−1.58947	−1.49766	−1.44428	−1.41600	−1.40710
.4540	0	.51046	2.06247	∞	−4.31441	−2.73708	−2.22262	−1.97925	−1.85005	−1.78491	−1.76488
.5878	0	.34911	1.05685	3.22439	∞	−5.73646	−3.53335	−2.82827	−2.51033	−2.36233	−2.31828
.7071	0	.27224	.73259	1.67673	4.59422	∞	−7.55951	−4.61041	−3.70046	−3.33496	−3.23228
.8090	0	.22951	.57977	1,18224	2.43642	6.35690	∞	−10.17771	−6.27367	−5.17695	−4.90194
.8910	0	.20419	.49669	.95382	1.75803	3.46676	8.90569	∞	−14.59886	−9.43808	−8.47927
.9511	0	.18920	.44984	.83532	1.45735	2.58738	5.06961	13.24395	∞	−24.56797	−18.64159
.9877	0	.18124	42561	.77664	1.31929	2.23798	4.00223	8.15130	23.10187	∞	−73.19713
1.00	0	.17874	.41808	.75876	1.27851	2.14041	3.73593	7.20978	17.22166	71.52164	∞

TABLE V.—FUNCTION P AGAINST x FOR $\tau=60°$

x_1 \ x	0	0.1564	0.3090	0.5878	0.8090	0.9511	1.00
			$\lambda=\frac{1}{2}$				
0.1564	2.2478	1.9613	1.4980	0.8830	0.5696	0.4113	0.3600
.3090	1.5673	1.4980	1.2413	.7646	.4963	.3580	.3046
.5878	.9259	.8830	.7646	.5146	.3280	.2230	.1866
.8090	.6084	.5696	.4963	.3280	.1946	.1146	.0826
.9511	.4482	.4113	.3580	.2230	.1146	.0446	.0213
1.00	.3986	.3600	.3046	.1866	.0826	.0213	0
			$\lambda=1$				
0.1564	2.2463	2.0200	1.5000	0.8834	0.5700	0.4200	0.3734
.3090	1.5655	1.5000	1.3134	.8267	5300	.3800	.3300
.5878	.9228	.8834	.8267	.6069	.3900	.2567	.2134
.8090	.6039	.5700	.5300	.3900	.2400	.1367	.1000
.9511	.4425	.4200	.3800	.2567	.1367	.0567	.0267
1.00	.3924	.3734	.3300	.2134	.1000	.0267	0
			$\lambda=2$				
0.1564	2.1727	2.2333	1.5200	0.8667	0.5333	0.3667	0.3133
.3090	1.4928	1.5200	1.2667	.7700	.4900	.3367	.2867
.5878	.8488	.8667	.7700	.5367	.3667	.2500	.2067
8090	.5295	.5333	.4900	.3667	.2433	.1467	.1067
.9511	.3678	.3667	.3367	.2500	.1467	.0600	.0267
1.00	.3177	.3133	2867	.2067	.1067	.0267	0

TABLE VI.—FUNCTION P AGAINST x FOR $\tau=120°$

x_1 \ x	0	0.1564	0.3090	0.5878	0.8090	0.9511	1.00
			$\lambda=\frac{1}{2}$				
0.1564	2.2825	1.6693	1.2393	0.8000	0.5377	0.3960	0.3547
.3090	1.6020	1.2393	.9860	.6460	.4360	.3160	.2813
.5878	.9606	.8000	.6460	.4280	.2777	.1893	.1640
.8090	.6431	.5377	.4360	.2777	.1693	.0977	.0777
.9511	.4829	.3960	.3160	.1893	.0977	.0360	.0167
1.00	.4333	.3547	2813	.1640	.0777	.0167	0
			$\lambda=1$				
0.1564	2.4163	1.8234	1.3900	0.9067	0.6500	0.5100	0.4600
.3090	1.7355	1.3934	1.1100	.7567	.5300	.4134	.3634
.5878	1.0928	.9067	.7567	.4967	.3434	.2534	.2067
.8090	.7739	.6500	.5300	.3434	.2067	.1300	.0934
.9511	.6125	.5100	.4134	.2534	.1300	.0634	.0300
1.00	.5624	.4600	.3634	.2067	.0934	.0300	0
			$\lambda=2$				
0.1564	2.4794	1.8934	1.5133	1.0267	0.7267	0.5600	0.5067
.3090	1.7985	1.5133	1 2800	.8800	.6067	.4534	.4000
.5878	1.1555	1.0267	.8800	.6000	.3934	.2667	.2200
.8090	.8362	.7267	.6067	.3934	.2334	.1334	.1000
.9511	.6745	.5600	.4534	2667	.1334	.0534	.0267
1.00	.6244	.5067	.4000	.2200	.1000	.0267	0

TABLE VII.—FUNCTION P AGAINST x FOR $\tau=180°$

x_1 \ x	0	0.1564	0.3090	0.5878	0.8090	0.9511	1.00
			$\lambda=\frac{1}{2}$				
0.1564	2.1518	1.5686	1.1586	0.7106	0.4653	0.3220	0.2786
.3090	1.4713	1.1586	.9320	.5973	.3920	.2753	.2320
.5878	.8299	.7106	.5973	.3986	.2573	.1736	.1386
.8090	.5124	.4653	.3920	.2573	.1600	.0986	.0680
.9511	.3522	.3220	.2753	.1736	.0986	.0470	.0220
1.00	.3026	.2786	.2320	.1386	.0680	.0220	0
			$\lambda=1$				
0.1564	2.3063	1.6867	1.2667	0.8100	0.5600	0.4100	0.3634
.3090	1.6255	1.2667	.9934	.6534	.4534	.3300	.2934
.5878	.9828	.8100	.6534	.4367	.2934	.2034	.1767
.8090	.6639	.5600	.4534	.2934	.1934	.1100	.0834
.9511	.5025	.4100	.3300	.2034	.1100	.0133	.0200
1.00	.4524	.3634	.2934	.1767	.0834	.0200	0
			$\lambda=2$				
0.1564	2.4060	1.7433	1.3000	0.8400	0.5933	0.4633	0.4200
.3090	1.7251	1.3000	.9933	.6533	.4600	.3466	.3066
.5878	1.0821	.8400	.6533	.4200	.2733	.1966	.1633
.8090	.7628	.5933	.4600	.2733	.1600	.1000	.0733
.9511	.6011	.4633	.3466	.1966	.1000	.0400	.0200
1.00	.5511	.4200	.3066	.1633	.0733	.0200	0

TABLE VIII.—FUNCTION P AGAINST x FOR $\tau=240°$

x_1 \ x	0	0.1564	0.3090	0.5878	0.8090	0.9511	1.00
			$\lambda=\frac{1}{2}$				
0.1564	1.8785	1.4720	1.1153	0.5693	0.2800	0.1220	0.0680
.3090	1.1980	1.1153	.9320	.5450	.2853	.1287	.0720
.5878	.5566	.5693	.5453	.4066	.2413	.1220	.0773
.8090	.2391	.2800	.2853	.2413	.1573	.0787	.0453
.9511	.0789	.1220	.1287	.1220	.0787	.0320	.0120
1.00	.0293	.0680	.0720	.0773	.0453	.0120	0
			$\lambda=1$				
0.1564	2.0296	1.5867	1.1833	0.6767	0.3967	0.2400	0.1833
.3090	1.3482	1.1833	.9633	.5933	.3600	.2234	.1767
.5878	.7071	.6767	.5933	.4067	.2567	.1633	.1267
.8090	.3872	.3967	.3600	.2567	.1567	.0900	.0633
.9511	.2258	.2400	.2234	.1633	.0900	.0433	.0200
1.00	.1757	.1833	.1767	.1267	.0633	.0200	0
			$\lambda=2$				
0.1564	2.1927	1.7033	1.3033	0.8167	0.5300	0.3700	0.3167
.3090	1.5118	1.3033	1.0967	.7300	.4767	.3300	.2767
.5878	.8688	.8167	.7300	.5200	.3433	.2200	.1800
.8090	.5495	.5300	.4767	.3433	.2167	.1267	.0933
.9511	.3878	.3700	.3300	.2200	.1267	.0567	.0267
1.00	.3377	.3167	.2767	.1800	.0933	.0267	0

TABLE IX.—FUNCTION P AGAINST x FOR $\tau=300°$

x_1 \ x	0	0.1564	0.3090	0.5878	0.8090	0.9511	1.00
$\lambda=\frac{1}{2}$							
0.1564	1.4198	1.4933	0.9400	0.3100	−0.0600	−0.2734	−0.3400
.3090	.7393	.9400	1.0566	.4566	.0766	−.1534	−.2434
.5878	.0979	.3100	.4566	.4400	.2233	.0233	−.0634
.8090	−.2196	−.0600	.0766	.2233	.2100	.0866	.0133
.9511	−.3798	−.2634	−.1534	.0233	.0866	.0466	.0066
1.00	−.4294	−.3400	−.2434	−.0634	.0133	.0066	0
$\lambda=1$							
0.1564	1.4296	1.3467	0.9567	0.2433	−0.0967	−0.2700	−0.3200
.3090	.7488	.9567	.9067	.4100	.0333	−.1600	−.2133
.5878	.1061	.2433	.4100	.4333	.1833	.0167	−.0367
.8090	−.2128	−.0967	.0333	.1833	.1900	.0900	.0367
.9511	−.3742	−.2700	−.1600	.0167	.0900	.0567	.0200
1.00	−.4243	−.3200	−.2133	−.0367	.0367	.0200	0
$\lambda=2$							
0.1564	1.6794	1.9600	1.3000	0.5534	0.1734	−0.0100	−0.0600
.3090	.9985	1.3000	1 1200	.6334	.2834	.0867	.0234
.5878	.3555	.5534	.6334	.5234	.3000	.1434	.0800
.8090	.0362	.1734	.2834	.3000	.1434	.0967	.0534
.9511	−.1255	−.0100	.0867	.1434	.0967	.0467	.0200
1.00	−.1756	−.0600	.0234	.0800	.0534	.0200	0

TABLE X.—FUNCTION $\frac{dP}{dx}$ AGAINST τ FOR $\lambda=\frac{1}{2}$

x_1 \ τ (deg)	60	120	180	240	300
$x=0$					
0.1564	2.2667	−3.3333	−6.0000	−2.2667	3.3333
.3090	.2667	−1.8667	−1.9333	−.2667	1.8667
.4540	--------	--------	--------	--------	--------
.5878	−.4133	−1.0267	−.8333	.4133	1.0267
.7071	--------	--------	--------	--------	--------
.8090	−.3300	−.7333	−.4800	.3300	.7333
.8910	--------	--------	--------	--------	--------
.9511	−.3017	−.5733	−.3000	.3017	.5733
.9877	--------	--------	--------	--------	--------
1.00	−.2600	−.5400	−.2600	.2600	.5400
$x=1.00$					
0.1564	−0.9367	−0.8633	−0.9333	−1.0133	−1.190
.3090	−.8767	−.7467	−.7933	−.9967	−1.340
.4540	--------	--------	--------	--------	--------
.5878	−.7300	−.5800	−.6183	−.8533	−1.4133
.7071	--------	--------	--------	--------	--------
.8090	−.5850	−.4700	−.4867	−.6650	−1.1567
.8910	--------	--------	--------	--------	--------
.9511	−.5033	−.4100	−.4000	−.4733	−.6700
.9877	--------	--------	--------	--------	--------
1.00	−.4767	−.3967	−.3693	−.4333	−.4333

TABLE XI.—FUNCTION $\frac{dP}{dx}$ AGAINST τ FOR $\lambda=1$

x_1 \ τ (deg)	60	120	180	240	300
$x=0$					
0.1564	5.0667	−8.6667	−10.3333	−5.0667	8.6667
.3090	.7667	−1.9333	−3.4667	−.7667	1.9333
.4540	--------	--------	--------	--------	--------
.5878	.2133	−.9667	−1.1000	−.2133	.9667
.7071	--------	--------	--------	--------	--------
.8090	−.0533	−.6933	−.7500	.0533	.6933
.8910	--------	--------	--------	--------	--------
.9511	−.1400	−.6400	−.5200	.1400	.6400
.9877	--------	--------	--------	--------	--------
1.00	−.1667	−.6200	−.4800	.1667	.6200
$x=1.00$					
0.1564	−0.9567	−0.8533	−0.8400	−0.9533	−1.0300
.3090	−.9733	−.7933	−.7600	−.8667	−1.0733
.4540	--------	--------	--------	--------	--------
.5878	−.8133	−.6267	−.5767	−.6600	−.9533
.7071	--------	--------	--------	--------	--------
.8090	−.6633	−.5100	−.4600	−.4833	−.6467
.8910	--------	--------	--------	--------	--------
.9511	−.5967	−.4633	−.4100	−.4033	−.3333
.9877	--------	--------	--------	--------	--------
1.00	−.5533	−.4467	−.3800	−.3633	−.2900

TABLE XII.—FUNCTION $\frac{dP}{dx}$ AGAINST τ FOR $\lambda=2$

x_1 \ τ (deg)	60	120	180	240	300
$x=0$					
0.1564	11.3333	−8.833	−16.3333	−11.3333	8.833
.3090	2.8000	−2.400	−5.6667	−2.8000	2.400
.4540	--------	--------	--------	--------	--------
.5878	.6833	−.9333	−1.2000	−.6833	.9333
.7071	--------	--------	--------	--------	--------
.8090	.2533	−.6667	−.7667	−.2533	.6667
.8910	--------	--------	--------	--------	--------
.9511	.2000	−.5867	−.6333	−.2000	.5867
.9877	--------	--------	--------	--------	--------
1.00	.1600	−.5467	−.5667	−.1600	.5467
$x=1.00$					
0.1564	−0.9733	−0.9067	−0.7733	−0.7467	−0.8000
.3090	−1.0533	−.7600	−.6400	−.7200	−.8400
.4540	--------	--------	--------	--------	--------
.5878	−.9467	−.6600	−.5000	−.4800	−.7200
.7071	--------	--------	--------	--------	--------
.8090	−.7200	−.5667	−.4867	−.4067	−.5467
.8910	--------	--------	--------	--------	--------
.9511	−.6200	−.5000	−.4500	−.3600	−.4267
.9877	--------	--------	--------	--------	--------
1.00	−.5600	−.4867	−.3800	−.3400	−.2333

TABLE XIII.—FUNCTION $-x\frac{dP}{dx}$ AGAINST x FOR $\lambda=\frac{1}{2}$

x_1 \ x	0.1564	0.3090	0.5878	0.8090	0.9511	1.00
			$\tau=60°$			
0.1564	0.399	0.890	1.044	0.964	0.933	0.9367
.3090	.194	.570	.877	.787	.810	.8767
.5878	.105	.261	.526	.623	.695	.7300
.8090	.074	.159	.375	.460	.532	.5850
.9511	.055	.124	.309	.379	.448	.5033
1.00	.050	.111	.280	.347	.417	.4767
			$\tau=120°$			
0.1564	0.526	0.662	0.785	0.834	0.859	0.8633
.3090	.316	.457	.609	.690	.731	.7467
.5878	.162	.269	.411	.508	.562	.5800
.8090	.117	.200	.321	.406	.453	4700
.9511	.085	.154	.266	.342	.391	.4100
1.00	.075	.142	.249	.328	.375	.3967
			$\tau=180°$			
0.1564	0.507	0.679	0.736	0.823	0.908	0.9333
.3090	.264	.465	.611	.663	.752	.7933
.5878	.118	.238	.394	.482	.579	.6183
.8090	.064	.149	.273	.377	.454	.4867
.9511	.044	.106	.208	.285	.358	.4000
1.00	.041	.101	.184	.260	.334	.3693
			$\tau=240°$			
0.1564	0.397	0.6999	0.924	0.987	1.0090	1.0133
.3090	.147	.431	.771	.905	.973	.9967
.5878	.008	.091	.381	.663	.816	.8533
.8090	−.020	.025	.159	.400	.598	.6650
.9511	−.018	.002	.059	.228	.4015	.4733
1.00	−.014	−.008	.042	.194	.363	.4333
			$\tau=300°$			
0.1564	0.6200	0.9070	1.1330	1.216	1.209	1.1900
.3090	−.2030	.3380	1.0800	1.3222	1.350	1.3400
.5878	−.2074	−.1591	.3590	1.021	1.360	1.4133
.8090	−.1372	−.2385	−.1734	.402	.970	1.1567
.9511	−.1175	−.2148	−.2933	−.025	.465	.6700
1.00	−.0940	−.2042	−.3245	−.067	.284	.4333

TABLE XIV.—FUNCTION $-x\frac{dP}{dx}$ AGAINST x FOR $\lambda=1$

x_1 \ x	0.1564	0.3090	0.5878	0.8090	0.9511	1.00
			$\tau=60°$			
0.1564	0.450	0.943	1.020	0.990	0.964	0.9567
.3090	.130	.463	.970	.918	.940	.9733
.5878	.050	.163	.568	.778	.811	.8133
.8090	.038	.117	.348	.602	.660	.6633
.9511	.035	.105	.290	.468	.570	.5967
1.00	.029	.099	.270	.427	.528	.5533
			$\tau=120°$			
0.1564	0.515	0.711	0.817	0.849	0.853	0.8533
.3090	.318	.480	.640	.7295	.778	.7933
.5878	.167	.292	.466	.559	.610	.6267
.8090	.124	.228	.375	.464	.501	.5100
.9511	.106	.191	.336	.426	.460	.4633
1.00	.095	.179	.318	.404	.440	.4467
			$\tau=180°$			
0.1564	0.518	0.668	0.770	0.814	0.834	0.840
.3090	.307	.470	.622	.7105	.748	.760
.5878	.162	.283	.419	.510	.560	.577
.8090	.110	.191	.319	.403	.4496	.460
.9511	.087	.158	.2705	.350	.395	.410
1.00	.080	.147	.2505	.326	.369	.380
			$\tau=240°$			
0.1564	0.442	0.733	0.890	0.937	0.9505	0.9533
.3090	.205	.460	.688	.794	.8500	.8667
.5878	.068	.198	.415	.565	.6400	.6600
.8090	.022	.095	.256	.379	.456	.4833
.9511	.002	.052	.163	.274	.364	.4033
1.00	.0006	.039	.134	.235	.324	.3633
			$\tau=300°$			
0.1564	0.241	0.967	1.1580	1.1033	1.0533	1.0300
.3090	−.051	.298	1.1266	1.2224	1.1300	1.0733
.5878	−.175	−.259	.516	.995	1.0330	.9533
.8090	−.128	−.244	−.205	.314	.6067	.6467
.9511	−.108	−.230	−.330	−.087	.215	.3333
1.00	−.109	−.214	−.308	−.080	.185	.2900

TABLE XV.—FUNCTION $-x\frac{dP}{dx}$ AGAINST x FOR $\lambda=2$

x_1 \ x	0.1564	0.3090	0.5878	0.8090	0.9511	1.00
$\tau=60°$						
0.1564	0.880	1.019	1.061	1.040	0.9985	0.9733
.3090	.097	.723	.834	.939	1.023	1.0533
.5878	.035	.282	.448	.642	.861	.9467
.8090	.027	.110	.305	.509	.6615	.7200
.9511	.021	.081	.235	.422	.568	.6200
1.00	.017	.067	.210	.384	.514	.5600
$\tau=120°$						
0.1564	0.473	0.655	0.856	0.922	0.918	0.9067
.3090	.260	.480	.781	.882	.8195	.7600
.5878	.142	.301	.583	.750	.700	.6600
.8090	.117	.239	.442	.560	.5775	.5667
.9511	.1035	.221	.379	.462	.495	.5000
1.00	.0942	.210	.358	.441	.477	.4867
$\tau=180°$						
0.1564	0.551	0.707	0.752	0.740	0.7550	0.7733
.3090	.373	.516	.581	.612	.631	.6400
.5878	.220	.327	.419	.465	.491	.5000
.8090	.153	.256	.332	.379	.451	.4867
.9511	.124	.200	.281	.327	.394	.4500
1.00	.122	.197	.262	.301	.351	.3800
$\tau=240°$						
0.1564	0.439	0.689	0.893	0.914	0.832	0.7467
.3090	.208	.406	.708	.814	.788	.7200
.5878	.077	.200	.460	.646	.585	.4800
.8090	.043	.119	.322	.489	.452	.4067
.9511	.033	.100	.278	.3996	.391	.3600
1.00	.029	.091	.262	.381	.376	.3400
$\tau=300°$						
0.1564	0.847	1.087	1.202	1.121	0.943	0.8000
.3090	.046	.482	1.000	1.118	1.039	.8400
.5878	−.149	−.040	.481	.862	.837	.7200
.8090	−.127	−.161	.162	.498	.5585	.5467
.9511	−.107	−.160	.045	.281	.412	.4267
1.00	−.100	−.140	−.008	.166	.230	.2333

TABLE XVI.—VALUES OF $\sum -x\frac{dP}{dx}$ AGAINST x FOR 3-BLAD AND 6-BLADE PROPELLERS

[For 3-blade propeller, $\tau=120°$ and 240°; for 6-blade propeller, $\tau=60°$, 120°, 180°, 240°, and 30

x_1 \ x	0.1564	0.3090	0.5878	0.8090	0.9511	1.00
3-blade propeller; $\lambda=\frac{1}{2}$						
0	0	0	0	0	0	0
.1564	.923	1.361	1.709	1.821	1.868	1.8766
.3090	.463	.888	1.380	1.595	1.704	1.7434
.5878	.170	.360	.792	1.171	1.378	1.4333
.8090	.097	.225	.480	.806	1.051	1.135
.9511	.067	156	.325	.570	.7925	.8833
1.00	.061	.134	.291	.522	.738	.8300
3-blade propeller; $\lambda=1$						
0.1564	0.957	1.444	1.707	1.786	1.8035	1.8066
.3090	.523	.940	1.328	1.5235	1.628	1.660
.5878	.235	.490	.881	1.124	1.250	1.2867
.8090	.146	.323	.631	.843	.957	.9933
.9511	.108	.243	.499	.700	.824	.8666
1.00	.0956	.218	.452	.639	.764	.8100
3-blade propeller; $\lambda=2$						
0	0	0	0	0	0	0
.1564	.912	1.344	1.749	1.836	1.750	1.6534
.3090	.468	.886	1.489	1.696	1.6075	1.5067
.5878	.219	.501	1.043	1.396	1.285	1.1400
.8090	.160	.358	.764	1.049	1.0295	.9734
.9511	.1365	.321	.657	.8616	.886	.8600
1.00	.1232	.301	.620	.822	.853	.8267
6-blade propeller; $\lambda=\frac{1}{2}$						
0	0	0	0	0	0	0
.1564	2.4490	3.837	4.622	4.824	4.918	4.9366
.3090	.718	2.261	3.948	4.367	4.616	4.7534
.5878	.1856	.6999	2.071	3.297	4.012	4.1949
.8090	.0978	.2945	.9546	2.045	3.007	3.3634
.9511	.0485	.1712	.5487	1.209	2.0635	2.4566
1.00	.0580	.1418	.4305	1.062	1.773	2.1093
6-blade propeller; $\lambda=1$						
0	0	0	0	0	0	0
.1564	2.166	4.022	4.655	4.6933	4.6548	4.6333
.3090	.909	2.171	4.0466	4.3654	4.446	4.4666
.5878	.272	.677	2.384	3.407	3.654	3.6303
.8090	.166	.387	1.093	2.162	2.6733	2.7633
.9511	.122	.276	.7295	1.431	2.004	2.2066
1.00	.0956	.250	.6645	1.312	1.846	2.0333
6-blade propeller; $\lambda=2$						
0	0	0	0	0	0	0
.1564	3.190	4.157	4.764	4.737	4.4465	4.200
.3090	.984	2.607	3.904	4.365	4.3005	4.040
.5878	.325	1.070	2.391	3.365	3.474	3.3067
.8090	.213	.563	1.563	2.435	2.7005	2.7268
.9511	.1745	.442	1.218	1.8916	2.260	2.3567
1.00	.1622	.425	1.084	1.673	1.948	2.000

THE THEORY OF PROPELLERS

III—THE SLIPSTREAM CONTRACTION WITH NUMERICAL VALUES FOR TWO-BLADE AND FOUR-BLADE PROPELLERS

BY THEODORE THEODORSEN

National Advisory Committee for Aeronautics

Report No. 777, 1944

SUMMARY

As the conditions of the ultimate wake are of concern both theoretically and practically, the magnitude of the slipstream contraction has been calculated. It will be noted that the contraction in a representative case is of the order of only 1 percent of the propeller diameter. In consequence, all calculations need involve only first-order effects. Curves and tables are given for the contraction coefficient of two-blade and four-blade propellers for various values of the advance ratio; the contraction coefficient is defined as the contraction in the diameter of the wake helix in terms of the wake diameter at infinity. The contour lines of the wake helix are also shown at four values of the advance ratio in comparison with the contour lines for an infinite number of blades.

INTRODUCTION

Since reference is often made to the wake infinitely far behind the propeller, it is desirable to establish certain relationships between the dimensions of the propeller and those of the wake helix at infinity. The present paper considers the relationship of the propeller diameter and the wake diameter, or the problem of the slipstream contraction.

The discussion is restricted to a consideration of first-order effects, that is, to the determination of the contraction per unit of loading for infinitely small loadings only. It will be seen that the contractions are indeed very small, of the order of a few percent of the propeller diameter, and that the high-order terms are therefore not of concern. The interference velocity accordingly is neglected as small compared with the stream velocity. The wake helix lies on a perfect cylinder and the pitch angle is everywhere the same. It is noted that the assumption of zero loading corresponds to that used by Goldstein for a different purpose.

SYMBOLS

R tip radius of propeller

r radius of element of vortex sheet

Δr contraction

Δr_0 total contraction or contraction at $\frac{h}{R}=0$

τ angle between starting point of spiral line and point P

H pitch of spiral

θ angular coordinate on vortex sheet

$h=H\frac{\theta}{2\pi}$

λ advance ratio $\left(\frac{H}{2\pi R}\right)$

x ratio of radius of element to tip radius of vortex sheet (r/R)

v_R radial velocity

V advance velocity of propeller

w rearward displacement velocity of helical vortex surface

$\overline{w}=\frac{w}{V}$

p number of blades

κ mass coefficient

$c_s=2\kappa\overline{w}$

Γ circulation at radius x $\left(\Gamma=\frac{\pi c_s \lambda V R}{\kappa}K(x)\right)$

$K(x)$ circulation function for single rotation $\left(\frac{p\Gamma\omega}{2\pi V w}\right)$

ω angular velocity of propeller, radians per second

y_1 radial velocity at point P due to a doublet element at θ,x except for a constant factor

$$\left(y_1=\frac{[\theta\cos(\theta+\tau)-\sin(\theta+\tau)]\,[1-2x^2+\lambda^2\theta^2+x\cos(\theta+\tau)]}{[1+x^2+\lambda^2\theta^2-2x\cos(\theta+\tau)]^{5/2}}\right)$$

$$y_2=\frac{K(x)}{p}\sum_n y_1 \text{ where } n=0,\ 1,\ 2,\ \ldots\ p-1$$

$$Y_1=\int_0^1 y_2\,dx$$

Y_2 angle of contraction, except for a constant factor $\left(Y_2=\int_\theta^\infty Y_1\,d\theta\right)$

Y_3 contour line of contraction, except for a constant factor $\frac{c_s}{\kappa}\frac{\lambda^3}{4}\left(Y_3=\int_0^\infty Y_2\,d\theta\right)$

$\frac{\Delta r_0}{R}$ total contraction in terms of radius $\left(\frac{c_s}{\kappa}\frac{\lambda^3}{4}Y_3\right)$

$\frac{\Delta r_0}{R}\frac{\kappa}{c_s}$ contraction coefficient $\left(\frac{\lambda^3}{4}Y_3\right)$

$$z_1=\sin\phi\left\{\tan^2\phi\left(x^{-1/2}-x^{1/2}\right)E(k)+2x^{1/2}[F(k)-E(k)]\right\}$$

$$w_1=\left[\left(\frac{2}{k}-k\right)F(k)-\frac{2}{k}E(k)\right]^{x=1}$$

THEORY

The radial velocity is obtained by using the Biot-Savart law and integrating over the entire surface of discontinuity. If Δr_0 is the total contraction, the problem is to determine the ratio $\frac{\Delta r_0}{R}$ for various numbers of blades at several advance ratios. Simple expressions referring to zero loading are used throughout.

The radial inward velocity dv_R' at the point P is calculated. (See figs. 1 and 2.) This velocity results from an element

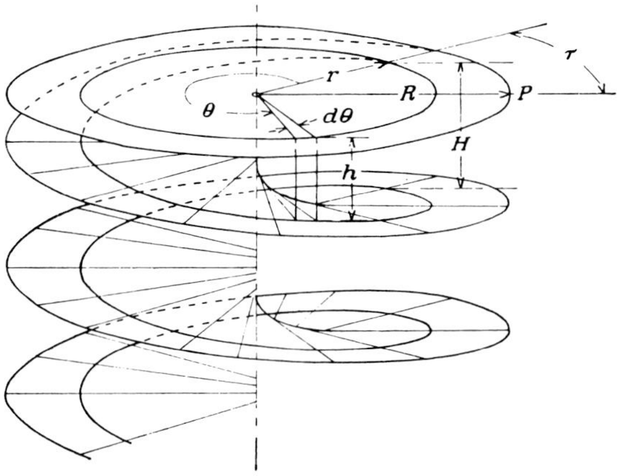

FIGURE 1.—Geometric relationships of wake helix.

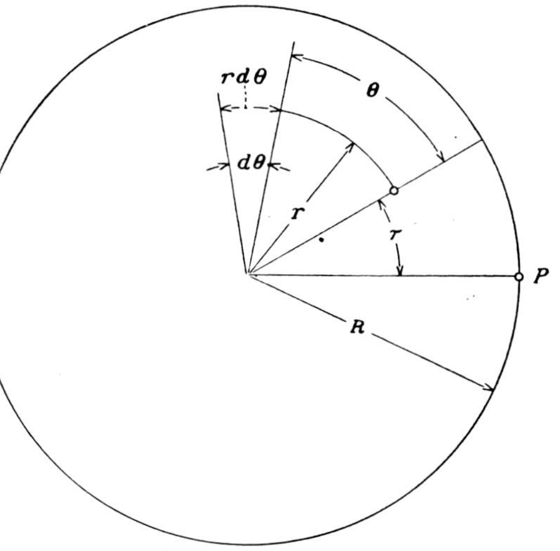

FIGURE 2.—Plan view of wake helix showing geometric relationships.

of circulation $f\,ds$, which is located on a spiral of radius r that starts in a plane perpendicular to the axis and containing the reference point P. The angle between the starting point of the spiral line and the point P is designated τ. The spiral extends below the plane to infinity. If the pitch of this spiral is designated H, the element at a projected angle θ from the starting point of the spiral is then at a distance h below the reference plane where

$$h = H\frac{\theta}{2\pi} \tag{1}$$

By introducing the nondimensional quantities

$$\left.\begin{aligned} \lambda &= \frac{H}{2\pi R} \\ x &= \frac{r}{R} \end{aligned}\right\} \tag{2}$$

in the Biot-Savart law, the following expression is obtained for the radial inward velocity dv_R' due to an element on the wake helix of strength f:

$$dv_R' = -\frac{1}{4\pi}\frac{f\,d\theta}{R}\lambda x\frac{\theta\cos(\theta+\tau)-\sin(\theta+\tau)}{[1+x^2+\lambda^2\theta^2-2x\cos(\theta+\tau)]^{3/2}} \tag{3}$$

By differentiating equation (3) with respect to x, the field of a doublet element on the helical vortex sheet is obtained, the doublet element consisting of two neighboring singlet elements each of strength f. Setting $f\,dx$ equal to Γ and dividing through by the stream velocity V gives

$$d\frac{v_R}{V} = -\frac{1}{4\pi}\frac{\Gamma\,d\theta}{RV}\lambda\frac{[\theta\cos(\theta+\tau)-\sin(\theta+\tau)]\,[1-2x^2+\lambda^2\theta^2+x\cos(\theta+\tau)]}{[1+x^2+\lambda^2\theta^2-2x\cos(\theta+\tau)]^{5/2}} \tag{4}$$

where v_R is the radial velocity at the point P.

Equation (4) may be written in the form

$$d\frac{v_R}{V} = -\frac{1}{4\pi}\frac{\Gamma\,d\theta}{RV}\lambda y_1 \tag{5}$$

where

$$y_1 = \frac{[\theta\cos(\theta+\tau)-\sin(\theta+\tau)]\,[1-2x^2+\lambda^2\theta^2+x\cos(\theta+\tau)]}{[1+x^2+\lambda^2\theta^2-2x\cos(\theta+\tau)]^{5/2}} \tag{6}$$

The function y_1 is plotted against $\theta+\tau$ for four values of λ and various values of τ and x in figures 3 to 6. With

$$\begin{aligned} \Gamma &= \frac{2\pi Vw}{p\omega}K(x) \\ &= \frac{2\pi V^2\overline{w}}{p\omega}K(x) \\ &= \frac{\pi VR\lambda c_s}{p\kappa}K(x) \end{aligned} \tag{7}$$

where

$$\begin{aligned} c_s &= \frac{2\kappa w}{V} \\ &= 2\kappa\overline{w} \end{aligned} \tag{8}$$

substitution in equation (5) gives

$$d\frac{v_R}{V} = -\frac{\lambda^2}{4}\frac{c_s}{\kappa}\frac{K(x)}{p}\,y_1\,d\theta \tag{9}$$

If the point P is at a distance $h=H\frac{\theta}{2\pi}$ below the propeller, integrating equation (9) over the wake yields

$$\frac{v_R}{V}=-\frac{\lambda^2}{4}\frac{c_s}{\kappa}\int_{-\theta}^{\infty}\int_0^1\frac{K(x)}{p}\sum_n y_1\,dx\,d\theta \tag{10}$$

It is noted that, with equally spaced blades, the function

$$\sum_n y_1 \tag{11}$$

is an odd function of θ and

$$\sum_n\int_{-\theta}^{\theta} y_1\,d\theta=0 \tag{12}$$

Equation (10) can therefore be rewritten as

$$\frac{v_R}{V}=-\frac{\lambda^2}{4}\frac{c_s}{\kappa}\int_{\theta}^{\infty}\int_0^1\frac{K(x)}{p}\sum_n y_1\,dx\,d\theta \tag{13}$$

Let

$$\left.\begin{aligned}y_2&=\frac{K(x)}{p}\sum_n y_1\\ Y_1&=\int_0^1 y_2\,dx\\ Y_2&=\int_\theta^\infty Y_1\,d\theta\end{aligned}\right\} \tag{14}$$

Values of Y_1 and Y_2, multiplied by a constant factor for convenience in plotting, are given in tables I to IV for two-blade and four-blade propellers for which λ and θ take on various values. These functions are plotted against θ in figures 7 and 8.

Equation (13) becomes

$$\frac{v_R}{V}=-\frac{\lambda^2}{4}\frac{c_s}{\kappa}Y_2 \tag{15}$$

Now

$$\frac{v_R}{V}=\frac{dr}{dh}=\frac{d\frac{r}{R}}{d\frac{h}{R}}=\frac{1}{\lambda}\frac{dx}{d\theta} \tag{16}$$

Therefore

$$\frac{dx}{d\theta}=\lambda\frac{v_R}{V}=-\frac{\lambda^3}{4}\frac{c_s}{\kappa}Y_2 \tag{17}$$

whence

$$\frac{\Delta r}{R}=\frac{R_2-R_1}{R}=\frac{1}{R}\int_{R_1}^{R_2}dr=\int_{x_1}^{x_2}dx=-\frac{\lambda^3}{4}\frac{c_s}{\kappa}\int_{\theta_1}^{\theta_2}Y_2\,d\theta \tag{18}$$

If R_2 is the radius at the propeller and R_1 is the ultimate radius of the wake ($\theta_2=0$, $\theta_1=\infty$),

$$\frac{\Delta r_0}{R}=\frac{c_s}{\kappa}\frac{\lambda^3}{4}\int_0^\infty Y_2\,d\theta=c_s\frac{\lambda^3}{4\kappa}Y_3 \tag{19}$$

where

$$Y_3=\int_0^\infty Y_2\,d\theta$$

Values of Y_3 are given in tables V and VI and are plotted in figure 9 for two-blade and four-blade propellers for which λ and θ take on various values.

After all substitutions are made, the complete multiple integral for the total contraction is obtained as

$$\frac{\Delta r_0}{R}=\frac{c_s}{\kappa}\frac{\lambda^3}{4}\int_0^\infty\int_0^\infty\int_0^1 K(x)\frac{1}{p}\sum_n y_1(\theta,x)dx\,d\theta\,d\theta$$

(See figs. 10 and 11.)

INFINITE NUMBER OF BLADES

For purposes of comparison, it is useful to obtain the contraction for the case of an infinite number of blades. By resolving the circulation into components parallel to and perpendicular to the axis of the wake, the helical vortices can be replaced by a system of vortices parallel to the axis and another of ring vortices having centers on the axis. Only the ring vortices contribute to the radial velocity.

The field due to a vortex ring of strength f and radius $r=Rx$, located at a distance h below the reference point P, is given by Lamb (reference 1, p. 237). In the notation of the present paper it is

$$\psi_0'=-\frac{fR}{2\pi}x^{\frac{1}{2}}\left[\left(\frac{2}{k}-k\right)F(k)-\frac{2}{k}E(k)\right] \tag{20}$$

where $E(k)$ and $F(k)$ are the complete elliptic integrals and

$$k^2=\frac{4x}{\left(\frac{h}{R}\right)^2+(1+x)^2}$$

As before, a doublet ring is obtained by differentiating equation (20) with respect to x. By setting

$$f\,dx=\frac{\Gamma}{H}$$

the following expression is obtained for the field of a doublet ring:

$$\psi_0=\frac{\Gamma}{8\pi}\frac{R}{H}k\left\{x^{-\frac{1}{2}}\frac{k^2}{1-k^2}E(k)+x^{\frac{1}{2}}\left[2F(k)-\frac{2-k^2}{1-k^2}E(k)\right]\right\} \tag{21}$$

In order to obtain the effect of the entire vortex system, equation (21) is integrated with respect to h/R and x as

$$\psi\left(\frac{h}{R}\right)=\int_0^1\int_{-h/R}^{\infty}\frac{\Gamma R^2}{8\pi H}k\left\{x^{-\frac{1}{2}}\frac{k^2}{1-k^2}E(k)+x^{\frac{1}{2}}\left[2F(k)-\frac{2-k^2}{1-k^2}E(k)\right]\right\}d\frac{h}{R}\,dx \tag{22}$$

The radial velocity

$$v_R=\frac{1}{R^2}\frac{\partial\psi}{\partial\frac{h}{R}}$$

Equation (22) may be written in the form

$$\psi\left(\frac{h}{R}\right)=\frac{R^2}{8\pi H}\int_0^1 \Gamma \int_{-h/R}^{\infty} \Phi\left(\frac{h}{R}, x\right) d\frac{h}{R}\, dx \tag{23}$$

so that

$$v_R=-\frac{1}{8\pi H}\int_0^1 \Gamma\, \Phi\left(-\frac{h}{R}, x\right) dx$$

$$=-\frac{1}{8\pi H}\int_0^1 \Gamma\, \Phi\left(\frac{h}{R}, x\right) dx \tag{24}$$

Now

$$\frac{\Delta r}{R}=\frac{1}{R}\int_{\infty}^{h} \frac{dr}{dh}\, dh$$

$$=\int_{\infty}^{h/R} \frac{v_R}{V}\, d\frac{h}{R}$$

$$=\frac{1}{8\pi HV}\int_0 \Gamma \int_{h/R}^{\infty} \Phi\left(\frac{h}{R}, x\right) d\frac{h}{R}\, dx \tag{25}$$

By substituting

$$\Gamma=\frac{\pi c_s \lambda V R}{\kappa} K(x) \tag{26}$$

where $K(x)$ is the horizontal component of the circulation coefficient, which may be expressed as

$$K(x)=\left(\frac{x^2}{\lambda^2+x^2}\right)^{3/2} \tag{27}$$

the following equation is finally obtained:

$$\frac{\Delta r}{R}=\frac{c_s}{16\pi\kappa}\int_0^1\left(\frac{x^2}{\lambda^2+x^2}\right)^{3/2} dx\int_{h/R}^{\infty}k\left\{x^{-1/2}\frac{k^2}{1-k^2}E(k)+x^{1/2}\left[2F(k)-\frac{2-k^2}{1-k^2}E(k)\right]\right\}d\frac{h}{R} \tag{28}$$

For convenience in using the Legendre tables, the second integral is written in the form

$$\int_{h/R}^{\infty} z_1\, d\frac{h}{R} \tag{29}$$

where

$$z_1=\sin\phi\left\{\tan^2\phi\left(x^{-1/2}-x^{1/2}\right)E(k)+2x^{1/2}[F(k)-E(k)]\right\}$$

and

$$\left(\frac{h}{R}\right)^2=\frac{4x}{\sin^2\phi}-(1+x)^2$$

or

$$\phi=\sin^{-1}k$$

(See fig. 12 for plots of z_1 against h/R.)

The final expression is

$$\frac{\Delta r}{R}=\frac{c_s}{16\pi\kappa}\int_0^1\left(\frac{x^2}{\lambda^2+x^2}\right)^{3/2} dx\int_{h/R}^{\infty}\sin\phi\left\{\tan^2\phi\left(x^{-1/2}-x^{1/2}\right)E(k)+2x^{1/2}[F(k)-E(k)]\right\}d\frac{h}{R}$$

(See table VII and fig. 13.)

INFINITE NUMBER OF BLADES FOR DUAL ROTATION

The contraction for a dual-rotating propeller with an infinite number of blades is next obtained. In this case $K(x)=1$, and the radial velocity is

$$v_R=-\frac{\Gamma}{2\pi H}\left[x^{1/2}\left\{\left(\frac{2}{k}-k\right)F(k)-\frac{2}{k}\,E(k)\right\}\right]_{x=0}^{x=1}$$

Since the value at the lower limit is zero and $K(x)=1$ for an infinite number of blades, it follows by substituting the value of Γ that

$$\frac{\Delta r}{R}=-\frac{c_s}{4\pi}\int_{h/R}^{\infty} w_1\, d\frac{h}{R}$$

where

$$w_1=\left[\left(\frac{2}{k}-k\right)F(k)-\frac{2}{k}\,E(k)\right]^{x=1}$$

(See table VIII and fig. 14.)

CONCLUDING REMARKS

The contraction coefficients are given for two-blade and four-blade single-rotating propellers at four specific values of the advance ratio. The calculations involve triple integrations and are therefore somewhat laborious and susceptible to numerical errors. Until more convenient methods are devised to perform this integration, it is hoped that the values given in this paper will serve the purpose. It is well to notice the small magnitude of the contraction. A four-blade propeller with normal loading and advance ratio is shown to have a total contraction in terms of the radius of less than one percent. The first-order treatment embodied in the paper is therefore adequate for all technical purposes.

Langley Memorial Aeronautical Laboratory,
National Advisory Committee for Aeronautics,
Langley Field, Va., *October 10, 1944.*

REFERENCE

1. Lamb, Horace: Hydrodynamics. Sixth ed., Cambridge Univ. Press, 1932.

TABLE I.—FUNCTION $\frac{\lambda^3}{4}Y_1$ FOR TWO-BLADE PROPELLER

θ (deg)	$\frac{\lambda^3}{4}Y_1$	θ (deg)	$\frac{\lambda^3}{4}Y_1$		
	$\lambda=\frac{1}{4}$		$\lambda=\frac{1}{2}$	$\lambda=1$	$\lambda=1\frac{1}{2}$
50	−0.000291	1	−0.000138	----------	−0.000683
100	.000148	2	−.000213	−0.000282	−.001088
130	.001966	3	−.000293	----------	−.001367
150	.004813	4	−.000382	----------	−.001232
170	.006679	5	−.000488	----------	−.001283
200	.005052	6	−.000570	−.000923	−.001316
220	.002008	7	−.000682	----------	−.001358
250	.000730	8	−.000789	----------	−.001358
300	.000450	9	−.000898	----------	−.001350
350	.001305	10	−.000984	−.001792	−.001358
400	.000622	20	−.001139	−.001571	−.001367
500	.000270	40	−.000999	−.001286	−.001080
550	.000400	60	−.000802	−.000862	−.000759
600	.000145	80	−.000339	−.000324	−.000354
650	.000031	100	.000460	.000312	.000084
700	.000149	120	.001730	.000709	.000274
750	.000175	140	.003131	.000809	.000347
800	.000058	160	.003351	.000740	.000321
900	.000079	180	.002658	.000492	.000132
		200	.001544	.000237	.000100
		220	.000625	.000093	.000073
		240	.000160	.000014	−.000015
		260	−.000056	.000003	.000008
		280	.000049	−.000013	.000036
		300	.000213	−.000004	.000047
		320	.000363	.000004	.000036
		340	.000390	.000008	.000030
		360	.000343	.000031	.000001
		380	.000232	.000008	−.000003
		400	.000113	−.000003	.000004
		420	.000027	.000020	.000007
		440	−.000011	6.000011	
		460	.000014		

TABLE II.—FUNCTION $\frac{\lambda^3}{4}Y_1$ FOR FOUR-BLADE PROPELLER

θ (deg)	$\frac{\lambda^3}{4}Y_1$	θ (deg)	$\frac{\lambda^3}{4}Y_1$		
	$\lambda=\frac{1}{4}$		$\lambda=\frac{1}{2}$	$\lambda=1$	$\lambda=1\frac{1}{2}$
0	0.000500	1	----------	----------	−0.000273
10	−.020680	2	----------	−0.000001	−.000250
30	.097700	3	----------	----------	−.000088
60	1,251120	4	----------	----------	.000083
65	1.858120	5	−0.004211	----------	.000251
70	2.879450	6	----------	.000002	.000501
75	3.849270	7	----------	----------	.000704
80	4.594600	8	----------	----------	.000905
85	4.987600	9	----------	----------	.001263
90	4.538300	10	−.011374	−.000013	.001432
95	3.549380	20	.006150	.001786	.002984
100	2.685010	40	.137004	.006466	.005328
110	1.330560	60	.363018	.006423	.003108
120	.821510	80	.342699	.004174	.001577
160	1.017150	100	.218548	.002161	.000532
200	.902770	120	.112735	.001281	.000298
250	.436960	140	.091686	.000865	.000224
300	.323530	160	.075117	.000535	.000214
350	.217700	180	.058218	.000345	.000166
400	.154190	200	.040861	.000224	.000078
450	.154010	220	.030023	.000176	.000101
500	.119570	240	.024839	.000130	.000066
.550	.038450	260	.021139	.000100	.000057
600	−.029500	280	.017093	.000062	.000048
		300	.014048	.000042	.000037
		320	.011174	.000032	.000025
		340	.009069	.000016	.000002
		360	.007762	.000032	.000004
		380	.006439	−.000018	
		400	.004650	−.000041	
		420	.003748	−.000003	
		440	.003884	−.000004	
		460	.004428		

TABLE III.—FUNCTION $\frac{\lambda^3}{4}Y_2$ FOR TWO-BLADE PROPELLER

θ (deg)	$\frac{\lambda^3}{4}Y_2$	θ (deg)	$\frac{\lambda^3}{4}Y_2$		
	$\lambda=\frac{1}{4}$		$\lambda=\frac{1}{2}$	$\lambda=1$	$\lambda=1\frac{1}{2}$
0	8.138900	0	0.377250	−0.004494	−0.003135
20	8.159900	2	.377650	−.004435	----------
40	8.219400	4	.378580	−.004280	----------
60	8.291400	6	.380140	−.003990	----------
80	8.351400	8	.382320	−.003490	----------
100	8.358900	10	.385170	−.002790	−.002466
120	8.223900	20	.402420	.000595	−.001651
140	7.745900	30	----------	----------	−.000876
160	6.570900	40	.437620	.006355	−.000189
180	4.917900	50	----------	----------	.000407
200	3.412900	60	.467020	.010675	.000907
220	2.512900	70	----------	----------	.001302
240	2.232900	80	.486770	.013075	.001577
260	2.202900	90	----------	----------	.001717
280	2.245900	100	.485670	.013075	.001724
300	2.215900	120	.453070	.011070	.001504
320	2.026900	140	.373150	.008050	.001129
340	1.734900	160	.267250	.004870	.000718
360	1.404900	180	.169400	.002470	.000444
380	1.108400	200	.102200	.001070	.000313
400	.890900	220	.067320	.000470	.000207
420	.780400	240	.055310	.000280	.000178
440	.745400	260	.053460	.000270	.000189
460	.740400	280	.052810	.000280	.000162
500	.674400	300	.048820	.000290	.000112
540	.504400	320	.040500	.000290	.000065
580	.324400	340	.028630	.000260	.000025
620	.246400	360	.016630	.000150	.000007
660	.231400	380	.007610	.000090	.000007
700	.189400	400	.002400	.000080	.000006
740	.112000	420	.000420	.000070	
780	.030000	440	.000100		
820	−.006000				
860	−.004000				

TABLE IV.—FUNCTION $\frac{\lambda^3}{4}Y_2$ FOR FOUR-BLADE PROPELLER

θ (deg)	$\frac{\lambda^3}{4}Y_2$	θ (deg)	$\frac{\lambda^3}{4}Y_2$		
	$\lambda=\frac{1}{4}$		$\lambda=\frac{1}{2}$	$\lambda=1$	$\lambda=1\frac{1}{2}$
0	0.024414	0	0.017258	0.007918	0.005175
10	.024414	2	.017259	.007918	.005107
20	.024416	4	.017261	.007918	.004728
30	.024380	6	.017266	.007918	.004084
40	.024256	8	.017276	.007918	.003214
50	.023969	10	.017287	.007918	.002343
60	.023338	20	.017317	.007908	.001099
70	.021958	40	.016676	.006873	.001235
80	.019333	60	.013899	.004520	.000902
90	.016049	80	.009902	.002668	.000675
100	.013540	100	.006845	.001594	.000541
110	.012166	120	.005099	.001014	.000404
130	.010889	140	.004010	.000644	.000314
150	.009821	160	.003112	.000407	.000240
170	.008444	180	.002383	.000255	.000173
190	.006951	200	.001859	.000157	.000135
210	.005703	220	.001486	.000091	.000102
230	.004773	240	.001186	.000087	.000073
250	.004082	260	.000949	.000049	.000052
270	.003528	280	.000741	.000028	.000035
290	.003035	300	.000596	.000010	.000020
310	.002594	320	.000472	−.000002	.000009
330	.002216	340	.000363	−.000010	.000003
350	.001887	360	.000271	−.000019	
370	.001612	380	.000192	−.000021	
390	.001376	400	.000132	−.000013	
410	.001166	420	.000087	−.000001	
430	.000959	440	.000046		
450	.000754				
470	.000550				
490	.000367				
510	.000205				
530	.000075				

TABLE V.—FUNCTION $\frac{\lambda^3}{4}Y_3$ FOR TWO-BLADE PROPELLER

θ (deg)	$\frac{\lambda^3}{4}Y_3$	θ (deg)	$\frac{\lambda^3}{4}Y_3$		
	λ=1/4		λ=1/2	λ=1	λ=1 1/2
0	0.048613	0	0.015944	0.002141	0.000602
20	.044739	2	.015800	.002154	------
40	.040850	4	.015656	.002168	------
60	.036926	6	.015511	.002180	------
80	.032975	8	.015366	.002191	------
100	.029007	10	.015221	.002201	.000748
120	.025056	20	.014474	.002217	.000855
140	.021248	30	------	------	.000921
160	.017800	40	.012913	.002111	.000950
180	.015057	50	------	------	.000944
200	.013062	60	.011197	.001852	.000910
220	.011670	70	------	------	.000854
240	.010549	80	.009382	.001490	.000780
260	.009501	90	------	------	.000695
280	.008448	100	.007525	.001094	.000607
300	.007392	120	.005732	.000728	.000439
320	.006381	140	.004148	.000437	.000303
340	.005483	160	.002927	.000243	.000208
360	.004734	180	.002099	.000136	.000148
380	.004139	200	.001594	.000087	.000111
400	.003664	220	.001277	.000065	.000086
420	.003268	240	.001049	.000055	.000066
440	.002903	260	.000837	.000047	.000048
460	.002459	280	.000632	.000039	.000030
500	.001882	300	.000441	.000031	.000017
540	.001318	320	.000276	.000022	.000007
580	.000922	340	.000146	.000014	.000002
620	.000651	360	.000066	.000008	.000001
660	.000425	380	.000021	.000005	.000001
700	.000232	400	.000005	.000002	
740	.000085	420	.000001		
780	−.000006				
820	−.000005				

TABLE VI.—FUNCTION $\frac{\lambda^3}{4}Y_3$ FOR FOUR-BLADE PROPELLER

θ (deg)	$\frac{\lambda^3}{4}Y_3$	θ (deg)	$\frac{\lambda^3}{4}Y_3$		
	λ=1/4		λ=1/2	λ=1	λ=1 1/2
0	0.067786	0	0.033572	0.010513	0.005286
10	.063525	2	.032969	.010236	------
20	.059264	4	.032367	.009960	------
30	.055006	6	.031764	.009684	------
40	.050757	8	.031162	.009407	------
50	.046549	10	.030558	.009131	.004389
60	.042420	20	.027537	.007750	.003532
70	.038450	30	------	------	.002766
80	.034832	40	.021584	.005158	.002131
90	.031732	50	------	------	.001650
100	.029167	60	.016211	.003155	.001297
110	.026892	70	------	------	.001040
130	.022885	80	.012055	.001916	.000856
150	.019263	90	------	------	.000722
170	.016059	100	.009157	.001185	.000618
190	.013358	120	.007100	.000738	.000465
210	.011148	140	.005512	.000453	.000343
230	.009303	160	.004265	.000267	.000243
250	.007765	180	.003314	.000151	.000173
270	.006435	200	.002574	.000086	.000122
290	.005288	220	.002003	.000052	.000080
310	.004300	240	.001545	.000022	.000049
330	.003461	260	.001165	−.000000	.000029
350	.002748	280	.000863	−.000012	.000015
370	.002138	300	.000634	−.000019	.000006
390	.001621	320	.000452	−.000021	.000002
410	.001181	340	.000307	−.000019	
430	.000823	360	.000196	−.000014	
450	.000532	380	.000116	−.000008	
470	.000306	400	.000061	−.000002	
490	.000153	420	.000023		
510	.000052				

TABLE VII.—CONTOUR LINES—SINGLE-ROTATING PROPELLER

h/R	$\frac{\Delta r}{R}\frac{1}{c_s}$	h/R	$\frac{\Delta r}{R}\frac{1}{c_s}$	h/R	$\frac{\Delta r}{R}\frac{1}{c_s}$	h/R	$\frac{\Delta r}{R}\frac{1}{c_s}$
	λ=1/4		λ=1/2		λ=1		λ=1 1/2
4.0	0.00045	4.0	0.00060	4.0	0.00058	4.0	0.00032
3.0	.00263	3.0	.00226	3.0	.00188	3.0	.00148
2.0	.00747	2.6	.00350	2.6	.00292	2.6	.00226
1.6	.01148	2.2	.00545	2.2	.00424	2.2	.00332
1.2	.01796	1.8	.00838	1.8	.00626	1.8	.00487
.8	.02888	1.4	.01266	1.4	.00937	1.4	.00726
.45	.04733	1.0	.01963	1.0	.01446	1.0	.01107
		.8	.02499	.8	.01812	.6	.01768
		.6	.03247	.6	.02312	.45	.02330
		.4	.04312	.4	.03053		
		.2	.05997	.2	.04233		
		.1	.07388	.12	.04985		

TABLE VIII.—CONTOUR LINES—DUAL-ROTATING PROPELLER

h/R	$\frac{\Delta r}{R}\frac{1}{c_s}$
10.00	0.000060
9.50	.000141
9.00	.000244
8.50	.000368
8.00	.000513
7.50	.000680
7.00	.000867
6.50	.001074
6.00	.001472
5.50	.001898
5.00	.002355
4.50	.002873
4.00	.003716
3.50	.004671
3.00	.006183
2.50	.008889
2.00	.013390
1.75	.016370
1.50	.020350
1.25	.025820
1.00	.033490
.75	.044930
.50	.062340
.45	.066120
.40	.070340
.35	.075070
.30	.080400
.25	.086370
.20	.093230
.15	.101230
.10	.110680
.05	.123220

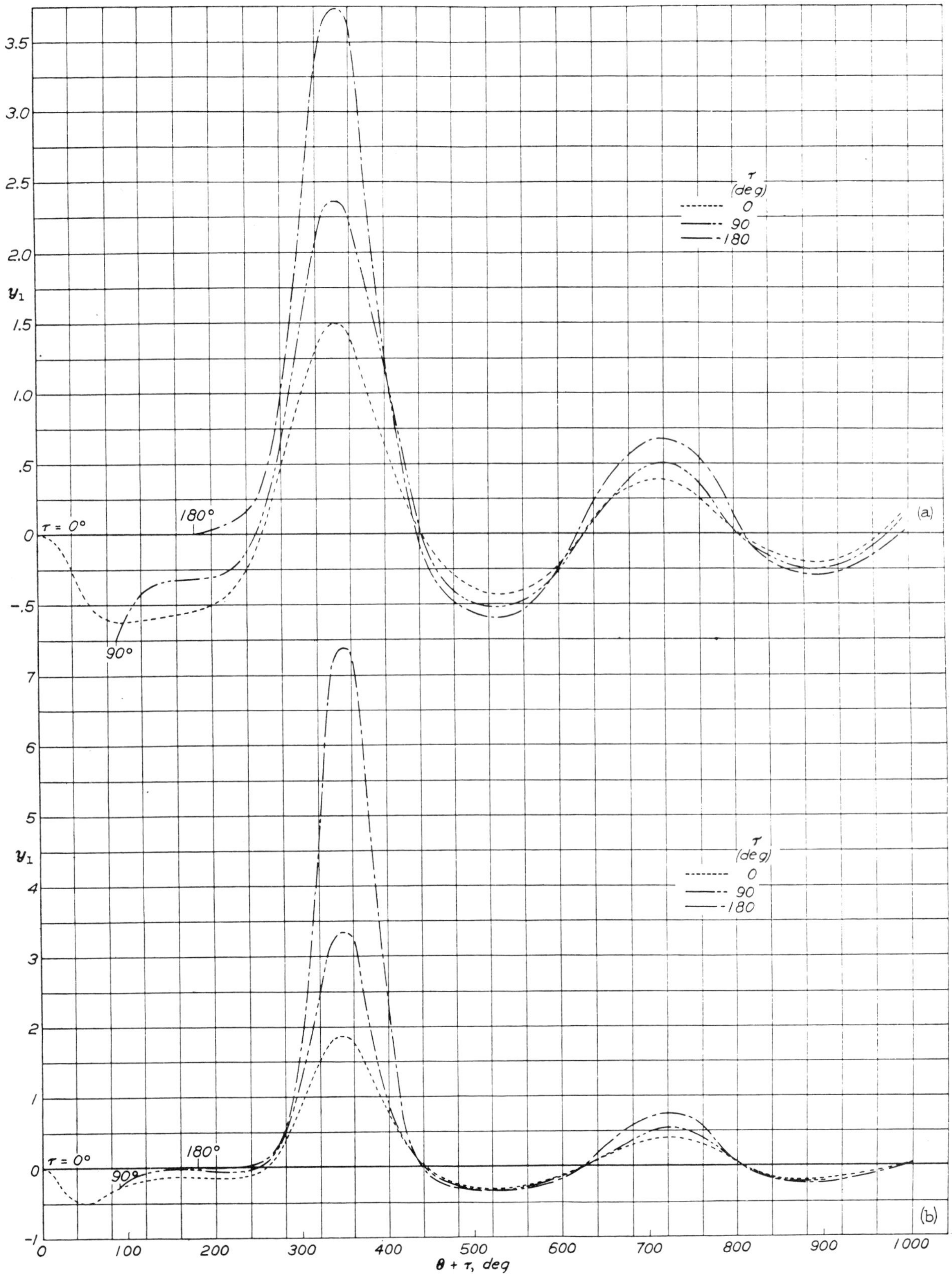

(a) $x=\frac{1}{4}$.

(b) $x=\frac{1}{2}$.

FIGURE 3.—The function y_1 for $\lambda=\frac{1}{4}$ and four values of τ.

737880—47——2

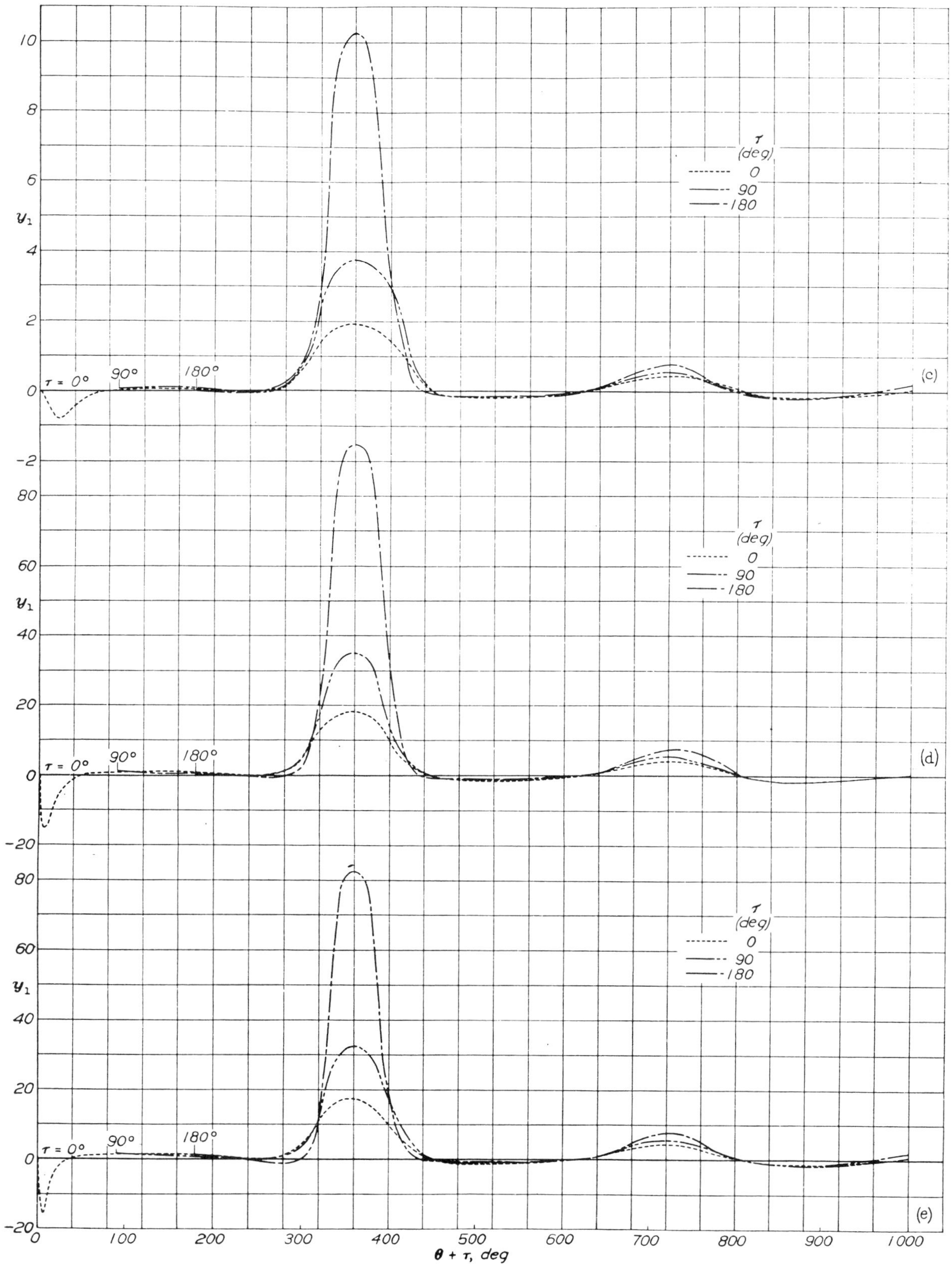

(c) $x=\frac{3}{4}$.

(d) $x=\frac{7}{8}$.

(e) $x=\frac{15}{16}$.

FIGURE 3.—Continued.

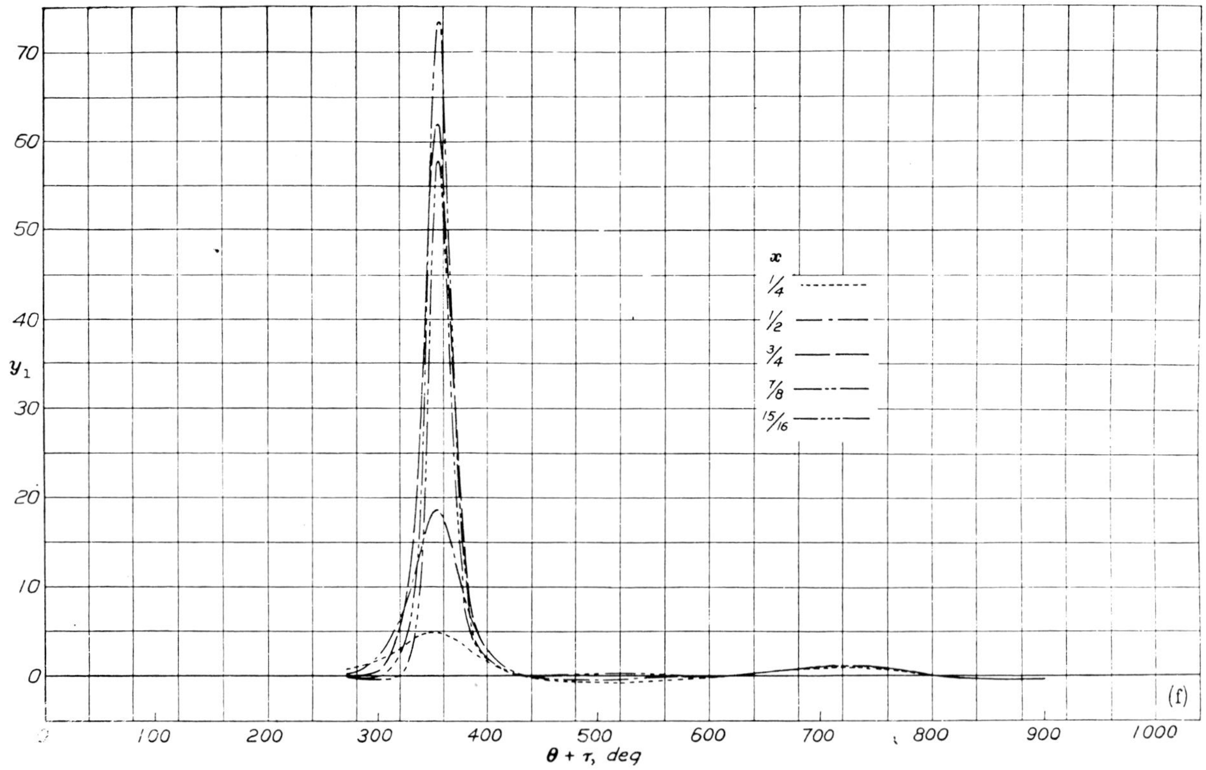

(f) $x=\frac{1}{4}, \frac{1}{2}, \frac{3}{4}, \frac{7}{8}$, and $\frac{15}{16}$; $\tau=270°$.

FIGURE 3.—Concluded.

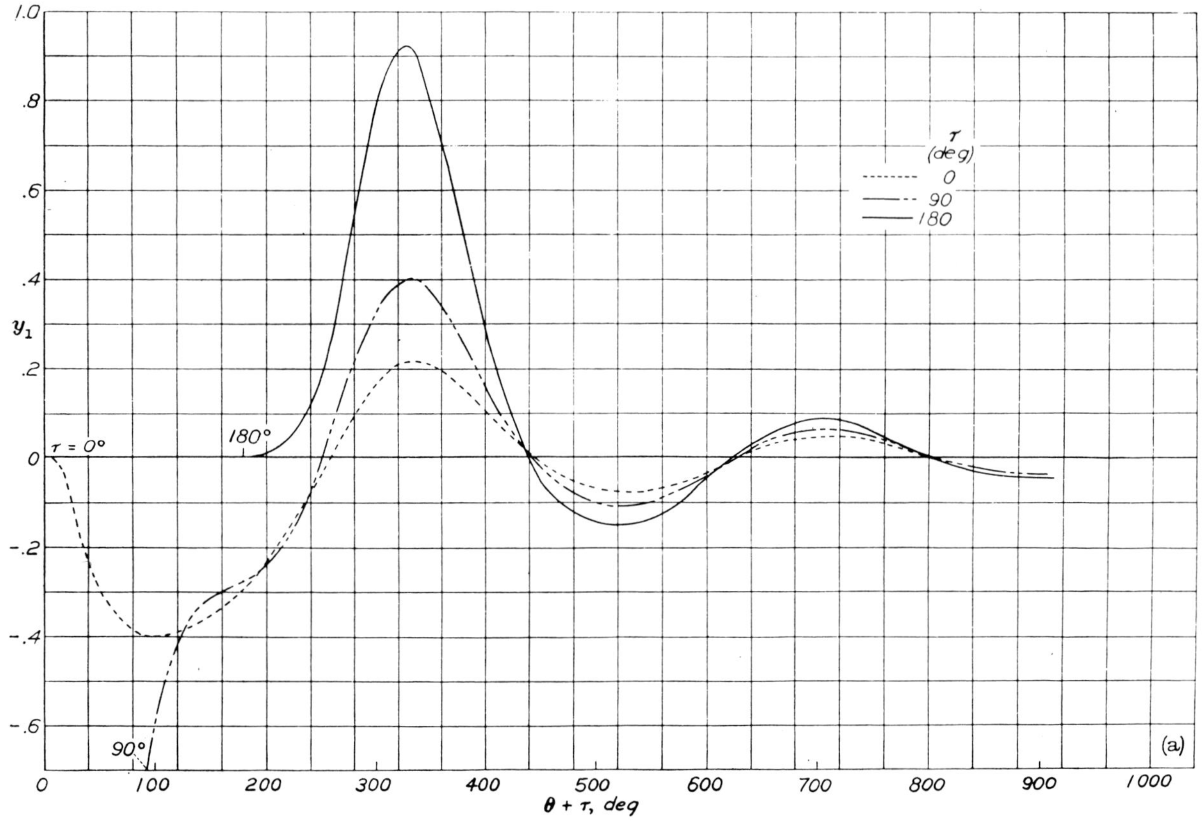

(a) $x=\frac{1}{4}$.

FIGURE 4.—The function y_1 for $\lambda=\frac{1}{2}$ and four values of τ.

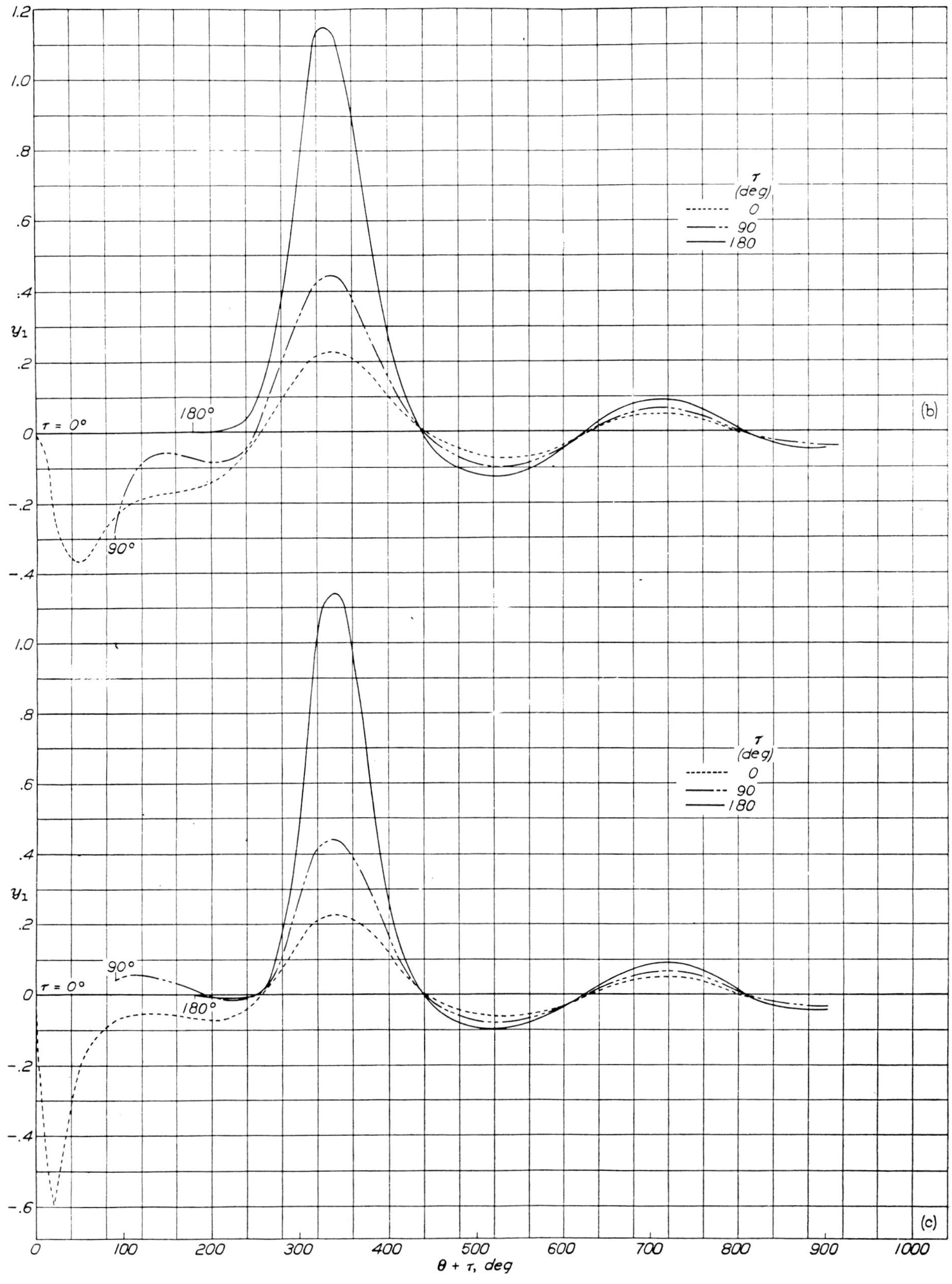

(b) $x=\frac{1}{2}$. (c) $x=\frac{3}{4}$.

FIGURE 4.—Continued.

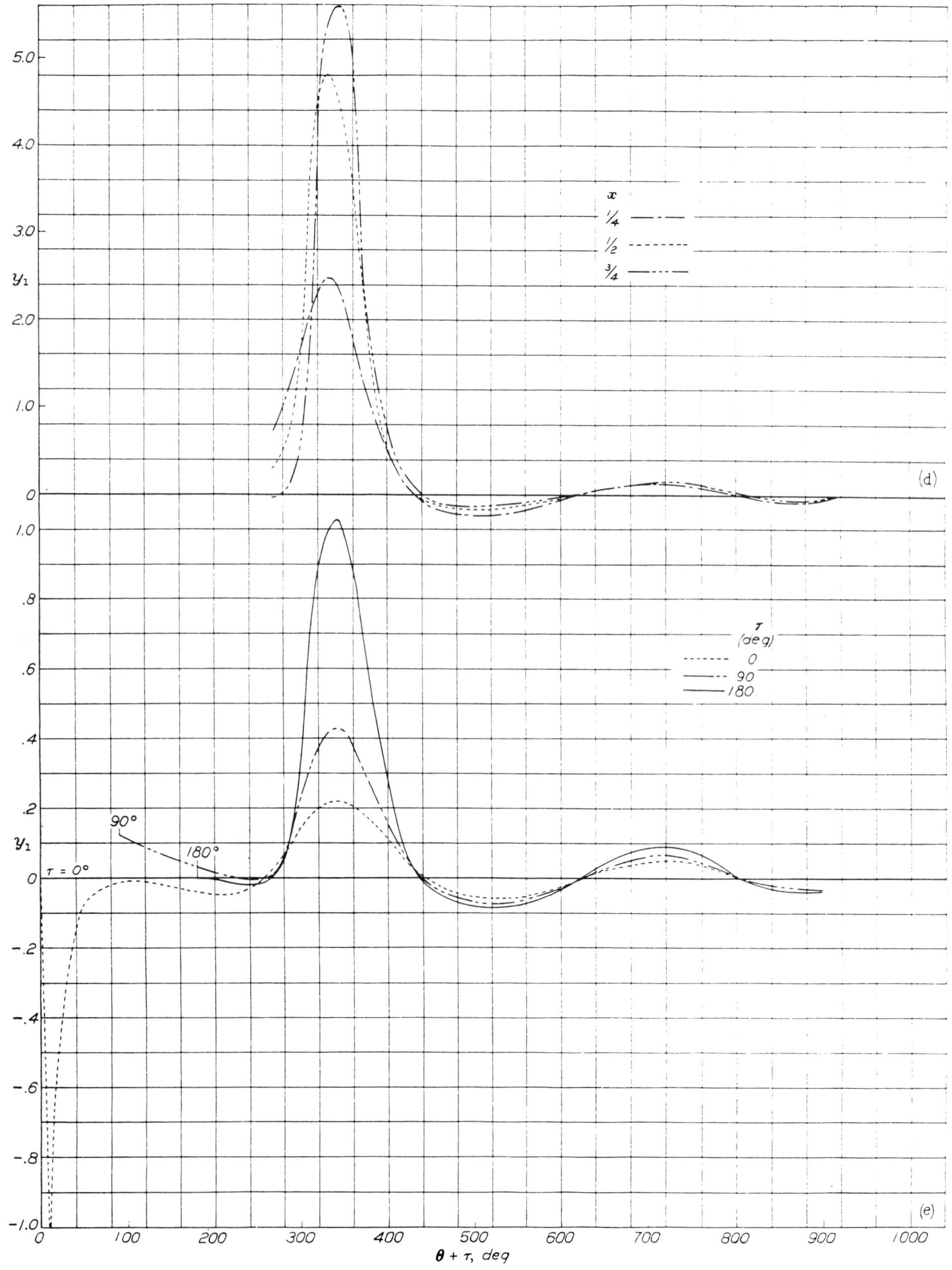

(d) $x = \frac{1}{4}$, $\frac{1}{2}$, and $\frac{3}{4}$; $\tau = 270°$. (e) $x = \frac{7}{8}$.

FIGURE 4.—Continued.

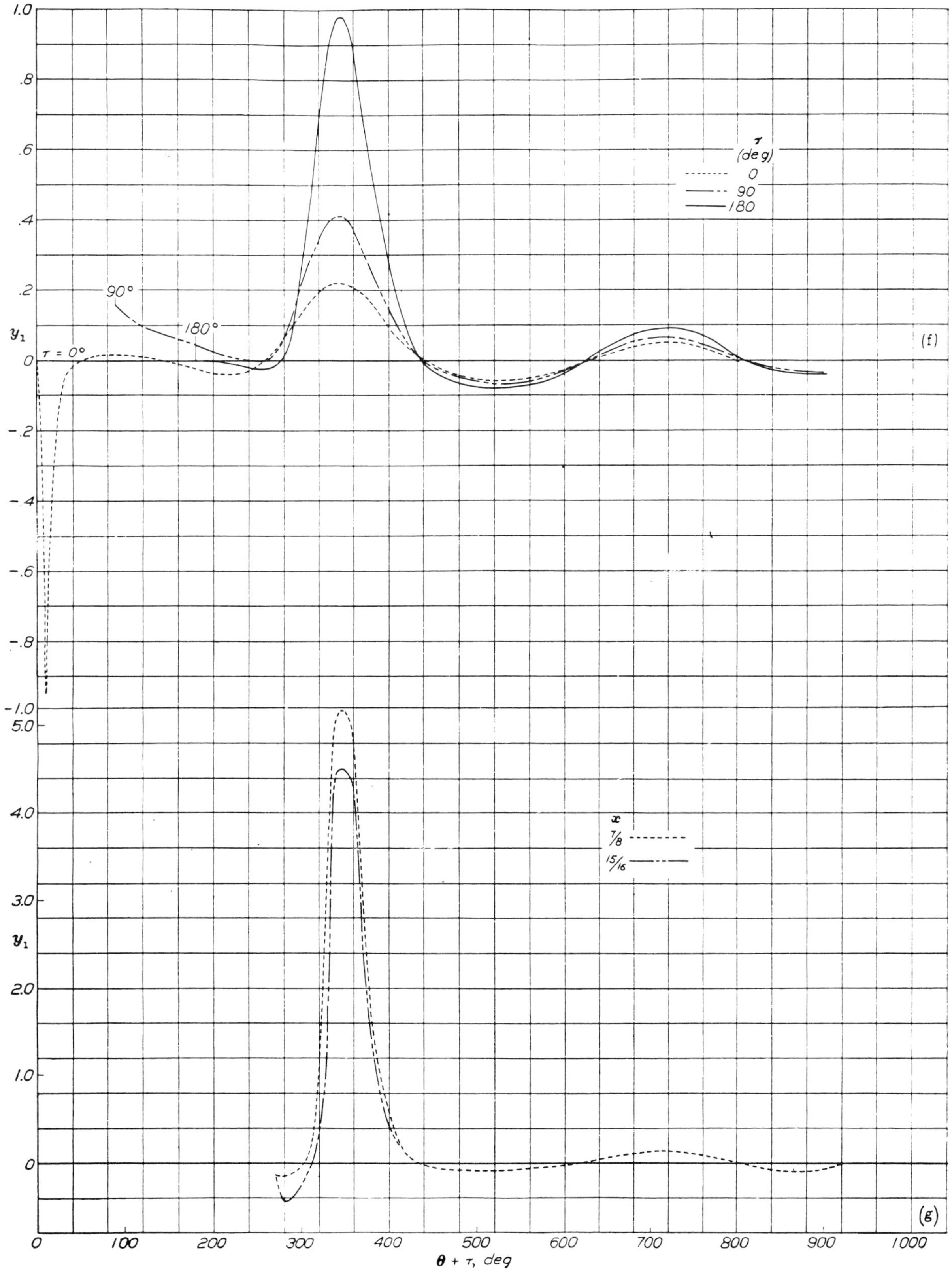

(f) $x=1\frac{5}{16}$.

(g) $x=\frac{7}{8}$ and $1\frac{5}{16}$; $\tau=270°$.

FIGURE 4.—Concluded.

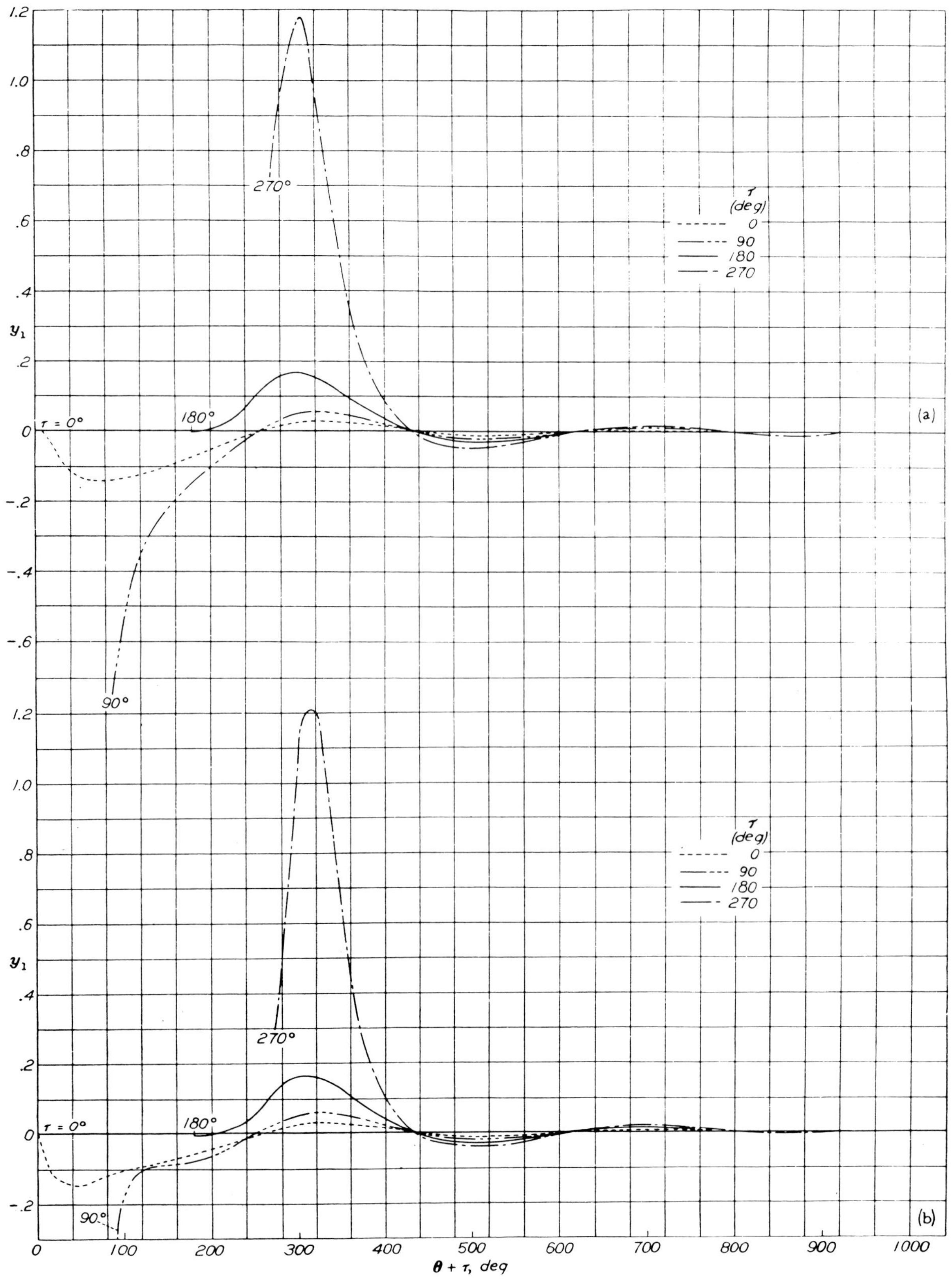

(a) $x = 1/4$. (b) $x = 1/2$.

FIGURE 5.—The function y_1 for $\lambda = 1$ and four values of τ.

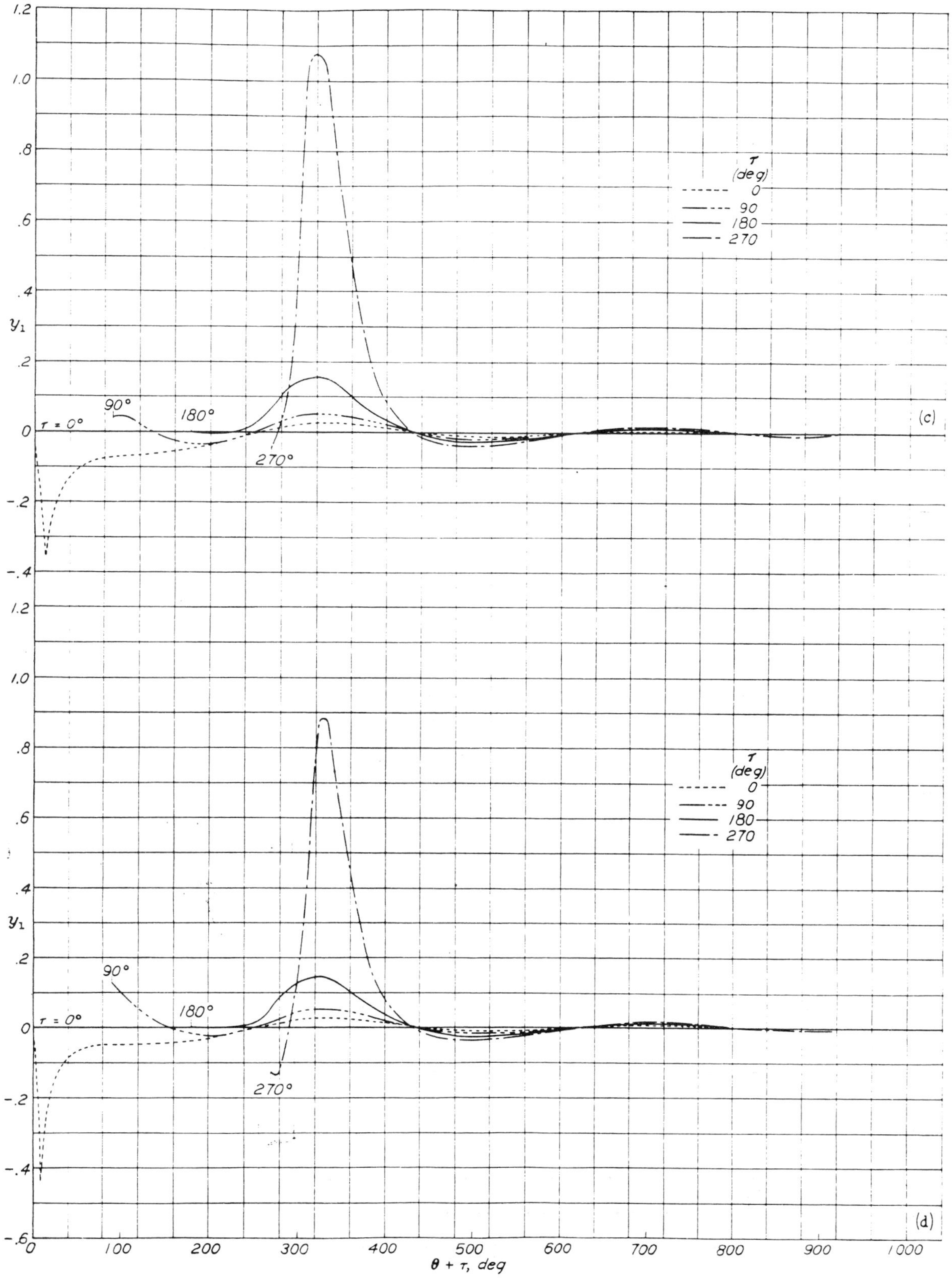

(c) $x=\frac{3}{4}$.

(d) $x=\frac{7}{8}$.

FIGURE 5.—Continued.

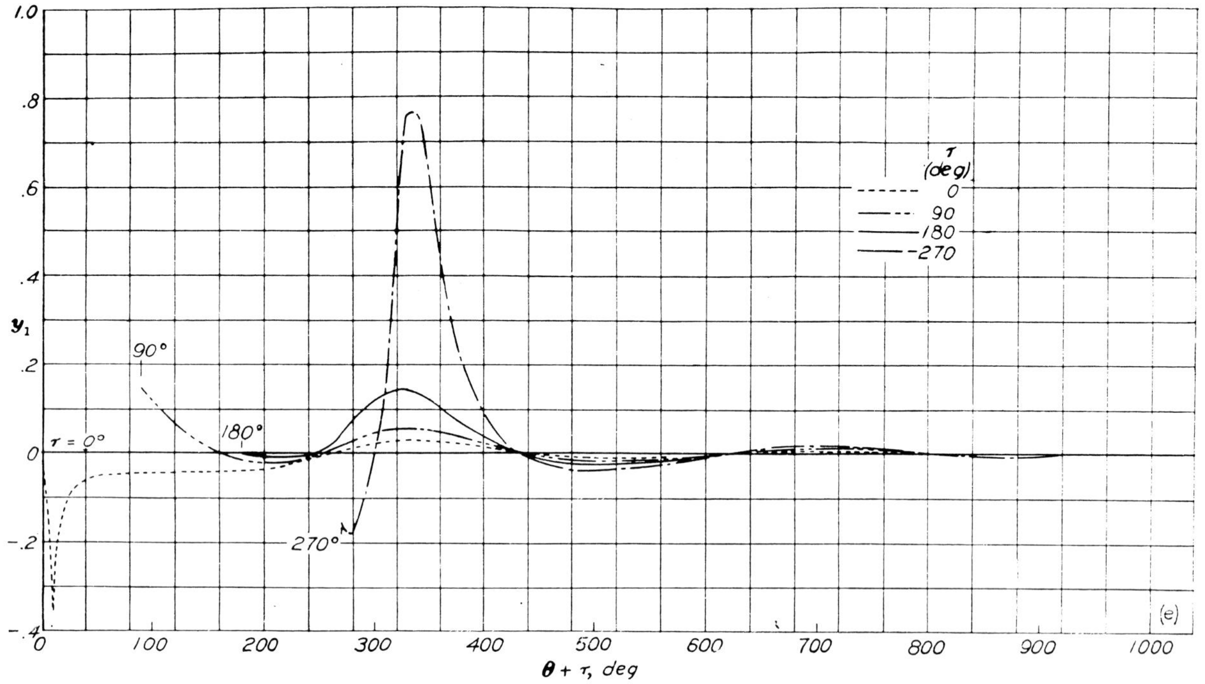

(e) $x = 15/16$.

FIGURE 5.—Concluded.

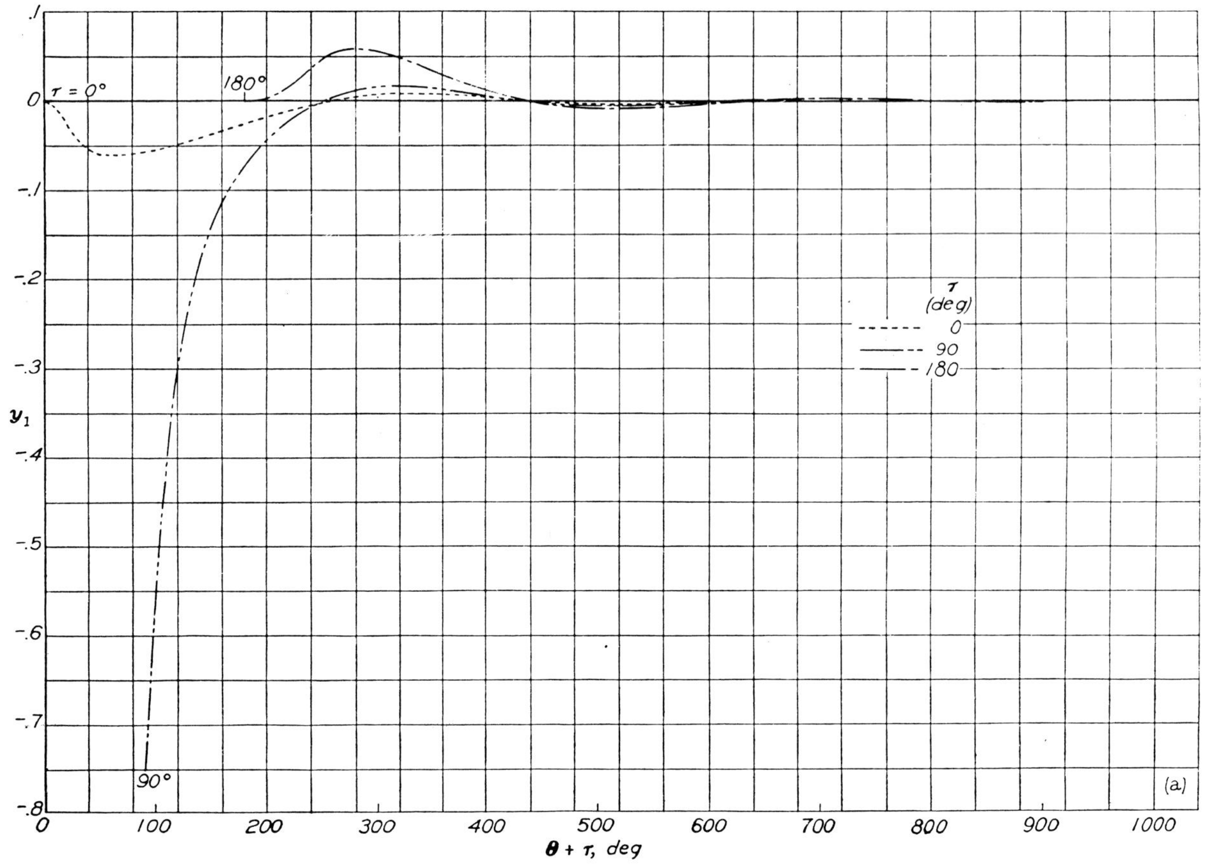

(a) $x = 1/4$.

FIGURE 6.—The function y_1 for $\lambda = 1\frac{1}{2}$ and four values of τ.

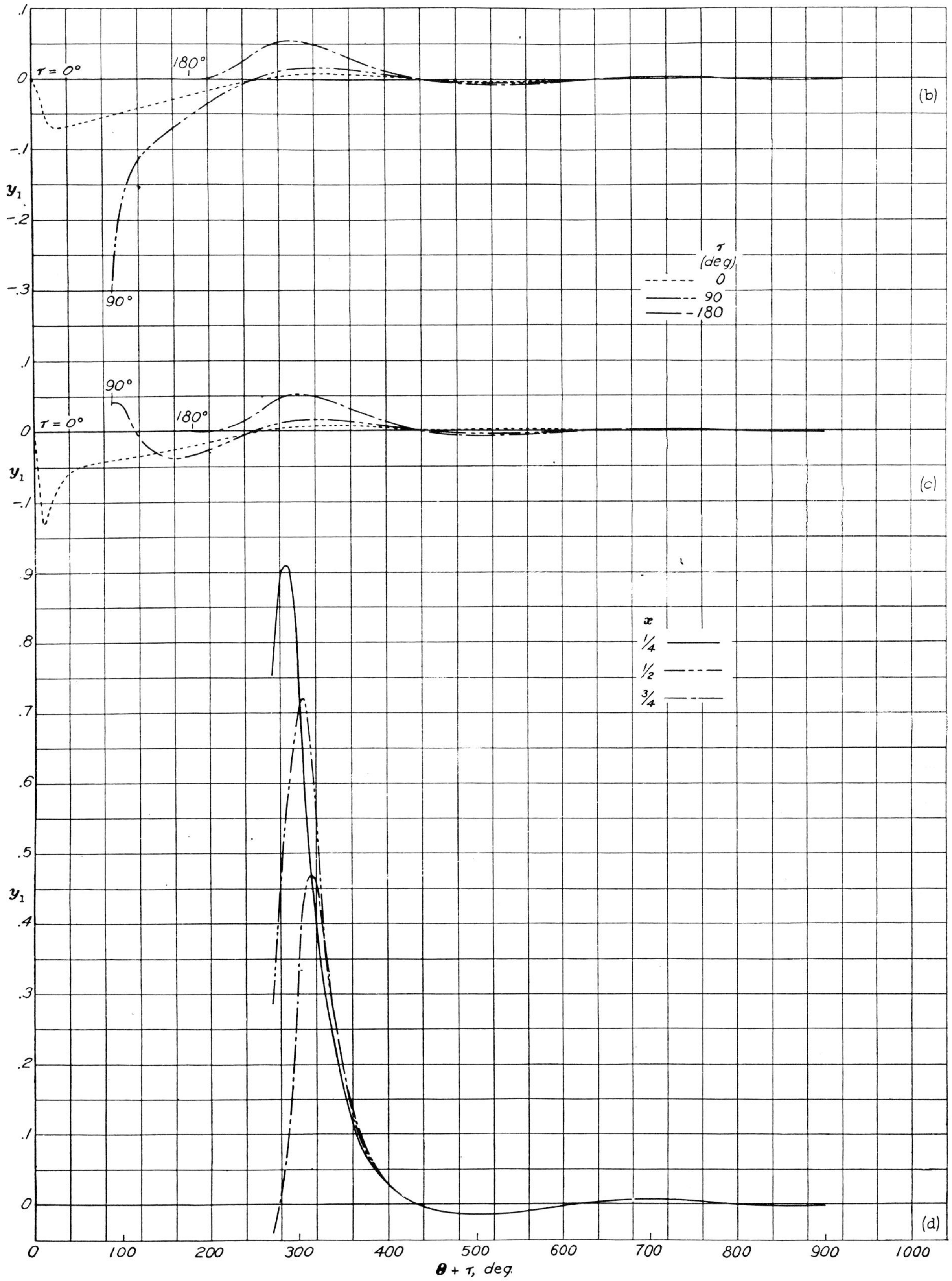

(b) $x=\frac{1}{2}$. (c) $x=\frac{3}{4}$. (d) $x=\frac{1}{4}$, $\frac{1}{2}$, and $\frac{3}{4}$; $\tau=270°$.

FIGURE 6.—Continued.

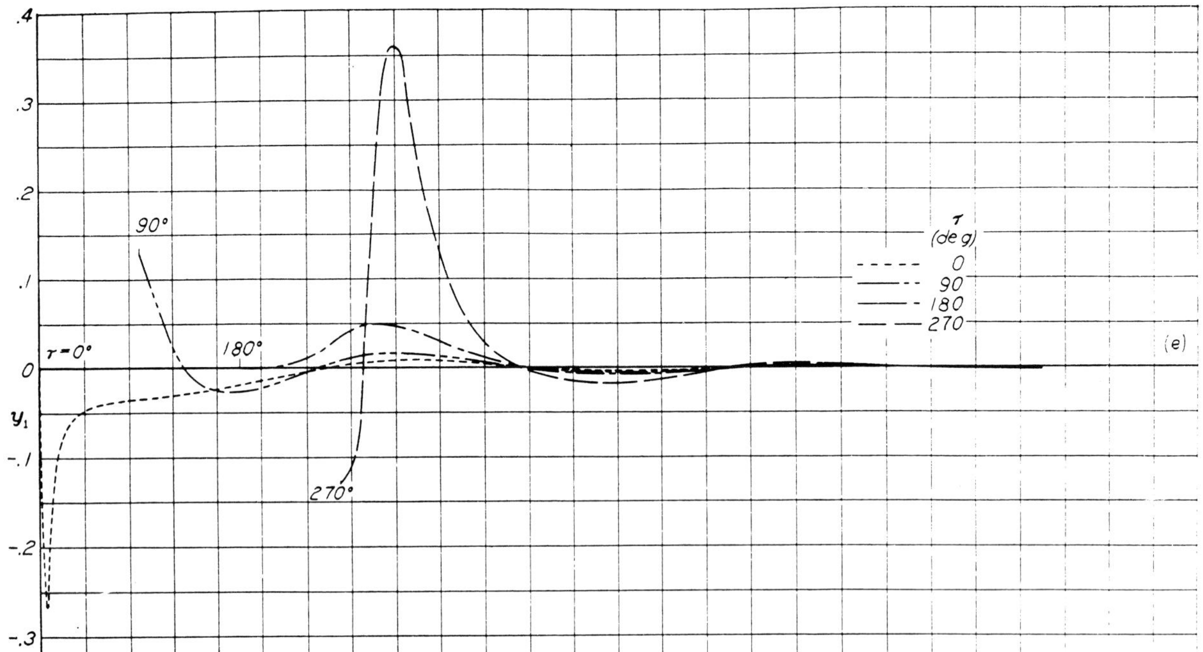

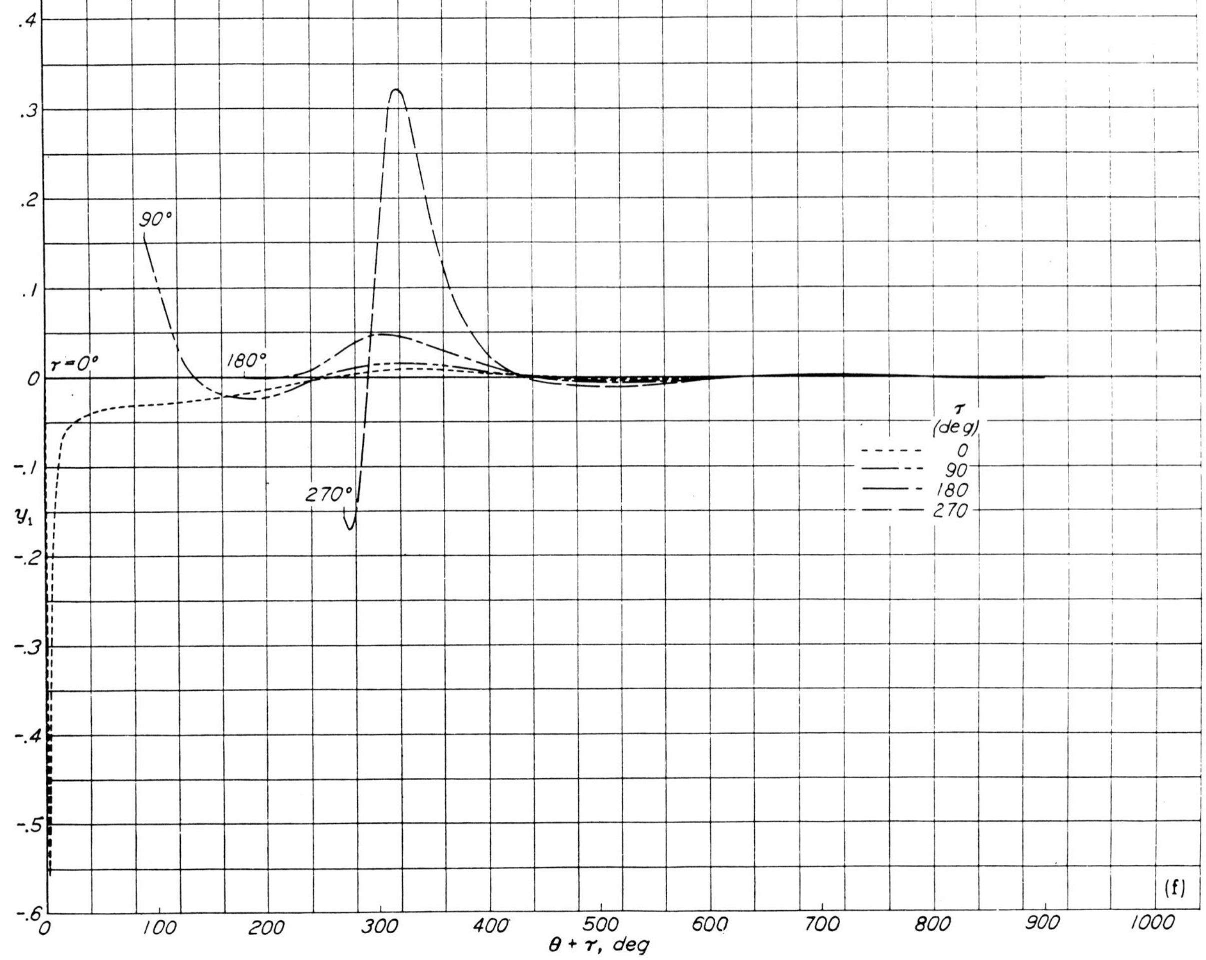

(e) $x = 7/8$.

(f) $x = 15/16$.

FIGURE 6.—Concluded.

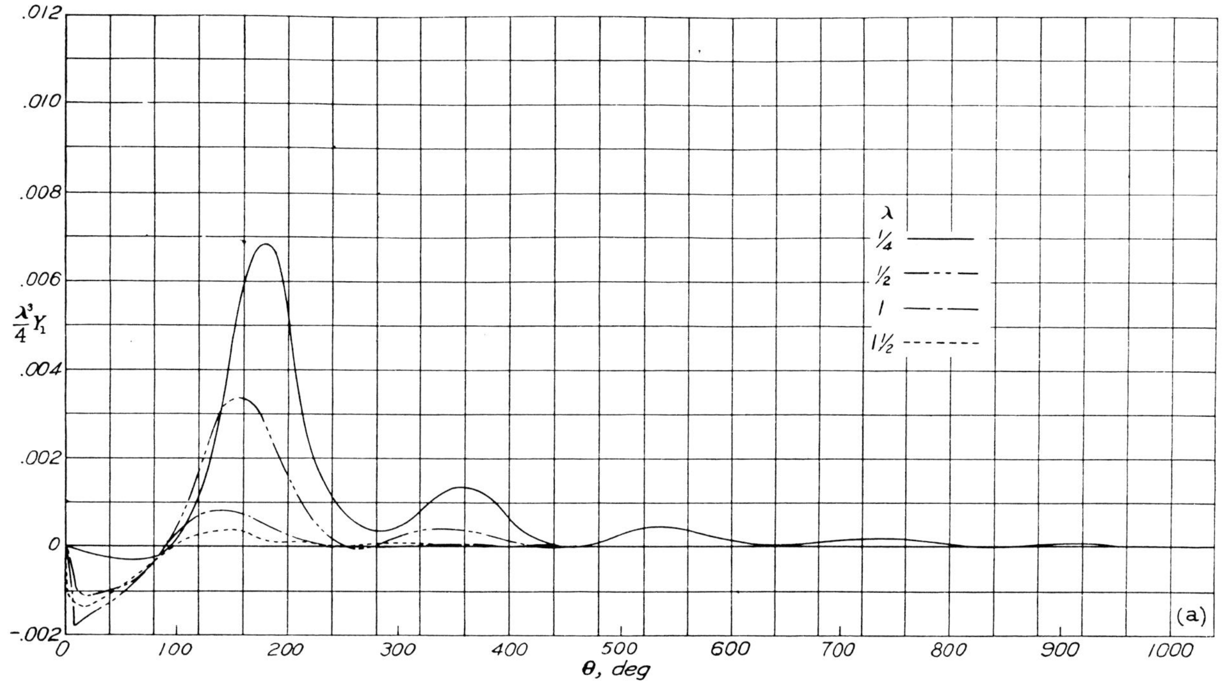

(a) Two-blade propeller. (See table I.)

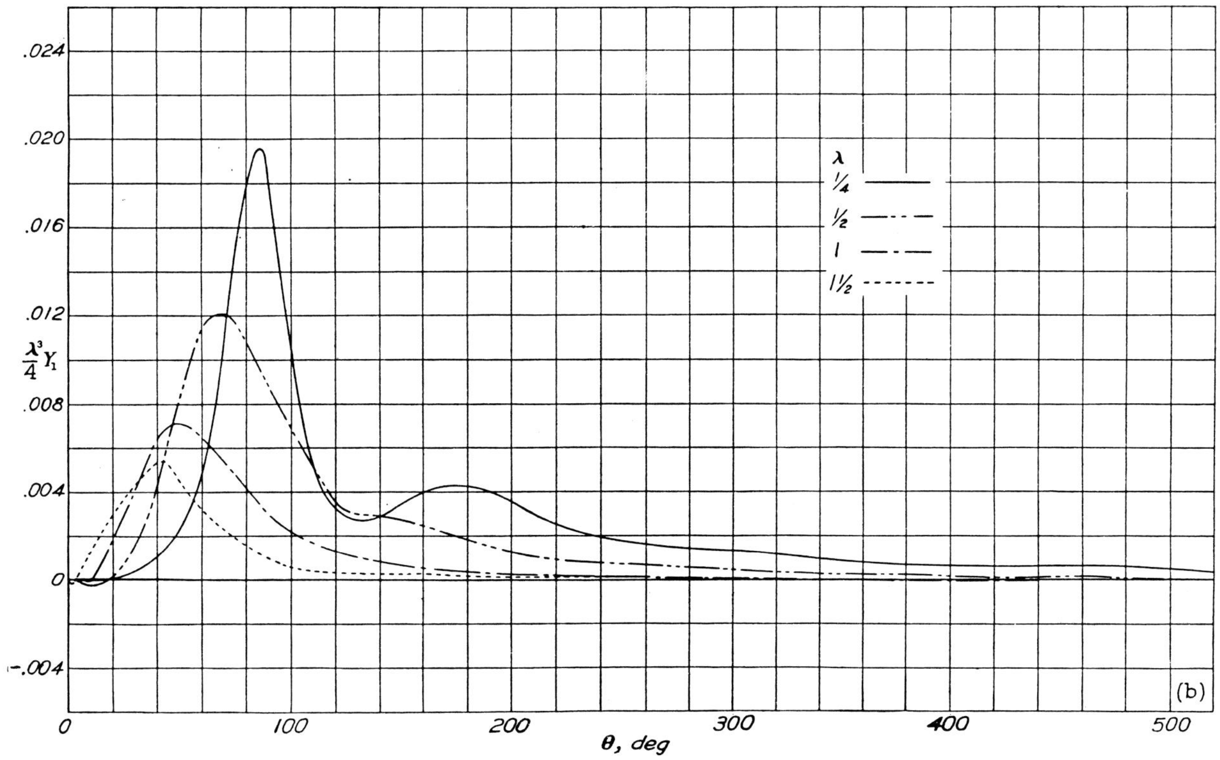

(b) Four-blade propeller. (See table II.)

FIGURE 7.—The function $\frac{\lambda^3}{4}Y_1$ against θ for four values of λ.

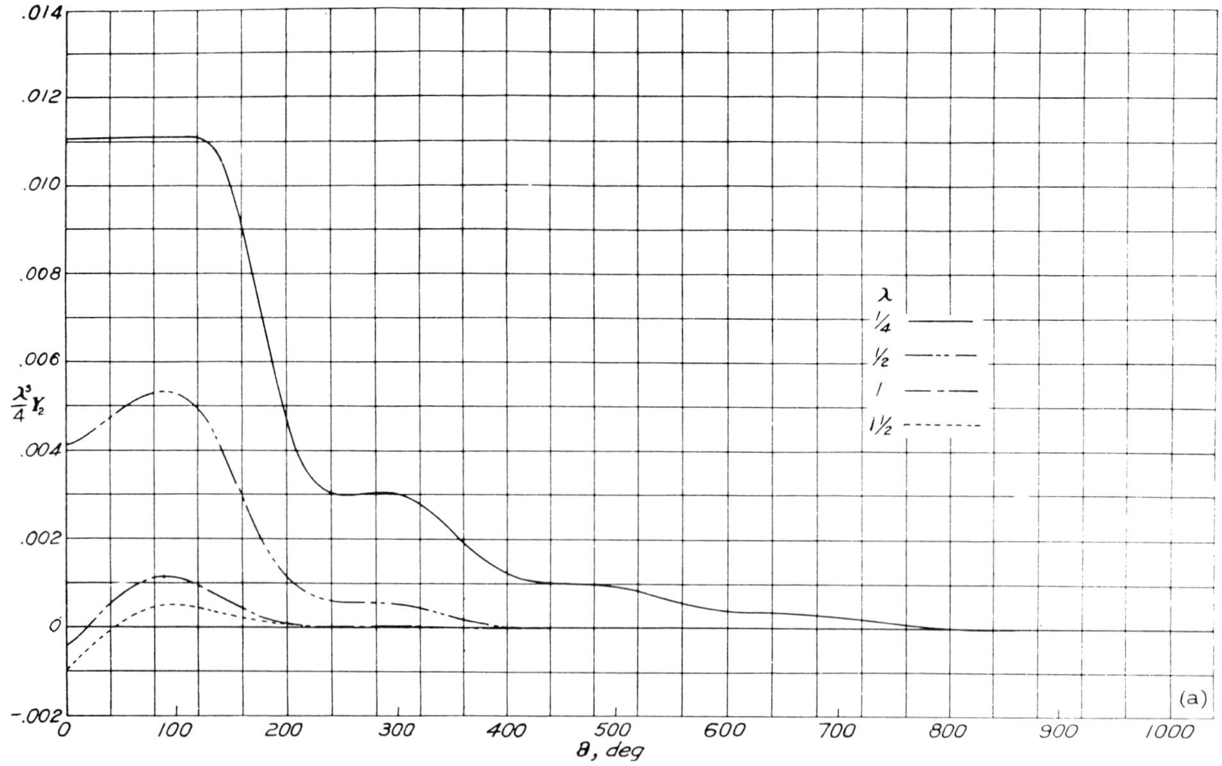

(a) Two-blade propeller. (See table III.)

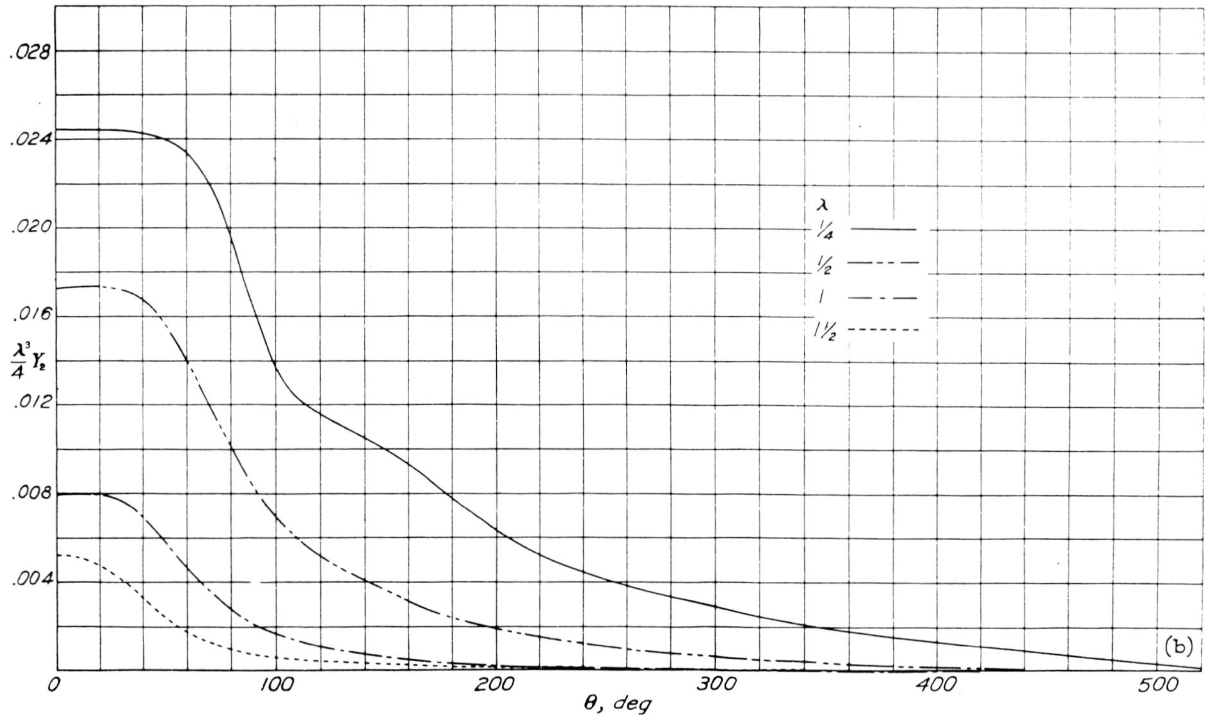

(b) Four-blade propeller. (See table IV.)

FIGURE 8.—The function $\frac{\lambda^3}{4}Y_2$ against θ for four values of λ.

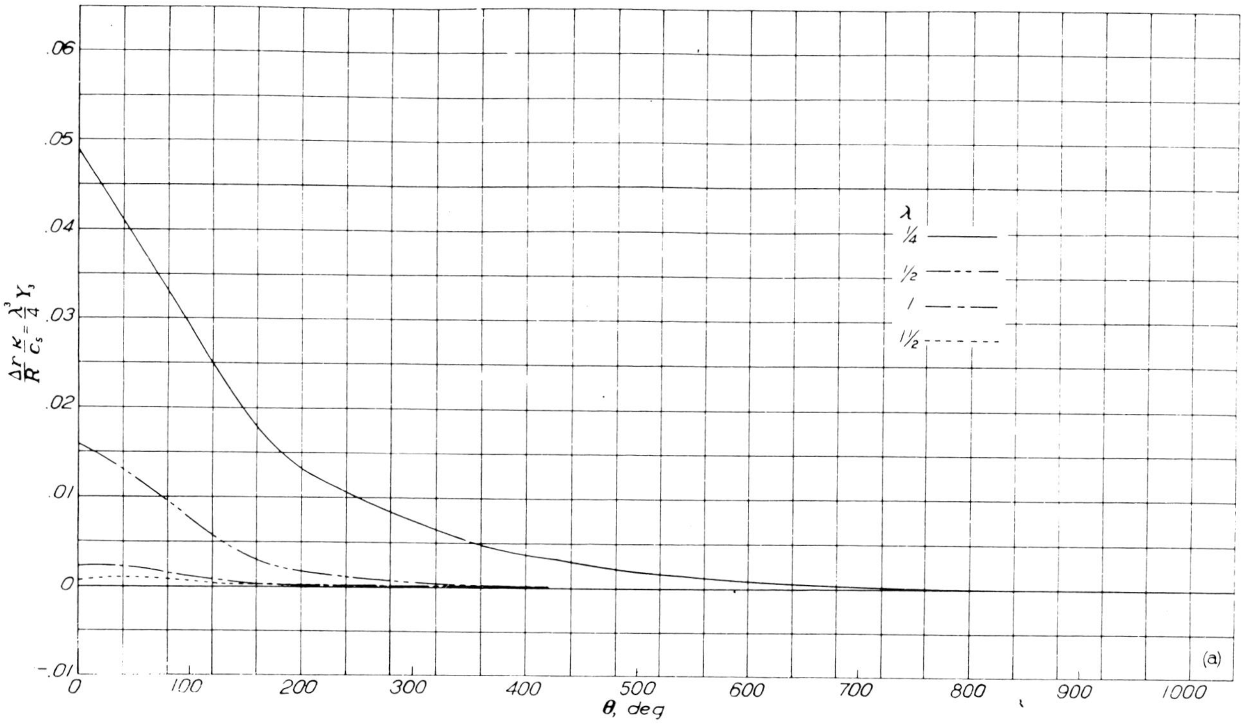

(a) Two-blade propeller. (See table V.)

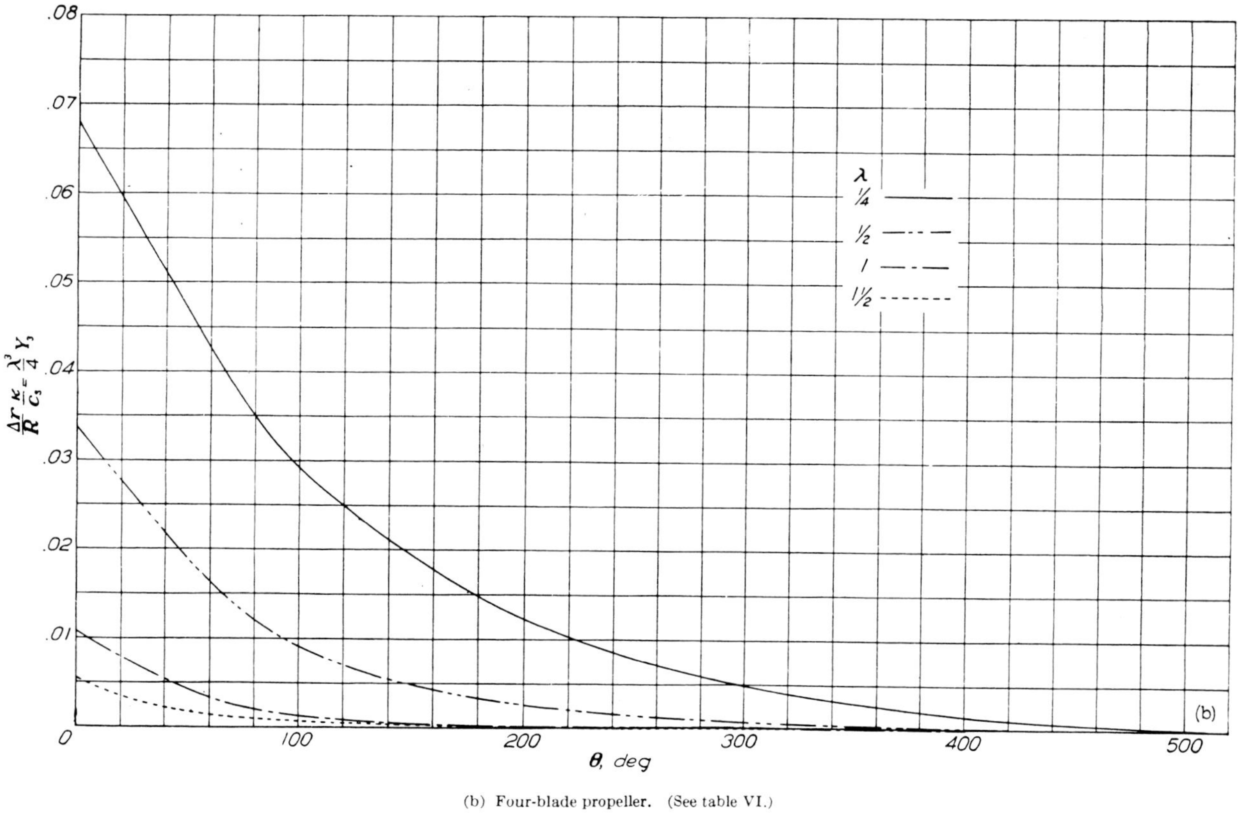

(b) Four-blade propeller. (See table VI.)

FIGURE 9.—The contour function $\frac{\Delta r}{R}\frac{\kappa}{c_s}=\frac{\lambda^3}{4}Y_3$ against θ for four values of λ.

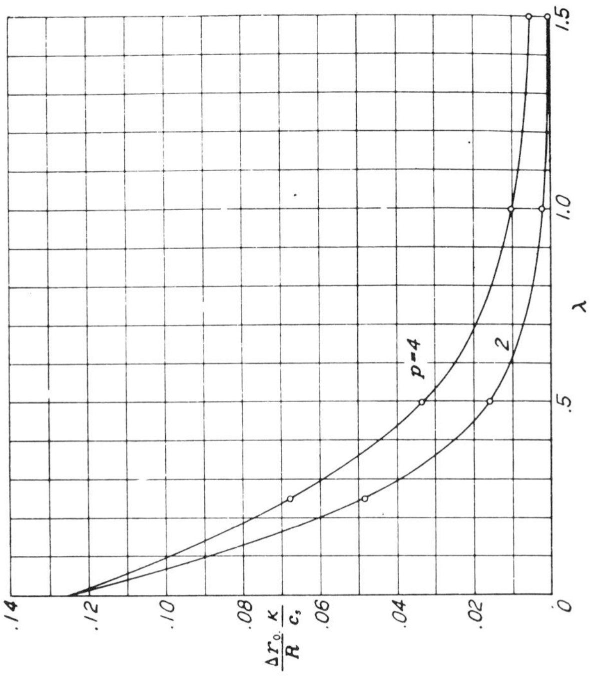

FIGURE 10.—Contraction coefficient $\frac{\Delta r_0}{R}\frac{\kappa}{c_s}$ against λ for two- and four-blade propellers.

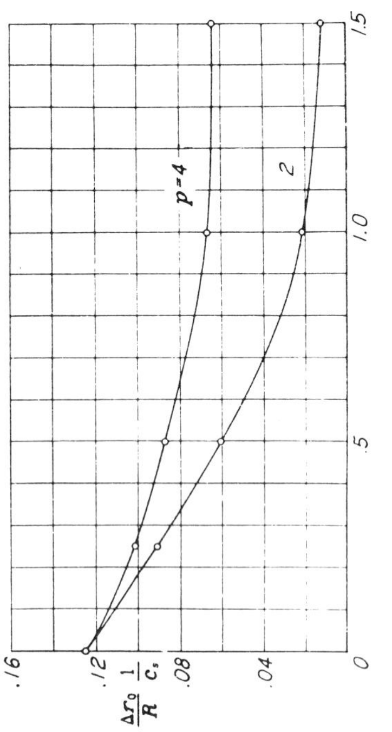

FIGURE 11.—Contraction coefficient $\frac{\Delta r_0}{R}\frac{1}{c_s}$ against λ for two- and four-blade propellers.

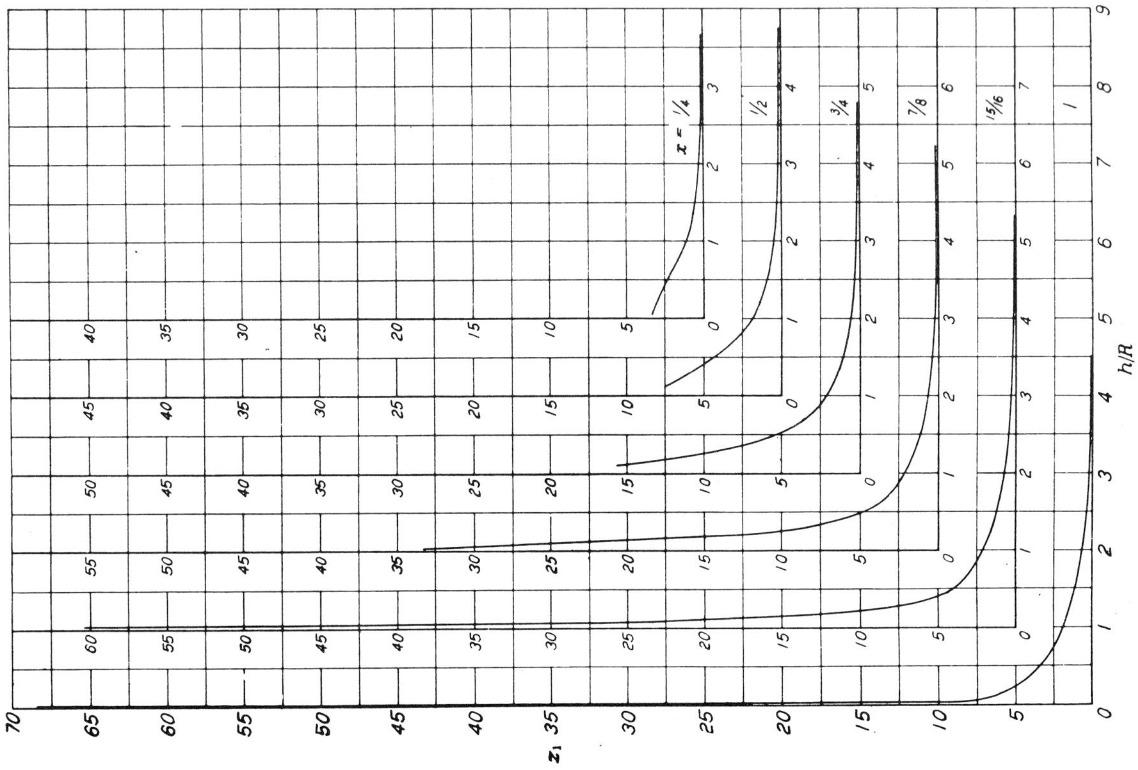

FIGURE 12.—The function z_1 against h/R for several values of x.

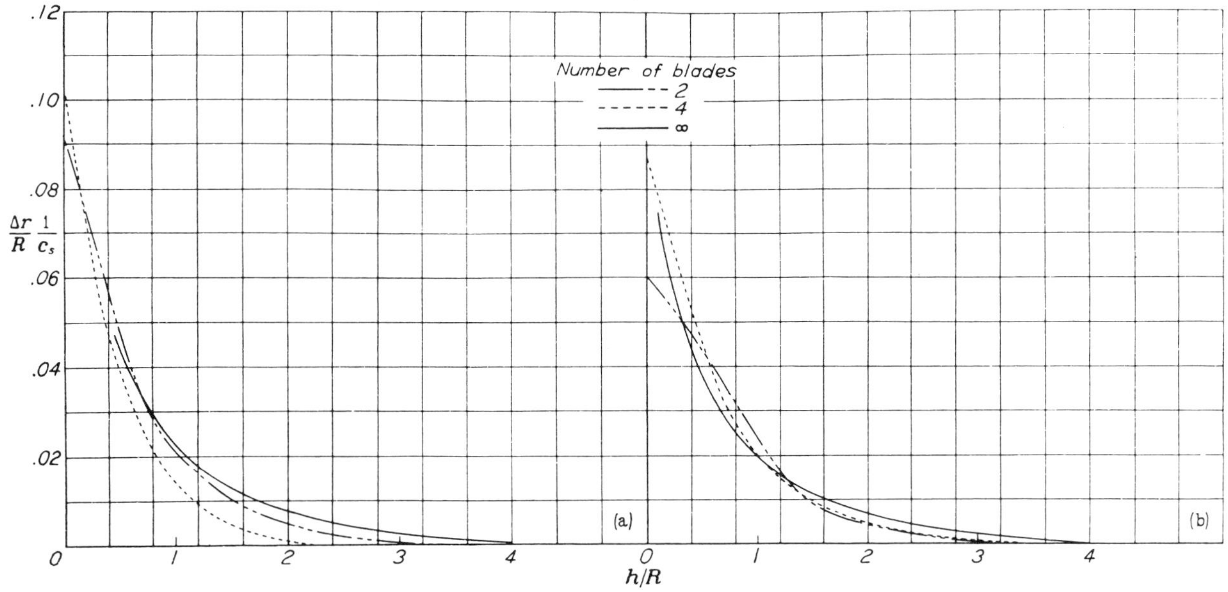

(a) λ=¼. (b) λ=½.

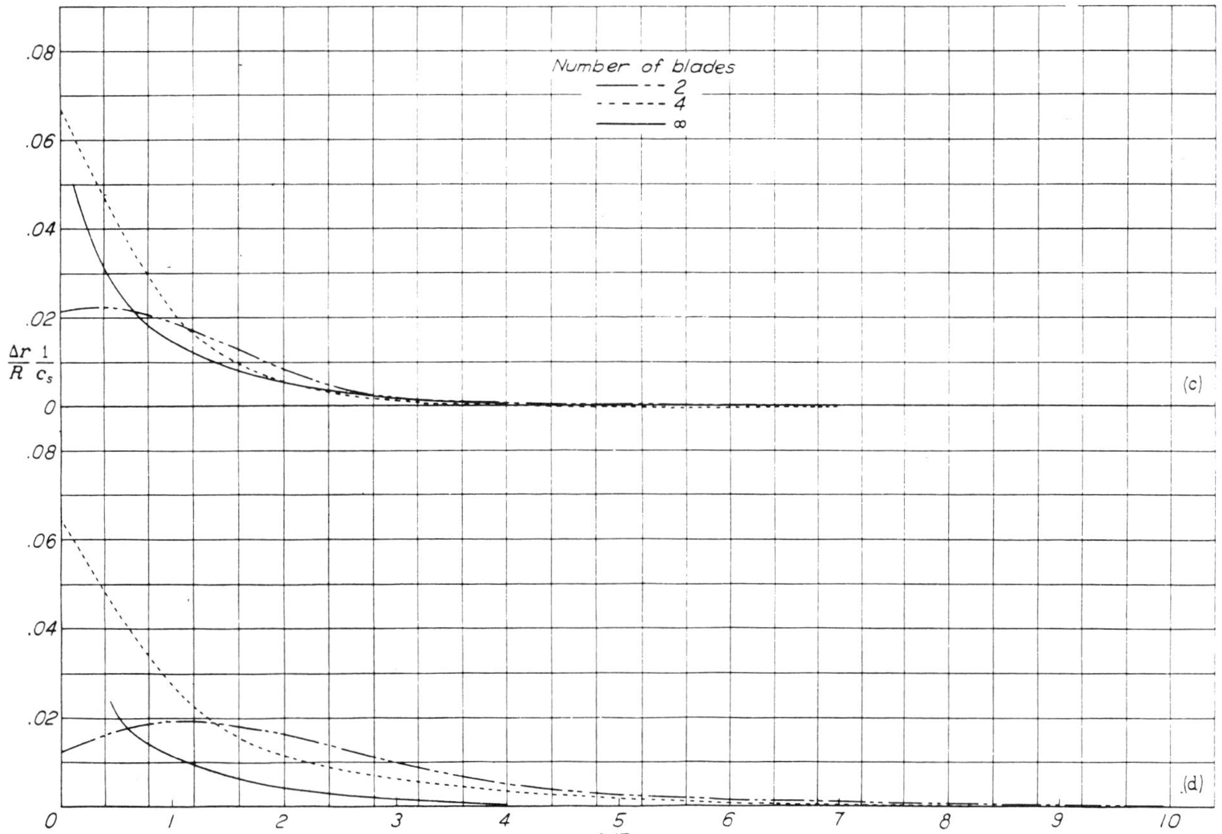

(c) λ=1. (d) λ=1½.

FIGURE 13.—Contour lines of wake helixes. (See table VII.)

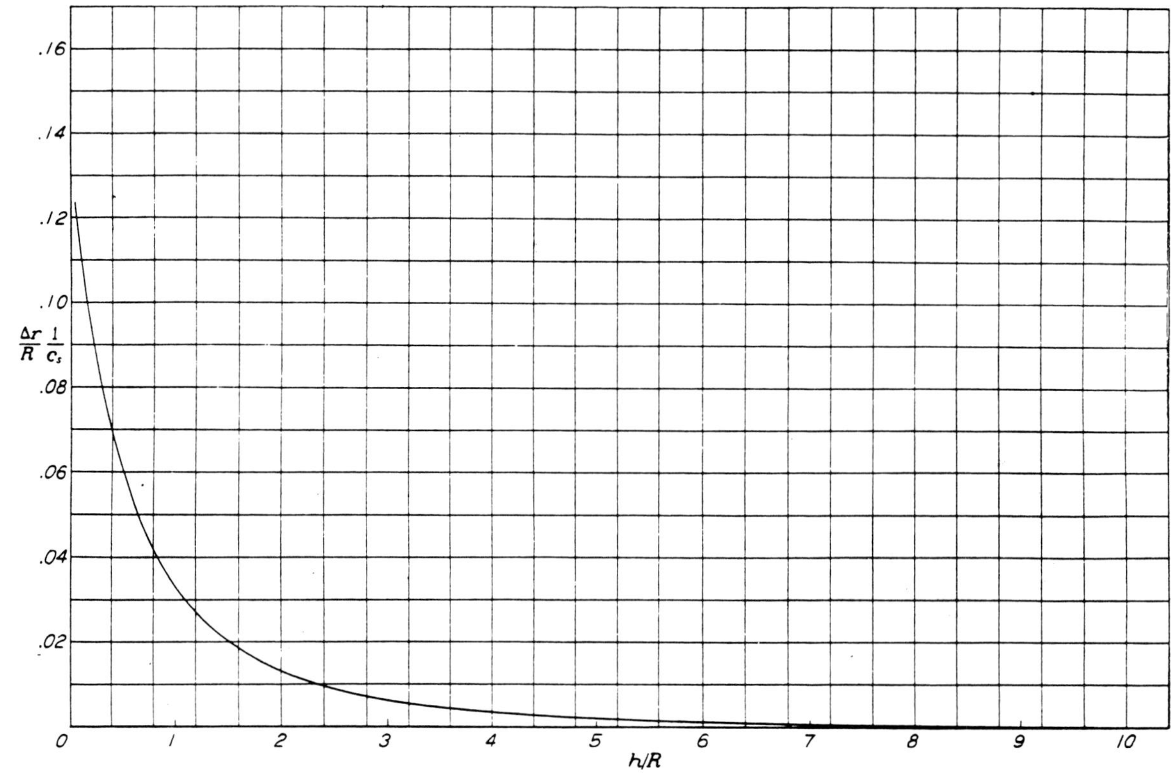

FIGURE 14.—Contour lines of wake for $p=\infty$. Dual rotation. (See table VIII.)

THE THEORY OF PROPELLERS

IV—THRUST, ENERGY, AND EFFICIENCY FORMULAS FOR SINGLE- AND DUAL-ROTATING PROPELLERS WITH IDEAL CIRCULATION DISTRIBUTION

BY THEODORE THEODORSEN

National Advisory Committee for Aeronautics

Report No. 778, 1944

SUMMARY

Simple and exact expressions are given for the efficiency of single- and dual-rotating propellers with ideal circulation distribution as given by the Goldstein functions for single-rotating propellers and by the new functions for dual-rotating propellers from part I of the present series. The efficiency is shown to depend primarily on a defined load factor and, to a very small extent, on an axial loss factor. Tables and graphs are included for practical use of the results. The present paper is the fourth in a series on the theory of propellers.

INTRODUCTION

The thrust, the energy loss, and the efficiency of a propeller are given completely and uniquely by the condition of the wake far behind the propeller. Detailed knowledge of the propeller required to create the particular wake pattern is not needed; in fact, the propeller is not uniquely determined by the wake pattern. An element of lift may be transposed in a direction tangent to the vortex surface in such a manner as to maintain the identical vortex pattern far behind the propeller.

Several equivalent propellers may thus exist—all with the same vortex surface far behind the propeller. Such quantities as the diameter, the pitch, and the rate of advance of the surface of discontinuity far behind the propeller are therefore of a more fundamental significance in many respects than the similar quantities referring to the propeller. At any rate, it has been found convenient for the present theoretical treatment to consider all quantities as referring to the conditions of the ultimate wake. Only in the final stage of the actual design of the propeller are the interrelations of the propeller and the ultimate wake of concern. For the present investigation only knowledge of the ultimate wake is required. The thrust, the various energy losses, and the efficiency are dependent only on the ultimate wake.

The present paper is the fourth in a series on the theory of propellers. The first of the series (reference 1) deals with a set of new functions for the thrust distribution of dual-rotating propellers. The second (reference 2) concerns the axial interference velocity, and the third (reference 3) treats of the contraction of the propeller wake.

734647—47

SYMBOLS

θ	angular coordinate on vortex sheet
R	tip radius of propeller
x	nondimensional radius in terms of tip radius
z	axial coordinate
p	number of blades of propeller; also, pressure
Γ	circulation at radius x
ω	angular velocity of propeller
V	advance velocity of propeller
w	rearward displacement velocity of helical vortex surface (at infinity)
λ	advance ratio $\left(\frac{V+w}{\omega R}\right)$
$K(x)$	circulation function for single rotation $\left(\frac{p\Gamma\omega}{2\pi(V+w)w}\right)$
$K(x, \theta)$	circulation function for dual rotation
κ	mass coefficient $\left(2\int_0^1 K(x)x\,dx \text{ or } \frac{1}{\pi}\int_0^1\int_0^{2\pi} K(x, \theta)x\,d\theta\,dx\right)$
F	projected area of helix (at infinity)
S	control surface (at infinity)
σ	volume of wake region
ρ	density of fluid
v	interference velocity
v_z	axial interference velocity
v_r	radial interference velocity
v_t	tangential interference velocity
ϕ	velocity potential
T	thrust
H	pitch of wake helix $\left(2\pi\frac{V+w}{\omega}\right)$
ϵ	axial energy-loss factor
ϵ_r	radial energy-loss factor
ϵ_t	tangential energy-loss factor
E	energy loss in wake
η	efficiency $\left(\frac{TV}{TV+E}\right)$

c_s specific loading factor referred to wake at infinity $\left(\frac{2T}{F\rho V^2}\right)$

a apparent induced displacement velocity at propeller disk

MASS COEFFICIENT κ

In reference 1 the concept of a mass coefficient κ was introduced. By definition

$$\kappa=2\int_0^1 K(x)x\,dx$$

where

$$K(x)=\frac{p\Gamma\omega}{2\pi(V+w)w}$$

and x is the nondimensional radius of the wake. In more general terms to include also dual-rotating propellers, κ may be defined by

$$\kappa=\frac{1}{F}\int_F K(x,\,\theta)dS$$

where $K(x,\,\theta)$ is a function of both the radius x and the angle θ or the time t. The coefficient κ is thus the mean value of the circulation factor $K(x,\,\theta)$ over the area of the wake cross section.

It is shown in the following discussion that the momentum

$$\rho\int v\,d\sigma$$

contained in the space σ enclosed between two infinite planes perpendicular to the axis at a distance between them equal to the distance between successive surfaces of discontinuity is equal to

$$\kappa wF$$

The designation "mass coefficient" originates from this relation. The mass of air set in motion with a velocity w is of the cross section κF or, if the column F is considered to be in motion, it will attain the mean velocity κw; hence the term "mass coefficient" is used for κ. Reference 1 gives the circulation function $K(x)$ or $K(x,\,\theta)$ and the mass coefficient κ for all significant cases of single- and dual-rotating propellers. It may be seen later that the mass coefficient κ times w is not exactly identical with the thrust coefficient $\frac{1}{2}c_s$ because κ refers to a certain momentum and not to the thrust.

GENERAL CONSIDERATIONS OF PROPELLER WITH IDEAL CIRCULATION DISTRIBUTION

Expressions will be given for the thrust and energy loss for both single- and dual-rotating propellers. The discussion is restricted to the case of the ideal circulation distribution. In this case, the surface of discontinuity moves backward as a rigid surface at a constant rate of motion w. The equation of motion may be written in the form

$$p-p_0+\frac{1}{2}\rho v^2+\rho\frac{\partial\phi}{\partial t}=0$$

where the subscript 0 refers to the condition at infinity with the medium at rest. Because of the stipulation that the entire field moves backward as a rigid body, the relation

$$\phi=f(z-wt,\,x,\,\theta)$$

exists and, consequently,

$$\frac{\partial\phi}{\partial t}=-w\frac{\partial\phi}{\partial z}$$

Since $\frac{\partial\phi}{\partial z}=v_z$, it follows that

$$\frac{\partial\phi}{\partial t}=-wv_z$$

and the equation of motion for this type of rigid-pattern displacement flow is, in general,

$$p-p_0+\frac{1}{2}\rho v^2=\rho wv_z \tag{1}$$

CALCULATION OF THRUST

In calculating the thrust of the propeller, it is convenient to employ an imaginary control surface, which encloses the propeller but is infinitely distant from it. The control surface may be chosen as a cube with infinitely long sides and with the propeller at the center and the wake directed perpendicular to one wall S, crossing it in the middle and extending infinitely far beyond or outside the control surface. Let the center of the wake be the z-axis. By methods of classical mechanics, the instantaneous thrust is obtained as

$$T=\int[p-p_0+\rho(V+v_z)v_z]dS$$

Introducing equation (1) transforms this integral to

$$T=\rho\int\left[(V+w)v_z+v_z^2-\frac{1}{2}v^2\right]dS$$

Since the thrust may vary with time as is the case for the ideal dual-rotating propeller, an integration must also be performed with respect to time. This integration results in the expression

$$T=\frac{1}{t}\rho\int_0^t\int_S\left[(V+w)v_z+v_z^2-\frac{1}{2}v^2\right]dS\,dt$$

Since ϕ and therefore the velocities v and v_z are functions of $z-wt$, this integral may be obtained as a volume integral taken over a volume of an infinite cross section S and a length along the axis z equal to the distance between successive vortex sheets. This distance is

$$\frac{H}{p}=2\pi\frac{V+w}{\omega p}$$

where p is the number of blades. The integral thus becomes

$$T=\frac{1}{\frac{1}{p}H}\rho\int_\sigma\left[(V+w)v_z-\frac{1}{2}v^2+v_z^2\right]d\sigma$$

Now

$$\int_\sigma v_z d\sigma=\int_F\phi\,dS=\int_F\Gamma\,dS$$

where the surface integral is taken over one turn of the vortex surface with dS as the projection on the surface S perpendicular to the axis z. With

$$\Gamma=\frac{2\pi(V+w)w}{p\omega}K(x,\theta)$$

the following relation is obtained:

$$\frac{1}{\frac{1}{p}H}\int_\sigma v_z d\sigma=w\int_F K(x,\theta)dS$$

This relation may be transformed by the introduction of the mass coefficient κ (see reference 1), which is defined as the mean value of $K(x, \theta)$ over the projected wake area

$$\kappa=\frac{1}{F}\int_F K(x,\theta)dS$$

Then

$$\frac{1}{\frac{1}{p}H}\int_\sigma v_z d\sigma=\kappa wF$$

For the second integral occurring in the expression for the thrust, a similar treatment yields

$$\frac{1}{\frac{1}{p}H}\int_\sigma v^2 d\sigma=\kappa w^2F$$

Finally, by definition of a quantity ϵ, which may be recognized as the axial energy-loss factor, the third integral is

$$\frac{1}{\frac{1}{p}H}\int_\sigma v_z^2 d\sigma=\epsilon w^2F$$

This integral is obviously the expression for twice the axial energy loss contained in the volume σ between successive vortex sheets. Since $v_z^2<v^2$, it is evident that $\epsilon<\kappa$ and $\frac{\epsilon}{\kappa}<1$.

By use of these three expressions, the thrust may be written in the simple form

$$T=F\rho\left[(V+w)\kappa w+\epsilon w^2-\frac{1}{2}\kappa w^2\right]$$

$$=\rho F\kappa w\left[V+w\left(\frac{1}{2}+\frac{\epsilon}{\kappa}\right)\right] \qquad (2)$$

CALCULATION OF ENERGY LOSS IN WAKE

By methods of classical mechanics, it can be shown that the expression for the instantaneous energy loss in the wake is

$$E=\int_S\left[\left(p-p_0+\frac{1}{2}\rho v^2\right)v_z+\frac{1}{2}\rho v^2V\right]dS$$

By use of relation (1) this expression becomes

$$E=\rho\int_S\left(v_z^2w+\frac{1}{2}v^2V\right)dS$$

734647—47——2

By integrating over time and transferring to a volum tegral as was done for the thrust, the expression is change

$$E=\rho\frac{1}{\frac{1}{p}H}\int_\sigma\left(v_z^2w+\frac{1}{2}v^2V\right)d\sigma$$

Replacing the integrals $\int_\sigma v_z^2 d\sigma$ and $\int_\sigma v^2 d\sigma$ as before gi finally

$$E=\rho F\kappa w^2\left(\frac{\epsilon}{\kappa}w+\frac{1}{2}V\right)$$

EFFICIENCY

With the thrust and the energy loss known from equati (2) and (3), the efficiency defined as $\eta=\frac{TV}{TV+E}$ is given

$$\eta=\frac{\rho F\kappa w\left[V+w\left(\frac{1}{2}+\frac{\epsilon}{\kappa}\right)\right]V}{\rho F\kappa w\left[V+w\left(\frac{1}{2}+\frac{\epsilon}{\kappa}\right)\right]V+\rho F\kappa w^2\left(\frac{\epsilon}{\kappa}w+\frac{1}{2}V\right)}$$

or

$$\eta=\frac{\left[V+w\left(\frac{1}{2}+\frac{\epsilon}{\kappa}\right)\right]V}{(V+w)\left(V+\frac{\epsilon}{\kappa}w\right)}$$

With the introduction of a nondimensional quant $\overline{w}=\frac{w}{V}$, the efficiency becomes finally

$$\eta=\frac{1+\overline{w}\left(\frac{1}{2}+\frac{\epsilon}{\kappa}\right)}{(1+\overline{w})\left(1+\frac{\epsilon}{\kappa}\overline{w}\right)}$$

which is the exact expression for the ideal efficiency of t heavily loaded single- or dual-rotating propeller. T efficiency is a function of the velocity ratio w/V infinit far behind the propeller and is dependent on only one oth parameter ϵ/κ, which is the ratio of the axial loss to the tot loss.

By introducing the specific loading factor c_s in equ tion (2), the following expression is obtained:

$$\frac{1}{2}c_s=\frac{T}{F\rho V^2}=\kappa\overline{w}\left[1+\overline{w}\left(\frac{1}{2}+\frac{\epsilon}{\kappa}\right)\right]$$

Substituting the quantity c_s in equation (4) gives

$$\eta=\frac{\left(\frac{1}{2}+A\right)\left(\frac{1}{2}+\frac{\epsilon}{\kappa}\right)^2}{\left(\frac{\epsilon}{\kappa}+A\right)\left(\frac{1}{2}+\frac{1}{2}\frac{\epsilon}{\kappa}+\frac{\epsilon}{\kappa}A\right)}$$

where

$$A^2=\frac{1}{4}+\frac{1}{2}\frac{c_s}{\kappa}\left(\frac{1}{2}+\frac{\epsilon}{\kappa}\right)$$

This formula shows the efficiency as a function primarily the parameter c_s/κ with a slight dependence on ϵ/κ. T efficiencies from the formulas given are plotted as functio of $\overline{w}$ and c_s/κ in figures 1 and 2, respectively; numeri values of the efficiencies are listed in tables I and II.

TABLE I

PROPELLER EFFICIENCY

$$\left[\eta=\frac{1+\overline{w}\left(\frac{1}{2}+\frac{\epsilon}{\kappa}\right)}{(1+\overline{w})\left(1+\frac{\epsilon}{\kappa}\overline{w}\right)}\right]$$

w \ ϵ/κ	η						
	0	1/100	1/10	1/5	2/5	3/5	1
0	1.0000	1.0000	1.0000	1.0000	1.0000	1.0000	1.0000
.05	.9762	.9762	.9760	.9759	.9757	.9754	.9751
.10	.9545	.9545	.9541	.9537	.9528	.9520	.9504
.15	.9348	.9347	.9338	.9329	.9311	.9294	.9263
.20	.9167	.9165	.9150	.9135	.9105	.9077	.9028

TABLE II

PROPELLER EFFICIENCY (IN SERIES FORM)

$$\left[\eta=1-\frac{1}{4}\left(\frac{c_s}{\kappa}\right)+\frac{3}{16}\left(\frac{c_s}{\kappa}\right)^2-\frac{1}{16}\left[\frac{5}{2}+2\frac{\epsilon}{\kappa}-\left(\frac{\epsilon}{\kappa}\right)^2\right]\left(\frac{c_s}{\kappa}\right)^3+\ldots\right]$$

c_s/κ \ ϵ/κ	η						
	0	1/100	1/10	1/5	2/5	3/5	1
0	1.0000	1.0000	1.0000	1.0000	1.0000	1.0000	1.0000
.1	.9767	.9767	.9767	.9767	.9767	.9766	.9766
.2	.9563	.9562	.9561	.9560	.9559	.9558	.9557
.3	.9377	.9376	.9373	.9370	.9366	.9362	.9360
.4	.9200	.9199	.9192	.9186	.9174	.9166	.9160
.5	.9023	.9022	.9009	.8995	.8973	.8958	.8945

It is of some interest to give the exact expression for η as a function of $\overline{w}$ and of c_s/κ in the form of infinite power series. These series are

$$\eta=1-\frac{1}{2}\overline{w}+\frac{1}{2}\left(1-\frac{\epsilon}{\kappa}\right)\overline{w}^2-\frac{1}{2}\left(1-\frac{\epsilon}{\kappa}-\frac{\epsilon^2}{\kappa^2}\right)\overline{w}^3+\ldots \tag{6}$$

and

$$\eta=1-\frac{1}{4}\frac{c_s}{\kappa}+\frac{3}{16}\left(\frac{c_s}{\kappa}\right)^2-\frac{1}{16}\left(\frac{5}{2}+2\frac{\epsilon}{\kappa}-\frac{\epsilon^2}{\kappa^2}\right)\left(\frac{c_s}{\kappa}\right)^3+\ldots \tag{7}$$

The very small dependence of η on ϵ/κ, particularly in equation (7), is evident.

INDUCED VELOCITY AT PROPELLER

If the efficiency is written in the form

$$\eta=\frac{1}{1+a}$$

the quantity a gives the apparent induced displacement velocity at the propeller disk. From equation (4)

$$a=\frac{\frac{1}{2}\overline{w}+\frac{\epsilon}{\kappa}\overline{w}^2}{1+\overline{w}\left(\frac{1}{2}+\frac{\epsilon}{\kappa}\right)} \tag{8}$$

or, in power series in $\overline{w}$,

$$a=\frac{1}{2}\overline{w}-\frac{1}{2}\left(\frac{1}{2}-\frac{\epsilon}{\kappa}\right)\overline{w}^2+\frac{1}{2}\left(\frac{1}{4}-\frac{\epsilon^2}{\kappa^2}\right)\overline{w}^3+\ldots \tag{9}$$

or, in terms of c_s/κ,

$$a=\frac{1}{4}\frac{c_s}{\kappa}-\frac{1}{8}\left(\frac{c_s}{\kappa}\right)^2+\frac{1}{16}\left(\frac{1}{2}+\frac{\epsilon}{\kappa}\right)\left(\frac{5}{2}-\frac{\epsilon}{\kappa}\right)\left(\frac{c_s}{\kappa}\right)^3+\ldots \tag{10}$$

FINAL REMARKS

Exact formulas for the ideal efficiencies have been developed. The efficiency is given simply as

$$\eta=f_1\left(\overline{w},\frac{\epsilon}{\kappa}\right)$$

or

$$\eta=f_2\left(\frac{c_s}{\kappa},\frac{\epsilon}{\kappa}\right)$$

It has been shown by series developments and graphs that the dependence of η on the parameter ϵ/κ, which is the axial loss in terms of the total loss, is very small, particularly in the second formula. For this reason the numerical value of ϵ/κ need not be known to a high degree of accuracy. It can be shown that ϵ/κ is approximately equal to κ and, for most practical purposes, this approximation is sufficient. On the other hand, the formulas are exact and the value of ϵ must be obtained to the degree of exactness actually desired. Values of ϵ for single-rotating two-blade propellers are given as an example in the appendix.

Langley Memorial Aeronautical Laboratory,
National Advisory Committee for Aeronautics,
Langley Field, Va., *October 12, 1944.*

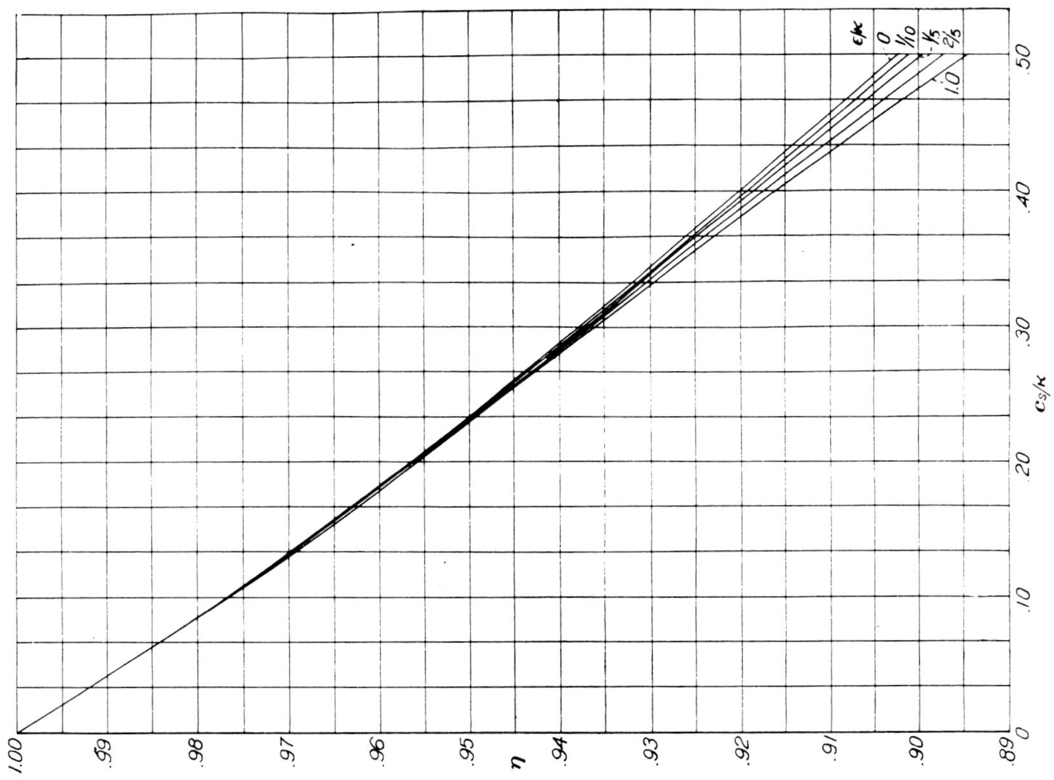

FIGURE 2.—Propeller efficiency.

$$\eta=\frac{\left[1+\sqrt{1+\frac{c_s}{\kappa}\left(1+2\frac{\epsilon}{\kappa}\right)}\right]\left(\frac{1}{2}+\frac{\epsilon}{\kappa}\right)^2}{\left[\frac{\epsilon}{\kappa}+\frac{1}{2}\sqrt{1+\frac{c_s}{\kappa}\left(1+2\frac{\epsilon}{\kappa}\right)}\right]\left[1+\frac{\epsilon}{\kappa}+\frac{\epsilon}{\kappa}\sqrt{1+\frac{c_s}{\kappa}\left(1+2\frac{\epsilon}{\kappa}\right)}\right]}$$

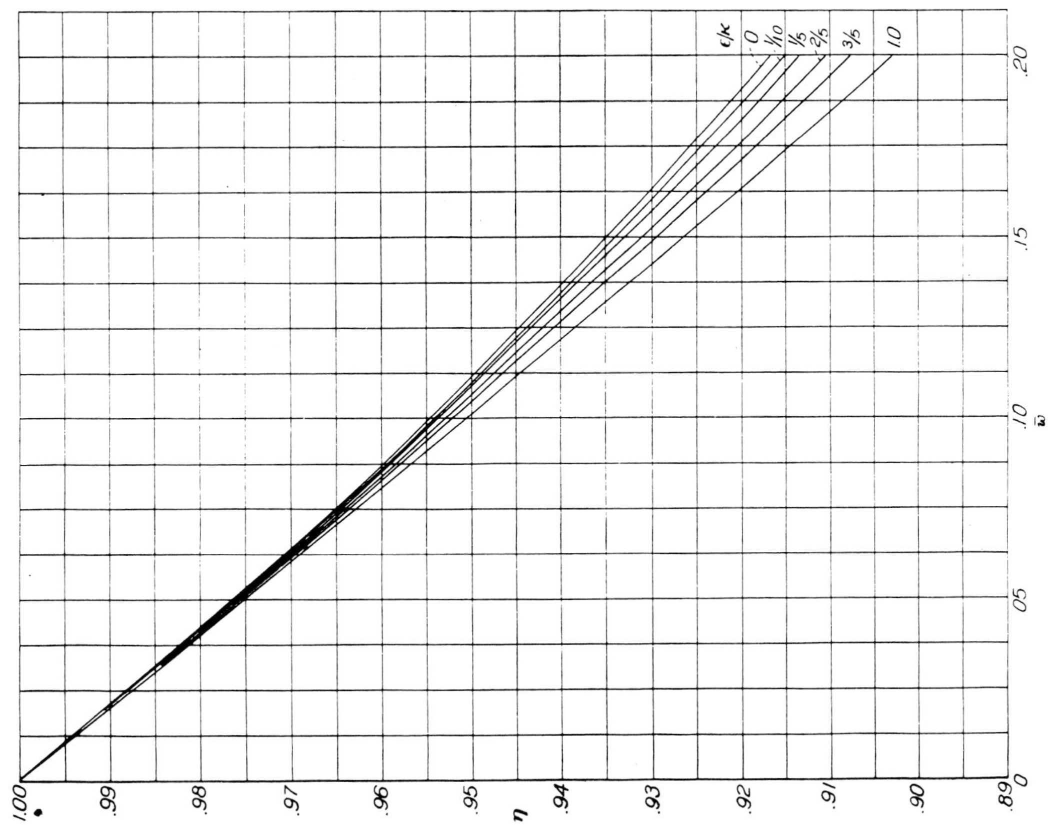

FIGURE 1.—Propeller efficiency.

$$\eta=\frac{1+\bar{w}\left(\frac{1}{2}+\frac{\epsilon}{\kappa}\right)}{(1+\bar{w})\left(1+\frac{\epsilon}{\kappa}\bar{w}\right)}$$

APPENDIX

DETERMINATION OF AXIAL LOSS FACTOR ϵ

It is seen from the efficiency formulas that the axial loss ratio ϵ/κ enters as a parameter. Since the dependence is very small, it is sufficient to know an approximate value of ϵ/κ. It is concluded from the following discussion that the loss ratio ϵ/κ is only slightly greater than the numerical value of the mass coefficient κ, since this relation holds for the known case of an infinite number of blades and shows reasonable agreement also in the case of a two-blade propeller for $\lambda=\frac{1}{2}$. Until the loss ratio has been obtained by direct calculation, the practice of putting $\frac{\epsilon}{\kappa}=\kappa$ is considered satisfactory for all purposes.

Axial, tangential, and radial loss factors are defined for single-rotating propellers by

$$\epsilon=\frac{1}{w^2F}\int_S v_z^2dS$$

$$\epsilon_t=\frac{1}{w^2F}\int_S v_t^2dS$$

and

$$\epsilon_r=\frac{1}{w^2F}\int_S v_r^2dS$$

respectively. Further, the total loss factor is given as

$$\epsilon+\epsilon_t+\epsilon_r=\kappa$$

In figure 3, $\frac{d\epsilon}{d(x^2)}$, $\frac{d\epsilon_t}{d(x^2)}$, and $\frac{d\epsilon_r}{d(x^2)}$ are plotted against x^2 for the case of a two-blade propeller with $\lambda=\frac{1}{2}$. These plots were made by using the functions and constants given by Goldstein for the velocities v_z, v_t, and v_r. The curves, upon integration, yield the values

$$\epsilon=0.0925$$

$$\epsilon_t=0.0768$$

$$\epsilon_r=0.0932$$

The sum of these three,

$$\kappa=\epsilon+\epsilon_t+\epsilon_r=0.2625$$

is very nearly equal to the value of κ obtained from figure 3 in part I (reference 1). It is noted that the radial loss, which has been neglected in all previous discussions of this subject, is the largest of the three losses.

In the case of an infinite number of blades, the formulas for $\frac{d\epsilon}{d(x^2)}$ and $\frac{d\epsilon_t}{d(x^2)}$ can be integrated explicitly to give

$$\epsilon=1+\frac{\lambda^2}{1+\lambda^2}-2\lambda^2\log\left(1+\frac{1}{\lambda^2}\right)$$

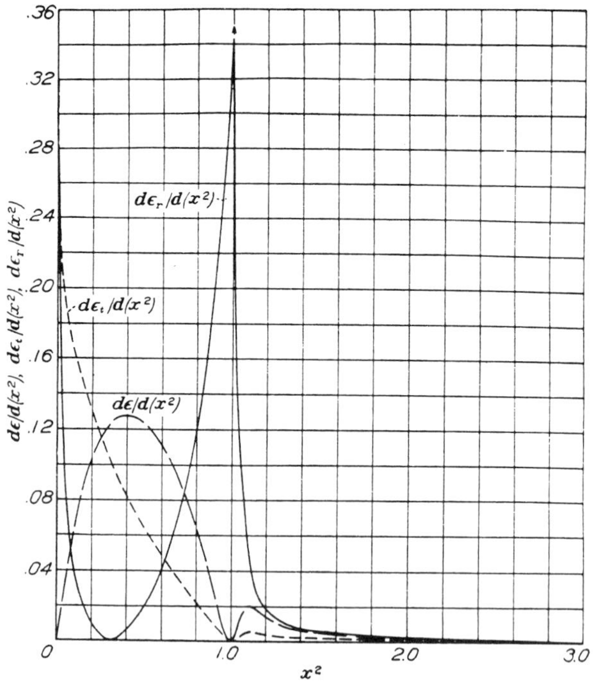

FIGURE 3.—Distribution of axial, tangential, and radial energy losses for two-blade propeller with $\lambda=\frac{1}{2}$.

$$\epsilon_t=-\frac{\lambda^2}{1+\lambda^2}+\lambda^2\log\left(1+\frac{1}{\lambda^2}\right)$$

and

$$\epsilon_r=0$$

The total energy loss is then

$$\kappa=\epsilon+\epsilon_t=1-\lambda^2\log\left(1+\frac{1}{\lambda^2}\right)$$

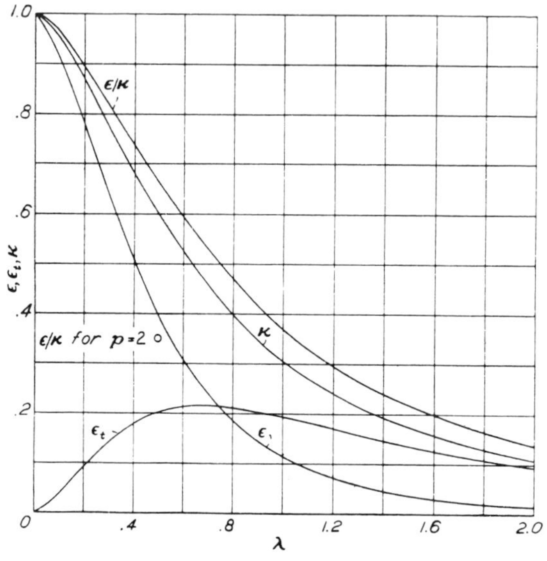

FIGURE 4.—Loss functions for an infinite number of blades.

The functions ϵ, ϵ_t, and κ are plotted against λ in figure 4. A plot of the function ϵ/κ is also shown in figure 4. The value of ϵ/κ for a two-blade propeller with $\lambda=\frac{1}{2}$, which is obtained from the given data, is shown by a point in figure 4. It is noted that, for the case of an infinite number of blades, ϵ/κ is slightly greater than κ; whereas, for the two-blade propeller with $\lambda=\frac{1}{2}$, $\frac{\epsilon}{\kappa}=0.35$ and $\kappa=0.2625$. The quantity ϵ/κ may therefore be tentatively estimated as somewhat greater than κ.

REFERENCES

1. Theodorsen, Theodore: The Theory of Propellers. I—Determination of the Circulation Function and the Mass Coefficient for Dual-Rotating Propellers. NACA Rep. No. 775, 1944.
2. Theodorsen, Theodore: The Theory of Propellers. II—Method for Calculating the Axial Interference Velocity. NACA Rep. No. 776, 1944.
3. Theodorsen, Theodore: The Theory of Propellers. III—The Slipstream Contraction with Numerical Values for Two-Blade and Four-Blade Propellers. NACA Rep. No. 777, 1944.

NOTE ON THE THEOREMS OF BJERKNES AND CROCCO

BY THEODORE THEODORSEN

National Advisory Committee for Aeronautics

Langley Memorial Aeronautical Laboratory, NACA Technical Note No. 1073, Washington D.C., May 1946

SUMMARY

The theorems of Bjerknes and Crocco are of great interest in the theory of flow around airfoils at Mach numbers near and above unity. A brief note shows how both theorems are developed by short vector transformations.

INTRODUCTION

The flow field at supercritical velocities may be obtained by inserting the required shock wave or waves and adjusting the fields to satisfy all boundary conditions. If the shock waves are inserted by proper procedure, there will exist a potential field up to the first shock wave and a field with rotation extending between and behind the shock waves. The theorems of Bjerknes and Crocco (Ref. 1) refer to such rotational fields.

SYMBOLS

$\bar{q}$	fluid velocity vector
ρ	density
p	pressure
R	gas constant
T	absolute temperature
T_0	stagnation temperature
k	adiabatic constant
r	distance from axis of symmetry
S	entropy
c_p	specific heat at constant pressure

THEOREM OF BJERKNES

The equation of motion of a fluid for the stationary case is

$$\bar{q} \times \text{curl}\bar{q} = \frac{1}{\rho} \nabla p + \frac{1}{2} \nabla q^2 \tag{1}$$

For a perfect gas

$$p = \rho RT$$

and

$$\frac{1}{2} q^2 = c_p(T_0 - T)$$

where T_0 is the constant stagnation temperature and c_p is the specific heat at constant pressure. Equation (1) hence transforms to

$$\frac{q \times \text{curl}\bar{q}}{T} = R\frac{\nabla p}{p} + c_p \frac{\nabla(T_0 - T)}{T} \tag{2}$$

The right-hand side of Eq. (2) is seen to be

$$\nabla(\log p^R - \log \nabla T^{c_p}) = \nabla \log\left(\frac{p^R}{T^{c_p}}\right)$$

$$= R \nabla \log \frac{p}{\frac{k}{T^{k-1}}} = \nabla S$$

where S is the entropy. Thus

$$\frac{\bar{q} \times \text{curl}\bar{q}}{T} = \nabla S \tag{3}$$

which is the theorem of Bjerknes.

THEOREM OF CROCCO

The theorem of Crocco may be obtained from the theorem of Bjerknes by a vector transformation. Since $T = p/\rho R$, the left-hand side of Eq. (3) may be written

$$\rho\bar{q} \times \frac{\text{curl}\bar{q}}{p} R$$

Take the curl of this expression, omitting the constant R:

$$\text{curl}\left(\rho\bar{q} \times \frac{\text{curl}\bar{q}}{p}\right) = \rho\bar{q}\ \text{div}\left(\frac{\text{curl}\bar{q}}{p}\right) - \frac{\text{curl}\bar{q}}{p}\ \text{div}\ \rho\bar{q}$$

$$+ \left(\left(\frac{\text{curl}\bar{q}}{p}\right) \cdot \nabla\right)\rho\bar{q} - (\rho\bar{q} \cdot \nabla)\frac{\text{curl}\bar{q}}{p}$$

For two-dimensional flow the three first terms on the right of this equation are identically zero since the vector curl $\bar{q}$ is perpendicular to the vector $\bar{q}$ and since div $\rho\bar{q} = 0$. With reference to Eq. (3) it is therefore seen that

$$(\rho q \cdot \nabla)\frac{\text{curl}\bar{q}}{p} = 0$$

or that curl$\bar{q}/p$ is constant along the streamlines. The useful result obtained then is that the rotation remains proportional to the absolute pressure p along each and all streamlines. This is the theorem of Crocco.

Similarly, for flow with rotation symmetry, the following expression may be written:

$$\rho\bar{q}r \times \frac{\text{curl}\bar{q}}{pr} R$$

where r is the radius from the center of symmetry. By the same reasoning curl$\bar{q}/pr$ is shown to be constant along each streamline. This expression, when translated into words, means that the rotation along a streamline is proportional to the pressure times the distance from the axis of symmetry.

Langley Memorial Aeronautical Laboratory
National Advisory Committee for Aeronautics
Langley Field, Va., August 14, 1945

REFERENCE

[1]Crocco, L.: Eine neue Stromfunktion für die Erforschung der Bewegung der Gase mit Rotation. Z.f.a.M.M., Bd. 17, Heft 1, Feb. 1937, pp. 1–7.

NOTE ON THE THEORY OF HURRICANES

BY THEODORE THEODORSEN

National Advisory Committee for Aeronautics

Published in *Journal of the Aeronautical Sciences,* Vol. 19, No. 9, September 1952.

THERE ARE certain interesting consequences of the new theory of turbulence* applying directly to the theory of hurricanes. These are: Hurricanes are created by the "collapse," in a universal pattern, of a large-scale boundary layer of considerable horizontal extension. Contrary to the situation in a small-scale boundary layer, where the more or less symmetrical "horseshoe" develops, only the counterclockwise branch of the vertical motion will generally appear in the northern hemispheres, since there is no longer complete symmetry because of the action of the Coriolis forces. Evidently, the required boundary layer develops by the passing of an air mass over extensive smooth surfaces such as the oceans or plains. The boundary layer becomes superlatively unstable, or, one may say, there obtains under such circumstances a greatly delayed transition. Then, let us say that somewhere on the surface below the air mass an obstruction occurs; the transition takes place violently, since the lower critical may have been passed by a thousand-fold. Turbulence develops behind the obstruction and produces an extensive retarded air mass. This situation is then mathematically equivalent to the existence of a portion of a large vortex extending from the ground over the upper boundary of the disturbed air mass and down to the ground on the other side of the retarded air mass. As the Reynolds Number is far above the critical, the vortex develops with great intensity by the universal turbulent mechanism; the horizontal portion of the vortex is moved downstream and upwards as shown in the new theory of turbulence. Clearly, the counterclockwise arm will develop most easily and, at least for large dimensions, will appear alone. Thus, the creative mechanism of hurricanes is entirely similar to the mechanism of turbulence.

*The Second Midwestern Conference on Fluid Mechanics, March 17, 1952. Theodore Theodorsen, "Mechanism of Turbulence."

MECHANISM OF TURBULENCE

BY THEODORE THEODORSEN

Presented at the Second Midwestern Conference on Fluid Mechanics

1952

Abstract

By an examination of the equation of motion it has been found possible to describe the physical properties of the mechanism responsible for the creation of turbulence. Turbulence is characterized by a definite three dimensional secondary flow pattern. The physical magnitude of such a pattern is shown to be proportional to a certain significant distance such as the distance to the boundary of the flow or to such dimensions as the diameter of a pipe. Thus the basic reason for the Karman similarity law and the power law for pressure drop and heat transmission may be accounted for. As a corollary it is further found that strictly two-dimensional flows are stable; a proof is indicated for the parallel two-dimensional flow of the Orr-Sommerfeld type. In the latter case, a small three-dimensional effect is required to maintain a disturbance.

The proposed mechanism provides transfer of momentum and heat by a large scale secondary flow the pattern of which is similar everywhere, and not by a gradient mechanism visualized by earlier theories. The transfer is due to large scale structures of horseshoe or ring shape with a strong material current directed along a well defined axis which forms an obtuse angle with the mean velocity vector in the plane of the largest gradient. The mechanism also yields the skewness noted in shear flow and is consistent with the observations on intermittency.

Introduction

As apparently the turbulent fluctuations are definitely three-dimensional it is of some interest first to clear up an apparent contradiction, namely the results of the Orr-Sommerfeld equation which relate to a disturbance in a strictly two-dimensional parallel flow. The excellent experimental work by Schubauer and Skramstad (Ref. 1) leaves no doubt that the predicted disturbances are observable and reproducible. It is also noted that the authors are aware of the three-dimensional nature of the flow as comments are made to this effect.

In the following we shall first study the two-dimensional equation of motion and then take up the three-dimensional case. It will be shown that it is possible to extract from the equation of motion information on the origin of turbulence.

Two-dimensional Disturbance, Parallel Flow

Equation of motion in two-dimensional flow:

$$\frac{\partial \omega}{\partial t} + q \cdot \nabla\omega = \nu \nabla^2 \omega \quad \text{or} \quad \frac{D}{Dt}\omega = \nu \nabla^2 \omega \qquad (1)$$

Let $\omega = \omega_o + \omega_1$ where ω_o represents the steady parallel flow and ω_1 is a small disturbance.

Let us specify that the boundaries, $y = 0$ and $y = y_c$, remain stationary or have a fixed prescribed velocity. For instance, the lower boundary may be fixed while the upper has a given velocity, q_c, as in the usual treatment of the boundary flow in the Orr-Sommerfeld equation.

Then

$$\int \omega_1 \, dA = 0 \qquad (2)$$

Let us further specify that the tube connects two chambers with pressures p_1 and p_2, respectively, and that these pressures be kept constant. As the cross-section of the (long) tube is constant, then

$$\int \omega_1 \, ds = 0 \qquad (3)$$

This relatinn states that the force on the tube wall remains constant and equal to the available pressure exerted at the inlet and outlet. Since no external forces are applied to cause a disturbance of the medium within the tube, this equality of the forces follows from principles of mechanics.

In the layer of the wall one may also integrate the pressure drop along the tube from beginning to end, and one gets, similarly,

$$\int \frac{\partial \omega_1}{\partial n} \cdot ds = 0 \qquad (3b)$$

By similar reasoning one may see from the equation of motion that all the higher derivatives taken along the wall integrate to zero

$$\int \frac{\partial^m}{\partial n^m} \omega_1 \, ds = 0 \qquad (3c)$$

Since ω_o is to represent the equilibrium flow one has further everywhere:

$$\nabla^2 \omega_o = 0 \qquad (4)$$

Let us transform Eq. 1 by multiplying by ω which is now a scalar quantity. One obtains:

$$\frac{\partial}{\partial t}\left[\frac{1}{2}\omega^2\right] + q \cdot \nabla\left[\frac{1}{2}\omega^2\right] = \nu\omega \nabla^2 \omega \quad \text{or}$$

$$\frac{D}{Dt}\left[\frac{1}{2}\omega^2\right] = \nu\omega \nabla^2 \omega \qquad (5)$$

Let us consider a large fixed volume of the medium as an infinitely long pipe

$$W = \frac{D}{Dt}\int \frac{1}{2}\,\omega^2\,dA = \nu\int \omega\,\nabla^2\,\omega\,dA \tag{6}$$

Since the cross-section of the volume considered is small compared with the extension in the direction of the flow, it makes no difference in reality whether one considers a fixed volume of the medium $(\frac{D}{Dt})$ or a fixed volume of space $(\frac{\partial}{\partial t})$.

Let us finally introduce the substitution $\omega = \omega_o + \omega_1$ in the right hand side of Eq. 6.

One has then

$$W = \nu\int (\omega_o + \omega_1)\;\nabla^2\,(\omega_o + \omega_1)\,dA \tag{7}$$

Here $\nabla^2\,\omega_o = 0$ by Eq. 4. The term,

$$\int \omega_o\,\nabla^2\,\omega_1\,dA\,,$$

may be changed into a surface integral. The expression may be rewritten

$$\int (\mathrm{div}\,(\omega_o\,\nabla\,\omega_1) - \nabla\,\omega_o\,\nabla\,\omega_1)\,dA \tag{8}$$

From Eq. 4 it is seen that $\nabla\omega_o$ is constant everywhere, and one gets the surface or, in this case, line integral for the second term

$$-\,\nabla\omega_o\int \omega_1\,ds = c\int \omega_1\,ds \tag{9}$$

This integral is zero because of Eq. 3 which specifies that no external forces are to be applied.

The first term of Eq. 8 may be changed directly to a surface (or line) integral

$$\int \omega_o\,\frac{\partial\,\omega_1}{\partial\,n}\,ds \tag{10}$$

Here ω_o is constant along the wall and the integral is again zero because of Eq. 3b.

One gets, therefore, for Eq. 7

$$W = \frac{D}{Dt}\int \frac{1}{2}\,\omega^2\,dA = \nu\int \omega_1\,\nabla^2\,\omega_1\,dA \tag{11}$$

One has, therefore, the very specific statement that the quantity representing the total of the original flow and the superimposed disturbance dissipates at a rate equal to the rate of dissipation of the secondary flow alone.

This may be seen if one considers the main flow $\omega_0 = 0$; in other words if one imposes the identical disturbance ω_1 on the same medium within the same boundaries at rest, Eq. 6 would read simply

$$\frac{D}{Dt}\int \frac{1}{2}\,\omega_1^2\;dA = \nu \int \omega_1\,\nabla^2\omega_1\;dA \qquad . \qquad (12)$$

The quantity on the right side represents the dissipation in a closed space which is well recognized and is causing the disturbance to diminish.

It has now been proven that a disturbance of the Orr-Sommerfeld type will decrease with time. The rate of decrease, as shown in Eq. 11 is exactly the same at each instant as the one calculated in Eq. 12, which latter gives the rate of decrease in a closed space of equal dimensions. The main flow has the sole effect of disturbing the pattern but does not transfer any energy. This statement will be obvious when three-dimensional disturbances are considered. At each instant, therefore, the dissipation proceeds as if the disturbance were imposed on a medium at rest. Regardless of the instantaneous configuration of the disturbance, this dissipation is negative, that is, ω_1^2 will decrease with time. One therefore concludes that strictly two-dimensional flows of the Orr-Sommerfeld type are stable and the disturbances will decrease with time at a rate each instant equal to that of a two-dimensional disturbance in a fluid at rest.

Because of the omission of the higher order term in the Orr-Sommerfeld treatment, it may be regarded as physically real only if one inserts a force equal and opposite to the higher order term disregarded. The term usually neglected $q_1 \cdot \nabla q_1$ may be written as $\frac{1}{2}\nabla q_1^2 - q_1 \times \text{curl}\, q_1$ and the work done on the medium as

$$E = (q + q_1)\left[\frac{1}{2}\;\nabla q_1^2 \;-\; q_1 \times \text{curl}\, q_1\right]$$

where q is the velocity of the main flow. The term $-\,q\left(q_1 \times \text{curl}\, q_1\right)$ is an alternating term affecting the flow. The term

$$E_1 = \frac{1}{2}\,q\,\nabla q_1^2 = \text{div}\; q\,\frac{1}{2}\,q_1^2$$

supplies the net energy permitting q_1^2, the amplitude of the disturbance to increase along the x-axis.

There is also an increase in the dissipation. This increase is hidden by the fact that the insertion of the extraneous forces must be compensated by an extra pressure gradient along the channel. This extra pressure gradient is not apparent in the equations in which the mean velocity is merely kept constant. This last condition is evidently a physical impossibility, since the pressure gradient required is higher in the center of the channel.

The Orr-Sommerfeld picture is inherently incorrect in two respects: the force, F, which provides the necessary energy, and the gradient, ∇p_1 , which compensates for the extra dissipation, are missing. In fact there is no mechanism available to provide the extra energy $\frac{1}{2} q_1^2$ or the extra dissipation (curl $q_1)^2$ These energies are both small, but of course absolutely necessary to satisfy the energy balance. Thus no solution is possible.

Three-dimensional Disturbance

We shall continue the two-dimensional treatment given above but with one significant modification which actually corresponds to a three-dimensional treatment. It will be evident why the particular modification is important. The modification is as follows:

Let there be sinks of uniform strength in the (two-dimensional) region considered. This assumption corresponds to a statement

$$\text{div } q = - c$$

where q is the two-dimensional velocity vector and c is a positive constant.

To make the equation of motion cover such disappearance of mass, one may write

$$\frac{1}{m} \cdot \frac{D}{Dt} m q = - \frac{\nabla p}{\rho} + \nu \nabla^2 q \qquad (13)$$

since the mass is not constant within the particle of fluid considered, we may write

$$\frac{1}{m}\left[m \frac{Dq}{Dt} + q \frac{Dm}{Dt}\right] = - \frac{\nabla p}{\rho} + \nu \nabla^2 q$$

Now $\frac{1}{m} \cdot \frac{Dm}{Dt} = \text{div } q = - c$ and is kept constant. One has therefore

$$\frac{Dq}{Dt} - q c = - \frac{\nabla p}{\rho} + \nu \nabla^2 q \qquad (14)$$

Transforming as usual, by taking rotation of q = ω, one gets for such a two-dimensional case

$$\frac{\partial \omega}{\partial t} + q \quad \nabla \omega - c \omega = \nu \nabla^2 \omega \qquad (15)$$

If one multiplies by ω one has for such scalar quantities

$$\frac{1}{2} \frac{\partial}{\partial t} \omega^2 + q \nabla \frac{1}{2} \omega^2 - c \omega^2 = \nu \omega \nabla^2 \omega \qquad \text{or}$$

$$\frac{1}{2} \frac{D}{Dt} \omega^2 - c \omega^2 = \nu \omega \nabla^2 \omega \qquad (16)$$

Taking a volume integral for a fixed quantity of particles one has

$$\frac{1}{2} \frac{D}{Dt} \int \omega^2 \, dA = c \int \omega^2 \, dA + \nu \int \omega \nabla^2 \omega \, dA \tag{17}$$

This equation gives the statement regarding the mechanism of turbulence. The value of c is, as we shall find, a positive quantity differing from place to place but with a well-defined positive mean value. We shall call this factor the turbulence factor, for convenience in further discussion.

The last term in Eq. 17 may be written:

$$\nu \int \omega \nabla^2 \omega \, dA = \nu \int \left[\nabla^2 \frac{1}{2} \omega^2 - (\nabla \omega)^2 \right] dA \tag{18}$$

Equation 17 then reads

$$\frac{1}{2} \frac{D}{Dt} \int \omega^2 \, dA = c \int \omega^2 \, dA + \nu \int \left[\nabla^2 \frac{1}{2} \omega^2 - (\nabla \omega)^2 \right] dA \tag{19}$$

Now let us consider a two-dimensional region where $\nabla^2 \frac{1}{2} \omega^2$ is negative; that is, there is a peak or maximum of $\frac{1}{2} \omega^2$ in the region. The viscosity term simply gives the rate at which $\frac{1}{2} \omega^2$ is lost by conduction $\nabla^2 \frac{1}{2} \omega^2$, and by internal destruction $(\nabla \omega)^2$. The rate lost by conduction simply adds up to the rate of $\frac{1}{2} \omega^2$ lost or gained by the boundary. This is a definite value. For laminar flow and $c = 0$, the rate at which the quantity $\frac{1}{2} \omega^2$ is gained at the boundary corresponds to the rate of internal destruction $(\nabla \omega)^2$.

For the case of $c > 0$ or turbulent flow, let us say in a state of fully developed equilibrium, one sees that the term

$$c \int \omega^2 \, dA \tag{20}$$

must be equal in magnitude to the net destruction which from Eq. 17 reads

$$\nu \int \omega \nabla^2 \omega \, dA$$

It can be seen that this equilibrium occurs at a certain Reynolds number

$$R = \text{constant} \tag{22}$$

We shall next indicate the actual mechanism of turbulence. This mechanism is again apparent from the equation of motion. The proof above, regarding the stability of two-dimensional flow, may be shown to apply to flows in which the vector rot q is perpendicular to the "streamlines" as also in the flow in circular pipes. The proof is quite identical with the proof for strictly two-dimensional flows.

We shall therefore seek the solution to the turbulence problem in the three-dimensional case. The complete equation of motion may be written

$$\frac{\partial \omega}{\partial t} + q \cdot \nabla \omega = \omega \cdot \nabla q + \nu \nabla^2 \omega \qquad (23)$$

We need here only consider the non-compressible flow since the mechanism is thus fully revealed.

Let us multiply each term of Eq. 23 by the vector ω_s which is the component of the rotation vector along the direction of the mean streamlines, which are considered to have small or zero curvature.

The result is again a scalar relation:

$$\omega_s \frac{\partial \omega_s}{\partial t} + \omega_s q \cdot \nabla \omega_s = \omega_s \omega \nabla q_s + \nu \omega_s \nabla^2 \omega_s, \text{ or}$$

$$\frac{D}{Dt} \frac{1}{2} \omega_s^2 = \omega_s \omega \cdot \nabla q_s + \nu \omega_s \nabla^2 \omega_s \qquad (24)$$

In this equation it is noted that the dissipative term on the right does not contain the velocity, q. The dissipation of $\frac{1}{2} \omega_s^2$ is therefore at each instant dependent on the value of ω_s regardless of the values of q and ∇q.

In fact, if one considers the main flow stopped for one instant the disturbances expressed by ω_s will remain unaltered. The quantity

$$\omega_s \nabla^2 \omega_s \qquad (25)$$

will therefore at each instant have the same value whether it is embeded-ded in the main flow or in closed vessel of identical shape. It is known that, in the latter case, the quantity

$$\frac{D}{Dt} \int \frac{1}{2} \omega^2 \, dV \qquad (26)$$

(taken for the whole vessel) will decrease with time, and that the terms on the right side of Eq. 24 are negative. It may be seen further that the turbulence factor, c, in Eqs. 14 and 20, is equivalent to ∇q_s in Eq. 24.

Evidently the term

$$T = \omega_s \omega \cdot \nabla q_s \qquad (27)$$

is therefore the nucleus of the turbulence problem. If the right side of Eq. 24 is to remain constant or increase, T must attain a sufficiently large value to become equal or exceed the quantity (26)–or the negative value of the net dissipation in a closed vessel at each particular instant.

At the first glance, one might believe that the quantity would average out to zero. However, the structure of turbulent flow is such that this is not the case. One might note that all that is necessary is that ω_s is in phase generally with $\omega \cdot \nabla q_s$. This condition is satisfied immediately by the structure indicated next.

Note that the turbulence term (and Eq. 24) contains the vector q only in the vector gradient $\omega \cdot \nabla q_s$. This quantity has three components: $\omega_s \nabla q_s$, $\omega_z \nabla q_s$, and $\omega_n \nabla q_s$. Here ω_s is already defined as the component of ω directed along the mean flow lines. As we shall only study the transfer mechanism we shall restrict ourselves to the case where ∇q_s is zero along the streamlines. The quantity ∇q_s is also considered zero in the direction perpendicular to the streamlines and parallel to the boundary.

This leaves as the dominant quantity in the turbulence term

$$T = \omega_s \, \omega_n \, \nabla q_s \tag{28}$$

where ω_n is the component of ω in the direction of the largest gradient ∇q_s. In fact ω_n may be defined more generally as the component of ω in the direction of the largest gradient. One can readily see that the product $\omega_s \, \omega_n$ reaches a maximum at an inclination of 45° with the direction of the main flow.

Equation of Motion in Three Dimensions

We may bring out three different forms of the turbulence term.

One has $\dfrac{\partial \omega}{\partial t} + \text{curl } (\omega \times q) = - \nu \text{ curl curl } \omega$. Multiplying by ω

$\dfrac{1}{2} \dfrac{\partial}{\partial t} \omega^2 + \omega \text{ curl } (\omega \times q) = - \nu \, \omega \text{ curl curl } \omega$. But

$$\omega \text{ curl } (\omega \times q) = \text{div} \left[(\omega \times q) \times \omega \right] + (\omega \times q) \text{ curl } \omega$$

We see, by considering saturated turbulent flow in a circular pipe, that the divergence term disappears. Generally the divergence term expresses simply the quantity ω^2 crossing the boundary. One has, therefore, using time or space averages,

$$\frac{1}{2} \frac{\partial}{\partial t} \omega^2 + (\omega \times q) \text{ curl } \omega = - \nu \, \omega \text{ curl curl } \omega \tag{29}$$

The term $(\omega \times q)$ curl ω (Fig. 5) is the turbulence creating term, and has the proper sign throughout the structure or secondary flow shown in Fig. 1. By another transformation, again leaving out the divergence term, one obtains for the averages

$$\frac{1}{2} \frac{\partial}{\partial t} \omega^2 + q \, (\omega \cdot \nabla \omega) = - \nu \, \omega \text{ curl curl } \omega \tag{30}$$

The term $q \, (\omega \cdot \nabla \omega)$, shown in Fig. 6, is another form of the creative term. It is again seen to have the proper sign in the structure of the horseshoe. Introducing ω_s, the component parallel to q, and noting that $\nabla (q \, \omega_s)$ averages out, one has finally

$$\frac{1}{2} \frac{\partial}{\partial t} \omega_s^2 - \omega_s \, \omega \cdot \nabla q = + \nu \, \omega_s \nabla^2 \omega_s \tag{31}$$

with the creative term as shown earlier. Finally, it is of interest to remark that in the state of turbulent equilibrium the vector ω is on the average neither created nor destroyed. The quantity ω^2 is both created and destroyed.

Mechanism of Turbulence, or the Physical Structure of the Secondary Flow

We are now in position to indicate the structure or pattern of the turbulent flow. We shall first concentrate our attention on the shear flow, as obtained in boundary layers and pipes. A slight modification of the same considerations will permit applications to jets, to wakes, and finally (in the limit) to homogeneous flows.

Physical vortex lines are necessarily continuous, that is they have no beginning and end. They can be shortened or lengthened at will, provided the required work is extracted or supplied.

We shall provide the structure shown in Fig. 1, which shows a wall-bound vortex horseshoe inclined in a downstream direction.

The triple product in Eq. 28 is positive everywhere. The vortex line along the horseshoe or "tornado" of the turbulence in Fig. 1 is seen to provide the proper condition. In the right hand branch of the horseshoe, the quantity $\omega_n \nabla q$ is positive everywhere since the vortex points inward; ω_s is also positive, since the tornado must lean to leeward during its entire lifetime, as we shall indicate. For the left branch, the signs for the quantities $\omega_n \nabla q$ and ω_s are both reversed and the product therefore is again positive.

Thus, in a state of equilibrium, there is equality between the dissipative term and the creative term. As the Reynolds number increases, the representative dimension of the vortices responsible for dissipation must decrease more or less inversely as the value of R.

One has, therefore, the following description of the process. The medium, in the case of shear flow, is composed of primary structure of horseshoe vortices. These vortices are similar in structure, and the representative dimension is proportional to the distance to the boundary. The horseshoe vortex is inclined, on the average, 45° with the flow direction, with the front of the shoe downstream.

There is a concentrated flow of the transferable quantity through the center of each horseshoe and directed perpendicular to its plane. The forward angle of the plane of the horseshoe increases with the Reynolds number.

The horseshoe vortices are distributed evenly throughout the region. The total area of the vortices penetrating a certain plane corresponds to an intermittency factor. The concentrated mass transport through the center of the horseshoes, with a small and distributed velocity in the opposite direction, gives the skewness observed in shear flow. It is also evident that this type of flow is not a gradient type transfer. The portion of the medium passing through the center of the horseshoe moves a distance which is in the order of the dimensions of the horseshoe. The mixing length is quite comparable to the distance to the wall. This is due to the fact that the life of each vortex horseshoe (in term of distance) is approximately equal to the distance to the wall.

To follow the life story of one horseshoe, it appears with its plane perpendicular to the wall, embracing a region of low velocity medium adjacent to the boundary. The strength of the vortex is proportional to the deficiency in velocity of the embraced region.

Next, the horseshoe is pulled downstream, following very nearly the main flow. The horseshoe is during this period exposed both to a drag force exerted by the main stream and to a cross force pulling the horseshoe away from the wall towards the center of the stream. Except for an unimportant dissipation of the main vortex structure, the work extracted from the main stream is equal to the work absorbed by the horseshoe vortex. The most intense transfer of energy occurs, as indicated, when the vortex structure is inclined approximately 45° with respect to the main flow. Since dissipation is unimportant in this process, one has here a simple explanation for the Karman similarity postulate (1930). To restate what we have been saying: all energy is transferred to large vortices just after their birth, involving a short period of their life.

This brings us to the next stage in the life period of a single horseshoe vortex. Beyond an angle of 70° the rate of energy transfer becomes smaller and smaller, and the first vortex is necessarily replaced by a new horseshoe vortex. The new vortex virtually devours the old one, as the latter is spun around the center line of the new horseshoe structure.

There is thus a secondary structure within the primary horseshoe pattern. It is this secondary structure that is responsible for most of the dissipation as there is a layer-like disposition of the earlier vortices forming a certain fine structure. This fine structure may be considered as secondary fluctuations of the primary fluctuations. The secondary structure is dissipating rapidly, while the primary structure on the average remains intact. One should note that the secondary structure covers a wide range of scale, with the shortest wave lengths near the center line of the horseshoe and the longest wave lengths in the medium between the primary vortices.

We shall next apply our theory to certain considerations in regard to the lower critical Reynolds number and later to the problem of transition.

Lower Critical Reynolds Number

The lower critical Reynolds number is defined for a pipe as the Reynolds number below which one cannot maintain turbulent flow, whatever the imposed disturbance. In other words, all disturbances, no matter how large, will die out. From Eq. 24 one gets the expression

$$R = \frac{-\omega_s \nabla^2 \omega_s}{\omega_s \omega_n \nabla q_s} \tag{32}$$

and the problem is to indicate the lowest value of R permitting the existence of a horseshoe vortex structure such as that shown in Fig. 1.

At the lower critical number, let us say that turbulence is just barely being maintained. The dissipation of the longitudinal vortices must be fairly uniform all over the space. Using very rough figures, let us assume that a horseshoe vortex in a circular tube reaches, on the average, 1/4 diameter from the wall, and that the diameter of the vortex shank or bundle is 1/20 of the diameter of the tube. The horseshoe thus may fill say 1/15 of the volume. With ∇q_s about 3, based on mean velocity and the diameter of the pipe, one obtains a value

$$R = \frac{20^2}{\frac{1}{15} \cdot 3} = 2000$$

Although the assumptions are rough, they are entirely reasonable. The figure is close to observed values obtained by experiments.

Boundary Transition

Without large imposed disturbances, turbulence will be due to irregularities at the boundary.

Let there be an irregularity in the flow at the wall of a general dimension Δy, and let the velocity gradient be du/dy and the Reynolds number

$$R = \frac{\frac{du}{dy} \cdot \Delta y^2}{\nu} \qquad (33)$$

At the proper value of this Reynolds number, a small vortex is formed. If it is strong enough and has sufficient life, it will upset the boundary layer sufficiently to create a larger and oversaturated vortex, that later is followed by a still larger and more oversaturated horseshoe vortex, and so on.

The critical point is thus the life story of the first vortex and whether or not the first has a successor. This process should be studied by observations and mathematical calculations.

Quite evidently, if the quantity Δy is small enough, the critical number (referred to as the pipe-diameter or the layer thickness) will exceed any given value. Thus one has not a problem of stability but simply one of a Reynolds number of a wall-created disturbance. If this disturbance reaches a certain magnitude it will set off an explosion-like succession of larger disturbances.

Comment on the Two-dimensional Linearized Stability Problem

Applying the results indicated to the treatment of the Orr-Sommerfeld equation, one may conclude at once that all cases are stable; in other words, all disturbances will damp out after a certain interval of time. The solution really does not involve time but rather the distance x, only. The so-called damped case does not represent a case of damped vibrations but merely a stationary case with the amplitudes decreasing exponentially with x. Similarly, the "unstable" case is nothing but a stationary case with the amplitudes increasing with x. The "neutrally stable" case should merely be referred to as the case of constant amplitude. Briefly, if one linearizes the two-dimensional flow, one is able to obtain stationary solutions, for which the amplitude need not be constant but may increase or decrease exponentially with the distance. We shall now state, as a direct result of the above investigation: all cases of solution of the Orr-Sommerfeld equations are damped, i.e., the amplitudes at all points are decreasing with time. We may further state: this damping does not appear in the Orr-Sommerfeld equation which in consequence permits only stationary solutions. As shown, the actual damping is at all points proportional to the square of the amplitude, the larger amplitudes therefore damping at a higher rate.

Remembering that the Orr-Sommerfeld equation is strictly a stationary case under all circumstances, one may draw some very interesting conclusions. With no energy furnished to the stream, no waves will appear under any circumstances. However, if one furnishes the energy proportional to the square of the amplitude all along the x-axis, one will get a response maximum at the proper frequency. Near transition, there is little doubt that the Orr-Sommerfeld two-dimensional case may appear physically in a three-dimensional pattern. Schubauer and Skramstad (Ref. 1) comment on the three-dimensional nature of their observed flow pattern. The flow, therefore, is pictured by a succession of horseshoes, as shown in Fig. 1, but with a mean symmetry plane quite like the two-dimensional Orr-Sommerfeld pattern. Thus the amplitude may increase in the x-direction, provided only that the very minute energy constant times amplitude squared, is furnished by the mainstream. This is evidently the case, and the process becomes similar to the three-dimensional problem described earlier. If a single impulse were imposed, an explosion might occur, but since a succession of oppositely acting forces are produced there is created an Orr-Sommerfeld field, with amplitudes increasing with x. In the two-dimensional case, however, the net loss (not shown) is actually proportional to the amplitude squared; the pattern with amplitude increasing in the x-direction, will therefore die out more quickly than the one with amplitude constant. Again, one must repeat that the two-dimensional case is always stable. If a certain energy is present or furnished at a point, this energy will only suffice for a short distance downstream.

Different, however, is the three-dimensional case. While it is true that the loss for a given three-dimensional pattern is again proportional to the amplitude squared, the constant is now somewhat larger. One might therefore readily conclude, erroneously, that the three-dimensional pattern is more stable. On the contrary, the three-dimensional flow has the property of being able to transfer energy from the main stream to the secondary flow. Referring to our earlier fundamental equation,

$$\frac{1}{2} \frac{D}{Dt} \omega_s^2 = \omega_s \omega_n \nabla q + \nu \omega_s \nabla^2 \omega_s$$

it is seen at once that this applies directly to an Orr-Sommerfeld three-dimensional pattern. The most "unstable" case merely means the case with the "softest" pattern. Thus the term $\omega_s \nabla^2 \omega_s$ is a minimum. The cross section of this three-dimensional flow should resemble the two-dimensional solution, with the frequency nearly the same. In the "neutral" cases, the two terms of the equation become equal and the disturbance remains constant. In the "damped" case, the wave length is too long or too short, the pattern is no longer "soft," and the friction term prevails. So we see that the experimental results are completely in accord with the three-dimensional theory, thus explaining the inherent contradiction of the two-dimensional theory that all cases are definitely stable. Briefly, the flow pattern prescribed by the Orr-Sommerfeld equation is correct. Firstly, the pattern is still sufficiently descriptive for a not-so-small three-dimensional related disturbance; secondly, the conclusion usually drawn from the Orr-Sommerfeld equation is qualitatively correct only if applied to such a three-dimensional pattern.

Comment on the Turbulence-Creating Mechanism

The treatment given above will not be complete without reference to the energy problem. How is energy transferred from the main stream to the secondary flow? Evidently some such energy transfer must take place. We know that in a closed container all eddies will very soon die out. The picture is again very simple. The "handle" shown in Fig. 1 has a low pressure along its centerline as a consequence of the spiral motion around this line. Now, as the handles are pulled downstream with the main current, there will result a lift force crosswise, pushing the vortex farther out into the main stream. The handle will continuously become longer and thinner. Because of the low internal pressure, work will be performed on it at the expense of the main stream energy. Note that the handles do not have any random distribution but always lean downstream during their period of life.

We shall indicate for some other occasion that the loss is, to a large extent, independent of the coefficient of friction and becomes proportional to the square of the velocity. The strange situation thus exists, in which the work done by the pressure on the handles or contaminations is dissipated immediately by the intense laminar motion around the core of such handles.

Motion of a Particle in Turbulent Flow

The turbulence-creating mechanism has been indicated by a discussion of the equation of motion. One finds, in conclusion, that such mechanism is lacking in two-dimensional flows and that, as a consequence, all two-dimensional flows are stable.

Normally, the dissipation is proportional to the viscosity and to the square of the velocity. We shall now indicate a new relationship intimately related to the mechanism of turbulence. Let us consider a short element of the "thread of turbulence." This element is shown in

Fig. 3. As explained before, there will be a lengthening of the element and a corresponding decrease in the cross section. The velocity for points within the element may be written as $q_R + q$, where q_R is the motion of the center of the element away from the center of curvature in the osculating plane of the centerline of the "thread" and q is the velocity relative to the centerline of the element and in the plane perpendicular to it. There are many elements like the one shown in a turbulent flow; in fact, these elements are the typical elements of turbulent flow; and the space is nearly "saturated" with threads containing such elements. It is within these threads that the most intense dissipation takes place, a dissipation which is many times greater than the dissipation of the "steady" flow.

The cross sections of the rings look more or less alike except for size. Since the energy that may be stored in one thread is small, as compared with the energy transmitted through it, all rings will be very much in equilibrium or in a steady state. The life of a thread, without energy absorption, is of the order of 10 to 1000 times shorter than the life of a thread normally absorbing energy from the main stream. We shall consider the condition of fully developed turbulence far away from the lower critical value of the Reynolds number.

One has the relation for any steady state

$$q\nabla H = \nu q \nabla^2 q \tag{34}$$

For normal Poiseuille flow, it is seen that the drop ∇H is proportional to the viscosity and to the velocity q to the first power.

With the element of turbulence, the situation is significantly different. One has here the relation

$$\nabla H = \rho\, q_t \times \text{curl } q \tag{35}$$

where q_t is the tangential velocity. Since the term on the right side of Eq. 34 is the loss per element, one sees at once that this loss is now proportional to the velocity to the third power. The quantity q_t is as follows

$$q_t = q_R \quad \frac{1}{2} \frac{r}{R}$$

where q_R is the velocity of stretching, which is proportional to the main velocity. One has for Eq. 35

$$\nabla H = \rho\, \Delta q \frac{\Delta q}{\nu} = \sim (\Delta q)^2 \frac{1}{\nu}$$

$$\text{The dissipation} = q\nabla H = \sim q_R \frac{1}{2} \frac{r}{R} \nabla H = \sim \frac{1}{2R} q_R (\Delta q)^2 = \sim c q^3$$

Evidently, the mean magnitudes are not entirely independent of Reynolds number. The dissipation of the turbulence elements is seen to be independent of the viscosity and proportional to q^3 . Actually, there is also some normal laminar flow in between the turbulence elements which will produce dissipation in normal manner.

Logarithmic Law

It is seen at once that the turbulence pattern, or the softest pattern, must depend entirely on the distance from the wall as the Reynolds number is not involved. The "collapse" or birth of a disturbance will occur when the average velocity gradient exceeds a certain value. But since velocity must be measured with reference to the velocity at the point, and since distance must be measured in terms of distance from the wall, one gets for the gradient the statement,

$$\frac{d\,\frac{\Delta u}{u}}{d\,\frac{\Delta y}{y}} = \text{const} \quad \text{or} \quad \frac{du}{dy} = n\,\frac{u}{y} \quad \text{which gives} \quad u = y^n \cdot \text{const.}$$

This is the Karman law of similarity.

Transition

Quite evidently a problem of stability is not involved. Transition will only occur beyond the point at which the lower Reynolds number has been reached and then only when sufficient disturbance is available to continue a certain chain of events. If care is taken to delay the disturbance, the transition may be postponed beyond any limit.

Note that the lower critical number is intimately connected with the local gradient as the essential variable. It is obviously advantageous that the local gradient is not large, away from the boundary, since the critical Reynolds number is then lowered. In other words, "full" velocity profile is necessary to delay transition. It would be important to obtain a description of the life story of the first horseshoe vortex sufficiently strong to create a successor, and to give the exact strength necessary for such a vortex to create a succession of vortices. It is evident that the further beyond the lower critical number the less strength will be required. The necessary strength may vary inversely as the excess Reynolds number over the critical value.

Conclusions

1. Turbulence may only have a three-dimensional pattern. The typical structure is indicated.
2. The primary turbulent structure is similar in pattern and differs only in scale.
3. Because of the similarity, the Karman similarity law follows, also the formulas for pressure drop and heat transmission in pipes.
4. Dissipation is almost entirely due to the secondary structure, which in turn is due to the winding up of the previous vortices.
5. The significant term in creating turbulence is the quantity $(\omega \cdot \nabla \omega) q$ and the proposed primarv structure may be defined as the structure giving the greatest average value of the creative term $(\omega \cdot \nabla \omega) q$ and the least value of the primary dissipation.

6. All two-dimensional flows are stable and the dissipation equals at each instant the dissipation that would occur if the same disturbance were imposed on a medium at rest within the same boundaries.
7. Cylindrical pipe flow is stable, but flow in a diverging pipe may exhibit disturbances of the Schlichting type.
8. Experimental research should be conducted on the first vortex appearing at transition.
9. Mathematical research should be performed on the life story of the first horseshoe vortex and on the conditions for a following chain of successive vortices.
10. Cyclones and tornadoes are examples of large scale "turbulence." The creative mechanism is identical.

References

1. G. B. Schubauer and H. K. Skramstad "Laminar Boundary Layer Oscillations on a Flat Plate," NACA Tech. Rep. No. 909 (1948).

2. Theodore von Karman "Progress in the Statistical Theory of Turbulence," Marine Research (Sears Foundation) 7 (3) (Nov. 15, 1948).

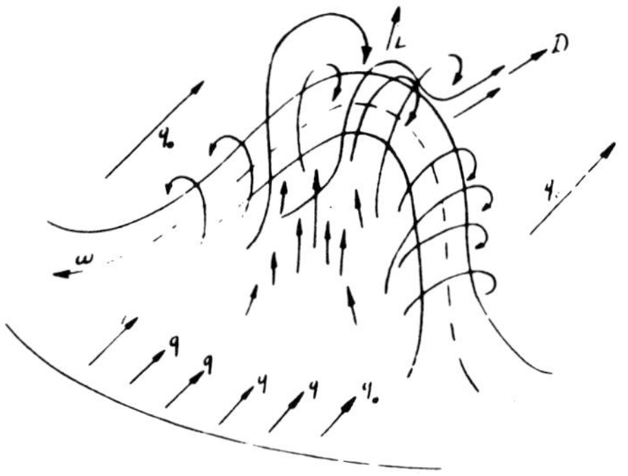

Fig. 1 Primary structure of wallbound turbulence. Note concentrated current through center-region of horseshoe pattern representing the "Reynolds stresses" and giving the "mixing lengths" of Prandtl.

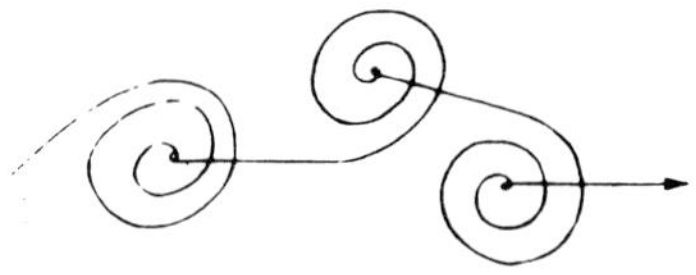

Fig. 2 Motion of a particle indicating basis for pressure drop in turbulent flow proportional to square of velocity.

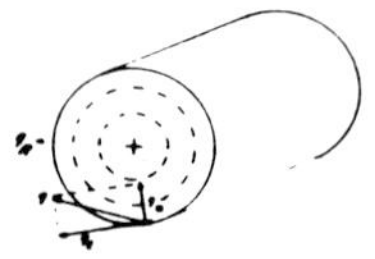

Fig. 3 Element of vortex. q_R is radial "stretching" velocity, q is velocity relative to centerline of element itself.

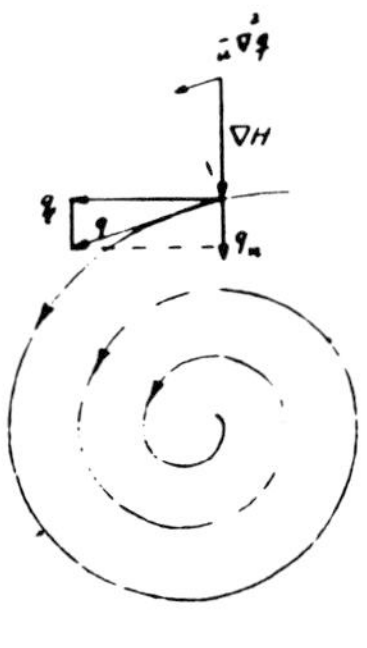

Fig. 4 Typical element indicating the process of transmitting work by compression of an element of horseshoe or ring pattern.

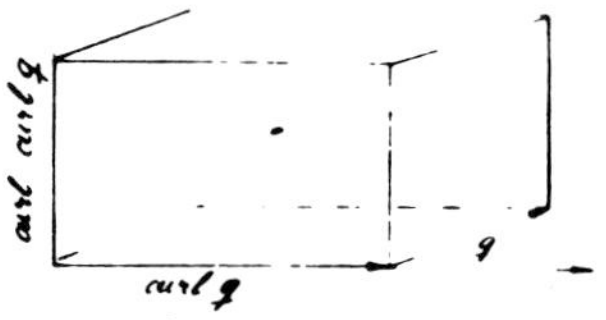

Fig. 5 Triple product (ωxq)curl ω, the turbulence creative term.

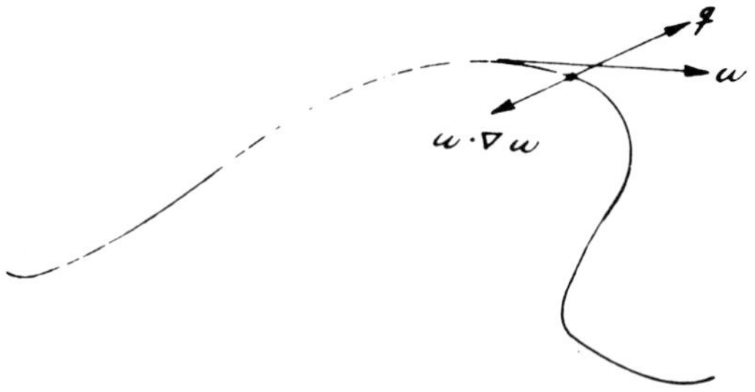

Fig. 6 Triple product ($\omega \cdot \nabla \cdot \omega$) q (Another form of the turbulence creative term).

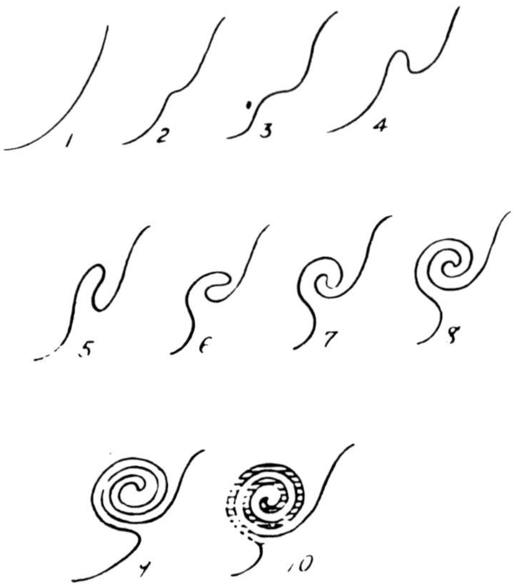

Fig. 7 Cross-section of horseshoe. Steps in development of horseshoe or turbulence pattern. Fine structure contains remains of previous vortices.

THE STRUCTURE OF TURBULENCE

BY THEODORE THEODORSEN

Fairchild Engine and Airplane Corporation

Published in *50 Jahre Genszschichtsforschung: Ludwig Prandtl,* Friedr. Vieweg & Sohn, Braunschweig, 1955, pp. 55–62.

Summary: Turbulence is directly related to the existence of a shear or boundary layer. In such a layer there exists under equilibrium conditions a balance between the creative and destructive processes. The author has shown that to account for the creative process there existes a definite structure, characterized as a universal element of turbulence. This element, because of an obvious resemblance in form, has been termed the "horseshoe". The predicted structure constitutes a nonstationary solution of the equation of motion. The main horseshoe is the shear transmitting element. It is shown that its surface is covered by a multiple arrangement of ever smaller order horseshoes. Reports on experimental work will be available in the near future, as will also a kinematographic record showing the development of the basic horseshoe structure in a boundary layer.

I. INTRODUCTION

It has been tentatively established that turbulence is characterized by a unique and universal flow pattern. For the past several decades it has been tacitly assumed that real turbulence as it occurs in nature is too complex to make a useful problem of direct research and most work was directed towards an artificially defined turbulence. The inherent complexity of the terms of the equation of motion did not permit more than a general recognition of effects and no general solution of the flow pattern of turbulence was attained. As a matter of fact, the early authors were just as close to a solution as were later authors. The situation was further aggravated by the fact that most authors were accustomed to the idea that there was a perfectly random motion of particles and that no basic pattern should or could exist. This very idea, that there was a random particle motion somewhat similar to the motion of the molecules in the laminar flow, persisted from the beginning. That this "particle" was of a certain size was shown by early measurements on correlation but this was about as far as the experimental evidence could usefully reach. It was not realized that a simple universal flow pattern existed and was the cause of the observable correlation.

Equally disconcerting was the nonconclusive result obtained on the transition from laminar to turbulent flow. Two lines of thought were apparent from time to time. The first school contended that the laminar flow was unstable in a classical sense and that an infinitely small disturbance would suffice to cause the transition. The fact that transition never seemed to occur at the expected *Reynolds* number was explained by even more mysterious theories. The observable disturbances prescribed by the *Orr-Sommerfeld-Tollmien* theory of small disturbances and later extended to include effects of heat transmission, appeared not properly related to the problem of transition and no clear relationship was ever established. All that could be said was that some connection could not be ruled out. The second school of thought contended that the transition could occur only due to a *finite* disturbance. It was observed, for instance, that laminar flow under proper conditions may be extended beyond any high value of the *Reynolds* number. This fact is clearly contrary to any assumption of instability in a normal sense. It appears to the writer that this contention is fully supported by the facts shown in the following. The flow is inherently stable against both two- and three-dimensional disturbances, provided the three-dimensional disturbances remain below a critical *Reynolds* number, based not on the main flow but on the disturbance itself. In regard to two-dimensional disturbances in the pure sense, these appear to dissipate as will follow from the conclusion of the present theory.

II. THEORY OF THE TURBULENT FLOW MECHANISM

In the following will be given a condensed but adequate description of the Turbulent Flow Pattern. The abstract is from the original presentation at the Second Midwestern Conference on Fluid Mechanics at Ohio State University, April 17, 1952 (Ref. [1]).

Starting with the equation of motion in the usual form

$$\frac{\partial \vec{q}}{\partial t} + \vec{q} \cdot \nabla \vec{q} = -\frac{1}{\varrho} \nabla p + \nu \nabla^2 \vec{q} \quad \text{or with}$$

$$\vec{q} \cdot \nabla \vec{q} = \frac{1}{2} \nabla \vec{q}^2 - \vec{q} \times \operatorname{curl} \vec{q} \tag{1}$$

$$\frac{\partial \vec{q}}{\partial t} - \vec{q} \times \operatorname{curl} \vec{q} = -\nabla \left(\frac{1}{2} \vec{q}^2 + \frac{p}{\varrho} \right) + \nu \nabla^2 \vec{q}$$

Nothing is gained in the elementary representation to consider ϱ variable. It is therefore treated here as a constant $\varrho = \varrho_0$. The quantity $\frac{1}{2} q^2 + \frac{p}{\varrho}$ may be denoted by H, the total head per unit of mass.

Thus

$$\frac{\partial \vec{q}}{\partial t} - \vec{q} \times \operatorname{curl} \vec{q} = -\nabla H + \nu \nabla^2 \vec{q}$$

where $\vec{q}$ is the velocity vector and $\nu =$ the viscosity coefficient $\frac{\mu}{\varrho}$. As a temporary digression we may multiply scalarly with $\vec{q}$ and get the work relation

$$\vec{q} \cdot \frac{\partial \vec{q}}{\partial t} = -\vec{q} \cdot \nabla H + \nu \vec{q} \cdot \nabla^2 \vec{q}, \quad \text{or}$$

$$\frac{\partial}{\partial t} \left(\frac{q^2}{2} \right) = -\vec{q} \cdot \nabla H + \nu \vec{q} \cdot \nabla^2 \vec{q}$$

Using the symbol $\frac{D}{Dt} = \frac{\partial}{\partial t} + \vec{q} \cdot \nabla$, the equation may further be written

$$\frac{D}{Dt} \left(\frac{q^2}{2} \right) = \operatorname{div} \left\{ -\vec{q} \frac{p}{\varrho} \right\} + \nu \vec{q} \cdot \nabla^2 \vec{q}$$

But $\vec{q} \cdot \nabla^2 \vec{q} = - \vec{q} \operatorname{curl} \operatorname{curl} \vec{q} = \operatorname{div} (\vec{q} \times \operatorname{curl} \vec{q}) - (\operatorname{curl} \vec{q})^2$. Thus the equation may be written

$$\frac{D}{Dt}\left(\frac{q^2}{2}\right) = \operatorname{div}\left\{- \vec{q}\frac{p}{\varrho} + \nu \vec{q} \times \operatorname{curl} \vec{q}\right\} - \nu (\operatorname{curl} \vec{q})^2 \tag{2}$$

The terms are here easily given physical significance. The first term on the right side relates to the surface forces: $- \vec{q} p$ is the work done on the element or region by the pressure-force and $\nu \vec{q} \times \operatorname{curl} \vec{q}$ is the work due to the viscous surface forces. The second term represents the loss due to dissipation within the element considered. It is here of interest to ask the question under what circumstances the first term maintains a positive value at all times or the circumstances under which the time average of the first term remains positive for a given region. In view of other developments it is postulated here that there exists a fundamental flow pattern for which the *time-average of the divergence term remains positive*. However, with the equation of motion in this form the pattern is not readily discernible and we shall proceed to show that with the equation in a more convenient form the proposed universal flow pattern becomes evident.

III. EQUATION FOR THE SCALAR QUANTITY ω^2

By taking the curl of the terms of equation (1), one has the conventional form

$$\frac{\partial}{\partial t}(\operatorname{curl} \vec{q}) - \operatorname{curl} (\vec{q} \times \operatorname{curl} \vec{q}) = \nu \nabla^2 \operatorname{curl} \vec{q}$$

or with $\operatorname{curl} \vec{q} = \vec{\omega}$

$$\frac{\partial \vec{\omega}}{\partial t} - \operatorname{curl} (\vec{q} \times \vec{\omega}) = \nu \nabla^2 \vec{\omega}$$

To obtain scalar quantities we shall multiply by $\vec{\omega}$. Thus

$$\frac{\partial}{\partial t}\left(\frac{\omega^2}{2}\right) - \vec{\omega} \cdot \operatorname{curl} (\vec{q} \times \vec{\omega}) = \nu \vec{\omega} \cdot \nabla^2 \vec{\omega}$$

But $$- \vec{\omega} \operatorname{curl} (\vec{q} \times \vec{\omega}) = \operatorname{div} [(\vec{\omega} \times \vec{q}) \times \vec{\omega}] + (\vec{\omega} \times \vec{q}) \operatorname{curl} \vec{\omega}.$$

Also $$\vec{\omega} \cdot \nabla^2 \vec{\omega} = - \vec{\omega} \cdot \operatorname{curl} \operatorname{curl} \vec{\omega} = \operatorname{div} (\vec{\omega} \times \operatorname{curl} \vec{\omega}) - (\operatorname{curl} \vec{\omega})^2.$$

The equation may thus be rewritten

$$\frac{\partial}{\partial t}\left(\frac{\omega^2}{2}\right) + \operatorname{div}\{(\vec{\omega} \times \vec{q}) \times \vec{\omega} - \nu (\vec{\omega} \times \operatorname{curl} \vec{\omega})\} + (\vec{\omega} \times \vec{q}) \operatorname{curl} \vec{\omega} = - \nu (\operatorname{curl} \vec{\omega})^2 \tag{3}$$

We need only call our attention to the equilibrium case of turbulence that is a case in which the turbulence level remains constant along the stream. The divergence term $(\vec{\omega} \times \vec{q}) \times \vec{\omega}$ will then have a time average of zero since $\vec{q}$ equals to zero along the wall or enclosure.

There remains then only:

$$\frac{\partial}{\partial t}\left(\frac{\omega^2}{2}\right) = - (\vec{\omega} \times \vec{q}) \operatorname{curl} \vec{\omega} + \nu \operatorname{div} (\vec{\omega} \times \operatorname{curl} \vec{\omega}) - \nu (\operatorname{curl} \omega)^2 \tag{4}$$

The equation states certain physical facts with regard to the creation and annihilation of the physical quantity ω^2. The first term on the right hand side of the equation represents the expression for the *creation* of the quantity ω^2. The author originally adopted the name of the *turbulence creating term*, the turbulence being this time measured by ω^2 (or in terms of ω^2). The second term on the right side represents the conduction of ω^2 from the enclosing walls. It is further also easy to verify that the term $(\vec{\omega} \times \vec{q}) \cdot \mathrm{curl}\, \vec{\omega}$ is absent in laminar two-dimensional or symmetrical flows. Thus the designation as turbulence term is justified. In fact, the term is intimately connected with the structure introduced in the following. No such structure can exist in the two-dimensional flow. Hence there is no turbulence-creating term in the latter case.

IV. CONDITIONS NECESSARY TO OBTAIN A POSITIVE TURBULENCE TERM

The scalar quantity $T = (\vec{q} \times \vec{\omega}) \cdot \mathrm{curl}\, \vec{\omega}$ is composed of the three vectors $\vec{q}$, $\vec{\omega}$ and $\mathrm{curl}\, \vec{\omega}$ (see Fig. 1).With a random distribution the quantity is evidently equal to zero. Since the quantity T must be positive for any kind of equilibrium turbulence it is immediately evident that a certain structure, not of a random nature, must exist. Fortunately it is very simple to identify the required structure that will fulfill the requirement of a positive value of the quantity T.

Consider a bundle of vortex lines, or what may be called a vortex tube. The vector ω is thus directed along its axis and the vector curl $\vec{\omega}$ lies in a tangential

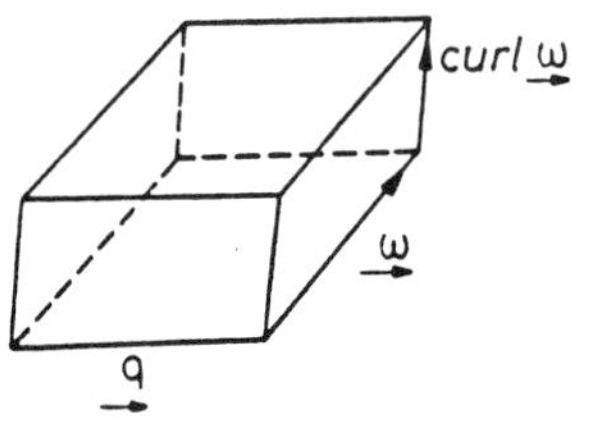

Fig. 1. Scalar quantity $T = (\vec{q} \times \vec{\omega}) \cdot \mathrm{curl}\, \vec{\omega}$ (the turbulence term)

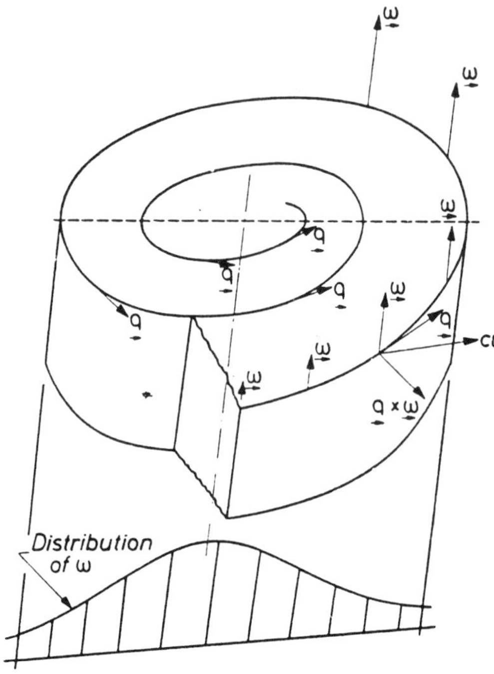

Fig. 2. Vortex tube (right leg of horseshoe in Fig. 3). The vector $\vec{q} \times \vec{\omega}$ has a tangential component (along curl $\vec{\omega}$)

direction along a closed path containing the center of the bundle. Fig. 2 shows a slice through one leg of the vortex bundle. With the velocity vector q directet along a circular path the value of T would obviously be zero since $\vec{q} \times \vec{\omega}$ is then radial. However, with a spiral flow direction, the vector $\vec{q} \times \vec{\omega}$ has a tangential component along curl $\vec{\omega}$ and the value of T is thus seen to be positive *if and when the positive direction of the streamlines is inclined inward towards the center of the vortex tube*- (It is recommended that the reader verify to his own satisfaction that T is positive under the condition shown in Fig. 2 and only then. This fact is of paramount importance in the theory.) Conversely, of course, T is negative if and when the velocity vector is generally in an outward direction. (With the previously common assumption of specially defined turbulence, characterized by a random motion, the quantity T would on the average be zero by definition.) We shall therefore introduce what may be called *natural or shear turbulence.* This is to be characterized by a definite structure continually produced and in which the mean quantity T is always *positive.*

To discuss the necessary conditions further it may be seen that a positive T calls for a *shrinking* vortex tube. The *expanding* tube is ruled out. One may conclude that the structure contains *elements of shrinking vortex tubes.*

V. INTRODUCTION OF THE HORSESHOE STRUCTURE

To follow up this initial requirement, it is seen that a force must be exerted along the length of the tube in order to produce the radial shrinking since the vortex tube otherwise would be in equilibrium with the surrounding medium and no shrinking would take place. It follows quite uniquely that there must exist a structure which the author originally introduced (Ref. [1]) as the "horseshoe". In Fig. 3 is reproduced the figure used in the original paper. A brief description of the action is in order. The horseshoe represents the universal element of the structure of turbulent flow. In consists simply in a vortex bundle or tube attached to the wall or solid boundary at the two "ends" and forming a loop or horeshoe extending into the boundary "layer". Since of course the vortex tube has no "ends" it may better be described as a bent vortex line. The loop protruding into the stream is exposed to the normal lift and drag forces which it *resists* by virtue of the low pressure core of the vortex. Or, conversely, because of the presence of the low pressure along the core of the vortex it resists the external action of the mainstream and thus is exposed to the normal lift and drag effect, acting on any *restrained* vortex element. To obtain the proper action it is evident that the plane of the horseshoe is inclined *downstream*. Again it is necessary to point out that this required condition in natural turbulence is strictly contrary to conventionally used random arrangement in which upstreampointing vortex tubes are as equally probable as those pointing downstream.

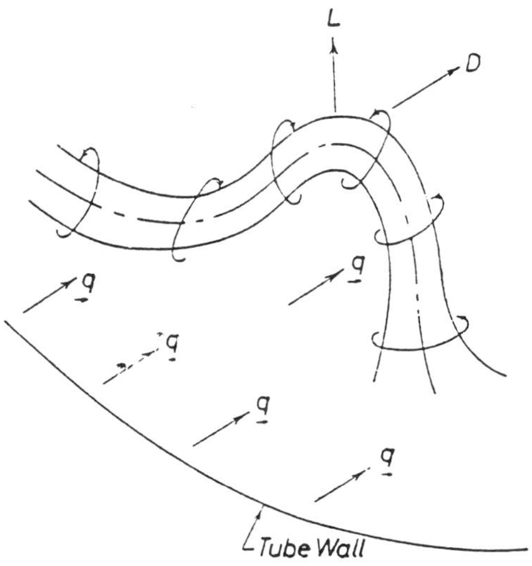

Fig. 3. Primary structure of wallbound turbulence (Presented at the Secound Midwestern Conference on Fluid Mechanics, March 17, 1952)

Thus the universal element of the turbulent structure is a horseshoe or loop-shaped vortex tube or, more generally stated, a bent vortex tube slanting in a downstream direction only. It is in place to point out that the existence of this universal element of the turbulent structure has been amply established by several independent experimenters. It appears to be entirely in accordance with the structure predicted by theory in Ref. [1]. We shall return later to a few further remarks on the experimental findings. (The reader may note that the circulation and the relative

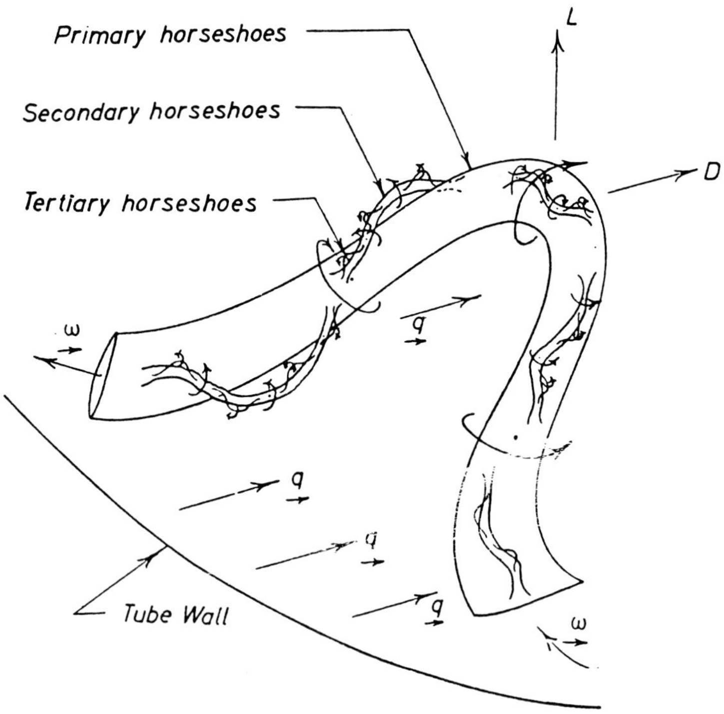

Fig. 4. Horseshoe of large *Reynolds* number

velocity produces the forces shown as lift and drag in Figs. 3 and 4. The horseshoe resists this force and provides the shearforce.)

It is, finally, in order to note that the proposed structure yields the positive value required for the divergence term in equation (2). This is explained fully in Ref. [1].

It is of interest to state that the flow pattern associated with the horseshoe may quite evidently be considered as the simplest and therefore the most efficient flow-pattern to produce a given "dynamic" shearforce. Granting that a shearforce may be produced both by a molecular momentum exchange and also by a macroscopic momentum exchange, it is contended that the most efficient macroscopic momentum exchange is produced by the proposed flow pattern.

VI. DETAIL LIFE STORY OF THE HORSESHOE STRUCTURE OR THE UNIVERSAL ELEMENT

So far we have merely discussed the equilibrium structure of natural turbulence. We are further concerned with the full life story of the individual element. This may be given as follows. By inspecting equations (2) and (4) it is at once obvious that for geometrically similar structures there is a lower limit below which the viscous term exceeds the creative term T. This minimum size is defined as the microhorseshoe to follow earlier usage corresponding to the term microturbulence. The *Reynolds* number of this horseshoe based on the existing gradient and the maximum dimension in direction of this gradient is in the order of 300—500. This horseshoe is consumed entirely by viscosity and its surface is not covered by secondary horseshoes as is the case at a large *Reynolds* number. Conversely, in contrast to the case of the microhorseshoe, the horseshoe with a large *Reynolds* number (of the horseshoe) is not dissipated by viscous effects but by the action of secondary "horseshoes" of smaller size covering its entire "surface". The secondary horseshoes are in turn not devoured by friction but mainly by the action of their own system of "planetary" horseshoes of a lower order and so on until the microsize horseshoe finally is reached. These are devoured by viscous effects only. There is thus a multiple arrangement of ever smaller horseshoes continually devouring the next larger one. Only the largest horseshoe, which is the shearproducing horseshoe, is directly produced and reproduced by the mainflow. It alone furnishes the shearforce and taps the energy of the mainstream. The size is, of course, not necessarily uniform but may vary about a certain mean value. A large *Reynolds* number horseshoe is tentatively shown in Fig. 4. Shown are the secondary horseshoe on the surface of the main or "shear" horseshoe. Also shown are the third order horseshoes on the surface of the second order. These may be the final horseshoes of minimum size or microhorseshoes.

It is finally of interest to remark that the velocity vector at any point thus is given by the location and "age" of the horseshoe structure. In normal circumstances each location is equally probable, while the probable age is given by the life story of the structure. With the flow pattern of the horseshoe known as a function of time, all the correlations may therefore be calculated.

The transition may be given as follows. If and when a vortex tube near the boundary experiences a local bending away from the wall, one of two definite alternatives will obtain: 1) The "tube" may again straighten out by diffusion or 2) it may experience a stumbling action and become what is virtually a discrete vortex with a loop projecting into the stream and exposed to a lift force which is seen to act in a direction *away* from the wall (Fig. 5). The energy contained will continually increase until the "boundary layer" is penetrated. Whether alternative 1 or 2 takes place is decided entirely by the *Reynolds* number of the original disturbance, measured by the dimension of the original bent tube and the existing gradient at the wall. The magnitude of the original disturbance is then not zero but rather a definite finite quantity related to the *Reynolds* number of the microhorseshoe.

It is in order at this point to bring up the relationship to the well-known *Tollmien* waves oserved first by *Schubauer* and *Skramstad* [Ref. 2]. What relation, if any, exists between the horseshoe structure and the two-dimensional stability problem? The writer makes the following observations. Two-dimensional flows cannot exhibit instability as the "creative" term T is missing. Therefore, all two-dimensional flows are *stable*. That is, all imposed *two-dimensional disturbances must die out*. This statement appears contradictory to the fact that the predicted frequencies were actually observed. The contradiction may be dissolved by the simple postulate that the *Tollmien frequencies* are perfectly significant not in regard to strictly two-dimensional waves, but rather in regard to the quite different problem of the optimum relative disposition of the horseshoes in the turbulent structure. Each *Tollmien* "wave" is therefore simply to be interpreted as the region of the *impending* birth of a horse-

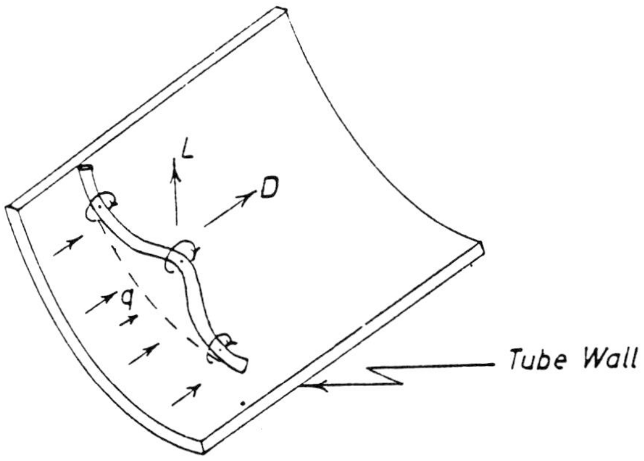

Fig. 5. Slightly bent vortex tube in boundary layer at transition. Note force away from wall

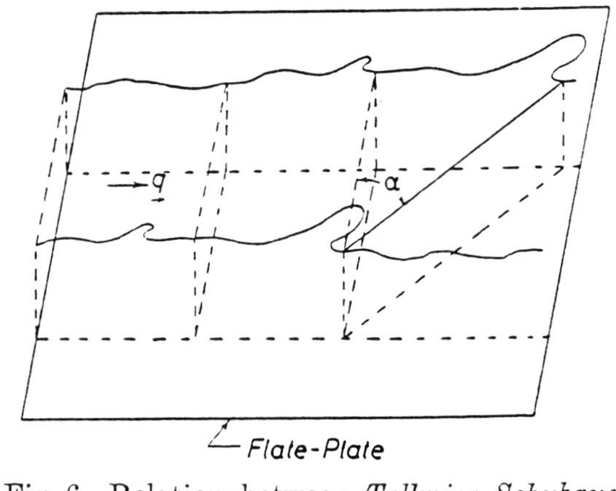

Fig. 6. Relation between *Tollmien-Schubauer* wave and the "horseshoe" in normal transition. Spacing frequency of horseshoe is connected with the "wave" which also has a third dimension

shoe. In other words: to calculate the spacial disposition of the horseshoes one obtains a definite optimum spacing and this spacing will correspond to the wave length of the *Tollmien* waves. It is probable that the treatment should be extended also to consider lateral spacing. In the end one may obtain the complete theory of the relative arrangement of the horseshoe pattern a behind point origin including the characteristic angle of lateral "contamination" (see Fig. 6).

VII. EXPERIMENTAL VERIFICATION OF THE THEORY

Experimental verification of the basic structural pattern of turbulence was first obtained by *Weske* and *Plankholt* using a tripping device proposed by the writer. The original result established beyond doubt the existence of the predicted pattern. Work is a present being continued by *Weske* at the University of Maryland and excellent technique has been developed for the detail measurements of the basic flow pattern.

Interesting results have also been obtained by *Harrington* and his co-workers at Rensselaer Institute. The, latter have established the appearance of the characteristic structure in *free* transition and have shown the independence of the original "cause". Reports of these experiments will soon be available.

Photographs of preliminary experimental horseshoe patterns are given in the Figs. 7 and 8.

Thus the predicted general flow pattern of turbulent flow and its basic structural element has been further established by experiments.

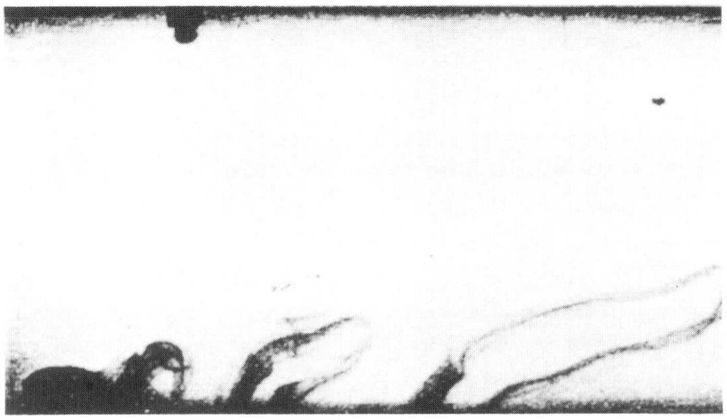

Fig. 7. Creation of turbulence structure "the Horseshoe". $R = 2{,}000 - 3{,}000$

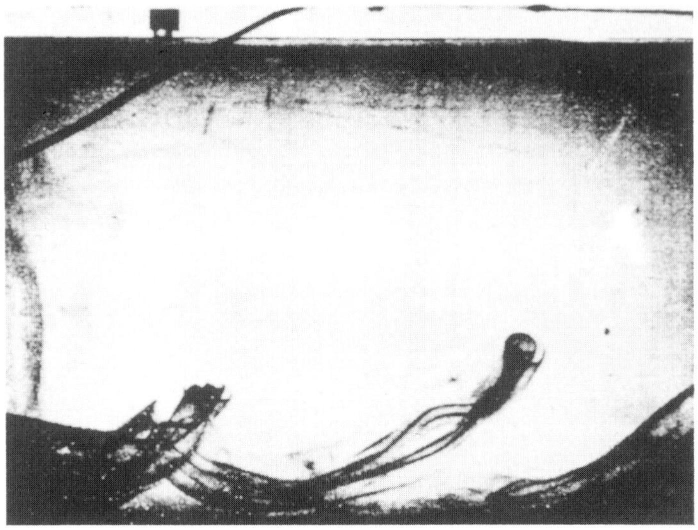

Fig. 8. Notice spiral layers in structure of "the Horseshoe". $R = 2{,}000 - 3{,}000$

References

[1] *Theodorsen, Theodore:* Mechanism of Turbulence. Proceedings of the Second Midwestern Conference on Fluid Mechanics, Ohio State University, 1952.

[2] *Schubauer, G. B.* and *Skramstad, H. K.:* Laminar Boundary Layer Oscillations on a Flat Plate. NACA Tech. Rep. No. 909 (1948).

Eingegangen am 11. 6. 1954

THE STRUCTURE OF TURBULENCE

BY THEODORE THEODORSEN

Originally published in *Fluid Dynamics and Applied Mathematics*, Diaz and Pai *Eds*.,
Gordon and Breach, New York, 1962. Reprinted with permission.

SUMMARY—It is shown that it is possible to write the equation of fluid motion with the vorticity ω as the variable in a short and exact form. The rate of change of the quantity ω^2 is shown to be composed of two parts only; one part, the creative term is proven to be positive under all circumstances, the second part always negative. It is further shown that turbulence necessarily must *comprise vortex loops* with radially pointing elements and that such vortex loops must be *under continual elongation*. The proofs were not included in the earlier presentations, (Refs. 2 and 3) only the necessity of the existence of the flow pattern was indicated.

For an incompressible viscous flow we write for the Euler equation of motion

$$(\partial \mathbf{q}/\partial t)+\mathbf{q}\cdot\nabla\mathbf{q}=-(1/\rho)\nabla p+\nu\nabla^2\mathbf{q} \qquad (1)$$

where $\mathbf{q}$ is the velocity vector, ρ the density and p the pressure. (Ref. 1, Chapter XI, Equation 4.)

With

$$\mathbf{q}\cdot\nabla\mathbf{q}=\tfrac{1}{2}\nabla\mathbf{q}^2-\mathbf{q}\times \text{curl } \mathbf{q}$$

one obtains

$$(\partial \mathbf{q}/\partial t)-\mathbf{q}\times \text{curl } \mathbf{q}=-\nabla[\tfrac{1}{2}\mathbf{q}^2+(p/\rho)]+\nu\nabla^2\mathbf{q} \qquad (2)$$

By taking the curl of each term of this equation there results with curl $\mathbf{q}=\omega$

$$(\partial\omega/\partial t)-\text{curl } (\mathbf{q}\times\omega)=\nu\nabla^2\omega \qquad (3)$$

To obtain scalar quantities we shall multiply each term of the equation by ω. One obtains thus

$$(\partial/\partial t)(\omega^2/2)-\omega\cdot\text{curl } (\mathbf{q}\times\omega)=\nu\omega\cdot\nabla^2\omega \qquad (4)$$

With the relation

$$\text{div } \{(\omega\times\mathbf{q})\times\omega\}=\omega\cdot\text{curl } (\omega\times\mathbf{q})-(\omega\times\mathbf{q})\cdot\text{curl } \omega$$

equation (4) reads

$$(\partial/\partial t)(\omega^2/2)+\text{div}\{(\omega\times\mathbf{q})\times\omega\}+(\omega\times\mathbf{q})\cdot\text{curl } \omega=\nu\omega\cdot\nabla^2\omega \qquad (5)$$

We shall first consider the second term

$$\text{div } \{(\omega\times\mathbf{q})\times\omega\} \qquad (6)$$

The mean value of this term is zero, as has been pointed out before. (See page 57 of Ref. 2).

However, a more precise final equation results by further contraction of the terms of Equation (5).

The argument of the divergence term may be rewritten

$$(\omega\times\mathbf{q})\times\omega=-\omega\times(\omega\times\mathbf{q})=\omega^2\mathbf{q}-(\omega\cdot\mathbf{q})\omega \qquad (7)$$

Taking the divergence

$$\text{Div}\,(\omega^2\mathbf{q}) = \mathbf{q}\cdot\nabla\omega^2 \quad , \quad (\nabla\cdot\mathbf{q}=0) \tag{8}$$

$$\text{Div}\,(\omega\cdot\mathbf{q})\omega = \omega\cdot\nabla(\omega\cdot\mathbf{q}),(\nabla\cdot\omega=0) \tag{9}$$

But

$$\nabla(\omega\,.\,\mathbf{q}) = \omega\,.\,\nabla\mathbf{q}+\mathbf{q}\,.\,\nabla\omega+\omega\times\text{curl}\,\mathbf{q}+\mathbf{q}\times\text{curl}\,\omega$$

Thus

$$\text{Div}\,(\omega\cdot\mathbf{q})\omega = \omega\cdot(\omega\cdot\nabla\mathbf{q}+\mathbf{q}\cdot\nabla\omega)+\omega\cdot(\mathbf{q}\times\text{curl}\,\omega) \tag{10}$$

$$(\text{since } \omega\times\text{curl}\,\mathbf{q} = \omega\times\omega = 0)$$

The first term on the right side of the equation may be transformed to

$$\omega\cdot(\omega\cdot\nabla\mathbf{q}) = \omega^2(d/ds)q_s \tag{11}$$

where s is taken along the vortex line ω (in the same direction).

The second term may be written

$$\omega\cdot(\mathbf{q}\cdot\nabla\omega) = \mathbf{q}\cdot\nabla(\omega^2/2) \tag{12}$$

The divergence term (the average value of which is zero) may now be reintroduced in Equation (5) using relations (7), (8), (10), (11), and (12).

One has then

$$(\partial/\partial t)(\omega^2/2)+\mathbf{q}\cdot\nabla(\omega^2/2)-\omega^2(d/ds)q_s-\omega\,.\,(\mathbf{q}\times\text{curl}\,\omega)$$
$$+(\omega\times\mathbf{q})\cdot\text{curl}\,\omega = \nu\omega\cdot\nabla^2\omega$$

It is now the merit of developing the divergence that the two last terms on the left hand side cancel and one may introduce the derivative which gives the rate of change for a given element of the fluid

$$(D/Dt)(\omega^2/2) = (\partial/\partial t)(\omega^2/2)+\mathbf{q}\cdot\nabla(\omega^2/2)$$

With such simplification Equation (5) is transformed to the simple form

$$(D/Dt)(\omega^2/2) = \omega^2(d/ds)q_s+\nu\omega\cdot\nabla^2\omega \tag{13}$$

This equation is more precise than Equation (5) used before as it does not give mean values of a stationary turbulent flow only but is actually *an exact restatement of the equation of motion.*

We shall now proceed to prove that for a stationary turbulent flow, which is the only case that has been considered before, the first term

$$\omega^2(d/ds)\mathbf{q}_s \tag{14}$$

which can again be identified as the "creative" term, *is always positive*, and that the other term

$$\nu \omega \cdot \nabla^2 \omega \tag{15}$$

which may be termed the "destructive" term, *is always negative.*

It is, of course, evident that it is sufficient to prove either case alone, since $(D/Dt)(\omega^2/2)$ must remain zero for stationary flows. We shall, therefore, show by an exact treatment that the term (15) is always negative. The proof proceeds as follows.

Let us write div $\omega = 0$

$$\begin{aligned}\omega \cdot \nabla^2 \omega &= \omega \cdot \text{curl curl } \omega \\ &= \text{div } (\omega \times \text{curl } \omega) - (\text{curl } \omega)^2 \end{aligned} \tag{16}$$

We know that for equilibrium laminar flow the two last terms are equal since $\nabla^2 \omega$ is then zero. The problem is to show what happens in the case of equilibrium turbulent flow. For simplicity in the treatment we shall restrict ourselves to the case of a circular cross section of the channel.

The mean value of the divergence term is obtained by the equation

$$\int_V \text{div } (\omega \times \text{curl } \omega) dV = \int_S (\omega \times \text{curl } \omega) dS \tag{17}$$

The mean value over the cross section is thus simply given by

$$(\omega \times \text{curl } \omega) 2\pi r / \pi r^2 \tag{18}$$

Now the volume or surface integral of the second term

$$\int (\text{curl } \omega)^2 dF \tag{19}$$

has the property that if the line integral

$$\int_F \text{curl } \omega \cdot d\text{F} = \int \omega \cdot ds = \text{ const.} \tag{20}$$

is of *a given fixed value*, Equation (19) gives a minimum *if, and only if, curl ω is a constant* over the cross section. (The condition (20) means that $\omega = \partial v / \partial r$ is constant on the wall or that the pressure drop

$$\mu (\partial v / \partial r)$$

is fixed.)

Thus to prove the statement one may write Equation (19) with curl ω as a constant and equal to the value at the wall plus an arbitrary value curl $\Delta\omega$ which is subject to the condition (20) with $\Delta\omega = 0$ on the wall. Then one has

$$\int \{ (\text{curl } \omega)_w + \text{curl } \Delta\omega \}^2 dF \tag{21}$$

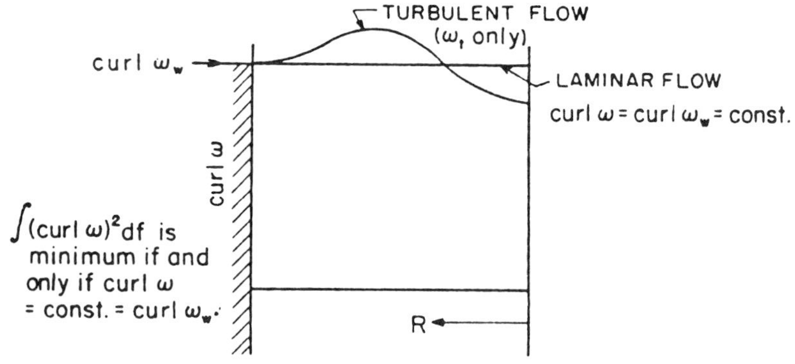

Fig. 1. Curl ω *vs* radius.

It is seen that because of condition (20) the product disappears, and since (curl $\Delta\omega)^2$ is always positive the value of curl ω must be constant and equal to the given value at the wall. Then and only then *is the minimum value of the integral obtained.* It may be seen that this particular case represents equilibrium laminar flow. In fact, with curl ω = C the two terms of Equation (16) are equal and of opposite sign.

We can next make the important and useful statement: The first term in Equation (16) does not depend on the internal flow condition but only on the value of ω and curl ω on the wall. The *mean value for equilibrium laminar or turbulent flow* is given if we write

$$\omega \cdot \nabla^2\omega = [(\text{curl } \omega)_w]^2 - (\text{curl } \omega)^2 \qquad (22)$$

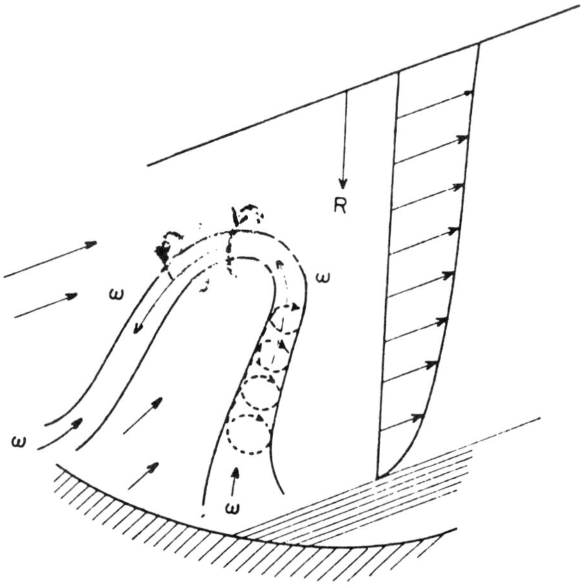

Fig. 2. Stretching vortex "horseshoe"

But we have already proven that curl ω_w *is the smallest possible value under any circumstances.* (See Fig. 1.) Only in the case of steady laminar or parabolic flow does the expression become zero. Since (curl $\omega)^2$ may be written

$$(\text{curl }\omega)^2 = [(\text{curl }\omega)_t]^2 + [(\text{curl }\omega)_r]^2 + [(\text{curl }\omega)_a]^2 \qquad (23)$$

the radial and axial terms are in addition to the tangential term which *alone* makes the expression (22) negative.

We may now use relation (22) to write equation (13) in the form

$$(D/Dt)(\omega^2/2) = \omega^2(dq_s/ds) + \nu[\{(\text{curl }\omega)_w\}^2 - (\text{curl }\omega)^2] \qquad (24)$$

It has thus been shown in general that for equilibrium turbulent flow the viscosity term is always negative, reaching zero only in the case of steady laminar flow.

Therefore, the creative term

$$\omega^2(dq_s/ds) \qquad (25)$$

is always positive. The turbulent flow is thus constituted as to make relation (25) positive by providing the proper mechanism. It can be seen that the term (dq_s/ds) is *always positive for a stretching vortex element.* Since neither a tangential nor an axial vortex will change its length, it may be seen at once that only a *radially pointing* element can be subject to stretching. Since a vortex line has no beginning or end it must *necessarily always form a loop.* This leads to the horseshoe structure as originally given in Reference 3. (See Fig. 2.) At higher Reynolds numbers there is not only loops of horseshoes at the largest gradient near the wall but similar loops will form internally as bent vortex lines[2] whenever or wherever the required local value of the Reynolds number of the "impending" pattern is exceeded. The essential and fundamental idea is always the stretching of the vortex lines. At very high Reynolds numbers there will also be a multiple arrangement of higher order vortices as pointed out earlier in reference 3.

REFERENCES

1. H. Lamb, *Hydrodynamics,* Dover Publications, New York, 1945.

2. Th. Theodorsen, "The Structure of Turbulence," *50 Jahre Grenzschichtforschung,* ed. H. Gortler and W. Tollmien, Friedr. Vieweg & Sohn, Braunschweig, 1955.

3. Th. Theodorsen, "Mechanism of Turbulence," *Proc. 2nd Midwestern Conf. Fluid Mech.* The Ohio State Univ., 1952.

RELATIVITY AND CLASSICAL PHYSICS

BY THEODORE THEODORSEN

1976

INTRODUCTION

This paper presents a new theory of light and the universe; in developing it, methods are employed for deriving the basic equations of relativity (shown boxed in) without invoking curvatures of space and artificial time.

This paper first describes a method for obtaining the well-known relativity expression for the increase in mass with velocity by purely classical means and shows that it relates only to masses with velocities induced by an externally applied force. In this phase of the work, the scalar form of the mass-energy relation is used.

The familiar mass-energy relation, $E = mc^2$, is then generalized into its tensor form wherein the mass is represented by an ellipsoidal tensor and the velocity of light, squared, by the inverse tensor. This complies with the ellipsoidal tensor representation of gravitational fields. These terms vary in magnitude with the distance and orientation from a massive body, such as the sun. Here is the crux of the paper. With this one assumption of the tensor form of the mass-energy relation there can be derived the important relativity relationships, and the cumbersome concepts of curved space and artificial time are avoided.

First, by using the calculus of variations, the expression for the geodesic of a light ray is derived. The same result is obtained by applying the law of constancy of angular momentum.

Then, the expression for the precession of the perihelion of Mercury is obtained using the tensor form of the mass-energy relation, the laws of conservation of energy, and the constancy of the angular momentum. Again, the result is the same as that arrived at by using relativity concepts and postulates.

The velocity addition theorem is also obtained using only Newton's law of action and reaction.

Speculation on the possible nature of the continuum concludes the paper.

PROPULSION BY EXTERNALLY AND INTERNALLY PRODUCED FORCES: THE TWO MASS-VELOCITY RELATIONS

In analyzing the relation of velocity and mass two different cases of propulsion are considered in the following. If the source of the energy supply is *external* to the body we shall term it Case I; if *internal*, we shall term it Case II. In Case I the mass increases as energy is supplied to the body from the outside, but in Case II even as the velocity is increasing, the mass of the body remains constant, as will be shown.

Using conventional nomenclature for Case 1 gives—

$$Fdt = d(mv)$$

The energy supplied from the source is then—

$$dE = Fvdt = Fds = vd(mv)$$

and by the mass-energy relation—

$$Fvdt = Fds = c^2dm$$

Thus also:

$$c^2 dm = vd(mv)$$

Multiplying by m on both sides and integrating yields the following:[1]

$$\boxed{m = m_0 \frac{1}{\sqrt{[1-(v/c)]^2}}} \qquad (1)$$

where m_0 is the value of the mass at $v = 0$. This is the well-known relativity expression for the increase in mass with velocity. It is, however, valid only *if and when the propulsive force is externally produced*. An electron exposed to the force of an electrostatic field is a typical example.

We shall next consider Case II, that of internal propulsion. An example is, for instance, a train on a horizontal track propelled by the energy of a battery inside the train. Let us consider the absolute magnitudes involved. One has, as above—

$$|Fdt| = |d(mv)|$$

But if—

$$m = m_0 = \text{const}$$

one then has—

$$|Fdt| = |m_0 dv|$$

and

$$|Fvdt| = |m_0 v dv|$$

On the left side of this equation is an element of the energy extracted from the battery and on the right side is the element of the corresponding velocity energy. The two elements are therefore equal but of opposite sign. Consequently the mass of the train remains the same, as postulated above: $m = m_0$.

For the velocity energy[2] of the train there is simply, by integration, and where $E_0 = m_0 c^2$—

$$E_v = m_0 \int v dv = \frac{1}{2} m_0 v^2 = \frac{1}{2} E_0 \left(\frac{v}{c}\right)^2 \qquad (2)$$

This is the fundamentally important formula for the energy in Case II. The velocity energy is exactly $E_v = 1/2)m_0 v^2$ *if and when the propulsive force is produced by internal conversion of energy*.

The importance of this Case II formula is that it applies to massive bodies and light particles in space: static energy is converted into velocity energy and vice versa. Thus the total energy is constant.

With the total energy $= E_0$, one has therefore:

$$E_0 = E_s + E_0 \frac{1}{2} \left(\frac{v}{c}\right)^2 \qquad (3)$$

and thus for the static energy,

$$E_s = E_0 \left\{1 - \frac{1}{2}\left(\frac{v}{c}\right)^2\right\}$$

Both Cases I and II are developed here in compliance with classical physics. *As shown, mass does not in certain cases increase with velocity*, and the statement from relativity that "mass increases with velocity" must therefore be qualified.

REDEFINITION OF THE MASS-ENERGY RELATION

It should be noted here that while the expression $E = mc^2$ was for all practical purposes introduced into physics by Einstein in his famous paper on special relativity (1905),[3] this relation nevertheless stands *independent of any theory* as a concrete physical law.[4]

In the previous pages we have employed the relation $E = mc^2$ in its original scalar form because this is applicable in cases where the variability of the velocity of light is of no concern. However, in other cases such as the calculation of the orbit of Mercury or the determination of the geodesic of a light ray where this variation is the essence of the problem, the tensor form of the relation must be employed.

The relation now may be written

$$E_0 = m_s c_s^2 \qquad (4)$$

where the subscript s refers to any direction with respect to the sun (or any appropriate massive body).

The mass m_s is represented by an ellipsoidal tensor and c_s^2 by the inverse tensor. These tensors vary in magnitude with the distance from the sun (or appropriate massive body). The product of the tensors is of course an invariant scalar E_0, which is the same in all directions. In the following we shall make use of this extended tensor form of the mass-energy relation.

THE GEODESIC OF A LIGHT RAY

A. Method of the Calculus of Variations

It is postulated that the energy of a light particle remains constant in space. Using angular coordinates r and ϕ with respect to the sun, write as follows:

$$E_0 = m_r v_r^2 + m_\phi v_\phi^2$$

For simplicity we shall put E_0 equal to unity. One has then—

$$\left(\frac{v_r}{c_r}\right)^2 + \left(\frac{v_\phi}{c_\phi}\right)^2 = 1 \qquad (5)$$

The light velocities c_r and c_ϕ are inherent properties of the continuum; v_r and ϕ are the instantaneous components in the radial and the tangential directions. It may be seen that[5]—

$$c_r^2 = \frac{c_\infty^2}{K_r} \qquad (6)$$

$$c_\phi^2 = \frac{c_\infty^2}{K_\phi} \qquad (7)$$

where K_r and K_ϕ are the principal dielectric constants of the medium with $K_\infty = 1$. Thus c_r^2 and c_ϕ^2 are inversely proportional to the terms K_r and K_ϕ. In the following light velocity is given in nondimensional form in terms of the velocity at infinity ($c_\infty = 1$) unless otherwise evident. In angular coordinates one has the following:

$$v_r = \frac{dr}{dt} = \dot{\phi}\,\frac{dr}{d\phi}$$

and

$$v_\phi = r\dot{\phi}$$

where $\dot{\phi} = d\phi/dt$. Equation (5) then reads—

$$\left\{\frac{1}{c_r^2}\left(\frac{dr}{d\phi}\right)^2 + \frac{1}{c_\phi^2}\,r^2\right\}\dot{\phi}^2 = 1 \qquad (8)$$

With F defined as the square root of the quantity in the braces, we may write—

$$F d\phi = dt$$

We may may now employ the calculus of variations in conventional manner to obtain the shortest path of a light ray. With—

$$\int_0^t F d\phi = t - t_0$$

the shortest path is then obtained by the solution of the equation,

$$\frac{\partial F}{\partial u} = \frac{d}{d\phi}\frac{\partial F}{\partial \dot{u}} \qquad (9)$$

where

$$u = \frac{1}{r}, \qquad \dot{u} = \frac{du}{d\phi}, \qquad \ddot{u} = \frac{d^2u}{d\phi^2}$$

After performing the indicated differentiations of the function F (see Appendix I) one obtains the relation:

$$\ddot{u} - \frac{1}{2}\,\dot{u}^2\,\frac{d}{du}\log\left(\frac{c_r}{c_\phi^2}\right)^2 = -\frac{1}{2}\left(\frac{c_r}{c_\phi^2}\right)^2\frac{d}{du}\left(c_\phi^2 u^2\right) \qquad (10)$$

This is the all-inclusive mathematical solution of the problem of the geodesic. It contains not only the Newtonian solution for a scalar field but also the relativity solution as obtained by Schwarzchild.[6] The solution is valid for any and all possible values of the light velocities.

Next we shall show how the identical solution is readily obtained by applying the physical law of the constancy of the angular momentum. The relation between this law and the geodesic is of fundamental interest.

B. Method of Constant Angular Momentum

Next let us introduce the physical restriction of a constant angular momentum. In classical physics one has—

$$\mathrm{h} = \frac{1}{c_\phi^2}\,r^2\dot{\phi} \qquad (11)$$

where $1/c_\phi^2$ is the tangential component of the mass tensor representing a particle of energy $E_0 = 1$, and $r\dot{\phi}$ is the tangential velocity.

In relativity $\mathrm{h} = \infty$.[7] Introducing the angular momentum h into Eq. (8) one has the following with $u = 1/r$, $\dot{u} = du/d\phi$, and $\ddot{u} = d^2u/d\phi^2$:

$$\left(\frac{c_\phi^2}{c_r}\right)^2\dot{u}^2 + c_\phi^2 u^2 = \frac{1}{\mathrm{h}^2}$$

By differentiation with respect to ϕ one obtains—

$$\ddot{u} - \frac{1}{2}\,\dot{u}^2\,\frac{\mathrm{d}}{\mathrm{d}u}\log\left(\frac{c_r}{c_\phi^2}\right)^2 = -\frac{1}{2}\left(\frac{c_r}{c_\phi^2}\right)^2\frac{\mathrm{d}}{\mathrm{d}u}\left(c_\phi^2 u^2\right) \qquad (12)$$

Thus the mathematical condition for the shortest path is perfectly equivalent to the physical restriction on the angular momentum. In other words, a light ray obeying the law on the angular momentum automatically traces the shortest path.

C. Derivation of Einstein's and Newton's Expression from Eq. (10) or (12)

If in Eq. (10) or (12) the values of the light velocities were known the path would be established. The variations are small, however—in the order of 10^{-8} at the orbit of Mercury, for instance.

Using Newton's scalar field with $c_r = c_\phi =$ Unity, one gets directly from Eq. (10) or (12)—

$$\ddot{u} + u = 0 \qquad (13)$$

This is the relation for a straight line in angular coordinates. The next-simplest field of radial symmetry is an ellipsoidal tensor field. This field is due to the effect of the Sun's gravitational force on the continuum. Employing the somewhat radical assumption of a "solid" (discussed later) continuum one gets for the respective strain components the following values (see Appendix II):

$$\tau_r = \left(1 - \frac{\mathrm{k}}{\mathrm{r}}\right)^2 \quad \text{and} \quad \tau_\phi = 1 - \frac{k}{r}$$

where $1/r = u$ and k is an integration constant.

In view of the Eqs. (6) and (7) one has then the equalities,

$$c_r^2 = \frac{1}{K_r} = \tau_r = \left(1 - \frac{k}{r}\right)^2 \qquad (14)$$

and

$$c_\phi^2 = \frac{1}{K_\phi} = \tau_\phi = 1 - \frac{k}{r} \qquad (15)$$

where the expressions are all given with respect to their values at infinity, c_∞, K_∞, τ_∞, or these quantities put equal to one. The continuum thus exhibits these surprisingly simple relationships between the dielectric constant, the stress tensor, and the square of the light velocity. The dielectric constant is seen to be inversely proportional to the gravitational stress tensor. This could be no accidental coincidence, but is evidently a significant physical fact. The continuum is also so constructed that the term with $\dot{u}^2$ is equal to zero with mathematical perfection; and the effect of this "disturbing" term has not been observed. It is thus seen that the gravitational fields play a dominant role in the properties of the continuum. The reference frame referred to later is also related directly to the gravitational fields.

The light velocities c_r and c_ϕ were introduced at the beginning of the development and the quantitative values established only at the end. The "disturbing" term with $\dot{u}^2$ is eliminated in consequence of the Eqs. (14) and (15) regardless of the value of the constant k. The term $\dot{u}^2$ does not appear in the Einstein solution, as squares of derivatives are a priori excluded. In this equation, $\dot{u}^2$ will be missing only if the ratio c_r/c_ϕ^2 equals unity. The value of $c_\phi^2 = 1 - (2m/r)$ where k is put equal to $2m$ to comply with the known physical relations [Eqs. (17) and (23)].

We insert this value in the Eqs. (10) and (12) and obtain the following:

$$\ddot{u} = -\frac{1}{2}\frac{\mathrm{d}}{\mathrm{d}u}\left\{(1 - 2mu)\, u^2\right\} \qquad (16)$$

or

$$\boxed{\ddot{u} + u = 3mu^2} \qquad (17)$$

where m is the mass of the Sun given in astronomical units as employed by Eddington[7]:

$$m = G\frac{m_1}{c^2} \qquad (18)$$

where G is Newton's constant, m_1 the mass in cgs units, and c the velocity of light at infinity. The numerical development of Eq. (17) may be found in footnote 7. It gives the angular deflection as 1.75 seconds of arc (in reasonable agreement with observations). It is of interest to note that the numbers 2 and 3 are actual integers in the preceding relations. Note by reference to Case II that only one-half of the total energy is in the form of velocity energy. This is in agreement with the fact that the static energy is equal to the velocity energy.

THE ORBIT OF MERCURY

It is postulated that the energy content of a body in space remains constant in its path of travel. We shall therefore apply Case II, the case of internal propulsion. With E_v and E_s as the velocity energy and the static energy, respectively, and with E_o put equal to unity,

$$E_v = \frac{1}{2}\left\{\left(\frac{v_r}{c_r}\right)^2 + \left(\frac{v_\phi}{c_\phi}\right)^2\right\} + \text{constant} \qquad (19)$$

and

$$E_s = -\frac{m}{r} + \text{constant} \qquad (20)$$

By addition, the total constant energy will be—

$$-\frac{m}{r} + \frac{1}{2}\left\{\left(\frac{v_r}{c_r}\right)^2 + \left(\frac{v_\phi}{c_\phi}\right)^2\right\} = \text{constant}$$

or

$$-\frac{2m}{r} + \left(\frac{v_r}{c_r}\right)^2 + \left(\frac{v_\phi}{c_\phi}\right)^2 = \text{constant}$$

In angular coordinates one has the following:

$$-\frac{2m}{r} + \left\{\frac{1}{c_r^2}\left(\frac{\mathrm{d}r}{d\phi}\right)^2 + \frac{1}{c_\phi^2}r^2\right\}\dot{\phi}^2 = \text{constant} \qquad (21)$$

Eliminating $\dot{\phi}^2$ by means of the relation for the angular momentum, Eq. (11), yields—

$$-\frac{2m}{r}+\left\{\frac{1}{c_r^2}\left(\frac{dr}{d\phi}\right)^2+\frac{1}{c_\phi^2}r^2\right\}\frac{c_\phi^4}{r^4}h^2=\text{constant}$$

$$-\frac{2m}{rh^2}+\left(\frac{c_\phi^2}{c_r}\right)^2\left(\frac{dr}{d\phi}\right)^2\frac{1}{r^4}+c_\phi^2\frac{1}{r^2}=\text{constant}$$

With $1/r=u$, $c_\phi^2/c_r=1$, and $c_\phi^2=1-2mu=\gamma$ one gets—

$$\frac{1}{h^2}\gamma+\left(\frac{du}{d\phi}\right)^2+\gamma u^2=\text{constant} \tag{22}$$

Differentiation with respect to ϕ and eliminating $du/d\phi$ yields—

$$\boxed{\ddot{u}+u=\frac{m}{h^2}+3mu^2} \tag{23}$$

This final result is again in agreement with that of the theory of relativity. With the extra term $3mu^2$ omitted one has Newton's formula:

$$\ddot{u}+u=\frac{m}{h^2} \tag{24}$$

where the mass m is in astronomical units [Eq. (18)].

Note that the term c_ϕ^2 appeared in the form $c_\phi^2=1-ku$. It may be verified that only for the value $k=2m$ is the result in agreement with the known physical facts.

The detailed calculation of motion of the perihelion of Mercury is given by Eddington.[7] This numerical calculation will for the sake of brevity be omitted here.

The path of a heavy mass is thus obtained here by the method of the constant angular momentum.

THE VELOCITY ADDITION THEOREM

The simplest procedure for obtaining this is by employing the method of Case II. For this problem the mass energy relation may be in scalar form. Let us assume we have an object equipped with an internal compressed spring. The energy in the compressed spring would upon release propel the body as a rocket. In compliance with Case II the mass m_o includes the mass of the object, of the spring, and the energy of the compressed spring.

We stipulate that the hypothetical spring is capable of delivering the same total impulse to the object whether the object be fired off from a state of rest or while the object is in a state of unaccelerated motion. If fired from a state of rest the impulse would be—

$$\int f\,dt=m_o v$$

If fired while in a state of unaccelerated motion, the impulse delivered would be of the same value. Consequently the momentum would also have the same value, though the mass and velocity would both have new and different values. Their product would nevertheless be equal to the product $m_o v$.

Now let us assume that we have some sort of platform equipped with an attached vertical section to serve as a backstop. Let us place our test object, with its spring compressed,on the platform with the spring against the backstop. Let us now give the platform with the test object on it a velocity of w. One realizes that if one were to release the compressive force of the spring against the backstop to give more forward velocity to the test object, the reactive impulse would push the backstop and the attached platform rearwards with the full momentum $m_o v$. In order to maintain the forward velocity of the backstop platform when the spring is fired, an equivalent momentum must be provided behind it. The state of motion of the platform will then remain unaltered, and the energy supplied for this purpose will go directly into the test object to increase its velocity. This added energy is then—

$$E=w\int f\,dt=wm_o v$$

This energy is added to the original energy $m_o c^2$ of the object at rest with the spring compressed, and one has for the total energy—

$$E_T=m_o c^2+m_o wv \tag{25}$$

and the mass is increased to—

$$m_T=m_o\left(1+\frac{wv}{c^2}\right)^2 \tag{26}$$

Since the two constant momenta can be added according to classical physics, one has, by addition, the following for the total momentum:

$$M_T=m_o w+m_o v=m_0(w+v)$$

and for the mass as shown in Eq. (26):

$$m_T=m_o\left(1+\frac{wv}{c^2}\right)$$

Thus for the resulting velocity, by division:

$$\boxed{v=\frac{w+v}{1+\dfrac{wv}{c^2}}} \tag{27}$$

From the foregoing it is apparent that *velocity has no separate and independent status. It is always the ratio of momentum and the associated mass.*

For the Fizeau case the velocity $v = c/\eta$ is the light velocity in a fluid medium of index η:

$$v = \frac{w + (c/\eta)}{1 + (w/\eta c)} \qquad (28)$$

For the limiting case $\eta = 1$:

$$v = \frac{w + c}{1 + (w/c)} = c \qquad (29)$$

For an observer on a raft floating on a fluid with velocity w in the same direction as c, the velocity of light is $c - w$,[8] in contradiction to the findings of the theory of relativity. This is a simple case of comparison of two velocities in accordance with classical theory. Both velocities are subject to measurement by means of ordinary clocks and measuring rods.

PRINCIPAL CONCLUSIONS

In the foregoing, Einstein's familiar expressions (boxed in) were derived without redefining the old physics concepts of Newton. One must conclude then that Newton's concepts of space and time remain viable in that they are entirely compatible with the results of Einstein. Furthermore, as a consequence of this incorporation of the tensor form of the mass-energy relation into classical physics, it appears that most classical concepts may be retained and that others such as those regarding light and gravitation may also be retained in a slightly altered form. Presently the velocity of light is classified as a "constant of nature," but as has been shown in this work, the velocity of light is not constant except under circumstances where there is no gravitational force.[9]

The fundamental laws of the propagation of light are proposed and presented here as follows.

1. REFERENCE FRAME OF THE UNIVERSE. *The universal reference frame is an orthogonal system composed of the equipotential surfaces surrounding all masses in the Universe and the gradient lines of the gravitation potential extending from their centers into space.*

2. MAGNITUDE OF THE LIGHT VELOCITY VECTOR. *The velocity of light with respect to points of the universal reference frame is a function of the potential of gravitation and the angle of the velocity vector with the gradient of the potential at any instant of time. The velocity of light obeys the laws of the propagation of light in a nonisotropic medium.*

3. REFERENCE FRAME OF THE EARTH. *The equipotential surface surrounding the earth and its gravitational gradient lines comprises the reference frame. The gradient lines of the earth move with it in translation, but not in rotation, as the frame is stationary or fixed with respect to a radial line from the center of the earth to the center of the Sun.*

It is pertinent to note here that the motion of the surface of the earth due to rotation relative to the reference frame is apparently far too small to have a detectable effect on electromagnetic phenomena. This is the reason why Maxwell's equations appear to be exactly true.

The universal reference frame is postulated to be permanently anchored to all the masses in the universe, but may be considered stationary in empty space. It is actually in a state of continuous distortion as it is everywhere "attached" to the stars, planets, etc., which are moving. But the relative distortions are of almost minute magnitude since the velocities of the bodies are small compared with the velocity of light. The lines of the frame or lines of the gravitational potential are crowded together in front of the advancing side of a body, and more sparsely spaced near the opposite side or in the "wake" of a body. In consequence, a light ray emanating from the advancing side of a planet, for instance, immediately reduces its velocity in response to local conditions while on the back or "wake" side, the light ray increases its velocity in response to those local conditions. A light ray approaching a heavenly body would respond to local conditions also.[9]

The earth and its reference frame or gravitational potential system, which extends some millions of kilometers into space, and which is fixed with respect to a radial line from the earth to the center of the Sun, revolves around the Sun in its potential system, which in turn is stationary with respect to a radial line from the sun to the center of the Milky Way, and so on. Though the earth and its potential system move together in translation, the earth rotates relative to its potential system. At the surface of the earth, it is speculated that the velocity of light as measured with respect to the reference frame in the east direction will prove to be different from that in the west direction by somewhat less than one km/s.[10]

On or in the vicinity of the earth the field of gravitation potential includes the field of the Sun, the self-generated field of the earth, and the effective field due to the centrifugal force. The balancing influence of the latter partially nullifies the effect of the field of the Sun; but both field effects are so small that the earth appears as if it were "alone" in space.

The maximum value of the velocity of light in the solar system occurs at "infinity" with respect to the Sun where the potential is maximum also.[11]

In regard to the laws of gravity, particles of light are not subject to mutual attraction or to the attraction of massive bodies, but are governed exclusively by the laws of transmission of light in an anisotropic medium. The anisotropy is caused by the strain system of the gravitational fields.[12]

Newton's Law of Gravitation applies to massive bodies (of constant energy content) but it does not give the total effect. A second law relates exclusively to motion in space, and I therefore propose the laws of gravitation to be stated as follows:

I. *This is Newton's law of gravitation applicable to massive bodies whether in motion or not.*

II. *Massive bodies in motion are additionally subject to, and particles of light are exclusively subject to, the classical laws of transmission of electromagnetic waves in an anisotropic medium.*

THE CONTINUUM

The continuum, the old ether, may be the real substance from which all Creation is made. At the beginning of the century, atoms were judged to be indivisible solid particles, and the continuum to be almost ethereal. Some decades later it was known that the atoms themselves were not only divisible, but in fact, almost void or empty. With the quantum theory, it became evident that even the remaining singularities, the protons and electrons were merely vibratory entities in the continuum. We know that light waves and these vibratory structures are electromagnetic in nature.

But rather than being ethereal, the continuum may be composed of a substance of enormous rigidity, with a very high modulus of elasticity. This concept is based on the fact that there is no observable time delay in the transmission of the gravitational force. Newton, Einstein, and this writer all give no allowance for time delay: Observations seem to be in agreement with this. In consequence of this apparent enormous rigidity there can be no appreciable energy stored in the continuum itself. It seems that a relaxed or strain-free continuum may have exactly zero energy content. Gravitational strain must by necessity contain (inherently) some energy, however minute. Thus one may say that the *continuum materializes under the strain of the gravitational influence.* The gravitational forces are supplied by the internal energy of the gravitating bodies themselves.

As the continuum probably contains almost no energy and therefore no mass, any compressional signal may have a high velocity. According to classical physics the velocity of the compressional waves must at least be greater, and probably greater by a high order, than that of the light waves. This is a problem of great interest to be solved in the future.

Another property of the continuum is that there is, of course, no friction or heat conduction whatsoever, not even any electric conductivity. Matter is manifested as vibratory entities in the continuum. Vibratory structures in ordinary cases may gradually intensify or dissipate, but the structures in the continuum of which physical matter is made change status only in finite steps. These structures lose or gain energy only in the form of electromagnetic waves.

This concept of the structure of the fundament of the universe is an inversion of the conventional one in that the continuum, normally considered to be empty or ethereal, is here considered to be "solid" in nature, and matter, conventionally thought of as being solid, is here considered to be mere vibrations in and of the continuum.[13]

APPENDIX I
DEVELOPMENT OF EQ. (10)

One has from Eq. (8):

$$\left[\frac{1}{c_r^2}\left(\frac{dr}{d\phi}\right)^2 + \frac{1}{c_\phi^2}r^2\right]\dot{\phi}^2 = 1$$

With $u = \frac{1}{r}$, $\dot{u} = \frac{du}{d\phi}$, one has

$$\left[\frac{1}{c_r^2}\left(\frac{\dot{u}}{u^2}\right)^2 + \frac{1}{c_\phi^2}\left(\frac{1}{u^2}\right)\right]\left(\frac{d\phi}{dt}\right)^2 = 1$$

or

$$F^2\left(\frac{du}{dt}\right)^2 = 1$$

where

$$F^2 = \frac{1}{c_r^2}\left(\frac{\dot{u}^2}{u^4}\right) + \frac{1}{c_\phi^2}\frac{1}{u^2}$$

Thus $F\,d\phi = dt$ and—

$$\int F\,d\phi = t - t_o$$

The shortest path (in time) is obtained by the calculus of variations, as follows:

$$\frac{\partial F}{\partial u} = \frac{d}{d\phi}\left(\frac{\partial F}{\partial \dot{u}}\right)$$

We proceed to develop the functions F^2 and F as follows:

$$F^2 = \dot{u}^2 A + B$$

$$F\frac{\partial F}{\partial \dot{u}} = \dot{u}A \qquad \text{(I)}$$

$$2F\frac{\partial F}{\partial u} = \dot{u}^2\dot{A} + \dot{B} \qquad \text{(II)}$$

From I:

$$F\frac{\partial^2 F}{\partial u\,\partial \dot u} = \dot u\dot A - \frac{\partial F}{\partial u}\cdot\frac{\partial F}{\partial \dot u} = \dot u\dot A - \frac{\partial F}{\partial u}\cdot\frac{\dot u A}{F} \qquad \text{(III)}$$

From I:

$$F\frac{\partial^2 F}{\partial \dot u^2} = A - \left(\frac{\partial F}{\partial u}\right)^2 = A - \frac{\dot u^2 A^2}{F^2} \qquad \text{(IV)}$$

Applying the calculus of variations yields the following:

$$\frac{\partial F}{\partial u} = \frac{\mathrm{d}}{\mathrm{d}\phi}\frac{\partial F}{\partial \dot u} = \dot u\,\frac{\partial^2 F}{\partial u\,\partial \dot u} + \ddot u\,\frac{\partial^2 F}{\partial \dot u^2}$$

$$F\frac{\partial \mathrm{F}}{\partial u} - \dot u F\,\frac{\partial^2 F}{\partial u\,\partial \dot u} - \ddot u F\,\frac{\partial^2 F}{\partial \dot u^2} = 0 \qquad \text{(V)}$$

For the first two terms of Eq. V:

$$F\frac{\partial F}{\partial u} - \dot u\left[\dot u\dot A - \frac{\partial F}{\partial u}\cdot\frac{\dot u A}{F}\right]$$

$$F\frac{\partial F}{\partial u} - \dot u^2\left[\dot A - \frac{\partial F}{\partial u}\frac{A}{F}\right]$$

$$F\frac{\partial F}{\partial u}\left(1 + \frac{\dot u^2 A}{F^2}\right) - \dot u^2 A$$

$$F\frac{\partial F}{\partial u}\frac{F^2 + \dot u^2 A}{F^2} - \dot u^2\dot A$$

$$\left[F\frac{\partial F}{\partial u}\left(2\dot u^2 A + B\right) - \dot u^2 A\left(\dot u^2 A + B\right)\right]\frac{1}{F^2}$$

We insert from Eq. (II)—

$$\left[\left(\frac{1}{2}\dot u^2\dot A + \frac{1}{2}\dot B\right)\left(2\dot u^2 A + B\right) - \dot u^2\dot A\left(\dot u^2 A + B\right)\right]\frac{1}{F^2}$$

$$\left[\frac{1}{2}\dot u^2\dot A 2\dot u^2 A + \frac{1}{2}\dot u^2\dot A B + \frac{1}{2}\dot B 2\dot u^2 A\right.$$

$$\left.-\frac{1}{2}\dot B B - \dot u^2\dot A\dot u^2 A - \dot u^2\dot A B\right]\frac{1}{F^2}$$

$$\left[\dot u^2\left(A\dot B - \frac{1}{2}\dot A B\right) + \frac{1}{2}B\dot B\right]\frac{1}{F^2}$$

$$\left[\dot u^2\left(\frac{\dot B}{B} - \frac{1}{2}\frac{\dot A}{A}\right) + \frac{1}{2}\frac{\dot B}{A}\right]\frac{AB}{F^2} \qquad \text{(VI)}$$

For the last term in Eq. (V) (without $-\ddot u$) we have the following:

$$F\frac{\partial^2 F}{\partial \dot u^2} = A - \frac{\dot u^2 A^2}{F^2} = \frac{AF^2 - \dot u^2 A^2}{F^2}$$

$$F\frac{\partial^2 F}{\partial \dot u^2} = A\,\frac{(\dot u^2 A + B) - \dot u^2 A^2}{F^2} = \frac{AB}{F^2} \qquad \text{(VII)}$$

From Eq. (V):

$$\dot u^2\left(\frac{\dot B}{B} - \frac{1}{2}\frac{\dot A}{A}\right) + \frac{1}{2}\frac{\dot B}{A} - \ddot u = 0$$

$$-\dot u^2\frac{d}{du}\log\frac{B}{\sqrt{A}} - \frac{1}{2}\frac{\dot B}{A} + \ddot u = 0 \qquad \text{(VIII)}$$

Insert the coefficients:

$$A = \frac{1}{c_r^2 u^4} \qquad B = \frac{1}{c_\phi^2 u^2} \qquad \dot B = \frac{1}{c_\phi^4 u^4}\frac{d}{du}\left(c_\phi^2 u^2\right)$$

Thus Eq. (10):

$$\ddot u - \frac{1}{2}\dot u^2\frac{d}{du}\log\left(\frac{c_r}{c_\phi^2}\right)^2 + \frac{1}{2}\left(\frac{c_r}{c_\phi^2}\right)^2\frac{d}{du}(c_\phi^2 u^2) = 0 \qquad \text{(IX)}$$

APPENDIX II
THE ELEMENTS OF THE STRESS TENSOR IN THE CONTINUUM

The stress tensor is here represented in ellipsoidal form. The gravitational field of the Sun is of spherical symmetry. The pressure of the field drops as one approaches its center (the Sun). One may write:

$$\pi\frac{\mathrm{d}}{\mathrm{d}r}\left(\tau_r r^2\right) = 2\pi\tau_\phi r \qquad \text{(I)}$$

where r is the radial and ϕ the angular coordinate; τ_r and τ_ϕ are the respective tensor elements. When $\tau_r = [1 - (k/r)]^2$ and $\tau_\phi = 1 - (k/r)$ and these are inserted into Eq. (I), the equation is satisfied:

$$\frac{d}{dr}\left[\left(1 - \frac{k}{r}\right)^2 r^2\right] = 2r\left(1 - \frac{k}{r}\right)$$

$$2(r - k) = 2(r - k)$$

This one has the solution that the tensor elements are—

$$\tau_r = \left(1 - \frac{k}{r}\right)^2 \text{ and } \tau_\phi = \left(1 - \frac{k}{r}\right)$$

where k is an arbitrary constant.

FOOTNOTES

1. Boxed-in equations are the same as those derived by relativity, the basic relativity expressions.

2. The terms static and velocity energy instead of the more usual terms potential and kinetic energy are intentionally employed. When a body is lifted from the surface of the earth the energy is not, as commonly understood, in the medium between the body and the earth, but is actually located in the molecules of the body itself. In other words, potential energy is ordinarily thought of as being external to the body rather than internal. To avoid this possible confusion, the term potential energy is deliberately avoided throughout this paper.

3. A. Einstein, *Ann. Physik* 17, 891 (1905).

4. Prior to Einstein's first published use of the Mass-Energy Relation, Hasenöhrl showed that contained radiation behaved as though it had a virtual mass of E/c^2. G. Joos, *Theoretical Physics* (Hafner, New York, 1950), p. 258.

5. G. Joos, *Theoretical Physics* (Hafner, New York, 1950), p. 362.

6. K. Schwarzschild, *Über das Gravitationsfeld eines Massenpunktes nach der EINSTEINschen Theorie,* (Akademie Der Wissenschaften Berlin, Sitzungsberichte, 1916) Vol. I, Part I., pp. 189–196).

7. A. S. Eddington, *The Mathematical Theory of Relativity* (Chelsea, New York, 1975), pp. 85–91.

8. The reader should recall that the conclusions of this paper are not dependent on the postulates of curved space and variable time. Only Newtonian Physics is employed.

9. I. I. Shapiro, *Scientific American* 219, (1), 31 (1968).

10. Experiment has shown that this figure must be less than 1/30 km/sec. J. P. Cedarholm, G. F. Bland and C. H. Townes, *Phys. Rev. Lett.,* 342 (1958).

11. H. A. Wilson, *Physics Review* 17, 54 (1921).

12. R. H. Dicke, *Physis Today,* 55 (1967).

BIBLIOGRAPHY BY SUBJECT

Wing Section Theory and Pressure Distribution on Airfoils

[1]"On the Theory of Wing Sections with Particular Reference to Lift Distribution," NACA TR-383, 1931.

[2]"Theory of Wing Sections of Arbitrary Shape," NACA TR-411, 1931.

[3]"General Potential Theory of Arbitrary Wing Sections" (with I. E. Garrick), NACA TR-452, 1933.

[4]"Airfoil-Contour Modifications Based on ϵ-Curve Method of Calculating Pressure Distribution," NACA WR-L-135, July 1944.

[5]"Measurements of Pressure Distribution on an Airfoil in the Mach Number Range Near Unity" (with A. A. Regier), NACA MR-L5H17b, Army Air Force, Bureau of Aeronautics, 1945.

[6]"Pressure Distributions for Representative Airfoils and Related Profiles" (with I. Naiman), NACA TN-1016, Feb. 1946.

Cowlings

[7]"Full-Scale Tests of NACA Cowlings" (with M. J. Brevoort and George W. Stickle), NACA TR-592, 1937.

[8]"Cooling of Airplane Engines at Low Air Speeds" (with M. J. Brevoort and George W. Stickle), NACA TR-593, 1937.

[9]"Full-Scale Tests of a New Type of NACA Nose-Slot Cowling" (with M. J. Brevoort, G. W. Stickle, and M. N. Gough), NACA TR-595, 1937.

[10]"The Fundamental Principles of NACA Cowling," *Journal of the Aeronautical Sciences*, 1938, pp. 169–174.

[11]"Test of Nose-Slot Cowling Installed on SB2U-1 Airplane" (with G. W. Stickle and W. H. McAvoy), NACA Memo, Dec. 1938.

Flutter

[12]"General Theory of Aerodynamic Instability and the Mechanism of Flutter," NACA TR-496, 1935 (reprinted 1940).

[13]"The Flutter Problem," *Fifth International Congress of Applied Mechanics,* Cambridge, MA, 1938.

[14]"Mechanism of Flutter—A Theoretical and Experimental Investigation of the Flutter Problem" (with I. E. Garrick), NACA TR-685, 1940.

[15]"Non-Stationary Flow About a Wing-Aileron-Tab Combination Including Aerodynamic Balance" (with I. E. Garrick), NACA TR-736, 1942.

[16]"Flutter Calculations in Three Degrees of Freedom" (with I. E. Garrick), NACA TR-741, 1942.

[17]"Miscellaneous Tests in Vacuum Sphere on Structural Damping of Airplane Wing Panels," NACA RB, Oct. 1942.

[18]"Effect of the Lift Coefficient on Propeller Flutter" (with A. A. Regier), NACA WR-L-161, July 1945.

Vibration and Flutter Testing of Prototypes or Actual Airplanes

[19]"Investigation of XPBM Wing-Flutter Model," NACA Memo for Bureau of Aeronautics, May 1939.

[20]"Flutter Analysis of the Brewster XF2A-2 Airplane," NACA MR for Bureau of Aeronautics, May 1940.

[21]"Preliminary Vibration and Flutter Studies on P-47 Tail," NACA WR-L-654, Aug. 1943.

[22]"Flutter Tests on SB2U Model in 16-Ft Tunnel" (with R. P. Coleman and N. H. Smith), NACA WR-657, Feb. 1943.

[23]"Flutter Tests of Modified SB2U Model in 16-Ft Tunnel" (with R. P. Coleman and N. H. Smith), NACA WR-742, Aug. 1943.

[24]"Flutter Tests of B-24 Fin-Rudder-Tab System" (with N. H. Smith), NACA WR-L-679, Sept. 1944.

[25]"Vibration Surveys of the P-40 Rudder and Fin-Rudder Assembly" (with A. A. Regier), NACA WR-L-652, April 1943.

[26]"Vibration Surveys of the P-47-B Rudder and Fin-Rudder Assembly" (with A. A. Regier), NACA WR-L-653, April 1943.

[27]"Vibration-Response Tests of a 1/5-Scale Model of the Grumman F6F Airplane in the Langley 16-Ft High-Speed Tunnel" (with A. A. Regier), NACA WR-L-743, 1944.

[28]"Vibration Response of Airplane Structures" (with A. G. Gelalles), NACA TR-491, 1934.

[29]"Propeller Vibrations and the Effect of the Centrifugal Force," NACA TN-516, 1935.

Propellers

[30]"Characteristics of Six Propellers Including the High-Speed Range" (with G. W. Stickle and M. J. Brevoort), NACA TR-594, 1937.

[31]"Theory of Propellers I—Determination of the Circulation Function and the Mass Coefficient for Dual-Rotating Propellers," NACA TR-775, 1944.

[32]"Theory of Propellers II—Method for Calculating the Axial Interference Velocity," NACA TR-776, 1944.

[33]"Theory of Propellers III—Slipstream Contraction with Numerical Values for Two-Blade and Four-Blade Propellers," NACA TR-777, 1944.

[34]"Theory of Propellers IV—Thrust, Energy, and Efficiency Formulas for Single and Dual Rotating Propellers with Ideal Circulation Distribution," NACA TR-778, 1944.

[35]"Effect of a Trailing Edge Extension of the Characteristics of a Propeller Section" (with G. W. Stickle), NACA WR-L-637, 1944.

[36]*Theory of Propellers*, McGraw-Hill, New York, 1948.

[37]"Theoretical Investigation of Ducted Propeller Aerodynamics," Vol. I and II, U. S. Army Transportation Research Command, Contract DA 44-177-TC-606, Aug. 1960.

[38]"Theoretical Investigation of Ducted Propeller Aerodynamics," Vol. III and IV, U. S. Army Transportation Research Command, Contract DA 44-177-TC-674, Aug. 1961.

[39]"Theory of Static Propellers and Helicopter Rotors," United Aircraft, Sikorsky Div. Rept., Sept. 1968.

[40]"Design of Static Propellers," United Aircraft, Hamilton Standard Div. Rept., May 1970.

Supersonic-Flow Studies

[41]"Extension of the Chaplygin Proofs on the Existence of Compressible Flow Solutions to the Supersonic Region," NACA TN-1028, March 1946.

[42]"A Condition on the Initial Shock," NACA TN-1029, March 1946.

[43]"Limits and Classification of Supersonic Flows," Univ. of Maryland, TN BN-23, March 1954.

[44]"Ramjet Compression, Combustion, and Cycle Efficiency at Hypersonic Inlet Velocities," Republic Aviation Rept., March 1961.

Turbulence

[45]"Note on the Theory of Hurricanes," *Journal of the Aeronautical Sciences,* 1952, p. 645.

[46]"Mechanism of Turbulence," *Proceedings of the Second Midwesterm Conference on Fluid Mechanics*, Ohio State Univ., 1952, pp. 1–18.

[47]"The Structure of Turbulence," Univ. of Maryland, TN BN-31, May 1954.

[48]"The Structure of Turbulence," *50 Jahre Grenzschichtsforschung* (Ludwig Prandtl Anniversary Volume), Vieweg, Braunshweig, FRG, 1955, pp. 55–62.

[49]"The Structure of Turbulence," Republic Aviation Corp. Rept, April 10, 1961.

De-Icing

[50]"Prevention of Ice Formation on Gasoline Tank Vents" (with William C. Clay), NACA TN-394, 1931.

[51]"Ice Prevention on Aircraft by Means of Engine Exhaust Heat and a Technical Study of Heat Transmission from a Clark Y Airfoil" (with William C. Clay), NACA TR-403, 1931.

Noise Research

[52]"A New Principle of Sound Frequency Analysis," NACA TR-395, 1931.

[53]"The Problem of Noise Reduction in Airplanes" (with A. A. Regier), NACA TN-1145, Aug. 1946.

Instruments

[54]"A Sensitive Induction Balance for the Purpose of Detecting Unexploded Bombs," NACA Memo, 1930.

[55]"Instrument for Detecting Metallic Bodies Buried in the Earth," *Journal of the Franklin Institute*, 1930, pp. 311–326.

[56]"Investigation of the Diaphragm-Type Pressure Cell," NACA TR-388, 1931.

Wind-Tunnel Design

[57]"The Theory of Wind-Tunnel Wall Interference," NACA TR-410, 1931.

[58]"Interference on an Airfoil of Finite Span in an Open Rectangular Wind Tunel," NACA TR-461, 1933.

[59]"Experimental Verification of the Theory of Wind-Tunnel Boundary Interference" (with A. Silverstein), NACA TR-478, 1934.

Flight-Path Optimization

[60]"Operation Analysis—Optimum Path of an Airplane—Minimum Time to Climb," Republic Aviation Rept., Feb. 1958 (revised May 1, 1958).

[61]"Minimum Take-off Distance of a Jet-Propelled Airplane," Republic Aviation Rept., Dec. 1959.

Fluid-Mechanics Studies

[62]"On the Propagation of Large Disturbances in a Gas; on the Combustion of Oil," Ph.D. thesis, The Johns Hopkins Univ., Baltimore, MD, 1929.

[63]"The Reaction of a Body in a Compressible Fluid," *Journal of the Aeronautical Sciences,* 1937, pp. 239–240.

[64]"Impulse and Momentum in an Infinite Fluid," in *Memorial Volume in Honor of the 60th Birthday of Th. von Kármán,* 1941.

[65]"Experiments on Drag of Revolving Disks, Cylinders, and Streamline Rods at High Speeds" (with A. A. Regier), NACA TR-793, 1944.

Miscellaneous

[66]"Elimination of Fire Hazard Due to Back Fires" (with I. M. Freeman), NACA TR-409, 1931.

[67]"Note on the Theorems of Bjerkness and Crocco," NACA TN-1073, May 1946.

[68]"Conclusion on Cascade Test Results from 'Institut für Stromungsforschung,'" Republic Aviation Rept., April 21, 1961.

[69]"Relativity and Classical Physics," *Proceedings of the Theodorsen Colloquium*, Norwegian Institute of Technology, Trondheim, 1976.